Praise for the First Edition of *Durham County*

"Jean Anderson's *Durham County* is a monumental history in every way. A vast and impressive piece of work, it not only supersedes all previous efforts but will hold a proud and lasting place among county histories in North Carolina. The solid research, the encyclopedic coverage, the lavish detail, the lucid exposition will make the book a rich mine of information and a touchstone for further research for the next generation and beyond."

—SYDNEY NATHANS, author of *The Quest for Progress: The Way We Lived in North Carolina, 1870-1920*

"Splendidly comprehensive and carefully researched, this book is unusual among county histories that I know in its sophisticated attention to national context and its sensitivity to all segments of the population. A superb book."

—ROBERT DURDEN, author of *The Dukes of Durham, 1865-1929*

"Destined to be the definitive history of Durham County for years to come."

—*North Carolina Libraries*

"*Durham County* deserves the widest possible readership. It offers an engaging perspective on familiar New South themes and an object lesson in bridging the enormous gulf that too often separates academic historians and lay readers."

—JAMES L. LELOUDIS, *Journal of Southern History*

Duke University Press gratefully acknowledges the generous support of these donors, who provided funds toward the production of this book:

The Mary Duke Biddle Foundation
Brenda and Keith Brodie
Steve and Edie Cohn
Duke Photography
Tom and Kim Miller
Office of Durham and Regional Affairs, Duke University
In Memory of H. Max Schiebel

Durham County

Durham County

A History of
Durham County,
North Carolina

SECOND EDITION,
REVISED AND EXPANDED

Jean Bradley Anderson

DUKE UNIVERSITY PRESS
Durham and London
2011

© 2011 Duke University Press
All rights reserved.
Printed in the United States of America on acid-free paper ∞
Designed by Chris Crochetière, and typeset in Charis
by BW&A Books, Inc.
Library of Congress Cataloging-in-Publication Data
appear on the last printed page of this book.

Frontispiece image: Barn at Horton Grove (1860), Stagville
Plantation Historic Site. Photograph by Joann Sieburg-Baker;
courtesy of NCOAH.

A people without history

Is like wind on the buffalo grass.

—TETON SIOUX PROVERB

Contents

Preface to the Second Edition   xi
Preface to the First Edition   xiii
Abbreviations   xvii

1 Land for the Taking: Prehistory–1740s   1
2 Moving In, 1740s–1771   15
3 The American Revolution   29
4 Eighteenth-Century Orange County, 1752–1800   38
5 The Rip Van Winkle Era, 1801–1840   51
6 Improvement Fever, 1840–1861   69
7 Origins of the Town of Durham, 1819–1861   85
8 Victory from Defeat, 1861–1865   97
9 From Bust to Boom, 1865–1880   108
10 A House Divided: An Independent Black Culture,
    1865–1880   130
11 A County at Last, 1880–1890   140
12 The Apogee of an Era, 1890–1903   169
13 Social Challenges, 1900–1917   203
14 The Face of Change, 1903–1917   223
15 Joining the World, 1917–1924   248
16 Elation and Depression, 1925–1941   281
17 World War II and the End of an Era, 1941–1945   321
18 The Old Order Changeth, 1946–1969   332
19 Civil Rights, 1954–1978   360

20 Rounding Out a Century, 1960–1981   379
21 City and County to Millennium's End   403

Appendix: Population Statistics and Officeholders   449
Notes   461
Bibliography   537
Index   561

Preface to the Second Edition

WHEN DUKE UNIVERSITY PRESS asked me to bring *Durham County: A History of Durham County, North Carolina* up to date for a second edition, I was hesitant; I was not sure that the 1980s and 1990s could supply sufficient material of interest; events of those decades were so recent as hardly to count as history. As I began to ponder them and compare life as it is today with that of 1980, however, I realized how much had happened to affect and change the way we live. Granted much of the change was not peculiar to Durham County, but there were aspects pertaining to this locale that warranted recording.

The fundamental economic shift from industry based on tobacco and cotton to medical and technological research—from a blue-collar to a white-coated workforce—was a complete break with the past. Equally dramatic has been our whole culture's growing dependence on computer technology and its almost endlessly innovative applications. This has produced a sea change, a break from pre-computer life as sharp as that of the automobile age from the horse-and-buggy era. The more I thought about changes the more I discovered topics that made the last two decades different and interesting.

Sources for research of recent times are somewhat different from those of the more remote past. There are far fewer books or studies that have analyzed and digested the raw materials of daily events. Collections of important primary documents have not yet been deposited in local repositories. Therefore I had to depend almost entirely on contemporary chroniclers and observers—newspapers, newsletters, and personal interviews—and with some reluctance, I was forced to consult the internet. Too recent to have undergone the usual winnowing that time performs, the last two decades have not yet been stripped of evanescent chaff; nor have their truly significant events, ideas, and persons become unmistakably identifiable.

Because of Durham's growth, it is now impossible to be in any way comprehensive in examining and recounting the myriad organizations and countless individuals who have recently played important roles in Durham's complex culture. The topics I have written about and the examples chosen to illustrate them must therefore be understood as representative. In gathering material from a variety of sources, I have had the help of many knowledgeable and generous friends, colleagues, and professionals of all sorts, including especially librarians and archivists. I have many reasons to thank Lynn Richardson of the North Carolina Collection of the Durham Public Library, and also Linda McCurdy of Duke University Rare Book, Manuscript, and Special Collections Library. They have been more than generous with their time and expertise. Sylvia Kerckhoff lent me her extensive collection of clippings covering her years on the city council and as mayor. She also kindly reviewed my summary of those years. Tom Gallie gave me his firsthand experience of the history of computer technology in the Triangle and closely reviewed my retelling of it. To both I owe many thanks. From start to finish I have benefited from the advice, encouragement, and careful attention of Valerie Millholland, Miriam Angress, and Fred Kameny, editors of Duke University Press. It is a pleasure to acknowledge the assistance of a host of others as well:

Jane W. Adams	Jane Goodridge	Robert A. Parker
Don Akin	Shelly Green	Carol Passmore
Cassandra P. Anderson	Guy Guidry	Patsy Perry
Susan Fox Beischer	Mary-jo Hall	Jack J. Preiss
Florence Blakely	John D. Hamilton	Milo Pyne
Gerald Boarman	Thomas F. Harkins	Deborah Craig Ray
Curtis Booker	Joseph Harvard	Hildegard Ryals
Dorothy Borden	Rebecca Heron	Herbert A. Saltzman
Reyn Bowman	Chris Hildreth	Walter Shackelford
Boyd D. Cathey	Melissa Jackson	Patrice Slattery
Howard G. Clark III	Robin Jacobs	Barbara Smith
Margaret Clark	Bill Jones	Don Solomon
Lisa Coombs	Bill Kalkhof	Frank Stasio
Philip R. Cousin, Jr.	Betsy Lash	Janice Stratton
Kim A. Cumber	Robert Lawson	Edie Thompson
Peter Denton	Bridget Madden	Jason Tomberlin
Patricia Dew	Myra Markham	Matthew Turi
Susy Dieter	Louise Maynor	Brandi D. Tuttle
Elizabeth Dunn	Kenneth McFarland	Vicki White
Jonathan Freeze	Rosemary Oates	
Thomas E. Frothingham	Angela P. Overton	

Preface to the First Edition

AMONG NORTH CAROLINA'S ONE HUNDRED COUNTIES, Durham is a Johnny-come-lately. Established in 1881, it takes its name from the City of Durham, which became the county seat. Over the century since the county's birth, during which the town repeatedly outgrew its original boundaries and asserted a robust and headstrong individuality, the young county has taken on its own character and almost obliterated the memory of its long minority as a part of the large and venerable old Orange County.

From its own establishment in the mid-eighteenth century, the County of Orange played an important role in the shaping and working out of the state's destiny. A forcing ground for such leaders as Archibald D. Murphey, Willie P. Mangum, William A. Graham, Josiah Turner, Jr., and Thomas Ruffin in its political heyday, the county produced a different kind of talent in the New South era. The new leaders—Robert F. Morris, John Ruffin Green, William T. Blackwell, Julian S. Carr, Washington Duke and his sons James, Benjamin, and Brodie, Richard H. Wright, George Watts, and Eugene Morehead—created in the eastern half of the almost entirely agricultural county a hustling tobacco industry with all its satellite trades. Soon secure in its own wealth and identity, with peculiar needs and aspirations, eastern Orange wrested autonomy from the legislature and in 1881 began an independent life under its own name—Durham County.

A very long chronicle of events preceded that independence, however, and belongs to the full story of Durham County. The history recounted in this volume begins, therefore, with the land and its first inhabitants, the Native Americans, and runs through the decades of early exploration and settlement into the vigorous antebellum period. It records the ending of that civilization in the Civil War and the evolution of a way of life based on a new economy that precipitated the change of a rural and agricultural society into an urban and industrial one. The history ends with the celebration of the county centennial in 1981. Two earlier histories—Hiram Paul's *History of Durham* (1883) and William K. Boyd's *Story of Durham* (1925)—centered on the town of Durham. *Durham County* is the first history of the whole county. It therefore offers much new material, based heavily on primary sources. Besides Paul's and Boyd's histories and many recent monographs on aspects of the county's social and political history, it also draws upon the work of dozens of Durhamites who have taken the trouble to gather and record historical facts about their families, churches, schools, organizations, and communities. Newspapers from 1820 to the present have provided contemporary windows through which to view the everyday life of the county. For recent times, personal memoirs, interviews, and oral histories have augmented the chronicle of facts. Details of all these source materials may be found in the notes and bibliography.

The aim of this history is comprehensive, but a single volume cannot possibly record every person, event, date, and name found in a county's annals. Despite its length, therefore, the present volume comprises only a selection from a much larger array of facts. Responsibility for what has been included must rest in part with the author, but frequently the availability or lack of materials rather than actual choice has determined the contents. Few families saved their papers and donated them to a public repository; few early churches documented their origins in written histories; few civic and social organizations left formal archives. Much of the county's earliest history is to be found only in public records: wills and estates, deeds, marriage bonds, tax lists, census records, and court and legislative papers. Even the public records are not complete. The surviving Durham Council minutes lack some early years and certain municipal records either did not survive or were never generated in the first place. Early Orange County deeds and county court minutes are also missing. This history is shaped, therefore, by the public documents that chanced to survive and by private papers in public repositories.

The general contours of one county history are much like another's; only in their particularities do they differ. What distinguishes one from another is the unique and fortuitous conjunction of time, place, and persons. Not every North Carolina town has had its Southern Conservatory or Trinity College, and though many have had tobacco and cotton mills, only one had simultaneously the Dukes and Julian Carr. Thus in tracing the development of Durham County, even while outlining the common pattern and placing it in a larger context, I have tried to highlight the exceptional detail, the departure from the typical that is the essence of the place. In treating the most recent decades, many of whose players are still alive, I have omitted much civic history because distance has not yet supplied the proper perspective from which to view it; time has not yet sifted the lasting from the ephemeral, the important from the trivial.

The impetus for this county history came entirely from the Historic Preservation Society of Durham. Without the society's commitment to the project, propelled in the undertaking by Margaret Haywood, Durham County would still lack a written history. Once the project was under way, both the city and county of Durham also contributed generous support.

NOW SOME PERSONAL NOTES. In writing the history I have benefited from the resources of several local institutions and the expert and gracious assistance of their staffs: the North Carolina Archives in Raleigh; the North Carolina Collection and the Southern Historical Collection of the University of North Carolina at Chapel Hill; the Manuscript, Reference, and Newspaper Departments as well as the general collection of the William R. Perkins Library of Duke University; and the North Carolina Room of the Durham County Library. Without them the project would have been impossible. I have also had the help of dozens of generous and patient individuals. Holding them all blameless for whatever errors this history may contain, I must express my thanks to all on whom I called for help. A few consistently encouraged me by their interest and voluntary involvement; they suggested sources of information, supplied new materials, obtained elusive facts, and generally repaired my ignorance. I am especially indebted to the late Mattie Russell, who strongly supported the project and blindly affirmed her faith in my attempting it; to the late Mildred Mangum Harris for her intimate knowledge of northern Durham County and identification of its material past; to Curtis Booker, who generously shared his encyclopedic knowledge and family papers concerning southern Durham County; to Rudolph and Edna Baker, who educated me in the families and communities of Oak Grove Township; to Mayme Harris Perry for the many oral histories she collected on my behalf and for acquainting me with Hayti's landmarks; to George and Mary Pyne, sources of all kinds of wisdom about the city and its past; to Dorothy Newsom Rankin for valuable information of many sorts; to Duncan Heron for sharing his geological expertise; to Marian O'Keefe for her help in rounding up photographs; to Anne Berkley of Durham County Library for all kinds of favors; to William E. King, who fostered this undertaking as both Duke University Archivist and head of the publications committee of the Historic Preservation Society; to William R. Erwin, Jr., who kept an eagle eye out for relevant new source materials and anything I might have overlooked in the extensive Duke University Manuscript Department collections; to Robert F. Durden and Carl L. Anderson, whose painstaking reading of the entire manuscript added immeasurably to its accuracy and readability. All of them have my profound gratitude.

In addition to those named above, I am indebted to the following persons for their assistance: F. Howard Alston, Del Amnott, John L. Anderson, Eunice Austin, Lenox Baker, Deryl Bateman, Susan Fox Beischer, Stanley Bergquist, Mary Christian Bernheim, Lydia Evans Beurrier, Robert L. Blake, Allan H. Bone, Robert H. Booth, Shirley Hanks Borstelmann, Benjamin Boyce, Edward Boyd, David Bradley, Elneda Britt, Carolyn Brown, Mrs. Hubert Browning, Isabelle Budd, Marshall Bullock, Ollie Nichols Carpenter, Mildred C. Cartee, Nancy Clark, Theo Clegg, Josephine and William A. Clement, A. J. Howard Clement, Dale Coats, Shirley Colton, Dorothy S. Colvin, William T. and Patricia Coman, Edward E. Cooke, Ruth Couch, Dana Courtney, Albert G. and Mary Cox, Lois Cranford, Bernice Crumpacker, Theresa Damiano, Vincent Damiano, Helen Davis, Frank A. De Pasquale, Maude Wilkerson Dunn, W. W. Easley, Vivian A. Edmonds, Daniel K. Edwards, Gillian M. Ellis, Louis and Maggie York Fara, John Fletcher, John B. Flowers III, Gayle Fripp, Cynthia Gardiner, Mary Louise Powe Gardner, Virginia Ghirardelli, James F. Gifford, Jr.,

Lucille Glenn, Hazel Godwin, Elise Evans Green, Louise Hall, Lisa Harpole, William A. Harrat, Ann Harrison, Marjorie Harrison, Edith Hassold, James R. Hawkins, Egbert and Margaret Haywood, James J. Henderson, Nannie Mae Herndon, Glenn Hinson, Betty and Louis Edward Hodges, Carson Holloway, Harriet Hopkins, Ned E. Huffman, Mrs. Wilmer Hunt, James Huskins, Patricia Hutchings, Cyrus M. Johnson, Jr., Ruth Wilkerson Johnson, John Maynard Jones, A. C. Jordan, Tommy W. Jordan, Margaret Keller, Dorothea Kohle, Thomas Krakauer, Peter Kramer, Nancy Laszlo, Lottie Riley Lawrence, Carol Layh, Mrs. Otis Lee, Harriet Leonard, Henry S. Lougee, Mrs. Caroline Mack, C. C. Malone, A. C. Maheshwary, Annie E. Markham, Charles B. Markham, Myra Clark Markham, Steven Massengill, Priscilla Gregory McBryde, Kenneth McFarland, Loring McIntyre, Evelyn McKissick, Fred McNeill, Jr., Brooklyn T. McMillon, Margaret Finney McPherson, Lyda Moore Merrick, Ruth Mary Meyer, Jane Mickey, Jacqueline Morgan, Montrose Moses, Harold Mozingo, Anthony Mulvihill, William D. Murray, Sydney Nathans, Albert Nelius, Margaret Nygard, Alison O'Reilly, David A. Page, Janice Palmer, Doris Parrish, Benjamin Patrick, Frances and Lewis Patton, Jessie Pearson, Norman Pendergraft, Erna Idalina Ripley Perry, E. K. and Sibyl Powe, Ella Fountain Pratt, Phyllis Link Randall, Katherine Harris Reade, Constance Renz, Samuel O. Riley, B. W. C. Roberts, Thomas Rogers, Hildegard and Clyde Ryals, Isabelle Samfield, Terry Sanford, Jr., Carolyn and John Satterfield, Richard J. Sauer, Marion F. Scott, James H. Semans, Barbara Semonche, Walter and Florence Shackelford, Catherine Stroud Shaw, Bertha Shipp, Miriam Slifkin, Amanda Mackay Smith, Barbara Soper Smith, Edwin G. Southern, Elna and Asa Spaulding, Nancy P. Speers, Phebe Stanton, R. Edward Stewart, Janice Stratton, Nelson Strawbridge, Lucy Durham Strickland, Shirley Strobel, Edmund S. Swindell, Jr., Patricia Sykes, James R. Tabron, Roxie Dark Taylor, Norwood A. Thomas, Jr., Janice Tice, Doris Belk Tilley, Laura Torain, Vera Carr Twaddell, Garry E. Umstead, H. Trawick Ward, Nancy Palmer Wardropper, Richard L. and Ruth Watson, Constance Merrick Watts, Ruby West, Mr. and Mrs. C. B. Weatherly, Bailey Webb, Mena Fuller Webb, Ran Whitley, Hugh E. Whitted, Jr., Erma Whittington, Nancy Williams, St. Clair Williams, John Woodard, and Julia Wray.

In accepting the task of writing a county history I had rather special motivation. When I first lived in Durham, I longed to know the past of the place I was discovering. Those I questioned assured me that Durham had no history before the Civil War. Graveyards on vacant lots, not completely overgrown, and here and there an antebellum farmhouse in the landscape told me otherwise. Paul's and Boyd's histories only whetted my appetite. My compelling desire to know the history of Durham, city and county, must be my excuse for saying "yes" when asked to do the job.

I offer the result diffidently, for I am keenly aware of its deficiencies and my own audacity as a native of neither Durham nor the South. Perhaps the love I have for both will excuse my presumption. If further justification be needed, let it be the conviction I share with Shirley Abbott, who so eloquently voiced it in *Womenfolks,* that "the past matters, that history weighs on us and refuses to be forgotten by us, and that the worst poverty women—or men—can suffer is to be bereft of their past."

Abbreviations

DCDB	Durham County Deed Books, Durham County Courthouse, Durham, N.C.
DMH	*Durham Morning Herald*
D.U. Archives	Duke University Archives, William R. Perkins Library, Durham, N.C.
DUMD	Duke University Manuscript Department, William R. Perkins Library, Duke University, Durham, N.C.
DU-RBMSCL	Duke University Rare Book, Manuscript, and Special Collections Library
Herald	Durham *Morning Herald*
H-S	*Herald-Sun*
N&O	Raleigh *News & Observer*
NCC	North Carolina Collection, University of North Carolina Library, Chapel Hill
NCCU	North Carolina Central University, Durham
NCOAH	North Carolina Office of Archives and History, Raleigh
OCCM	Orange County Court Minutes: Minutes of the Court of Pleas and Quarter Sessions, North Carolina Office of Archives and History, Raleigh
OCDB	Orange County Deed Books, Register of Deeds, Hillsborough, N.C.
OCR	Orange County Records, North Carolina Office of Archives and History, Raleigh
OCW	Orange County Wills, North Carolina Office of Archives and History, Raleigh; Orange County Will Books, Orange County Courthouse, Hillsborough, N.C.
SHC	Southern Historical Collection, Louis Round Wilson Library, University of North Carolina, Chapel Hill
SOHP	Southern Oral History Program, Louis Round Wilson Library, University of North Carolina, Chapel Hill
UNC	University of North Carolina, Chapel Hill

Land for the Taking:
Prehistory–1740s

1

DURHAM COUNTY, NORTH CAROLINA, was created on 28 February 1881 by a legislative act that was ratified by a referendum of its inhabitants on 10 April following.[1] Durham County, like counties in general, exists for the convenience of its inhabitants and at their expense. It supplies the services of local government in a central location. County boundaries, like Durham's, are usually arbitrary, with little reference to geographical or historical considerations. Boundary lines exist only on paper until some legal question requires their surveying.[2] Thus a county has only a political and fiscal reality when first created, and, like a newborn child, comes into the world with no formulated character or individuality. Only over time do these develop in the interaction of the people and the place so as to give the land its own peculiar stamp and the people a sense of unity and identity.

Long before the County of Durham existed, however, the people were there, working, improving, exploiting the land to eke a livelihood from it, pitting their ingenuity against its potential to build a better life for themselves. The history of that relationship of land and people is the history of Durham County.

GEOGRAPHY

In its present configuration, Durham County is roughly a rectangle with an eastern bulge, its east and west long sides lying roughly on a northeast to southwest axis like its rock foundation. Its area of 296 square miles, or 188,928 acres, ranks it among the smaller counties in North Carolina while its location close to the state's center at north latitude 36 degrees and west longitude 79 degrees places it in an advantageous crosscurrent of trade and travel.[3]

For farmers, which is what the early settlers were, two factors are crucial: weather and soil. Durham's climate is always described by the bland adjective "moderate," but "moderate" is a relative term and describes only the results of Durham's averaged-out statistics compared to those of the world at large. It fails to

Map 1. An outline map of Old Orange County as it was established in 1752, showing portions taken from it to form other counties. The dotted line represents the original boundary between Orange and Wake (1770) counties. The darker gray area shows Durham County's boundaries at its establishment in 1881. The lighter gray area represents Carr Township, the portion of Wake County added to Durham County in 1911.

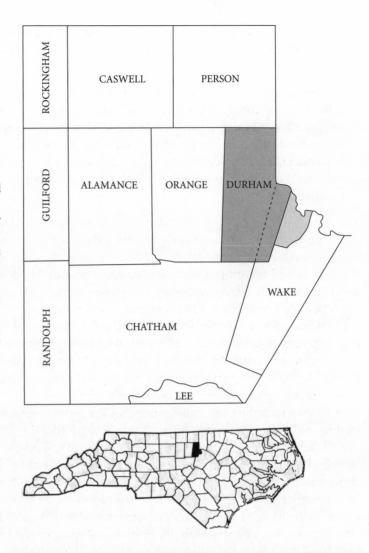

convey the intemperate swings of hot to cold and drought to rain the native knows. Winters, it is true, are short and summers hot and long, the temperature only occasionally falling below 20 degrees in winter and rising above 90 degrees Fahrenheit an average of fifty times a summer. Six to seven inches of snow a year is average based on a variation of from a foot and a half of snow one year to a trace the next; and rainfall is so locally and seasonally variable that averaging becomes meaningless. A range of anywhere from twenty-eight to fifty-one inches a year indicates no shortage.[4]

The frost-free season is over two hundred days a year, from mid-April to late October, but freaks of weather destroy expectations, and fruit trees blandished into bloom by early springlike days are often blighted by late frost. This frequent occurrence was noted over two hundred years ago by a Revolutionary War soldier from Pennsylvania sent down to join General Nathanael Greene's forces in South Carolina.[5] Lt. Enos Reeves spent two nights at Mount Tirzah in Caswell County (now Person County), just over the Durham County border in March 1782. The day he arrived the fruit trees were in bloom, but he awoke next morning to a whitened world.

> The peach trees were in full blossom, and covered with snow; you could see a blush of red through it, which to me was a lively resemblance of beauty in distress, and in distress they truly were, for a like accident happened [to] them about a week before I marched and killed the most of them. It is a mere accident in this Country to have a good fruit year, on account of the changeable weather, which is some days like Summer and the next perhaps as cold as winter.

Reeves had precisely the right word to describe Durham's climate: changeable.

Though probably few of the early settlers had ever lived in so southern a latitude before, with the advantages it promised for farming, they saw another promise in the soils lying beneath the forest wilderness. Compared to the mostly worn-out and often stony or chalky soils they had known in their native countries of England, Scotland, or Ireland, what they found was a richness beyond belief, virgin land millions of years old with topsoil many inches deep. Although they must have found the prolonged summer heat trying, they could only have been delighted by the frequent and unfamiliar warm, sunny days, free of the dampness of northern Europe, and with the gently to steeply rolling, well-watered land described by an early explorer as "the Flower of Carolina."[6]

Soils vary with the rocks from which they are formed. An analysis of Durham's geology presents a somewhat different view from that of the explorer or early settler and sets it apart from most other Piedmont counties in the state.[7] Two-thirds of Durham County lies within the morphological phenomenon known as the Durham Triassic Basin. Created over 200 million years ago by volcanic action in the Late Triassic period, many geologists believe, the basin forms a narrow trough, part of a series along the eastern seaboard, trending northeast to southwest and varying in width from five to twenty miles. The east-central and southern parts of the county lie within this basin and differ perceptibly from the northern and west-central third, which is underlain by the Carolina Slate Belt formed likewise by volcanic action six hundred million years ago. At that time the southeastern part of the North American continent is thought to have been a sea with largely single-celled organisms—algae. Evidence of multicelled organisms, however, was discovered in 1975 in fossils in the northern part of Durham County on Little River in the South Lowell area. The fossils, the oldest yet found in the western hemisphere, represent annelid worms. Their imprints, some almost a foot long, were discovered by Lynn Glover III, a professor at Virginia Polytechnic Institute. The marine worms lived on the shores of the volcanic islands that are supposed to have existed here in precambrian times. The section of rock in which they were found, metamorphosed volcanic rock of the Slate Belt, was removed for permanent custody to the Smithsonian Institution.[8]

This general description of Durham's geology, however, must be modified to suggest its actual complexity. Dikes and sills, igneous formations, largely of feldspar and pyroxene, have intruded the basin sediments, and chemical weathering has resulted in a wide variety of rock components and conglomerates, while the rocks of the Slate Belt have their own pyroclastic debris with intrusive quartz veins. The result of this geological pudding is a like mixture of soils with varying agricultural capabilities. Into the basin's trough over the millennia have washed the soils weathered from rocks on either side of the basin to be mixed with the soils of the Triassic rocks. Mostly sedimentary in origin and strongly weathered because of the warm, humid climate, the basin soils are acidic, leached out, and lacking in natural fertility.[9]

Innocent of rock and soil analysis, the settlers saw only the agriculturally desirable terrain, never rising above 730 feet (the highest point just southwest of Mount Lebanon Church) in the northwestern part of the county or falling below 230 feet above sea level (the lowest point lying just half a mile east of Barbee's Chapel) in the southwestern part of the county.[10] They found ample rivers and streams flowing through sometimes steep gorges and sometimes flat marsh and meadowland. But the overwhelming presence was the forest—endless, dark, filled with bird and beast and deep soil and huge timber. The aboriginal forest up to early historic times when the first settlers knew it provided a richer, more varied forest cover with far more edible fruits and nuts and more species of game animals than are found in the Piedmont today. Here were all the raw materials to sustain life and to provide the surplus for progress. Hardwoods and some conifers were the original tree cover of Durham County, the hardwoods along the streams and the conifers on the ridges. Longleaf pines originally grew in the county and were still to be found in the southeastern section in 1915. While a mixture of hardwoods and pines still covers 67 percent of the county, none of it is first growth; and because of subsequent changes through long years of man's intervention, much of it is scrub growth lacking the luxuriousness of the primeval forest the settlers found.

CAROLINA'S BEGINNINGS

Abortive or short-lived attempts to colonize the land now known as North Carolina started with Raleigh's expedition in 1584 and continued sporadically through most of the seventeenth century. Only in 1663, with King Charles II's gift to eight nobles and supporters of a grant in the New World from the 31st to the 36th parallel and from the Atlantic Ocean west to the South Seas, did settlement begin in North Carolina that was to prove permanent and finally lead to a single, consistent, and comprehensive government under the British monarchy. The Lords Proprietors, as those who received this land were called, had broad powers to develop a colony as they wished, powers equivalent to those exercised by the Bishop of Durham in England but with a few important limitations. They had to guarantee to settlers the same rights that Englishmen enjoyed at home, representation by freemen in lawmaking and liberty of conscience in religious matters.[11]

A restrictive economic policy imposed by the mother country and the Lords Proprietors' attempts to impose a medieval political and social order, however, resulted in resistance, even rebellion, by the early settlers and chaotic government for many years. Lack of a unified land policy created discord and discouraged large-scale immigration. For some years even before the 1663 gift to the Lords Proprietors, individual Virginians had been moving south into the Albemarle area of Carolina, buying land from the Indians, viewing the unexplored territory as merely an extension of the Virginia colony. Thus it was the Albemarle Sound area and the valleys of the rivers that emptied into it that were settled first, while only slowly did the tidal rivers south along the coast attract new settlers. But government for private ends did not encourage public prosperity. Disillusioned in their hopes for the gigantic land company they had started, the Proprietors' efforts languished, and their interest eventually narrowed to a small portion of their holdings, the development of the coast of what became South Carolina in 1710 when North Carolina was separated from it and assigned its own governor. In 1729 the heirs or assigns of all but one of the Lords Proprietors were willing to sell back their land to the then king, George II.[12]

THE GRANVILLE DISTRICT

The unwilling heir was John Carteret, more familiar under his later title, Earl Granville.[13] His refusal to relinquish his title to the land led to the necessity of laying off his one-eighth of the original land grant from the rest of the colony which the king now owned. In 1743 Earl Granville was awarded the entire upper half of North Carolina, an area of twenty-six thousand square miles from the Virginia line sixty miles to the south and from the Atlantic Ocean to an indefinite western boundary that was continually extended as the surveyors worked their way westward. As it happened, this was by far the most populated and prospering section of the colony, with much of the finest land. Land now in Durham County fell within this Granville District, so that it was from Granville's agents that settlers in this area acquired their land grants. Since immigration into North Carolina was primarily from the north and northeast, it was the northern sections of North Carolina that were taken up first; thus it was Earl Granville who reaped the first profits and not the royal colonial government. This situation put a strain on the fiscal operations of the colony, for the royal governor was responsible for administering the entire colony; Lord Granville's rights extended only to the land and its revenues, not to its governance. With the revenues collected from only the sparsely settled lower half, the governor was hard put to pay the costs of government. For the settlers, too, the Granville District caused problems. They had to deal with Lord Granville's often unscrupulous agents, who were eager to exploit the perquisites of their office for private gain. The settlers frequently brought charges of corruption and extortion against the agents (Francis Corbin particularly aroused their wrath), and on more than one occasion took action against them when their grievances went unheeded. The land office was not only corrupt; it was inefficient and kept few records of the entries and grants the inhabitants had paid for.[14]

The land grant situation was further complicated by large royal grants to Henry McCulloh, the Scots speculator and sometime colonial official under the British Board of Trade, which had responsibility for affairs in Carolina. One such grant for

1.2 million acres in 1737 was surveyed in twelve square tracts, of which five were located within the Granville District. One of the five included land that would become part of Durham County. It covered the headwaters of the Neuse River as far south as Ellerbee Creek and east into parts of present Wake and Granville counties. The confusion and contention over the respective land grants of Granville and McCulloh as well as the abuses of the Granville land grant office created financial and legal hardships for the first settlers.[15]

EXPLORATION OF THE BACKCOUNTRY

While eastern North Carolina was in the throes of uncoordinated, private colonization, the Piedmont, usually referred to then as the "backcountry," was being explored and exploited from Virginia. A few accounts of explorers and traders reveal the land and its native peoples as they were at the end of their long period of undisturbed possession. Already the ravages of disease and alcohol introduced by the Europeans had taken their toll, and the traditional tribal enmities and consequent warfare had been exacerbated by the pressures of advancing European settlement all along the eastern seaboard of America. Movement of Indians from the northeast and south exerted pressure, too, on the tribes in the Carolina Piedmont, causing them to relocate in turn. Originally large and mighty tribes had been reduced and demoralized through these causes, and remnants had regrouped for protection, risking a merging of traditions and loss of cultural integrity. The landscape, on the other hand, was almost unchanged since before even the Indians' arrival, though minor modifications had occurred. Animals seeking salt licks, water holes, and fording places, and Indians following their prey or traversing their blazed paths on the ridges had threaded the forest with trails which the explorers and traders made use of.

Primary among the trails was an ancient route known to the Europeans as the Indian Trading Path or the Occoneechi Trail. It led from present Augusta, Georgia, to the Catawba Indians near the North Carolina border, northeast across North Carolina (passing through what would become Durham County) to Fort Henry, an important trading post in Virginia now known as Petersburg, on up to Bermuda Hundred on the James River.[16] Its five hundred miles, roughly paralleling the route of Interstate 85 today, served many backcountry tribes in their intertribal traffic and their trade with the newcomers. Settlement near the Trading Path was a convenience for the Indians who served as guides to the Europeans or participated in the trading; consequently their villages were often to be found close to the Trading Path.

The first European account of the land that is now Durham County is in the travel record of a German physician, John Lederer. Perhaps acting as an agent for Virginia's Governor Berkeley, he came down the Trading Path in 1670 seeking out the Eno Indians. This was the tribe described in 1654 by another Virginia governor, Francis Yardley, as a "great nation" that had resisted most valiantly the advances of the Spanish.[17] Like the Shakori and Adshusheer Indians with whom they were later found allied, the Eno have been tentatively identified as members of the Eastern

Sioux.[18] It was in present Durham County that the Eno Indians lived in their village called Eno Town.

Lederer's description of the Oenochs, as he called them, begins with their land:

The Country here, by the industry of these Indians, is very open, and clear of wood. Their Town is built round a field, where in their Sports they exercise with so much labour and violence, and in so great numbers, that I have seen the ground wet with the sweat that dropped from their bodies: their chief Recreation is Slinging of Stones. They are of mean stature and courage, covetous and thievish, industrious to earn a peny; and therefore hire themselves to their neighbours, who employ them as Carryers or Porters. They plant abundance of Grain, reap three Crops in a Summer, and out of their Granary supply all the adjacent parts. These and the Mountain-Indians build not their houses of Bark, but of Watling and Plaister. In Summer, the heat of the weather makes them chuse to lie abroad in the night under thin arbours of wilde palm. Some houses they have of Reed and Bark; they build them generally round: to each house belongs a little hovel made like an oven, where they lay up their Corn and Mast, and keep it dry. They parch their Nuts and Acorns over the fire, to take away their rank Oyliness; which afterwards pressed, yeeld a milky liquor, and the Acorns an Amber-colour'd Oyl. In these, mingled together they dip their Cakes at great Entertainments, and so serve them up to their guests as an extraordinary dainty. Their Government is Democratick; and the Sentences of their old men are received as Laws, or rather Oracles, by them.[19]

The significant details to note here are their cleared fields for agricultural use and their reputation as porters and suppliers of grain for their neighbors. The statement that they reaped three crops in a year has been thought exaggeration or even fabrication to make a wonderful tale more wonderful. Actually it is confirmed by a John White drawing of the Indian town of Secoton at the end of the sixteenth century. The caption he wrote for his drawing explains the depicted plantings as "their rype corne," "their greene corne," and "corne newly sprong."[20] In other words they staggered their harvest to get fresh provisions over a longer period. He noted too that they built storage structures beside their wattle and daub houses to keep their corn and mast dry.

At the time of Lederer's meeting with the Eno Indians, the Occoneechi Indians were located on the Roanoke River approximately where the trading path crossed the Carolina-Virginia border.[21] The Occoneechi later moved southwest to the Eno River near present Hillsborough as a result of the Susquehanna Indians' incursions and the treachery of the Occoneechi's English allies after their joint victory over the intruders. A cursory mention of the Eno Indians, substantiating Lederer's location of their town, occurs in a letter of Abraham Wood to a friend in London in 1673.[22] Wood, an important trader at Fort Henry, sent out small parties to buy Indian trade goods. One of his agents, James Needham, was killed by an Occoneechi guide, Indian John, in 1673, but another in the party continued the expedition and returned safely with the furs and skins they had purchased. This party stopped at Eno Town both going and returning.

The fullest account of the Eno Indians and their confederates and neighbors is that of John Lawson, surveyor general of the Carolina colony. Lawson made himself acquainted with the land and natives of the backcountry more intimately than any other explorer. He had an eye, too, for the flora and fauna, for the climate and geography, and their implications for settlement. In 1709 he published in London the first history of North Carolina and a travel account of his exploration of the backcountry of North and South Carolina in 1701. The book includes as comprehensive a listing of animals, birds, reptiles, fish, trees, shrubs, and flowers as he could discover for himself or from informants; and his descriptions of the native tribes, particularly those of the Indians he knew best around Pamlico Sound where he lived at Bath—their customs, beliefs, even some vocabulary lists—make up an invaluable record of the whole colony as it existed at the beginning of the eighteenth century.

Of primary interest here is his passage through the area of present Orange and Durham counties. The excerpt that follows begins with Lawson and his party starting out on a winter day from the Haw River, where they had spent the night, for Occoneechi Town on the Eno River:

As soon as it was day, we set out for Achonechy-Town, it being, by Estimation, 20 Miles off, which, I believe, is pretty exact. We were got about half way, (meeting great Gangs of Turkies) when we saw, at a Distance, 30 loaded Horses, coming on the Road, with four or five Men, on other Jades, driving them. We charg'd our Piece, and went up to them: Enquiring, whence they came from? They told us, from *Virginia*. The leading Man's name was *Massey*, who was born about *Leeds* in *Yorkshire*. He ask'd, from whence we came? We told him. Then he ask'd again, Whether we wanted any thing that he had? telling us, we should be welcome to it. We accepted of Two Wheaten Biskets, and a little Ammunition. He advised us, by all means, to strike down the Country for *Ronoach*, and not think of *Virginia*, because of the *Sinnagers*, of whom they were afraid, tho' so well arm'd, and numerous. They persuaded us also, to call upon one *Enoe-Will*, as we went to *Adshusheer*, for that he would conduct us safe among the *English*, giving him the Character of a very faithful *Indian*, which we afterwards found true by Experience. The *Virginia*-Men asking our Opinion of the Country we were then in? we told them, it was a very pleasant one. They were all of the same Opinion, and affirm'd, That they had never seen 20 Miles of such extraordinary rich Land, lying all together, like that betwixt *Hau*-River and the *Achonechy* Town. Having taken our Leaves of each other, we set forward; and the Country, thro' which we pass'd, was so delightful, that it gave us a great deal of Satisfaction. About Three a Clock, we reach'd the Town, and the *Indians* presently brought us good fat Bear, and Venison, which was very acceptable at that time. Their Cabins were hung with a good sort of Tapestry, as fat Bear, and barbakued or dried Venison; no *Indians* having greater Plenty of Provisions than these. The Savages do, indeed, still possess the Flower of *Carolina*, the *English* enjoying only the Fag-End of that fine Country. We had not been in the Town 2 Hours, when *Enoe-*

Will came into the King's Cabin; which was our Quarters. We ask'd him, if he would conduct us to the *English*, and what he would have for his Pains; he answer'd, he would go along with us, and for what he was to have, he left that to our Discretion.

The next Morning, we set out, with Enoe-Will, towards Adshusheer, leaving the *Virginia* Path, and striking more to the Eastward, for *Ronoach.* Several *Indians* were in our Company belonging to *Will's* Nation, who are the *Shoccories*, mixt with the *Enoe-Indians*, and those of the Nation of *Adshusheer. Enoe-Will* is their chief Man, and rules as far as the Banks of *Reatkin.* It was a sad stony Way to *Adshusheer.* We went over a small River by *Achonechy*, and in this 14 Miles, through several other Streams, which empty themselves into the Branches of *Cape-Fair.* The stony Way made me quite lame; so that I was an Hour or two behind the rest; but honest *Will* would not leave me, but bid me welcome when we came to his House, feasting us with hot Bread, and Bear's-Oil; which is wholesome Food for Travellers. There runs a pretty Rivulet by this Town. Near the Plantation, I saw a prodigious overgrown Pine-Tree, having not seen any of that Sort of Timber for above 125 Miles. . . .

Our Guide and Landlord *Enoe-Will* was of the best and most agreeable Temper that I ever met with in an *Indian*, being always ready to serve the *English*, not out of Gain, but real Affection; which makes him apprehensive of being poison'd by some wicked *Indians*, and was therefore very earnest with me, to promise him to revenge his Death, if it should so happen. He brought some of his chief Men into his Cabin, and 2 of them having a Drum, and a Rattle, sung by us, as we lay in Bed, and struck up their Musick to serenade and welcome us to their Town. And tho' at last, we fell asleep, yet they continu'd their Consort till Morning. These *Indians* are fortify'd in, as the former, and are much addicted to a Sport they call *Chenco*, which is carry'd on with a Staff and a Bowl made of Stone, which they trundle upon a smooth Place, like a Bowling-Green, made for that Purpose, as I have mention'd before.[23]

The as yet undiscovered location of Adshusheer, fourteen miles from Achonechy (Occoneechi), within the bounds of present Durham County, is the most tantalizing fact in this narrative, which teems with significant information about the natural surroundings: the prevalence of wild turkey, bear, and venison; the beauty and bounty of the Hawfields; and the shift in terrain and tree cover just slightly to the east. Indian culture, too, is richly described: their food, music, beliefs, manner of living, and intertribal relations: the alliance of the Shakori, Adshusheer, and Eno, and their close cooperation with the Occoneechi. The character of Enoe-Will and his willingness to serve the English is an important portrait, for he is the first inhabitant of Durham County known by name. Will's estimate of Lawson as "very well affected to the Indians" adds a note of historical irony to the passage, for within a decade Lawson was to die at the hands of the Tuscarora Indians.

The Eno Indians represented only one of the numerous backcountry tribes whom Lawson met on his journey; and Lawson's is almost the last record of these tribes before their amalgamation with other groups north and south and their ultimate disappearance as distinct tribes from the historical record. The Occoneechi and Eno Indians were among the groups long thought to have been resettled for their protection and that of the host colony at Fort Christanna on the Meherrin River in Virginia in 1715 by the Virginia governor Spotswood, where they remained until the Indian school closed in 1723. Sometime after that, it was claimed, some of the Occoneechi took refuge with the Cayuga Indians in upstate New York. Others possibly went west or south.[24] The decline and dispersal of the Piedmont tribes in their final years was so complete that they faded out of historical records entirely. The Eno Indians are mentioned finally with other tribes in 1743 as having joined the Catawba Indians in South Carolina.[25] A detail in Lawson's account (their guide's errand to buy rum from the English) foreshadows the last glimpse of Will in the historical record. He is Shacco Will in William Byrd's "A Journey to the Land of Eden." There he is seventy-eight years old and trying to interest Byrd in a silver mine on the Eno River, with whose environs he seems intimately acquainted. Byrd paints a sad picture, perhaps an embellishment of his own, but consonant enough with the facts of the Indians' decline after their contact with the white man's culture. Byrd ended his interview with Will by giving him a bottle of rum with which "he made himself very happy and all the Familey very miserable by the horrible Noise he made all Night."[26]

ARCHAEOLOGY

Sketchy as the historical record is of the Indians who once frequented or inhabited Piedmont North Carolina, it has provided archaeologists with clues and facts of time and place around which to construct a more comprehensive understanding of the vanished peoples. Archaeological excavation throughout the Piedmont during the last fifty years has provided a chronology for the cultural sequence of Indian occupation.[27] It has identified Paleo-Indian (12,000–8,000 B.C.) Archaic Indian (8,000–500 B.C.), and Woodland Indian (500 B.C.–A.D. 1700) cultures, and within these broad time spans has differentiated even more finely early, middle, and late periods of both the Archaic and Woodland cultures.[28]

THE PALEO-INDIANS REMAIN LEAST-DEFINED because their population was small, dispersed, and simply organized; and the soils of the Southeast are not conducive to the preservation of floral and faunal remains. Few sites have been excavated and in those sites few remains discovered. That their economy was based on hunting and gathering is clear. Long-held suppositions that Paleo-Indians in the Piedmont hunted now-extinct Pleistocene mammals such as bison, mammoth, and mastodon and changed their habitation seasonally to follow their food supply have been brought into question recently. The same doubt exists in regard to the Archaic Indians. The absence of differentiation in their recovered tools suggests that their prey did not vary much in size from Paleo- to Archaic Indian times or within each of the periods; tools required for hunting megafauna might be supposed to differ from those used for other prey. Observation of the present Piedmont terrain and knowledge of its flora and fauna in prehistoric times have made evident that the rich alluvial floodplains have always supplied all the ingredients of the known Indian diet. Seasonal migration would have been therefore unnecessary.[29]

More detailed information is known about the Archaic Indians; they have left evidence of themselves everywhere. Expanding population and a more settled lifestyle, particularly in the Late Archaic period (2000–500 B.C.), are reflected in the number of sites and the length of their occupation. Though great diversity of culture and more complexity of social structure are evident, the economy of the Archaic Indians continued to be based on hunting and gathering.[30]

Only with the Woodland Indians (500 B.C. up to the beginning of European contact, about A.D. 1500) are significant changes observable: the introduction of pottery, of the bow for hunting, of agriculture to supplement hunting and gathering, and indications of more permanent villages. Signs of social differentiation are found in burial practices and patterns.[31]

Though still largely uninvestigated, Durham County's Indian heritage is exceedingly rich. Two factors are responsible: the Indian Trading Path or Occoneechi Trail, which completely bisected the county, attracting all manner of Indians over its course into the mid-eighteenth century, and the extensive system of watercourses in all parts of the county that provided the native peoples with hospitable terrain for their subsistence. The historical records make it clear that two Indian towns, Adshusheer and Eno Town, and the tribes they represent were located in the county; and concentrations of archaeological remains in many locations speak of other nameless Indians before them.

THE EURO-AMERICAN IMAGINATION has always been haunted by the alien Indian culture; it has prompted surface collecting of Indian relics probably since the first settlements and has found putative burials and shrines in every large collection of rocks. Local tradition dies hard; one such rock formation to the north of Mason Road in Durham County still retains its Indian status in the popular imagination despite its relegation to folklore by experts.[32] Authentic sites, however, have been identified all along the principal rivers and creeks, particularly where joined by lesser streams, through clusters of lithic and pottery remains found by both amateurs and experts.

Many sites along the Eno and Flat rivers within the bounds of the Falls of the Neuse Reservoir area, several along New Hope Creek, and still others on the Eno River east of Roxboro Road are among the most promising as yet unexcavated locations.[33] A number of surface and subsurface archaeological surveys have been done at specific sites in conjunction with road, bridge, or dam building. Unfortunately, examinations of this kind are necessarily limited in extent and time. Neither does this kind of survey usually produce sufficient evidence on which to build a detailed reconstruction of the particular Indian culture represented.[34]

Only one site in Durham County has been sufficiently tested to permit more than cursory description, and as yet that site possesses only potential value. It lies on Flat River within the Falls reservoir bounds and has been examined more than once within the last fifteen years. The first testing (1970) and consequent examination (1974) suggested to the archaeologists that it was the Adshusheer of Lawson's account.[35] The third examination (1975–76) led to its identification with Lederer's Eno Town.[36] A cluster of five related tracts where the old Oxford highway formerly crossed Flat River, the site has suffered by road- and bridge-building and long agricultural use.

Despite these disturbances, the cumulative work has found there evidence of intact subsurface deposits: middens, hearths, burials, structures, pits with "floral and faunal remains, carbonized wood for radiocarbon dating, ceramics, lithic artifacts and débitage, and trade items from European contact."[37] The stone remains show use of this site from Early Archaic through Late Historic times. The questions the site raises—the length of occupation by specific cultures, the variety of cultures represented, the role of the Eno Indians in the early historic period and their relation to the other Piedmont tribes, the nature of their architecture, food, tools, trade, and religious beliefs—archaeological digs may someday answer. The location of this site on the once heavily traveled Trading Path at the forefront of the cultural clash and exchange in the seventeenth and eighteenth centuries suggests the richness of its value as a key to the past. Additionally, and quite by chance, its present inclusion in the Stagville Historic District, where the state maintains a site for the teaching of plantation history, particularly its slave culture, gives it a unique significance and role to play in Durham County's future.[38]

What full-scale excavation of Eno Town would mean to the understanding of Durham County's own Indian cultures may be imagined from the results of a current excavation on the Eno River just outside Hillsborough, the site of Lawson's Occoneechi and the Eno Indians' nearest neighbor. Archaeology is a comparatively young discipline and its application in Piedmont North Carolina is younger still. The Archaeological Society of North Carolina was formed as recently as 1933; and the first extensive excavation of a Piedmont site only began in 1935. Professor Joffre L. Coe of the University of North Carolina was the trailblazer. He first located the site near Hillsborough and excavated it over the years 1938–41.[39]

This early work revealed a palisaded village of round houses, 22–25 feet in diameter, with shallow pits for fireplaces. One burial was found beneath the dirt floor of a house, the body in a flexed position, typical of the historic period, accompanied by a pot and pipe. Most of the projectile points were from the Late Woodland period, small and triangular, but a few older ones, stemmed and larger, were also found there. Tools such as bone awls, knives with stems, and shell beads were rare. The clay of the pottery was mixed with sand and some mica, and showed a stamped, cord-marked, or net-impressed decoration. One large amphora with a pointed bottom was the most striking object uncovered.[40]

What was not found there—English trade goods—posed a serious objection to the site's identification with Lawson's Occoneechi village. The current excavation has supplied an answer to the problem. It has uncovered, only a few hundred yards from the original excavation site, another site of rich promise.[41] Already several burials have yielded a variety of trade goods: scissors, bottles, metal and glass buttons, lead shot, a pewter porringer and pipe, and glass beads, among other things. Remains in the middens, hearth, and storage pits have revealed the diet of the inhabitants.[42] It consisted of white-tailed deer, box turtle, wild turkey, and miscellaneous birds. There was evidence that Indians of the site had consumed one bear and one pig. Corn had become an important staple in their diet, and grapes were their most common fruit. Work on this site has contributed immeasurably to the knowledge of proto- and prehistoric Piedmont cultures.

Between Lawson's 1701 journey and the arrival of the first settlers in the 1740s, Piedmont Carolina's history is a blank. Two documents bear on the subject, however: William Byrd's account of the North Carolina-Virginia boundary survey in 1728 and Edward Moseley's 1738 map of the Carolinas. Both reflect a terrain that until then had undergone only the slow modifications of nature's work, before it was to be changed swiftly, utterly, and irrevocably by a swelling flood of foreign intruders with a culture that had little or no respect for nature or Native Americans except as exploitable benefactions.

A land dispute between the colonies of North Carolina and Virginia had been occasioned by Charles II's second charter to the Lords Proprietors in 1665, which extended Carolina's northern boundary northward, well overlapping Virginia's original grant. Thereafter each colony claimed the land in the extension, and each granted land to settlers within the disputed area. Sporadic attempts throughout almost seven decades to resolve the difference had come to nothing. Finally a survey by a joint commission made up of North Carolinians and Virginians (including Byrd), an Indian guide, surveyors, and support staff undertook the project in 1728.[43] After reaching Hyco Creek in present Person County, the North Carolinians refused to go farther, claiming that they were fifty miles west of any settlement and that the survey could be continued when the need arose. In other words, no land had then been taken up west of present Warren County. Moseley's map confirms that situation geographically. It shows only one trail cutting across the backcountry, the Indian Trading Path, and in the vast interior no white habitation. To be sure, Byrd's purchase of 20,000 acres on the Dan River which he had coveted and bought at the time of the survey, and Governor George Burrington's 30,000-acre grant in the Hawfields are duly indicated. Of the coastal settlements, the Cape Fear area shows the farthest penetration inland, possibly one hundred to one hundred fifty miles, where Moseley indicates Welsh and Palatine settlements.[44]

Moseley estimated the Indian population in terms of its fighting men. The Cherokees were the most numerous with four thousand fighting men, but that number included two groups in South Carolina. The North Carolina Cherokees were deep in their mountain fastness. Others were negligible: the hostile Tuscaroras had begun an exodus after their defeat in 1712, and the friendly Tuscaroras had made peace with the government of North Carolina and been given a reservation in present Bertie County to which they had retired. Moseley estimated these Indians and the hostile Meherrin Indians to number three hundred fighting men in all and fast declining.

In his office as surveyor general of the colony, Moseley was in a position to know precisely where lands had been taken up and where settled. As a commissioner of the dividing line survey, he saw firsthand that the Indians were all but gone from the backcountry, having either retreated to the mountains or joined with larger groups to the north or south. The Europeans had what they wanted at last—the backcountry for the taking.

Moving In, 1740s–1771

2

FIRST LANDOWNERS

Aside from Lord Granville, who was in a class by himself, speculators with good connections, surveyors, and crown officials were the first owners of land in Carolina's backcountry. They took advantage of their positions to obtain grants as investments. Henry McCulloh had well over a million acres; Governor Burrington had a smaller grant in the Hawfields; Governor Gabriel Johnston had tracts on the Little and Eno rivers; William Churton, Lord Granville's surveyor, obtained land for himself in Orange County and obligingly allowed Francis Corbin, Granville's agent in the land office, to obtain land in his, Churton's, name as well, probably to cover up Corbin's crassness.[1] Churton, however, was different from the others in that he actually lived on his land in Orange County, held various town and county offices, and made his home in Hillsborough, the county seat he had laid out (in the time-honored tradition of surveyors) on his own land.[2]

Within present Durham County's bounds Henry McCulloh stood alone in this class. Aside from his hundred thousand acres at the headwaters of the Neuse, straddling present Person, Granville, Wake, and Durham counties, the rest of the area was available to the rank and file of settlers who wanted land to farm and live on. Between 1729, when all the Lords Proprietors but Granville had relinquished their rights to the Carolinas, and 1746, when the Granville land office opened in Edenton, grants to land in what became the Granville District were issued in the king's name; but the westering tide of settlers had not yet reached as far as present Durham County, and few crown grants have come to light for land in what is Durham County today.

While the first speculators were anticipating the rush to settle the backcountry, settlement from the east of North Carolina was proceeding slowly until the 1740s, when the pace quickened. As a result of the increase the legislature added new counties: Edgecombe and Northampton in 1741, Granville and Johnston in 1746, and Anson and Duplin in 1750. By 1751 Governor William Tryon reported to the British Board of Trade that "inhabitants flock in here daily, mostly from Pennsylvania and other parts of America, and some directly from Europe. They commonly seat themselves toward the West and have got near the mountains."[3]

As counties were added, their western boundaries were understood to extend to the western boundary of the colony. Thus land grants in present Durham County might have been made and registered in a variety of counties to the east depending on the date. The earliest known grants date from the late 1740s and comprised land primarily in the northwestern part of the county. The key factor in population growth seems to have been roads, important then as they are now to population distribution and commercial success.

Newcomers to the backcountry came by four routes. First was the small but continuous drift from the more eastern North Carolina counties. These settlers were generally English in origin, though there were Irish and Scotch-Irish among them. Not directly off any boat but descendants of earlier settlers in North Carolina or other English colonies, they moved short distances, looking always for fresh land within reach of the established limits, merely extending the ragged edge of the frontier by hacking out homesteads farther to the west. The Indian Trading Path brought a similar group of newcomers, usually from Virginia, but also from the middle colonies. Throughout the seventeenth century, a tide of Highland Scots in succeeding waves moved up the Cape Fear River, eventually populating ten counties of present North Carolina at the headwaters of that navigable stream. If any of these immigrants drifted as far north as present Durham County, theirs was a negligible and unnoticed influx.

In the 1740s and following, immigrants of two other origins began to arrive in the backcountry by the fourth route in such numbers that they seemed the overwhelming majority—Germans and Scotch-Irish. They had been arriving by boatloads for decades in the middle colonies of Pennsylvania, New Jersey, and Maryland, so that newcomers in the 1740s found these colonies so filled up that available land was either too expensive or situated on the western frontiers where hostile Indians were a menace to white settlers. Many chose instead to follow the Great Philadelphia Wagon Road, which ran from the city west through Lancaster and York counties, and then they turned southward into the Valley of Virginia where sometimes they established settlements on the Virginia frontier in Augusta and Rockbridge counties; but these, too, were well populated by the 1740s. Another consideration for those who had risked their lives to escape imposed religious conformity at home was that Virginia had an established church, the Church of England, which maintained a tighter hold over the lives of the Virginia settlers than did the same church in North Carolina, where land was abundant and cheap, liberty of conscience guaranteed, and the Indians were isolated in their mountain fastness. Many chose to push on to this new Eden. They turned eastward through the Staunton Gap and crossed the Dan River into North Carolina. At that point they dispersed, fanning out throughout the headwaters and valleys of the Yadkin, Catawba, and Haw rivers. A few even found their way to the headwaters of the Eno River in Orange County.[4]

Religious persecution had been the primary cause of the German Protestants' migration to America, but allied to this had been economic and political discrimination as well. The Scotch-Irish were people of Lowland Scottish or, less frequently, northern English origin, who had been encouraged to resettle in England's northern Ireland province of Ulster in the late 1600s. There they had been too successful for their own good, developing cattle and sheep production and linen and woolen manufacture. The English government and absentee English landlords had responded with economic restrictions and rack rents. Severe religious and civil proscriptions in the Test Act of 1704 further curtailed their rights. Ripe for the attractions of promotional literature and propaganda of ships' captains engaged in the profitable transportation of emigrants to the New World, the Scotch-Irish were easily persuaded to seek refuge and a better life in America.

Durham County's geographical location in relation to these migration routes determined who would settle there. Too far north to receive the Highland Scots who entered at Wilmington, and on the easternmost rim of the great sweep of backcountry available to the Scotch-Irish and Germans arriving by the Great Wagon Road, Durham County received almost entirely those moving west from the older North Carolina counties or traveling down the Indian Trading Path from Virginia— a predominantly English mix. Among the first to take up land in present Durham County were William Reeves, who received 400 acres where Ellerbee Creek runs into Neuse River (1746), Hugh Wood, who received 400 acres on Little River (1747), Patrick Boggan, 650 acres, and James Ray, 350 acres, on opposite sides of Little River (1749), William Strahorn [sic] 320 acres on the southwest side of Flat River (1749), and William Boggan 419 acres on Little River. John Patterson was established on New Hope Creek in the 1740s.[5] It is clear from a grant to Michael Synnott in 1752 that he had already taken up residence some time before that, for his grant is described as "including his mills."[6] All these grants were issued by either McCulloh or Granville and were located in then Granville County. Bladen County, too, was the designated site of some early grants of land actually in Durham County today—for example, grants to Joseph and William Barbee.[7] John Ellerby (Allaby), who received grants in Bladen County in an area that was later Anson County, may have first taken up land in present Durham, for Ellerbee Creek must take its name from the family.[8]

Almost nothing is known of these first settlers. The Pattersons are traditionally said to have come from Maryland.[9] If William Strahorn was a relative of the Gilbert Strayhorn (Strain) who took up land first in the Hawfields and then on New Hope Creek in the 1750s, he must have come from Northern Ireland via Pennsylvania.[10] The Rays and Woods were probably English. Neither Patrick nor William Boggan remained here long. A William Boggan from Chester, Pennsylvania, who took up land in Rowan County in the late 1750s, is probably the same William Boggan who was earlier in Orange. Patrick Boggan of Orange died in 1757. Possibly the Patrick Boggan of Anson County, the brother-in-law of Thomas Wade, founder of Wadesboro, was William's son, for the Boggans of Orange are also found closely associated with Wades in deeds and tax lists.[11]

Michael Synnott was an Englishman who first appears in records of Bertie

County in 1748. He was well established by 1752 on eastern Orange County land as the owner not only of mills on the Eno River but of a large tract, his homeplace, on the Trading Path, where he "kept tavern" and took in travelers. It was there that the Moravian Bishop Spangenberg and his party found accommodation on their way to survey the land that eventually became known as Wachovia. When one of the "brothers" in the group fell ill and could not continue, he and another "brother," who was left behind as nurse, remained at "Captain Sennet's" [sic] while Synnott himself proceeded west with the Moravians and the surveyor, William Churton. A few years later another party of Moravians coming to join the settlement at Wachovia camped by Tar River and were visited by Synnott's son "who lives here on Tar River; he recalled that some years ago Br. Horsefield stayed for some time with his father."[12]

Though these are the names in the surviving grants, undoubtedly many others of whom no record survives took up land about the same time. Evidence of this may be gathered from the names of chain carriers or adjacent landowners mentioned on surveys made in connection with grants. For example, William Boggan's survey of 1751 shows Benjamin Cole and John Dunagan [sic] as chain bearers.[13] Dunnagan is also named as an adjacent landowner. It is clear that these families, too, were already settled here. The 1750 Granville County tax list adds to the list of those known to have been established in the area at that early date. It names, for example, Thomas, Charles, and George Gibson, Henry Webb, junior and senior, John and Hugh Wood, William Bowling, Thomas and John Dunagan, Benjamin Cate, Francis Day, William Daniell, James Bowie, and William Forrester, all found a few years later in Orange County records.[14] The process of obtaining a land grant—first to record an entry for land, then to receive a warrant to survey it, next to have the survey made, and finally to get it issued and recorded in Granville's land office and in the county in which the grant lay at the time of issue—was lengthy and uncertain. Careless if not dishonest land agents often bungled the process or failed to record the results.

ORANGE COUNTY ESTABLISHED

With such large additions to the population of the backcountry in the late 1740s, governmental machinery was necessary both for the settlers' convenience and the colonial government's better control. In the spring of 1752 a bill to establish a new county formed from parts of Granville, Johnston, and Bladen counties was introduced in the legislature.[15] The county was to be named Orange and its congruent parish, Saint Matthew's—a vast area that included the present counties of Orange, Person, Caswell, Alamance, Chatham, and Durham, and parts of present Guilford, Randolph, Rockingham, and Wake. Its northern boundary was the Virginia line, its southern the same as that of the Granville District, and its western, still undetermined, extended as far as the colony's until 1753 when Rowan County was established to its west. The eastern boundary, described in the legislative act, ran from the Virginia line at Hyco Creek south to the Eno River, thence the south side of Eno downstream to where Horse Creek runs into the Neuse River, thence south to the southern boundary of the Granville District.[16] Orange County's June Court of 1752 made provision for surveying the eastern boundary.[17] As neither of the adjacent counties, Johnston and Granville, participated in the running of the line, it was not strictly a legal boundary. In any case it was soon altered. In 1761 the legislature reannexed a slice of Orange to Johnston County; the new line ran south from the southwest corner of Granville County.[18] Just nine years later Orange lost territory on three sides when Wake, Chatham, and Guilford counties were formed. By that act Orange's eastern boundary was established as what is now approximately the western boundary of Durham County's Oak Grove township.[19] From that time on, Orange County was whittled down periodically, but its eastern border remained unchanged for a hundred years. During that century the families whose names and fortunes were to become identified with the area that is now Durham County took possession of their lands and established religious, economic, and family ties with their neighbors. The county in which they had their homes and the local government that controlled their lives, to which they paid taxes, gave their labor for building and maintaining roads, served their time in militia and on juries, and looked to for justice, order, and protection, was Orange County. Based largely on laws promulgated in 1715 and only slightly modified from time to time, the county government as first established was to prevail almost unchanged up to the end of the Civil War.

Power was in the hands of the justices of the peace, who were nominated by the county representatives to the General Assembly (usually justices themselves) and appointed by the governor, at first colonial and later state. The justices were men of property, the most prosperous and respected in the county, and traditionally appended "esquire" to their names as a token of their office. Because they were appointed for life and were a self-perpetuating body, and because they appointed or nominated candidates for all local offices—sheriff, constables, overseers of the roads, and many others—they could run things very much to their own liking. The court they presided over had administrative and judicial functions touching every phase of settlers' lives.[20]

Sixteen men were appointed justices in the newly formed Orange County, and as far as can be determined not a single one was from the eastern section, now Durham County. Not until June 1757, when Robert Abercrombie was appointed to the court, was this area represented. Abercrombie was joined by Tyree Harris in 1763 and by Joseph Barbee in May 1764.[21] The reason for this lack of representation may have been the sparsely settled character of the area or simply the lack of political influence because of its distance from the county seat. Justices of the peace made up the commission responsible for initiating and building roads in the county. In the June and September courts of 1759, new roads were ordered to be built leading northeast and southeast from Hillsborough to Halifax County and Kinston, respectively, through eastern Orange County.[22] Until then the Indian Trading Path alone served traffic in eastern Orange. Maintenance of the roads, though ordered by the courts, was never sufficient to overcome the effects of the weather, and most were almost impassable in wet weather. There were of course farm paths used very locally, but these had no official status and were not under the court's jurisdiction.

The lack of roads was a serious drawback to development; farmers who wished to market surplus crops needed roads on which to transport them to markets in Virginia and Cross Creek (later Fayetteville).

The justices wielded power in the selection of important county officers. Foremost of these was the sheriff, whose job brought prestige and sufficient emolument to be coveted. He was responsible for elections and the collection of taxes. As his pay was a cut of the taxes, there was some expectation that he would perform his duty assiduously. He was also at the head of county law enforcement and the management of prisoners and the jail. Serving under him, besides a deputy or two, were the constables. Tyree Harris, appointed in 1766, was the only sheriff chosen from the eastern part of the county until the end of the century. Constables, who actually collected the taxes and did the police work, were chosen from every section of the county. Eastern Orange was assigned two constables in 1754: Thomas King for the Flat and Little River areas, and William Barbee "in the lower part of Enoe and parts adjacent."[23]

The register of deeds and the clerk of the court were equally desirable posts, for their incumbents, too, collected their salaries from the business they transacted: the recording of deeds, wills, marriages, estates, lawsuits, court minutes, and all the business of the court which the minutes detailed. The courthouse gang grew rich. Neither of these powerful offices was ever filled by a representative of eastern Orange, undoubtedly because it required constant attendance at the courthouse and thus residence in Hillsborough. The lawyers battened noticeably on this legal commerce. An early traveler in the backcountry remarked that the practice of law was "peculiarly lucrative and extremely oppressive."[24] Thus every courthouse town early attracted its bevy of lawyers to reap the profits.

Though the lucrative or influential jobs did not fall to eastern Orange inhabitants, the justices did appoint overseers for the existing roads in every part of the county. At the September 1753 term of court, John Dunnagan was appointed to oversee the Indian Trading Path from the Granville County line to Michael Synnott's. Mark Morgan, John Patterson, and William Rhodes oversaw different lengths of the Cape Fear Road in the same year.

At their first court in September 1752, the justices of Orange County laid the basis for carrying out their duties by levying a tax of one shilling on every taxable person. Age, infirmity, and indigence naturally excluded a portion of the population, though only a very small percentage of these made up the first settlers anywhere. White women, children, and Indians also were untaxed. Slaves of working age and free blacks of both sexes were taxed. At the October 1754 term of court, "Alexander Mebane, Esq. late Sheriff of this County came into Court and exhibited a list of Eleven hundred and thirteen Tythables on oath; which he had received and collected while he was Sheriff in the years 1752 and 1753."[25] This list was probably not very different from (if it is not indeed the same as) the first surviving tax list, customarily dated 1755, which contains the same number of taxables and supplies evidence of the settlers then in Orange County.[26] It substantiates Matthew Rowan's statement to the British Board of Trade in 1752: "In the year 1746 I was up in the Country that is now Anson, Orange and Rowan Countys, there was not then above one hundred fighting men; there is now at least three thousand for the most part Irish Protestants and Germans and dayley increasing."[27]

Naturally only a small number of the 1,113 "tythables" lived in what is now Durham County, but of families long associated with this county the Barbees, Beasleys, Bohannons, Bumpasses, Canadys, Cardens, Dennys, Dunnagans, Fowlers, Lawses, Morgans, Parkers, Pattersons, Rhodeses, Rogerses, Staggs, Wilkersons, and Woods were already here. The list records 130 blacks, of whom four families were free mulattoes: Gideon and Micager Bunch; Thomas Colens (senior and junior), John Colins, Samuel Colens and son, Charles; George, Majer, and Thomas Gibson; and Moses and Mary Ridley. The list included 724 separate households, of which only 9 percent owned slaves. Of the 64 slave-owning families none had more than ten slaves. In eastern Orange Mark Morgan had the most, six; Joseph Barbee had five; Duncan Bohannon and Henry Webb had four each; James Forester, Nathaniel Kimbrough, and Joseph Wade had three.[28]

As soon as Orange County court was established in one place, a county seat was laid out. Referred to as Orange Court House until it received its first name of Corbinton in 1754, the town was later called Childsburg (1759) and finally Hillsborough (1766), which it has remained.[29] The town grew from the first, attracting the people who needed court services and the lawyers to serve them; the inns and taverns to supply food, drink, and lodging; blacksmiths and saddlers (the service stations of that day); carpenters and brickmasons; merchants and mantuamakers; doctors and ministers—all interdependent for goods and services. On a frontier there was work for all. Those with skills or capital could prosper.

Among the administrative duties of the justices was the licensing of ferries, mills, and taverns. To run a tavern or inn required only a few spare rooms for use as a bar and bedrooms where travelers might sleep luxuriously alone or share the rooms and beds with as many as could be crowded into them. The earliest recorded taverns (as well as inns) in Orange County were on the Indian Trading Path. Michael Synnott and Patrick Boggan were granted licenses at the September court 1753, though both had probably been providing accommodations before the county was formed. Two travelers besides the Moravians recorded stopping at Boggan's: the Reverend Hugh McAden, who traveled from group to group of Presbyterians living in the backcountry, and John Saunders, an agent of a merchant in Suffolk, Virginia. Two miles after crossing Flat River with difficulty on 6 September 1754, the latter arrived at Boggan's "w[h]ere we put upp for the Night, and both ourselves and horses fared well, having good beds and clean sheets. . . . Got good tea and toast and butter in the morning for breakfast and the horses got good Corn and Oats." Then he continued on his way ten miles to Synnott's. When Patrick Boggan died in 1757, Henry Webb, whose eleven hundred acres adjoined the west bank of Flat River, supplied the hospitality on that leg of the Trading Path. At Webb's death in 1759 Thomas Stagg filled the breach at his dwelling—a site that soon came to be called Stagville. Judith Stagg continued the business a while after her husband's death.[30]

Besides licensing inns and taverns, the justices issued the prices that they could charge. For example, a hot meal with small beer cost eight pence, lodging for the night with a good bed and clean sheets cost four pence. A horse's stabling also cost four pence and his oats and corn one shilling per peck. His pasturage cost four pence for twenty-four hours. Various kinds of rum and rum mixtures were the most common drinks sold, but wines such as claret and Madeira were also served.[31] Not everyone with a tavern license had room to put up travelers. But hospitality was the rule in frontier America. Almost anywhere a traveler arrived at nightfall he could count on being sheltered and fed. What he received was as chancy for him as what he gave in return was for his hosts. If he had to lie on the floor next to the fire or share a bed with the children, it was as much as he could expect. The settlers were glad of any extra cash that came their way and of the contact a traveler brought them with the world outside their acreage. "In Pioneer countries," Isak Dinesen wrote, "hospitality is a necessity of life not to the travellers alone but to the settlers. A visitor is a friend, he brings news, good or bad, which is bread to the hungry minds in lonely places."[32]

FRENCH AND INDIAN WAR

The news that travelers would have brought in the 1750s would have been of rising fear on the frontiers of all the colonies. The conflict between England and France for possession of the new continent was reaching serious proportions. The main battles of the French and Indian War (1754–63) took place in Canada and the northern colonies, but a source of the conflict was the possession of the Ohio valley, and as the owner of that vast area of the fur trade, Virginia was brought into the fighting. Possession of all the colonies, however, hinged on the result.[33]

The Indians were enticed to attack by both sides, and the settlers on the frontiers of each English colony were victims of the strategy and suffered from the Indians' frustrations and changing sympathies. Colonial militia in the South were poorly trained and equipped; most of the fighting, therefore, was done by British regulars and some "provincials" hired for short terms of service and for particular objectives. The Orange County militia, however, was called out several times, and North Carolinians from all counties served in the provincial troops. Indians, too, Catawba and Cherokee, were enlisted, for if they had been successfully recruited by the French, the backcountry would have become a battlefield. Fortunately, the Catawbas remained loyal to their traditional friends, but the Cherokees caused the colonies grave concern and eventually warfare. At first they performed their role as mercenaries faithfully, but twice on returning to their homes from service in Virginia they plundered frontier settlements. Later in the war, when the conflict in the South had evolved into what was regionally known as the Cherokee War, the Overhills Cherokee Indians and some from the Middle settlements attacked the English. Settlers on the edge of the North Carolina frontier were repeatedly forced to flee to the palisaded Moravian town of Bethabara or Salisbury in Rowan County to escape scalping parties. Troops from England aided by colonial troops and some Indian scouts finally defeated the Cherokees and brought an end to the Cherokee War. The defeat of the French on the Saint Lawrence by the fall of Montreal in 1760 assured victory to the English and paved the way for possession of the continent.[34]

The impact of this on Orange Countians, aside from those who either served in the militia on the frontier or as provincials who served out of the colony, was the reappearance among them of the long-gone Indians. They needed no reminders that these others had lived there before them, but most settlers had probably never seen them. Blazed trails and cleared fields, occasional stone artifacts or European trade goods in the soil of their gardens, and the ubiquitous projectile points lying exposed and alien in their newly plowed fields made their daily presence felt. Now once again there was Indian traffic on the Trading Path as the Indians journeyed to and from Virginia as mercenaries.

Tension and uncertainty between colonists and Indians in their uneasy alliance during these years are reflected in the colonial records. At a provincial council meeting in May 1757, commissioners were appointed in Granville, Orange, Rowan, and Anson counties "to Provide necessaries for the Indians in Alliance with us on their March in the Service of the Public from their Several Nations to and from Virginia or any part of this Province." The commissioners were allowed "eight pence per Diem for each Indian that shall be found with necessaries."[35] The Orange County court had already in March 1757 made provision to reimburse citizens who found themselves entertaining Indians. Hospitality was not really a choice when a whole band suddenly turned up in the front yard. In June 1757 William Reed as deputy clerk of court reported claims amounting to two pounds one shilling for "dyating" fifty-six Catawba Indians and corn for eleven horses. In March 1758 he reported a claim for one hog delivered to Captain Bull and his company of Cherokee Indians on their journey to Virginia.

Not all relations with the Indians were harmonious. In the March 1757 court, Captain Snow, a friendly Catawba Indian, accused Michael Synnott of harboring a horse stolen from him a few years previously. The court heard the testimony and decided in the Indian's favor.[36] With the end of hostilities, however, the Catawba and Cherokee Indians retired to their respective lands, on the border of North and South Carolina or across the Appalachian mountains, and no longer troubled the Orange County settlers.

Instances occurred of isolated Indians, not part of tribal groups, living among the white settlers either as slaves or servants or even independent farmers. The will of John Alston, proved in 1760, contains evidence of such a case. John Alston, a member of the eastern Carolina Alston family, early settled in Orange, bringing his immediate family with him. To his son James he left a tract of land on Ellerbee Creek with the proviso that Indian Ben, who was living on it, "shall have the use of the place for four years paying an equal part of the expenses and dividing the profits equally with my son James Alston."[37] After leaving this single footprint in the historical trail of Durham County, Indian Ben, like the other natives of the land, is found no more.

WAR OF THE REGULATION

The French and Indian War was not the only disturbing event in the early years following Orange County's formation. While population increased steadily from the continued influx of new settlers, abuses of government caused growing unrest among them. In the 1760s a groundswell of discontent and frustration took form in the Sandy Creek Association, a leading faction of the Regulator Movement centered in what is now northeast Randolph County but was then in Orange. While not the only county involved in the movement, Orange County was the home of the most vehement protest and the center of violence.[38]

Historians have painted the Regulators in different hues all the way from dark, radical, ruffian malcontents to shining challengers of colonial exploitation. They have been portrayed as forerunners of the Revolutionary patriots; as participants in an east-west controversy in which the richer east wielded power unjustly over the more populous west; as alien immigrants, Scotch-Irish, Welsh, and German, against the English establishment; as the underdogs in a class struggle between the entrenched elite and the oppressed rank and file of farmers. In Orange County the Regulators' eleven broadsides and a petition to the governor exactly defined their grievances: inefficient, irresponsible, unjust, and dishonest local government and government representatives. They wanted the courthouse gang to be accountable to the people for the taxes they collected and the fees they charged; they wanted "regulation"—legally fixed, known charges and reins on corruption. High taxes (instituted to pay for the French and Indian War but never removed); a new tax to pay for the sumptuous governor's palace; the requirement that taxes and fees be paid in specie; exorbitant quitrents, contested land titles, and inaccurate surveys in the Granville District; extortion in fees by the local courthouse gang; and inequitably applied laws imposing militia, jury, road-building, and road-repair duties made up the litany of their complaints. Herman (Harmon) Husband, a pamphleteer, leader, and spokesman for the Regulators in Orange County, estimated that as much as one-twelfth of a man's yearly labor was consumed by these last duties. If they had been exacted evenly, fairly, and without regard to persons, no one would have had cause for complaint. The law specified that white males sixteen to sixty years of age were to perform these obligations, but those exempt became an ever larger group: political officeholders, men of wealth or social position, petty officials such as constables or road commissioners, schoolmasters, clergymen, attorneys, physicians, and operators of mills and ferries. This left a pool of mostly young, landless, uneducated, poor, or uninfluential farmers who could ill afford the expense of traveling to court, spending days there as witnesses or jurymen, or neglecting farmwork to drill at a muster or labor on the roads.[39]

Orange Countians were not alone in organizing against abuses in local government; Granville and Halifax county factions had already led the way, and Mecklenburg, Johnston, Cumberland, Rowan, and Anson counties also contained strong groups of agitators. Orange County's protest began in August 1766 when the Regulators called a meeting at Maddock's (later Hart's) mill near Hillsborough to discuss their grievances with local officials. Thomas Lloyd, an assemblyman for Orange, approved the meeting as reasonable. Edmund Fanning, the most hated of the courthouse gang, called the meeting an insurrection. The officials failed to appear. After a futile attempt to appeal to the legislature, the Regulators prepared a petition to Governor Tryon and his council in May 1768, signed by 474 inhabitants of the county, outlining the abuses they wanted corrected.[40]

That their charges were justified is clear. Tryon admitted in a private letter that sheriffs had embezzled more than half the money they had collected and were unable to account for their collections; he warned officials and lawyers against overcharges and ordered that the list of fees allowed by law be published. Increases in the Regulators' numbers and incidents of violence prompted Tryon to attend the September 1768 term of superior court in Hillsborough accompanied by militia. Edmund Fanning was tried and convicted for taking excessive fees but was fined only a paltry sum. Thirty-seven hundred Regulators were present at that term of court, for besides Fanning a few of their number were tried for riot, inciting to rebellion, and like charges growing out of disorders that had occurred earlier in Hillsborough. Although Tryon pardoned most of the accused, tensions continued to rise, for nothing had really changed. Fanning, prime target of the Regulators' hostility by virtue of his multiple offices—assemblyman, register of deeds, judge of the court, colonel in the militia—resigned as register of deeds as a result of his conviction, but was elected assemblyman from the borough of Hillsborough in the 1769 elections, the first representative of the newly established pocket borough.[41]

In any controversy, once factions have been polarized, distrust and suspicion grow, communication stops, rumors thrive, divisions widen, and reason flies away. Thus even the cool reasonableness of Ralph McNair, acting as intermediary for the Regulators in the initial stages of the protest, failed. He wrote to Herman Husband:

> I assure you my Dear Sir you will [find] Coll: Fanning quite different from what he has been represented and I'm certain he would find you very different from the accounts he has heard of you. The storys that have been told backwards and forwards are really amazing and I am now convinced that nothing but downright mistake has been the cause of all the late disturbances.[42]

When the hotheads of the movement carried it beyond the reach of reasonable men, McNair became a witness against them.

The spreading of Regulator support into new areas and the Hillsborough riots during the September 1770 term of superior court precipitated the final drama. The Regulators had entered the town in huge numbers and disrupted the court proceedings by attacking Fanning and hounding the judge, Richard Henderson, from the scene. Fanning's house was cut from its sills and its contents dragged into the street and destroyed. When the assembly met in New Bern in December and January 1770/71, the assemblymen worked to correct the laws, calm the protestors, and put down the insurrection. Tryon's council urged him to resort to military means to stop the disorder. The assembly passed the Johnston Riot Act, which allowed the trial of rioters in any county regardless of where the riot had taken place, and declared anyone an outlaw who had not responded to a court summons within sixty days. The Regulators' reaction was increased definace, refusal to pay their taxes, and threats of violence against lawyers and judges who attempted to convene court.[43]

In May 1771 Tryon and an army of militia troops marched from New Bern to confront the insurgents and force compliance with the laws. As Tryon's army neared the large number of Regulators that had massed beyond Great Alamance Creek, the Regulators asked for another hearing. Attempts at negotiation failed, and Tryon resorted to force. In short order the colonial troops overwhelmed the Regulators, superior in number but inferior in discipline and arms. Colonel Fanning, leading a detachment of Orange County militia comprising 137 men and a number of officers and drummers, must have felt a measure of satisfaction. Casualties on both sides were light: nine killed and sixty wounded on Tryon's side, nine killed and an unknown number wounded on the Regulators'. One prisoner, James Few, was summarily hanged in accordance with the new Riot Act, for Few had not answered a court charge within the prescribed time limit. The other prisoners were sent to Hillsborough while Governor Tryon and his army marched west to stamp out any remaining resistance, destroying the homes and farms of many Regulators as they went. Over six thousand Regulators accepted Tryon's offer of pardon in return for surrender of arms and submission to the laws of the land. Hundreds of others, disheartened or their property destroyed, eventually moved over the mountains to Tennessee.[44]

On his return to Hillsborough Tryon had the prisoners tried. Twelve were convicted of treason; Tryon pardoned six and hanged six. During the trials the army was encamped by the Few plantation just east of the town; adding to the woes of that family, the army horses and cattle were allowed into the planted fields to destroy the crops as retribution for James Few's involvement with the Regulators. The family shortly afterward moved to Georgia, where their fortunes improved, and in time the North Carolina legislature voted them compensation for damages.[45]

The effect of all this on eastern Orange was probably no more than a general anxiety and unrest. A letter from William Johnston, a merchant of Hillsborough and plantation- and store-owner in the Flat River area, to Richard Bennehan, his partner, suggests that a few inhabitants of the Flat River area were Regulator sympathizers, but there is no evidence of any group that might have rendered aid to the cause. Of the hundreds of signatures on the Regulator petition to Governor Tryon, not one can be clearly identified with the families of eastern Orange.[46] Several factors may explain the absence of Regulator support there. Predominantly English in origin and correspondingly Church of England in religious affiliation, they must have felt no inherent affinity with the Scotch-Irish, Welsh, and German dissenters who made up a large segment of the Regulators. Even if they shared the Regulators' indignation at abuses of power, they probably found civil disobedience both alarming and repugnant. In addition, distance from the centers of Regulator enthusiasm and leadership, compounded by poor roads, aggravated their separation. Lack of communication and access may have left the settlers in eastern Orange poorly informed of the course of events and powerless to participate in them.

A single event during the controversy brought the action within the present borders of Durham County: Tryon's march to Hillsborough. His army traversed a portion of southern Durham County, and—some historians believe—built a road as they went. The road has been identified by some with present Cornwallis Road.[47]

Arriving in Wake county with his troops, Tryon found that at a point about four miles south of the present city of Raleigh the existing road ended, and there was only a bridle path into Orange County. By his order an extension was cut directly over hill and dale to Hillsboro. It ran about four miles south of the city of Durham, and remains of it can still be seen. This road was called by Tryon the Ramsgate road. Tradition has identified it with a road taken by Lord Cornwallis, British general in the War of the Revolution, in his retreat after the battle of Guilford Court House; but the maps of the time show that Cornwallis did not march through the region now included in Durham county.[48]

Tryon's journal, order book, and correspondence supply ample documentation of his activities and those of his troops day by day, but little in them substantiates the building of a road through Durham County. Although one unit of his army was made up of "pioneers," a corps of engineers for building bridges or roads on a march, they undoubtedly had enough to do to repair an existing road, possibly the route from Hillsborough to the Johnston County line ordered to be laid out by the court justices in 1760. Unquestionably they had heavy work cutting trees to allow the bulky wagons and artillery pieces that Tryon brought with him to pass along the ill-maintained trails of the backcountry; his progress, however, was too rapid to accord with the supposition that he was actually building a road as he went. Tryon's records of his expedition give the details of camping sites, passwords, and events on the march. His army left Theophilus Hunter's lodge on 7 May 1771, and marched twelve miles to Jones's on Crabtree Creek in today's Morrisville area. Next day, 8 May, the army marched to John Booth's on New Hope Creek near the mouth of Third Fork Creek.[49] On that march Tryon stopped at Charles Abercrombie's store where he bought ribbon, writing paper, and twelve broad axes "for the pioneers."[50] Charles Abercrombie (John Booth's son-in-law), his father, and his brother Robert owned large tracts of land in eastern Orange County. Two of Charles's were located where the city of Durham now lies; on one of them, it has been assumed, his muster ground lay.[51] It does not seem possible, however, that his store was in this location as well, for Tryon's route across the county was farther south, possibly a route that more closely approximates the old stage road from Raleigh to Chapel Hill if not Cornwallis Road. Somewhere on this established artery must have stood Abercrombie's store.

Abercrombie's was not the only store in eastern Orange. William Johnston, the Scots merchant mentioned above, had come to America in 1760 and to Orange County no later than 1763, when he received a land grant from Lord Granville. Also in that year he petitioned the court for a slight alteration of the road that ran through his plantation on Little River—the Indian Trading Path. After first establishing a store in Hillsborough in partnership with James Thackston, he branched out in 1767 with another store on his plantation. This did well enough to justify its continuance. He negotiated with Richard Bennehan, a young man who worked in the Petersburg store of Edward Stabler, and persuaded him to assume the management of the Little River store and to take a one-third share of the business.[52] This store thrived under Bennehan's care and continued in that advantageous location until Johnston's death in 1785. If other stores existed in eastern Orange by 1771, they have not left any traces in the records.

One other effect of the Regulator movement on Orange County was its reduction by dismemberment. At the 1770/71 meeting of the legislature, bills were passed to create new counties out of the sections where Regulator strength was greatest as a way of dividing the disaffected citizenry into separate areas under tighter governmental control. Thus Guilford was created out of Orange's western side, Wake out of the eastern (to separate the Regulator forces in Johnston from those in Orange), and Chatham out of the southern.[53] Petitions from the inhabitants of these areas for the creation of new counties in order to relieve them of long and expensive journeys to courts or musters gave the lawmakers sufficient excuse for an action that well suited their own ulterior purposes.[54] The creation of these counties also resulted in greater representation of the backcountry in the legislative body, another political gesture toward conciliation. Though the Regulator movement itself was quashed, some of its principles became permanently incorporated in the government of North Carolina and, more important, in the minds of the inhabitants.

The American Revolution

3

OT ON THE HEELS OF THE REGULATOR MOVEMENT came the American Revolution, actually a civil war. Many of those who had opposed the Regulators now found themselves in the position of fomenting opposition to official governmental policy, supporting resistance, and advocating rebellion. The shoe was on the other foot. Again economic stringencies were at the root of the problem, but this time it was planters, merchants, and professional men who were feeling the pinch. For all, there was as well a sense of personal injury that comes from restraints externally imposed and from abridgment of freedom which reflective men saw as abuse of power.

American colonial history discloses a tendency from the earliest times toward separation from the mother country. The makeup of the population—with so large a proportion of religious and political dissenters who strongly objected to church or state interference with their lives—made it inevitable.[1] Since economic issues had also been primary among the propelling forces for their emigration, they could certainly be counted on to resist threats to their economic independence and well-being. The Sons of Liberty, who forced the repeal of the Stamp Act, and the Regulators, who achieved a measure of governmental reform, had demonstrated this sensitivity to infringement of their liberty. It was in character, therefore, for the colonial leaders to react with indignation and resistance when, after decades of neglect during which the colonies had gone their own way, developing their own policies and procedures, the British government began to enforce trade regulations and to use taxation of the colonies to remedy ills at home. The Tea Act of 1773 (which gave a monopoly on the tea trade in the colonies to the East India Company) was only one of a series of restrictive measures imposed on the colonies. The Stamp Act of 1765 and the Townshend Act of 1767, which imposed revenue taxes on certain items, had already raised colonial ire to the boiling point so that cumulatively they spurred colonial cooperation and alienation from England.[2] Once embarked on a course of concerted resistance, the colonies were quickly carried on the tide to full rebellion. First committees of correspondence were set up to establish intercolonial communication, and then provincial congresses were called to deliberate action. These extra-legal meetings were the first serious step to open defiance, for they replaced the colonial assemblies that the royal governors failed to call or dismissed.

But there was no unanimity of opinion in any colony, and lines were never clearly or permanently drawn between the political partisans, Whig or Tory, or the warring factions, patriot or loyalist.[3] Complex factors governed preference: attachment or animosity to England; prudence or impetuosity of character; familial, religious, and social affiliations; economic expedience; and political ideology; and these were often conflicting. North Carolina was composed of many different groups whose position in the confrontation could not be predicted: the inhabitants of the backcountry with a traditional distrust of the eastern elite's influence in the colonial government; the ex-Regulators, who had paid a price already for civil disobedience; the German and Scotch-Irish enclaves, whose religion and culture separated them from the coastal English; Moravians and Quakers, whose pacifistic tenets prevented their participation in armed confrontation; Highlanders, who kept to themselves and had, like the Regulators, taken an oath of allegiance to the Crown; blacks and Indians, who had no stake in either outcome and might easily be recruited by the British.[4] The leaders of the provincial congress must have eyed this conglomeration of peoples with some dismay. How would they rally sufficient support from so varied a population to offer resistance on the vast scale required?

Because of the wide spectrum of political beliefs, the leaders in every colony had to grope their way toward consensus. But practice in self-government in the colonies had strengthened independence of mind and action. The French and Indian War had already given the colonies a taste of continental cooperation and a sense of common purpose.[5] In the Carolinas the Regulator controversies had made the inhabitants aware of political issues; the leaders of the opposing factions had been forced to articulate beliefs and principles concerning government and the governed. The colonial assembly had begun to reflect more accurately the people it represented, and its leadership was learning how to channel factional loyalties into support of general objectives. In a word, Americans were becoming politically savvy. This was the situation at the beginning of the American Revolution before any shots had been fired.

It was England's actions that provided the mortar to bind the disparate groups. To retaliate for the Boston Tea Party, Parliament imposed the Coercive Acts—a collection of laws that strengthened parliamentary control over the government of Massachusetts—and by substituting General Gage as governor of the colony as well as commander-in-chief of British forces in America, imposed actual military rule.[6] When British troops finally attacked the very citizens they were there to protect, and more troops from England were sent to control the citizens of other British colonies, the bond was complete. In North Carolina anti-British sentiment was further spread by the Privy Council's disallowance of the establishment of Queen's Museum, a Presbyterian college in Mecklenburg County, and of the bill allowing court attachment of property of defaulting debtors living in England.[7] Despite their differences, colonists found there were common causes around which all could rally. The opening shots at Lexington and Concord were only the sparks applied to a continental tinderbox. War quickly followed.

Although no major battles were fought on Orange County soil, the inhabitants suffered the usual ills of war: shortages of money, manpower, food, and supplies of all kinds, and the immeasurable toll of worry and heartache. The Loyalists, in addition, suffered confiscation of their property and became refugees in their own country or fled to foreign lands. The soldiers on both sides endured physical hardship, disease, disability, or death. Though spared the carnage of major battles, Orange Countians experienced a series of events that swept them very much into the current of the conflict, for Hillsborough became both a military and political center. The first event that brought Orange County directly into the action was the meeting in Hillsborough of the Third Provincial Congress in 1775. There, too, the General Assembly met in 1778, 1780, and 1782. There Baron DeKalb and his army camped and foraged in 1780, soon followed by General Gates both before and after the disastrous defeat at Camden. There came General Greene to relieve Gates, and there Governor John Rutledge of South Carolina carried on his government in exile. In 1781 General Charles Cornwallis and his army occupied the town for five days, the soldiers paving the intersection of Churton and King streets by day but pillaging by night in the surrounding countryside. Smallpox visited the town that year, no doubt brought by the soldiers. That year and the next brought Colonel David Fanning's raids, including his daring capture of Governor Burke with some of his council. Hart's mill, having been taken over by Cornwallis's forces, was raided by Captain Joseph Graham. This skirmish, another with Tarleton's forces at Clapp's mill on Alamance Creek, the Battle of Lindley's Mill, and Pyle's Hacking Match brought actual fighting into the county. None of it took place in eastern Orange, but the inhabitants could not have known from day to day when a battle might occur in their area. From 1782 to 1784 Hillsborough was the capital of the infant state, at the heart of all the frenetic activity of a government at war. There met the Committee of Safety, and later the Board of War, and late in the war industries were set up there for shoe, paper, and arms manufacture to supply critical needs.[8]

When the delegates to the Third Provincial Congress trooped into the little town of Hillsborough in 1775, they were actively setting out to win the support of the backcountry to the Whig cause. Congress's meeting there emphasized the importance of the region's participation to the Whig cause. Delegations were appointed to meet with the Moravians, former Regulators, and Highlanders with the hope of winning their support, or at the very least, nonintervention. With the first two groups they reported success, though with the Regulators it was only partial, but, as the aftermath showed, they failed completely with the Highlanders. Another result of this Congress was the decision to raise and equip two regiments of provincial troops and six battalions of Minutemen, a kind of home guard, and, to finance this, to print 50,000 pounds in bills of credit. A provincial council was created to carry on the government when the Congress was not in session.[9]

The prelude to the final break with England came at the Provincial Congress in Halifax in April 1776. The representatives instructed the North Carolina delegates to the Continental Congress to concur in a vote for independence, and a committee was asked to draft a temporary constitution for an independent state. No agreement was reached on a document until the following Provincial Congress in November, again at Halifax. The election of delegates to this meeting became a near riot in Orange County because of the crowds who turned out to vote and their impassioned opinions about the constitution to be written. The first slate of delegates elected was rejected because of irregularities in the election, and a new election was held. The second group of delegates missed all the debate on the state constitution, but they did arrive in time to vote for the adoption of the Bill of Rights and the constitution the following day. Of the five Orange County delegates, one man was elected both times: John Cabe, who owned large tracts of land now in Durham County.[10] Orange County's delegates were instructed to attempt to incorporate certain principles in the document, some of them radical for the time: that power was entirely derived from the people, that there should be no established church and complete freedom of religion, and that no officeholder should be permitted to hold a position in more than one branch of the government. These they achieved, but a final provision, that the new constitution be ratified by the people, failed. The constitution that the delegates adopted tended toward democracy in theory, but in actuality established a landed oligarchy. Throughout, however, it reflected the lessons North Carolina had learned under the royal governors. For all its defects it was to serve the state for sixty years.[11]

The comings and goings of armies and government officials disrupted the accustomed isolation of Orange County during the next six years. At first the traffic on the two or three roads leading to Hillsborough through the eastern section must have been a welcome novelty, but it soon came to herald a most unwelcome and increasing burden. With many men away in the army, keeping the farm going at home and producing enough food to feed the family became a daily task for each inhabitant. When in addition came the burden of feeding masses of troops and the swollen population of Hillsborough, many families must have found themselves frequently close to the sharp edge of hunger. One historian has written of the militia's marches and countermarches that they "had stripped the land as clean as would a plague of locusts."[12] Thomas Burke, a victim of the practice, wrote to General Gates in July 1780, "[I] find it absolutely necessary to stay some time to prevent what remains of my property from falling prey to the wasteful ravages of the Troops in and about this neighborhood. No provision has been made for their reception, and they arrived in circumstances of great distress for want of every species of provision and forage."[13] It is not surprising, therefore, that Cornwallis, when he returned there later the next year after the Battle of Guilford Courthouse, could not remain long, for the countryside had been stripped bare of supplies. He was forced to move on to a less thoroughly plundered place. His orders, always gentlemanly and gracious in tone, clearly convey what must have been the common behavior of visiting troops whether royal or patriot: "Lord Cornwallis is very sorry to be again obliged to call the attention of the officers of the Army to the repeated orders against plundering."[14] From his headquarters in Hillsborough on 22 February came a similar order: "It is with great concern that Lord Cornwallis hears every day reports of the soldiers being taken by the enemy, in consequence of their straggling out of camp in search of whiskey."[15] Another fragment of evidence comes from the son of a Revolutionary soldier, Thomas Ross, who related that his father remembered how Cornwallis's soldiers stole the horses from the millboys at the Abercrombie mill on the Eno.[16]

Besides this drain on their supplies, the residents of Orange County felt the war's effects in other ways. New laws, new duties, and new taxes affected them. The preparations for war involved the raising of provincial troops, minutemen, and militia; training of troops with men of all ages made constant use of the muster grounds. Until 1774 tax collection districts corresponded to militia districts and were known by the captains' names. In that year, however, General Butler of the Hillsborough Military District divided the county into sixteen newly drawn districts with their own names. The land now in Durham County became Saint Mary's and Saint Mark's districts, corresponding roughly to the northern and southern sections of the present county.[17] In 1778 Charles Abercrombie was appointed to list the property for taxation in the districts of Saint Mary and Saint Mark.[18] In 1777 the new state levied a property tax of one-half penny on a pound evaluation or twenty-one cents on a hundred dollars evaluation. This tax increased steadily through the war years until by 1781 it had reached twenty dollars on every one hundred dollars evaluation, reflecting the runaway inflation and the devalued currency. The phrase "not worth a continental" was coined at that time, "continental" referring to the paper money issued by the Continental Congress in Philadelphia.[19]

At the August 1777 term of Orange County court, the justices issued notices to all merchants trading with Great Britain or their factors, agents, or storekeepers that they must take an oath of allegiance to the new state. Anyone who refused was required to leave the state within sixty days or go to jail.[20] Prisoners in the county jail for any reason were encouraged to join the Continental Line to gain their freedom. Even loyalists could change their minds and be released to enlist.[21] In 1778 the oath was required of all males sixteen years old and up. William Cain was appointed to administer it in Saint Mary's District, and John Tapley Patterson in Saint Mark's.[22] Many Orange Countians proved to be loyalists, but of those identified none lived in eastern Orange, though some may have owned land there. For example, James Monro, a Scots merchant in Hillsborough, owned a large tract on the Eno River. Monro, however, later changed his mind and returned to Orange County.[23]

All through the war loyalists were leaving and returning to North Carolina and Orange County, trying to save their property from confiscation. Some, however, emigrated to England, some to Nova Scotia, New Brunswick, and Ontario in Canada, and some to the Bahamas, West Indies, or even East Florida.[24] Many Quakers, too, found it expedient to leave. They moved westward not only because of the penalty they paid for pacifism and the distress they endured during both the Regulator and Revolution crises, but also because of chattel slavery, to which they were vehemently opposed, and which promised to remain an integral part of life in North Carolina.[25] The removal of neither the loyalists nor the Quakers, however, had much effect on eastern Orange, for few if any of them had lived there; its residents had always been and continued to be predominantly in the mainstream of North Carolina's evolving culture. Those who refused to fight for whatever reason were required to pay a threefold tax. In eastern Orange, John Tapley Patterson, John Redman, and John Scarlett paid such a tax.[26]

The position of blacks during the Revolution was ambiguous. Free blacks in North Carolina, for the most part mulattoes, had participated on almost equal terms with whites in the civic life of the colony. They could own land and vote and had been expected to serve in the militia and on the road maintenance crews just as had white men. Consequently, numbers of free blacks bore arms in the Patriot cause. A tally of the army in 1778 showed fifty-eight blacks from North Carolina in the Continental Line.[27] Although these soldiers have not been identified, possibly among them were free blacks from eastern Orange County.

For enslaved blacks, the Revolution offered unparalleled hope and opportunity for freedom. When it became known that any slave joining the British forces would gain his freedom, slaveowners knew they would have to double their vigilance to hang on to their human property. Richard Bennehan, a merchant in eastern Orange, on his departure with the militia wrote to his storekeeper, "It is said negroes have some thoughts of freedom. Pray make Scrub sleep in the house every night and that the overseer keep in Tom."[28]

In addition, the Patriots knew that the British would encourage slave revolts, and that the slaves were quite capable themselves of conspiring violently against their masters to achieve liberation. A third threat to slaveholders and aid to bondsmen was the moral stand adopted by the Quakers against slaveholding: the Yearly Meeting directed its members to free their slaves. Many thousands of slaves did escape to the British, and some slave insurrections were plotted, though none was ultimately successful. Many Quakers did free their slaves, contrary to North Carolina law, which reserved that power to the county courts. As a result, some of the freed slaves were captured and returned to slavery.[29] These internal conflicts compounded the chaotic conditions of the war years.

Though little personal testimony has survived of the war experience of civilians, a great deal is known about that of the military. For example, a letter of Richard Bennehan's expresses the urgency and uncertainty of the unseasoned recruit about to set forth to his first battle. He wrote in February 1776 from Hillsborough to James Martin, the clerk at the Little River store:

> We are this moment going to march & we thought by way of Wake Court House, but when under arms, our Rout was altered & we are going directly among the Scotch men who are embodied in Cumberland County near X Creek [Cross Creek, now Fayetteville] & it is said to the am't of ab't 3,000 men under good officers & regulations.[30]

Bennehan was among the troops led by James Thackston, colonel of the Hillsborough District. Their original orders to join battle with a contingent of loyalists marching toward Wilmington were changed, and they were redirected to Cross Creek where other loyalists were ordered to gather round the Royal standard. Thackston's objective was to prevent the town's becoming a refuge for the first group when they discovered their way to the coast blocked. Bennehan missed fighting in the famous Battle of Moore's Creek Bridge by the change in orders. He expected a hard battle at Cross Creek, however, from its loyalist defenders, and had made provision for his effects in the event of his death. His letter continued:

> My friend James, should anything prevent my ever returning, my will and all my cash, papers, etc. are in my Little Blue Trunk standing on the chest of drawers. Mr. Johnston, who is now in his bed very sick, begs your care and attention to his mill dam and everything about his plantation.[31]

The raising of six continental regiments, provided for by the provincial Congress of April 1776, was needed because militiamen could not be counted on for long terms of service (the usual militia tour was three months), and militiamen lacked the training and discipline of regular troops.[32] Continental enlistments were for two and a half years. Each regiment was to have 728 men divided into eight companies, each company with a "captain, two lieutenants, one ensign, four sergeants, four corporals, two drummers or fifers, and seventy-six privates." Each man's pay (one shilling a day for provisions, an advance of three pounds, and an enlistment bounty of forty shillings) was to be docked ten shillings to cover the cost of his uniform. What his rations should be was also stipulated by the Congress, but reality must quickly have altered regulations.[33] As inflation grew rampant and supplies quickly dwindled, the army was lucky to have anything at all. Throughout the war shoes were particularly hard to come by and quickly worn out, hence the army's takeover of a shoe factory in Hillsborough and the exemption of cobblers from the military draft to keep them at work. The Provincial Congress established a quota of supplies that each county was to furnish the troops. Orange County was to provide "73 hats, 306 yards of linen, 146 yards of wool, 146 pairs of shoes, and 146 pairs of stockings."[34]

Although militiamen were considered inferior fighters to the Continental troops, they took part in every engagement and often fought valiantly. The Third Provincial Congress in Hillsborough reorganized the militia when they set up six military districts in the colony. Each county was to form five divisions from its population of men aged sixteen to sixty—four of regular companies of no fewer than fifty men, and a fifth of aged or infirm men. Instead of the old system of mustering once or twice a year, they were to muster every month and to be fined ten shillings for absences. The rank and file were to receive two shillings and sixpence a day in actual service, an amount later raised to eight shillings. The rank and file and noncommissioned officers were also to receive a $20 bounty at the time of enlistment.[35]

No list has been compiled of soldiers in the Revolution from the area that became Durham County. Though an incomplete list has been attempted for Orange, it is not possible to know in every instance which men actually lived in eastern Orange. A tentative list would include the following: Robert Ashly, Richard Bennehan, Jacob Bledsoe, Lewis Bledsoe, George Carrington, James Carrington, Benjamin Carroll, John Daniel, Lewis Deshong, William Dilliard, James Dollar, Jonathan Dollar, William Dollar, Hardeman Duke, William Duke, Edward Ferrell, Davis Gresham, John Harris, Benjamin Herndon, James Herndon, Zack Herndon, Isaac Hicks, William Hodges, William Hopkins, George Horner, Thomas Horner, Moses Leathers, John McFarling, Thomas Marcum, William Ray, Jesse Rigsbee, John Rhodes, William

Rhodes, Elisha Roberts, Thomas Ross, Thomas Scarlett, John Sherron, Lazarus Tilley, and John Woods.[36]

Veterans who applied for pensions from the United States government were required to prove their service by discharges, or, lacking such, by a detailed statement of their participation. If their widows or children applied in their names, much genealogical information also got into their records. A brief summary of the typical service of the Orange County soldier may be found in the narratives of four young men of eastern Orange. Moses Leathers, who lived in the Eno River area, enlisted in the Sixth Regiment of the Continental Line under Captain Archibald Lytle and Colonel Gideon Lamb. Leathers fought at the battles of Brandywine and Germantown. When Leathers's two-and-a-half-year term of service was up, he was discharged at King's Ferry on the North River in New York and made his way home. He next volunteered in the militia and fought in the disastrous Battle of Camden under General Gates.[37] Like Leathers, William and Hardeman Duke of the Flat River area enlisted in the Continental Line under Captain Lytle and were marched to Wilmington and thence to Charleston, where William well remembered bathing in the sea, no doubt a novelty to a backcountry youth. After a furlough at home, both went to Valley Forge with Washington, where they were inoculated against smallpox. Convalescence from the mild case of the disease that inoculation produced prevented their leaving Valley Forge with Washington, but they later rejoined his army in New York and fought in the Battle of White Plains. They too were discharged on the North River in 1778.[38]

George Carrington had a somewhat different series of experiences. A native of the Flat River area, he enlisted as a substitute for Solomon Mangum under his brother Captain James Carrington and was put in charge of a battle wagon. The driver was Elisha Roberts, a boy whom George's father, John Carrington, had raised. While the wagons and wagoners remained safely behind the lines, James Carrington and his soldiers fought in the Battle of Stono Ferry. George's next tour of duty, again with his brother James, found him at the siege of Charleston, where he was taken prisoner. He was soon paroled, returned home, and shortly after volunteered to fight the Tories in a light horse company under Captain John McFarling (McFarland), a friend from his childhood in the Flat River area. They marched to the Haw River and patrolled its banks looking for Tories. They fought under Colonel Robert Mebane in the Battle of Lindley's Mill against four or five hundred Tories, where in George Carrington's words, "we had a hard fight & gave them a good beating though our number was much smaller than theirs." Recruited by McFarling yet again, they had ridden only as far as William Cain's when the company was disbanded as too few to fight the Tories.[39] As George Carrington's account makes clear, anyone who wished not to fight could hire a substitute to go in his stead. Thomas Ross was Fred Geer's substitute and fought at the siege of Savannah. Richard Bennehan, too, later in the war hired Ezekiel Kinchey to serve for him in the "state legion."[40]

Independence was gained at great cost. The Revolutionary War left in its wake economic, physical, and emotional exhaustion. The very nature of the conflict—a civil war—had increased the last component significantly. With neighbor against neighbor, even brother against brother, the intricate social fabric was violently torn apart. The loyalists either were forced to leave their homes and property to begin lives all over again in a strange place or stayed and took the consequences, often personal attack and the destruction of property by their own militiamen. Hundreds of refugees were set adrift by the armies of the Americans or British as they alternated possession of the terrain. On all sides families lost fathers, sons, or brothers who had been their sole economic support. Hundreds of thousands of acres changed ownership, and new settlers came to replace those who left. The heirs of Lord Granville were the heaviest losers of land. They lost the entire Granville District, almost half of North Carolina, when it was confiscated by the state. Later long-drawn-out lawsuits to gain compensation proved futile. British merchants, too, lost heavily, for American debts were for the most part uncollectable as states refused to pay. Ultimately merchants had to seek compensation from the British government. Like white Americans, thousands of slaves gained freedom, and free Americans of both races, now reborn as citizens of a new nation, were gaining a sense of national pride in a fusing of interests with other ex-colonists in a novel and common endeavor—building a nation.

Eighteenth-Century Orange County, 1752–1800

4

LAYING THE FOUNDATIONS

In the meantime the settlers had been laying the foundations of a society that was beginning to assume its own character and strength. They had already built homesteads, mills, and churches, and through their institutions, traditions, and inter-marriages had begun to develop a social structure that survives to this day.

In 1761 Governor Dobbs stated that immigration into the colony had completely ceased during the previous seven years, an effect of the French and Indian and Cherokee wars. What growth had occurred, and it was considerable, was due, he said, to natural increase.[1] Though immigration had undoubtedly been much reduced, Dobbs's view of the matter was not entirely accurate. Not a few land grants were issued by Henry McCulloh in the years 1758, 1759, and 1760, of which the largest number were around the headwaters of the Neuse—undoubtedly because this, his most eastern tract, was well away from the area of Indian attacks.[2] Population figures for Orange County in 1766, moreover, show a large increase over the figures from the first tax list of the county: whites numbered 3,324, blacks and mulattoes, 649.[3] Astonishment at the growth of population in the Carolina backcountry was expressed as far away as Connecticut, where a newspaper reported in 1767, "There is scarce any history . . . which affords an account of such rapid and sudden increase of inhabitants in a back frontier country, as that of North Carolina. To justify the truth of this observation, we need only to inform our readers, that twenty years ago there were not twenty taxable persons within the above mentioned County of Orange; in which there are now four thousand taxables."[4] Orange County was the most populous in the colony. Another impediment to immigration had been the closing of Lord Granville's land office between 1766 and 1773.[5] Though settlers were unable to get title to Granville lands during those years, they nevertheless continued to arrive and settle, buying land from earlier grantees or waiting to obtain title when the office reopened. When the Revolution began and the new state took over the granting of land in the former royal colony as well as in the confiscated Granville District, a tremendous backlog of land transactions to record and a huge number of new entries to grant resulted in the state's doing quite literally a land-office business.

Who were the newcomers to eastern Orange and whence had they come? From histories of some of the families, from the names they bore, and from public documents it seems clear that the largest number of them came from Virginia, where they had been established a generation or more, though some few did come from colonies farther north. By tradition the Bowlings, Cains, Hopkinses, and Suitts are said to have come from Maryland; the Allens, Cabes (McCabes), and Umsteads from Pennsylvania. The Umsteads, Foglemans, and Links were some of very few originally German families to settle in eastern Orange, although large numbers settled in the Haw River valley and westward on the land now found in Rowan, Davidson, Mecklenburg, and Cabarrus counties. From over the border in Halifax County, Virginia, came the Carringtons, Kennons, Links, and Lipscombs, while from Goochland Parish came the Bilboas (originally a Huguenot family), Couches, Dukes, Harrises, Holloways, Trices, Parrishes, and Masseys. From Bristol Parish came the Dezerns (another Huguenot family), Morelands, and Vaughans. From Middlesex County came the Barbees (who had arrived in the first wave of immigration), Markhams, Morgans, Rhodeses (likewise early arrivals), Ferrells, Greshams, Guesses, Nicholses, Shepherds, and Worthams. From Caroline County came the Herndons, Leighs, Mays, and Pattersons. The Glenns came from Louisa County. The Valley of Virginia counties of Augusta and Rockbridge supplied the Shieldses, McCowns, and Lynns. Though previously in Sussex County, Virginia, the Mangums drifted into Orange from Warren County, North Carolina; the Alstons came from Halifax County and the Colcloughs from Granville County, North Carolina. The latter had been previously in Stafford County, Virginia. The Rogerses came from New Hanover County, Virginia, but they had earlier been in Rhode Island. The Tilleys, Shieldses, and McCowns had come from Ireland to Virginia and the Turrentines from Italy to Ireland before arriving in North Carolina.[6] While the population in eastern Orange County remained, therefore, predominantly English, there was beginning to be more of a mix with a larger element of Scotch-Irish.

A case has been made that the northern part of Durham County was settled by a more affluent population than the southern part, a conclusion based on a comparison of the 1790 tax districts of Saint Mary's and Saint Mark's.[7] A closer look at these lists, however, does not support such a conclusion. To begin with, because the area and population of Saint Mary's were much larger than Saint Mark's, a comparison of the raw figures is meaningless. Saint Mary's contained 237 white taxables, of whom 173 owned land totaling 61,619 acres; Saint Mark's contained 138 white taxables of whom 92 owned land totaling 39,965 acres. The average acreage per landowner was 356.2 acres in Saint Mary's but 434 acres in Saint Mark's. Further, a count of the taxable slaveowners shows that 48 percent of taxed whites owned slaves in Saint Mark's District, compared to only 33 percent in Saint Mary's. Examined another way, 8 percent of landowners in Saint Mark's (seven men) owned 1,000 or more acres, while in Saint Mary's only 6 percent (ten men) owned that much. What is a clear difference between the districts is that Saint Mary's contained John Carrington, Jr., Richard Bennehan, and William Cain, who owned far more than the average number of both acres and slaves. The presence of these men brings up the averages in Saint Mary's District considerably, presenting a distorted picture. Probably a fair description would be that the yeomen in Saint Mark's District were a more homogeneously prosperous group than that in Saint Mary's, while the group in Saint Mary's included both a few very wealthy men and a larger proportion of landless men (37 percent) than Saint Mark's (33 percent).[8]

Another difference between the districts lay in their geography. The three rivers, Eno, Little, and Flat, with their fertile valleys and well-drained ridges, made Saint Mary's land suitable for a variety of agricultural uses. Saint Mark's, on the other hand, lay almost entirely in the Triassic Basin where drainage was poor; and though New Hope Creek and its tributaries supplied large quantities of rich bottom land, some of it was so low and of such soil as to be wet, even swampy, much of the time, and thus not truly arable. In addition, farmers involved in the production of staples for the market economy required access to commodity markets. The distribution of roads favored Saint Mary's, with its main artery to Virginia and network of local cart roads on the dry ridges. On the other hand the terrain worked to Saint Mark's disadvantage and made all its roads impassable much of the time. The geographical advantages of Saint Mary's probably account for the development there of the large-scale farming and notable prosperity of the larger planters.

Before leaving the comparison of populations, a look at the settlers in the areas of Wake County that later became Durham County might be instructive. Though it is impossible to find tax lists exactly congruous with the acreage of Cedar Fork, Oak Grove, and Carr townships (the areas taken from Wake County to help form Durham), tax lists approximating those areas of western Wake suggest the population makeup. The districts of Captains William Warren, Thomas King, and John Barbee in 1793 show combined totals of 247 white taxables, of whom 202 were landowners with a total of 72,500 acres. These numbers give an average of 359 acres per landowner. Thirty-eight percent of them owned slaves. Six percent of them (twelve men) owned over 1,000 acres.[9] Thus the population as regards land- and slaveholding was very much in line with the adjoining districts of then Orange County.

While waves of new settlers moved into Orange County, another, smaller stream moved out. During and after the Revolution emigration was noticeably heavy, either to South Carolina and Georgia or west to Tennessee and beyond. The Greene County, Georgia, deeds, for example, show familiar Orange County names: Abercrombies, Booths, Cains, Peelors, Trices, and Greshams. Often it was the younger or landless branches of families who moved, hoping for better opportunities in a new frontier. Another reason for emigration was the availability of military bounty land in Tennessee for those who served in the Revolution or for those who bought bounties from veterans. Still another element that moved on was made up of debtors fleeing the arm of the law, chronic drunkards or generally shiftless men, or even petty criminals who knew how to take advantage of a frontier society.[10] As Simon Suggs said, "It is good to be shifty in a new country."

Hardiness of muscle and spirit was required of those who undertook the arduous and risky move into a wilderness or frontier; they were forced to leave behind most of what they owned and bank on health and luck to carry them through the long journey on rugged roads to a new and untested environment, there to reestablish themselves quickly enough to get a crop in the ground and a shelter over their heads before another winter rolled around. One family's move is described by William Few, brother of the Regulator:

> My father . . . purchased lands on the banks of the river Eno, in the county of Orange. Those lands were in their natural state. Not a tree had been cut. The country was thinly inhabited, and the state of society was in the first stage of civilization. My father employed a man to build a house on his lands, and returned to remove his family. After selling his lands in Maryland and such of his goods and chattels as were not moveable, the remainder were placed in a wagon drawn by four horses and in a cart drawn by two horses. In the autumn of 1758 he set out for North Carolina with all his family and property. There a new scene opened to us. We found a mild and healthy climate and fertile lands, but our establishment was in the woods and our first employment was to cut down the timber and prepare the land for cultivation. My father had taken with him only four servants, who were set to work, and every exertion was made to prepare for the ensuing crop.[11]

As Few's narrative makes plain, getting a crop planted was vital to the newcomer's survival. Clearing a field for it was backbreaking work, first felling trees and then burning off the land, and finally breaking up the sod. If a farmer had sufficient cleared land to plant a staple, he chose wheat or tobacco, usually not both. Tobacco was grown only by those farmers with many hands to help, for it was a labor-intensive crop. Since wheat was bulky, it was usually ground into flour before being marketed. With the money from a staple, a farmer could obtain items that he could not supply himself, such as coffee, sugar, and rum. Almost every farmer had swine; they ran free in the woods foraging for themselves. Only crops were enclosed. If swine were to be sold at market, they were trotted there on the hoof, even as far as Petersburg and northward. Animal herds were usually small by necessity; comparatively little cleared land was available for pasture in the early days.[12]

Folk housing—utilitarian, unself-conscious, the kind most settlers lived in—took two forms in eastern Carolina and the Piedmont. Both were one-room structures with lofts above. One form was of sawn lumber usually constructed sixteen by sixteen feet, the other of logs, sixteen by twenty-four feet. Log houses were a part of Scandinavian and German tradition which the Scotch-Irish were quick to adopt when they met with it in Pennsylvania or the other middle colonies. The English adhered to their own tradition.[13] As the first settlers were predominantly English in eastern Orange, the prevalent form of housing was probably the square, sawn variety. Possibly the oldest of the few structures that survive from the later eighteenth century is the Horton cottage at Stagville. Believed to date from about the 1770s, it is built of pit-sawn boards, two to three inches thick and ten inches wide, dovetailed at the corners. Extremely wide pine boards sheathe the inside walls and weatherboarding, the outside. The engaged front porch shows a coastal influence;

Piedmont houses usually had no porches at that time. The ceiling beams in its original one room, sixteen by sixteen feet, are beaded, a refinement not typical of the average yeoman farmer's dwelling. The cottage, which originally stood in another location on the same tract, was moved to its present site in front of a row of slave houses at Horton Grove for use as an overseer's house when the Cameron family was developing Horton Grove slave quarters in the mid-nineteenth century.

Although probably more substantial than average, the Horton cottage is not the finest type of eighteenth-century structure to survive in Durham County; the William Cain house, Hardscrabble, can claim that distinction. A large, double house, both sections dating from the eighteenth century, it stands high on a hillside on the old Trading Path, or Hillsborough to Oxford road. The front section, 28 by 42 feet, contains heavy Georgian paneling and mantels throughout the six rooms, plastered and ceiled above the wainscoting. The back section of four rooms, slightly smaller with lighter Federal-style decoration, contains, nevertheless, structural details that suggest an earlier date than the front. Evidence exists that at least one of the sections (and perhaps both) was built by Samuel Hopkins and Martin Palmer in 1790.[14]

Somewhere between the grandeur of the Cains and the modest but refined simplicity of the Hortons stands the Richard Bennehan plantation house at Stagville. The smaller wing, approximately twenty-five feet square, was built in the late 1780s, probably just after the building of the Stagville store in 1787. One large room with a shedroom behind it and a loft above made up the original structure. Again Georgian paneling below the chair rails and plastered walls and ceilings above show simple but fine construction. In 1799 a larger section was added consisting of one large room and a broad hall with staircase downstairs, and a large and a small bedroom upstairs. Only slightly more ornate than the original section, the height and lines of the addition give dignity to the house to match the standing of its owner.

One other eighteenth-century house, which stood until the 1970s, should be remembered for its rarity among dwellings of its time in Orange County—Tyree Harris's brick house. Probably built in the 1760s, it was about twenty feet square, of half-timbered construction with the exception of the rear, chimney wall, which was entirely of brick; within, it had one room downstairs and one upstairs, though it later acquired an addition. Bennehan bought the brick house from Harris in 1776 and moved there with his bride after adding some outbuildings and repairing others, but he made no alterations in the house. He called the place Mount Union because of its location at the confluence of the Eno and Flat rivers.[15]

Though most early houses have disappeared, estate records reveal their contents, reflections of the life lived in them. When a man died, if he had left no will, his administrator was required to give the court an inventory of his possessions, which were then sold at auction by the sheriff and the proceeds distributed among the heirs. Slaves were sold along with other possessions, but land was divided, if possible, among the heirs without a sale. The estate inventory of Joseph Bohannon of Saint Mark's District is typically modest, showing only the bare essentials for his own and his wife's needs. He owned no land, possibly because he was a young man just starting out in life, but possibly also because he practiced a craft—joinery.

Besides his joiner's tools his possessions included three "horse kind," three saddles (one a woman's), a slave boy named Denby who probably worked alongside his master at his craft, 136 feet of black walnut plank (his raw materials), and half interest in a whipsaw (an important tool of his trade) with John Patterson, probably his partner. Inside his house Bohannon had a walnut chest, a table, and a bedstead with feather bed and bedclothes. No children or relatives shared his home, but he did have a wife. The objects she worked with were listed as his: a loom, a linen wheel and slay, two iron pots, a frying pan, four dishes, six plates, six spoons, two earthen plates, one punch bowl, one teacup, one tin cup, two forks, two basins, some pewter, and a box iron and heater. He and his wife, Patty, also kept some livestock to supply their needs: eight geese, thirteen head of cattle, and eight head of hogs. Besides these, Bohannon owned a Bible and two razors.[16]

In contrast to this modest estate is that of Patrick Boggan, the innkeeper on the Trading Path, who died in 1757.[17] He ran a farm as well as a hostel, and both occupations are reflected in his inventory. For his farm he had seven horses, twenty head of cattle, two hogs, ten sheep and three lambs (for their wool and mutton), one wagon and gear, one plow with plow irons, four broad hoes, two mattocks, an axe, a pair of hand millstones, one grindstone, three sickles, and a branding iron. His farming comprised both livestock and crops, one of which was probably flax, for he owned a flax wheel, two hackles, a chuck reel, and a set of spools for linen and woolen spinning and weaving. The quantity of his household possessions reflects accommodations for transient guests: five bedsteads, "three feather beds and furniture," two tables, two tablecloths, two walnut benches, five chairs, a chest, three iron pots, a brass kettle, a tea kettle, a set of tea ware, twelve plates, nine trenchers, twelve spoons, nine knives, seven forks, four mugs, six dishes, six basins, two wooden platters, a butter pot, a churn, a stool, two hand towels, a case of bottles, two candlesticks, two chamber pots, a box iron, and many other miscellaneous items. The listing of six "broak" horses suggests they too may have been part of his equipment as an innkeeper, spare horses to ride or to pull a vehicle when needed. He also had four saddles.

A few possessions related to his tavern: five barrels, three hogsheads, two pails, five noggins, two piggins, seven bottles, a funnel, five kegs, a bung borer, brass scales and weights, a pair of money scales, and a tickler, a tool for extracting bungs from casks. Even his clothes were not exempt from the auction block: two coats, three jackets, a great coat, two pairs of breeches, a pair of trousers, three pairs of stockings, a pair of shoes, a pair of garters, four shirts, and a hat. A pair of spectacles and a Bible completed Boggan's worldly goods.

MILLS

Grist- and sawmills were vital industrial components of the eighteenth-century agricultural economy. They supplied the farmer with cornmeal for his daily bread and lumber for his farm buildings; they made possible his participation in the market economy with his corn, wheat, and lumber. A settler with more resources than average was quick to request permission to build a merchant or public mill if his land offered a good mill seat. Anyone could build his own mill on his own land, but if he hoped to serve the neighborhood commercially, he was required to get the court's approval.

Michael Synnott's mill on the Eno River, constructed even before he received the grant of land it stood on in 1752, was the first on record in Orange County and was located a short distance upstream from the now reconstructed West Point Mill.[18] Synnott was the kind of man about whom legends develop. One longtime resident of the area, himself a miller, related that Synnott "got drownded. He was a bachelor and he kept all his change in the mill. He had ½ a pot of gold and silver. The water rose up and carried him in and tumbled the mill into the deep hole. More people been diving to get that pot of gold. They say they've never found a bottom, the water's so deep."[19]

In 1778 Charles Abercrombie and William Thetford applied for a license to build a mill at Shoemaker's Ford, exhibiting a petition from the neighborhood for the mill. The court required an investigation to see whether the millpond would "overflow the Mill of any other person," surely an oblique reference to Synnott's mill a short distance upstream.[20] At the end of the eighteenth century George Carrington, the Revolutionary War veteran, owned Abercrombie's mill. It was possibly Carrington who built the house that stood until recently on the knoll east of the mill and whose Flemish bond chimney has been saved. Huge stone boulders formed the cellar and foundation of the two-story house. Much later the addition of a back wing and Victorian roof and porches so disguised the age of the house that it was unwittingly demolished in the 1970s.

A mill's location was an integral factor in its success or failure. It required first of all a site where bedrock could offer a secure footing for the mill foundation, preferably sufficiently high above the stream to escape the worst of the sudden flooding in Piedmont streams. Next it needed a site within a burgeoning farm population accessible by roads on both banks of the stream and by a good ford so that farmers could reach it from both sides. Abercrombie's mill had an optimal site. It began with an excellent ford and soon had roads approaching it on both the north and south banks. In 1786 the court ordered a new road laid out from Abercrombie's mill to Hillsborough, supplying it with yet another large area of potential custom.[21] The lack of a ford and main roads leading to it probably accounted for the Synnott mill's short life, while Abercrombie's continued uninterrupted under different names and ownerships into the twentieth century.

Many other mills were built in eastern Orange on all three rivers and some of the larger streams. Just before his death in 1785, William Johnston had one built on Little River at Snow Hill plantation by George Elliot and Joseph Brittain. George Newton obtained permission in 1777 to build a mill on the south fork of Little River, a location that later became well known under the name of South Lowell Mills.[22] Other mills were James Vaughan's on Dial Creek in the Flat River area (1780), Samuel Daniel's on New Hope Creek (1783), Isaac Hicks's mill on Eno (1791), William Cain's on Little River (before 1795), and George Herndon's, date and site unknown.[23] Vaughan's was probably on the site later known as Nathaniel Harris's mill where Dial Creek ran into Flat River, now covered by Lake Michie. After having reversed itself twice on Hicks's petition, the county court granted him permission for a public mill. In 1793 Hicks sold his tract presumably with a mill to John Kennon, who three years later sold it to Charles Kennon. In 1806 it was bought by Richard Bennehan and remained in that family throughout the rest of its existence, last known as Red Mill.[24] Cain's mill remained in that family until Thomas R. Cain sold it to his partner Samuel H. Johnson, who continued to run it until 1908. Along with many other mills on all the rivers, it was destroyed by an unusually severe rain storm and the consequent flooding.[25] Johnson Mill Road preserves the memory of the mill and its location, just downstream from the bridge over Little River. Herndon's mill is known from his will, probated in 1796, by which he left to his wife five hundred acres and a gristmill, probably on Northeast Creek.[26]

Unknown are two mills shown on the Collet map of 1770: Gibbs mill on Flat River and Wads mill on Little River.[27] Gibbs mill was probably the forerunner of Crabtree's mill, for "Gibb" could have been the mapmaker's misnomer for "Gibson," the owner of the tract where Crabtree's mill was later located. Wads mill probably represents a misspelling of the name Wade. Land on Mountain Creek and Little River containing a gristmill was sold to settle John Wade's estate.[28] Clues to still other mills are found in stream names mentioned in land records.[29] These may all have been small, private mills which could be built on creeks whose small and variable flow would suffice for the needs of one family. Public mills collected a toll for their services, an amount regulated by law, and often produced handsome profits for their owners. The laws of 1715 stipulated a miller's toll as one-eighth of the total of ground wheat and one-sixth of ground corn.[30]

Mills played more than an industrial and economic role in the building of that early society. They played a social role as well, offering isolated families a place to meet their neighbors and to exchange news, opinions, encouragement, and information, and where they could hear the harangues of county politicians and list their taxables with the sheriff's constables. The millpond offered a swimming and fishing hole to the men and boys, and the thunder of the intricate machinery and glorious rush of water over the wheel added wonder and pleasure to their flat, work-ridden lives. In later decades, as mechanical improvements occurred and the functions of the mills multiplied, they would assume an ever-growing importance in the settlers' lives.

CHURCHES

Also performing the function of community centers, though in a more restricted way, were the churches. Few churches or meetinghouses, as they were more usually called, existed in present Durham County in the eighteenth century. Members of the Church of England, the established church in North Carolina, were supplied with churches by the Colonial government. The first Orange County church was at Hillsborough at least by 1764, and soon two chapels were built, one to the north and the other to the south of it, missing by only a few miles becoming part of Durham County's history.[31] Anglicans in eastern Orange could take their pick of these. Those of dissenting beliefs, who carried their religion as part of their baggage, were quick to establish religious groups in the neighborhoods they settled. Since eastern Orange lacked both Scotch-Irish and German settlements, it had no early dissenter congregations such as Eno and New Hope Presbyterian churches in present Orange County. The Separatist Baptists, too, established churches in the 1750s, but though Shubal Stearns made hundreds of converts in Randolph County and adjacent areas, his influence did not extend to eastern Orange. After the Revolution, when dissenting groups at last formed churches in present Durham County, they first built brush arbors of boughs supported by poles, and afterward rough buildings of frame or logs dignified by the name of meetinghouses. No regular preachers cared for these congregations; they managed the services themselves with occasional visits from itinerant preachers. The need to be their own teachers and preachers as well as jacks of all trades developed in these early settlers an independence of mind that tended to reject authority and hierarchy in church matters even if they had not already been indoctrinated by dissenting beliefs before their arrival in the back-country. It is not surprising, therefore, that so many were attracted to the Baptist fold, or to the more regulated but equally plainspoken and self-reliant Presbyterian and Methodist persuasions—the three denominations with the most members in Durham County today—when their accustomed Anglican services were no longer supplied. Durham County can, however, claim one eighteenth-century Anglican structure—its existence inferred from the slimmest of evidence—a private chapel built by William Johnston on his home tract near the graves of his wife and their five small children.[32]

The vacuum left by the demise of the Church of England during the Revolution began to be filled by itinerant preachers of the Methodists and Baptists who came in the middle 1770s. Francis Asbury, the most famous, first came to North Carolina in 1780. On that visit he preached at Hillsborough in William Courtney's tavern to about two hundred people, whom he described as decent and well behaved. Of his mission he wrote, "Hitherto the Lord has helped me through continual fatigue and rough roads, little rest for man or horse, but souls are perishing—time is flying—and eternity comes nearer every hour."[33] This sense of urgency kept him on the road over forty-five years, traveling 270,000 miles and preaching 16,425 sermons. Also on his first visit he preached at Neuse preaching house in present Durham County, where four hundred people gathered to hear him. He recorded that "these people have had an abundance of preaching from the Baptists and Methodists, till they are hardened."[34] From names recorded by Asbury the meetinghouse can be generally located in the Fish Dam Ford District of then Wake County. It very possibly evolved into Kimbrough's meetinghouse, which some thirty years later was in the same neighborhood.[35] Another eastern Orange meetinghouse may have been established shortly after Asbury's visit. In 1781 James Trice of St. Mark's District left property in his will to be converted to cash "to the use of Bilding of a meeting house in this neighborhood where my Executors shall think most convenient for the use of the Publick."[36] A third eighteenth-century meetinghouse was built on the land of Richard Rhodes, who in 1794 gave for the purpose two acres in what is today Brag-town. When he sold his tract to Abraham Anderson, he reserved the acreage for the meetinghouse, and when Anderson sold the same tract he excepted "two Acres for the use of the Congregation and place of publick worship by the name of the Eno Meeting house."[37] The congregation soon after allied itself with the Primitive Baptists. The third building of this congregation still stands on the same two acres that Rhodes originally deeded.[38]

One other church still active in Durham County had its roots in the eighteenth century—Mount Bethel United Methodist Church in Bahama. Traditionally, Nathaniel Harris has been credited with its founding in 1750.[39] Actually, Nathaniel Harris did not come to Orange County until the late 1750s and died in 1775, while no evidence for a meetinghouse in that area can be found until the 1780s. A long deposition of James Walker, Jr., concerning a disputed boundary line, discloses the origins of Mount Bethel Church. It was Archer Harris, the son of Nathaniel, who is there credited with the establishment of a meetinghouse. Walker said that the Methodist itinerant preachers came to their neighborhood in 1780, and that Archer Harris was converted and became a lay preacher. Walker further said that when Stephen Wilson bought Charles Carroll's land in 1784, "the Methodists had a Meetinghouse on the land, and moved the Meetinghouse" with Wilson's consent to the land of James Walker, Sr.[40] Thus the meetinghouse was built sometime between 1780 and 1784. In 1812 Archer Harris gave two acres of land to John Wilson, John McFarling, and Nathaniel Harris (his son), "trustees of a meeting house standing at the Cross Roads between the Harris's and John McFarlings . . . for the only proper use and benefit of a meeting house."[41] Five or six years later the congregation was incorporated into the Methodist Church and assigned to the Granville circuit. The church was long called Crossroads Meetinghouse because of its location at the junction of the roads from Raleigh to Roxboro and Oxford to Hillsborough. Now called Mount Bethel, the present edifice, the sixth, stands at the same intersection but on a different corner, separated from its graveyard.[42]

Unlike early churches, early schools have left no traces in the records. Life was so demanding of time and energy in the early years that none were left over to give to educating children. Self-sufficient as the settlers were in every other respect, home schooling was probably the prevailing system, if any attention at all was given the matter. The first kind of organized school to develop in rural areas was the "old field" or subscription school. A group of neighbors would band together to hire a teacher for their children, one of them donating for use as a schoolroom an old structure in an abandoned field. They shared the cost of the teacher's salary, a very small sum, for a three- or four-month course of lessons, usually held during the season of the year when farm work was least demanding and the children's help most easily spared. Though a simple enough solution in principle, its practical application could often be difficult; the farmers lived so far apart that a group of children within walking distance of one another was not easy to find. Not a few such schools were organized, nonetheless, and William Few described one that he attended in Orange County just over the present Durham-Orange line.

In the year 1760 a schoolmaster appeared and offered his services to teach the children of the neighborhood for twenty shillings each per year. He was employed, and about thirty scholars were collected and placed under his tuition;

in the number I was enrolled. . . . This schoolmaster was a man of a mild and amiable disposition. He governed his little school with judgment and propriety, wisely distinguishing the obedient, timid child from the obstinate and contumacious; judiciously applying the rod when necessary. He possessed the art of making his pupils fear, love, and esteem him. At this school I spent one of the most happy years of my life.[43]

SLAVERY

Chattel slavery, which developed along with agriculture, had become entrenched in the lives of these settlers by the end of the eighteenth century. In 1665 the law allowed fifty acres of land to each settler for each slave that he brought into the colony, thus encouraging the ownership and importation of slaves.[44] The exhausting work of clearing the wilderness for planting could hardly have been done without slave labor. In the Piedmont, settled late by yeoman farmers rather than planters committed to large-scale commercial farming, the slave population grew more slowly than in the coastal plain. Nevertheless black population growth far exceeded white in eighteenth-century Orange County. The 1755 tax list shows that blacks then made up a very small proportion of the total population, perhaps under 5 percent.[45] The population figures of the 1790 census show two thousand slaves to some ten thousand whites, and the 1800 figures show 3,327 slaves to 12,222 whites, yielding black percentages of the total population of 21 percent and 27 percent respectively.[46]

Laws concerning slaves—restricting their activities, mobility, and legal rights; giving masters complete control over their persons, while at the same time prohibiting inhumane treatment, maiming, or killing—were changed from time to time as the institution became ingrained in the society and as social attitudes toward slavery solidified. There was nothing static in the relationship of the colonists and their slaves, and the customs and circumscriptions associated with the antebellum period, the last phase of the institution, did not come into being all at once.[47] They took decades to evolve and were influenced by events, movements, and practices in the country at large—for example, the system of indentured servants so prevalent in early colonization efforts, religious opposition to slavery among certain sects, the Revolution and its potent ideas of inalienable individual rights, technological improvements in cotton culture, the closing of the slave trade, the emancipation and abolition movements, slave revolts, and the South's nearly complete economic dependence on agriculture.

The regimen under which slaves lived is generally known. They worked from dawn to dusk six days a week, were permitted off the plantations only with passes, and could not hold unauthorized meetings, carry or possess arms, or engage in commerce with whites. Their quarters were routinely inspected by patrollers appointed by the court (these were the hated "pattyrollers" of the slave narratives), who searched for stolen goods or secreted weapons and made sure the curfew was enforced. Slaves could be hired out if they were not needed as servants or field hands, and a skilled slave was often more valuable to his master if he was allowed to practice his craft. Although the master would then take all or a portion of his earnings, a slave might also practice his craft on his own time, thereby earning enough eventually to buy his freedom and even that of his wife and children from a willing master. On large plantations where the slaves numbered more than a family or two, they were usually quartered in a row of log cabins or one-room frame houses with mud floors and plank shutters. The houses were damp and chilly in winter, heated only by a fireplace where food could be cooked, and stifling in summer. Sometimes they were built as double cabins flanking a central chimney, the saddlebag type of cabin construction. On the Bennehan-Cameron plantations, where the masters understood the relation between hygiene and disease, they practiced not only periodic cleaning-out of houses and relocation of quarters but genuine improvement in the construction of slave housing over the years. The slave houses at Horton Grove and Shop Hill on the Stagville plantation, built in 1851 by Paul Cameron according to the specifications of Duncan Cameron, give Durham County the only complete unit of slave quarters surviving in the state. Each two-story frame structure with brick infill for insulation contains four rooms each seventeen feet square, two to a floor. These houses, six of which still stand, represent the Camerons' best efforts to supply healthful quarters for their huge number of slaves. Shaded by oaks, erected on high pilings, and provided with wooden floors, whitewashed walls, and larger-than-usual rooms, these houses may have advanced the health of the families assigned to them.[48] But even under the most benign management, it must be said, the slaves' basic needs were met barely sufficiently rather than amply.

Because of lack of evidence, much less is known about slavery on the yeoman farmer's farm, where at most one or two black families lived out their isolated existences. Instead of occupying a cabin in a row at the quarters on a large plantation, separated from the master's big house, supervised by an overseer, with little or no personal contact with the master or his family, the slaves of a yeoman farmer lived in a cabin not very different from their master's, in the same yard. The wife and children of the master labored in the fields alongside the black family. Faced with common dangers from the natural environment—accident, disease, or death— these families had more to unite than to separate them. General lack of education and illiteracy were common to both. A bare minimum of earthly possessions characterized their homes. The food on their tables and the clothes on their backs were hardly distinguishable. Depending entirely on the temperament and inclination of the white master, their daily association may have been either troubled or harmonious, but a totally individual matter.[49] For the slaves, nevertheless, however well they were treated, they bore in equal measure with plantation slaves the frustration and psychological fetters that loss of freedom imposed. It might be argued that their lot was less cruel, less noticeably harsh, and by small degrees more tolerable than that of plantation slaves. On the other hand, it might equally be argued that separation from others of their kind made racial identity and cultural continuity more difficult. Plantation slaves had at least numbers to reinforce their customs, their ethnic integrity, and sense of self and to share the burden of helplessness or rage that frustration engendered.

It is clear from the letters of plantation women that some were sensitive to the psychological plight of their slaves and tried to treat them with kindness and consideration. Mary Ruffin Cain, the wife of William Cain, Jr., wrote to her daughter Minerva away at school in 1833:

> You ought to learn to treat your father's domestics (who are daily employed in adding to your *comfort* and *gratification*) with much feeling and give them as little trouble as possible, for place yourself in their situation, and how do [you] think you would bear it? Always bear in mind that you will have to answer at the bar of God, for your conduct towards them, and that they have souls to be saved as well as we, and therefore ought not to be provoked to get angry or to do wrong—you had for several years an excellent example in your cousin Martha Moore's conduct towards servants. Even now when she comes to see us, she never fails to say How do you do? to them, and *always* speaks kindly to them.[50]

Free blacks increased as well as slaves. Besides natural increase in those already free, former slaves increased the number by obtaining freedom in a variety of ways.[51] Masters who had children by slave women were sometimes prompted by natural feeling to free the women and their children. Slaves who served in the Revolution were sometimes freed, and slaves who rendered some notable service to their masters could be emancipated. Some masters were moved by Revolutionary ideals to act on their principles and free their slaves. Many other slaves ran away and were never retrieved. The growing presence of free blacks complicated the status of both free black and slave, hardening the color line, and establishing caste as well as race as economic and social determinants in the culture. From the some dozen free blacks named in the 1755 Orange County tax list, their numbers grew to 101 in 1790 and 108 in 1800.[52] Except for a few of their names, nothing is known of free blacks in eighteenth-century eastern Orange.

After fifty years of strenuous effort in the backcountry, the Europeans, with the forced help of Africans, had tamed a wilderness. They had completely dispossessed the Native Americans, a race and culture alien to them; they had accommodated themselves to a new climate and natural environment; they had built the rudiments of a stable society and replaced an irksome, unresponsive government with one of their own devising, if still not democratic at least accessible and more accountable to the people. The chance to progress and prosper was theirs. Space to expand, freedom to choose, and an ordered society in which to function offered these newcomers, now settled, all they could have hoped for when they pulled up stakes and risked all. Time would show what they did with this good fortune.

The Rip Van Winkle Era, 1801–1840

5

T HE EVOLUTION OF THIS ORDERED SOCIETY took place in difficult times. From the end of the Revolution until the end of the century, serious problems threatened the life of the young nation. They were financial and economic because of the huge cost of the war, inflation, the disruption of foreign and domestic trade and commerce, and debt, public and private. They were governmental, as the experiment in democracy picked a careful way, holding in principle to its ideals while often compromising in practice as it organized the government. How to write a national constitution that would satisfy all the partners; how to balance the needs of the federal union, once established, against the claims of the states' autonomy; how to defend the nation and conduct foreign policy to avoid war, which at that time would have spelled doom for the young country; how to adjust the inherited judicial and legal systems of England to the new demands of a federal system and its governmental machinery; and similar momentous tasks became the daily work of the novice rulers. Finally, the problems were also political, as all these issues tended to divide the population into opposing camps. The Federalists predominated from George Washington's undisputed election as president until he left office at the end of the 1790s. They stood for a strong central government capable of defending itself against foreign powers, particularly France and England, which wished to manipulate the new nation for their own opposed ends and were thus serious threats. The Federalists also tended to be slave- and landholding men and to be sympathetic to the interests of their class (the market economy, international and coastal trade, and transportation of goods), failing to mask their disdain for the opinions of the rest of the citizenry. They adopted fiscal policies that produced revenues for defense, and they established a national bank.

Against their policies grew another faction, represented by Thomas Jefferson and the Republican Democrats. These men stood for popular government; they believed in the common man and distrusted the elite, and they advocated economy in national affairs. They resisted the growing power of the central government and insisted on states' rights. For the first thirty to forty years of the new century this was the dominent point of view, carried to new extremes under the banner of Jacksonian democracy and its hero, Andrew Jackson.

In North Carolina, the Federalists had held power at the beginning of the 1790s, but public support was never enthusiastic and Federalist viewpoints were never dominant. The Federalists soon lost office, and by the beginning of the new century Democratic views prevailed along with the party, to the exclusion of any other. The long sway of this philosophy led to serious consequences for the state because of its own peculiar problems. Together they were responsible for a period known as the Rip Van Winkle era, an epithet particularly appropriate for North Carolina's condition. Stagnation in every form characterized life in the state. The problems were agricultural, economic, geographic, political, and cultural. The Piedmont shared with the mountain region the ignominy of being the poorest section of the poorest state in the nation. Exhausted soils and antiquated farming methods yielded poorer and poorer returns for the state's primarily agricultural economy. Geographic barriers to transportation impeded cultural and agricultural progress alike. The lack of ports, navigable rivers, and passable roads forced farmers who grew staple crops and wished to participate in the market economy to expend half their profits transporting their produce to markets in South Carolina or Virginia. Those who sold their produce in neighboring states also spent the profits there for supplies they needed, draining the state further of credit and specie. Isolation fostered provincialism, prejudice, and ignorance.[1]

Government in North Carolina was ostensibly democratic but in practice oligarchic, the landowning class holding the reins at both the state and local levels. After the demise of the Federalists' power in 1808, one party alone, the Jeffersonian Republicans, held sway, and lacking a challenging opposition, contributed to the state's backwardness. The prevailing political views of the landowners were represented in the United States Congress by Nathaniel Macon for thirty-seven years. Distrustful of government (the least government was the best) and a passionate defender of states' rights, he voted against federal involvement in or expenditures for internal improvements, education, or other national development. With little formal education, he believed that education should be a private matter paid for by those who could afford it. This widely held opinion translated into the shocking statistic of the 1840 census: one-third of the state population was illiterate; one-half, if blacks and children were included.[2] Hampered by cultural malnutrition, a depressed economy, an over-conservative government, exhausted soils, and falling land prices, hundreds of families left the state. Ambitious, intelligent youths with pluck and energy realized that conditions at home offered them no hope or opportunity for advancement. By the time of the 1850 census one-third of native North Carolinians were living in other states.

THE STAGVILLE PHENOMENON

Orange County reflected the general stagnation, but also other early-nineteenth-century movements, events, and social trends. The Great Revival in religion, for example, took fire in Orange County; the army recruited a number of its young men for the War of 1812; and the slow evolution of demographic patterns resulted in incipient communities around such focal points as churches, stores, or mills.[3] It was also in Orange County that Archibald DeBow Murphey lived and practiced law and politics, crusading for the solutions that he saw for North Carolina's problems: mass education, political reform, and internal improvements. At the same time technological advances such as Whitney's cotton gin were revolutionizing cotton culture, the federal government was opening up for settlement new lands in the Deep South ideal for cotton growing. In eastern Orange, as elsewhere, ambitious sons of long-established families were striking out on their own in new territory. Their exodus and the depressed land values made possible a phenomenon that occurred in present Durham County: the creation by Richard Bennehan, his son, Thomas, and his son-in-law, Duncan Cameron, of a huge and profitable plantation complex certainly unique in the Piedmont. Many of their neighbors, for example William A. Tharpe, the Alveses, Bledsoes, Cains, Davises, and Harrises, who owned large acreage on the rivers, were eager to sell their lands and try their luck elsewhere; the partnership of Bennehans and Cameron was just as eager to buy their lands at the current low prices.[4]

The Stagville store, established in 1787 and the basis of Richard Bennehan's wealth, continued to thrive and to increase its usefulness to the neighborhood. In addition to its primary retail function, it supplied the services of a bank (lending money, taking mortgages on land and slaves, and extending credit) as well as those of a factor (accepting commodities for resale elsewhere). It held auctions of land and slaves on which it had foreclosed, sold the services of stud horses to improve the neighborhood stock, and housed a post office opened in 1807. Bennehan put his store profits into land and slaves. After his daughter's marriage in 1803 to Cameron, the source of whose lucrative income was the law, Bennehan conceived a plan to capitalize their money by pooling all their resources under one management.[5] The partnership of Bennehans and Cameron by careful management and patient additions of land built up a plantation complex, comprising about thirty thousand acres at its height, that included stores, mills, blacksmith shops, tanyards, and distilleries. The scale of this enterprise and the progressive methods of agriculture introduced by Cameron's son Paul after 1837 made the partnership a highly profitable undertaking. The number of slaves, close to nine hundred before the Civil War, was sufficiently large to clear new land every year and maintain its productivity.[6]

The long-term effects of this enterprise were two. As the plantation's borders moved outward, engulfing tract after tract of adjacent land, a general depopulation of the area occurred. The nearest neighbors were farther and farther away, while on the plantations themselves the black population continued to grow, leaving the Camerons, their overseers and families, and a few miscellaneous clerks or managers of the stores and shops to form a small white minority. This single ownership through several generations preserved the land unchanged and undeveloped, and prevented the natural growth of population, roads, commerce, and communities that was taking place in the rest of the county.

THE GREAT REVIVAL

A noticeable slump in religious interest and fervor after the Revolution and through the 1790s caused the ministers and members of the existing churches deep concern. Their belief in the centrality of God in all things, however, made them view the religious doldrums as part of God's plan, a purposeful withholding of His grace, and they felt sure that a religious revival would eventually occur.[7] The long and fervently held hope made the revival, when it came, run through the populace like wildfire. The cultural aridity of frontier life, the isolation, and the settlers' sense of their vulnerability to danger, disease, and death readied the becalmed backcountry populations for the new winds of pulpit oratory: emotional, personal, spellbinding, and aggressively earnest. This kind of delivery had first been brought into North Carolina in 1755 by Baptist preachers, but over the years it had been adopted by other denominations. Now, responding to the blast, the religious current flowed everywhere like a tidal wave covering the whole South.[8]

In North Carolina the first signs of what was to come occurred at the Crossroads Presbyterian Church in then Orange County in the summer of 1801, and immediately thereafter at Hawfields Presbyterian Church not far away.[9] Quite suddenly and to the surprise of all, a spontaneous emotion swept the congregation, producing tears, faintings, shakings, shoutings, despair, or ecstasy. Word of the occurrence traveled fast, and crowds grew as the hysteria spread. The result was the phenomenon known as revivals. A church would arrange for a protracted meeting and provide a series of services often held by ministers of more than one denomination. Families would pack provisions into their wagons and prepare to camp out around the meeting grounds, where their days would be filled with exhorting, praying, singing, and preaching until, under this unrelenting bombardment and the hypnotic effect of mass emotion, huge numbers of the congregation would be moved to one or another manifestation of religious experience. Though arising first in the Presbyterian churches in Orange County, the Methodist and Baptist congregations were very soon caught up in the same enthusiasm. Within a few years, however, the Presbyterian and Baptist ministers became alarmed by the excesses of these revivals and backed away from them, while the Methodist clergy embraced them all the more closely as exactly suited to their theological needs.[10]

Only two churches in present Durham County were organized within the years of the Great Revival (1801–5): Camp Creek Primitive Baptist Church in 1803 and Cedar Fork Baptist Church in 1805. The surviving minutes of Camp Creek record that it was organized 30 June 1803 by Elder George Roberts, Reubin Pickit, and William Brown with a membership of about three dozen.[11] In 1812 John Wilburn gave "to the Baptist Body belonging to the new meeting house called Wilburns meeting house" one and a half acres of his home tract lying on the waters of Camp Creek "for the only use of said meeting house which was built by subscription and is free for the ministers of every Christian denomination to make use of in preaching the Gospel of Jesus Christ."[12] The ecumenical impulse reflected in this deed typically permeated religion in those years during and following the Great Revival. Among members named in the surviving minutes, which begin in 1852, are the

Monk, Hampton, Horner, Cozart, Blalock, Roberts, Ashley, Holeman, Ellis, Moize, and Peed families. Two black members were free: Fanny Day and Elizabeth Evins. At the end of the nineteenth century all the black members withdrew and formed their own congregation, Moore's Grove Primitive Baptist Church four miles west of Stem on land given by Sam Moore. Like Camp Creek, this church was disbanded when the United States Army requisitioned the entire area to build Camp Butner in 1942.[13]

Cedar Fork Baptist Church was established 22 April 1805 by Elders George Roberts and Roland Gooch from the Flat River Association. The first structure, built on the land of Lewis Herndon, was of log, with the usual gallery for black members, of whom there were fifty in 1859. The first minister was Ezekiel Trice, who served thirty-five years, starting with a salary of forty dollars per year. Tradition says that a second structure was built in 1834 on land donated by Joseph Jones to the church deacons Edmund Herndon and John Hill.[14] Among the papers of Zachariah Herndon, brother of Lewis and Edmund Herndon, however, is a bill dated 1822 from the carpenter John Hudgins for building a sawmill, apple mill, store, ginhouse, and a meetinghouse. Another in 1827 records his putting four windows in the meetinghouse.[15] If these relate to Cedar Fork church, then the second meetinghouse was built in 1822, and the one built in 1834 would have been the third.

After the Civil War the church was forced to consider a separation of its black and white members. A report on the matter stated,

> We see they [the black members] are inclined, very much inclined, to independent action in religious matters as well as everything else, and seem to have no heart to worship God (even at churches where their memberships are) with the white race. . . . We would, therefore, recommend that the Colored members of this church be requested to withdraw from the church, and organize churches of their own race and color, where they can worship God without restraint and embarrassment.[16]

Shiloh Church, now just over the Wake County line, is the church the black members formed when they withdrew. At that time the whole area including the Cedar Fork community was part of Wake County. It was peopled by Sorrells (Searles), Pages, Terrys, Stones, Marcoms (Markhams), Beasleys, Barbees, Kings, and some of the numerous Herndon family. Cedar Fork Township, originally in Wake County, is now in Durham County's Triangle Township, and the old Cedar Fork community is called Nelson, a name originated in the 1880s for the railroad station there.

One other Primitive Baptist Church was organized before 1840: Mount Lebanon, still situated on the tract where it began, at the corner of Milton Road and present Guess Road. The first building faced Milton Road, for Guess Road did not then exist. In 1839 two acres for this church were deeded by Joseph Armstrong and George T. Coggin to James Latta, Demsey Woods, and Thomas Latta, but a building had already been erected.[17] A reference to Mount Lebanon Church is found in an undated letter of Paul Cameron to his father: "On Sunday last at a Baptist Meeting House just this side of Mr. Cains, Mrs. White [Cain's daughter] had a young negro man cut-to-pieces by a slave of Mr. Lipscombs—the boy is yet alive and but little hope of his recovery."[18]

In the same neighborhood in 1811 was a church known as Cain's Chapel, undoubtedly built by William Cain for the use of his family and his many slaves. It was probably Episcopalian, for the wife of Duncan Cameron (a pillar of the Episcopal church) wrote to him in June of that year, "Doctor Hall spent last evening with us; he is I think quite an agreeable, and appears to be a truly pious man; he gave us most excellent prayers last night, and this morning my brother [Thomas Bennehan] went with him to Cain's Chapel where he was to preach."[19] Cain's Chapel seems to have been short-lived, for in 1818 an Episcopal minister in Wilmington asked Duncan Cameron to help the "faithful remnant" of Episcopalians in the vicinity of old Saint Mary's Chapel (Cain's neighborhood) reorganize a church. The Reverend Adam Empie wrote that there were seventy males "who are either Episcopalians in principle or favorably disposed towards the Episcopal Church."[20] A church was organized and a new structure must have been quickly erected, for services were already being held in 1818.[21] Though the new Saint Mary's Chapel, situated on the same tract of land as the colonial chapel, is not in Durham County, it is so close to the boundary line that certainly some of its members were drawn from present Durham County.

The gradual resurrection of the Episcopal Church is seen in another action of Duncan Cameron. In 1825 he began to build a chapel at Fairntosh, his own plantation adjoining Stagville, where he had established his family in 1810 by building a large, simple, but elegant house in primarily Georgian style and the usual complement of outbuildings, all of which stand today. The chapel was completed by 1826 and consecrated the following year under the name Salem Chapel. Cameron promised to add one hundred dollars a year to the salary of the regular minister of Saint Matthew's Parish for services once a month at Salem. Obtaining the services of a minister even once a month was difficult, but Salem Chapel continued to be used by the Cameron family and their slaves until the 1840s, when William M. Green, who had conducted the services, was appointed Bishop of Mississippi and left the state.[22]

During the Rip Van Winkle period three Methodist churches joined old Mount Bethel in serving eastern Orange's population. These were Fletcher's Chapel, Andrews Chapel, and Orange Grove, the last more familiar now as Trinity United Methodist Church in the city of Durham. Fletcher's Chapel was formed in 1825 after a rousing camp meeting on the land of Wiley Fletcher near its present location in Oak Grove Township. Though no building was erected until 1837, the people in the community requested that they be included in the rounds of Jacob Hill, a Haw River Circuit rider. After the first church had been built, Wiley Fletcher deeded the land it stood on (two and a half acres) to the church trustees: Perryman G. Richmond, Wiley Fletcher, Abner Peass, Willis Roberts, and John Barbee.[23] A community had already begun to form there with a store and blacksmith shop on the main road from Raleigh to Roxboro. The church structure, 60 by 30 feet, was internally divided by a center pole to separate men and women as they sat in the pine pews. The white-painted church trimmed in red was lighted by candles and heated by two wood-burning stoves. Separation of the sexes was discontinued and oil lamps replaced candles about 1900.[24] Besides the Fletchers, Barbees, and Robertses, other families in the area were the Suitts, Ferrells, Halliburtons, Holloways, Rogerses, and Nicholses.

The John Nichols house, built about 1812, is still standing on Jimmie Rogers Road. A hall-and-parlor-plan house with a porch across the front, it retains most of its original features.[25] John Nichols's great-grandson, John Thomas Nichols, recorded in his diary on 4 July 1872, "Helped to dig grave . . . at the old grave yard at C. J. Rogers where my Great Grand Father John Nichols, who was killed by the running away of horses hitched to a waggon, was burried."[26] Calvin J. Rogers, whose wife inherited the Nichols house, was sheriff of Wake County, 1848–50, and a representative in the legislature, 1866–67.

Southeast of Fletcher's Chapel was another group stimulated by itinerant Methodist preachers of the Raleigh circuit. A log schoolhouse on the land of Thomas Cozart was used for their meetings in the 1830s and known as Chapel Church, later Andrews Chapel Church. A deed for two acres from Cozart to the trustees in 1846 names them as John I. Lee, Jonas Marshall, Joseph M. Cozart, John R. Moore, W. L. Alston, C. W. Page, and Simon Pope. Andrews Chapel Church stood beside its own graveyard and that of the Cozart family on Olive Branch Road until it was moved to its present site on the Leesville Road. There the old Chandler Schoolhouse was converted into the present sanctuary.[27] Some of the early settlers in the area were named Massey, Kimbrough, Delk, and May. The 1809 tax list shows that in the area of present Lynn Crossroads, David Delk ran a tavern and owned over a thousand acres and seven taxable slaves.[28] Later, families named Lynn, Beavers, Weaver, Shaw, and Evans moved into the area. In 1840 a post office called Kelvin Grove was established in that general vicinity, which is now included in Carr Township.[29]

Trinity United Methodist Church also resulted from a revival meeting, held at a place called Orange Grove on the Hillsborough to Raleigh road close to the then Wake County line. Two itinerant preachers, Willis Haynes and David Nicholson, are credited with its founding and the building of the first church structure in 1830. Two years later William R. Herndon deeded one acre to the church trustees—Herndon himself, Daniel G. Rencher, David Roberts, Willis Roberts, Ezekiel Hailey, and John W. Hancock—to be used for a Methodist church and an academy. Hancock became the teacher in this academy; Malbourne A. Angier was one of his students. In 1835 Jefferson Dilliard, for reasons unknown, burned down the building, but it was soon rebuilt.[30] In 1860 the little Orange Grove congregation moved with the changing drift of population to a half-acre tract in the village of Durham's Station, formerly included in Dr. Bartlett Durham's home tract of close to one hundred acres. Doctor Claiborn Parrish, a devout Methodist, then owner of the Bartlett Durham tract, reserved the acreage for the church.[31]

COMMUNITIES

Churches often acted as magnets for other public services. Mount Bethel and Cedar Fork churches can be credited for the present communities of Bahama and

Nelson that eventually grew around them. The stability of these communities received considerable economic reinforcement later in the century when railroads chose them for stations. In the early nineteenth century, as the network of wagon roads grew, stores and taverns as well as churches took advantage of roadside locations to woo the public. Farmers with a little capital and an advantageous site could increase their incomes by enterprises of this kind.[32] As a result, crossroad hamlets and even villages began to dot the landscape. A stimulus for improving the roads was the establishment of stagecoach routes and increased postal service throughout the state. Early in the century, stage lines ran coaches from Raleigh to Hillsborough and Chapel Hill, and by the 1830s from Raleigh to Roxboro past Stagville. Duncan Cameron's daughter Mary Anne wrote to her brother Paul, "The Stage Horn excites a considerable commotion among the little negroes and Master Dan immitates the sound very well."[33] If the traffic was sufficient and the neighborhood growing, a store-cum-tavern (most stores had licenses to retail liquor) within a few years might find itself the heart of a community, on the map with a post office. A post office in that era, like a railroad station later, tended to stabilize the store and community in which it was placed. Among such sites in Durham County were Stagville (1807), Dilliardsville (1823), Red Mountain (1825), Midway (1826), Fish Dam (1826), Herndon's (1827), Leathers Crossroads (1830), Round Hill (1832), Flemington (1833), Prattsburg (1836), Lipscomb's (1838), and West Point (1839).[34]

Fish Dam, like Stagville, was a Bennehan enterprise, established in 1802 when Richard Bennehan built a store at the river crossing, with a blacksmith shop and quarters for an overseer and the slaves who would farm the large adjacent tracts. The main road from Raleigh to Roxboro crossed the river at the ford, so that there, as at Stagville, Bennehan tapped a ready-made traffic.[35]

Midway (1826), known variously as Buffalo Hill (1837) and Dial Creek (1851), on the east side of Flat River, was the location of the "storehouse" of Samuel Garrard and Willie M. Shaw. Garrard and Shaw established the business in 1823 but dissolved it three years later. Both men died in 1828, Garrard after thirty years in the Methodist ministry, Shaw as a young man of twenty-six.[36] Midway post office was moved to the Ellison G. Mangum and Orford Moize store located on the Bahama-Moriah Road, possibly at the corner of Hampton Road where the firm of Ellison G. Mangum and Company later stood, and probably where earlier had been the firm of Willie and William P. Mangum, the uncle and father, respectively, of the statesman Willie P. Mangum. The elder Willie Mangum died in 1809; William P. Mangum continued the business alone until his bankruptcy in the early 1820s. Willie P. Mangum's financial difficulties began at that time because he had signed promissory notes for his father. The business of Ellison G. Mangum, the illegitimate son of Taylor Duke and Chaney Mangum, sister of William P. Mangum, was notably successful. In 1858 the post office was moved again, to a two-room structure on Captain Addison Mangum's homeplace, one room of which was his law office and the other the post office. Its name was changed to Flat River. Also located on the Bahama-Moriah Road a short distance from Hall Road, the building remains to this day, though Mangum's dwelling beside it is now gone.[37]

Two other northern Durham County communities, Red Mountain and Round Hill, evolved at this time. Both places take their names from geographical features in an area where Flat River cuts down between high hills that by comparison with the more usual gently rolling terrain seem unusually prominent. The name Red Mountain appears as early as 1825, when a post office was established there in the store of John J. Carrington, who served as postmaster. After Carrington's financial reverses and consequent move to Tennessee, Abner and Harrison Parker went into business at Red Mountain, and the post office continued in their store.[38] Round Hill post office was established in 1832 in a store run by William Horner, the father of the famous educator James Hunter Horner.[39] The geographical closeness and frequent intermarriage of the families in these communities resulted in much duplication of family names. In general, however, in Red Mountain lived the Parkers (the large family of David Parker, who had a tannery to supplement his farm income and who was the father of Abner and Harrison Parker), the Joneses, Hopkinses, Carringtons, and Horners.[40] By midcentury the Bowlings, too, were established there. At Round Hill, south of the crossroads where Mount Bethel Church stands, lived Doctor Claiborn Parrish (son of Allen and grandson of Ansel[m] Parrish) and various branches of the Harris, Duke, King, Tilley, and Ball families.[41]

In these two communities on the west side of the Flat River, Colonels Abner and Harrison Parker and D. C. Parrish long acted as the unofficial leaders, justices of the peace, and officers in the militia as well as merchants. In conjunction with their stores, like other storekeepers in other areas of the county, they dabbled in financial transactions such as lending money and buying promissory notes at discount ("note-shavers" was the disparaging term for them); through the advantage of a little capital, they were able to prosper. Besides serving as post offices, their stores were used as polling places and for tax collections, militia musters, and political rallies, earning their owners quasi-official status. As a consequence, these men became through the manifold kinds of business transacted on their premises the repositories of all local information, public and private, and bosses in their neighborhoods. Over the years, because of large families with many intermarriages, a tight web of kinship covered the county, often extending into neighboring counties. This closeness bred strong emotional ties that were handed down through the generations like the lands the families owned. This characteristic of early rural settlements, once typical of the American landscape anywhere, has persisted much longer in the South and helps to give the whole region today its particular character.

To the west of Bahama another neighborhood was growing around Leathers Crossroads near the north fork of Little River where a road from Hillsborough met the road from Cain's mill. At that crossing was the Leathers family "storehouse." In 1830 Elizabeth N. Leathers was selling a tract of 210 acres along with a dwelling house, outhouses, the store, and two good wells. She offered to accept a wagon as part payment, a fact which suggests that she was intending to emigrate. Some time later John B. Leathers owned a store there, both alone and in partnership with James Latta.[42] In this neighborhood, as the name indicates, the Leathers family predominated, but there were also Lattas, Tilleys, Cogginses, Armstrongs, and a spillover of families from the periphery of Round Hill and Red Mountain. In mid-century the community lost its identity by becoming absorbed in the better-known enterprise of South Lowell Mills.

In the southern part of the county entirely different networks of kinship and less well-documented business ventures were developing. The Hillsborough *Recorder* kept its readers well informed about happenings in the northern part of present Durham County, but little news from the southern part found its way into the newspaper columns, probably because few inhabitants of that district ventured regularly to Hillsborough over the execrable roads and little if any news of them and their doings reached the editor's desk. They went instead to Chapel Hill, as the roads did, a much nearer community. The Herndon clan, south and southeast of what is today the city of Durham, owned considerable land. Zachariah Herndon, a physician, established partnerships with other men to run commercial enterprises while he practiced his profession, allowing him to reap commercial profits without spending time at the trade. By 1801 he had established a store on his lands lying on Northeast Creek and bordered by the road to Chapel Hill. In 1826 Herndon had his son Rhodes as a partner, and the next year their clerk, P. Henderson Owens, was taken into partnership. In 1834 Herndon deeded twenty-seven acres to his sons, Zachariah, Jr., and Rhodes, but retained for himself lifetime use of all the buildings except the store and cotton gins. By 1835 (the year the elder Herndon died) the firm was known as Herndon and High, Isaiah S. High having been taken into the business. The Herndons sold out to High, who immediately took a deed of trust on the property to raise money.[43] In 1839, however, he wished to sell and advertised the property known as Herndonsville: "It is well known as a fine stand for a country store; it has a good dwelling, a store, two gin houses and gins with all their geer, a good dairy."[44] Another store with the name Herndon's was located farther to the north near Prattsburg. It was run by William R. Herndon and had the benefit of a post office from 1827 to 1836.[45]

No other southern Durham community was granted a post office in this era, probably because nothing resembling a community nucleus could be identified. Again geography stood in the way. Nonetheless, intermarriage and the spreading density of settlement created a sense of community as on Flat River. Slightly south and to the west of the Herndons lived the extensive Barbee family, cousins of the Herndons and the Rhodeses. There, too, had settled in the 1780s John Leigh, whose son Sullivan bought up several of the Barbee tracts.[46] Richard Stanford Leigh, Sullivan's son, is of interest because of his material legacy to Durham County history. At the time of his marriage he received from his father five hundred acres on which he built a two-room frame house in 1835, now modified by internal changes and external additions. Sheathed and ceiled with wide pine boards and its board and batten doors hung on large H and L hinges, this house is the oldest house in the county, until recently still owned by the original family but now in public ownership. In the yard stand historically important outbuildings: two slave houses, one with a stick chimney, a dairy raised on legs and pine-panelled, with water pipes under the floor to cool the dairy products, a smokehouse, carriage house, and corn crib.[47]

Richard Stanford Leigh owned in his prime just short of one thousand acres, the measure of a planter, and sixteen slaves. In 1860, though his main crop was corn, he also grew 125 bushels of wheat, three bales of cotton, and the usual Irish and sweet potatoes, beans, and peas. He kept some livestock, from which he got meat, dairy products, and wool; bees provided honey and beeswax. Two wives bore him twenty children, whom they were able to educate well and rear in comfortable circumstances.[48] The kind and quantity of their possessions testify to that. Along with their farm buildings, quantities of furnishings, furniture, farm implements, and family papers survive. The Leigh farm is today the most important historic resource in southern Durham County.

Two other post offices, more than likely housed in stores during this period, were Lipscomb's (1838) and Flemington (1833), later Brassfield (1856). The former was located on the home plantation of William Lipscomb where the Lipscomb house, much altered and expanded, stands at the crossing of Roxboro and Mason roads. A Christian church is said to have existed at Flemington, perhaps the nucleus of the community that developed where Robert Fleming had settled in the eighteenth century.[49] Located in Cedar Fork Township, an area dubbed the "dark corner of Durham County," this hamlet died despite its location at the hub of several roads and its possession of a railroad station in the 1870s.

Two other communities also developing in this era, Dilliardsville and Prattsburg, in almost the same place but with a decade or more between them, probably looked neither more nor less promising than those already discussed. They were, however, to have a quite different history, for they were the tiny forerunners of the city of Durham (see chapter 7).

MILLS

As important as churches and stores in the development of communities and community feeling were the old mills. They remained industrially preeminent until the introduction of steam power freed manufacturing from the riverbanks. Besides running saws and grindstones, the mills expanded to include carding machines for the preparation of wool and cotton for spinning, and tilt hammers for primitive forge work. The first spinning factory in North Carolina was established in 1815 by Schenck and Warlick in Lincoln County, but if a group of Orange County men had succeeded in their efforts, that county might have initiated the textile industry in the state. On 28 May 1813, Dr. John Umstead was chairman of a public meeting in Hillsborough to formulate plans for a cotton and woolen factory to be known as the Hillsborough Manufacturing Company. Apparently the required amount of stock was never subscribed, for no subsequent notice of the company exists.[50] Perhaps the War of 1812 had begun to affect the economy and discourage investment, or perhaps investors were not ready to gamble hard-earned money on so new an enterprise.

The mills along the Eno River during the first four decades of the nineteenth century were McCown's, Carrington's (later Sims's), Cameron's New Mill, and Bennehan's (earlier Hicks's and Kennon's), which ran from 1806 to the end of the century. On Flat River were Crabtree's, Nathaniel Harris's, Umstead's, and James

Walker's mills; along Little River were Robert Harris's, Cain's, and Lipscomb's. New mills appeared on the larger creeks as well: Bennehan's on Panther Creek, Samuel Southerland's and Duncan Cameron's sawmills on Ellerbee Creek, and John Garrard's mills on Mountain Creek, Zachariah Herndon, too, had a sawmill, possibly on Northeast Creek or one of its many tributaries.

In 1813 John Cabe's daughter Rachel married Moses McCown, who the same year was given by Cabe a large tract of land downstream from his own and, two years later, half ownership in a tilt hammer that Cabe built on the tract.[51] The McCown house, originally three rooms downstairs and two upstairs, of heart pine inside and out, still stands near the Cole Mill Road crossing of the river. It was enlarged and altered by Samuel Sparger in the early twentieth century. Oral tradition tells of John Cabe's nine beautiful daughters, all of whom are said to have married millers. Truth, however, has been altered to fit fancy, for a miller for each of them cannot be found in the records. Rachel, however, married two, for McCown died in 1829, and in 1831 Rachel married Herbert Sims, a widower who had inherited land on Flat River from John Carrington, his former father-in-law. In 1817 Sims had bought the extensive mill lands (over one thousand acres) of his brother-in-law George Carrington, who had overextended himself and from 1808 on floundered ever deeper in a financial morass.[52] Carrington's application for a Revolutionary War pension describes those troubled times and their results:

> His mind is so shattered & his memory is so frail, that he cannot trust it—that misfortune with mismanagement brought his private affairs into confusion, which terminated in the entire dispersion & destruction of the whole of his estate & in this helpless condition he was rendered much more helpless & his situation more deplorable & wretched by the visitation of God in the destruction of his intellect for a considerable time. That in the years 1818 & 1819, as he thinks, there was an entire alienation of mind for the most of the time & that ever since, his mind & memory have been so weak & treacherous that he cannot, nor can his friends, trust them & yet he has always been temperate or reasonably so.[53]

A gristmill, store, dwelling, and tavern had been part of the complex under Carrington ownership, but Sims expanded its operations to include a sawmill, blacksmith shop, cotton gin, stills, and post office.[54] As guardian to his stepchildren, Sims continued to operate the old McCown mill as well. He played a responsible role in the affairs of the county: he was a colonel of the militia, a veteran of the War of 1812, a justice of the peace, and a representative in the General Assembly (1838). The importance of Sims's mill community was recognized by the government in establishing a post office there in 1839, called West Point for reasons not known. The postmasters were in order John W. Hancock, James S. Leathers, Herbert Sims, Jr., and John C. McCown, who held the office when it was discontinued in 1866 after the Civil War. The year before, General Sherman had used West Point as a point of reference in establishing a dividing line between the Union and Confederate forces during the peace negotiations.[55]

Cameron's New Mill, so called to distinguish it from either Cameron Mills in Person County or, more likely, Cameron's sawmill on Ellerbee Creek, was built in 1834, a three-story millhouse 35 by 40 feet, with two waterwheels 15 feet in diameter. There, too, at the same time, Duncan Cameron built another sawmill, 42 by 14 feet.[56] Although Cameron's New Mill was a public facility, it was too far removed from a well-populated neighborhood to be very useful. Its prime value was its convenience to the Camerons in grinding their own huge crops of wheat and corn. Situated just upstream from the present Oxford highway crossing of the Eno River in the Triassic Basin, and thus vulnerable to severe flooding and the raging waters of freshets, it suffered repeated damage throughout its existence.

Richard Crabtree probably built his mill on Flat River soon after his purchase of four acres from William Parrish in 1816. The deed mentions a millseat, and it is likely that the tract he bought had been the Gibbs millsite of Collet's 1770 map. Crabtree's will, written in 1841 and probated in 1849, devised his saw- and gristmills; presumably they continued to run throughout his lifetime.[57] Remains of the mill, stone foundation with arches and head and tail races, are visible on the site, which is now in Hill Forest of the University of North Carolina.

No evidence remains, however, of Nathaniel Harris's mill downstream on the east bank at the mouth of Dial Creek, because the damming of Flat River created Lake Michie, whose waters have flooded the site. Harris's mill was in existence by 1834, for an ad in the newspaper for flaxseed to be ground at this mill appeared in that year under the name of Robert Harris, Nathaniel's son, Archer's grandson. Nathaniel actually sold Robert the large tract around the mill in 1836, but he reserved for himself the mill and three acres. In the same year Robert Harris sold the land and established himself at another set of mills, for grist and flaxseed oil, on the south fork of Little River at the old George Newton mill site.[58] Robert Harris was an ingenious mechanic, but possibly unstable. Soon after assuming the running of this second mill complex, he emigrated with his family to Tallahatchee County, Mississippi, and in 1841 committed suicide, leaving a wife and three small sons. In 1837 Nathaniel Harris sold his own mill on Flat River to Carter N. Waller of Granville County. On the same date he sold to Squire D. Umstead another small tract of twenty-five acres adjoining the mill tract and upstream on both Dial Creek and Flat River. Some time after 1850 (Waller's mill was still operating in that year), Umstead established his own mill on Dial Creek and Flat River at a site that would be today north of the bridge across Lake Michie at Bahama. The old Harris-Waller mill would be just downstream from the bridge where Dial Creek meets Flat River.[59]

Tradition in the Bahama area of the county credits James Walker with a mill on the east side of Flat River downstream from Harris's mill, at the same site where Walker's daughter Sallie later ran a mill. Though his will makes no mention of a mill and directs his executors to sell all his lands and slaves and divide the proceeds among his heirs, clearly Walker must have owned a mill at one time: John Lockhart and Bedford Vaughan, Walker's executors, sold fifteen acres and a mill "adjoining Walkers old place" to Sally [sic] Walker in 1856. Walker had died in 1855 at the age of eighty-eight; his active days must therefore have been some twenty or more years previously, suggesting that his mill must have been built in the 1830s. The site of Sallie Walker's mill is shown on the L. Johnson map of Durham County (1887) as south of the old Nathaniel Harris mill (then called [Addison] Mangum's) and north of Haywood Tilley's mill. A 1920 map of the county shows the Jock bridge crossing where Walker's mill traditionally stood.[60]

Tilley's mill had been the site of a gristmill for a very long while. In 1807 Elisha Umstead was operating a mill there and continued to do so at least until 1848. In the earlier year Thomas D. Bennehan, writing to his father, recounted the damage done by a July flood: "Last week Flat River was as high as it has been this winter; it carried off Umstead's Mill Dam entirely & I am told there is not a vestige of it left. The [mill]house is safe."[61]

Robert Harris's departure left his mill on Little River in limbo. He had probably leased it from Joseph Armstrong, for no record exists of his purchase or his administrators' sale of the mill. John B. Leathers was given the mill by his father-in-law, Joseph Armstrong, and continued to run it until the 1850s, when he sold it for a short time to John A. McMannen.[62]

Cain's mill continued to be run by the Cain family: after William's death in 1834 it was operated by his son William, Jr., and after the latter's death, by his son Thomas Ruffin Cain. Little is known of Lipscomb's mill on Little River. William Lipscomb intended to leave it to his son John along with Anderson, the slave miller, but by 1860 he had already advanced it to John. When John D. Lipscomb died intestate in 1875, his lands were divided among his heirs, each of the four receiving a share of the mill.[63] Within the memory of those now living, a mill on the same site was known as Berry's mill.

It would be hard to overestimate the importance of mills in an agricultural society—as meeting places for individuals and groups, as commercial centers offering manifold services, as lines of communication with the world beyond the farms. Against a backdrop of working machines, fascinating and challenging, the people met, bought provisions, collected mail, paid taxes, and cast votes; they learned from the broadsides nailed to the walls of strayed animals, estate sales, runaway slaves, militia musters, quack medicines, and camp meetings; they listened to politicians make their pitches and exchange promises for votes; they fished, swam, and swapped horses, views, and news. Through it all the separate and lonely farmers came to understand the community and society that they were creating and of which they were a part.[64]

SCHOOLS

Except for academies and seminaries in towns, little is known about schools in this period. That rural schools existed is proved by the fact that two-thirds of North Carolina's population was literate in 1840; rural schools just did not get into the records. There can be no doubt, however, that schools were deplorably insufficient. The local and temporary subscription or old field schools, which had developed in the eighteenth century, continued to prevail. The term of these schools was short—three or four months—and the instruction elementary. Almost anyone with the rudiments of an education could set himself up as a teacher. In 1832 Willie P.

Mangum referred to "the school in the neighbourhood" as a temporary solution for his daughter's education, but he hoped to make arrangements with the free black educator John Chavis for a school on his plantation if he could round up enough support from his neighbors.[65] Chavis—by tradition a soldier in the Revolution, a graduate of Princeton and the Academy at Lexington (later Washington and Lee University), licensed to preach by the Lexington Presbytery, and a renowned teacher of both white and black children—had probably numbered Willie P. and his brother Priestley Mangum among his students. He maintained a strong affection for both, and his stance as mentor, freely scolding, instructing, or praising them and addressing each as "my son" in a familiarity of manner unique in black-white relations, strongly supports the probability.[66] In a long career Chavis taught schools primarily in Granville and Wake counties, but he taught at least one in Durham County on Ellerbee Creek near Eno Primitive Baptist Meeting House in 1825 and 1826. It was a school for girls and had in the latter year twenty-two students from six to twenty years of age.[67]

Less well known than Chavis are several other teachers who taught in eastern Orange. One who, like Chavis, ran a school wherever he could find employment was Lotan G. Watson. For one year he acted as private tutor to Duncan Cameron's sons. Later he studied medicine and, at his death in 1849, was a professor at Transylvania University medical school in Kentucky.[68] John W. Hancock, who ran the academy for boys at Orange Grove, also taught girls, among them Mary Jane and Patsy Dilliard, Jefferson's sisters. Thomas Flint, a Virginian, a Revolutionary War veteran, and the author of a grammar book published in Hillsborough in 1827, was another man who spent most of his life as a teacher. He, too, reputedly taught Willie P. Mangum and was for some years the teacher at the Piper-Cabe schoolhouse. In 1821, at his plantation on Ellerbee Creek he boarded and taught pupils, among them Termesia Rhodes, a granddaughter of John Cabe. Termesia was sent to Chavis's school in 1822, and in 1823 Silas M. Link, better known later as the county surveyor, was her teacher. John Marcom, too, must have run a school. Guardians' accounts reveal that he taught Adeline Herndon, charging 66⅔¢ per month or $3.42 for five months in 1839.[69]

Thanks to Archibald Murphey and his supporters, who knew how desperate the cultural climate was in North Carolina, the fight for public schools was kept alive. It became a priority when the Whig Party came to power in the late 1830s. In 1839 the legislature passed an act establishing common or public schools for all white children between the ages of five and twenty-one. In the Orange County referendum on schools, only three precincts voted against them. Thereupon Orange County was divided into fifty-one school districts five miles square, and a school committee of three men was appointed for each district. The committees were to obtain school buildings and teachers for the children in their districts, the number and size of schools varying with the school population. The court imposed taxes for their support, a poll tax of five cents and a property tax of two cents for each hundred dollars' valuation of land. Nine school board members were appointed by the county court, of whom only Silas Link was from eastern Orange.[70] At first, organization was slow and inefficient. Where parents were eager and school committees zealous, schools were established and students recruited, but where prejudice continued against free education because it smacked of charity, or where the more influential men in a district preferred education to remain a preserve of those who could pay for it, schools were slow in coming. Poorly qualified teachers, inadequate equipment, and one-room schoolhouses that were often abandoned cabins, drafty, leaky, dark, and uninspiring, were more likely to quench than feed any spark of ambition to learn that the children possessed. Only over time did a system evolve that could address the deficiencies, raise the standard of teaching, and encompass all the children. Though North Carolina was at last on the road to recovery by 1840, much harm had been done. Deprivation in the physical environment—a lack of creature comforts or technological conveniences—is quickly rectified; cultural malnutrition, on the contrary, is crippling, and if the nutrients come too late, the victims may never recover. Generations of North Carolinians suffered, and generations were required to catch up.

POLITICS

Even before the Whig Party became the vehicle of Orange County's political power, a few statesmen surfaced from the maelstrom of opinion as leaders with clear vision for public good. In the Colonial and Revolutionary periods William Johnston played an important role in eastern Orange County, as did Duncan Cameron during the Federal period. Johnston's influence was felt in the Provincial Congresses, in the government of the town of Hillsborough, in the county militia, and on the Committee of Safety for the Hillsborough District. Although a supporter of the American side in the Revolution, he was no flaming patriot. He remained a loyal friend of Edmund Fanning, at the same time proceeding calmly and objectively along the course he saw as best for the new country. Cameron, an unswerving Federalist, served eight terms in the state legislature and succeeded to the leadership of Archibald Murphey's internal improvements committee. He was looked on as the political boss of Orange County throughout the early decades of the nineteenth century.[71] High-principled, aristocratic, and authoritarian, he well understood where progress lay, but did not always recognize the means to achieve it.

Both Murphey and Cameron were instrumental in fostering the career of the region's preeminent statesman, Willie P. Mangum, for they early saw in him qualities of intellect and leadership that could further their objectives. Mangum was born in 1792 into a family of comfortable circumstances; he was a son of William Person Mangum and a grandson of Arthur Mangum, a pioneer planter in the county. Soundly educated in school and university, Willie P. Mangum possessed an inherent talent for oratory, great personal charm, and an elegant, tall bearing that gave him a winning edge on the hustings. If he had pursued his law practice or remained on the judicial bench, he would have won both prosperity and esteem, but he was ambitious for success in a wider arena. Elected to the state legislature at the early age of twenty-six, he progressed to the U.S. House of Representatives in 1824 when he was just over thirty. In state matters he supported the Murphey program of public expenditure for education and internal improvements, but not with federal funds; on national issues he was less consistent, first opposing Andrew Jackson, then supporting him, and finally repudiating him for his stand on South Carolina's nullification issue and the United States Bank. After Mangum's election to the Senate in 1830, he remained in that chamber with only a few years' interruption until 1853. Because of William Henry Harrison's death in his first year as president, Mangum, as president *pro tempore* of the Senate, missed by a hair's breadth becoming president when the new President Tyler narrowly escaped death in the accidental explosion of a gun on the USS *Princeton* in 1844.[72]

Advantageously and happily married to William Cain's daughter Charity, Mangum regretted his long absences from home. His financial affairs suffered from his neglect and imprudent investment, though his wife managed his plantations carefully. He was too generous to his friends and too casual with his creditors. William Cain repeatedly rescued him financially. Duncan Cameron said of him, "He may have some money in Washington—he never has any at home."[73] Nonetheless, Mangum built for his family a handsome house, Walnut Hall, in the Greek Revival style on the site of an earlier home; he planted it with specimen trees and plants bought in Washington. A fire destroyed the house in 1933. The huge walnut trees that gave it its name are gone.

The formation of the Whig party in 1834 brought to North Carolina a two-party system once again. Though there had been throughout the 1820s and 1830s pro- and anti-Jackson forces, the emergence of a clearly defined Whig program gave the voters a clear alternative to the Democratic Republicans. An amusing letter to Mangum concerning the events at a country sale, written by a neighbor, the young miller Robert Harris, reflects the ardor of that new partisanship.

> Those contrary republicans and Devlish clan that you have around you when at home—the Boullings, Dukes & Carringtons—formed a sort of Jackson club and possessed themselves of His leading principle War & bloodshed. They commenced their work upon our humble wagon maker Haywood Gooch and there was not a man on the ground but what was afraid to go to his relief but our noble spirited Col. D. C. Parrish who rushed in at the risk of his own life and succeeded in rescuing him by taking the wolves on his own back. They had Dr [Doctor] under their feet for ten minutes or more endeavoring to beat and stamp him to death, and his cowardly friends Strong enough and a plenty of them was a fraid to interfere till at length Some disinterested persons insensed with Such out dacious conduct rushed in, over powered them, and saved Parrish.[74]

To channel their support legitimately, in the next decade the partisans formed political clubs, which served to bring public attention and debate to local and national issues. These clubs educated an electorate expanded in 1835 by the reformed state constitution—discussed in the following chapter—and helped translate the Piedmont's views into new legislation. Orange County became conspicuous in the state for the number and quality of its leaders. The attention paid to them, the interest politics commanded in those years, and the presence of so admirable a national figure as Mangum, could not help stimulating Orange Countians to take pride in their county's political prominence and to participate in the political action. From lethargy and indifference, the spirit of the age had proceeded to engagement and concern. The Rip Van Winkle era was over.

6

Improvement Fever, 1840–1861

T HE IMPETUS TO IMPROVEMENT came from Orange County. Archibald Murphey's adherents and disciples were finally able to enact his program when they came to power with the rise of the Whig party in the mid-1830s. Their first achievement was the constitutional convention, which resulted in a new state constitution in 1835. The people were at last allowed to vote for governor. Representatives to the legislature were to be apportioned by population instead of allocated two to a county; borough representation was scrapped; and provision was made for amending the constitution and for referenda to confirm amendments.[1]

Energy and optimism characterized this era of the county's history. The new provision for the establishment of public schools, though not a concept supported by all, was nevertheless tonic to the population. Along with the first scattered, poorly taught, poorly supervised public schools, new private schools and academies were spurred into being. If even the poorest children were to be educated, it behooved well-to-do parents to provide equal if not better schools for their children. Other aspects of Murphey's plans were implemented as well, particularly improvements for internal transportation. Among the many enterprises chartered for this purpose was the Neuse River Navigation Company, which would have made possible commercial water traffic upstream to Smithfield and accommodated lighter craft by means of canals and locks up to Hillsborough.[2] Though nothing came of this endeavor, other navigation companies were formed and made improvements, dug out channels, and built canals and locks. Some plank roads were also constructed, though not nearly so many as were chartered. Two companies chartered in 1855, whose roads would have crossed Durham County land if they had been built, were the Chapel Hill and Durhamsville Plankroad Company and the Chapel Hill and Morrisville Plankroad, Tramroad, and Turnpike Company.[3] Improvement fever was contagious, and while many new ventures in industry were financed by surplus cash from the advancing agricultural economy, some were flukes of inspiration.

THE SOUTH LOWELL VENTURE

One such venture in northern Durham County might well have become the nucleus of a modern metropolis but for the accident of geography. South Lowell in present Lebanon Township first emerged under its ambitious new name in 1845. A newspaper advertisement announced that John A[rchibald] McMannen had bought the North Carolina rights to Young's Smut and Screening machine (a machine that separated diseased from healthy grain), and that inquiries about the machine might be sent to Holden's Enoe Mills or South Lowell Mills.[4]

Born in Virginia in 1812, McMannen had been brought to North Carolina as a child by his parents, John and Hannah McMannen, and like his father was trained to be a cooper. He was also a lay preacher of the Methodist Church and but for lack of formal training would probably have been ordained to the regular ministry, a career that would have exactly suited him.[5] In 1843, however, he conceived a scheme for spreading the gospel and incidentally earning some money. He planned an engraving, short on illustration and long on text, contrasting the pilgrimages through life of the sinner and the Christian. He found an artist, Matthew Ball, to execute his ideas and then proceeded to copyright the result and print it. The engravings were sold either printed on paper and framed in mahogany (two dollars), or printed on satin and framed in gilt (eight dollars).[6] It was a resounding success. This odd venture enabled McMannen to emerge from obscurity and play a role in the history of Durham County with his colorful personality, ambition, imagination, and willingness to take risks for the sake of his dreams. His quite ordinary failings—lack of formal education or a sense of prudence or proportion—were stumbling blocks throughout his life, but his talents were in a class by themselves.

McMannen used the proceeds from the engraving to purchase the patent for the smut machine and to invest in their manufacture at John B. Leathers's mill (renamed South Lowell, no doubt after the town in Massachusetts, with its reputation for grand-scale milling and for prosperity). Again McMannen struck it rich. These machines were of vital interest to millers because they made it possible to keep blighted grain from contaminating the final product. The newspaper reported in 1854 that McMannen had already sold $125,000 worth of the machines. As a result of this activity, South Lowell was put on a mail route and received a post office at the mills in 1846. In 1853, McMannen was able to buy the mill and the tract it stood on from Leathers, along with a large tract of land between the north and south forks of Little River lying north of the road. On the bank of the north fork he built a substantial house (still standing) for his wife, Elizabeth Latta, daughter of James, and their ten children.[7]

The mills' prosperity and the climate of the times inspired the neighborhood to its next improvement: the South Lowell Male Academy, which opened in February 1849 with the Reverend James A. Dean as headmaster. Dean had solid qualifications: A.B. and M.A. degrees from Wesleyan College in Connecticut and ordination by the North Carolina Conference of the Methodist Church.[8] Located across the road from McMannen's house, the school offered three curricula: elementary education ($10 a term), the higher branches of English ($12.50), and the classical course ($17). The trustees were McMannen, Drs. A. W. Gay, James S. Leathers (a brother of John B. and son of Fielding), and Richard Blacknall, and D. C. Parrish. The school was immediately successful. The very next year the trustees let bids for the building of a brick dormitory, 40 by 22 feet, one room below, two rooms above, to accommodate the numbers of students who wanted to come to the school from around the state.[9] The same year a girls' school, the South Lowell Female Academy, was established under the direction of Miss Emma Patterson, and McMannen boarded some of the girls in his house. Besides McMannen and James Leathers, the trustees were John B. Leathers, Silas M. Link, and George T. Coggin. The Reverend A. Arnold advertised that he could board up to thirty students at the hotel in the village (the old Elizabeth Leathers house at the corner of Rougemont and South Lowell roads) for $6.50 a month for room, board, and washing; lights were extra. The school could soon boast a library of close to two hundred volumes; it became the center of all cultural activities in the area: the South Lowell Lyceum, the Temperance Society, religious meetings, and miscellaneous events such as a course in Hebrew by an ex-Harvard professor.[10]

A few documents give a more intimate view of the South Lowell Academy. James Gill, a student, wrote home: "Mr. McMannen is preacher, a very fine man and has [a] very likely daughter and she performs well on the piano. Mr. Mc and two of his sons are fiddlers. They play with the piano and it makes very nice music. . . . Our principal [then Charles Harris] is a lawyer and competent man and much of a gentleman in all respects; he gives lectures on friday evenings on various important subjects." Another South Lowell Academy student was Ellison G. Mangum's son Adolphus, who went on to Randolph Macon College, was ordained a Methodist minister, and later became Professor of Mental and Moral Philosophy at Chapel Hill. His diary, kept during his college years, tells much of northern Durham County people. Mangum was particularly fond of McMannen, "his hearty laugh," and "the flights of fancy of his fruitful imagination." "I love Mc devotedly," he wrote, "& wish him a happy life and a happy Eternity. His fireside is a pleasant home to me & I long for him to steer clear of his difficulties and prosper in all things."[11] McMannen did considerable preaching, marrying, and burying in the area, but his "fruitful imagination" and rash ambition led him into more real estate ventures than his manufacturing business could support, even though the size of his business was such that in 1856 he had "twenty-two experienced hands" working for him. Nevertheless he was unable to meet the interest payments on his loans when they fell due, and eventually debt overtook him. D. C. Parrish and John B. Leathers repeatedly lent him money, but he was finally forced into bankruptcy.[12]

From 1845 to the Civil War South Lowell thrived. In 1856 Dr. Edward Scott advertised a medical school there, which, however, was short-lived. Scott became a captain in the Confederate army and died at the age of thirty-three while in service. The South Lowell neighborhood was well supplied with physicians. Besides Scott there were James S. Leathers, A. W. Gay, Richard Blacknall, Edwin M. Holt, and John A. McMannen's sons Charles T. and Leroy Dewitt McMannen. Holt and the two McMannen brothers were graduates of South Lowell Academy. Charles T. McMannen, as ambitious as his father, later patented the American Tar Mixture, an ipecac and wintergreen concoction that had much success as a panacea.[13]

So Methodist a community was not without church services. Besides McMannen's services at the academy there was nearby Union Grove Church, also built at McMannen's instigation at his earlier location on the old Hillsborough to Oxford Road. William Lipscomb built the church on his own land, possibly in the late 1830s, with the understanding that he would be repaid, but the Civil War wiped out any hope of that. Lipscomb then turned the building into a dwelling and sold it. Adolphus Mangum often preached at Union Grove Church in the 1850s. Frequently Norman Dunnegan, a Primitive Baptist, preached there as well.[14]

IMPROVEMENT ELSEWHERE

South Lowell's cultural springs flowed into the neighboring communities of Red Mountain and Round Hill. Though long supplied with a church, Mount Bethel, Round Hill had as yet no school. With five daughters to educate, D. C. Parrish, inspired by his friend McMannen's success, set up a female seminary on his plantation at Round Hill in 1850, taught by the aptly named Martha (Patty) Duty, an eighteen-year-old miss from Granville County. By 1858 Dr. Edwin M. Holt, a scion of Alamance County's manufacturing family, was chairman of the Round Hill school's executive committee. Holt had married into Harrison Parker's family and established a medical practice at Round Hill. He later built a house on the corner of Orange Factory and Roxboro roads (still standing) where he lived the rest of his life, a trusted doctor of the whole countryside. One South Lowell patient recalled him in her nineties: "He was a nice-looking man; I just loved him."[15]

Red Mountain also needed a school. John P. Bailey, whom a South Lowell graduate, Addison Mangum, described as "dull as a meat ax," left his assistant headmaster's job at the academy in 1854 and with his wife opened Red Mountain Female Academy. Its promoters were Abner Parker, John Lockhart, Richard Holeman, Richard Blacknall, and George W. Jones; Willie P. Mangum donated the five acres on which it was built. In 1856 Meriwether Lewis (possibly a relation of the explorer) and his wife were principals. The only church in the community was on the plantation of David Parker and was known as Shady Hill Meeting House; it was probably built in the early 1840s.[16]

Adolphus Mangum's diary is a window into the northern part of the future Durham County of the 1850s; it allows glimpses of many aspects of society: its poor, prosperous (no one was rich), young, old, insane, and intemperate; its churches, schools, stores, homes, and social organizations; its politicians and community leaders, its humble and obscure. As he rode horseback from one place to another in his summer vacations, looking up friends, visiting relations, and attending local events, he observed and faithfully recorded all he saw: a tax gathering or a muster at Red Mountain at the store of his Parker uncles, Harrison and Abner; political speeches at Midway store (his father's business); a "topsyturvy fandango" of the blacks that followed a political rally; and the drunken fights that arose from the freely dispensed liquor of the politicians. Mangum enjoyed revisiting the scenes of his school days, and often rode over to South Lowell. He laughed at the schoolboy humor chalked on the spittoons in Mr. Whittier's and Mr. Waterman's classrooms, "Remember me" and "Unsolicited Contributions thankfully rec'd." He noted the stores in Round Hill village: Parrish and Company (D. C. Parrish and Williams Harris's undertaking), Sweeny's, William Moize's tailor shop, and Leathers and Latta at South Lowell.[17] He observed and described his home, too. One evening in July 1856, he sat in the passage between the two houses that made up Locust Grove, watching the moonlight on the trees and listening to the evening sounds.

> There is an old porch in front on the west end which is enveloped by a luxuriant vine called "Virgin Bower." The South side of the passage is approached by an aperture lined overhead and on either side with spreading multifloras [illegible] Rose vines, dahlias, crocus, hydrangea, snow-ball, chrysanthemum, flax, geranium, cypress, Jessamine (which winds its way up the corner of the old building) and a variety of small roses and flowers all interspersed. [He goes on to describe the yard.] Near the avenue stands an old appletree, which not being a favorite shadetree or fruit tree, is alone permitted to stand because planted by my mother's hands—Back towards the west are two borders filled with different sorts of flowers—& right at the west end stands a large spreading Cedar & locust tree. Near this stands a favorite tree called the wild cherry, the prettiest of the species I have ever seen & esteemed the most beautiful of all the trees in the yard.[18]

Mangum also described a local Fourth of July celebration. "They had a long table nearly one hundred yards long running up into the woods in a semicircular form. Col [Abner] Parker was marshall of the day & we had a procession in the following order: Ministers of the Gospel, Sons of Temperance, Union Volunteer Company in their uniforms, citizens generally, Orators of the day, Chaplain & Reader of the Declaration of Independence." Squire D. Umstead read the Declaration, and then all the company went to the table and ate a dinner prepared by Major Bedford Vaughan. The site of the celebration was in a field close by the Flat River Union Church, which had been formed, probably in the 1840s, by Baptists who had withdrawn from Primitive Baptist churches because of the latter group's antimissionary stance. It was located on Elisha Umstead's land on the east side of Flat River. Lewis Roberts was the first clerk; some of the early members besides Umstead were Henderson Tilley, Bedford Vaughan, Willis Ashley, John King, William B. Parrish, and William Bowling. In 1856, after Umstead's death, it moved to Granville County and took the name Knap of Reeds.[19]

Cultural ambition was not confined to the northern part of the county. The Fletcher's Chapel Church area also wanted a college preparatory school and in 1853 established Morning Sun Academy. The trustees were Mark Tate, manager of Cameron's Fish Dam store, Dr. Thomas Hicks, Peleg Rogers, Robert Halliburton, and Calvin J. Rogers. Principals of the school in the early years were Thomas Jefferson Horner, Alexander C. Jones, A. J. Jones, and A. P. Pickard.[20]

While private schools of this caliber were few, some progress was made in setting up the new free district schools, and the old system of subscription schools still continued. The names of a few teachers in that first decade of public schooling are known: Burwell Freeman, William Furlong, Alsey B. Holland, Edwin Horner, Archibald Hunter, Frank Jones, N. M. Lane, Jonathan Laws, Thomas Laws, Joseph Mangum, Rufus Massey, James F. Rogers, Sidney Scott, Francis Stagg, and John Tilley.[21] School teaching was a precarious livelihood, so that it attracted those who either aimed higher and needed money to continue their education, or those unfit for other kinds of work—the elderly and the handicapped.

None of the private schools survived more than a few decades at most; nor did the churches Union Grove or Flat River Union (at their original sites) or Shady Hill. But other churches organized in these years are still active: Mount Hebron, which became Duke's Chapel Church (1840); Rose of Sharon, which became the First Baptist Church of Durham (1845); Berea Baptist Church (1855); Masseys Chapel Church (1855); Mount Tabor Church; and Sandy Level Church. Mount Hebron's founding is attributed to William J. Duke, Washington Duke's oldest brother. Zealous, impassioned in his faith, untutored but hard-working, he was an exhorter and lay preacher in the Methodist Church and, like McMannen, would gladly have done church work full-time. The oldest of Taylor and Dicey Jones Duke's ten children, he was obliged with only a meager education to make his own way in the world and to help his younger brothers after his father's financial problems cost the elder Duke his home and farm. Stories about Willie Duke have been handed down in affectionate memory: how he loved to sing "The Old Ship of Zion" and how he prayed for rain: "O Lord, send us some rain. We need it. But don't let it be a gully-washer. Just give us a sizzle-sozzle."[22]

In 1840 Duke set aside one acre of his land for a church. The structure known as Mount Hebron was built of logs, 30 by 35 feet, with siding and wooden shutters, and was situated on the road to Roxboro. After many years, agitation developed in the church over the question of moving it. Some members were determined to keep it where it was; others were just as determined to move it. In 1879 Duke deeded the land to the church trustees, perhaps hoping to quell the controversy. Nevertheless in 1885 a new church was built on the Old Oxford Highway on land deeded to the trustees by John L. Markham, and the old site and church were auctioned off. Perhaps to soothe Duke's wounded feelings, the name of the church was changed to Duke's Chapel.[23]

The origins of the other Methodist churches, Masseys Chapel and Mount Tabor, are less well documented. John Massey is said to have been the principal donor of the former, which in a 1903 reconstruction stands on the original site on the Fayetteville road close to the Chatham County line.[24] Although the Mount Tabor Church history records its establishment in the 1870s, it is at least two decades older. Adolphus Mangum mentioned in his diary that he preached the funerals of Johnny and Adolphus Moize at Mount Tabor Church in 1856. Washington S. Chaffin, a Methodist minister on the Granville circuit in 1862, regularly preached at Mount Tabor. His diary records his first sermon there on 11 January, after which he took dinner at Addison Mangum's house just down the road from the church. "I guess he has made money slowly but surely. The country around Mount Tabor, I think, is beautiful." On the way home from his visit on 4 July he met up with a rabid secessionist, whom Chaffin described as "the kangaroo class of politicians—jumps well, is long legged, & depends more upon his activity than on his judgment."[25]

The Baptists founded Berea Church in the southern part of the county in the mid-1850s. In 1857 Coslett and Martha Herndon donated four acres to Willis and Charles G. Marcum [sic], George M. Shepherd, Mordecai Sears, and H. J. Pearson on which to build a "Missionary Baptist Church of Christ in connection with the Raleigh Baptist Association." It too remains on its original site on the Fayetteville road. An earlier church in this area may have been a forerunner of Berea. In 1848 George W. Vickers sold a large tract of land to Chesley P. Trice, the location of which is described as "beginning at a stake in front of the meeting house" on Vicker's line.[26]

In 1853 a group of Baptists on the present Junction Road organized a congregation known as Sandy Level Church, located about halfway between present Joyland and Gorman. To honor Columbus Durham, a former pastor (1876–88), its name was changed to Durham Memorial Baptist Church when it was moved to its present location on Holloway Street in 1939.[27]

The church founded in these years that has grown and prospered most, known first as Rose of Sharon Baptist Church and later as First Baptist Church, began in 1845 in the schoolhouse at Piney Grove, one mile south of West Durham. In 1846 George W. Rhodes (having just previously moved to Tennessee) sold two and one-half acres to Noah Trice and William Whitaker, trustees, for "a House or place of worship for the use of the members of the Missionary Baptist Churches." The site adjoined Strayhorn land; Andrew Turner witnessed the deed. Surveys made by the North Carolina Railroad Company in 1850 show Rose of Sharon Church by the railroad right of way adjoining Bartlett L. Durham's land.[28] These landowners' names— Strayhorn, Durham, Turner, and Rhodes—identify a place on the ridge between the New Hope Creek and Eno River watersheds that would soon have a name of its own and a role to play in the lives of the people of eastern Orange.

OTHER INDUSTRY AND AGRICULTURE

South Lowell was not the only place in the county where manufacturing was attempted. Other ventures were a woolen factory, a cotton factory, and a window sash and shutter factory. The first was a project of John Cabe's grandsons, Robert M. and John Cabe Shields. They bought acreage half a mile downstream on the Eno River from the old Cabe mill (then in the possession of their father, William T. Shields) on which to build a woolen factory. Their aunt Martha Moderwell took a mortgage on the acreage, buildings, and equipment which gave them the capital ($3,500) they needed for the project. In 1852 the Hillsborough *Recorder* announced the factory, about to start, and hoped it would spur local farmers to raise sheep. Although Robert Shields died that year, his brother continued to run the business with new partners and the money they put into it: William Nelson in 1854 and John D. Lipscomb in 1856. The county fair of 1854 exhibited three samples of cloth from the Alpha Woolen Mills (the name the Shieldses had given their factory); the samples were black, brown, and steel-mixed.[29] In 1857, much in debt, the business was advertised for sale. Martha Moderwell took possession and then leased the factory to another nephew, Charles J. Shields, who took as his partner a Pennsylvania native and experienced factory superintendent, Benjamin P. Sykes. By March 1859, however, the partners had a falling-out, deliberately contrived by Shields's meddlesome father. Charles Shields took a new partner, his brother-in-law Lorenzo Bennett, son of James Bennitt [sic]. In 1860, with a capitalization of $6,000 and eight employees, five women and three men, whose total wages per month were $61, it turned out 1,200 yards of "jeans, etcetera" worth $3,000. The death of both partners in the Civil War put an end to the business. Not even its site on the river, known locally as "factory bottom," reveals anything of the Alpha Woolen Mills. The railroad siding later called Funston, close to the Bennett Place, was also known as "woolen siding," a vestige of the Bennett and Shields enterprise.[30]

The cotton factory was destined for a much longer run. John C. Douglas, William Lipscomb's son-in-law, and John Huske Webb, son of Hillsborough's Dr. James Webb, formed a partnership in 1850 to build and operate a factory to spin thread and make cloth. They bought land on Little River downstream from Lipscomb's mill and erected in 1852 what they called Orange Factory, because it was at that time the only cotton factory in Orange County. A letter from Thomas C. Dixon, a member of the crew engaged in its construction, described it as ninety-four feet high from the roof projection to the brick foundation. Dixon, a Quaker, thought his fellow workers a rough lot. "We have a very bad company some to drink & all to sware, Fiddle & dance play cards and so on."[31] He wrote of having gone to church one Sunday at Lipscomb's (that is, Union Grove) and of a Ba[t]chelor family that was coming to do the cooking for the crew and then to work in the completed factory. The 1860 census names Virganetta Batchelor and three daughters, all spinners, and a son, a carder. That year the factory, capitalized at $30,000, produced 140,000 pounds of cotton yarn worth $28,000. The thirty women workers earned a total of $225 a month and the twenty men $640. The machinery was run by both water and steam.[32]

Besides the huge factory, Webb and Douglas erected a gristmill, with a dam on Little River that served both operations, and workers' houses perched in neat rows on the hillside above the factory. One habitation larger than the others, a boarding house for single workers, was known as the "twenty house." A general store, a schoolhouse, and eventually a log church completed the village. Skilled workmen were the wheelwright, William Holloway, the machinist, George Pickard, and the blacksmith, William Richard. At first the factory made only thread, but during the Civil War, when three-fourths of its work was government contracts, it made cloth for Confederate uniforms.[33]

In 1864 the factory was bought by William H. Willard, a native of Massachusetts, who had come south in his youth to improve his health and had stayed to engage in manufacturing, banking, and other business enterprises. In 1866 a dispute arose between him and Paul Cameron, a near neighbor, when Cameron accused Willard of buying produce stolen from his plantations by his ex-slaves. Cameron apologized to Willard before a suit for slander went to court, but Cameron's overseers, and

George Pickard, who had been factory superintendent for twelve years, substantiated Cameron's claims that he had lost many hogs, sheep, and bales of cotton to the factory, principally under the previous owner.[34]

In 1873 Willard sold the factory to Sidney Willard Holman, possibly a relation, who took a mortgage of $45,000 on the almost 700 acres including the factory, village, and surrounding farmland. Holman ran the general store and superintended the factory. By the end of the decade it had 42 looms and 1,300 spindles producing ginghams and seamless bags. In 1887 began the factory's palmiest days. That year Willard repossessed it, serving as president and treasurer of the renamed Willard Manufacturing Company until his death in 1898, while W. C. Holman was vice-president, Sidney Holman was superintendent, and Albert Gallatin Cox was assistant superintendent and manager of the store, newly rebuilt after a fire. The factory was then making rope, twine, hosiery yardage, and seamless bags with the sweepings it bought from the weaving, spinning, and carding rooms of Durham's Pearl Mill, among others. In 1887 the Lynchburg and Durham Railroad was incorporated and established on its line, a mile from the factory, a station called Willardville.[35]

Willard devised the factory to the children of his daughter Hannah and her husband Samuel A. Ashe. In 1904 and 1905, after unsuccessfully trying to interest Benjamin N. Duke in buying it in partnership, Cox bought the company with James B. Mason, who became president. They called the new enterprise the Little River Manufacturing Company. Mason also bought the old William Lipscomb place as his home, which he proceeded to enlarge and alter to its present form; and Cox bought 207 acres on which he built a house for his family. Cox is credited with the second church in the village, which replaced one built on land donated by Willard, and for a later structure in 1898, known first as Orange Factory Methodist and now as Riverview Methodist Church. In 1916 Little River Manufacturing Company was sold to J. A. Long of Roxboro, who renamed it Laura Cotton Mill and made yarns and striped convict cloth. In 1938 Laura Cotton Mill was sold for $4,000 to Roxboro Cotton Mill, its useful days and profitable operation long past. The mill workers continued to live in the mill houses, but the place had lost its vitality and continued its slow decay until the rising waters of the now dammed Little River claimed it.[36]

Scattered throughout the countryside were many small industrial establishments for leather tanning, wheat threshing, cotton ginning, wool carding, blacksmithing, and the like. One of these was the window blind (shutter) and sash factory established by Robert Fulton Webb on his plantation off the present Moriah-Bahama Road. Webb, a native of Baltimore, is said to have met John A. McMannen there and to have been influenced by him to come south to Orange County. Here he met and married Amanda Mangum, daughter of Ellison G. Mangum. Besides the blinds and sashes, Webb made other wooden products, including picture frames, which he exhibited at the first Orange County fair in 1854. At that fair, too, George Pickard, the Orange Factory machinist, showed what he could do with metal: he exhibited a carving set, a razor, a chisel, and cotton spools, the latter probably among the many items he designed in his work at the factory.[37]

Along with these innovative industries, new and old mills along the river banks continued to operate. On the Eno were the old mills, McCown's, West Point, and

Bennehan's. Though McCown's ground $6,000 worth of flour in 1860 and West Point only $4,800, the miller at the latter mill made $16 a month compared to $12 for McCown's miller. The Bennehan mill ground $19,000 worth of flour that year and employed two men, whose wages totaled $30 a month. One new mill had been established, that of William W. Guess in 1848 at the present Guess Road crossing of the river. This mill produced $6,000 worth of flour in 1860 and paid its miller $15 a month. On Little River the South Lowell Mills were again in John B. Leathers's possession, paying two millers a total of $36 a month but producing only 400 barrels of flour worth $2,400. Lipscomb's mill produced the more usual $6,000 worth of flour. Neither Cain's on Little River nor Cameron's on Eno reported earnings in the 1860 census year.[38] They were probably temporarily out of repair, a common condition of mills on Piedmont rivers.

On Flat River old mills under new owners and a few new mills ground the wheat that was being grown in ever larger quantity. At Red Mountain George W. Jones, who operated a store there at mid-century, applied for a permit to construct a mill in 1850. The commissioners appointed to look into the matter reported that such a mill would be "of immense value in the neighborhood." An acre of Benjamin Hester, who owned land on the opposite bank, was condemned for the project. Although the mill was built in 1850, it is not included in that year's census or in that of 1860. Jones sold it in 1870 to his Bowling in-laws, who operated it for many years. It is the only original mill structure still standing in Durham County. Crabtree's mill was owned by Harrison Parker in 1860; it ground $3,600 worth of flour that year. The miller earned $25 a month. Squire Umstead's and Nathaniel Harris's mills, though unreported in the 1860 census, were still operating, and were later run by Umstead's sons and Harris's nephew, Addison Mangum, respectively. Sallie Walker was operating her father's mill, and ground 600 barrels of flour worth $3,600 in 1860. Two years later, in the midst of the Civil War, she sold the mill to David and William L. Allen of Granville County for $3,000. By 1870 it was being run by the partnership of Hargrove and Meadows.[39]

Elisha Umstead's mill had been bought by Bedford Vaughan and his partner Henry C. Sweeny of Granville County along with two large tracts of Umstead land. In 1856 they were forced to take a mortgage on the property: 58 acres on which the Union Mills stood, and 135 acres on which the Union store and a tobacco factory stood. "Union" in both names recalls the Flat River Union Church that had earlier also been there. At a foreclosure sale John Lockhart bought Union Mills and leased them to Haywood Tilley, Bedford Vaughan's son-in-law, who reported their production in 1860 as 6,260 barrels of flour worth $34,000, obviously a thriving business. During the Civil War Lockhart was murdered by slaves, and the mill was sold in the estate settlement to Tilley. The mill stood about where the dam for Lake Michie is now located.[40] It could be approached by a road from the present Cassam Tilley Road, named for one of Haywood Tilley's sons.

In addition to flour, each of these mills also ground corn in great quantity, for corn was the daily diet of man and beast as well as a staple crop. Flour, however, was a lucrative product for marketing. Fayetteville, North Carolina, and Petersburg, Virginia, had long been flour markets for Orange County farmers. After the building of the railroad, however, they were able to ship by rail to Norfolk, Virginia, as well. A letterhead for the firm of Rowland and Brothers of Norfolk advertised that they were exclusively flour agents and boasted as customers in Orange County Webb and Douglas (Orange Factory), P. C. Cameron, W. W. Guess, J. A. McMannen, George W. Jones, and Shields and Nelson (who presumably marketed the flour from Cabe's old gristmill). Orange County ranked fifth in the state in 1840 and seventh in 1860 in the quantity of wheat grown. In the latter year it grew 157,794 bushels of wheat, a sharp increase over the 1840 and 1850 figures of 87,579 and 93,338 bushels respectively.[41]

Other staples of Orange County farmers were tobacco and cotton. A comparison of the quantity of tobacco grown in the county as recorded in the 1850 and 1860 censuses reveals the large increase in its growth in the decade. In 1850 Orange County farmers grew 194,275 pounds; by 1860 the figure was 1,159,764 pounds. The building of the North Carolina Railroad in the early 1850s, which enabled farmers to get their produce to new markets, and the gradual increase in the number of local factories, small though they were, spurred its popularity as a staple. In 1860 two Orange County factories were listed in the census as processing tobacco (worth $34,000), though neither was in eastern Orange. One, however, and perhaps two, was operating there (see below). If Bedford Vaughan's factory had ceased after its sale to Lockhart, by 1870 Vaughan was back in the tobacco business again with a host of others.[42]

Though cotton was grown extensively in North Carolina throughout the nineteenth century and well into the twentieth, neither climate nor soil favored it in Orange County. Paul Cameron, a scientific farmer and promoter of progressive techniques, remarked in his old age after a lifetime of growing cotton in both North Carolina and the Deep South that "any man who will plant cotton in N.C. needs a guardian."[43] Before the Civil War the best land in the area could produce only one bale (four hundred pounds) to an acre. Though many farmers grew it, they were not dependent on it. In 1850, those who grew it reported an average crop of one to four bales. The exceptions were William N. Pratt, a shrewd businessman and entrepreneur, who reported 80 bales, Paul and Thomas Cameron, 65 and 75 bales, respectively, and John Lockhart, 7 bales. In 1860 the farmers who grew cotton averaged 2 or 3 bales (and most farmers did not grow it), while Paul and Thomas Cameron grew 400 and 80 bales, respectively, Fendal Southerland grew 20, and Mordecai Sears grew 6. The reason for the much larger production of Southerland, the Camerons, and Pratt was their ownership of cotton presses. Orange County cotton production was 253,473 pounds in 1840, 922,000 pounds in 1850, but only 339,200 pounds in 1860.[44] Presumably most of those seriously interested in growing cotton on a large scale had by then moved to states in the lower South.

FREE BLACKS

That emigration was still continuing is shown in the population statistics for those decades. The 1820 census of Orange County had shown 16,777 whites, 6,153 slaves, and 562 free blacks. The 1850 census figures reflect an Orange County only half its former size; the formation of Alamance County from Orange in 1849 removed the prosperous, more industrialized half of the county. In 1850 the diminished Orange County counted 11,428 whites, 5,255 slaves, and 443 free blacks, totaling 17,116. The Alamance figures for 1850 were 7,921 whites, 3,196 slaves, and 327 free blacks, totaling 11,444. The 1860 Orange County figures show, however, that despite births and some immigration, the emigration was still going on. There were only 11,311 whites, 5,108 slaves, and 528 free blacks.[45]

Free blacks were an anomalous group in slavery days. They were few enough not to seem to pose a threat to the white social order, but their free status, though recognized by law, had no place in the social structure of a slave state. They competed with difficulty with whites for work as farm laborers or, if they had skills, as artisans, even though some were highly adept. Most, however, were farmers like the majority of whites, subsisting on their own land or as tenants on another's. Of the free blacks on the first tax list of Orange County (1755), only the Bunch family apparently remained through several generations. The numbers of free blacks increased with the decades. The increase was slow but steady: 116 free blacks were residents of Orange in 1800, 332 in 1810, and 562 in 1820. Despite four decades of natural increase (and allowing for the removal from the rolls of a number of free blacks with the formation of Alamance County) by 1860 their number had risen only to 528.[46]

Though few remained from the first group of black settlers, the next wave of immigrants, probably just after the Revolution, like the white immigrants of that era, proved remarkably stable. The 1790 census for the parts of Wake County now in Durham County lists Locklear, Pettiford, Macklin, Stewart, Tabourn (Tabun, Tabon), Evans, and Hedgepeth families—the names of free blacks found six decades later in those areas. In the Durham sections of Orange County in 1800 (no 1790 census survives for Orange) appeared the names Bird, Heathcock, Weaver, Revell, Jones, and Jeffries; these are repeated in each successive decade. Following 1800 some free black families of Granville, Person, and Wake counties came into Durham and became very numerous; among them were the Days, Basses, and Chavises. The Day family, of whom the most illustrious was Thomas Day, an expert furniture maker of Milton, Caswell County, still has many branches in the area. The Chavis family, too, had an illustrious member in John Chavis, the noted educator of both black and white children. Much intermarriage among free blacks developed a network of kin exactly like that among white families in the area.

Legal changes prompted by Nat Turner's rebellion in 1831 restricted the rights of free blacks, making their lot even more difficult than it had been before. They could no longer preach, teach, assemble, or move freely. Some of their legal rights, for example, the right to bear arms or to vote, were curtailed, and the prevailing climate for them was one of suspicion and aversion.[47] The general improvements of the era therefore conferred only limited benefits on free blacks. Since most of them in eastern Orange and western Wake were farmers, they did enjoy the improved agricultural conditions of the period. Free blacks with skills usually congregated in towns, for planters and yeoman farmers commonly depended on slaves for whatever skilled work was necessary on the plantations. The Camerons, for example, trained slaves as millers, smiths, coopers, shoemakers, tanners, and mechanics. Although eastern Orange and northwestern Wake had no towns, there were nevertheless some skilled free blacks scattered throughout the area. The 1850 census lists Howard Chavers (Chavis) as a blacksmith, William Day and Stanford Walden as mechanics, Frederick Mathews and Jefferson Robertson as carpenters, John Evans as a brickmason, Abraham Scott and Jefferson Chavis as millers, James Waller and B. Mitchum as ditchers, Hinton Goins as a shoemaker, Jesse Jenkins as a stonecutter, and Thomas Harris as a lawyer, a rarity indeed.[48]

The picture the census records paint of the seventy years before the Civil War was of a rural society without geographical segregation of whites and blacks. Free black farmhouses and tenant houses were scattered around the farms and along the roads interspersed with whites' houses, whether poor or prosperous. Their very sparseness precluded any concerted efforts of free blacks to establish schools or other cultural organizations parallel to the whites' in the age of improvement, though they continued as usual to be nominal members of the white churches in their neighborhoods.

SOCIAL PROBLEMS

Despite general improvement in the farm economy in the antebellum years, the widened possibility for education with the establishment of public schools for whites, the beginnings of industry, and the stability of life in the now well-knit communities established around the churches, mills, or country stores, not all was well. Life was still precarious for all, vulnerable to the chance of illness and death that could remove the breadwinner of a family, leaving orphan children, elderly widows, or other helpless dependents. In colonial days the poor had been the responsibility of the parish, and special taxes had been levied for their support. Under the state constitution, wardens of the poor under the supervision of the county court, who appointed or elected them, took over this responsibility. Taxes continued to supply the necessary funding.[49] Orphans left unprovided for were bound out to men and women who were responsible for training them to be self-supporting, teaching them the elements of reading, writing, and arithmetic, and taking care of their needs until they reached their majority, twenty-one for boys, eighteen for girls. In return, the labor of the children belonged to the masters. The courts tried to be conscientious in administering this system, and not infrequently removed children from masters who reputedly ill-treated them. Originally the care of the elderly, insane, or infirm poor had been undertaken by individuals eager to increase their earnings; the court paid them a small amount for their service. How compassionate or adequate this care was can be readily imagined. In 1789 Orange County was one of a group of counties empowered by the legislature to build almshouses for their poor. Early in the nineteenth century the idea of providing land around the almshouse on which the inmates could grow their own food was conceived, and the plan was adopted. The poorhouse, as the almshouse came to be called, was not large enough to accommodate all who needed it. The overflow was placed in private homes as before; those who took in the poor were paid to provide daily care.[50] In 1832 twenty-one persons were housed in the poorhouse. In 1838 a tax of two cents on the poll and five cents on each $100 valuation of land was allotted for the support of the poor. The next year the amounts were fifteen cents on each poll and six and one-half cents on $100 valuation of land. Twenty years later the amounts were only a fraction more. By 1846 there was an overflow of fifty-six persons unable to be accommodated in the poorhouse. The number was small, however, in relation to the total population, and the expenditure for their care was minuscule. In 1860 paupers in the state numbered only 1,922 out of a population of 992,622, and the amount spent on them was $83,486, not thirteen cents a day per indigent person.[51]

In 1838 and 1843 the county built additions to the poorhouse farm specifically for the insane, who until then had been housed indiscriminately with the white and free black, old and infirm. The second structure was 20 by 26 feet, with four rooms and a passage running along one side.[52] In 1848 when Dorothea Dix made her inspection of facilities for the insane in North Carolina, the Orange County jail, which also housed some insane, got a good report, but the poorhouse she judged "neither clean, nor comfortably furnished."[53] She continued:

> A little expenditure by the County, and a little care would render the establishment more comfortable. There were six insane there in close confinement, and much excited. The most violent, a man long a maniac and caged, was clean, but so noisy as to disturb all the premises; a large part of the time the room in which his cage was built, could be made light, but was commonly dark and close "to keep him more quiet"! A negro girl, a most pitiable case, was in the opposite building; and a white woman, also, in a separate compartment, vociferous and offensive in the extreme. In a passage between their cells or cages was a stove in which fire was maintained when necessary. The place was very offensive. The keeper could not altogether be blamed for this; he was hired to direct a poor-house, and not qualified to rule a madhouse, and should not be expected to do it.[54]

In 1847, when Thomas D. Bennehan died, he left one thousand dollars to be used for a Christian and benevolent purpose. Duncan Cameron, his executor, decided to donate the sum to the county as an endowment for the poorhouse. Perhaps Dix's candid criticism brought such conditions to the attention of the better-off inhabitants of the state and resulted in an improvement of conditions. In 1853 the Hillsborough newspaper published a story about the poorhouse and commended its superintendent, Sampson P. Moore, for his efforts to make the buildings more cheerful by painting them.[55]

Besides these depressing solutions to the problem of paupers and the insane, there was another alternative, which the people themselves probably preferred. If they had a roof over their heads, some went on living as best they could, supplementing local handouts by scrimping and working at whatever they could, too proud and independent to accept the charity or the shame of confinement in the poorhouse. Undoubtedly many who were really in desperate straits went unnoticed by the authorities. Such a case was described in Adolphus Mangum's diary.

A neighbor, old Mrs. King, was found frozen to death in her small cabin, where she had been caring for an idiot daughter. The next day the daughter, too, was found dead, having wandered out of the cabin down to a dry creek, perhaps in search of help, water, or kindling. She too had died of exposure.[56]

This period of internal improvements and cultural and humanitarian reform—the legislature acceded to Dorothea Dix's plea for a hospital for the insane, and established a school for the blind as well—also stimulated a spirit of self-improvement and social cooperation evidenced in the formation of small groups united by a common purpose. As easier economic conditions supplied leisure, the people found ways to use it profitably. Fraternal orders, political groups, reform societies, and self-improvement organizations were established. Debating societies became popular as education became more democratic. At universities, debating societies with Greek names had long played the role later adopted by fraternities of helping to give the raw wood of youth the polished finish of mature men, able to behave, think, and speak with propriety. In the South special advantages adhered to public speaking, and the art was raised to a high level of performance. Political careers depended largely on this skill, but it was also an expected attainment of a lawyer, preacher, or landed gentleman. Those who were beginning to feel the deficiencies of their educations made an effort to remedy them. Round Hill, under D. C. Parrish's influence, formed a debating society in the 1840s. On one occasion George W. Jones, whose career included not only merchandising but schoolteaching and practicing law, gave such a fine oration there that people clamored to have it printed. Quite naturally South Lowell Academy organized a lyceum, which presented speakers on uplifting topics, drawing its audience from the local farm folk as well as the school community. The Rough and Ready Club was another Flat River group, this one political, interested in supporting Taylor's candidacy for president. The Whigs later sustained their political efforts by a regularly formed local organization, the Flat River Whigs.[57]

The social evil most pervasive and obvious was alcoholism. It had, of course, always been part of frontier life, and alcohol consumption on both sides of the Atlantic in the eighteenth century had been staggering, but the problem grew with the population, and the prevalence of alcoholic beverages grew with the proliferation of stores and taverns for its sale. The medicinal use of spirits, too, aggravated the problem. Liquor was an all-purpose drug used as an analgesic, soporific, tranquilizer, and tonic. The temperance movement, which had begun in the early years of the nineteenth century, began to take hold in the backcountry in the 1840s. Local groups were formed, sometimes as neighborhood clubs, sometimes as church groups, and became local chapters of the national organization, the Sons of Temperance. Mount Hebron Temperance Society, founded about 1842, seems to have been the earliest in eastern Orange. W. W. Guess was president, James Stagg (Willie J. Duke's son-in-law), recording secretary, and John W. Hancock, corresponding secretary. On the standing committee were William J. and Washington Duke and "Baldy" (Archibald) Nichols. The Round Hill society (organized no later than 1845), which met at Mount Bethel Church, had among its members D. C. Parrish, Williams and Marcus Harris, Harrison and Jesse Parker, William Piper, and Squire D. Umstead. So great was the interest in this organization's efforts to alleviate the problem that the Hillsborough newspaper devoted the entire front page of one weekly issue to the national society's constitution.[58]

Adolphus Mangum's diary and correspondence contain much evidence of the problem in the neighborhood. Mangum commented on a neighbor he found already intoxicated early one morning in his father's store and on the drunken fights at political rallies. After one rally he wrote, "I saw enough drunkenness in those two days to convince a friend of the necessity of prohibition to the happiness of man and the gratifying success of our country."[59] The problem affected the genteel as well as the ragtag and bobtail of society. E. G. Mangum wrote to Adolphus about their cousin Willie P. Mangum, then the eminent president pro tempore of the United States Senate, "He was, last Thursday, beastly and insensibly drunk at home in the presence of Col. Parker, Sam D. Morgan, and Hinton Mangum." Mangum's failing was no secret in Washington either. A friend wrote to Duncan Cameron expressing concern for Mangum's political career because of his intemperance, and urged Cameron to try to get him home.[60]

LIFE IN THE ANTEBELLUM DECADES had been made easier in many respects. Opportunities had widened for education and employment, and the climate for mental, spiritual, and moral cultivation had improved. The railroad was uniting the east and west and destroying geographical barriers. For the white population, at least, a period of progressive and productive living with some leisure and extra cash had come at last. Government had assumed with the people's consent more responsibility for their economic and personal well-being. Despite occasional drought or floods, agricultural problems were receiving some amelioration: the railroad, new roads, a state agricultural society and fair for the dissemination of new knowledge, and, in the 1850s, better weather. Many a farmer may have shared Paul Cameron's feeling at midcentury that in a few years he would have "all matters here in a mighty nice fix."[61]

Origins of the Town of Durham, 1819–1861

7

TWO SMALL COMMUNITIES, Dilliardsville and Prattsburg, were the actual forerunners of the city of Durham; both were post offices in the early nineteenth century. Their stories begin with roads: the Hillsborough to Raleigh road and the Roxboro to Fayetteville road, mere cart tracks winding through boundless forests that alternated with scattered homesteads and fields. William Dilliard, previously a Wake County landowner and possibly the son of Henry Dilliard, bought land in Orange County in 1819 just where these roads crossed. It had belonged to Absalom Alston, whose ownership is preserved in the name Alston Avenue, and consisted of 450 acres.[1] In the course of the next few years Dilliard acquired other tracts, so that when he died in 1824 he left close to 1,000 acres. He also left a widow, Lydia, and thirteen children, seven of them minors. His older daughters had already married into local families; his sons-in-law were Reuben Barbee, James Trice, and James Lewis, indicating that his family was well incorporated into the neighborhood.[2]

Since Dilliard represents a kind of founding father and little is known about him, his possessions will have to speak for him. His landholdings and personal possessions delineate a prosperous farmer with claims to gentility. He owned twelve Windsor chairs and a Windsor armchair besides six "common chairs," six "sitting chairs," one large armchair, and three painted chairs. He also owned twelve silver teaspoons and six silver tablespoons. The larger pieces in his house were eight beds, a walnut chest, a sideboard, three tables, two mirrors, and a carpet. That he owned a family carriage was a hallmark of his status. An oxcart and a wagon aided his farming operations. A cotton gin and press, over nine thousand shingles, and a copper still indicate additional sources of his income. A broadside distributed by Willie P. Mangum in his 1823 political campaign against General Barringer discloses that "Mr. Wm. Dilliard's" had been a site on their electioneering circuit. Dilliard himself was postmaster.[3]

That paper and another headed "Dilliardsville" from the widow Lydia Dilliard are evidence of the existence of the little community that soon lost its identity. After Lydia's death in 1831, many of her children sold their shares of inherited land and emigrated to other states. When the court-appointed commissioners had laid off her widow's dowerland, they had described it as lying on the Fayetteville Road. When the same tract was sold after her death, it was described as fourteen miles from Hillsborough on both sides of the road leading from Hillsborough to Raleigh, clearly the crossroads known today as Dillard and Main.[4] The Dilliardsville post office was closed in 1827 and the mail sent to a new office, Herndon's, a store on the Hillsborough road owned by William R. Herndon, who had supplied the land for the Orange Grove Church. It seems likely that the oldest Dilliard son, known variously as William J. and Jefferson, was the Jefferson Dilliard accused of burning down the Orange Grove Church.[5]

Herndon's store lost the post office in 1836 when it was transferred to Prattsburg; a community with a rowdy reputation, it took its name from William N. Pratt, who had bought the Dilliard dowerland in 1832 and purchased another large tract of 450 acres known as the Dilliard old place in 1846.[6] On the first he established a store which drew to itself the traffic on the nearby main roads. It also drew attention of another kind. A court case in 1833 indicted Pratt for "keeping a disorderly house for his own lucre and gain at unlawful times as well on Sundays as on other days" for "evil disposed persons of evil name and fame and conversation to come together." There his customers upset the "peace and dignity of the state" by "drinking, tipling, playing at cards and other unlawful games, cursing, screaming, quarreling and otherwise misbehaving themselves."[7] This was a reputation that took the community a century to live down. Pratt had much earlier purchased land from John Scarlett in what is today the Mount Hermon Church neighborhood of Orange County. In that deed Pratt is described as "of Hillsborough." Over the years he bought many other large tracts of land between his tracts at Prattsburg and his Scarlett plantation. At Prattsburg he ran a large general store where the post office was located, a cotton gin and press (which had belonged to Dilliard), and a blacksmith shop. After Thaddeus Redmond joined the business, shoemaking and repair were added services. The railroad survey made in 1850 shows Prattsburg as a cluster of buildings not a mile to the southeast of the railroad station, situated on the north side of the Hillsborough road not far from the surveyed track.[8]

Pratt's reputation was that of a hard businessman, careful of money and quick to take advantage of debtors. Though he never married, it was common knowledge that Polly Redmond was the mother of the two children he acknowledged as his even in his lifetime. Before his death he deeded to her 225 acres, a tract called the James Browning plantation, in words reminiscent of the marriage vows, "for repeated acts of kindness shown to myself and family both in sickness and in health." To his two sons, William Thaddeus Redmon[d] (called Thad) and James K. Redmon[d], he gave 240 and 160 acres respectively. Thaddeus received the old Hardin Couch mill on Ellerbee Creek (in what is now the Croasdaile neighborhood) which he later ran as Redmond's mill. Both were also bequeathed personal property: clothing, guns, a gold watch, and household furnishings. Pratt made his will long before he died in 1867. In it he provided $2,000 with which Thaddeus was to receive classical schooling and a university education at Chapel Hill. By the time the will was probated Thaddeus was grown, married, and no longer able to take advantage of the provision even if he had wished to.[9]

William N. Pratt is remembered with derision in Durham lore because of one miscalculation in a long and successful career devoted to money-making. When he was approached by the North Carolina Railroad for land on which to build a station, he set his price too high, and they asked elsewhere. His motive, it is supposed, was fear that a station on his land would frighten his customers' horses and damage his business.[10] His shortsightedness soon resulted in a competing cluster of commercial enterprises near the station, built on land freely given. Prattsburg faded from the scene.

The man who had seen and seized the opportunity was Dr. Bartlett Leonidas Durham. Durham had moved in late 1847 or early 1848 to the land that was to become Durham's station. Though no deed exists for this purchase, other documents attest to his ownership of land at this location at so early a date: his petition to the county court in May 1848 to make the new section of the Hillsborough road through his land the public road and to close the old section; a deed of 1849 recording a sale of land described as "near to Durhams Station on the North Carolina Railroad"; and another deed of 1850 describing the land in question as on the road leading from Hillsborough to Raleigh and adjoining land of B. L. Durham.[11]

It is customary to ascribe prescience to Bartlett Durham in the purchase of his land. The railroad, however, was not incorporated or its route begun to be determined until 1849. That a railroad was to be incorporated and its route laid through his property a year or more after he bought it was simply a stroke of luck. Although the survey engineer had some leeway in mapping out a route and in choosing stations between the main ones authorized in the legislative bill—Goldsboro, Raleigh, and Charlotte—there never seems to have been any doubt of the course it would take from Raleigh to the present Durham area. The Hillsborough road had long since found the ridge; the railroad track had only to follow the Hillsborough road, taking care to avoid the "Brasfield hills."[12]

Durham's eagerness to see a station established close to his property is understood in terms of his livelihood. Like merchants, doctors have depended on population density for the most efficient and remunerative use of their services. Durham must have been overjoyed to supply three acres for a station and warehouse and a right of way across his land for the tracks. The other landowners along the proposed route were no doubt equally glad. After the tracks were laid a few landowners complained that they deviated from the survey and were too close to their dwellings, and they received payment for damages. These, however, were minor problems. The majority of landowners saw in the railroad a lifeline.[13]

The question of whose land Durham purchased in late 1847 or early 1848 is exceedingly vexed. The only recorded purchase of land by Durham is that of the John Shepherd tract in 1852. A possible clue comes from a statement in the obituary of Fred C. Geer that Geer loved to tell the story of "how the property of George Rhodes was bought by Dr. Durham."[14] Rhodes left Orange County in the mid-1840s for Tennessee, probably because of financial reverses. It was George Rhodes's land that

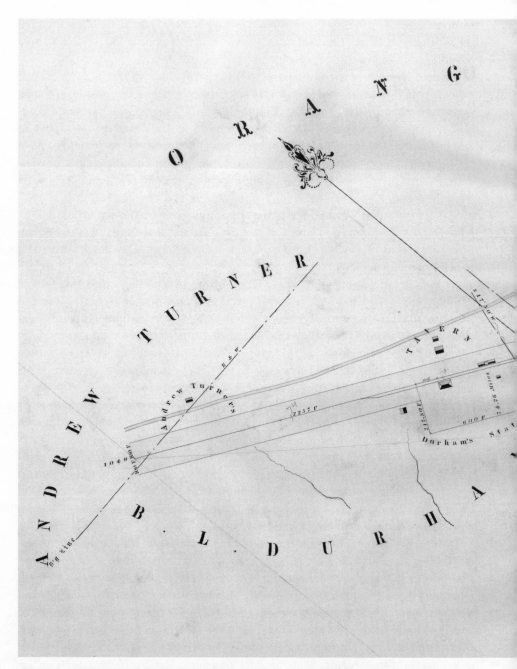

North Carolina Railroad Survey Map (1850), book 3, p. 19, NCOAH, North Carolina
Railroad Company Collection. Rose of Sharon Church (later First Baptist Church) is
shown adjoining B. L. Durham's land and the land donated by Durham to the railroad. Adjoining the church property to the east is William N. Pratt's land, previously
William Dilliard's. The following page of the survey (not shown here) places Pratt's
store (Prattsburg) approximately 3,300 feet east of the church property.

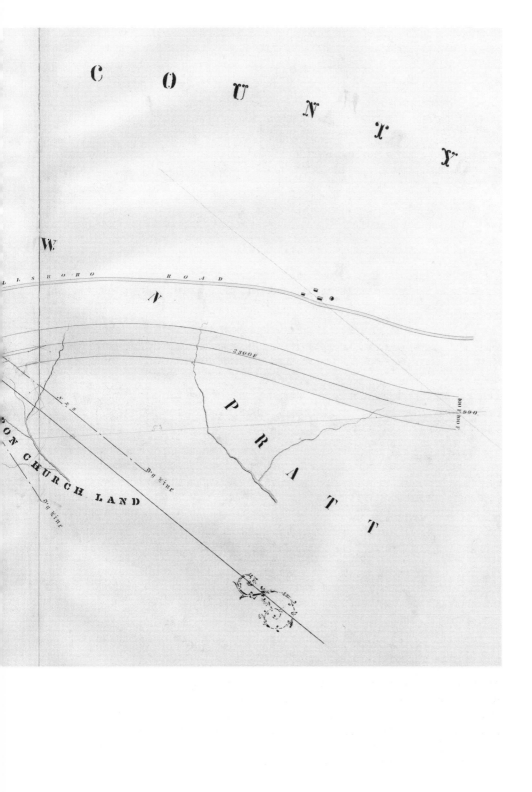

C O U N T Y

W

N

LLSBORO   ROAD

2800F

N

800 F 800 F

P R A T T

4 8 8

ON CHURCH LAND

Dg Line

Dg Line

Rose of Sharon Church bought in 1846 when it moved to its first Durham site of two and a half acres; it is more than likely, therefore, that Durham's land, directly adjoining the church, as the railroad survey map shows, had also been Rhodes's land, corroborating Geer's story.[15] In 1846 Andrew Turner, too, bought George Rhodes's land, a hundred acres at a sheriff's sale. The railroad survey map discloses that in 1850 Turner owned a large tract of land on the north side of the proposed railroad right-of-way at Durham's station. One can safely surmise that Turner had resold to Durham the southern part of his hundred-acre tract, and from this portion Durham gave the railroad the three-plus acres in 1849. Apparently Durham did not bother to record his purchase. Unfortunately, to compound the difficulty, the deed that transferred Durham's acres to the railroad was lost. Many years after Durham's death his executors and heirs made the railroad another deed to replace it. The second deed conveyed three acres and a right-of-way across Durham's tract.[16]

Bartlett L. Durham was born 3 November 1824 to William L. and Mary Snipes Durham, who lived near the Chatham County line southwest of Chapel Hill on the Antioch Church road. His earliest Orange County ancestor was Matthew Durham, whose son William Lindsey Durham was Bartlett's grandfather. Where he gained his medical knowledge is not known. The family believed he had taken a course at Jefferson Medical College in Philadelphia in November 1845, but neither Jefferson nor the medical school of the University of Pennsylvania in the same city has a record of him. He could, nevertheless, have taken a course without having been recorded on their regular rolls. Most of his training he undoubtedly received as the student of a local doctor. It is possible that Dr. James Webb of Hillsborough had been his mentor. A deed of 1847 records that in 1838 or 1839, when William Durham's possessions were sold to satisfy a debt, Webb bought the lot and returned everything to Durham because the possessions had been sold at far less than their worth. Webb said he would take payment for what he had spent and return to Durham's children a deed for the possessions, thus protecting them from further attachment. Bartlett Durham might already have been apprenticed to Webb, a fact that would explain Webb's interest in the family.[17]

Although Durham set in motion vast changes by his auspicious gift of land for a station, he did not long live to see the results. A hero larger than life, he blazed through little more than a decade at that place called Durham's Station before burning out. A tall man weighing over two hundred pounds, he was remembered in local lore as "a jovial fellow. On moonshiny nights he would get a group of boys together and serenade the town." Thaddeus Redmond remembered one occasion when he and his brother Jim, Ed Lyon, L. Turner, and Dr. Durham went out together. "We had some horns, a fiddle and a banjo. We went by a barroom and got some liquor" before waking up the town. Redmond also related how Durham knocked around with women, or would go on a spree and get in a fight. Redmond remembered being treated for typhoid fever as a child by Durham. The doctor was deeply concerned about his patients and assiduous in his ministrations until he saw that a case was hopeless, when he would disappear for a week or two and drown his sorrow in drink.[18]

One of the women that he seems to have serenaded was Susan Ann Clements, who, after Durham's death of pneumonia on 2 February 1859, brought a charge of bastardy against his estate. She claimed that her son born ten months before (March 1858) and named Romulus for another eponymous hero, was Bartlett Durham's. The lower court that heard the case decided against her on the ground that the defendant was dead and could not defend himself. Appeal to the superior court reversed the decision, and Durham's estate was ordered to give her money for the child's support. Another appeal, to the Supreme Court, reversed that decision, and Susan Ann Clements was left to fend for herself. Durham's legal heirs were three sisters, one of whom was married to Francis A. Stagg. Stagg had begun a career with the railroad as agent at Durham's Station. The Staggs were the parents of James Edward Stagg, who married Washington Duke's granddaughter Mary Washington Lyon. In that way an even more famous family was knitted into the kinship of the founding father.[19]

Bartlett Durham's medical practice and moonlit highjinks were not his only interests. In 1850 he was nominated and elected by the Democrats to represent Orange County in the legislature. During that session he introduced a bill to incorporate a division of the Sons of Temperance in Orange County, a stance about which he must have felt some ambivalence. In 1852, although he at first declined nomination to a second term in office, he was finally persuaded to run and was reelected. During this session he introduced a bill to incorporate the Hillsborough Academy.[20]

By 1852 Bartlett Durham was in business with Malbourne Angier; they were licensed to sell spirits in a general store on the Hillsborough road on the north side of the railroad adjoining Pratt's line. Durham city's first historian, Hiram Paul, states that the first store in Durham was owned by Bartlett Durham, John W. Carr, and James Matthews with Angier as clerk. This probably preceded the Durham and Angier partnership. Charles T. McMannen later bought this store and sold it in 1857 to Solomon Shepherd, Thomas Ferrell, and David M. Cheek, who ran it as Shepherd, Ferrell, & Cheek Co. Cheek soon sold his share to his partners, and the next year Shepherd and Ferrell sold out to Riley Vickers. Six days later Vickers sold the half-acre back to Malbourne A. Angier, who remained at that site, "the old red corner" of Main and Mangum streets, so long that his name is traditionally associated with it. The partnership of James Pratt, brother of William, and John W. Hancock also ran a store at Durham's Station, but not for long; they soon became indebted to William Pratt.[21]

Where Bartlett Durham lived is uncertain. Boyd's history called Durham's house Pandora's Box and located it on the north side of the tracks at the east end of the lot where the Carrs' silk mill later stood on Corcoran Street. Lewis Blount, who grew up in Durham and drew from memory a map of the hamlet as it looked in 1867–68, labeled the annex to Robert F. Morris's hotel Pandora's Box but shows it in a different location, north of the hotel which stood facing the station. The railroad survey map shows Durham's house as south of the tracks and adjoining the railroad lot on the west. Another source, Thaddeus Redmond, said that Durham boarded with Andrew Turner, whose house stood where the Liggett and Myers tobacco factory now stands at Main and Duke streets. It seems certain that Durham first lived where the railroad survey shows his house; conceivably he later boarded at both the hotel annex and at Andrew Turner's.[22]

Others soon began to capitalize on the little boom the station had started. Ironically William Pratt, whose land extended to the proximity of the station, was one. In 1853 he offered to sell land lying on the east side of present Mangum Street at the west end of his large holdings. He advertised one-acre lots running north and south near the Rose of Sharon Church about thirty yards from Durham and Angier's store and two hundred yards from the depot.[23] In 1855 a more ambitious plan was put forth in the newspaper by South Lowell's entrepreneur, John A. McMannen, with his usual flair for large undertakings:

Proposals for Building a Town

The undersigned having purchased the property at Durham's Station, on the Great North Carolina Central Rail Road, is now making arrangements to lay off a town in half acre lots, and proposes to give away, and make a full right and title to every other lot in the place, provided the individual who accepts the proposal will bind him or herself in a bond with good security, to build a certain class house on the same in the course of twelve months from the time they enter into the bond. Persons who feel interested, will address the undersigned at South Lowell, Orange County, N.C., who will forward to them a plan of the town, number and location of the lots, terms, etc.

This place is located in a fine, healthy section of the County, twenty-five miles west of Raleigh and twelve miles east of Hillsborough, and twelve miles north of Chapel Hill. Merchants and mechanics, and business men in general, will find this proposal worthy of their prompt attention. The terms will exclude the sale of ardent spirits, and all persons of questionable character. Persons who make application will please state the business they wish to engage in etc.

John A. McMannen
South Lowell, N.C. May 26 [1855][24]

The land McMannen proposed to develop in this way, probably south of the tracks and away from the incipient town around the station, where there already existed not only a store that sold spirits but a tavern as well, was the tract that Bartlett Durham had bought in 1852 at a sheriff sale as the land of John Shepherd, containing about one hundred acres. No sale to McMannen is registered, but Durham's estate papers record the fact and the sequence of events that it precipitated.[25] McMannen as usual had sensed a good thing, but again his reach had exceeded his grasp, and his prohibition of ardent spirits spelled doom to his dream. There were no takers. He unloaded the land on his friend John B. Leathers, who sold it to Henderson May in 1858. McMannen had unfortunately made only the down payment on the purchase price of the land, and in 1857 Durham brought suit for the rest of the money. By that time McMannen's financial affairs were in colossal disorder. He owed over $5,000 on some fifteen debts. He lost his prosperity in South Lowell and everything else he owned. Fortunately his friends stuck by him, and by the time Pratt's lands were sold in 1867 to settle his estate, McMannen was back in the marketplace, again buying land. Though his 1855 plan was frustrated, his friend D. C. Parrish, who seems to have purchased land around the station, saw to it that McMannen got five acres on the railroad from the station tract by deeding it to Elizabeth Latta McMannen. He also deeded to McMannen's son Dr. Charles McMannen and his son-in-law John Lockhart fifteen acres adjoining Mrs. McMannen's land. Thus originated the tract of land with the address McMannen Street, formerly the section of Mangum Street south of the railroad. It was not until the late 1860s that the McMannen family actually built their own large house at the top of this street adjoining the railroad and on the highest point of land, whereby it became known as "The Heights."[26]

The railroad survey, beautifully mapped, is unequivocal proof of where things stood geographically at midcentury.[27] The station and warehouse are shown close to Bartlett Durham's and Andrew Turner's houses; a tavern lies on the Hillsborough road near the station but north of the track. Pin Hook, in what is now West Durham, and Prattsburg, less than a mile east of the station, are also shown. Another mile and a half east of Prattsburg, the Orange Grove Church lies close to the then Wake County line. All landowners along the tracks are identified. Running from west to east across what is today Durham County, the map shows the following landowners or sites: William T. Shields (who then owned John Cabe's homeplace straddling the Orange-Durham line), James Bennett [sic], Henry Neal, William Pratt, Joshua Horn, Archibald Borland, Rebecca Hicks (for whom Hickstown was named), again Pratt, Isaac Pool, Anderson Copley, Pin Hook, Israel Turner, John Turner, Moses Turner, Andrew Turner, B. L. Durham, Durham's Station, Rose of Sharon Church, and yet again William Pratt, Pratt's store, Riley Vickers, G. W. Barbee, James Malone, Orange Grove Church, Jacob Bledsoe, the then Wake County line, Winny Brassfield, Anderson Cheek, Michael Green, Henderson Morris, John G. Thompson, again Green and Morris, G. Tryce, W. George, Yancy Rochelle, Brassfield, William George, Hugh Lyon, Hiram Witherspoon, John Page, William Booth, James Green, J. Trice, and the Cedar Fork Church.

In collecting local history in Durham around the turn of the century, Professor John Spencer Bassett of Trinity College discovered colorful tales of the Pin Hook neighborhood (later the Erwin Cotton Mill area) and of a settlement known as Peelers Crossroads, where Neal Road crossed the old Hillsborough road. Anthony Peeler, the patriarch, had received a Granville grant in 1754, and his son Benjamin, a state grant south of his father's in 1795. Both Ellerbee Creek and the Hillsborough road ran through Benjamin's tract. Tradition held that Benjamin Peeler took in travelers and killed them in order to gain possession of their horses, which he sold in Raleigh. Their bodies he threw down a well. He was abetted in this evil by two sons, Pet-Tich-Eye and Redwine. As the 1823 will of Samuel Peeler shows, it was he who had a son named Anthony Redwine Peeler; probably Pet-Tich-Eye was the nickname of another son.[28]

Of the settlement at Pin Hook, Bassett had little better to report. The shiftless of society, usually addicted to vices of one sort or another, tended to congregate there, attracting others of their kind. A rough and brawling place with grog shops and brothels, it offered wagoners a campground and well, along with its other attractions. At the time of the railroad survey in 1850 Pin Hook was owned by Anderson Copley, whose father had got it from the Turners and William Pratt. William Turner had a license to retail spirits at Pin Hook in 1850. It seems likely that Pin Hook's unsavory reputation was of earlier date, possibly during Pratt's ownership, given the character of his Prattsburg property. A story in the Hillsborough newspaper in 1871 reflected its already established character. "There is a place called Pin Hook in this county and it is remarkable for a race that was run there many years ago by a man and a woman. They wore no clothes and ran for a quart of liquor."[29]

From 1850 to 1860 growth in the hamlet of Durham was slow but steady. The station and its volume of business required more public services: more stores, grog shops, campgrounds, and other accommodations. It was the opportunity to supply this last requirement that attracted to the town another of its better-known inhabitants, Robert F. Morris. Morris appeared on the Orange County scene first in Hillsborough, where he owned a variety store in 1847. The same year he was granted a license to retail liquor at the Hillsborough House, the old Faddis's Tavern of the eighteenth century. In 1848 he was licensed to "hawk and peddle" goods in Orange County. In 1850, then thirty-six years old, he was the hotel keeper of the Hillsborough House. He bought his first property for ten dollars at a sheriff sale in 1851: two hundred acres of William Copley's land near the Pin Hook area. Sometime in the early 1850s, recognizing the opportunity for his services in Durham, he moved to the tract of land that Andrew Turner had owned and took his chances running a hotel there.[30]

The great increase in the growing and processing of tobacco in the United States made the next milestone in Durham's history inevitable. Small tobacco factories such as those in Hillsborough or Bedford Vaughan's on Flat River had led the way. Although the station first stimulated the cultivating and shipping of tobacco around Durham, the real profits were to be made in manufacturing, for the processed product brought far more than the raw. It also made sense to build a factory close to the station to save carriage costs. A Virginian, Wesley A. Wright, was the first to establish a factory at Durham for processing tobacco. He began, it is said, in 1858 with his partner, Thomas B. Morris, Robert's son. Their product, Wright claimed, was labeled Best Spanish Flavored Durham Smoking Tobacco. They used a flavoring formula concocted by Wright, which he subsequently patented. In 1861 he moved the operation to John Barbee's farm two miles from Durham. There one of his customers was Fred C. Geer, who testified at a later trial concerning the copyright of Wright's label that Wright sold tobacco in barrels or loose but always unlabeled. Geer said that after buying the tobacco from Wright, he hauled it home, and then Wright came and flavored it with the tonka bean. James W. Cheek sold the tobacco (still without a label) for Geer at the depot. The next year Wright had been obliged to go into the Confederate army and terminate his career in Durham.[31]

The lawsuit in which Geer was a witness brought to light much early history of tobacco production in Durham. It was instituted in the 1870s by another Virginia tobacconist, Lewis Armistead, against William T. Blackwell. In 1870 Armistead had bought from Wright his flavoring formula and label. To prove to Armistead his title to "Best Spanish Flavored Durham Smoking Tobacco," Wright had drawn up a paper stating his claim and brought it to Durham to get the signatures of men who had known him in his Durham days. He succeeded in getting the signatures of Presley J. Mangum, William Mangum, Riley Vickers, Solomon Shepherd, W. Y. Clark, and Nash Booth. At the trial the truth emerged that the signatories had not known what they were signing. William Mangum said he couldn't read but signed what Wright told him the paper stated, that Wright was the first to make smoking tobacco in Durham. "I can't read writing unless it is very good; I am a very poor scholar," were Mangum's words. Riley Vickers didn't bother to read the paper. He did not know what the tobacco was called. P. J. Mangum said he was running an engine at the time and read only a few lines. He never meant to testify that Wright was the originator of the Durham brand of tobacco. Solomon Shepherd said that he had been sick and was very feeble, and the paper was badly written. Nash Booth said he hadn't read it. Blackwell successfully defended his right to the name Durham and to the label, which pictured a bull in profile, in the first of many such suits, and Wright has shown up as guilty of fraudulent claims and practices. The trial also made plain the ignorance and ingenuousness of the farmers he duped. Durham would soon lose its greenhorn character with the emergence in its midst of one of the most sophisticated and formidable business minds in an age of financial tycoons. Already the seeds of a gigantic industry had taken root and would emerge in their own good time.[32]

They could take root, however, only because the ground had been prepared by the establishment of the railroad. Progressive minds in the state had long recognized how vital it would be to North Carolina's economy. As early as 1828 discussions had centered on how a railroad might be built through the center of the state. The suggestion was made that political candidates be judged by the stand they took on the building of a railroad. The regressive fiscal policy of the state government in the Rip Van Winkle era, however, made the undertaking of anything so expensive as a railroad an impossibility. With the Whig ascendancy, change occurred, and the impossible became thinkable. Finally only the difficulty of reaching a consensus on the funding and routing of the railroad delayed the reality. At last on 27 January 1849 the legislature passed the bill to establish the North Carolina Railroad to run from Goldsboro through Raleigh to Charlotte, with private subscribers providing one-third and the state two-thirds of the necessary $3 million capitalization.[33] Surveys were begun on 21 August 1850, and in the following May the results were given to the railroad's board of directors. Stockholders, usually planters, contracted to build the railroad, each agreeing to build a few sections in return for railroad stock and cash: two-fifths in stock and three-fifths in cash. Paul Cameron, for example, built several sections east of Hillsborough, supplying the materials himself and using his own slave labor. The construction of the total length was completed on 29 January 1856 at a cost of $500,000. Six passenger cars were purchased that year, as well as a number of engines with classical names—Ajax, Ixion, Sysiphus, Midas, Apollo, Pactolus, Ulysses, and Cyclops. The line had been completed as far as Durham by 1854, and in 1855, while he was trying to establish a town, John A. McMannen was the railroad agent at a salary of $150 a year. When his dream collapsed and he moved back to South Lowell, Francis A. Stagg got the job at a salary of $300, presumably because of the increased volume of passengers and freight. The earnings from Durham's Station in 1856 showed $2,780.05 in freight and $2,699.70 in passenger receipts. The passengers numbered 2,878.[34]

The inhabitants of eastern Orange, along with the rest of the state, shared in the benefits brought by the railroad. The reduction of transportation costs stimulated production; towns and factories grew up around stations; land values, travel, and mail service increased. Distance between places and people decreased, spurring unity and state pride. The railroad put money in the farmer's pocket and light in his mind. It was high noon in the antebellum South. Dilliard and Dilliardsville, Pratt and Prattsburg, Durham and Durham's Station, Wright and his factory—each played a part in the as yet uncertain drama unfolding on the ridge between the Eno River and New Hope Creek. The railroad itself played the leading role. Yet it would be the Civil War with its ignominious defeat that suddenly would turn a commonplace history into an American epic.

Victory from Defeat, 1861–1865

8

ORANGE COUNTY WAS AGAIN SPARED the brunt of warfare in a fratricidal contest during 1861–65. Only one skirmish, in the last days of the war, is known to have taken place on its soil. In all other afflictions of the Civil War, however, it was a full participant.

North Carolina's position in the Confederacy was ambivalent. A majority of her people had been reluctant to leave the Union, fully committed as they were to its preservation and proud of its accomplishments. Prudence gave way to passion in a long series of political events that led to war, probably because the men then offering the most forceful leadership led the South toward confrontation. The few voices of reason and peace could not be heard above them, and after strenuous efforts by men such as Thomas Ruffin and William A. Graham to alter the course and find peaceful solutions, South Carolina made alternatives impossible by firing on Fort Sumter. North Carolina accepted her geographical fate and fell into line, joining her fellow southerners in the Confederate States of America. The causes of the war were many and complex and are still being debated. The issue of slavery, which is now popularly seen as the cause, was not at the time the only point of contention. Nor was the initial goal of the northern forces to free the slaves, as is generally supposed. Differences in political philosophy and economic policy fueled the controversy as well. As the North developed and prospered commercially and industrially, and immigration and urbanization changed its social and cultural patterns, its differences from the South became more and more pronounced. Almost unchanged, the South clung to its agricultural and rural way of life with the conservative and provincial beliefs and dogged individualism that that kind of culture fostered. Extreme sensitivity to outside criticism, absolute adherence to the policy of states' rights, and an unswerving conviction of the South's moral, cultural, and ethnic superiority characterized the planter mentality that ruled the South.[1]

North Carolina joined the Confederacy in May 1861 and reaped the whirlwind. She lost 40,000 men from wounds or disease and contributed far more than her proportionate share of men and supplies. The financial drain was enormous, and the scars of sacrifice, deprivation, and physical and emotional exhaustion were long-lasting. As at the start of any war, patriotism and enthusiasm in a common cause sent thousands of volunteers off to join the army.[2] This gallant spirit, sustained by many throughout the war, together with the heroic efforts of the men in battle and the sacrifices of families on the home front have come to symbolize the South in its vain struggle against a vastly superior force in numbers and supplies. Like any lost cause, that of the Confederacy took on a mythic glamour and nostalgic sanctity that adheres to it to this day. Over 125,000 North Carolinians fought in the Civil War in addition to home guard and militia units. No exact roster of Orange Countians has been completed, but tentative estimates range between 1,500 and 2,000 men up to August of 1864. With its many small cotton and woolen mills, North Carolina undertook to clothe its own units, the only Confederate state to do so.[3]

Even before the war started, preparations had begun. Robert Fulton Webb had organized the Flat River Guards early in 1860 when anger against the North began to rise. Webb served as captain, William K. Parrish as lieutenant, W. P. Hampton as second lieutenant, William Emmett McMannen as third lieutenant, and Dr. E. M. Holt as surgeon. This unit eventually became Company B of the Sixth North Carolina Regiment. Alvis Kinchen Umstead remembered as an old man how he marched in the Flat River Guards to Willie P. Mangum's home, Walnut Hall, to say goodbye. Mangum had been paralyzed by a stroke and was carried out to the shade of a tree where his daughter Pattie interpreted his efforts at speech to the company. "Boys, God bless you every one, but you can't succeed. Their resources are too great for you." Prophetic words, if hardly the kind to inspire departing troops.[4]

After their leave-taking, the Flat River Guards marched to Durham on 21 May 1861 and took up quarters in the little wooden Methodist church, the ancestor of today's Trinity church. (Members of the Orange Grove congregation had moved to town and just the year before had erected the frame building.)[5] Hardly a month later at Manasses, young William Preston Mangum, a member of the Flat River Guards through his illustrious father's urging, was among the first casualties. Other wounded were Mangum's cousin Simeon Carrington, David Roberts, Guilford Laws, Sam Turrentine, and Allen Tilley. Immediately after the battle, numbers of friends visited the troops on various errands: to take food and clothing to the soldiers, help nurse the wounded, boost their spirits, or retrieve the bodies and possessions of the dead. The Mangum family heard from some of them about young William's plight. A small Bible he had carried in a breast pocket had prevented immediate death from the bullet that struck him, but he died a week later, probably of infection. Another Flat River guard also died from that engagement, Van Buren Oakley. Willie P. Mangum died under the blow of his son's death.[6]

Other companies attracted eastern Orange County men. The Orange Guards, a Hillsborough unit, was organized by Pride Jones, originally as Company A, then Company G of the Twenty-seventh North Carolina Infantry. Its rolls contain many familiar names, among them William ("Tip") Lipscomb, Charles J., James S., and William Thomas Shields, Lorenzo Bennitt, and Thomas R. Cain. Bennitt and Charles

Shields died of disease; James Shields was killed in battle. The ailing Tip Lipscomb was fetched home at his anxious grandfather's insistence in 1863 and Wilson Brown sent in his place. The unit began its service at Fort Macon in May 1861 and surrendered at Appomattox Courthouse under Lee in 1865.[7]

The Orange Light Artillery (Company G of the Fortieth Regiment) was organized by Captain William Cameron, a cousin of Paul Cameron and a physician. This company included among the more familiar names on its roll Dr. James F. Cain, James W. Blackwell, Hardy Massey, George Piper, Joseph H. Shields, John W. Rigsbee, O. K. Proctor, Herbert H. Sims, Jr., James E. Lyon, Felix D. Markham, Presley J. Mangum, Simeon Hester, Dudley Parker, and Samuel, William, and John W. McPherson. It was nicknamed the Church Bell Battery because it had two large howitzers and two smaller pieces of artillery made from Hillsborough church bells.[8]

Company K of the Forty-first Regiment enrolled a college student from Chapel Hill, later to be one of Durham's most illustrious citizens, Julian Shakespeare Carr. First known as the Orange Cavalry, Company K was commanded first by Josiah Turner, Jr., then by William A. Graham, Jr., and finally by John P. Lockhart. John Thomas Nichols and J. C. Ferrell of the Oak Grove area belonged to Company D of the Thirtieth Regiment, Captain Eugene Grissom's company.[9] Nichols, the oldest of nineteen children of Henry Walter and Margaret J. Halliburton Nichols, kept a sketchy diary of only a half-dozen entries during his army service when he snatched time to write. He gave much more space to the love poems he wrote or received. One of his few war entries is dated 9 November 1861:

> Still times in camp [Wyatt] this morning; health moderately good in the Reg. and as for myself my health is better seemingly than it has been for several days. C. M. Rogers is on the mend; he has been very sick with the yellow jaundice. Capt. E. Grissom & Dr. Smith has been at Wilmington for the last 2 days. Capt. has returned to Smithville verry sick. We rec'd a report that fort Royal was taken by the enemy. . . . My health is verry delicate. I have had a verry severe attack of the jaundice and have been verry sick for several days past.[10]

Nichols's concern with health reflects the army's serious problem with disease, which was responsible for almost half of North Carolina soldiers' deaths.

Captain William Johnson Freeland organized the Durham Light Infantry, Company C of the Sixth Regiment, also known as the Orange Grays. In this unit were William G. Guess, Dr. William J. Hugh Durham, William Jasper Christian, William T. Gresham, John Wesley Barbee, Reuben Brassfield, Jefferson Browning, James Carrington, James T. Ferrell, Matchurine Herndon, Kinchen, John N., James, and William J. Holloway, James E. Lyon, Rufus Massey, John and Sterling Proctor, John Cabe Shields, and James K. and William Thaddeus Redmond. Freeland was wounded at Seven Pines, had his leg amputated at the thigh, and died in the hospital. In later years, when Thaddeus Redmond was asked whether he had been at Gettysburg, he replied, "I was there, and they like to killed me there." Although he was wounded and suffered disability the rest of his life, he came of tough stock; he died at ninety-three.[11]

Durham men were members of assorted other units. Company I of the Sixth

Regiment, first known as the Cedar Fork Rifles, was organized under Captain Richard W. York in the Cedar Fork area of then Wake County. Dr. Edward M. Scott commanded Company D of the First Regiment, and B. W. Matthews served in Company E of the Forty-seventh Regiment. J. W. Latta was captain of a special company known as the Bridge Guards with the duty to protect the North Carolina Railroad. They were later part of the Sixty-sixth Regiment.[12]

A few men went into the Confederate Navy, among them Washington Duke and J. W. Hamilton of Durham. Hamilton at first served on the battleship Fredericksburg, and was later transferred to the Fourth Battalion and sent to guard Richmond. Duke was drafted in September 1863 and transferred to the Navy at Charleston. When Richmond was threatened, he was one of many seamen sent to the James River squadron. There he was captured late in the war and imprisoned in New Bern until the surrender.[13]

On the home front, the families of soldiers were the first to experience the effects of war. Without the men to keep the farms running, the burden fell on women, children, the old, or the physically unfit for military service, since little more than one-quarter of Orange County's families owned slaves. Seventy-five percent of slave-owners owned fewer than ten slaves, and only three or four families owned more than one hundred slaves. Suffering due to food shortages soon became widespread. The county immediately made plans to aid the needy with food. John Norwood and Paul Cameron were appointed by the court to manage the gathering and distribution of food to soldiers' families. Acting as their agents were Squire D. Umstead, D. C. Parrish, Harrison Parker, and John Burroughs. By means of special taxes, the county at first raised money to pay for supplies for soldiers' families and others in need. The shortage became so acute by 1862 that it was beyond the means of the county to handle. The Union blockade and the invasion of eastern North Carolina shut off the supplies from the North on which the South had so long depended, and the disruption of transportation facilities made impossible the distribution of whatever supplies existed within the state. Hoarding and speculation exacerbated the shortages. The soon-rampant inflation (close to 7,000 percent) put even what supplies there were out of reach of all but the wealthiest. Lack of manpower, particularly millers, blacksmiths, and tanners, further crippled production. The Confederate government, forced to impress supplies, made itself very unpopular. Poor weather and the resultant poor crops added to the woes of the homefront.[14]

With a portion of the population consistently opposed to secession, a growing number goaded by hunger and poverty to long for peace at any price, and the ever-present problem of deserters (eventually 23,000 men and 400 officers from North Carolina alone), Governor Vance had difficulty counteracting falling morale and organized opposition. The Heroes of America, popularly known as Red Strings because of their emblem, while apparently not a problem within Orange County, were numerous elsewhere in the state and openly hostile to the continuance of the war. In April 1863 Vance warned that many would starve unless speculation in the necessities of life stopped. He forbade the exporting of salt, bacon, pork, beef, corn, meal, flour, wheat, potatoes, shoes, leather, hides, cotton cloth, yarn, and woolen cloth. To encourage compliance with the law and to discourage private speculation, sixty-eight county magistrates resolved in August 1864 that they would sell to the county corn agent for the support of needy soldiers' families one-tenth of their surplus wheat and corn crops at prices fixed by the North Carolina commissioners and would ask all farmers to do the same. They asked those who were not farmers to contribute money for the same purpose.[15] By January 1865 the situation was even worse. A special session of the county court authorized $25,000, soon raised to $40,000, for the purchase of 8,000 bushels of corn, but Orange County had to supply it; the Confederate government by this time had all it could do to feed the soldiers. At this time 600 women and 800 children were on the Orange County relief rolls—19.7 percent of the adult white women in the county, and 35 percent of the white children under eight. Possibly some of these were refugees from eastern North Carolina and southern Virginia, who continued to arrive in Chapel Hill, Hillsborough, and even Durham's Station.[16]

As the Confederacy's situation went from bad to worse, a large sector of the population could only have rejoiced: the roughly 350,000 slaves in North Carolina, who caught a glimmer of their coming freedom. How the slaves responded to war conditions varied with their proximity to the battle lines. They had of course always been viewed by whites as the enemy within the gates, but during the Civil War they became a particular cause for watchfulness, and with reason. As the northern armies invaded the coastal areas, large numbers of slaves walked off the local plantations and fled to the Union lines, where they were immediately freed and given jobs similar to those of their former existences. To prevent this loss, planters with numerous slaves in the coastal plain moved them inland, far removed from the fighting, for safekeeping. Although the majority of slaves, lacking the opportunity to flee to the Union battle lines, won a reputation for faithfulness to their white masters by keeping to their tasks to the end, many of them exhibiting genuine affection and concern for the white women and children left defenseless at home, some became recalcitrant and uncooperative as the Union troops neared.[17]

Willy-nilly, many slaves were employed in the Confederate cause: laboring in ironworks, factories, or mines; building fortifications, or serving in army camps as cooks, wagoners, or body servants to young masters. Some of Paul Cameron's slaves were conscripted for work on the fortifications around Wilmington. He was so concerned about losing them by escape, disease, or maltreatment that he sent an overseer to care for them. In the end he lost them all, both those at home and those hired out, an investment he calculated at $443,000.[18]

Jubilee came at last to eastern Orange, and memories of those days, permanently fixed in slave narratives, document the swift course of events that led from slavery to emancipation. Sometimes the arrival of General Wheeler's cavalry heralded the end, for Confederate forces were as notorious for plundering as Union. When the Union forces arrived at a plantation, bent on collecting food and valuables, they informed the slaves of their freedom almost as an afterthought as they rode off to the next plantation. If, on the other hand, the master or mistress anticipated the Yankees' arrival, they called their black families together and formally told them they were free.

Sarah Debro, a slave whom Polly Sutherland White inherited from her father,

William Cain, Sr., described her experiences during the war, at its end, and in the aftermath.[19]

I was about waist high when de soldiers mustered. I went with Mis' Polly down to de musterin' field where dey was marchin'. I can see dey feets now when dey flung dem up and down, sayin', "Hep, hep, hep." ... Marse Jim [nephew of Polly White] was cavalry. He rode a big hoss, and my Uncle Dave went with him to de field as his bodyguard. He had a hoss, too, so if Marse Jim's hoss got shot dere would be another one for him to ride. ...

I 'members when Wheelers Cavalry come through. Dey was 'Federates but dey was mean as de Yankees. Dey stole everything dey could find and killed a pile of niggers. Dey come round checkin'. Dey ask de niggers if dey wanted to be free. If dey say no, dey let dem alone. Dey took three of my uncles out in de woods and shot dey faces off.

I 'members de first time de Yankees come. Dey come gallopin' down de road, tromplin' down de rose bushes and messin' up de flower beds. Dey stomped all over de house, in de kitchen, pantries, smokehouse, and everywhere, but dey didn't find much, 'cause near about everything done been hid. I was settin' on de steps when a big Yankee come up. He had on a cap and his eyes was mean. "Where did dey hide de gold and silver, nigger?" he yells at me. ...

When de War was over de Yankees was all round de place, tellin' de niggers what to do. Dey told dem dey was free, dat dey didn't have to slave for de white folks no more. My folks all left Marse Cain and went to live in houses dat de Yankees built. Dey was like poor white folks' houses, little shacks made out of sticks and mud with stick and mud chimneys. Dey wasn't like Marse Cain's cabins, planked up and warm. Dey was full of cracks, and dey wasn't no lamps and oil. All de light come from de lightwood knots burnin' in the fireplace.

Few personal records document the war years for the white inhabitants of eastern Orange County, but two women, one of whom later lived in Morrisville, Wake County, and the other in Chapel Hill, have left clear pictures of the lives of the families at home. Mary J. Grierson, daughter of a planter near Concord, remembered that "the negroes were faithful and planted the fields and gathered the crops—they served in house and kitchen; many of them went with their masters to the army as body guards and cooks. The *Advance* (a specially built blockade runner) ran the blockade from Wilmington and brought blankets, shoes, and ammunition for the soldiers and blue muslin and brown calico—never but these two colors—the latter at $15 a yard."[20]

Grierson made plain the privations caused by inflation: a pound of tea from Charleston cost $200, a barrel of flour $800, a spool of thread $20. During the last days of the war a plug of tobacco cost $500. Her father owned a cotton mill and dyed the cloth with oak bark, walnut hulls, and cedar, and used rusty iron in vinegar to set the dyes. Family carpets, piano covers, and heavy draperies were cut up for army blankets. "All pieces of cloth that would make a bandage, large or small, was wound in a roll and all linen rags were scraped for lint and sent to the army." In the last year of the war shoes were made from cloth with attached wooden soles. Many different vegetables were tried as substitutes for coffee: wheat, rye, sweet potatoes, and okra seed; sassafras was a common substitute for tea. Ink was made from oak balls, soda from burst corn cobs, and saltpeter from the dirt under smokehouses.[21]

From Cornelia Phillips Spencer came similar testimony.

I speak now of Central North Carolina, where many families of the highest respectability and refinement lived for months on cornbread, sorghum, and peas; where meat was seldom on the tables, tea and coffee never; where dried apples and peaches were a luxury; where children went barefoot through the winter, and ladies made their own shoes, and wove their own homespuns; where carpets were cut up into blankets, and window-curtains and sheets were torn up for hospital uses; where soldiers' socks were knit day and night, while for home service clothes were twice turned, and patches were patched again.[22]

News was slow in traveling from the battlefields in those days, and Chapel Hill was more removed than Durham from any traffic that might bring it. At least the railroad came from east and west to Durham with daily reports from other areas of the state. Cornelia Spencer described the uncertainty and waiting during the last days of the war when newspapers had suspended publication and civilians did not know what their fate would be at the hands of the Union forces. "We sat in our pleasant piazzas and awaited events with quiet resignation. The silver had all been buried—some of it in springs, some of it under rocks in the streams, some of it in fence-corners, which, after the fences had been burned down, was pretty hard to find again; some of it in the woods, some of it in the cellars. There was not much provision to be carried off—that was one comfort."[23] On a Sunday in April 1865 a dozen Union soldiers quietly rode into town from Raleigh; after assuring the residents that there would be no pillage, they retired to their camp for the night. Next morning, Easter Monday, 17 April, she wrote, "General Atkins, at the head of a detachment of four thousand cavalry, entered about eight A.M. and we were captured."[24] It was a quiet ending to four years of fear, anxiety, and everyday want— fear of whom the next battle would wound or kill, anxiety about provisions for faraway soldiers and family at home, want of sufficient fuel and food to satisfy the simplest physical needs. Exhaustion and relief must have been the dominant feelings of all on that Easter Monday morning. One Durham resident, Mary R. Holeman, in later years wrote a poem about those anxious days.

I seemed to see Kilpatric's men,
Hear drums begin to beat—
They've come to Durham's station now
Listen—to tramping feet.[25]

For Durham the war's importance was its ending at James Bennitt's farmhouse three and a half miles west of town on the Hillsborough to Raleigh road. Although General Robert E. Lee had surrendered the Army of Northern Virginia, comprising twenty-six thousand troops, at Appomattox Courthouse, much larger numbers of southern troops were still in the field. General Sherman had had enough experience in the South to understand how much time would be spent, how many lives would be lost, how much suffering and expense would be involved in tracking down and fighting the remaining armies. Consequently, by the time he entered Raleigh on 13 April he was in a mood to negotiate with General Joseph Johnston. He had already captured Fayetteville and destroyed the Confederate arsenal there, a severe blow to the South; he had won the battle of Bentonville the third week in March. With the occupation of Salisbury on 12 April, General George Stoneman had completed his famous raid on western North Carolina, a raid that wreaked havoc on rail lines, bridges, factories, and supplies, all vital to continued warfare. For the South, General Lee's surrender had been symbolic of the defeat of the Confederacy, and few men had heart for further futile fighting. Exhaustion of spirit, supplies, and fighting men were evident to everyone. All knew that although the Confederate armies could pursue a pattern of strategic retreat and guerrilla warfare all over the vast southern region, forestalling Confederate defeat for months or years, the North's superiority in numbers and supplies would in the end decide the outcome, and the Confederacy would be forced to capitulate. Durham's geographical luck again dealt her a high card in the historic game about to be played. Sherman in Raleigh and Johnston in Greensboro made arrangements to meet. Sherman took the train to Durham and Johnston moved his headquarters temporarily to General Wade Hampton's office in Hillsborough, and from these points the generals marched to their rendezvous.

Because by chance the house of James and Nancy Bennitt was that place of rendezvous on 17 April 1865, their names became permanently fixed in the history of North Carolina. As General Sherman left Raleigh that morning, he was handed a telegram informing him of Lincoln's assassination. Telling no one, he continued to his meeting and after arriving at Durham station went to General Kilpatrick's headquarters in Dr. Richard Blacknall's house south of the railroad warehouse lot. Together with a small escort the two generals set out on horseback to the west along the Hillsborough road. Like the small group riding to meet them, they carried a white flag. A temporary truce had been declared to allow for the negotiations. With General Johnston rode General Wade Hampton.[26] Sherman's account is probably as close to the truth as anyone can now come to the events of that meeting:

> We shook hands and introduced our respective attendants. I asked if there was a place convenient where we could be private, and General Johnston said he had passed a small farm-house a short distance back, when we rode back to it together side by side, our staff-officers and escorts following. We had never met before, though we had been in the regular army together for thirteen years. . . . He was some twelve or thirteen years my senior, but we knew enough of each other to be well acquainted at once. We soon reached the house of a Mr. Bennett, dismounted, and left our horses with orderlies on the road. Our officers, on foot, passed into the yard, and General Johnston and I entered the small frame-house. We asked the farmer if we could have

the use of his house for a few minutes, and he and his wife withdrew into a smaller log-house, which stood close by.

As soon as we were alone together I showed him [Johnston] the dispatch announcing Mr. Lincoln's assassination, and watched him closely. The perspiration came out in large drops on his forehead, and he did not attempt to conceal his distress.[27]

Johnston instantly realized that Sherman's position was now a delicate one. Though Lincoln had given him authority at City Point, Virginia, where they had met just three weeks previously, to make peace with Johnston and to negotiate not just military but political terms, neither of them could know what the Congress and new executive would approve. They could only arrive at some tentative agreement and wait for Washington's reply. This they achieved in meetings on 17 and 18 April, drawing up a treaty along the lines that Grant had dictated to Lee. The terms included the immediate parole of soldiers on their swearing loyalty to the United States and depositing their arms in designated places, amnesty for all southerners, the continuation of the established state governments and the states' immediate reinstatement in the Union, and full participation in the rights of citizenship for all the inhabitants.[28]

When the treaty terms reached Washington, Sherman was in immediate trouble. He was denounced and accused of insubordination by the secretary of state, Edward M. Stanton, for trespassing on matters of state. With the rejection of the agreement in Washington, Jefferson Davis instructed Johnston to continue the war. Just before the truce was due to expire, Johnston disobeyed orders and requested to meet with Sherman again to arrange surrender terms. When the two generals met for the third time and eventually signed somewhat altered and exclusively military terms, a whole week had passed during which detachments from both armies were encamped around the countryside. For the period of the truce Sherman had ordered a separation of the troops by establishing a line of demarcation between them that would run through Tyrrell's Mount in Chatham County, Chapel Hill, Durham's Station, and West Point. He strictly forbade any vulgarity, rowdyism, and petty crime, and assured them that "the general hopes and believes that in a very few days it will be his good fortune to conduct you all to your homes."[29] His hopes were well founded; the peace was concluded on 26 April at the third meeting at the Bennett farmhouse. Johnston surrendered 36,000 soldiers in North Carolina and over 52,000 in Georgia and Florida. Very soon afterward the two remaining armies in Alabama and Louisiana also signed surrender agreements, and the war was over.[30]

Like their house, the Bennitts formed only part of the backdrop for the two main players in the drama. For the onlookers, however, the Bennitts and their house had been touched by history. Representative of the predominant class in North Carolina, the Bennitts were yeoman farmers owning no slaves, industrious, versatile, never very far from the thin line between debt and solvency. James Bennitt, a native of Chatham County, was married to the widow of Richard Pierson, Nancy Leigh Pierson, a cousin of Richard Stanford Leigh. At first a sharecropper,

Bennitt had become a landowner only in 1846 when he purchased the place in Orange County that has become known by his name. He sold off almost half of his original 325 acres soon after he purchased them from Willis Dilliard. Besides self-sufficient and diversified farming, the Bennitts turned their hands to anything that would bring in extra cash: selling watermelons, plugs of tobacco, spirits, meals, or a night's lodging; engaging in shoemaking, tailoring, and hauling passengers and produce. The war years were hard on them; they lost their son Lorenzo, who served in Company G of the 27th Infantry Regiment, and their son-in-law Robert Duke, a younger brother of Washington Duke and a member of Company E of the 46th Infantry Regiment.[31]

The cabin's role in history was instantly recognized. The initials of soldiers who wanted to record their presence at the historic place were carved all over the siding and even inside on the beams. There the family continued to live out their unpretentious lives. James Bennitt was moved to write to the governor to complain that the table on which the generals had signed the treaty had been removed with a promise that he would be paid ten dollars and a horse, but he had been unable to collect them. He died in the late 1870s, his widow in 1884. Brodie Duke, the oldest surviving son of Washington Duke, bought the place from Bennitt's granddaughter in 1890 and had a shell of rough wood built over the exterior to preserve its deteriorating siding. The Bennitts' daughter, Eliza, had married Brodie Duke's uncle, but the site held more than familial or historical interest for Brodie. He saw it as a marketable investment: he authorized its sale at the Columbian Exposition of 1893 in Chicago but found no buyer and finally sold it to Samuel Tate Morgan after 1908.[32] Morgan, son of Samuel Davidson Morgan, a well-to-do planter of the Fish Dam (now Redwood) area of Flat River, valued the site's historical importance. He had long wished to own it and to place a memorial marker at the site, but he died in 1920 without fulfilling that purpose.

The importance of the Bennett place affair to Durham's history lies in what occurred during the final weeks of the war and the peace negotiations. Confederate forces had streamed west from Bentonville through Durham, retreating with Johnston toward Greensboro, but thousands were still in the vicinity. Durham's Station was the headquarters of General Kilpatrick, and around the town and on the outlying farms swarms of his soldiers were also encamped with nothing to do. Hiram Paul, relating events that had occurred less than twenty years before, must be believed when he said that Durham was neutral ground during the truce and that the soldiers of both armies fraternized, "swapped horses, ran foot races, shot at targets, and, around the same camp-fires, told hairbreadth escapes, spun camp yarns, and had a 'good time' generally," and, when the peace was declared, "literally smoked the pipe of peace."[33] With a plug of tobacco selling at five hundred dollars, as Mary Grierson recalled, a storehouse full of processed tobacco such as stood near the station at Durham would not long remain unobserved or inviolate. The storehouse of J. R. Green's little frame tobacco factory was soon plundered of its entire contents, and Green counted himself a ruined man. Actually the theft proved an advertising scheme on a scale beyond his wildest dreams. The stolen delights of the unfamiliar bright-leaf tobacco that the soldiers enjoyed in the leisure of the spring days and the euphoria of the war's end left indelible memories. When the thousands of soldiers had scattered to their homes all over the Union, they sent back to Durham's Station for more tobacco and continued to ask for it, spreading its reputation far and wide, intent on recapturing the pleasure and mood of those days. To the small hamlet of Durham, the captors had become captives.[34]

From Bust to Boom, 1865–1880

9

WHEN THE SOLDIERS DEPARTED at the end of April 1865, leaving J. R. Green's business a shambles, the future must have seemed very uncertain for townspeople and farmers alike. Although they had been spared actual battle and, for the most part, destruction of property, bridges, and railroad by the timely truce, there was still much to feed their sense of hopelessness and depression. The war had depleted their stores and made their money worthless, and defeat had disrupted their government, their economy, and their whole social structure.

RECONSTRUCTION

Animosity toward the North that would survive indefinitely, resentment of all outside interference, and distrust of foreigners developed at this time all over the South. Southerners understood that the North's superiority in resources of men and materials had directly caused their downfall. They resented defeat by northern armies filled—as they believed—not only with Negro troops but with myriads of European immigrants. The large infusion of immigrants made the North different from the South and, in their view, inferior. To the bitterness of defeat were added fear and ignominy: fear of the freed slaves—350,000 in North Carolina—possibly hostile and certainly destitute people unaccustomed to freedom; ignominy in being ordered to treat blacks as political and social equals. A reporter for the *Nation* who toured the South immediately after the war informed its readers that "all native Southerners, the poorest and most degraded equally with the rich, and people of the most undoubted unionism as well as secessionists, unaffectedly and heartily despise the Negroes."[1] While this generalization is too sweeping, there was some basis for the statement; certainly there was a general feeling of superiority and disdain on the part of most whites. No such harsh feeling is evident, however, in a letter from Durhamite George R. Marcom to his brother Benjamin in January 1866;

it expresses merely apprehension about the ex-slaves' conduct and objective realization of their economic plight.

> Christmas has past off very quiet with us, more so than was antisipated in regard to the Freedmen. They conducted themselves very well and most of them have made contracts for the present year. In fact a grate many have left and gone South and west—so many that I believe labor will be scearce. A good number of wimman & children is hear yet strowling about—and I dont see any chance for them to live and I think some of them is bound to starve, but they are free. . . . Perhaps it was right for Slavery to be abolished; sometimes I think [God] so willed it or it would not have bin done.[2]

As this letter in part suggests, the response of the freedmen to freedom was to test it by going wherever they pleased, working or not working, taking whatever food was at hand, and casting off servility to whites. This behavior was both feared and resented by whites, particularly by former masters, who saw in it both insolence and irresponsibility.

Southerners also generally despised the carpetbaggers, who included not only northern men and women who came south in the service of the government or charitable organizations, or on their own to help restore normalcy to a defeated and disoriented people, but also capable politicians such as Albion Tourgée and unscrupulous opportunists eager to take advantage of the situation for their own benefit. Carpetbaggers of the most hated variety, because of their political activity on behalf of the Republican Party, were employees of the federal government's Freedmen's Bureau, primarily a relief agency established to help ex-slaves and impoverished whites with food, clothing, shelter, and medical care. It also gave special attention to helping blacks find work, obtain fair contracts from employers (often their former masters), and receive legal aid and schooling. Along with its relief work, however, it ensured votes for the Republican Party by encouraging black participation in the political process, enlisting blacks in local chapters of the Union League on an equal footing with white members, and indoctrinating them in their civil rights.[3]

Without the Freedmen's Bureau, Radical Republicans claimed, ex-slaves would have soon again been subjugated economically, socially, and politically by the white majority; it is safe to say that without it they certainly would have been far more disadvantaged than they actually were, struggling in a hostile world. In the same year that the U.S. Congress passed the Civil Rights Act of 1866, giving blacks equal justice under the law, the North Carolina legislature enacted a "black code." It made blacks' marriages legal, allowed training for them in various occupations, and recognized their contracts as legally binding, but it denied them equal justice. When the United States Congress passed the Fourteenth Amendment, assuring all males twenty-one years of age the rights of citizenship, the North Carolina legislature rejected the amendment overwhelmingly. Although North Carolina legislators had voted to annul the ordinance of secession and had accepted the Thirteenth Amendment, which abolished slavery, they refused to grant blacks the right to vote. Other southern state legislatures acted similarly. As a result, in 1867 Congress resorted to a series of Reconstruction acts and to military rule.[4]

Under Reconstruction North Carolina was obliged to write a new constitution (1868) that made no distinction in the rights of blacks and whites. With blacks exercising their voting rights (military supervision saw to that), the Republicans took control of the state government in 1868 and held it until 1870, while Republican Governor Tod R. Caldwell was continued in office until 1874. During these years blacks filled minor political posts and began to assert themselves with dignity and pride, rejecting the humble and obsequious behavior to whites that had always been required of them. Weak local authority, widespread poverty, and political dissension led to a rise in crime and violence. In addition, the period 1867 to 1870 saw the formation and activities of vigilante groups all over the South, loosely identified generally as the Ku Klux Klan, though actually comprising variously named societies such as the Invisible Empire, the White Brotherhood, and the Constitution Union Guards. Prompted by a vacuum in local authority, these groups, apologists argue, intended to supply the lacking law and order, though they may, in fact, have sought to undermine what little there was. Their aim was allegedly political: to combat Radical Republicanism, gain power, and to maintain white supremacy. These results were achieved, whether or not the Klan and its allies were more than a little responsible. They also vowed to protect southern womanhood. The Klan's masks, hooded robes, secrecy, sudden nighttime appearances, and tricks were formulated to suggest that they were the spirits of the dead Confederates returning from the grave to punish whites who cooperated in establishing the new social order and to prevent blacks from exercising their new rights. As time went on, however, they did more than merely frighten their victims. The Klan rode at night with muffled horses' hooves to their victims' homes and dragged them from their beds to beat, mutilate, or kill them. Favorite objects of Klan attack were black or white northern schoolteachers of freedmen and the schoolhouses in which they taught, which often served as meeting places for the local Union Leagues.[5]

Orange County was one of the areas in which the Klan was most active. William L. Saunders, a resident of Chapel Hill and afterward secretary of state, was Grand Dragon of North Carolina. Not a few members of the old planter class were Klansmen, and many, like respectable southerners everywhere, at first viewed the Klan with favor. When Congress finally began to investigate it and its fellow secret organizations, public opinion, shocked by the violence, had swung against the groups. Klansmen killed five blacks in Orange County and attacked numerous others, among them the inhabitants of the poorhouse. Many blacks fled the area permanently rather than risk the consequences. Because so many incidents attributed to the Klan occurred in Orange County, in 1870 Governor Holden asked Pride Jones of Hillsborough, a former Klansman, to attempt to disband the organization there. Born into the planter class, Jones had been the colonel of an Orange County unit in the war and held widespread respect.[6] The turnabout in opinion is reflected in a newspaper report of a Klan hanging of a black man at Graham in adjoining Alamance County:

Such deeds as this will not only prevent Northern men coming here and settling, but it will drive off desirable population, disgrace society and tarnish
the escutcheon of the state. We feel proud that it did not occur in Orange. Let
her continue to respect and venerate law and good order, without which we
shall relapse into a state of barbarism.[7]

Not all the violence that occurred in those years was definitely tied to the Klan.
Retaliation for Klan activity and the general atmosphere of violence and disorder
both before and after the Klan's establishment led to barn burnings and other vandalism, often mistakenly attributed to the Union League. The newspaper reported
in 1870 that Bedford Vaughan's tobacco factory near Stagville had been burned
with a resulting $6,000 loss. Another incident, blamed on the Flat River Union
League, concerned James Carrington and his daughter, who claimed that they were
prevented from passing on the Oxford highway by one Peter Leathers, a black.
Republicans of eastern Orange County who suffered attacks of one sort or another
during Reconstruction were James B. Mason, William Maynor, Sidney Upchurch,
Andrew J. and Nathaniel King, and Washington Duke, whose son Benjamin many
years later conceded that his father had endured "many petty persecutions and
almost ostracism socially." The Klan's effect was to weaken and demoralize Republicans and to continue economic, political, and social discrimination against
blacks.[8]

Although the new state constitution was altered after the Conservatives returned
to power, following the end of military rule and the demise of the Freedmen's Bureau, the new system of county government that it incorporated remained in place,
albeit with some modifications made in 1877. Instead of a county court presided
over by justices of the peace in whom all local power rested, the new constitution substituted a commission of five members, which became the administrative
and legislative arm of the county; the county was divided into townships and each
township given some local autonomy with locally elected magistrates, clerk, constable, and school committee. The county court was abolished, and the superior
court or its clerk assumed the judicial powers of the former justices. The constitution as written provided for the election of five commissioners, who served two-
year terms, and for the election of all county officers: sheriff, clerk of court, register
of deeds, surveyor, and the like. It was the first provision of the system that the
returning Conservatives eliminated in 1877 and which was not restored until 1896.
Instead, the justices of the peace were allowed to appoint the commissioners.[9]

In the first election under the new constitution in 1868, two Durham men were
elected Orange County commissioners: Robert F. Morris and William N. Patterson.
The first county commission requested the county surveyor, Silas Link, to draw up
a county map showing the newly organized townships and school districts, for the
new constitution had guaranteed four months' schooling each year for every child
aged six through twenty-one. The townships of eastern Orange became Mangum,
Durham, and Patterson. In 1877 Mangum was divided at Little River; the newly
created township south of the river was named Lebanon for the old meetinghouse
there.[10] In August 1869 the following officials were elected in the townships:

Mangum: Addison Mangum, A. M. Latta, magistrates
                Richard Lunsford, clerk
                J. B. Leathers, constable
                S. H. Turrentine, R. F. Webb, A. M. Leathers, school committee
Durham: M. A. Angier, Major Green, B. C. Hopkins, magistrates
                Archibald Nichols, clerk
                M. H. Turner, constable
                R. D. Patterson, J. W. Marcom, H. H. Sims, school committee
Patterson: R. S. Leigh, A. B. Gunter, magistrates
                W. T. Patterson, clerk
                J. B. Marcom, constable
                H. S. Marcom, W. T. Barbee, W. R. Marcom, school committee[11]

The town of Durham was formally establishing itself, too, and was beginning to respond to the new prosperity that demand for its tobacco was bringing. The town as it was then is very quickly described.[12] The nucleus was still Robert Morris's clutch of frame buildings, hotel and annex, double log kitchen, blacksmith shop, office, barn, stable, and feed house on the tract now bounded by the railroad, Corcoran, Main, and Mangum streets. Across the tracks were the railroad depot and warehouse and James W. Cheek's house (the former Rose of Sharon Church), and to their west were Green's factory and the house of his partner, Dr. Richard Blacknall. To Cheek's east and south was the tract of John A. McMannen. Morris's tobacco business (reorganized in 1865) and Green's were providing the vital spark which kindled the recovery to come.[13] Solomon Shepherd, A. M. Rigsbee, William Mangum, and Calvin O'Briant ran bars, J. W. Cox, a tailor shop, and the Mangum brothers, William and Presley J., a sawmill, cotton gin, and carpenter shop, in which the post office was located. James Whitt and Squire Bull, the latter a black man, were shoemakers. Other blacks living in the town were Lewis Pratt (W. N. Pratt's former blacksmith), Solomon Geer, and George Bradshaw and their families. W. K. Styron, J. W. Cheek, and M. A. Angier ran general stores. Four doctors served the area: Blacknall, W. J. Hugh Durham (a young cousin of Bartlett Durham), Thomas Hicks, and Thomas Vickers. The Methodist and Baptist churches and the common school and academy buildings represented the cultural cornerstones, religion and education, on which Durhamites would continue to build.[14]

So closely hedged with farms was the town that some townsmen could pursue both rural and urban occupations. The nearest farms were those of Jesse and Fred Geer, Jim Redmond, Green, Mangum, O'Briant, Lyon, A. M. Rigsbee, Morris, Angier, Strayhorn, and Mrs. Orpah May. On the other hand, D. C. Parrish, John A. McMannen, and Richard Blacknall had forsaken farming entirely. McMannen moved his smut machine manufacture to the large tract of land he owned on soon-to-be McMannen Street. Blacknall practiced medicine and in the early 1870s opened a pharmacy. Parrish, always involved in a variety of occupations besides farming —political, religious, civic, and military organizations—used his old skills as an iron- and leather-worker and opened a carriage factory.[15]

As Durham continued to act as a magnet, drawing off from older communities their most enterprising citizens, the incipient towns languished and never became more than crossroad villages. Durham's growth and the problems arising from it spurred Orange County officials to have the town incorporated in 1866. A few months later the United States Congress invalidated all acts of southern legislatures under their existing governments. In 1869 the new legislature passed a second bill for incorporation, and the residents of Durham held an election on 4 August 1869 for town commissioners and a magistrate of police, later denominated a mayor.[16] Those elected were James W. Cheek, magistrate, Robert F. Morris, A. M. Rigsbee, W. K. Styron, W. Y. Clark, and William Mangum, town commissioners or aldermen. Together they chose J. T. Farthing as town clerk and Andrew Turner as constable.[17]

The aldermen then drew up bylaws for the town, an area to extend one-half mile in each direction from the station warehouse. Principally concerned with order and the moral tone of the town, the aldermen's chief problem arose over the vexed question of retailing spirits. At first determined to limit liquor sales to a few licensed taverns run by responsible men, they were soon tempted by the money made from licenses to grant them to all who applied, thereby perpetuating Durham's prewar reputation as "a roaring old place."[18] A protracted contest followed, with the Temperance faction giving the other town aldermen a hard time. Finally A. M. Rigsbee, the Mangum brothers, and Calvin O'Briant were voted licenses. Presumably Rigsbee and Mangum abstained from voting. When D. C. Parrish joined the town board, the laws began to reflect his biases: a new ordinance prohibited card playing in the mayor's office; a new street running south from the railroad was to be called McMannen Street for his old friend, through whose land it would run; the sale of liquor within fifty yards of Main Street was prohibited. As this last ordinance would have effectually banished the cluster of saloons on and near the corner of Main and Mangum streets, John S. Lockhart, Parrish's son-in-law, soon after got the law repealed. Five days later, Julian S. Carr, another Parrish son-in-law and newly sworn alderman, reinstated the ordinance with the provision that only a two-thirds majority vote could repeal it. Thus the battle went on, the laws changing with the makeup of the town board.[19]

Stores, peddlers, and factories as well as taverns required operating licenses, and the sale of these licenses also helped defray the town's expenses. The aldermen set the tax rate at $0.50 per $100 evaluation of property and $2.25 on every poll. John A. McMannen, D. C. Parrish, and Sterling Proctor were appointed the town's first tax assessors. With the tax money, the town provided for the creation and maintenance of streets, which the aldermen had the duty of naming.[20]

The story of the laying out of Main Street in 1869 conveys the primitive state of the town in the 1870s, "There are men, young yet," a reporter wrote in 1896,

who remember the Saturday afternoon when Robert F. Morris, M. A. Angier, Col. D. C. Parrish, Morgan Closs, Washington Duke, Solomon Shepherd, Atlas Rigsbee, J. W. Cheek, Frederick Geer, and Col. W. T. Blackwell, with Brown Jordan as ploughman, and two big mules laid out Main Street, beginning at Esquire Angier's store running east through an old field. When the work was done, and two long furrows on either side about a mile long showed where the street was to be, the less credulous of us gathered just as the sun was setting to criticize such foolishness, and to guy the "Fathers" with sarcasm as to the price of corner lots and exasperating questions as to how they proposed to people their newly made town. But they builded better than they knew, and every one of them lived to see their new laid street built on and occupied from end to end.[21]

At the town board meeting following this achievement, Morris moved that Main or Pratt street be established "as it is now plowed."[22]

The aldermen felt no need for a town hall until 1878. In that year A. M. Rigsbee built on his corner a brick store one hundred feet long to replace an earlier frame one, and the second story was fitted out to serve as a town hall. They had quickly recognized, however, the need for a guardhouse, and years before had bought land for one from M. A. Angier.[23] The aldermen's problems were relatively minor because they took no responsibility for the serious economic and cultural needs of the people, particularly the large number of freedmen just beyond the town limits, learning self-reliance as they worked out new patterns of survival and established social institutions to supply their needs.

EDUCATION

The collapse of the Confederacy had wiped out the Literary Fund by which North Carolina had supported its school system since 1839. Because the legislature between 1865 and 1868 was unwilling to vote money for schools, the school system was in general disarray. In 1868, however, the Republican legislature appropriated $100,000 for schools that were to be established or reestablished in the new townships under the direction of the superintendent of public instruction, an office provided for in the new constitution. Each county was to receive fifty cents from the state for every child within its borders. Therefore a census of schoolchildren and existing school buildings was undertaken. In Orange County the inventory counted only forty-three schoolhouses "in badly deteriorated condition" to serve the 3,667 white children. Black children, numbering 2,235, would now also have to be accommodated. Sixty-three new buildings, at a cost of one hundred dollars each, and fifty dollars for the repairs to each existing building was the estimate for putting Orange County's children to school. Though the plans were well-intentioned, general poverty postponed the establishment of any adequate system. For many years no provision was made for building or maintaining schools. Furthermore, there was no compulsory school law, and teachers were often unqualified for their jobs.[24]

The Freedmen's Bureau, assisted by religious organizations, and the Peabody Education Fund, started by a Massachusetts-born philanthropist to establish schools for blacks and whites in the devastated South, stepped into the breach between the state's plan and its implementation. Chapel Hill and Hillsborough received schools for freedmen, set up by the Friends (Quakers) of Philadelphia. The only school for freedmen in present Durham County was one under the aegis of the Methodist

Church (possibly assisted by the Freedmen's Bureau), located in what later became known as Hayti.[25]

Besides the public schools for whites supported by the county with the limited funds of 1868, there were a few private schools. An academy in town was chartered in 1865 by M. A. Angier, Solomon Shepherd, John Ruffin Green, Robert F. Morris, and others, but a school had been operating on the site since the early 1850s. B. C. Hopkins continued and expanded the school as the Durham Male and Female Academy in 1868. Hopkins announced that the children of ministers and "dismembered Confederate veterans" would be taught free. W. H. Rowland, J. B. Williams, and L. T. Buchanan were other early principals of the Durham Male Academy. In 1870 a Mrs. Colton established a primary school for boys and girls on Liberty Street opposite Mrs. J. T. Womble's Durham Female School.[26]

In the northern part of the county the old South Lowell Academy continued under a series of principals. In 1878 the Red Mountain Male and Female Academy was established by R. B. Blalock in the old store-cum-post office that had been Abner Parker's old stand. Its instruction, which was to be strictly nonsectarian, included primary, secondary, and commercial curricula. Across Flat River, Willie P. Mangum's daughter Martha had undertaken to pay her father's debts and support the family by beginning a female academy in January 1863. It had a long and successful run with only a short interruption into the 1890s. Hardly a mile away, the Mangum Male Academy had also been established by 1871 with A. H. Stokes as principal. It was short-lived. In 1879 Frank W. Roberts was running the Round Hill Academy.[27]

In the Wake County portions of later Durham County, private schools were being established as well. Cedar Creek Academy was started soon after the war in a two-room structure, the upper one used by the Masons, the lower one by the school. This building burned in 1875, but was replaced by another with the same arrangement. In 1893 a new school was built, which became part of the public school system after 1894, taking the name Nelson, that of the post office established there in 1885. In the Oak Grove area at a place called Dayton, the present site of the Olive Branch Baptist Church but then a Nichols family preserve, Dayton Academy was founded in the middle 1870s. Its constitution specified in 1878 that no subject of a sectarian character or tendency would be tolerated. Among the school's early teachers were J. C. Hocutt, George Perry, and the Rev. J. F. MacDuffie. When the school closed in the middle 1890s, the building was moved to the late Dr. R. E. Nichols's land.[28]

RELIGION

Religious zeal continued during and after the war. Williams Harris of the Flat River family, a Methodist lay preacher, reported on a revival at "Durhams" in the fall of 1863, which lasted sixteen days and converted sixty-eight whites and thirty blacks. Guest preachers such as Professor Phillips from the university and the Reverend Jesse H. Page, a Methodist chaplain with the Seventeenth Regiment, helped spell the sponsoring pastors.[29] In the town, congregations found themselves outgrowing their small frame structures. Both Methodists and Baptists replaced theirs in the 1870s with much larger brick buildings. The Baptists topped their 1878 building with a steeple 140 feet high. The same year the Methodists began their new building which countered with a 200-foot spire.[30]

In the countryside new congregations formed as well. A group had been holding services in a brush arbor called Hopkins Grove for a number of years when the Durham Baptists organized it as a mission in 1878. Nash Cheek from the Durham congregation ran a Sunday school there, and the next year Simpson Browning and Columbus Durham, the Durham church's pastor, secured two acres for the group and oversaw the building of a church called Rose of Sharon, a name that had just been discarded by the Durham church, newly named the First Baptist Church. In the Fish Dam neighborhood a congregation calling itself first Belvin Baptist Church and later Mount Calvary held services in the 1860s in the Colclough schoolhouse, but it soon died out. In the 1870s, as a response to the veteran Baptist preacher Columbus Durham's concern, Jesse Howell was sent to the people at Fish Dam; after a succession of services, a revival held in August 1879 resulted in a new organization called Roberson Grove Church. A. G. Ferrell and J. P. Roberson professed faith at this revival and by their efforts a church building was almost immediately supplied on Roberson's land by carpenters paid by Ferrell. The first regular pastor, in 1880, was R. A. Patterson. The current church building, the third, stands on the same land on a site only a short distance from the old Colclough school site.[31]

West of Durham in today's Lakewood area, another Baptist congregation was organized by the efforts of the Durham church. Yates Baptist Church, named for the missionary to China Matthew T. Yates, began as a brush arbor in 1877 on land owned by Jane Rigsbee Anderson, who was encouraged by her brother Thomas J. Rigsbee to make it available to the group. Still another Baptist congregation, Pope's Chapel, was formed in the 1870s and built on Sidney Pope's land in 1875. This group was organized in 1891 into Ephesus Baptist Church.[32]

The Methodists organized McMannen's Chapel and Calvary Methodist churches in the 1870s. A rift in the Durham church, whose minister, John Tillett, held stricter views than some of his parishioners, may have been the origin of McMannen's Chapel. A number of members withdrew and formed their own church in 1870, among them the R. F. Morris, John A. McMannen, and John and Gray Barbee families. Under McMannen's leadership they held services at Lipscomb's crossroads. Either this group or another under McMannen's leadership moved to land donated by Henry T. Neal in 1878, where they built a small church and named it for John McMannen. Mrs. Brodie L. Duke, McMannen's daughter, presented the church with a Bible and hymnal. Of Calvary Church almost nothing is known except that it was located near Stagville plantation, possibly on land originally part of the Brick House Farm on the east side of Flat River. In 1870–71 the church was in the charge of the strict John Tillett and in 1884 of J. T. Lyon. Later the congregation moved to the Butner area of Granville County and was discontinued when Camp Butner was built during the Second World War.[33]

In the 1870s, too, another religious group organized for the first time in what would become Durham County. Richard Blacknall and his family were for many decades the only Presbyterians in eastern Orange. By 1871 they were able to muster enough fellow sectarians in Durham to hold services, first in the Methodist church and then for five years in a public hall. By 1874 they were numerous enough to organize. By 1876 they had built a frame structure on the corner of Roxboro and Main streets, a location they still maintain. Their first regular minister was H. T. Darnall. By 1880 they had forty-three members. The Episcopalians had not formally organized in the 1870s, but they were meeting, and a minister named Hughes was holding services once a month for them in the Good Templars Hall.[34]

The 1860s and 1870s were years in which blacks were first forming their own congregations, withdrawing from the white churches of which they had been members, or organizing entirely new congregations among the new black settlements. They wanted not only to direct their own religious lives, but to worship in a different kind of service, with more congregational participation and more unrestrained emotional expression. Barbee's Chapel in the southern part of the county was established by former slaves of Willis Barbee, a bachelor physician, son of Christopher Barbee, and inheritor of The Mountain, Christopher's home in present Durham County. When he died in 1869, he left one hundred acres of his home plantation and everything on it to his ex-slave Harriet and her children, whom he had presumably fathered. It was on this land that the freedmen built their church.[35]

Southwest of town another black congregation was forming. In June 1875 Charles G. Markham and his wife, Mary, sold an acre of land for one dollar to Thomas and Dallas Daniel, Edward Mitchell, Eldridge Parrish, and Benjamin Kornegay as trustees of Markhams Chapel Missionary Baptist Church. The site was on the old Chapel Hill road southwest of Durham near its present location.[36]

In 1874 a group in Red Mountain acted on a desire to worship together and began services, informally gathering under trees, in barns, or in a brush arbor. Led by the Reverend John Mitchell, they eventually built a log cabin on land that lies today just back of the white Red Mountain Baptist Church. When the latter church was organized in 1880, the black congregation was forced to relinquish the land and move across the road, where they built a second structure. The present structure of New Red Mountain Baptist Church is its sixth, the fifth on that site.[37]

Three other congregations vitally important to black history in Durham were also formed in the 1860s, two of them located south of the railroad tracks opposite old Prattsburg. These became Saint Joseph A.M.E. Church and White Rock Baptist Church, both at the heart of the black culture that was developing along with the white. The third was in Hickstown, the old Pin Hook area (see chapter 10).

THE TOBACCO INDUSTRY

Underlying all this expansion lay the vitality of the burgeoning tobacco industry, which made possible a relatively swift recovery for Durham and its environs from the defeat and devastation of war. The lesson that the South had learned from the war was that besides superiority of numbers and supplies, industry had made the difference. The South had long been dependent on the North for manufactured goods, the North's resources had won the war, and industry had given the North enormous wealth and the advantages wealth buys. The conquered, true to historical form, now aped their conquerors. Therefore in the South and in Durham a new kind of community leader was in the making—the industrialist—whose new source of wealth would give him previously undreamed-of power. In Durham the tobacco magnates were to supply the vision, the leadership, and the particular character of the social superstructure, which they would underpin with substantial funding.

Robert F. and Thomas B. Morris with Wesley A. Wright had been Durham's tobacco pioneers. After Wright's withdrawal, Dr. Blacknall became the Morrises' partner in an undertaking that was small but that inspired others, such as John Ruffin Green (1840–69). After Green's father, Major Green, had moved his family from Person County to the old James Leathers tract on the Eno River in 1856, the younger Green had begun to grow and peddle tobacco. He saved his money and on his father's farm he began a factory, which burned before it was completed. He then went to Durham, bought the Morris and Blacknall factory, and continued to run it throughout the war. The plunder of his manufactured tobacco during the peace negotiations might have resulted in his giving up tobacco manufacture, except that almost at once requests for his product began to flow in to the station agent and town officers, and soon his factory was humming again. He had the good sense to see a need for a specific name and trademark for his product. His lucky hit on a trademark over a lunch of oysters with his fellow manufacturer, James Y. Whitted of Hillsborough, is local lore. Whitted pointed to the bull's head on the Coleman's Durham brand mustard jar, suggesting that Ruffin might make similar use of a bull as his trademark. A refugee buggymaker from New Bern painted a profile portrait of a neighbor's bull to hang over the door of the factory, and Green stamped his product "Genuine Durham Smoking Tobacco," the words accompanied by the bull's picture. The success of Green's trademark can be measured by the host of imitations and resulting lawsuits for infringement of copyright.[38]

Green had a number of partners in his short business career. The first was a war refugee from Onslow County, Captain William P. Ward, who bowed out after the destruction of the warehouse in 1865. Next followed R. A. Jenkins, who put up Green's product in Williamsboro, Granville County; James Edward Lyon in 1868; and William Thomas Blackwell and James R. Day, fellow Person Countians, in 1869. Blackwell and Day had been tobacco jobbers in Kinston, buying tobacco from Green and peddling it throughout the surrounding counties. With the prospect of a settled organization and increasing business at last in his grasp, Green died of tuberculosis at Sparkling Catawba Springs in July 1869. Blackwell then bought the factory, the name, and the brand from Green's heirs, and the next year took a new partner, Julian Shakespeare Carr (1845–1924), whose father bought a one-third share in the business. The company was at last on its way. In 1869 the factory force was less than twelve and the output only 60,000 pounds a year; by 1883 the annual product was over five million pounds and the company employed 900 hands.[39]

Green was not alone as a tobacco manufacturer in the 1860s, either in the town or in the surrounding countryside. As it became increasingly clear that the tobacco industry was continuing to expand and to provide ever larger profits, anyone who could put together a little capital gave industry a whirl. In 1866, Robert Morris with his son Edward W. Morris and William H. Willard formed another partnership, R. F. Morris and Son. Their product was "Spanish Flavored Eureka Smoking Tobacco." From 1867 to 1870 there were others engaged in manufacturing: on their farms, Washington Duke, Bedford Vaughan, and W. D. Lunsford; and in town, Brodie L. Duke, Zachariah I. Lyon and Company, Lockhart and Parrish, Link and Hughes, Durham and Mangum. The 1870 census recorded Vaughan's product as 7,000 pounds of chewing tobacco worth $1,610 and 3,000 pounds of smoking tobacco worth $690.[40] In 1867 Z. I. Lyon and his son J. E. Lyon had begun to manufacture tobacco on their plantation not far from Durham. After a year with Green, the younger Lyon rejoined his father in the manufacture of "Pride of Durham," in their new factory at the corner of later Pettigrew and Pine streets under a reorganization that included James W. Cheek and Frederick C. Geer. Lyon also made "Plucky Durham," "Our Durham," and "Cut and Slash" Smoking Tobacco. After trying manufacturing for a time, beginning in 1869, John S. Lockhart moved instead into warehouse management. Isaac Newton Link, son of the county surveyor, joined his brother-in-law, Dr. W. R. Hughes, who was already operating the manufacturing firm of W. R. Hughes and Company. Link bought him out in 1876, but sold out himself in 1881. Brodie Leonidas Duke had moved to town in 1869, where he began to manufacture his own brand, "Semper Idem." Nothing is known of Durham, Mangum and Company but the name; the firm was still in operation in 1872 when it was listed as a member of the Durham Tobacco Board of Trade, a kind of business guild to which both manufacturers and warehousemen belonged. Established in 1872 in the interest of protecting and improving the tobacco business by cooperation among its many members, the association listed forty members in 1875.[41]

The most important manufacturer before 1870 and the long distance winner by any measure was, of course, Washington Duke. Duke's immediate forebears were plain yeoman farmers. His father, Taylor Duke, son of John and Dicey Jones Duke, lost his home tract overlooking Little River in the 1820s after several years of straitened circumstances, and Washington was bound out to William James Duke (1803–83), his eldest brother, to learn farming. After reaching the age of eighteen, Washington Duke began to farm on rented land. His marriage in 1842 to Mary Caroline Clinton, daughter of Jesse and Rachel Vickers Clinton, eased his way, for the Clintons were prosperous, and when Jesse died in 1847 the young Dukes inherited land and cash. With a portion of this inheritance Duke bought additional tracts of land, one of which, on Ellerbee Creek, became the Duke homestead. The front section of the house he built in 1852 contained two rooms in each of two stories. An ell at the back containing a dining room and kitchen was added about 1860. The Fish Dam Road ran by the front gate, and clustered round the main house were eventually three factories from the different stages of his business's growth, a wellhouse, and a smokehouse. Across the road were stables and barns.[42]

By his first marriage Duke had two boys, Sidney Taylor (1844–58) and Brodie Leonidas (1846–1919). After Mary Caroline's death in 1847, Duke married Artelia Roney in 1852 and added three more children to his family: Mary Elizabeth (1853–93), Benjamin Newton (1855–1929), and James Buchanan (1856–1925). Both Sidney and Artelia died of typhoid fever in the summer of 1858, but the widower and his children continued to live at the homeplace with the help of a black woman, Caroline, whom he had bought in Hillsborough for three hundred dollars in 1855. As he was not listed with any slaves in the 1860 census, Duke probably freed or resold her soon afterward. When Duke was drafted for military service, his younger children were sent to their Roney grandparents, and Brodie, too underweight for regular service, was attached to a company serving at the Confederate prison in Salisbury. On Duke's return in the spring of 1865 the family was reunited at the homestead, and the tobacco manufacture was begun.[43]

After his rise to fame and fortune Washington Duke (1820–1905) told his own story to a reporter:

I began life in Orange as a country boy with nothing. I never inherited a dollar. Up to the breaking out of the war I had been farming thirty years. I had worked hard in the fields, made on the farm nearly everything I needed, and by close economy I had bought and paid for my farm and had stocked it well. . . .

I made only one crop of cotton which I sold at five and a half a hundred [$.055 per 100 pounds]. This crop didn't pay and I never made another. . . . I went into making tobacco in 1859 and 60. We knew nothing then of the present methods of curing, and my crops were sun cured. The first year the crop was wonderfully fine and was sold for between 8 and 10 cents a pound.

Before the war I hauled fodder and flour to Raleigh on wagons, once I remember through mud that came up in some places to the axles of the wagon wheels, and again through rain and snow. I slept in camps or in the wagon more than once when the snow was on the ground. The fodder would bring me 60 cents a hundred, and flour $4.50 a barrel. . . .

About the time the war broke out I had made up my mind to quit farming and go to manufacturing tobacco. In carrying out this resolution in 1863, I sold everything, even my horses, stock and crops, and agreed to take pay for them in tobacco. I even traded my plantation, agreeing to take pay in tobacco to be delivered yearly for six years, but afterwards had to take it back. Some of my friends thought I was very unwise. I had quite a quantity of tobacco stored away and when the armies came along they took most of it.

When the war was over I found myself at Newbern, and after being released from Libby prison, with only a five dollar Confederate note, sold that to a Federal soldier for fifty cents, and walked home, 134 miles, to my farm near Durham. I said to my boys, when I got back home: "The war is over. For people who will do their duty and stick to their business, there never was a better opportunity in the world for men to make their fortunes."[44]

He planted a crop of tobacco and in a log cabin began to process the stored tobacco that the soldiers had not carried off. His three sons helped on rainy days when no farming could be done, hauled some of it to Durham to Captain Ward, Green's partner, and had it put up into plug tobacco. Then Duke peddled it in the small towns of eastern North Carolina along with some smoking tobacco they had made. He received anywhere from fifty to sixty cents a pound in the years 1867 to

1870. He reckoned his profits at about fifteen cents a pound on 25,000 pounds of processed tobacco each of those years. He worked mainly sun-cured tobacco from Orange and adjacent counties, using more bright than dark tobacco.[45]

In a second log cabin, 20 by 30 feet, Duke carried on the various steps of hand processing smoking tobacco: beating, sifting, packaging, and labeling it. He called his product "Pro Bono Publico," giving, as one Durham author has said, "an inkling of the regard in which unschooled 'Wash' Duke held the language of erudition."[46] An eyewitness account of the final steps in the preparation of tobacco for market shows the family on a cold, snowy evening around a large fireplace, Duke's daughter, Mary, working at a table filling little cotton bags with tobacco, tying bows in the drawstring tops, and pasting on the bags yellow labels on which she had written in pen the now well-known trade name.[47]

After testing the waters for a few years, his sound business sense and years of sad experience in farming prompted Duke to stay with tobacco manufacture and give up the farm. In 1869 his son Brodie, the first of the family to move to town, took possession of an old log hut on what became Main Street close to where later the Liggett and Myers factory was built. He used the one downstairs room as his factory and slept in the loft, maintaining like his father a pinchpenny existence, eating ash cakes and cornmeal and drinking only branch water. After his father took the plunge, moving to town sometime between 1872 and 1874, the elder Duke built in 1874 a modest frame building with a partition dividing it into two sections to house both his own and his son's operations. Very soon, however, Washington Duke was able to replace this structure with a fine three-story building, forty by seventy feet, beside the railroad and east of present Duke Street.[48]

The 1870s saw a new rush of riders jump on the industrial merry-go-round. R. T. Faucette started in 1871 with plug tobacco and then switched to smoking tobacco with a brand called "Favorite Durham." Webb, Roulhac and Company (James Webb and W. S. Roulhac) moved from Hillsborough to Durham in 1874. Paul Cameron bought a partnership for his young son Duncan in this firm, but these young men were novices and soon gave up the field to their more experienced competitors. William L. Lipscomb and his brother-in-law John W. Dowd went into business in 1874 on Dillard Street and expanded their operation when they took over the business of the dissolved Webb, Roulhac firm in 1876. In that year the R. F. Morris firm was yet again reorganized and began the manufacture of snuff along with smoking tobacco. Their cheap brand was "Maccaboy" and their expensive brand "Ladies Choice Scotch Snuff." J. R. Day took another stab at manufacturing, going into business with his brother W. P. Day in 1878. They sold out to a New York firm two years later.[49]

Other manufacturers tried their luck in the 1870s. Richard Harvey Wright (1851–1929), another major figure in the development of Durham industry, appeared on the scene in the early 1870s. Born in Louisburg to Thomas Davenport and Elizabeth Glover Wright, he was apprenticed to James T. Hunt in Oxford after his father's early death. He next became Hunt's partner, running a large country store at Tally Ho. When the store burned and their investment was wiped out, Wright started again in Hillsborough. Shortly afterward he moved to Durham to manage a store under the name Hunt and Wright, and in 1875 he began a small tobacco manufacturing business on Main Street near the Dukes, producing "Genuine Orange County Bright Leaf Smoking Tobacco." In that year as well, Alexander Walker, another Person Countian, formed a partnership with Thomas G. Cozart and George Bauer (of Cincinnati, Ohio) to manufacture tobacco, but this plan never seems to have got beyond the organizing stage. Toward the end of the decade two other entrepreneurs attempted the Durham industrial scene: Lucius Green, son of John Ruffin Green, in 1877 and E. H. Pogue in 1879. Green put up a small building, seventy by thirty feet, and manufactured "O. K." and "Indian Girl." Pogue, who had already had a successful business in Hillsborough, built a four-story frame structure in which he made cut plug and twist chewing tobacco and a smoking tobacco called "Sitting Bull." Martin and Reams was also a Durham firm in the 1870s as was Hunt and Thomas.[50]

The increase in the tobacco crop and factories resulted from the enormous demand for the area's particular kind of tobacco—brightleaf, so called for its rich yellow-gold color. A combination of seed, soil, and curing process had resulted in a variety especially well suited to smoking tobacco, which was growing in popularity and supplanting plug. In 1839 Stephen, a slave of the Caswell County Slade brothers, accidentally hit on the new curing process when, in an emergency, he substituted charcoal for wood to fuel the fire in a curing barn. The particular seed that produced brightleaf, which had been developed after years of experimentation by enterprising farmers, needed poor, sandy soil, well endowed with silica, and turned the desired color when dried by the intense but controlled heat that charcoal-fueled fires gave. When in the 1870s a refinement of the curing process replaced the open fires in tobacco barns with a system of flues to conduct the heat from fires under the barns, without the smoke and its impurities, all the constituents were in place to produce a consistently high-grade product.[51]

The new factories provided a convenient outlet for the local crop so that Durham farmers, no longer required to transport tobacco to Virginia to be sold, trundled it to Durham instead and earned larger profits. Naturally the suitability of the land for tobacco determined who could grow it. Paul Cameron was, of course, in a class by himself with the huge amount of land and labor at his disposal. The 1860 census reported his crop as 30,000 pounds, the largest grown in the county. His neighbor, John D. Lipscomb, was next with 15,000 pounds. Joseph Woods, Lipscomb's brother-in-law, and Robert F. Morris grew thirteen and twelve thousand pounds respectively. The best tobacco land in the county was east of Flat River. The largest producers in that area were Cynthia Carrington, Ellison G. Mangum, David Parrish, Squire D. Umstead, and Willie P. Mangum. The west side of Flat River was not far behind. There Benjamin Hester, John B. Leathers, Harrison Parker, Henry T. Gates, George W. Jones, Isham and D. C. Parrish, Henderson Tilley, Thomas Cameron, and Dr. James F. Cain produced anywhere from four to ten thousand pounds.[52]

The loss of their slaves at the end of the war cut deeply into the productivity of the large landowners. Thus there were no more 30,000-pound crops. But because of the convenience of the factories, many farmers with suitable land gave some acreage to the crop if they had not done so before. Those who had, now increased their plantings. North Carolina grew 16,640,000 pounds of tobacco in 1870 and 38,820,000 pounds in 1880. The former slaves, who had labored to grow the tobacco, now found jobs in the factories. They were used in many of the manufacturing processes, particularly the most unpleasant and demanding of strength and endurance. In 1869 there were seven factories in Durham, employing ninety-eight hands, producing products worth $134,330. Ten years later there were fourteen factories, with 870 employees, producing $996,000 worth of processed tobacco. The use of tobacco had greatly increased during the war, but a change in its use was also taking place. The students at Chapel Hill, whom Green saw as his particular clientele, were "discarding the quid for the pipe." Durham had the product to fill the bowl.[53]

It should be noted that Durham was not the only place where tobacco manufacturing was taking root in North Carolina. Small farm factories had existed all over the Piedmont even before the Civil War. By 1870 North Carolina had ninety-eight tobacco factories in twelve different counties, Granville leading the pack with thirty-nine; even Rockingham and Stokes counties had more than Durham. In 1881–82 seven other counties contained more factories than Durham, Davie County at the top of the list with 29. It was the energy and genius of the particular men involved in Durham's leading companies, Carr and the Dukes, however, and the keen competition among them, that accounted for Durham's eventual supremacy as the tobacco capital not only of the state but the world.[54]

Carr, the son of John Wesley Carr, a prosperous merchant of Chapel Hill, was no ordinary mortal. Though small of stature, he had large ideas, great generosity and public spirit, a genius for business, a Confederate veteran's soul, and all the tastes of a bon vivant. Born in easy circumstances, he had none of the cramping pecuniary inhibitions of some self-made men. He dressed with flair in the highest fashion, usually, in his later years, in striped trousers and a cutaway coat with a flower in his lapel. He enjoyed equally the making and spending of money. Along with self-indulgence and vanity, however, went high spirits, geniality, and gallantry, which eased his dealings with his fellow men—not to mention women.[55]

The phenomenal rise of the Bull Durham company after Carr's arrival was due primarily to his business acumen and aggressive use of advertising. The imagination he brought to the job and the scale on which he implemented his ideas were completely in character. He set out to spread the name of Bull Durham the world over, and he achieved his goal. Unlike his partners, he had the advantage of education and the help of a successful father to launch him in business. A stint at the university had added confidence and polish, and his experience in the Civil War as a private had perfected his skill in dealing with all manner of men. Though young, he was no novice when he joined Blackwell and Day, having already had a year and a half in business with an uncle in Arkansas. Gregarious by nature, the loyalty he felt to his brothers in arms he continued to translate to his later associations. He became particularly proprietary about Durham, and contributed whenever he could to its improvement and prosperity. He made liberal gifts to Trinity United Methodist Church, to Trinity College, which he was able to help move to Durham, and to a variety of civic organizations. Nor was his charity narrowly focused; it swept over every aspect of Durham life. In short order Carr put Blackwell's business on a rising course and Durham on the world map. Day sold out in 1878, leaving Blackwell and Carr to steer the industry to new heights.[56]

William T. Blackwell (1839–1903), called the father of Durham by the town's first historian, was quite as chauvinistic about the place as Carr—and as generous. Like the Green family, he came from the Woodsdale community of Person County. Poverty and a scant education denied him the finesse and advantages of Carr, but he had a close acquaintance with tobacco from seedbed to market that made him a knowledgeable buyer of leaf. Blackwell worked hard and with Carr's help brought his company to the first rank of manufacturing, making a fortune in the process. It was his boast that he had owned well over three hundred houses in Durham, most of them built by him to house the workers Durham needed for its booming industry. Generous in his business practices, he charged rents only 10 percent above costs. When he withdrew from the Bull Durham company in 1883, he started the Durham Bank and invested its funds in real estate. His liberality, however, was his downfall; he lent money too widely, too generously, and too incautiously. His bankruptcy in 1888 caused the closing of sixteen other businesses whose money was invested in his bank. He lost every penny of his large fortune, sacrificing himself to repay his creditors. He was never able to get back on his feet, and many letters to Benjamin Duke reveal both his desperate circumstances and Duke's generosity to his pathetic appeals for money up to his death in 1903.[57]

Besides the economic boost of his tobacco factory, Blackwell gave Durham a second business boom when he established a tobacco warehouse in 1871. Until Durham had its own market, farmers were obliged either to peddle their leaf at the factory door or send it to the markets in Virginia where they could expect to receive a better price but at some cost and trouble to themselves and some damage to the product. Blackwell built his warehouse on the northeast corner of later Pettigrew and Blackwell streets opposite his factory. The first sale took place there on 18 May 1871, and Blackwell purchased the first lot. That year the warehouse handled 700,000 pounds of tobacco; the next year the amount was 2 million pounds. With a local market the factory could be sure of a steady and ample supply of tobacco and a chance to buy only the best leaf for their purposes. The farmers, too, profited. Their prices were better in a competitive market where more than one factory bid on the lots. Competition also encouraged the farmers to cure, grade, and prepare their leaf with greater care.[58]

The success of the first warehouse bred others. During the next decade firms that owned or managed the warehouses formed, split, changed partners, and regrouped like sets in a square dance. W. T. Blackwell and Company built a second warehouse on the north side of Main Street in 1872, the Durham Warehouse, managed by H. A. Reams and Alexander Walker. In that year as well T. B. Lyon and W. D. Lunsford put up the Farmers Warehouse on the site where Union Station later stood, only to relinquish it to J. E. Lyon and Edward J. Parrish the following year. H. A. and I. M. Reams built their own structure in 1876 at Main and (now) Corcoran streets, 40 by 160 feet, which was taken over by W. A. Lea and Thomas Decatur Jones in 1880.

The Planters, built by Henry W. Wahab and Company, and the Banner, built by Lea, Corbett and Company, joined the scene in 1876 and 1879.[59]

In 1879 D. C. Parrish's son, Edward James Parrish (1846–1920)—who had been the auctioneer in Durham's first warehouse, capitalizing on his experience as a Methodist exhorter—built his own warehouse on the northeast corner of what became Mangum and Parrish streets. Like his brother-in-law Julian Carr, Parrish had grandiose plans; he erected a brick structure 56 by 225 feet, the biggest and best warehouse in the state at that time. It had sheds on both its long sides, which could accommodate one hundred wagons, and a basement for storage and sleeping accommodations for farmers. Its roof, like the others', was riddled with skylights to allow buyers to judge leaf color accurately in natural light. Its stables (at the southeast corner of later Church and Parrish streets) could hold many hundred horses. Parrish hired Jim Barnes, a black "tooter," to blow a tin horn six or eight feet long for fifteen minutes before a sale to call the buyers from all over town.[60] Clyde Singleton told of going with tobacco from Person County:

We'd leave home one morning, spend the night on the road, and get into Durham the next afternoon. We'd take our tobacco to Cap'n Parrish's place; he had a warehouse on what is now Parrish Street—they named the street after him. When we'd get close to town he'd have a pair of big mules waiting to hitch on and haul us in to the warehouse. The mud in the streets sometimes would be knee-deep to a mule. He had stalls for the horses and mules and quarters for farmers, though some would sleep in their wagons. Everybody brought their provisions and cooked their victuals.[61]

The marketing business opened a whole range of new jobs and brought new workers to Durham: laborers to handle the leaf at the warehouses, brokers, auctioneers, buyers, clerks, draymen, and hostlers. Opportunities and population multiplied in tandem. Auctioneering became a new skill. At first performed by natives such as Parrish and Garland E. Webb, a son of Robert F. Webb, it soon attracted specialists who developed the chant and lingo associated with it today. At the end of the 1870s the Barham family came to Durham with their special auctioneering style. Claudius Augustin Winfield Barham and J. Q. A. Barham began their Durham careers in the Wilkerson Brothers and Banner warehouses respectively. C. A. W. Barham set a record by selling 693 piles of tobacco in two hours and seventeen minutes. "He can talk the shingles off a meeting house," the paper wrote. The experienced style was relaxed and apparently effortless, requiring five to eight years to perfect. A visiting auctioneer would be asked to sell a few rows like a visiting minister being asked to pray. One expert "had the prettiest, softest voice, clear as a bell, and his lower jaw would be going like a sewing machine. When he came out on the floor his clothes were pressed as if he was going to preach, and he wore a high starched collar with the tie tight at the top."[62]

Prize rooms (tobacco storage houses), which held tobacco for later resale or packed it for shipment, also sprang up. Some of the early firms were those of

Thomas Decatur Jones, who married into the Southgate family, Thomas H. Martin, Kramer and Webb, Pinnix and Walker, and Lockhart. Other less respectable middlemen were attracted to the market as well. Pinhookers swooped in and took their profit when farmers were ignorant or careless in preparing tobacco for sale. They would buy up cheaply the ill-sorted and ill-prepared lots that the factory buyers rejected, resort and rearrange the tobacco and then resell it at a profit.[63]

COMMERCE

Despite the ebbtide to town because of the tobacco industry, growth occurred in the countryside too. The community and commercial centers, stores and mills, changed hands, expanded, and proliferated, but otherwise remained much the same. The water mills were still operating, usually under new names but in the same places. The 1870s saw the introduction of turbine wheels into the milling business, and many of the old mills switched over to the newer technology. Steam, however, was also becoming available, and in very short order it made the water mills obsolete. More and more mills were set up in town, freed from the riverbanks where they had stood for so long. The mills of William K. Parrish, James Lunsford, Addison Mangum, Richard Stanford Leigh, Robert Patterson, John Cabe McCown, William Lipscomb, Thaddeus Redmond, William Bowling, John W. Dowd, William and Presley J. Mangum, John G. Russell, and the Morgan brothers are found in the records of these decades. A few had stores attached to the mills, but other stores had come on the scene.[64]

At Red Mountain George W. Jones had competitors in the businesses of R. C. Hill and P. A. Flintom. At Orange Factory, which was now producing handsome plaids, ginghams, and ticks, and where the wholesomeness of the village life was praised by the newspaper and credited to Holman's management, both A. G. Cox and S. W. Holman ran general stores. W. H. Moize had also opened up a shop there called Billy Button, obviously a tailor shop. J. Penny's and S. Penny's stores were located in Oak Grove, while in the Fish Dam area F. M. Barbee and Duane Carpenter tried their hands at merchandising. A Dayton post office had been established in 1868 in the Nichols store on Patterson Road (then the old Roxboro to Raleigh road) with Rosanna Marshall as postmistress, followed in 1874 by John T. Nichols. His diary for 1875 expands the picture of the Dayton community, which included the Mount Pleasant Lodge No. 157 (Masonic) and a brand new Grange hall belonging to the newly founded chapter of the National Grange of the Patrons of Husbandry. He was master of the Grange and W. R. Nichols, secretary. The Grange hall was used for preaching and the Dayton Academy for meetings and lectures of various kinds, including the worship services of the Olive Branch Baptist Church after its organization in 1876. S. J. Allen soon after provided an acre on which to build a sanctuary.[65]

Besides their primary function, the new stores filled a need for sociability, countered isolation, and provided a forum for cracker-barrel philosophers and politicians to hone their opinions and share their frustrations. Idling for hours 'round a potbellied stove in winter, the farmers nattered and chewed and spat and socialized, a kind of comfortable fraternity that the more restless and ambitious go-getters scorned. The contrast in philosophy is seen in a remark of Brodie L. Duke, who despite his later weaknesses for women and liquor, began with the same strong Puritan work ethic as his more famous brothers and father. In reply to a reporter's question in 1902 about the basis of the Duke success, he answered defensively: "Why did we succeed? Because we worked day and night and did not waste our time sitting at some stove in a country store indulging in trivial conversation, and finding fault with those who had not buried their talents."[66]

By the end of the 1870s new stores and services had multiplied apace. In 1878 R. G. Dun (later Dun and Bradstreet) rated some seventy businesses or industries in Durham. Only the Blackwell tobacco company and the Davis, Blackwell printing company were given top ratings. Among the newcomers in the middle 1870s were two Jewish merchants and their families, the Goldsteins and the Mohsbergs. They were a new element in Durham's hitherto homogeneous population. If their history was like that of other Jewish merchants, after their arrival in New York or Charleston, they had probably begun as peddlers, traveling through the country selling inexpensive and portable wares until they had saved enough to invest in their own businesses in a place that seemed destined to grow. Apparently Durham struck the fancy of A. Mohsberg and J. Goldstein in 1875, when they opened grocery and dry goods stores in Durham. These families were the vanguard of others who came in the 1880s and in the years that followed.[67]

A vital addition to Durham business was the founding in 1878 of a bank by Eugene Morehead, son of the former governor. He had come to Durham when he was offered the job of stamp agent for the U.S. Department of Internal Revenue. The necessity of paying over large amounts of money for tobacco purchases, supplies, stamps, freight, and payrolls in the tobacco business made crucial the availability of cash and credit. Gerard S. Watts of Baltimore became a partner in 1884, and after Morehead's death in 1889 the firm was reorganized as the Morehead Banking Company with new capital and stockholders, among whom were A. M. Rigsbee, J. S. Carr, J. W. Markham, A. H. Stokes, F. C. Geer, W. M. Morgan, and Paul C. Cameron. Morgan told Richard Wright that it was a separate and distinct company, paid nothing to the old bank for its goodwill and business, and assumed none of its obligations.[68]

Atlas M. Rigsbee, who replaced his wooden store with a brick two-story building in 1878, was the son and grandson of successive Jesse Rigsbees (whose land lay where Duke University's West Campus is now built). A. M. Rigsbee kept his farm, but turned his attention more and more to town real estate and commerce.[69] As stores and other enterprises were built along the newly laid-out Main Street, businesses occupied their lower floors, while halls for lectures, meetings, church services, recitals, or entertainment in general might occupy the upper. The upper floor of Rigsbee's store had been made into the town hall; the Knights of Pythias, a fraternal order, had a hall over Halliburton's store; other halls were Stokes, Matthews, and Duke, all situated along Main Street over businesses with those proprietors' names. In 1876 the hall of the Good Templars, a strong temperance group, was the site of a citizens' meeting to discuss the organization of a fire department. In that year, too, a new Masonic lodge was organized at the urging of James Southgate, who had opened an insurance agency in Durham the year before. Other fraternal orders already in existence besides the Templars and Knights were the Eno Lodge of the Ancient Free and Accepted Masons, organized about 1860, and the Odd Fellows.[70]

Among the numerous new services the town was offering were newspapers. In 1872 Caleb B. Green, a brother of John Ruffin Green, started the weekly *Tobacco Plant.* Since 1820 Orange County had benefited from the superior journalism of Dennis Heartt and his Hillsborough *Recorder,* but Green's paper had a Durham focus, chronicling daily life, pointing the way to improvement, encouraging and boosting a sense of pride, and forging a community spirit that would ultimately bear fruit in the struggle for independence in the early 1880s. Another Durham paper begun in the 1870s, but short-lived, was the Durham *Herald* edited by T. C. Woodburn. John D. Cameron had tried to edit a newspaper as early as 1845, and announced a sheet with the imposing title *The Regulator.* Cameron took over the Hillsborough paper in 1871 and moved it to Durham in 1874. In 1881 he sold it to E. C. Hackney. All the newspapers harped on the same themes—growth and prosperity. The *Herald* virtually exulted, "Still they come—we mean to our Durham—strangers locating here every day—Come on, we have room for all who come."[71] Two years later, 1878, the *Tobacco Plant* enumerated the results. The town population was 2,700 (a figure that changed with every writer); sixteen factories employed six hundred hands and used 5 million pounds of tobacco a year. Four warehouses sold 810 million pounds. The town amenities were three white and four black churches, twenty-three dry goods and grocery stores, four shoe shops, and four blacksmiths.[72]

A tax list for 1875 gives a detailed picture of the town and who had settled in it. It reveals as well who still lived in the countryside and their property and distribution in the new townships of eastern Orange. Mangum Township had 437 taxables, of whom 189 owned land. Of the 248 landless taxables exactly half were black. Thirteen percent of landowners owned more than three hundred acres of land. There were 6 black taxable landowners. Patterson Township held 268 taxables, of whom 136, or 51 percent, owned land; the landless numbered 132. Thirty-four percent of landowners owned over three hundred acres. Five landowners in the township were black. Durham Township is difficult to compare with either Mangum or Patterson because it contained the town, whose lots were owned by a large number of the residents. If these town property owners are included, 452 taxables (61 percent) owned land out of a total 741, a far higher percentage than rural landowners alone. Landless taxables numbered 289, 109 blacks and 180 whites. Only 10 percent of landowners had more than three hundred acres. There were twenty-two black taxables who owned rural land, nine others owned town lots.[73]

A comparison of the 1875 tax list with a voters' registration list for Durham precinct made in 1868 reveals exactly who had moved into or near town in the seven-year period. The newly elected Republican state administration had ordered voting registration lists to be drawn up in accordance with the new constitution for the election to be held in the fall. Washington Duke as a staunch and prominent Republican was given the job of drawing up the list for Durham Precinct. It recorded the names of all males over twenty-one years of age of both races, listing 412 whites and 205 blacks.[74] Who some of the whites were and their occupations have been suggested in the previous discussion. So large a black presence in or near the town now requires closer examination.

10

A House Divided:
An Independent
Black Culture,
1865–1880

FOR THE SLAVES, emancipation was a messianic experience, an apparent
fulfillment of a divine promise as well as a long-cherished hope. Jubilee it
seemed, and it took getting used to. The euphoria was accompanied by a
longing to reunite families, to know the pleasure of moving about freely from place
to place, to cease to labor under someone else's yoke, to relax. As Pauli Murray
described it in *Proud Shoes*, "It was a time for walking off the plantation with all
their belongings in a little bundle slung over the shoulder, for testing the ultimate
limits of their freedom."[1]

From a former master's viewpoint it was chaos. Paul Cameron wrote: "At Fairntosh and Stagville all are going to the devil or dogs as fast as they can—wont work—
destroying stock, outhouses, enclosures!"[2] In another letter he wrote again, "Just
now not one is at work—a sort of Carnival all at the marble yard & on the River
banks."[3]

For the ex-slaves reality broke in quickly when the food was gone. Under the
watchful eye of the Freedmen's Bureau they were encouraged to make contracts,
often with their former masters, either for annual wages or a share of the crops
and shelter. Thus many ex-slaves found themselves living in the same cabins,
working the same fields, often under the same overseers, but with the prospect
of earnings. As the system worked out, sharecroppers and wage laborers obtained
credit at the local store to buy whatever food, clothing, or supplies they needed to
keep them going until the crops were harvested and wages paid. While in theory
this was a workable system, in practice the merchants' greed far outreached the
croppers' ability to pay up; they were charged exorbitant interest for credit (up to
60 percent), and it took a good harvest just to break even.[4] More often than not the
croppers added a past year's debt to a new year's purchases and went ever deeper
into debt.

The system had advantages for both worker and farmer. Since the workers received no money until the crop was harvested, they were unlikely to walk off the

farm in search of better jobs; since they were paid in crops, the farmer could hire them without the necessity of paying cash, a desperately short article in Reconstruction North Carolina; since the amount of money the crop brought bore some relation to the amount of work and care given it, there was incentive for croppers to work hard and conscientiously. The advantage to the croppers was that they were their own masters and could work at their own rate and on their own time; their children could go to school or help in the fields; their wives could work at home or elsewhere.[5]

In the late 1860s and all through the 1870s agricultural prices reflected the depressed economy, fertilizer was beyond the budget of many farmers, and the crops dwindled from year to year. At their liberation, however, the freedmen could not know how things would work out, and hope attended their labor.

Not all the ex-slaves chose to continue farming. If a freedman had been trained in a skill, he often continued to practice it, hiring himself out to his former master or setting himself up independently in a community where his services were needed. Blacksmiths, coopers, carpenters, and shoemakers performed vital roles. In the growing towns work related to building trades, traditionally black work, was often well paid. Where competition was not too keen these artisans might count on good custom. But the depressed economy (1873 was a notably bad year) made any business precarious, and assurance of sufficient trade to provide support for a man and his family was problematic. For ex-slaves without skills who also chose to leave farming and chance finding work in growing towns, the move held even greater risks. Freedmen might be desperately poor on the farms, but the likelihood of their starving there was minimal. When they moved to town they were entirely cut off from this lifeline. One ex-slave summed up its chanciness metaphorically, "I tells you, Sister, when a nigger leaves de farm an comes to town to live he sho is takin a mighty big chance wid de wolf."[6]

The 1860 census recorded 5,108 slaves and 528 free blacks in Orange County. Though many free blacks had settled in the villages of Chapel Hill and Hillsborough, there was no comparable cluster in the vicinity of Durham or anywhere else in eastern Orange.[7] In 1870 when enumeration by township gave geographical meaning to the figures, Orange's three eastern townships contained a total of 2,170 blacks, of whom 1,063 were in Mangum Township (where whites numbered 1,402), 698 in Durham Township (1,625 whites), and 409 in Patterson Township (683 whites). By 1880 the totals by township were: Mangum, 1,061 (1,293 whites); Lebanon, recently formed from Mangum, 75 (729 whites); Patterson, 754 (1,293 whites); and Durham, 2,372 (3,135 whites).[8] The free blacks in eastern Orange were almost without exception farmers or farm laborers. They were scattered throughout the countryside without any discernible segregation from the white majority. The land they owned tended to be poorer than the whites' because such land had originally been cheaper and more available, and because over the years black farmers had not been able to afford expensive fertilizers to replenish the nutrients that yearly crops extracted from the soil. Otherwise they lived down the road or across the stream from white neighbors in peace and often in friendliness.

A close reading of the 1860 census shows that the part of the town of Durham now known as Hayti did not then exist. The first documented use of the name Hayti in Durham is found in a deed of 1877 in which a lot was sold "near the town of Durham in the settlement of colored people near the South East end of the Corporation of said town known as Hayti."[9] The origin of the name in this context is a mystery. Conjecture has attributed it to whites as a name for any black settlement, and to blacks as an expression of their admiration of and hope of emulating the independent island nation. The use of the term as a convention of mapmakers for any predominantly black community was current as early as 1867. A map of New Bern and vicinity in that year identified the black settlement across the Trent River from the town proper as Hayti, even though it had a name, James City.[10] Gray's "New Map of Durham, 1881," showed Hayti so labeled extending south from the angle formed by South Railroad (Pettigrew) and Fayetteville streets.[11] As the deed quoted above makes clear, Hayti lay outside the town limits of Durham, a spatial separation favored by both races at that time. In addition blacks escaped the burden of municipal taxes. Across the tracks yet close to the town, Hayti could conveniently supply the workers needed for tobacco factories and related industries and businesses.

Landowners in what became Hayti were primarily Malbourne Angier, Minerva Fowler, and Sterling Proctor, but others such as Robert F. Morris, the heirs of William N. Pratt, and Andrew Turner also owned scattered tracts there. The willingness of these landowners to sell to blacks made possible the settlement that became Hayti. Another determinant in the blacks' location was the use that Edian Markum (later Markham) made of the small parcel of land he bought from Minerva Fowler in 1869, which seems to have formed the nucleus for the later growth.[12] On the land that lay exactly in the angle formed by Pettigrew and Fayetteville streets (labeled "Hayti" on the 1881 map), Markum organized a church and school. He was in Durham at least by 1868, for his name appears on the voter registration list taken late in that year. By his own account he came to Durham as a missionary of the Methodist church to the newly emancipated blacks "when Governor Holden was in office [1865, 1868–71]." At that time he said, "there was not a colored Methodist in the place."[13] Markum's school was undoubtedly the freedmen's school, referred to in the previous chapter, listed in the commissioners' 1868 reports.

Conflicting evidence about Edian Markum's life makes the truth difficult to ascertain. His son wrote that Edian Markum was born in slavery in Elizabeth City, Pasquotank County, in 1824.[14] Despite this statement, Markum's family had in its possession a freedom certificate that it claimed was Edian Markum's, made out in the name of Edian Spelman and certifying by the county court that the bearer had been born free. Spelman was a free black surname and all the Spelmans in Pasquotank County seem to have been freeborn.[15] Markum said that he had been born in Edenton, had run away at about age sixteen or eighteen with two Quakers to Ohio, and had gone on to Canada.[16] Whatever the truth of his origins, Markum had gone to the North, learned to read and write, and there felt the call to minister to his fellow blacks. At the end of the Civil War, like many other literate blacks in the North, he had come south to preach and teach. He obtained land and built a brush arbor and soon after a small cabin beside it. In 1870 he deeded the land to the small group he had organized into a congregation and went on with missionary work elsewhere, leaving his successors, C. C. Cobeal, Billany Paine, Lewis Edwards, and George Hunter successively, to carry on his good work. Under Hunter's pastorate the first frame church was built, and under the Reverend W. D. Cook, the second. Markum had called the church Union Bethel; when it joined the A.M.E. denomination it became Saint Joseph.[17]

Edian Markum later returned to Durham; he lived on land he still owned next to the church and continued to preach informally. With his wife Mollie (or Millie) Walden, he raised three children of their own, Maggie, William Benjamin, and Robert, as well as three foster children.[18] In 1893 he was superannuated by the bishop, unjustly he felt, to make room for younger men. A newspaper reporter who interviewed him in 1898 described Markum as the most interesting of the black preachers in Durham.[19]

Others who acquired land in Hayti in 1869 or the years following were Charles Amey and his son Monroe Jordan, who bought adjacent tracts on Fayetteville Street from Robert Morris and Andrew Turner in 1871 and 1872, respectively. David Justice bought two tracts totaling over sixteen acres along the railroad east of its junction with Fayetteville Street. Jasper Jones bought land adjoining Justice and Jordan in 1871, and in the same year Cornelius Jordan bought land on Fayetteville Street. In 1877 John O'Daniel, a former Carr slave reputed in the black community to be Julian Carr's half-brother, bought a tract on Fayetteville Street where he lived the rest of his life. Unlike other early black settlers, he eventually shared in the industrial boom of black business that occurred around the turn of the century. Of these earliest black landowners only O'Daniel had not been a Cameron slave.[20]

The community around Markum's church grew, but other tracts south of the railroad and westward were also being settled by freedmen. On South Street Henry Russell settled on land purchased from Sterling Proctor in 1877. George Bradshaw bought a small tract on Willard Street from Morris. Between Duke Street and Vickers Avenue and parallel to them Abner Banks laid out Banks Street on land bought in 1869 from Sterling Proctor. A little farther west, in the area of present Carroll Street (at first called Cameron Street), Proctor sold Luke Cameron a tract adjoining Abner Banks's. Still farther west was the large tract (ninety-three acres) from which Maplewood Cemetery was carved out in late 1874. In 1873 Dempsey Henderson had bought it from Morris's heirs for $600 and had proceeded to sell off small lots in the present Kent Street and Lyon Park area.[21] On present Kent Street, then part of Chapel Hill Road (the Hack road), the Fitzgerald brothers bought land in 1879. Richard B. Fitzgerald and his brother Robert, the latter of whom had come south first to teach the freedmen in Hillsborough, had established themselves as brickmakers at their University Station farm. A commission to supply the bricks for the new state penitentiary had given their business a boost. In Durham Richard Fitzgerald bought a large tract with a good vein of clay for brick in the vicinity of later Gattis and Wilkerson streets, at that time adjoining land of J. W. Gattis and Jesse Rigsbee. Here he began a brickyard and built an eighteen-room house shaded by a grove of maples and magnolias. His business prospered, and he became the leading brickmaker of Durham.[22] On Kent Street Richard Fitzgerald built with his own bricks a handsome church called Emmanuel A.M.E. Church about 1888 and donated it to the congregation.[23] Richard Fitzgerald also built the brick building that stands on the corner of Chapel Hill and Kent streets as well as many other buildings in town. In the 1890s Robert Fitzgerald moved from Kent to Carroll Street and attempted to carry on his own brickmaking business. Unscrupulous workers, however, took advantage of his increasing blindness, and he soon retired. The cemetery encroached as the years passed, and the blacks who lived around it were forced to relinquish their land and homes as it grew. Still they held on where they could, and the neighborhood with its church maintained its stability and continuity of families into the present century.[24]

Within the town limits Willis McCown and Solomon Geer owned a lot on the corner of Main and Roxboro streets. Lewis Pratt owned land where the first and second courthouses later stood. Squire Bull, the shoemaker, also lived in town but owned no land.[25] Of these early black landowners the following were already in the Durham precinct in 1868 when Washington Duke made up the voter registry: Amey, Banks, Bradshaw, Henderson, Jones, both Jordans, Justice, Lunsford, McCown, Meaks, Pratt, Russell, and Sears. Many of these men were kin from intermarriage during their families' bondage on the Bennehan and Cameron plantations. Charles Amey's name (or its variant, Amis) was that of his ancestors' early owners, the father and brother of Mary Amis Bennehan. Amey's wife was Elizabeth Jordan. Their son Monroe chose his mother's surname. Monroe Jordan's wife was Anna Meaks, daughter of Albert and McKinza Justice Meaks. Cornelius Jordan was married to Phillis Banks and Luke Cameron was married to Silva Banks. Other family names of Cameron plantation blacks, many still to be found in Durham County, were Bell, Brandon, Cain, Campbell, Davis, Dickenson, Dixon, Dunnagan, Edwards, Goodloe, Hart, Haskins, Jeffries, Latta, Laws, Nichols, Parks, Peaks, Ray, Sears, Sowell, Staples, Strudwick, Umstead, Veasey, Walker, Watson, Weaver, Williams, and Yarbrough.[26]

Besides long association on the Cameron plantations and kinship, many of this group had another bond—their religion. In 1883 Candis Laws, David Justice and his wife Netta, Charles Amey and his wife Betsy, Lemuel Sowell and his wife Kate (Sparkman), Johnson Ray and his wife Elizabeth, Benjamin Johnson and his wife Sarah, Isaiah Sparkman, Jasper Jones, David Lunsford and his wife May, Robert Justice and his wife Gracy, Bradford Hughes and his wife Roxana, Cornelius Jordan and his wife Ann, Frank Sears and his wife Mary, and Meridith Latta and his wife Emeline transferred one-eighth of an acre of land to Robert Justice and Frank Davis, deacons of the Colored Primitive Baptist Church in 1883.[27]

For Freedmen in the vicinity of Durham, the expanding tobacco business acted as a magnet. Unskilled labor was wanted for processing tobacco, and many former field hands made the move to town. But factory work was not their only opportunity, and early black settlers worked in a variety of jobs, for a few had skills and experience that fitted them for other occupations. Cornelius Amey, Lewis Goodloe, Bradford Hughes, Abner and Monroe Jordan, John Justice, David Lunsford, Johnson Ray, and Henry Russell worked in tobacco as leaf handlers, stemmers, factory hands, or general laborers. Charles Amey became a driver; Abner Banks and Luke Cameron first got jobs as railroad workers and then as house carpenters;

John Cameron was a boxmaker; Daniel Goodloe was first a railroad worker and then a blacksmith; Dempsey Henderson was first a cook and later a gardener; Jasper Jones was a railroad engineer; David Justice was first a carpenter and later a factory worker; Frank Sears a grocer; and Frank Sowell a minister. Cornelius Jordan continued to farm after his move to town, but his grandson Matthew Christmas was by the late 1880s the headwaiter at the Hotel Claiborn. Their wives and daughters, if they worked, were children's nurses (Sarah Husband), sack stringers (Emma Henderson), washers (Fannie Haskins), cooks (Fannie Husband and Emma Jordan), waitresses (Candis Laws), or general domestics (Katie Sparkman). Judy Banks, Abner's sister, got a job taking care of the railroad station, a post she kept forty years. A newspaper article about her in 1926 recalled that "she was possessed of pronounced gentility and a fine sense of humor." She was also fond of her pipe. She had acquired her genteel manners in the Camerons' house, where her mother, Silva, was a house slave.[28]

Outside their families, the main interest of blacks (and whites, too, for that matter), was their church. As one scholar has written,

> The Church has been, and continues to be the outstanding social institution in the Negro community. It has a far wider function than to bring spiritual inspiration to its communicants. Among rural Negroes the church is still the only institution which provides an effective organization of the group, an approved and tolerated place for social activities, a forum for expression on many issues, an outlet for emotional repressions, and a plan for social living. It is a complex institution meeting a wide variety of needs.[29]

This was particularly true of the decades immediately following emancipation. The church gave shape, meaning, and support to ex-slaves' lives.

Assistance in these efforts began to come from other social organizations, particularly fraternal organizations, which also provided burial and health insurance. The oldest of the lodges in Durham is Doric Lodge of the Free and Accepted Masons. The first black lodge of this order, chartered in Boston in 1784 by the Grand Lodge of England, was the inspiration of Prince Hall, who had been initiated into an army lodge in Boston in 1775. Through Hall, who acted as Grand Provincial Master in America, many other lodges were organized. Neither the organizer nor the earliest members of the Durham lodge are now known.[30]

Black preachers developed a particular authority within their congregations that grew out of a "well-developed oral tradition whereby the spoken word was the repository of the history and folk wisdom of the culture."[31] Their tradition of oratory, too, made a drama that provided emotional release for the worshipers and carried a message of ever-appealing comfort. Each sermon was a mounting expression of emotion, uttered with increasing speed and rising pitch to an explosion of words in a sustained, intoned chant, full of repetition of phrases that invited audience participation and punctuation with "amens," "hallelujahs," and other exclamations.

The centrality of black churches to the people's lives gave the earliest churches in Hayti great importance and influence in the growth of the black community. At the same time that Markum was forming his church, a Baptist group was meeting for a similar purpose. The White Rock Baptist Church began with services held in the home of Mrs. Margaret Faucette in 1866 at what became Pettigrew and Husband streets. A few of those who attended these services, conducted by the Reverend Samuel Hunt, were Mrs. Sallie Husband, Joshua Perry, Goskin Lee, and the latter's wife, Malissa.[32] Their first frame structure, on a lot 100 by 150 feet, built under Hunt's leadership at Pettigrew and Coleman streets, was on land purchased in 1877 from Cornelius Jordan, who deeded it to John W. Cheek, Henry A. Reams, Edward Dolby, Thomas Garwood, Willis Moore, and Samuel Hunt as trustees of the Colored Missionary Baptist Church.[33] A simple frame building sufficed until 1890, when plans for a more spacious and elegant structure took shape under the Reverend Allen P. Eaton's leadership. Sufficient money was eventually raised, the cornerstone laid in 1893, and the structure, which could hold a thousand people, completed three years later. At the first service in the new building, Professor W. H. Pegram of Trinity College preached, and half the seats were reserved for white visitors. Among those specially invited was Washington Duke, to whom Eaton made no bones about the reason: "because you have given us more cash money than any man."[34]

Saint Joseph's growth paralleled the Baptist congregation's. The 1890s saw that group too replace a frame structure with one of brick (supplied by Richard Fitzgerald's brickyard), begun in 1891. Samuel L. Leary, who had been brought to Durham by the Dukes to build tobacco warehouses, was the architect employed to design the church. His most ambitious project, Trinity College's first building in Durham, met with an accident almost fatal to Leary's career. The central tower collapsed just before the completion of the building in 1891. No structural errors manifested themselves in Saint Joseph's church, however, and the building stands to this day, an exuberant expression in color and line of a talent that gave Durham a few prized landmarks. A stained-glass window memorializes a white patron, Washington Duke, for his contributions to the building of the church. Funds for the purchase of an organ were raised by John O'Daniel, John Merrick, James Weaver, Agnes Saterfield, W. G. Pearson, and the Reverend J. E. Jackson. The congregation moved to a new location in 1973, but the old building was taken over by the Saint Joseph's Historic Foundation, which saved it from demolition during urban renewal in the 1970s.[35]

New Bethel Baptist Church, another black church formed in these years, grew out of a Sunday school started in 1877 in an enclave of blacks on the south side of the railroad tracks near the old Pin Hook area.[36] Now known as the Crest Street area, the community of blacks and whites was then called Hickstown and included both sides of the tracks. Only Hicks Street is left as a reminder of the neighborhood that took its name from the white family of Hawkins Hicks, the common-law wife of Jefferson Browning. Browning died in 1863, leaving all his property to his three sons by her, James, Payton, and Dudley; Hicks sued for dower and got it. She died in 1916 at the age of eighty-five after a long and eccentric life.[37]

Other pockets of black settlement to the east and later to the north of the town completed a kind of ring around the corporation. A pocket called Smoky Hollow, east of the town's boundary in what later became Edgemont, was notorious for its rowdiness and crime. In the late 1880s the newspaper editor waged a campaign to get the landlords who owned the tenements there and in other unsavory districts such as Moccasin Bottom to oust their unruly tenants or risk having their names printed in the paper. The land on which Durham is situated rises and falls abruptly: the higher land laced with eroded hollows and run-off gullies, the bottomland along branches. On cheap and available land the poorest blacks built their shanties. Thus the community developed with alternating black and white neighborhoods spreading out from the town, while the land in the town itself, the most expensive, was almost entirely white-owned. Pauli Murray's *Proud Shoes* described the situation she remembered from her Durham childhood:

> Shacks for factory workers mushroomed in the lowlands between the graded streets. These little communities, which clung precariously to the banks of streams or sat crazily on washed-out gullies and were held together by cowpaths or rutted wagon tracks, were called Bottoms. It was as if the town had swallowed more than it could hold and had regurgitated, for the Bottoms was an odorous conglomeration of trash piles, garbage dumps, cowstalls, pigpens, and crowded humanity.[38]

As the black presence became a large and permanent part of Durham town life, the two races developed ways of dealing with each other that were superficially polite and calculated to allay fear and anger on both sides. Leaders of both races reinforced through lip service the myth of harmonious race relations. It was whistling in the dark. Under the surface ran ambivalence in feeling and attitude that the apparent cooperation concealed. Of first importance was maintaining peace and preventing outbreaks that might erase black progress, however small, or upset the industrial applecart for the large manufacturers, who needed a reliable and constant pool of black labor. During slavery's many generations, the races had evolved a modus vivendi, each knowing what to expect of the other and what the other expected. The accommodation in some instances was so close a fit that in the memory of some of the freedmen, interviewed during their last years in the Great Depression, their lives before emancipation, viewed through a mist of nostalgia, seemed halcyon compared to the harsh economic struggle, uncertainty, dislocation, and emotional stress of their new condition. One old ex-slave reminisced, "Ole Marster dead en' gone en ole Mistis too, but I 'members 'em jes' lak dey was, when dey looked atter us whenst we belonged to 'em or dey belonged to us, I dunno which it was."[39]

The joy of emancipation was quickly adulterated by unforeseen difficulties: white backlash, institutionalized racial discrimination, and segregation. Reconstruction, which brought the Republicans to power and blacks to minor positions of authority, government jobs, and even to the legislature, was a shocking experience to many whites who had always viewed blacks at worst as a subhuman species, and at best as children. When the Conservatives, soon to be called Democrats, regained political power, the freedmen's chances for equal rights faded. Most whites were determined to have no more of that. They deluded themselves for decades with beliefs such as those expressed in 1873 by the Hillsborough newspaper editor in response to Senator Sumner's plea for social equality for blacks: "The sensible colored man of the South desires no such obliteration of natural lines. He is wise enough to know how deeply they are drawn, and how impassable they are. . . . There is that in nature, there is that in history, there is that in experience, which tells of an ineradicable distinction which no laws can reconcile."[40] The longer the old leadership remained in office, the firmer and more binding became the laws devised for keeping blacks in their place. Among the freedmen one faction of leaders advocated a course of political moderation in seeking their civil rights. They counseled that if blacks educated themselves, proved themselves self-reliant, law-abiding, and economically independent, whites would in time willingly cede them their rights. This was the theory underpinning Booker T. Washington's self-help philosophy.[41] Realists among the blacks, however, foresaw a different chain of events. After their dreams of forty acres and a mule evaporated, and in their stead came low wages and crop liens, they understood that without political rights they would be forever socially and economically disadvantaged. In need they could no longer turn to the old master for shelter and food, or to the old mistress for clothing and medical care. They were strictly on their own. Competition with white labor in the job market hardened animosities. The gulf grew between the races.[42]

Symptomatic of the situation was the case of Lewis Pratt, William N. Pratt's former slave and blacksmith, to whom he had willed the land on which Lewis Pratt lived and worked and which happened to be in the town. When Lewis Pratt died in the 1870s, land values within the town limits had begun to boom, and segregation of the races as policy had already begun. Lewis Pratt's son, Lewis Jenkins, was deprived of his inheritance. The denial of the land to Jenkins rested on a legal technicality: Morgan Closs in drawing up William Pratt's will had failed to use the words "in fee simple" to describe Pratt's gift of land to Lewis Pratt. That it had been William Pratt's intention to give the land outright to Lewis Pratt, his contemporaries well understood. For that reason John Burroughs, Pratt's executor, had not attempted to deprive Jenkins of the land until Closs, John A. McMannen, and Robert F. Morris, who had known Pratt's intentions, were dead. Burroughs admitted this under oath.[43] Thus had race relations declined. Instead of noblesse oblige, which had motivated the better sort of whites' relations with blacks, many whites were now confederates in a concerted effort to restrict blacks' freedom and rights. An advertisement in 1876 for William Mangum's White Man's Saloon spelled it out: "We have divided our house and keep room exclusively for white gentlemen and a separate department for colored persons."[44]

At the same time that a gulf was growing between the races and old prejudices were being confirmed in each new generation of whites, the blacks in Durham were holding their own, even making progress in their now separate but parallel culture. In the closing decades of the century they took charge of their own destiny in a way that became a model for the country. It has often been said that the black business efflorescence could not have occurred without the acquiescence of the white establishment, and that Durham as a new community had not been retarded by antebellum traditions that persisted in older southern towns.[45] Durham's freedom from that past has been used to explain both white and black economic burgeoning.

The causes are probably more complex than this. Certainly in men such as Julian Carr a belief in white supremacy and paternalistic responsibility to blacks precluded any other relationship between the races, and in the white population as a whole racist attitudes and behavior continued as usual. What made a difference in Durham was probably a combination of attitudes. First, there was in Durham as in other New South cities an acceptance of work, even manual work, as the proper and honorable business of daily life. Work became the new morality. Even Paul Cameron, the quintessential planter, had no illusions about the new order. Always a hard worker himself, he advised his children that in the new South they would have to work with their hands or their heads in order to survive.[46] Along with this work ethic, adherence to the dogma of Christian charity, the brother's keeper commitment, was nurtured in the mainline religious denominations, Methodist and Baptist. If paternalism was not the style of Washington Duke, Christian charity was. The results were similar. But perhaps most characteristic of Durham was still a third attitude, an easygoing tolerance, a live-and-let-live philosophy that may have been the psychological expiation for unrestrained moneymaking. The 1890s saw colossal new fortunes built on hard work and business ingenuity, subsidized by an underpaid and overworked labor force. Paradoxical beliefs existed side by side. Whites forced political restrictions and social separation on blacks at the same time that they voted them educational opportunity and winked at their economic advancement. Resentment coexisted with laissez-faire, and civil injustice with altruistic concern. A strong, self-sustaining, and dynamic black culture thus was able to emerge and flourish alongside these contradictory white impulses and unresolved conflicts in a house divided.

A County at Last, 1880–1890

11

GOVERNMENT

Despite the political and social turmoil of Reconstruction, industrial impetus carried Durham forward. Exponential growth of population, commerce, and industry made absolutely clear the difficulties and disadvantages of being fourteen miles from the county seat. To search titles, record deeds and mortgages, register marriages, probate wills, argue cases, serve on juries, witness at trials, transport criminals to jail, or confer with the incarcerated required a trip to Hillsborough. Four-fifths of the legal instruments recorded in Orange County were from Durham. Those involved in legal business could lose whole days at a time because of train scheduling; one train left Durham in the morning and another did not return till night. Most inconvenienced by the distance were lawyers and their clients, who paid for the time and travel.[1]

Although the move by Durhamites for separate governmental identity seemed to spring suddenly into public notice, it had been mooted in private for some time in legal and industrial circles. Nothing had been made of it in the political election of 1880, but only a few months later, in January 1881, Caleb B. Green, a representative for Orange County in the legislature, introduced a bill for the establishment of a new county to be called Durham. It would comprise the eastern townships of Orange County, parts of the Cedar Fork and Oak Grove townships of Wake County, and small portions of both Chatham and Granville counties. Citizens in the affected areas presented petitions to the legislature requesting the action proposed in House Bill 119.[2]

As a Durham resident and owner of the *Tobacco Plant,* Green was in a prime position to rally support for his bill. Obviously he had not instigated the move but was acting for a group of powerful businessmen. Among the most important were William T. Blackwell, Julian S. Carr, Edward J. Parrish, and Jonathan Cicero Angier, son of Malbourne Angier and brother-in-law of James B. and Benjamin Duke—all connected in some way with the tobacco business. As their guide and front man to head the lobbying campaign in the legislature they hired Thomas C. Fuller, who had the able assistance of his soon-to-be-licensed son, Williamson W. Fuller, Augustus Merrimon, and John Manning. David G. McDuffie's new map of the proposed Durham County was an effective tool in the presentation of their case.[3]

On the home front others were busy collecting signatures on petitions and whipping up enthusiasm at rallies in support of the bill. Bennehan Cameron reported to his mother that at one such meeting Jimmie Cain tried to speak against the measure and was hooted and hissed from the platform, whereupon Edward Parrish, in the mold of his father as the defender of the underdog, got up and shamed the audience for their disgraceful behavior.[4] Almost immediately strong opposition to the bill was organized despite its surprise introduction. The commissioners of Wake County, led by W. R. Poole, and the Raleigh Board of Trade were dead set against the bill and did their own lobbying in the legislature, presented petitions against it through Representative Smedes, and held a large rally, organized by Walter Clark, W. H. Bagley, B. C. Manly, J. A. Jones, Thomas H. Briggs, and R. B. Tucker. Dr. Richard Lewis wrote to Paul Cameron asking for money to fight the bill in the two vulnerable townships of Wake, reminding him that he had most at stake in those areas.[5] Cameron was in the anomalous position of owning large tracts in Orange, Wake, and the proposed Durham counties as well as substantial property in Hillsborough and Raleigh. He sent his son Bennehan to Raleigh to lobby against the bill independently.

In the debate on the issue the proponents had the best arguments: the huge population growth in Durham, the magnitude of the tobacco industry, and the tobacco poundage derived from the eastern townships of Orange on soils very different from those of the western townships. Statistics for the most recent year showed that $1.65 million worth of leaf tobacco had been traded and $2 million of manufactured tobacco produced in Durham. From a reputed 256 persons living in the hamlet of Durham in 1870, the town had grown to upward of two thousand persons (*Branson's Business Directory for 1884* gave the population as three thousand), not including the considerable clusters of blacks in Hayti and the other pockets of population ringing the town. Such growth had inevitably brought with it a huge increase in squabbles, drunkenness, and crime, and the arm of the law was neither long enough nor strong enough to cope with the situation. Frenzied activity in building was reflected each week in the newspaper columns. "The Town is enlivened by the clink of the trowel, the music of the hammer, and the song of the laborer," the paper rhapsodized.[6]

The opponents had psychological advantages on their side: the natural antipathy to change characteristic of most societies; Orange's long and illustrious history, which was a matter of pride and a heritage not lightly to be discarded; and not unreasonable fears of the tax burden that might come with a new county. On the tax matter some assurance was forthcoming. Wake County had incurred considerable debt, and its citizens were fearful that the removal of numerous taxpayers from its rolls would increase the burden on those remaining. Full assurance was given, however, that if the new county should come into being a proportionate share of Wake's debt would be carried over to the new county along with the former residents of Wake.[7] This left only the taxes that the new county would itself impose as unknown quantities.

In the legislature the bill did not have plain sailing. Although it passed its three readings in the House without serious trouble, in the Senate it became hopelessly entangled in parliamentary procedure and was strongly buffeted by stiff opposition. Early in the debate the bill was amended to delete the portions of Granville and Chatham from the proposed county, and the political plot was thickened by the introduction of a bill for the incorporation of Vance County. At a crucial moment a shift in sentiment resulted in the Durham bill's passage on 28 February 1881.[8] A proviso written into the bill required ratification by the voters of the proposed county. The vote held on 10 April resulted in 1,739 for and 297 opposed to the new county; therefore Governor Thomas J. Jarvis proclaimed the county established on 16 April.[9] Whatever discussion and disagreement there may have been about the name to be given it had been settled before the bill's introduction. Those who had wished to call it Mangum, to honor the proposed county's most famous statesman, Willie P. Mangum, gave way to the more powerful faction, those connected with the town of Durham, the tobacco industry, and in particular the Blackwell Company, whose chief product was so closely identified with the name Durham. Durham as the new county's name was included in the bill.[10] Its boundaries were described as follows:

> Beginning at the north-east corner of Orange county, thence with the Orange and Person line north eighty-seven degrees, west, eight miles, to the corner of Mangum and Little River townships of Orange county; thence south ten degrees west, twenty-five and one-quarter miles, to the Chatham county line, at the corner of Patterson and Chapel Hill townships; thence with the Chatham County line south eighty-seven degrees east, seven miles, to the Wake County line; thence the same course four miles, to a point in Wake county in Cedar Fork township; thence a line parallel to the Wake and Orange line north fifteen degrees east, thirteen and one-half miles, to the corner of New Light and Oak Grove townships; thence continuing the same course two and one-quarter miles, and following the dividing line between said townships to the Granville county line, at the corner of the aforesaid townships; thence with the Wake and Granville line to their corner on Neuse river, in the Orange county line; thence with the Granville line about north nine and three-quarter miles to the beginning.[11]

The new county's townships retained their old names. The law designated voting precincts and provided for the surveying of the new county and for the appointment of justices of the peace, who would elect five county commissioners. They in turn would elect county officers; name and define the electoral districts; provide voting procedures, officials, and machinery; build a courthouse, jail, and poorhouse; and transact all other kinds of business that the rights and privileges of counties made possible, among which were the collection of taxes, maintenance of roads, bridges, and public buildings, and the granting of licenses.[12]

On 1 May, the justices of the peace elected Alvis Kinchen Umstead, Washington Duke, Gabriel A. Barbee, John T. Nichols, and Sidney W. Holman as commissioners. The commissioners met for the first time the next day in a room over John Markham's store and elected Umstead their chairman and William T. Patterson clerk of the court. At their second meeting they elected James R. Blacknall, a son of Dr. Richard Blacknall, as sheriff, Dr. Albert Gallatin Carr, Julian Carr's brother, as coroner, and the following men as constables for the six townships: D. L. Belvin (Durham), J. S. Penny (Patterson), T. M. Barbee (Oak Grove), W. H. Morris (Cedar Fork), John W. Parker (Mangum), and W. S. Terry (Lebanon). Their first concern was to equip themselves for work. They purchased a minute book, court dockets, and furniture for the courtroom: a dozen chairs, four tables, a water bucket, dipper, pitcher, goblet, and half a dozen pens and holders. At first they rented a room from Col. D. C. Parrish for county office space, but in October they decided to rent Stokes Hall for the courtroom and four other rooms in the same building as county offices. During their first sessions they continued to fill county jobs: J. J. Ferrell was made clerk of the superior court and probate judge, Dr. William M. Lowe, register of deeds, and George W. Jones, superintendent of common schools. When Ferrell died in the summer, they appointed William J. Christian in his place.[13]

Their most serious business was the purchase of land for a poorhouse. After much vacillation, they bought a 138-acre tract from W. A. Wilkerson for $1393.75 and built a frame house on it. Brodie L. Duke, who owned a furniture store, sold them furnishings for both the courtroom and the poorhouse. In March 1882 the commissioners decided to build a house of correction on the same tract. Prison labor could be used to maintain the grounds and building, to clean, and to cook as well as to raise the food needed for their own and the poorhouse inmates' use. To superintend the establishment the commissioners appointed John W. Evans at a salary of $240 per annum. All these matters were decided harmoniously and without dissent.[14]

The commissioners, however, like their town counterparts, fell out over the question of liquor licenses. "After a fair and full discussion it was ordered that no License should be issued to sell Spirituous Liquors in the County of Durham." They had been persuaded to this stand by their chairman, teetotaler Umstead. They did, however, grant S. R. Carrington a license to retail beer, against Umstead's wishes, and as new applicants came before them, they granted beer licenses to them as well. In June the question was brought up for reconsideration and discussion was refused. By August, however, their resistance worn down, the commissioners granted full liquor licenses to eight applicants. After a serious disagreement over another matter, Umstead resigned in a huff. Duke replaced him as chairman, and young Duncan Cameron, another son of Paul Cameron, was appointed to fill the vacancy. The way was open to grant liquor licenses.[15]

SCHOOLS

Just as the push for independence had come from townsmen, so did that for a graded school. Again Green presented the bill in the legislature. It passed both

House and Senate readings without hitch. It did not pass into law, however, until a referendum had been held. The call for this election was delayed, probably because the sponsors needed time to drum up enough support for the measure to ensure its passage.[16] Although other North Carolina towns had already established graded schools, the people of Durham were not wholeheartedly in favor of them. At the root of the opposition, much of which came from Republicans, was objection to the taxes necessary to support such a school. Many felt it was unfair to tax everyone to pay for the education of some, particularly when a number of citizens could well afford to send their children to the private schools already established in the town. Some saw the graded school as a threat to the private schools. Still another objection was to the method of funding as racially discriminatory: the law stipulated that additional poll and property taxes collected from white inhabitants would be used for a white school, those collected from blacks, for a black school. Because there were few black landowners in the town and because the value of their holdings was comparatively small, taxes paid by blacks would be inadequate to fund a building, teachers, and equipment comparable to those funded by white taxpayers, and also proportionately more burdensome. Finally, among the opposition was a faction that objected to any kind of government involvement in education. Among those who opposed the graded school, banded together, and distributed broadsides were Washington Duke, Robert E. and J. E. Lyon, A. K. Umstead, William Mangum, Edward J. Parrish, M. A. Angier, W. W. Fuller, John S. Lockhart, and A. M. Rigsbee. They presented their arguments forcefully but without rancor or inflammatory prose. They simply stated that though they supported the concept of graded schools as an improvement over the public schools then established, they felt that the time was not ripe for them and that the present bill was faulty in being burdensome and racially discriminatory. Higher taxes would increase rents in the town where rents were already too high and where houses were needed. They advocated increasing the area of the town to take in more population to help spread the cost and to increase the town tax base.[17]

In objecting to the bill's discriminatory aspect, they said, "We of Durham, have always professed to do full justice to the colored people, and in fact went so far as to elect the chief white Republican of the county [Washington Duke] Commissioner for the county, in consideration of the solid vote given by them to support the new county." They next showed that the amount raised by taxes on blacks in the town would amount only to $9.20. "Would not that run a big School?"[18]

The advocates nevertheless were undeterred and finally petitioned the aldermen to set a date for the vote. The referendum was held in May and the act was passed into law by a two-thirds majority. Those who backed the graded school proposal and carried it to victory were, besides Green, William T. Blackwell, J. B. Whitaker, Jr., John M. Moring, George W. Jones, J. F. Freeland, D. C. Mangum, N. A. Ramsey, and T. C. Oakley. The aldermen elected the following men to the Durham Board of Education and Learning: Eugene Morehead, J. B. Whitaker, Jr., and Julian Carr. Because Carr declined to serve on the board, citing his conflict of interest—he was president of the Methodist Female Seminary—Bartholomew Fuller, a lawyer recently moved to Durham from Fayetteville, was elected to replace him. These men together with the district school committee's three members—D. C. Gunter, William Maynor, and T. C. Oakley—formed the Durham Graded School Committee. E. W. Kennedy became superintendent of the graded school and Charles D. McIver, his assistant. Richard Wright's factory building on Main Street just east of the Duke lands was rented for use as a school. Morehead donated one hundred dollars to provide textbooks for poor children.[19]

In 1885 the graded school opponents were heard from again. Atlas M. Rigsbee obtained a restraining order for the collection of taxes for the graded school. He cited the discriminatory basis of the school bill and wanted its constitutionality tested in court. A referendum in the town on a bond issue to raise $15,000 to build a graded school had already passed. The court declared the law unconstitutional in 1886, and the bond money had to be returned. During the delay for new legislation to be written and enacted, William T. Blackwell offered to carry the costs of the school himself to keep it open. The school commissioners, Eugene Morehead, S. F. Tomlinson, and E. J. Parrish, joined by Robert F. Webb, appealed to the citizenry for contributions to share the burden with Blackwell. By this means the school continued through 1886–87. After a new, nondiscriminatory law was passed, another referendum was held, which again resulted in a vote for the school. Again Rigsbee and his cohorts called a halt by questioning whether a majority of qualified voters had actually been polled. The voting rolls contained the names of 980 persons, while only 410 had voted for the graded school. Immediately the rolls were examined and purged of 180 names of those who were either no longer resident in Durham or deceased. That made the number who had voted for the measure a legitimate majority. When Rigsbee sued again about the legality of the procedure, he lost.[20]

During the litigation the school committee had run what amounted to a subscription school. It also established a school for the town's black children in the Primitive Baptist Church. The next year the black school was moved to a small tobacco prize room on Red Cross Street, which burned down in 1886. In November 1887 the newspaper reported the completion of a new brick school for black children.[21]

James C. Biggs, a relation of the Southgates, who attended the graded school during its first years, described the town in those years. Two homes, he said, still retained their windmills, and stepping stones were placed in the mud streets at corner crossings to help pedestrians to cross. Durham seemed to his family "a crude town, raw and alien to all they knew, but an incredibly good location in which to establish a business." Biggs also recalled the "moonlight school" for the factory workers who thirsted for education. In the spring and summer of 1888 and 1889 all who wished to come to evening classes were taught free by volunteer teachers, including Biggs's mother and John Spencer Bassett.[22]

Though Rigsbee had chosen high ground on which to contest the graded school, his motives may have been somewhat mixed. In 1881 he had built and promoted the Baptist Female Seminary on Mangum Street. Rigsbee's Methodist allies had equally mixed motives since they were supporting the Methodist Female Seminary, also established in 1881. Last, there was a new Durham Male Academy, different from the one chartered in 1865 but with the same name. The trustees had secured the

Reverend James A. Dean as principal, the former headmaster of the South Lowell Academy. By then he had a long and varied career behind him, which included not only a short presidency of the Ohio Wesleyan Female College and Mansfield College, and several pastorates in Massachusetts, Connecticut, and Rhode Island, but also translations of scientific articles from French and an edition of Gibbon's *Decline and Fall of the Roman Empire*. He stayed in Durham only a year before moving on to the presidency of New Orleans University, a black college. In 1887 Professor H. W. Reinhart took over as principal of the Durham Male Academy with thirty-five boys under his tutelage. That same year Charles D. McIver opened the Durham High School for boys and young men, and William Gaston Vickers, with years of teaching experience, opened a school on his huge tract of land southwest of Durham, which comprised the later Morehead Hill and Forest Hills neighborhoods.[23]

According to the 1881 State Board of Education report, the new county had forty-six school districts and 4,159 school-age children, while the county superintendent, George W. Jones, reported that there were only fourteen teachers, seven white and seven black, thus fourteen schools in actual operation. He admitted that "the county is behind but a better day is coming." That better day was long delayed. Obviously the subscription schools and private academies had to take up the slack, at least for white children. Besides those enumerated, there was a sprinkling of such schools around the county. In Oak Grove Township, for example, Duane Carpenter donated land for a subscription school opposite his home; it had sometimes as many as sixty students at a time although the structure contained only one room. This was the Morning Sun Academy, another new school with an old name, taught by Addison Cicero Weatherly (c. 1859–1939) whom Willis Carpenter described as "a splendid teacher but too strict and stern." Corporal punishment was as usual in the school as in the home, for many Christians interpreted the Bible literally and teachers had traditionally underscored their teaching with a fundamental caning. Nor was the rod the only instrument employed. A pre-Civil War teacher, Abel Jackson, had a long pole with a nail on the end of it with which he could easily reach any child whose eyes strayed from his book or slate. If a child lied, Jackson applied hot pepper to his head. Many teachers would probably have concurred with the advice of the old schoolmaster Thomas Flint: "cripple their shins and send them a-howling."[24]

THE TOBACCO INDUSTRY: CIGARETTES

Competition was heating up in the tobacco industry. Both the leading firms underwent reorganization, gearing up for new levels of production. In 1878 the Dukes took into the firm George Washington Watts of Baltimore, son of Gerard S. Watts, who had come to Durham to obtain the agency for the Duke products and ended by buying a fifth interest in the business for his son. The new firm was called W. Duke Sons and Company. In 1880 Washington Duke wished to withdraw from the firm, and his share was sold to Richard Harvey Wright (1851–1929) for twenty-three thousand dollars. Wright lacked the cash to pay for it, however, and Duke accepted mortgages on Wright's property until he could pay the debt. Wright was aggressive and ambitious like James B. Duke, and became the main salesman for the firm while James B. Duke managed the manufacturing, Watts the finances, and Benjamin N. Duke the correspondence. Wright soon circled the globe setting up agents for Duke products.[25]

At the Bull factory changes were also occurring. Blackwell pulled out in 1883 and the Philadelphia firm of E. M. McDowell and Company bought into the business, but wishing to retain the Blackwell name, they applied for a new charter from the legislature to form a corporation to be called Blackwell's Durham Tobacco Company. Julian Carr remained in the business, and as owner of a controlling amount of stock in the corporation, became its president. In 1887, the company reorganized again as a stock company called Blackwell Durham Cooperative Tobacco Company. Reuben Rink, alias Jules Koerner of Kernersville, a "celebrated fresco and ornamental painter," was hired to repaint the Blackwell factory and to replace the two big, crudely painted bulls adorning the front of the building with two more finely drawn figures. In 1891 the company took back its old name of Blackwell Durham Tobacco Company.[26]

Two new manufactures, both arising within the tobacco industry, gave Durham new momentum in the 1880s: the introduction of cigarettes (in 1880 by the Blackwell Company and 1881 by the Dukes) and the establishment of a cotton factory to make cloth for tobacco bags in 1884, both Carr initiatives. Cigarettes had been popular in Europe since 1860 and had been manufactured in New York since 1863 when Americans began to adopt their use. They were hand-rolled by European immigrants who had been trained in the work in their homelands.[27] When the Blackwell Company began production of cigarettes with eighty-two workers, it hired David Siegel of New York to superintend their manufacture. The following year, 1881, the Dukes hired his brother J. M. Siegel to superintend cigarette production in their factory, still striving to keep up with the Bull factory. The Siegel brothers, born in Kovno, Russia, had long experience in every phase of the work. They brought from New York a contingent of about three hundred Polish Jews experienced in hand-rolling to make the cigarettes in both factories. It has been assumed that the Jewish community in Durham traces its origin to these cigarette rollers. In fact, a few Jewish merchants had already settled in Durham in the 1870s, for example, the Mohsbergs, Goldsteins, and Gladsteins; in 1880 Nachman and Lehman had opened a clothing store. Instead of adding substantially to this small core, most of the rollers stayed only a short while before returning to New York. The details of their sojourn in Durham are not documented, but they seem to have been discontented with their pay and working conditions. A number of the workers belonged to the Knights of Labor and were not silent about superintendents' assaults on employees. Washington Duke's later comment on the episode was that "they gave us no end of trouble."[28] Although within a year almost all had returned north, the Siegel brothers remained longer and started up their own business in 1884, manufacturing "Cablegram" cigarettes.[29]

Duke (and presumably the Blackwell company acted similarly) advertised for "twenty-five white girls to make cigarettes."[30] The girls were taught by the few remaining New Yorkers. One Duke factory girl, Laura Cox, who had begun working at the age of eight, described the work. Six girls were seated around one of a series of tables; in the center of each table lay a pile of tobacco prepared for rolling. It was covered by a damp cloth to retain moisture. From this pile each girl would take enough for one cigarette, an amount called a monkey, and lay it on a ten-inch square of marble (according to D. C. Christian) or pasteboard (according to Cox) called a kleunky, where it was then rolled in a paper and the edges carefully secured by a paste made of flour and water applied by a hollow, pencil-like tool. A handful of completed cigarettes would then be held between the fingers and the edges trimmed. One worker could roll about two thousand cigarettes a day; she was paid fifty-five cents per thousand. If she made the more expensive cigarettes with mouthpieces, a fad of the time, she was paid sixty-five cents per thousand.[31]

As brightleaf tobacco became the preferred sort with smokers, the demand for Durham's products increased but Duke sales did not gain on Blackwell despite dynamic Duke salesmen such as Wright and Edward F. Small. Insatiable ambition to overtake the Bull prompted James B. Duke to gamble in 1884; he installed the newly invented but as yet unperfected Bonsack cigarette machine in the Durham factory. The smoking public was thought to have a prejudice against machine-made cigarettes, but Duke saw the machine as the only means to achieve his ambition. Able to perform the work of forty-eight handrollers, the machine became the decisive factor in the company's sprint to fame.[32]

For some years James E. Bonsack had been working on a machine to roll cigarettes, and though one had been tried out in the Richmond factory of Allen and Ginter, Bonsack had not been able to persuade any manufacturer to commit himself to machine production, principally because the machine did not yet work perfectly. In 1884, however, Duke agreed to lease one, and it was installed in the factory along with an operator and mechanic, William T. O'Brien. After O'Brien had worked on the machine and ingeniously corrected its defects, it performed satisfactorily. Under a secret contract with the Bonsack company that gave more favorable terms to the Duke firm than to its competitors, more machines were soon added, and by 1889 Duke was turning out 823 million cigarettes a year. The last handrollers left the Duke factory in 1888. The inability of the Knights of Labor to contend with the introduction of machines and the firing of their members contributed to the organization's decline in Durham.[33]

Intensive advertising abroad as well as at home supplied the necessary markets for the sudden overproduction caused by the change to machines. At about the same time the federal government cut the tax on cigarettes, and Duke again gambled by immediately reducing the cost of a pack of cigarettes by the full amount of the tax. He sold "Duke of Durham," their first brand of cigarette, for five cents per package of ten cigarettes.[34] James B. Duke's invention of the sliding box in which to package the cigarettes solved another problem, that of a container that would give easy access to the product at the same time that it supplied sufficient protection. Duke of Durham was soon joined by a variety of other brands to suit all pocketbooks and tastes.[35]

In the crucial year 1884 James B. Duke again risked failure by starting a branch factory in New York City, and moved there himself to oversee the business. He felt they could better supply the northern markets from that base, where there was an experienced labor supply. In the following six years Duke strengthened his position to such an extent by strategic maneuvering, shrewd negotiation, and jockeying for position in Bonsack contracts, that by 1890 he had persuaded his four largest competitors (the Allen and Ginter, Kinney, Kimball, and Goodwin companies) to form with the Dukes a company to which they would all sell out, taking in exchange a proportionate share of the new stock and creating so large and powerful a combine that their remaining rivals would be virtually eliminated. Thus was established the American Tobacco Company, capitalized at twenty-five million dollars. James B. Duke, thirty-three years old, was named president. The year 1890 found the Dukes at the top of the heap at last. In that era of fierce competition, unrestrained and ruthless business practices, and frenzied combinations, James B. Duke proved himself one of the most astute and audacious dealers of them all.[36]

In 1884, however, just as the Dukes were on the verge of overtaking the Bull, internal strife caused by Richard Wright almost sabotaged the whole enterprise. The Duke company needed more capital to launch its gamble on the Bonsack machine, to construct a larger factory to house the expanded operation, and to commence manufacturing in New York. Anticipating the expiration of the old partnership in 1884, the partners drew up a new agreement, and each of them but Wright agreed to increase his share of capital; Wright had not yet paid off his debt to Washington Duke and was in no position to ante up more capital. The Dukes offered Wright a variety of accommodations that would have enabled him either to remain in the firm without coming up with the additional capital or to sell his own interest to them, but he refused each offer, preferring to play his own game. The danger to the firm was that at the contract's expiration in 1884 Wright could dissolve the firm and sell his interest to another company, or find sufficient outside funding to take over the company himself. When the other partners drew up a new agreement without Wright in 1885, Wright took legal steps to have a receiver appointed and the firm sold. Wright's aim appears to have been to scare the Dukes into an advantageous settlement out of court. In any case this is what he achieved, receiving for his interest a much higher price than he had been offered before. The company was saved. Wright, who immediately joined a Virginia competitor, the Lone Jack Company, as manager and principal stockholder with close links to the Bonsack company, nevertheless continued to harass his old partners.[37]

THE COTTON INDUSTRY

As early as 1874 there had been discussion in Durham about building a cotton factory to supply cloth for tobacco bags. Although each of the large factories already maintained its own bag manufactory, the cloth had to be purchased elsewhere. Julian Carr realized that a cloth factory could supply all the cloth needed for the Bull company as well as for other companies in the town. The Blackwell company used 92,000 yards of cloth a month to make the 70,000 to 80,000 bags a day it needed. This operation gave employment to many women in the factory itself and to women working in their homes, who performed the stringing and tagging of the bags. Durham was just then becoming a market for raw cotton. The newspaper estimated that Orange County probably grew in excess of three thousand bales a year. James W. Cheek, a general merchandiser, advertised himself as a cotton factor as well. Obviously Durham was beginning to supply enough local cotton to make a cloth factory profitable.[38]

In 1884 Carr formed the Durham Cotton Manufacturing Company, capitalized at $130,000, with J. M. Odell as president, J. A. Odell, W. R. Odell, and William H. Branson as secretary, treasurer, and manager. Carr was the main stockholder. The Bull factory was its largest customer. Growing steadily over the years, it expanded its production from cloth for tobacco bags to chambrays, ginghams, domets, brown sheeting, and colored goods. Built on Pettigrew Street in East Durham, the mill was a four-story brick building, 75 by 150 feet, with weave sheds, a picker building, and engine and boiler rooms. In 1886 the plant was described in the *Manufacturers' Record* as one of the most extensive and finest of plants in the country. "A magnificent Watts-Campbell Corliss engine of 300-horse power, driving 8,568 spindles, the largest number in the state, and 200 looms" won the reporter's admiration. Other machines, such as Dann's warper, a Worthington steam pump capable of throwing five hundred gallons of water a minute (to be used in case of fire), and Edison incandescent burners gave the factory the advantages of the latest technology. The mill employed two hundred primarily white workers. When a boiler explosion in 1899 killed Branson, William A. and J. Harper Erwin took over management of the business with a large increase of capital.[39]

In 1887 Carr incorporated a second firm, the Golden Belt Manufacturing Company, in his own, his wife's, and T. B. Fuller's names. This factory did not make cloth, but only bags in which to sell tobacco, flour, cornmeal, salt, and the like. It netted him annually $7,500, or 20 percent on the invested $50,000, a small but profitable operation. But this company, like the cloth factory, continued to expand, and by 1900 it had forty-eight machines producing 10,000 bags daily. The finishing work of clipping the stacks of bags apart, turning them right side out, stringing them, knotting the strings, and putting them up in twenty-five-package lots was still done by women and children in their homes earning thirty to forty cents per thousand bags. An expert could do two thousand a day, the average worker about five hundred. Some steps of this operation continued to be a household industry in Durham through the early decades of the twentieth century.[40]

NEW BUILDING

The construction industry strove to keep pace with manufacture. Like an adolescent constantly outgrowing his clothes, Durham was bursting at the seams. Builders and carpenters, masons and plasterers, and even an architect or two hustled to fill the need. W. H. and Hill Carter Linthicum, architects and builders, came to Durham in 1880 from Virginia. The father, W. H. Linthicum, died in 1886, but his son, Hill Carter, made a career as a leading architect in Durham until his death in 1919. He was responsible for organizing the North Carolina chapter of the American Institute of Architects and Builders Association. The 1870s and 1880s saw the start of substantial construction, reflecting a desire of the owners to display their affluence as well as their taste. J. J. Ward wrote to his cousin in 1884, "I never saw nor heard tell of a town thriving any faster than Durham."[41]

Land values climbed precipitously in the eighties: Samuel A. Thaxton bought thirty-eight acres in 1884 and two years later sold less than five acres for more than the whole tract had cost him. Some entrepreneurs, seeing an avenue to quick profit, formed land or real estate companies, bought up farm tracts adjacent to the town boundaries, and sold them off in building lots. Others went a step farther and constructed buildings. A building and loan association formed in 1887 bought land on the east side of Alston Avenue with the intention of erecting one hundred houses. The Durham Land and Security Company was incorporated by Dr. J. L. Watkins and R. I. Rogers. William T. Blackwell started the Durham Real Estate Agency with Lucius Green, Frank P. Burch, and W. S. Halliburton. The Enterprise Land Company of J. C. Angier and W. A. Guthrie bought land stretching from Fayetteville Street on the east to Morehead Hill on the west as well as property in the town. In 1890, J. S. Carr, Col. A. B. Andrews, and Richard Wright formed the Durham Consolidated Land and Improvement Company by buying out the Enterprise, West End, and Durham Land companies. J. B. Warren and C. A. Jordan, who began the Trinity Land Company about 1891, sold out to Carr and formed a new company known as Morgan, Watkins and Company.[42] Those who could afford town land took advantage of the shortage and constructed business and dwelling houses, profitable investments that rented even before buildings were completed. For Richard Wright, Linthicum and Bethell erected an office building with a mansard roof and ornamental glass at the corner of Depot (later Church) and Main streets. The elder Linthicum also built a new factory near Main and Roxboro streets for Z. I. Lyon and Company, replacing their wooden one burned in 1884, and a handsome brick smokestack for the Blackwell factory. The three sons of another Durham contractor, C. M. Van Noppen, were hired to paint the stack. Expert steeplejacks, Leonard, Charlie, and Johnnie, all in their teens, also painted the two-hundred-foot steeple of Trinity Church. Construction was a hazardous business: their father died the following year from a fall from the Wright Building he was then constructing.[43]

New residential areas beyond the town limits were started at this time and earlier ones expanded. Morehead Hill, named for one of its first prominent residents, was begun on land purchased from William Gaston Vickers. Eugene Morehead and George Watts built large houses there in 1880. On Chapel Hill Street between Willard and Lea (Duke) streets, Benjamin Duke built a mansion (1887–88) beside his former home catercorner to William T. Blackwell's 1875 mansion, contrasting the high styles of the two decades.[44] In the 1880s larger and finer houses began to replace the earlier ones. At the corner of Willard and Chapel Hill streets, James Southgate's daughter Mattie and her husband, Thomas Decatur Jones, built a brick mansion in 1888. In each of the principal rooms on the first floor a different wood was used for the wainscot and mantel—walnut in the parlor, golden oak in the dining room, cherry in the smoking room, mahogany in the bedroom—and all but the bedroom had crystal chandeliers. The house, with its nine rooms downstairs and six upstairs in addition to servants' quarters, made a significant contribution to

Durham's growing residential landmarks. Here the widowers James Southgate and his son, James H. Southgate, along with the latter's children, joined Mattie Jones's family to live out their lives after her husband's early death in 1889.[45]

Farther to the west, between Chapel Hill Street and the railroad, William Albert Wilkerson developed Green Woods (now comprising Wilkerson and Burch streets and South Buchanan Boulevard), where he built his own and other ample houses, high-roofed against the summer heat, lavish with porches to catch the summer breezes, and rich in ornamental carpentry. Though untrained as an architect, Wilkerson learned how to make his own blueprints for houses he built, as his son Albert Ernest Wilkerson was later to do, and often worked with architects on larger structures. He built the Bartlett Mangum house on Chapel Hill Road; the Bishop's house on the East Campus of Duke University; Main Street Methodist Church; Washington Duke's house, Fairview, on Main Street; the W. T. O'Brien house on Burch Street; and many other less expensive houses.[46]

The Blacknall brothers, sons of Dr. Richard Blacknall, acquired large tracts of land in West Durham and built their own houses there. James Blacknall first used his tract as a farm. When he sold off the land, he made its old windmill over into a fifteen-room house in 1887. Richard D. Blacknall, a druggist, built a brick house in Queen Anne style. It originally stood at the corner of Anderson Street and Erwin Road but was moved in 1986 to a lot on Alexander Street when Erwin Road was widened for the expressway. The area in which the Blacknalls chose to build came to be called Caswell Hill or Heights and extended along the crest of land on the south side of the railroad tracks from opposite the present East Campus of Duke University almost to Hickstown. There Dr. J. L. Watkins and John C. Angier had already built their houses.[47]

These were the years when Hickstown was given a spurt of growth by Durham's voting to go "dry." Hickstown was incorporated in 1887 to protect it from a similar fate, and it immediately became a source of alcoholic beverages for Durham with many stores and saloons. A few Durham merchants, whose profits came from liquor sales moved to Hickstown, S. R. Carrington and William Mangum among them. Hickstown's reputation was not enhanced by this development. Two years later a group of residents of Caswell Heights, led by Blacknall, protested Hickstown's incorporation to the legislature, for the rowdiness was getting out of hand much too close to their own quiet bailiwick. Protesting with Blacknall were his near neighbors J. W. Brooks (for whom later Brookstown was named) and J. W. Swift (hence Swift Avenue).[48]

East Durham, too, expanded in the late 1880s because of Carr's cotton factory. Samuel Tate Morgan, a commission merchant, bought and sold all kinds of grain, provisions, and country produce, but his main product and source of future prosperity proved to be fertilizer. He established the Durham Fertilizer Company around 1881, using a waste product of the tobacco factories—the potash-rich tobacco stems—to make fertilizer. Through growth and consolidation of all the fertilizer companies in Virginia and North Carolina, in 1895 he formed the enormously profitable Virginia-Carolina Chemical Company, with headquarters in Richmond. The Durham Woolen and Wooden Mills Company, which made bobbins, shuttles, and other equipment for use in cotton factories was also built in East Durham in 1884 by John C. Angier, his brother-in-law Alvis H. Stokes, Morgan, Morehead, Carr, and James Blacknall. Richard Wright and Dr. J. L. Watkins bought the factory in 1888 and put a new mansard roof on it. The business did not thrive, and Wright sold it in 1891 to a Rhode Island firm that came in, dismantled it, and carried off the machinery. The editor of the *Daily Globe* had some fun at Wright's expense, writing, "A few more such citizens as Mr. Wright and a few more enterprises as the removal of the wooden mills and we shall soon have a city of mammoth proportions." All this industry in East Durham required houses for the workers and stores to supply their needs. A post office was established in 1887 in the cloth factory, and Branson was appointed postmaster. The newspaper editor could well exult, "East Durham is on a boom."[49]

When another bona fide architect arrived in Durham about 1886, the material culture of the town took on new elegance. He was Byron A. Pugin, who designed some notable buildings, including the University of Virginia chapel, but whose antecedents and professional qualifications are unknown. His name suggests a family relationship with the English architect and designer, Augustus W. N. Pugin, who worked with Sir Charles Barry on the Parliament buildings in London. Although the Pugin family seems never to have heard of Byron A. Pugin, it is not impossible that he was an illegitimate son of the famous architect. Byron Pugin's death certificate in Georgia, which gives that state as his birthplace, names no parents.[50]

Byron Pugin built many structures in Durham. Possibly the first was a house for J. E. Lyon in Redmond's Grove (in the Ramseur Street area), which contained twelve rooms, one bathroom, two small dressing rooms, lots of gables under a slate roof, a double veranda in the rear, and porches all around. At the same time, Pugin was erecting for E. J. Parrish the Parrish Building on Mangum Street, three stories high with terra-cotta ornamental tile, plate glass windows, and art glass over the door. Pugin was also the architect for Parrish's new furniture "emporium," handsome enough to live up to its name: pressed brick, gold and terra-cotta trimmings, plate glass, and a galvanized decorative cornice along the top of the third story. In 1887 as well Pugin supplied plans for stores of John C. Angier and Rufus Massey at the corner of Main and Church streets.[51]

Benjamin Duke was pleased with Pugin's work. In May 1887, he contracted with W. F. Remington to build a residence for him at the corner of Chapel Hill and Willard streets according to plans drawn by Pugin. This house, the Terrace, contracted to cost $8,000, remained Benjamin Duke's Durham home until it was replaced in 1908 by Four Acres at the same location.[52] After settling in at the Terrace, the Dukes found an occasion to throw open their new house for their friends and fellow townspeople in June 1890 when Brodie Duke, a widower since 1888, remarried, and the Benjamin Dukes entertained the newlyweds at a soirée.

In due time each guest found his way to the refreshment room, and a thing of beauty it was too. In the center of a large table was a miniature lake, around the edge of which ferns and water lilies seemed to grow. . . . Here ribbon water ices, cream and other delicacies were served in the cutest souvenirs. All this time grand strains of music filled the whole house, and made all hearts joyful.[53]

Pugin's most prestigious commission in Durham was the designing of the first county courthouse. The importance of the job may be judged by the fanfare surrounding the laying of the cornerstone. E. J. Parrish's Durham Light Infantry and band led the parade. Then followed Bennehan Cameron, chief marshal, and his assistants—all mounted: William Haywood McCabe, Thomas Holloway, T. A. Noel, S. F. Tomlinson, Thomas Rigsbee, and Albert Gallatin Cox. Dignitaries in the procession included the mayor, J. F. Freeland, the head of the town councilmen, M. A. Angier, and Thomas W. Mason, the chief speaker, escorted in a carriage by lawyer James S. Manning. The fire-hose company, led by Chief Dick Blacknall and the Colored Fire Company, led by Captain Sidney Carson, added panache. The Masons, who were to perform the ritual anointing of the stone with oil, wine, and fruits of the field, brought up the rear.[54]

The Masons had been long established in Durham—Eno Lodge, No. 21, had been organized in 1860—but other fraternal orders, too, flourished in the 1880s and 1890s when there were few competing organizations for small groups interested in mutual welfare and community improvement. In 1876 a second Masonic lodge was organized by James Southgate (1832–1914), an enthusiast of such organizations and of every good cause. A native of Virginia and a graduate of the University of Virginia, he had first chosen to teach and headed in turn the Norfolk Male Academy, the Louisburg Female Academy, and the Olin High School in Iredell County before switching to the insurance business as an independent agent. Looked on as little better than gambling with fate or God, insurance was only slightly more profitable than education, and Southgate was receptive to Julian Carr's offer of the Bull Durham Company's custom if he moved to Durham. In 1876 Southgate arrived and brought to Durham the gentility, cultivated tastes, and community-focused energies of his whole family. Besides organizing lodge No. 352, he was also involved with the Durham Chapter, No. 48, of the Royal Arch (R.A.M.); the Durham Council, No. 7; the Durham Commandery, Knights Templar; and the Knights of Pythias, No. 31. The Odd Fellows had Golden Link Lodge, No. 114, by the 1880s, and a second lodge in 1894, when the Durham Council, No. 588, of the Royal Arcanum was organized. The Benevolent and Protective Order of Elks organized a lodge in 1900. These orders had their halls on the second floor of Main Street stores, where more substantial, two-story buildings had begun to replace the original one-story frame stores and shacks.[55]

By far the most sumptuous building constructed in the 1880s was Julian Carr's Somerset Villa, begun in 1887 and completed the following year. The architect was John B. Halcott of Albany, New York, who had built the New York state capitol building. He also accepted smaller jobs in Durham, planning stores for Jones and Kramer in the fashionable mode of brownstone trimmed in terra-cotta with plate glass and iron trimmings. Carr spared no expense to acquire the latest improvements in domestic comfort and the best products of every description for fitting out and furnishing his house. The large cities of the eastern seaboard supplied him with nothing but the best, from door handles to carpets to lighting fixtures. Of more than usual interest was a stained-glass window depicting the story of Rosa Hartwick Thorpe's poem "Curfew Must Not Ring Tonight." It was designed and made by the Boston firm of Redding, Baird and Company.[56] Mrs. Cornelia Phillips Spencer wrote to Paul Cameron about the house.

> You have heard of Mr. J. S. Carr's timely gift of corn to the county. He certainly does do good with his money, & nobody can begrudge his possession of the finest house in the state. He invited me & Mr. and Mrs. Love [her son-in-law and daughter] to come to D[urham] & take lunch with him, & go over his new house. We went, the last week of Mar. & found the house & its fittings well worth a visit.
>
> Some one has wondered why Mr. C. should choose to put such a house & such furniture in such a place as Durham. I think he gets more good of it there than he could elsewhere. In W[ashington] City there are hundreds as fine— many finer—but here it is unique, & he can share his pleasure in it with his own folks & his old friends & neighbors. It is worth fifty dollars to him to have a hack full of Chapel Hill people drive up to his door, & be shown all round.
>
> I was very much pleased with Mrs. Carr's appearance. Perfect good-breeding & propriety marked all she said & did—, & she is so handsome that if it had been otherwise, we would have condoned all failures in consideration of her beauty.
>
> The furnishing of that house is all on the costliest scale. I imagine that there are not many houses in this country where the fittings up of the bathrooms are of solid silver—where the hand-painting on the walls of *one* bedroom occupied six men for seven or eight weeks—where the lace curtains for one window cost $500, one sofa cost $750, and one lamp $150 etc. etc.[57]

Mrs. Spencer confessed that she would rather put $100,000 into an institution for boys and girls in North Carolina or connect her name with the university for all time rather than spend such an amount for lace curtains and satin and plush and Sevres china and cut glass. "At least, I think so *now*: if I were tried, I might not turn out so well."

Carr surrounded his mansion with equally magnificent gardens under the supervision of Reuben Hibberd, a young Englishman, who also erected greenhouses of his own and opened Durham's first florist business on the corner of Dillard and present Ramseur streets. Somerset Villa replaced Carr's mid-1870s mansion, Waverly Honor, which was removed to a site across Dillard Street by the railroad to make way for its successor. James Southgate took a lease on Waverly Honor for his son, James Haywood Southgate, who married Kate, Bartholomew Fuller's daughter, in 1882.[58]

RAILROADS, PUBLIC SERVICES, AND BANKS

The 1880s was also a time of scrambling for railroads, and Durham's new wealth helped in the race. The old North Carolina Railroad, up to this time Durham's only link with the outside world, had been leased since 1871 to the Richmond and Danville Company. The tobacco industry's expansion was inhibited by a lack of more ample facilities, so that it was from them that the push came. Although the Durham Railroad Company, incorporated in 1880 by W. T. Blackwell, J. E. Lyon, H. A. Reams, B. L. Duke, J. S. Lockhart, and F. C. Geer, failed to carry out its plans, two other lines, incorporated in 1885, were constructed: the Durham and Roxboro and the Durham and Clarksville, followed in 1887 by the incorporation of two more: the Durham and Northern and the Durham and Southern. Much the same group of entrepreneurs was involved in all four enterprises, the most prominent being Blackwell, Carr, E. J. Parrish, and Eugene Morehead. A line to Lynchburg was effected by linking three shorter lines; the Durham and Roxboro was Durham's contribution. The county and Duke each subscribed $100,000 to what became known as the Lynchburg and Durham Railway. Despite this support, the railroad terminal (at Ramseur Street) was a mile from the Duke factory. The owners of the tracks through the center of the town, the Richmond and Danville and the Durham and Northern, were not inclined to let a third company horn in on the freight business. Consequently when the railroad was completed in 1890, Brodie L. Duke promoted the building of a belt line to connect the Duke factory with the Lynchburg and Durham line to the north of the city.[59]

The Durham and Clarksville road, for which the city subscribed $50,000, was completed in 1888 and leased to the Richmond and Danville Railroad. Early in 1889 the Durham and Northern was completed, for which the town had subscribed $100,000. The terminal for this line (at Dillard Street) was also a mile from the Duke factory. Undeterred by the threat of litigation they would incur, the townsmen themselves laid the tracks in the right-of-way of the North Carolina Railroad on the night of 9 April 1889 by moonlight, under the supervision of the Durham and Northern engineers. The next morning all the workmen were arrested. The local magistrates heard the charges and dismissed them. That night the same workmen completed the laying of the tracks to the Duke factory. The injured railroad sent workers in to tear up the track but were stopped late in the day by a restraining order from the federal district court. Again the decision was in favor of the Durham and Northern line. This did not end the local litigation, however, for the Richmond and Danville would not give up the fight. They contested the right of the town to grant a right-of-way on land then leased to another authority. This brought the town into the legal proceedings, trying to prove its right to grant the right-of-way. Despite temporary settlements the contention flared anew in 1895 when the Southern Railway bought the Richmond and Danville corporation. In 1903, in renewed litigation, the decision went against the town and consequently against the old Durham and Northern line, by then merged with the Seaboard Air Line Railroad. Finally that company negotiated a lease of the track from the Southern. Samuel Morgan, writing to Morehead at the height of all the railroad building, had cause to say, "Well, the Town is on a regular 'Birmingham Boom' and they say will be the R R center for N.C. It looks like it now."[60]

Later, short lines were built, primarily for the convenience of the lumber industry: the Durham and Southern (1906) built by Benjamin Duke to connect with the

Seaboard Air Line at Apex and the Atlantic Coastline at Dunn, and the Durham and South Carolina (1905), also connecting with the Seaboard Air Line.[61] While these lines gave Durham ample freight facilities, none was a through line for passenger service.

This was also the era in which municipalities began to supply their citizens with new services: water, fire protection, public transportation, and communication. In the 1870s and 1880s the town suffered a series of fires that eventually forced the establishment of both a municipal water supply and some rudimentary fire protection. When insurance for property on Main Street became almost impossible to obtain because of so many losses through fire, the aldermen at last took action. They authorized the purchase of a fire truck with ladders, hooks, and buckets, but no firefighting brigade to use them. A volunteer company, the Durham Chemical Fire Company, was formed in 1880, not the first informal organization to try to fill an ever more pressing need. A revised town ordinance in 1882 instructed the aldermen to organize two fire companies, one a hook and ladder company, the other a bucket and hose company, both under the supervision of a chief engineer and, remotely, of three fire commissioners. In 1882 the Durham Chemical Fire Company under Captain R. D. Blacknall paraded its new uniforms, led by the Durham Cornet Band. As the city still had no water besides wells or springs scattered around the town, the fire brigade's capacity to act was considerably hampered. The companies were made up of volunteers, exemption from poll taxes their only compensation. They made their own regulations and elected their own captains. Excelsior Fire Company No. 1 was a white group, a hose company. A black hook and ladder unit, captained by Peyton H. Smith, performed the more daring and dangerous firefighting maneuvers. The fire commissioners rented a building for a fire station in 1888 and considered paying firemen. In 1891 Firehouse No. 1, described as one of the best equipped in the state, was built for $3,000 at Mangum and Holloway streets according to the plans of Samuel L. Leary. It had an electric alarm system and in its tower an 829-pound bell, cast in Baltimore. In the middle 1890s, two additional white companies were formed: the Golden Belt Company and the Independent, both hose companies. All the units were under Chief Walter C. Bradsher and included about sixty-five men.[62]

In 1896 the Dukes authorized J. B. Warren, the superintendent of the Duke factory, to offer the town the use of the building then occupied by the Independent Hose Company for a new city fire company, and promised one hundred dollars a month to feed the horses. The city accepted the offer and agreed to buy a new truck and two horses, and to employ a driver. By 1903 the city had built a second fire station, a two-story brick building that replaced the one donated by the Dukes at the corner of Main and Duke streets. The Dukes donated $4,000 toward its construction. Designed by the Charlotte firm of Hook and Sawyer, it was equipped with a hose wagon, a steam engine, and handsome, well-kept horses. The fire department, professional and completely under city authority since 1909, was motorized in 1915 when the first gasoline-engine trucks were purchased.[63]

Most crucial to the firefighting effort was the water supply that the town contracted for in June 1886 with A. H. Howland of Boston. A private system was decided upon because the town was not wealthy enough to issue bonds and build its own. Howland was given a thirty-year franchise, but a city engineer was to approve equipment and installation. Water pressure was to be sufficient to provide ten streams of water, each one hundred feet high, from ten fire hydrants. The city had the option of buying the company within twenty years. In 1886–87 a one-hundred-foot dam was built at a point where Nancy Rhodes Creek empties into the Eno River, now the Cole Mill Road area. Howland was assisted by W. F. Ellis, seventy-five laborers, and two blacksmiths. Also under construction was a storage basin 8,300 feet away on top of Huckleberry Hill, which gives its name to the residential area of Huckleberry Heights. A pond behind the dam was to hold 6 million gallons, the hill reservoir, 3.5 million gallons. Water was pumped from the pond to the reservoir. As the needs of the city grew, this system was expanded over the following forty years.[64]

The Durham Water Company, formed in November 1886, ran the business and maintained the waterworks. Eugene Morehead was president, W. W. Fuller, attorney, and Howland and Ellis, managers. In 1887 Howland and the city could not agree on the size of water pipe to be installed. After repeated delays the town accepted the water system in April 1888 even though it did not meet the standards specified in the original contract. Repeated wrangling about insufficient pressure and unsatisfactory service culminated in action when disastrous fires in 1894 and 1895 made the company's shortcomings obvious to all. Suits against the company finally brought about its demise, but it had been in financial trouble before: it went into receivership first in 1893 for unpaid bills of the McNeal Pipe and Foundry Company. S. W. Holman, at that time local manager of the Durham waterworks, resigned, and John C. Michie was appointed in his place. When dead fish were found floating in water too muddy to drink, a new filter was installed and the reservoir bottom was cemented over.[65]

A bizarre sequel was the staged suicide of Howland in January 1894. He jumped off a Fall River Line steamer on his way to Boston. Libel suits were thought to be at the bottom of his action. A month later he was discovered in New York under an assumed name and his ruse laid bare. A month before his "suicide," he had taken out a $50,000 life insurance policy and was hoping to collect on it. When the water company went into receivership again in 1898 it owed $194,000. Then new arrangements for water service were made between the city and another Boston man, John D. Hardy, who had been treasurer of the company as early as 1893. The new company did not much reduce the general dissatisfaction. The city finally bought the whole system in 1916 after a comprehensive survey by Gilbert White, an independent engineer. At that time the city decided to establish Flat River as its main water supply and built a dam and water supply system there, though it continued to use parts of the old Eno River system.[66]

The Durham Street Railway Company was chartered 6 March 1887 with W. T. Blackwell as president, J. S. Carr as vice-president, and R. D. Blacknall as secretary and treasurer. A. W. Howland contracted to build it and ran the track from Redmond's Grove up Main Street to Blacknall's stables just a little beyond the town limits. By July the horse-pulled cars had arrived. The drivers handled no money;

the passengers deposited their fares in a box as they entered. Carr and Wright's Durham Consolidated Land and Improvement Company, which purchased the franchise from the Penn Construction Company in 1889, soon ran into financial difficulties. Carr suggested they refurbish the cars to make them look "as bright as a new pin." Interruption of service seems to have followed, and the city threatened the company with the removal of the tracks unless they were relaid. Too many broken wagon wheels and serious accidents resulted from tracks projecting several inches above the street level. Afraid of losing the town franchise, Wright made promises of improvement but did nothing. Finally, the company was allowed to keep the franchise after promising to organize and operate an electric line. The Durham Traction Company was formed 4 February 1901 with Wright as president, Carr, as vice-president, and J. S. Manning, H. A. Foushee, and Samuel Register as directors. A powerhouse was built on a vacant lot near the Bull factory. The electric cars began to run in June 1902.[67]

The Durham Electric Lighting Company, organized in 1885 by Carr, Morehead, and Watts, obtained the exclusive right to supply electricity for the town for fifteen years. Their powerhouse was on Peabody Street near Roxboro Street. By 1888 the company was not only supplying limited street lighting, but was also serving a few homes and businesses. Julian Carr's sumptuous house, for example, had electric lighting, call bells, and burglar and fire alarm systems. Wrangles over rates and service characterized this arrangement too. To increase their profit, the company supplied lights only on moonless nights, a saving that the city thought should be reflected in the charges. The Durham Traction Company bought the Durham Electric Lighting Company with its city franchise. In 1900 another electric company was formed, the Durham Light and Power Company, and given a fifty-year franchise to supply electricity to manufacturing plants and to distribute gas as well. Carr and Watts had formed the Durham Gas Company in 1888; thus these two electric and gas companies were in direct competition for a limited market. In 1905 the Traction Company and the Light and Power Company ended their rivalry, agreeing that the Traction Company would supply electricity and the Durham Light and Power Company would supply gas. This latter company was absorbed by the Carolina Power and Light Company in 1911. The next year yet another power company was incorporated to serve Durham, the Southern Power Company, a creation of B. N. Duke, and managed by R. L. Lyon and Jones Fuller. As it was also chartered to operate street cars, amusement parks, and the like, it hoped to take over all the old Carr and Wright interests. To avoid that ignominy, in 1913 Carr and Wright sold the Durham Traction Company with all its subsidiary services to Henry L. Doherty and Company of New York, a corporation with franchises in more than one hundred cities. Immediately Wright bought the Interstate Telephone and Telegraph Company.[68]

The telegraph had first come to the South in the late 1840s; it arrived in Durham with the railroad in 1854. The first commercial service, however, was that of Western Union in 1880, located on Corcoran Street. In 1894 the Postal Telegraph Company opened an office, also on Corcoran Street. The companies operated independently throughout the country until 1944, when the United States Congress merged them.[69]

A proto-chamber of commerce, known in its local version as the Commonwealth Club, made the first efforts to obtain telephone service in Durham in 1888. Apparently it succeeded, for Southern Bell Telephone and Telegraph Company began operation in Durham that year. Complaints about charges resulted in the securing of a competing company, for subscribers to the Bell company had all agreed to use the new company if one could be established. The Interstate Telephone and Telegraph Company was organized by Louis A. Carr (no relation to the native Carr family but a newcomer from Baltimore), J. S. Carr, and George W. Watts. The new company, in operation by June 1894, charged $30 a year for a business phone and $20 for a residential phone, compared with the Bell company's corresponding rates of $48 and $36. In 1903, the Interstate bought the Bell facilities, and by 1913, when Wright acquired the company, it had a clientele of 1,363 subscribers. Complaints about poor service were endemic to Durham's public services. After having agreed in a newly negotiated contract with the city to put his maze of unsightly wiring on the main streets underground, a move that had to take place before the streets were paved, Wright made no move to comply. By 1919 anger was running so high against the Interstate that subscribers threatened to form a new company. The newspaper joined the fray, singling out the telephone, traction, and gas companies as the worst of the public service vendors. Wright's tenacity proved stronger than the city's; he never buried the wires. Wright sold out in 1933 to the Theodore Gary Company, which ran the local company as the Durham Telephone Company. In 1955, the newly formed General Telephone Company of the Southeast bought the local company and two years later made Durham its headquarters.[70]

All this growth, particularly the tremendous industrial expansion, required a huge financial undergirding; this was provided by the creation of local banks. As mentioned, Durham's first bank had been established in 1878 by Eugene C. Morehead, a son of the governor; in 1884 William T. Blackwell led a flurry of new ventures with the establishment of a second, the Bank of Durham. 1887 saw the incorporation of three more institutions: the Fidelity Trust Company and Savings Bank, the Durham Savings Bank and Trust Company, and the First National Bank of Durham. The Fidelity Bank was a B. N. Duke project that included M. A. Angier as president, and Watts, both Carrs, J. W. Blackwell, Lucius Green, A. H. Stokes, and S. F. Tomlinson, among others. The other two banks were Carr projects and included many of the same directors: the Carrs, Watts, Fuller, and Parrish. At the end of 1888 Durham's economy was shaken to its foundations by the collapse of the Bank of Durham, which carried down with it a number of prominent citizens and well over a dozen businesses. O. R. Smith, informing Wright about local affairs, summed up the momentous year:

> Durham is on a Bust—got more than she knows what to do with, and needs a guardian untill she becomes of age, or takes the "pledge"—she has been drunk with excitement for six months. The Tobacco Exposition—Sam Jones [a revivalist who had caused a religious convulsion and a frenzy of conversions], the election [that had firmly entrenched conservative Democrats], and her increase of business were more than her youthful nerves could stand—and

now she has the delirium tremens of Bankruptcy with two dollars in hand for every one she owes, a youthfull indiscretion she will out grow, before she arrives at the years of virility.[71]

The election Smith referred to had generated much party rancor, followed by arson and near murder. Besides the Democratic candidates there had been Republican and Third Party candidates, the latter perceived as radical. The Third Party advocated woman's suffrage, labor unions, prohibition, and what the Democrats termed "Negro rule." Its supporters were D. C. Mangum, Jordan Emerson, T. H. Burgess, C. C. King (editor of a labor newspaper, the *Craftsman*), Thomas W. Laws, G. A. Rhodes, E. G. Jordan, Page Warren, C. F. Vickers, Marion Terry, and a number of prominent blacks such as Richard Fitzgerald, W. G. Pearson, and William Holloway. E. G. Jordan, a blacksmith by trade, had come to Durham in 1885. He was a leader in the Knights of Labor and stirred enthusiasm in the ranks of both white and black labor. He was nominated as a radical candidate for constable but was defeated. He ran for town alderman on the dry ticket and when the town voted to go "dry," his popularity ran high for a time. But the backlash came swiftly. After the election in which the Democrats regained local power, the house of C. B. Green, the county Democratic Party leader, was set on fire, and rumors circulated that blacks incited by Jordan were to blame. A mob led by William Bradsher took Jordan under cover of night with the intent to drive him out of town and hang him. When E. J. Parrish heard what was happening, his good judgment, sense of fair play, and aversion to mob tactics sent him after the carriage; he insisted that the captors return Jordan to his family and provide the whole family with train tickets for the following day. Parrish's personal courage and respect in the community carried the day, and the incident passed without dire consequences.[72]

It is clear, however, that below Durham's new prosperity and veneer of respectability the old raw frontier spirit was very close to the surface. A few men with superior intelligence, genius for business, and plain decency bolstered by a simple but firmly seated religious faith held the reins; they were responsible for the incredible progress the town had made and for whatever moral and cultural efforts its people had undertaken. Contrasts abounded. In front of the new mansions were impassable muddy streets. The same air that wafted music from Stokes's hall carried the stench of garbage. Many years later Dr. Isaac M. Manning would look back to the 1880s and "glancing out the window on Corcoran Street" recall that "in 1887 it was lined with warehouses and that the street was covered with watermelon rinds and other rubbish. There were no sewers or waterworks. Typhoid fever and dysentery were taking a heavy toll. There were no adequate health laws or hospital facilities. Durham smelled to high heaven."[73]

ORGANIZATIONS: SECULAR AND RELIGIOUS

Growth brought complexity of social structure and its attendant problems. Along with new business and commercial opportunities and jobs in industry and construction, it brought both gains and losses in the quality of life. Health hazards and social problems multiplied, but the influx of people with differing backgrounds and experience brought new ideas and new leaders. Increase of income freed the better-off, moreover, for a variety of new cultural and social activities to promote their own or society's improvement.

The first purely cultural group was the Durham Literary Society and Lyceum, begun in November 1880. Bartholomew Fuller, a Fayetteville lawyer who had moved to Durham to work for the Blackwell Company, was the first president, and other organizers were Watts, Southgate, Morehead, Tomlinson, H. T. Darnall, and James Dike.[74] Dike had left a promising career as a teacher in the Boston Latin School and had come south in hopes of restoring his failing health. He ran a bookstore, which stocked not only the best in literature but music and music supplies as well.[75] Men like Dike felt a need for the exchange of thought and knowledge with like-minded men and women that the Lyceum could provide. The group immediately began to buy books with the aim of starting a public library and reading room. By May 1881 they had one in operation; members had free access to it, but outsiders paid a small fee.[76] In 1882 two musical organizations made their debuts, the Mozart Musicale and the Durham Glee Club. The former's officers were J. B. Whitaker, Jr., Mrs. Morgan Closs, W. S. Halliburton, and Uriah M. Wahab. It met once a week, and anyone could join. Celestia (Lessie) Southgate, who had the advantages of talent and training, began her long musical career by teaching instrumental and vocal music in the Methodist Female Seminary. In 1886 she opened the Durham School of Music and in 1888 organized the Saint Cecilia Society, long a vital musical influence in the cultural life of the town.[77]

Around the problems of alcoholism groups had rallied since the 1840s. Baptist and Methodist churches had been bulwarks against the making and sale of spirituous liquors, and their members were for the most part solidly in line behind them. The Good Templars, too, had been active in Durham since the 1870s. Prohibition was very much a political issue at this time. The legislature had voted for statewide prohibition in 1881, but a referendum had failed to sustain it, notwithstanding Will Rogers's later witticism that North Carolinians would vote dry as long as they could stagger to the polls. The Central Prohibition Club was organized in 1886 to get prohibition enacted into law by grassroots action. T. M. Stephens, John V. Rigsbee, and Horace N. Snow were its officers. The Woman's Christian Temperance Union organized a chapter in Durham in 1886 and set up a reading room for men stocked with books, papers, and periodicals. In 1888 a Local Option Club was formed with Professor H. W. Reinhart as president, Snow as secretary, and an executive committee made up of Watts, Southgate, Burkhead (the editor of the *Tobacco Plant*), and others. This movement was successful; by 1903 more than half of North Carolina's counties prohibited sales and manufacture of alcoholic beverages. In 1909 the state legislature made the entire state "dry."[78]

In addition to the established fraternal orders, freemasonry of other sorts existed. The doctors established the Durham Medical Society at least by 1880. Their main concern was the need for a hospital for the poor (the rich could pay for nursing and medical treatment at home), and they offered to lead a campaign to raise the necessary funds and to donate their advice and services when such a hospital had been established. They donated one hundred dollars to get the campaign going; the Knights of Pythias gave fifty dollars more, but six months later the effort was dead. However, Dr. Albert Gallatin Carr, Julian Carr's brother and the first county coroner, kept the idea alive.[79]

Farmers who had joined the Patrons of Husbandry in the 1870s were caught up in an even more promising organization at the end of the 1880s when the Farmers' Alliance movement reached North Carolina. Beginning in the state in 1887, it had gained 90,000 members in 2,147 chapters by 1890. Their aims were to encourage farmers to aid, support, and trust one another, and weld themselves into an effective group that could make their views known and listened to. Among their accomplishments were a cooperative food store, a cooperative tobacco warehouse, and even a tobacco manufacturing company. Individual chapters were formed, such as those at Dayton and Morning Sun academies, by Pleasant Massey, who went around the county explaining to the farmers the benefits to be gained from membership. A countywide alliance of local units was headed by John T. Nichols.[80]

In 1888 A. F. Murphy formed a local chapter of the Ancient Order of United Workmen Ehrlich Lodge No. 4. John Spencer Bassett was its state organizer in 1894.[81] Teachers, too, got together to further their interests; the Teachers' Assembly (1887) came out strongly for equal pay for women as their first aim, an effort the newspaper supported.[82]

In 1884 George W. Watts organized and became the first president of the Commonwealth Club, a voice for the concerns of the industrialists and a means for them to act in concert in the building of a better Durham. They fought to get railroads and attract new industry and to publish Durham's strengths. The club was still functioning in 1910.[83]

In this era women first attempted autonomous action within church auxiliaries and missionary societies. The women of Trinity Church formed an auxiliary in 1882 and those of the First Baptist Church in 1887. The work of these groups is so important to the church and so much taken for granted today that it is hard to imagine the opposition they initially generated. Public roles for women violated both cultural tradition and religious doctrine. Nevertheless women defied the scriptures, holding meetings in the church and speaking at them. It was shocking to men to see women emerge into the public world and function in it. Very soon after the formation of these societies came the creation of women's organizations to operate outside the church, such as a chapter of the King's Daughters organized in 1890. A nonsectarian society with many chapters here and abroad, it utilized the growing leisure of middle- and upper-class women in various charitable endeavors.[84] The secularization of both social and charitable impulses, hitherto encompassed by churches, greatly increased in this decade.

A new direction for Durham men was the organization in 1890 of a purely social club, the Golden Belt Club, with pleasure its only goal. Modeled on fashionable urban men's clubs, it would supply members a reading room, game rooms for pool and billiards, and smoking rooms. In explaining its role, a reporter stated that the YMCA took care of a large group of unmarried men in the town, but that an even larger group, "and they among the best," felt the need "of social intercourse without the restraining influence which the semi-religious character of the YMCA would naturally place upon them."[85] This was a declaration of independence indeed. It was also a sign of the times and a measure of Durham's sophistication and wealth.

Nevertheless, new, religious-inspired organizations came on the scene, the Salvation Army (1887) and the YMCA (1888). The former began with two workers, both from Massachusetts, and met with some success converting souls and salvaging lives. It definitely filled a need: the county and city governments made no provision for the poor and needy beyond the doors of the county home. The YMCA began with fanfare, for big guns were behind it, among them Southgate, Leo Heartt, Watts, and E. J. Parrish. It immediately picked up 120 members, and Parrish offered a lot on Church Street for a building and $250 as the start of a building fund. Surprisingly, the organization ran into opposition from local ministers and was discontinued in 1894 with a large debt to pay off.[86]

New churches, too, were organized in this decade, both in town and in the countryside. A Primitive Baptist congregation was formed by members of Eno and Lebanon churches that had moved to town; they built a church in 1881 on Roxboro Street with Elder T. Y. Monk as their minister. The Christian Church congregation purchased a lot in 1887 at Queen and Liberty streets on which to build a sanctuary. The Blackwell Baptist Church (later Second Baptist Church and now Temple Baptist Church) grew out of a Sunday school started in 1886. W. T. Blackwell, W. J. Christian, J. V. Rigsbee, J. A. Tatum and others were the organizers in 1888. It was named in honor of William T. Blackwell's mother, for the Blackwells were the main contributors.[87]

Sunday schools were incubators for two other town churches, Main Street Methodist (now Duke Memorial) and East End Methodist (now Carr), both outgrowths of Trinity Church missions, one in Duke's tobacco factory and the other in Carr's cotton mill. The Reverend T. A. Boone of Durham Methodist Church (not named Trinity until 1886) was responsible for these efforts, and Amos Gregson was appointed first pastor of both. East End, a frame church costing $3,000, was built in 1886, and the next year the Reverend John H. Hall was assigned to it. William H. Branson became the Sunday school superintendent. At the other end of town, Gregson began services on 1 May 1886 in Duke's factory, forming Bethany Sunday School. Its members grew in a short time from 100 to 224. The Duke family and others of Trinity's congregation transferred their memberships to the new organization. Brodie Duke gave land at the southeast corner of Main and Gregson streets for the first building, which Benjamin Duke suggested be called Main Street Methodist Church, a name it held until 1912 when the present church (1907–14) at Chapel Hill and Duke streets was built and named Memorial Methodist Church (Duke Memorial after 1925) to honor Washington Duke. The Dukes were the principal donors for this church, which cost over $175,000.[88]

During these years the Sunday school of Trinity Methodist Church was involved in a curious relationship with a young Chinese boy whose adopted name was Charles Jones Soong.[89] His later fame and success are the stuff of legend. As a young seaman, he had come into the port of Wilmington and there marked his conversion to Christianity with baptism. The Reverend T. Page Ricaud of Wilmington sent him to Trinity Sunday school, for Charlie felt called to go into missionary work in his homeland, and he wished to be educated for the task. Trinity Sunday school, of which Julian Carr was superintendent, took on the responsibility of supporting and educating him. He was first sent to Trinity College in Randolph County and then to Vanderbilt University to be trained for the ministry, but all his vacations were spent with the Carrs in Durham, where he established lasting ties with them and the Southgates.

After Soong's return to China he spent some years in missionary work, proving an invaluable aid to American missionaries there. At the same time, he was establishing himself financially and politically by a judicious marriage and by becoming secretary to the nephew of Li Hung Chang, one of the most influential men in China. Soong played an integral role in the revolution that overthrew the Manchu dynasty and founded what has facetiously been called the Soong dynasty because of the success and prominence of his four children, whom he sent to the United States to be educated. His son became governor of the Bank of China, one daughter became a medical social worker, another married China's first president, Sun Yat-sen, and the third became a world figure by her marriage and political partnership with Chiang Kai-shek, leader of Nationalist China after the Kuomintang broke with the Communists in 1927. Tradition has woven many stories into the history of Soong's Durham sojourn that cannot be documented, but the plain truth of the matter is that he developed close associations with several Durham families during his formative years to whom he felt a lifelong attachment and gratitude.[90]

Another Sunday school was the beginning of Angier Avenue Baptist Church. In 1886 R. T. Howerton of the First Baptist Church undertook to organize a Sunday school among the settlers just east of the town. He arranged for services in the old Oak Grove school building. In 1889 the members decided to organize a church, East Durham Baptist Church, and built a building at the corner of Angier Avenue and Driver Street. Among the charter members were Mrs. Jane Gray, Mrs. F. D. Hudson, and Mrs. A. W. Renn, who donated the land. The present church was built in 1924 on the same site.[91]

An Episcopal mission organized by the Reverend Joseph B. Cheshire of the Chapel Hill church became Saint Philip's in 1880 when a sanctuary was built on Main Street near Dillard. The first church warden was Charles M. Herndon and the treasurer was Colonel Robert F. Webb.[92]

In the county a group of Baptists who had been meeting in Hayes schoolhouse organized a church called Bethesda (1884), from which the community in Oak Grove Township takes its name. At Red Mountain another group of Baptists organized a church through the efforts of Mrs. William Bowling (née Bettie Tapp). It too began as a Sunday school, meeting in the woodshop of Mrs. Bowling's husband, Captain William Bowling (1817–1907), who donated five acres on which by 1881 Red Mountain Baptist Church had been built. It is said that lumber for the structure was taken from the abandoned Shady Hill Baptist Church. The first Red Mountain Church stood until 1923, when a new church was erected by the Bowlings' children and others. Another Sunday school, organized in the 1880s in the southwest corner of the county, became Ephesus Baptist Church in 1891. Influential in its formation were Sidney M. and George E. Pope, L. W. Leigh, and Pleasant Massey.[93]

GROWTH IN THE COUNTY

The rural population was still expanding despite the pull of Durham, "sucking the very life-blood from the slow old-fashioned towns nearby."[94] A map of the county published in 1887 (copyrighted by Lemuel Johnson but now generally known as the Southgate Map) shows many new place names. Many of these were stations and water stops on the railroads then being built. In Mangum Township, the post offices of Luster (1880) at Bowling's mill and Lyndover (1882), on Roxboro Road near the Person County line, came into being. Bowling's or Lyndover Academy was established in 1887 one mile south of the Lyndover post office on the Hillsborough to Oxford road. Its supporters were Simeon Bowling, superintendent, and W. R. Clark, Dr. J. A. Wise, John Poole, Dewitt Blalock, R. J. Tilley, P. A. Flintom, and Thomas Carver. It was first leased to the local public school, which needed a building, and then used for its own school session. Despite Hasten Bowling's steam sawmill and Bowling's and Cothran's saw- and gristmills in the area, both the Luster and Lyndover post offices were discontinued in 1903 and 1904, respectively, a reflection of the dwindling activity and population. A third post office in the same area, Bowling, established in 1888, lasted only until 1897, when the name was changed to Rougemont (the French version of Red Mountain) to identify a new station, the post office, and an aspiring community. The railroad depot there drew to itself all the commercial activity of the area, and the old names and places were superseded by the new.[95] Old Round Hill, the former Parrish stronghold, was now known as Hunkadora (1881) with Radford Stagg as postmaster. Stagg had acquired the D. C. Parrish farmhouse, one room of which is thought to be incorporated in Stagg's house still on the site. When the railroad was completed in 1890 and stations established along its route, "Hunkadora" may have seemed too frivolous a name for its new dignity; the station became Bahama in 1891, a name popularly explained as a combination of the first syllables of the family names Ball, Harris, and Mangum, prominent and prolific families in that place.[96]

Below Bahama the same railroad line (last owned by the Norfolk and Western Railroad) established a station at Willardville to serve Orange Factory, and a post office with the same name opened in 1891. South of Willardville another station was situated at Fairntosh and gave Paul Cameron what he had long dreamed of—a railroad at his door. In the 1880s, under the supervision of his sons, Duncan and Bennehan, a new Stagville store and post office were established.[97] To the west on the Roxboro to Durham road another post office, Galveston, was opened in 1888 in the store of William T. Cole. On the same road farther south, old West Point Post Office was reborn as McCowns in 1883. Still farther south a new community, Bragtown, came into being around 1880 when John S. Carden was appointed postmaster. Alone among these communities, however, Bragtown has continued to grow and retain its identity even within Durham's city limits.[98]

In Cedar Fork Township near Cedar Fork Church, a post office and station, hardly more than a water stop, were established on the old North Carolina Railroad and called Nelson, possibly the name of a railroad official. Cedar Fork Post Office, 1860–66, and Llewellyn Post Office, 1882 only, were earlier names for Nelson.[99]

PUBLICATIONS

Attempts to keep the populace informed and to give them a sense of cohesion and local pride were undertaken by the semicommercial, semicultural newspaper business, which had its own burgeoning in the 1880s. Besides Caleb B. Green's *Tobacco Plant* (1872–89), a conservative, tactful paper with a Democratic political cast, there were several other substantial journalistic endeavors and a handful of short-lived ventures. John D. Cameron's *Recorder*, except for a year in Hillsborough (1895) edited by Mrs. Al Fairbrother, continued under E. C. Hackney's and Zeb V. Council's successive editorships until 1911. There was also James Dike's *Daily Dispatch* (1880), a more literary venture that did not survive; the *Daily Reporter* (1885), David W. Whitaker's creation; the *Methodist Advance* (1880–87), published by a minister of Trinity Church, Frank H. Wood; the *Church Messenger*, an Episcopalian paper, the work of the Reverend E. N. Joyner; the *Durham County Republican* (1884); the *Daily Progress* (1888), a third party paper; the Durham *Workman*, labor's organ owned and edited by Hiram Paul; the *Sun*, which began in 1889 under James A. Robinson, a veteran newspaperman, and which has survived many an editor and financial crisis to the present; and the *Globe*, a daily paper begun by Edward A. Oldham in 1889. Oldham bought the *Tobacco Plant* from J. S. Carr and gave it a new format and name, but shortly afterward sold it back to Carr. In December 1890 Carr sold it to Al Fairbrother, then of the *Omaha Bee*, who came like a sharp northern wind into the temperate and tepid newspaper climate of Durham. His impact was felt in the early 1890s, when he shook up the town with outspoken criticism of prominent (and up to then sacrosanct) persons, used humor to puncture pomposity, and exposed social ills wherever he found them.[100] Carr would never have sold him the *Globe* if he had known what Fairbrother would do with it.

SEEN AS A WHOLE THE 1880S PROVIDED much change for the people of eastern Orange. To begin with, they finally had their own county, symbolized in the large, dignified Pugin courthouse. By the end of the decade a number of new rail lines had cut their way across the farmland, dotting the landscape with depots and water stops and new place names. A huge increase of population streaming into the town of Durham from other counties and from older communities within the new county changed the character and social fabric of the town, and put an end to the chances of outlying communities for further growth. The town, whose population doubled in the decade, began to fill up with substantial business and residential structures, and almost as many people now lived around the periphery in new neighborhoods. Growth created dislocation, physical and social, brought a host of new problems, and exacerbated the old ones. Though much that was ugly, unhealthy, and unsavory needed correction, the town had now reached a point where it could devote extra time, money, and attention to its problems and, at last, to cultural improvement. The county could end the 1880s with a feeling of pride and optimism. Robert Winston, who chose to move to Durham and practice law, characterized the place he found: "It must be admitted, Durham's industrial enterprises far surpassed her aesthetic equipment. It was several years before we Durhamites turned our attention to the finer things of life." He added, however, "When we did get down to culture . . . we made her hum."[101]

This decade, which saw the building of what was in reality the infrastructure of Durham's future, closed with the laying of a cornerstone for what would be the most vital and far-reaching construction project of all—Trinity College.[102] The little institution, which had been struggling along for fifty years in Randolph County, would slowly work like yeast in a loaf to help bring the youthful society of Durham during the next hundred years to full maturity.

The Apogee of an Era, 1890–1903 12

PURSUING CULTURE

Julian Carr's belief that "nothing elevates and refines a community like schools" made him an enthusiastic participant in the little group that brought Trinity College to Durham. Carr had already been a substantial supporter of the Randolph County institution. In 1887 he had given it ten thousand dollars in securities to form an endowment (the largest gift it had received to that time); with two other trustees he had been keeping the college afloat since 1885. As chairman of the search committee Carr had also been instrumental in choosing for the college its new president, John Franklin Crowell (1857–1931), in 1887. A Pennsylvanian by birth, an Evangelical, and a Yale graduate, Crowell was not a likely choice to be president of a small, southern, Methodist college. Yet his presidency was to prove crucial because he was imbued with the newest philosophy of higher education springing from German universities and, forceful and fearless, he was prepared to put his ideas into action. He wanted to overhaul the curriculum. Instead of classical languages, he saw more value for the college student in modern languages, just as he believed that the curriculum should have some relevance to the workaday world. Crowell advocated the new science based on Darwin's and Spencer's theories and the new social sciences and history; he stressed seminars and research in laboratories and libraries instead of entire dependence on lectures; and he believed in the freedom of universities to investigate and teach as they saw fit. Most of all he was convinced that the place in which all this could best take place was a city or town where the financial support a college needed and the "creative forces of modern society" were to be found. Crowell was determined that Trinity should move from its isolated location and persuaded the Methodist Conference to agree to a move at its convention in 1887; to that end he entertained offers from North Carolina communities.[1]

Crowell had already decided on Raleigh with its offer of $35,000 when Durham began to negotiate even higher stakes. Robert F. Bumpas, the minister of Main Street Church, and E. A. Yates, the presiding elder of the Durham District, have been traditionally credited with spurring Washington and Benjamin Duke's interest in getting Trinity to Durham. "I have thought of the day," Bumpas wrote to Benjamin Duke in 1898, "I went to your house after dinner and found you lying on the lounge in the hall, and you told me you were thinking of buying the Park [Blackwell's] and building an orphanage for the Methodist Church. When I suggested that you have Trinity College moved to Durham, you agreed to consider the matter." Then he went on to remind Duke of their visit to Carr and of Washington Duke's promise to Bumpas to give $85,000 to achieve the move.[2]

The Dukes, like other Durhamites, had felt their civic pride wounded by the Baptists' decision not to locate a female seminary in Durham because of Durham's unsuitable factory- and mill-town atmosphere. The elder Duke was willing to match Raleigh's offer and add $50,000 to it for an endowment. Carr, equally sensitive to the civic slur and with already strong ties through donations and service to Trinity, would not be outdone in generosity, particularly by the Dukes. He offered the 67.5 acres of Blackwell's Park (then in his ownership) to the college. The land had been bought from Archibald Nichols by James W. Blackwell, William T.'s brother, in 1880–81 and made into a racetrack with stables and grandstand for the breeding and racing of fine horses—"the finest race track in the state." William Blackwell had bought the whole complex from his brother by 1886 and had probably sold it to Carr when bankruptcy overtook him. The promised money and land were sufficient to persuade Crowell to move the college to Durham.[3]

Washington Duke's expectation that all good Methodists would rally round and help support the college was soon disappointed, and his and his son's gifts alone managed to keep the college open during the next hard years. More than contributors failed them. Samuel L. Leary, whom they had chosen to build the huge main building (eventually named for the elder Duke), apparently miscalculated the weight and stresses of the central tower, and on the eve of its completion it collapsed. For Leary it was the crash of his reputation and career. Because of the collapse, Trinity's move was delayed a year, and the college did not open in Durham until the fall of 1892.[4]

Besides the main building, much else had to be built to house the college. A huge building called the College Inn (later Epworth), a kind of student union, dormitory, chapel, and mess hall all under one roof, was designed by a Washington architect, built by Richard Baxter Bassett (the father of later Professor John Spencer Bassett), and paid for by Washington Duke. Also built at that time was a third building known as Crowell Science Hall, named for Crowell's wife, who had died during the period of transition to Durham, and built with money from her estate. To the east of the main building six small faculty houses were also built by Bassett for married teachers. To make an attractive entrance to the campus, a gateway of rounded iron double arches designed by Reuben Hibberd, the grounds manager, was erected in 1896, a gift of B. N. Duke.[5]

Trinity's first years were financially difficult. Crowell had to pay the teachers from his own pocket during one crisis, and Washington or Benjamin Duke came to the rescue whenever called upon to do so. Carr, too, donated from time to time; in 1897 he gave $10,000 for a chair in philosophy (named for him). By the end of the decade, however, Duke gifts had established an endowment, and several additions to it had secured Trinity financial stability at last. At the same time the honeymoon was over. The college had materially changed the character of the town, as the city fathers had hoped it would, but it had also brought notoriety, dissension, and division, which they had not bargained for.[6]

With the arrival of the college, a new cultural uplift became evident. Faculty members began to preach in church pulpits, joined local clubs, lectured in Stokes Hall on intellectual topics, and participated in the life of the town. The business and professional men welcomed them gladly, and the faculty families were delighted by the warmth of the hospitality accorded them. The college arranged for a public series of guest lecturers and artists. A professor of political science from Princeton was one of the speakers; a reporter wrote that Woodrow Wilson was not much of an orator but he was "the brainiest American of the present decade" whose speech "bristled with thought." New clubs with an academic slant were formed: the Shakespeare Club (1895) and the Canterbury Club (1896); town and gown, men and women were represented in both. Young men formed the Young Men's Literary and Debating Club in 1896 and held public debates at the courthouse. Another group was organized to perform amateur theatricals. It managed to stage Handel's oratorio *Esther* as a masque in 1894 with James H. Southgate as King Ahasuerus, Minnie Happer as his queen, and Mamie Dowd as her attendant.[7]

Although women were participants in many of these groups, their continuing efforts toward independence led them in 1896 to form their own club, the Up-To-Date Club, actually the inspiration of Mattie Southgate Jones and Mrs. Leo D. Heartt. Twelve charter members planned the course of study: modern thought and inventions and inventors. They elected Mrs. Brodie Duke president. Two other entirely female organizations were the Tourist Club, organized in 1900, and a chapter of the United Daughters of the Confederacy in 1899. Mrs. A. G. Carr headed the UDC while Mrs. Duke, who withdrew from the Up-To-Date Club, organized the former.[8]

The verve for uplift of the 1890s created a market for newspapers. Besides the old *Recorder* and recent *Sun,* there was the notorious *Globe,* which succeeded the *Tobacco Plant* in 1889, after the latter was sold to Edward A. Oldham. It went through a series of editors and owners for a year before being bought by Al Fairbrother in December 1890. After his memorable three years as editor and another two under different editorship, the daily became a weekly, leaving four newspapermen out of work and making room for another daily paper. The unemployed quartet, J. H. King, J. T. Christian, W. W. Thompson, and Zeb V. Council, started the *Globe Herald,* very soon changed to *Morning Herald.* After the first two owners sold out and Thompson sold his share to Edward T. Rollins in 1896, there began the almost century-long association of the Rollins family with the *Herald* and after 1929 with the venerable *Sun.*[9]

An idea whose time has come is not dependent on the work of one group to translate it into reality, but on the general climate of acceptance. For years the concept of a public library had cropped up in one group after another—first in 1881 in the Lyceum and next in the WCTU with its reading room. When the Methodist churches established their Epworth Leagues, they, too, wanted to establish public reading rooms. The Trinity League in 1894 discussed acquiring the YMCA library when that organization became defunct, but decided that the time was not ripe. The very next month, however, Main Street Methodist Church's League set aside "a cozy, comfortable reading room" in the church with current periodicals and one hundred or more volumes, open every evening from 7:00 to 9:30 and free to the public. In June 1895 the newly founded Canterbury Club discussed establishing a free library and asked key business and professional men to write articles in support of the idea. The city government agreed to contribute to its maintenance if one were built. Other groups such as the Social Science Club and the Graded School committee also favored the idea. Lalla Ruth Carr stirred up interest among other men's and women's groups. A mass meeting at the courthouse resulted in a permanent organizing committee made up of the Reverend L. B. Turnbull and Professors Edwin Mims and C. W. Toms. Miss Carr offered a building lot at Five Points valued at $2,500 to which Mrs. Thomas H. Martin added a fifteen-foot strip to enlarge the available area. Other groups sent in money.[10] George Pegram wrote to his mother, "I see that Durham is about to get a public library. It took Raleigh three months to get $2,000, while it seems that Durham gave three times that much in one night. Therefore Durham is more than three times as *literary* as Raleigh. I doubt that, but the library is a good thing anyway."[11] Women formed themselves into soliciting committees and with the trustees went to work to raise money. When the library was built and opened in early February 1898, the aldermen promised fifty dollars a month for operating expenses. The frame library, looking more like a private house than a public building, was the first free library in the state and the first supported from public funds. A report on its second anniversary boasted of 4,500 volumes and an average circulation of sixty books a day. Mrs. F. L. Weddell was in charge the first year and Miss Sally R. Henderson the second.[12]

Not to be outdone by the larger municipality east of them, West Durhamites wanted a public library too. W. M. Yearby, who had elegantly redecorated his drugstore there, donated a room over his store for the library, "handsomely fitted up."[13]

Lessie Southgate's music school attracted many imitators, particularly after she married Thomas J. Simmons in 1891 and moved to Georgia. Vernon Darnell, who had taught piano and organ in Lessie's school, continued to teach on his own, and several other new teachers advertised their services as well: Miss Willie Smoot, Miss Nola Woodward, and Miss Annie D. Peay. Recitals by their students provided almost the only musical entertainment besides the traveling professionals who periodically performed in Stokes Hall.[14]

Around the end of the century opportunities to hear good music increased with the establishment of two new enterprises. Gilmore Ward Bryant, a native of Bethel, Vermont, and a musician of long teaching experience, had been teaching at Peace College in Raleigh for four years when he decided to come to Durham to drum up support for starting a conservatory. After receiving encouragement from leading citizens, he presented his plans to Benjamin Duke, who agreed to provide a building and renovated his father's old house for the purpose. The Southern Conservatory of Music opened in the fall of 1898 with forty pupils. Howard Foushee, a representative in the legislature, secured a charter for the school in January 1899. The following summer, enrollment was running so high that the school had to seek larger quarters. The Dukes agreed to build a school and employed Charles C. Hook and Frank McM. Sawyer, architects of Charlotte, to design the building as a memorial to Mary Duke Lyon, Washington Duke's only daughter, who had died in 1893 of pneumonia after a long bout with tuberculosis.[15]

The tripartite, Italianate building with porches, flat arches, and twin towers was erected on the southwest corner of Main and Duke streets. The center section contained the auditorium for performances. The towers held stairways to the gallery, ticket offices, and cloakrooms. The north wing held the living quarters for fifty resident young ladies (culture was for women, a prevailing notion in those years): kitchen, pantry, dining room, bedrooms, baths, parlors, and reception room. The south wing included a vast practice hall capable of holding twenty pianos, small practice rooms, and classrooms. The dominant feature of the practice hall was a large stained-glass window depicting Saint Cecilia at the piano and above her a large harp surrounded by scrolls of musical excerpts from Mendelssohn, Mozart, and Beethoven. Hook suggested its biblical inscription: "And lo, thou art unto them as a very lovely song of one that has a pleasant voice and can play well on an instrument."[16] The new building opened in 1900 and the school flourished. Young women in Durham and throughout the South benefited from the quality of its instruction, and Durham began to enjoy steady offerings of good music by the conservatory faculty and other professional artists whom the Bryants brought to Durham.[17]

Perhaps the enthusiastic response to the conservatory encouraged the aldermen to build a municipal building to house the city government, a market, and a public auditorium. Such a combination of functions had long been traditional throughout the state. The new building, designed by Sawyer and Hook and built in 1902–3, could hold 1,500 persons in its second-floor auditorium. On the ground floor, offices for the city occupied one side of the building while a market for meats, vegetables, and dairy products occupied the other. After severe damage in a fire caused by faulty wiring in January 1909, it had to be largely rebuilt, again by Hook and Sawyer, on a slightly different plan. This second Municipal Building or Academy of Music retained the city offices, but the space the market had formerly occupied was appropriated by the rebuilt theater to increase the size of the stage and seating capacity. Hook had accurately described it beforehand: "It so far eclipses anything in this section, anything in the state, that I have no place in mind which gives you an idea how fine it will be. . . . It will be a gem." It served until 1924, when it was torn down to make way for the Washington Duke Hotel.[18]

ENTERTAINMENT

Until the construction of the first academy in 1902–3, Stokes Hall or Opera House (at the northeast corner of Main and Corcoran streets) was described as "the chief and only place of amusement in Durham." Mallory and Hackney were then its managers. In it played the Durham orchestra, acclaimed in 1900 as long the best orchestra in the state. At that time another orchestra was being formed with many of the old players under the direction of Donovan Richardson, a violinist. Another musical organization of the day was the Durham Choral Society, which also performed in Stokes Hall. Throughout the 1890s touring theatrical companies brought plays to Durham, among them *Kathleen Mavourneen, Pygmalion, East Lynn,* and *Uncle Tom's Cabin,* a surprising favorite despite its sensitive subject.[19]

High culture was, of course, not the general fare. Much more common were the ice cream parties, skating parties at the rink, "germans" for those who danced, or excursions to the various nearby mill ponds for those who picnicked or fished. Another kind of diversion that interested a large number of residents, and which was to become an annual event beginning in 1891, was the flower show organized by the ladies whose tastes ran to horticulture. Pleasure knew no bounds, however, when a circus came to town, "the gladdest day of all the year," one reporter called it.[20]

Nothing characterized the changed ambiance and exuberance of the opulent nineties quite as much as the new Hotel Carrolina, which J. S. Carr built in 1893 at Peabody and Corcoran streets facing the railroad. It replaced an earlier Carr hotel, the Claiborn, built on the same site by 1885 and named for Carr's father-in-law, Doctor Claiborn Parrish. The new hotel, in the luxury class and, at the time of its building, the best in the state, had seventy rooms centrally heated and ventilated and lighted by its own electric plant. Its public rooms were the height of elegance, not to say ostentation. The main hall and office were salmon and blue, the ladies' reception room light blue and ivory and furnished in Empire style; the gentlemen's reading room was Louis XV and the main parlor Louis XVI, in ivory and gold. The rooms were frescoed primarily by North Carolina artists, and the dining room, which could serve one hundred diners at a time, was hung with tapestries against soft green walls decorated with heraldic designs. It all cost $85,000. In gratitude, the leading citizens of the town, who had been unable to raise the money to capitalize a hotel for the town by their own efforts, fêted Carr at a dinner in the hotel. "No one does so much for Durham as he does," an editorial stated, "or does it with such graciousness." The hotel had a relatively short existence; it burned to the ground in 1907 while Carr was away from town. He sent two hundred dollars to the firemen in recognition of their efforts to save his prize hostelry.[21]

Durham had had a number of lesser hotels and boarding houses, beginning with Robert Morris's in 1858. In 1876 Durham had acquired the Grand Central Hotel, owned and operated by L. L. Hassell. There were also the Durham House, in front of the Baptist church, and later the Hopkins House, at Liberty and Cleveland streets, both operated by Alexander and Susan Hopkins, who had come from Granville County. The latter hostelry survived into the 1920s. The Driver House on Church Street south of Main was another early hostelry, run originally by J. T. and Nancy Driver. The Yearby House, like the other "houses," though called a hotel was actually a boardinghouse. It stood on Main Street between Roxboro and Church streets and was built at a time when only wooden shacks lined that part of Main Street. At the end of the 1890s, on the site of the Presley J. Mangum house at 326 Main Street, was built the Sans Souci. It was presided over by Mrs. Octa Thomas and later by Mrs. Lena Hessee. The Sans Souci was demolished in 1926 to make room for the Johnson Motor Company.[22]

SOCIAL PROBLEMS

While the 1890s had an opulent side for a privileged minority, the decade actually brought distress to many more, especially farmers and the urban poor. Increase of social problems—poverty, disease, and crime—was made shockingly clear by the economic depression and severe cold of 1893. The old rowdy areas of Smoky Hollow and Sugar Hill became scenes of more frequent and more violent crimes. At the beginning of January a dead baby was found in a trash dump at the edge of Smoky Hollow. A week later a black woman was found frozen to death. Churches began to send out relief committees to discover those suffering from cold and hunger and to make appeals for help from the general citizenry. Ever the paternalist, Julian Carr sent out his own team to distribute alms. In the space of one day, through all these efforts three hundred persons had been assisted with food, fuel, and clothing, but the size of the problem had already outgrown the only resource, private charity.[23]

The winter continued with a spate of robberies and more tragedies. January ended with a series of deaths within the town center that shocked the whole community out of any sense of complacency. They occurred in poor families living in the cellar of O'Briant's store, where a number of homeless people had sought shelter. A young mother of six children was found dead just one day after another young woman and her infant. To obtain help, the latter woman had some weeks before made an affidavit before a judge that James Norwood, a member of the state legislature from Orange County, was the father of her unborn child. The judge had sent a notice to Norwood to appear before him, but Norwood had never come, and the mother and infant perished. In February, Smoky Hollow was back in the news with a brutal murder, and the seamy life of that area was revealed in a court testimony. In April the town matrons could stand no more. They called a meeting of Smoky Hollow landlords in order to find out who owned the neglected dwellings and to try to persuade them to clean up their properties and take responsibility for the people to whom they rented.[24]

The *Globe* editor, Al Fairbrother, found these matters fair game. He gave no quarter to Norwood or to the kind of justice meted out to those protected by wealth or position. The town health officer, Dr. N. M. Johnson, ordered O'Briant to clean up his building and get rid of vermin, excrement, and garbage. Fairbrother called on women to organize a charity to take over the relief of the poor and needy on a continuing basis. The young women of the town met the challenge the next year and formed the Provident Club. Through Carr's generosity they obtained office space in the new First National Bank building in which to collect and distribute contributions of every kind. They assured possible critics that they would not interfere with regular church channels of charity but would reach those outside the arms of the church. The founders and officers of the group were Lida Carr, Mamie Heartt, Mabel Tomlinson, and Margaret Morehead. They could rightly be called the fore-runners of the Charity League, afterward the Junior Service League.[25]

The too-rapid growth of the city, the large influx of strangers in the factories and mills, and unhygienic living and working conditions created problems that the simple municipal government set up in Reconstruction times could no longer han-dle. Though the town had a water supply and one main sewer, it made no provision for the collection of garbage or for cleaning the mud- and manure-mired streets. Most people thought the role of government should be limited, and they actually resisted government interference, as they called it, in their lives. That the question was very much in their minds is seen in the topic the Trinity College Literary clubs chose to debate in 1896: "Resolved that the modern tendency of governments to increase their functions is dangerous to civilization." Efforts by the city and county, therefore, to expand their roles and address some of the more critical problems were often resisted.[26]

In no area was this more true than in medicine and the treatment of illness. The germ theory of disease had finally won acceptance, but remedies had not yet been found for most infectious diseases. If diagnosis was much improved, treatment was still largely palliative. An indication of the cultural lag in lay information was the popular response to poisonous bites. Up to 1900 and beyond, when someone was bitten by a presumably rabid dog, a "madstone" was instantly sent for. The Rever-end Alexander Walker, a lay preacher originally from Person County and a man-ager of the Bull factory, owned a madstone and generously lent it wherever it was needed. The porous stone was applied to a bite, where it would adhere, supposedly absorbing the poison until the wound was clean or the stone full, after which it would fall off. In 1900 came a change with the report of a child's death from rabies even though the madstone had been applied. The same year another story told of a number of persons bitten by a mad dog, which was killed immediately and its head sent to Raleigh for examination. Those bitten were also sent to Raleigh to receive "the Pasteur treatment." But folklore dies hard; in 1903 a child bitten at Stagville was said to have recovered when the madstone was used, and in 1912 the editor felt compelled to write a long essay about the folly of the madstone, obviously still in use.[27]

More credible but equally useless were many patent medicines of the day, con-sistently advertised (and purchased) to cure everything from coughs to impotence. Among the Durham entrepreneurs in this field were Charles McMannen, who con-cocted the American Tar Mixture for coughs and sore throats, which his brother John A. McMannen, Jr., manufactured; John M. Sears, with a cure-all for every-thing from ulcerated eyes to neuralgia, sour stomach, and corns; and H. G. Coleman with a Tobacco Oil Liniment and Medicated Tobacco Soap. Another tobacco cure was patented by General Thomas L. Clingman and manufactured by E. J. Parrish, J. S. Carr, and W. T. Blackwell, who organized the Clingman Tobacco Cure Com-pany. Leonidas L. Polk, the illustrious Populist candidate for president, editor of the *Progressive Farmer,* and commissioner of agriculture for North Carolina, made up and patented a medicine to cure diphtheria, in the manufacture of which he tried to interest the Dukes. Benjamin Duke, however, had already put money into a treatment of nearer interest to him: the Keeley Institute in Greensboro for the treatment of alcohol and drug addiction, which had been established in 1892. Brodie Duke had benefited from Dr. Leslie E. Keeley's cure in Dwight, Illinois, in 1891–92, and had been instrumental in establishing the Greensboro operation. The directors included Durhamites Leo Heartt, A. K. Umstead, J. B. Warren, J. F. Slaughter, George Watts, and Alexander Walker; the medical director was Dr. W. J. Hugh Durham.[28]

Meanwhile the physicians were concerning themselves with other medical problems. They recognized that contaminated water threatened the general health of the populace, and having pushed the aldermen to obtain a pure water supply, they were now advocating a comprehensive sewage system. In July 1894 the town health officer, Dr. Neal P. Boddie, and the county health officer, Dr. John M. Manning, declared that the city should devote its attention to a sewer system rather than to paving streets, because an epidemic of typhoid fever was in the making. Despite the urgency of the plea no action was taken; a year later there was still no sewer system.[29] Water was responsible for more than typhoid. Malaria was a scourge each summer in rural areas, particularly where marshland and still water provided mosquitoes with breeding grounds.

The first town government had been authorized to appoint a board of health consisting of two persons. At their May 1872 meeting the aldermen had appointed Dr. W. J. H. Durham and Captain Freeland to the board. They had recommended an ordinance requiring the regular cleaning of privies, the clearing of trash and refuse from town lots, the draining of certain pools, and ditching to prevent others' forming. The powers of this board were unfortunately only advisory; when the councilmen adopted the recommendations and formulated ordinances to give them the force of law, they aroused so much opposition that they weakly ignored violations rather than incur citizen wrath. In 1875 the town had appointed a health officer, provided for in the revised city charter that year, to enforce the statutes, but the situation had not improved even as late as the 1890s.[30]

The decade ended with another disease scare when John C. Angier's driver, Tom Lucky, came down with smallpox. Lucky and his family were removed to the pest-house at the poorhouse farm. Trinity Park (the college campus), not far from Caswell Heights where the Angiers lived, issued an ordinance of quarantine against all persons living on the south side of the railroad tracks between Milton Avenue and Erwin Mills and south to Burch Street, an area that included Brookstown and Caswell Heights. Erwin Mills followed suit. The city passed a law the following year stating that all persons must have been vaccinated within seven years, excluding only those to whom vaccination might prove injurious. A fine was threatened for noncompliance. Nonetheless, three years later the city was still unable to enforce the ordinance: it was seen as an infringement of personal liberty.[31]

On another medical front, however, progress was made. Although Dr. A. G. Carr's own efforts to found a hospital had failed, his example had influenced his patient George Watts in 1894 to give a hospital to the town. Watts had himself experienced the comfort and care of expert hospital nursing, and he saw that a hospital would be an important contribution to the people of Durham "to whom he felt gratitude." At that time many people looked on a hospital as a place to go to die; therefore rejoicing over the gift was somewhat tempered. Watts hired the Boston firm of Rand and Taylor to design the hospital, which when built consisted of a central administrative building, forty by forty feet, flanked by two patient wings, one for men and one for women, connected by glazed colonnades—all frame. In the basement were housed a laundry and an autopsy room. The hospital was built on four acres at the intersection of then Guess Road (now Buchanan Boulevard) and Main Street. It catered to whites only, and many of its beds were reserved for charity patients. Watts donated the hospital to the county at a meeting at Stokes Hall on 21 February 1895.[32]

Watts's philanthropy in Durham has been overshadowed by James B. Duke's later munificence, but at the time of Watts's death in 1921, his obituary correctly stated that he was the greatest philanthropist that North Carolina had produced. He had built not only the first hospital and its replacement (1908–10), costing well over a million dollars, later additions to the hospital, and three consecutive sanctuaries for the First Presbyterian Church, but he had also built Watts Hall and the chapel at Richmond's Union Theological Seminary, made large donations to Elizabeth College in Charlotte, to missionaries in Cuba, Korea, and Africa, and to Davidson and Flora Macdonald colleges and Barium Springs Orphanage in North Carolina.[33]

A CRITIC TAKES AIM

It is difficult to reconcile the Watts of these humanitarian impulses with the picture Fairbrother drew of him in his *Globe* attacks, or to write off his charity as a sop to an uneasy conscience. The editor first attacked Watts in 1891, in relation to an alleged fraud committed by the Durham Fertilizer Company: the sale of many bags of fertilizer without revenue stamps. Watts's links with this company were as a director and brother-in-law of its co-owner (with Samuel Tate Morgan), Louis Carr. Less than a month later Fairbrother reminded his readers that although Watts had agreed to take up the whole issue of bonds to finance the graded school, he had reneged when he discovered that instead of 6 percent, they paid only 5 percent. If Fairbrother had been content to denounce something once, he might have got away with that, for people have short memories. But he hammered away at the same themes again and again. He went too far in November 1893 in reporting the outcome of Richard Wright's unsuccessful suit against the Dukes. "It seems that Watts, as we believe is his habit, and as has been shown in the *Globe* as to his style in general, played double. . . . No honest man would believe as sorry a creature as George Watts," whom he then finished off with the characterization of a "polite Presbyterian liar."[34]

Fairbrother was immediately visited by a delegation protesting his treatment of respectable citizens. He apologized but was very soon giving his side of the story and casting aspersions on the delegation's credibility in characterizing themselves as representative of Durham. Fairbrother clearly had to go. He was forced to sell the paper and prevented by an injunction from publishing any other paper in the state.[35] There was concern that he would take up a position in a nearby town and continue his barrage of grapeshot against the city fathers.

Watts was not the only one at whom Fairbrother took aim. The superintendent of the graded schools, Edwin W. Kennedy, Robert I. Rogers, Holman, the water company, A. M. Rigsbee, the city aldermen, revivalists, and slum landlords all took his fire.[36] Along with this sniping he injected large amounts of fun and spoofing into his newspaper, and there were larger topics to engage his attention. One of them was the way of life for the workers in the new mill villages. All former farm people, they had given up the isolation of the farm and its contest with poor soil and increasing debt in favor of known wages for all the family, nominal rents for housing superior to tenant farms, in a sociable village with compatible people. For many of them life had never been so endurable. A store (often run by the company) supplied their daily needs, and the company provided a church for Sunday worship. On the face of it there seemed to be little to complain about. Keen observers like Fairbrother, however, saw inherent evils in the arrangement, which became apparent to the workers only over a span of years.

> The cotton mill at East Durham which has worked hands till 8 o'clock at night, and started the hands from sleep at 4:30 in the morning and given men like Odell a chance to get very rich, and fellows like the creature Branson a chance to get fat off of human toil—well the concern, we learn, has sold its company store, and will hereafter pay by the week and let the poor devils spend the little they get whenever and however they may please.
>
> This is business, and the fewer concerns which monkey with human toil as this thing at East Durham has done, the better for communities and the better for all men except those who receive their bread absolutely from the sweat of other men's brows.[37]

Fairbrother alludes to the poor wages, long hours, curtailment of freedom, and general exploitation of the workers. He could have added the more telling indictments that would be the weapons of the fight for reforms after the turn of the century: the deprivation of schooling for the children of these families and the health hazard to them all. A third evil more clearly seen in retrospect than by the workers was the paternalism by which the mill managed not just the working hours of its laborers but their private lives as well. Morality, religion, recreation, health, and welfare—all in time came to be areas of management's concern and control. The result was a large population that had no experience and often no desire to make its own decisions or direct its own lives. Dependency, obedience, and unquestioning acceptance of authority formed the other face of paternalism.

THE COTTON INDUSTRY

After Carr had led the way, the Commonwealth Club members decided to establish a cooperative cotton factory, actually a stock company, which they incorporated in

1890 as the Commonwealth Manufacturing Company. The heaviest investors were Brodie Duke, J. S. Carr, and Richard H. Wright. Correspondence between Carr and Wright in 1892 discloses that the mill manager, Holman, managed the mill badly and Carr wanted to get out of the enterprise. He told Wright that Brodie Duke was prepared to take it off their hands and give them seventy-five cents on the dollar for their shares. Reluctantly Wright acceded, and Brodie Duke took it over as the main stockholder. The factory, which made yarn and hosiery, was small, beginning with only 6,400 spindles and 58 knitting machines. By 1892 Duke had a larger textile venture also under way. He incorporated the Pearl Cotton Mills in 1892 (named after his daughter) and built a three-story factory 89 by 225 feet, with picker, engine, and boiler rooms, in which 10,000 spindles and sixty looms eventually manufactured wide sheeting. The mills were located on the Beltline Railroad, part of which he had completed in 1891. Duke owned very large acreage in North Durham, which he wanted to develop. He built housing beside the mill for two hundred workers and a small church. He completed plans for this mill and its environs as a boom town by incorporating North Durham. Of that little municipality he was elected mayor; the commissioners were R. B. Boone, Edwin Thompson, W. L. Cooper, F. C. Geer, and H. E. Seeman. Unfortunately Brodie Duke was caught short in the financial crisis of 1893 and lost everything. Since the Pearl Mills had not then been completed, the stockholders decided to complete them. In 1894 Mabel Duke, another of Brodie's daughters, set in motion the machinery run by a 300-horsepower Corliss engine. The reorganized company elected George Watts president and Branson secretary, treasurer, and general manager.[38]

Apparently when Brodie Duke went bankrupt, Benjamin Duke took over his shares of the Commonwealth Mill. By 1900 Brodie Duke was president again and probably in possession of his original holdings, thanks to the rescue by his brother. The factory then had 7,000 spindles and 140 employees making colored hosiery and underwear yarns.[39]

Benjamin Duke, acting for himself and others of the family, was soon following Carr's and his brother's lead. In April 1892 he incorporated the Erwin Cotton Mills. Operations began 16 June 1893. Benjamin Duke had been persuaded to this move by William A. Erwin, a member of the Holt family of the Alamance County textile mills; consequently he was hired by Duke to be secretary and treasurer of the company and to run the mills. In their preliminary negotiations Erwin had promised Duke that his financial return would be 40 percent of his investment. A man highly praised by his former employers and with long experience in the business, Erwin was given full responsibility for the mills' success or failure, and because of that Duke gave the new enterprise the Erwin name. The new company bought several adjacent tracts of land in West Durham across the tracks from the Blacknalls' property and built a brick factory 75 by 347 feet, two stories high, with a picker building, dyehouse, boiler room, and engine house. Rows of neat houses beside the factory were built for the workers, who in 1895 numbered 375. The factory then had 11,000 spindles and 360 looms producing fine muslin, chambrays, camlets, and denims. The workers were provided with a building for a Sunday school, and Erwin set aside a tract of land in front of the factory for a park.[40]

Two hosiery companies joined Durham's textile industry in 1895; George W. Graham, Paul Cameron Graham, and George P. Collins, heirs of Paul Cameron, started the Durham Hosiery Company, and J. S. Carr, the Golden Belt Hosiery Company. The latter company, using both cotton and silk, was set up to make ladies' and children's stockings and men's socks, 750 dozen pairs a day. The factory was located on Mangum Street in the Parrish Building, in which the First National Bank had begun its existence. Both companies limped along until they merged in 1898 and were incorporated in that year as the Durham Hosiery Mills, a firm destined for success. Special tariff protection for hosiery, the Dingley Tariff Act of 1898, and the Spanish-American War were fortuitous coincidences for the new company. Carr established the Carolina Hosiery Company in New York as a commission firm to sell the products from the Durham textile and hosiery mills as well as those from other places.[41]

There was rejoicing that Carr's mills were to be built in Smoky Hollow, for they would wipe out at last the "dark hole of iniquity and infamy." Charles H. Norton got the construction bid to build the 385-by-103-foot building and a bag factory 161 by 78 feet. A cotton house 148 by 79 feet and an engine and boiler house 121 by 47 feet were part of the original complex of brick buildings trimmed with granite. A reservoir 200 by 60 feet was also included in the plan. New streets with floral names and rows of pretty cottages, it was hoped, would erase the old image with the old slum. As the newspaper phrased it, "Edgemont will be the beautiful industrial silkworm that will come from the Smoky Hollow cocoon."[42]

TAMING THE BULL

Julian Carr's switch to the textile industry gave him a new financial base as his interest in the tobacco company declined. After the Blackwell Company's reorganization in 1883 and 1887, it failed to pursue the aggressive policies that had kept it not only competitive but ahead of the pack. Up against the might and money of the American Tobacco Company, it soon faltered. Carr recognized the inevitable and went forward to meet it. As early as 1891 there were rumors of a merger of the Blackwell Company and the American Tobacco Company. In 1892 more rumors accused the Dukes of forcing Carr's company to join the trust. B. N. Duke publicly denied this, stating that Carr's associates had in fact approached the American Tobacco Company in New York with an offer to sell, which had been refused. Carr was at the time toying with becoming a candidate for office and was making political hay of his antitrust stance. A long statement by Duke reveals that though Carr claimed that he had had nothing to do with the negotiations, he had in fact agreed to receive stock in the American Tobacco Company and remain as manager of the Blackwell company after its sale.[43]

No merger took place at this time. In 1896, Carr once more approached the American Tobacco Company, offering this time to sell the Golden Belt bag manufacturing company. Again the offer was refused. In 1898, however, the Blackwell Company was bought by the Union Tobacco Company, and three financiers of that company, Thomas F. Ryan, P. A. B. Widener, and W. S. Elkins, soon afterward obtained control of the stock and resold it to the American Tobacco Company. Many people in Durham were incensed that a northern company had been able to get control of the Blackwell firm, the original source of Durham's phenomenal success. William A. Guthrie, Carr's brother-in-law and holder of one share, took the lead in fighting the takeover and petitioned the legislature for the appointment of a receiver and a rechartering and reorganization of the company. The American Tobacco Company then obtained a bill of equity and brought suit against Guthrie and other minority stockholders. When the case was heard the judge ordered the company into receivership and appointed as receiver Percival Hill, the representative of the American Tobacco Company who had come to Durham to forestall Guthrie's action. The company was next advertised for sale at auction and was bought by the American Tobacco Company for $4 million. Guthrie refused to give up. In 1906 he, George R., and James W. Blackwell, incorporated the Blackwell Durham Tobacco Company of New Jersey and sued the American Tobacco Company, which they claimed had no right to the name or the brand of the old company. The case was summarily dismissed.[44]

The people of Durham lost more than control of their factory. Perhaps symbolic of a new age was the demolition of the structure at the corner of Carr and Pettigrew streets in which Durham had held its very first tobacco auction in 1871. Also symbolic of the end of an era was the death of Mrs. B. N. Duke's father, Squire Malbourne Angier, on the last day of the year 1900. Honest ambition, hard work, steadiness, and pluck like his would no longer suffice to compete in the new industrial world of high finance and high stakes. The Dukes had mastered the new world, but the Dukes were not to be long in Durham. In 1900 Benjamin Duke decided not to build an elegant new house in Durham but to follow the firm to New York. He bought a large house at the corner of Eighty-second Street and Fifth Avenue and moved permanently, though he always maintained a home in Durham. Other civic leaders, too, were drawn off by the giant American Tobacco Company and the Dukes, who were always good judges of men; Durham was being drained of its talent just as it had once drained its neighboring communities.[45]

The Bull factory's bankruptcy was a reflection of troubled economic times. Julian Carr, like many others in 1893 and afterward, sustained financial reverses. As a remedy for the national insolvency, he proposed to the U.S. House Ways and Means Committee a large increase in the tax on manufactured tobacco. Anguished cries came from fellow manufacturers, who were outraged by what they perceived as his treachery. Carr was not afraid to stand by his principles, popular or not. "My theory is," he explained, "tax the luxuries and allow the necessaries to go as near free of taxation as it is possible."[46] Carr never lost the esteem of his peers, however, and in 1896 they elected him president of the newly organized Southern Tobacco Manufacturers' Association.[47] Carr was not a simple man to understand. Along with his profession of religious convictions and moral principles, lavish generosity, and concern about others in need, he was touchy, vain, and volatile, with a sometimes uncontrollable temper. Nor did he hesitate to protect his interest or to foreclose on his brothers-in-law J. S. Lockhart and E. J. Parrish, who had badly overextended themselves in real estate and lost heavily in the depression of 1893. Lockhart moved to Danville, where he continued to engage in the tobacco business, and the Dukes finally came to Parrish's rescue.

Although Parrish lost his real estate, most of it either sold at auction or taken over by Carr, J. B. Duke helped him manage his large debts and in 1899 hired him to go to Japan to represent the American Tobacco Company's interest there. The Japanese government had a monopoly on the importation of tobacco and imposed prohibitive tariffs on manufactured products. To circumvent these regulations, the American Tobacco Company bought a controlling interest in the Japanese Murai Brothers Company and needed an executive there to oversee the manufacture and marketing of its products. Parrish proved to be the perfect choice. He was experienced, polite, convivial, honorable in business, conscientious to a fault, and determined to prove himself to Duke. Part of his salary was deducted regularly to pay off his debts, but when he returned permanently to Durham in 1904, after the Japanese government had taken over the tobacco industry, he was clear of debt and once more financially flush. He had also won the American Tobacco Company favorable terms in the final negotiations, largely through his own popularity and esteem. He was a genuinely likable man and came home a hero, decorated by the Japanese government.[48]

Despite the bitterness of their business competition and the ignominy for Carr of losing the Blackwell Company to the American Tobacco Company trust, Carr's urbanity enabled him to maintain with Benjamin Duke the usual social relations of surface amicability. Typically he closed a letter to Duke in 1896 by inviting Duke to come out and spend a night at his farm, adding, "bring Angier with you." The farm mentioned was his country estate of over one thousand acres outside Hillsborough, which he called Occoneechee. Originally the home of James Hogg and afterward of Hogg's daughter Robina, who had married William Norwood, Carr added a double-storied portico to the front and a wing to the back of the old farmhouse, which stood on a bluff overlooking the Eno River. He built fine barns for livestock and with the latest agricultural methods was making Occoneechee a model farm. In 1893 he was elected president of the state Agricultural Society.[49]

The nineties saw a nostalgic interest in rural property as it became fashionable for rich men to buy places in the country—farms, hunting lodges, retreats—wishing to escape the very towns they had worked so hard to build up. Benjamin Duke bought many small tracts and put together a farm of over two thousand acres, the Meadows, near University Station on the old road to Hillsborough. John T. Hogan, his farm manager, regularly sent him rather discouraging reports on the farming operations. In 1895 Duke added a large frame house (still standing) with wide porches facing the road to Hillsborough near University Station. In the next decade, James H. Southgate built on the top of a nearby hill a two-story log house in which he entertained friends with his magnificent view of the countryside by day and the stars by night. The young members of the Fun-Lovers Club were entertained by Southgate once in their giddy youth and remembered it thirty years later as "the grandest place with cozy corners galore. There were thirty of us at University Station. . . . We sat around a big log fire and Mr. Southgate was grand to us. We all kissed him good-bye."[50]

The plight of the farmer was responsible for the success of Populism, a third-party political movement that swept onto the scene in the 1890s and shook up the status quo before weakening from internal division and fading away. It left in its wake a resurgence of racial hostility that was felt in the South through most of the twentieth century. Behind the creation of the Populist Party lay the ever-worsening agricultural economy and the desperate farmers. They had been steadily ignored since the 1870s while more and more of them lost their land and became either tenants and sharecroppers or workers in mills and factories. Farmers were unable to cope with the continually falling prices of farm products, high tariffs, freight rates, fertilizer costs, and a system of credit that pushed them always further into debt, favoring as it did the creditor over the debtor. Their patience exhausted, they welcomed the Farmers' Alliance that came into the state in the late 1880s as a ray of hope, and they joined in droves. The alliance program was not at first political; it called for cooperation and mutual trust in working out economic and social solutions to farm problems and sponsored cooperative ventures of various types. Bad management, insufficient capital, and hostility from merchants and banks, however, prevented their enterprises from succeeding, and the alliance itself declined as an effective organization after a political split in its ranks. Its ideas and criticism were sound, nevertheless, and had a tremendous political impact.[51]

Its leadership looked first to the Democratic Party, to which most alliance members belonged, to achieve its goals, but when Democratic legislators voted down a bill they had promised to pass, the agrarian radicals in their midst separated from the Democrats and formed the Populist Party to pursue the goals they sought. They saw as vitally important the regulation of railroads to eliminate rebates and rate discrimination, to reduce freight charges, and to force railroads to pay their share of taxes; they also pushed for the subtreasury plan—government storehouses and credit—to enable farmers to sell at top prices and borrow on their crops at little cost.[52]

The new party was an immediate threat to the Democratic Party that had ruled the state, if only by a small majority, since the end of Reconstruction. In Durham County it attracted those who had been most active in the Farmers' Alliance and those who had earlier belonged to what was called the Third Party. The result was great political confusion through the 1890s as the Populists gained strength, and both Democrats and Republicans tried to join hands with them to benefit from their support at the polls. Though the new party was composed largely of former Democrats and some Republicans, it did not attract the Dukes because of its prime tenet that trusts were a cause of the farmers' poverty.[53]

Conservative Democrats saw the Populists as radicals. In 1892, when the Republican Party offered no election slate, Frank L. Fuller, a Democrat, appealed successfully to the Dukes for support in his campaign for the legislature. He described his opponent, P. H. Massey, as "conceited, bigoted, boastful, arrogant, and blasphemous," "at heart an anarchist," and "an enemy of capital and thrift." This was Patrick, not Pleasant H. Massey, the ardent Methodist who preached tirelessly without compensation all around the county to Baptists and Methodists alike and organized the local farmers into Alliance chapters.[54] On the other hand, to an independent thinker like Robert Winston, a birthright member of the planter class and a Democratic member of the General Assembly in 1884, the Democrats were more to be feared. They were undemocratic, self-serving, and repressive of blacks. Local councilmen and commissioners were amateurish and slipshod; lacking budgets and audits, they failed to account to the citizens for the spending of their tax money; they muddled along while the magnitude of their problems outgrew their capacity to deal with them. Winston was heartened when "the toilers became articulate."[55]

An articulate leader of the Populists was Leonidas Polk, North Carolina Commissioner of Agriculture and publisher of the *Progressive Farmer,* who was expected to become the party nominee for president of the United States in 1892. His sudden death a few weeks before the convention, however, left the party temporarily floundering and dealt a blow to its election hopes that year. In the 1894 state and local elections, the Populists had a chance at capturing the reins. Their choice for governor, William A. Guthrie, a brother-in-law of Carr, outlined their party's national goals: unlimited coinage of silver, abolition of the national banks, a graduated income tax, election reforms including the election of senators by popular vote and the return of power to the people in choosing county commissioners, extension of the public school system, more funds to education, and equal rights and equal protection for all. Durhamites who supported the party were Pleasant Massey, J. T. Cash, J. W. Ferrell, J. E. Cole, D. C. Mangum, A. M. Leathers, William Gaston Vickers, William Jasper Christian, John V. Rigsbee, T. J. Holloway, W. W. Woods, and Dr. Y. E. Young. Thomas Settle, a Republican, was the Populist and Republican parties' choice for the House of Representatives. A Populist alliance with the Republicans swept some of each party into office. Only one Democrat won on the local Durham scene. While in office in 1895 the Populists enacted much good legislation. They returned local government to the people with a new election law that also set up fairer procedures; they restricted the legal interest rate to 6 percent; they made large appropriations to state colleges and normal schools, and increased the property tax allocated to public schools.[56]

The 1896 election was more confused than the earlier ones because the Populists supported Republicans on the local level, joined the Democrats on the national scene to support William J. Bryan for president, and nominated their own candidates for governor, lieutenant governor, and auditor. They won many offices, but the Republican candidate for governor, Daniel L. Russell, won out over Guthrie and the Democrat in a three-way race. The new county commission included A. D. Markham, J. B. Warren, and W. D. Turrentine; other winners were clerk of superior court, W. J. Christian; county attorney, Howard A. Foushee; register of deeds, W. W. Woods; sheriff, Felix D. Markham; county treasurer, T. J. Holloway; and coroner, Dr. M. P. Ward—a mixture of Populists and Democrats except for Warren, a Republican. In 1898 the Republicans and Populists agreed to fuse again, and divided up the county offices in their slate of candidates, but the Democrats built their campaign around a surefire issue, white supremacy, and won handily. During the short time that the Republicans and Populists were in power, the black presence had again become politically noticeable at the polls. Though this effect was seen only in minor offices, it was enough to rekindle in white southerners' breasts the fear smoldering there from Reconstruction days, the specter of "Negro domination." When the Democrats, purposely capitalizing on this emotion, shouted fire, many joined the hue and cry. The election result was overwhelming.[57]

Once back in office, the Democrats went to work to entrench themselves and limit as much as possible the influence of black votes on any future election. The means they devised to this end was a constitutional amendment that would require a poll tax and a literacy test for voters. The dilemma this posed for them was how to eliminate the blacks without also eliminating the illiterate whites. The "grand-father" clause, an amendment to the state constitution, was the solution. By this clause anyone who had been entitled to vote on or before 1867 or his lineal descendant, despite an inability to read, could continue to vote, provided he registered before the last day of 1908. The amendment was passed in the summer of 1900.[58]

In his 1900 campaign for governor, Charles Aycock at first campaigned on the race issue as a believer in white supremacy and the disfranchisement of illiterate blacks. But Aycock soon made education for all the main plank of his platform, a cause that found much general support. Education in North Carolina was much in need of improvement. Insufficient schools, poorly qualified teachers, rundown facilities, lack of books, and a short school year resulted in miserably educated children. Although Durham County had the best-supported school system in the state, it was only the best of a bad situation, and voters were finally recognizing both the importance of education to economic security and the inadequacy of what was generally available to them. Thus the Democrats had an unbeatable combination of issues in their 1900 campaign, with education and racial discrimination cutting across party lines.

The Populists in Durham County, however, did not give up without a fight. Some of them spoke out against the injustice to blacks of the constitutional amendment, but this issue seriously divided them; the Democratic position won adherents from both the Populist and Republican parties. When the anti-amendment Populist candidates staged a rally in East Durham, the crowd became unruly and threw eggs at the speakers. Epps Walton, a candidate for state representative, told them that there was race prejudice in North Carolina, reminding them that God made the colored man and asking whether he was to be disregarded. Speaking at another rally, D. C. Mangum said, "My God! Talk about negro domination, I have never seen it." He warned the crowd that if the amendment passed, "an office-holding oligarchy" would be fastened on the people of North Carolina, words that proved true. It took courageous men to espouse an unpopular viewpoint and speak out against injustice.[59]

The editor of the *Sun* was not, however, among them. That paper blatantly sided with the Democrats and indulged in ugly journalism during the campaign. Sticking by one's race was made to seem the ultimate loyalty; justice did not enter into the question. The newspaper reported at length the campaign of the Democrats, who held a parade led by J. D. Pleasants, flourishing a "white supremacy" banner and followed by a band and a white float with sixteen young ladies all attired in white carrying small white flags. Streamers on each side of the float proclaimed, "Protect us with your vote." Victor S. Bryant was the main speaker to a crowd of three hundred.[60]

Despite the enormous Democratic victory, a few fusion candidates won magistrate races in the county: G. A. Barbee and Stanford Pickett in Patterson Township, W. H. Perry, A. M. Sorrell, and Sam Davis in Oak Grove Township, and James Henderson and Thomas Lipscomb in Lebanon Township. With victory in hand, the *Sun* adopted a very different tone. In place of hostility and insults, it spoke with arrogance and paternalistic condescension: "The unlettered and unlearned colored man will then [1902] cease to be a voter and a disturbing element in the political life of this state." In voting for black disfranchisement, the paper hypocritically explained, "The white people bear no ill will towards the negro. They do not propose to harm him, or hurt him in any way, but on the other hand protect him and save him from his white allies who have traded on his vote and secured offices [for him] to rule over white people." It concluded on this ringing note: "North Carolina belongs to white men and they intend to rule her, and rule her peacefully."[61] White women, who as members of the disfranchised majority of the population might have been expected to have a different view of the subject, held their peace and bided their time.

BLACK BUSINESS

During the very years when racial fires were burning hottest, when Democrats were wresting back control of the state, disfranchising blacks and openly violating their rights, and when most whites were blinking at lynchings if not approving them, the black sector of Durham was making strides in business that would shortly give the lie to the white supremacy argument. Just as a small group of white entrepreneurs had harnessed opportunity and ridden it to success, a similar group of remarkable blacks cooperated in new dreams and made them reality. The most prominent were John Merrick (1859–1919), Dr. Aaron McDuffie Moore (1863–1923), William Gaston Pearson (1859–1940), James E. Shepard (1875–1947), Richard Burton Fitzgerald (c. 1842–1918), and Charles Clinton Spaulding (1874–1952). Many others were associated with them and lent money and effort, but this group provided the leadership, initiative, and daring.

Merrick, the son of an ex-slave and a white man, learned bricklaying as a boy and worked first in Chapel Hill and later in Raleigh. His next job as a bootblack in a barber shop led to his picking up a new skill. John Wright, a barber in the store, persuaded him to move to Durham, where Wright intended to go into business for himself. Soon after the move in 1880, Merrick bought half interest in Wright's business and then the entire enterprise, opening his own store on 6 March 1882. Over the course of a decade the business expanded until it included five shops, three for whites and two for blacks. Although he had no formal education, he had learned to read and write, and with his native intelligence, perseverance, and knack of getting along with whites he had all he needed to launch and succeed in larger undertakings.[62]

Because of Merrick's position as Washington Duke's barber, an association that provided trips to New York and glimpses into the world of business tycoons, much has been conjectured about Duke's role in his success. Duke has been credited with bringing Merrick to Durham and even with supplying the idea that in 1898 grew into the North Carolina Mutual and Provident Association (later the North Carolina Mutual Life Insurance Company). It is doubtful that Duke did more than encourage Merrick in whatever ideas he conceived, perhaps giving him practical advice on how to put them into action. Merrick's experience with the Royal Knights of King David, a semi-religious fraternal and beneficial society for health and life insurance, was probably a much more direct influence. Merrick, Wright, W. A. Day, J. D. Morgan, and T. J. Jones had bought the society lock, stock, and barrel in 1883. Through the years as treasurer of the society, Merrick learned much about the insurance business in relation to blacks.[63]

At that time their short life expectancy and often precarious health made blacks poor insurance risks. In 1900 life expectancy for black men at birth was 32.5 years and for women only a year longer. Yet for those same reasons they badly needed insurance, and white companies either refused to insure them or charged exorbitant premiums and paid reduced benefits. Merrick found willing investors in 1898 and founded the North Carolina Mutual and Provident Society with fellow investors Moore, Pearson, D. T. Watson (a tinsmith), Shepard, E. A. Johnson (a lawyer and dean of Shaw University Law School), and P. W. Dawkins. When it was actually incorporated, T. O. Fuller, a black representative in the North Carolina legislature, and N. C. Bruce became incorporators while Dawkins's name was removed. Fuller had faced many delays and political hurdles to effect the incorporation, unquestionably because of white blocking tactics, but with the charter finally in hand the business began 1 April 1899. Merrick became president, Moore treasurer and medical director, and Watson secretary and office manager. That first year the company did so poorly that it lost money, and many of the investors withdrew. A reorganization left only Merrick and Moore as principals; a young cousin of Moore's, Charles Clinton Spaulding, was hired to keep the office.[64]

Spaulding had had a series of jobs: dishwasher, bellhop, and butler, working part-time in Judge Winston's household while he attended Whitted School. After graduation he managed a grocery company for a year before accepting the job at the Mutual. Both Spaulding and Moore were natives of Columbus County and descendants of free blacks with a long landholding and farming tradition. In common with Merrick, they had driving ambition and mental and physical energy. Dr. Moore brought to the business professional medical training; his judgment on the issuance of policies was critical to the business's success. Merrick and Moore saw the company as a way to help their fellow blacks. Their other livelihoods, moreover, freed them to risk the venture, for they could dip into their own pockets to keep the business solvent during times of crisis.[65]

Given the racial climate that demanded the separation of the races, blacks were thrown more and more on their own resources. Fortunately, in Durham indifference had a prettier face: tolerance, which W. E. B. Du Bois after his 1912 visit identified as what made Durham different from other places in the South. "I consider the greatest factor in Durham's development to have been the disposition of Durham to say 'Hands off—give them a chance—don't interfere.'" This attitude characterized both Washington Duke and Julian Carr. Although Moore with his normal and medical school education, his innate reserve, independence of action, and conservative demeanor, was not typical of blacks of their acquaintance, they found in Merrick a man adroit at conforming to their ideal Negro—deferential, good-humored, obliging—and at the same time capable of playing his own game, clever, and adept at his trade. He could exploit the white man's sense of superiority in an advertisement such as one he inserted in the newspaper in 1900 for his "Old Reliable, Nine Chair Barber Shop," in which he boasted that he had sterilized not just the mugs, towels, and razors, but "the whole shop, negro and all." Judge Winston, a keen observer of character, contrasted Merrick and Spaulding. He saw Merrick as old-fashioned, kind, contented, plump, pleasant-looking, jolly, gracious, and willing to kowtow to white men, while Spaulding, a new type, was lean, Cassius-like, and seldom smiled. "He sought no tips. All he asked of life was an open field and a fair chance. He was strictly business."[66]

Merrick invested the profits from his shops in real estate, and built houses with lumber from old tobacco warehouses that Duke contracted with him to remove. Moore, too, had other irons in the fire. He was instrumental in persuading George Watts of the need of a hospital for blacks. Watts, whose hospital had excluded blacks, was thinking of adding a wing for them. Moore, however, made him understand that black doctors needed a hospital in which to practice and care for their own patients. The black population was expanding as fast as the white, and one wing would not long suffice. Watts conveyed his concern to the Dukes, as did Dr. Albert Gallatin Carr, their doctor; Merrick, their barber; W. H. Armstrong, Washington Duke's butler; and Mrs. Addie Evans, his cook.[67]

Benjamin and James Duke agreed to build a hospital and located it at the corner of Proctor Street and Cozart Alley. President Kilgo of Trinity College wrote to Benjamin Duke about the laying of the cornerstone 4 July 1901, "Your father and I had a big time with the negroes on the fourth. They were laying the corner-stone of the Lincoln Hospital and asked me to make them a speech, which I did. I gave your father credit for the hospital, and everybody shouted over it; but afterwards he told me 'Ben and Buck are building this.'" Washington Duke's name, however, is included with his sons' on the cornerstone. Their purpose in giving the hospital is stated on a plaque, which embodies one of the favorite and significantly misleading myths of the post–Civil War South. "With grateful appreciation and loving remembrance of the fidelity and faithfulness of the Negro slaves to the Mothers and Daughters of the Confederacy during the Civil War, this institution was founded by one of the Fathers and Sons. . . . Not one act of disloyalty was recorded against them."[68]

Merrick became president of the hospital board of directors, and Moore, the acknowledged founder, was made superintendent. A frame structure accommodating fifty patients was the first hospital. The first annual report (1902) submitted by W. G. Pearson, secretary, showed that the hospital had treated seventy-five patients, of whom eight had died of pneumonia. In 1910 a nurses' training school was added, which became very useful in providing nurses for the community. Despite the addition of a wing, within a short time the hospital had been outgrown, and by the time of World War I, the facilities were both cramped and outmoded. Recognizing the need, the Dukes again assumed the responsibility and in 1921 offered $75,000, which was matched by the city, county, and black and white citizens, to build a much larger, well-equipped hospital. The Dukes, Watts, and John Sprunt Hill donated the home tract of the A. H. Stokes estate on Fayetteville Street between Linwood Street and Massey Avenue, on which a brick building designed by the architectural firm of Milburn and Heister was erected for $150,000. The buildings of the original hospital were donated in 1925 to the black Ministers' Alliance to be used for an old people's and orphans' home. John C. Scarborough, the donor, who had moved to Durham in the 1890s from Kinston, said it had been the dream of his life to do something for the unfortunate ones of his race in Durham. The concept was later expanded to include a day nursery, the origin of the Scarborough nursery.[69]

Like Merrick and Moore, the other black leaders had multiple business interests. In 1895 Moore had as partners in establishing the Durham Drug Company (a drugstore) Pearson, Fitzgerald, Shepard, and J. A. Dodson. Fitzgerald, besides his brick manufactory, was president of the Coleman Cotton Mill in Concord, Cabarrus County, organized by a group of black businessmen with the help of Washington Duke. Fitzgerald was also president of the Real Estate, Mercantile, and Manufacturing Company, incorporated in the spring of 1899 with Peyton H. Smith of Durham and D. A. Lane of Washington, D.C. The company operated a general merchandise store as well as a tobacco factory, producing "New Durham" and "The 1900" brands of tobacco. In 1901 Shepard ran a real estate loans and investments business.[70]

RELIGION

While business and industry were new fields of endeavor for blacks in the South, churches, their first institutions, remained at the center of their lives. The two largest and most prosperous black congregations were Saint Joseph's, Merrick's church, and White Rock Baptist, Moore's church. Both churches were rebuilt in brick in the 1890s. White Rock Baptist was completed in 1896 under the inspired leadership of their minister, Allen P. Eaton, who has been called "a spiritual giant." Increasing wealth and education, however, were becoming divisive factors in the black community; those lucky enough to obtain them were turning away from the old forms of worship to more intellectual, restrained, unemotional services, and they wanted their clergy to be educated men. When this shift occurred in White Rock Baptist Church, Eaton left his old congregation and started Saint John Baptist church on Dunstan Street in 1898. More modest congregations had been organized in the 1880s, and others were added in the 1890s. A second Baptist church on Shanty Row (1881), Mount Vernon Baptist on Ramsey Hill (organized as a mission by Pastor J. B. K. Butler in 1880), another A.M.E. church on Chapel Hill Street, and a Primitive Baptist church on Fairview are listed in the 1889–90 city directory. Other Primitive Baptist congregations were Mill Grove, five miles north of town, and a church at 505 Fayetteville Street, both organized in 1883. Elder Luke Webb was pastor of both. A Durham Primitive Baptist Association (Colored) was formed in 1888. The first black Holiness church of the Pentecostal faith, Gospel Tabernacle United Holy Church, began in 1884 at the home of the Reverend C. C. Craig on East Piedmont Avenue.[71]

Saint Mark A.M.E. Zion Church was founded in 1890 by A. Williams, Mrs. Flora Colley, Jordan Wilson, Jerry Richmond, Gaston Bynum, Mrs. Sarah Marsh, and Herbie Richmond. They bought a lot at Pine and Pickett streets for their first small frame building. Offshoots of this church were Mount Olive at Thaxton and Powe streets (1917) and Kyles Temple on Dunstan Street (1929), both A.M.E. Zion congregations. The Presbyterians, after a successful money-raising campaign by their minister, the Reverend L. D. Twine, in 1893 built a frame church at the corner of Pine and Poplar streets. Later named for its first preacher, it is now known as Covenant United Presbyterian Church and is located on Lincoln Street. The formation of the East Durham Colored Methodist Church grew out of a Sunday school started in a log hut by the Reverend A. W. Adkins from Granville County, who, in a tradition that continues all over the South to this day, had bought the land and built the church himself. Adkins, a tobacco worker, also organized the Independent Order of the Knights of King Solomon, perhaps in imitation of Merrick's successful Knights of King David. Mount Calvary Christian Church (1898), West Durham Baptist (1892) on Ferrell Street (later at Gattis and Thaxton streets), and Union Baptist (1899) were also organized in the 1890s.[72]

Of more than usual interest was the church provided by the Reverend Moses Hester at his house in Brookstown across the railroad tracks from Trinity. Hester had been born in slavery but had educated himself and felt a call to preach. A basement room, where the hill sloped away from the house, gave space for his Sunday services, which he announced by the ringing of a bell mounted on a post at one corner of his porch. Another bell just like it at another corner rang factory hours as a service for his neighbors. The whitewashed house had green and red striped doors and window frames. Dedicated in 1893, he called the church Berea. A mixed audience attended the services, the few whites drawn by curiosity and Hester's personality. Among them one Sunday was Professor Jerome Dowd, who recorded the experience and in 1940 could still quote Hester's words: "The mountains were God's thoughts piled up and the seas were his thoughts imbedded." One professor said to Hester after the service, "I notice you are not much of a Methodist; you didn't take up a collection," to which Hester replied, "Bless you, I'm no pauper. I never takes up any collection. The Lord provides for me." Hester died in 1908, and his funeral and burial took place at New Bethel Baptist Church at Hickstown.[73]

Another out-of-the-ordinary man called to religious work was James A. L. Trice, son of John Trice, a farmer with ten children, living near Durham. When only eight years old, James Trice went to work in the factories to help support the family. In 1888, at age eighteen, he joined the Baptist church, where he was greatly attracted to religious work. Further inspired by the visit of two missionaries in 1890, he decided to devote his life to evangelizing. His fellow workers formed missionary societies in the factories to support his work. In 1890 he went to Freetown, Sierra

Leone, under the auspices of the International Missionary Alliance of New York. He delighted a huge mixed audience three years later with a lecture in the courthouse on his African work.[74]

Watts and the Dukes contributed to his support, and Trice wrote them about his progress. Trice and his wife, who then had a little girl of their own, started a home for orphan Temne children and kept ten little girls and one boy, but hoped to build accommodations for them in a separate building. In 1898 Trice became the United States vice-consul, B. N. Duke having lent him the money for the fifty-dollar bond. By 1900, however, the Missionary Society was no longer providing support, and Trice was disenchanted. He had made friends with the chieftains, had learned the native language, and intended to go on with his church work and school but needed to find another source of income. He considered making brick or starting an import-export business. With Duke's help he tried the latter, representing various U.S. firms including the American Tobacco Company, but within two years he was $2,500 in debt. Lack of capital and credit, damaged or inferior goods, expenses, delays, and shipping losses all contributed to his failure. He next moved to northern Nigeria, where he worked until 1905 with the customs department. In his last extant letter he told of planning to come back home the following summer in order to put his children in school.[75]

In the countryside, black farmers near Bahama organized a Baptist church called Mount Calvary in 1893 under the auspices of the Reverend C. H. Mayse. After meeting initially in a log cabin, they used a public schoolhouse, Brown Hill School, on the railroad about a mile south of Bahama for their services. Like so many others, this church evolved from a Sunday school, which had been started in 1892. The first minister of Mount Calvary was the Reverend J. M. Taylor, but it was under the Reverend J. C. Lyons that the congregation began to build a church. Money to build the current sanctuary (1939), a white frame building with two towers with pyramidal caps, was raised by the "God's acre" plan. Each farmer set aside one acre of land from which the produce, when sold, yielded money for the building fund. The women, too, contributed money from the sale of poultry and eggs. Sam Thompson, a local carpenter, did the actual construction.[76]

As willing to live and let live in religious matters as they were in racial, white Durhamites hardly blinked when Roman Catholics and Jews established houses of worship in the 1890s. Bishop Haid of the North Carolina Roman Catholic Diocese had vainly asked B. N. Duke's help in 1892, but by 1896 Father Prendergast of Raleigh was holding regular services in a room in the Durham YMCA. Soon afterward the small group of worshipers rented the second story above J. R. Gooch's store on Corcoran Street and caused some protest because a church in that location would prevent the sale of liquor. In 1905 when the first Roman Catholic church, Saint Mary's, was built on Chapel Hill Street on land donated by William T. O'Brien, there were 110 Catholics in Durham. There had been Catholics in Durham, however, since the 1870s. Mrs. James Lawrence, wife of the inventor of a cigarette-packing machine for the Blackwell company who moved to Durham in 1871, first held services at her house. In the late 1870s the number grew with the addition of a group from Lockhaven, Pennsylvania, who had attempted but failed to start a colony in Orange County and had drifted into town. In 1881 William T. O'Brien came to Durham with the Bonsack machine. In 1909 Francis O'Brien (no relation to the Durham family), the first priest, started a school (at first called Saint Mary's and later Saint William's), run by three Dominican sisters from Newburg, New York. Although he faced an uphill battle in financing such an undertaking in so uncompromisingly Protestant a part of the country, and although the school had a very slow beginning, it soon won a place in the community. In new quarters on Burch Street behind a new church (1957) on Chapel Hill Street, the school is now called Immaculata, and the church, the Church of the Immaculate Conception.[77]

The Jewish residents had set up a Hebrew cemetery adjoining Maplewood Cemetery in 1884, but they could not afford to build a synagogue until 1892. They, too, at first rented quarters for services, over Maddry's store at 102½ Main Street. Besides the early comers such as the Goldsteins, Mohsbergs, Maxes, and Gladsteins, there had now arrived the Siegels, Jacob Levy, Myer Summerfield, Joe Smolensky, Samuel Lehman, Isaac Gradwell, M. Greenberg, E. Cohen, M. Haskell, A. Bernstein, and Rabbi D. Rosenthal. In a kind of ecclesiastical musical chairs, the Jews bought the Christian Church building at Queen and Liberty streets just after that congregation bought the newly vacated Main Street Methodist Church building from the Methodists, who had decided to build anew on Chapel Hill Street. The Beth-el Synagogue remained at the Liberty Street site until 1918, when the city decided to cut through Queen Street. Then the Hebrew congregation built a new structure (1921) on land at the corner of Holloway and Queen streets. In 1957 they moved again, to the corner of Markham and Watts streets.

Although there was a degree of religious tolerance in Durham, there was a limit to what Durhamites perceived as acceptable divergence from their own mainline denominations. Therefore there were complaints when Mormon missionaries began to use school buildings to hold religious services. Appeals to the county commissioners soon put a stop to the practice.[78]

The Protestants, however, were thriving. Textile mills were responsible for a handful of new churches; to provide churches for mill workers was part of the owners' paternalistic duties. Industrialists, like planters, felt that sermons were an effective means by which to inculcate in workers the virtues of loyalty and morality and attitudes that equated labor with godliness. If not exactly as calculated as brainwashing, the brand of religion thus provided did have a similar effect. Benjamin Duke provided a Methodist church near the Erwin mill. A congregation was organized in 1894 called West Durham Methodist Church (changed to Asbury in 1944), resulting from a revival held there by Reuben Hibberd. In 1896 Duke deeded them the land and contracted with W. A. Wilkerson for a structure like that of Bethany Church, which he had recently built on Guess Road. Also in West Durham, a Baptist church was organized the same year by a group from the First Baptist Church. They originally built a structure on Main Street, but after it was destroyed by a storm in 1897, they built a second church on Alexander Street. In 1936 they built a new church, renamed Grey Stone Baptist Church, at Athens and Nixon streets, designed by the Durham firm of Atwood and Weeks.[79]

Branson Methodist Episcopal Church was organized for Commonwealth Mill workers in 1900 and first known as Commonwealth Methodist Episcopal Church. Hibberd was again responsible (with W. T. Cole) for its formation, and Brodie Duke gave the land while B. N. and Washington Duke donated money for the building. In 1922 a new church edifice was named Branson to honor William H. Branson, the mill manager who had been killed in a boiler explosion in 1899. A Presbyterian mission was also started in the Commonwealth Mill section. A Baptist group from Carr's Edgemont community established a church in 1902, and the Reverend J. M. Arnette was appointed its pastor.[80]

North Durham was growing apace as well. In 1898 Hibberd established a Methodist mission at Pearl Mill known as Cunniggim's Chapel, built by Brodie Duke. Later called Pearl Mill Methodist Church, it continued at that site until 1924, when it moved to Gregson Street. It was discontinued in 1927 and its wooden structure sold for $7,000. A Presbyterian mission, Pearl Mission, begun under the Rev. L. B. Turnbull's ministry, became Second Presbyterian Church in 1902; in 1917 its building was moved to land donated by Brodie Duke at the corner of Duke and Trinity streets where seven classrooms and other improvements were added. This church eventually moved to the corner of Trinity and Gregson and became Trinity Avenue Presbyterian Church. The neighborhood around Mangum and Roxboro streets also needed a church, and Hibberd again became the sparkplug for the undertaking. From a mission organized as a Sunday school in the 1880s, Hibberd formed a church in 1890. In 1902 B. N. Duke supplied money for a church building at the corner of Mangum and Cleveland streets. It was named Mangum Street Methodist Episcopal Church South. Arnette was called to serve this group in 1907. When a new site (the old Dr. J. T. McCracken homeplace on Trinity Avenue) and a new structure were decided on in 1916, the church was renamed Calvary United Methodist Church. The old sanctuary was sold to the Universalist congregation, which in turn sold it to the Holloway Street Christian Church. In 1927 the McKay Drug Company acquired the building.[81]

James B. Warren (1850–1913), also a Methodist, superintendent of the American Tobacco Company plant, a county commissioner, and city councilman, in the early 1890s donated land for a church on Guess Road three miles from town. Money for a building was donated by the Duke family and others. At first called Warren's Chapel, the official name of Bethany was given by the Reverend Dr. Yates at the dedication ceremony in the fall of 1892. Because of insufficient support the services lapsed for ten years until the congregation was revived in 1902 by a young divinity student at Trinity.[82]

Other Methodist churches were built at this time. North of town on Roxboro Road, Mount Sylvan Methodist Church was built in 1891 on land donated by Sallie E. Cole. James B. Mason gave land across the road for a new, larger church in 1924. Zachariah Dickie, James E. Bowling, and other trustees of Rougemont Methodist Episcopal Church, South (organized c. 1875), bought two acres in 1891 for that congregation's first sanctuary. W. B. Ellis (died 1894) directed in his will that a church be built on his land on the east side of the Flat River. By 1901 his executors, John

W. Umstead and Adolphus and Marcus Tilley, had overseen the building of Ellis Chapel.[83]

No one could say that religion in the South is anything but flourishing today, yet the 1890s saw the zenith of religious fervor. Secular interests such as the newly formed men's and women's clubs that began to increase in the nineties continued in the new century, and more and more people found interests outside the church to occupy their spare time. Eventually, the automobile and movies transformed the way people lived. Changes in behavior and thought were reflected in the churches and their forms of worship. While they enjoyed their heyday, however, they gave people an outlet that was joyous and social as well as constructive and restorative. An old woman remembered the old-time religion and contrasted it with that of today. "Then, you could hear music a long ways. Now folks get in a church and shut the door—You can't hear whether they're singing or not. You could hear them in that church at the crossroads [Mount Bethel Methodist Church]—in those days—half a mile away. They had the windows up and the doors open. Why has it changed? Movin' with the time, the fashion, I reckon."[84]

EDUCATION

Unlike the churches, education in the South was anything but thriving and had become a topic of much concern in the 1890s, long before Governor Aycock chose educational improvement as his main campaign promise. North Carolina public schools in 1897–98 averaged 63 school days a year, compared to 172 days in Massachusetts and 179 in Connecticut. The whole field of education was in ferment as educators debated the new theories and methods. Women and education, coeducation, blacks and education, funding for education, intercollegiate sports—all were vexed questions for educators.[85]

Education for women had gained ground with the establishment in 1891 of the State Normal and Industrial School (later the Woman's College of the University of North Carolina) by Charles D. McIver, who had once taught in Durham and was a tireless campaigner for education for women. One canny farmer, who moved from Durham to Arkansas early in the nineteenth century, understood the importance of education for women, whose civil and legal rights were restricted. Noah Trice wrote to his brother Pleasant in 1859 and asked about their sister Priscilla: "I fear some body has done rong with that girl and her property. Property is not very certainly safe for girls, not so much so as a good education would be."[86] Another advocate of education for women was N. A. Ramsey, who wrote in his *Durham Almanac* for 1896,

> Our Women are fully equal intellectually to our men, and far superior in all other respects. Where the state gives ten dollars for the education of our *boys,* she gives only one dollar for the education of our *girls,* and there are more girls in the state than boys. Did you ever think of this solid disgraceful fact? If you never did, think about it a little, and if you are a gentleman, the more

you think about it the madder you'll get. This gross wrong cannot be borne much longer.[87]

Washington Duke thought about it, and the same year gave Trinity College $100,000 for an endowment fund on condition that women be admitted on an equal footing with men. From time to time Trinity had been admitting and graduating a few women day-students, who had been taught in the same classes with men. With the endowment Duke intended women henceforth to be residential students with their own facilities on campus and with the same opportunities for study that the men enjoyed. Duke knew what education could mean to women, for he had sent his daughter Mary with James and Benjamin to New Garden Boarding School (known after 1889 as Guilford College). The year after their father's gift to Trinity, Benjamin and James gave Guilford College, which had always been coeducational, money to build a science hall in memory of their sister.[88]

Public education had become an issue because it was the victim of inconsistent local support: by the 1890s much inequality existed between one school district and another, between one-room country schools and city graded schools, between black and white schools in which only the length of the school terms was the same. In 1894, for example, both white and black schools of the county ran an average of under twenty-two weeks. Education for blacks was a political football. Some whites said, "Educate a Negro and spoil a field hand." Others, with the skewed view of that time, conscientiously believed that education was a way to control the alleged beast in the black man. Republicans saw education as his right. Blacks wanted to run their own schools while Fusionists wanted township committees of education set up with both black and white members. In 1899 the State School Superintendent, Charles Mebane, a Fusionist, succeeded in setting a precedent of state appropriations to schools to supplement local taxes. Each year thereafter saw ever-larger sums of state money go to education. Julian Carr, although a loyal Democrat, supported the Fusion school bill and offered $500 to the county that had the largest percentage of qualified voters in favor of extra taxes for schools. In 1900 Durham County spent the highest amount per capita on schools of any county in the state: $2.80 from county funds, $0.14 from the state.[89]

Another incendiary topic, intercollegiate sports, was always in the news. President Crowell of Trinity was a strong advocate of intercollegiate sports at Trinity, while President Kilgo, his successor, was just as strongly opposed. In the late 1880s Paul Cameron had foreseen the dangerous drift of such sports and their extraneous nature to education. He wrote,

> For one I want all this inter-Collegiate games broken up: they will end in bitter rivalrys, bitter words & perhaps hard blows. Besides it occupys so much time that should be given to books & imposes expenses & charges on the boys that many of them cant afford—I wish to see all their contest to be for intellectual superiority, not of foot exploits. Let them take as much exercise as they please on their own campus—but not go off to exhibit as gladiators.

Professor William H. Pegram and other faculty members wrote about their concerns to Benjamin Duke, who apparently did not sympathize with them. The next year he and his father donated two hundred dollars to the football team.[90]

In the town the graded schools were at last getting their own buildings. In 1892 was built the first graded school for white children, named Morehead for Eugene Morehead, a member of the first Graded School Committee. Designed by Leary, located on Dandy Street, and heated and ventilated throughout, the brick building consisted of two stories and basement, holding ten classrooms, an auditorium for one thousand students, and a library of eight hundred books. Until 1896 this school had only nine grades. The first graded school for black children, built in 1893 at Ramsey and Proctor streets, was named Whitted for the first principal of the black graded school, James A. Whitted. The school had first used the Primitive Baptist Church and next a prize house on Red Cross Street, in which locations it had had only six grades. In its new location it had nine. To this school in 1896 Benjamin Duke donated one hundred desks and, the next year, chairs for what William Gaston Pearson, the principal, referred to as the school chapel. A second graded school for whites, Fuller (named for Bartholomew Fuller, another member of the first Graded School Committee), was built in 1899 on Cleveland Street on land of which part was owned and donated by A. M. Rigsbee and where the first academy and Masonic Hall still stood. The new school's top class, the sixth, had a homeroom with a carpet, dotted-swiss curtains, and a canary in a cage.[91]

A new superintendent of the graded schools was appointed in 1894: Clinton W. Toms, who made himself very popular by the dedication and energy he brought to the job. He and teachers W. W. Flowers (who succeeded Toms as superintendent in 1897) and R. L. Wharton opened a free night school for mill workers. West Durham began to raise money in 1898 for a graded school; B. N. Duke contributed $250. By 1900 both East and West Durham had graded schools operating nine months a year. The West Durham school resulted from a consolidation of Piney Grove school on Swift Avenue and Northside school in West Durham, north of the railroad tracks. West Durham's consolidated school was in a new twelve-room frame building on Swift Avenue.[92]

Four secondary schools were available in the town all through the decade and a fifth joined them at the end. The four schools initially operating were the Durham Female Institute under Professor Middleton's authority, the Methodist Female Seminary under Miss C. W. Carpenter, the Male Academy under Professor L. T. Buchanan, and Miss Florence Fleet's school, held at John L. Markham's home to teach girls Latin, German, French, and music. Trinity Park School, a high school under the aegis of Trinity College, was opened in September 1898 on the campus. A high school had been established in 1891 at Trinity, Randolph County, and conducted by the Reverend John F. Heitman, a brother-in-law of Julian Carr, but in that rural setting it had thrived no better than the college. In 1895, after Trinity College had joined in founding the Southern Association of Colleges and Secondary Schools, which set standards for preparatory training and college admission, it realized the necessity of bridging the gap between current public graded school work and college work. For that purpose Trinity Park High School was established for both girls and boys and housed in a brick building (Asbury, now destroyed) at the northwest corner of the campus. Resident female students were lodged in the Mary Duke building along with the women college students. In that first year there were five girls in the high school and eighteen in the college. Other private homes where students could live were scattered about nearby. The first headmaster was Joseph Francis Bivins (1874–1904), a graduate of Trinity, who died tragically in 1904 by falling off a moving train. The school was closed in 1922.[93]

Public school districts proliferated as the population grew and as people became willing to tax themselves for the support of additional teachers and schoolhouses. But as old school districts were subdivided, the funds available for teachers and books and the length of the school term tended also to be reduced. New districts and schools and even some new private schools appeared in the county in this decade. Patrick Henry Academy in the Massey's Chapel area, run by Professor W. A. Massey, was begun with eighty students. J. E. Latta was the teacher at Piney Grove Academy, apparently a different school from Piney Grove in West Durham.[94] A subscription school, Milton Hill on Milton Road, was fondly remembered by Mary Lucy Russell Harris, who began her schooling there at five years of age. Milton Hill was a one-room log structure with a huge fireplace at each end:

> The teacher sat (when she sat) in a chair in one corner near the fire. The opposite corner was filled with wood and those boys who chewed tobacco sat on top of the wood so they could spit in the fire. . . . There was a long window reaching across one side of the room. Underneath the window was a sloping desk and underneath that a bench. This was the writing desk! A dozen boys and girls could sit there and write in their copy books. On a small shelf by the door was a water bucket and dipper. . . . We had no desks but plenty of benches and children. I'd say that on rainy days when the boys couldn't work in the fields there must have been sixty of us.[95]

The education that this kind of school offered, exactly the same as that available for generations, was sufficient for the demands of farm life, but it could not prepare children for the complex urban world that was developing near them, and of which many would eventually be a part. The gulf between the county and city schools grew ever wider, handicapping the rural child socially and economically for many years before the differences were finally all but eliminated. Durham was fortunate in its city school superintendents and in the caliber of its teachers. The upper grades were taught by men who often had the same qualifications as college teachers, and who were called professors. Their presence in the community along with that of the college teachers gave Durham a cultural advantage that the city fathers had sought, one that helped to balance the ever-increasing segment of overworked, underpaid, and uneducated mill and factory workers.

THE KILGO-GATTIS AND BASSETT AFFAIRS

Two causes célèbres threatened not only the reputation but the stability and future of Trinity College at the end of its first decade in Durham. A central figure in both was Trinity president John Carlisle Kilgo (1861–1922), a great preacher, a fighter, and a man who inspired fierce partisanship or enmity. One of those he irritated was another difficult man, Judge Walter Clark of the state supreme court and a Trinity trustee. Robert Winston described him as a socialist who posed as a champion of the people, without emotion or friendship. On the other hand, Judge Shuford described Kilgo as "a manipulator and ecclesiastical politician, a man who manipulates bodies and gets positions for himself and others. He also has the reputation of being a vindictive man." Those two—Kilgo and Clark—could hardly have avoided a confrontation. It erupted in their correspondence over Kilgo's leadership of the college away from its traditional southern Democratic, conservative moorings, his attacks on the state university, and his close ties to the Dukes. The precipitating incident was Kilgo's having won trustee approval of a faculty tenure plan over Clark's objections during Clark's absence. Clark accused Kilgo of malfeasance in office. In June 1898 Kilgo gave the correspondence to the trustees and they endorsed Kilgo's actions, all but one calling for Clark's resignation from the board. Clark was furious to have been judged without a hearing.[96]

When the press got wind of the controversy, Clark's charges became vituperative and more personal. Feeling that he had been defamed and that Trinity's progressive leadership and academic freedom were being attacked through him, Kilgo demanded an investigation. During the course of it, defending himself in fine oratorical form, he spoke the words that resulted in the long-drawn-out lawsuit brought against him by a superannuated Methodist minister and Durham bookseller, Thomas Jefferson Gattis. Gattis was suspected of having been Clark's source for his slanderous accusations against Kilgo (accusing Kilgo of being a puppet of the Dukes, who had paid him private gratuities); he became the target of Kilgo's scathing wit: "Behind a pious smile, a religious walk, and a solemn twitch of the coattail, many men carry a spirit unworthy of them."[97] A printed report of the proceedings was Kilgo's undoing. Gattis sued for slander. Despite two lower court verdicts against Kilgo, a large award to Gattis for damages, and four appearances in the state supreme court, the case was finally dismissed because Gattis could not prove malicious intent on Kilgo's part. Nevertheless the costs were high. The public had been polarized, the Methodists had been divided, and Trinity had become the real focus of the attack.

The Dukes' gifts and ties to the college at a time when Populism was winning great support for its stand against trusts injected political rancor into the proceedings, the more so since rich Republicans such as the Dukes were never regarded with favor by strong southern Democrats anyhow. Winston, as Kilgo's lawyer, very close to the heat and aware of the influences at work, described the case as "an effort to use the courts to destroy new and progressive Trinity College and Kilgo, its president; to utilize the ill-will of tobacco farmers to blast the reputation of the Republican Duke family and eliminate them from public life." Trinity had become "a stronghold of liberalism in the South and the Lion in the pathway of Bryanism. It must be restored to the old order, to Clark, to General Carr and to Josephus Daniels. It must be wrenched from the hands of the Dukes and Kilgo and Few and Bassett and Mims and Flowers" (the last four its most outspoken professors). Carr's long rivalry with the Dukes probably led him to finance Gattis's defense. If Kilgo had lost the case, Winston believed, there would have been no Duke University, because the Dukes' association with the college would have ceased.[98]

Winston's reference to Trinity College as "progressive" had much supporting evidence, none perhaps more convincing than the college's independent course in racial matters. When Booker T. Washington had visited Durham to speak at the Colored County Fair in October 1896, the college invited him to come to the campus and speak to the students and faculty, the first southern white college to do so. He and a few black citizens accompanying him were courteously received, Washington related, and his speech was heard with enthusiasm. The students gave him a college cheer as he departed.[99]

The political and social climate that surrounded the Kilgo case and made it more than a legal issue also complicated the Bassett affair that followed on its heels. Professor John Spencer Bassett's connection with Trinity and the Dukes, the dangerous racial hostility of radical whites to blacks, the low boiling point of southerners on racial questions in those years, the progressive racial stance adopted by Trinity, and the divisiveness and sentiment against the college that the Kilgo-Gattis case had engendered combined to cloud the issue with anger, enmity, fear, and desire for revenge. Political history from 1898 through the election of 1900 explains the explosiveness of the racial issue. Radical white fear and hatred had been translated into Democratic votes everywhere, and, in some places, into violence. By 1900 the Populist party had fallen apart from internal dissension, and the Republicans had soon after adopted a "lily-white" face, leaving blacks with no political advocate at all. The first few decades of the new century thus became the nadir in race relations; blacks were not only politically and socially shackled; they were physically endangered as well. Lynching, though at its height in 1892, declined only very slowly in the next decade and became in the South almost entirely a weapon against blacks.[100]

This was the political and racial situation in the fall of 1903 when Professor John Spencer Bassett, editor and founder of the *South Atlantic Quarterly,* described it in an article called "Stirring Up the Fires of Race Antipathy." The article revealed him as an orthodox conservative on the race question—believing in the inferiority of blacks—but also as realistic in foreseeing their eventual political and industrial equality. His article inquired into the causes of the recent heightened hostility between the races and blamed as one of them the recent exploitation of the race issue by the southern Democrats to win votes. With the blacks' economic and educational progress and increasing resistance to oppression, Bassett predicted their eventual parity with whites in the life of the country. As an example of their progress he pointed to Booker T. Washington as probably the greatest native southerner after Robert E. Lee. Bassett must have known that his article would evoke heated discussion, and this was probably his aim in writing it, but he was surely not prepared for the storm that actually followed. Immediately the old battle lines formed—the Dukes, Kilgo, and Trinity on one side against the *News and Observer* editor Josephus Daniels, the Democrats, and Confederate flag-wavers on the other. The outrage of Bassett's critics was reflected in newspapers all over the South. In time, however, the uproar was reduced to a single issue: the right of a college professor to say what he thought—in other words, academic freedom.[101]

A similar furor had engulfed an Emory University professor, Andrew Sledd, for an *Atlantic Monthly* article of July 1902. As a friend of Sledd's father-in-law, Bassett had undoubtedly thought much about the matter and decided exactly where he stood. His scholarly principles were already well known. In starting the *South Atlantic Quarterly* he had stated that it was to be dedicated to "the cause of enlightenment" and to rebuilding "the intellectual life of the South."[102]

While hostile newspapers led the chorus calling for Bassett's resignation or dismissal, James H. Southgate, as chairman of the board of trustees, and B. N. Duke were deluged with letters from Trinity alumni in other parts of the country. Many eyes were on the trustees as they deliberated what to do. Walter Hines Page, an alumnus, wrote persuasively to Duke: "It is of the highest importance that a professor from Trinity College should be allowed to hold and to express any rational opinion he may have about any subject whatever; for this, of course, involves the question of freedom of speech." In another letter Page wrote, "When you win this fight, you may forever afterwards be sure that Trinity College will be free—and everybody will know that it is free." When the trustees met to decide whether or not to accept Bassett's resignation, the other professors, too, had letters of resignation penned and ready to deliver if Bassett's were accepted. As it happened, the trustees voted nineteen to seven to refuse Bassett's resignation and the day was saved. Page's prediction was correct. The Bassett case has become a national landmark of academic freedom.[103]

W. B. Dukeman wrote to B. N. Duke to congratulate him on the outcome: "The College has made a great deal of capital out of a controversy which was purely accidental and not of its seeking by simply showing backbone at a critical time." Not bending under pressure is the mark of a character fully formed, firmly based, sure of itself and its principles—the mark, in fact, of maturity. Durham had reason to applaud and be proud. Months before Bassett's article appeared, Walter Hines Page, as a proxy for James B. Duke in dedicating the new library, Duke's first major benefaction to the college, had enunciated Trinity's and its patron's belief in intellectual freedom. Page quoted what Duke had told him to say to the students on that occasion: "Tell them every man to think for himself." Then Page had dedicated the library "to free thought, reverent always, always earnest, but always free."[104]

THE 1890S WERE THE APOGEE OF AN ERA. It began with the formation of the American Tobacco Company, which made the Dukes among the richest men in the nation, and ended with Benjamin Duke's move to New York. In between, the textile industry grew apace in the local economy, and mill villages offered a new way of life for erstwhile farm families. Social ills overwhelmed local government. The material expression of new wealth changed the town's ambience, and the coming of Trinity College gave substance to its cultural ambitions. Clubs competed with churches for the extra time that prosperity provided. Women found ways to utilize their talents and banded together for self- and social improvement. The failed

Confederacy, now somewhat receded into history, took on a glamour that it had not had in reality, and the myth of plantation civilization and the southern cavalier helped salve psychic wounds and isolate the South in a web of romantic illusion. The last tangible symbol of the Confederacy, the remains of Jefferson Davis, transported from New Orleans to Richmond for reburial, gave the people of Durham a moment to recall the suffering of the war and its aftermath before leaving them to the dream. In May 1893 Julian Carr called on the citizens, white and black, to close their businesses and come to the station and stand bareheaded in tribute as the train carrying the remains passed through the town. The schoolchildren would strew flowers along the tracks and the Durham Light Infantry would march to the station and fire three rounds over the car with Davis's remains. When it stopped in Durham, Davis's daughters appeared on the rear platform to acknowledge the tribute, but there was no shooting—just great silence—and then the train rolled north.[105]

Social Challenges, 1900–1917

13

W HEN THE TRAIN CARRYING the Benjamin Dukes rolled north to New York in June 1901, Durham's days of naive delight in its success were temporarily over.[1] The new century would see continued development and enormous expansion along lines already established; it would see some innovation in accordance with Durham's genius; and reform would be carried forward, with only occasional stoking, by the momentum achieved in the previous decades.[2] Of the principals who had engineered the achievement—Blackwell, Carr, Morehead, Parrish, Watts, Wright, and the four Dukes, among others—only Carr, Watts, and Wright remained at the controls. Washington Duke was enjoying his twilight years in retirement, Blackwell, a broken man, would soon be dead, Morehead was long dead, Parrish was far away in Japan earning more than laurels, and Brodie Duke's personal demons were absorbing his energies.[3] In the new century, Durhamites would continue to broaden their interests beyond religion and politics to social concerns; they would gradually increase their personal and economic security as responsibility for the more serious problems that come with growth—poverty, crime, and health—were consigned to government. A proliferation of experts in many fields would be necessary to handle the increasing complexity of social, governmental, and business affairs; responsibilities still locally managed, such as education and roads, would need supplemental funding.

INDUSTRY, UNIONS, AND SOCIAL WORK

The loss of the original strong individualists who had shaped the town's development created a vacuum into which others could move, sometimes with equal impact, sometimes not. William A. Erwin, to whom Benjamin Duke entrusted his family's textile interests, proved to be a giant of the pioneer stripe. Like the Dukes, he gathered around him as deputies able administrators who took their places in the community as well as the business world—for example, his brother, J. Harper

203

Erwin, and his brother-in-law, E. K. Powe. Watts brought to Durham his son-in-law, John Sprunt Hill, a native of Faison, Duplin County, who, after settling in Durham in 1903, founded the Durham Bank and Trust Company and the Home Savings Bank; he became president of both. Richard Wright always included his brother, Thomas Davenport Wright (c. 1854–1901), in his businesses, but the latter was plagued by ill health and incapable of the sustained effort necessary to success. Despite other partnerships in the development of his machine manufacturing and real estate empire, Richard Wright lived very much to himself, frequently involved in lawsuits, dogged by his own ill luck. He lost his first business with all his investment by fire; in his first year of marriage his wife died, to be followed three years later by the child whose birth had killed her. He next lost a foot through an accident with his horse. This series of early blows was probably more than a little responsible for his difficult personality. He nevertheless left his mark in Durham's history with the Wright Machinery Company (begun as Wright's Automatic Tobacco-Packing Machine Company in the 1890s), the Wright Refuge, and Bonnie Brae Farm. Business shrewdness and the capacity for hard work he had in plenty, enabling him to corner the Bonsack machine sales rights in foreign lands just at the time that cigarette manufacturing was switching over to machinery. He followed that triumph by obtaining in the 1890s the exclusive rights to the North American sale of the tobacco package wrapping machine manufactured by the Rose brothers in Gainesborough, England. Wright's company concentrated on perfecting, improving, and selling new inventions as labor-saving devices continued to refine manufacturing.[4]

The textile industry also expanded. In the early years of the new century, B. N. Duke and his associates controlled the Erwin Mills, Pearl Mill, and the Durham Cotton Manufacturing Company, rotating the top offices among themselves.[5] The Dukes and Erwin invested elsewhere as well. Erwin took over as president of the Cooleemee Cotton Mills (which the Duke faction had bought in 1901), and ran the factory at Duke (now Erwin) in Harnett County, which the Dukes and Watts built in 1902.[6] Toward the end of the decade they were ready to build again, and Erwin tantalized the city fathers by refusing to say where, the threat of building elsewhere acting as a defense against the city's need to expand and take in West Durham. A delegation of businessmen, professionals, and local officials visited Erwin and all but begged him to build the new factory in Durham. Despite protestations of being both overwhelmed and touched by such wooing, Erwin played hard to get. He told them frankly that the factory would be built at the place offering the most advantages to the company. They understood what this meant and accepted the condition. As the accommodating suitor Durham got the new mill, and the city refrained from embracing West Durham until 1925.[7]

Julian Carr and his family were also active in these years. Carr's money was invested in the Durham Hosiery Mills and the Golden Belt Manufacturing Company. He was fortunate in having as his associates his four sons and his nephew, William F. Carr, who were trained in business. Julian Carr, Jr. (1876–1922), was particularly ingenious and conscientious in pursuing new policies to elicit the cooperation of employees, such as granting them participation in both the management and profits of their work. Educated at the University of North Carolina with an additional year at Harvard Law School, young Carr assumed the management of his father's business in 1900. One of his first concerns was the waste cotton generated in the manufacture of hosiery and sold at a very low price. He wanted it reused to make rough socks for children and thus earn a profit. Lacking available labor, he took the unconventional step of hiring black labor to run a new operation in a reconverted furniture factory. For this he met with prejudice and criticism. A white myth about blacks maintained that blacks were incapable of running machinery; that further-more the rhythmic noise would put them to sleep. White millworkers saw the hiring of blacks as a threat, robbing whites of potential jobs. Actually Carr was gambling because free black labor in textile mills was untried. He entrusted recruitment to the capable John O'Daniel and within eighteen months had the factory on a pay-ing basis, its workers producing a dozen pairs of socks per machine per hour, the same rate as white laborers. The work force presented many problems, to be sure, to which the company adjusted with wisdom and flexibility; it accepted without complaint workers' absences because of church revivals, protracted meetings, or circuses.[8]

With this experiment in 1903 the Carrs entered a course of expansion that re-sulted in a chain of sixteen mills.[9] In 1909 they bought two mills in Chapel Hill, the Alberta from Thomas Lloyd and the Blanche Mill from the Pritchard brothers and W. E. Lindsey. These two combined became the fourth mill in the chain to manufacture hosiery; the name Carrboro was given to the community that devel-oped around them. In 1912 the Carrs added another mill on Elm Street behind the Angier Avenue plant, to spin yarn for the hosiery mills. Even before this addition the Durham Hosiery Mills were reported to be the largest in the world, employing 950 workers, mostly women and girls. The new mill was expected to add 150 to 200 more. The younger Carr's history of the enterprise reveals how little of their own capital they initially worked with, and how with prudence and integrity they con-verted a small, mortgaged knitting mill into the nucleus of a $6 million enterprise. The tricks of this conversion were largely financial, but there was also a strong ele-ment of social responsibility that strengthened the human cooperation on which it was built.[10]

In 1910 the Carrs planned to expand the Golden Belt Company with a three-story brick addition 120 feet long and to create two hundred new jobs. This company was already a large operation, comprising both a cloth manufactory and a plant to make the cloth into bags. A total of seven hundred people, mostly women and girls, worked there, and hundreds more worked in their homes turning, stringing, tying, and tagging the manufactured bags.[11]

The war that broke out in Europe in 1914 had a depressing effect on the cotton market, although it stimulated the production of hosiery. European markets now had different priorities, and cotton began to pile up in American warehouses. Dyes used in cloth and yarn production, which had been imported from Germany, were unobtainable. By the later teens, however, improvement began in other parts of the textile industry. B. L. Duke's Commonwealth Mills, which had been idle for four years, were now overhauled, and under John Pugh's superintendence they were again set in operation in 1916. Dr. E. H. Bowling and his partners, J. W. and J. H.

Emory, also started a small knitting mill in 1916 located on Gurley Street in the northeast section of town. In 1918 the North State Knitting Mills, of which Carr was president, were enlarged from 85 to 450 machines capable of making up to 2,500 pairs of white socks a day.[12]

As impatient of little fish in the pond as was James B. Duke, in 1919 Julian Carr bought the Bowling-Emory Knitting Mill outright; he turned it into another black-operated plant named the John O'Daniel Hosiery Mills to honor O'Daniel, who had recently died. He also bought eleven acres of Edward J. Parrish's Eastern Heights land on which to build fifteen houses for the seventy-five to one hundred workers. W. F. Carr was made general manager.[13]

Textile mills were not exempt from unionizing efforts, and though labor unions never noticeably thrived in the South, sporadic efforts to unionize workers met with some success. These were almost entirely effected by outside organizers, either worker-inspired to teach fellow employees how to protect themselves against the uncertainties of life and employment, or by northern companies and workers who feared the competition presented by cheaper products of southern firms that had the advantages of both access to the raw materials and cheap labor. Unionizing, the northerners reasoned, would raise wages and consequently raise the prices of southern goods. The Noble Order of the Knights of Labor, organized in Philadelphia in 1869, was the first union in Durham. Its chapters organized geographically rather than by skills and open to both sexes and races, the Knights early worked to equalize the pay of men and women and curtail the working day to eight hours. The order found the climate in the South distinctly hostile to its efforts; both workers and employers viewed strikes as contrary to the will of God. Furthermore, they distrusted northern organizers and feared the strong Roman Catholic infusion in unions with large numbers of immigrants. Individualistic to the core, southern workers also recognized the right of employers to hire whomever they wished at whatever wages.[14] Nevertheless by 1888 Durham had five assemblies of the Knights of Labor. Of particular interest is the involvement of Hiram V. Paul, Durham's first historian, who edited a labor journal, the *Durham Workman*. In 1882 in another labor paper, the *Journal of United Labor,* Paul wrote that the whip "is freely used on the backs of helpless little children in the Duke factory. The Knights of Labor will take the matter in hand and call upon the friends of humanity to aid them in putting an end to such outrages." Fearing the effect on his business of these charges, James B. Duke went in person to the order's Philadelphia headquarters to iron out the matter of the allegation. He promised that the whipping would stop if the Knights would cease their attacks on his factory.[15]

The Duke factory had additional labor troubles. The Polish Jews who had been brought down to roll cigarettes objected to the introduction of the Bonsack machines, rightly seeing in them the end of their own employment. Almost no details of this controversy survive, but B. N. Duke's later correspondence refers to documents relating to the troubles of 1884, 1885, and 1886, among them articles by labor agitators calling for a boycott of Duke brands because of the use of machines. Another incident in the Duke factory implicated Junius A. Strickland of the Knights of Labor. Chicago police investigating an anarchist bomb incident found a letter from

Strickland claiming that the red flag would fly over Durham. The Knights of Labor dismissed Strickland and disavowed any connection with anarchists. Within a few years, however, after a peak membership of one thousand members, the Knights of Labor faded from the Durham scene.[16]

In 1900 a new wave of union organizing hit Durham. During the dog days of August it was reported that a labor organizer had infiltrated the Erwin mill and signed up 191 members there. The management denied any knowledge of it. The same week the Reverend J. F. Austin spoke to a crowd in the courthouse encouraging unionization. Conflicting versions of the firing of workers at the mill next reached the paper.[17] An editorial added some background to the incident. The unionized workers had some time before asked to meet with Erwin to explain to him their reasons for wishing to join the union—to provide a kind of mutual aid when workers were sick and unable to work. They felt that Erwin should have been more friendly to their concern, but he had adamantly refused to meet with them. No doubt he felt that it was his prerogative to take care of them in need and wanted no interference with his "family." By the end of August the striking workers and their families were feeling the pinch and beginning to suffer from lack of food and medicine. Erwin said he would relieve all cases of hardship, that he had not known of their distress. The role of the forgiving father was clearly to his liking. The newspaper applauded his statement, adding, "There is nothing that Mr. Erwin would not do for the betterment and uplifting of humanity. By this generous act of his he shows that he has not the slightest hard feelings towards any of his former employees on account of the recent labor troubles in his mill."[18] The significant word here is "former." No more was heard about unionizing Durham cotton mills for a while.

Some workers did unionize, however, and sporadic strikes by groups of men and women sometimes won small concessions, though they sometimes lost them their jobs entirely. Clerks, bricklayers, plumbers, printers, telephone exchange operators, and even tobacco workers at the Bull factory staged such protests. In 1913 East Durham weavers struck and subsequently lost their jobs, while three years later weavers in the Golden Belt factory and menders in the Chatham Knitting Mill, a Carr subsidiary, struck for higher pay. Thomas B. Fuller, who had been superintendent of Golden Belt since 1881, dismissed their complaint, saying that their wages were as good as any in the state.[19] Perhaps to forestall agitation in the other mills, J. S. Carr, Jr., who supervised the Carr textile empire, increased wages in the existing eight hosiery plants, granting a 7½-percent rise in pay; he reduced work hours by two each week, and increased lunchtime from forty minutes to an hour. Large government orders that came at this time occasioned optimism in the company. Erwin Mills, too, raised its wages by from five to fifteen cents a day about this time, citing the constantly increasing prices that were causing hardship for millworkers. The next year Erwin Mills awarded bonus pay as well as wage increases to all its employees. Prices for cotton were nonetheless steadily declining.[20]

Agitation from another source concerning the age and hours of workers created a storm of controversy between reformers and industrialists that was not resolved until the 1930s. As early as 1895 a bill had been introduced in the state legislature to restrict the workday to nine hours and to prohibit the employment of children under fourteen years of age. A compulsory education bill was introduced about the same time. Erwin Mills then operated eleven hours a day six days a week and employed children twelve years of age and up who could read and write. B. N. Duke was against legislating matters that he felt could be better settled between employer and employee. He was nevertheless willing to abide by what the workers wanted, but he was certain they wanted the longer hours to earn more money. He also felt that too many restrictions scared away northern investors. Both bills were reported out of committee unfavorably.[21]

While the number of women working in mills rose 50 percent, a decline occurred in the number of working children. In 1896, 6,046 children worked in the mills; in 1899, only 3,470 children were employed. The arguments against child labor were that the children were not only deprived of an education but were also mentally and physically stunted. One critic thought that the mill experience was more damaging to girls than to boys because they learned nothing of the domestic arts, were given a taste of independence, and thereafter were spoiled for settling down to housekeeping on a farm. They enjoyed the company and liberty that millwork gave them. New legislation in 1913 left unchanged the ages and hours but prohibited night work except between seven and nine in the evening. In 1916 a federal child labor law raised the required age to fourteen for children who worked in mills and factories. Julian Carr said he intended to abide by the new law and felt that child labor regulations were not properly a state matter. The principle of states' rights, he said, was too often a cloak for delay or nonaction. In the Carr mills the slogan was "humanity first and dividends second."[22]

The alternative to restricting the age of workers was to require education. Compulsory education had been one of the Populists' aims and was still a live issue. Many people objected to government interference in matters of education, and many millworkers favored child labor because they needed the additional income working children contributed. In 1904 the average weekly wages in Carr's Golden Belt Manufacturing Company were $6.40 for men, $4.46 for women, and $2.60 for children working eleven-hour days six days a week. Many of the millworkers had not had any education themselves and did not understand the need for it. In time, however, great numbers of workers came to favor compulsory education, and it became law in 1907. It did much to reduce further the number of children in the mills.[23]

Washington Duke was pained by anyone's being deprived of an education, and his early example of supplying night school for his tobacco workers was followed by Erwin in the cotton mills. In 1899 he offered them eleven weeks of free instruction, of which forty to fifty workers took advantage. In another educational effort, Mrs. Erwin, her daughter, and her sister Mrs. Leak regularly read to the women millworkers in their homes, and women of the West Durham Presbyterian Church (newly organized primarily through the efforts of the Blacknall family and later appropriately named for Richard Blacknall) formed sewing classes for the children.[24]

These modest gestures of concern were the forerunners of a much larger program that began in the second decade of the new century and probably accounted for the comparative quiet that permeated the mills during these prewar years. The Carrs pioneered social work in the South among their millworkers. In 1911 they hired Katherine Gilbert of Philadelphia, a trained nurse, to look after the sick and attend to sanitation and health matters in the mill village. The same year they instituted a profit-sharing plan for Durham Hosiery Mills employees. East of the mill they set up a park and playground with a bandstand for the band, a group of twenty-six workers whose instruments, instruction, and uniforms were supplied by the management. Rewards were offered for suggestions about ways to increase efficiency in the mills, and a health and life insurance fund was created for old employees. In 1914 the company initiated a kind of credit union for its employees, issuing small loans at 6 percent interest over six months. The Golden Belt company began to care for its workers too. In 1915 it built a community center with an auditorium to double as a gym, baths, and classrooms where domestic science and other subjects were taught. In another paternalistic move in 1919 the Carrs hired Milburn and Heister to build a dormitory for two hundred factory girls at the corner of Ramseur Street and Parrish Place. The building was to include eight reception rooms where the girls could receive visitors.[25]

Erwin Mills was not slow to follow the Carrs' lead. In 1916 James B. Duke suggested that a profit-sharing plan be instituted at Erwin Mills; the same year Ella Mae Howerton was placed in charge of a number of projects to improve life for the workers. Her hiring had resulted from the work of the Welfare Club organized by a group of volunteers working through women's committees in the West Durham churches and backed by the mill management. After forming a mothers' club, a girls' club, a library, and a nursery, the volunteers persuaded William Erwin to provide half the money to continue the programs if they provided the other half. Since their work was very much in harmony with his own aims, he readily agreed and provided a building for their use. Miss Howerton was hired and given two assistants, Beulah Arey to teach a cooking class, and Olivia Johnson to run a day nursery. The public library furnished books and magazines for the Welfare Club library, and sewing circles made baby clothes. The club also built and equipped a fenced playground.[26]

The endeavor closest to Erwin's heart, however, was Sunday school work, and this led him in time to build a church. To his thriving Sunday school, started in 1894 in the hall over the company store and post office, he had early added Friday evening church services. Finally, with contributions from all his brothers and sisters, he built Saint Joseph's Episcopal Church, despite the fact that most millworkers were not Episcopalians. The small Gothic Revival structure, named to honor their father, was completed in 1908. The year before, Erwin had joined John C. Angier and E. K. Powe on Caswell Heights; his large house, Hillcrest, stood at the corner of Swift Avenue and Pettigrew Street.[27]

In tobacco manufacturing the Duke firm was still forging ahead. The 1890s had seen extraordinary competition and then consolidation of the American Tobacco Company and its rivals. The Duke-led faction eventually controlled four-fifths of the industry, excluding cigars. The financial maneuvering that accompanied these

transactions was as complex as the network of companies manufacturing cigarettes, snuff, smoking and chewing tobacco with their related industries for production, packaging, and retailing.[28] Because cigarettes constituted a minor part of
the tobacco industry in America, Duke was challenged to extend his dominion into
other fields. First, he invaded the chewing-tobacco arm of the industry and bought
factories engaged in the business, at the same time using hard-hitting tactics to win
over the jobbers, wholesalers who managed the distribution of tobacco products.
Within a few years American had a respectable share of that market. Realizing
the futility of cutthroat competition dependent on price undercutting to win, the
plug companies decided to combine in 1898 and formed another monopoly called
the Continental Tobacco Company. Although the American Tobacco Company
owned less than a majority of the shares of the new corporation, James B. Duke
was elected president. Fielding Lewis Walker, Jr., managed the Durham office of
this company.[29]

Duke next wanted to expand his control of the industry globally. In 1901, the
year that the old Blackwell Company fell under the hammer to American, James
B. Duke bought two factories in Germany and then went on to Saint Petersburg in
Russia to look for others. His most formidable competition, however, was the Imperial Tobacco Company of Great Britain and Ireland, an amalgamation of British
companies formed in 1901 to protect themselves from Duke and his associates, who
aimed to buy them up one at a time, having already got control of the Liverpool
firm of Ogden's, Limited. Striking back, Imperial obtained a license to manufacture
in the United States, giving farmers hope that with competition they would receive
better prices for their tobacco. At the height of the Imperial-American struggle for
mastery, the Imperial company opened a warehouse for redrying and shipping tobacco in Durham itself and hired four hundred workers under the management
of William M. Fallon, a partner in the leaf brokerage firm of Fallon and Martin,
which Imperial bought along with the plant on Morris Street. Foiled in his takeover attempt, Duke proposed a combination of the two massive corporations to
divide their respective markets, Imperial alone to supply the United Kingdom while
American supplied the United States and Cuba. With this agreement the British-
American Tobacco Company was organized in 1902. In 1903 the British-American
Tobacco Company, too, opened Durham offices, and C. W. Toms was appointed its
agent.[30]

Duke's extraordinary activity in the early years of the century produced a
short-lived if runaway victory. In 1907 the U.S. government brought suit against
the American Tobacco Company under the Sherman Antitrust Act and four years
later was awarded the verdict. The gigantic company, comprising sixty-five corporations, was eventually reduced to four main companies: American, Liggett and
Myers, R. J. Reynolds, and P. Lorillard. In Durham the old Bull company remained
under American, and the Duke company became a subsidiary of Liggett and Myers.
Locally, the factories had gone on as usual during the first decade of the century.
However, as James B. Duke had claimed, competition was good for business, and
after the division the tobacco companies considerably increased both production
and profits. New warehouses were built and the old factories expanded.[31]

While the antitrust suit was still pending in 1908, an independent tobacco manufacturer, the Khedivial Tobacco Company of New York, had the temerity to attempt
a branch manufacturing operation in James B. Duke's backyard. The former factory
of Z. I. Lyon Company at Pine and Pettigrew was leased for the purpose by W. L.
Walker, formerly of Durham and owner of a controlling interest in the Khedivial
firm. The company gave further offense by calling its product Walker's Durham.
The American Tobacco Company took umbrage and threatened a suit. Walker's
effrontery knew no bounds: he hired R. N. Lee, a former superintendent of Duke's
plant, and George Burch, longtime head of the flavoring department at the Bull
factory. A fire at the Khedivial factory in 1910 put an end to the upstart company in
Durham.[32]

Having scaled the summits in the tobacco industry, James B. Duke's interest
shifted to a new challenge—electric power. The Duke brothers invested $25,000
in the Catawba Power Company in 1902. The concept of developing hydroelectric
power for the industries of the Piedmont was large enough to appeal to J. B. Duke,
and the brothers continued to study plans and gather information before investing
heavily. The chief engineer of the Catawba Company, William S. Lee, was an expert
on the subject and the kind of hard-driving, ambitious man of vision that appealed
to the Dukes. Under his tutelage they saw an opportunity to achieve something big
for their region by way of electric power. They incorporated the Southern Power
Company in 1905 at $7.5 million capitalization, taking over the Catawba Power
Company as part of the deal. The Duke investment in power plants and in the textile companies that used their power rapidly increased. The Dukes organized the
Southern Public Utilities Company in 1913 to supply power to individual subscribers, not only manufacturing companies, but communities, transportation systems,
and small businesses as well.[33]

Word of the Dukes' plans excited Durham in 1910 when the brothers and Lee arrived in town. The paper reported that they would bring electric power to the mills
and were thinking of buying Wright's Traction Company (they had just bought the
Charlotte transportation company). Their visit bore fruit in 1911 when the Southern
Power Company began to provide electricity for the Durham textile factories. A
newspaper reporter became eloquent over the event:

> The power was turned onto the Durham line Saturday. From the water driven
> generators on the Rocky Creek below Great Falls, S.C., the mysterious energy
> flashed over the lines from tower to tower, over hill and valley, through the
> fields of ripening corn and the forests in which the leaves are turning red
> and gold into the sub-station located on the hill just beyond the Pearl Cotton
> Mill.[34]

The distance was 175 miles, the longest distance over which electric power had
ever been transmitted, the paper boasted. These cautious moves into electric power
were the foundation of the vast Duke Power Company that would come into being in the 1920s, bringing with it an even vaster cultural and economic bonus for
Durham.

POVERTY AND PUBLIC HEALTH

The mills' social welfare work was a late and partial response to a larger and long-standing problem. How to provide for the poor and sick of the community baffled town authorities and responsible citizens because no satisfactory, comprehensive system had been worked out either to collect funds, identify the needy, or distribute alms in a society that had outgrown old usages. The Provident Club girls were very soon out of their depth, for they had no training for the work. Their organization disbanded as a result of the crisis of 1902 when the winter was particularly difficult and many people's basic needs went unmet. Although the Reverend Thaddeus Troy, a retired Methodist minister, had been designated city missionary, one of whose duties was the care of the poor, he could not possibly manage the job himself. Led by the Reverend W. L. Cunningham, pastor of Main Street Church, and Thomas B. Fuller, a group of concerned citizens formed the Associated Charities in 1902 to receive and distribute donations of food, fuel, clothing, and money, and appointed Troy to manage the work. Their efforts were not entirely successful because their office was hard to find (over the store of Pridgen and Jones) and was open only a few hours each day. At the same time the already established charities—the Salvation Army, the King's Daughters, fraternal and church organizations—continued their own efforts. By 1908 the city was persuaded to contribute $275 to the Associated Charities. A decade later its donation was ten times that amount. Mrs. R. D. Blacknall followed Troy as secretary of the Associated Charities in 1908; Jennie Langston, a secretary of J. S. Carr, followed her in 1910.[35]

In 1913 Captain W. M. Bouterse of the Salvation Army, an experienced and much-liked man intimately acquainted with Durham's poor, was hired by Fuller to assume the job of secretary of the Associated Charities. Criticism of his double role forced him to resign just at the time that a new state law provided for a county department of public welfare, and Durham County established a Welfare Department. But townspeople were not receptive to the plan, and, sticking to the old system, they hired the Reverend H. A. Forrester, a Holiness preacher, to replace Bouterse. More interested in spiritual revival than bodily survival, he neglected his job of collecting and distributing supplies, kept no records, and antagonized local officials. Strangely, when a Board of Charities and Public Welfare was set up, and the work of the Associated Charities and that of the county Welfare Department were combined under it, Forrester was appointed its new superintendent. In the one year of his incumbency he did succeed in having a Durham cottage established at the Stonewall Jackson Training School, a rehabilitation program for juvenile delinquents. The next year, 1920, however, W. E. Stanley took over the post and made it a professional and full-time job.[36]

Public welfare included more than the problems of poverty. Closely related were health and crime. Urbanization and industrialization were responsible for serious health hazards during these years, for example, a disease new to Durham, pellagra. The history of this disease in Durham could start, like so many other Durham histories, with the Carrs. They branched out into another industrial area in 1901 when they established the Carrolina Roller Mills to produce flour and cornmeal.

These mills occupied the 1882 prize house of Rowland and Cooper on McMannen Street; their products were "Peerless" flour picturing Robert E. Lee on the bag, and "Banner," with the Confederate flag. The machinery represented the latest technological advances in the refining and processing of grain. Ironically, improved milling methods were in part responsible for the scourge that visited the South in the early decades of the new century. The first death from pellagra in Durham occurred around 1906, but only in 1910 did the disease become sufficiently alarming to be reported in the papers. One reason was that it was early recognized as a disease of poverty, and families in which it occurred would try to conceal the fact. Doctors would frequently certify another cause on the death certificates of pellagra victims to spare the families' feelings. Pauli Murray wrote about her family's consternation when her grandmother was diagnosed as having the disease: "Down our way, having pellagra was only a little less disgraceful than having 'the bad disease,' as folks called gonorrhea and syphilis. People thought it came from dirt and filth and that only ignorant poverty-stricken country folks got it."[37]

The doctors were completely mystified by the disease and jumped from one to another theory to explain its nature. Spoiled cornmeal, the sand fly, or an organism in the blood were some of their hypotheses. In the summer of 1911 more people died of pellagra in Durham in July and August than of any other cause. In September there were 150 cases being treated. In eleven southern states that month 10,300 cases were recorded. The U.S. Public Health service was asked to investigate the matter. Meanwhile, in Durham Dr. Edwin H. Bowling, a son of Captain William Bowling of Flat River, was constantly in the news because of his concern with the disease. He practiced in East Durham where most of his patients were poor and many had pellagra. He claimed that his treatment was successful 90 percent of the time. He attended a conference on pellagra and reported back on the various papers he had heard. One he described proved to hold the correct solution, but he did not know that at the time. He reported that a doctor in Panama named Deeks attributed the disease to Americans' diet, naming the huge quantity of sugar that they ate and flour produced by the new refining methods. He advocated returning to the old-fashioned "rockground" flour as the Germans had lately done. He also mentioned that Americans' diet should include more fruit, green vegetables, and meat.[38] A local doctor who hit on the secret was a black physician from Chapel Hill, Edward Caldwell. He prescribed lean meat, fresh vegetables, and milk, and began curing his cases, upon which "the white folks sat up and took notice. Before long they were sending for him to come to their places after dark. . . ."[39] Dr. Caldwell understood that the limited diet of poor blacks—cornmeal and grits, fatback and molasses—was responsible for the disease.

With more than his share of pellagra cases, Dr. Bowling anguished over their lack of care. Watts Hospital refused to accept them because the other patients believed pellagra to be contagious. Only the workhouse or insane asylum would take them, the latter because the last stage of the disease was insanity. He asked the city to agree to contribute to the upkeep of a hospital that would admit pellagra victims and volunteered to build, equip, and run it himself if he could get city support. The city and county representatives met to discuss the matter, but they would go no farther. The County Medical Society met and approved the plan. A few citizens such as Reuben Oscar Everett, a young lawyer, spoke for it, but John Sprunt Hill spoke out against the plan, ostensibly because it would be a private hospital run for gain, though he may also have feared competition with the family-backed Watts Hospital. No hospital was built for pellagra victims. Instead, in October 1912 a group of investors acting independently secured the old Corcoran Hotel on the corner of Corcoran and Chapel Hill streets and remodeled it as Mercy Hospital for contagious diseases. It did not admit pellagra cases. In July 1914 Dr. Bowling appeared again before the aldermen asking that isolation wards be set up at Watts and Mercy hospitals for pellagra cases, a request repeated by Dr. Caldwell, who told them that half his patients suffered from the disease. Mercy Hospital did not long survive; it closed at the end of 1915 for lack of support.[40]

Studies of pellagra by a U.S. Public Health doctor very soon confirmed that pellagra was related to diet, but it was not until the 1930s that the lacking nutrient in the victims' diet was actually identified as nicotinic acid, found in red meat, fresh vegetables, and dairy products. With this clue, Drs. William Perlzweig, David and Susan Gower Smith, and Julian Ruffin at the newly founded Duke University medical school, developed a treatment for the disease. Changes in the way many southerners lived had affected their diet and made them vulnerable to the disease: cash-crop farming, which appropriated all a farmer's land and energies to money crops; the move to town where livestock was prohibited and space was lacking for vegetable gardens; and the new roller mills that eliminated vital nutrients.[41]

In the first years of the new century the city and its rudimentary health department had been inching toward more efficient methods of organization. In 1907 a health committee was established, and Dr. T. A. Mann was appointed health officer. In the same year the aldermen enacted an important ordinance. After 1 January 1908 physicians and midwives would be required to record all births within the city along with information about each child: name, sex, color, place of birth, physical condition, names of parents, including the mother's maiden name, and the parents' place of residence. Furthermore, the health officer would be required to inform the aldermen each month of deaths within the city, and burial of the dead would require a permit from the chief of police after presentation of a death certificate containing information similar to that on a birth record. These laws represented a tremendous step forward, for until this kind of information became available, nothing was known about birth and death rates, statistics on diseases, increase or decrease in numbers of cases, environmental factors influencing health, and the like. The state of North Carolina did not adopt such laws until five years later.[42]

Another progressive medical event of 1907 was the decision to build a new Watts Hospital. Ten years after the original hospital opened, George Watts realized that his hospital was sadly deficient for its purpose, and in 1907 he announced that he would donate a new hospital. After buying a 56-acre tract north of Trinity College abutting the new macadam road (later Broad Street), he built a hospital on the plans of Kendall and Taylor, Boston architects, costing a million dollars, half for the building and the other half for an endowment. Of Spanish mission architecture in brick and stucco with a red tile roof set in a grove of large trees, the hospital opened in December 1909.[43]

In 1909 the city substituted a Board of Health for the old health committee. The personnel were almost unchanged, but they now had a budget and sanitary policemen to enforce the health ordinances. This board drafted a sanitary code covering a variety of concerns, including the preparation and sale of meats and milk. It also listed current cases of tuberculosis within the city.[44] A smallpox epidemic that began in 1910 and worsened through 1912 actually precipitated the creation of a combined county and city health department, a concept that Dr. Bowling strongly urged, if he did not originate it. Dr. Arch Cheatham was appointed the first full-time superintendent of public health and began his service in 1913. In 1915 Cheatham was joined by Dr. J. H. Epperson as a staff bacteriologist. Epperson replaced Cheatham in 1922, and served until his death in 1958.[45] Slowly the department gained the citizens' confidence and submission, and under Dr. Epperson it developed into an organization that was respected for its leadership throughout the state.

The superintendent's first report in 1914 brought to light facts on which the city and public were forced to act. It showed the death rates of whites and blacks, ten and twenty-three per thousand population, respectively. That the black rate was over twice that for whites reflected blacks' inadequate diet, medical care, and living conditions. The superintendent warned that this should concern whites because of their close association with blacks who worked in their homes as cooks, nursemaids, and laundresses. He recommended that a black registered nurse be added to his staff to work with the black population, to care for the sick and needy, and to instruct mothers in child care and housekeeping, work parallel to that of his white nurses with the white population. He reported on the agency's other concerns: garbage collection (15 tons each week), emptying of privies (2,700 a week), examination of dairies (161), and of animals for slaughter (1,052), inspection of meat markets, restaurants, and hotels. Cheatham tabulated the number of visits by the white nurses to those sick with tuberculosis, typhoid, whooping cough, pellagra, scarlet fever, diphtheria, mumps, and measles. Although the health department was not a charity-distributing organization, he stated, they could not ignore need where they found it and consequently referred all such cases to the organizations in the city that regularly handled them. The itemization of diseases revealed that in Durham County tuberculosis was the leading killer of both whites and blacks, as it was nationwide, followed by pellagra and kidney disease.[46]

Tuberculosis was one of many public concerns of the Civic League. The League was the creation of Mattie Southgate Jones in 1909 to provide an organization to identify problem areas for civic improvement. Made up of both men and women, it influenced town leaders to recognize and act on their concerns. It was inevitable, however, that it would run into conflict with the business establishment. One of the League's first endeavors was to establish city parks; another was to improve the town's appearance by the removal of unsightly wires, poles, and signs that had made Main Street a jungle. They sponsored yearly cleanups for the removal of trash, debris, and refuse. They went further and actually beautified ugly spots by the addition of plants and flowers. During their ten years of existence they were successful in getting the telephone company to forbid the use of its poles for the tacking of handbills, and they made some gains in the battle against tuberculosis. They were successful in persuading Brodie Duke to donate land for a park, but they were defeated by Richard Wright when they asked him to clean up his vacant lots. His answer: "It seems to me there are plenty other places that might be beautified to advantage without interfering with business property in the most expensive real estate section in the town where lots must be used for business purposes."[47]

The battle against tuberculosis was very close to Mrs. Jones's heart because she had lost her husband and son to the disease, which had long been a scourge of young adults. Many families in the county, rich and poor, had known its blight. Duncan Cameron had lost four daughters to it; Mary Duke Lyon, two sons and a daughter-in-law; Abner Parker, his entire family; and many another family, such as the Greens, Joneses, and Moreheads, was touched by it. After Robert Koch's discovery in 1882 of the tubercle bacillus, some attempts were made to isolate cases to prevent contagion. The better-off could afford to send a family member away to the sandhills, or mountains, which became popular sites for sanitaria in the last decades of the nineteenth century for the supposed efficacy of pine-tree effluvia and mountain sun and air. The huge problem was where to accommodate the new masses of city dwellers unable to afford such cures. Crowded together in limited space, one family member after another would succumb to it. The state supplied only one hospital for treatment of tuberculosis cases.[48]

So concerned were Durhamites about the problem that a meeting was called in 1908 to discuss possible means of action. By 1911 the Civic League had joined the battle and was selling Red Cross seals, part of a national endeavor to raise money for research and treatment. By 1914 the league ladies were working to get a tuberculosis hospital for the county, and successfully appealed to Brodie Duke for a building site.[49] The Lincoln Hospital report of 1916 reported on the problem among blacks and urged that a hospital be built for all tuberculosis cases. That year, in desperation, Lincoln Hospital added a wing for the purpose, very much helped in this move by the league and others. George Watts contributed $500 and Erwin, $100. The next year Dr. Cheatham's report included much commendation for the excellent progress being made in the black community against disease in general. Blacks had organized the Negro Civic League in 1912, and thereafter a Business Men's League, Mothers' Club, Ladies' Board of Lincoln Hospital, Federation of Women's Clubs, and the Ministerial Union, all of which dealt with health care incidental to their larger concerns. That year as well, the legislature passed a bill allowing any county to establish and maintain a tuberculosis sanitarium. With this license the league ladies set to work again to get such a facility.[50]

In the second decade of the new century other medical problems surfaced. Hookworm, which was found to infect one-third of the county's population in 1910, was successfully dealt with by the Health Department. In 1914 the state typhoid fever rate was three times that of the national average. The Health Department again went to work, and with free inoculations and widespread education about its prevention it soon had the disease under control. But medical problems that only continued to worsen were infantile paralysis (polio) and drug addiction.[51]

A new peril, death from peritonitis after surgery, came with the first decades of the new century.[52] The cause was the increasing diagnosis of appendicitis and its surgical treatment. At first, Durhamites with appendicitis had the option of sending for a specialist to operate on them or taking their chances with a local doctor. Benjamin Duke's daughter Mary was operated on in 1907 by Dr. Gill Wylie of New York, who came to Durham to perform the operation. Others frequently sent for Dr. J. W. Long of Greensboro. By 1912 Durham's Dr. Joseph Graham, who had begun to perform appendectomies in 1908, announced that he was limiting his practice to surgery.[53] Specialization within the medical profession, as in so many other areas, began in this period. With practice, surgeons' techniques improved, and mortality in these cases declined.

So innocuous a holiday as New Year's Day also presented an annual public health problem. Durhamites still wanted to welcome it with firecrackers, a remnant of the tradition of New Year's shooters. To allow the townspeople to join in the general noisemaking, the prohibition against fireworks within town limits had to be lifted for the 24-hour period of New Year's Day except within the city center. The aftermath, unfortunately, was always a rash of wounds and burns that too often progressed to tetanus infections, for which there was no scientific remedy. The *Sun* tried to help by publishing a "remedy" that consisted in burning woolen cloth and directing the smoke to the wound twenty minutes at a time for several applications. Later, when firecrackers had become an accompaniment to Independence Day celebrations, Dr. Wilburt Davison recalled, "Fourth of July tetanus deaths of those days were appalling."[54]

BLACK ACHIEVEMENT AND NEW BARRIERS

In black Durham, the new year was celebrated somewhat differently. Emancipation Day, commemorating Lincoln's proclamation of 1 January 1863, was remembered every year with speeches, the reading of the proclamation, music, and a parade. The participants customarily assembled in the courthouse, where a prominent black, sometimes John Merrick, presided over ceremonies marked by decorum and, in those years, probably not the usual joy. In later years it became traditional to sing the Negro National Anthem, "Lift Every Voice and Sing," written in 1901 by James Weldon Johnson to music composed by his brother J. Rosamond Johnson.[55] The difference in the New Year's celebrations was symptomatic of the separation of the races and the difference in their cultural heritages. This separation, however, fostered the independent culture developing in black Durham at this time. Both in business, which underpinned its progress, and in education, advances were made before World War I. The success of the Mutual company encouraged other endeavors and, as in the white culture, the same few men provided the leadership.

When some of E. J. Parrish's property was auctioned off in 1901, John Merrick bought up lots that had belonged to the Parrish stables on Parrish Street and in 1905 built a substantial two-story building with the help of loans from Benjamin Duke's Fidelity Bank and George Watts's Home Savings Bank (founded in 1904). Into this new edifice the Mutual moved its offices in 1906 along with other smaller black enterprises such as the Royal Knights of King David and the Odd Fellows (chapter founded 1905). About the same time Merrick bought adjacent lots and in 1908 filled them with new enterprises: a movie house, a café, and a tailoring shop. In the Mutual building itself the upper floor was rented out for offices for black doctors: F. T. Page, J. N. Mills, A. M. Moore, C. H. Shepard; E. W. Canada, a lawyer; Merrick, Pearson, and W. S. Ingram, the secretary of the Odd Fellows Chapter. The business of the Mutual had so grown that it now required two stenographers, fifteen clerks, and twelve agents in the field, all under the direction of J. T. Goodloe, the office manager.[56]

After hearing two Raleigh promoters speak on the advantages of a building and loan organization, Richard Fitzgerald and William G. Pearson decided that a bank was really what was needed first and raised ten thousand dollars in subscriptions to fund the undertaking. Dr. James E. Shepard wrote a charter, and in 1907 the legislature incorporated the Mechanics and Farmers Bank, which opened in August 1908 in the Parrish Street building. Fitzgerald was elected president at the organizational meeting, Merrick, vice-president, and Pearson, cashier.[57]

The Mutual launched other business ventures in new directions in this period: publications, a drugstore, a hosiery mill, and a real estate company. The newspaper, the *North Carolina Mutual,* edited by Irwin H. Buchanan, was a house organ to keep the Mutual's agents informed. In 1906 the company started the *Durham Negro Observer,* also edited by Buchanan, but, like its forerunner the *Advance,* of 1901, it did not pay and ceased publication the same year. Also in 1906 the company bought from the True Reformers, then in decline, their newspaper the *Reformer* and hired its editor, W. S. Young, to continue editing it. In 1911 Young bought the paper from the Mutual and continued to publish it until 1918.[58] The Bull City Drug Company was incorporated in 1908; the drugstore it owned was located on Parrish Street and managed by Dr. S. T. James from Laurenceville, Virginia. Dr. Charles H. Shepard, a brother of James E., was president of the company, while Spaulding and Pearson were respectively secretary and treasurer. An earlier company, organized in 1895 as the Durham Drug Company by Moore, Pearson, Dodson, Fitzgerald, and Shepard, in 1901 became the Fitzgerald Drug Company.[59]

The success of the Carrs' mill worked by blacks prompted Merrick to establish a second black textile mill in 1910. The Mutual contributed five thousand dollars, and the mill was already in operation when Booker T. Washington visited Durham late that year. He wrote enthusiastically about the mill and about black Durham's progress, attributing it not only to the ambition and thriftiness of the Negro and to the leadership of men like John Merrick, but also to the attitude of the leading whites. He cited particularly Carr and Washington Duke, who by their generosity to black endeavors—a hospital, churches, and schools—and their humane employment policies had tried to foster a harmonious interracial climate. The Durham Textile Mill made socks, seventy-five pairs a day, on eighteen machines run by twelve women and two men. Many other workers were engaged in its other operations. Charles C. Amey, a graduate of the Agricultural and Technical College (for blacks) in Greensboro, was the manager. The mill closed in 1916 because of a slump in textile production due to the war in Europe, but also because of lack of a market for its goods. The owners were too involved in other endeavors to give it the attention it required.[60]

The Merrick-Moore-Spaulding Land Company came into being because the state insurance commissioner advised the Mutual Company that too much of its money was invested in real estate. To comply with the law yet retain the property, the real estate company was set up in 1910 and much of the property transferred to it. After Merrick's death the company became the (Edward R.) Merrick-McDonald-Wilson Company and later Union Insurance and Realty Company.[61]

Another insurance company, obviously a Mutual imitator and competitor but hitherto not mentioned in the history of black Durham, was the Carolina Mutual Life Insurance Company of Durham, organized in 1903 with its home office in Raleigh until 1905 when it was moved to Durham. It was made up of some of the same organizers as the North Carolina Mutual, those who pulled out of the older company at the time of its reorganization in 1899. Pearson was president of this second company, Shepard, vice-president, and Dr. J. A. Dodson, a druggist, was secretary and treasurer. The general manager was G. W. Powell, and among its directors were John A. Dancy, Moore's wife's uncle and Recorder of Deeds for the District of Columbia, and S. H. Vick, ex-postmaster of Wilson. In 1908 an advertisement for the company claimed that it had 250 agents in the field and twenty-two branch offices.[62] The fate of this company is unknown.

William Gaston Pearson (1859–1940), who was involved in so many of these enterprises, had got his start in life through the generosity of Julian Carr. After hearing the young Pearson give a stump speech in 1883, Carr had offered to pay his way at Shaw University. He knew Pearson's mother, Cynthia Ann Pearson, originally a Florida slave owned by Gray Barbee and married to a slave of William Pearson. Until the founding of Saint Joseph's A.M.E. Church she had been a member of Trinity. Carr was not mistaken in Pearson's abilities. He won the orator's medal at Shaw in 1883 and went on after graduation in positions of leadership from one achievement to another until he won the Harmon award in 1928. He started the Bankers Fire Insurance Company (1920) and the Southern Fidelity and Surety Company (1926) and was principal of first the graded school and then the Hillside Park High School for thirty years. A right-hand man to Spaulding, Pearson benefited as the company prospered and became a wealthy man, but he never gave up his teaching or his dedication to the uplift of his race.[63]

James Edward Shepard (1875–1947) was another man of exceptional drive and devotion to his people. Son of the Raleigh minister Augustus Shepard (d. 1911), he too was educated at Shaw, taking a degree in pharmacy. His father had begun his ministerial career as a representative of the American Baptist Publication Society and had organized the Baptist State Sunday School Convention of North Carolina in 1872, becoming its first president. Later he accepted the pastorate of the White Rock Baptist Church, a move that brought his own talents and those of his children to Durham. James Shepard followed his father into Sunday school work and into the ministry. In 1907 he traveled all over Europe and Africa on Sunday school work, finishing up his tour at the international Sunday school convention in Rome. His travels undoubtedly stimulated his desire to provide religious training for American blacks. Very soon after his return he investigated ways to implement his idea.[64]

In 1908 he put together a prospectus to raise money for a Bible school modeled on that at Northfield, Massachusetts, to train Sunday school teachers and missionaries. The plan included the teaching of languages and some medicine as well as biblical studies. He proposed to build the school on a 280-acre tract at Irmo-South, ten miles from Columbia, South Carolina, where there were already three buildings formerly belonging to the South Carolina Industrial Home. Another possible site offered him was twenty acres at Hillsborough. His fundraising met with some success; by 1909 he had raised $1,000 and decided on Durham as the location of the National Religious Training School and Chautauqua, as he chose to call it. The Merchants Association in Durham, always alive to prospective advantages to Durham, had cooperated in the effort and had persuaded Brodie Duke to sell the school twenty acres on Fayetteville Street and donate the proceeds to the cause. By July the concept had widened to include courses on agriculture, horticulture, and domestic science, obviously concessions to pressure from white backers who did not want to lose their black labor pool through education for only white-collar jobs. Mass meetings to stimulate interest brought prominent speakers: D. A. Tompkins, Dr. James H. Dillard, and Rabbi Abram Simon among them. Julian Carr was treasurer of the organization, Shepard, president, and Moore, secretary.[65]

In 1910 the first buildings, costing $20,000, went up—two dormitories, a dining room, and an auditorium—and the school opened in July. Judge Jeter Pritchard and R. B. Glenn agreed to raise money for an endowment by touring the North, where Mrs. S. P. Avery of Hartford, Connecticut, had already donated $4,000 to the cause. Despite the initial enthusiasm, the money raised was insufficient to support so ambitious an undertaking for long. Shepard had to borrow repeatedly to keep the school going. One of his creditors, G. C. Farthing, went deeply into debt in 1912, forcing the repayment of his loans. The school property was auctioned along with all the Shepards' private property, household furnishings, and library. Nonetheless the school continued to function, and that spring the president of the Southern Railway spoke at the commencement exercises giving the only advice to blacks that whites, determined to maintain the status quo, were capable of: "Above all . . . avoid creating in the minds of your pupils dissatisfaction with the opportunities that are open to them."[66] The opportunities he meant were agriculture and domestic service. At the auction of the school property Thomas M. Gorman, Carr's personal secretary, bid it in for Carr for $25,000, and funds were found to keep the school open. In 1923 the state took over the school with its thirty-three acres and sixteen faculty members, as it had already done with the black colleges in Winston-Salem and Elizabeth City. Shepard was retained as president.[67]

This notable achievement—the establishment of a black educational facility by black initiative—took place at a time when race relations in the South could hardly have been worse. Yet underneath the apparent acquiescence of blacks in the white-supremacy scheme of things, changes were taking place. Frustration and anger were becoming manifest in a rising black crime rate (in which cocaine dependence figured) and in increasing emigration to the North. Although a prosperous black entrepreneurial class was quickly coalescing in Durham, sustained by new business and the professions and reinforced by a network of kinship as intermarriages took place among the successful families, the large mass of black labor bore the brunt of racial hostility. Their pay was pitifully low and their opportunities almost nil. Black exodus to the North and West, which had begun during Reconstruction, accelerated after 1900, increasing with each decade. The black leadership, which in essence was the Mutual leadership, at the apex of the social hierarchy, was looked to by the white community as responsible for the entire black community, to ensure that there was no rocking of the boat. This small group of men understood that their own liberty and success were hostage to the whites for peace between the races. They saw their job as keeping the lid on black anger, going to the rescue in crises, and finding ways to help the impoverished mass of blacks in their need, sickness, or hopelessness. They tried to discourage black emigration, knowing that a plentiful black labor supply was prerequisite to staving off white interference. It was a difficult maneuver they were expected to perform, and they did it exceptionally well.[68]

What made race relations particularly explosive around the turn of the century and beyond was the widespread acceptance by southerners and, in fact, by much of the white southern leadership, of the Radical view of blacks. Having arisen about 1890, this aberrant concept portrayed blacks as retrogressing physically and morally, a view for which corroboration was claimed in the pseudo-science of the day. An increase in the black crime rate coincided with a new white fear, no longer that of mass black uprisings against whites, but of individual rapes by black males of white women. Lynching, which had occurred sporadically for over a century and which historically had had no racist aspect, at the same time became more and more a crime committed by whites against alleged black transgressors, particularly rapists. Because Radicalism found easy acceptance, it was effectively used in political contests. In Durham Julian Carr exemplified the Radical view. Despite his paternalism toward blacks, an attitude that translated into real help in the form of money, food, and attention, he could never rid himself of Radical notions. In 1917 he proclaimed, "We are sitting on the lid in Dixie and in spite of the world, the flesh and the devil, we propose to keep unpolluted the red blood of the Anglo-Saxon. We have plighted troth that we will pass down to our posterity and these to their posterity, the blue eyes and the flaxen hair of our precious children and to keep this troth inviolate."[69] This was pure Radical rhetoric.

The Radical viewpoint had a strong propagandist in the North Carolina minister and popular novelist Thomas Dixon. In 1905 his novel *The Klansman* came to Durham in the form of a play. The Dixons came with it and were guests of the Louis Carrs. The newspaper comment on the play—blatantly racist like the novel, which portrayed a Negro as a brute and a rapist—was that it presented the Negro "as we know him."[70] The play returned to Durham in 1908, a year after the inauguration of the Jim Crow railroad laws, and the Durham *Recorder* candidly reported that it revived people's prejudices, which were already apparent enough without encouragement. When *The Klansman* came yet again to Durham as the movie *Birth of a Nation,* it was shown at the Academy of Music against the protests of blacks, who understandably feared it would inflame passions and precipitate violence against them.[71]

The black population did not meekly accept all the inequities visited on it. In 1914 a delegation of prominent blacks visited the Railroad Corporation Commission office to complain of the Jim Crow service the railroads supplied, using old wooden cars sandwiched between the newer steel ones, subjecting those in the wooden cars to extreme danger in the event of an accident. They requested all wood or all steel cars on every train. Their request was prompted by experience, a head-on collision of a freight and passenger train near Hamlet in the summer of 1911. The passenger train had been loaded with Durham Sunday school members on an excursion to Charlotte sponsored by Saint Joseph A.M.E. Church. In the collision the wooden cars had splintered and compacted like accordions, killing seven passengers and injuring twenty-five. The event had profoundly disturbed the black population of Hayti and had become part of their oral culture. When Professor Frank Brown of Trinity, who organized the North Carolina Folklore Society in 1913, was collecting ballads of the Durham locale, he came across "The Hamlet Wreck," composed by workers in the tobacco stemmery at Liggett and Myers and written down by two of them, Franklin Williams and William Firkins.[72]

Blacks had always sung at their work, as slaves in the fields and freedmen in the factories, transforming daily burdens to bearable songs. Like churches of the same period, factories had their windows open, and voices joined in haunting melody soared out of the steaming workrooms to those listening in the streets. From this diversion developed quartets of the better musicians who began to compete in public entertainments. The Durham Dulcet Quartet, for example, competed against the Winston-Salem All Stars Quartet in March of 1908 and won the palm. This tradition continued right up to the Second World War. The parents of Shirley Caesar, the Gospel singer, came to work in the Liggett and Myers factory in 1926, and her father formed a quartet called Just Come Four. Their four oldest children, aged seven to thirteen, still too young to work in the factory, also formed a quartet. Most of the groups sang a cappella, but a few were accompanied by guitars. The music they sang, both in the stemmeries and in the quartets, was "Christian music," not blues. This form of black culture, while no longer part of the work place, flowered in other soil—in black churches and in the professional entertainment world—and continues in the mainstream of American culture to this day. Similarly, from their musical heritage, a small group of musicians of the poorest class of blacks brought to flower in Durham in the early decades of the century a regionally distinct form of the now widely popular music known as the blues (see chapter 16).[73]

Richard Bennehan (1743–1825). Portrait attributed to John W. Jarvis. Courtesy of Walter
E. Shackelford, photographer.

Duncan Cameron (1777–1853). Portrait by William Garl Browne. Courtesy of North Carolina Collection Photographic Archives, Wilson Special Collections Library, UNC.

Willie Person Mangum (1792–1861). Portrait by William Garl Browne. Courtesy of North Carolina Collection Photographic Archives, Wilson Special Collections Library, UNC.

Hardscrabble Plantation House (eighteenth century). Courtesy of Historic Preservation Society of Durham.

John Nichols House (c. 1812). Photograph by Thomas C. Rogers, Jr. Courtesy of Historic Preservation Society of Durham.

Bennehan House (1787, 1799), Stagville Plantation Historic Site.
Courtesy of Kenneth McFarland, photographer.

Fairntosh Plantation House (1810, 1817). Courtesy of Kenneth McFarland, photographer.

John Archibald McMannen (1812–75). Courtesy of Mary-jo Hall.

Slave cabin with stick chimney, Leigh Farm.
Courtesy of Curtis Booker.

Richard Stanford Leigh (1809–98). Ambrotype courtesy of Curtis Booker.

Duke Homestead (1852), Washington Duke on the porch. Courtesy of DU-RBMSCL, Semans Family Papers.

The Bennett Place c. 1875, probably James Bennett at the gate. Courtesy of NCOAH.

Barn at Horton Grove (1860), Stagville Plantation Historic Site.
Photograph by Joann Sieburg-Baker; courtesy of NCOAH.

West Point Mill in flood, 1908. Photograph by Hugh Mangum;
courtesy of Eno River Association.

Robert George Fitzgerald (1840–1919) during the Civil War. Courtesy of North Carolina Collection, Durham County Library.

John Thomas Nichols (1840–92) during the Civil War.
Courtesy of DU-RBMSCL, J. T. Nichols Papers.

Bartlett Leonidas Durham (1824–59). Portrait by unknown
artist. Courtesy of DU-RBMSCL, W. T. Dixon Papers.

William Mangum House and family. Courtesy of DU-RBMSCL, W. T. Dixon Papers.

Houses of E. J. Parrish (right) and Caleb B. Green. Courtesy of DU-RBMSCL,
E. J. Parrish Papers.

Somerset Villa (1888). Courtesy of DU-RBMSCL, W. T. Dixon Papers.

Edward James Parrish (1846–1920). Courtesy of DU-RBMSCL, E. J. Parrish Papers.

Parrish's Warehouse (1879). Courtesy of DU-RBMSCL, W. T. Dixon Papers.

W. T. Blackwell and Company Factory (1874, 1880). Courtesy of DU-RBMSCL, Picture Collection.

Washington Duke (1820–1905) and his granddaughter Mary Duke (later Biddle).
Courtesy of DU-RBMSCL, Semans Family Papers.

William T. Blackwell (1839–1903). Courtesy of North
Carolina Collection, Durham County Library.

Julian Shakespeare Carr (1845–1924). Courtesy
of DU-RBMSCL, Picture Collection.

Benjamin Newton Duke (1855–1929) and Sarah Pierson Angier Duke (1856–1936).
Courtesy of DU-RBMSCL, Semans Family Papers.

The Southern Conservatory of Music (1900) as drawn by Hook and Sawyer, Architects. Courtesy of DU-RBMSCL, B. N. Duke Papers.

Duke Factory (1884) in mourning for President William McKinley, 1901. Courtesy of DU-RBMSCL, Picture Collection.

Old Watts Hospital (1895). Courtesy of North Carolina School of Science and Mathematics.

George Washington Watts (1851–1921) on the steps of Watts Hospital with the 1898 graduating class of nurses. From left: Mrs. Troy, superintendent of nurses; unidentified school official; Annie Ferguson; Eva O'Hagan (later Mrs. Sol Mason); Lily Cowan (later Mrs. D. C. Mitchell); and Miss Florence McNulty, superintendent of the hospital. Courtesy of North Carolina Collection, Durham County Library.

Thomas Decatur Jones (1852–1889) and Mattie Southgate Jones (1864–1936). Courtesy of DU-RBMSCL, Southgate-Jones Papers.

Edian Markum (Markham) (1824–1910). Courtesy of St. Joseph's A.M.E. Church, Durham.

White Rock Baptist Church (1896, 1910). Courtesy of North Carolina Collection, Durham County Library.

St. Joseph's A.M.E. Church (1891). Courtesy of Milo Pyne; photograph by George C. Pyne, Jr.

North Carolina Training School and Chautauqua (c. 1910–20). From left: Parkhurst Cottage, boys' dormitory; Chidley Hall; and Avery Auditorium. Courtesy of North Carolina Central University, Office of Public Relations.

James Edward Shepard (1875–1947). Courtesy of DU-RBMSCL, Picture Collection.

John Sprunt Hill (1869–1961). Courtesy of Annie Watts Hill Foundation.

Lowes Grove Farm Life School (1913). From left: Lowes Grove Baptist Church; boys' dormitory; the Little Red School House (in the trees); and the high school (1911). Photograph from *Annual Report of the Public Schools of Durham County, 1913–1914*. Courtesy of Curtis Booker.

Lincoln Hospital (1901). Courtesy of North Carolina Collection, Durham County Library.

Merrick House (John Merrick on the balcony). Courtesy of North Carolina Collection, Durham County Library.

Richard Burton Fitzgerald (1842–1918) and family. Courtesy of North Carolina
Collection, Durham County Library.

Office of the North Carolina Mutual and Provident Association (after 1919
North Carolina Mutual Life Insurance Company). From left: Dr. Aaron
McDuffie Moore, John M. Avery, John Merrick, Edward Merrick, and Charles
Clinton Spaulding. Courtesy of North Carolina Collection, Durham County
Library.

Commonwealth Cotton Mill employees (1880s). Courtesy of DU-RBMSCL, Picture Collection.

Bahama School. Courtesy of DU-RBMSCL, Picture Collection.

Red Mountain Baptist Church (c. 1910–20). Courtesy of Robert A. Parker.

St. Philip's Episcopal Church (1907). Courtesy of Milo Pyne;
photograph by George C. Pyne, Jr.

Camp Creek Primitive Baptist Church congregation, 1942. Photograph by Benjamin F. Patrick. Courtesy of SHC, Benjamin M. Patrick Papers, UNC.

North Carolina Mutual Life Insurance Company (1921). Courtesy of NCOAH.

Corcoran Street, Durham, 1926. From left: Geer Building, First National Bank Building, Durham Hosiery Mill, and Post Office. From *Durham, North Carolina: A Center of Industry and Education* (1926). Courtesy of Curtis Booker.

James Buchanan Duke (1856–1925). Courtesy of
DU-RBMSCL, Semans Family Papers.

John Carlisle Kilgo (1861–1922). Courtesy of D.U. Archives, DU-RBMSCL.

William Preston Few (1867–1940), inauguration photograph, 1910. Courtesy of
D.U. Archives, DU-RBMSCL.

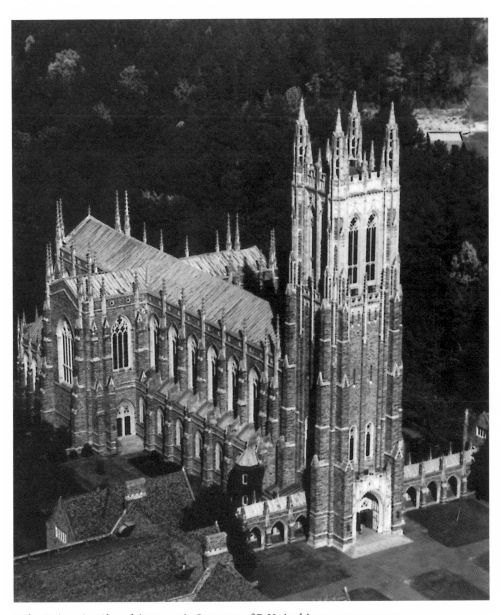

Duke University Chapel (1930–32). Courtesy of D.U. Archives, DU-RBMSCL.

Washington Duke Hotel (1925). Courtesy of North Carolina Collection, Durham County Library.

Mamie Dowd Walker (1880–1960). Photograph by George C. Pyne, Jr. Courtesy of Milo Pyne.

Pettigrew St. in Hayti, 1930s. Courtesy of North Carolina Collection, Durham County Library.

Pauli Murray (1910–85), lawyer, writer, and first black woman ordained in the Episcopal Church. Courtesy of North Carolina Collection Photographic Archives, Wilson Special Collections Library, UNC.

Successive editors of the *Merrick-Washington Magazine for the Blind*. Seated from left: John Washington, Lyda Moore Merrick (1890–1987), and Charlotte Hackett; standing from left: Margaret Wisenton and Ila Blue. Courtesy of North Carolina Collection, Durham County Library.

Louis Austin (1898–1961). Courtesy of North Carolina Collection, Durham County Library.

Burroughs Wellcome Company building (1972), Research Triangle Park. Courtesy of GlaxoSmithKline. Used with permission.

National Humanities Center (1979). Photograph by Joann Sieburg-Baker. Courtesy of National Humanities Center.

Durham Skyline with the SunTrust and Peoples Security buildings.
Courtesy of Durham Convention and Visitors Center.

Durham Bulls Baseball Park. Courtesy of Durham Convention and Visitors Center.

American Tobacco Company buildings in process of rehabilitation; old air-conditioning watercourse. Courtesy of Durham Convention and Visitors Center.

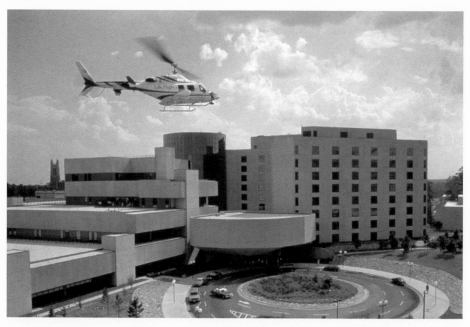

Duke University Hospital-North with Life Flight helicopter.
Courtesy of Durham Convention and Visitors Center.

Terry Sanford presenting a "blue devil" statuette to Mary D. B. T. Semans.
Courtesy of DU-RBMSCL, Semans Family Papers.

Coach K. (Mike Krzyzewski). Photograph by Jon Gardiner.
Courtesy of Duke Photography.

John Hope Franklin (1915–2009). Photograph by Chris Hildreth.
Courtesy of Duke Photography.

Chancellor Julius Chambers with Justice Willis Whichard of the State Supreme Court and Benjamin Ruffin (1941–2006), chairman of UNC Board of Governors. Photograph by Robert Lawson. Courtesy of North Carolina Central University, Office of Public Relations.

Reynolds Price. Photograph by Les Todd. Courtesy of Duke Photography.

The Iris Fountain, Doris Duke Center, Sarah P. Duke Gardens. Photograph by Les Todd. Courtesy of Duke Photography.

Magic Wings Butterfly House, North Carolina Museum of Life and Science. Courtesy of Beth Mauldin.

Three Coquerel's sifakas (*Propithecus coquereli*) in one of the forested natural habitat enclosures of the Duke Lemur Center. Photograph by David Haring. Courtesy of Duke Lemur Center.

The Face of Change, 1903–1917

14

TOWN AND COUNTY GROWTH

The ballooning of Durham's population in the first two decades of the new century made significant changes in the town and its surroundings. In 1900 the town counted 6,679 residents; ten years later the number was 18,241. Much of this rise is accounted for by the extension of the city limits in 1901, which quadrupled the town area. Some residents included in the new figure had long been settled on the periphery of the town; many more, however, were newly arrived in town, drawn away from the countryside. Thus in 1910 emerged a new demographic picture of Durham County that signaled the end of an old era and the beginning of a new, marked by an urban majority. In 1910 only 49.3 percent of Durham's population was still rural.[1] For the swelling crowd in the town new services had to be supplied, and the face of the city, its material culture, and the way its people lived radically changed. This was obvious in buildings, entertainment, and transportation.

The revolution in transportation was three-pronged: the establishment of an electric trolley service over six miles long, the improvement of roads, and the coming of the automobile. The Durham Traction Company (owned by J. S. Carr, A. B. Andrews, and Richard Wright) made possible new residential areas out of town but within walking distance of trolley lines. Improvement of the roads encouraged mobility and increased settlement along the main arteries leading from town; and the automobile, while not at first the common possession it would soon become, profoundly changed the habits of the residents, eventually leading to the virtual abandonment of downtown as a place to live.[2]

Except for Carr's pocket park at Ramseur and Dillard streets and a more ample one at Erwin Mills—both privately owned—there were no open places for Durham's residents to amuse themselves until after the turn of the century. The newly formed trolley company, aware of what had happened in Raleigh and Charlotte, saw an opportunity to increase its revenue by establishing an amusement park at the west end of the trolley line. In 1902, the year it began operation, the company secured from W. H. Proctor and Nancy Rigsbee twenty-seven acres beyond the cemetery that would provide a western terminal for its cars as well as the necessary space to develop a park with a merry-go-round, a roller coaster, a lake for swimming, a rink for roller skating, a pavilion for dancing, and a casino for summer stock performances. A baseball park at the eastern terminal was already established to attract riders in that direction, but actually the trolleys themselves were sufficient amusement. The open-sided summer cars rollicked along at such speeds when they first began to run that the town felt obliged to put a limit on them. The aldermen decreed a six-mile-an-hour limit, but vociferous protest succeeded in relaxing the restriction to fourteen miles an hour. Still, it was fast enough to create a breeze and provide a cool ride away from the stuffy city.[3] Besides the chance to swim in the heat of the day and to dance to live music in the cool of the evening, patrons were drawn to the Runkel Stock Company productions. The company performed in a large frame building, innocent of paint or ceiled roof but capable of seating an audience of eight hundred, where an occasional snake might drop from the bare rafters to enliven the show. After the Runkels' son died following an operation for appendicitis, for which his mother blamed a Durham doctor, the town held memories too bitter for the family to return. No other company successfully filled the Runkels' shoes, but for many summers trolleys packed with joyful riders continued to carry Durhamites to Lakewood Park.[4]

The development of the park was a direct spur to residential development in the same vicinity, logically named Lakewood. As the park bordered the main road to Chapel Hill, this thoroughfare attracted new houses, some of them large and ornate in the Queen Anne style in an exuberance of variety. Captain Joseph R. Renn, a conductor on the rail line from Henderson to Durham and stationmaster of the Union Station after its construction in 1905, had already settled on that stretch of the Chapel Hill Road in the 1890s. Another who built there after Lakewood Park was established was Captain Leonidas James (c. 1845–1923), a native of Noble County, Ohio, who bought the defunct North State Lumber Company Ltd. of Michigan in 1901 and renamed it the James Lumber Company. He developed the northeast corner of the county now known as Redwood, probably named for the large red oaks that grew there. Besides the sawmill and a handsome residence for his family, James built a general store, managed by his wife, for the colony of lumberjacks. James himself became postmaster of the new office in 1901. On land purchased in Lakewood in 1905 he built a house at the corner of Chapel Hill and House streets where he lived until his death in 1923. James Street is named for him.[5]

Redwood also acquired a school in 1901, replacing the Colclough school (itself later replaced by Roberson Grove Church) and Cedar Grove School (replaced by Mount Zoar Church). Redwood earned a dubious reputation in those early years when dissension over school hiring broke out among the neighbors. So uncontrolled did the anger become that the antagonists resorted to poisoning one another's livestock and eventually burned down the school in 1912. The first teachers were the Reverend Charles A. Sigmund and Maggie Ward. In 1912 the teachers were Joe Massey, Beulah Bragg, and Lilly Carpenter. Redwood School was soon rebuilt;

it continued until 1927 when it was consolidated with Mineral Springs School and two younger schools: Southview and Southview Annex, both in Carr Township.[6]

The automobile appeared on the streets of Durham in 1901. The first of the new-fangled contraptions was owned by George Leonidas Lyon, Washington Duke's grandson. That the automobile caught on quickly is seen in the opening of a car agency in 1902 by C. W. King, who sold Milwaukee cars costing between $750 and $1800. By 1907 cars had become so common that the city had to establish a speed limit. When a child was killed by a car that year, the rate was lowered from ten to eight miles per hour on Main Street. Two companies that ran cars between Chapel Hill and Durham were in business in 1908, the Durham Auto Company and the Bull City Transit Company. Unfortunately, the road between the towns was so bad that they could not run in wet weather. The town's first taxi service began in 1909 with one cab. Before the advent of public transportation, a man who worked in the city had to live within walking distance of his workplace or own a horse and carriage. While the coming of the trolley in the 1880s had liberated masses of people to live out of town, they were limited in their choice to areas near trolley routes. With cars available, however, a road was the only requirement, and the new freedom was intoxicating.[7]

Since few young men could afford a motorcar, George Lyon must have been the envy of every young blade in town. Besides possessing an automobile, he was a sportsman and a crack marksman. In 1908 Lyon won the eastern championship in trap shooting. In 1912 he successfully defended the title of world champion that he had won the previous year and represented the United States in the Stockholm Olympics. Unfortunately, he had early contracted tuberculosis, the same disease that had killed his mother, and he died in 1916 at the age of thirty-five.[8]

The motherless Lyon children had lived at Fairview with their grandfather during their childhood, but in 1900 George Lyon, then married to Snowden Carr, a daughter of Louis A. Carr, built a fine house in the Morehead Hill enclave of George Watts's friends, relatives, and associates. A few years later John Sprunt Hill and his wife moved into the former Watts house, which had been moved across Duke Street to make room for Harwood Hall, Watts's stone mansion built in the late 1890s. In 1909–10 both James E. Stagg, Benjamin Duke's secretary (like Hill just returned from a sojourn in New York), and Victor Bryant built large houses at the corner of Vickers and Duke streets. Stagg's house, Greystone, designed by Charles C. Hook, is reminiscent of the Benjamin Duke mansion Four Acres, also Hook's work, built in 1908–9 at the corner of Duke and Chapel Hill streets. In 1910 John Sprunt Hill obtained from his father-in-law the former house and grounds of L. A. Carr (Watts's brother-in-law) in the next block of Duke Street and hired the Boston firm of Kendall and Taylor to build an elaborate Spanish-style villa which was completed in 1912 and still stands today. With a few more grand houses built in the middle teens, for example those of Howard Foushee and John M. Lipscomb (another Louis Carr son-in-law), the Morehead Hill section had become the best new address in Durham.[9]

The oldest elite neighborhood, where Edward J. Parrish and Julian Carr had staked out their homesites in the 1870s, and genteel neighborhoods in nearby blocks of Main, Dillard, Cleveland, Mangum, Liberty, Holloway, and Roxboro streets were still developing. The house at the northwest corner of Dillard and Main, for example, where William ("Tip") Lipscomb had lived, was first remodeled by Williamson W. Fuller, and after Fuller moved to New York as general counsel to the Duke company in 1895 it was remodeled by Robert W. Winston, the latter naming it Eldon Hall. After Winston's move to Raleigh as a law partner of Governor Charles Brantley Aycock, the house was bought by C. W. Toms, who later sold it to John Buchanan. That vicinity was still very much a Carr preserve in the first decades of the century; the A. G. Carrs lived on the southwest corner opposite Somerset Villa, the elder Mrs. Carr on Main Street, T. M. Gorman, Carr's secretary, also on Main Street in a brand-new mansion, and Richard Wright in Parrish's old mansion (1876) at the northeast corner of Dillard and Main.[10]

Brodie Duke, going his own way as usual, in the 1880s had established his home on a large tract of land now lying between Duke and Gregson streets. In 1901 he began to develop the land lying between his own estate and the college. He laid out a grid of streets from Lamond to Urban and from Guess Road (now Buchanan) to Duke Street, the neighborhood now known as Trinity Park. While the Morehead Hill and Dillard Street areas were notable for their mansions, the Trinity Park area, which was close to a trolley line and populated by middle- to upper-income professionals and businessmen, was characterized by a great variety of houses, some large and pretentious but none presuming to the name of mansion.[11]

Still another alternative to living in town was that chosen by Edward J. Parrish. On his return from Japan in 1904, he tested New York life, as other American Tobacco Company executives had done, but in a short time he returned home, broader of girth and whiter of hair, and sporting a new goatee, but with the old dignity. His return to Durham had not been certain, however; while abroad, Parrish had written to W. W. Fuller, "Sometimes I almost decide that I will not make Durham my future home. My relations with the Colonel and Doctor [his brothers-in-law Julian S. and Albert G. Carr] cause me to think I may not. (This confidential)."[12]

Undoubtedly the trouble in Dr. Albert Gallatin Carr's family brought Parrish back to Durham. Quite as much a town character as his wealthier brother, Dr. Carr had been a bulwark to the Wattses and Dukes and everyone else who benefited from the ebullience of his personality and the efficacy of his bedside manner. After earning his degree at Jefferson Medical College in Philadelphia in 1870, he had first settled temporarily in Cary before moving to Durham. There he had devoted himself to his profession with consuming interest and energy, and even taken courses at Johns Hopkins medical school to acquaint himself with the new uses of the microscope. At times afflicted by what his family called a nervous disease, he would become irrepressible, spend money lavishly, go deeply into debt, work without rest, and upset those around him with his frenzied activity. In one such episode his son appealed to Benjamin Duke to help get his father home. Without warning A. G. Carr committed suicide in January 1905.[13]

The shock was almost as great to the town as it was to his family; in spite of his eccentricities, he had been generally esteemed. Edward Parrish probably rushed to Durham to give his sister, Carr's widow, whatever support he could render. Parrish's return at this sad time actually proved propitious for his finances, for it was the beginning of a time of expansion and prosperity for the town and state. The Democrats, again in power, were determined to reform more than the deplorable school system. The prosperous atmosphere in Durham catered to new enterprises for which money was available, and construction and real estate were flourishing. Parrish could not have failed to observe the changes that had already occurred in the new century foreshadowing the expansion to come. He did what he had done before and invested in land: lots on Elizabeth Street, McMannen Street, Main Street, Hickstown, in Albright (a new black area along Holloway Street), a tract on Chapel Hill Road (WaWa Yonda), another tract in Lebanon Township, and much else besides. For himself he planned to build a handsome house on Main Street adjoining the courthouse, only a block from his former home. In 1907, however, perhaps influenced by Southgate's example and certainly by Carr with Occoneechee Farm, he changed his plan and bought the farm that had belonged to his sister and brother-in-law, the John Lockharts, then owned by another sister's relations, the Moores. For his sisters he called the estate Lochmoor. The tract lay on the road to Roxboro south of the Eno River and had been part of the Horton estate when the Lockharts acquired it in the 1870s.[14]

In the country Parrish set about building a gentleman's estate, greatly expanding the old two-story farmhouse with frame additions and unifying the whole facade with a huge double-storied classical portico and open and closed porches supported by pillars. A captain's walk crowned the main section. He developed his farm with the choicest of shrubs, flowers, and fruit trees, beehives, livestock, and domestic animals. His taste, like Carr's, ran to quality as well as grandeur, and he stinted no expense to complete the new farm's utility or beauty. Characteristic of his attitude was a letter he wrote in 1905 ordering a dog: "Now, I do not want simply a fair dog; I want the best dog."[15]

In line with the return-to-the-country movement that began in the middle 1890s was the trend in the new century to establishing clubs in the country for hunting. Quail Roost Shooting Club was formed around 1902 by a group of wealthy Durhamites and some of their business acquaintances from Baltimore and New York. Under its first president, William T. O'Brien, accommodations were built for housing the hunters and their families, who might wish to spend weeks at a time. The group acquired hunting privileges over three thousand acres of adjacent land in both Durham and Person counties, and the club remained active until World War I. The corporation was dissolved in 1926, and George Watts Hill acquired the land and converted it into a prizewinning dairy farm, part of which later became a conference center and retreat when Hill donated it to UNC. It has now been returned to private ownership.[16]

A similar attempt to convert Huckleberry Springs into a private club was not successful. The land had been owned originally by Nancy Rhodes, a descendant of Benjamin and Elizabeth Cabe Rhodes, and the creek in that vicinity with her name was the site of the Durham waterworks' first dam. For many years, when the springs belonged to Sheriff Blacknall, they had been used for picnics or stag barbecues. Among Blacknall's guests were John Sprunt Hill, J. S. Cobb, Jones Fuller,

C. W. Toms, the Duke brothers, J. F. Wily, J. H. Mahler, Moses McCown, and Jefferson Riley. George Lougee, nicknamed "Old Brunswick," would cook the barbecue and the men would pitch silver dollars at a line, a game they called crackaloo, while they imbibed more than the pure spring water. In 1907 a group was formed to build a clubhouse there and hunting rights were acquired on a thousand acres, but the plans went no farther. A few years later the land was bought by John Jefferson Riley and his brother-in-law T. J. Walker.[17]

The water bubbling from the springs was especially prized, and the Rileys proceeded to capitalize on it. They established bottling works and sold the water, a profitable venture. Judge Sam Riley, Jefferson's son, in his nineties attributed his long life to the water and remembered delivering it in a cart through the town streets when he was a boy. A demijohn or five-gallon jar cost a quarter. An advertisement for the water recommended its use "to feel safe from typhoid and malaria this summer." The first decades of the new century were popular times for springs because many people feared the contaminated well water of crowded towns and disliked the treated water in the municipal system. Not far from Huckleberry Springs on the Cole Mill road, Dr. Robert L. Holloway established Rivermont Springs on his land, and T. N. Allen sold water from a spring at the Duke Homestead. It was also in this decade that the mineral springs on today's Mineral Springs Road were discovered and first enjoyed.[18]

In the early years of the century, landmarks that characterized the city's twentieth-century face were taking shape. In 1905 alone three hundred buildings were added to Durham, but residential building was only a minor part of the construction occurring in those years, particularly in town. The Golden Belt Manufacturing Company and the Durham Hosiery Mills bulked larger and larger in East Durham, massive, brick structures surrounded by auxiliary buildings and clusters of millhouses. In the center of town the six-story C. C. Hook and Sawyer Trust Building (1904) became Durham's first skyscraper; its near neighbor, the Temple building, was put up in 1909. In 1914 Durham's banks housed themselves impressively in new structures: the First National Bank, designed by Milburn and Heister, at Main and Corcoran; the ornate Italian palace-like (Frederick) Geer Building opposite, designed by A. C. Blossom, housing the Fidelity Bank on its street level; and the marble temple of the Citizens Bank at Main and Mangum streets. The Academy of Music (or Municipal Building) in both its versions added elegance to the cityscape. Although the Federal Building (1906) containing the post office was later demolished, as was the Milburn and Heister railroad station (1905), the high school (1904), later altered as the city hall, remained. Saint Philip's Church (1907–8), the YMCA (1908), the Malbourne Hotel (1915), Parrish's Arcade complex (1909–11), and the second structure of the First Presbyterian Church anchored the eastern end of Main Street. To the block of Morris Street north of the new high school was erected the Imperial Tobacco Company's imposing Romanesque Revival building (1916) designed by the Richmond firm of C. C. Davis Company.[19] Farther west were the twin Watts and Yuille tobacco warehouses (1904), the present Brightleaf Square, and on Chapel Hill Street the massive Memorial Methodist Church (begun

1907). At the west end was Saint Joseph's Church (1908) and the additions to Erwin Mills. Many blocks to the north in yet undisturbed farmland rose the new Watts Hospital (1909).[20] All of them large and substantial, with architectural integrity and style, Durham's new buildings reflected a society in which solidity, ambition, and substance counted for much.

The urban magnet, while drawing heavily from the old communities, did not totally deplete their strength. The oldest established places—Bahama and Red Mountain/Rougemont—continued to grow and were enjoying their palmiest days. (J. D. C.) Turner and Hill, A. W. Tilley, and W. E. Hall had stores in Bahama, and Simeon Bowling, (H. E.) Carver and Company, S. F. Gates, C. L. Suitt and Company, and W. M. Bowling had stores in Rougemont. Carver's store had expanded in the 1890s, when its business required four clerks. Now Carver also owned sawmills and bought tracts of timber from which he made crossties and lumber. Bahama began a new enterprise too. Following World War I the sons of A. K. Umstead started the Bahama Milling Company at the heart of the village. They sold the operation in 1928 to Benjamin Bradley Mangum, who continued it.[21] With a few exceptions all the other communities lost their vitality and began to fade, if not to disappear completely. Yet in the southeast, along present Alston Avenue, a new community sprang into life in the new century: Lowes Grove, straddling the boundary between Cedar Fork and Patterson townships in what had become known as the "dark corner of the county" because of its sparsity of population and lack of good roads to either Durham or Raleigh.

The progenitor of the Lowe family, from whom the new community took its name, was Stephen Lowe, a bricklayer who had come into Wake County from Bute County in the 1770s. His descendants spread out, buying land in the same general area. His grandson Edmund Lowe (d. 1885), a Confederate veteran, and Edmund's wife, Patsy Sorrell Lowe, were instrumental in organizing the Sunday school and informal church services that resulted in the formation of Lowes Grove Baptist Church and consequently the community that developed around it. They and their neighbors at first belonged to Cedar Fork Church, but roads, weather, and distance from the church often prevented their attendance at services. In 1889 members of the Lowe, Hopson, Green, and Haley families with the help of the Reverend Dolphus Barbee met and organized a Sunday school. Because Mrs. Patsy Lowe was paralyzed, they met at the Lowe plantation, first on the porch or in the house and later in an outbuilding in a grove in front of the house, hence the name. Later still they moved to the public schoolhouse.[22]

Another group three miles south of Lowes Grove had been inspired to the same purpose and in 1879 had organized a Sunday school known as High Point. Members of the Barbee, High, Lewter, and Markham families had taken the lead in this effort. In 1907 the Reverend Robert E. Atkins began to preach to them regularly. With contagious determination he persuaded them to form what they named High Point Baptist Church, despite opposition from the members of Cedar Fork Church, who believed that the competition would weaken the older organization. Unable to raise sufficient funds to build a church, however, they soon saw the wisdom of joining the group at Lowes Grove, which by then had the schoolhouse to meet in. The merged congregations kept the Lowes Grove name. Pleasant Massey, who had faithfully preached to the Sunday school for many years, continued to serve at the congregation's request. Eighteen months after the church was organized in 1909, the original nineteen members had grown to sixty-five, and by their contributions of labor and money, with a few outside donations such as Julian Carr's fifty dollars, a frame church 54 by 34 and 18 feet high was built on an acre of land donated by Robert Rigsbee. When an elementary school was planned for this tract in 1925, the old church was moved across Alston Avenue. A foundation with basement rooms for the Sunday school was dug at that time, and the old frame building, moved to the foundation, was stuccoed over. The present structure was built on the same site in 1948.[23]

A dubious tradition once credited the Lowes with the donation of a school site as well. However the land was obtained, by 1896 the county had established a school at Lowes Grove: a one-room building moved from the Nelson community and at its new site known as the Little Red Schoolhouse. In 1910 the community voted an extra tax to improve the facilities. With this money the county bought more land and built a larger building with three classrooms, cloakrooms, an auditorium, and a library. The second decade of the century added new courses to the curriculum; the inclusion of domestic science and shop reflected the philosophy that education could also be practical. Lowes Grove School was the first in the county to institute a separate department of domestic science, taught by Geneva Cheatham. In 1913 the state legislature passed the Farm Life Bill for Durham County, allotting $2,500 for expert instruction in domestic science and agriculture, along with a bill fixing six months as the minimum school year. Lowes Grove School, which was already on a nine-month schedule, seized the opportunity, and, closely followed by Bahama, became the first Durham community to apply for the farm-life program. In 1913, assured of receiving the funding, it began to build a dormitory for the students who would live at the school at the county's expense. Students from other counties could attend for two dollars a month. To make itself self-sustaining, in 1915 the school bought additional acres on which to raise marketable crops. By 1922 two hundred students were enrolled in the farm-life school, and its fame had spread all over the country through an article in *Collier's* magazine. The voters overwhelmingly approved a supplemental tax to fund a new building and set to work on the county's first brick school.[24]

Lowes Grove also profited from the agricultural reforms that John Sprunt Hill was vigorously promoting, one of which was the system of rural credit unions that he had seen on a European tour of investigation. With evangelical zeal he preached the new gospel around the state, detailing all that was wrong with farming in North Carolina. One fault was that farmers were paying almost 40 percent more than cost for their supplies because of credit charges. A cooperative credit system could radically reduce this expense. In 1915 the legislature passed the McRae Rural Credits Bill, which set up a plan for short-term loans to farmers. Seconding Hill's concerns was Professor J. M. Johnson, who conducted a farmer's institute at Lowes Grove that summer and told the local farmers hard truths about agriculture in Durham

County. The average farm contained only thirty acres and netted only $497 a year. A fifty-acre farm should yield $1,000. It was not so much the small acreage as the poor productivity and planning that were at the root of the problem.[25]

In December 1915 the Lowes Grove school, bankers, and representatives of the state Department of Agriculture together formed the Lowes Grove Credit Union, the first rural credit bank in North Carolina and one of the first in the nation. Among the twenty-four farmers and businessmen who joined immediately were T. W. Barber, G. H. High, J. H. Markham, W. B. Hopson, T. L. Pendergrass, J. L. Morehead, T. B. Pierce, and Hill himself. Loans at 6 percent, cooperative buying, and the exercise of thrift set the Lowes Grove farmers on a sound economic program that prospered from the start. Its success and that of the school brought further development and prosperity to the community. In 1919 it was the first community in the county to apply for incorporation under the enabling legislation. A charter granted in August 1919 allowed it to form a local government, levy taxes, and issue bonds for roads, schools, libraries, and other public services. A board of directors made up of three qualified voters formed the governing body. They were G. W. Barbee, chairman, J. S. Woods, secretary, and J. H. Shipp, C. C. Fletcher was made a special policeman for the school district, and G. W. Ellis was elected magistrate to enforce the ordinances and regulations.[26]

Besides the church, school, and credit union, other new developments were forging a sense of community. One was the building of a station and siding in 1916 on the Durham and Southern Railroad, built by the Dukes in 1905 to run from Durham to Dunn straight through Lowes Grove. A cart road opened by the people themselves before the Civil War had been so poorly maintained it was no longer passable. Now to enable the farmers to transport their produce to the Durham markets, the county was persuaded to build a macadam road (1907), and the dark corner of the county was finally brought into the light. Sid Hopson opened a general store in the area in 1908, and when a telephone line was put into place in 1913, the sense of isolation vanished.[27]

Rural free delivery, established by the federal government in 1902, was blamed by many country storekeepers for the decline in their business and the slow shrinking of crossroads villages. The C. M. Miller map of 1910, however, documents new place names, post offices, railroad stops, schools, and stores. Centered at the intersection of present Cheek and Burton roads, for example, Gorman had become a place in its own right with the establishment of a post office with that name in 1892. In 1903 a lively organization of young Gorman men, the Fletcher Packhouse Debating Society, held regular meetings to debate current issues. Its president was J. D. Fletcher, and its secretary, D. H. Stallings. There, too, J. E. Suitt ran a general store and operated a sawmill and cotton gin, services that attracted local farmers. Crowding on Gorman were two other railroad stops: Holloway Station (named for the numerous Holloway family of that place) on the Oxford and Clarksville line, about a mile to the north, and Burton (possibly from the family name Halliburton), a stop on the Seaboard Airline Railroad about a mile to the south.[28]

Lillian, in the center of what in 1911 became Carr Township, took its name from a schoolhouse close to Carpenter's store and Penny's gin. White's Cross Roads lay where Cornwallis, Rigsbee, and Erwin roads intersected three to four miles west of Durham. A schoolhouse with that name stood on the site where the Burroughs family later built their farmhouse (still standing) in the 1920s, a short distance southeast on Cornwallis Road at its intersection with a cutoff to Rigsbee Road. Southeast of Durham on Angier Avenue, a quarter mile beyond today's city limits, was a Southern Railroad stop called Bilboa where a store and post office were established in 1904. R. M. Jones ran the notably profitable general store. While Bilboa had no debating club or church to flaunt its name, it did have a chapter of the Junior Order of United American Mechanics.[29]

CIVIC AND SOCIAL ORGANIZATIONS

When business and industrial magnates detected a flagging of the municipal leadership and entrepreneurial spirit in 1902, they organized a club whose function was to attract new business and industry to Durham and to prod the city government to civic improvement. They held a meeting at the courthouse to form a Chamber of Commerce and Industry, of which Robert Winston was elected president and W. A. Slater, J. D. Pridgen, and J. Harper Erwin first, second, and third vice-presidents, respectively. An executive committee and seventeen subcommittees organized the work of the chamber. The immediate concerns were Durham's lack of a suitable station (to replace the shacks provided by the railroads), a city park, and streets in the newly incorporated parts of town. With the help of Jones Fuller in the legislature, a bill was passed enabling the railroad corporation commission to require the railroads to build a station in Durham. Union station was already becoming a reality when the chamber elected new officers two years later and announced a new goal: a Carnegie library for the town. The Durham Chamber of Commerce was incorporated in 1906. Under its new president, Edward J. Parrish, the good roads program became its goal.[30]

Perhaps the old animosity between the brothers-in-law prompted Carr to form in 1907 what he described as a commercial club, of which he became president; J. M. Manning, vice-president; R. H. Sykes, secretary; and T. M. Gorman, treasurer. It began with seventy-nine members, and in Carr style aimed high, intending to provide spacious and comfortable rooms, in effect all the amenities of a gentleman's club. Carr had first called it the Cavaliers Club, but this name did not stick. Instead, the old Commonwealth Club was reborn. The members rented space in the new Trust Building and fitted up a library, card room, billiard and pool room, buffet, and kitchen. Although both Duke and Carr interests were heavily represented among the charter members—J. E. Stagg, Watts, William A. Erwin, and Angier B. Duke, as well as Carr and Wright—Parrish's name is not to be found either among the officers or board of governors.[31]

Whether or not Carr's new club undercut the effectiveness of the chamber, the older group faded from the scene, and its role was assumed in 1912 by a third group calling itself the Commercial Club. They demonstrated their commitment by immediately hiring an experienced executive secretary. Carr's son Claiborn was president, and W. F. Carr, W. W. Flowers, T. B. Fuller, W. D. Carmichael, and Samuel W. Sparger made up the executive committee. One of their first goals, echoing the Civic League's campaign, was to get rid of the jungle of wires and poles on Main Street. They published a brochure to advertise Durham's attractions, and in 1915 regularized their status by reorganizing as a chapter of the state Chamber of Commerce, which had been established in 1912. Almost immediately this group, too, lost its initial drive, but enough interest was sustained to keep it going. James H. Southgate, one of the promoters of the changeover, was president after the reorganization as he had been before it.[32]

With its hiring of Burke Hobgood as executive secretary in 1917, the Chamber of Commerce got its roots firmly planted at last, but it had a very shaky beginning. To stimulate interest, in 1913 the Commercial Club mounted a slogan contest for a gigantic sign to be erected on the tallest building in the town in view of all the incoming trains. A sign was designed for the winning slogan, "Durham Renowned the World Around": a rectangle some forty by thirty feet surmounted by a globe with the words *Progress, Success, Health,* and *Wealth* alternating with the slogan as the 1,230 electric bulbs flashed the messages to the night sky in colored lights. Here was a bid for fame by the same means Carr had used to promote Bull Durham: blazing the name before the world. The sign was erected on the Wright Building at Church and Main streets because the words were not legible at the Trust Building's height. Donated by Wright's Traction Company, the sign was unveiled with speeches, reminiscences, and boosterism of the most blatant form.[33]

Younger and sportier Durhamites under John Sprunt Hill's influence organized a country club. Hill, a golf enthusiast, had built a nine-hole course on his country estate Croasdaile, a huge tract extending from Rose of Sharon Road south to Hillsborough Road. He and his fellow players E. B. Lyon, J. R. Weatherspoon, E. R. Leyburn, J. M. Lipscomb, J. L. Morehead, J. E. Stagg, H. C. Barbee, W. M. Fallon, and S. W. Sparger had formed a local team. Several members of this group incorporated the Durham Country Club in 1912. Hill made available to them his golf links and two acres for a clubhouse near present Club Boulevard and Hillandale Road and offered to sell other small tracts for summer homes near the club. They built a Dutch colonial two-story building comprising a central section flanked by wings with a 94-foot porch across the front. Membership was open to any who wanted to join, for the group hoped the club would represent "the turning of a new page in the social history of the city in that it would bring the workers of the city, the makers of Durham history, into closer contact with one another and Durhamites will learn to know one another better under the most favorable conditions."[34]

E. J. Parrish was elected temporary chairman while the stock was being offered for subscription, and Hill was elected president at the organizational meeting following. The next year Hill offered to the club the ownership of his adjacent golf links if the club would maintain them. He also stipulated that the links be available to any white person who paid fees, whether or not a club member. Apparently there were not as many players as expected. Hill soon took back the maintenance of the links to enable the club to reduce its membership fee from $25 to $16 a year.

Heavily in debt by the end of 1914, the corporation sold the club to Hill with all its improvements. Its short life, however, was long enough to leave its name on the road it abutted: Club Boulevard.[35]

The prewar years hatched a clutch of other new organizations, patriotic, fraternal, and social. The Elks (1900), Manataka Tribe of Red Men (1901), Maple Camp of Woodmen of the World (1901), the Confederate Veterans' John Manning Camp (1902), and new chapters of the Junior Order of United American Mechanics. The JOUAM had been started in Philadelphia in 1845, part of the then-current nativist movement. Its initiates were expected to answer "yes" when asked, "Are you willing to do all you can to prohibit the landing upon our shores of the ignorant, pauper, and criminal hordes of the Old World?" Primarily a small life insurance beneficial society, in North Carolina it concerned itself with orphans. It was the first of several groups between 1901 and 1917 to collect donations of money and land on which to establish an orphan asylum in Durham. Following the JOUAM, the Red Men, the Knights of Pythias, the North Carolina Children's Home Society, and the Woodmen of the World tried and failed in the same attempt. The Children's Home Society came closest to success, having decided on a site offered by Oswald Kinion Proctor on present Miami Boulevard and a plan for an orphanage to be called Joyland. Although no asylum was ever built there, the name for the area stuck.[36]

Other clubs formed in these years were the Durham Golf Club (1900), Durham County Fair and Driving Association (1901), Cotillion (1902), Volkamenia (1903), Durham Art Club (1904), Durham Gun Club (1904), Pandora Club (1904), Halcyon Literary Club (1910), Eclectic or New Canterbury Club (1910), Patriotic Order of Sons of America (1910), General Davie Chapter, DAR (1911), Roundabout Club (1912), American Association of University Women (which began as a chapter of the Southern Association of College Women in 1913), Rotary Club, Auction Bridge Club, Campus Club (for faculty wives), Wide-Awake Circle (for Jewish girls), Equal Suffrage League, Young Men's Club (all in 1915), Boy Scouts (1916 and again in 1919), and the Dorcas Club (1917). The Equal Suffrage League was organized and led by Mrs. Edward J. Parrish after Senator Hobgood of Guilford County had successfully introduced a bill to enable women property-owners to petition for the ballot with the same literacy requirement as that for male voters. Many men willing to support the right of white women to vote were afraid of the effect that black women voters might have if suffrage were extended to women. Despite the active support and campaigning of such men as Judge Walter Clark, Professor Archibald Henderson, and attorney R. O. Everett, Durham women had to wait for the passage of the Nineteenth Amendment in 1920 to claim their right to vote.[37]

The Sheltering Home Circle of the King's Daughters, made up of two young women from each of eight town churches, made a lasting contribution to Durham during these years. They first planned to build a home for victims of Smoky Hollow, a euphemism for prostitutes, or as an editor called them, "soiled doves." When wiser heads persuaded them that they were not suited for this endeavor, they redirected their efforts to another needy group, elderly women of slender means. Brodie Duke gave the Daughters $500 and the promise of two lots when they were ready to build a home. By 1911 they had raised enough money for an $8,000 building to accommodate sixteen women. After the home was built and proving its value, the city began to contribute larger and larger sums, although most of the women paid for their own living expenses. By 1922 so great was the need of this service that the King's Daughters planned another, larger home. Brodie Duke had died in 1919, but his brothers gave $35,000 to the building fund. The Colonial Revival brick and limestone structure on the original lots, opposite Duke University's east campus on Buchanan Boulevard, which opened in 1925, could accommodate thirty-six women. The Daughters' original objective was incorporated into the wider plans of the Salvation Army, which in 1917 opened a shelter for prostitutes in a building on Morris Street.[38]

Accommodations for another sector of the population were also acutely needed after the Carrolina Hotel burned in 1907, for Durham suddenly found itself with no first-class hostelry. Lesser hotels hoping to capitalize on the lack spruced themselves up. The Corcoran was enlarged and redecorated. E. H. Murray refurbished the Saint Helen Hotel as the Hotel Murray. Parrish, however, tried hardest to cash in on the opportunity. He had long owned land adjoining the courthouse. On it he had already built in 1909 an elegant small theater and a series of shops—the Arcade—facing Main Street. Between the Arcade and the courthouse and extending across the backs of adjacent lots he now built a hotel, also called the Arcade, which opened in 1911. Since it faced the station, convenient for travelers, most of whom were salesmen, he first made it a commercial hotel, furnished with mahogany furniture and brass beds. The next year, however, Parrish enlarged it, tearing down part of Lyon's old boarding house on Roxboro Street to obtain extra space. A new dining room facing the station, all glass on its outside wall, with three floors of bedrooms above, filled the new addition, making sixty-two rooms and two dozen bathrooms in all. The old dining and commercial rooms became reading and writing rooms and a palm room with a fountain. Further expansion took place to the west by building behind the courthouse to Church Street. A garden with seats for guests adjoined the station, luring travelers into this oasis.[39]

The change of character from commercial to luxury-class hotel was unquestionably Parrish's attempt to hold his clientele in the face of serious competition by a new hotel across Main Street. Through the efforts of the Merchants Association, the Commercial Club, Watts, B. N. Duke, and their Fidelity Bank, money was raised in 1912 to erect a first-class hotel on the corner of Roxboro and Main streets. When Taurus was announced as the name for this new venture, the town matrons objected. The hotel received instead the name Malbourne, unquestionably to memorialize B. N. Duke's father-in-law, Malbourne Angier, as Carr had honored his own father-in-law in naming his first hotel the Claiborn. The Malbourne had 125 outside rooms with steam heat, telephone, and hot and cold water, and fifty private bathrooms. The architect, Charles M. Robinson of Richmond, had designed a brick building on a granite base with a massive copper cornice, ornamental iron balconies, and marquees over the Main and Roxboro street entrances.[40]

The Arcade hadn't a chance against the Malbourne. In 1912 Parrish sold the franchise of his hotel to Hubert J. Latta, who changed the name to Lochmoor to honor Parrish and give it a classier name; but nothing could save it, and in 1914 it was bankrupt. E. I. Bugg, who was then leasing the Malbourne, took over the Lochmoor, closed the dining room, and used the rest of the building as an annex. In 1921 Steve Changaris leased it from the Malbourne and redecorated it. The dining room had been used as the public library for a year or more while a new library was being built, but Changaris now returned to it its original function. In 1919 Parrish had almost concluded a sale of the hotel to the city and county for $55,000, but the county backed out. Two months later the Elks bought it for $65,000. Many years later, again needing space, for the second courthouse was by then outgrown, the county decided to buy Parrish's old hotel from the Elks and this time stuck to the deal, obtaining it for $50,000 in 1943.[41]

GOVERNMENT

Meanwhile the old courthouse's fate was equally uncertain in the second decade of the new century. While the city anguished over water, sewage, streets, and contagious diseases, the "County Dads" (Fairbrother's epithet) shilly-shallied over the courthouse. It had long before become too small for the myriad offices the county now needed. No one seemed able to decide whether to tear the building down and build anew on the same site or to start fresh in another location. Only after the commissioners learned that they could buy additional land adjacent to the courthouse did they decide to rebuild on the old site. The Young Men's Club took a prominent part in spurring the commissioners to action. Frank Milburn of the firm of Milburn and Heister presented acceptable plans that persuaded even Carr to abandon the old building, and a new courthouse was built in 1916. The Masons anointed the cornerstone in which the first cornerstone's contents were again immured along with a new box of representative items. A massive, dignified building with a jail on its top floor (a Milburn characteristic), it was used for more than five decades until abandoned for a new building across Main Street in 1978.[42]

The increased space that the courthouse needed was directly related to the growth and complexity of government. Whether city or county, local government was growing ever larger in people's lives. Besides compulsory education, vaccination against smallpox, and age and hour restrictions for working children (legislation frequently seen as usurpation of parental rights), new laws dictated the behavior of adults—from the use of intoxicants to driving their cars and muzzling their dogs—in the interest of public health, safety, and welfare. But the increased interaction of people and government also provided benefits. As voters began to understand the results of this cooperation, they were more willing to give up money or freedom for the desired good.[43]

Besides the new Department of Health and the municipal and court buildings, local government achieved major fiscal reforms. Salaries were inaugurated for all court officials in place of fees extracted from the public. City firemen no longer had to volunteer their services, risking life and limb, but became salaried. The old magistrate's court was replaced by a recorder's court, and the blue laws were eased. Tobacco, soft drinks, and cigars could be bought on Sundays, but drugstores still had to close during church hours. When the municipal building burned and was rebuilt without the city market as part of the complex, and a new city market was built at the corner of Foster and Watkins (now Morgan) streets, the smell of fish was once and for all removed from city business. These changes, instigated by dissatisfaction with the old system, paved the way for more efficiency and professionalism in local government.[44]

The historian R. D. W. Connor spoke at Trinity College advocating, among other things, the need for experts to deal with the complexity of modern government. A Durham lawyer and representative in the state legislature, Sumter C. Brawley, took the initiative and drew up for the city a bill for a new, commission form of municipal government. Many prominent men (including Julian Carr) supported the change, citing Durham's backwardness: a lack of beautiful public buildings, of an adequate water supply, of generous parks and playgrounds, and of well-paved streets. The city was financially naive as well: until 1913 it had never had a budget; if it ran out of funds, it borrowed. Dr. William H. Glasson of Trinity was made head of a committee charged with drafting a new charter for Durham. A mass meeting in 1915 to introduce the proposed charter approved the document, and J. Ed Pegram shepherded it through the legislature. In March 1915, however, a general referendum defeated it by ninety votes. Misinformation and failure to vote were the reasons given for its defeat, but city employees and ward politicians doubtless feared losing their jobs if a more streamlined and efficient system were adopted, and they lobbied against it.[45]

In 1917 the legislature passed a bill allowing municipalities to choose from a variety of forms of local government, and the new Durham charter was again put to a vote and again failed. Acrimonious debate had preceded this vote, suggesting that the opposition was losing ground. R. O. Everett, in favor of the new form, called opponent John Sprunt Hill "the greatest straddler on earth"; Jones Fuller called Hill "the self-appointed manager of this town." The Chamber of Commerce took the matter up and after close study proposed a modified system of eight councilmen with staggered terms, and a manager hired by the councilmen. In 1921 it was again put to a vote and this time passed, possibly because women were voting for the first time. In the new city government six of the eight aldermen were elected from specific areas or wards, while two were aldermen at large. All candidates were voted on by all the voters, a racist provision to prevent blacks from electing one of their number to the council. A mayor was elected independent of the city commission, but he held little power, while the city manager was given managerial power and authority over hired experts to head departments concerned with streets, water, fire, police, and finances. In June 1921 Robert W. Rigsby was engaged as Durham's first city manager.[46]

Julian S. Carr had long been the local boss of the Democratic party. Although he lost his bid for the United States Senate in 1900 to Furnivall M. Simmons, he was elected to the State House of Representatives in 1910. One of his most important bills provided state aid to counties for roadbuilding and maintenance and for buying better equipment. Both he and his friend Bennehan Cameron were very much in the forefront of the good roads movement. They saw to it that Durham formed a chapter of the association in January 1911. While Cameron was a representative in the legislature in 1915–16, Durham and Wake counties received federal funds to build a highway between Raleigh and Durham. Cameron also made sure that Durham was included in the route of the proposed Quebec-Miami International Highway. The railroads, too, were behind the good roads movement, for they assumed that with better roads farmers could more easily get their crops to the stations to be shipped to distant markets and thus increase railroad freight revenues. Ironically, it was to be the network of good roads throughout the nation that eventually doomed all railroads as trucks took over the freight industry. In these early years, however, the immediate goal was "to get the farmers out of the mud." Many good arguments sold the program: good roads meant less wear and tear on vehicles, teams, harness, and gear; cheaper hauling; more profitable crops; higher land values; and better schools and churches from improved incomes. The slogan was, "a good road brings prosperity and happiness." In conjunction with new roads came better bridges to replace the old wooden ones that were washed away year after year by freshets and floods.[47]

A newspaper reporter had fun describing such a freshet in 1901:

> Jupiter Pluvius reigns. Let the web foot rejoice and the finney tribe be glad. Let dust cry aloud, "My name is mud!" Let the cisterns and the wells be filled. . . . The weary plowman rests, and the loafing farmers pile their dripping saddles in the country merchant's store. . . . The owner of upland corn and wheat hath a gold mine and the bridge builders shall not lack for work. Eno River arose out of its bed and made a summer tour across the country. New Hope did not spring eternal in the human breast, and the dweller on its bottom knows now "where he is at." For the flood doth "rearrange and shift" his possessions, his wheat hath the corn field a-top and the melon patch doth seek the delta at the gulf. Hay shall be a mighty crop in the land, nor shall the beast of any field lack for drink. . . . Great is Jupiter Pluvius![48]

New bridges of substantial steel and concrete were built well above the destructive waters. The county commissioners in 1914–15 put new bridges at the Fish Dam, Bacon Rind, and Stagville crossings of the Flat River and over New Hope and Third Fork creeks. Four more bridges were completed in 1916 at Monk's Ford over the Little River, at Geer's (originally Guess's) mill and Cole's mill over the Eno, and at Addison Mangum's mills over the Flat River.[49]

Carr presented other bills: one to enable the school board to build a school in West Durham; a bill for a rail line between Durham and Chapel Hill, the old line built in 1873 from University Station to Chapel Hill never having paid; and a bill to annex to Durham County a section of Wake County adjacent to Oak Grove Township west of the Flat River. The residents there wished to join Durham County because Raleigh was too far away. They also commonly used Durham markets in which to sell their crops. There being no objection from Wake County, this object was easily effected, and a new township named for Carr (because of his part in bringing it into existence) was added to Durham County in 1911. Carr had also introduced bills to charter the Durham and Danville Railroad and to substitute the commission form of government for towns in North Carolina, which had paved the way for the eventual change in Durham's city government.[50]

A disastrous fire in 1914 revealed the inadequacies of the municipal water system. A water main broke on Mangum Street and the water pressure was insufficient to fight the fire, which burned out most of the block between Mangum and Church, Main and Parrish streets. Even before the fire, however, the inadequacies of the water system were under discussion. John C. Michie of the water department had asked the town to decide about its future water supply before the contract with the old company expired. Rumors abounded that the big corporations were opposed to a municipally owned company because it would eliminate the possibility of profit for private enterprise. Objections came from citizens opposed to the $500,000 in bonds that would be required to finance a city-owned system. George Watts, T. B. Fuller, J. B. Mason, William A. Guthrie, John M. Manning, J. Ed Stagg, George B. Lyon, and William G. Bramham signed an advertisement against the bonds. They argued that the paving of city streets should come first and (their real reason) that private enterprise could run a water system more efficiently.[51]

Dr. Bowling thrust himself into this debate, contending that the city should own its water system. He supported the Flat River as a better water source because of its purity as contrasted with the Eno, which flowed through Hillsborough, where it became the conduit for the town's sewage and industrial waste. A. K. Umstead asked cogent questions in print and resorted to a court injunction to try to stop the new project. John D. Hardy of the Boston firm that owned the water system, very much under attack, defended his conduct of the company. In 1914 the company was already in receivership, never having made a cent of profit. Before the city finally decided to buy the old plant and build a new one on the Flat River, there were many rancorous meetings and personal confrontations. The city had hired Gilbert C. White of Charlotte, an independent engineer, to assess the old plant and place a fair value on it along with recommendations for a renovated or newly built water system. White recommended a new system with a contingency reservoir surrounded by a park. Following his advice, the city purchased from J. S. Hill acreage for the reservoir and park adjacent to the country club. Hardy hired Jones Fuller to defend the company's rights in the wrangle with the city and impugned White's honesty in his charges for the new water system plans. J. S. Hill got into the fight and harshly criticized the report of a New York firm of engineers, offending the firm representative personally and refusing to apologize when requested to do so. He later sued the city over the legality of the water bonds issue, but he lost the case in the Supreme Court. While Hardy asked $500,000 for the old system, he eventually settled for much less, and the city proceeded to build a new dam and water plant on land it had bought for the purpose from Bennehan Cameron on both sides of Flat River.[52]

EDUCATION

North Carolina's school system was in need of all the help it could get. The state led the nation in illiteracy from 1890 to 1910, and school enrollment and attendance were very low. As already noted, in 1900 Durham County spent the largest sum of money per student in the state, that amounting to $2.80, to which the state added $0.14 per child. In 1902 Durham County had thirty-four white and seventeen black public schools in operation, almost all of them one- or two-room structures with one or two teachers. In the county, as opposed to the city, the teachers were mostly young, inexperienced, and poorly qualified (with some conspicuous exceptions such as A. C. Weatherly and C. W. Massey), and all were poorly paid. But Aycock's campaign promise and the climate of general reform began to benefit the schools as well.[53]

Legislators attempted to lengthen the school year and broaden the school curriculum. School libraries were required and practical training—domestic science and shop—was added. Special school district taxes and supplemental county taxes helped to raise the quality of schoolhouses and teaching alike. In 1905 the East and West Durham school districts became the first in the county to vote additional taxes for their schools. By 1910 ten others had done so, and the trend quickened. The movement to provide students with free textbooks arose in these years as well. The enactment in 1913 of compulsory education for children eight to fourteen years old for whatever school term was provided by their district was an improvement over the 1907 law requiring only four months.[54]

One bright spot was the city school system, particularly Durham High School, which the state Superintendent of Education visited in 1908 and rated top-notch. City teachers were the highest paid in the state and the system the best managed. Durham High School, by then in its new building on Morris Street, had the finest building and equipment in the state. It had four hundred students, almost half of whom were boys, an exceptionally high proportion, attributed to the number of male teachers on the staff. In 1915, the city passed a bond election for two new schools, one of which was a replacement for the Morehead school that had burned that year.[55]

The city offered other educational resources as well. In 1915 the Knights of Pythias sponsored a free night school (W. M. Upchurch, principal) for those not enrolled in the hosiery mill school. More than two hundred applied for admission. Mrs. Walter Lee Lednum had begun her business school in 1914, first in the Lochmoor Hotel, and later in the old Central Hotel on Main Street (previously the Sans Souci boarding house). Those living in the city had obvious educational advantages, particularly if they were white.[56]

The schools for blacks, however, were greatly inferior, particularly those in the county. Charles H. Moore, state inspector of colored schools, reported on Durham County's black schools in 1916 after visiting thirty-five counties in the state. He had found twenty one-teacher schools and one two-teacher school in Durham County. "In no other county did I find the school houses upon the whole in such an inferior condition as I find them in this county for the colored school children."[57] No schoolhouses had been built within ten years, only two of the twenty-one had ever been painted, only one-third had desks, and the rest had only shaky benches cast off from white schools. The only good thing he found to say was that the school term was longer than in most other counties. The legislature had required school libraries in 1901, and Julian Carr eagerly donated ten dollars to each white school in the county. By the end of 1902 only four white schools still lacked libraries, while in 1919 only slightly more than half of black schools had yet been given libraries. The law that allowed self-imposed taxation within school districts for extra support (designed to add quality to whatever education a county could provide) worked great inequity in the schools. The defining of districts was gerrymandered to separate white and black school districts, with the result that each race taxed itself for its own schoolhouse. Obviously the blacks could not muster the same kind of financial support for their schools as the whites.[58]

By 1912 there were forty-nine schools in the county, but the overcrowding was still severe. A bond issue was proposed to remedy the situation, and Carr, then chairman of the county Board of Education, lobbied hard for it. When the $50,000 issue passed, the county immediately began to build new schools. At the same time a policy of consolidation of school districts was adopted, a move that resulted in the pooling of resources and improvement in buildings and quality of education. With new roads and the introduction of public transportation for schoolchildren that accompanied consolidation, one large school could easily take the place of a handful of small neighborhood ones. With the large-scale replacement of old schools and the consolidation of many small districts by 1916, the county school situation was much improved over its 1908 situation, at least for whites.[59]

Concern for children's labor and schooling was accompanied in these years by an entirely new concern—their recreation. The chamber of commerce took the lead in a drive to obtain playgrounds. With the donation of land at the corner of Duke and Main streets by Brodie Duke, private funds were raised to make the playground a reality in the summer of 1916. W. W. Card, a Trinity College athletics teacher, was hired to supervise the playground, which opened in mid-August. Thus almost no aspect of life went unimproved in those prewar years. Working conditions, health, education, recreation, culture—all had the center stage for the first time in history, not only because the needs in these areas were so conspicuous, but also because experts were educating the general public to the importance of each to the strength of the whole social fabric.[60]

URBAN AMENITIES

Durham's cultural aspirations, which had taken wing at the end of the old century, did not flag. Music continued to be its favorite among the arts. Three new music schools joined the Southern Conservatory in supplying the demand for voice and instrumental instruction. Miss Daisy Robbins began her long-enduring school in 1905 in which she was soon joined by her sister, Alberta R. Wynn. Both sisters had studied and continued to study abroad or in New York with well-known teachers. Their school was chartered in 1909 as the Durham School of Music. Miss Mary Holman, who had studied at the New England Conservatory of Music, opened her Select School of Music, upstairs over a store at Five Points, in the early teens. Felicia Kueffner (later Sears) began her Piano and Vocal School in 1917 and the next year changed its name to the Progressive Music School. The Southern Conservatory continued to have more applicants than it could accommodate. In 1905 Howard Foushee had appealed to Benjamin Duke for permission to rent the Main Street Church building for additional dormitory space; he had had to turn away more than two dozen girls for the year 1905–6 and was already filled for the following term. In 1912 there were 169½ students, the half having been a young lady from Stem who had time for only half a lesson between trains.[61]

Delight in making one's own music by playing or singing alone or in groups was soon to decline, as modern technology provided inexpensive access to first-class performers for the rising standards of taste, as well as more passive entertainment. Phonograph records, player pianos, and visiting professionals created an audience no longer satisfied with the homegrown article. In 1911 a group of town and campus music-lovers formed the Durham Festival Association to bring well-known performers to Durham. The association enlisted subscribers for a series of performances, and proceeded to engage first-rate artists. Walter Damrosch and the New York Symphony gave the first scheduled concert.[62] Vaudeville theaters that presented incipient cinematographic wonders along with the usual stage revues were widely patronized. In 1908 Durham had three theaters, the Edisonia, the Electric, and the Bon-Ton (for black patrons), joined the following year by the Dixie and the Arcade. With rapid improvement in motion picture technology, vaudeville became only auxiliary to the film and in time disappeared completely. During the teens the Paris, Grand, Strand, Orpheum (later Rialto), and the Rex (in Hayti) were built, garishly opulent picture palaces befitting the make-believe world they served.[63]

Next to music, Durham's interest in the public library satisfied its cultural needs. Having distinguished itself by establishing the first public library in North Carolina and the first supported by public funds, Durham next led the state in hiring a professional librarian. Lillian Baker Griggs, forced by widowhood to train for a career, enrolled in the Library School of the Carnegie Library in Atlanta (now part of Emory University), and took her degree in 1911. When the board of the Durham library, headed by Thomas B. Fuller, hired her the same year, they were novices all round, not sure what to ask or expect of one another. The library had suffered from lack of skilled management and organization. Mrs. Griggs was given carte blanche. The newness of the institution and of the profession gave her scope for innovation, and during her thirteen years' tenure she made the library a leader in the field while she became an integral member of the community and by her personal and professional influence fostered the library's development and usefulness. She instituted a rental collection of current fiction, the fees for which supported purchases for the regular collection. She instituted branch libraries for the East and West Durham mill populations and weekly story hours for children in schools and at the main library. She extended book-lending to county residents, thereby earning county support. In 1916 she supervised the conversion of Dr. Moore's library for blacks to a public facility with city support. One of her last accomplishments for Durham, besides the building of a new Carnegie library (1921), was the acquisition of a bookmobile in 1923 to transport books to rural schools and communities, one of the first such programs in the nation. Because the Kiwanis Club almost alone raised the necessary funds and financed the building of the book truck, it was called Miss Kiwanis.[64]

The black library, mentioned above, had been the creation of Dr. Aaron Moore, who had founded a Sunday school library at White Rock Baptist Church in 1913. He had encouraged other churches to use it, but sectarian rivalry deterred them. In an effort to make it more widely useful, he moved it out of the church into a building at Fayetteville and Pettigrew streets. Mrs. Hattie B. Wooten was the first librarian and the board of trustees was made up of Moore, J. M. Avery, M. T. Norfleet, C. C. Spaulding, Mrs. S. V. Norfleet, E. D. Mickle, Dr. Stanford L. Warren, W. S. Pearson, and J. A. Dyer. In 1917 the city and in 1918 the county began to contribute to its support, and both white and black donors helped to increase and develop the collection. A report in 1919 noted that the year had begun with 1,942 volumes and ended with 2,389. Later named Stanford L. Warren Library to honor Dr. Warren, who was chairman of its board for many years and who led the drive for its new building (1940), it became part of the county system.[65]

RELIGION

Religion continued its hold on all sectors of the population, resulting in new congregations and expansion of old; Edgemont Presbyterian Mission became Fuller Memorial Church (1909); and West Durham Mission became Blacknall Memorial Church (1916). The First Presbyterian Church was rebuilt (1916) and in 1922 added a church house adjoining it. Edgemont Baptist Church (1902) burned in 1913 but was rebuilt by 1915 under the leadership of the Reverend Charles C. Smith. Lakewood provided itself with a new Baptist Church (organized 1912) in 1914, and North Durham (organized 1907), now Grace Baptist, built a new church on land donated by Frederick Geer. Gorman (1916) and Bahama (1912) Baptist churches were also organized in these years, and the old Roberson Grove church was rebuilt. Besides Memorial Methodist Church's imposing new building, smaller Methodist congregations added churches to the landscape: Calvary (1916), Lakewood (1913), and Rougemont (1911). W. A. Erwin had the Presbyterian, Methodist, and Baptist churches of West Durham painted pea green.[66]

Former Cameron slaves and their descendants organized Cameron Grove Baptist Church (1901), first located on the Cameron plantation but later moved to Bragtown. Saint Matthew Colored Methodist was organized in 1902. It burned in 1949, and after receiving funds for rebuilding from Bishop C. H. Russell of the National Council, the church was renamed Russell Memorial. Other new black Baptist congregations begun in this era were North Side, Goodhope, later Mount Zion, and Ebenezer (all 1909), Olivet (1913), Mount Olive (1916), Henderson Grove (1917), and Free Will (1918), later Gethsemane. White Rock Baptist Church was remodeled and enlarged.[67]

New sects appeared too. A revival conducted by S. B. Williams in 1907 resulted in the formation of a Wesleyan Methodist Church the next year in the home of J. E. Conway. The first minister of the thirty-member congregation was the Reverend W. H. Hawkins. Their first church structure, at the corner of Ninth and Knox streets, was not built until 1917. A Universalist preacher, Thomas Chapman, spoke to a group in Kearn's Hall on Angier Avenue on a September afternoon in 1905 and organized a Sunday school and a church. Arthur Roberts was the first minister. In 1918 the Universalists bought the old Mangum Street Methodist Church building when that congregation built Calvary.[68]

A unique religious mission began in Durham in 1906 under the auspices of Saint Philip's Church and S. S. Bost, its minister. A group of deaf-mutes, interested in the Episcopal Church, was formed into a Sunday school with the help of the Reverend Oliver Whidlin. Roma Fortune, a member of the group, was assigned to act as interpreter, and as his interest grew he assumed the role of religious instructor and pastor, teaching and preaching as well as ministering to the sick and dying. When he decided to train for ordination, his place was taken by Robina Tillinghast, who continued in the post many years, attracting new members to the group and serving other groups throughout the state. By 1916 the Durham mission had attracted close to seventy-five members, enough to warrant its own minister. The Reverend Roma C. Fortune was assigned to them in 1918, and in 1930 they laid the cornerstone of their own church, Ephphatha, only the second such church in the country.[69]

For the Episcopal church in Durham these years were the most productive in its history. In 1906 Saint Philip's congregation was ready to rebuild. The old frame structure was moved to the back of the lot to make way for an elegant new sanctuary. Designed by Ralph Adams Cram of Cram, Goodhue, and Ferguson, it represented his special talent for the Gothic Revival style, most notably exemplified in his Cathedral of Saint John the Divine in New York City. The new church was completed in 1907.[70]

Besides the elaborate new Cram structure for Saint Philip's and Erwin's new Saint Joseph's, the Episcopal Church established two missions. One grew out of a Sunday school started by a group from Saint Philip's in a hall over a drugstore on Driver Avenue. The Burcham family, the only Episcopalians in East Durham, and a number of children affiliated with Baptist or Methodist churches in the area were the first members. They used the East Durham school for their meetings until Colonel J. Harper Erwin donated a lot on Hart Street on which to build a chapel. Because money for the building (1901) was provided by the Brotherhood of Saint Andrew, the church was named St. Andrew's. In 1956, when it became a diocesan mission, it was assigned its own minister and proceeded to build the present small stone sanctuary on Park Street.[71]

The second Episcopal mission, Saint Titus, was organized in Hayti in 1909. A very modest frame building with a wooden cross at one edge of the ridgepole was built at the corner of Pine and Proctor streets. This served until 1927–29 when another structure was built at Fayetteville and Umstead streets. After the second church burned in the 1960s, the present sanctuary, located on Moline Street, was built. One of its early ministers, also traditionally acknowledged as its founder, was the Reverend John E. G. Small from Barbados, who married Sarah Ann, a daughter of Robert G. Fitzgerald.[72]

The proliferation of saloons and public drunkenness spurred an interdenominational drive for prohibition. Streets where saloons flourished were distinctly unpleasant if not menacing. Both the Baptist and Methodist churches organized against them, and through hundreds of petitions kept the issue alive in the legislature until they achieved their goal. In 1881 and 1886 Durham County had voted against prohibition and for the local option plan, but it reversed itself in 1887 and 1888. Trials of bootleggers (illegal manufacturers) and blind tigers (retailers of illegal liquor) began to jam the court dockets, proving that people were not drinking less; they simply no longer reeled about the streets. In 1903 the legislature passed the Watts bill prohibiting the manufacture of liquor in all rural areas—a blow to bootleggers—but Durham city voted to remain wet at that time. Nonetheless arrests for drunkenness in Durham fell from 40.3 percent of all arrests in 1903 to 16.1 percent in 1913. To help the church people in their campaign for prohibition, Carrie Nation, the indefatigable saloon-smasher, came to town in 1907. The newspaper reported that she was fully up to standard and "made herself as obnoxious as possible." By 1908 prohibition had become so widespread through local option (90 percent of the state) that the next step had to be statewide prohibition to prevent the few remaining wet counties from flooding the dry ones. Prohibition became statewide following a vote in 1908, anticipating the national swing by over a decade.[73]

SPORTS

A more healthful leisuretime activity was sports, and the most popular was baseball. Like music, baseball had at first been played by anybody, usually in a mowed field on a summer afternoon, but this pastime, too, was being transformed into a spectacle for the masses while the experts, soon to be professionals, took over the playing field, and the ordinary man threw down his glove and sat back to watch. Teams of better-than-average players, usually black, had been formed as early as the 1870s. The Eno Bottom Rangers of Hillsborough challenged the Durham Base Ball Club to a game in Durham in 1875. The rough and boisterous behavior of the early teams occasionally resulted in injuries and even death. George Lipscomb died after a game against Hillsborough's team as a result, the newspaper claimed, of too much redeye whiskey and sun.[74]

A Durham Athletic Association, formed in the late 1890s, marked the beginning of professional baseball in Durham. Virginius Ballard, who had been secretary-treasurer and manager, resigned in 1900 and was succeeded by William D. Carmichael. In 1901 Durham had one of the eight teams making up the Virginia-Carolina League. The Durham Bulls Club was founded the next year but unquestionably had its origins in the earlier team. Soon a number of nonprofessional town teams played scheduled games. The hosiery mill had a team in 1907, and two black teams played a game at George Lyon Park in 1908, the year in which Durham tried to get another professional team together. Their efforts failed because they lacked a good playing field with the necessary facilities. In 1909 the traction company provided a baseball park on Driver Avenue. The first games at the new park were played in 1910 when a Durham city league was formed, comprising teams from East and West Durham, the hosiery mill, and the YMCA. Soon new contestants were found in teams from rural communities such as Gorman and Nelson. In 1912 a new Athletic Association was chartered as a stock company to raise money to support a professional team. James A. Kelly of Wilkesboro was hired as manager, and the Durham team joined a Carolina League. When South Carolina withdrew, a new league was formed, which continued until World War I, when Durham's team stood in first place.[75]

Durhamites enjoyed no other spectator sport in those days, for football had been under interdict at Trinity College since the departure of Crowell, who had introduced it. Crowell had believed in sports as physically and mentally conditioning and as a builder of good faculty-student relations and morale. Trinity had played its first football game against a Chapel Hill team in 1888 and won. After Kilgo's advent football was countenanced for only a few months, for the Methodist church was against games on the grounds that they produced injuries, brawls, and sprees, and led the students into immorality. William Preston Few, who succeeded Kilgo in 1910, did not delay in saying where he stood on the issue. During the inaugural festivities, which were marked with new pomp and prestige—the presidents of Harvard, Chicago, and Clark universities saw fit to attend, attesting to Trinity's academic stature since the Bassett affair—Few outlined in his speech the dangers to education that the world at large represented. The temptation to grow large, he warned, for the sake of public importance and the introduction of intramural sports to garner public support and attention were both inimical to educational values. For the student, time and effort spent on sports was a perversion of the educational purpose. Equally subversive was education for obtaining wealth. Greed, Few told the audience, was already abundant in the world without fostering it in college students. The purpose of education was to mold character and to develop the whole man.[76]

At first the students held their peace, but soon began to murmur and then to agitate and finally to protest. They distributed handbills all over town and had their question flashed on the screens of movie houses, "Why Can't We Play Football?" When they held a rally round the statue of Washington Duke, the dean dispersed them. They later marched downtown, 250 strong, and rallied at the post office. The following Sunday in chapel Dean Cranford in no uncertain terms let them know what was what. "No amount of the game, five or ten minutes, either varsity or interclass, will be tolerated at this institution. Any man who plays will be expelled."[77] In 1917 another set of undergraduates staged a bolder, far more dangerous protest by building a bonfire so big that the city, seeing the glow, assumed the college was on fire and sent the fire department to deal with it. The trustees lifted the ban on football in 1918, and in 1920 the Trinity football team had the pleasure of defeating Guilford in the first game of its resurgent career.[78]

While Few's views of the conduct and purpose of higher education were essentially unimpeachable, the administrators were dependent on much outside money to run a first-class institution, and were forced to compromise their independence from worldly contamination to find ways of appealing to potential donors. Trinity's campus had continued to expand during the early years of the century. Besides the new library, James B. Duke's gift, East and West Duke Buildings and the dormitories Jarvis, Aycock, and Alspaugh had been completed by 1912. The campus was enclosed with a granite wall, a gift of Benjamin Duke in 1915. Departments of law and education were added to the curriculum and became independent schools in 1904 and 1910, respectively. The former was headed by Samuel F. Mordecai, a Raleigh lawyer and one of the most colorful characters on campus. Kilgo's dream of a college for women remained unfulfilled until the 1920s, but it was given priority in Trinity's plans, and money-raising campaigns by alumni and other groups brought it ever nearer fulfillment.[79]

One of Trinity's and Durham's red-letter days occurred in October 1905 when President Theodore Roosevelt, on a tour through the South, stopped his train before Trinity's gates and spoke to the students and assembled crowd. They had prepared an old flatbed car as a speaker's platform, covered it with a fine Persian carpet, decorated it with bunting, and made it comfortable with a weathered oak armchair. Undeterred by the protests of his bodyguards, who wished him to remain on the train, the president strode the hundred yards to the improvised platform and spoke for twelve minutes on a theme Professor Bassett had provided him. He told the students that they represented academic freedom, the right to seek the truth and to hold the private judgments it dictated.[80]

Trinity had taken its place as an intellectual beacon in the land. Bassett had made plain the direction that Trinity should choose in order to fulfill its role: "Make your stand for scholarship; it is what Trinity needs most and what the South needs most. They need it more than influence or numbers or even religion." By 1917 Trinity could feel that it was shaping up, a claim that Durham, too, might make with its fine buildings, solid industrial base, cultural amenities, and social reforms. Although the old engineers were largely replaced, Durham County might still claim to be bowling along the right track.[81]

Joining the World, 1917–1924

15

WARTIME

Wars of any size or duration often become watersheds in social history. The Spanish-American War of 1898–99, however, made almost no change in the daily lives of most Durhamites. If one sector of the population felt it more than another, it was the blacks. For the first time they were made to feel that they too had a country to fight for; some were admitted to the armed forces, not as body servants to young masters but on terms similar to those of white recruits. Company H of the Third Regiment of volunteers was led by Captain Peyton Smith, who many years before had headed the black hook and ladder company of volunteer fire fighters.[1]

John C. Michie was captain of the local white company, Company I, First North Carolina Volunteers, and as an engineer was chosen to oversee the work of laying out Camp Glenn at Morehead City for a training camp. The company of about eighty men was given a sendoff when it left Durham for training camp in April 1898. Later, when the unit was finally on its way to Florida to join the forces being sent to Cuba, it was involved in a train accident, in which William Matthew Barbee was killed and a few others injured, among them J. M. Colclough and John Harris. Although a few Durham men did get to Cuba (after the fighting was over)—for example, Joe Hicks and Sid Rochelle—none was killed in combat. A monument to Durham's white veterans was erected at Maplewood Cemetery, and the Joe Armfield Veterans Post was organized. By 1908 the following veterans were already buried at Maplewood: William Matthew Barbee, Luther G. Stone, George M. and Samuel Eubanks, Rufus V. Stem, Samuel Henderson, Ira McDade, John D. Andrews, E. J. Remington, James Bowles, Albert L. Gates, John Strickland, and George Bennett.[2] Among the participants from Durham County in that short martial interlude was one famous name, that of Choctaw, Bennehan Cameron's prize racehorse, which he presented to General Fitzhugh Lee, Robert E. Lee's nephew, to ride in victory through the streets of Havana. Choctaw afterward returned quietly to pasture at Fairntosh.[3]

Whatever small stir the Spanish-American War made in Durham County life was quickly forgotten in a much more significant experience that changed forever the people and the way they lived their lives—World War I. The United States was sucked into the cauldron of world politics once and for all in 1917, and the nation took its place as a world power. In North Carolina, enthusiasm for the war effort quickly rose to fever pitch, evoking cooperation on a scale previously unknown. The state contributed over 86,000 men to the armed forces and lost close to 2,500 through combat, wounds, or disease. Black soldiers made up almost one-fourth of North Carolina troops. Their presence in the army and in some menial naval jobs (they were not admitted to the marines) was controversial and created problems of every sort. The South did not want northern or armed blacks in its midst and did not approve of their having their own officers. Some hostile communities caused near-riots, but Durhamites seem to have accepted the situation without public protest, whatever private reservations they harbored.[4]

The matter of black recruits was a sensitive issue and handled with great care, particularly the selection of men for officers' training. The Chamber of Commerce conferred with black leaders to recruit the best type of men between the ages of thirty and forty-four. C. C. Spaulding met with nine representative blacks to compile a list of eight names of candidates for officers' training, who, if accepted by the army, were to be sent to Fort Des Moines, Iowa. The men they recommended were E. G. Gray, a contractor, teacher, and graduate of Hampton Institute; William Ashley, a graduate of Yale and teacher of history at the National Training School; G. L. Bullock, a graduate of the Briggs school at Enfield and a teacher of manual training at the Whitted school; E. Moore, a skilled mechanic; Lewis Spaulding, an insurance agent who had been a noncommissioned officer in the Spanish-American War; Charles T. Fitzgerald, a brick manufacturer and son of Richard B. Fitzgerald; J. M. Bullock, another Briggs school graduate and teacher; and William L. Wilson, a Hampton Institute graduate and teacher at Bennett College.[5]

In the early days of the war, rumors circulated that black soldiers would join the Germans, but C. C. Spaulding instantly quashed them. Moreover, two hundred blacks held a demonstration of loyalty called by Captain Peyton Smith, at which the North Carolina Mutual band furnished music, and the participants ringingly passed resolutions of loyalty to flag and country and offered their services to the nation. Eventually, in March 1918, a group of ninety-five black recruits from Durham, joined by others from Person and Granville counties, was selected to go to Camp Grant in Rockford, Illinois, for their basic training. A special service at White Rock Baptist Church preceded a parade with band to the station. Two months later two dozen more Durham blacks were added to the recruits at Camp Grant.[6]

White volunteers were concentrated primarily in two local units, while a few others and draftees were scattered throughout the services. The volunteer units were Company M (the old Durham Light Infantry Company organized by Captain J. F. Freeland in 1878), the Third Regiment of the National Guard, under the command of Captain W. E. Page, which was incorporated into the 120th Infantry of the 30th Division, and Battery C, Durham's unit of North Carolina's 118th Field Artillery, also the 30th Division. A recruiting rally was held for Company M at the

Banner warehouse, and by the end of a week it had reached its full complement of 150 men, a number increased to 250 before it left Durham. As Company M had only just returned from the Mexican border expedition, many of the men were already in fighting trim. This group was among the forces that broke the Hindenburg line in 1918. Battery C comprised 91 men and four officers and participated in the Argonne battles of 26 September and 7 October 1918. Both units were honored in farewell ceremonies, which included the presentation of a mirror and razor to each man by the Chamber of Commerce, Merchants' Association, and Rotary Club.[7]

Wyatt T. Dixon, a volunteer in Battery C, kept a daily account of his war service from his enlistment in July 1917 through the unit's quartering in the Star Brick warehouse, training at Camp Sevier, convoy to England and thence to France, seventy-eight days at the front (all the time under fire), sojourn in Luxembourg, return to Newport News, welcome parade in Raleigh, and final mustering out in March 1919. With remarkable luck the unit lost but two men: Willie Sims from meningitis while in training camp and Charles B. Wills from pneumonia in Luxembourg. Company M was not so fortunate. Eleven were killed in action, thirty-one were wounded, and thirteen were gassed.[8]

Regular recruiting machinery was set up for drafting men into the armed forces. Durham County had twenty-six precincts at which men aged twenty-one to thirty-one were required to register. Numbers assigned to registered men were drawn in Washington, D.C., to determine the order of call-up. About one in five men examined was taken into the service, slightly better than the one in six national average. The students at Trinity College and in the high school chafed because they were not part of the action. A petition for military training by 250 Trinity students resulted in the offering by Professors Flowers and Hall, graduates of the Naval Academy, of three hours of drill a day for three college credits. Drill later became a substitute for physical education and was required along with classroom work in military training and tactics. In the summer of 1918 Trinity was approved for a Student Army Training Corps, and 80 percent of the student body enlisted. The government paid their tuition and fees and provided uniforms. Two companies of high school students were also formed and given drill and elementary military training.[9]

Men over thirty-one were as impatient as the students and immediately formed a Home Guard, which drilled under Captain Michie. Civilians in general, however, fought the war on the home front with special liberty loan, war bond, and Red Cross drives to supply money to fund it. When food became scarce or too costly to buy, they grew what they could in their backyards. Trinity College planted twenty acres in vegetables. Many women volunteered for Red Cross work and rolled bandages. Customers carried their own packages home from the stores. Labor became scarce, production increased, taxes on cigarettes, cigars, and tobacco more than doubled, and women began to take on work that they had never been allowed to do before. They drove trucks, milk wagons, and grass mowers. Black women replaced teenage boys as sackers in the factories, one phase of the tobacco-packing process. The latest child labor bill, which prohibited children under sixteen in industry, was expected to eliminate these workers in any case, so that the labor shortage caused by the war accelerated plans for replacement of the child workers. The child labor law was later found unconstitutional, but women were at the machines to stay. The U.S. Congress passed a daylight saving bill, following the lead of Britain and France, which was expected to save millions in fuel costs.[10]

Some Durhamites served in administrative capacities. Julian Carr was appointed to the food administration in Washington, while William Erwin was appointed food administrator for the county, regulating the prices of scarce commodities. In January 1918 Erwin announced that flour would cost $12.50 a barrel and sugar $10 a pound. J. S. Hill was president of the county Board of Agriculture and chairman of the county Food Conservation Commission. Bennehan Cameron was chairman of the state Transportation Committee of the North Carolina Council of Defense. Mrs. John S. Hill was president of the local Red Cross chapter, charged with organizing and coordinating the many phases of its work. She and her husband donated an ambulance to the chapter for use in France, and other Durhamites raised sufficient funds for a second ambulance. A sizable number of Durham doctors and some Watts Hospital nurses joined the services for overseas duty. Dr. Joseph Speed was the first doctor to sign up. Others were B. U. Brooks, A. A. Woodard, B. M. Watkins, M. N. King, N. D. Bitting, and T. C. Kerns.[11]

On 14 July 1918 were reported the first two deaths of Durham men, Junius F. Andrews of the navy and George O. Hamlet of the army. Soon, however, Durhamites were to share with their fighting men a daily threat to their lives—an epidemic of Spanish influenza. In September 1918 it broke out in army camps in the United States and by October was rampant in the civilian population. Stores, schools, churches, and mills closed either because of their crippled work force or as a preventive to further spread of the disease. The first Durham death from influenza was that of C. R. Kidd of West Durham, an area especially hard hit. J. S. Carr, Jr., as chairman of the County Commissioners, was responsible for dealing with the problem. He called on school principals for help and designated certain schools to be used as emergency hospitals for flu cases. He sent out a call for fifty nurses to care for the sick. All public meetings, including church services, were prohibited. Funerals could be held only in the cemeteries. By the middle of October the epidemic was tapering off after infecting 2,308 townspeople and 400 in the county. Trinity College had 200 cases. By November the Board of Health statistics showed 4,076 cases, with a higher death rate among whites than blacks. The number of deaths was not disclosed.[12]

A relieved populace welcomed the armistice in November 1918. Their first consideration was a memorial for the servicemen who had died, numbering about forty-four. General Carr suggested that the Frank Fuller property at Main and Roxboro streets be turned into a public park with a community building and a memorial monument. A public referendum on the park, to be built with tax money, defeated the proposal. Although local recognition was postponed, the government was already handing out military medals for exceptional service. Hubert Teer, who had been wounded, was decorated; Luther H. Barbour, twice wounded, was awarded the Distinguished Service Medal. John B. Hayes won a similar medal and a Military Cross; Bruce Mason won a Croix de Guerre from the French government; Sidney W. Minor, who had commanded the sixtieth brigade, of which Company M was a part, was awarded a Distinguished Service Cross, as was Lawrence Stanfield for extraordinary heroism in action. Charles W. Perry and Edward T. McGhee were cited for bravery and recommended for a Service Cross. Elbert Chappell was cited for conspicuous and unfaltering devotion to duty.[13]

Besides a memorial service held in May 1919 for those who had died in the war, a huge homecoming celebration in April let Durhamites mark an end to a short but trying period in their history. Fifty thousand turned out to see the parade that celebrated both the war's end and Durham's semicentennial. Main Street was decorated with flags and bunting, a luncheon for veterans was given at Lakewood Park, Colonel Sidney W. Minor and Lieutenant Colonel Sidney C. Chambers of the 113th Artillery spoke, as did Governor Thomas W. Bickett, boxing bouts entertained the crowds, and a masquerade ball topped off the festivities in the evening. A war memorial was finally set up at the corner of the courthouse square in November 1921.[14]

A period of social and economic adjustment followed the war, and the Chamber of Commerce tried to anticipate the returning soldiers' needs and prepare to deal with them. They deliberated the kinds of temporary employment that might be found for them and suggested setting up an employment bureau to facilitate their hiring. The result of their efforts was the establishment of the Red Circle Club in April 1919 to provide a meeting place, rooms for reading, smoking, and recreation, and help in finding employment. William G. Bramham (who had been president of the chamber) was chairman of the new club.[15]

The problems of returning servicemen were of short duration. Much larger and more lasting results were the extension of the powers of the federal government and changes in social customs and attitudes that the war brought about. The government had temporarily taken over the railroads and the telephone and telegraph systems. It had determined the prices of essential foods and regulated their distribution. It had passed legislation described as a civil rights bill for the armed forces, which protected soldiers and their families from the loss of insurance or their homes because of nonpayment of taxes, mortgages, or premiums. It continued to control food prices and extended its jurisdiction to clothing under the National Food Administration after the war was over. The exigencies of wartime necessitated actions by the government that would have been unthinkable and unacceptable in earlier times and accustomed people to continually expanding federal control of their lives.[16]

WOMEN

Women were eager to contribute to the war effort. Although mechanisms were set up to facilitate their participation, the state provided no funding, and male opposition to their efforts limited their accomplishments. At the national level a Woman's Committee was added to the Council of National Defense, and each of the state councils was directed to establish a women's committee that would in turn organize the counties and coordinate efforts on the local scene. In Durham County Caroline Fuller was appointed chairman. Organizations working with her were the Red Cross headed by Mrs. Hill, the State Library Association represented by Lillian Griggs, and the North Carolina Suffrage Association represented by the local chairman, Mrs. John Cunningham. The work of the Woman's Committee was of many kinds, some already mentioned: war-funding drives, Red Cross work, victory gardens, canning clubs, oversight of working conditions of children and women in industry, recreation and health in army camps, and many other efforts to improve or safeguard life on the home front. Women were invited to register so that the community would know the kinds of skills and help it could count on, but comparatively few responded, afraid of what might be expected of them. Besides the reluctance of women to register, the women's committee in North Carolina was handicapped by receiving no aid from the all-male Council of Defense. If not openly hostile, the men were clearly condescending and uncooperative. That the women accomplished so much is the wonder. Their most successful effort was in food production through the promotion of victory gardens and canning operations. North Carolina's food production figures quadrupled in the years 1917–18. Learning the techniques of food preservation by canning proved extremely popular and resulted in many classes and clubs for the purpose.[17]

The women who actively supported the work of the Woman's Committee, despite disappointment and discouragement, nevertheless acquired knowledge and skills that they carried over into similar work in the years following. They educated themselves quickly about social issues, and they learned political and practical strategies to accomplish their goals in the face of male opposition. The fight for woman suffrage made this very plain. Although it had long been under way when the war came, war conditions accelerated the pace of the battle and strengthened the women's case. R. O. Everett, in dedicating a women's building at the state fairgrounds in 1917, stated a verity that applied directly to the women's movement: "Every liberalizing movement has found its origin or culmination in some hour of national peril."[18] The labor shortage caused by the war, which enabled women to join men in the workplace and prove their capability to fill responsible jobs, and the experience and self-confidence earned through these opportunities combined to force the issue.

The Durham Chamber of Commerce, cognizant of the responsibility that women had shouldered in the war and the contribution that they could make, decided in 1918 to open its membership to them and to include a few women on its board of directors. The first women elected to the board were Mrs. L. A. Tomlinson as a vice-president along with five new directors: Mmes. T. M. Gorman, Y. E. Smith, M. T. Atkins, J. C. Angier, and H. E. Seeman. Four of the six new members were absent for their first meeting; their record of attendance did not improve because they could not manage evening meetings. Consequently, in the following year, a reorganization took place that resulted in a women's division of the chamber, of which Mrs. I. F. Hill, Mrs. C. M. Carr, and Mrs. Victor Bryant were officers.[19]

Woman suffrage won acceptance in the United States Senate in June 1919 and became the law of the land by constitutional amendment in 1920 after ratification by a sufficient number of states. North Carolina was not among them. Despite suffrage planks in both the Democratic and Republican platforms in 1920, the state legislature defeated yet again the suffrage amendment in both the House and Senate. Nevertheless, women continued to work their way into local party affairs, and in 1920 two women were appointed to fill vacancies on precinct committees: Mrs. Parrish in place of her ailing husband on the Bragtown committee, and Julia Carver, daughter of County Commissioner H. L. Carver, on the Rougemont committee. The County Democratic Convention, having in 1920 gone so far as to invite women to attend, actually chose fourteen as delegates to the state convention and appointed women to every committee. These political pioneers were Mmes. T. D. Jones, J. S. Cunningham, S. P. Mason, F. A. G. Cowper, W. R. Murray, E. G. Muse, E. J. Parrish, J. E. Stagg, and a trio of young women: Sallie Ferrell, Sallie Beavers, and Lida Carr Vaughan. In October of that year, women could, rhetorically speaking, thumb their noses at the state politicians and register to vote, the Nineteenth Amendment having been ratified. The federal government having overridden civil injustice, women were now legally on a footing with men where voting rights were concerned, but that was only the beginning of a long struggle, for in almost every other area of their lives women were still circumscribed in power and action by custom and prejudice. Even getting women registered to vote required overcoming their long-ingrained passivity in public affairs.[20]

The state convention of the League of Women Voters met in Durham in 1924 and defined its goals for the coming year. At the top of the agenda was registration of women to vote. The women were also concerned about juvenile justice and wanted a separate juvenile judge (not the judge of the Superior Court as provided for in the existing system), a trained probation officer, and a mental health clinic to deal with juvenile offenders. Additional concerns of the league were limiting the work day for children to eight hours and the extension of the school year to eight months. It also worked for equal justice for women in sentencing and for their right to serve on juries. Durham had no chapter of the league, but Durham women could join the state organization founded by Gertrude Weil of Goldsboro in 1920. At least one Durham woman was a member, Mary Octavine Thompson Cowper (Mrs. F. A. G. Cowper), who served as executive secretary of the state league in 1924, editor of its bulletin, and regional director of the southeast for the national league. In 1924 she also became executive secretary of the North Carolina Legislative Council of Women, whose main effort at that time was campaigning for the secret ballot and the elimination of polling abuses. Indicative of her personal interest was the symposium on juvenile courts that she conducted at the 1924 state convention, hosted by the Durham Woman's Club.[21]

When the League of Women Voters with the cooperation of the YWCA agitated for an investigation of child labor in the textile industry, the women were brought into direct conflict with Durham industrialists, often their own husbands or friends. The local YWCA chapter had been organized in 1916 to fill the needs of single working women, to give them a place to live and socialize and to supply them with educational, religious, and cultural programs, but it was not actually up and running until 1920. During its first two years the YWCA supported two summer programs that proved very popular. One was a camp at the old pump station on the Eno River.

Two hundred women and girls who otherwise would have had no summer vacation benefited from the opportunity for rest, recreation, good food, and a wholesome atmosphere at very reasonable rates. The other program, for which the Durham YWCA was one of many sponsors, was the Bryn Mawr Summer School for industrial and office women workers held at Brevard, North Carolina. In 1920 the YWCA had outgrown its rented rooms at 303½ West Main Street and began a campaign for its own building. Mrs. J. C. Angier led the effort to raise twenty thousand dollars. The YWCA's cooperation with the League from 1923 to 1926 to investigate child labor, however, almost sabotaged the building campaign. Benjamin Duke, usually the most generous of men, joined the other industrialists in refusing to contribute because of the women's involvement with the proposed investigation. Kemp Plummer Lewis, by then manager of Erwin Mills, was alarmed by the women's bitterness and their threat to abandon the fund effort and openly place the blame on the industrialists for its failure. That, he wrote, "would have given the ladies and all their friends a sledge hammer to knock us in the head."[22] Believing with the other industrialists that the YWCA headquarters in New York was controlled by radicals, he arranged a meeting with Mrs. J. E. Stagg, Mrs. C. W. Toms, Jr., and Mrs. I. F. Hill and persuaded them of the error of their ways so that eventually they reached a compromise. The men would contribute privately to the building fund and the women would drop their call for an investigation. Kemp Lewis reported that he had shown them where their interest lay.[23]

Less militant in their feminist purpose were women's clubs that came into being at this time. Durham women who had chosen or been forced to support themselves in the business world, usually in clerical and secretarial jobs but also as teachers and administrators, banded together in 1919 to form a Business Women's Club. Sallie Ferrell was president, Sallie Beavers, secretary, Grace McBroom, treasurer, and Barbara Drum and Maggie Clark, first and second vice-presidents, respectively. A few years later a group of Durham women decided to form the Durham Women's Club. Mrs. W. J. Brogden was elected president, and Mrs. W. H. Glass, Mrs. C. H. Livengood, Mrs. Randolph G. Adams, and Mrs. Burke Hobgood were the other officers. One hundred fifty women attended the first meeting held in the Piedmont Club, a male preserve, and heard Randolph Adams speak on the history of the Woman's Movement. An astonishing total of 294 women were admitted as charter members. The local group became a chapter of the larger Federation of Women's Clubs the same year.[24]

The enthusiasm with which some women seized new opportunities for community service and self-liberation was upsetting to the ultraconservative segments of Durham. A Temple Baptist minister harangued his congregation against the ways of the world, particularly the newly independent young woman. After quoting Isaiah, who described the daughters of Zion as walking with "stretched forth necks and wanton eyes, mincing as they went and making a tinkling with their feet," he compared them to modern girls, "good for nothing little frizzle-headed, painted and powdered, mincing, chocolate-eating primpers out hunting husbands."[25] Though only a small number of Durham women would have fitted this description of "flappers" of the 1920s, and certainly a minority of local women of any age were pressing for further gains, the times had indeed changed and women's lives would henceforth be different.

Women were showing up in places they had never been before. One such place was among the exhibitors at the state fair, an innovation pushed through by R. O. Everett, a declared supporter of woman suffrage, when he was president of the North Carolina Agricultural Association. Another place was on local school committees. Since the passage of a legislative act to allow women to serve on school district committees, the state had been urging their appointment, because they naturally took more interest in children and were better informed about them than men. Lillian Fuller, Frank Fuller's daughter, was elected to the Bragtown district school committee that year. More such appointments followed, and in July 1918 John W. Umstead, a Bahama farmer, businessman, father of a later governor, and chairman of the county school board, declared that as far as he was concerned women should have any office they desired. "Work of women in the World War . . . has completely changed him from an anti-suffrage advocate to one of the warmest supporters the women ever had," the newspaper reported.[26] Some other early appointees to school committees were Mrs. Dave Patterson, Mrs. J. B. Mason, Mrs. E. J. Parrish, Mrs. K. R. Mangum, and Mrs. Pleasant Massey. Lillian Fuller was unique in another way. She had studied agriculture at Cornell University in New York and was running her own farm along scientific lines. Recognized for her expertise, she was also secretary of the Durham Board of Agriculture. At about the same time, two women were appointed to labor boards set up by the federal government to arbitrate problems between labor and management, Mrs. J. E. Stagg and Mrs. J. J. Baldwin.[27] With so many new fields of action opening up to them, women who had a taste for independence and power in civic affairs were unwilling to take any more backseats.

RACIAL UNREST

Although the war brought no immediate changes for the better in race relations, it provided salutary new experiences for whites and blacks to build on in the long battle for racial equality. Blacks who had served overseas learned for the first time what it was like to be treated as equals by whites. Black servicemen, who had risked their lives in battle, were in no mood to submit again without objection to the humiliating treatment they received at home. It became, therefore, much harder in the postwar years for black leaders to keep the lid on frustration and anger when they reached the boiling point.

Frightened by race riots that were breaking out in many large cities across the nation, the formation of a new Klan, and the continuing incidents of lynching, even of blacks in military uniform, the insurance magnate C. C. Spaulding moved on two fronts: he directed his agents in the field to counsel blacks to get together with whites friendly to them to calm the fears of both, and at home he arranged a meeting with white leaders at the Colored Odd Fellows Hall on Mangum Street to keep the lines of communication open. White speakers at that meeting cited, as usual, the good feeling between the races in Durham and voiced hope for better times soon and reassurances that violence would not erupt here. It was whistling in the dark. The chartering in 1915 and remarkable subsequent growth of a new Invisible Empire of the Knights of the Ku Klux Klan gave legitimate grounds for black fears. Started by Colonel William J. Simmons, a professor of southern history at Lanier University in Atlanta, it included three men who had belonged to the original Klan, giving it in southern eyes some legitimacy and respectability; it professed ideals most southern whites subscribed to: patriotism, Christianity, white supremacy, and sanctity of the home and womanhood.[28]

Durham was ambivalent in its reaction to the new Klan, an indecision reflected in the *Herald,* which conceded that while there were at present no conditions that warranted such an organization, it did not rule out the possibility of such a need in the future. It defended the old Klan from charges of night ridings, burnings, and the like as false accusations stemming from the hatred of the North for the South. The Klan in Durham tried to ingratiate itself with the public. It made surprise visits to churches, masked, garbed, and silent, disrupting services to donate money to good causes. One Sunday morning it interrupted Trinity Methodist Church's service to donate $300 to the Wright Refuge, a home to be built for neglected children. It used its dramatic techniques to create a sense of mystery and power and to instill awe and fear. It staged parades, held public initiations, and addressed audiences in the Academy of Music to improve its public image and spread its ideals.[29]

Despite its best efforts, the Klan made enemies, among the first, surprisingly enough, the local chapter of the United Daughters of the Confederacy. That group had planned a large celebration for the Confederate veterans' reunion in 1921 when the Klan announced it would have a parade down Main Street on the same day. The women were furious at this interference with their own plans and protested so successfully that the King Kleagle canceled the Klan's parade. The *Herald* began to think that perhaps the Klan was not something to stand behind. It quoted the words of a Florida judge, William B. Sheppard: "It is not within the province of secret societies to say who is or is not a desirable citizen. . . . There is a law here that can be brought to bear upon any group of people or secret organization which administers justice in the woods."[30] In 1923 an effort was made in the North Carolina legislature to unmask the Klan by the Milliken bill, aimed at all secret societies. Unfortunately, the higher principles which influenced many voters against vigilante action were overwhelmed by their racist fears, and after passage in the House, the bill lost in the Senate. In that year it looked as though the Klan was winning its popularity campaign when the Imperial Wizard, introduced by the mayor, Dr. John M. Manning, spoke at the Academy of Music to an enthusiastic audience.[31]

How impotent law enforcement agencies were against popular support of the Klan became shockingly clear to Durhamites in 1920, when a black Durham laborer was lynched for alleged assault of a white girl in Person County. An angry crowd took the presumed attacker from the sheriff's custody and hanged him on a tree in a black cemetery. The *Herald* reported: "The lynching party performed its task quietly and in a well organized manner."[32] A few days later, sickened by the local news accounts, editorials, and readers' letters about the case, Nello Teer, owner of a road construction company in Durham, whose roots in Orange County went back to post-Revolutionary days, courageously wrote to the paper about what he labeled a "ghastly mistake." He explained that Edward Roach, the lynched man, had worked for him on a project near Roxboro, and on the day of the assault had fallen ill and been excused from work by the foreman. On his way to Mount Tirzah station to catch a train back to town, he had been apprehended, not told what the charges were against him, prevented from communicating with Teer, who could have cleared him, and promptly taken in hand by a masked mob and executed. Teer said he was motivated to make the statement "in the interest of truth and justice . . . with the hope that this fearful crime may shock our people as to make its like again an impossibility."[33] Although the state offered a $400 reward for the apprehension and conviction of each member of the mob, no one came forward to inform on the culprits. That probably surprised no one. By 1922 there had been 3,436 lynchings in the nation within thirty-two years, of which only twelve had been successfully prosecuted. Repeated efforts by Congress to pass an antilynching bill were always thwarted by southern members.[34]

Some segments of the Durham population were troubled by the state of race relations and made efforts to improve them. Trinity students, for example, made an annual visit and donation of money to the Wall Street Church to show the love they bore "Uncle" Tom Hopson, a veteran Trinity janitor and minister of the church. The Wall Street neighborhood, today's Walltown, located north of the Trinity campus adjoining Club Boulevard, had been settled by George Wall (d. 1930), another Trinity janitor and bellringer for fifty years. An account of the 1921 visit told that the delegation of fifty students was welcomed by John Love, a printer connected with Trinity "with a command of language that would have credited any speaker," and the students in response expressed the hope that there would soon be "complete understanding between the white and colored races of the South."[35]

Besides the Klan there were other factors to try the courage of blacks in the South and to make them look for a foothold elsewhere. The exodus of many to the North and West, which had begun as a trickle in earlier decades but which was becoming a flood by the time the United States entered World War I, was a direct result of dangerous race relations and social and economic conditions. A high death rate and incidence of disease, a depressed farm and industrial economy, tenancy, inferior schooling, and Jim Crow laws had created for blacks an impossible trap from which there was no escape except through migration, an uncertain alternative. No exact numbers are available on the size of the black exodus from Durham, and even estimates on the number who emigrated from the entire South vary widely, from one million up to 1918 to the more conservative but certain gain of 330,000 blacks in the states of the north and west for the decade ending in 1920. A meeting in Richmond by southern blacks to discuss the problem reported figures from the Bureau of Negro Economics of 300,000 who had left the South in 1917 alone.[36]

The Corporation Commission took up the matter of Jim Crow accommodations in 1920 and complained to the railroads that they were not equal to white accommodations, the condition on which they were permitted to be separate. Blacks were assigned only wooden coaches, and no provision was made for eating or sleeping facilities. The separation of the races had become so complete that everywhere in the South duplication of public accommodations was provided: black and white restrooms, drinking fountains, railroad cars, waiting rooms, hotels, and restaurants. Blacks were confined to balconies in theaters and to the back seats of city buses. The story is told of a Durham white man's remarking to a black employee, "John, it is going to take a lot of money to build better schools for Negro children — it's going to be expensive business," to which the black man replied, "Cap'n, intolerance is always expensive."[37]

The black leadership in Durham tried to address these problems through a variety of approaches. In 1922, when most blacks were still staunch Republicans, they formed the Colored Voters League to encourage blacks to vote not for "platforms and parties" but for "men and measures." J. C. Scarborough, the owner of a black undertaking establishment, was elected president; Dr. Stanford Leigh Warren, R. McCants Andrews, Dr. J. N. Mills, and William O'Kelly were the other officers. The ballot was almost the only tool that blacks possessed with which to exert influence and shape policy, but few of them in this century had been permitted or dared to use it. The formation of the league was the start in Durham of a long struggle that won its greatest victory in the 1960s.[38]

Spaulding and his associates attempted to establish new financial institutions to strengthen the black economy, recognizing that black prosperity was one of the most important weapons against white prejudice. Spaulding's watchfulness to avoid tainting the Mutual's name by any connection with questionable ventures failed in these years when an escaped arsonist from Kentucky came to Durham in 1920 and blazed a trail of brilliant success and deception through the black business community. Wanti W. Gomez established himself as a credible entrepreneur first in the role of independent agent for the Mutual, then as initiator of the Bankers Fire Insurance Company (1920), for which, through the Mutual's contacts throughout the South, he was able to raise capital in short order. Of that first successful black fire insurance company William G. Pearson was president, Spaulding and Moore, vice-presidents, John M. Avery, treasurer, and Gomez, secretary. This company became a permanently solid, thriving institution. Gomez's most grandiose but last scheme was a national bank. The National Negro Finance Corporation (1924) was conceived as a borrowing pool for black business, committed to investing its money in the purchase of bond issues for black schools and recreation programs. Dr. Richard R. Moton gave the organization a national cast and prestige as the titular head, while it was really run by Durhamites Spaulding, Gomez, Avery, and Pearson. In 1926 Gomez disappeared as mysteriously as he had come and was never heard of again. He took with him the funds of one of his enterprises but left untouched those of the Bankers Fire Insurance Company and the Finance Corporation.[39]

Unrelated to Gomez's projects, the Mutual Building and Loan Association was organized in 1921 by Richard L. McDougald, another Columbus County native and bookkeeper in the Mechanics and Farmers Bank, to encourage black home ownership. The next year the Merrick-Moore-Spaulding real estate company reorganized and added McDougald to its leadership, becoming the Merrick-McDougald-Wilson

Company, and continued under its new name to manage the Mutual Company's real estate. In 1915 Pearson established and headed the Peoples Savings and Loan Association and in 1920 the Fraternal Bank and Trust Company, but neither survived long.[40]

HEALTH

The health of blacks became cause for alarm in this era. In 1920 the death rate for whites in North Carolina was 11.8 per thousand population, but 17.4 for blacks. The rates for the city of Durham were 10 per thousand for whites and 29.9 for blacks. Infant mortality showed the same discrepancy. Even as late as 1927–28 almost a third of black babies in Durham died in their first year of life. At the other end of the life cycle the story was no different. Only 12.1 percent of blacks lived past the age of sixty. Worst of all, statistics for 1927–28 showed that 64 percent of blacks died before the age of forty. In 1926 the Durham Business League, a local chapter of the national organization founded by Booker T. Washington in 1901 and begun in Durham about 1916, ordered a survey of the health and living conditions of blacks in Durham. The investigation reported that 80 percent of blacks lived in rental housing, substandard, cheaply constructed, overcrowded, badly lighted and ventilated, and lacking in sanitary arrangements. Surface privies were standard fixtures in black neighborhoods. The difference in black and white health was attributable to blacks' poor housing, lack of sewerage, years of poor nutrition, and general medical neglect.[41]

Because improvement in the health of the black population was very much in its interest, the Mutual Company in 1921 set aside the whole second floor in its new building as a medical department under Dr. Moore's direction. In 1925 Dr. Clyde Donnell, a graduate of Yale and Cornell, was in charge of the health extension work. The company bought the very latest in medical equipment and treated as many as sixty persons a day in the examining, X-ray, and operating rooms.[42]

Black leadership had the help of whites in a related approach to the problem, an interracial effort (interrupted by the war) to replace the completely inadequate Lincoln Hospital. This effort was now urgent because of the destruction by fire of part of the old building in 1922. J. S. Hill led a successful building fund drive after the Dukes agreed to donate $75,000 in matching funds. Hill, the Dukes, and Watts had in 1917 supplied the purchase money for the four acres of the Alvis H. Stokes homeplace, Stokesdale, on Fayetteville Street for a new facility. After the new building opened in 1925, B. N. Duke gave $25,000 for a nurses' home in memory of his son Angier, who had died in 1923; and the family of Dr. Moore, who died the same year, equipped and furnished the home in his memory.[43]

Durham's Health Department, one of the most progressive in the state under its superintendent Dr. Arch Cheatham from 1913 to 1922, was keenly aware of the city's special problems. Besides its high infant mortality and death rates, Durham also had the highest number of deaths from tuberculosis for blacks and the highest number of total typhoid cases, of which the majority were blacks. To combat infant mortality, the Health Department introduced an ordinance regulating midwifery. Since almost all black births were unattended except by midwives—and many white births, too, were supervised only by midwives, who, up to 1923, were unregulated—the new regulation affected a large number of cases. It required that midwives be registered, and to qualify they had to be of good moral character, free of tuberculosis and of venereal and other disease, and to have passed a required course in midwifery. They were also required to administer nitrate of silver to the eyes of newborn infants and to register their births. Black nurses were added to the Health Department staff to visit each newborn's mother and instruct her in child care. To combat infant diarrhea, which caused many deaths, the Health Department set up a ten-gallon pasteurizer and provided pasteurized milk for sick babies.[44]

The Health Department also addressed community-wide problems with clinics for drug addiction, dental disease, and tuberculosis. The narcotics clinic was Dr. John M. Manning's innovation to take care of addicts whose source of drugs had been cut off by the 1915 federal narcotics regulations. For those who had been dependent on drugs for many years, deprivation posed a serious health risk. Manning arranged to administer maintenance doses to known addicts, numbering, he thought, about thirty persons, who, with the exception of two veterans gassed in the world war, had been users for ten to twenty years. One was a Confederate veteran who had used morphine since the Civil War. Manning's humanitarian gesture brought unexpected consequences. The size of the problem overwhelmed his resources. The clinic closed after two months, but many months later Manning was indicted by the federal government for violation of the narcotics law. The Durham-Orange Medical Society, the Lincoln Hospital board, and the city council rushed to his defense with resolutions of commendation for his civic sense and irreproachable Christian character. At his trial he explained that he had written the government asking what should be done about long-term addicts when the Harrison law went into effect and had received no reply. He had then taken it upon himself to deal with the situation, possessing as he had a license for the dispensing of morphine. He was immediately acquitted.[45]

The dental clinics were begun in 1919, the first in the state, and provided free dental care for white children six to twelve years of age. They also treated the county convicts. In 1928 the state Board of Health together with the city and county paid the salary of a black dentist to care for black schoolchildren, and this arrangement, with the help of federal funds, was continued until 1935.[46]

Dentistry had been practiced in Durham since the 1870s, when Dr. J. Davis and his brother advertised their services. Dr. L. B. Henderson was practicing in Durham by 1881, and in the 1890s J. C. Brown, W. H. Edwards, and Isaac N. Carr were on the scene. Edwards came from Wake Forest, while Carr, a native of Wilmington, had practiced since 1879 in Tarboro before moving to Durham. One of Carr's skills was a cure for baldness involving the implantation of hair bulbs, a Turkish technique, as he described it, originated by Dr. Meneham Hodara. After 1900, Carr was joined by his son George, and other new names appeared in the advertisements: Dr. Emmett W. Shackelford from Virginia, Dr. J. T. McCracken, and Dr. H. E. Satterfield. The Durham County Dental Society for white dentists was formed in 1908. Black dentists joined the Old North State Medical, Dental, and Pharmaceutical Society, formed in 1887. The Old North State Dental Society was organized in 1919, but in 1928 it joined the older society as the dental section.[47]

Tuberculosis clinics were an attempt to identify cases early and start treatment before the disease was hopelessly advanced. Clinics were held for whites and blacks, but the latter refused to take advantage of them. A nurse for tuberculosis cases was added to the Health Department staff in January 1923 to supervise the 110 known patients. The number of cases discovered at the clinics persuaded the county commissioners to establish a tuberculosis sanitarium if the voters approved. A Durham County Tuberculosis Society, headed by W. A. Erwin, was formed in 1924 to lead the educational campaign preparatory to the vote on the hospital. Despite the acute need, the vote went against the hospital, possibly because it would have treated only whites, and Durham County did not get a tuberculosis hospital until 1944. In any case, the state death rate from the disease showed a decline in 1921, probably as a result of measures already adopted by Durham's and other health departments. Testing of cattle for tuberculosis, for example, had begun in a somewhat unorganized way in 1915, thus identifying a very frequent source of the disease in humans. By 1921 dairy licenses were supplying enough money to hire a veterinarian to test the herds and destroy the infected animals. Ordinances instituted in 1919 that required either disposable cups and spoons or sterilization of the utensils at soda fountains also helped to prevent contagion.[48]

The Health Department had help from other organizations in its efforts. The Red Cross had established baby clinics at the mill villages of East Durham, Edgemont, and West Durham, under the care of Dr. B. U. Brooks, Durham's first pediatrician, who gave an hour a day to each clinic. It later established one at Lincoln Hospital when the new facility opened. Durham became the first place in the state to offer this care.[49]

Long-range and large-scale remedies were also being considered—a full-scale medical school and hospital. Word got around that the Rockefeller Foundation had decided to establish a medical school with its own hospital somewhere in the South and that the Baptists intended to build a hospital as well. Efforts to secure either of these for Durham, however, were forgotten in the enthusiasm that greeted a proposal of President Few of Trinity College. He wanted to expand UNC's two-year medical course to a full-fledged, jointly sponsored medical school and to build it in Durham where an improved Watts hospital could serve as its teaching facility. The university had already been exploring ways of making its medical program a four-year course. Both the North Carolina Medical Society and the university trustees gave tentative approval to the plan, and the newspapers were full of editorials, articles, and letters touting it. It had first been the dream of Trinity's Crowell to establish a medical school in Durham; George Watts had taken up the idea after that; again in 1920 Watts and Few had discussed the possibility of making Durham "a hospital, medical, and public health center," and Mrs. Watts had followed up with an offer of land for the necessary buildings. Now John Sprunt Hill proposed that Durham should raise $300,000 to build additions to Watts Hospital and $500,000 to build the medical school. Hill insisted, however, that the school be independent of the university and that Watts hospital remain independent of the school. R. O. Everett presented a different plan, which met with more general approval. He proposed that Durham submit to the state a plan for a $10 million facility, including school and hospital, the city and the state to share the expense. The UNC trustees would not agree to the Durham plan, and a much more modest proposal was finally presented to the legislature. President Few had, of course, kept James B. Duke informed of the debate, hoping, not without reason, that he would be challenged to present a solution. When he finally did in 1924, all other discussion became moot.[50]

Two years later Durham gained another hospital when Dr. Samuel Dace McPherson (1873–1953) assumed the responsibility and financial risk of establishing his own eye, ear, nose, and throat hospital. It opened in March 1926, long before the projected Duke Hospital was completed. Over many years McPherson's hospital continued to increase in size, expertise, and prestige, becoming a valuable resource as well for the training of physicians in its specialties. After World War II, Samuel Dace McPherson, Jr. (1919–1998), joined the practice and became a pioneer in microsurgery of the eye. After his retirement the institution was sold and continued under the name North Carolina Specialty Hospital.[51]

AGRICULTURE

Farmers found themselves caught in an agricultural crisis caused by long- and short-term factors: the depressed economy, the one-crop system, exhausted soils, antiquated farming tools and methods, and the credit noose, in whose squeeze they almost always were caught. In 1920, 43.5 percent of Durham County farmers were tenants, a figure which rose to 45.2 percent by 1925. Of Durham County blacks engaged in farming only one-fourth owned their own farms. Tenancy went hand in hand with illiteracy, credit dependency, poor housing, absence from school, and rootlessness. One-crop farming encouraged tenancy and buying on credit, which could amount to anywhere from 20 to 71 percent in additional costs per year. Durham farmers had repeatedly been told of the extent of Durham County's dependence on imported food as a result of one-crop farming, and its relation to their dependence on credit, but they were slow to change their ways. About 75 percent of Durham's cultivated acreage was planted in cash crops: 19 percent in tobacco, 14 percent in cotton, and 41 percent in corn. The patriotic duty and economic necessity to grow food during the war, however, influenced some farmers to diversify their crops. B. N. Duke's farm at University Station, for example, was suitable for tobacco, but in 1917 and 1918 it concentrated entirely on stock, forage, and food. In 1915 it had produced 2,000 pounds of pork, but in 1917 it produced 10,000 pounds. It grew cow peas and soybeans as well as wheat and corn. Some farmers received seed free from their congressmen as an inducement to grow food crops.[52]

Those who persisted in one-crop farming found some help in cooperative measures. Tobacco farmers improved their position somewhat by joining the Tobacco Growers Cooperative Association; as many as 50 percent of Durham County tobacco farmers were members by 1921. Through it, farmers were paid a standard price they could count on and were no longer at the mercy of middlemen, who were naturally opposed to the organization. While tobacco prices soared in 1919, because of the war and inflation, to $56.96 per hundred pounds, the next year the price dropped to $24.61 per hundred pounds. Cotton growers had already felt the effect of plunging prices. In addition, they faced increased freight rates (until a long court case adjusted North Carolina's rates to equal Virginia's in 1921), a shortage of labor because of the black exodus, and the resulting higher wages for farm laborers. In 1922 R. O. Everett succeeded in forming the Cotton Commission, an organization representing all the cotton-growing states, to consider their common problems, find remedies, and work more closely with the U.S. Department of Agriculture in eradicating and controlling pests. In 1923 the boll weevil, which had earlier invaded the Deep South, spread to Durham County to add to the farmers' troubles.[53]

Soon, with the help they were receiving from the Durham County Board of Agriculture, the Cooperative Association, farmers' institutes, and county agents, farmers began to obtain better yields. Then another problem confronted them: overproduction, which caused further declines in farm prices and sent them more deeply into debt. The 1922 production figures for North Carolina were 110 percent above the previous year's. But if farmers' prospects grew dimmer, they now made up less than half the population of Durham County: hundreds of families had left the land and moved to town to take up what seemed a more secure life as wage-earners in the cotton mills or tobacco factories.[54]

PUBLIC WORK

In the postwar years unions were once more challenging the industrial status quo. The industrialists had been running just ahead of the organizers by instituting more and more reforms, but in 1918 tobacco factory employees were at last being organized by the Tobacco Workers Union, backed by the American Federation of Labor. Management responded at first in the usual way. At the Sovereign cigarette factory a machine operator was fired because of his activity on behalf of the union, and members of a committee that went to talk to the manager about the situation were also fired. At the American Tobacco Company both blacks and whites were involved in unionizing efforts. At first city and county officials successfully intimidated the white group so that they were afraid to go to meetings and soon lost their charter. The company chose to handle the blacks differently. It ignored their efforts to organize and instead granted Christmas bonuses, admitted a few to operative positions, and raised their wages. In 1919, however, union efforts were proving successful, and management changed its tactics. When black machine operators at the Liggett and Myers plant went on strike for an increase of pay, they were fired. Undeterred by this setback, however, they persevered, and by August 1919 some three hundred workers in the two major tobacco companies had joined the union. The same month workers at both American and Liggett and Myers had their working hours reduced to nine hours daily and were given time-and-a-half pay if they chose to work a tenth hour.[55]

Arthur Vance Cole (1880–1976), the leader of a white tobacco local, tried to deal with labor's traditional racial and gender divisions. He invited women to enlist and encouraged blacks to continue their efforts to organize. The factory officials, on the other hand, knew that preventing such a combination was in their interest, and they counted on the usual racial alignment to prevent interracial cooperation: white workers made common cause with their employers, who upheld white supremacy, rather than with their fellow employees, while black workers saw white workers as rivals for jobs. Cole ultimately lost his job at American for his efforts, and the local collapsed.[56]

Other workers also attempted to organize in 1919. The International Textile Workers Association formed a local with thirty charter members under the direction of Marvin L. Ritch, a football coach, lawyer, and union organizer. He was fighting for a 48-hour week and a minimum age of sixteen years for factory workers. By August the textile union reported eight hundred members from the Edgemont mills alone. The Durham Traction Company workers were also busy unionizing. So successful was the total response that the next year a central labor union was formed with representatives from the various locals. A. V. Cole of the Tobacco Workers Union was elected president, E. D. Morris of the textile workers, vice-president, B. C. Kelly, also of the textile workers, treasurer, W. W. Barrow of the typographical union, secretary, and R. A. Lassiter of the carpenters' union, sergeant-at-arms. The unions represented, besides those already mentioned, were the electricians', street railwaymen's, and printers'.[57]

The war was partly responsible for union successes, because it had managed to breach the South's isolation. Thousands of southern workers as soldiers met workers from other sections and learned how they lived and worked and what they earned. In addition, the shortage of labor caused by the war and the black exodus temporarily placed southern workers in a good bargaining position. The soaring cost of living, however, at the same time forced the workers to strike for better wages, and they were able to make some modest gains. As soon as the depression hit in 1921, however, the situation was reversed. Harsh cuts in working hours and wages left many workers begging for work of any kind. Money for union dues was an expense they could not afford. When they struck in these years, they soon discovered that the unions had insufficient funds to support the effort, and eventually the strikes were forced to collapse. The unions' weakness disillusioned many southern workers, and once again the impetus toward unionizing ceased.[58]

Despite temporary union success, welfare work and social programs at both the Carr and Erwin mills staved off permanent organization at this time. At the Carrs' mills this accommodation to workers' needs culminated in a plan conceived by Julian S. Carr, Jr., which he called industrial democracy. He had always been passionately concerned for the welfare of his workers, but it seems a little more than coincidence that he instituted his plan of worker participation in the administration of the mills just at the time that the U.S. government announced its plan to film the Durham Hosiery Mills as the ideal example of industrial harmony. The film was to tour the country to educate both workers and industrialists in ways to work toward the best interests of both and to counteract the growing appeal of bolshevism. It is true nonetheless that Carr had long been searching for a way to bring his workers more fully into the mills' management. The scheme he devised was modeled on the United States government with a senate and house of representatives composed of workers and the executive branch represented by the mill officers and directors. The frequent meetings of the two houses gave workers ample opportunity to voice suggestions and complaints and institute changes in their routines. It was probably at their suggestion that 150 employees of the Durham Hosiery Mills met daily for twenty minutes of singing during lunch time in the looping room of Mill No. 1. A piano had been installed and the workers sang whatever they chose.[59]

When the Depression began to close in on the mills, the Carr workers voted themselves repeated cuts in pay, and the mills were forced to curtail operations. In part of 1921 the mills were shut more than they were open, alternately closing one week and operating three days the following week. Occasional government contracts for socks kept the workers swinging between depression and optimism, but conditions finally became desperate and many of the workers were forced to quit in order to find work elsewhere. The industrial democracy scheme faltered when so many of the representatives in the senate and house had left the mill that it could no longer function. The death of J. S. Carr, Jr., in March 1922 doomed the system completely. While it was in operation, however, from late 1919 to early 1921, progress was made toward lighter, more sanitary workplaces and a more equitable adjustment of the pay scale. Fire ladders and back porches, paint inside and out, and electricity were added to the village houses to make them safer and more comfortable and cheerful. The mills saved $40,000 during the first year of the plan's operation, of which half was returned to the workers either as bonuses or as maintenance of the industrial democracy operation. Because of the personal and emotional investment he had in his workers, J. S. Carr, Jr., ranks high among industrial leaders. Unlike those of the older generation, he understood the difference between paternalism, which substituted benevolence for decent pay, and enlightened cooperation between labor and management. He understood that it was "the people, not machines, that make the goods."[60]

At Erwin Mills, the philanthropic spirit reached its apex in the building of Erwin Auditorium, a large brick and stone edifice designed by Hill C. Linthicum to house all the mills' social and recreational programs. It was paid for with what would otherwise have been distributed to the employees as bonus money. Completed in 1922, it immediately became a center for the West Durham community. The auditorium, which could accommodate one thousand persons, was used for concerts, plays, flower shows, meetings, lectures, and, best of all, movies twice a week for only a dime (a nickel for children). The building also housed a library, showers and dressing rooms, a bowling alley, and, later, a swimming pool and cafeteria. The baby clinic, cooking and crafts classes, scout meetings, and the night school offered additional benefits to the mill villagers. And all this irresistible fare was topped off with a cherry: a soda fountain. C. B. West was appointed director of the facility, and Miss Rosa Warren supervised the women's programs.[61]

The workers' responses to the mills' social programs have been well documented through interviews with dozens of mill workers. Their housing was clean, well maintained, inexpensive (usually about twenty-five cents per room per week), and convenient. They liked the sociability of the village. They had space in their yards for vegetables and flowers. "The auditorium was almost our home. We had a recreation center. We had a band and band concerts. Miss Rosa Warren would fix all kinds of games and things. . . . Christmas was a wonderful time. Everybody got an apple and an orange and a stick of candy."[62] Besides playgrounds, tennis courts, and shower stalls (where later the Blue Light Restaurant stood) workers remember in the park a kind of zoo that included an eagle, a bear, and monkeys. Presumably the latter gave the name Monkey Bottom to the large open fields and residential area in the hollow on the south side of the tracks between Swift Avenue and Oregon Street. The mill people seem not to have felt any social stigma because of their jobs or their isolation in villages. As Bessie Buchanan, a worker at Erwin Mills, described it, Durham had hundreds of tobacco and hosiery workers as well as cotton mill workers so that together they made up the majority of the population. "It was all more like just one group."[63] But a stigma did attach, however, to those who lived in the hollow called Monkey Bottom. Although the mill houses on Case and Oregon streets adjoined Monkey Bottom, they were not in it. It was a kind of no-man's-land with scattered shacks of human outcasts or hangers-on of the mill society. Erwin and his subordinates saw to it that morality prevailed in the villages—transgression meant expulsion—and the unfortunates who could not abide by the rules had to fend for themselves and live as they could. It was these people who lived in Monkey Bottom. A villager summed up the attitude of the workers when she said, "A person don't ever know what they'll be brought to in this life, but I sure hope I'll never have to move to Monkey Bottom."[64]

Memories about the mill at West Durham almost always center on the character of William A. Erwin. The workers remember that he addressed them in his Fourth of July speeches as "my people," and he could explain how to tighten their belts when the First World War came along: "Have as many slices of bread as usual but cut them thinner." He could even make them understand why a cut in their salaries was necessary; as one former employee put it, "He was a convincing man."[65] Another man remembered that "Erwin was a thoughtful person and he did have his employees in mind. I think he did all he could as a person for them. . . . You'd be surprised how much of his own personal money he would use to help sick employees. W. A. Erwin was a man who considered the employee along with the business."[66] Erwin convinced them that he had their welfare at heart in his operation of the mill. A candid letter he wrote in 1926 to Kemp Lewis, eventually his successor as president of the company but for many years his manager of the mills, contrasts somewhat with Carr's priorities and reveals the balance Erwin tried to strike between the competing claims of workers and investors: "I urge upon you to keep in mind that we cannot let go the cordial enterprising spirit which it has cost us much to establish in our villages and in the hearts and minds of those serving our Company in a responsible way, for the spirit and soul of our business is the life of our business and has roots deeper in same than what we call 'policy.' We must treat everybody right, but must keep in mind that our stockholders come first."[67] Arthur Cole said of Erwin, "His mill villages are better than most other companies', and the ones at Erwin are specially good. But he preaches baths, swimming pools, and that kind of thing and then won't pay a wage that is anything near even a living wage."[68] It was the private person inside the businessman who tried to do the right thing and won for Durham its good industrial reputation. The conclusion of the North Carolina Child Labor Commission Report in 1924 commended "the fine spirit of cooperation shown by the manufacturers of the county." It praised the personnel and health departments of some of the larger industrial plants "which contributed largely to the upbuilding of the health and moral conditions of the employees," and the manufacturers' "strict adherence to the letter and spirit of the law." It concluded, "Durham has one of the best, if not the best, record of any manufacturing city in the state in respect to child labor conditions."[69] It was equally true of Durham's labor conditions in general. The credit was due to the conscientiousness (even if watered down by concern for stockholders) of men like B. N. Duke, William A. Erwin, and the J. S. Carrs, father and son.

GOVERNMENT

Although Erwin could control his villages, his influence was much less in the city of Durham, and when the movement to extend the city limits got under way there was nothing he could do to stop it. The new council-manager city government that the citizens had voted in 1921 embarked on new paths, reforms, and general housecleaning, raising a good bit of dust. Unfortunately the postwar depression coincided with its tenure, and immediately forced a pay cut of 10 percent on all city officials and employees and a tax rise from fifty-five to eighty-six cents per hundred dollars of property valuation on property owners. One reason behind the city's desire to expand was its need to increase its tax base. The Chamber of Commerce, Merchants Association, and Real Estate Board favored the move but met strong and vocal opposition from residents and property owners in the areas proposed for annexation. The businessmen said that manufacturers and distributors took no notice of a town Durham's size when they looked for places to expand into. If Durham hoped to attract these tax-generating establishments, it needed a larger population. The mill villagers feared that their rents would rise, and factory owners naturally fought against taxation by the city, particularly when they were already strapped financially and operating only part-time. Thomas Fuller Southgate reminded a mass meeting called to discuss the issue that Durham was morally bound to Erwin by a promise not to encroach, which had been given him at the time he agreed to build a second mill in West Durham. A resident of East Durham remarked that the burden of city taxes would make home ownership impossible for the man of small means. After the city had gathered information of every sort in order to weigh the pros and cons fairly—the effect of extension on schools and the health department, the specifics of the promise to Erwin, and the like—the whole effort was temporarily halted when the representative to the legislature, R. O. Everett, who was dead set against the move, refused to introduce the necessary legislation.[70]

The possibility of the extension of the city limits forced attention to future growth and its problems as Durham's difficulties with traffic, street maintenance and paving, and the extension of sewer, water, and gas lines were seen in relation to its mushrooming suburbs. If Durham were to expand into already developed neighborhoods, how could the fundamental urban amenities be made compatible to existing facilities? Realignment of streets, addition of pipes for city water, sewer, and gas, and repaving after their installation would obviously prove a duplication of efforts and a terrible waste of taxpayers' money. Governance over developers' plans was needed to assure that their standards matched city standards and meshed with city plans. The new city manager advocated planning and zoning, new concepts in Durham and by their nature unpopular. He included in his educational campaign the requirement of city parks as part of a comprehensive plan. The city council went along with the recommendation and established a commission on zoning with the authority to develop a city plan, an ordinance to implement it, legislation to permit it, and an educational campaign to educate citizens to accept it—a very large order indeed. This thankless task fell to Judge R. H. Sykes, chairman, Mrs. I. F. Hill, C. E. Boesch, and Holland Holton.[71]

When Rigsby made his plea for city parks, he was only requesting what others had unsuccessfully asked for since the 1890s. Erwin and Carr had supplied their employees with parks early in the century. Wright had developed parks at each end of the trolley line, and the Rotarians had developed the pocket park in the city center. J. S. Hill had urged the development of parks and had given the old Angier homeplace on Umstead Street to the blacks as a public park. The city had included a park in its plan for the reservoir at Hillandale Road in 1915, but only because the reservoir would need a buffer and the extra land would be otherwise unused. Gaston Vickers offered a park at Vickers and Cobb streets in 1917, but the city refused it on the grounds that his street-paving requirements would be unacceptable to the taxpayers. The new city government responded to the manager's plea only under considerable pressure from outside forces. Seven civic groups established a playground commission in 1924 for the purpose of making the existing six playgrounds (located at five white schools and one black) more efficient by additional equipment and supervision. They appealed successfully to the city for $3,000 to carry out their plans. The following year, 1925, the city formed the Recreation Department under the supervision of Clarence R. Wood. Perhaps the U.S. government's plans in 1924 to establish two national parks in North Carolina, in the Blue Ridge and Smoky Mountains, gave the city fathers the reassurance they needed to forge ahead.[72]

Progressive state legislation in these years—state construction and maintenance of county roads, the requirement of a medical certificate to marry, care of the insane and alcoholics in state hospitals, and the elimination of the poll tax as a voting requirement—moved the state forward and by some of its actions removed from county shoulders costly burdens that they had only weakly borne. It left local governments freer to deal with their more specific needs. Although R. O. Everett balked at introducing a bill for city extension, he was willing to fight on other fronts with legislation for the consolidation of the city and county school systems, the establishment of a medical school and a tuberculosis hospital, and a force of rural police to patrol the roads for bootleggers, speeders, and joyriders.[73]

After two years in the job, the city manager was proving his worth in the enormous sums he was saving the city by his fiscal and departmental reforms. In the process he and two councilmen looked into the city's contributions to charity and the Welfare Department and found chaos. The council ordered an investigation, which was carried out by Dr. J. F. Steiner of Chapel Hill. After reviewing every organization concerned with charity, his report cleared certain agencies and condemned others. The Watts and Lincoln hospitals, the Salvation Army, Wright Refuge, YMCA, YWCA, and Traveller's Aid Society were commended for their work; the city's money given to them seemed well spent. The Welfare Department itself, on the other hand, was inefficiently run and fiscally irresponsible. Reorganization was long overdue. The report also criticized the duplication of the Welfare Department's efforts by religious, fraternal, and civic organizations, whose contributions accounted for 65 percent more than the entire community chest budget. Steiner said that their efforts were inefficient, since charity was not their main function, and that they lacked coordination.[74]

What the report did not recognize was that usually it was these very organizations that first recognized the needs of the community and undertook to address them, leading eventually to the city's assumption of the responsibility. They took the lead because local government defaulted. It was the Rotary Club, for example, that began a school lunch program in 1924 for poor children, made loans to high school boys to enable them to remain in school, and persuaded the YMCA to establish a summer camp for boys on the Eno River at Roxboro Road, at first called Camp Rota-Y-Ki (a name that reveals the Kiwanis' participation) and later called Camp Sacarusa. It was industry's welfare work that at length led to the city's establishing a welfare department. And it was Richard H. Wright, at Judge Wilbert Young's urging, who donated $10,000 in matching funds and a $50,000 endowment to establish a temporary home for neglected children. The Wright Refuge opened in the fall of 1923. Later called the Wright School, the facility was operated by the state for emotionally disturbed children. Clearly, strong individuals through private action or religious, fraternal, and civic organizations still led the community in the 1920s.[75]

Although the Steiner report angered many citizens, it resulted in some improvements. In 1925 the County Council of Social Agencies was formed to coordinate all social welfare programs and to let each of the organizations know what the others were doing. Reorganized, too, and rebuilt was the county home. The old poorhouse farm with its collection of cabins to house the indigent, ill, criminal, and insane was itself a scandal. With some of the ill and the insane now become state responsibilities, its function and services could be better defined. To finance a new facility the county commissioners were at length persuaded to sell off some of the tract, of which only one-third was in use. A tripartite brick building 230 feet long, designed by G. Murray Nelson, was begun in 1924, a momentous year in which Durham was to emerge from its old chrysalis and take wing as a major city.[76]

One organization that had worked hard for Durham and now handed over its myriad projects to others was the Civic League or Association, of which Mrs. Jones had served as president throughout its ten-year existence, 1909–19. She felt that its work could now be done better by newer organizations that had come on the scene. The educational work could be handled by the PTA, the community singing by the YWCA, the home economics work by the public schools, the Law and Order League by the Federated Ministers Association, the public health work by "the best organized Public Health department in the State," and care for the city's appearance by the city itself under its new management. Christmas seals and tuberculosis work would be continued by a board of twelve league women.[77]

The Civic League's emphasis on the city's aesthetic ambiance—efforts to clean up trash from vacant lots, to spruce up the railroad margins with flowers, to tidy up the streets by the removal of overhead wires and store signs—heightened citizen awareness of how the city looked. The league's successes in this line were usually only temporary, for beauty is not a popular cause, especially when it competes with commercialism, but the league may have had some influence on the character of the construction that went on at this time. Much money was spent on good architecture in the downtown area. A group of handsome buildings was added to the cityscape, the public library among the most attractive.

Over General Carr's strong objections, in 1916 the library board had set in motion efforts to secure Carnegie funds with which to replace the outmoded and outgrown facility. As chairman of the board, Carr may have felt it beneath his dignity or that of any southerner to beg northern philanthropists for help, and he refused to attend meetings when the board persisted in that course of action. Thomas B. Fuller, the vice-chairman, came to the rescue as he had in other crises: in the severe winter of 1902 when he had helped found the Associated Charities, and in the 1918 and 1920 influenza epidemics when he had worked night and day to help the victims in practical ways. After persuading the city and county to agree to the requirements of the Carnegie grant, the trustees sold the old library for $21,000, which not only paid for the new lot but added to the building and book funds as well. Designed by Edward L. Tilton of New York and built by Norman Underwood, the new building opened in 1921. Carr forgave his renegade board and continued his support for the rest of his life; he requested that at his death, instead of flowers, people donate books to the library.[78]

C. C. Hook's synagogue at Queen and Holloway streets (1919), a Home Savings Bank at Main and Market (1921), Richard Wright's Franklin Court Apartments at Main and Dillard (1921), the Masonic Temple at Main and Roxboro (1922), the renovated high school building converted to a city hall (1923), the Alexander Motor Company building (1924), and the continually rising framework of the new Washington Duke Hotel (1925) designed by Stanhope S. Johnson of Lynchburg, Virginia, gave Durhamites much that was new to look at and take pride in. Before the close of 1924 plans were already made for two more Milburn and Heister landmarks: the King's Daughters' new home (1925) and a theater attached to the city hall (1926), formally known as the Durham Auditorium but later called the Carolina Theatre. Durham could boast that $3 million worth of buildings had been added to the scene in 1924 alone.[79]

There were new churches too: Branson Methodist (1922), Watts Street Baptist (1923), a new Angier Avenue Baptist Church (1924), Oak Grove Free Will Baptist Church on Colfax Street (1923), and in the city center, plans for a new Trinity Methodist Church to replace the 1894 structure burned in 1923. The form that this structure would take caused much discussion and disagreement in the congregation. Carr wanted a spire to rise 205 feet, surmounted by a lighted cross twenty feet high, like that of a Methodist church he had seen in Detroit. Bennehan Cameron offered red sandstone from his own plantation as his contribution. Carr favored this material over the architect Ralph Adams Cram's recommended Indiana limestone, which would soon show discoloration from the weather. Finally, Cram's plans were chosen, including a spire, but as construction proceeded and funds ran low, it became clear that the spire would have to be sacrificed. (Only in 1985 was Carr's wish fulfilled when the Cram church finally received a spire.) Mrs. Caleb Green (Kate Morris, the daughter of Robert Morris) was chosen to lay the first foundation brick of the 1925 structure, possibly as a senior member of the congregation but also possibly as a concession to the times.[80]

Two more purely social men's clubs were organized in these years, the White Elephant Club and the Piedmont Club. The White Elephant charter members, C. E. and J. E. Roberts, R. B. Abbott, Clem Warren, McCory Webster, and W. S. Markham, hoped to put up a building equipped with a swimming pool, a bowling alley, pool and billiards tables, and a reading room. Piedmont Club members had similar ambitions and realized them with the erection of a three-story building in the corner between Main and Chapel Hill streets at Five Points. It contained all the amenities of a gentleman's club of that era, including a ballroom and adjoining kitchenette on the third floor, which were inaugurated with a reception and ball in 1921. Judge Sykes was the first president, Dr. Foy Roberson, vice-president, and J. M. Markham, secretary-treasurer.[81]

Popular culture in Durham began to reflect worldwide trends. The two-step and tango came to Durham in the dance craze that caught up the postwar generation of young people. The phonograph and player piano (middle-class families commonly possessed one or both of these new inventions) easily supplied the music, so that even in the face of ecclesiastical disapproval, dancing became a common pastime. The new music, jazz, a unique contribution of American blacks to world music, in its gradually evolving styles beginning with ragtime, expressed irresistibly the spirit of the times. North Carolinians had been shuffled up in the American pack during the war, and in the aftermath participated in a much freer interchange between southerners and the rest of the nation. The daily newspapers reflected the broader perspective: national and world events now claimed the columns of the first page, the result of the Durham *Herald*'s subscription to the Associated Press news service in 1919.[82] Gone from its columns were the trivia of community happenings—picnics and hayrides, who visited whom on Sunday afternoon, and who was confined with illness. As a result, the continuum of daily life in rural parts of the county dropped out of the historical record. The comic strips took on a new importance, appearing not as one or two isolated strips but massed on a page or more. The newspaper began to sort itself out into sections: women's pages had begun in the new century's early decades, and a sports section developed with the rising attention to athletic events of not just local but national interest. Technological improvements of all kinds were also reflected in the new format. Movies and photography in general had widened the lens of the individual viewer, creating an interest in far-flung events and peoples, and pictures could now be transmitted and published quickly to accompany the stories gathered by the news services. Any local sheet could now plug into world events if it could pay for the service.

Although the war had interrupted minor league baseball in Durham, the interest and support were still there waiting for William G. Bramham and other enthusiasts to form another association. This they did in 1919, creating the Piedmont League, of which a new Durham Baseball Club became a member. From the Durham Bulls team almost immediately emerged a star player, Leo Mangum, who was hired by the Pittsburgh Pirates in 1920 and farmed out to lesser clubs. In his first season with Pittsburgh, Mangum was loaned to the Albany Lawmakers, where he pitched four no-hit games, and during the three following seasons he played for the Minneapolis Millers, where he became Mike Kelly's pitching ace. In midsummer 1924 Mangum was sent to the Chicago White Sox. In winter he would coach the Durham YMCA basketball team.[83]

By 1926 support for the local team had resulted in the construction of a new ball park, El Toro, as it was called, on Morris Street. A few Durham men had put up the $160,000 facility, one of the best fields in the minor leagues. Their support was justified when the Bulls won the Piedmont League pennant in 1930. The Depression, however, brought difficult times because of the debt on the park. In 1933 the J. S. Hills gave the city $20,000 to buy it from the Homeland Investment Company (a Hill-controlled firm), which then owned the property. They asked only that the name be changed to Durham Athletic Park and that if the property were ever sold the proceeds be used to buy additional recreational land. They also expressed the hope that it would not be used on Sundays for commercial games. In the same year Bramham, who had been president continuously of the Piedmont League, was elected president of the National Association of Baseball Leagues. Although fire destroyed the park in 1939, it was rebuilt, and in 1941 the Brooklyn Dodgers, who owned the Piedmont League franchise, came to Durham for a spring training exhibition game. Five thousand fans witnessed the Dodgers defeat the New York Yankees, 5-1. Playing in that game were two all-time stars, future Hall of Famers Joe DiMaggio, who scored the Yankees' only run, and Peewee Reese, shortstop of the Dodgers.[84]

CULTURE UNDER FIRE

Education was still causing concern in spite of all that had been achieved since 1900, and improvements were being introduced. Teacher training classes began in 1919 under the supervision of Holland Holton and Matilda Michaels, with the help of men like Few, Mims, Boyd, and Brooks to teach the classes. A twelfth grade for high school was required by law beginning in the school year 1919–20. Parent-teacher associations took their places in the schools, after having begun as mothers' clubs in 1914. A vote on a city school-bond issue passed by a large majority, allowing the city to buy the former B. L. Duke homestead on Duke Street for two new school buildings, Durham High School and Carr Junior High School.[85]

When the Ayers report of the Russell Sage Foundation was released in 1920, it caused consternation. It showed that the North Carolina school system was fourth from the bottom in the nation. E. C. Brooks, then state superintendent of education, rushed to the state's defense, claiming that the report had not included the latest improvements in the system, notably the twelfth year for high schools and the rise in teachers' salaries. The same year the General Education Board, also reporting on North Carolina schools, showed that the average seventh-grader could read only at the fifth-grade level while the average city school child ranked little better. Although nothing was said specifically about Durham city or county schools, the conclusion was plain for all North Carolina schools. They needed better facilities, better-trained teachers, and better teacher salaries. Durham had still more humble pie to eat in 1923 when Charles L. Coon, superintendent of Wilson County schools, accused it of hypocrisy in boasting of its unexcelled educational advantages on billboards set up on roads entering the county. "Why don't you quit putting up signs which are a white lie?" Coon inquired. He then went on to criticize the inequality in Durham school facilities. Some children sat on pine planks while others had fine desks, some attended school six months and others nine. He warned the people, "If you let your children grow up in ignorance you will go to hell as rapidly as a blue pig can fly." What he advocated was a countywide system with equally distributed resources.[86]

Undoubtedly these reports were the reason that county school buildings and equipment began to receive some attention. The Rosenwald Fund (established by the Sears Roebuck official Julius Rosenwald), part of whose concern was to help black schools with buildings, libraries, and equipment, awarded money to a number of Durham county schools that raised the required matching funds. Schools at Lyon Park, Walltown, Hickstown, Pearsontown, Bragtown, Lillian, Hampton, and Rougemont were all replaced by Rosenwald-funded buildings, three- and four-room structures strictly utilitarian in design. In 1924 the newspaper nostalgically noted that only one log schoolhouse remained in the county, the school for blacks at Stagville, which was hoping to qualify soon for Rosenwald aid. The first schools for whites had long before been replaced, but many of the newer structures, too, were now outmoded. Auditoriums of eight white schools were condemned as firetraps in 1923: Lowe's Grove, Nelson, Mineral Springs, Redwood, Glenn, Bahama, Rougemont, and Patrick Henry. The consolidation of districts, begun some years before, was accelerated. Redwood, Glenn, and Mineral Springs schools, for example, were combined with South View in a new building located at Mineral Springs. Mangum Township consolidated its high school classes at Bahama in a new brick building designed by Atwood and Nash, Durham architects.[87]

Under this barrage of criticism, the city, too, went about making improvements. The old Whitted school for blacks at Ramsey and Proctor streets, decaying and rat-infested, burned down in 1921 and was replaced by a 28-classroom building on Umstead Street. The city high school for whites instituted the first cooperative class in the state in 1916–17. Designed to discourage boys' dropping out before graduation because of either economic necessity or boredom, it allowed them to work part-time, alternating work and school, sharing jobs with other boys. These students were taught in special classes and at a faster pace. The innovator and teacher was Miss Maude F. Rogers, who continued to teach the class for thirty-four years.[88]

Under Superintendent Frank M. Martin, a program for underweight primary school children was begun. Chosen from the third to sixth grades, the children attended what was called the Open Air Class. They received almost individual instruction from Ila L. Howerton and progressed at their own pace. They also were given nutritious lunches and snacks and afternoon naps. The following year the program was expanded to twelve classes of twenty children each. Parents of the children met once a week for instruction in diet and food preparation. Only two other states had such a program, California and Massachusetts. By 1929 the numbers of underweight children showed a marked decline; the program was succeeding.[89]

Its schools were not the only aspect of Durham's culture under fire. A *Herald* editorial was harsh in its criticism of its culture in general. "In material things it [Durham] is a leader. Industry flourishes here as in few other places. . . . But, Durham has developed in a lopsided fashion, and is not making any progress in rounding up its life. There is too strong a spirit of commercialism, while the intellectual and esthetic side has been neglected, except by the few."[90] It cited the 2 percent of the population who took all the initiative in making the community a better place to live. It cited, too, the poor borrowing record of the library and the poor attendance at first-class musical or theatrical performances. Its inhabitants were afraid of the words classic and classical. Durhamites' tastes needed educating. It was true that fine efforts were being made along these lines, but it was also true that a kind of fatigue or malaise afflicted the town and its leadership. Earlier, a long list of Civic League goals had included the development of parks, an architectural plan for Durham, illustrated lectures of an informative kind, and circulating art galleries and museums; the last item on the list had been "give inspiration to city officials." These alert women with the good of the community at heart had detected the acedia afflicting its culture.[91]

The Southern Conservatory was a bellwether of the situation. With but two years of its lease to run in 1921, Bryant was concerned about the school's future. He thought that the lease would not be renewed, and in view of the outmoded structure and facilities, he was tempted by offers from other cities to locate elsewhere. He asked Durham for a solution that would enable the school, at one time the centerpiece of town culture, to remain there. He received no response. He therefore decided to build a new school south of the city on Alston Avenue on a ten-acre plot where tennis, basketball, and croquet could be accommodated. A bus could transport town students to and from school, for most of the students were local. Among the 315 enrolled students in 1922, only 40 were boarders. The new building's cornerstone was laid early in 1923, and the beautiful old conservatory was razed in June 1924.[92]

The cultural decline was reflected in newspaper comments. The Kiwanis Club, which donated the bookmobile to the library in 1923 to extend library services to rural communities, and the Lions Club sponsored a series of performances in 1922 and 1923 to bring the best of music to the city and try to cultivate popular taste. Of these the newspaper commented, "For the first time in the history of big music ventures in Durham, the efforts of the organization putting on the concert were successful." When a choral society was about to be organized late in 1924 the newspaper commented, "This city is far behind the other cities of the state from a musical standpoint"—sad commentaries on a city that had once regarded itself as in the vanguard of musical cultivation.[93]

A few churches meanwhile were beginning to emphasize a better quality of music in their services. The First Presbyterian Church hired William Powell Twaddell as a full-time music director in 1921 to play the organ, direct the choir, develop boys' and girls' choirs, and possibly form a choral society. Concurrently, Twaddell became director of music in the city schools. He had been director of music both at Temple University in Philadelphia and Saint Agnes's Episcopal Church in New York. From 1922 to 1924 Twaddell was also organist and choir director at Temple Baptist Church, where the new minister was the Reverend Trela D. Collins, with whom he had been associated in Philadelphia. Twaddell was also music director at Saint Philip's Church from 1937 to 1946. Music in the schools expanded dramatically in these years with the formation of bands, orchestras, choirs, and glee clubs. State contests encouraged serious application, and Twaddell was spectacularly successful in training Durham's high school chorus and soloists, who won the contests year after year.[94]

Along with frank criticism and positive response had come an effort to achieve a clearer perception of Durham's situation measured against her fast-receding past, a time to take stock. As part of this critical exercise the Chamber of Commerce commissioned William K. Boyd, a Trinity professor, to produce under their supervision a history of the town and environs to be researched by him and his students. The chamber also undertook other historical projects, for example the Bennett Place memorial. The chamber wished to place a commemorative marker at the site, and the Morgan heirs who owned it agreed. Before anything was done, however, the cabin burned to the ground in October 1921. Reuben Oscar Everett and Frank L. Fuller introduced legislative bills authorizing a monument at the site and appropriations for its maintenance. The state agreed to give fifty dollars a year toward its maintenance, provided the Morgan family donated a marker and the land. Designed by W. H. Dacy—two pillars representing the North and the South, joined by an architrave with the word *Unity* inscribed—a monument was eventually erected.[95]

When Julian Carr, R. O. Everett, Bennehan Cameron, and James E. Lyon planned an extensive dedication ceremony, opposition came from an unexpected source, the United Daughters of the Confederacy and the local organization of the Civil

War veterans. The ladies of the Julian Carr Chapter of the UDC explained that they had wanted a marker placed quietly and without fanfare. They objected to so much publicity for the place where their ancestors had had to admit defeat. Carr and Lyon argued that the monument was a memorial to two ideals—to the indissoluble union and to the indestructible states. The monument would also celebrate Durham's prosperity, which had resulted directly from the presence of both armies in the area. Neither the UDC nor the veterans were persuaded, and they refused to participate. Nonetheless the ceremony, presided over by Cameron, passed off with dignity on 8 November 1923 when General Carr, acting for the Morgans, donated the memorial and the land to the state. Although it was an occasion for reconciliation, it was almost completely ignored by the federal government and the northern press. The following year, through R. O. Everett's efforts, a stone pavilion that had been erected by the Rotary Club on an empty downtown lot was moved to the Bennett Place. In 1925 Durham County agreed to accept and maintain the site. Soon public apathy and more pressing problems—depression and war—eclipsed the site, and it became one of the least-known and least-visited in the state.[96]

That was not the end of the story. Starting in 1923 and from time to time thereafter, the desirability of reconstructing the Bennett house was raised in the press, but only in 1961 was the ambition realized. A chance gift of money to reconstruct the house came in 1958 from a daughter of Frederick L. Bailey, a former Erwin Mills agent. In 1960 Charles Pattishall, a Durham businessman, Civil War buff, and member of a committee appointed to oversee the reconstruction, observed that the old William Haynes Proctor house, about to be demolished on the corner of Palmer Street and Chapel Hill Road, consisted of two frame-covered log structures from the early nineteenth century, one of which closely resembled the old Bennett house. The committee set to work and with the cooperation of a number of persons was able to acquire the old houses. One of the buildings was found to fit the old house foundation almost exactly. The other was reworked to match the old Bennett kitchen, and finally a smokehouse was built. In July 1961 the whole complex became a state historic site.[97]

While the chamber was focusing on the Bennett Place, the UDC was trying to elicit support for a different kind of Confederate memorial. As a result a statue of a soldier, its pedestal inscribed with the veterans' names, was erected on the courthouse lawn in 1924.[98]

Obviously it was a time of testimonials to the living and memorials to the dead, and two other Durham figures were recognized in these years for their roles in Durham's past. In 1920 the town celebrated its most illustrious citizen's seventy-fifth birthday. The stores and factories closed, the governor came, and the city presented Julian Carr with a loving cup three feet high. William G. Pearson, representing the black community, presented him with a gold-headed engraved cane. Pearson made the audience laugh when he said "he knew the General when he made the Bull Durham so strong that he drank water in the far northern lakes and groveled his tail in the sands of New Mexico."[99] The next year Carr was elected Commander-in-Chief of the United Confederate Veterans; in 1923 he was awarded an honorary LL.D. from the University of North Carolina.[100]

Carr wished to see another city father, Bartlett Leonidas Durham, honored with an oil portrait and a grave marker. Early in 1924 General Carr presided at his last public function, the unveiling of Bartlett Durham's portrait, painted by P. Phillips of New York from a photograph supplied by Mrs. J. Ed Stagg, whose husband was Durham's nephew. In March Carr went to Washington to have his tonsils removed, but his throat had not healed when he went the following month to Chicago to visit his daughter Lida Carr Flower. He arrived with influenza, which progressed to pneumonia, and he died at the end of April.[101]

A week later the town witnessed the biggest funeral it had ever known. The business section was draped in black, and Somerset Villa was thrown open for the public to pay its respects as Carr's body, dressed in his Confederate general's uniform with a white carnation in his lapel, lay in state. The funeral procession included 150 cars. Josephus Daniels said of Carr, "His sunny nature, his perennial youth, his courtesy, chivalry, his public spirit, his simple faith made a radiant and useful life."[102] No words, however, could describe the loss his death would mean to the city in character, color, imagination, and enterprise. He was unique, and much of what Durham had become and achieved was due to him. His death marked the end of an era that had encompassed the high noon of planter civilization, the Civil War, Reconstruction, the New South industrial efflorescence, and reconciliation with the rest of the country in another war. Carr's town, into which he had poured himself and his considerable resources, was about to pass into history along with him. A new era lay ahead.

DUKE UNIVERSITY

The *annus mirabilis*, 1924, had opened on a note of optimism. Judge Sykes published a summary of encouraging statistics. The tax evaluations for the city and county showed $58 and $82.5 million, respectively, while Durham's industrial output was $80 million. The federal government received $43 million from tobacco revenue taxes; 40 million cigarettes were produced every day, along with 2 million bags of tobacco, and 264,000 pairs of hosiery. The city tax rate was $1.05 per $100 valuation while the county's was $0.92. Its two hospitals contained 202 beds, and the annual death rate had declined to 12.8 per thousand.[103]

Later, at the start of Trinity's 1924–25 school year, President Few was quoted as saying, "Every phase of the college this year is expected to experience success. Never before have all indications pointed toward a more promising year."[104] Clearly, he knew something he wasn't telling. It was no secret, however, that James B. Duke had plans for Trinity College, and behind the scenes for a number of years Few had been feeding him with ideas. Of late Duke had been talking more openly about his interests. As early as 1920 rumors were published that he intended to donate all his stock in the Southern Power Company to Trinity as an endowment. By the early 1920s the Duke family had already donated $4 million to Trinity for various purposes, most recently $25,000 for a new gymnasium, $50,000 for a law school building, and another $50,000 for a school of religious training, in addition to $1 million for endowment. The *Wall Street Journal* interviewed Duke in 1923, no doubt with the intention of ferreting out some indication of what the aging Duke intended to do with his fortune.[105] He was there quoted as saying, "It doesn't do any good to make money any more, as the government takes it away from you as fast as you can make it," a rather general complaint of multimillionaires at that time, the income tax having begun in 1913. He complained that he was not getting a sufficient return on the money he had invested in electric power. He deflected the reporter's prying with trivial answers. He told the reporter that "a man can get more enjoyment and real entertainment out of 15 cents worth of tobacco than anything else he knows of." He was actually already involved in a financial decision which would be crucial to Durham. Unless the Southern Power Company, which had already been allowed to raise its rates in the recent past, were permitted to raise them again, he threatened to quit hydroelectric power in North Carolina. In early January 1920 the rise was granted and the way was clear for him to complete his plans for Trinity College.[106]

James B. Duke would not be hurried, however, and Few endured frustration as he waited for Duke to act. Clinton W. Toms, president of the American Tobacco Company—a close confidant of Duke and trustee of Trinity—acted as liaison between Duke and Few, tactfully keeping them both informed of the other's concerns and hopes and advising Few when and how to advance his cause. From his earlier campaign for a medical school, during which Duke was made aware of North Carolina's medical deficiencies, Few was able to develop a concept that inspired Duke to act—majestic, comprehensive, and irresistible. The concept was of a university, named for the Duke family, at the heart of which would be a strong college of liberal arts surrounded by a constellation of professional schools, including a medical school and teaching hospital. Few even sent Duke a model draft of such an institution. It was a plan that Duke could accept, and he incorporated it into a larger design of his own devising. During the last days of the plan's refining, Duke gathered his closest associates and advisors about him in Charlotte and requested that they remain with him until a finished document had been drawn up. Besides a few Charlotte businessmen, hovering, encouraging, suggesting, were George G. Allen, Alexander Sands, William R. Perkins, Toms, and, at times, Robert L. Flowers and Few.[107]

Before the formal announcement of the plan was to be made public, the news leaked out, and on the morning of 9 December 1924 the *Herald* headlines incorrectly read, "$40,000,000 for Duke University." From the news story Durham learned that if Trinity College would assume the Duke name, it would become a full-fledged university and a principal beneficiary of a new Duke Endowment created by the document formulated at Charlotte known as the Duke indenture. The $40 million was to be given to the Duke Endowment, the income of which would be distributed annually to specified educational, religious, and medical institutions of both races in the two Carolinas. Duke University would receive 32 percent of the yearly income of the Endowment. Although the announcement of the indenture was the first public notice of Duke's intentions, Duke and Few had been doing a lot of private thinking and conferring, even going so far as to investigate architectural styles and building locations. After the announcement of the plan, people in Durham remembered having caught sight of stakes stuck in the ground on the campus marked "site for medical building," "site for law building," before they had been quickly removed.[108]

While still reeling from Duke's astonishing news, Durhamites had a more immediate concern. On that very day they were to go to the polls to vote on the city limits extension. Feeling suddenly set apart like winners of an unexpected windfall, their sense of importance and good fortune must certainly have played a role in their decision in the voting booths. To encompass so vast a concept as a great university and the wealth that was to follow in its wake required an enlarged conception of the city, required, in fact, an extension of the city limits to include the campus and its adjacent lands now certain to be developed. It was not surprising under the circumstances that the people voted for extension to give Durham a size and importance commensurate with its new role as the home of Duke University. Was not the Washington Duke Hotel, even then rising toward its sixteenth floor, a symbol of Durham's new aspirations?

Although Trinity's trustees had yet to act on Duke's offer, there was not much doubt about the outcome. On 30 December, the day the trustees met and voted acceptance, they and President Few attended the regular luncheon meeting of the Rotary Club. On his entrance Few was given a standing ovation. A spirit of cooperation between town and gown and soaring hopes of better times—even splendid times—in store filled the company with heady delight that spilled over into the singing of a closing hymn, "Praise God from Whom All Blessings Flow." J. B. Duke's view of his magnificent gesture, however, was more sober. When interviewed after signing the indenture at his legal residence in New Jersey on 11 December, he said his intention was to furnish leaders for the South. When asked whether luxury wouldn't spoil people, he explained, "There will be no luxury. Nothing makes people so unhappy as luxury. Satisfied ambition is an awful thing."[109]

With the affirmative vote for the city extension, Durham became overnight the fourth largest city in the state. More important than the potential prosperity for the city, however, was the blow struck for culture in the creation of Duke University. The country as a whole might count the world war an important watershed, but the Duke indenture marked Durham County's own private watershed, which divided it from its small beginnings and phenomenal adolescent growth, cut it loose from a past of isolation, outmoded sentiments, customs, and parochial contentment to shove out onto uncharted waters. The eyes of the country were now not only on Durham but on the state as well. A *New York Times* article, picked up by the Durham *Herald,* described the state's progress as "the romance of an awakened people" and showed how it had pulled itself up by its own bootstraps out of "mire, illiteracy, and poverty" to rank sixth in national prosperity, fourth in agriculture, and threatened to dislodge Massachusetts from the first place in cotton manufacturing. The year had certainly fulfilled its promise, and Durham had joined the world at last.[110]

Elation and Depression, 1925–1941

16

BUILDING THE UNIVERSITY

As Durham County, with greatness thrust upon it, prepared to watch the building of a university in its midst, it could not foresee that shortly it would be distracted by a crisis of unforgettable dimensions: the Great Depression. While the one would benefit the county and its people, the other would bring long-lasting injurious material, social, and psychological changes. The year 1925 opened with the American academic community's eyes on Durham. "There was an almost apocalyptic expectation that something extraordinary was arising in the South," Mason Crum remembered, and every teacher in the nation wanted to teach at Duke University.[1] The Duke indenture had spelled out James B. Duke's purposes, specifying which aspects of education would be emphasized. He "endeavored to make provision in some measure for the needs of mankind along physical, mental, and spiritual lines. . . ."[2] He considered education the greatest civilizing force next to religion and wanted the university to produce "preachers, teachers, lawyers, and physicians because these are most in the public eye, and by precept and example can do most to uplift mankind."[3] Next to these he ranked chemists, economists, and historians for their help in developing resources, increasing wisdom, and promoting happiness. In implementing Duke's plans, the trustees advised pursuing quality in students rather than numbers, excellence in the university rather than size.[4]

Aware that the university's development would affect the town and that good relations between them were essential, Robert L. Flowers, the vice-president, called a meeting to discuss with town leaders how best to capitalize on the Duke windfall, "to bring Durham to greatness."[5] Town and gown had tended to go their own ways as each pursued its private goals and met its particular problems. Both the Kilgo-Gattis and Bassett cases had contributed to the separation because of the political, religious, and philosophical issues that enveloped them. The joint raising of funds in 1920 for the James H. Southgate memorial building (1921), however, had stimulated a renewed cooperation, and now both parties wished to further that spirit. Within the year three professors were chosen presidents of important civic clubs: Dean William H. Wannamaker of the Rotary, William T. Laprade of Kiwanis, and J. M. Ormond of the Lions. Town and gown were re-embracing in the glow of their common good fortune.[6]

For its own sake, of course, some university action had to be unilateral. Acquisition of land for the new university, for example, was accomplished as secretly as possible. In 1923 and 1924 Few already had agents buying land north of the campus, preparing for the large expansion he knew was to come and hoping to avoid the inflationary prices that would follow the announcement of Duke's intentions. Although some canny landowners suspected what was happening and sold their land at inflated values (in response to which J. B. Duke threatened to build the university in Charlotte), many Durhamites seemed totally unaware of this proceeding. Nor did they suspect what was happening when Murray Jones, a local realtor acting for Duke, bought up tract after tract of what was to become West Campus and Duke Forest, eventually totaling more than 8,000 acres. President Few had explored the neighborhood and found the forests of pines and hardwoods northwest of town that he felt would meet with Duke's approval.[7] A reporter who noticed the large amount of land changing hands in early 1925 wrote, perhaps disingenuously, "It was another big buy in that section of the county where engineers are busy laying off lines apparently for some mammoth development."[8] In May, Jones registered deeds of sixty-seven separate tracts worth about $1 million, and the First National Trust Company transferred to the university land amounting to sixty-two tracts worth $2 million.[9] Much of the land lay along Rigsbee Road and included the old Rigsbee and Pickett family farms.

The architectural firm of Horace Trumbauer of Philadelphia, which had built James B. Duke's New York mansion, was chosen to design the new university buildings long before the indenture was completed. Duke and his architects had visited the college early in 1924 to consider the many questions the grand scheme posed. In June 1925 building plans were revealed, and in July it was announced that the Trumbauer firm would design eleven buildings on the old Trinity campus, eventually to be made a woman's college, and sixteen buildings on the new campus to the west of town where the men's college would be built. James B. Duke took particular interest in the architecture, stone, and siting of the buildings, testing many possibilities before making choices. He insisted that the chapel be the central building of the new campus, and he gave great attention to the natural setting, marking trees that were to be saved before construction was begun, and to the landscaping in general. The stone that eventually was chosen, Huronian slate from a quarry in Hillsborough, was found by a scouting team of Professors Few, Frank Brown, and Robert Flowers. The very hard Cambrian stone covered 350 acres to a depth variously estimated at 80–200 feet and contained colors ranging from dark blue through lighter blues to greens, purples, browns, yellows, and black. Architectural work on the buildings was delegated to Julian Abele, the chief designer of the Trumbauer firm and the first black graduate of the University of Pennsylvania's School of Architecture.[10]

Those closest to James B. Duke in these months of momentous decisions knew of the illness that incapacitated him in July 1925, but his death in October was nevertheless a shock to everyone. Although directly attributable to pneumonia, Duke had been ill for some months with what was called pernicious anemia. A more recent review of the facts in the case has termed it aregenatory anemia. The immediate effect on Durham was a scramble to prepare for the influx of visitors who would attend the funeral ceremonies. The Washington Duke Hotel, scheduled to open later in the month, was hastily prepared for their reception. A private train of seven cars brought the body from New York along with Duke's widow, his daughter, Doris, and many friends and associates. The body lay in state in one of the parlors of the East Duke building, and for the funeral procession an honor guard of students lined the streets from the campus to Memorial Methodist Church where the services were held. Speculation was rife over what Duke's death would mean to the new university. When the will was recorded, it showed that Duke had increased the amount specified in the Duke indenture for building the university and considerably more than doubled the original $40 million given to the Duke Endowment.[11]

An unforeseen windfall affected some Durham County residents. Duke left $2 million to be divided among the legitimate heirs of his parents' brothers and sisters. Obviously he had had no conception of what difficulties he would create for his executors by this legacy. They took two years to identify the rightful heirs after investigating hundreds of claims and finally awarded 196 individuals proportionate shares but denied 525 others. Thirty-five of the lucky ones were Durham County residents who received $359,281.50 of the bequest. Duke's estate was estimated at $150 million, of which the greater part was left to Doris.[12]

For the next decade the development of the university was the focus of change in Durham as the old campus gained its handsome Georgian structures, the forest was cleared for building after building on the new campus, and professors to head the new departments and swell the faculty ranks were announced. "DUKE TO HAVE GREAT MEDICAL SCHOOL," the headlines trumpeted in October 1925. Dr. Wilburt Davison, assistant to the dean of the Johns Hopkins medical school, was chosen as dean of the new school, and he is generally credited with laying the foundation of a medical facility that by the 1980s ranked as one of the best in the nation. His iron control disguised by informality and easy personal relations enabled him to keep close tabs on every angle of the organization. Working within financial constraints, he chose young men, usually Hopkins-trained, as department heads, a gamble that paid off. Ambitious like Davison, together they built a medical center of respect and renown. Eight million dollars was available for building the university; by Duke's will an additional ten million was given to the Duke Endowment, four million of which was to be used for building the medical facilities. The income of the remainder was to go to the university as a whole. Although accounts vary as to the exact amount Duke provided for land and buildings, the Duke Endowment gives the figure as $17 million. The total Endowment was $90 million.[13]

But fame accrued to the university faster through the hiring of William McDougall, an internationally known psychologist and physician, than through its medical center. McDougall had been a British army doctor in the world war, particularly involved with shell-shock victims, and he soon gained attention for Duke through his interest in and support of psychical research. McDougall, staunchly backed by Few, brought Joseph Banks Rhine to Duke in 1927. Rhine and his coworker and wife, Louisa, had become interested in the work of Oliver Lodge and Arthur Conan Doyle and wanted to explore "the rim of the great problem of the nature of life."[14] Rhine, who had intended to go into the ministry before taking a Ph.D. in biology, was both morally and ethically convinced of a supernatural power in the world, but at the same time was sufficiently the scientist to wish to find laboratory proof for his conviction. "Even if the claims of religion for man's spiritual nature proved to be unsupportable," he felt, "it would be better to *know* than to hope or to trust in authority."[15] Through Rhine's experiments in parapsychology, Duke University became identified in the popular mind with psychical research, an activity that naturally led the Rhines perilously close to the fraudulent world of spiritualism, poltergeists, and legerdemain. The tension between faith and skepticism caused by Darwin's theories and more recent scientific discoveries had brought turmoil to both scientific and theological circles. Rhine's work had waiting disciples everywhere, people who found themselves torn between the rational dictates of science and the emotional appeal of faith in the supernatural, particularly the concept of life after death; and they had an almost fanatical hope for Rhine's success.

First as an honorary postdoctoral student and eventually as a regular member of the psychology department, Rhine's connection with Duke attracted notice everywhere. The choice of his book *Frontiers of the Mind* by the Book-of-the-Month Club in 1937 and a series of radio programs on the subject at the same time vaulted him into national prominence and brought Duke, in Few's view, welcome attention. But in certain academic circles uneasiness, even disapproval, was mounting. Also in 1937, Duke University Press began to publish the *Journal of Parapsychology* (edited by McDougall and Rhine), which dealt with Rhine's experiments in extrasensory perception, psychokinesis, clairvoyance, telepathy, and other occult phenomena. Rather soon his colleagues and other scientists across the country decried the mantle of scientific legitimacy that Duke was providing Rhine's studies and those of his students, who were receiving master's and even doctor's degrees for their work in these areas. President Few and McDougall were attracted to his work and respected him personally, but because of the dissension, they wisely found independent funding for him in 1947. Eventually his connection with the university was severed completely when his work had attracted sufficient outside support to guarantee its continuance. He established his own Foundation for Research on the Nature of Man (FRNM) in the former Dean Wannamaker house opposite the East Campus, where the foundation continued its investigations even after Rhine's death in 1980 and his wife's in 1983.[16]

Construction of the West Campus began with the Student Union building, for which Doris Duke laid a ceremonial cornerstone in 1928. In July 1930 the medical school and hospital building was opened with accommodations for four hundred beds and three hundred medical students. The same fall the cornerstone for the chapel was laid.[17] The awesome beauty of the centerpiece of Duke's plan more than fulfilled its purpose. Visitors came, many of them critical of an institution that could be bought with tobacco money and of a university that was now springing full-blown into life out of J. B. Duke's and President Few's heads. Even a few alumni were enraged by what they saw as Duke's presumption, one arguing with Few that "nothing short of a *miracle* can ever establish a truly great university in a place like Durham."[18] But "fools, that came to scoff, remain'd to pray." The magnificent chapel, 275 feet long, with a 210-foot tower reminiscent of Canterbury Cathedral, is one of the finest examples of Gothic Revival architecture in the world. The British novelist Aldous Huxley, a sympathetic supporter of Rhine's work, saw "nothing boring or mean about Duke." He found it "picturesque and grandiose," and "genuinely beautiful."[19]

The ornamental stonework of the chapel was designed by John Donnelly, the stained-glass windows by G. Owen Bonawit, New York artists. James B. Duke's close friends and associates William R. Perkins and George G. Allen donated the fifty bells of the tower carillon, made in Loughborough, England. Landscaping for the entire university was entrusted to the Boston firm of Olmsted Brothers, founded by Frederick Law Olmsted. One of the final embellishments to the chapel was the memorial chapel, to the left of the chancel, to which the bodies of Washington Duke and his sons were transferred and entombed in sarcophagi of white Carrara marble. The tombs are adorned with sculptured figures of the three men carved by Charles Keck, who also made the statue of James B. Duke, complete with cane and cigar, which now stands in front of the chapel. Friends of Duke, inspired by James A. Thomas, representative in China for the British-American Tobacco Company and a loyal friend of Trinity and Duke, donated money for these sculptures.[20]

So different in their natures, yet devoted to one another and to the religion that nurtured their generous impulses, the Duke brothers, Ben and "Buck," pursued their differing goals through hard work. James B. Duke, whose genius for business made everything possible, was relentlessly ambitious and, in some eyes, even ruthless. His retiring and modest brother, also a shrewd businessman, was more overtly committed to helping people. He correctly identified his own forte when he playfully wrote to a young protégée, "I am a pretty good judge of folk."[21] Their father, whose simple faith and harsh experience gave moral strength to his character, instilled his own values in his sons and reconciled his unswerving Methodism with a dogged perseverance and tolerance for others in a philosophic synthesis: "A proper ambition is God's call to a higher life."[22] His practical advice for the South was "Take a rest on politics and prejudice for a few years; quietly turn in and build factories; put wheels in motion; utilize the bounties of nature and create employment for the unemployed; have vacant places for those who come to locate with us."[23]

Benjamin Duke died in 1929, and although he had not been in Durham since 1923, his ties to the college and region remained strong. Because of his self-effacing nature, the extent of his philanthropy was not generally known. Small southern sectarian colleges and a wide array of churches, hospitals, and orphanages were the objects of his benefaction. Trinity College, of course, always received the largest share. After his son's accidental death in 1923, for example, he established the Angier B. Duke scholarships in his memory. President Few understood what Benjamin Duke had meant to the progress of Trinity College, even to its survival. He had been largely responsible for directing James B. Duke's interest to Trinity that resulted in the munificent gift. William Few wanted to create as a memorial to Benjamin Duke an institute for graduate studies separately funded and named for him. Although he received encouragement for the plan from James B. Duke's associates, they were concerned with their own schemes, and Few was forced to drop the project. A spectacular memorial to Benjamin Duke was eventually made, however, in the donation to the chapel in 1976 of a Flentrop tracker organ, sixty feet high, mounted in a loft at the back of the chapel, its red and gold case ornamenting that wall.[24]

Benjamin Duke's children, Angier Duke and Mary Duke Biddle, made large gifts to Trinity during their lifetimes. The latter reintegrated her own life with that of Durham and Duke University after her divorce in 1931 from Anthony J. Drexel Biddle Jr. and spent much of each year in Durham. In 1935 she bought the James O. Cobb house in Forest Hills for her Durham home. That she was a perceptive and shrewd person was already discernible in the sprightly young girl of 1896 who wrote to her father in New York on April Fool's Day about her playful successes in Durham. "I have had a right good time today April-fooling people. I fooled Mrs. Robinson, and Brother, and many other people. I don't think you can fool any body much up there."[25] In 1956 Mrs. Biddle established the Mary Duke Biddle Foundation to manage her philanthropy. The foundation was to support religious, educational, and charitable activities in the states of New York and North Carolina. One-half of the annual income was to go to Duke University for religious, scientific, literary, or medical purposes. Her lifelong interest in music and gardening is reflected in particular support to music in the university and to the Sarah P. Duke Gardens. The Duke Gardens were started by Mrs. Benjamin (Sarah P. Angier) Duke at the suggestion of Dr. Frederic M. Hanes. After her death in 1936 her daughter, Mary Duke Biddle, carried on the project as a memorial to her mother. Initially based on the plans of the noted landscape architect Ellen Shipman, over the years the gardens were much expanded and became a tourist destination because of their exceptional beauty and horticultural variety.[26]

It was probably at Mrs. Biddle's urging that the university repurchased the old Washington Duke homestead when it came on the market in 1931. Washington Duke had sold his farm to William P. Newton of Greensboro in 1883. In 1903 when it was again for sale, two Durham lawyers futilely suggested to Benjamin Duke's secretary that one of the Dukes might wish to buy the place "where W. Duke Sons and Company was born." The farm was partitioned, and the 140 acres containing the house were bought by T. N. Allen, who subsequently bottled and sold spring water there. At the time of the 1931 purchase from Allen's daughter, the newspaper described relics remaining from the Dukes' occupancy: the flowered wallpaper put on by the twelve-year-old Mary [Duke Lyon], the kitchen safe with its painted glass panes and hand-etched designs, and a wooden bench made by one of the family. The university held the homestead until 1974, when it was donated to the state as a historic site. A museum of tobacco culture and manufacture run by the Tobacco History Corporation, Inc., was added to the homestead to supplement the farm buildings in interpretation of the site.[27]

Vice-president Robert L. Flowers was correct in foreseeing that the university would change Durham. Charles B. Markham, as both assistant treasurer of the university and native of the town, told the Kiwanis Club in 1937 that Duke was injecting into the Durham economy about $4 million a year.[28] Its intellectual contributions were harder to measure. It continued to bring to Durham in ever-greater abundance the best musicians, artists, lecturers, and scholars in every field to enrich life there beyond any calculation.

LABOR UNREST

The George Fuller Construction Company of Washington, D.C., was employed to construct the new buildings on the old campus. As it hired only union members, Durham, whose construction workers were for the most part non-union, could not supply the necessary labor. Although this prompted the formation of a number of local unions and stimulated the membership of local workmen in those already formed, the Fuller Company had already brought organized workmen to Durham, and their presence was a disturbing element to local industrialists who heard rumors of union organization among its workers by the American Federation of Labor. Kemp Lewis, manager of Erwin Mills, and the managers of Durham Hosiery Mills and Liggett and Myers hired an agent from the Railway Audit and Inspection Company of Atlanta to infiltrate the mills and factories and relay to them information about organizing efforts. They learned that the tobacco factory was about 20 percent organized, and that though a good many workers at Erwin Mills were dues-paying members of unions, there were no meetings going on. The unionizing flurry in the building trades, however, made possible once more a central labor union, chartered by William Green, president of the American Federation of Labor. John A. Peel, a local carpenter, was elected president. Seven unions were affiliated with it, including barbers, electricians, carpenters, hosiery workers, printers, and stagehands and movie projector operators. The membership was swelled by the number of northern workmen in the city. The university very soon corrected its public relations blunder by establishing its own construction company under the direction of A. C. Lee, the engineer who had advised James B. Duke in his electric power endeavors; this company employed almost entirely local, non-union workmen. The northern workmen departed, and local workmen deserted the unions in droves so that once again the central union lapsed until it was reborn in 1934.[29]

Not the workers themselves but the federal government eventually confronted the industrialists successfully, changing for all time the old paternal mold of industrial relations. With the advent of the Roosevelt era and the National Industrial Recovery Act of 1933 (NIRA), which set up the National Recovery Administration (NRA), workers in every sector of American business and industry were granted the right to bargain collectively, to form and belong to unions with impunity. Immediately after NIRA became law, the Tobacco Workers International Union (TWIU) formed Local 176 at Liggett and Myers on 17 June 1933 under the leadership of E. L. Crouch. Ernest Latta, one of the charter members, had tried to organize a chapter in 1929, but the firing of men who joined halted his attempts. Local 183 at the American Tobacco Company was also formed at this time, both locals only for whites. In 1934 a chapter for stemmery workers of Liggett and Myers, Local 194, was organized at the black YWCA. By 1939, 95 percent of Liggett and Myers's production workers as well as a majority of leaf workers were members. The company opposed the union until 1939, when a paralyzing strike ended with an increase in workers' wages and the company's acceptance of the union as a permanent feature.[30]

In the textile and hosiery plants the road to unionization was stormier. In March 1934 a meeting to organize textile workers was held at West Durham High School. Again, Lewis resorted to spies to learn what was happening in the mill. By March the United Textile Workers Union agent had had varying success, greatest at Golden Belt, limited at Durham Hosiery Mills where he had set up Bull City Textile Local 2155 (one of seven in Durham), and apparently none at all at Erwin Mills. The Golden Belt mill closed down in late May 1934, throwing 150 to 200 workers out of jobs a week after the union had been organized there. The company placed the blame on lack of orders. In August the situation became more inflammatory because outside agitators came in and, according to Lewis, "poisoned the people and made them feel that we are their enemies instead of their friends, all based upon misrepresentation of the most drastic kind. We are now being drawn into a general strike, with no credit whatever being given to us for having treated the people fairly."[31]

In September a general strike was called, later described by a West Durham resident as "the worst strike here that ever was." During that year oscillations in the mills' work between cutbacks and overproduction resulted in further pay reductions and enormous unrest among the workers. Wages at Erwin Mills had fallen 63.5 percent between November 1920 and May 1932. Hindsight accused the union leaders of a power play to whip up sentiment for their own purposes with the workers as pawns in their hands. The general strike, which was called for Labor Day, 3 September, and ended almost three weeks later, involved fifty-two hundred workers from Erwin Mills, Golden Belt, Durham Hosiery, and East Durham Cotton manufacturing plants, but there was no violence, not so much as a fistfight. It began with a memorial service in Pine Hill Cemetery at the grave of Clem Norwood, who had been killed on picket duty by strikebreakers in Philadelphia. The four thousand who attended the service pledged themselves to a "great fight against the evils of poverty amid plenty, oppression in a democracy, and against all social greed, selfishness, and bigotry."[32] They dedicated themselves to peace in industry based on justice. Other workers continued to join the strike in sympathy until there were seven thousand out on strike in Durham. Norman Thomas, the Socialist Party leader and ex-Presbyterian minister, spoke to a throng during the strike, strengthening their sense of purpose. Albert Beck, who had engineered the union organizing, directed the strike activities in a North Mangum Street building donated by Richard Wright for strike headquarters. Local merchants offered food, credit, and tents. When the strike ended, however, the workers discovered that they had gained nothing. They returned to the same wages, hours, and workloads as before. The experience, in fact, probably set back the cause of organized labor in Durham because of its failure to achieve results. It disenchanted its members once more, and lost them.[33] The federal government negotiated a settlement and followed it up with the Winant Report, which recommended an investigation of the textile industry supervised by the Bureau of Labor Statistics. The women's clubs that had continued to battle for the investigation after the YWCA leaders had backed down must have felt a quiet triumph in this late victory. The state commissioner of the Department of Labor in the biennial report covering July 1934 to June 1936 urged the adoption of the NRA textile code, which included a forty-hour week and an eight-hour day; he acknowledged the "disgrace of having the longest legal work-day for women of any civilized country, excepting only Japan. No other state or nation has an eleven-hour day for women."[34]

The end of the 1934 strike did not bring an end to union activity. Small, intermittent strikes occurred throughout the decade. At the Durham Hosiery Mills, where the Carrs would not recognize the union, a strike was called in July 1935. Scabs resorted to violence to break through the picket lines and slashed two union officials, Bonnie Glenn, president of Local 93, and Ernest Latta of the Liggett and Myers Tobacco local. Mayor W. F. Carr, president of the hosiery company, led a number of workers through the lines unmolested. Erwin Mills had a one-day strike of its battery fillers in 1937 and in 1939 in its bleachery department. In 1939 as well, Golden Belt avoided a strike by negotiating a contract with the local union representatives that continued the forty-hour week, eight-hour day, time-and-a-half wages for overtime, double pay for Sundays and holidays, a week's vacation with pay, and a pay raise. That year North Carolina ranked forty-seventh among the states in percentage of unionized workers and later slipped to last place. That was also the year in which management fully accepted unions and collective bargaining as inevitable. The Durham Hosiery Mills and Golden Belt Manufacturing Company adjusted their pay scales to conform to federal minimum wage standards. Despite setbacks, labor had won the battle, chiefly because the federal government had stepped in, first with the NRA industrial codes, then with its investigations, and finally with the establishment of the National Labor Relations Board, which was authorized to adjudicate between employers and labor when negotiations were deadlocked.[35]

OTHER CONSTRUCTION

The expansion of Trinity College to a full-fledged university brought an influx of outsiders to a hitherto homogeneous society—workmen to build it and employees to work in it. By 1927 there were already small enclaves of foreigners. The 1930 census showed the town with more than 0.7 percent foreign-born residents, or 361 in a population of over 45,000. Of the minority groups the Greeks numbered fifty-nine; Russians, fifty-five; Italians, forty-one; English, thirty-one; dwindling down through other nationals to two Indians, three Chinese, and one Japanese. In 1927 the town had eighteen restaurants and two confectionaries run by Greeks. When George Niccaulu was asked why he went into the food business, he explained that meringues reminded him of the clouds of home, grape juice the sea, cakes with icing the temples, "so, to keep from dying of homesickness I opened a restaurant. Now I make new clouds, new seas, new temples every day." Another foreign group that became a permanent part of the community was composed of northern Italian stonemasons, who came to build the Tudor-Gothic structures on the new campus, and other skilled craftsmen such as Antonio Germino, an ironworker and tool-maker, who eventually operated the Southern Tool and Manufacturing Company on Duke Street. Among the masons were Peter Ferettino, Luigi (Louis) Fara, Tony Citrini, Tony Berini, Pete Giobbi, Pete Yon, and John Rosazza.[36]

New faculty and their families, although not of a foreign culture, did bring different ideas and interests to Durham. Mostly from other areas of the country and with a variety of backgrounds and experience, they were "new blood in a hitherto more or less ordinary Piedmont town."[37] A faculty wife and native southerner saw the situation from both sides. "For though town and gown do not exactly mix (each privately considers the other a trifle bizarre), they do mingle enough to receive flashes of insight into alien habits of thought."[38] Some of the new residents built homes in Forest Hills and Hope Valley, two recently developed neighborhoods. The former was the conception of the New Hope Realty Company, managed by W. J. Griswold and planned in 1917 to comprise 242 acres extending from Pine Street west along University Drive, then called Hope Valley Road. E. S. Draper, the landscape architect who had planned Charlotte's Myers Park, was hired to lay out winding streets, playgrounds, and parks with 331 building lots for whites, 115 for blacks, and 22 farms. When the company went bankrupt, it was bought by the First National Trust Company in 1922, and the project was trimmed to 160 acres. In 1923 five miles of streets, city water and sewer pipes, a golf course, swimming pool, and clubhouse were added. Lots were sold, and new houses, many designed by the Durham architect George Watts Carr, were built. The clubhouse burned in 1927 but was rebuilt the next year and the club reorganized. In the Depression the development again went bankrupt and was bought by John Sprunt Hill, who donated to the city the clubhouse and pool and thirty-nine acres of the floodplain for a public park in 1932, Forest Hills Park.[39]

The Hope Valley project, which also attracted some of the new faculty, was begun in 1926. The first public announcement of the projected development by the Mebane Company (Jesse Mebane was one of the chief investors) focused on the golf club that was to be at its heart. Gilbert C. White, C. M. Carr, John Buchanan, and a few Greensboro businessmen formed the local committee of the corporation. A $50,000 clubhouse, restricted to three hundred members, was designed by Aymar Embury (the designer of the Mid-Pines Club at Pinehurst) and opened in July 1927. The winding roads, originally intended to have had Indian names associated with the area—Eno, Cherokee, Occoneechee—and chosen by public contest, were given English placenames, no doubt thought to be more elegant and certainly more in keeping with the English cottage architecture typical of the original houses built along them.[40]

Between these two residential areas, Dr. Lyle Steele Booker attempted to lay out and develop a smaller enclave (117 acres) east of Cornwallis Road and south of University Drive, now known as Rockwood. Called Booker Heights in 1925, the tract had been called Cornwallis Heights by its previous owner, Julian Carr. The Alamance Insurance and Real Estate Company took over its development, but had sold only half the lots in 1929 when it went bankrupt and returned the unsold lots to Booker. Although some faculty families bought land in this development as well, Duke University soon began to allocate sections of its vast land holdings for faculty housing beginning with the old section of Pinecrest Road, where the first five faculty houses were built in 1930. Offered especially generous lots well below the market price and subsidized expenses, new faculty were attracted to Durham and jumped at the opportunity to build their own houses in a neighborhood protected by special covenants from undesirable development and outside buyers. In 1940 lots on Cranford Road and west along Anderson Street were made available for faculty housing.[41]

Suburban development had been going on a long while, largely to accommodate a swelling population, but a much more fundamental change occurred in the 1920s. Formerly prime residential areas in town were being turned to commercial use as center city property became more and more expensive. Well-heeled residents were selling out at tremendous profit, preferring to live in tastefully planned remote neighborhoods to remaining city-pent in their grand, old-fashioned town dwellings. Once the exodus started, it became a fashion. Symbolic of the times was the fate of the Julian Carr property. As his estate was gradually settled, his homeplace in the center of town was put on the block after the family's offer of the house and grounds to the Woman's Club had been refused. Somerset Villa with its seventeen rooms and ten baths was much too large for anyone's needs and much too old-fashioned for anyone's taste in the 1920s, and the Woman's Club was in no position to maintain it. The property was divided into fifty building lots and sold at auction in 1925. C. McM. Carr bought the house for $1,050. The property as a whole brought $187,627. The loss of the Carr mansion reflected a changed world. Suburbia had replaced urban living, convenience had supplanted grandeur, and anything Victorian was out of fashion.[42]

The stimulus to construction that the building of the university brought to Durham carried over into the early Depression years and mitigated the effect on the people of Durham of the general economic collapse. While elsewhere in the nation construction halted, in Durham it merely slowed. Two ambitious projects completed in the first year of the Depression were the Snow and Kress buildings, planned and begun in 1929. The Snow Building was designed by George Watts Carr in the Art Deco style for Mrs. H. B. Lane, the widow of Horace North Snow. The S. H. Kress Building at the southwest corner of Mangum and Main streets, also in the Art Deco style, was the first air-conditioned building in Durham.[43] Two other landmarks built during the Depression, both designed by the Durham firm of Atwood and Weeks and erected with federal funds, were the post office at the corner of Chapel Hill and Rigsbee streets and the armory or civic center on the southeast corner of Morgan and Foster streets. The post office was formally dedicated by Postmaster General James A. Farley in 1934 with considerable hoopla, befitting a project that had provided so many with jobs during the blackest days of the slump. The combination armory-civic center, an arrangement devised by the Chamber of Commerce, met with opposition but was finally constructed around the old city market. It incorporated as much as possible the building materials of the old market.[44]

Also built in this era but financed entirely with private funds was the structure that still dominates the entire cityscape, the seventeen-story Hill building at the northwest corner of Main and Corcoran streets. Built by John Sprunt Hill to house his business and banking interests, it was designed by the same architects that built the Empire State building, Shreve, Lamb, and Harmon. The largest local building constructed in this period, its projected cost was $900,000, a hefty sum to pour into the sagging economy.[45]

Also constructed were new facilities for the tobacco companies, the only industry to maintain momentum in Durham during the Depression. Increase in the use of tobacco, as always in times of stress, pushed production to new levels. The American Tobacco Company enlarged its plant on Blackwell Street in 1938 and built eight warehouses on Ellis Road, adding to the thirty-two already strung out along the former estate of Y. E. Smith. Liggett and Myers, too, needed additional storage and in 1934 added ten warehouses to its collection on Broad Street, where it already had twenty. The auction houses were likewise feeling cramped. In 1938 alone the Planters, Star Brick, Liberty Number 1, and Banner were enlarged, and Liberty Number 3 was constructed, giving Durham three times the amount of auction house space it had had a decade before. To relieve the bottleneck in the auctions themselves, a third set of buyers was added in 1933 to speed up the auctioning.[46]

The churches, too, enjoyed brisk building phases both before the Depression and again at the end as the economy brightened. The monumental new First Baptist Church, designed by Reuben H. Hunt of Tennessee and begun in 1925, took its place at the head of Chapel Hill Street, filling the vista with its majestic portal and pedimented porch. Trinity Avenue Presbyterian, Asbury Methodist, and Mount Vernon Baptist churches began brick structures in 1925, 1926, and 1940, respectively, while Duke's Chapel Church revealed its family connection by the use of the university's quarry stone for its new sanctuary, begun in 1926. Built according to plans of the Horace Trumbauer firm and assisted by $15,000 from Benjamin Duke and $10,000 from the Duke Endowment, the church was completed in 1927 at a cost of about $50,000. Saint Paul's Lutheran Church, a congregation formed in 1923, and the West Durham Baptist Church, renamed Grey Stone Baptist, also built stone churches in 1929 and 1936 respectively.[47]

In the county a number of new buildings replaced the old ones; rebuilt were Olive Branch Baptist Church (1926) and Cedar Fork Baptist (1932), and Roberson Grove dedicated its new church in 1939 after the destruction of an earlier building three years before in a storm. Both Gorman Baptist and Sandy Level Baptist (Durham Memorial) began new sanctuaries in 1939, and Bethesda Baptist the next year. Newly organized congregations were Braggtown Baptist in 1938 and Holloway Street Baptist and Mount Bethel Presbyterian at Huckleberry Springs in 1941. Two denominations that had been in Durham for several decades obtained a firmer foothold: the Church of Jesus Christ of Latter-day Saints, more familiarly known as the Mormons, built a chapel on Holloway Street in 1932, and the Christian Scientists purchased their first church property, at 406 Cleveland Street.[48]

THE GREAT DEPRESSION

When the United States plunged into the Great Depression at the end of 1929, everyone was caught off guard. Among the causes blamed for the crash have been imbalance in the economy between the rich urban and the impoverished rural populations and unrestrained, improperly backed financial speculation.

The year in Durham began sadly with the death of Benjamin Duke on 8 January. Although he had been away from Durham for many years because of a long and undiagnosed illness (in hindsight thought to have been Ménière's disease), his death marked the breaking of one more link with the past, the loss of a town father who had been responsible in part for Durham's special destiny. With a fortune less than his brother's, he had nevertheless given away large sums all through his life, primarily to Trinity College, which had received about two and a half million dollars. Richard Wright's death in March removed from the scene the last of the original tobacco pioneers. Dissension among his heirs concerning the provisions of his will carried the litigiousness that had characterized his life even beyond the grave. Drawn up in 1921, the will antedated his philanthropic interests, so that both Louisburg College and the Wright Refuge were disappointed in their expectations of further assistance. Wright's sister Mary Wright assumed responsibility for the refuge, however, and gave it $100,000 in 1930 and contributed to its maintenance and operation until she died in 1932.[49]

In June 1929 the federal government found itself with a $200 million surplus because of startling increases in tax revenues, reflecting extraordinary prosperity in some sectors of the economy, though certainly not in agriculture or textiles. Waves of selling, however, had begun to topple the stock market in May, as stockholders, who had bought on margin, hurried to cash in on the greatly inflated prices. In October the nervousness of those who had invested imprudently rocked the market, and in one hour losses on paper totaled $5 billion. On the last day of the month the stock market had its blackest day; stock prices plummeted, many men were ruined, and fortunes dissolved in air.[50]

Durham's experience in the 1920s and 1930s was not that of the nation as a whole. A depression in agriculture and textiles had already gripped the South beginning in the early 1920s; from 1928 to 1932 farm income in North Carolina decreased further to 65.7 percent of its pre-Depression level, but because of the building of Duke University with its large outlay of money in Durham and because of the tobacco industry, which expanded exponentially, Durham's experience of the Depression was somewhat cushioned and of shorter duration than that of the rest of the nation. It was nevertheless a time of emotional stress and financial difficulty for many people, particularly those who even in the best of times lived on the brink of poverty.[51]

The first to feel the pinch were the blacks, and their plight was revealed to the rest of the city by the Welfare Department which suddenly felt the strain on its services. The Health Department, too, noticed that infant deaths and cases of tuberculosis and pellagra were increasing. Help came from the federal and local governments, charitable organizations, and individuals. The Health Department began to distribute concentrated milk donated by manufacturers. The federal government's relief money supplied hot lunches for 200 schoolchildren, but it was inadequate: Durham had 700 to 800 children in the city schools who qualified for help. To the poor in general the federal government began distribution of surplus food through a community relief store, but local merchants complained because such food giveaways cut into their own business. As a result, the relief commissary was phased out, and those who qualified for food were given cash to use in the regular stores. The Red Cross distributed 200,000 pounds of flour, providing one thousand families with three months' supply. It also distributed free clothing. Wholesale prices, which had advanced 100 percent, added further hardship to the average person. Realizing that they were receiving the bulk of relief funds (69 percent) while making up only 29 percent of the population, the black community met in December 1932 to organize a relief drive to raise $5,000.[52]

The crux of all Depression problems was unemployment, resulting in a staggering number of people without any source of income. Gifts of food and clothing were only stopgap measures; what was needed was jobs. As industry faltered and businesses shrank or closed entirely, as commercial institutions failed and capitalists went bankrupt, as men lost their jobs and then their homes, unable to pay taxes or mortgages, armies of people were suddenly without any means of support, hungry, and homeless. The governor formed a Council of Relief and Unemployment to attack the problem and appointed M. E. Newsom of Durham to head it. One of its solutions was temporary, largely cosmetic work for jobless men paid for in food. Government on every level was forced to devise work that would at the very least prevent starvation. To enable the state to assume some of the burden for care of the unemployed and to institute work programs, Governor O. Max Gardner also proposed a pay cut of 10 percent for all state employees, a measure that affected professors at the university and teachers in the schools as well as all other government workers. As a private university Duke was not required to cut its salaries, but it later followed suit when its endowment income fell drastically. The Chamber of Commerce established an employment bureau in the city market office under the care of Ethel Carr Lipscomb, bringing together employers and employees with some success.[53]

Only after the election of Franklin D. Roosevelt in 1932 did the federal government devise larger measures that more nearly addressed the desperate needs of the unemployed. With Federal Emergency Relief Administration (FERA) funds, the National Re-employment Service was started in every state in the spring of 1933. The local employment office became a federal service and moved to new quarters on Morgan Street across from City Hall, again under the direction of Ethel Lipscomb. It was allocated $30,000 for unemployment relief and $5,000 for free hospitalization. In 1935 the legislature established a state employment bureau. In 1938 when unemployment compensation became law, the work increased enormously, and the staff grew from seven to sixteen employees. FERA funds also supported canning projects, and a canning shed was built in which county workhouse inmates and unemployed women canned vegetables. Mrs. J. E. Cole with twenty assistants instructed housewives in the process in their homes. Other FERA projects were dried milk packaging, rug weaving, and road building.[54]

Another federal innovation in 1933 was the Civilian Conservation Corps. Young men from eighteen to twenty-five years of age could join for a year's service, live under army supervision, and work at reforestation and park service projects. They were paid $30 a month, of which all but $5 was sent directly to their families since their own needs—shelter, food, and clothing—were supplied. Durham's CCC Camp Edward L. King was built in 1933 on a sixty-acre site, leased from the Wright heirs, on Club Boulevard east of Roxboro Road. At the start it accommodated 108 men. By September 1934 the men had built forty-five miles of truck trails through the Duke, UNC, and Hill forests making fire lanes, two hundred bridges, and a fire tower, and had planted a timber crop. The camp closed in August 1934 but was revamped for a new contingent a year later and renamed Camp Julian S. Carr. New buildings were built, and the men, who now numbered close to two hundred, worked on gully control and soil erosion projects. In 1938 the second camp was closed and, amid clamorous protest by Durham officials, prepared for a third group, all blacks. The newspaper and church groups criticized the intolerance of the city leaders, who soon regretted their hasty first reaction. The farmers made it known that they had benefited from the work of the camp and were eager to see it continued regardless of the color of the men. Two hundred blacks were established at the camp under the Department of Agriculture's Soil Conservation Service to instruct farmers and build terraces to prevent soil erosion. In 1940 the camp was moved to another location near Chapel Hill, though still in Durham County. The old camp was rented to the National Youth Administration (NYA) and used for vocational training.[55]

Besides encouraging the formation of unions, as mentioned earlier, the NRA improved working conditions and levels of compensation for all. Depending on voluntary cooperation rather than coercion, it encouraged the adoption of industrial and business codes that designated fair hour, wage, and price scales and stated the rights of employees to collective bargaining. There was surprising compliance with the codes, objectionable as they may have seemed to many employers. Businesses and industries that accepted them were awarded blue eagle emblems to be prominently displayed as badges of patriotism. The public was encouraged to sign pledges to deal only with businesses in compliance. The government was fighting a war against poverty, and those who cooperated with its efforts were good soldiers. Because of the NRA codes, the barbers' work week, for example, declined from the traditional 72–85 hours a week to 52 or 54 hours. The price of a haircut rose from 20¢ to 35¢. Banks and stores accepted the forty-hour week and a minimum salary of $14 a week. Grocery stores accepted the 48-hour week for their employees but refused to curtail their hours to the suggested number. They insisted on opening at 7 A.M. and staying open later on weekends. By September 1933 the newspaper reported compliance by 586 of 825 Durham employers. Minimum hours created new jobs—1,763 full-time and 118 part-time—in businesses that operated more than forty or forty-eight hours a week. Thomas Dixon, who spoke in Durham under the auspices of the West Durham Baptist Church, called NIRA the most important legislation since the Magna Carta.[56]

Signs of an easing of the Depression were reported in January 1934. M. B. Fowler, chairman of the Central Relief Committee, stated that relief rolls had decreased from 12,000 in March 1933 to 4,000 at that time. His organization had distributed $600,000 in food, clothing, fuel, and salaries in its three years of existence. Construction in 1933 doubled over the previous year's level, as did the price of cotton. Tobacco went from $11 to $19 for a hundred pounds. Optimism, however, was premature. Although temporary upswings occurred in industrial orders, by the winter of 1935 the unemployed were protesting at FERA headquarters for higher wages and more food. When their wages were cut again in July, they complained so bitterly that a state investigation of the local office was ordered.[57]

Many aspects of FERA work were taken over by the WPA (Works Progress Administration) when it was created in 1935. Its workers were hired for a minimum of 130 hours a month but at a one-third cut in wages, resulting in pay of 20¢ an hour. In December 1935 direct relief was abolished as FERA was phased out, causing immediate hardship to 300 families on the relief roles. Churches stepped in to collect $5,000 and clothing for those affected by the cut and for the 450 employees coincidentally thrown out of work in November by the closing of Durham Hosiery Mill No. 1. One of the first effects of the WPA felt in Durham was the distribution of four rail carloads of food consisting of dried and canned fruit, vegetables, and meat. It also set up nursery schools for children of relief clients to enable the parents to accept work. White children were sent to Southside School and blacks to White Rock and Saint Mark's churches in Hayti. Many construction projects in Durham County were the result of WPA contributions of labor: a third of the $750,000 cost of the new sewage treatment plant; almost half of the $280,000 cost of the new North Carolina College buildings; and 30 percent of the $130,000 needed for the new Whitted, Bragtown, and Bethesda schools. WPA funds financed a job-training program of the state employment service for black women on relief. If accepted in the program they received 240 hours of training as domestics at the Harriet Tubman YWCA and were paid $27 a month while enrolled. The training was also available for those not on relief, but they received no pay. In 1938 the WPA was the number one employer in the nation.[58]

A government innovation that remained a permanent part of national life was the social security system. Begun in 1935, it at first covered only the indigent aged, dependent children, and the blind. In 1940 it was extended to many kinds of workers as a compulsory pension system, contributed to in employees' working years by both employers and employees. A Social Security office serving six counties was opened in Durham in 1938, under the management of Mrs. Nina Horner Matthews, who served until 1971.[59]

The problem on the farms was not unemployment but stemmed from a combination of factors. Acreage under cultivation in Durham County in 1930 was the same as it had been in 1850, but the number of farms had vastly increased; the size of the average farm had shrunk to about twenty acres, far too small to produce an adequate annual return. The number of tenant farmers increased as farmers lost their land or young men unable to purchase land joined the work force. This number peaked in 1935, when 54.5 percent of farmers in North Carolina were tenants. By 1940 the number had dropped to 49.3 percent. Overproduction and depressed prices and markets combined in the 1930s to make it harder than ever for farmers to survive. While farm agents, farm-life schools, demonstration programs, and educational and informational services helped farmers produce ever-better harvests, their efforts were useless unless the crops could be sold at reasonable prices. The federal government had already introduced crop quotas, and these became ever more necessary during the Depression. The large oversupply of tobacco in 1932 and its low market price resulted the following year in Durham County's huge vote in favor of tobacco quotas. Well over 90 percent of Durham farmers signed up for tobacco reduction, and close to 70 percent for cotton. Farmers were paid $17 an acre in 1934 for each acre removed from cultivation. In 1937 farm income was at its highest level since 1930, and that situation again brought overwhelming approval in 1938 and 1939 of the cotton and tobacco quotas. Just as the tobacco farmers began to feel more confident, the war that broke out in Europe in 1939 caused a new setback. European factories were being diverted to war production, their warehouses were well stocked, and tobacco farmers found their market seriously diminished. At the same time, however, the market for wheat and other grains doubled from 1937 to 1941.[60]

A new farmers' cooperative, Durham Farmers Mutual Exchange, was established in 1930. John Sprunt Hill offered the old John O'Daniel Hosiery Mill building on Gilbert Street for the operation and agreed to renovate the building and pay the salary of a manager the first year. Increasing from 200 to 900 members by 1935, the cooperative served many nearby counties and increased the volume of its business 25 to 28 percent a year. A curb market begun in 1930 and operated by the women's advisory board and the county farm and demonstration agents gave farm women an additional source of income through the sale of poultry, eggs, baked and pickled goods, and fresh flowers and vegetables in season.[61]

Because of its comparatively better economic position, Durham had to cope with transients. The unemployed from other counties flocked to Durham hoping to find work. The Welfare Department and the Salvation Army were overwhelmed by appeals for help; they could not handle the needs of legitimate residents, let alone wave after wave of transients. Police were urged to ask them to move on. When this approach did not work, the city designated an old hotel on Church Street as a transient bureau, affording them temporary shelter and help.[62]

Unemployed persons banded together in Durham and formed associations to air their needs, share their problems, and lobby for help more efficiently. Make-work in the community was devised for them and allotted according to need. In February 1933 Professor Newman I. White of Duke's English department set up the Labor and Materials Exchange, approved by the Central Relief Committee, along lines already established in other parts of the country. Labor was exchanged for supplies—clothing, shelter, food—and small amounts of money. Space was provided in the city market where the unemployed could gather to play checkers or read and perform the sewing, barbering, shoe repairing, and woodworking that they bartered for supplies. Donations of clothing, laundered and cleaned free by local laundries and cleaners, were also sold in a kind of flea market. Operated very flexibly with extremely limited funds and with whatever each day offered, the exchange responded successfully to individual needs. It was forced to suspend operations, however, after only six to seven months because free space was no longer available.[63] By this time other federal relief measures were being tried, and with the expanding tobacco industry and government-subsidized and private construction, Durham began to feel the easing of its economic pains.

LOCAL GOVERNMENT

The extraordinary proliferation of federal government agencies was observed with dismay by many, but to many others the new social programs became lifelines. State and local government, too, underwent similar growth in this period, assuming larger roles in the lives of North Carolinians. Because of the deplorable economic conditions, the state expanded its control in a variety of ways. In 1931 it took over the care of all roads. It had already assumed responsibility for primary roads in 1921, but now it included county roads as well. Durham County was unique in owning its own road-building equipment with which it had created 1,250 miles of first-class roadways. J. S. Hill, who had been a state road commissioner for ten years—during which time he had procured for Durham more state roads than other counties felt it was entitled to—was "solidly and singly" against the state takeover of roads, claiming that the tax would not cover the cost. At the same time, of course, the state assumed responsibility for prisoners, the labor force customarily used for roadwork. As a solution to unemployment the state proposed to spend $6 million to complete 300 miles of roads linking each county seat with every other. The state assumption of road building and maintenance lifted a heavy burden from the county and enabled it to reduce taxes.[64]

The county's other onerous burden was the school system. In 1931 a bill to add a one-cent sales tax was proposed to allow the state to run the schools for a uniform six-month year, but though it passed in the House, it was defeated in the Senate. Two years later a bill establishing a statewide state-supported eight-month school term passed, and a few months later a three-cent sales tax was adopted (exempting some essential foods) by which the school system would be financed. Besides lessening a tax burden of the counties, state control did much to equalize the quality and quantity of schooling available to all the children in the county. The same year, however, city voters passed a supplemental school tax to preserve Durham city schools' nine-month school term, creating a disparity again between the city and county schools. The state drastically reduced teachers' salaries, which had already been cut several times before, to help reduce its deficit. Some salaries dropped from $2,000 a year to $720 over the Depression period. With the last cut, a salary of $1,000 a year was decreased to $672. Yet these cuts were in accord with the wishes of some of the population, for example, the Taxpayers League, a group headed by Harry W. Lehman, which played watchdog to government expenditure of tax monies. Along with many other recommendations, such as the cutting of teachers' salaries, the league advised the consolidation of Durham city and county governments. By the end of the decade, however, opinion was swinging the other way, and along with the restoration of teachers' salary cuts came efforts by blacks to equalize the pay of white and black teachers. In 1941 both these efforts began to show results.[65]

On the local level government was showing muscle in other ways. In 1925 the town of Durham, with its greatly expanded territory and tangle of roads and outlying neighborhoods, wisely called in a planner, Herbert S. Swan of New York, to diagnose its growing pains and prescribe a cure. A year after Swan had done his work and had drawn up a zoning map to accompany an ordinance, they were presented for approval by Judge Sykes's committee, which had authorized them. A new building code was drawn up by the building inspector, J. T. Still, with many specifications to insure safety and health; no building, for example, was to be higher than fourteen floors to protect small buildings' access to light.[66]

New regulations and restrictions were not accepted without opposition, and both zoning and building codes met with the usual lamentations. S. C. Brawley advanced the argument that zoning interfered with the individual's right to do as he chose with his own property, failing to recognize that in a democracy one person's right cannot be allowed to infringe on another's. Frank Fuller bluntly maintained that opposition to zoning came from a few people who were denied permission to build filling stations on their property. The opposition introduced a bill that called for a referendum on Durham's zoning ordinance, certain that a vote would defeat the ordinance. The bill, however, was killed in committee. The building code was tested in court through a violation by a local contractor, who had built houses in a black neighborhood twelve feet apart with wooden window frames. The code allowed as little as six feet between houses provided the building materials were metal or fireproof. The contractor had also rented the houses without a permit signed by the building inspector. The code's legality was upheld and the contractor fined. The Chamber of Commerce asked for a joint chamber-city study committee to investigate the city's establishing a planning department. As a result of the committee's recommendation, such a department was finally established in 1944.[67]

County government was embarrassed by scandal. When the sheriff who had held office for twenty-three years, died in 1930, his accounts were found to be $176,000 short, a loss that the county had to absorb. Some of his closest friends had not paid taxes for a half-dozen years. Awareness of fiscal laxity in sheriffs' departments some years before had resulted in a governor's commission in 1926 to streamline county government. The report of the commission, headed by Eugene C. Brooks, recommended a county manager to handle financial matters. Some counties, the committee found, had made no reports in twenty years. Following up on the recommendation, the *Herald* had published articles by Paul Wager that analyzed the possible varieties of county manager systems and those already tried in North Carolina. Following the sheriff's office disclosure, Durham County adopted the manager form of government and hired one of its commissioners, Dallas W. Newsom, to fill the new job. He retained his seat on the commission only until the November election. Widespread reorganization, particularly in fiscal matters, and the appointment of a tax supervisor, J. Q. Davis, to remove tax matters from the sheriff's department, soon followed. Newsom inherited a county debt of $2.5 million, but within a decade he was able to reduce the county indebtedness by half, absorb the sheriff's department loss along with another smaller deficit, materially lower the tax rate, and close each year of the decade with surpluses as high as $30,000. Until his hiring, the county had been forced to borrow at the end of each year to meet its obligations, but in 1941 Newsom reported a surplus of over $95,000.[68]

While still in the housecleaning mood, some city and county leaders suggested combining certain operations of the two local governments for efficiency, particularly the tax offices. In 1932, after a two-year study, a chamber committee headed by Justin Miller, dean of Duke University's law school, recommended complete consolidation of the governments. During the same period a commission to study the feasibility of consolidation of the two school systems had also been at work. Support for consolidation was found insufficient to justify the cost of a referendum on the issue, however, and the effort was scrapped, only to be taken up again in 1936 at the urging of George Watts Hill, then a member of the city council. This effort, too, foundered. Twice more, in 1960–61 and 1974, consolidation was proposed and each time lost in a referendum. The last vote had been preceded by careful planning and preparation, exhaustive study, and wide discussion of the issues, and had gained strong support. E. K. Powe III headed the Charter Commission that drew up the plan of consolidation. Floyd Fletcher led the forces supporting the plan, which included Mayor James Hawkins, three councilmen, two county commissioners, state senator Kenneth Royall, state representative H. M. Michaux, the *Herald* and *Sun* newspapers, the Junior League, the League of Women Voters, the Chamber of Commerce, and the Committee on the Affairs of Black People (DCABP). Arrayed against this formidable strength were three county commissioners, eight councilmen, the Farm Bureau, and most county residents, many of whom had recently fled the cities after the racial integration of the schools began. The contest turned on a racial issue; although consolidation of the schools was not made part of this plan, fear that the next step would be school consolidation caused its defeat.[69]

An innovation affecting both city and county was the separation of the Juvenile Court from the Superior Court in 1934 and the appointment of a special judge to administer it. Various women's groups had long advocated such a move, but it was the American Association of University Women (AAUW) that was finally successful. Both city and county appointed study groups that concurred with the AAUW's advice. Ignoring the recommendation of the Juvenile Court Commission chaired by John Bradway, a law professor at Duke University, to appoint G. Frank Warner, former secretary of the YMCA, to the new judgeship, the city and county chose instead Mrs. Mamie Dowd Walker, a move that later caused political repercussions. Once separated from the Superior Court and with its own judge free to give it her whole attention, the Juvenile Court began to make strides. Her years of experience on both the city recreation and education boards made Judge Walker an ideal choice, and she brought a dedication and imagination to the job that made the Juvenile Court an influence for good in the troubled area of juvenile delinquency. She initiated whatever programs she felt would help, insisting that the court address the child's needs as the cause of his misdeeds. She drew into her work every civic group that could aid in any way: churches, schools, health and recreation departments, police, and the resources of Duke University. This had a two-way benefit: it acquainted a large cross-section of the populace with the problems of the juvenile court and recruited their help in finding solutions.[70]

Judge Walker established schoolboy and schoolgirl safety patrols, black and white coordinating councils, and eventually a youth home to shelter the delinquents while their cases were studied. How badly the latter was needed became public knowledge when a black boy held at the detention center at the county home hanged himself. At that time white children were housed on the second floor and black children in the basement, each child locked in his room without washing facilities and served in isolation by regular prisoners. Judge Walker asked for a center with a homelike atmosphere entirely protected from contact with adult prisoners. Also at her request a crime bureau in the police department was set up to work with the juvenile court, athletic and recreational clubs, and the Welfare Department. When without warning G. Frank Warner was appointed in Judge Walker's stead in 1941, there was a public outcry that did not cease until she was reinstated the following year. She had won the support and affection of both the black and white communities, who knew what her work had accomplished. Her court had become a model for others around the country. In 1968 the court was superseded by the Juvenile Division of the Fourteenth Judicial District court.[71]

In the 1930s governmental programs for parks and recreational facilities often received substantial funding. These programs were viewed not only as necessary antidotes to the effects of urbanization but as vital components in the fight against a rising crime rate, particularly juvenile delinquency. Although Durham had finally set up a Recreation Department under the authority of a Recreation Commission in 1925, it had done relatively little to develop facilities for recreation until the Depression. Then George Watts Hill, as head of a committee to study the matter, persuaded the city council to fund summer recreation programs at the city schools and parks and to develop facilities for this purpose. The John S. Hills donated thirty-five acres in the Goose Creek area for black and white parks. These became East End and Long Meadow parks. C. R. Wood applied for Reconstruction Finance Corporation funds to establish five recreation centers at the schools, which would supply the heat, light, and janitorial services. When development of the Duke Park area was undertaken in 1934, opposition led by Richard Wright II, and Basil Watkins resisted it; Marshall Spears, then chairman of the recreation commission, stood his ground, and in the end a pool, tennis courts, swings, and other facilities were added. Also in 1934 J. Harper Erwin offered to the city the Durham Cotton Manufacturing Company park with its pool and bathhouse. In 1935 Wood planned for a city-county recreation site at the old pump station on Eno River and asked for $200,000 to add twelve cottages, picnic and camp grounds, a baseball diamond, swimming and boating facilities, two dams, a bridge, and play areas, but the city refused to fund it. WPA funds helped to develop both Hillside and Long Meadow parks; swimming pools were added to both in 1937. The next year a park and bird sanctuary were established on Ellerbee Creek on some sixteen acres, later expanded to over twenty-four acres, given by J. Frank and Ruby Day Barfield and O. B. Wagoner. The Hills also gave a small park at the corner of Branch Alley and Proctor Street, the site of the old Whitted School. Although the Hills' donation in 1939 of the entire 149 acres and the facilities of the Hillandale Golf Course was to the Durham Foundation, it became for all practical purposes a city park. The heirs of Richard Wright donated seventeen acres for a park on Anderson Street in 1941 after a WPA project had extended and opened that street for development. All these parks or playgrounds lay within the city limits, and others were added from time to time as new neighborhoods developed.[72]

A vast area of parkland outside the city boundaries was acquired with the old (1915) and new (1926) waterworks and reservoir on the Flat River amounting to close to 350 acres. There boating and fishing were allowed. In the late 1950s additional acreage was added to the Lake Michie land through the acquisition of Spruce Pine Lodge, a handsome summer place built by Mrs. J. E. Stagg during the Depression.[73]

It was the Depression that taught Durham the value of parks. The impulse to explore and enjoy the natural environment had obvious appeal when free entertainment was at a premium. Under the auspices of the city Recreation Department, a hikers club was formed in 1931 to provide outings to nearby sites. Professor Hugo L. Blomquist of Duke's Botany Department lent his expertise in identifying the trees and flowers the seventy-five members encountered. The interest evoked by this activity inspired Ernest Seeman to form a comparable organization at Duke. Ernest was the son of Henry E. Seeman, a Canadian who had moved to Durham in 1880 and who had eventually started a steam printery and branched out to publish educational literature, including the *South Atlantic Quarterly*. The young Seeman was also a publisher: from 1925 until 1934 he headed Duke University Press. He was also an amateur naturalist and jack-of-all-trades, who wanted to share his discoveries in Durham's hinterlands. He invited selected faculty and students at the university for a hike. The appreciative response resulted in the Explorers' Club, which enjoyed excursions under his direction not only in the Durham vicinity but to the coast and the mountains as well.[74]

A constant concern of the city and county from 1927 through 1941 was an airport. Forward-looking leaders saw that airports would soon become vital factors in the American transportation system; their job was to move public opinion to accept that fact and agree to the expenditures necessary to obtain one. A *Herald* editorial in 1927 noted that Raleigh was building an airport; Greensboro, Winston-Salem, and High Point had joined forces to build one; and Wilmington already had one. It urged that Durham make an airport one of its immediate goals. The Chamber of Commerce took up the cause, and a year later the city and county agreed to buy a hundred acres for the purpose near the county home, if the electorate would approve the necessary bonds. George Watts Hill, then a city councilman, opposed this method as an unnecessary expense. He thought private investment should build and own the airport, but the chamber argued that an airport should be, like highways, a public facility publicly financed and owned.[75]

In 1929 private investors opened a small airport on the Raleigh road in East Durham for recreational flying, but its runways (1200 feet long) were too small for commercial use. In 1931 Duke University offered land near the Bennett Place (Funston Siding) on a fifty-year lease, which the city and county accepted. A few months later, however, the whole question was again up in the air; a military officer advised that the tract's location and a high-tension wire running through it made it unsuitable. His countersuggestion of a 40-acre site adjoining the county home, if additional acreage could be bought to accommodate 2,500-foot runways, was found infeasible. Other options were a tract offered by Thomas D. Wright east of his home, Bonnie Brae Farm, and a tract of fifteen acres on Ellerbee Creek offered by the city. Nothing was decided.[76]

In 1936 the city and county bought 140 acres north of the county home for $40,000. A WPA grant of $140,000 was obtained through Durham's congressman, William B. Umstead. The Department of Commerce approved the location. With everything at last seeming to move forward, public sentiment perversely turned and opposition grew; fear of the cost, fear of an airport as a target in wartime (war in Europe then seemed inevitable), doubts about the size of the tract, and the pressure of more urgent needs for the money troubled the voters. The bond issue to approve the financing was roundly defeated.[77]

Eddie Rickenbacker, the World War I ace, who had been promoting airports and aviation all around the country, suggested that Raleigh and Durham pool their resources to build a facility between them. This proved constructive advice. Raleigh's airport was too small and could not be further developed, while Durham could not afford to undertake an airport alone. A joint committee was formed and a new plan considered. The result was the Durham-Raleigh Aeronautics Authority, a four-man committee of the two city and county managers authorized to purchase land and construct and operate an airport. In 1941 the authority bought 891.7 acres in Cedar Fork Township of Wake County on the advice of the Civil Aeronautics Administration. War having at last been declared, the airport land was leased to the U.S. government in July 1942, and the U.S. Army Corps of Engineers was charged with developing it for military use. The government bought almost a thousand more adjoining acres for use as a camp. By the spring of 1943 three runways were ready for use, each 4,500 feet long and 150 feet wide at what was called Raleigh-Durham Army Air Base. The first airline to receive authorization to use the airport was Eastern Airlines, which relocated its operations from the abandoned Raleigh facility in 1943. The new airport was returned to civilian ownership in 1948, including all 1,840.9 acres and the numerous service buildings and equipment that the army had added.[78]

By 1953 three major airlines were using Raleigh-Durham Airport: Eastern, United, and Piedmont. The old combination army mess and barracks was used as a terminal until 1955, when a new one-story terminal was built and one runway was extended to 5,500 feet to accommodate larger planes. Regular jet service began in 1965 after improvements were made to runways, control tower, and lighting. The later history of the airport has been one of continued expansion and improvement as the area developed and the population grew, and commercial aviation for passengers and goods expanded dramatically. By 1985 close to 3 million passengers used the airport annually; by 2000 that number was 10.4 million.[79]

PUBLIC HEALTH

In this period the medical profession had to cope with a variety of new stresses. Durham had a national reputation in the 1920s for dope-peddling, and the situation was worsening. A federal investigation in 1925 resulted in indictments against six doctors, all of whom had dispensed morphine to addicts in violation of the narcotics law. One and a quarter million doses of sixty grains each had been dispensed in Durham over an eighteen-month period, although there were only fifteen or sixteen known addicts in the town. One addict, his wife, and his mother-in-law had been living in a doctor's house and had been given five dollars a month and illegal drugs in return for domestic services. The morphine traffic was not eliminated by these arrests. In 1932 a narcotics agent still described Durham as "one of the chief centers of illegal 'dope' traffic in North Carolina." He hinted that physicians were still at the root of the problem; they wrote enough morphine prescriptions to supply three cities the size of Durham.[80]

Watts Hospital, which had consistently finished each year in the red, found itself in 1929 with a severe drop in revenue for several reasons. First, of course, was the economic depression which made people reluctant to incur medical expenses and to pay for those they did incur. That year the hospital had only a 48 percent occupancy rate. Its medical staff, a small select group with a virtual monopoly on the hospital's use, had created divisiveness and ill-feeling within the profession and thereby limited the use made of the hospital. To rectify the situation, the hospital added an associate staff of twenty doctors, who had the privilege of using the hospital for their patients. George Watts Hill also successfully petitioned the city to increase its annual donation to $12,000 to help cover the ever-rising costs of charity patients. The hospital opened an outpatient clinic in 1931, free to charity patients except for laboratory fees, and in 1932 reduced its inpatient charges as well, lowering the rate for ward beds, for example, from $3 to $2 a day. In 1934, still facing financial crisis with a $25,000 deficit, the hospital was forced to charge even its charity patients $1 a day. A new director for the hospital, Sample Forbus, who had been trained in hospital administration at Strong Memorial Hospital in Rochester, N.Y., was employed in 1935; but even he could not solve what was a nationwide problem of rising medical costs due to the increasing use of expensive technology and a much augmented, now primarily poor, population. More stringent operating budgets meant more crowded conditions in the hospital and overwork and underpay for the employees. By 1943, the hospital's black employees were working seventy hours a week, while white workers worked fifty-four hours.[81]

Another measure to address the hospital's annual deficits was a plan worked out by Dr. Wilburt Davison as chairman of a Chamber of Commerce study committee to set up a medical insurance or prepaid hospitalization plan. Called the Durham Hospital Association, it was to begin in May 1929. The committee was unable to get the insurance needed for the plan, however, and the stock market crash in late

1929 completely quashed the scheme. A more comprehensive plan called Hospital Care Association, devised by Davison and George Watts Hill in 1933, began operation with a loan of $68,000 from the hospitals. Only the fourth such nonprofit plan incorporated in the nation, the yearly cost to the subscriber at that time was only $18 a couple. This plan evolved into the present Blue Cross and Blue Shield of North Carolina after a merger in 1968 with Hospital Saving Association of Chapel Hill.[82]

Crippled children's needs received attention in 1930 when Dr. Arthur R. Shands, an orthopedic surgeon at Duke Hospital, appealed to the Durham Shrine Club on their behalf. There were 9,000 cripples under sixteen years of age in North Carolina and some 318,000 in the nation, while there were only 9,000 beds in all to accommodate them. In 1938, through Dr. Shands's influence, Miss Grizelle Norfleet of Winston-Salem offered $5,000 a year to run a facility for crippled children. An old house on Fifth Street (later Sedgefield) in Durham was obtained for the purpose, the first such place south of Baltimore. Under the supervision of the Duke Department of Orthopedics, specifically Dr. Lenox Baker and Dr. R. B. Raney, who donated their services, the children were given therapy and taught how to care for themselves. The facility lasted about four years until the shortage of help and the difficulties of rationing during World War II made it impossible to continue. When the war was over, through the North Carolina League for Crippled Children, Dr. Baker, and others interested in the cause, a bill was introduced in the legislature to establish a state facility for children crippled by cerebral palsy. Because Duke Medical School had the only department of orthopedics in the state, the obvious location for such care was Durham. Dr. Flowers, president of the university from 1941 to 1948 and Dr. Baker's father-in-law, gave ten acres of university land on Erwin Road for the new hospital, and the North Carolina Cerebral Palsy Hospital opened in 1950. In 1981 the hospital became the Lenox Baker Children's Hospital.[83]

Another effort on behalf of children was the Open Air Camp, the creation of the Woman's Club in cooperation with the Health Department. Its purpose was to prevent tuberculosis in children at risk through malnutrition. Mrs. Mary Stagg donated to the club the old E. H. Bowling mill on the Eno River at Guess Road (formerly Guess Mill) and adjoining buildings which were renovated with volunteer labor for the use of thirty children, a director, and aides. There the children lived under careful supervision, assured of a healthy diet, rest, and exercise. Begun in 1930, the camp was continued each summer until 1939 when the water quality in the river became unsuitable. That year Mrs. Stagg repurchased the site and gave it to a special board of trustees to hold for the Board of Health and to operate under their aegis.[84]

The Lions Club recognized the unmet needs of another group of handicapped persons—the blind. To provide them with skills for employment, in 1936 the Lions taught the blind to cane chairs and make rugs, doormats, and mattresses. The operation moved from one place to another until 1938, when the club renovated the former Knitwell Hosiery Mill on East Main Street at Hyde Park Avenue where it established permanent quarters. Seventy percent of the industry's production was sold to the federal government and a substantial share to the furniture industry, which bought the mattresses and mattress covers. The work force, 75 percent blind and many additionally handicapped, was assisted by sighted supervisors. At first the Lions had to finance the work by fund-raising campaigns, but within a few years the industry became entirely self-supporting.[85]

During most of the 1920s North Carolina's birthrate was the highest in the nation. In 1927, for example, it stood at 28.8 live births per 1,000 population. Its infant mortality rate was also high and continued to increase during the Depression. Although by 1934 the birthrate had dropped to second place, infant mortality in that year rose from 66 to 76.3 deaths per 1,000. Only four states had a higher rate. The national rate was 54 per 1,000 in 1939 when North Carolina's rate was 65 and Durham's 67 per 1,000. Diseased parents, inadequate prenatal care, and a large percentage of illegitimate births made the figures for blacks even more alarming. North Carolina pioneered a health service for blacks in 1935 with money supplied by the Rosenwald Fund. A black physician, hired by the state, visited city after city, working with the existing agencies on whatever local health problem was most pressing. Another attempt at a solution was the proliferation of well-baby clinics. In 1937 when Dr. Angus McBryde, a pediatrician who established a practice in Durham in 1935, was put in charge of a new clinic at the Lyceum Building of Pearl Mill, the city already had four other such clinics for white babies and two for blacks, and the county had clinics in Bahama and Oak Grove.[86]

The catalogue of diseases that commonly afflicted children lengthened in the 1930s when polio became more and more prevalent during the late summer. While in August 1931 six cases were recorded, by mid-September 1935 forty-two cases had been reported, and the Durham-Orange Medical Society advised against the opening of the schools at the scheduled time. That year North Carolina had 675 cases, the worst year until 1943. Some years were entirely free of cases, but others were bad enough to close the swimming pools and cast a pall of anxiety over the summer.[87]

WOMEN'S WORK

Women's clubs persevered in causes related to women and children. Besides continuing to call for an investigation into the working conditions of women and children, they called for new uniform marriage and divorce laws and a maternity bill to provide day-care centers for children of working women. Accusing the clubs of being dictated to by their national organizations, a *Herald* editorial described the maternity bill as "a piece of rank socialism and conforms to the principle which has been adopted by Soviet Russia for the care of its young." Mrs. Willis J. Brogden of Durham was elected second vice-president of the State Federation of Women's Clubs in 1929 and made district chairman. Determined in their aims, they were unperturbed by rhetorical salvos and continued to pursue what they were convinced were important social changes for those whose needs had been largely overlooked.[88]

The American Association of University Women's social studies committee, headed by Mary Octavine Thompson Cowper, recognized that nursery schools were badly needed for children of low-income families. Their purpose was not only to provide day care for children of working women, but to supply the advantages of real instruction in the preschool years at a price that underprivileged families could afford. The WPA had already established three nurseries for children of families on relief, and nursery schools for children of middle-income families had been around a long time. The AAUW's plan was for a nursery school with minimal charges, five or ten cents a day, supported and administered by them and staffed by paid trained teachers and volunteer assistants. They incorporated the Durham Nursery School Association in 1938 with Mrs. Cowper as president. In May 1938 the association opened a nursery school in a house on East Main Street with thirty-six children under the supervision of three professionally qualified teachers, Mrs. Robert Peck, Mrs. Charles C. Smith, and Mrs. John A. Wall, and three assistants. Two years later, when the association had three hundred members and forty-six children were enrolled in the school, it moved to a larger house on Hyde Park Avenue. A mothers' club and a monthly clinic for preschool children in the neighborhood were added to the program. In 1944 Mrs. Cowper started a second school, Southside Child Care Center, for the convenience of Erwin Mills workers. After Mrs. Cowper's retirement, Mrs. Hollis Edens, the wife of Duke University's president, led the drive that renamed the second school in her honor. The association, still further expanded and still privately managed, later became an agency of the United Fund.[89]

Kindergartens, too, were becoming a necessity, and while their inclusion as part of the public school system would wait many decades, they were available under a variety of auspices. In 1940 the city Recreation Department set up two free kindergartens for children aged four to six, one at the Lyceum building, which had been built by Pearl Mills as a community center for its operatives earlier in the century, the other at Long Meadow Park in East Durham. In September 1934, Vera Carr Twaddell began a kindergarten, which grew over the years through the primary grades into a secondary school, applauded for its strong academic and musical instruction. Mrs. Margaret Wannamaker Kennon, at the request of Dr. Holland Holton of Duke's Department of Education, started the Little School on East Campus. Comprising a kindergarten and two primary grades, it was used for observation by education students. When it outgrew its quarters, it was moved to the former Wannamaker home. Renamed the New School, it continued until 1943. Another venture under the psychology department was begun after the war, providing classes half a day for three- and four-year-olds. This school eventually added primary grades, and in the 1980s the Duke School for Children became an independent entity in its own quarters in Monkey Bottom, land purchased from the university. Many other nursery schools and/or kindergartens, earlier and later, were established by churches as a service to their parishioners.[90]

Other women's groups had varying success with their programs. A Durham chapter of the Business and Professional Women's Club was started as early as 1921–22. This club lapsed, and a new organization, formed under the auspices of Dean Alice Baldwin of Duke's Woman's College in 1935, attracted a substantial membership. In 1936 Mrs. Walter L. Lednum, an organizer of the local chapter and head of a successful business school in Durham since 1914, became editor of the *Tar Heel Woman*, the magazine of the State Federation of Business and Professional Women's Clubs, and moved it to Durham. Kathrine Robinson (Mrs. R. O.) Everett, the first woman graduate of the law school at the state university and a practicing attorney in Durham, was the first president of the Durham chapter, followed by Mrs. J. Franklin Barfield, the bookkeeper for two tobacco warehouses, then a job usually filled by a man. The Durham Garden Club was organized in 1929 with twenty-two members, and by 1935, with close to one hundred members, it set out to beautify the city. While garden clubs sprouted thereafter in neighborhood after neighborhood, the Woman's Club fell victim to the Depression. It had bought William K. Boyd's house on Buchanan Boulevard as a clubhouse in 1926, but ten years later, with economic hard times and dwindling membership, it failed to keep up the mortgage payments, and Dr. Boyd repossessed the property.[91]

Another business and professional women's group was the Altrusa Club, an international organization similar to the Rotary Club for men. The Durham-Chapel Hill chapter was organized in 1934, but when Chapel Hill formed a new chapter in 1947, the first group became the Altrusa Club of Durham. Interested in community and vocational service, it was instrumental in getting the Goodwill Industries begun in Durham; it cooperated with the Botany Department at Duke University to plant and landscape the grounds of the Cerebral Palsy Hospital. In 1934 the Altrusa Club, with the PTA Council, of which Emetta Seeley was president, and the Durham chapter of the AAUW, decided that Durham needed a girl scout program. A troop had been formed as early as 1926 by Leah Boddie but had been disbanded shortly afterwards. Mrs. Seeley went to New York state for the required three months' training; on her return she organized the Durham County Girl Scout Council, chartered in 1935 and made up of four troops. The next year five more were formed, and the organization began to receive community fund money, thereby guaranteeing its survival. Dr. Lois Stanford was elected the council's first president. In 1955 the Bright Leaf Council, the first regional supervisory group, was formed, which included Durham and five nearby counties, black troops as well as white. Girl Scouting in Durham's black community was begun in the late 1940s under the leadership of Julia Warren, Mildred Amey, Emma Butler, and Rose Butler Browne. J. C. Scarborough donated land on Fayetteville Street for a camp site, later named for his wife, Daisy E. Scarborough.[92]

The Charity League, a respected and hard-working group of young women, under Mrs. Victor Bryant's leadership in 1938, was made a chapter of the Association of Junior Leagues of America and its name changed to the Junior League of Durham. The local league had begun in 1928 as the Red Cross Motor Corps, a group of ten volunteer drivers for clients and staff. Two years later, calling themselves "the Charity League," the women expanded their service to the community. During the depression the league was responsible for the distribution of free milk for babies, and it set up the Durham Babies Milk Fund as a separate organization in 1935. The league contributed over $7,000 and ten volunteers to support the work of the fund the first year. The Milk Fund performed a variety of tasks. It served 248 families, dispensing large quantities of milk, cod liver oil, medicine, groceries, fuel, and clothing with the help of volunteers from the Charity League, the Hayti Mothers' Club, and many other organizations that donated services or goods. Because of the diversity of its work, the name of this organization was changed in late 1936 to the Family Service Association in preparation for joining the Family Welfare Association of America. Among the women who had supervised the Charity League and established the Babies Milk Fund and who continued to oversee the Family Service Association were Mmes. Douglas H. Sprunt, president; A. P. Wiggins and D. Saint Pierre DuBose, vice-presidents; and Victor Bryant, treasurer. Mrs. John Sprunt Hill, a charter member of the Red Cross, founded a Durham chapter of the Needlework Guild in 1931 to sponsor the making and collecting of clothing for the poor.[93]

BLACK PROTEST

Ferment in all aspects of black culture began to manifest itself by pressure at the barriers that confined it. New organizations focused attention on civil rights and tested existing traditions; though hard economic times ground down bodies, they could not crush spirits that persevered in traditional channels with new inspiration and energy. The first challenges to segregation showed what gains could be made by a little pressure. Widespread use of the ballot also proved to be a trustworthy weapon if enough blacks could be persuaded to use it. Achievements by blacks in mainstream American entertainment, particularly music and sports, were serving as models for emulation and pride. Black art and artists had emerged on the world stage. Such singers as Marian Anderson, Roland Hayes, and Dorothy Maynor gave concerts in Durham's city auditorium to critical acclaim.[94] The level of their artistry entirely eradicated any remaining stereotypical impressions of black entertainers of earlier decades. In addition, the national, even worldwide acceptance of Negro spirituals, jazz, and the blues won for blacks not only a place but serious attention in the world of music. From the gains of the 1920s and 1930s would come the success of the 1960s.

In 1927 and 1929 fact-finding conferences on the status of blacks took place in Durham. Black and white experts in many fields, W. E. B. Du Bois, for example, assessed the situation, specifying areas for praise and blame. The consensus was that black churches could do more for the community: their facilities could be put to more frequent use; they could more actively address social problems; and they could encourage their congregations to greater interest and participation in the solutions. Specific areas of concern were the movement of farm families to the cities and the lack of jobs in areas formerly exclusively black now being filled by white labor. Blacks needed encouragement to enter industry where opportunities were greater because there the color line was tending to disappear. Blacks were most notably absent from business and financial firms and totally missing from wholesale merchandising. The importance of the press was noted in creating an atmosphere of cooperation and conciliation between the races. The stand that the press had taken on lynching was seen as responsible for the change of opinion against it. The press could do much to root out evils and treat racial issues honestly. This analytic approach to race relations and black concerns demonstrated a new determination to face the ugly reality and try to change it.[95]

Black acquiescence was disappearing in Durham. The Negro Business League began to ask for "equal opportunity to share and enjoy rights and privileges of citizenship." A deputation before the city council requested paved and lighted streets, police protection, improved school facilities, and representation on the city boards of health, education, and welfare. This was a logical if unforeseen result of the extension of the city limits to include more of Hayti. The previous extension of 1901 had included primarily the business section of Hayti, but the more recent extension included many residential areas where blacks felt acutely the lack of city services and civil rights that white citizens took for granted. Although little came of the request, a precedent had been established, and appearances before the council became easier and more frequent, and pressure mounted on the council to heed the requests.[96]

In 1935 Frederick K. Watkins, known as the "movie king" because he owned movie theaters in Hayti, and Philip Escoffery, a West Indian lawyer, led a contingent before the council to ask for two black policemen, a black detective, and additional protection. The council responded with the assignment of two white policemen to share a regular beat in Hayti. The next year another delegation led by C. C. Spaulding requested a policeman for traffic duty near black schools and the inclusion of blacks on juries. Names of blacks had traditionally been included in the jury pool, but officials supervising the drawing had consistently rejected them as unfit whenever they were drawn. The *Carolina Times* kept the jury issue alive with an editorial after noting that no black jurors were included on the slate drawn for the August court in 1937. Two weeks after Spaulding's appearance another delegation again pressed for civil rights and requested a twelfth grade for Hillside Park High School. In 1937 the additional grade was added at Hillside as a one-year experiment to give the students opportunities for vocational training courses. This rationale revealed that whites still would not accept blacks' ambition for a college education or their right to college preparatory schooling.[97]

The most courageous attempt to gain black civil rights was in the area of higher education. In North Carolina the attack began on the graduate level, for blacks seeking admission to white professional schools could legitimately claim that there were no black institutions providing such training. If a black wished to become a doctor, pharmacist, or lawyer, he or she had to apply to a white institution or go out of state. In 1933 some blacks felt that the admissions policies at the state university should be tested, and in Durham this feeling was translated into action by Conrad Odell Pearson (1902–84), a nephew of W. G. Pearson and a Howard University–trained lawyer. With the help of Cecil McCoy, another lawyer, and S. C. Coleman, a newspaperman, he located a man willing to participate in a test case: Thomas Raymond Hocutt, a graduate of North Carolina College, who had worked in a drugstore for some years and now wished to become a pharmacist. Hocutt applied for admission to the pharmacy school in Chapel Hill and was eventually denied admission on a technicality: the transcript of his college record was not included in his application papers. James E. Shepard, a member of what Pearson called the "status quo people," had refused to send the transcript. The university refused to accept the transcript when it was sent to them by Hocutt.[98]

Behind Shepard's reluctance to cooperate with Pearson was a long struggle to keep his institution afloat. It had passed through some difficult times always on the edge of financial ruin. In 1916 it had been saved by a timely gift from Mrs. Russell Sage, and in 1921, again desperate, Shepard had offered it to the state, which turned it into a college for training black teachers. In 1925 it was changed to a liberal arts college and, with significant help from B. N. Duke, renamed North Carolina College for Negroes. In 1929, however, cause for anxiety arose anew when a bill was introduced in the legislature to close the college and give the proceeds from its sale to the Agricultural and Technical College at Greensboro. Blacks and whites in Durham, among them John Sprunt Hill, rushed to its defense, again arguing the importance of training black teachers within the state. The bill to close the college was defeated.[99] Through all these vicissitudes Shepard, an astute politician, had carefully maintained a cordial if deferential relationship with leading whites in Durham and in the legislature, and he was not willing to jeopardize this accord by challenging them on so sensitive a point as the integration of state graduate programs. Thus with Shepard's help, the university was able to scuttle the Hocutt challenge.[100]

The next step was to try the case in the courts. Lawyers for C. C. Spaulding tried to get Pearson and McCoy to drop the case; the state attorney general told Pearson that if he would drop the case, money would be appropriated for Hocutt to get his training out of state. Pearson, however, persisted for the sake of principle. William H. Hastie, a brilliant, soft-spoken lawyer appointed by the National Association for the Advancement of Colored People (NAACP), argued Hocutt's case, while Victor Bryant defended the university. Bryant won the case. This was only the first of many cases that Pearson was to manage on behalf of black students denied admission to the university, but Pearson never again made the mistake of trying such a case in a state court; he chose a federal court instead. For his many successes Pearson is credited with integrating both the university law and undergraduate schools at Chapel Hill, either by obtaining admission for students by a settlement or by winning court decisions in the students' favor.[101]

In 1938 a U.S. Supreme Court decision required that state universities admit blacks to graduate or professional schools unless equivalent instruction were available at black institutions. When the Durham newspaper carried this news, the reporter correctly surmised that this ruling would result in the expansion of North Carolina College for Negroes. Shepard's institution soon received a law school. The state pumped money into the campus, adding $250,000 worth of buildings, even-handedly distributing contracts among the town architects Atwood and Weeks, George Watts Carr, and R. R. Markley. Law professors from Duke and Chapel Hill were engaged to teach in the new school, which was scheduled to open in 1939. Only one applicant qualified that term, however, and the opening was postponed till the next year.[102]

Efforts to seek justice either in or out of the courts at this time were of two sorts. The more conservative North Carolina Mutual leadership chose traditional channels and personal appeals to state and local leaders where their own prestige would count, while younger men such as Pearson or those without traditional ties in the community to hamper their actions used the courts and other direct challenges.

When the test case for Hocutt was reported in the *Herald,* Spaulding and Shepard were first accused of instigating it, a charge they were quick to deny. A *Herald* editorial then took back the accusation and expatiated on the situation: "We think, and they [Spaulding and Shepard] agree, that a law suit is not the proper means of gaining for the Negro race admittance to a law school operated by the state. They prefer to pursue more tactful methods and we support their positions."[103] Spaulding knew how to capitalize, however, on the fear that the more radical blacks stirred in white leaders, disposing them to compromise or concession. Spaulding used the Hocutt affair to speak out on other issues that troubled him: inequality of black and white teachers' pay and the inferior schools and schooling provided for blacks. He felt free to explain the radical viewpoint without seeming to share it:

> There is a growing feeling on the part of Negroes in North Carolina that the white people, as represented in the lawmakers, are not treating them right and that there is little hope of fairness to be expected from them so far as appropriations and other things are concerned. . . . The younger element of Negroes in North Carolina do not believe in the leadership of the older Negroes. They think that the older Negroes represent the servile type and that a more aggressive leadership is needed. . . . The Negro is simply asking for justice in the courts, fair treatment on public carriers, and a just share of public funds.[104]

Free to pursue the new, aggressive methods was one outsider, the Reverend Miles Mark Fisher, a sterling example of the new breed. Fisher came as pastor to White Rock Church in 1933, an advocate of the social gospel and an entirely realistic crusader for black rights. He had a strong educational foundation, with degrees not only from Morehouse College in Atlanta and the Northern Baptist Theological Seminary in Chicago but also master's and doctor's degrees from the University of Chicago. He gradually wrested control of his church from the Mutual leadership by filling vacancies on the board with his own appointees, thereby enabling him to carry out programs that the old leaders had thwarted. He organized church members into districts and had them meet monthly to discuss their concerns. He lent the church for meetings of the Tobacco Workers Union, Local No. 194. He built recreational facilities for the youth of the church and a community center behind the church with supervised activities for boys. The center was cited in Judge Mamie Walker's 1938 report as having contributed "more than anything else to the decrease of juvenile delinquency among Negro children of the community."[105] A softball league of sixty boys was an outgrowth of his efforts; each player was required to attend a Sunday school regularly to join. Fisher invited visiting artists to perform in the church and established cooking schools, a Boy Scout troop, and a nursery school. He also organized the local chapter of the NAACP. So inspiring were his sermons that even standing room was not available when he preached.[106] For heady new wine like this, old bottles were inadequate.

Fisher's message was for those already at work, as evidenced in the Negro Business League and other groups who were not afraid to confront the city council with their needs. The Harriet Tubman YWCA, within three years of its formation, was already so successful it was in need of larger quarters; its brick building on Umstead Street became a well-used community resource. The Daisy E. Scarborough day nursery and temporary orphanage opened in 1926 in the old Lincoln Hospital building and became of ever-increasing service in the community. With the encouragement of Judge Walker of the Juvenile Court, a facility similar to Fisher's center, the John Avery Boys' Club, was provided in 1940. It was begun by the Negro Citizens Committee headed by C. C. Spaulding and located first at 418 Fayetteville Street before moving to the old quarters of the Harriet Tubman branch of the YWCA at 508 Fayetteville Street. William J. Kennedy, Jr., destined to follow Spaulding as head of the Mutual, was the club's first president. From 1945 to 1982 it was under the direction of Lee Smith. It provided two hundred boys six to eighteen years old with sports, arts and crafts, manual training, typing, and a clinic.[107]

The prestige that men like Spaulding and Shepard had earned among the white leadership still counted for much, however, and they, too, when they could effectively do so, lent their support. In 1935 they sent a letter to the Recreation Committee suggesting that a much higher amount be requested from the WPA than the $39,000 the city had slated for Hillside Park. They cited Raleigh with its smaller black population and a $125,000 WPA grant as cause for their sense of injustice. They urged that Durham ask for $100,000 to develop the park with a swimming pool, gymnasium, and other equipment because Durham completely lacked such facilities for blacks. The request was partially granted: Hillside Park got a swimming pool in 1937 mostly financed by WPA funds. Spaulding and Shepard again put their prestige on the line when they wrote to Dean William H. Wannamaker of Duke University, chairman of the city school board, asking that Whitted School be completed according to plan as a high school. Primarily WPA funds had built it, but it was unfinished. Shepard based his request on his students' need for a place to practice teach. Overcrowded conditions and dilapidated facilities were also brought to the school board's attention. East End school was so overcrowded that each teacher had fifty-one students in a class; the East Durham school had one drinking fountain for three hundred children, no cafeteria, four toilets in the basement, and iron stoves to heat the classrooms. By September 1937 Whitted school had been completed, and the East End school had a four-room addition. A new East Durham school was built in 1939.[108]

If city-owned buildings were deficient, privately owned rental properties were unimaginably worse. The problem of substandard housing in Durham had its first airing in 1937 when a new federal program provided funds for slum clearance and subsidized construction of low-rent replacement housing. The United States Housing Authority had come into being in December 1934, and the local office was set up under the direction of R. L. Lindsey. He immediately announced a housing survey to assess Durham's situation, identify substandard housing, encourage owners to upgrade their property, and make available loans at low interest for new housing. This last provision was of particular interest to Durham, which suffered from a low-rent housing shortage. His plan excited the usual controversy. While many acknowledged that some rental property, yielding its owners as much as 30 percent return on their money, was unfit for human habitation, others saw government housing as competition hurtful to their interests. Because of strong opposition by "slum property owners," the local committee decided against applying for some of the half-billion dollars available from the federal government for new housing. The *Herald* was fearless in its reporting of this pussyfooting. "Several members of both the city council and the board of county commissioners are known to be heavily interested in 'shanty property' and it is unlikely, those making the survey said, that they would support a movement which might seriously destroy or curtail their earnings."[109]

The state planning board, in cooperation with the WPA and the Durham city and county governments, finally undertook the housing survey. The newspaper kept the issue before the public, reminding Durhamites that other cities were receiving millions of dollars for slum clearance and low-rent housing while Durham continued to grumble about government interference. While the survey was in progress, some of the more sensational facts were reported in the press. It revealed, for example, that a former mansion of eleven rooms provided housing for ten families. The city appointed a slum clearance commission chaired by Daniel K. Edwards. Offers of help in identifying the most serious slums came from various interested groups: the Junior League through its president Mrs. J. O. Cobb, black social and fraternal organizations represented by J. J. Henderson, and local real estate agencies. The survey showed that almost two-thirds of city housing was substandard—9,367 of Durham's 15,334 dwelling units—because of overcrowding, disrepair, or lack of plumbing. It also showed that blacks suffered most from these conditions—four-fifths of the black population lived in substandard dwellings. The conclusion was that the city desperately needed new housing, but since privately built housing was profitable only for rents beyond the means of most renters, publicly subsidized housing was the only answer. Edwards requested that a local housing authority be established, but the matter went no further until 1949, when Edwards was elected mayor and set up the Durham Housing Authority himself.[110]

Of incalculable importance to the black community was the formation in 1935 of the Durham Committee on Negro Affairs (DCNA). Accounts of its founding differ. C. O. Pearson claimed that he and James D. Taylor first saw the need for an organization that would work more informally for the same causes that the NAACP pursued through the courts, and that would engage the entire community. Encouraged by Richard Lewis McDougald, they approached C. C. Spaulding, who also gave their idea his blessing and called an organizational meeting at the Algonquin Tennis Club on 15 August 1935. Other accounts attribute the suggestion to the Reverend George A. Fisher of Raleigh, who had helped form a similar organization there. Fisher brought his own organization to the attention of Spaulding, who immediately sent invitations to a meeting to 150 blacks representing every aspect of black life. All accounts agree that Spaulding called the meeting and was elected president of the new organization. Rencher N. Harris presided over another mass meeting two years later in the new Hillside High School auditorium to inform the community of the organization's aims. Thurgood Marshall, then a Baltimore attorney, was the main speaker.[111]

C. O. Pearson had been appointed at the start to head the DCNA's political division. Its concern was black voting. Louis Austin and R. McCants Andrews had begun to register black voters in the 1920s, but in 1928 Durham still had only fifty registered blacks. The Independent Voters' League had then taken up the task. Under Pearson's leadership, one thousand blacks were registered by the end of 1935, and by 1939 over three thousand or 68 percent of eligible blacks were registered. In 1943, when John S. Stewart stepped down as head of the DCNA after fourteen years in office, Durham County had the highest black registration in the state. An unusually large number of blacks went to the Democratic Party precinct meetings in May 1936, and nine of them were named delegates to the county convention: James Taylor (also elected chairman of the courthouse precinct), T. D. Parham, J. H. Wheeler, W. J. Kennedy, Jr., E. G. Spaulding, W. D. Ellis, H. M. Michaux, G. W. Cox, and H. C. Davis. In 1938, for the first time in Durham's history, blacks entered candidates in the primaries, hoping to increase black interest in voting. M. Hugh Thompson, a lawyer, was nominated for county commissioner, and Louis Austin, already one of two black magistrates, bid for a place on the board of education. Although the DCNA dared not touch the larger issue of segregated public schools and accommodations, it did achieve much by the political power it gained. Little by little it won for blacks positions on commissions and boards, a few public offices, a fire station manned by blacks, a few black policemen, and recreational facilities, together forming the thin end of the wedge.[112]

The fact-finding conference's estimate of journalism's role in race relations was amply substantiated by the black editor Louis Austin of Enfield, North Carolina. As sports editor of the *Standard Advertiser* in Durham, he was urged by R. L. McDougald to buy a controlling share in the paper and become its editor. The then editor, E. G. Harris, was not doing the job that McDougald saw was needed. McDougald lent Austin $250, enabling him, with Alexander Barnes, to buy control of the paper in 1927. He changed its name to the *Carolina Times*. An indefatigable crusader for justice and civil rights, Austin was of a new class of blacks who kowtowed to no one, and he made the paper an unrelenting crusader for all black causes, including in his coverage news that bore on race relations from all over the nation. While he reported facts without regard to white sensibilities, he was also a fair fighter. His handling of the Vernon Farrington case, possibly the first resistance by a black in Durham to the Jim Crow law on buses, demonstrates this aspect of his character. When Farrington sat down beside a white off-duty policeman, he was assaulted. The policeman was fined five dollars and suspended without pay from his job for four days for an "unprovoked and unwarranted attack upon a Durham citizen." Austin followed his report of the case with an editorial aimed at defusing an issue that had angered the black community. He charitably blamed the policeman's violence on his limited education and the narrow views of his environment and recommended that the court record against him be erased. Justice had been served and there was no virtue in vindictiveness.[113] Louis Austin fed his readers a bracing diet, strengthened their resolve, and raised their self-esteem.

Racial pride received an invigorating infusion when Joe Louis, the "Brown Bomber," won the world title in boxing by knocking out James J. Braddock in June 1937. Mayhem immediately broke out in Hayti. Bricks were hurled, car windshields broken, false alarms sounded—bringing fire engines racing into the streets—and even some shots fired. Fire Chief Frank Bennett appealed to C. C. Spaulding, who immediately went straight into the heart of the fray and quieted the rioters. The next day he met with the DCNA and issued a statement regretting the incidents, calling on parents of the unruly youths to mete out appropriate punishment. Little harm was done. Some blacks had merely celebrated overexuberantly; to a depressed people it was a landmark in their renewal of hope.[114]

Blacks were not alone, however, in their new crusade for their due rights. An ugly incident between another policeman and a "blockader" (an illegal liquor brewer or seller) attracted attention when the black man was shot and killed by a policeman, whom he had hit with a fruit jar while resisting arrest. Though the officer was charged, the case was dismissed in court, provoking a barrage of letters demanding a grand jury investigation. Among the writers were Frank Porter Graham, president of the university at Chapel Hill, Howard Odum, respected head of the Institute for Research in Social Science, and his colleagues, Rupert Vance, Robert House, and Guion Johnson. The DCNA was not shy in calling the killing "injustifiable homicide."[115] Rumblings from the depths of society's faults warned of volcanic action to come.

CULTURE, POPULAR AND HIGH

Music-making is at the heart of black culture. One strain of black music, the blues, came to national prominence through recordings in the 1920s and 1930s, developing in different parts of the country characteristic variations. At that time Durham was a center of the Piedmont blues, a variety that has been described as "unlike the sultry, mournful music of the Mississippi Delta. . . . [It is] enthusiastic foot-tapping music. Despite slow bluesy moments it is distinguished by a ragtime energy accentuated by the rhythmic rapping of a washboard and punctuated by the whoops and calls of the harmonica."[116] Created, developed, and perpetuated by untutored musicians, blues dealt with the predicament of working-class blacks, their woes and consolations. The blues represented a change from the usual folk music of rural get-togethers—corn shuckings, log rollings, and log cuttings—where square dances and frolics dictated fast, country music. The blues thrived in urban conditions where the usual social restraints of kin and church were removed and replaced by a disorienting, fast-paced, competitive society, moral laxity, and unfamiliar terrain. In the eyes of respectable blacks, blues music was sinful, both the guitar that played it and the topics it dealt with; no one who sang and played it would ever get to heaven.[117]

Attracted to the bustling tobacco towns were laborers and musicians alike, particularly when the Depression made work hard to find. Most musicians worked at unskilled jobs by day and made music at night, but for a select group of handicapped men for whom music was a living, Pettigrew Street in Hayti and the warehouses in central Durham became their workplaces. The acknowledged masters of the Durham blues were Blind Boy Fuller (Fulton Allen), Blind Gary Davis, Blind Sonny Terry (Saunders Terrill), Bull City Red (George Washington), and Richard and Willie Trice. The names of their predecessors and contemporaries are forgotten; these men are known because of their recordings. James Baxter Long, who managed the United Dollar Store in Durham, was responsible for that. He sought out, coached, and rehearsed the best musicians and took them to New York to record their music. Although Long's efforts were motivated in part by self-interest—he took a large cut of the profits—he was an expert in this variety of music and understood what would sell. Blind Boy Fuller, who recorded well over a hundred different songs for Long under the Perfect Record Company label, was usually heard with Bull City Red on the washboard and Terry on the "harp," as the harmonica is called. The recordings were made within a short span, 1935–41, and say much about the time and place and the musical tradition of which they were a part.[118]

Besides the warehouses where bored farmers waiting to sell their tobacco or those already flush from completed sales gladly pitched their money into the musicians' hats, house parties were the best source of income. Also called "chittlin' struts" or "piccolo struts," parties were held all over town. Anyone could open his house and, with music, bootleg liquor, food, and a place to gamble or dance, could get a party going. The musicians might be hired for a fee or invited to pass a hat. Their lives were always financially precarious, and the Welfare Department or the Blind Industries frequently contributed to their survival. Terry was almost the sole exception in this respect. He rose to the top of the New York entertainment scene where he appeared in such musicals as *Finian's Rainbow* and in *Cat on a Hot Tin Roof*, and for years teamed with Brownie McGhee as one of the most successful blues duos, nationally and internationally. Fuller's was the more usual fate. Always on the fringes of society, in the gray area just beyond the law, Fuller lived a life of economic uncertainty and deprivation. His bad temper and a handy pistol, which he was not shy of brandishing, landed him in court in 1938 for shooting his wife. He escaped punishment by a verdict of accidental shooting. "Big House Bound," one of Fuller's best-known songs, is based on the incident. He died in 1941 while still in his thirties.[119]

Interest in the bluesmen revived in the 1960s during the civil rights movement, and much information about them in Durham and elsewhere was learned through interviews and rediscovery of the old recordings. Although no longer fed by the spontaneous creative outburst of black experience in Durham, Piedmont blues music was a vital part of that culture through the first four decades of the century. Sonny Terry described its dual function. "It's the kind of music that kept a whole lot of folks alive 'cause others liked it well enough to pay to hear it. Not only money, but it helped them to get over the hard things in their lives."[120]

For one youth—Reginald Mitchiner, who grew up in Durham in the twenties and thirties and was interviewed years later for the Southern Oral History Project—life in Hayti, then at full throttle, seemed nourishing and rich. Black businesses did not completely monopolize Fayetteville and Pettigrew streets; Mitchiner recalled that amid the welter of stores, the two-block stretch of Pettigrew called "Mexico" held candy shops and restaurants run by Greeks and Jews. He loved the corner drugstores where young blacks spent their idle hours and loose change. "I hung out around Doc Pearson's store at the corner of Fayetteville and Elm in Hayti. Everybody from all over town would come through there sometime on Sunday, either by that corner or the corner at Glenn Street. People from the East End, West End, or East Durham would come to Hayti, because they ain't living if they don't come to Hayti."[121] He liked working in the tobacco factories, too, because they sang all day long. "When you'd raise a song in your section, you got anywhere from a hundred to a hundred twenty-five folks singing with you. It was always spirituals." But Mitchiner liked other kinds of music too. He remembered the dances in the warehouses where Duke Ellington, Eubie Blake, and Benny Goodman would play and just about "blow the top off the building." He thought "Benny Stewart . . . was a whiz! She could stroke the 88s with the best of them—with Jimmy Gunn and Lanky Cole. They could walk a keyboard."[122] Live entertainment was still plentiful in the 1930s, but piccolos (the local word for jukeboxes) were becoming more common. "The piccolo business was a big business, up to World War II. Any house could have a piccolo, and they did. A lot wouldn't have it, because that was one way to draw the police, having a piccolo in a private dwelling—something was spooky there."

The blues formed only a part of Durham's musical diet in the depression years. Mention has already been made of the black singers Hayes, Anderson, and Maynor, whose concerts brought luster to the city's music. Both opera and drama, provided by touring companies, were a part of Durham's cultural scene. Duke University was partly responsible for the high caliber of the visiting artists, for their artists series brought to Page Auditorium Metropolitan Opera singers such as Mary Garden, John McCormack, Kirsten Flagstad, and Ezio Pinza as well as the Philadelphia Orchestra, the Ballet Russe de Monte Carlo, and instrumentalists E. Power Biggs, Arthur Rubinstein, Josef Hofmann, and Sergei Rachmaninoff. The university encouraged its students to make music too. During the early thirties originated the annual concert of Handel's *Messiah,* consisting during the first years only of excerpts but later of the entire work. John Foster Barnes, the men's glee club and choir director as well as campus impresario, mounted annual productions of Gilbert and Sullivan operettas from about 1936 through 1941. The Theatre Guild resurrected the custom in 1962, producing three annual shows; but after 1964, the Durham Savoyards, Incorporated, was organized and continued the tradition. From the university bands and orchestras emerged three young men who later won fame as popular orchestra leaders in the big band era: George E. "Jelly" Leftwich, a Durham native, Les Brown, and Johnny Long.[123]

Another black musician of national reputation was Nell Hunter, a native of Memphis, Tennessee, who was married to Dr. A. S. Hunter, a Durham physician. She had studied music and vocal pedagogy in Chicago before going abroad for training. She concertized in America during the 1920s and in the Depression was appointed assistant director of the Federal Music Project of the WPA in North Carolina, and later state choral director for the National Youth Administration. In 1939 she and her chorus gave a command performance at the White House during the visit of Great Britain's King George and Queen Elizabeth.[124]

The white community produced a nationally known singer, too, at this time. During her high school years, Lucille Brown (Browning became her professional name) came under the tutelage of William Twaddell, who recognized her talent and found support to finance professional training for her at the Juilliard School in New York. In 1932 she began to study with Madame Marcella Sembrich, the Polish coloratura and former Metropolitan Opera diva. Browning made her debut at the Metropolitan Opera in *Hansel and Gretel* in 1936, and she sang regularly with the Falstaff Opera Company in Philadelphia. Two years later when only twenty-five years old, she had sung twenty roles with the Met in over eighty performances.[125]

The development of radio as popular entertainment came in this period. The first demonstration in Durham of the wireless telephone, as the newspaper called it, was given in 1921 both at the Durham Public Service Company and at William M. Piatt's residence. The audiences listened to a band concert broadcast from what would become Pittsburgh's KDKA, the first commercial radio station in the country. In 1926 the Lions Club discussed raising money to buy a station for Durham but decided nothing. The next year the *Herald*-owned station, WKBG, went on the air in Chapel Hill with a broadcast of a choir concert. In 1934 George Watts Hill with other businessmen bought the franchise of the Wilmington station WRAM and moved it to Durham. Under the call letters WDNC it became the city's first radio station, broadcasting from above the B. C. Woodall Company on Chapel Hill Street. In 1935 the Hill group sold it to the *Herald* company, which has owned it ever since. WTIK, affiliated with the Tobacco Network, was added to Durham after the Second World War in 1946 and soon became identified with country music; the same year saw the organization of WDUK, an American Broadcasting affiliate. In 1948 WSSB, affiliated with the Mutual Broadcasting System, was started, offering news, sports, and country music, and in 1950 the managers of WTIK and WDUK, Floyd Fletcher and Harmon Duncan, combined their stations, retaining the letters WTIK. The national networks, with chains of stations throughout the country, became responsible for most of the programs during radio's heyday in the 1930s and 1940s, but their quality and audience declined markedly after the invention of television and its general affordability following the Second World War. Duncan and Fletcher pioneered television in Durham in 1954 with their station WTVD organized as a stock company, Durham Broadcasting Enterprises.[126]

Another form of popular culture in the 1920s and 1930s that became big business was spectator sports. The football stadium was the first new structure completed on the West Campus of Duke University. Wallace Wade, with a spectacular record of winning teams behind him, was brought from Alabama to Duke in 1931 as athletic director and head coach. During the next sixteen years Duke won 110 football games out of 143 played. Wade brought the Duke team to national attention in 1938 when they were unbeaten, untied, and unscored on, a record that won them an invitation to play in the Rose Bowl in California on New Year's Day 1939. Although Duke lost to Southern California 7–3, the players received heroes' welcomes both from the town and the university. When they were again invited to play in the Rose Bowl after another triumphant season, war broke out before the game was played. Because of fear of possible Japanese attacks on the West Coast, the game was moved to Durham and played there on New Year's Day 1942. Again Duke lost, this time to Oregon State, 20–16.[127]

Although by 1941 the Depression was well behind them, the people of Durham, like those in the rest of the country, had had a sobering experience, one that transformed their views of money, work, and government as it transformed the role of government in people's lives. The introduction of wonder drugs, nylon and other synthetics, and air-conditioning—the importance of the last cannot be overestimated in the development of the Sunbelt—had begun to change their lives. At the same time they had seen a university take form and in its own way shape them and their town. Life in Durham would never be the same again.

World War II and the End of an Era, 1941–1945

17

ORLD WAR II, which began in Europe in 1939 but which had been brewing through the 1930s, became, for as long as it lasted, the central fact of life for all who served in it. For most other people as well the war altered, colored, circumscribed, and directed the course of their lives. From 1933 when Hitler in Germany and 1937 when the Japanese in China began to act out their nefarious dreams, the United States little by little lost its inclination and ability to steer clear of world politics and international involvement. For some years it seemed possible to preserve legal neutrality while contributing money and goods where its sympathies and interest lay. In hindsight, however, American participation was clearly inevitable if Nazis, Fascists, Communists, or Far East zealots by concerted action were not to enslave much of the earth. The Japanese bombing of the American naval base at Pearl Harbor, literally out of the blue on 7 December 1941, was the decisive act that brought the United States into the war. Totally unexpected by the Americans—Japanese negotiators were at the time in Washington—the air raid found most of the Pacific fleet a sitting duck and seriously crippled American defense despite President Roosevelt's measures to prepare the country for war.

American moods in 1939 had ranged from strict isolationism, which had found a standard bearer in Charles A. Lindbergh and his America First organization, to extreme interventionism, which advocated jumping into the fray at once. Americans had given little thought to Japan; it was Europe that had their attention. From the moment of the bombing in December 1941, however, the mood of the country was almost as one in its determination to fight. There was as usual a sizable number of conscientious objectors, who opposed war for any reason, but as a respected historian has said, of all the wars the United States has been engaged in, it fought World War II with the fewest regrets.[1]

Bringing the American people to the point of accepting preparations for war and defense had been a difficult task, but from the start they had been eager to help the victims of aggression with humanitarian aid. First in Durham had been the drive, headed by George Watts Hill, to raise funds for Finland, where heroic ski troops were battling the numerically overwhelming Russians. By summer 1940, plans were formulated to bring thousands of European children to homes in America to escape the expected civilian bombing. At the head of the Durham Committee for the Care of European Children was the Reverend John H. Marion, who had hoped to bring one hundred children to Durham. As it turned out, only two came, not through the Durham organization but through private negotiations and the American Society for the Protection of Refugee Children. They were Shirley and Richard Baker from England, who lived from 1940 to the war's end with the Frederick Bernheims, both Duke faculty members.[2]

When Congress passed the first peacetime draft law in the nation's history, men between the ages of twenty and forty-four were required to register. Three draft boards of three persons each (one a physician) were established in Durham, and twelve thousand Durham men registered for the draft. A lottery in October determined the order of their call-up. Two army contingents, one white and one black, left for training at Fort Bragg in December 1940. World War II was the first in which blacks were recruited in all units, but at the start segregation still prevailed. In 1944, after the Normandy invasion, the War Department issued an order abolishing racial segregation in recreational and transportation facilities at all army stations. It was obviously impossible organizationally to maintain segregation within a huge army in foreign lands moving from place to place, shuttling to hastily improvised facilities just behind the battle lines. Already in the summer of 1940 the National Guard was calling up its units for training. The Durham Machine Gun Company of 121 men left for a year's training at Camp Jackson in South Carolina. By the end of March 1941 about five hundred men had joined the armed services, well over half of them volunteers. The government also ordered the registration and fingerprinting of aliens, a task delegated to the post office, and imposed taxes on cigarettes, beer, liquor, and amusements to help pay for the enormous buildup of military equipment.[3]

In 1940 and 1941 private civilian efforts were directed toward raising money for the British War Relief Society, whose state headquarters were in Durham under the direction of James G. Clark. Mrs. George B. Ferguson wrote a radio play in which, among others, Professor Gifford Davis, Mrs. Nello Teer, and young Banks Anderson took part. Wool for knitted socks and sweaters was distributed to volunteer knitters. The proceeds from Duke's annual Gilbert and Sullivan production of 1941 were donated to the society. The Red Cross accepted the responsibility of making 33,300 surgical dressings under Mrs. Foy Roberson's direction. Other women responded to the National Park Service's request for hospitality and recreation for British seamen and officers stationed at Camp Crabtree (now Umstead Park) while their ships were being repaired in eastern ports.[4]

The huge expansion of Fort Bragg near Fayetteville offered lucrative jobs to Durham's skilled workers, particularly plumbers, of whom the Durham union supplied 500 at the peak of building operations in 1941. Covering 130,000 acres and accommodating 160,000 men at the height of the war, Fort Bragg was easily one of the largest and most functionally comprehensive army installations in the nation. In general, wages increased dramatically in all skilled and unskilled industrial jobs. While some areas of the economy, like agriculture, were still struggling, the Great Depression for most families was definitely over.[5]

Durhamites accepted with good grace the National Youth Administration training center at the old CCC facilities on East Club Boulevard. This center was equipped by the federal government to train auto mechanics, metal workers, machinists, carpenters, radio repairmen, and photographers in groups of two hundred men every six months. The first such program in the nation, it enlisted men rejected for service for physical reasons; their nutrition and health therefore received particular attention while they were being trained. The government supplied $72,000 and Durham, $22,550 to set up the center. The men were paid $35 a month, out of which they were required to pay $23 for food and lodging. When the program ended, the facilities were turned into a rapid treatment hospital for venereal disease under the management of the U.S. Public Health Service. It was capable of treating two hundred inpatients at a time at government expense. The purpose was probably twofold: to reclaim for the draft pool the large number rejected because of venereal disease and to remove and treat infected prostitutes from the city streets to safeguard the soldiers at the newly built Camp Butner.[6]

Durhamites did not accept with equal grace, however, the news that the government would establish an army camp of large dimensions within its borders. The land chosen for the camp was not only the best in the county and would be thus lost to tobacco and other agricultural production, but also the camp would uproot a great number of families, many of whom had lived on their land for generations. The vulnerable farmers accused the Chamber of Commerce, which had worked to secure the camp, of wanting to line the pockets of merchants at their expense. Some suggested that huge waste tracts in Person County between the Virginia–North Carolina line and Roxboro would provide less costly terrain and avoid use of agricultural land. Residents of Ellis Chapel, Copley's Corner, Flat River, Umstead's Corner, and Mangum's Store communities—those threatened by the proposal—resisted in every way they could. The County Land Use Planning Commission, headed by Vestal C. Taylor, manager of Fairntosh Plantation, opposed the government's plan, and Taylor along with J. A. Newton and the Bahama minister Millard Dunn were part of a delegation that went to Washington to protest.[7]

Undeterred, the army went ahead with its plans and acquired acreage in Durham, Granville, and Person counties. Plans for the relocation of 1,325 families and their churches went forward; of that number four hundred families and 125 farms were in Durham County. A force of 16,000 men was gathered to build the camp, two thousand of them from Durham, and the Durham engineering firm of William M. Piatt was given the construction contract. Stores in town stayed open late Friday evenings hoping to catch in their tills as much of the $500,000 weekly payroll as possible. Named for a Tar Heel general, Henry Wade Butner, Camp Butner was formally dedicated and opened by Colonel H. W. Huntley, the post commander, in August 1942. Built as an infantry training camp, it became the home over the war years of the 78th or "Lightning" Division, Third Infantry, Thirty-fifth Division, and Eighty-ninth Division under Major General Thomas D. Finley. It also housed prisoners of war. Old-time Bahama residents well remember the young German boys who were permitted to work on the local farms and at other jobs unrelated to the war effort.[8]

When the camp was in full operation, Durham was a city transformed. Four thousand off-duty soldiers on any day could be seen on the city streets. Accommodations for their recreation became the largest of Durham's war responsibilities because it was the headquarters for all Camp Butner off-base activities. The United Service Organizations (USO) established centers with facilities provided by the government in sites donated by the city. Three USOs for white servicemen were eventually in operation in Durham: the first at 310 East Main Street, a second at Morris and Hunt streets, and a third on Dillard Street in the former residence of C. C. Thomas. Glenn Thistlethwaite directed the activities with the help of a committee appointed by the YMCA. A USO for black servicemen was set up at 1201 Fayetteville Street on a site owned by the Merrick-Moore Memorial Park Association, and Frederick Watkins's home served as a club for black officers. The USOs provided meeting rooms, reading rooms, showers, restrooms, checkrooms, kitchens, snack bars, sleeping quarters, libraries, radios, stages, telephones, typewriters, phonographs, and dance floors.[9]

Other organizations pitched in to help with hospitality. The Chamber of Commerce found accommodations for eight thousand additional residents, as Durham suffered an acute housing shortage with 23,000 families crowded into 17,085 units. It found halls for ping-pong, pianos, and parties; it supplied maps, magazines, and birthday cakes ordered by absent relatives. The Red Cross used its surgical dressing quarters as a Sunday morning canteen for coffee and doughnuts. The YWCA helped recruit local girls, carefully screened, to entertain the GI Joes and provided a place where they could play games and dance. The Colored Elks operated an open-air garden at 910 Fayetteville Street, organized by Frederick Watkins. At the train station the Travellers Aid Society set up a lounge to serve transients, under the direction of Mrs. Bayard Carter and Mrs. Clinton W. Toms. A similar service for blacks in the colored lounge was directed by Mrs. E. W. Butler. They distributed cookies, magazines, cigarettes, and postcards. The Exchange Club also operated a lounge and canteen on the site of the former bus station at Rigsbee and Orange Streets, serving civilians as well as servicemen.[10]

Men from Camp Butner and the vocational training program were not the only war-related additions to Durham's street scene. In 1941 the navy set up an ROTC program at Duke University and in 1943 added a Naval College Training School (usually referred to as a V-12 program). Duke also housed an Army Finance School begun in 1942, but it was moved to Fort Benjamin Harrison, Indiana, in June 1944. So many new customers to fill the merchants' coffers, so much war construction to occupy builders and craftsmen, government contracts for industry, and general acceleration of the economy added up to staggering statistics for 1942. Industrial workers at Camp Butner earned $44 million, while debits to individual bank accounts—a measure of economic vitality—reached the unprecedented total of almost $700 million. Durham's own industrial payroll increased 27.4 percent over the previous year and 44.8 percent over 1940.[11]

The war had brought prosperity to Durham, but it was a mixed blessing. Off-duty servicemen could be troublesome in large numbers. Reginald Mitchiner reminisced about Durham during the war: "It had fallen to a low ebb after the Depression in the early thirties, and folks had been trying to come out and bloom again, but then come World War II and that was really a shot in the arm."[12] He remembered particularly its effect on Hayti, his part of town:

> If you find any veteran of World War II that was ever stationed at Butner, he'll ask about Hayti. Because any veteran stationed there had Hayti indelibly imprinted on his conscience. They was running buses in from Butner to Durham—it was a regular shuttle. No sooner had they got off of duty out there than they converged on Durham. Taxi drivers made money like nobody's business. A man driving a taxi around then was averaging from $150 to $200 a night, especially around pay day. . . . The place was jumping, because there were clubs and joints of all descriptions everywhere. It turned into a Vegas strip almost. . . . The soldiers made business better in every category, licensed or unlicensed. If you get a bunch of guys that will only be here for a little while, they'll pay double for everything they get, only they want it right now . . . whatever it was from booze to women. The MPS had to patrol all the time, cause it was hairy. . . .
>
> Now the place tries hard to elevate its image, but there's always that undercurrent when they're reaching back to the days when it wasn't so nice.

Something of the atmosphere Mitchiner described is reflected in the newspapers. In May 1943 a reporter described a Saturday night in Durham: "A tidal wave of khaki engulfed the city last night."[13] The Camp Butner soldiers poured into town swamping the movie houses, the telegraph offices, the ice cream parlors, the skating rink on Rigsbee Avenue, the bowling alleys, the train and bus stations, and the ABC stores where the supply of whiskey had vanished by noon. A similar invasion of soldiers the previous month had resulted in a riot in Hayti when a black soldier tried to buy liquor with more than one ration book and refused to turn the books over to the ABC clerk when ordered to do so. The soldier drew a knife; the ABC clerk drew a blackjack and gave chase up Fayetteville Street. Others joined the fray throwing bricks and cement. A bus driver and two policemen were injured, a soldier knocked unconscious, autos damaged, car tires ripped, and property stolen or destroyed. Local police restored order with tear-gas bombs and the help of a machine-gun unit from Butner. The state guard was mobilized and waited in readiness at Durham Athletic Park through the night. The judge who fined various participants made it clear that it was the duty of citizens to quiet things down, not stir them up.[14] Spontaneous incidents like this one as well as organized protests occurred in many parts of the country. Soldiers newly released from their routine discipline and in search of excitement felt little tolerance for business as usual and even less for the humiliations of the past.

A hospital unit was recruited at Duke Hospital, headed by Duke chief surgeon, Dr. Clarence E. Gardner, and largely staffed by Duke personnel. Its fifty-eight medical and dental physicians as well as many nurses were ordered to England where the unit was set up near Norwich as the Sixty-fifth General Hospital. Among the Durham group were Drs. Thomas T. Jones and Isaac Manning, Jr., and nurses Kathleen Godwin Smith and Mary Elizabeth Brooks. Capable of accommodating one thousand patients, the hospital served the wounded from the Eighth Air Force and endured a heavy workload after the Allied invasion of Normandy in 1944. Because of the number of nurses needed overseas, hospitals at home suffered a crucial shortage. The federal government addressed the problem two ways: by providing nurses' aide training under the WPA and funds for additional dormitories at hospitals with nurses' training programs. Both Lincoln and Watts hospitals in Durham benefited by new buildings.[15]

The toll of suffering and loss of life in the war was great, but compared to other nations, whose civilian populations endured years of bombing, displacement, invasion, or occupation by foreign forces, America suffered least. Still the casualties and deaths mounted as the months passed through D-day, the huge invasion of France on 6 June 1944, through V-E day, the end of the war in Europe on 8 May 1945, to V-J day, the surrender of the Japanese on 15 August 1945. At the end of 1944 Durham County had lost close to one hundred men and one woman. Although no figure has been given of the number from Durham County who served in the armed forces, a conservative estimate would be close to ten thousand.[16]

Various memorials have been erected to these service personnel. The Exchange Club (organized in Durham 27 October 1941) kept track of casualties and deaths. At the courthouse it placed a memorial plaque with the names of those from Durham County killed in World War II. Erwin Mills mounted its own plaque for employees killed in the war. In 1986, the plaque was removed to Oval Drive Park. A stadium (1960) was the county's war memorial.[17]

As in the First World War, civilians were pressed into activities related to the war effort, and many took jobs for absent workers. Women entered the work force in enormous numbers, often filling positions or performing work previously reserved for men, encouraged to do so as their patriotic duty. Two women applied for taxi driver licenses in 1942. The Police Department hired its first woman, Mrs. Fannie Walters, as a dispatcher. Hosiery workers were among those retrained for war production, for the mills could no longer obtain raw silk for stockings and either had to close down or retool. Durham Hosiery Mills and Golden Belt Manufacturing Company were hard hit, and Georgetown Silk Mills on East Pettigrew Street was liquidated in October 1941. Some hosiery workers were retrained in sheet metal classes at the NYA and Durham High School; others were retrained for airplane woodworking.[18]

Food production was a crucial occupation, and farmers were short of help. The government therefore promoted the growing of "victory gardens" as it had in World War I. Everyone with a plot of ground put it to use, and women were encouraged to produce and preserve more food. A community cannery was opened at Oak Grove where the Rural War Production Training Program provided users with free facilities and materials, except for the tin cans they used. Oak Grove School agriculture students built the cannery.[19]

Civilians endured the usual inconveniences and shortages of wartime. Gasoline, tires, shoes, sugar, meat, and coffee were rationed, and stamps for their purchase were issued equitably. As was to be expected, black markets in restricted products were not long in arising and became a wartime phenomenon. To combat runaway inflation, the federal government established rent and price controls. Fred H. Davis was appointed local rent director. Besides dedicating a portion of their paychecks to the purchase of war bonds (probably the most widely supported war effort), all sectors of the population helped in the salvage of vital scrap materials—tin, brass, iron, rubber, rope, and aluminum. Periodic collections of these materials were stimulated by contests, and prizes were awarded for the greatest poundage. Durham County collected well over 600,000 pounds of scrap rubber in its first drive in 1942. To save rubber and gasoline, some bakeries and dairies reverted to horse and wagon for deliveries.[20]

During the first months of the war, fear of enemy attack prompted the setting up of civilian watchers, who constantly monitored the movement of planes in the event of an attack. Taking turns at three-hour shifts, two operators were constantly on duty. The city manager was in charge of the control center. Fear of sabotage of war industries dictated other cautionary measures. Extra policemen and firemen were added to factories engaged on government contracts, for example, the Wright Machinery Company and Erwin Mills. Blackouts and air raid drills became routine occurrences. Murray Thornburg was appointed local director of defense training. Clinton W. Toms, Jr., was civilian defense coordinator and ordered the first black-out test in April 1942. The first air raid drill had already taken place in December 1941. Sirens were mounted on buildings in various parts of the city to sound the alarm and all-clear signals. Even after the war, when the cold war with Russia prolonged defense measures, the sirens continued to be tested weekly. The Pearl Harbor attack was not easily forgotten.[21]

Women assumed important duties of leadership in civilian defense. Mrs. Frank L. Fuller, Jr., Mrs. Samuel Sparger, and Mrs. Mary B. Robbins conducted air raid instruction classes. Mrs. Kenneth Clark was executive secretary of the Durham County Civilian Defense Council (OCD) from January 1942 through April 1944. Dr. Lois Stanford was appointed to head the mobilization of women trained in nursing and medical care. Women students at Duke University were given courses in cartography, general engineering, and technical drawing, skills which they could put to immediate use upon graduation. Besides the volunteer work of collecting salvage, aiding in nurseries, canning vegetables, carpooling, and hostessing at USO and YWCA parties, women could also become professional service personnel by entering either the WAACS (Women's Army Auxiliary Corps), the WAVES (Women Accepted for Volunteer Emergency Service), WAFS (Women's Auxiliary Ferrying Service), or general nursing service with various hospital units. Mary Frances Ivey was the first Durham WAVE, Mrs. Oscar Barker, among the first WAACS, and Nola M. McCloud, the first black WAAC. By March 1943, sixty-two Durham women were serving in the WAACS.[22]

The Red Cross stepped up its quota of surgical dressings. Durham's quota for 1944 was 500,000 bandages, and by July the volunteers working day and night had not completed half; but the Normandy invasion in June, which spurred an increase in volunteers, solved the problem. Besides the room at City Hall provided for this activity, the Red Cross had a room in the basement of the Stanford Warren Library in which black women were also engaged in the rolling of surgical dressings. The Red Cross also managed a sewing room at Watts Street Baptist Church where volunteers from all religious sects and sections of the city worked to make clothing for the homeless and displaced persons in Europe.[23]

Some social problems caused by the war had to be addressed immediately, particularly the care of children of working mothers. The Durham Emergency Child Care Center, Inc., with, naturally enough, Mrs. Cowper at its head, received federal funds to set up additional child-care facilities. Southside School cared for young schoolchildren before and after school hours, while Y. E. Smith School cared for preschoolers as well. Three nursery schools for blacks received federal funding: the well-established Scarborough Nursery as well as Burton Nursery School (and child-care center) and Pearson Child Care Center for school-age children. Durham Nursery School, Mrs. Cowper's creation, and Durham Baptist Church nursery school both received funds for the care of preschool children. The Durham Social Planning Council, an organization developed by the Community Chest, directed its attention to the needs of teenagers, also left without home supervision when their mothers took war work. The council tried to obtain facilities for supervised entertainment—for example, the USO clubs (at times when servicemen were not using them), schools, and churches—with the cooperation of PTA and church group volunteers. Many new Boy Scout and Girl Scout troops were formed.[24]

With so much time and energy absorbed by the war, little was left over to devote to peacetime and domestic concerns. Only essential construction—that already begun, or that related to the war effort—was permitted. As a result, the housing shortage, which had developed before the war, grew steadily worse and precipitated an enormous building boom when peace came at last. Some few civic improvements, however, occurred during the war. The old Knights of Pythias building was rebuilt for the Edgemont Community Center, and the Masonic building at Main and Roxboro streets changed into the Health Department. A tuberculosis hospital, for which so many people had fought for so long, finally became a reality in March 1944. The old prison facility on Newton Road, which had become unnecessary when the state took over the care of prisoners, was renovated as a sanitarium able to accommodate fifty-six patients, half white, half black. Profits from the ABC stores were appropriately used in adapting the building to its new function: many longtime alcoholics developed tuberculosis. Though on the decline, the number of cases in Durham County was still very high, particularly among blacks. The statistics for 1941 showed 134 new cases, eighty-seven black and forty-seven white, and the same year accounted for forty-three deaths, thirty-five black and eight white. Dr. A. Derwin Cooper of the Health Department staff was appointed resident physician.[25]

Better nutrition for the general population played into the declining tuberculosis rate. Helpful in this respect was a new technological invention, the preservation of food by freezing, which brought the possibility of better year-round nutrition nearer reality. A better method than canning to preserve food in respect to flavor and the preservation of nutrients, the freezing of foods became a new industry and increased variety in the diet. Nello, Dillard, and Hubert Teer saw a related business opportunity in the new product. They started the Quick Freeze Locker Company, which rented space to farmers to store frozen products in bulk.[26]

The housing crisis was not peculiar to Durham and became a top priority everywhere when hundreds of thousands of returning soldiers and their new families had nowhere to live. In Durham, as in other college towns and cities, besides native veterans returning to their homes, the GI Bill, which financed veterans' education, brought additional ex-servicemen to attend Duke University and North Carolina College for Negroes. Extraordinary measures had to be devised to meet the need. The federal government made available to local governments surplus materials, which included temporary housing such as Quonset and Nissen huts and other prefabricated structures. Trailers (later called mobile homes) became a common emergency solution until more permanent housing could be built. Local governments quickly found available land for "victory villages" and purchased the surplus dwellings to rent to veterans. The city of Durham leased for two years two tracts for trailer camps, fifteen acres for seventy-eight trailers for white veterans and their families (in East Durham) and two acres for twenty-two trailers for black (adjacent to Hillside Park), serviced by city water and sewer. Both colleges also provided temporary housing on their campuses for the veteran students who needed it.[27]

Trailers did not disappear, however, when construction caught up with demand in the postwar years, and among the general public they became a permanent solution for low-cost housing. Their popularity stemmed not only from their low cost; being mobile, they could also be moved and set up almost anywhere. At first only stringencies of soil and water restricted their placement. When they became permanent features in the landscape, new laws had to be devised to accommodate them. More restrictively handled by Durham County and city than by many other North Carolina areas, they could only be placed in areas designated by the zoning regulations of the county or city. In 1960 North Carolina had 19,133 such homes. By 1970 the number was 77,542. That year Durham County had 804 trailers, of which sixty-two were within the city limits.[28]

The problems posed by trailers were among the first issues faced by the Durham city planning department, which was established in 1945. A planning department had long been advocated but its creation had hitherto been prevented, although a City Planning Commission had been established in 1922 and subdivision regulations and a zoning ordinance had followed in 1926. A new zoning ordinance was adopted in 1951. The first few planners to head the city department had no particular qualifications for the job and were solely interested and expert in traffic and road problems. Watts Hill, Jr., however, a member of the city council in 1955, was dissatisfied with the department and managed to persuade other councilmen that a change was in order. Paul Brooks, who in 1955 became the fourth city planner, provided that change. His first assignment, the location and planning of new fire and police department buildings, for which Durhamites had voted a bond issue in March 1956, resulted in a 44-page booklet detailing a long-range plan for a combined city and county government complex; it was too ambitious for their needs as they saw them, and both city and county boards turned it down. Brooks's plan was not without its supporters, however; to prepare the ground for its future acceptance, Mayor R. Wensell Grabarek asked for a long-range capital improvement commission, and James R. Hawkins, later Grabarek's successor, headed a Downtown Development Association, inspired by the Merchants Association, to find ways to revitalize the center city.[29] Planning had come of age.

Other changes took place in the city government both during and after the war. An age-old request of Hayti's inhabitants was heeded in 1944 when two black policemen, James B. Samuel and Clyde Cox, were added to the city force. North Carolina's four other large cities had already hired black policemen with good results. In the same year, the old Recreation Department, no longer under the Recreation Commission, was made a full-fledged city department. In 1945 further organizational change was effected when the rules for electing councilmen were changed. Six of the twelve representing the city at large and six more, each representing one of the six city wards, were to be voted on by all the voters. Councilmen's terms were for four years, the mayor's for two. The 1943 local election had seen a woman candidate for a ward seat for the first time. Miss Ethel Meacham from the third ward was not unexpectedly defeated by the incumbent. Some things hadn't changed. Mayor William F. Carr, who had already held the office many years, was re-elected in 1943 and continued in office till 1949.[30]

Durham County, also reacting to pressures of growth, in 1949 became the second North Carolina county to receive legislative authority to zone land and the first to exercise it. A Planning Commission was set up the same year, but a zoning ordinance was not completed and adopted until 1956. The county electrical and plumbing inspections department performed the planner's duties from 1956 until 1962, when George Jackson was appointed the county's first planner and head of the new Durham County Planning Department.[31]

Public needs found new help. The Recreation Department in 1943 added a program for the blind, supplying books and magazines in Braille. Special recreation for them was also planned and supervised by Mrs. Sarah K. Garth. Nine years later Mrs. Lyda Moore Merrick, daughter of Dr. Aaron Moore and daughter-in-law of John Merrick, was inspired by a blind friend, John Washington, to help the blind in her community. Because materials for the blind in the Stanford Warren Library contained little of interest to blacks, Mrs. Merrick started a Braille magazine, which contained excerpts from leading black magazines and newspapers. She chose the materials herself, had them translated into Braille, and published them quarterly in the *Negro Braille Magazine.* She and her husband bore the major expense of the publication, and she alone carried the whole project from 1952 until 1971. Later it became the responsibility of the trustees of the Stanford Warren Library, who changed the name to the *Merrick-Washington Magazine for the Blind* and published it semiannually.[32]

A voice of reason was heard in civic and political deliberations when a Durham chapter of the League of Women Voters was chartered in 1947 after a year of informal existence. Among the charter members were Mrs. John Ohlson, president, and Mmes. Louis D. Cohen, Joseph G. Pratt, J. V. Bell, and J. B. Rhine. In 1951 the group became a member of the state league (reestablished in that year after a hiatus) at a convention held in Durham.[33] Reason in polity would be crucially needed in the social upheavals of the next decades.

The difficulties ahead, however, were undreamed of in the euphoria and abandon of Durham people when the war ended. The worst seemed over when Germany capitulated on V-E day (8 May 1945). Servicemen in the European theater of war expected to be transferred immediately to the Pacific for what was thought would be a long-drawn-out fight. The stunning explosion of the atomic bomb over Hiroshima on 6 August and over Nagasaki on 9 August, however, brought sudden realization that the end was near. It came on the evening of 14 August with President Truman's announcement of the unconditional surrender of the Japanese; and although the following day was declared V-J day, the official end of World War II, no one waited to celebrate. In the early evening hours in the late summer light of 14 August, the people streamed into the city streets and unleashed in uninhibited and irrational joy the tensions and emotions of the long war years. Powerless, even if willing, to restrain the jubilation, the police could only look on as an informal parade of cars filled to overflowing, riders perched on hoods, fenders, running boards, and roofs, drove down the streets, ignoring stop signs, honking, shouting, yelling in a frenzy of delight. Whistles blew; fireworks exploded; people on the streets danced, hugged one another, threw their arms around stray servicemen, and generally went haywire in Durham's "maddest demonstration of all time."[34]

The Old Order Changeth, 1946–1969[1]

18

A CHANGED WORLD AND ITS DISLOCATIONS

The war accelerated the rate of change in the South as in the world, causing the usual stresses of adjustment. Change led toward an always greater role by the federal government in addressing the needs of the people and to a global perspective in foreign policy and commercial ties. The Korean and Vietnam wars, which the United States fought from 1950 to 1953 and 1965 to 1975, respectively, would have been impossible in the 1930s. They were corollaries of the cold war with the Soviet Union that bred a policy of interventionism abroad and an irrational hatred of Communism at home; a consequence of the latter was distrust and character assassination of individuals suspected of leftist sympathies. McCarthyism, the name given the phenomenon, left traces in state legislation that were later causes for embarrassment and regret. At the same time President Kennedy's Peace Corps (1961) continued the process of broadening Americans' experience of foreign lands, but it was fueled by a new sense of responsibility to underdeveloped nations, in particular those of the Third World, coupled with a political motive of winning new nations for democracy, or more candidly, preventing their falling within the Russian sphere of influence. The astonishing recoveries from extreme devastation and economic ruin of both West Germany and Japan through the adoption of the victors' weapons—in this case heightened efficiency and quality in industry and high technology, combined with their people's ingenuity and capacity for hard work—clearly showed which way the world was wending.

President Eisenhower's programs, controversial because to some conservatives they smacked of socialism—federal aid to education and medical care for the aged—were developed in the new Department of Health, Education, and Welfare (1953), headed by a cabinet level director, Oveta Culp Hobby, who had also been head of the Women's Army Corps and was thus used to breaking new ground. Health, education, and welfare became and remained central concerns of government at

32

all levels. The Servicemen's Readjustment Act of 1944, known informally as the GI Bill of Rights, among other provisions gave all veterans the opportunity for further education and training. Similar provisions were made for both Korean and Vietnam veterans so that huge numbers of young people during a score of years were able to acquire a college education and professional training who would otherwise never have had them. The Supreme Court decision (1954) in *Brown v. Board of Education of Topeka, Kansas* during Eisenhower's administration and the landmark legislation of Kennedy's New Frontier and Johnson's Great Society were courageous advances in areas of civil rights, health, and the everlasting fight against poverty. That man does not live by bread alone the federal government acknowledged by its recognition and support in 1965 of the humanities and the arts in civic life. The second half of the twentieth century witnessed, therefore, a series of fundamental changes in social attitudes and governmental policies, which created a society unlike any that Americans had known before.

Politics reflected the changes. The "solid South" tradition in voting ended when the southern Democratic Party ceased to be the party of white supremacy. Instead, it became more and more the party of intellectual liberals, organized labor, old-line Democrats, for whom the name commanded loyalty, and of blacks; a party that espoused liberal concepts, the welfare state, and real democracy, completely confounding some old allegiances.[2] The Dixiecrats of 1948 and the Democrats for Nixon twenty years later evidenced the political disaffection of most of the old ultraconservative white supremacists and states' righters, who in some cases would soon ally themselves with the Republican Party.

State government was more responsive to the changes than was local government, where the electorate remained doggedly conservative. The election of Kerr Scott as governor in 1948 signaled the change in North Carolina, followed by the appointment to the Senate of Frank Porter Graham to fill the unexpired term of J. Melville Broughton, and Scott's 1954 election to the Senate, successfully managed by Terry Sanford, then a state senator, after a bitter campaign into which the racial issue had seriously intruded. Although the Truman years saw a large number of North Carolinians in important government posts at home and abroad, many traditionally Democratic Tar Heels became frightened by the liberal swing of the federal government, and began to leave the Democratic Party.[3] Still, the state government continued the policies Scott had initiated. William Bradley Umstead, the only Durham County native to fill the state's highest office, continued his predecessor's policies of support for schools and other public institutions. But Umstead's final illness, which began immediately after his taking office, curtailed any effective leadership he might have given. His death in 1954 brought to the office Luther Hodges, a practical businessman, who had worked in the Truman administration as chief of the Economic Cooperation Administration office in West Germany and was therefore in tune with the nation's foreign trade policies, although his racial views were relatively more provincial.[4]

When Terry Sanford won the governorship in 1960, after two bitter primaries in which the race issue was paramount, the state was clearly on a progressive course. Significantly, Durham County gave its vote to I. Beverly Lake, who represented the reactionary position. Like Aycock, Sanford became identified with educational advancement through his initiatives in that field, many of which were continued by his successors: the inclusion of food in the 3 percent sales tax to raise additional money for schools (1961); increased pay for teachers; the establishment of a state system of community colleges, vocational training centers, and technical institutes; the creation of the Governor's School (1963), a summer program for gifted children; the establishment of the North Carolina School of the Arts (1965), free professional training in the arts for talented high school students; and the expansion of the Consolidated University of North Carolina. Paradoxically, the 1963 legislature, which instituted so many progressive educational measures, passed the Speaker Ban Law, prohibiting known Communists, advocates of government overthrow, or those who had pleaded the Fifth Amendment when questioned regarding Communist or subversive activities, from speaking at state-supported institutions. Until declared unconstitutional in 1968 by a federal court, the ban was a cause of consternation and protest in academic and progressive lay circles.[5]

In Durham, too, politics reflected mounting urgencies. Veterans returning from the Second World War found a county that despite all the change already apparent in the country still clung to its outmoded cultural and material shell. Many people who had not been away were also beginning to feel that changes were needed, particularly in leadership: complacent, reacting instead of leading, and dedicated to the status quo. A third element of the population agreed—the trickle of newcomers that grew into a flood in the 1970s and 1980s. All these groups realized that the old forms and usages could no longer serve new needs. Long before, a poet had written in another time of crisis words familiar to every hymn-singing Protestant in Durham:

> New occasions teach new duties; Time makes
>   Ancient good uncouth;
> They must upward still, and onward, who would
>   Keep abreast of Truth.[6]

It was now time to turn the words into action; but that was easier sung than done.

The problems that Durham faced in the 1950s and 1960s were primarily social and economic, but the solutions were inevitably political. Primary of course was the civil rights movement and the legal sanctions the federal government provided to assure its progress (see chapter 19). In Durham, responses were shaped by the historical relationship between the black and white communities and by the mettle of Durham's leaders. Because local government consistently failed to address growing racial unrest and economic stagnation, the 1950s have sometimes been described as "the doldrums" in Durham's history; on college campuses they brought a new age of conformity and conservative attitudes and aims of quick riches on corporate ladders. But the 1950s were also the seedbed for the social revolution of the 1960s.

New political alignments and demographic changes in Durham were reflected in the 1949 election. A coalition of labor and blacks, welded by John Leslie Atkins, together with a small but growing group of liberals, was able to elect as mayor Daniel

K. Edwards, a veteran with a new perspective yet a moderate with roots in Durham. Two years later the same combination made history by electing two women to the city council, Kathrine Robinson Everett and Mary Duke Biddle Trent (later Semans), Benjamin Duke's granddaughter, a hard-working idealist committed to improving Durham. Another voice of conscientious commitment joined the council with the election the same year of Emanuel J. Evans, affectionately known as "Mutt" Evans, as mayor. Still more progressive, in 1953 the first black councilman, Rencher Nicholas Harris (1900–1965), a real estate appraiser and candidate of the DCNA, was elected with the help of the liberal Voters League for Better Government.[7]

The black/labor alliance split, however, on the rock of racial equality; it did not survive the Supreme Court ruling on schools in 1954, which frightened many white southerners back under their security blankets of white supremacy. The court decision made real the prospect of racial equality (the breaking of a taboo that was to some white southerners unthinkable) and growing black power. One result was an influx of poor whites into the Klan and another, an eventual mass exodus of the better-off whites to the suburbs. "White flight," as the latter was called, enabled many children to enroll in county schools where, if integration were to be actually effected, the racial mix would be predominantly white. This left the city with a black majority in the school population and enough black political clout to achieve greater electoral gains, an important first step. To effect social change, however, would require sit-ins, boycotts, threats of violence, litigation, and the intervention of the federal government.[8]

Besides the racial issue, Durham faced the challenge of Durham's needy, clearly described in a speech to the Community Chest in January 1952 by Howard E. Jensen, a Duke professor of sociology, who candidly set out what he called "Durham's Unmet Needs." The chest had once more failed to meet its goal in raising money for Durham's varied social programs, a failure in charity and in understanding. Later expanded into ten articles published by the *Herald,* Jensen's speech listed Durham's ills as class and race opposition, juvenile delinquency, emotionally disturbed children, and inadequate measures to supply the medical, emotional, and physical needs of the poor. The city needed experts to assess and deal with emotionally disturbed children and family problems. It needed more nursery schools, kindergartens, and recreational centers. It needed tighter laws against drug abuse, the first indication of a growing national problem. In Jensen's assessment of the agencies he surveyed, the Health Department came off best, but it, too, required more money than it was given.[9]

At the end of the decade came another volley of criticism from a series of *Herald* articles. Reviewing Durham's poor economic situation, the articles answered the question "Is Durham Lagging Behind Other North Carolina Cities?" with a resounding "yes." Unlike Jensen, Russell Clay, the poser of this question, indicted Durham's outgrown and outmoded man-made environment as the cause of its economic failure. Narrow streets unequal to the volume of traffic, parking problems, and ugly and deteriorating buildings were both the cause and the result, he said, of Durham's backwardness. In the center city nothing had changed since the end of World War II.[10] His indictment was based on a report released by the Downtown Development Association, which shocked the citizens with its pessimistic statistics and shook the city out of its complacency.[11] The report incited the city to hire a consultant, Julian Tarrant of Richmond, who unveiled a plan in September 1959 for a governmental center to be built on the tract of the Planter's Warehouse, which had burned to the ground in 1944. When Wense Grabarek, then a councilman, discovered a million-dollar surplus in the city budget, the council, although refusing to build any new buildings, voted to repair the old ones and to buy the warehouse site.[12]

E. J. Evans, mayor from 1951 to 1963, elected with Atkins's support the first time, felt defensive under these attacks and tried to put a brighter face on things by citing the accomplishments of the 1950s under his leadership: the $750,000 YMCA building on Trinity Avenue, the off-street parking garage between Main Street and the railroad at Corcoran, the ongoing urban renewal, better water and sewer facilities, a newly established black fire company in Hayti (1958), and the Wellons Village Shopping Center. Evans was always positive and optimistic, though he had presided over difficult times, masterfully holding together with genuine consideration for others and inherent civility disparate factions with their conflicting interests and needs. At a time when so much needed attention and resources were lacking, there was little Evans could do but keep people working together, mindful of the general good rather than their individual priorities. While he succeeded in maintaining dignity in city government and humanitarian values in solving its problems, he only delayed the social upheaval that could not be contained indefinitely. More than a third of the city population was being denied its proper place in the established order; its talents were frustrated. Despite Evans's pride in Durham's pioneer efforts in sewage treatment and water purification, larger issues were not being addressed, and he could not refute Clay's conclusions. They were based on telling statistics: industrial employment in Durham had dropped 19 percent between 1947 and 1959, the city had declined from second to fourth place among manufacturing cities in the Piedmont, and had fallen from third to last place as a wholesaler. The average weekly wage was $64.41, the lowest of the five Piedmont cities.[13]

Evans's point that new construction was a sign of vitality had some validity. Because building had dramatically slowed or halted during the Depression and war years, an effort to catch up in the 1950s produced a building boom. The major portion of the construction, however, was not in the heart of Durham but at its edges. By annexation of areas where development was taking place and of a few already well-settled suburbs, the city was able to increase its tax base.[14] Evans's allusions to Wellons Village and urban renewal were ironic, for these blossoms of Durham's economic flowering held the seeds of its destruction. The phenomenon of suburban shopping centers, a logical consequence of the population's move to the suburbs in the 1930s and in the postwar years, was a serious blow to the life of cities everywhere. Forest Hills Shopping Center, begun by George Watts Hill in 1955, was Durham's first suburban collection of stores, but Wellons Village Shopping Center (1959) was much larger, with many more kinds of stores and therefore much more of a magnet to local residents. Shopping centers offered everything in one place. As the trend continued, the bigger and better clothing and department stores left downtown Durham and moved to the shopping malls. Lakewood and Northgate shopping centers were built in 1960, South Square in 1975.[15] The city seemed doomed commercially. Clay had hoped that a radical rebuilding program would save the center city and had advocated many of the cosmetic and traffic remedies that were later tried without noticeable improvement: pedestrian malls, facelifted buildings, more offstreet parking, one-way traffic, easier ingress and egress, a loop road around the city center, and an expressway for transient traffic.[16] Nothing helped.

DEVELOPMENT FOR HEALTH

Instead of the center city, the area near Duke University saw much of the postwar development, a direction that continued through the 1970s as the medical center grew. There was an urgent need for housing for medical students and residents, who had long outgrown their quarters in a building adjacent to the hospital and who were now likely to be married and with families, a new phenomenon in the student population. The university supplied the land for the construction of Poplar Apartments (1950–51) by the J. A. Jones Construction Company of Charlotte. Although primarily meant for hospital and medical school personnel, other university employees found in these 250 units convenient and affordable housing. In the next decade additional apartments were added in the adjacent Holly Hills development, which comprised 104 units.[17] The facilities for Duke's student nurses were also outgrown. In 1950 a new dormitory for nurses, Hanes House, was begun; named for the donor Elizabeth P. Hanes, it accommodated offices, classrooms, and quarters for 260 students at Trent Drive and Erwin Road.[18]

As early as 1938 Durham had hoped to attract one of the veterans hospitals the federal government was planning to build. It achieved this goal in 1946. Duke University made more land available on Erwin Road not far from its own hospital, realizing that such a facility would open wider opportunities for learning and employment for its own students, interns, and medical staff. Strikes and political wrangling delayed the project both before the groundbreaking in 1950 and during the three years of its construction. The hospital finally received its first patient in 1953. A five-story addition increased the size of the Veterans Hospital in 1965, and further expansions occurred in following years.[19]

Along the same stretch of Erwin Road, the Methodist church administration built a retirement home in 1955. After the need for such facilities became obvious in the war years, retirement homes and nursing care units changed living patterns for the elderly. Older people now preferred to be independent of their children and, if unable to remain in their own homes, to move to retirement homes or communities where they could be assured of care if needed and medical services for their increasing health needs. In 1946 the Methodist Conference founded the Methodist Retirement Homes and obtained thirty-nine acres for a facility in Durham. The first building (1955) contained forty rooms; the M. M. Fowler Building provided a hundred more in 1950; and the Joseph F. Coble health care facility of 123 beds was added in 1976. The home's proximity to Duke Medical Center made high-quality care available.[20]

In the meantime Duke University, recognizing a need as well as fulfilling James B. Duke's intention for it, gradually but dramatically expanded its health ministry to the community and the region, adding many research laboratories and special treatment centers, an eye hospital (1972), and, led by Dr. William G. Anlyan, a $90 million new hospital, Duke North (1980), with over 600 beds to become a major health center of the Southeast. The Duke teaching staff of nurses and doctors, which had numbered 220 in 1950, by the mid-1980s had risen to 900; the entire university payroll, which included about 16,000 persons, amounted to well over $193 million a year.[21] At the same time Durham's economy was shifting from dependence on industry to research, education, and medical services. Though textiles and tobacco still provided a substantial contribution to the town's wealth into the 1970s, they began to show signs of decline. In the 1980s Erwin Mills and American Tobacco were sold, and Liggett and Myers's production was significantly curtailed.[22]

Accessory to this shift was a maverick in Durham's economic picture that could not have been predicted. It stemmed from the arrival from Germany in 1934 of Dr. Walter Kempner to practice and teach at Duke Medical School. In the course of his treatment of hypertension and heart and kidney disease, he hit on specific dietary elements as contributory factors in these disorders and devised the now famous rice diet as part of the medical therapy. Free of salt and fat and comprising principally rice along with fruit, fruit juices, and vitamin supplements, taken with as much exercise as consistent with each patient's capacity, the diet proved conspicuously successful. That many of Dr. Kempner's patients lost significant poundage on the diet suggested its applicability to the treatment of obesity as well. The program grew so large that special eating houses outside the medical center were set up for Kempner's patients where their meals could be strictly supervised and their health monitored daily. Kempner's diet became as famous as Rhine's laboratory.[23]

When Kempner retired in 1972, his program was continued in the medical center. A somewhat modified regimen was also directed by the medical center as a community outpatient service, the Dietary Rehabilitation Center, which stemmed from early attempts by Dr. Siegfried Heyden to teach good dietary habits through a diet lunch-a-week program for the medical center personnel. Over the years other weight-loss programs with slightly different therapeutic approaches and costs were established in Durham by former participants in the Kempner program so that patients who did not succeed on one regimen could try another. Durham has profited in no small way from the nearly five hundred patients a year that these obesity clinics served. It was estimated that these visitors spent $2 million on hotels and apartments alone and over $4 million more on other necessities and luxuries.[24] One man's poison is another man's meat.

EDUCATION

The federal government contributed to the building boom in Durham by its aid to education and roads. As early as 1939 North Carolina realized that something had to be done to raise teachers' salaries. Black teachers in the city, paid even less than white, organized in 1943 to press for equal pay. Frank G. Burnett, principal of

Burton school, was elected president of the new organization, and Mrs. Mildred W. Amey and Mrs. Katherine C. Thomas were vice-presidents.[25] At the same time Josephus Daniels, the editor of the Raleigh *News and Observer*, was urging that the school year be extended to nine months, the increase to be paid for by the huge state surplus.[26] Because North Carolina ranked nationally fifth from the bottom in 1946 in the amount spent on schooling per pupil ($51.62), in 1946 the federal government proposed to allot the state $300 million over ten years to bring that figure up to $85.52, principally by raising teachers' salaries.[27] School construction, which had lapsed during the war, now resumed, trying to catch up with the growing population and to repair the many old buildings in the system. Governor Kerr Scott, who by his election in 1948 had dislodged the complacent state establishment—a coalition of bankers, lawyers, and manufacturers that had run the state for fifty years—was a new broom in government and able to get the General Assembly to vote $25 million for school building and repair.[28]

Among education's advances at this time was Durham Academy's expansion and achievement as a secondary school of distinction. Organized in 1933 by Mrs. George Watts Hill for her own young children and those of her friends, it grew with the children, adding a grade a year and was taught according to lesson plans developed by the Baltimore Calvert School, which Mrs. Hill had attended. Because of this connection, the school was called the Calvert Method School and paid a fee to the mother institution for each child enrolled. Its first principal was Miss Margaret McGary, formerly of the Morehead School, and its first classes were held in the Forest Hills clubhouse. Through the Hills' generosity, it soon moved into the old John Sprunt Hill house on the east side of Duke Street, where it remained until 1965. In 1937 the Hills built an annex for a kindergarten and the next year incorporated the school. At that time Mrs. Dallas Pickard became headmistress, a post she held for almost twenty years. In 1946 the school purchased the Hill house and kindergarten facility for $15,000 and struggled to pay its way through tuition alone. In 1957 the link with the Baltimore school was broken, and the school was free to adopt its own teaching methods and course work under its new name, Durham Academy.[29]

The board of Durham Academy soon realized that its inadequate facilities were limiting enrollment and academic programs. With the help of many loyal alumni, parents, and donors, the board raised enough money to buy land and build a new school on Academy Road in 1965. The final step in Durham Academy's evolution was taken in 1972 when the school offered for the first time a complete high school in its own new buildings on Ridge Road near Pickett Road. An anonymous donation of $1 million in 1975 enabled the school to provide the quality education it had striven for.[30]

ROADS

The state legislature's money for schools, however, was small compared to the $200 million the legislature voted for road building. The federal government, wishing to complete a nationwide network of first-class roads, also allocated money for this purpose. North Carolina's share was $11.5 million, part to be spent on new highways, part on secondary roads.[31] The highway between Chapel Hill and Durham and Interstate 85 was part of the result. High wages and general prosperity in the postwar period made the price of a car at last within the reach of almost anyone, and with new roads reaching into the farthest mountain recesses and out to the sandy Outer Banks engineered a result that changed the country and the country-side forever. Freedom never known before, freedom from isolation and freedom to explore, contributed to the knitting up of a pluralistic society. Automobile own-ership incidentally created new cultural phenomena—shade-tree mechanics and drag and stock car racing, plebeian sports that attracted the newly mobile.

RELIGION

Churches, too, needed new buildings. Some expanded their existing facilities, some organized new congregations in new suburbs, and some established themselves for the first time in Durham. Baptists were far and away the largest denomination, and the Southern Baptists in the 1940s added Holloway Street (1941), Alston Ave-nue (1944), Guess Road (1945), Immanuel (1942), Faith (1946), and Calvary (1948) churches, followed in the 1950s by Westwood (1950), Plain View (1950), and Park View (1952) in those new developments. Baptists of other varieties also organized churches so that those who professed every shade of belief could find congenial church homes. Other mainline denominations also built in this era: Saint Luke's Episcopal Church (1956); Northgate, a Presbyterian church (organized in 1944 and built in 1953); Saint Paul (1943), Maybrook (1949), and Epworth (organized in 1951, built in 1955), all Methodist churches; and Grace (1942), a Lutheran church. Roman Catholics formed a second congregation with a mission on Alston Avenue (1942) on a sixteen-acre tract. The very old Pentecostal Holiness congregation (1908), the first of that denomination in Durham, moved to a new sanctuary on Hyde Park Avenue (1943), changing its name to suit its location.[32] Completing the list of old, established congregations that built or rebuilt in this era was Beth-El congrega-tion, which constructed a new synagogue in Trinity Park in 1957. A second Jewish congregation, Judea Reform, was organized in 1961. The mainline black denomi-nations, too, were growing in this period. Morehead Avenue Baptist Church was added in 1946, and by 1953 there were at least fifteen other black Baptist congre-gations within the city limits: White Rock, Mount Vernon, Mount Gilead, Mount Zion, New Bethel, Ebenezer, First Calvary, Gethsemane, Jacob's Well, Saint John of Walltown, Saint Paul, Northside, Orange Grove, Union, and West Durham.[33]

Denominations new to Durham were the Society of Friends, organized as an independent meeting in 1943 but with no meetinghouse until 1953; the Greek Or-thodox Church, organized in 1945 but unable to build until 1955 when Saint Bar-bara's came into being; and the Unitarian, organized as a lay-led fellowship in 1949. Only after the Unitarians' alliance with a third Durham flowering of Universalists in 1966 did the joint congregation purchase its own buildings in 1976, and in 1986 a new church on Garrett Road was constructed to meet the needs of a growing population.[34]

The Friends had been meeting informally since 1937, primarily a group of Duke

University people under the leadership of Dr. Elbert Russell. Although the Society of Friends had been the first organized sect in North Carolina after the established Anglican Church, with a monthly meeting organized as early as 1678 in the northeastern part of the state, only one group had existed earlier in this vicinity: Eno, a short-lived preparatory meeting established in the eighteenth century just north of Hillsborough.[35] The peculiarly religious disposition and tolerance of the people of the region allowed for wide varieties of religious experience and expression, not entirely explicable by differences in racial stock, cultural origins, or geographical isolation.

The religious bent of the local population was always predominantly conformist and conservative, even in its Protestantism. When Durham people were attracted to fringe sects, they leaned toward the emotional and anti-intellectual. An example of this is seen in a religious curiosity that made Durham its home in the late 1940s. In the summer of 1947 the cult of snake-handling became part of the services held at the Zion Tabernacle, located a block from Main Street and Sears Roebuck. Under the tutelage of their pastor, Colonel Hartman Bunn (Colonel was a given name), the congregation in the simple frame structure began to practice the apocryphal biblical prophecy "They shall take up serpents." When the police got wind of it, the city council hastily wrote an ordinance against snake-handling, and the police raided a service and confiscated two poisonous snakes. *Life* magazine, too, became interested in Durham's snake-handling sect, and after learning of a snake-handling convention to be held in Zion Tabernacle in the fall of 1948, it obtained permission to take pictures. It later published some sensational photographs: copperheads and rattlers freely wrapped around a visiting preacher's head or held by members of the congregation while people hummed, chattered, spoke in tongues, danced, and generally hypnotized themselves into a religious frenzy in which faith cast out not only fear but reason. The congregation's interracial makeup, the character of Bunn—mild-mannered, soft-spoken, unexcitable—and the unfamiliar behavior of the participants, workers in the cotton mills, the tobacco factories, and Wright Machinery Company, utterly confounded the authorities. Snakes were again confiscated and arrests made. Bunn appealed the charges and challenged Durham's ordinance on the grounds of its interference with religious liberty, but the state Supreme Court upheld its legality. Those who continued to practice snake-handling had to do it elsewhere. When Bunn returned to Durham and Zion Tabernacle in 1955 and broadcast once a week over WTIK, snakes were no longer in evidence.[36]

While religious fervor continued in the South and in Durham so, too, did the perennial prohibition question. During the war the Durham Allied Church League launched a campaign to abolish the ABC stores, led by F. A. G. Cowper, who cited the enormous increase in women imbibers as a reason to support the cause. Allied against this group was the Durham Ministers' Association, which may have had scruples about alcoholic beverages but had even more reservations about the results of legislated prohibition. Even so conservative a Presbyterian as John Sprunt Hill accepted the chairmanship of the executive committee on liquor control, preferring state-controlled sales to the ills of prohibition.[37] Durham continued for many years to sell liquor by the bottle yet prohibit its sale by the drink, so that the local phenomenon of brown-bagging came into general use. A patron of a restaurant who wanted a drink before or with his dinner could provide it from a well-disguised bottle of his own supplying. Yet the old order passed, and even this "good custom" was found corrupt. Liquor by the drink was voted in and became law in 1978.[38]

URBAN RENEWAL

Having enjoyed a decade of building, the city embarked on over a decade of demolition euphemistically called urban renewal. The phenomenon was nationwide and the principle sound. But in its application its purpose was shaped to the uses of the local leaders, uses not always in the best interests of the people it affected. Originating with the federal government, the plan offered America's decaying inner-city neighborhoods, as Reginald Mitchiner put it, "a chance to bloom again." With a combination of financing—two-thirds federal, one-third local—the opportunity seemed too good to ignore. After the North Carolina General Assembly approved the concept in late 1957, Durham's planning director, Paul Brooks, requested students at the University of North Carolina at Chapel Hill's Department of City and Regional Planning to do a study to show how Durham might take advantage of this opportunity. They responded with a plan for a 200-acre blighted area of Hayti that could be renovated for $600,000. The city council was persuaded of its merit, and the newspapers pushed the idea. In 1958 the city created the Durham Redevelopment Commission with Robinson O. Everett as chairman and Brooks as acting executive director until Ben T. Perry III was appointed in 1962.[39] The commission eventually oversaw seven different projects. Most lending and realty companies as well as construction, architectural, and legal firms, who could expect to reap benefits from its execution, supported the undertaking. To raise the required local funds, a bond issue was proposed amounting to $8.6 million, a sum which included funds not only for urban renewal but a great deal more for other improvements. Among the power brokers lobbying for the plan was the DCNA, a group as enthusiastic as the Board of Realtors, Chamber of Commerce, Central Labor Union, Durham Council of Architects, and the League of Women Voters. They realized that black business, too, would participate in the lively exchange of money when the buying and selling of land and the borrowing and lending of money got under way. In addition, Hayti stood to gain, with other decaying areas of the city, in finding itself completely rebuilt. The people who would lose their homes and businesses were assured that they would be fully compensated and that better or equal accommodations would be provided for them. Those who opposed the plan objected in principle to federal intervention in local affairs, the use of federal money, government condemnation of private property, and the likelihood of increased taxes from the bond issue, or they were sentimentally attached to their homes and neighborhoods, however unattractive or run-down others thought them. A small majority approved the bond issue; a 3 percent shift in the vote would have rejected it.[40]

It is a fact of American life that the areas of cities most likely to be called slums— where the needs of people are greatest and the people themselves most helpless to meet them because of lack of money, education, health, or training, and where crime, illness, and vice are most prevalent—happen often to be black neighborhoods. Black areas, therefore, were most often the targets of urban renewal. Unfortunately, the result did not match its promise, for a number of reasons related to leadership, local management, unforeseen side effects, and alleged racial bias. The latter charge was made by many knowledgeable blacks who claimed that urban renewal everywhere became a means to remove black neighborhoods, disperse black power, and destroy black unity. Many felt that poor blacks were hoodwinked by their middle- and upper-class leaders. The other side of the argument emphasized that however valuable Hayti was as an expression of black culture and vitality, the fabric of the neighborhood was badly run down (like that of downtown Durham) and that only a few of its many small businesses were more than shoestring operations, precariously surviving from year to year. Among the exceptions were the *Carolina Times* and the Service Printing Company. The real strength of black business was firmly based and handsomely housed in downtown Durham. In any event, what occurred in Durham was correctly called "urban removal." The bitterness caused by Hayti's destruction was compounded by the failure on the part of Durham's leaders to fulfill their promise and rebuild a better Hayti. Twenty-five years later the land that had bustled with life was still a wasteland overgrown with weeds.

Besides the initial Hayti project, an additional area near North Carolina Central University, then still North Carolina College, and other black neighborhoods were chosen for complete demolition. To help supply inexpensive housing for displaced inhabitants whose incomes made them ineligible for public housing, yet who could not afford to purchase on the open market, Dr. Clyde Donnell, Rencher N. Harris, and F. W. Scott incorporated in 1963 the Lincoln Hospital Foundation, a nonprofit, non-stock corporation.[41]

White leadership was much more concerned with the inner city, where its interests lay. Telephone, electric, gas, sewer, and water lines were all renewed and buried. The amenities Clay had advocated were added: a traffic loop around the center city, one-way streets, trees, fountains, pocket parks, off-street parking garages, and, over much of the demolished Hayti area nearest downtown, a huge expressway to carry traffic to and from the new Research Triangle Park and Raleigh. Amid these improvements, however, the city streets lay in ruins as building after building went down before the bulldozer. The speed of this process, too, was a snail's pace. Year after year went by with many city streets torn up and impassable. Merchants complained, as well they might, for ever fewer people wanted to hazard the jumble of construction machinery, blocked streets, and unfamiliar driving and parking routines to shop downtown when the newer shopping centers could meet all their needs. As one shop after another closed or moved to the suburbs, no new tenants replaced them. After fourteen years had gone by, and the city was supplied with its new amenities, it was ready for new investors to come along and rebuild; it waited in vain. Standing isolated were the banking and financial institutions, the new City Hall (1978) and Judicial Building (1978), parking garages, and automobile franchises.[42]

The expressway and six other projects, with all the related improvements, had cost $41.6 million, of which the federal government had supplied two-thirds. The people most affected, owners of condemned property who had had to move and relocate, numbered 4,057 households and 502 businesses. Old neighborhoods were destroyed that could not be rebuilt.[43] The low-rent apartments or tract housing that took their places were physically more comfortable, but the neighborly ties, integral authenticity, and rootedness of places that had grown organically by their own vitality were gone. Bitter disenchantment was the general harvest. The commission bore the brunt of all the criticism as it intensified through the years. It was probably unfairly blamed, too, for the additional disaster that hit the town in 1966 when the Southern Railroad discontinued passenger service through Durham. The commission was accused of coveting the old station property for new building. The city did nothing to oppose the railroad action, although the newspapers, the Chamber of Commerce, and Duke University fought the closing strenuously. Besides the loss of rail service, many people regretted the loss of the architecturally interesting old station as they saw many old landmarks disappearing before their eyes. When Mayor James Hawkins pushed the button to implode the Washington Duke Hotel in 1975, they could tolerate no more.[44] The pain of losing one's built environment was greater than anyone had anticipated. As buildings disappeared, the few that were left became dearer and harder to part with. The shocks of urban renewal everywhere and a deep nostalgia for what was gone may, in fact, have had much to do with the tide of historic preservation that swept the country in the bicentennial years, touching Durham, too, with notable results. This was perhaps the saving grace of urban renewal.

HOUSING PROBLEMS

Tied in with urban renewal was a wide spectrum of problems related to housing: the acute shortage caused by the ban on building during the war, increased demand resulting from marriage and baby booms, slums and slum landlords, racial discrimination and inequities in rents, difficulties in the financing of new housing, and the need to upgrade or replace substandard housing. A variety of Congressional acts and the agencies they created began to address a national problem. Durham soon witnessed their local application. When Daniel K. Edwards became mayor in 1949, he set up the Durham Housing Authority to take advantage of federal help with housing problems. A minimum housing code was drawn up by which to judge already constructed property and require conformity of landlords, a big step toward the eradication of substandard housing if enforced. Theoretically, if housing did not meet the requirements, it either had to be upgraded or torn down and replaced by authority housing. The Building Inspection Department was responsible for the code's enforcement, and it invariably chose to require upgrading, giving the landlord time within which to make the repairs, and extending the time limits repeatedly rather than taking steps to demolish the structures.[45] When old housing began falling to the bulldozers in 1962, however, and low-cost housing was needed more than ever, the civil rights movement was also under way, and the Housing

Authority became embroiled in a much wider battle as a focus of black resentment. The homes and neighborhoods of the poorest blacks were being taken from them, and the location and rents of new housing became burning issues. Blacks accused the authority of placing subsidized housing in only the southeastern section of the city, well away from prosperous white areas, in effect intending to create a black ghetto. Such placement, they further charged, had a political motivation as well: it prevented blacks from infiltrating white voting precincts where their votes would dilute white power. The privately financed replacement housing of the urban renewal program charged rents that many blacks could not afford. Consequently, they moved into old, formerly white neighborhoods with decaying dwellings, whereupon landlords immediately raised the rents.[46]

One instance of this caused a storm of protest. A landlord bought a number of houses in the Edgemont community and raised the rents of every unit as much as $22 per month, although he had made no repairs or improvements to justify the increases. The Edgemont Community Council, made up of representatives from the neighborhood under the aegis of Operation Breakthrough, a federally funded agency, was determined to resist, and complained to the city inspector, who after inspecting the property notified the landlord of all the improvements required in his many substandard houses. The landlord did absolutely nothing. The inspector was caught between the impotence of the city department to enforce its own code and members of the city council, whose business profited from real estate. The irate tenants did not give up easily, steadily pressuring both the landlord and the council for action. The newspaper gave the controversy wide exposure, and as the city kept extending the time limits for the required repairs, the city officials and the landlord began to look worse and worse.[47]

The location of low-cost housing caused another battle when the authority proposed to build yet another project at the southeastern edge of Hayti in 1967. A new school, Rencher Harris Elementary School, was then being built there, revealing how much behind-the-scenes planning had already taken place. When protesters resorted to demonstrations that threatened to get out of hand, the Housing Authority realized how vulnerable it was and feared to go ahead with its plans for the Bacon Street development. Having discarded two alternative locations in white areas because of white protest, it had little choice but to decide on the fourth possible site, the Damar Court Apartments on Moreene (Dairy) Road. At the same time Duke University, which owned a number of recently built married student housing units directly across Morreene Road from the Damar Court Apartments, entered the controversy by offering to sell the authority its married student housing. Although made as a gesture toward racial harmony, some saw Duke's offer as self-serving: it would have been difficult, the argument went, for Duke to rent those units so close to a low-cost housing development.[48]

The Housing Authority, despite internal bickering and external buffeting, achieved results. Its first construction was Few Gardens (1953) and a portion of McDougald Terrace (1954), providing 487 units between them. In 1959 the authority in an agreement with the Redevelopment Commission (urban renewal) built 650 additional units. It afterward built a variety of housing in many different areas of the city and two high-rise low-rent developments for the elderly. The first was Oldham Towers (1969), built on Richard Wright's Franklin Court Apartments site and named for Carvie Oldham, the controversial executive director of the Housing Authority and butt of much racial animosity. The second was Henderson Towers (1978), named for James Jackson Henderson, a long-time black member of the authority board and eventually its chairman.[49]

Despite much improvement through federal housing laws and financing and the many antipoverty programs of Lyndon Johnson's administration, housing problems did not go away. In fact they remained much the same. A report in 1976 found that in Durham one in five families occupied substandard housing; three-fourths of the substandard housing was rental property, and most of it was occupied by blacks who were charged higher rents than whites in better accommodations.[50]

Another measure to supply low-cost housing, the inspiration of a Chamber of Commerce committee but unacknowledged because of divided membership opinion on the question, was the formation in 1968 of a nonprofit corporation, Durham Investment Company. An interracial group of business people put up $65,000 and decided to build one hundred single-family dwellings on a forty-acre tract adjoining the Durham Industrial Development Corporation park, a neighbor that might be expected to create jobs for the houses' occupants. The houses were to be sold for $10,000 to $12,000 each. Mary D. B. Trent Semans was made president of the corporation, placing its integrity beyond question. Those credited with its conception were J. J. Henderson, Ben Ruffin, Floyd Fletcher, James R. Hawkins, and John H. Wheeler.[51]

THE RESEARCH TRIANGLE AND NEW INDUSTRY

A germ of Durham's shift of economic direction, which resulted in the greatest boom since the early days of the tobacco industry, was planted in the 1950s. The origin of the Research Triangle Park has been traced to two independent ideas; the earliest one was the unfulfilled dream of Howard T. Odum, who hoped to found an institute independent of the university at Chapel Hill but drawing on its resources and that of its satellite colleges to research, compile, and disseminate knowledge in the social sciences. Odum even identified the present site of the park as the location for his institute. His idea died aborning.[52] The other idea was conceived by Romeo Guest, a Greensboro native, business entrepreneur, and head of a construction company. He had noticed the cluster of industrial research laboratories in the vicinity of Harvard, MIT, and other colleges in the Boston area, and thought more industry might be attracted to North Carolina by a similar reciprocally beneficial arrangement established in the Carolina Piedmont, where many institutions of higher learning were concentrated. He, too, picked the present park location as the best available site.[53]

Guest began to talk up his plan to large corporations and local state and college officials. Walter Harper, head of the Department of Conservation and Development, Chancellor Carey Bostian of North Carolina State University, Malcolm Campbell and William Newell of the School of Textiles, Harold Lampe, dean of Engineering, and Brandon Hodges, a paper company executive and former state treasurer, listened sympathetically. When Luther Hodges became governor and the plan was presented to him, he seized the initiative, for it fitted in exactly with his own blueprint for North Carolina. A successful businessman of mixed conservative and moderate political tenets, he wanted to attract more industry to the state. Hodges set up the Research Triangle Development Committee in 1955 (the name Research Triangle had been Guest's inspiration), with Robert M. Hanes as chairman. Dr. George L. Simpson, Jr., who had coincidentally worked with Odum on his plan many years before, was appointed executive director and charged with developing plans to sell the concept. Another committee under Lampe set about compiling a list of research facilities in three universities of the Triangle: North Carolina State University at Raleigh, the University of North Carolina at Chapel Hill, and Duke University at Durham.[54]

The initial efforts were frustrating and unproductive. A temporary recession in the economy, the deaths of Hanes and Brandon Hodges, and the general reluctance of corporations to commit their money to so uncertain a project combined to prevent progress. In late 1958 the three universities incorporated the Research Triangle Institute, a nonprofit organization, to conduct research and market it to industry. In 1958 George Watts Hill, Archie K. Davis, and G. Akers Moore, Jr., were added to the institute board, Hill becoming president of its board of governors. Davis suggested changing the whole concept from a moneymaking to a nonprofit organization; with this change their efforts began to succeed. Two million dollars was quickly raised, and the Research Triangle Foundation was incorporated in late 1958 to receive the money. Davis became its president.[55]

Meanwhile, Karl Robbins, an ex-textile manufacturer, had agreed to put a million dollars of his own into the real estate project, and Guest had been authorized to buy up to five thousand acres. Together they formed Pinelands, Inc., a private company incorporated in September 1957, to own and develop the property they bought. William Maughan, a forester at Duke, was hired to do the actual buying, and as in the acquisition of land for Duke University, prevention of inflation of land values was achieved by keeping secret the Pinelands connection with the publicized Research Park. The heirs of A. M. Rigsbee sold almost one thousand acres to the project, the largest tract in the bundle of parcels that finally made up the approximately 5,500 acres of the Research Triangle Park. Land in the "dark corner" of the county was still comparatively cheap and used for farming, if at all, and the average price was little more than $200 per acre. In 1958 when development did not meet Robbins's expectations, he and Guest agreed to transfer the land they had bought to the foundation at cost. Then the foundation gave the institute $500,000 and 157 acres to begin its operation.[56] Although industrial companies were slow in coming, after the announcement in 1959 of Chemstrand's intention to build in the park, others took the risk and planned their new research facilities there. In the 1960s, to spur development, Governor Daniel K. Moore gave the federal government more than five hundred acres on which to locate various research agencies. The National Center for Health Statistics, the Air Pollution Control Office, and the Environmental Protection Agency all built facilities in the park. IBM began its move to the park in 1965. When the Burroughs Wellcome Foundation moved its headquarters to the stunning building designed by Paul Rudolph in 1970 the park's future success was well assured. Later a coalition of business corporations, the three universities, and private initiative was able to secure the National Humanities Center for the park (1978).[57]

The technological explosion and its industrial applications resulted in the arrival of many new "high-tech" companies either in the park or on its periphery, bringing to southern Durham County an almost unmanageable development of all kinds and unprecedented prosperity. When the institute began to sell land to its corporate tenants in 1959 the price was $2,000 an acre; in the late 1980s it was $45,000. By then it was the largest research park in the nation, its workers numbering 27,000, and its payroll exceeding $400 million.[58] The towns at the angles of this triangle were direct beneficiaries of its success, but they also reaped a less beneficial harvest of economic success—unrestrained construction, proliferation of population, strains on local services, roads, and schools, and the ugly face of cheap commercial enterprises, which suck at the edges of new wealth. The whole area lost the unspoiled, rural ambiance that held so much attraction for the newcomers of earlier decades as well as the native population.

Concurrent with Guest's inspiration of the park and its development was an independent attempt to spur industrial development in Durham County by the establishment of the Durham Committee of 100, a Chamber of Commerce idea. Thomas Yancey Milburn, an architect and member of his father's firm, Milburn and Heister, had retired to Durham in 1950 and was appointed to the post of executive director of the new committee in 1955. Milburn was credited with the high-pressuring of key persons about the Research Triangle plan that resulted in Governor Hodges's assuming statewide leadership and launching the enterprise. Among Milburn's many other efforts to attract new industry to Durham was the Durham Industrial Development Corporation (DIDCO), which acquired 294 acres of the old Gray Barbee property close to Durham, with which to lure new industry. DIDCO built facilities to order for the industrial tenants, among them the Durham Drapery Company and Owens-Illinois Glass Company. When Milburn retired in 1962, the committee ceased to function; it was no longer needed.[59]

Another attraction for industry after 1958 was the presence of an educational training center, as it was then called, in which many industrial skills were taught, some especially tailored to serve the new industries. The center resulted from both state and federal legislation. In 1957 the legislature had provided for the establishment of industrial education centers throughout the state to encourage vocational training, and the next year Congress passed the National Defense Education Act, which funded similar training. Durham put up $500,000 to buy a large tract from DIDCO, whose tenants could profitably utilize the center to train new employees. Before it was built, classes were begun in the two city high schools and in Erwin Mills, General Telephone Company, and Duke Hospital, where courses related to the needs of those establishments could be conveniently taught.[60]

A behind-the-scenes crisis occurred over the perennial race question. Frank Fuller, then chairman of the city Board of Education, was strongly opposed to admitting blacks to the program, while a school board member, Rencher N. Harris, the first black appointed to the school board (1958), was just as strongly determined that they should participate. Watts Hill, Jr., who had fathered the legislation in the House and was a keen promoter of new industry in Durham, recognized the importance of the center as a drawing card and took upon himself to arbitrate the impasse. He knew that the blacks could defeat the whole program if they were excluded; furthermore, he was in the vanguard of the effort to win for them equal opportunity.[61] A compromise was reached in the decision to restrict the high schools' facilities to their student bodies but to open the center's classes to persons of either race over the age of eighteen. It is ironic that from the start it was assumed that only men would be admitted. By the 1980s the center comprised four buildings on 63 acres along Lawson and Cooper streets and served well over 12,000 students, men and women, yearly. From its first designation as Durham Industrial Education Center, its name was changed in 1965 to Durham Technical Institute and in 1986 to Durham Technical Community College.[62]

The black community picked up the idea of an industrial park, and in 1968 with part of a $1 million grant to Durham from the Office of Economic Opportunity (OEO), United Durham Incorporated was established by Leander Medlin, Jeannette Watson, R. Edward Stewart, Carrie Carlton, Nathan Garrett, and Walter Umstead. When the corporation did not succeed as its incorporators had hoped, they restructured it and formed UDI Community Development Corporation in 1974 as a nonprofit organization. With a federal grant for the extension of city sewer lines into the area in 1977 came the approval by the city of the first phase of an industrial park. It comprised ninety-one acres between Cornwallis and Fayetteville roads, fifteen acres of which were reserved for offices and the rest for industries.[63]

OLD INDUSTRY

The decline of Durham's old industries was not dreamed of in 1950. All through the 1940s they had enjoyed vigorous health due to the war, they had expanded plants and production, and they continued to be responsive to changing times. Military contracts had required Erwin Mills to add a third shift; the company began to sell off its mill village housing to the workers; and it was learning to accommodate to a strengthened union. The decision in 1942 to sell its housing was beneficial to workers and company alike. The much higher wages that employees earned during and after the war enabled them to become homeowners. Houses that had cost $375 to build were sold to the workers for $2,000 each, and were reselling in 1975 for ten times that amount. The company no longer had to make repairs on the houses or pay insurance or property taxes, taxes that had doubled in 1925 when West Durham was taken into the city limits. The company changed its manner of dealing with its employees as well. A short strike in 1940 was the last in which its old management practices were evident: the usual firings did not result in an end to the strike. The federal government stepped in, reinstated the workers, and forced the company to reach an agreement with the union, Local 246.[64] Throughout the war years and into the 1950s and 1960s Erwin Mills and most other factories in Durham were the targets of strikes, a trend that occurred all over the country as unions tested their strength and won concessions in their demands for higher wages, better working conditions, and fringe benefits.[65]

Erwin Mills took a notable step in 1943 under the progressive leadership of William Ruffin, then secretary-treasurer, when it hired a Duke University economics professor, Frank T. DeVyver, as vice-president for personnel and industrial relations. An expert in labor relations, DeVyver had already befriended the local union, attended its meetings, and gotten to know its leaders. In his new position he immediately set up a personnel department (up to then employees had been hired at the gate) and a grievance procedure, and he became responsible for negotiations with the union, to which over half the employees then belonged.[66] He had plenty of opportunity to exercise his skills in the following decades. Two strikes in 1945 (one lasting a week and the other five months) were on the whole harmonious. There was no violence, and the company went to great lengths to express its goodwill. During the longer strike it guaranteed the loans the employees had made to buy their houses for as long as they were on strike, and it strung up wires to the factory gates where the pickets were camping to give them lighting at night. Both sides wanted to continue the working relationship and understood that with time they would reach an agreement. The strikers wanted a minimum wage of $0.65 an hour, a 45-minute lunch break, a week's vacation for employees with less than five years' employment and two weeks for those with more. To all these demands the company finally agreed, as well as recognizing the union as the workers' exclusive bargaining agency.[67]

Unfortunately, the 1951 strike, called by the national union, was an entirely different affair. Although there were no deaths or injuries, several attempts were made to blow up portions of the mills. Twice the company appealed to the courts for relief from the violence. In 1955 yet another strike occurred when the company hired blacks as cloth doffers without first discussing this innovation with the employees. The mills had had difficulty finding workers who would do the backbreaking work. At DeVyver's behest, the company sat down with the union and representative workers to explain the problem, and the strikers agreed to the change. Eventually the mills were completely integrated.[68]

William Ruffin, who succeeded Kemp Lewis as president of Erwin Mills in 1948, had already been with the mills twenty-seven years. He had begun as a weaver after graduation from college and had worked his way through a variety of jobs before entering the administrative end of the business. He was sensitive to the workers' views and needs and liked working with them. He was the first southerner to become president of the National Association of Manufacturers (1950–51). While he was president of Erwin Mills, the families that still held the majority of the stock decided to sell out, and Burlington Industries bought their controlling interest. It eventually sold the business and machinery to the J. P. Stevens Company in 1986. Within a short time, Stevens halted manufacture and sold off the inventory.[69] High labor costs, inefficient and outmoded manufacturing plants, and foreign competition from less-developed countries contributed to the nationwide decline of the textile industry and, in Durham, to the closing of the old Erwin Cotton Mills in 1986.

Different factors, however, were at work in the decline of Durham's tobacco industry. In 1944, at the height of World War II, Durham produced one-fourth of all cigarettes made in the United States.[70] In the postwar period both Liggett and Myers and American Tobacco expanded their Durham facilities, introduced new brands of cigarettes, and enjoyed a large share of the market. Change came in the 1960s, and one cause can be traced to the early 1950s, when tobacco companies began to come under attack as makers of a product injurious to health. There was actually nothing new about such charges. In 1826 a friend of Duncan Cameron had told him that the use of tobacco caused a cough, bloody expectoration, prostration, circulatory disturbances, and narcotic and stimulant effects.[71] In 1872 the editor of the Hillsborough *Recorder* wrote, "A boy who smokes early and frequently, or in any way uses large quantities of tobacco, is never known to make a man of much muscular energy, and generally lacks muscular and physical, as well as mental power."[72] It was not just a coincidence that long years before, cigarettes had been called "coffin nails." Reports published in the 1950s, however, citing the ills of cigarette smoking, were based on scientific studies and medical statistics and showed that lung and other cancers were occurring in ever-increasing numbers of heavy smokers. The U.S. Department of Public Health finally made its own studies and published the results of its investigation in the surgeon general's landmark report of 1964; it condemned cigarettes as the major cause of lung cancer and other respiratory diseases.[73]

By the late 1960s the tobacco companies began to diversify their holdings, at the same time proclaiming through the American Tobacco Institute, the industry's lobby, that there was no scientific proof that tobacco or any of its components caused cancer. Manufacturers were nevertheless very much handicapped by the government's requirement that cigarette packages carry a health warning, by the odium of separating smokers from nonsmokers in public places, and by a later surgeon general's warnings of the hazards of "passive smoking" (the inhalation by nonsmokers of air contaminated by cigarette smoke). The American Lung Association claimed that cigarette smoking was killing 350,000 Americans a year, more than the combined battle deaths in World War II and the Vietnam War.[74]

Locally, the war on tobacco had clear repercussions. Liggett and Myers dealt Durham's industrial economy a blow in 1979 by moving its corporate headquarters to New York. It thereafter diversified its holdings through ownership of companies making wines, liquor, pet foods, and watchbands as well as tobacco products, calling itself the Liggett Group, Incorporated. In 1980 the Liggett Group with all its subsidiaries was sold to Grand Metropolitan Limited of London. In 1986 Liggett and Myers was sold again, thereafter closing down much of its tobacco production and retiring or firing hundreds of Durham employees. American Tobacco in the same year announced that it would close and sell its Durham plant. It seemed inevitable that the city that Bull Durham built might no longer make tobacco.[75]

As a direct result came the decline in the cultivation and auctioning of tobacco.

Durham farmers planted far less than they were entitled to. The carnival atmosphere that once pervaded Durham in the fall as the warehouses filled up, the city streets were clogged with farm wagons or trucks, and the stores hummed with buyers enjoying the first fruits of their labors was totally absent. Instead of the thirteen warehouses that Durham possessed in the 1950s, only one auction house remained in 1986, the Planters Warehouse on East Geer Street, no longer in the center of town. Instead of 1947's 50 million pounds of tobacco, Planters could hope for only 4 million pounds in 1986. The long tradition of auctioneering, which had begun with Edward J. Parrish, closed with Durwood Thomas, Durham's last auctioneer.[76]

OTHER HEALTH ISSUES

Another health issue arose in Durham in the 1950s, the question of adding fluoride to the city water supply to fight tooth decay. The Health Department was already backing the suggestion in 1951, and after the city council approved the move, the city expected to add the chemical within a short time. Town doctors and dentists recommended the measure, as did the state Board of Health.[77] A public hearing was held in August, and to the city's astonishment a crowd turned up to object. Leading the fight against the proposal was a town lawyer, R. M. Gantt. His objections were two: the cost of the sodium fluoride, and its long-term effects on adults and older people. So much feeling against the proposal unsettled the councilmen, and when the vote was taken, it was defeated seven to five. (One councilman was absent.) Those who had braved the crowd and voted in favor were Watts Carr, Jr., Mary D. B. Trent Semans, Mayor Evans, Kathrine Everett, and E. R. Williamson. In 1957 the issue was brought forward again, with a similar fate.[78] Probably the most prominent citizen to object was John Sprunt Hill, who in his later years was usually on the conservative side of a question. In the winter of 1962 a third city council was asked to consider the measure. The arguments were still the same. Wade Brown, the head of the water department, spoke about the costs; $3,700 would pay for the equipment installed and $6,500 a year would pay for the chemical, a small sum measured against the cost of dental care for children with carious teeth. Despite assurances from local doctors, there seemed to be no convincing evidence to the other objection: fluoride had not been tried long enough to know what its effects were on the older population. The council at last voted approval, and in May 1962 fluoride was added to the city water.[79] In the succeeding quarter-century, the incidence of caries in Durham children's teeth markedly declined.

A very different public response greeted another public health measure. Polio epidemics, which grew steadily more frightening as the years passed, were suddenly brought to an abrupt halt by the research of Dr. Jonas Salk in 1955 and Dr. Albert Sabin in 1961, both of whom developed vaccines against the disease. Salk developed a vaccine that used dead organisms of three different strains of the disease and gave immunity to the paralysis that could occur with infection. Dr. Sabin, on the other hand, used living organisms and produced a vaccine for each of the three varieties which were then combined and administered orally. This method provided complete immunity to the disease over a much longer period. To immunize as many people as quickly as possible, the Durham-Orange Medical Foundation decided to make the vaccine available free and administered it in saturated sugar cubes. An estimated 68 percent of the population turned out.[80] Very soon polio, like smallpox, was conquered in the United States.

OTHER COUNTY MATTERS

Although the public presented little resistance to polio immunization, not all county problems were so harmoniously solved. Durham County had as manager for thirty-five years (1949–84) Edmund Slade Swindell, Jr., a man not only skilled in finance and public relations, but fiscally and politically conservative, and thus in tune with his board. As one of his first duties, the commissioners asked him to prepare the way for a county land-use and zoning plan authorized by the legislature in 1949. The drawing-up of an ordinance and zoning map was only the first step in a process that would take seven years to accomplish. Swindell arranged informal meetings in all the county's communities to present the concept of a land-use plan, to educate the public about the need for the regulations, and to allow for public comment and advice. Poor attendance and lack of interest defeated the educational intent, so that when the ordinance and map were presented for adoption by the board of commissioners at a public hearing, a storm of protest broke. Frontier individualism again proclaimed its right to do as it pleased with its own property. One of the most vehement critics was John Sprunt Hill. Because of the furor, the commissioners took no action but let the matter rest. Only in 1956 did they once again hold a public hearing; in the face of opposition they adopted the regulations and set up a planning department to administer them.[81]

Two achievements of the 1960s were the county's entrance into the sewage treatment business and the building of a county hospital. The growth of the Research Triangle in the early 1960s and the desire of the county and city to secure more industry made provision for water and sewage imperative. Where growth was occurring (in the Research Triangle Park) the kind of soils and the shortage of a plentiful water supply created serious handicaps to their plans. All the water resources were located in the northern part of the county. A city-county committee with equal representation was set up to find solutions. The decision was to share responsibility for the facilities. The city would provide the water, since it was the only municipality in the county and already had a sophisticated water supply system, and would divide with the county the responsibility for sewage treatment: the city was responsible for the northern section, the county for the southern. To carry out this plan a number of new facilities for sewage treatment were built in the 1960s: four new city-owned plants in 1967–68 (the Eno River, Lick Creek, Sandy Creek, and Hope Valley plants, the last to be phased out since it lay in the floodplain of Third Fork Creek), and the county-owned Triangle plant off Highway 55 in 1966 to serve the Research Triangle, Parkwood, and the southeastern part of the county. Durham County was the first county in the state to own and operate a sewage treatment plant. The building of the Jordan Reservoir covering parts of Chatham and Durham counties, which went into operation in the 1980s, created a large additional water source for southern Durham County.[82]

Swindell's ability and tact were more sorely tested when the county had to deal with the ever-increasing costs and problems of health care. Watts Hospital was overcrowded and old-fashioned and could not be adapted for modern hospital requirements and equipment, while Lincoln Hospital, even more outmoded and inadequately equipped, was declining in use year by year at the same time that its expenses mounted. Neither Watts nor Lincoln operated within its budget. Blacks, who had always been admitted to Duke Hospital and who, in the early 1960s, were admitted to Watts on a limited basis, preferred the treatment they received in the white hospitals. A plan to build a new integrated Watts hospital was proposed, but it made meager provision for Lincoln Hospital's critical needs. Money to finance the undertaking would be raised by bonds. When a referendum on the bonds was held in 1966, the measure was roundly defeated, opposed both by blacks, who feared they were losing their hospital and understood that there was little in the new plan to answer their needs, and by whites, opposed to integration.[83]

Swindell then set up a Hospital Study Committee, racially balanced, to investigate the problems and find a more comprehensive solution. H. Spurgeon Boyce chaired the group, which hired a professional team to compile the information and advice they needed. When the committee had concluded its deliberations, it recommended to the commissioners a new acute care hospital, the conversion of the Watts and Lincoln plants to extended care facilities and related programs, and the consolidation of their organizations. The county was in a difficult position. The boards of Watts and Lincoln hospitals understandably did not wish to relinquish control and feared what might take their places. The black community did not want to lose its own hospital, and its doctors did not want to lose their hospital connections. The delicate negotiating over jealously guarded turf was long and often appeared hopeless. Eventually, however, a consensus was reached, and another bond issue to cover the committee's recommendations was put to a vote in 1968. This time it passed comfortably because of black support, and the new Durham County General Hospital for all became a reality in 1976. Lincoln Hospital became Lincoln Health Center, fulfilling a vital need for local primary health services, and the old Watts Hospital was closed.[84]

Repeated efforts, always frustrated, to come to a decision about a new public library occupied the 1960s and 1970s. Despite the grossly inadequate building on Main Street, which could hold only a portion of the library's books, a decision was deferred from year to year. Until 1965 library facilities were segregated. Control and funding came from both the city and county. Eventually the city and county agreed that the library should be a county responsibility and the city gave the land and old library to the county. Cooperation and agreement on a new facility were handicapped by both lack of money and disagreement among library board members about location and personnel. Two referendums on bond issues for a new building were defeated. Finally, under the leadership of Benjamin E. Powell, librarian of Duke University, who was chairman of the public library board of trustees from

1962 until his death in 1981, consensus was reached, and in 1976 a third referendum approved a bond issue. A new facility costing three million dollars opened in 1980 near the new governmental center on land cleared by urban renewal. The Stanford Leigh Warren branch on Fayetteville Street was not abandoned, a fear of the black community, but in fact received a complete renovation in 1985 and became a satellite library with its own board of directors in its refurbished old building.[85]

An antiquated courthouse was another county worry of long standing. Renovation seemed clearly impractical despite the additional space provided by a new office building (1967) beside the old courthouse, which relieved congestion for a while. Location was always a point of disagreement in addition to the perennial question of funds. Both sticking points were resolved in the early 1970s after independent studies were submitted by the Durham Civic–Convention Center Commission, the Downtown Revitalization Foundation, and the Bell Design Group. Two of their suggestions eventually adopted were a traffic loop around the inner city and a civic center in the area bounded by Chapel Hill, Roney, Morgan, and Foster streets; the civic center would include the old city hall, the Carolina Theatre, and convention accommodations. From these studies came, too, the plans for the new city hall on Mangum Street near Chapel Hill Street and the new judicial building across from the old courthouse, both financed by the federal revenue-sharing program.[86]

Fire protection for the county was achieved only gradually. The first step was the designation of a city truck, based at the Ninth Street fire station, to respond to county fire alarms. For this service the county paid several hundred thousand dollars a year. The truck's distance from most parts of the county, however, made adequate protection impossible. In 1960, a year after the Mangum School at Bahama was destroyed by fire, that community formed a volunteer fire company, the first in the county. Supported entirely by donations, the seventeen volunteers operated out of an old garage and used an overhauled Pepsi-Cola truck to fight fires. In 1964 they built their own station and acquired more professional equipment. Bahama's lead was followed by other communities: Bethesda in 1963, Parkwood in 1968, Lebanon in 1971, and Redwood in 1978. Eventually support for these companies was arranged by special taxes levied on property owners within the respective fire districts. Volunteer firemen were trained in emergency medical care so that they might respond to all kinds of accidents as well as fires. In 1980 a county fire marshal, a trained professional, was employed to coordinate and oversee the volunteer companies. He also instituted a countywide fire prevention ordinance. Durham soon achieved the highest fire protection performance rating of any county in the state.[87]

While the county was beginning to enjoy fire protection at last, the city was embarking on a new governmental structure that combined the administration of fire and police departments under one organization: public safety. A national trend in this direction had persuaded the city council that it was a more efficient use of manpower and tax money. Each employee was trained to perform two jobs, and each former fire and police station equipped to handle any emergency. A shortened response time resulted. After less than a year in office, the first public safety officer, Jacob A. Jessup, resigned and was succeeded in 1971 by Esai Berenbaum, a retired army colonel and assistant to the city manager Harding Hughes, whose idea the public safety program had been.[88] Some employees in both former departments refused to accept the new order, maintaining their opposition so long that in 1986 another council dismantled the system and reverted to the dual administration.[89] More expensive than the unified command, it nevertheless allowed for individual career preferences, urban administrators believed, and more concentrated training and higher proficiency in both fields.

SOCIAL REMEDIES

A great number of innovative and remedial social programs were tried, some originating during the war, some in the postwar era. Among the more successful were the Coordinating Council for Senior Citizens and the Goodwill Industries. In 1952 was formed the Golden Age Society, which evolved into the Coordinating Council for Senior Citizens. It was instituted through the help of the AAUW, the YWCA, the Altrusa Club, and the city Recreation Department. Frances Jeffers, a worker in the predecessor to Duke's Center for the Study of Aging and Human Development was its first president, Ann Johnson its first executive director. As its names indicate, it tried to meet the needs of older people in more than basic physical ways. Neighborhood centers all over the county, where senior citizens enjoyed companionship, a midday meal, crafts, games, and other pastimes, were a direct result of this organization's efforts.

An affiliate of Goodwill Industries of America (founded in Boston in 1902) was chartered in Durham in 1964, and as Goodwill Industries, Inc., began its work in 1966 in the old Coca-Cola bottling factory at Main and Buchanan streets. A contribution of thirty-five thousand dollars from the community funded its start. It provided rehabilitation, skills training, and job placement for physically, emotionally, or mentally disabled persons. From the collection and reselling or recycling of secondhand goods, Goodwill Industries earned 85 percent of its annual funds. At first confined to serving Durham County, its scope increased to include all of east central North Carolina.[90]

In response to the criticism voiced by Howard Jensen in his 1952 speech to the Community Chest, the Durham Youth Board was established to gather data on the needs of Durham's young and to help organizations already set up for their benefit. To counter his charges of community stinginess, a new organization, the United Fund (now the United Way), was established to handle the collection of voluntary contributions. Mrs. Semans was made its first president. With its goal of $395,246 for 1953 almost reached by the end of its first campaign, the fund lent hope of a better response to local needs.[91]

By far the greatest attention, however, was devoted to the poor, a group that included not only the old, the young, and the disabled, but many afflicted by other factors contributing to poverty: unemployment, illiteracy, the lack of salable skills, mental illness or incompetency, alcohol or drug addiction, substandard housing, and crime made up the tangled net in which the poor were caught. One focus of this attention was Smoky Hollow or Edgemont, the neighborhood with the longest history of social problems. The closing of the cotton mill there in 1938 had started a deterioration that worsened with the passing years; by the 1940s poverty and rising crime rates called attention to the neighborhood's plight. The campus church at Duke decided to sponsor a community center and, with the cooperation of the city recreation department, renovated the second floor of the old Knights of Pythias building for the purpose. Professor Howard Jensen was chairman of an advisory board set up to oversee the project. The Reverend and Mrs. Louis A. Mayo were made full-time directors of the center, which opened in 1941–42 and arranged activities for neighborhood children every afternoon and several nights a week. The suggestion for the project had come from the juvenile court as a measure to stem the increase in juvenile delinquency and to fill the vacuum left by the closing of a center run there in the Depression by the WPA. When the building burned in 1943, new facilities were built at Elm Street and Angier Avenue.[92]

Because of the determination of the Duke student volunteers, the program survived during the next fifteen years despite negligent directors, the conflicting philosophies of the Recreation and Welfare departments, a polio epidemic in 1944, which closed the center temporarily, and the failure of the city to meet its obligations to provide recreational facilities and supervision. In the 1960s new problems arose as the first black families, displaced by urban renewal, began to move into the previously all-white neighborhood.[93] White residents gradually moved out, and the neighborhood became predominantly black by 1968. Through Lyndon Johnson's Great Society programs in the 1960s, government money supplied a variety of new approaches to poverty, for example, the distribution of food stamps to needy families, begun in 1966 and administered through the Welfare Department.[94] Besides the Boy and Girl Scout troops, a preschool program, and supervised games and dances, many kinds of craft classes were added to the original program at the Edgemont center. Operation Breakthrough and the Youth Organization for Community Action later provided new programs at the center for children and young adults.

The last-named organizations began during Governor Terry Sanford's administration, through recommendations and a grant from the Ford Foundation, to which he had appealed for advice. First, at the foundation's suggestion, he set up in 1963 the North Carolina Fund, "an independent, non-profit, charitable corporation to receive and dispense moneys from other foundations" for local antipoverty programs.[95] The new fund invited communities to devise programs which addressed particular local needs and submit them for possible funding. Durham's plan, called Operation Breakthrough, concentrated on ways to break the cycle of poverty through education and job training, and won the fund's support. A corporation with the name Operation Breakthrough was set up in 1964 to receive and administer money and programs under a steering committee made up of chairman Everett H. Hopkins, Louise McCutcheon, Carlie Sessoms, Kenneth Royall, James Semans, Marion Thorpe, Victor Bryant, Jr., Robert L. Foust, and the mayor, R. Wensell Grabarek. After qualifying as a Community Action agency the following year, Operation Breakthrough was entitled to receive federal money authorized by the Economic Opportunity Act of 1964. With these and other federal and state funds, it continued a variety of programs to help all age groups. Operation Breakthrough made its headquarters in a building on Main Street in the Edgemont community and worked through the Edgemont Community Center to implement its first program, the Neighborhood Youth Corps. Its purpose was to encourage young people to complete their education and fit themselves for employment through training and the acquisition of salable skills. When the federal government began its Head Start program the same year, it was administered in Durham through Operation Breakthrough.[96]

In 1965 Howard Fuller came to Durham as an employee of Operation Breakthrough to coordinate community organization efforts in one particular area. A native of Milwaukee, with a master's degree in social work and himself a product of a deprived environment, Fuller easily shaped his work to the needs of the people he served. The North Carolina Fund made the program a separate entity under the name of the Foundation for Community Development in 1967, with Nathan Garrett as executive director and Fuller as director in charge of setting up neighborhood councils as sounding boards for the problems and frustrations of the inhabitants. Fuller trained the participants to organize, to develop leaders, and to present their grievances to decision-making bodies in order to effect changes. An intelligent organizer and charismatic speaker, he was ideally suited to the task. Passive roles as welfare recipients, he realized, had kept the poor in their dependent situation and did nothing to solve their problems. Equally effective as Fuller's assistant, and very much in the same mold, was the Durham native and NCC student Benjamin Ruffin. Both men were active in the civil rights movement in the 1960s and won prominence in the Edgemont Council's battle with its slum landlord, which resulted in appeals to the city Inspections Department, appearances before the city council, and marches on city hall.[97]

In 1969 Mrs. Inez Gooch, president of the Edgemont Neighborhood Council, was responsible for an innovative program financed by Operation Breakthrough. With the assistance of UNC seniors who intended to pursue careers in health care, she arranged classes one evening a week to disseminate information about health care and diseases. Soon realizing that the people who came needed more practical assistance, Mrs. Gooch obtained the use of an empty building and the services of volunteer medical and nursing students, first from UNC but later also from Duke, to operate a clinic once a week. Despite the loss of their building through arson, the work continued, increasing in 1969 to twice a week, and expanded to offer the services of volunteer pharmacists, laboratory technicians, dieticians, and dental students. The clinic served about fifty persons a night and referred those with more serious problems to the health department.[98]

Operation Breakthrough continued to expand, providing services to Durham's poor with money from various federal agencies as well as from the city, county, state, and private foundations. The federal government's alphabet soup proved Operation Breakthrough's main sustenance. The Office of Economic Opportunity (OEO), the Community Service Administration (CSA), the Department of Health, Education, and Welfare (HEW) and its successor, the Department of Health and Human Services (HHS), and the Department of Labor funded its programs. When the federal Comprehensive Employment and Training Act (CETA) funds became available to Operation Breakthrough in 1978, they further augmented its services.[99]

Hindsight reveals the 1950s as politically lackluster times, struggling to adjust to change and to deal with the first rumblings of social action that erupted in the 1960s. Urban renewal, the expansion of suburbs and their orientation around shopping centers rather than city centers, and political struggles between those who wished to hold the line and those who wished to move forward changed the face of Durham rather than its heart. But very deep and important changes in economic direction were being made that would come to fruition in the 1970s: the beginning of the Research Triangle and the decline of Durham's old industries. But all parochial concerns were engulfed in the 1960s in a national storm—comprehensive, well-organized, and powerful—the civil rights movement. Swept into it were not just government at all levels, but politicians, social workers, and laymen everywhere.

Civil Rights, 1954–1978

19

BLACK VETERANS RETURNING FROM WORLD WAR II had even more reason than white to feel Durham unacceptably backward. Like their fathers after World War I, they were angered by returning to second-class citizenship after experiencing comparative social equality and a sense of personal freedom abroad. After World War II they were no longer in a mood to accommodate, and they were in a better position to object. Black men on the home front had enjoyed better jobs and higher wages because of the war. Many black women had been trained for industrial and office work that had been previously closed to them and had earned in these new jobs far better pay than domestic work had yielded. Many black veterans were enrolling in colleges and aiming at middle-class careers. Besides feeling resentment about their racial handicap, blacks were determined to obtain the rights that had been denied them, moods that understandably threatened the white status quo.

The causes of the civil rights movement were the same everywhere—racial discrimination and injustice and segregation—but the local forms it took and the responses they met were different. The precipitating action of the postwar phase of the civil rights movement is usually thought to be the Supreme Court decision of 1954, *Brown v. Board of Education of Topeka, Kansas*. This was followed in the rest of the decade by only token integration and stalling by every conceivable means; the movement evolved into a more militant, even violent phase in the 1960s and achieved notable results. It should be remembered, however, that the struggle had fluctuated but been unceasing for almost a hundred years. In Durham, the modern phase of the struggle really began with the organization in 1935 of the DCNA (Durham Committee on Negro Affairs), which signaled an upsurge of effort. The DCNA's wide-ranging attention made it quick to seize any opening to advance blacks' rights. Its efforts in the 1940s to get blacks into jobs as policemen, managers of the ABC (alcoholic beverage control) stores in Hayti, magistrates, and, most important, to have them registered as voters were first steps in what later became a broad advance.[1]

By the late 1950s the DCNA was thought by young Durham blacks too conservative for effective leadership. They joined instead more militant groups such as local chapters of the NAACP (National Association for the Advancement of Colored People), CORE (the Congress of Racial Equality organized by James Farmer in 1942), the Southern Christian Leadership Conference (a passive resistance movement led by Martin Luther King, Jr.), and the Student Non-violent Coordinating Committee. Still, the DCNA continued to follow a course that had proved productive; it had countenanced forthright and uncompromising demands, often offensive to whites and beyond any expectation of immediate attainment, by John Wheeler and other outspoken leaders at the Mechanics and Farmers Bank in order to provide the more traditional and conservative leaders of the Mutual room to negotiate compromises with the white leadership.[2] In the 1950s and 1960s, it let the radical activists of the civil rights movement make stiff demands while it kept the channels of communication open with white leaders. How conservative the early leaders of the DCNA were, in their actions if not in their ideology, is seen in Spaulding's speech to a black audience in 1941; echoing Booker T. Washington's approach, he blamed racial discrimination on black ignorance, lawlessness, and failure to be dependable and productive. Spaulding had refused to condone the march on Washington that year to protest discrimination in the armed forces and defense work, feeling it inappropriate in wartime. Yet he was willing to co-sign a telegram to President Roosevelt the same year making the same complaint.[3] Dr. James E. Shepard, another conservative, appeared in 1944 on "Town Hall," a national radio program, to talk about race relations. He advocated letting each state handle its own problems and cited North Carolina as a civilized Christian community that believed in democracy and could be counted on to make "needed social, political, and economic adjustments."[4] These men continued to play the stabilizing role, soothing fears, preventing confrontation, and thereby lessening racial tension and maintaining the confidence of the white leaders. Young leaders questioned the efficacy of this approach and condemned it as too slow.

Racial incidents were inevitable during the war when black northern soldiers stationed in southern army camps refused to accept "Jim Crow" laws. Buses in particular became rings for interracial sparring.[5] In 1943 a city detective got into an altercation on a bus with a young black woman, Doris Elizabeth Lyon, who refused to move to a seat in the back and hit him on the head after he forcibly moved her. The next year a black soldier from Camp Butner was shot and killed by a bus driver for refusing to sit in the back of a Durham city bus. The driver claimed self-defense. The driver's acquittal did nothing to ease racial tension.[6]

All over the South a few concerned whites had been doing what they could to improve race relations. As early as 1906 an interracial group had been formed in Atlanta to deal with racial tensions. In 1919, also a postwar period of strained race relations, another group of white leaders had met to deal with the emergency of returning soldiers and were soon joined by black leaders. Under the influence of

Will W. Alexander this group formed a permanent organization, the Commission on Interracial Cooperation, "to promote interracial peace through interracial communication." Spaulding became treasurer of a North Carolina branch formed in 1928. The commission's aim was to eliminate discrimination, not segregation, and to obtain for blacks civil and political rights, economic opportunity, and equal justice in the courts.[7] By 1942, when the commission had lost its early vigor, one of its longtime leaders proposed a conference of southern blacks to discuss what whites could do to alleviate the potentially explosive situation. Meeting in Durham, this group made a list of demands that included the ballot, civil rights, employment opportunity, and access to public services. From this and a similar meeting of whites in Atlanta eventually came a new biracial organization in 1943, the Southern Regional Council. Howard T. Odum became its first president, and in the 1970s John Wheeler served a term as president.[8]

SCHOOL DESEGREGATION

The federal government ended segregation in the armed forces in 1948. As in the arts and sports, where black talent was first recognized and rewarded, in the military an individual's skill was more important than his color. This move by the government did much to counter racial prejudice. When another arm of the federal government let loose the thunderbolt of *Brown v. Board of Education* in 1954, southerners, though stunned, seemed resigned to accepting integrated schools as the law of the land. It has been argued that if white southerners had not had time to recover from their shock and rethink their position, desegregation might have been accomplished overnight and with a minimum of friction. But as time passed and each state began to devise schemes for delaying compliance, they found a lot of room to maneuver.[9]

From 1954 on, the civil rights movement became far and away the central action in all parts of the nation for two decades. Although local politicians in Durham preferred to ignore the situation, they were forced to respond to the crises that black unrest provoked. At every turn, whether addressing poverty, inner city decay, new construction, health care, or education, political leaders found themselves confronting the race issue. Even the Vietnam War, which bred intense opposition for other reasons, became a civil rights issue because of the disproportionate number of blacks drafted to fight it. Draft boards were anything but evenhanded in their application of regulations, and some were notoriously lax in granting exemptions. Certainly the most unpopular war that the United States fought, the Vietnam War consumed a decade of hopeless, senseless, and often brutalizing service of thousands of young men for a futile political cause. Anger about the war increased everyone's volatility and added to blacks' sense of outrage.

Rencher Harris, when asked to comment on the Supreme Court's decision, replied with some cynicism that integration had not worked any miracles in the North, and even though the ruling would not make any noticeable changes, he believed that equal opportunity was the right of every person. Harris's realistic assessment, quiet resistance under pressure, and genuine desire to find common ground with whites eventually lost him the confidence of the DCNA; they thought him too conciliatory to whites. In 1957, after he had served two terms on the city council, the DCNA refused to back him for a third term. They switched their support instead to John S. Stewart, president of the Mutual Savings and Loan Association, who won election. The next year Harris was appointed to the city school board where, for the next four years, he fought alone the battle for integration of the schools, a task he characterized as thankless.[10]

The states were allowed to decide their own response to the Supreme Court decision, and Governor Luther Hodges made the choice for North Carolina. Wishing to justify the choice of reluctant and slow compliance, he portrayed society as in danger of being torn asunder by black militants on one hand and redneck reactionaries on the other; he would pursue a careful middle course by taking the first halting steps toward compliance without inflaming white passions to rebellion, a course to which reasonable people of good will would adhere in order to prevent the closing of the schools as Virginia and Oklahoma chose to do. North Carolina's solution was the Pearsall Plan or Pupil Assignment Law (1955), named for the Hodges-appointed chairman of the committee that created it, Thomas J. Pearsall of Rocky Mount. By its regulations each local school board was given the authority to review and decide, each on its individual merits *other* than race, applications for reassignment in the public schools. Parents of either race had the option of applying for reassignment of their children to schools of their choice. Each school district also had the option to close its schools by a majority vote. Schools would remain segregated unless legally challenged. Hodges appealed to blacks to stick voluntarily to their schools in order not to disturb civic peace or close the schools, thus placing the burden of integrating the schools squarely on the blacks' shoulders. The Pearsall Plan became law in 1955, and blacks prepared to make use of it.[11]

Although there was very little action on the matter until the 1960s, school integration began in Durham in the late 1950s. A lawsuit against the school board in Durham had already been filed when the Supreme Court decision was handed down, making the case moot. In the summer of 1955, John S. Stewart, John H. Wheeler, J. Fred Pratt, M. H. Thompson, and D. E. Moore appeared before the city Board of Education and in a long, carefully reasoned, and calmly stated petition asked the board to devise a plan for desegregating the schools. The education committee of the DCNA took on the task of encouraging parents to ask for reassignment and of helping them prepare the many necessary papers. When reassignment was denied, the NAACP and DCNA took the responsibility for bringing and arguing court cases at no financial risk to the children's parents. Although reassignment was requested almost as soon as the Pearsall Plan became law, the school board found dozens of excuses other than race on which to base rejections, and the first school year for which the school board approved any reassignments was 1959–60, when it allowed 8 of 225 reassignment requests.[12]

For those young pioneers who began the integration process in the fall of 1959, enormous courage was required. Daily they faced the jeers and insults of many hostile schoolmates for the sake of a principle and a better education. Anita Brame and Lucy Jones, both of Walltown, assigned to Brogden Junior High School, were the first to cross the threshold of a white school, followed two weeks later at Carr Junior High School by Andree Yvonne McKissick and Henry Alonzo Vickers. Claudette Brame and Larry Scurlock were assigned to Durham High School, and Sylvester and Amos Williams were to attend East Durham Junior High. The school board found inadequate preparation a good reason for denying reassignment, but until Harris disclosed this to the press, the board kept it secret, because to use that excuse was to admit the truth of what blacks were claiming: the inequality of black and white schools. Members of the DCNA education committee, William A. Clement, Lee B. Fraser, and N. H. Barnett, took turns escorting the younger children to school every day during that first year. Violence had occurred in other places in the South in similar situations, and these men were determined to protect the Durham youngsters as much as possible, although they could, of course, do nothing about the harassment the students were subjected to at school or the humiliation of inadequate preparation.[13]

Children whose applications for transfer were refused turned to the courts for aid. Blacks well understood the role the courts played in giving legal sanction to politicians who favored integration but who didn't dare proceed on their own for fear of losing their constituency. Floyd McKissick, a native of Asheville, a civil rights lawyer in Durham and the first black student of the UNC law school, expressed their point of view: "Go ahead and sue me so I can do it."[14] In 1957 the mothers of Joycelyn McKissick and Elaine Richardson had brought suit to have them reassigned to Durham High School after they had been rejected by the school board. In October 1959 they won their case, and Joycelyn entered Durham High, from which she was graduated in the spring of 1960. A similar suit, which involved many more students denied reassignment, was filed in April 1960: *Warren H. Wheeler by his next friend John Wheeler and others v. the Durham City Board of Education.* Conrad O. Pearson, Floyd McKissick, J. H. Wheeler, and Thurgood Marshall were attorneys for the plaintiffs. The federal court ruled that integration was not required by the 1954 decision but that blacks could not be denied the right to attend any school.[15]

In 1960 a $6 million school bond election was proposed to fund the building of more schools to relieve the overcrowding, especially in black schools. Rencher Harris, backed by the DCNA, refused to support the bond issue unless the school board adopted outright a policy of integration. He knew that additional space and modern equipment would remove incentive and a valid argument for pupil reassignment and thus serve to perpetuate segregation. His tactic failed, however, and the bond issue passed. It was ironic, therefore, that one of the new schools built with the bond money was named for him when it opened in 1967 shortly after his death.[16]

In 1963 a federal court rejected the too gradual desegregation of Durham's schools and ordered a freedom-of-choice plan instead. The ruling was appealed. Meanwhile, in 1963–64 the city school board approved the transfer of well over a hundred black students from all-black schools to predominantly white ones. From that point on desegregation became more rapid, for a federal judge denied the appeal and reaffirmed the freedom-of-choice plan. In 1964 the city school board assigned students according to neighborhood, but transfers were to be allowed by choice unless precluded by limitations of space. This in effect continued separate black and white schools (since neighborhoods were segregated), and while it promised relief for those who utilized the bureaucratic process, it still left to blacks the often intimidating and burdensome initiative.[17] In 1970–71 came court-ordered integration of the schools, and as much racial balance as possible was achieved by pairing black and white schools and creating attendance zones for the two high schools. The city school population had dropped from fifteen thousand in early 1960 to about nine thousand in 1970 because of white flight and the proliferation of private "Christian" academies to avoid integration, and since the city school system was by 1970 predominantly black, integration was no longer an issue. In 1980, when the city school population was 85 percent black, a committee under the city's first black superintendent, Dr. Cleveland Hammonds, studied the city system and the integration question; it recommended that school assignment be only by neighborhood patterns without the option of reassignment. That remained the basis of assignment.[18]

During the years of school desegregation the Durham chapter of the Links had its eye on these vulnerable children. Chartered in 1958 by sixteen women leaders in the black community, among them Dr. Helen Edmonds, who served as president of the national organization in 1970–74, Mrs. Charles C. (Mae) Spaulding, Jr., Mrs. Charles D. (Constance) Watts, Mrs. William A. (Josephine) Clement, and Mrs. Alex M. (Hazel) Rivera, the Links instituted a series of projects to benefit minority children. One such project helped the academically talented who needed extra tutoring or emotional support in adjusting to their new, integrated schools and schoolmates. Another benefited culturally deprived youths. Through the years the Durham Links contributed scholarships and raised funds for sickle-cell anemia research, promoted social justice, and established programs to fight alcohol and drug addiction.[19]

The county schools escaped a desegregation crisis primarily because blacks delayed forcing the issue until several years after the city schools had begun integration, when the level of white anxiety was notably lower. Whites were in no danger of losing their majority, however, even if integration had taken place at once. In 1960 the county system was 71.89 percent white and only 28.11 percent black, with a total of 9,023 students. The negative vote in the referendum on consolidation of the city and county schools in 1960 further reduced white fears. Blacks, ironically, had strongly opposed consolidation because they feared that many black teachers and administrators would lose their jobs in the elimination of positions resulting from a more efficient system. As events turned out, no applications for reassignment were received by the county school board until the summer of 1963. Then a delegation of blacks led by Harold M. Fitts, Jr., appeared at the May meeting to request that the county devise a system for desegregating the schools. The board explained that it had received no requests for reassignment and promised to handle any reasonable ones it was presented. In June it received four applications and granted reassignment to three of them, refusing the fourth only because there was no seventh grade (the one to which the child had just been promoted) in the school to which he wished to be reassigned. Those permitted to transfer from Merrick-Moore High School to Jordan were David Curtis Jones, Roy Anderson, and Arthur McCullen. A year later the board approved twenty-eight requests, rejected five, delayed a decision on one, and approved one conditionally. Late that summer three more black children were given transfers.[20]

In February 1965 the county lawyer explained to the school board members that they must sign a nondiscriminatory statement or else lose federal funds, which then amounted to $175,000 a year. Part of these monies paid for the free lunch program for underprivileged children. All but one member agreed to sign. As a result of a court case, *Clarence Thompson et al. v. Durham County Board of Education et al.,* the county system was required to start desegregating the schools in the 1965–66 school year according to the freedom-of-choice plan. The board worked out a system of gradual integration, beginning with children starting school and those going into grades seven, eight, and ten. The following year the plan applied to those entering grades three, five, nine, and twelve, and the next year for those entering grades two, four, six, and eleven. In 1968–69 freedom of choice applied to all grades.[21] The percentage of black students increased in the county system as federal housing developments were built in the county, but after 1970 some rearrangement of school uses became necessary to maintain better racial balance where assignment by neighborhood (the plan that replaced freedom of choice) resulted in skewed numbers. For example, all the county's sixth grades were consolidated at Bragtown school, and all kindergarten children were assigned to Lakeview school, for both those schools would have been overwhelmingly black if they had remained neighborhood schools. Once having achieved complete integration, the school administration could get on with improving the quality of education in all the schools.[22]

A small drama came out of the school integration struggle that gave hope of future harmony. In 1971 a federally funded two-week program of meetings called Save Our Schools (SOS) was held. At daily sessions citizens could express their views, anxieties, and hostility, and by listening and talking, it was hoped, might arrive at solutions to facilitate integrating the schools without violence. Two unlikely cochairmen from opposing camps were appointed: Claiborne P. Ellis, a utilities serviceman at Duke University and head of the Durham Ku Klux Klan, and Mrs. Ann G. Atwater, a black activist from an Operation Breakthrough neighborhood council. Despite his racist views, Ellis was a basically moral and honest man and a law-abiding citizen. Convinced of the inferiority of the black race, he opposed forced integration and federal intervention. Realizing that if he did not participate in the SOS program the views he represented would not be voiced in that forum, he accepted the cochairmanship and promised to seek solutions in a "fair, honest, and respectful manner."[23]

The unlikely cooperation of the cochairmen and their dramatic contrast caught national attention. Following the charette (the name given to the series of meetings), they were asked to express their diverse views on television and in a documentary film, "Busing: Some Voices from the South," which they then accompanied to various East Coast cities where it was shown to explain their views. Audiences were amazed that Ellis and Atwater could communicate quietly, rationally, and without rancor. In 1972 Ellis could still claim that his views were unchanged, but he was actually undergoing soul-searching and a change of heart. By 1973 he was advocating the unity of black and white workers and trying to get Duke's black maintenance employees to join his union.[24] His communication and cooperation with Ann Atwater had changed his view of blacks.

On the Duke University campus, the struggle for integration in higher education was carried on very quietly behind the scenes. In 1948 the Divinity School students had petitioned for the admission of blacks as day students in their program. President Hollis Edens refused to act on that petition or on two subsequent ones in 1949 and 1951. By 1953 he felt he could mention the matter to the trustees, but he made no recommendation to them until 1954. A few graduate students, he thought, should be admitted, but he realized that the trustees were not yet ready to take that step. A group of faculty led by the provost chose to argue the issue on other than moral grounds, demonstrating how continued segregation would harm the university in faculty and graduate student recruitment, in applications for federal grants and subsidies, and in attracting professional association meetings to Duke. These were arguments with practical considerations that the trustees were bound to concede. In March 1961 they agreed to admit blacks to the graduate and professional schools, and in June 1962 they opened the undergraduate colleges to blacks.[25]

DESEGREGATION OF PUBLIC FACILITIES

School integration was only one aspect of the larger civil rights battle. The fear and friction that it generated, however, contributed to further decline in race relations. By 1957 Rencher Harris became so concerned that he wrote to Mayor E. J. Evans petitioning him to establish a biracial committee to consider problems facing all the citizens. He said, "Where formerly there was trust, there is now mistrust; where formerly there was faith, there is now suspicion; where formerly there was a candid discussion of problems on which there were differences of opinion, there is now silence."[26] Evans acted on the suggestion and established a Committee on Human Relations, of which he appointed the Reverend Warren Carr of Watts Street Baptist Church chairman and Rencher Harris a committee member. The selection of Carr was a good one; unafraid of controversy and eager for social reform, he had been a catalyst in his church for social service, a tradition that his successor, Robert McClernan, continued with conspicuous results. From that congregation came child care for retarded children, which developed into the Association for Retarded Children; the host houses program, free housing for financially strapped families of long-term hospital patients; the rape crisis center; Hassle House, a refuge and help line for drug abusers; and Threshold, a socializing and rehabilitation program for chronic mental patients. Considered a maverick by orthodox Southern Baptists, this church followed northern tradition in an active outreach ministry.[27]

The sit-ins that were so effective in breaking down segregation in restaurants began in 1960. The publicity that attended the sit-in of a group of Agricultural and Technical College students in Greensboro on 1 February 1960 was responsible for all the others that followed. The students, well-dressed, well-behaved, and committed to passive resistance, took seats at the "whites only" lunch counter at Woolworth's on Elm Street and, when refused service, repeated daily their silent but dramatic demonstration of what it meant to be black in the South. Actually, the technique was not new; it had been tried in Durham in August 1957 when the Reverend Douglas E. Moore of Asbury Temple with a few students from NCC entered the white section of the Royal Ice Cream Company store at the corner of Roxboro and Dowd streets and asked for service. When they were refused, they quietly sat down until arrested for trespass.[28]

Following the Greensboro sit-ins, the NAACP chapter at NCC, led by Lacy Streeter, Callis Brown, and other students from Durham Business College, Bull City Barber College, DeShazor's Beauty College, and Hillside High School, took up the effort and organized a boycott of stores with segregated lunch counters: Walgreen's, Woolworth's, and Kress's. During the students' visit to Woolworth's, 8 February 1960, the store refused to serve them and closed the lunch counter. When they moved on to Kress's the manager closed the store. A sit-in at Rose's resulted in the store's removing the counter stools, after which it served black and white together. In February, Martin Luther King, Jr., and Ralph Abernathy addressed a crowd at White Rock Baptist Church, strengthening the students' resolve. In March the students were encouraged by a visit from Roy Wilkins, who spoke to Durham's NAACP chapter. On the advice of McKissick, who not only had earlier participated in the movement but continued to play a large advisory role in its direction, the students organized picket lines for the Carolina and Center theaters (city-owned) and the bus station and petitioned the city for integrated recreational facilities.[29]

Black students had the support not only of the Ministerial Alliance but other local college students and professors who joined them in picketing restaurants and theaters. Careful police behavior, dismissal by judges of trespass charges against those arrested, and the closing of the counters and stores defused the potentially explosive situation. By the end of 1960 progress had been made in integrating retail services in Durham. On 24 March 1961 the NAACP chapter published a list of stores to be boycotted and stores to be patronized, a tactic that succeeded more than once, because by reducing merchants' receipts it produced leverage for negotiation.[30] By the end of 1960 Durham's lunch counters were integrated.

Freedom Highways or Freedom Rides were names given a protest campaign aimed at segregated facilities on highways that filled the summer of 1962. Howard Johnson's restaurant on the highway between Durham and Chapel Hill became the target of repeated sit-ins and demonstrations. During one sit-in there, supported by four thousand people, seven hundred were arrested. It occurred on 12 August 1962, the year in which McKissick organized a chapter of CORE in Durham. Roy Wilkins, executive director of the NAACP, spoke at a rally at Saint Joseph's Church along with James Farmer, the national director of CORE, and leaders from NCC, the local NAACP, and DCNA before proceeding by motorcade to Howard Johnson's and a 45-minute demonstration. The idea of "Freedom Highways" had likewise been tried earlier. In 1947 Jim Peck had first come to Durham on a pioneer "Freedom Ride" in which Floyd McKissick, then a student at NCC, also participated. Peck came again in 1962, at that time assigned to picketing Eckerd's in downtown Durham in the hope of persuading the management to hire blacks in other than menial positions. He was also part of a group that went to the S&W Cafeteria in the Home Insurance Company building on Chapel Hill Street and stood by the steam table until the restaurant closed rather than serve them. Advising the students of the 1962–63 sit-ins, in addition to McKissick, was a small group who had been participants in the 1960 sit-ins: John Edwards, Bruce Baines, Quinton Baker, Joycelyn McKissick, Vivian McCoy, and Walter Riley.[31]

The struggle intensified in 1963. On the night of Mayor Grabarek's election, 18 May, protesters held a rally followed by a march through the city and sit-ins at six eating places. After the arrest of 130 persons, hundreds of people swarmed around the courthouse, where the jail occupied the top floor, expressing sympathy and solidarity with those arrested. The NAACP and CORE announced that thirty days of mass demonstrations would begin on 20 May. It was clear that the protesters would attack on all fronts at once: schools, public accommodations, and fair employment practices. Mayor Wense Grabarek needed all the nerve and aplomb he could summon to deal with the situation, as he did, directly. He went in person, a slight, dapper man, always with a red carnation in his lapel, to a meeting of protesters, one thousand strong, held at Saint Joseph's A.M.E. Church. Habitually soft-spoken and immensely polite, he asked permission to enter and address them. Then, pointing out that by their demonstrations they had informed the community of their deeply felt grievances, he spoke about the danger of racial tension and division and promised to take positive steps to respond to their complaints. Finally, he asked for their support and understanding. Impressed by his coming, his tone, and his words, they accepted his sincerity and promised to halt demonstrations and give the mayor time to act on his promises.[32]

On 23 May 1963 Grabarek set up the Durham Interim Committee (DIC). Two of its eleven members, Asa Spaulding and John Wheeler, were black. He appointed Watts Carr, his opponent in the recent mayoral race, to chair the committee, among whose members were Watts Hill, Jr., Watts Hill, Sr., James Hawkins, and Harvey Rape, a cafeteria owner. Grabarek's mandate to the committee was to "resolve and reconcile" racial differences by trying to find ground for mutual agreement and voluntary acceptance by both sides.[33] Grabarek met repeatedly with McKissick, the students, and the restaurant owners to keep the lines of communication open and to try to reach agreement. On 21 May the Durham Restaurant Association had reaffirmed its segregation policy, although seven eating places had agreed to drop racial barriers immediately. Among these were Tops Drive In, Honey's, and Turnage's. The Interim Committee asked the food service businesses to reconsider their decision and to adopt a policy of serving bona fide customers of any race. As a prod to the restaurateurs and other purveyors of goods and services, more than seven hundred persons, mostly employees of Duke University, took an advertisement that filled a whole page of the Durham *Herald,* in which they pledged to support those merchants operating theaters, stores, hotels, motels, and restaurants who would adopt a policy of "equal treatment to all without regard to race." The Palms restaurant owner was forced to accept integration by Watts Hill, Sr., who threatened to call in a loan from Hill's bank if compliance was refused.[34]

These approaches were productive, for within the next few weeks the Interim Committee reported that many Durham motels, hotels, restaurants, and lunch counters were integrated. Quite voluntarily in June the city also integrated its swimming pools and other municipal facilities, including the public library. By fall, all theaters (except drive-ins) also dropped the color bar, while the Chamber of Commerce and Jaycees decided to open membership to blacks. Grabarek persuaded the city council to adopt the statement that discrimination because of race, color, creed, or national origin was contrary to the constitutional principles and policies of the United States, the city, and the county. Much of this positive response was achieved not only through black pressure but through personal persuasion by the mayor and other Durham leaders, who lobbied conscientiously and tirelessly behind the scenes. Part of Grabarek's success as a middleman was his leverage with both parties: in dealing with blacks the threat of a white backlash, in dealing with whites the threat of black riots and disorders, ironically the same strategy that Governor Hodges had used to delay school integration.[35]

At the same time work was progressing in other sensitive areas. The day after Grabarek's election, the activists had presented the city council a petition asking for more city jobs for blacks and a fair employment practices ordinance to guarantee fair hiring in the private sector. They also presented a list of requests concerning discrimination in employment to the Interim Committee on 24 May 1963. On 28 May the Industrial Education Center announced two areas of training—retail distribution and marketing—in which it would enroll qualified blacks. Many retail businesses pledged themselves to hiring solely on the qualifications of applicants, and, realizing how few blacks had had the opportunity to become qualified, they agreed to work with the Industrial Education Center to develop a training program. Six of Durham's banks, a few insurance companies, and Duke University also announced that qualifications alone, without regard to race, would determine their hiring choices. Industries working on federal contracts were obliged to adopt fair hiring practices to conform to federal law. By the end of 1963 forty-one retail stores, six banks, and three large insurance companies had also done so.[36]

OTHER GRIEVANCES

Although the battle was not yet won—1964 saw a continuation of sit-ins in a few places that held out against integration—at least the streets were peaceful again. To replace the DIC, which had done its job so effectively, Grabarek set up the fifteen-member biracial Committee on Community Relations, headed by Watts Hill, Jr. This was to hear and solve, if possible, further controversies as they arose and to advise the mayor when action was needed. In accomplishing so much so fast, the 1963 protests not surprisingly caused organized resistance. In 1963 the Durham County Citizens Council (DCCC) was formed to counteract the DCNA's influence in politics, to elect segregationists to the county commission and city council, and to keep Watts Hospital segregated. After two poorly attended visits by Governor George Wallace of Alabama, in his campaign for president, the group realized that it could not muster the support it had expected. All the candidates it had endorsed in the 1964 election lost except those that the DCNA had also endorsed. All the DCNA candidates won. After 1968 the DCCC faded out of existence.[37]

Agitation increased after the middle 1960s. Despite agreements, black employment in white businesses had not proceeded far. Discrimination in myriad guises continued. Black neighborhoods endured unpaved and ill-lighted streets, inadequate firefighting equipment, poor recreation facilities, unenforced building and housing codes, unresponsive public agencies, and general frustration. The racial confrontations of the last years of the decade were potentially far more explosive and violent than those that preceded them. College students or young social workers, supported behind the scenes by the "conservative" black business elite and professional groups, employed bolder and more strident attention-getting methods to accomplish what earlier tactics could not.

Operation Breakthrough's neighborhood councils provided the hitherto unrepresented poorest blacks information on how to make their complaints known. Their complaints almost all centered on the problems of housing and the frustrations they experienced with the Housing Authority, the Redevelopment Commission (the agency for urban renewal), and the city Building Inspection Department. The Edgemont neighborhood troubles were only one element in the total housing controversy. The Redevelopment Commission's habit of buying houses and allowing the former owners to continue to occupy them as renters but at rents excessive for substandard housing, or to evict them without supplying equivalent housing, or without demolishing the vacated properties properly angered those affected. Carvie Oldham, the executive director of the Housing Authority, seemed more interested in carrying out its regulations than in listening to the complaints of its tenants. Authoritative and inflexible, he infuriated blacks, who wanted a more responsive hearing and more representation on the governing boards. James Jackson Henderson had been the only black on the authority board for years. They were also tired of negotiating agreements that were not adhered to. Excessive utility charges, poorly maintained grounds and facilities, and unsatisfactory lease agreements added up to poor morale and daily irritations that they felt powerless to cope with.[38]

Howard Fuller, the black organizer and spokesman, after forming an Area Council of representatives of the neighborhood councils, quickly understood that an independent organization would better serve their purpose, and in 1966 he had the United Organizations for Community Improvement (UOCI) chartered. Mrs. Rubye Gattis, who had been chairman of one of the original five councils, was elected president of the new organization, which now included seventeen neighborhood councils. The UOCI helped get poorer blacks registered to vote and transported them to the polls. It encouraged them to attend city council meetings regularly and to protest the lax enforcement of the building code.[39] It encouraged a sense of shared purpose and strengthened their determination to make their complaints known.

They chose the long, hot summer of 1967 to be heard. As protests and black anger mounted, the mayor and council, alarmed that Durham would become another riot-torn Newark, took action to allay tensions. After the Bacon Street housing site march in July, which had left some broken windows downtown and other minor damage, Grabarek met with the protesters and formed an ad hoc committee to provide a forum for discussion with all parties to the controversy. Headed by councilman Eugene Carlton (thus known as the Carlton Committee), the committee was to study each area of complaint thoroughly and make recommendations to the council. The UOCI created a Citizens Action Committee from a cross-section of the black community to draw up a list of grievances, which it submitted to the city council. When the city council's two black members asked for a citywide conference on all the problem areas—housing, education, employment, welfare and health services, youth activities, and crime prevention and control—still another council committee was formed. After several demonstrations turned into near-riots, as white hecklers and racists, spoiling for a fight, confronted the demonstrators, and as lone arsonists repeatedly chose targets at random to vent their anger, the mayor called in the National Guard to prevent further violence. Many meetings were held between the UOCI and various representatives of white committees or agencies, some futile, some productive. Although the Bacon Street hotbox was removed when the Housing Authority purchased the Damar Court Apartments and Duke University graduate student housing, all other points of friction continued to heat up.[40]

The city school board's failure to adopt the Headstart and Neighborhood Youth Corps federal programs in 1966 provoked mass rallies and marches to the Operation Breakthrough and city school administration offices. Fuller addressed a rally at Saint Joseph's Church and helped organize plans for further protests, which were successful in persuading the school board to reverse its decision the following year. Many whites blamed Fuller for black unrest and the stirring up of racial hatred, but his role as constructive leader was defended by both Asa Spaulding, then president of the Mutual, and Watts Hill, Jr. Spaulding wrote, "I doubt seriously that removing Mr. Fuller from the Durham community would be a better cure of its ills than his remaining here as a reminder of its ills until they are cured."[41] Hill, then on the state Board of Education, said, "[Fuller] is the single person most responsible for there not being riots in Durham."[42]

Many small accommodations were made to black demands in that summer of 1967, but the housing issue continued to produce protest, violence, arson, civil disobedience, and fear of general mayhem. The following year proved just a continuation of similar incidents. When the Carlton Committee report was finally made public in the winter of 1968, it included many recommendations to the Housing Authority (but not the replacement of Oldham), the Recreation Department, the Redevelopment Commission, and city agencies. It also recommended the establishment of a permanent Human Relations Commission with an executive director to keep the channels of communication open and continue to work on problem areas as they arose. Three months later the mayor appointed another committee to investigate the need for a Human Relations Commission, provoking Councilman William T. Coman to blunt criticism of the action. Coman, who had served a year on the Carlton Committee and had headed yet another subcommittee investigating grievances, refused to condone further procrastination. "The council knows the need for a human relations commission, and it has failed to act, although $15,000 was made available in the budget for such a commission."[43] But no commission was formed.

The summer of 1968 saw the formation of another black organization to lead the protests. After much preliminary work, the Black Solidarity Committee for Community Improvement (BSCCI) was forged from many groups, presenting a united front of the widest range of representation yet achieved: the DCNA, UOCI, NAACP, and others. The chairman was A. J. Howard Clement III, an executive of North Carolina Mutual, a Durham native, and an articulate leader. This committee drew up a fifteen-page memorandum of demands, which it presented to the Chamber of Commerce and the Merchants Association on 27 July 1968. It also outlined the consequences of inaction, beginning with an economic boycott and, if necessary, progressing to public demonstrations, and finally to civil disobedience. The very next day saw the start of a boycott of Northgate Shopping Center, Model Cleaners, and the Coca-Cola Bottling Company. As time passed, more and more stores were targeted until all but two or three downtown stores were included. The discipline was remarkable and the tactic effective.[44]

The city, badgered by a worried Merchants Association, then headed by William L. Burns, in September 1968 established a Human Relations Commission made up of eight blacks and seven whites and chaired by a black, James Woodward. The black protesters were asked for their minimum conditions for ending the boycott, and they responded with nineteen items, of which four were satisfied by February 1969. Hayti would receive better fire protection, the Recreation Department would hire blacks in upper-level jobs, improve the facilities at W. D. Hill Center, and make use of school facilities for recreation during the summer months. It was claimed that the stores had lost an estimated $900,000 before the boycott ended on 16 February 1969. By that time the merchants had applied sufficient pressure on the chamber and other city groups to satisfy the BSCCI that progress was truly being made. The Chamber of Commerce devised the Matchup program to help find jobs for blacks and actively sought out instances of discrimination, injustice, or exclusion in business and civic affairs in order to eliminate them. In 1969 the OEO awarded a $1 million grant to Durham, part of which was used for United Durham Incorporated (UDI), of which Nathan T. Garrett became president. Two blacks were appointed to vacancies on the Housing Authority (albeit not the two the protesters requested), residents were allowed to participate in decisions for the W. D. Hill center reconstruction, a black was appointed assistant director of the Recreation Department, the Merchants Association chose Henry Hayes, a black, as policeman of the year, and black membership on the school board increased. The results of the two years of protest were significant. All areas of black complaint improved, some more than others, and paved the way for later successes. It is noteworthy, however, that almost all the gains, from school integration to fair employment practices, were achieved not through greater voting influence but through the courts, demonstrations, protests, boycotts, or threats of violence.[45]

BLACK POWER AND BLACK MUSLIMS

Elsewhere in the nation, however, cynicism was replacing hope for participation by blacks in mainstream America and turning the poorest blacks to different and often more extreme solutions. Experience of integration had disappointed and disenchanted many, for changed laws had not changed attitudes. Black power, as exemplified by Stokely Carmichael's faction, represented the wish of blacks to cultivate their own cultural and political unity in order to gain power and to deal with the white majority from a position of strength. A "black is beautiful" philosophy and separatist ambitions began to replace the urgent demands for integration of the earlier years. The Black Muslims (a group that appeared in Durham in 1961), also espoused an anti-integration philosophy. Led by Elijah Muhammad, they gained numbers of followers in the 1950s and 1960s until a power struggle between Muhammad and one of their preachers, Malcolm X, resulted in the latter's assassination in 1965. Basically a puritanical religious movement whose followers eschewed tobacco, alcohol, drugs, and gambling, its aim was to develop a separate society with its own economic foundation and cultural organization. A third group, the Black Panthers (1966), succeeded in stirring up racial animosity and a mood of violence everywhere. Their revolutionary philosophy to achieve what they called black liberation inflamed blacks to more violent acts, exhausted the patience of many sympathetic whites, and caused a backlash from authorities who had to deal with them.

Caught up in the separatist philosophy of the times, Fuller was attracted by Marxist ideology, black cultural nationalism, and the ideas of Malcolm X. He was able to convey his enthusiasm for revolutionary goals to some of the black students at Duke, and eventually in 1969 he made his allegiance very clear by establishing Malcolm X Liberation University in an abandoned warehouse on Pettigrew Street to train blacks to run their own businesses and industries and to develop their own skills and cultural traditions. Fuller urged adoption of a black manifesto demanding five hundred dollars in reparations from every white Christian church and synagogue in the nation as a means of financing his undertaking. The North Carolina Diocese of the Episcopal Church made a large donation to Malcolm X University, which incensed many church members, revealing the stresses and strains as well as the ideological splits in mainstream America as a result of the civil rights movement. The university struggled on without notable success and in 1970 was forced to suspend operation in Durham, whereupon Fuller moved it to Greensboro, where it did not long survive.[46]

After Malcolm X University moved away, a school much more in line with Durham's tradition came into the limelight. Started in 1947 by Lucinda McCauley Harris as a business school, it moved from its Pine Street home in 1970 to a new campus on Fayetteville Road and took the name Durham College. It was accredited as a junior college the following year. The same kind of financial inadequacies immediately beset it, however, and its poor facilities and, what was worse, its poor food upset the entirely black student body. They made their intolerance plain by ripping up the dining room. Nonetheless, one hundred students graduated in 1974. Under its president, James W. Hill, it carried on through the decade with HEW grants and managed to erect a few new buildings. Muhammad Ali spoke at the dedication of a new athletic facility in 1977. Losing its junior college accreditation, however, was a death blow, and the college closed in 1980.[47]

PROTEST AT DUKE UNIVERSITY

Whether or not Howard Fuller and Ben Ruffin were responsible for the black student agitation at Duke in 1968 and 1969 is now debatable, but these effective leaders and role models for numerous young activists undoubtedly abetted its occurrence. The black students at Duke University, who numbered fifty to sixty in those years, were involved in two crises, one a sit-in at the president's house and campus vigil after the assassination of Martin Luther King, Jr., in 1968, and the next year the take-over of Allen Building, the administrative center of the university. Although the assassination was the spark that set the students in action in 1968, they were also influenced by the long-smoldering disagreement between Duke's administration and its maintenance staff, many of whom were grossly underpaid blacks, concerning hours, wages, and union representation. Added to this was a general feeling of indifference and insensitivity on the campus to the blacks' situation, symbolized by the president's membership in the segregated Hope Valley Country Club. Stimulated by the assassination to press for changes, the black students and their white sympathizers decided on a protest march. The administration, in constant touch with the city officials in this time of uncertainty, was afraid what effect a march downtown might have on other blacks, whose anger was already at the boiling point. At first, the protesters, among whom were many whites, decided to march in Hope Valley but switched instead to Duke Forest, an area in which most of the faculty, including the president, lived. When the marchers found themselves outside President Douglas M. Knight's house as rain began to fall, they decided to make their demands in person and were admitted. There they stayed, waiting for satisfaction, unwilling to leave for two days.[48]

Finally, feeling that the most effective tactic was to leave the president's house, they moved back to the campus, where a thousand students camped that night on the lawn in the main quadrangle, and in the four days that followed were joined by many more.[49] They were addressed by militant young faculty members, sent supportive telegrams by Robert F. Kennedy and Nelson Rockefeller, and encouraged by the activist poet John Beecher. On Monday, 8 April, unionized members of the maintenance staff went on strike, and the protesters, showing admirable discipline, made the workers' goals their own. In the end the university agreed to a minimum wage of $1.60 an hour by 1969 and mechanisms for future communication: a Duke University Non-academic Employees Council and a Duke University Employee Relations Advisory Committee. The trustees refused to give in on union recognition and collective bargaining.[50]

The spirit of the following year's protest was entirely different; it stemmed from the black students' sense of alienation. On 13 February 1969, just as the university offices were opening for the day, a group of black students took over Allen Building; they carried in iron pipes and containers they claimed were filled with gasoline, with which they later threatened to destroy university records. After escorting the secretaries and officers out of the building and barricading the doors, they presented by telephone a list of thirteen demands to the administration, among which were the establishment of a black studies program, a black dormitory, and increased black enrollment. Sympathizing students stood outside the building, forming a human barricade for those inside. Fuller and Ruffin visited the students to advise them and support their efforts. Ironically, President Knight was that very day in New York, trying to get funding for a black studies program, but he returned immediately when notified of the crisis and in the late afternoon held a faculty meeting to inform the teaching staff of the situation. Meanwhile, Provost Marcus Hobbs and others in the administration had been meeting continuously and in midafternoon presented the students with answers to their demands, revealing almost total acquiescence. But the administration required acceptance or refusal of the terms within an hour and evacuation of Allen building or police would be called in and all students engaged in the takeover would be accused of trespassing and subject to dismissal.[51]

The occupying students were angered by the time limit attached to the proposal, for they had been waiting for over two years for the administration to address their demands, but it is not clear why they did not find the administration's terms acceptable. It is clear that the police had already been alerted and began to come on campus near the close of the specified hour. During the same hour the faculty meeting on East Campus produced only irritation and division, some professors suspecting that the meeting had been only a diversionary tactic while the hour for the police's arrival ran out. Knight's answers to their questions and his performance as a whole were judged weak and unsatisfactory by censurers and sympathizers of the protesters alike. Just before the police reached the main quadrangle, the black students had been persuaded by their leaders and the administration to leave Allen Building. A confrontation between student spectators and the police, who resorted to tear gas, was therefore both anticlimactic and unnecessary. Fortunately, the university records remained unharmed, and though there was minor vandalism inside the building, no irreparable damage was done. The students involved were dealt with lightly, and in the face of trustee and alumni displeasure at the leniency, Knight resigned six weeks later. His view of the situation was close to the mark: that the university was in danger of being torn apart by "mob tyranny masquerading as academic freedom and suppression of thought masquerading as patriotism."[52]

WOMEN IN ACTION

The tumultuous 1960s were not totally void of interracial goodwill and some notable achievements. Men and women of stature of both races quietly exerted their influence, leading the way to rapport and color blindness, which Rencher Harris called a spiritual blessing. When Asa Spaulding retired as president of the Mutual, for example, the Chamber of Commerce gave him its 1967 Civic Award and a standing ovation. Its warmth encouraged him to run for and win a seat on the county commission, the first black to do so. In that year as well Dr. Reginald Hawkins became the first black to run for governor of the state. In 1972 James M. Rogers, a teacher at Durham High School, won the chamber's Distinguished Achievement Award in recognition of his having been designated National Teacher of the Year.[53]

Another distinguished black citizen, Elna Spaulding, Asa Spaulding's wife, pioneered a new field in race relations. In 1968 she attended a national conference for women, sponsored by *McCall's* magazine, to discuss ways in which women might cooperate to prevent the violence that had invaded the civil rights movement and to facilitate peaceful social change. She returned to Durham determined to nurture the same spirit of interracial cooperation and to put into action the solutions they had discussed. Instead of confining her efforts to her own acquaintances, she advertised a meeting in the papers and called for women who shared her desires to attend. Expecting a few dozen to turn up, she was overwhelmed by the hundred who appeared at the YWCA to join her on 4 September, 1968. They came from all walks of life and both races. An organization called Women in Action for the Prevention of Violence was born. Mrs. Spaulding was fittingly elected president. The new members met in informal groups in one another's houses to become acquainted, establish mutual trust and understanding, and share anxieties and problems related to schoolchildren in Durham. The experience of meeting as equals was a new one for many of the women, and a biracial women's group was a unique approach to the social problems in Durham at that time. Their first goal was to help persuade the mayor to establish a Human Relations Commission, which was soon achieved. Their next assignment was to mediate between the Black Solidarity group and the Merchants Association. In the fall of 1970, when the schools were first completely integrated, they persuaded the school systems to hold an open house at each school with all the administrators and teachers present to greet the students and their parents, answer questions, open communications, and create trust. The schools had never opened more smoothly. Women in Action continued to be a catalyst for cooperation and a resource when problems occurred. Later, they set up headquarters at the Urban Ministries building, along with a variety of other social services, and maintained a helpline for women in crisis. In 1974 Mrs. Spaulding became the first woman county commissioner.[54]

CREST STREET

How much the civil rights movement had accomplished in giving blacks confidence and skill in standing up for themselves and in teaching whites to respect their rights was demonstrated in 1978. The state Highway Department, never notable for its human sensitivity, developed plans for a new road directly through a black community. The proposed route for the expressway continuation, the juggernaut that had flattened Hayti, was planned to obliterate the Crest Street neighborhood (the southern section of the former Hickstown). The biggest names in the business community, which included representatives of the Chamber of Commerce, the Merchants Association, and the Central Carolina Bank, turned out at a public hearing to express their support for the new road. It was essential, they felt, to solve the traffic tie-ups and bottlenecks in West Durham. The controversial route polarized the citizenry for and against the road. So numerous were those who wished to be heard on both sides that the hearings had to be continued at subsequent meetings, and blacks found many whites siding with them and critical of the state, which would destroy still another part of black Durham—an old, well-established community with a school, a church almost a century old, a grocery, and thickly clustered homes, small and deteriorated though many of them were, on an eroded hillside. The Crest Street community, where many residents had lived all their lives, was within walking distance of Duke and Veterans hospitals and Erwin Mills (then Burlington Industries), the employers of most of its residents.[55]

After the strident hearings, the upshot of the controversy was a compromise. The highway would be built, but the community would be preserved, though partially relocated and rebuilt. The school and church would remain, the classrooms reconstructed as twenty-one apartments for the elderly and the auditorium as a community center; some houses would be moved and improved while the remainder would be demolished and new ones built for those residents who wished to remain in the neighborhood. In addition, a site would be made for a new store, and the former graveyard would become a park with recreational facilities. Paved and guttered streets would replace the gullied and gutted dirt roads. The Durham Housing Authority and the City of Durham would share the costs with the Department of Transportation, a sum figured at close to $8 million. The state would of course pay for the highway construction (not included in the above figure) as well as for the removal and reinterment of remains from more than a thousand graves in the community cemetery. There would be no obliteration like Hayti's. The Crest Street neighborhood would survive.[56] That much at least the government had learned.

Rounding Out a Century, 1960–1981

20

T HE LESSONS OF THE 1960S AND 1970S concerned more than civil rights. They contributed as well to an improved understanding of women's rights, environmental and historic preservation, and the value of cultural and artistic activities. Durham shared this march toward enlightenment. In the arts particularly, it showed marked vitality. Progress was partly due to the discovery that cultivation of the arts was good business and the consequent support that the business community supplied. Social problems, however, had the spotlight. The Vietnam War generated passion and resistance through half the 1970s before coming to an inglorious close, leaving an enormously increased drug problem nationwide. The plight of Durham's disadvantaged grew worse as well—the ill, the illiterate, the addicted, the alienated, and the destitute—a situation it shared with the nation. Compassion to deal with these problems, however, was not lacking. The Volunteer Services Bureau and Durham Congregations in Action together with the Department of Social Services mobilized the abundant charitable impulses of Durham's people to supplement dwindling public moneys for these needs. A Chamber of Commerce poll taken in 1969–70 disclosed that instead of its traditional approach to economic development, over 90 percent of its members felt that the chamber should concern itself more with problem areas of daily life—schools, crime and juvenile delinquency, traffic congestion, and inadequate airport facilities—because these factors very largely influenced success in the recruitment of business and industry.[1]

POLITICS

Local politics of the 1960s and 1970s also became more complex and, in a way, more interesting, not only because of the social ferment but because the continuing switch of erstwhile Democrats to the Republican party added competition to elections, more discussion of issues, and more clear-cut choices between candidates.

Rising general involvement in political matters was evidenced in the League of Women Voters "Meet the Candidates" meetings, which had originally attracted very meager audiences but which grew in this period into standing room only events.

When Richard Nixon was elected president in 1968 many Republican candidates were carried into office on his coattails, but in the South the third party of Alabama's ex-Governor Wallace attracted voters who might otherwise have voted Republican. Blacks, who had traditionally adhered to the party of Lincoln until switching en masse to Roosevelt in 1936, began again to vote Republican, particularly the well-to-do, whose interests in big business coincided with those of the national party. In 1960 Asa Spaulding had started the Durham Negro Voters League to oppose the Democratic DCNA. Unanimity among blacks was harder to forge as their participation in political life grew, and gradations of political opinion developed among them. In 1972 the Concerned Citizens Forum, another black Republican organization, was formed. Its secretary was Helen G. Edmonds, a respected historian and professor at NCCU, who had been the first black woman to second the nomination of a presidential candidate when she endorsed Eisenhower in 1956. In 1972 Durham County had 56,745 registered Democrats and 10,405 Republicans. As Nixon won reelection, he again carried Republican candidates into office; this time many of them were in the South. Governor Holshouser became North Carolina's first Republican governor since Daniel L. Russell was elected in 1896. The reactionary Jesse Helms won a seat in the Senate, defeating Durham's own Nicholas Galifianakis, who had served two terms in the House of Representatives. That year, however, saw the DCNA's Democratic candidate H. M. "Mickey" Michaux, Jr., a Durham lawyer, become Durham County's first black representative in the state legislature. In 1972 the Democratic party, realizing the strength of its adversary, buried internal strife by electing as county chairman Lavonia Allison, a black woman and professor at NCCU.[2]

Diversity and competition grew. Three black candidates ran for seats on the city council in 1973—Ralph A. Hunt, Benjamin S. Ruffin, and Josephine Turner—though only Hunt won election. That year the Watergate debacle dampened Republican hopes, causing a definite lull in the Republican swing. In 1974 the Durham County Political Action Committee for Education (PACE) joined the scene, a frankly special-interest group intent on pressing teachers' concerns. In 1975 Susie Sharp became the first woman chief justice of the state Supreme Court, reflecting the new latitude for women's talents. The liberals had formed the Durham Voters' Alliance in the 1960s, and their viewpoint was beginning to prevail more frequently; the liberal effort to have school board members popularly elected rather than appointed, for example, succeeded in 1975, a year when the group was also successful in electing liberal council members. A decided trend to the left in the city elections in 1977 was reversed two years later when another conservative cycle began. A group called Citizens for Durham's Future emerged that year, supported by ex-mayor James Hawkins. Its backing of Harry Rodenhizer helped win his election as mayor. Thus the oscillations continued with the political power tilting first one way, then another, while significant action was often hamstrung by fragmentation. Every mayor found to his regret that what Durham needed was "more community unity; more trust and less suspicion; more pulling together and less pulling apart," as Asa Spaulding declared when he campaigned unsuccessfully for mayor in 1971.[3]

Durham County's representatives in the General Assembly proved to be effective leaders. Notable among these men were Willis Whichard, a Durham native, who served in both houses before election to the state Supreme Court bench, George W. Miller, Jr., Kenneth C. Royall, Jr., and Michaux, all of whom consistently pulled their oars if not always in unison. Perhaps the most far-reaching achievement of Durham's members was during the 1978–79 term, when Whichard was a senator, and Kenneth B. Spaulding, Miller, and Paul Pulley were representatives. In that session the legislature passed the bill to establish the North Carolina School of Science and Mathematics in Durham. Success was not due to the politicians alone, but to the cooperation of the Hill family and local work behind the scenes. Another pioneering educational concept, credited to Terry Sanford, the school created enormous interest among the counties competing for it. Durham County's offer of the twenty-seven-acre site of the old Watts Hospital and its fifteen buildings, amounting to an $8 million gift, was the winning bid. Opened in 1980 and capable of accommodating three hundred students, the free school provided an elite education for schoolchildren talented in these subjects. Besides the exceptional physical facilities, the educational climate supplied by the Research Triangle and surrounding universities, and the geographical position in the middle of the state were undoubtedly determining factors in Durham's favor.[4]

ENVIRONMENTAL CONCERNS

Durham County won a victory on the environmental front as well. In a classic case of grassroots power successfully pitted against a bureaucracy, the Eno River controversy consumed a small but vocal sector of Durham's population for seven years. The problem stemmed from plans developed by the Research Triangle Regional Planning Commission for the region's future water resources. Among the long-range solutions was the damming of the Eno River to supplement the Flat River reservoir as a water source for the City of Durham. The city accepted the plan without question; the Eno River had been the city's first water source in the 1890s. The city was propelled into land purchase for a new Eno reservoir sooner than expected when in 1966 a proposed housing development near the old pump station threatened the long-range plan. The city quickly bought the land in question and within a year or two began a concerted effort to purchase other land along the river that would be flooded by the projected dam, whose location was to be two hundred feet west of Guess Road. Much of the purchase money came from the Department of Housing and Urban Development (HUD) with the stipulation that it was to be used for open space purposes, recreation among them. At first no one seriously objected to the prospect of another large recreation area like Lake Michie for fishermen and boaters until a few landowners whose riverfront lands would be lost to the new lake banded together in 1966 to fight the project.[5]

The opposition that this group was able to build rode the crest of the worldwide environmental revolution that in the 1950s had acquired a new life and new disciples in response to the population explosion, technological and chemical advances, and developmental pressures of the postwar years. Scientific studies revealed the damage to nature and wildlife, water and soil, and to whole ecosystems from new pesticides used in farming and from massive topographical changes caused by new bridges, dams, roads, housing developments, and industries with their toxic wastes. As natural resources were depleted on commercially owned land, private interests eyed enviously the huge reserves of timber and minerals in the national parks. Thoroughly alarmed, national environmental organizations mobilized their forces to acquaint the public with what was happening in the country. Rachel Carson's *Silent Spring,* which appeared in 1962 and proved the grave threats of air, water, and soil pollution, shocked a large number of people into awareness and action. The federal government learned along with the public of the planetary crisis: natural resources were not inexhaustible, and technological advances had put into man's hands the means to destroy his world and himself with it. The list of endangered species of flora and fauna grew ever longer. Immediate measures were vital. Earth Day in April 1970 marked the beginning of a battle to halt the world march to self-destruction that man's ingenuity and arrogance had led. In 1970 Congress passed the Environmental Protection Act, which created the Environmental Protection Agency (EPA) and the Council on Environmental Quality. The state, anticipating the federal act, passed substantial legislation in 1969 to control coastal estuaries and air pollution. It was no coincidence that the battle for the Eno River came at just this time. Water was an endangered resource, as was the other resource that figured in the Eno controversy, identified by a ninety-year-old landowner on the river, Grover Cleveland Shaw: "They aren't making any more land."[6]

Led by the indomitable, articulate, and deceptively soft-spoken Margaret Rodger Nygard, a transplanted Britisher, the small group of Eno landowners recruited sympathizers in their effort to preserve a natural resource close to the city in its wild and free state. Its woods and banks alive with wildflowers, deer, possum, beaver, fox, and even turkey, the Eno River valley was still primarily untouched by development, although dangerously close to the spreading city. For city officials who had believed Durham's future water needs were solved, and who faced in the late 1960s many rather different imminently serious crises, the outcry from the Association for the Preservation of the Eno River Valley (chartered 1970) was only a nettling distraction.

The group at first floundered in political inexperience and made its personal pleas to deaf ears, but Mrs. Nygard developed a shrewd political sense and began to utilize many avenues to achieve her purpose. After first publicly questioning the choice of the Eno as Durham's prime water supply by casting doubt on the published figures for its projected water yield, the group lobbied to change the city's priorities so that it would tap alternate sources first. The group won its first significant advantage when Pearson Stewart, then head of the Regional Planning Commission, rearranged that body's priorities in a published report in 1968, promoting both another dam on the Flat River and a dam on the Little River before recourse to a dam on the Eno River. The group also won the support of the local press, gained members from all sections of Durham and Orange counties, and constantly kept the issue before the public. The association waged a sophisticated educational campaign, acquainting the public with the river's historical and natural resources—it led winter and spring hikes and seasonal rafting trips that ended in free refreshments around warming bonfires; gave slide shows with musical accompaniment; held photographic contests portraying river scenes; and sold annual calendars filled with local lore—to muster wide local support.

The association also benefited from the help and advice of the North Carolina Conservation Council, the Wildlife Federation, and the Nature Conservancy. The winning strategy was the concept developed in 1966 of a linear state park along a twenty-mile stretch of the Eno River, running from east of Hillsborough on both banks of the Eno River to its confluence with the Flat River, an area that would encompass all the land already owned by the city as well as much more. In response to the association's plan for a park, Mayor Grabarek, a master of politesse and political know-how, hoping to defuse the association's power, announced a plan the following year for a city park in the area between Guess and Roxboro roads. This, of course, would not preserve the Eno from a dam or its banks from submersion, and the association was unappeased.[7]

Two state government officials in Governor Robert Scott's administration (1969–73) had ambitions for the state park system that played into the association's hands. James S. Harrington, secretary of Conservation and Development, and Dr. Arthur Cooper, his deputy, very much wanted to enlarge the state parks system and were particularly aware of the need for parks near urban areas. They were receptive, therefore, to the concept that the association presented. They also recognized that they needed the help of the Nature Conservancy (a national organization that bought and held endangered lands until permanent solutions could be found for their preservation) in the overall acquisition of park lands to allow the state to move quickly and flexibly, and they hoped to bring the organization to the state. When the Eno River Association through its own initiative became the Nature Conservancy's first project in North Carolina, it acquired stature in state eyes and was seriously listened to. In persuading the state to adopt its imaginative plan, the association had the help of two key officials, both Durham residents: Thomas Ellis, superintendent of State Parks, and Thomas Hampton, chairman of the State Parks Commission. From time to time donations of land for a park along the river kept up the association's spirits and zeal.[8]

When the state conceded that a park near an urban center with the expected growth of Durham would be an important addition to its system, the association's battle was won. The state proposed to buy from the city all the land it had already acquired for the dam. The city was able to acquiesce gracefully in the higher power's plan through two fortuitous discoveries. One was that the original figures of the Army Corps of Engineers estimations of river flow were grossly inaccurate, as the association had contended; the second discovery, by Larry Amick, the city budget director, was that the Nello Teer Company quarry, a hundred yards from the Eno River east of Roxboro Road, would be completely mined by the year 2000 and would then be available for storing as much water as a dam on the Eno and at considerably less cost. Seven years after the battle began, the city abandoned its intended dam and accepted Amick's alternative. With the sale of city lands to the state the Eno River State Park was born.[9]

Incidental to the major battle, the association fought a short skirmish in 1969–70 over the site of an old gristmill, miller's house, and mill owner's farmhouse on the banks of the Eno at Roxboro Road. The cause had already been taken up by a few perceptive individuals acting alone, particularly Frank DePasquale, an architect who lived in the neighborhood. Ervin Industries, community and home-builders, had acquired ownership of seven hundred acres on the river abutting both sides of Roxboro Road. They planned a shopping center and large residential area on the east side, while reserving the west side for office buildings and condominiums. In anticipation of the changes, strip commercial development had already begun, threatening to destroy the natural beauty of the residential area. When Ervin Industries bulldozers were on the site and about to demolish the farmhouse, the Eno River Association halted the operation by calling for an environmental impact statement. Such a statement could be requested for any project involving federal funds that threatened to destroy areas of natural or historical value. Minute examinations of the sites and their merits then had to be made and the results weighed against the value of the proposed changes. Ervin Industries was not prepared for the delay or the public hassle and privately reached an agreement to sell the site on the west side of Roxboro Road to the city.[10]

The result was West Point on the Eno, a city park which comprised the land Grabarek had already promised as a park as well as the thirty acres bought from Ervin Industries and additional land either donated or bought with city or federal money. The park became a substantial public resource with both natural and historical value. The city established Friends of West Point, Inc., appointed William T. Coman its chairman, and created committees with members drawn from a variety of city and county organizations to undertake the multiple tasks of creating a park. Public and private money and volunteer labor built a new stone foundation for the mill. Mill machinery, moved by volunteers of the Eno Association, came from an old mill in Stuart, Virginia, donated by the owners. The Kiwanis Club paid for roofing the reconstructed mill and building the chimney with bricks donated by Southgate Jones from the recently demolished Thomas D. Jones mansion on Chapel Hill Street. The Junior League, with some help in funding and services from the city, took on the entire reconstruction and decoration of the McCown-Mangum house; the Board of Realtors supplied funds and volunteers for the erection of a picnic shelter; garden clubs planted gardens and landscaped the restored homeplace; the Nello Teer Company hauled tons of dirt free to the site; and I. Harding Hughes, the city manager, who had borne the brunt of the Eno Association's battering for years, ironically was able to build a dam on the river at last. He pitched into the restoration of the mill and put into the city budget the munificent sum of $200,000 to build a dam for a millpond and to divert the water into the millstream. The old buildings represented Durham's past through two hundred years; the park gave the public miles of unspoiled forest along a wild and free stream. Central to the interpretation of the complex, however, beside the serene millpond with its ducks and fishermen, was the reconstructed mill, which demonstrated how an early industrial operation functioned and thereby created with its myriad services a community center for a rural population.[11]

In the 1970s another dam proposal stirred up a different group of Durham County residents. The problem of a water supply for Raleigh was becoming acute as that city, too, grew enormously. The Neuse River was Raleigh's only large water resource, and something had to be done to increase its impoundment. The Army Corps of Engineers had planned a large dam on the Neuse to form what they called Falls of the Neuse Reservoir. The western portions of the reservoir would affect land on both the Eno and Flat rivers, thus involving Durham County. In 1972, as land for the project was being bought up, resistance grew from landowners and environmentalists alike. While the strongest protest came from Wake County residents, who were most injured, Durham County citizens complained as well. The loss of the most fertile crop and forest land in the three counties of Granville, Wake, and Durham and the destruction of wildlife habitats, amounting in all to 43,000 acres, seemed a high price to pay; but the need for water outweighed all other considerations. After bureaucratic delays of all sorts, the dam was built and the reservoir became a reality.[12]

WOMEN'S LIBERATION

When beatniks, flower children, and hippies were successively populating the street scene in surplus army and castoff clothing, beads, beards, and headbands, and civil rights, anti-Vietnam, and gay rights activists were shaking the assumptions underpinning the status quo, women joined in the cacophony of complaint. Women's liberation, the woman's movement under new guise and leadership, found itself with powerful arguments and the agents to plead them. Betty Friedan's *The Feminine Mystique* (1963) was only the first in an outpouring of polemics by militant feminists, articulate and often angry, on the status of women in the modern world. Still living under the disabilities of antiquated laws and outgrown traditions, and political, economic, and social handicaps, modern, middle-class American women did not hesitate to speak their minds. Strident, at times abrasive, and in some ways counterproductive, they nevertheless accomplished much in explaining to other women as much as to men the complex web of discrimination against women, often subtle and hard to recognize, in the tightly woven fabric of American culture.

Governor Terry Sanford established the Governor's Commission on the Status of Women in 1963 and appointed a Duke history professor, Anne Firor Scott, to head it. A report of the commission's findings was completed the following year and covered women's employment, education, health, welfare, and family and community roles. It also identified their problems and the private and public policy changes necessary to address them. A decade later, during the administration of Governor James E. Holshouser, Jr., another committee reexamined the problems and found some of the same and some different areas of concern. Employment practices and inequities in the law were still stumbling blocks, but social services, such as the need for rape crisis centers, were recommended for the first time. Women's bid for independence had triggered an increase in violence against them by men who perceived themselves threatened and hostile. Changes in the handling of rape cases by police and courts were also needed to provide victims with sympathy and support in place of suspicion and the presumption of complicity in the crime.[13]

The state actually lagged behind society in recognizing these problems. Many places had already seen the need and tried to meet it. In the early 1970s an informal women's group, made up of Duke students and employees and young wives and mothers, took up the topic of rape in one of their meetings because of a recent case on the campus. Led by Shirley Hanks Borstelmann and Doranne Meny, they resolved to do something about helping the victims. With the aid of volunteers, they set up a rape crisis telephone line in the home of one of the group, taking turns on duty. The kind of help they gave ranged from the therapy of a sympathetic ear to taking the victims to the hospital, or going to court with them. They lectured to church groups and professional clubs and health care personnel. One of their most frustrating battles was to persuade the local newspapers not to print the names of victims, for the shame and pain of publicity prevented the reporting of many such crimes to the police. The Durham police department was cooperative and supportive.[14]

After 1976, battered women, victims of domestic violence, a type of crime that formerly went unreported or at least unacknowledged by the police and courts, received similar attention. Simultaneously in Chapel Hill and Durham, those concerned about the crime got together to learn what they might do. The Chapel Hill group was made up largely of UNC professionals in research, mental health, and teaching, while the Durham group, led by Constance Renz, a graduate student, who had first brought the problem to YWCA members, comprised social service and legal aid workers as well as feminist activists and a few victims. The two groups merged as the Orange-Durham Coalition for Battered Women and in 1977 received a grant from the state Council on the Status of Women to fund a crisis telephone line, which later evolved into Helpline, run by an executive director and volunteers.[15]

The YWCA provided succor in all manner of ways for those caught in the riptides of social change, breaking out of its old image to answer the new needs of women. It sheltered the Women's Resource Center (1973) with a large library; a medical self-help program for women, with referral information about doctors responsive to their medical problems; the Battered Women's Coalition; Rape Crisis Center; TALF (Triangle Area Lesbian Feminists); and NOW.[16]

Like the parallel movement for black civil rights, women's liberation in Durham was not as vociferous or threatening to the status quo as in other places. Although the National Organization for Women (NOW) was formed in 1966, the Chapel Hill-Durham chapter was not organized until 1971 and never received the wide support it expected. The members tended to be comparatively young women and frequently only temporary residents, many of whom had experienced firsthand the disabilities that women labored under. Pat Smith, Sue Nelson, Judy McNeil, Marlyene Kilbey (who became a national officer in NOW), Jeannette Stokes, a student in the Duke Divinity School, Carole De Saram, and Harriet Hopkins were among the NOW supporters in Durham. Determined to effect reform on a wide front, NOW members first concerned themselves with the economic problems of women forced to earn their own living. These included child care, credit, and age and sex discrimination in the workplace.[17]

After the United States Congress in 1972 approved the Equal Rights Amendment, which would guarantee equal rights to all citizens regardless of sex, NOW chapters countrywide made its adoption by the states their main objective. In 1973 a sufficient number of women had joined NOW to divide the joint Chapel Hill-Durham group into separate chapters. Other groups—the League of Women Voters and professional women's clubs, Common Cause, the American Civil Liberties Union, the North Carolina Council of Churches, and the AFL-CIO, for example—joined with NOW in creating a state coalition to lobby for the amendment, ERA United. Gail Bradley, a prominent leader in the Durham and state leagues, was vice-president for public relations. Despite intense lobbying and strong support from the Piedmont, the enduringly conservative cast of the state's majority prevented ERA's adoption although it was presented in six biennial legislatures and lost by only a few votes in 1977. In 1971 the league, through its lobbyist Ruth Mary Meyer, persuaded state Senator Hargrove Bowles and Durham Representative Willis Whichard to introduce bills that would ratify the Nineteenth Amendment (Woman Suffrage) some fifty years after the fact. The league hoped that the legislators would recognize an analogy in the two situations and, taking a lesson from history, pass ERA with other progressive states. While both houses passed the Nineteenth Amendment without murmur and with some embarrassment, the lesson was not learned.[18]

The focus of the national NOW—on abortion reform, government-subsidized child care centers, equal pay for women, the removal of legal and social barriers to education, political influence, and economic power for women—while it covered all classes was principally on the economically disadvantaged. Many older Durham women, well-educated professionals, were not in sympathy with the confrontational tactics of NOW's approach. Therefore, in 1974, under the leadership of Betty Wiser of Raleigh (later a member of the state legislature), they formed a state chapter of the Women's Equity Action League (WEAL), an organization that appealed more to middle-class women through its rational, even-tempered, bi-gender approach. While most of its members were in Durham, it also included a few from Chapel Hill and Raleigh. Among its most active Durham members were David and Gail Bradley, Anneliesse Markus Kennedy, Elaine Martin, Marilyn Bentov, and Alice Greenlaw. During its short life it gave support to the ERA effort and effected local change—for example the inclusion of both husbands' and wives' names in telephone book listing.[19]

The same social conventions that limited women's freedom restricted men, just as slavery had enslaved masters as well as slaves. The concept of separate roles for men and women, notions of acceptable behavior, and appropriate kinds of work, and standards of achievement peculiar to each sex came under attack from the women's liberation movement. Obviously, one source for the inculcation of these norms was the education to which children were exposed at an early age. Amanda Mackay Smith, who came to Durham in 1972 and became an active member of NOW, WEAL, the Women's Political Caucus, and the YWCA, persuaded the state Board of Education to institute a program for teachers to examine their attitudes and teaching materials to see how they might reflect sex biases. She set up a program called New Pioneers, for which she traveled from county to county teaching teachers, sensitizing them to the subtle ways in which society fostered stereotyped conceptions and choices in its children. But eradicating sexism from the schools proved very slow work; while some counties were responsive to the new approach, were careful in the selection of schoolbooks, and made an effort to encourage equal treatment for its students, Durham County proved almost intractable.[20]

The changes that came about from all these efforts nationwide were many, but a conjunction of factors abetted women: the climate of protest and reform of every sort, the introduction of the birth control pill, and the Supreme Court ruling on the right of abortion, the two latter fundamental to women's sexual liberation. The ground that women gained became patent in higher education (particularly in the professions); in business and the workplace generally; in legislation concerning property, marriage, divorce, and inheritance; in sexual behavior and social matters. There were also losses to be recorded, notably the deterioration of the family, seen in the large increases in the number of divorces, abortions, illegitimate births, and emotionally disturbed children.

Just before the beginning of the women's liberation movement, the women's clubs of Durham received a gift from a man who would have been amazed by the direction their efforts would take. When John Sprunt Hill died in 1961, he left his magnificent Spanish Colonial Revival house on Duke Street as a memorial to his wife, Annie Watts Hill, and gave the use of it to the women of Durham. He had been impressed by his wife's dedication to the community and the service that she and women like her so freely gave (she had been a charter member of the Red Cross and the YWCA and the founder of the Durham chapter of the Needlework Guild), and he recognized their need of a place to meet. The Annie Watts Hill Foundation that his will established for the governance of the trust and the maintenance of the house specified only that the groups who used it should be nonpolitical and nonsectarian. It was a typically chivalrous gesture on his part and timely recognition of the role that women had played almost from the start in civilizing Durham. Hill House, coming as it did in the early 1960s, represented both the passing of an old order and the coming of a new.[21]

SOCIAL WORK

As more women entered the work force by choice or necessity, they were drained from the pool of community volunteers. Social concerns generated in the 1960s and 1970s, however, attracted a new source of workers: men, young and old. Retirees carried much of the load formerly borne by women of all ages, and men felt as much committed to serving society as women ever had. The need for them unfortunately grew ever greater. The number of families living in poverty, of black men unemployed, of women with young children in need of support, of mentally ill and alcohol and drug addicts—all had risen. Of this large group more and more slipped between the life nets that government had devised and were left to charity to save. Congregations in Action, a coalition of four downtown churches, came to the rescue with a series of social programs staffed by volunteers. Founded in the early 1970s, the coalition began by serving the needs of the elderly in the Oldham Towers high-rise apartment house, which housed many of those displaced by urban renewal. Unaccustomed to apartment living, many of the residents found themselves for the first time isolated from their accustomed neighborhoods and without gardens in which to grow a few flowers or vegetables, without house pets for company, without friends to drop in for a chat, without the spiritual and social support of their neighborhood churches. Members of Saint Philip's, First Baptist, Trinity Methodist, and First Presbyterian churches along with the Junior League devised ways to help them. Congregations in Action soon expanded its focus to include the Liberty Street Housing Project (another product of urban renewal), providing there a summer recreation program. As volunteers increased, their programs grew. By 1976 forty or more churches had joined the effort.[22]

In that year Nancy Laszlo, then president of Congregations in Action, set up and headed for five years the Meals on Wheels program, a project that had been successfully tried in other parts of the nation. By 1987 it served 250 hot meals to shut-ins daily. A soup kitchen, originally started by Saint Philip's Church, provided one hot meal a day for the homeless and destitute, originally in its own parish house, but after 1986 in the Urban Ministries building, a structure built to house a variety of social programs, including those of Congregations in Action. In winter it was used as a shelter for street people (a nationwide phenomenon of the 1970s and 1980s), a program supervised by the Presbyterian Council. The Methodists established a clothing cupboard, also housed in the new building, and, as mentioned above, Women in Action kept quarters there to help women in crises with immediate aid.[23]

One problem that increased dramatically and impinged on all others was drug addiction. Rising use of drugs in urban ghettoes spread during the 1960s and 1970s to middle-class youths. Drug use became a serious drain on society, not only because of the users' resort to crime to support the high cost of addiction but because of the serious side effects in physical and emotional harm that often resulted. By 1971 college youths had progressed from experimentation with marijuana, which, though a drain on personal resources, caused relatively little damage, to LSD or "acid," a far more potent drug frequently attended by alarming reactions. A combined town and campus group in Durham, made up of David May, the Baptist chaplain at Duke, "Hutch" Travor, president of the Duke student government organization, Anthony Mulvihill, a mental health professional, Dawn Hall, another Duke student, and Everett Ellenwood, a Duke psychiatrist, set up a crisis intervention center at Hassle House, a building donated by Watts Street Baptist Church. Their primary service was a helpline for people to call when they had a bad reaction. It also operated as a walk-in service for a few who needed more than a voice on the end of a line. A staff of one or two paid workers together with a large group of trained volunteers, many of them from Duke, performed a vital service in the community.[24]

With funding from the county under supervision of the Area Mental Health Board, Hassle House operated until the summer of 1982. It sent speakers into the schools to talk about drugs and repeatedly led a kind of one-day Outward Bound program, set up tutoring for potential dropouts in the Saint Theresa neighborhood, and, through the training and experience given its volunteers, attracted a host of young men and women to careers in the field. Hassle House's success was its undoing. The County Health Department persuaded the Mental Health Board that the program could be handled under its aegis more economically. When the county commissioners would not find other funds to keep it in business, Hassle House was forced to close. A comparable program set up later by the County Mental Health agency proved to be many times more expensive than Hassle House.[25]

While social problems grew worse, population growth and development continued apace and brought to Durham a prosperity that had been the ambition of the Research Triangle planners. Those who came to fill new high-paid jobs in the Triangle or in Durham's business or professional sectors brought with them a life-style that materially altered the way Durham lived. Their tastes demanded and their salaries commanded the best in material comforts. The result was the availability as never before of expensive housing, quality food, gourmet restaurants, and widely varying entertainment. For the first time Durham had a large, well-heeled middle class with uninhibited spending habits. The "gilded salariat," as one historian called the Research Triangle work force, and Durham's yuppies spent money as naturally as they breathed.[26] Their presence significantly abetted those who had been long engaged in the battle to enrich the quality of life with the magic of the arts.

CULTURE AT LAST

All over the South, as in America generally, prosperity watered a previously arid ground and was bringing about a cultural flowering in the old "Sahara of the Bozart." Art requires more than the artist to flourish. It requires money and a supportive atmosphere as well. The creation of the North Carolina School of the Arts in Winston-Salem in 1965 was a significant spur to artistic ambition and attainment in the state and a source of first-class artists. Durham began to develop its own symbiosis. Its first artistic stirrings had occurred much earlier, however, during many years when the few who wished to create or enjoy art, cultivate the best in American culture, or preserve and display it faced entirely uphill work. A stinging indictment of Durham that appeared in the *Atlantic Monthly* in 1940, while undoubtedly striving for journalistic sensation, nevertheless hit home in its criticism.

> [I]n Durham, as nearly everywhere else in the United States, the propagation of the arts, like the duties of spring cleaning and putting up pickles, is left to the ladies. . . . [I]n general Durham's men let their ladies absorb Duke's "advantages" while they root for its football teams. . . . In short, Durham's men — conscious of the fact that the South, with fifty percent of the nation's resources within its borders and a rapidly growing population is nonetheless the most poverty-stricken area of America — are out to get the business, and let him who will have the "culture."[27]

The postwar years changed all that. New sources of creative energy percolated in the community with better success, simultaneously working toward the establishment of museums and the formation of groups to encourage artistic endeavor.

Museums had slow work gaining the footholds they needed to assure permanence. Durham's oldest museum, the North Carolina Museum of Life and Science, began as the conception of Clarence Wood, the Recreation Department director, who in 1946 established at Northgate Park a small building to house a few stuffed animals and live frogs, snakes, and other little creatures that children are likely to be interested in. There was also an aviary for wild birds. Arthur Lucas, an employee of Wood in charge of the exhibits, applied for and received a grant in 1946 from the William T. Hornaday Foundation to develop a children's museum. The Children's Museum Association was chartered the same year by Robert Bruce Cooke, Howard Jensen, and Paul Dillard Gamble among others. In 1947 the association purchased the old Hester homeplace at the end of Georgia Avenue and moved the museum there. A few larger animals in cages outside—a fox, raccoon, rabbits—were added to the mice, fish, and talking parrot, shells, minerals, and other nature displays inside. Operating on a pittance from the city and a few donations, the museum offered many regular activities for children—story hour, nature study, and creative crafts and collecting clubs—as well as special events. The building and exhibits had seriously deteriorated by 1961 when the museum board took advantage of a developer's offer to buy the tract with available surrounding acreage for a new residential development.[28]

The city had already begun in 1958 to search for a place to move the museum and had obtained a tract of over eleven acres on what became Murray Street, where it erected a small metal building to house the exhibits (opened 1962). The Junior League took on the task of raising funds for an educational building in 1967, and the museum's development quickened through the late 1960s and following decades. Besides living and stuffed creatures and plant and mineral collections, the museum presented elementary science exhibits. An interest in space as a result of the federal space exploration program resulted in the museum's acquisition of artifacts related to space probes and moon trips under the imaginative leadership of the museum's director, Richard Westcott. He expanded the museum's scope in another direction as well by stationing life-size prehistoric animals, which he modeled himself, around the uncleared acreage through which a small railroad carried observers on a wildlife tour. A few faithful supporters gave attention and hard work to the museum's development, sustaining it through the bleak 1960s when its direction was uncertain and public support poor. After momentum for the museum picked up, it acquired retired vehicles of many sorts: an army tank, a railroad caboose, a fire truck, a jet fighter plane, and a double-decker London bus. The 1986 city and county bond referendums contained large funding for the museum's development and ensured an institution able at last to realize its potential.[29]

The three state historic sites in Durham County, already mentioned, came into being in this period: the Stagville Center, the Bennett Place, and the Duke Homestead, the last with its adjunct Tobacco History Museum (1977) displaying the tools, machinery, packaging, and marketing paraphernalia peculiar to the tobacco industry. The Bennehan House and Horton Grove Quarters of the Stagville Center provided comprehensive material for historical studies of antebellum plantation life unequalled in the state. The restored farmhouses of the Bennitts and Dukes, along with the "living history" days staged on their grounds periodically, demonstrated what life was like on yeoman farms in the 1860s and 1870s. The host of knowledge about the families who inhabited them added a personal and local interest to the more general history lessons such places could teach.

The first efforts to establish a museum for the fine arts stemmed almost entirely from Duke University. The Woman's College library, under its director Lillian Griggs, with the cooperation of the art department, occasionally held exhibits of paintings, drawings, prints, and furnishings; at the same time it built up a collection of art books and sponsored lectures and extracurricular classes to nurture art appreciation. In 1931 the Art Association of Duke University and a department of arts were formed. The association, led by Professor William K. Boyd, arranged a long-term loan of the art collection of Mrs. Margaret Barber of Missouri, which included furniture, paintings, manuscripts, and objets d'art. When the loan expired in 1956, Duke University arranged to purchase a number of the items. It had already been given in 1942 the fine collection of Chinese furnishings displayed in the James A. Thomas Memorial room of the East Campus library. The general public, however, was not then interested in any consistent or supportive way in art. When Hickory opened an art museum in 1944, a *Herald* editorial lamented that Durham, which could well support a museum, had none, a fact the paper blamed on the failure of leaders in the community to give art the attention and support it required.[30]

The need for an arts building, which would also serve as a museum, was pondered by successive Duke University committees from 1957 until 1966. Professor William Willis of the Classics Department repeatedly voiced his department's need for classical artifacts in its teaching. His persistence resulted in the acquisition of a small collection of classical vases, sculpture, coins, and manuscripts from private donors, alumni, and library funds. When Mrs. Ella Brummer, the widow of a New York art dealer and collector, in 1964 wished to donate a medieval collection to Duke, President Douglas Knight persuaded the trustees to accept the gift and provide space for its display. A further small classical collection donated by Mrs. Brummer in 1965 and a major collection purchased from her in 1966 formed the nucleus of the Duke University Museum of Art holdings. Opened in 1969 in a renovated science building on East Campus, the museum soon acquired small but good collections of African, pre-Columbian, and oriental art; a docent program funded by the Junior League helped make the museum's treasures accessible to the public.[31]

North Carolina Central University's inspiration for a museum came from its art department chairman, Edward N. Wilson, a sculptor. He presented a plan for a museum to then President Alfonso Elder in 1958. Although the time was not propitious for such an endeavor, he was given permission to use a classroom as a gallery. Ten years later, when Albert Whiting became president, he proposed the purchase of good reproductions of art to be hung in classrooms and public halls on campus and encouraged art exhibits, beginning with one to celebrate his own inauguration. In 1971 the art department found the opening it had been waiting for when a comprehensive art exhibit was proposed to be held in conjunction with the Pan-African Games, an event that was to bring to Durham the best athletes from many African nations to compete in the United States for the first time. Leroy Walker, NCCU's athletic director and later chancellor, took the lead in planning the event and had the cooperation of Duke's athletic department for the unusual meet. Wilson's plan for a museum was updated and submitted again, this time with some success, to the administration. Borrowed from public and private collections, many pieces of African art were assembled for the exhibit, and the administration allotted space for a permanent collection. In 1977 a large addition, in reality a new building, was constructed as a museum and dedicated by Governor James L. Hunt. The museum gradually acquired a small but significant collection of Afro-American art, and its exhibits added much to the vitality of Durham's art scene.[32]

An art museum had been a dream of a few amateur and professional artists in 1947 when they organized the Creative Art Group, of which Mrs. Bingham Dai was the founder. At the organizational meeting besides Mrs. Dai were Elizabeth Lyon, Rhea Wilson, Ruth Latty, Jeanne Whiteside, and Ola Maie Foushee. Soon after, Paul Gamble, Helen Kendall, Ann Basile, George and Mary Pyne and others joined the group, meeting once a week to paint under the critical eye of artists from local colleges, principally Gregory D. Ivey from the Woman's College in Greensboro. When this group heard of the efforts of A. M. Tidd, James W. Hamm, and Randy Jones to form an art guild, they immediately gave their support. The Durham Art Guild, Inc., came into being in July 1949 and opened membership to interested laymen as well as amateur and professional artists. Mrs. Whiteside was the first president and Tidd, vice-president. They met monthly, except in summer, and heard lectures on art, art history, and art processes. They donated their services to the community to judge art competitions in the schools and raise money to promote exhibits and classes. The growing professional sector of the community wanted more arts and crafts classes than the schools or Recreation Department could supply, and the Art Guild began to fill these needs. It also began an annual exhibit of local artists in 1949.[33]

From the 1950s on, new artists in both the university art departments and the community as a whole steadily emerged. Through its art department, North Carolina Central University contributed to Durham many practicing artists. Among them were Edward N. Wilson and Robert F. Kennedy, sculptors, Carlyle Johnson, a painter, and Isabel Levitt, who worked in many media including photography and ceramics. Although Ernie Barnes was a Durhamite born and bred and a graduate of North Carolina Central, he did not become a professional artist until he had concluded his professional football career and moved to California. Willie Nash, on the other hand, while also a product of the art department, taught at NCCU and continued to paint in Durham. Marianne Manasse, a refugee from Nazi Germany with her husband, who taught in the German department, first painted in traditional forms, but later successfully experimented with mixed media, a combination of painting and collage.[34]

Duke's art department similarly benefited the community. The painters Robert Broderson and Vernon Pratt, a Durham native, and the sculptor Frank Smullin won more than local recognition for their work. Artists in other departments made significant contributions. Irwin Kremen, a psychology professor, developed a second career with his collages, which were exhibited nationwide. Robert Blake, a medical illustrator, was a master of his craft and in his pictures captured much of the flavor of the rural Piedmont South. Susan Carlton Smith, a medical librarian, created from seeds, pods, leaves, twigs, and other natural materials extraordinary miniatures. Her books for children, illustrated with her own color drawings, translated the same magic to the printed page.[35]

Other artists in the community enlivened the art scene: Edith London, trained in her native Berlin as well as in Paris, with abstract images in paintings and collages; Primrose Paschal, with portraits; Nadine Vartanian, with watercolors and oils; Ann Basile, whose great promise was cut off by an early death, with oils; and Elizabeth Reeves Lyon and Nancy Tuttle May, best known for watercolors and collages. Sylvia Heyden distinguished herself in the art of tapestry weaving.[36]

While Durham had many practicing artists by the decade of the 1970s, it had not been devoid of native talent in earlier times, and contrary to the contention of the *Atlantic Monthly* article that the arts were the province of Durham's women, the 1930s produced a group of men who became professional artists. Both the time and the place, however, made earning a living by art impossible, so that if they intended to stick to their last they had to go elsewhere to survive. In that decade appeared Nelson Rosenberg, Eugene Erwin, Ralph Fuller, Jr., Murray Jones, Jr., and Nathan Ornoff. In 1932 Nelson Rosenberg, a graduate of Durham High School and Duke University, was painting murals on the walls of the Bureau of Standards and Measures in Washington. He had already had practice in New York working on the Rockefeller Center murals and teaching fresco classes.[37]

Gene Erwin, son of J. Harper Erwin, after finishing his schooling at Durham High School and the University of North Carolina at Chapel Hill, attended the New York School of Fine and Applied Arts (Parson's), spent a summer at Harvard, and won a Carnegie scholarship for study at the University of Iowa. There he concentrated on mural painting with Grant Wood. Erwin had begun an art school in Durham in 1934, but his study in Iowa interrupted that work. When he returned he painted a series of flowers of North Carolina for the state, a project funded by the WPA, and from 1936 to 1940 was associated with the North Carolina Federal Art Project, of which he became director in 1937. Erwin later moved to New York.[38]

Nathan Ornoff, Jr., a native of Norfolk, Virginia, but a product of Durham schools after his family's move to Durham in his early childhood, studied first with Mrs. Lucille Strudwick, who taught art at Durham High School from 1931 to 1933, and next at the Art Center Studio, a school run by Gene Erwin, Clement Strudwick of Hillsborough, and Ralph Fuller, Jr. Ornoff, too, was interested in murals, and when he was a student at the National Academy of Art in New York planned two murals for Durham High School, which were apparently never executed. After he returned to Durham in 1939 to find the Art Center Studio no longer in existence, he opened the Durham School of Art at 130 East Chapel Hill Street.[39]

Mural painting had fitted well into the government-funded art projects of the Works Progress Administration because it could be done on the walls of public buildings where the taxpayers could enjoy what their money had paid for. Artists who had not previously thought of painting murals were glad to oblige to get work. It was not surprising that Murray Jones, Jr., although first a painter and etcher, chose to try his hand at murals. Almost a contemporary of Erwin's, Murray won a University of Chicago fellowship and used it to study and paint in Tahiti. On his return he held an exhibit of his work at the Woman's College Library. During the war years he was for a time stationed at Fort Knox, where he painted a mural for the Jewish chapel.[40]

After a stint as a teacher, Ralph Fuller, Jr., found as the others had that Durham could not then support artists. He moved to New York, where he had a long career as a commercial illustrator. In later life he lived in Saint Croix in the Virgin Islands, where he, too, finally painted murals, in this instance for a church.[41]

In 1940 two newcomers to Durham, Kaj and Georgina Klitgaard, both Guggenheim winners, opened a school of art while Mrs. Klitgaard worked on a commissioned mural in Chapel Hill. She had a studio in Durham's Snow Building because she needed a large wall on which to mount her mural sections. Her husband, a retired sea captain and writer, supervised the art classes. Their sojourn was short. Another foreign-born artist who came to Durham but who elected to remain was Angus McDougall (son of the Duke psychology professor), whose métier was sculpture, a field in which he won modest success. One of his works, a bust of Frederick Douglass, is in the Douglass Memorial Cemetery in New York.[42]

Photography as an art form won late recognition in North Carolina. Photographers whose interest was artistic as well as hobbyists with different purposes formed an organization called the Duke-Durham Camera Club in the 1930s. Several decades later, pressure on the Durham Art Guild to recognize the work of photographers with a purely artistic intent resulted in the establishment in 1974 of the Durham Photographic Arts Society (later the North Carolina Center for Creative Photography). Notable by the 1970s for their work in this genre were Caroline Vaughan, John Menapace, Alex Harris, and Elizabeth Matheson.[43]

The history of photography in Durham really begins in the 1880s with commercial photographers such as William Shelburn and Charles Rochelle. By the end of the century commercial photography was a reliable livelihood, and Durham had Oliver W. Cole and Waller Holladay along with other less well-known practitioners. Hugh Mangum (fl. 1900–1910), a Durham native who used a packhouse near his family's home (now the McCown-Mangum house at West Point) as a darkroom, never maintained a studio in Durham; but his glass negatives, preserved and donated to the county by the Vaughan family, form an important photographic archive of Durham's past. Just after the turn of the century came Durham's first woman photographer, Kate L. Johnson, who was still active in the 1930s. From the 1950s on, James Whitley and Walter Shackelford, Durham natives, dominated the field of portrait and wedding photography.[44]

In 1923 a commercial photographer emerged who developed an extraordinarily successful enterprise. James E. Strawbridge, a Durham native, learned his craft by working with a photographic firm in Philadelphia whose business was photographing school groups. When Strawbridge returned home to set up his own business, he chose the same specialty and became the first school photographer in the South. In the early 1950s, after Strawbridge's sons had joined the business, they began a photofinishing service to develop and print during the summer months photographs taken by the general public, since the school work consumed only nine months of the year. From this secondary business, after its amalgamation in 1961 with two other small companies, evolved the largest photofinishing firm in the world, Colorcraft.[45]

The performing arts also found sponsors in the postwar decades. Jeanne Whiteside was instrumental in the formation of the Durham Theatre Guild. She was present at the meeting of drama enthusiasts in 1946 that resolved to incorporate the Durham guild. With William N. Hardy as president, the group went on to produce three plays in its first year of existence. Only lack of funds brought the guild to a halt in 1953. At the end of the year, however, with renewed determination it resumed its program, presenting thereafter at least three and sometimes as many as five plays a year. It also sponsored drama in the high school, where Mrs. Paul North helped form and oversee the Junior Players. Some of the guild members became successful professionals in New York, for example, Anita Morris, Jeff Chandler, and Alexander Molina. Charles B. ("Buck") Roberts, Jr., who began with the guild, always wanted to have his own company that would perform year-round. He first organized the Durham Star Playhouse in the late 1950s, and when it was discontinued, he founded in 1963 the Triangle Summer Theater, which became a professional company the following year and in 1965 took the name Triangle Repertory Theater. It was soon after discontinued. Drama, too, lacked public support in the 1960s.[46]

Music shared in the creative resurgence. Jane Wilkins Sullivan and Marian Wallace Smith organized the Durham Oratorio Society in 1949, a name that was changed to Durham Civic Choral Society when the group was chartered the following year. The founders, residents of Durham who had been members of a Raleigh oratorio society, mailed out invitations to which sixteen singers responded by attending an organizational meeting in the basement of the First Baptist Church. Allan Bone, a professor of music at Duke and choirmaster of Saint Philip's Church, became their first conductor. The group presented its first concert free to the public in December 1949 at the Baptist church. Like other societies devoted to the arts, in the 1960s the Choral Society experienced difficulty maintaining sufficient interest to pay its way and was almost forced to disband. In the middle 1970s, however, musical interest and expertise rose dramatically in the community, an improvement reflected in the society's subsequent vitality and virtuosity.[47]

The Durham Symphony Orchestra was a natural growth of the increase in the community of both musicians and musical taste. Made up of a mixture of amateur and professional musicians who wanted to make music, the Durham Symphony came into being in 1976 after Vincent Simonetti (who became its first conductor) advertised for interested musicians to come to an organizational meeting at Erwin Auditorium. Among those who responded were the Robert Wentzes, Dr. Dewey Lawson, Isabelle Samfield, Elizabeth Krynski, and Ernest Sunas. As the community expanded, the increasing number of musicians on which the orchestra could draw consistently raised the quality of its performances.[48]

From the start Trinity's and later Duke's sponsorship of all the arts stimulated community participation through performances, readings, lectures, exhibitions, and classes. With music, however, it struck a responsive chord in the community. With the upsurge of interest after the war came new university efforts. In 1945, at the suggestion of Katherine Gilbert of the art department, Ernest William Nelson of the history department founded the Chamber Arts Society. Supported in large part through the university communities of Durham and Chapel Hill, the Society brought quartets of the highest caliber to Duke in a series of five concerts each season. The first concert was given in 1945 by a group of string players of the Pittsburgh Symphony, which was in Durham to perform in the All-Star Series. The quartet called themselves the Carnegie Players for the occasion. Through many years, while he handled all the paperwork and, with the help of an equally dedicated committee, selected the performers, Professor Nelson expended much time and money to keep the society in the black. The music room in East Duke building where the concerts were held for so many years was later fittingly named the Nelson Music Room.[49]

In 1964 the University laid the groundwork for additional musical fare when the music department, in cooperation with the Mary Duke Biddle Foundation, brought the violinist Georgio Ciompi to Duke from the North Carolina School of the Arts. The following year he organized his own quartet, whose members, in addition to teaching, performed a series of free concerts each year. The Benjamin N. Duke Memorial Organ, commissioned in 1969 and built in the style of eighteenth-century French and Dutch organs, has already been mentioned. Frequent free concerts by world masters on the 5,000-pipe instrument added another dimension of excellence to Durham's music.[50]

The music department, established as an independent entity in 1960, made its mark in other ways. Allan Bone, in a span of over forty years, built up and conducted the Duke Symphony Orchestra, at the same time presenting countless concerts of orchestral and choral music both on and off campus. Through many years he cooperated with his colleague John Hanks, a vocal arts teacher, to conduct an opera workshop. From its classes emerged talented students who won national and even international reputations, for example, Michael Best, a Durham native and member of the Metropolitan Opera Company. Other Hanks students were Steven Kimbrough, whose career in Germany won him European acclaim, and William Stone of the New York City Opera Company. Durham children benefited from the Pre-Collegiate String School, started by the department and taught by Dorothy Kitchen, using the Suzuki method for small beginners. Her most notable success was her own son, Nicholas, who won acclaim from his earliest appearances.[51]

Because many groups interested in the visual and performing arts had come into being by the early 1950s, and all needed the support they could give each other, the president of the Theatre Guild called a meeting with the heads of the other arts groups in 1953, and together they formed an umbrella organization, United Arts; the next year the name was changed to Allied Arts of Durham. Its purpose, besides strengthening the position of the arts in Durham by sponsoring classes, performances, and exhibits, was to coordinate the various groups' calendars to prevent overlapping or duplication of activities. The Art Guild, Theatre Guild, Civic Choral Society, Duke University Arts Council, Chamber Arts Society, and the Durham chapter of the North Carolina Symphony Society were the original member organizations. The George Watts mansion, Harwood Hall on Duke Street, then empty, was used as headquarters, and the groups held their meetings and classes there until 1961, when the mansion was demolished along with its near neighbor, the Eugene Morehead house, to make way for the Blue Cross Blue Shield headquarters building. Little more than a block away the Howard Foushee house was standing empty, and Allied Arts, after a fund-raising drive, purchased the house and moved its activities there. In the 1970s the concept of arts councils spread across the land; like Allied Arts, they were umbrella organizations but with a community-wide orientation and more inclusive participation. Better able to prove its civic purpose, the Durham Arts Council (the name Allied Arts adopted in 1975) was gradually successful in obtaining money from local government to help fund its operations and to foster and stimulate the arts in the Durham community.[52]

Duke University could take credit for having stimulated creative writing in Durham. Not much evidence of activity in this genre was found outside the university community until the 1960s. Within its walls, however, one man inspired an extraordinary succession of students who made names for themselves in the literary world. William Maxwell Blackburn, born to South Carolinian missionaries in Persia, came to Duke in 1926 after graduate work at Yale and spent the next fifty years teaching literature and creative writing. His teaching first bore fruit after World War II when a book by his former student Mac Hyman, *No Time for Sergeants* (1954), became a major best seller and stage and screen success. Hyman was followed by a string of other students who became respected nationally known writers: William Styron, Reynolds Price, Fred Chappell, James Applewhite and Anne Tyler. Durham could claim only two of these writers beyond their student days: both Price and Applewhite returned to Duke to teach and write. Price's many novels and Applewhite's poetry won wide recognition, and some of their own students in turn began productive careers in Durham.

Quite apart from the Blackburn influence was a handful of Durham women who made their own way independently in the literary world. Notable among them were Helen Bevington, Frances Gray Patton, Pauli Murray, Mary Mebane, Mena Webb, Camilla Bittle, Sylvia Wilkerson and Ina Forbus—all but Bevington and Forbus were southerners, and of the southerners only Patton not a native Durhamite. Helen Bevington, for many years a teacher like her husband in Duke's English department, wrote among other things witty *New Yorker* verse and moving volumes of autobiography. Autobiographical, too, though presented thinly veiled as fiction, were Mary Mebane's books. Mebane, who grew up in the Mill Grove area of Durham, revealed not only the bitterness of an underprivileged childhood but also that of class and social discrimination within the black community. Pauli Murray's *Proud Shoes*, although it went far beyond Durham to trace her family's biracial origins, powerfully re-created the Durham she knew in the early decades of this century. Mena Webb wrote one novel, *Curious Wine*, a biography of Julian Carr, *The General Without an Army*, and many historical articles for the local papers. Camilla Bittle won success with several novels and many stories for popular women's magazines such as *McCall's*, *Good Housekeeping*, and the *Ladies' Home Journal*. Sylvia Wilkerson's early novels in the 1960s conveyed the flavor of the Piedmont South, but later, in California, she centered her interest and writing in automobile racing. In the 1950s and 1960s Ina Forbus translated her understanding and love of animals into small books for children in the tradition of Beatrix Potter.

It was the deft and humorous short stories of Frances Patton, however, the wife of another Duke English professor, that caught the attention of Hollywood. In 1955 a movie was made of *Good Morning, Miss Dove*, which premiered in Durham, a special occurrence, with a gala civic dinner at the Washington Duke Hotel to honor the author before the movie's first showing at the Center Theatre.

Congressional action of 1965 that established and funded both the National Endowment for the Arts (NEA) and the National Endowment for the Humanities (NEH) stimulated community programs in both fields. The changed attitude toward the arts made possible many kinds of innovative public programs. Creative Arts in the Public Schools (CAPS) began in 1972 to introduce all kinds of art into Durham schools through a team-teaching approach. Janice Palmer, with the help of Alice Alston, Dorothy Borden, and Pauline Silberman, originated the concept and worked through Ella Fountain Pratt, the successor at Duke to John Foster Barnes as campus arts entrepreneur, to interest Allied Arts in the proposal and solicit its backing. The First Presbyterian Church's donation of $1,000 funded the start of the work in the schools, and the NEA contributed major funding for the project during its beginning years. Using dancers, poets, and painters to explore a theme with a class, the children were urged to create their own poems, paintings, and dances all on the same topic, to stimulate their creativity and enrich their learning.[53]

Another innovative program with the arts in Durham came through Dr. James Semans, who became aware of the Hospital Audiences, Inc., program for patients in hospitals. In a New York hospital he found the arts and theatrical productions being used in the treatment of illnesses and drug addiction and decided to find a way to introduce the arts into Duke Hospital. With a grant from the Mary Duke Biddle Foundation in 1975, he instituted a small program with the cooperation of Allied Arts. After a feasibility study for establishing a full, in-house program at Duke Hospital, an NEA grant supplied the funds to implement it. Janice Palmer, with her experience in the CAPS program, was a natural choice to develop and coordinate it. Started in 1978, the endeavor soon developed into a many-pronged program that included art and humanities exhibits, performing arts, artists in residence, closed-circuit television for cultural and health films, and the purchase of paintings and sculpture of North Carolina artists for exhibition in patient and public areas of the hospital.[54]

With the arrival of the American Dance Festival, another of the performing arts was institutionalized in Durham. Its coming was the culmination of efforts by a group of enthusiasts who wished to foster interest in the art form through dance classes and performances. Members of this group who formed Dance Associates in

1969 were Dot Silver, Barbara Busse, Julia Wray, and Susanne White, soon joined by Ella Fountain Pratt, Dorothy Borden, Barbara Bounds, and Jacqueline Erickson. At first content just to bring together those with the same interest, they very soon began to establish dance classes through Allied Arts. The group learned to their amazement the potential support for the dance in the community when they sponsored A Day for Dancing at Erwin Auditorium in the early 1970s. On that day they presented dancing classes and demonstrations of all kinds of dance, expecting fifty to seventy-five participants. They were overwhelmed when six hundred showed up. With that kind of evidence to proceed on, in 1974 they established a summer program of classes called Loblolly on Duke's East Campus. A second series, Summerdance, under the auspices of Duke University in the summer of 1976, was set up for them by Vicky Patton, a dance enthusiast herself and assistant for special projects to Duke President Terry Sanford.[55]

For the sake of furthering this endeavor and on the advice of Nancy Hanks, a Duke trustee and then head of NEA, Vicky Patton visited the American Dance festival in New London, Connecticut, to discover how summer dance programs could be developed. In the course of her investigation she learned that the festival was planning to relocate, and she was inspired to lure them to Durham. With the support of Sanford, who believed with a writer a hundred years before that "art is the surest and safest civilizer," and after succeeding in interesting the festival director, Charles Rinehart, in Durham and Duke as a possible new home, Patton and the Dance Associates canvassed Durham's leaders and met with enthusiastic promises of financial support, particularly from the Liggett Group. Against stiff nationwide competition the women pulled off a coup: the American Dance Festival moved to Durham in 1978. Located on East Campus, during six weeks each summer it offered daily classes for dancers of every taste and level of ability and evening performances of professional dance troupes from all over the world.[56]

In the same summer of 1978 another cultural tradition began when the Carolina Cinema Corporation opened the doors of the long-closed Carolina Theatre for the showing of art films. Organized by Constance and Montrose Moses and a group of their friends, the corporation had two purposes: to bring good movies to a Durham audience that would otherwise miss them, and to save a beautiful building that was doomed to demolition. With a gift of $5,000 left over from the defunct Downtown Revitalization Program, they made the minimum repairs to render the building usable as a movie theater, and they persuaded the city fathers to preserve it until plans could be drawn and financing found for its inclusion in a proposed civic and convention center for downtown Durham. Since the city government had the same year moved into its new city hall and abandoned its old structure, the Durham Arts Council was able to lease the old city hall that summer and thus further the realization of a role for the arts in Durham's center.[57]

The implosion of the Washington Duke Hotel on 14 December 1975 shocked Durhamites. They had lamented the demolition of the railroad station and the fine homes of Eugene Morehead, George Watts, and others of the Morehead Hill neighborhood, and quietly regretted the destruction of the flamboyant wooden mansions on McMannen Street, which lost its name as well through urban renewal, but the hotel meant even more to many people. Since 1925 it had been the scene of happy civic and personal occasions of all sorts. One native described the 1970s:

An uneasy feeling crept into the thinking of many of us that somewhere along the way, much that was Durham's heritage had disappeared or was doomed. What had happened to our visible roots that had held us so firmly and securely in this hometown of ours? What did we have left that told the story of Durham—its love affair with tobacco and textiles and Old Trinity and the able men and women who built the foundation for Durham's growth and prosperity today?[58]

One who shared that feeling with many others but who did something about it was Margaret Haywood. Even before the hotel's demise, she and equally dedicated friends organized a society to save Durham's historical heritage. The Historic Preservation Society was chartered in 1974 and in a short time had close to six hundred members. The first of many achievements was its persuading the Liggett Group to donate the old Bennehan House at Stagville to the society for preservation. Because of its long use as a tenant house and the subsequent sale of the plantation to the Liggett and Myers Tobacco Company, the historic structure had deteriorated, and for years had stood empty and dangerously exposed to weather and vandalism. Through the society's efforts, within two years it was in the protective hands of the state and by 1977 was restored for use as a preservation technology center. Thereafter the impulse to preserve, restore, and adapt old buildings to new uses was significantly strengthened by the society's work. The renovation and adaptation of the Duke-built Yuille and Watts tobacco warehouses (1900–1904) to house specialty shops and offices under the inspired name of Brightleaf Square (1981), and the Bullington warehouse (1927) for condominiums (1982) were results of this influence. Strong financial incentives provided by new federal tax laws in the 1970s materially aided the spirit of historic preservation. That the nation was celebrating its bicentennial also bolstered the cause.[59]

Mrs. Haywood was the driving force in the Durham celebration of that important milestone. In 1974 Mayor Hawkins agreed to appoint a Durham Bicentennial Committee, and Herbert Bradshaw served as chairman. A range of events scheduled throughout the year culminated in a three-day folklife festival at West Point on the Eno, with entertainment for all: music from country to folk, from blues to rock, from blue grass to gospel; cloggers, buck and wing, and other dancers; ethnic and regional foods; traditional skills, crafts, and games—served up in a southern cultural barbecue.[60]

Having worked up an appetite and got into practice, everyone was ready when the Durham County Centennial came along in 1981. Paul Wright, a vice-president of the Central Carolina Bank, was chairman of the celebration committee. A week of festivities began with a two-hour parade on 26 April, the anniversary of Generals Johnston and Sherman's final meeting at the Bennett Place, and continued throughout the week with historical exhibitions at both Northgate and South Square malls, a ball with music supplied by Duke graduate Les Brown and his orchestra, plays, concerts, a dinner at Cameron Indoor Stadium with an ensemble of singers celebrating Durham's history, and musical jamborees at Lowes Grove and Orange Factory, all ending with fireworks at Northgate on Saturday night.[61]

Ultimately more important to the people of Durham than these exuberant but ephemeral extravaganzas to commemorate the past were the solid triumphs in preserving it that the Historic Preservation Society had already achieved: the saving of the Stagville house and quarters, of old Saint Joseph A.M.E. Church, and of the Pegram house, a residence from the old Trinity College faculty row; the commitment to an ambitious series of historical publications; a county cemetery inventory, organized and carried through by Doris Belk Tilley; and the financial support, encouragement, and recognition of a whole range of other salvage and restoration projects—in sum, the gift to Durham of its past.

Anniversaries are sobering times for looking back, judging decisions and actions, and totting up gains and losses. A moral and cultural score is a long-range tally and not reducible to numbers. An economic score is more easily reckoned. As Durham County rounded out its first century, its economic balance sheet gave satisfaction on many counts.

Fundamental to the cultural flowering that had at last come was a sound economic base, and this the numbers verified. The county could budget $71 million annually for expenses and the city $50 million more. Although Durham's traditional industries were declining, 135 industries could still be counted within its boundaries, many of them new, and with well-paid workers. Tobacco and textiles had yielded the palm to health care and education. Duke University with the largest payroll of any employer in the county, paid out in 1981 $180 million in wages and supplied $30 million more in fringe benefits. Concurrent with the university's contribution to the cultural life of the area was its even more significant participation in science and the humanities nationally. Duke had become a major university with a major medical center. Its fame redounded to Durham's credit. Among other large corporations with headquarters in Durham County were the North Carolina Mutual Life Insurance Company, Central Carolina Bank, Burroughs Wellcome Company, Colorcraft, the General Telephone Company of the South, and the international construction giant, Nello Teer. Durham had close to $500 million in bank deposits and $400 million more in savings and loan associations.[62]

For many of Durham's 150,000 residents, of whom two-thirds now lived within the city, the good life was within their grasp, and the results of the long conversion of once pristine Piedmont wilderness to prosperous urban area, still surrounded by ample though increasingly threatened countryside, forests, and streams, seemed entirely a cause for celebration.

City and County
to Millennium's End

GOVERNING AT THE MILLENNIUM'S END

The closing decades of the twentieth century brought great changes, challenges, and innovative solutions. The changes were profound and irrevocable. Advances in technology and science affected every aspect of life. Devastating discoveries—HIV/AIDS and global climate change—posed unprecedented challenges to the world, all inevitably shared by Durham. Despite several national business recessions the general economic movement was upward, certainly in Durham, with growth in commerce, industry, population, personal income, the built environment, and support for the arts and historic preservation, while Duke University and the Research Triangle Park continued to lead and fuel the forward march. In retrospect two events of 1980 foreshadowed the new character that Durham was quickly assuming: the opening of Duke University Hospital North and the decision of General Electric to build its new micro-electric center in the Research Triangle Park. Medicine, with manifold research ramifications, and new computing technology together would be Durham's economic dynamo, basis for pride, and source of new fame.

The new climate in the county was understood and encapsulated in a new slogan by Dr. James E. Davis (1918–97), a respected town surgeon who gained national recognition as president of the American Medical Association. He wanted the city to create a new image by capitalizing on its strengths: its five hospitals, two nursing schools, and myriad clinics and health professionals, "the most comprehensive range of high quality health services of any community in the nation."[1] He persuaded the city council to adopt his slogan for Durham: The City of Medicine.[2] With considerable support from the business sector he launched a campaign to publicize and validate the slogan by inaugurating a yearly formal dinner where awards were given to distinguished physicians or scientists who had made significant contributions to medicine. This slogan, unlike so many previous ones, caught on, having a credible base. Only the next year a new research facility for the National Institute of Environmental Health Services occupying 506 acres was dedicated in the Research Triangle Park. Dr. James Wyngaarden, who had left Duke to become head of the National Institutes of Health (NIH), gave the dedication.[3] The park won this national agency partly through the efforts of former governor Terry Sanford, then president of Duke. The same year Lincoln Health Center moved into its brand-new quarters. It offered primary care and mental, dental, and health education to almost twenty thousand patients. The city's emergency medical technicians for the southern part of the city were based there as well. This facility was an important factor in Durham's being named an All-American City in 1983.[4] Charles Markham, then mayor, said it was the high point of his service to receive the award from President Reagan in Washington.[5] The city was basking in good fortune.

LOCAL GOVERNMENT

The centennial celebration was hardly over when the local election in November 1981 gave the city council five new progressive members, among them two women and two African Americans, representing the first stage in bringing a liberal coalition to power.[6] With the election of 1983 the council gained five women and five African Americans. To complete the sweep, the election in 1985 and reelection in 1987 of Wilbur (Wib) Gulley as mayor enabled the council to act on previously unthinkable issues. When Gulley was succeeded by Durham's first African American mayor, Chester Jenkins, the liberal majority was able to wield power a decade before a reaction set in.[7] This strong representation of black members was certainly due to the considerable influence of the Durham Committee on the Affairs of Black People (DCABP, formerly DCNA). During these years Willie Lovett was chairman of the organization and Lavonia Allison, who eventually succeeded Lovett, was head of its political committee.[8] Allison earned the chairmanship of the DCABP in 1997 and went into the new century at the helm. Not hesitant to be confrontational, she was forceful, effective, and feared.[9]

This period was characterized by successful efforts to control growth, preserve the natural and built environment, and defend the civil rights of still marginalized segments of the population. The ample representation of blacks on the city council for the first time made attention to that last aim almost a certainty. The council also made administrative changes, such as rescinding the mayor's right to appoint committee heads and reestablishing independent police and fire departments after having given the combined Public Safety organization a fourteen-year trial.[10]

The most visible of the achievements during the decade was the effort to revitalize the city center. Empty storefronts, depressing streetscapes, and general inactivity had reached a critical point. In March 1982 a retired justice of the state Supreme Court, Willis Whichard, chairman of the Downtown Durham Development Corporation, and his board members presented the council with a workable plan, and the passage in June of that year of a $10.5 million bond issue paved the way for the council's action.[11] The city wanted to build a civic center and seek private investment to erect a hotel and office building on land it had bought up along Chapel Hill Street. Among several plans the council considered was one presented by Watts Hill, a vitally interested party because of his ownership of the empty city block where the Washington Duke Hotel had stood. His plan would have placed the new hotel on his block. The council rejected Hill's plan, despite its other attractive features, because it needed to recoup the money expended on land acquisition by reselling it to a hotel developer.[12]

Poorly written contracts, lack of oversight, foot dragging, reluctance of private investors to cooperate, irresponsible contractors, and other frustrations vexed the project, but by the end of the decade the city could boast a new civic center with a hotel on top and an office building over a city-financed garage (a concession to the builder) on the way. It had also guaranteed the restoration of buildings for the arts: the Carolina Theatre (1926) with the addition of two small adjoining movie theaters (completed in 1994) and old City Hall for the Durham Arts Council (completed in 1987).[13]

The hotel was the undertaking of Clingendael Investment Corporation (owned by Julius Verwoerdt). The office building was supplied by Frank Wittenberg, who built a fifteen-story tower of tinted glass, steel, concrete, and granite for offices and apartments, designed by Frank DePasquale. It was only the second skyscraper in the city center after the Hill bank building, built during the Depression. Peoples Security Life Insurance Company (1983), an amalgam of Peoples Life and the old John Sprunt Hill Home Security Life Insurance Company, occupied the tower, which exemplified the latest fashion in skyscrapers and added a completely new look to the cityscape.[14]

Orville Powell, the new city manager, hired in 1983 when Barry de Castillo resigned, took some of the blame for the rough course of the city's building effort, but he nevertheless survived to serve as a judicious and reliable city manager until 1997.

During the decade the council was also able to complete construction of the contentious freeway connecting the Research Triangle Park to I-85 in Durham, after having overcome the initial opposition and justifiable anger of the Crest Street neighborhood. (See chapter 19.) At the same time the city supplied over $2 million to restore and rehabilitate Old St. Joseph's Church in its new role as the Hayti Heritage Center for African American Culture (completed in 1991), one of the few landmarks in Hayti to survive urban renewal.

Construction outside the city center also presented the council with perplexing questions, revealing the inadequacy of city planning and existing building codes. In 1985 a developer from Texas, T. F. Stone, wished to build a seventeen-story building between South Square Mall and the Duke Forest residential area. Naturally protest followed. The majority of council members found the proposed building objectionable because it did not conform to the long-range plans on the books. Placing so tall a building on the outskirts of town was not only visually inappropriate to its surroundings but could well encourage further erosion of the center city. In the end the council had to approve the request.[15] Only a short time later, however, it adopted a new ordinance that dictated a ten-story limit for new buildings outside the city center, but too late to prevent the "green pickle," as the tall building came to be called because of its height and green glass sheathing.[16] That unpleasant lesson probably accelerated the merging of the city and county planning and tax departments, proposed in 1985 and accomplished in 1988.[17] Obviously more farsighted, careful, and comprehensive planning was needed to accomplish the council's purposes.

The city ran into no opposition with another development to the southeast, which it hoped would help Durham win a share of the fast-expanding work force of the Research Triangle. Durham had lamented that so many of the new workers tended to settle in Cary or the Raleigh suburbs. This was true partly because Durham city and county schools had poor reputations and partly because attractive, convenient housing in Durham was limited. The new development, Woodcroft, was to provide 2,700 houses or apartments built in stages on 750 acres of ground southeast of Hope Valley, foretokening the new direction of the city's expansion.[18]

The council's proudest accomplishment of 1984 was the passage of a water quality protection ordinance.[19] When it was presented for consideration to the council, Durham Research Properties, among others, came forward to object because the ordinance would restrict its plan for a huge development called Treyburn, to occupy 5,200 acres on the old Cameron plantation lands, abutting two water supplies: the Falls of the Neuse reservoir (completed in 1983) and Little River reservoir, then under construction and completed in 1987. This company was composed of Terry Sanford, Sr., Terry Sanford, Jr., Clay Hamner, Frank Kenan, and Thomas Keesee. Their ambitious enterprise was to be an industrial park with an adjacent upper-income residential community, built about a golf course and clubhouse. The partners strongly objected to the ordinance's prohibition of development within a mile of any major reservoir.[20] The city had an ally in the freelance photographer and computer consultant Jim Clark and his Save the Water grassroots organization. Clark, a Florida native who had been fighting environmental battles for a long time, was very vocal in his objections to the projected development and supportive of the new ordinance. While the city council later enacted exceptions to the ordinance that would accommodate Treyburn, it also eventually required an environmental impact statement, a result of Clark's advocacy.[21]

The sticking point for both council and company was whether sewer and water lines would be allowed within the critically sensitive one-mile limit. Without these lines the company could not accommodate industry. The compromise plan allowed the lines, much to conservationists' outrage but also to the city's advantage.[22] The county would buy from the city a small sewage treatment plant, have it moved to Treyburn, and pay for the installation of city water and sewer lines, but prospective users would pay for their use at double the rate of city users. In the future the city would be allowed to annex the development.[23] This last provision was to forestall an eventuality that had occurred the previous year when the state legislature passed a bill exempting the Research Triangle Park from being annexed by any municipality. Durham, which had built the water and sewer lines to the park, had fully intended to annex it and thus markedly improve the city tax base. The exemption was a severe blow.[24] The county, in which almost all of Treyburn lay, was to have an even stormier battle.

At the end of the 1980s the council proposed and finally passed another pro-environmental piece of legislation. It required a much more detailed procedure for the developers of major projects, namely an environmental impact statement, a public hearing, and approval by the council. The hearing on the draft proposal was unusually contentious. Developers were unhappy, particularly W. Clay Hamner, representing Montrose Capital Corporation (another partnership with Terry Sanford, Jr.), who threatened to take his developments elsewhere, feeling aggrieved because he had given Durham the restored tobacco warehouse complex Brightleaf Square, Treyburn, and the first phase of Erwin Square, an office tower between one-story rows of boutiques, and had rehabilitated the huge factory buildings of the former Erwin Mills for apartments. His resistance was for nought; this council was serious about the environment and good planning.[25]

Voters seemed willing to keep passing bond issues for constructive purposes, reflecting the mood of the times and the recovered and robust economy after a slump in 1981. In 1986 they passed another very large bond issue for many infrastructure improvements: sewer and water, solid waste disposal, streets, and a hydroelectric generator at Lake Michie, but also for the reconstruction of the Durham Arts Council building and improvements at the Museum of Life and Science.[26] Along with its support of the Arts Council and the restoration of the historic theater, this council had set up the Historic District Commission to oversee the city's new historic district ordinance. The commission was advisory but it would have an important voice in helping to preserve the city's historic structures.[27]

The council was able to promote many progressive social measures as well, including civil rights for the black minority and for homosexuals. The council proclaimed Martin Luther King's birthday a holiday and made mandatory for city-funded projects the hiring of a minimum number of minority- and women-owned firms or services.[28] Mayor Gulley stirred up one portion of his constituents to the point of promoting a recall election when in 1986 he issued a proclamation designating an anti-discrimination week with an eye toward the Triangle Gay and Lesbian Pride march in Durham. The airing of homophobic and mean-spirited opinions followed. Both newspapers' editorials criticized the mayor because the issue was so divisive. Gulley had Christian fundamentalists to combat as well as political conservatives. But eighteen ministers inserted an advertisement in the local newspaper to praise Gulley for his stand. The council unanimously condemned the KKK's intention to stage its own march as a protest, but because of the First Amendment it had to allow the KKK to proceed. The Gay Pride march went off without incident, drawing six hundred to one thousand participants.[29]

The council adopted a plan presented by its own public works committee to set up an urban trails and greenways committee that would develop walking and biking paths through historic areas and residential neighborhoods. Two council members who had supported the cause in its planning stages, Jane Davis and Sylvia Kerckhoff, became president and secretary of a twenty-two-member commission to plan and initiate the effort. The first section of the first proposed trail was to run from Rock Quarry Park to I-85. In 1988, noting the very slow progress of the effort, the planning department got approval for a plan that would add 5.6 miles of trails at a yearly cost of $802,000 for land acquisition. There was, of course, always the hope of generous donations of land for the purpose. The proposal's eventual aim was to supply 25 miles of trails for every 50,000 residents.[30]

The city made a major move when it agreed to take on the city transportation service, which had been run by the Duke Power Company for decades. It established the Durham Area Transit Authority (DATA) in 1989, purchased new buses, and substantially increased the efficiency of the service. While the service was never profitable, the city clearly had the responsibility to maintain it.

Steadily rising land values throughout the 1980s gave the council an ostensible reason for removing a contentious item from the agenda, but environmental issues really motivated its action. In 1980 a Northern Loop around Durham containing a portion known as Eno Drive was put on the long-range plan of the State Department of Transportation (DOT) to alleviate increasing traffic congestion to and from the Research Triangle. At its introduction opponents were vociferous and angry, because their neighborhoods would be torn apart and the Eno River would be threatened. Eno Drive would in part have paralleled the river and violated its seclusion, as well as making it vulnerable to noise, runoff of oil and gasoline, and noxious fumes. Although the city continued to acquire land for the bypass, by 1988 land values had risen so much that it became plain to the council member Sylvia Kerckhoff and her Public Works Committee that the city could no longer afford to purchase land for the corridor. She proposed instead that existing roads be widened to accommodate the traffic but not to constitute a bypass, and that Eno Drive as mapped be removed from the state's road plan. No money had been appropriated for the drive at that time. In 1991 the state Department of Transportation complied: Eno Drive as mapped would no longer be on the plan. The Eno River Association seemed to have won another long battle, but the war was not yet over. Alternative versions of Eno Drive continually reappeared, and each time one hydra's head was cut off another sprang up in its place. Eno Drive came up for consideration in 1992, 1995, and 1998; but it was finally taken off the books, and money appropriated in the 1990s was used for other roads.[31]

Another ever-increasing and serious environmental issue was trash disposal. Landfills were filling up fast; finding available land for new landfills and maintaining them was becoming almost impossibly difficult for the city and county governments. "Not in my backyard" was the inevitable public response. Recycling was one partial solution to the problem. In Durham a pioneer solar energy and recycling company called SunShares came into being in 1980. It was the inspiration of a visionary and astute business entrepreneur, David Kirkpatrick, a Duke University graduate who knew that similar firms were already in operation elsewhere and could be profitable. SunShares contracted with private individuals and businesses to collect and resell selected items: aluminum and steel cans, clean paper, newsprint, and glass bottles. Another start-up nonprofit company, Shimar Recycling, owned by Meredith Morley, offered a collection service for businesses and institutions in the Triangle area, and in 1987 Larry Shively and a partner took over and continued the recycling activities of SunShares. In 1988 the city and county contracted with SunShares for curbside collection in the city and at designated sites in the county.[32] The new routes increased collections by so much that by 1997 the company's revenues had grown from $40,000 to $3 million and its workforce from two to sixty-two.[33] Durham County was able to reduce its waste per capita by 11 percent in seven years, the best record of North Carolina's six most populous counties. As technology improved to handle increasing waste products, recycling caught on with the general public and became even more efficient and widely practiced.

Before the political pendulum swung the opposite way after all these progressive measures, in 1990 the county and city were able to pass what was then the largest bond issue in Durham's history. The referendum included $83.4 million for two sewage treatment plants and the expansion of the existing one, and $45.2 million for solid waste disposal and a new landfill. An additional $5 million were to be spent on watershed land acquisition, $3.4 million for parks and recreation, $3.2 million for urban trails and greenways, and $2.5 million for downtown sidewalks, lights, crosswalks, and other improvements.[34]

At the beginning of the 1990s a flagging of spirits from a short-lived economic downturn and a sense of pessimism took over, if only temporarily. New federal regulations without federal funding under the Reagan administration had exacerbated already strained budgets.[35] A variety of other causes contributed to the mood. The public rejection of a proposed new baseball stadium was expected to precipitate a domino collapse of planned structures related to the rehabilitation of the old American Tobacco complex.[36] If that plan failed, the city would find itself with acres of empty tobacco manufacturing company buildings. The city was also threatened with the loss of its minor league baseball team, the Durham Bulls.[37] The Durham Bulls Baseball Club, newly franchised in 1980 by Miles Wolff as a farm club of the Atlanta Braves, had just been sold to Jim Goodman, an entrepreneur from Raleigh who was expected to move the team there.[38] At the same time a spate of scandals involving local government was poisoning the public trust. The head of the Housing Authority, the Superintendent of Public Schools, some officers in the police department, and a city councilman were all facing criminal charges or investigation by the SBI.[39] Crime and drugs were a larger problem than ever; the collapsing schools were in limbo as merger with the county system was only in the planning stages. The city bid for the Thelonious Monk Institute of Jazz, which Governor James Martin and Senator Terry Sanford had backed, failed.[40]

The public reacted to all this bad news and to the long rule of a progressive city council by electing a new conservative group in November 1991. Harry Rodenhizer, who had been ousted in 1981, came back as mayor along with others of his political persuasion, strongly supported by the voters group Friends of Durham.[41]

The gloom soon lifted, for Durham had many reasons to feel optimistic as it began a long stretch of economic prosperity. *Fortune* voted the Raleigh-Durham area the best place for business in the United States,[42] and the city received an AAA bond rating.[43] American Airlines opened its hub at Raleigh-Durham Airport and initiated a direct flight to London in 1993. The map-maker Rand-McNally named the Raleigh-Durham area the third-best place to live in America.[44] Although Glaxo reneged on its intention to build opposite the tobacco complex, the city went ahead without public approval and built the baseball stadium on the repurchased Glaxo tract, along with a garage to serve it. The county also contributed a parking garage. Goodman built an architecturally compatible large building, Diamond View Office Tower, overlooking the stadium for the headquarters of his company, Capital Broadcasting, and kept his team in Durham. Although Adam Abram backed out of his proposed plan to develop 275,000 square feet of the American Tobacco Campus, Goodman valiantly stepped in to continue with it, and Duke University contracted to occupy another very large chunk of its potential 1 million square feet. New restaurants as well as apartments and loft apartments to be built in the complex would make city living possible again.[45] The gloom was gone.

While the first female mayor, Sylvia Kerckhoff (1993–97), was in office, two city council actions, one at the start of her term and the other at the end, gave her great satisfaction. The first was the creation of Downtown Durham Inc. in 1993. A nonprofit 501(c)(6) organization intended to promote and facilitate development and revitalization of the city center, it established a board of trustees representative of a wide range of investors and contributors, including local government, corporations, large and small businesses, educational institutions, the professions, the media, the arts, and preservationists. Under its director, Bill Kalkhof, the organization became a "deal-maker and facilitator for public, private, and public-private development," hewing to standards of appearance, safety, parking, and the like that could much enhance the chances of successful development. Steadily, if slowly, the city center began to show tangible results. The other action was the council's acceptance of a "living wage" law that would raise the minimum wage of workers on city contracts or payrolls to $7.55 an hour for entry-level jobs, far more than the federal minimum wage of $4.75 in 1996. Council meetings in September and December 1997 set the stage for passage of the ordinance in January 1998.[46]

The cityscape went on being renewed. The other huge tobacco manufacturing complex in downtown Durham, the abandoned Liggett and Myers site, was also slated for rehabilitation. West Village was the new name of the row of tobacco warehouses along Duke Street, planned in 1994 and begun in 1999, to contain two-bedroom apartments and retail space. Blue Devil Ventures (later Trackside Group LLC), the developer, was the corporate name of Thomas Niemann, Brian Davis, and Christian Laettner, the latter two former Duke University basketball stars turned professionals.[47] This project would bring several hundred more downtown residents.

One hindrance to downtown living was a general fear of crime. Although police statistics showed that most city crime took place in the northeast central section and that the center city had a very low crime rate, fear remained. Allied to crime was the ever-present issue of gun ownership and gun control. Both city and county government were called to deal with it again in this period, with rather different outcomes. Gun-control advocates never made much headway against the American fondness for guns and the strong gun lobby. The topic was politically sensitive. The assassination attempt on President Reagan in 1981, however, had given new impetus to advocates and temporarily softened resistance.

Closer to home, moreover, was Durham's unacceptably high homicide rate, which prompted a group of town ministers led by the Watts Street Baptist Church minister Mel Williams to introduce the topic once again and to form a religious alliance to combat it.[48] They wanted tighter controls on the possession and sales of guns, especially assault weapons. The day they presented their plea the thirtieth murder of the year occurred in Durham. The subject landed on both county and city agendas. Mayor Kerckhoff agreed that tighter restrictions might be needed. Nobody wanted to see guns in the hands of the mentally unstable, such as Reagan's would-be assassin, but that prospect seemed more remote to many than the prospect that innocent men, women, and children might fall prey to ordinary criminals with guns. On the other hand, many people felt the need for guns to protect themselves.

After a few contentious public hearings the city passed a new gun-control ordinance with many concessions to gun advocates. To win passage the council had to remove a ban on semiautomatic weapons and on displaying weapons in city streets, on sidewalks, and in alleys. The ordinance they passed prohibited guns on city property, at public assemblies, fairs, malls, and other public venues, on buses, at polling places, and in the possession of anyone under the influence of alcohol or drugs.[49] The county commissioners, after months of discussion, supported the right of law-abiding citizens to possess concealed weapons.[50] A few later confessed that they hadn't understood what they were voting for. A state law unique to Durham County had been passed by the general assembly in 1935, which allowed Durham County to require the registration of guns and issue permits for their possession. That law remained in effect.[51]

At almost the end of the century an unprecedented move by voters effected dramatic change in the city government. Voters were sufficiently riled up in 1998 to collect enough signatures to place on the November ballot a proposal to reduce the number of council members from thirteen to seven. The city council welcomed the proposal but changed the date to that of a special election on December 8th, and the proposal passed, breaking a seventy-four-year tradition.[52] This was not accomplished without heated public discussion. Many voters, including moderate Democrats on the council, felt that the black political organization and far-left Democrats held too much power to sway elections. At the officially scheduled forum to debate the plan, other reasons were voiced. The council's size, the largest in the state, required constituents and lobbyists to contact too many members, unnecessarily prolonged discussion at council meetings, encouraged squabbling over trivial matters to the detriment of more pressing ones, and made it difficult to attract well-qualified candidates. Resentment toward the council was heightened by its having recently awarded itself a 32 percent pay raise, which it then quickly reduced to 9 percent. On election day the 20 percent of voters who cared enough to go to the polls included 62 percent who wanted a smaller council. The reduction went into effect at the election of November 2001. Candidates representing and living in three newly drawn wards were to be voted on by all voters.[53]

Meanwhile the Board of County Commissioners successfully engaged many of the same issues that faced the city council, and with corresponding changes in personnel. Its first black female member, Elna Spaulding, had been elected in 1974 and served until Josephine Clement replaced her in 1986. Like Spaulding, Clement provided a quiet civility and common sense at often contentious meetings. In 1982 Bill Bell, a commission member since 1972, became the board's first black chairman and continued in that capacity for twelve years. In 1985 the first black county manager, Jack Bond, succeeded Edwin Swindell, who had served for thirty-five years. Becky Heron, who in 1982 became the second woman and the first white woman added to the board, in 1994 became its first female chairman. In 1986 women accounted for three of the board's five members—the first time they were a majority—and in 1990 they added a fourth member. The century-long male-only tradition was finally broken. As in the city, the shift in the board's makeup influenced its concerns, and during the 1980s and 1990s schools and the environment were very much in the foreground.[54]

It was fortunate that both governmental entities experienced simultaneous as well as similar change, since that made for better cooperation. The newly united city and county planning departments simplified and facilitated work on issues such as land and water ordinances. The commissioners had to approve measures pertaining to the watershed and major projects passed by the city council before they could become law. Many of the development issues before the city council were also on the county agenda; the huge Treyburn developmnent, before its partial annexation by the city, lay of course in the county and was a touchy item for the county commissioners as well. How to balance the investment of landowners with the public requirement of a safe water supply pitched pocketbooks against health in an emotional battle. In 1990 it was discovered that the maps used when the commissioners had approved the Treyburn development had been incorrectly drawn; it was even implied that the maps had been altered to accommodate the company. Treyburn had consequently been allowed to violate the watershed ordinance because seven miles of shoreline had not been included in the watershed. With the political pressure of Save the Water and the Southeast Neighborhood Association, Commissioner Deborah Giles led a crusade to have the maps corrected, and succeeded in 1992.[55] The seven miles of waterfront were restored, and control of the restricted territory was given to the Army Corps of Engineers.[56] At the same meeting the commissioners declared a moratorium on any kind of building within one mile of the shoreline until new zoning regulations could be drawn up.[57] Members of the same coalition had been fighting a proposed landfill site in their neighborhood. The city wisely backed off on that. The commissioners finally adopted new watershed regulations three years later after a very acrimonious meeting. With one exception, only houses were to be built within the critical one-mile area around the lake. The exception was Treyburn, which had already been zoned as a corporate park under the old rules and maps. Becky Heron, then chairwoman of the commissioners and long a champion of environmental issues, with other conservationists, was unhappy with the result, but compromised for more control over future development requests.[58]

Probably because of their experience with Treyburn and at the suggestion of Ellen Reckhow, who was elected to the board in 1988 and remained on it well into the twenty-first century, the commissioners established a City-County Environmental Affairs Advisory Board, made up of specialists who could help the commissioners make informed decisions and take some of the heat off them when they dealt with hot-button issues.[59]

A state grant to create an inventory of the county's natural and cultural resources resulted in an important tool to aid the planning department and board of county commissioners in directing and controlling growth. The push for this effort came from members of the Eno River Association: Margaret Nygard, Hildegard Ryals, Kenneth Coulter, and Becky Heron. The first section of the comprehensive inventory, called "Critical Lands," prepared under supervision of the Triangle J Council of Governments, was published in May 1985. It listed graveyards and historic, recreational, mill, and archeological sites. Ryals headed the large supervisory committee and is credited with the entire effort. Publication of the second and third sections, supported partly by county funding, followed at two-year intervals and covered natural areas, birds, animals, and other wild species and fish.[60]

Ryals followed up this effort in 1989 and the following years with the New Hope Creek Corridor preservation initiative, which proposed a conservation belt connecting the Eno River to Jordan Lake, a huge new water resource serving Wake County. Durham and Orange counties as well as Durham city and Chapel Hill agreed on a resolution to recognize the importance of preserving the New Hope Creek, its banks and tributaries. They set up an advisory committee to create a master plan, which they accepted in 1991, and to help them implement it.[61] The Triangle Land Conservancy stepped in when necessary to help save threatened tracts in the corridor. A huge tract of 2,200 acres of Duke Forest was fortunately already under protection when the effort began. The process of acquiring land or covenants to protect land, however, was extremely slow.[62]

Attention to the environment and conservation efforts of all kinds was becoming urgent as the words "global warming" gained currency a century after they were first articulated. When fully understood they conveyed a concept that eclipsed the disparate environmental anxieties of previous decades in its breadth and crucial implications for the future of the earth and civilization. When global warming was added to disappearing species, air and sea pollution, acid rain, eroding beaches, contamination of the food chain and droughts (1986 presented a severe one)—all evidence of a degrading planet as a result of human activity—the gravity of the earth's plight was frightening. The means of this revelation was the data-processing computer. With powerful new computers coming into wide circulation in the 1980s, huge quantities of data could be processed and integrated for the first time to create models of evolving changes, revealing the magnitude of the problem. Surprisingly, many people were unconvinced by the evidence—religious fundamentalists and other ultra-conservatives—and chose to treat the conclusion as a political convenience.

Durham got a taste of what the environmentalists predicted the future might bring in September 1996, when it was struck by Hurricane Fran. Coming only six weeks after another devastating hurricane, Bertha, which had raked eastern North Carolina but whose severe winds had also reached into the Triangle, Fran caught the attention of even the unbelievers. Though visited by hurricane damage before, Durham had not experienced anything like the breadth and severity of this storm.

It snapped off the tops of countless pine trees and toppled huge red oaks, which fell on power lines, roofs of houses, and cars parked in driveways, blocking streets and creating a tangle of dangerous downed wires. Duke Power Company sent for eighteen hundred of its workers elsewhere in the state and for a thousand workers of other companies from states as far away as Ohio, West Virginia, and Mississippi. It took as long as a week to restore power to much of the area. Twenty-two persons were killed statewide (three in Durham) and damage amounted to $22 million. Durham no longer felt immune to environmental changes.[63]

As important as the environmental issues were, the merger of the city and county schools in 1992 was almost certainly the most long-lasting and significant accomplishment of the Board of County Commissioners in the 1990s. As already mentioned, several of the city and county agencies had already been combined, and the effort to merge the entire city and county administrations had been voted down several times since the subject was first proposed in 1924.[64] In February 1991 Governor Martin precipitated the whole issue again by proposing that the state fund only one school system per county, thus forcing the merger of duplicating school administrations and helping to prevent the divisions along racial or economic lines that characterized the Durham school systems. He left to the counties themselves the alternative of funding redundant school systems.[65]

Obviously the schools merger opened a Pandora's box of emotions and problems and could not be effected without a fight. The city's black residents were immediately alarmed by the proposal, because they feared that their teachers and administrators would lose their jobs. The white residents of the county, many of whom had fled to the suburbs to avoid the schools' integration in the 1960s, were alarmed all over again; their particular fear was that integration could be achieved only by extensive busing, and they did not want their children having to ride long distances to school. Opposition to the merger for many rested on their belief in neighborhood schools, which had been more or less the ideal for a number of years for both blacks and whites.

The whole subject was inescapable when the city schools' situation became deplorable. Testing revealed that students in almost all the schools were performing below the national norm, and even below the state norm.[66] White flight still continued to erode the white presence in city schools, leaving a black majority that reached 90 percent by 1990.[67] With a tax base correspondingly eroding, the city schools were receiving less and less money and falling farther and farther behind. The situation reached a crisis in 1991 when the city school system budget was cut, and an irresponsible school superintendent was asked to resign.[68] The county commissioners came to the rescue when the city school board scheduled a furlough of three weeks without pay for the teachers because of a deficit of $1 million.[69] Great inefficiency and petty fraud in addition to lack of oversight by the school board had led to the situation.[70] The county commissioners voted in June to merge the two systems.[71] The state Board of Education twice rejected the merger, however, and only when the county sued the board and asked the legislature to intervene was the merger approved.[72]

Creating one large combined system was not easily achieved. Three school zones instead of the former districts were drawn with the aim of attaining more racial balance and at the same time preventing long bus rides for the students. A student was assigned to a school within his or her zone but had the right to request reassignment for a valid reason.[73] Magnet schools were to be developed to allow students with similar interests to be grouped together and to encourage school choice.[74] Nine magnet schools opened in 1996.[75] The first magnet school was the former Morehead Elementary, which became a Montessori magnet school for fifty four- and five-year-olds.[76] The old failing Durham High School was turned into a magnet school for the arts, eventually with great success.[77] A new seven-member school board for the merged system was appointed under the chairmanship of Nancy Yirtle.[78] Two new high schools, Riverside and a new Hillside, were built to ease the overcrowding in Jordan and Northern high schools.[79] A new superintendent of the school system, Ann Dellinger, was appointed in 1997, and eighteen months later schools were reporting sharply increased test scores. She proved to be an excellent administrator, but her long tenure was never free of political sniping by portions of the community.[80]

While the school administration gained savings and efficiency with the merger, the schools did not gain racial balance. Many remained almost segregated. Rogers Herr, for example, in a white neighborhood, in 2001 was 74 percent black, 16 percent white, and 10 percent Latino.[81] A referendum on school bonds in 2001 still generated much black opposition. Some still harbored fears that the money would be unequally distributed. The passage of the bonds, however, showed that among both blacks and whites enough voters had changed their attitudes and were learning to work together with confidence.

From the 1980s on, community colleges assumed greater importance as sources of vocational training for some students and as bridges to higher education for others. New technologies were evolving that demanded new skills in the workforce at the same time that colleges and universities were raising their tuition and entrance requirements, frustrating the hopes of high school graduates to pursue college degrees. The community college responded to both challenges. As well as offering job training in areas always needing workers, it contracted instruction for specific industrial needs; and it offered programs leading to an associate's degree that enabled recipients to transfer to institutions of higher learning.

Durham Technical Institute, which had evolved from an industrial training center in 1965, changed its name to Durham Technical Community College in 1986 when it was allowed to add a college transfer program. Phail Wynn, Jr., who had been president of the institute since 1980, became the first African American to head a community college in North Carolina. The school thrived under his leadership, serving 25,000 students each year and offering specialized career training programs. It also opened satellite campuses on Snow Hill Road near Treyburn and in Orange County.[82] At the same time Wynn lent his talents to many civic organizations, serving on the boards of the North Carolina Mutual Life Insurance Company, the Triangle Community Foundation, the Research Triangle Institute, and the Research Triangle Foundation. He was also president of the Greater Durham Chamber of Commerce and won many awards for civic service. In 2007 he became vice-president for regional affairs of Duke University.[83]

As a footnote to these decades, an initiative by city and county to form international bonds should be noted. In the 1980s the city embraced Sister Cities International, a movement motivated by a longing for world peace and cooperation among nations that encouraged cities to form partnerships with foreign populations, partnerships that were social for the most part but potentially economic as well. Until the cold war ended with the fall of the Berlin Wall in 1989, the western world lived for forty years with anxiety, witnessing an arms race and fearing that an international incident would spark an inferno of nuclear warfare. A few groups and individuals sought ways to lessen the tension by reaching across international boundaries to the Russian people. In Durham, Dorothy Borden was one of these. A member of the Episcopal Peace Fellowship and Congregations for Peace, she convened a meeting of the two groups to discover what they might do along these lines. She learned of Sister Cities International, which had grown out of President Eisenhower's People to People initiative. With the advocacy of a receptive mayor, Wib Gulley, and two council members, Jane Davis and Tom Campbell, the city and county governments agreed to a proposal that Durham participate in international partnerships. In fact, the city discovered during its research of the proposal that Durham's mayor James Hawkins, on his own initiative and without any fanfare, had enlisted Durham in a Sister Cities partnership with Durham, England, on a visit to England in 1976.[84]

The upshot of Borden's effort was the acquisition in November 1989 of Kostroma in the Soviet Union as a second sister city. The signing with the representative from Kostroma took place in Durham. For good measure Durham gained two other sister cities: Toyama in Japan, also in 1989 (Gulley went to Japan for the signing), and Arusha in Tanzania in 1991 (Mayor Chester Jenkins went to Africa for the signing).

Besides the benefits of international goodwill and, to be hoped, understanding, these alliances had cultural and commercial advantages. They promoted exchanges of many kinds between teachers, students, and civic and other organizations, as well as forming connections between commercial companies and churches. St. Luke's Church in Durham, for example, already had a link with Christ Church in Arusha; Toyama gave a pavilion to Duke Gardens; and in 1995 Dr. Patrick Kenan organized a trip by the Durham Savoyards to Durham, England, for a performance of music by Gilbert and Sullivan. Two choirs, the Mt. Olive Baptist Church gospel choir under Marlon West and the Jordan High School choir under Scott Hill, also visited and performed in Durham, England, under Sister Cities auspices. The gospel performance was so popular that the choir later returned independently.[85]

SCIENCE AND SOCIETY: ILLS AND SOLUTIONS

Computer Technology

The 1980s were a time of unforeseen changes, and the most crucial agent of change was computer technology, which came within reach of the average person for the first time, and changed the way the world worked quite as irrevocably as the gasoline combustion engine had done in the early years of the twentieth century. The breakthrough to mass adoption and mass production of personal computers made computers on desktops as common as telephones. The importance of this to Durham can be traced to events in the 1960s, and the inception of computer technology to World War II.

The desktop computer contrasted starkly with the colossal ENIAC machine that filled a whole room of the Moore School of Engineering at the University of Pennsylvania in the 1940s, but it was only another step in a long path of innovative advances. The war, and its urgent need for machines that could handle complex mathematical calculations with unimaginable speed, had greatly spurred the technology.[86]

The history of computer technology in Durham is linked to the giant company International Business Machines (IBM). When the company, which had been the leader in electrically driven punched-card data processing machines, turned its attention to computers in the early 1950s, it became dominant in the rapidly growing industry. In the 1970s IBM introduced its revolutionary System 360 machines, ranging in size from minicomputers to supercomputers. The computer pioneer responsible for this machine and its software was Frederick P. Brooks, born in Durham and educated at Duke (1953) and Harvard (1956). Despite his success and length of service at IBM, he was persuaded by the University of North Carolina to set up a department of computer and information science in 1964, and he remained at Chapel Hill for the rest of his career.[87]

Perhaps by coincidence, in 1965 IBM decided to move a large part of its computer operation to the Research Triangle Park after considerable enticements offered by North Carolina's governor and the park recruiters. So eager was North Carolina to make this important capture that it waived the rule prohibiting manufacturing in the park. The importance of this coup may be seen in the results. During the six years after the park's creation, only 214 of its almost 7,000 acres had been sold, but in 1965 alone a variety of companies purchased 1,035 acres, among them, of course, IBM's 400 acres. Announcements early in that year by both the U.S. Department of Health, Education and Welfare and IBM of plans to build facilities in the park undoubtedly inspired others to follow suit and gave the park the momentum it has maintained to the present. By century's end IBM, with 13,000 employees, was the second-largest employer in Durham County, after Duke University.[88]

A decade before IBM's move to the park, John J. Gergen and Thomas M. Gallie had introduced computers and computer science to Duke University. They received a grant from the National Science Foundation to fund an IBM System 650 computer and offered graduate-level courses. At that time computer science was spurned by most academics as "vocational training." In 1971, with help from Dean Marcus Hobbs of Trinity College and Dr. Eugene Stead of the medical school, Gallie was able to persuade Duke to set up a program in computing, which evolved into a full department of computer science in 1973.

By the mid-1960s Duke University's use of computers had so increased that the outmoded machine could not keep up with the university's needs. The other

Triangle universities were experiencing the same problem, and none could afford to buy one of the new, more powerful machines. A solution was found in 1965 when Brooks, Gallie, and James K. Farrell, who had introduced computing at North Carolina State University, joined forces to set up Triangle Universities Computation Center (TUCC) in the Research Triangle Park. With their efforts combined and the three universities sharing the costs, these pioneers obtained a very large IBM System 360 computer connected by telephone to smaller 360s at each institution.[89]

TUCC set up the North Carolina Computation Orientation Program (NCCOP) to make limited computer access available free of cost for one year. NCCOP hired young "circuit riders" to visit the colleges as they entered the computer age. Soon these institutions obtained their own computers and developed their own computer courses. Computers of all kinds began to proliferate at Duke, UNC, and NC State. No longer necessary, TUCC went out of existence in the mid-1990s.[90]

In 1980 the three Triangle universities and the Research Triangle Institute formed the Microelectronics Center of North Carolina (MCNC) to conduct research in the fabrication of integrated circuit chips and to spread knowledge and use of the latest computer-based technology to all the regional universities and colleges, research institutions, public libraries, and medical centers. Governor James Hunt persuaded the General Assembly to make an initial grant of more than $40 million to MCNC.[91]

Other manufacturers of component parts, hardware and software, flocked to the area, drawn by IBM's success. The enormous activity in the industry inspired entrepreneurs and start-up companies in every aspect of the technology to market their innovations. Red Hat Inc., for example, began its meteoric success in the Triangle in the mid-1990s, offering the Linux operating system and other open-source software.[92]

An incalculably valuable and revolutionary outgrowth of computers was of course the internet, along with the World Wide Web (1989) and the field of information technology (IT) as a whole. The internet joined all places in the world and incomparably advanced knowledge. Global trade and international interchanges of every description resulted from the instantaneous communication and exchange of information that the internet made possible. Besides conquering distance and time, computers could control almost every mechanical operation. Their application in research was profound. They made possible medical discoveries and technologies such as ultrasound and magnetic resonance imaging, cyto- and lasik surgery, and a host of other noninvasive diagnostic tools. They could analyze, calculate, and organize data of a magnitude and complexity beyond imagining. They made possible the twentieth century's triumphal ending achievement: the decoding of the human genome. Because computer technology innovation, intrinsically connected with research of all kinds, now drives the economy of the Research Triangle Park and Durham County, the city and county are poised to be for the foreseeable future in the right place at the right time.

As IBM attracted other computer-related companies to the park, so the move there in 1970 of Burroughs Wellcome's corporate headquarters became a magnet for pharmaceutical and biomedical companies; and again the move there in 1982 of the National Institute of Environmental Health Sciences (NIEHS) brought health-related companies and medical research laboratories in its wake. Of the seventy biotechnology companies in North Carolina in 1992, a third of them were clustered in the Research Triangle Park, and other companies continued to come.[93] By the year 2000 there were 140 companies of all kinds in the park. Although the corporate giants were the flashiest tenants and the business sector investment was huge, the park's incorporators, the three universities, made sure that its character remained intellectual and its purpose the furtherance of human knowledge.[94] The universities' establishment of the Triangle Universities Center for Advanced Studies Inc. (TUCASI) made their intentions perfectly plain. It was under TUCASI's aegis, for example, that the National Humanities Center (1978), discussed earlier, was formed.

The first tenant, the Research Triangle Institute, also helped to establish and maintain the park's character. Called the centerpiece of the park, it earned fame for its prolific scholarly research. In 1980 it had over a thousand employees and earned $47 million in research contracts; by 2000 the earnings were $200 million. The institute's research dealt principally with environmental and medical problems, dictated by governmental and social needs.[95] From its laboratories in 1988, for example, came the discovery of the therapeutic use of taxol (made from the Pacific yew) by Monroe Wall and Marsakh Wani. Licensed for use in 1992, taxol proved to be a breakthrough, if not a cure, in the treatment of ovarian cancer; it doubled the survival rate of those treated with it.[96] Further fame was brought to Durham when three park scientists were honored with Nobel prizes in physiology or medicine: George H. Hitchings, Jr., and Gertrude Belle Elion of Burroughs Wellcome in 1988 and Martin Rodbell of the National Institute of Environmental and Health Sciences in 1994.[97]

Nothing has stimulated scientific research as much as the Bayh-Dole Act (1980). Almost made to order for Durham's economy, it accelerated the already existing triangular relationship of government, research laboratories, and industry. The act, really an amendment to the patent laws, enabled universities and researchers to patent the products of their publicly funded research and thus to share in the substantial financial rewards with the companies that leased from them the rights to manufacture and market their products. Among those profiting from the legislation were, of course, Duke University scientists. Cooperation of the companies in the park with the Duke laboratories had long been mutually beneficial, actually the raison d'être of the park's establishment, and the Duke researchers had long enjoyed government funding for their work. To its credit, state government immediately saw the opportunity that the new law offered and established the North Carolina Biotechnology Center (1982) in the park "to facilitate research, business and education in biotechnology."[98] The establishment of this center along with the

Microelectronics Center of North Carolina (1980; see above) proved to be perceptive and forward-looking moves that put North Carolina in an advantageous position to ride the crest of the new economy.

Duke laboratories contributed a number of medical successes. A widely hailed
product was the nicotine patch invented by Dr. Jed E. Rose. In three months of
marketing it yielded $300 million in sales.[99] It is not a little ironic that the institu-
tion built on a tobacco fortune should be the creator of a product to cure tobacco
addiction.

Many researchers at Duke have set up small companies concentrating on research of very specific diseases, for example Sphinx Pharmaceuticals (1987), taken
over by Eli Lilly and Company in 1994 and tripled in size, Enzyme Technologies
Research, and Macronex Inc., in search of remedies for autoimmune diseases.[100]

In 1997 medical trials at Duke Medical Center ended with good news for "bubble"
children and their parents. From time to time newspapers had told heart-rending
tales of children born without immune systems, who were forced to live in sterile
isolation. Even with that precaution, those children usually fell victim to opportu-
nistic infections and died. Although a cure had been found in bone marrow trans-
plants from siblings with perfectly matched marrow, preceded by chemotherapy,
Dr. Rebecca Buckley of Duke found an easier cure that was almost completely effective. From trials conducted at Duke from 1982 to 1997 she proved that the children could be saved with only half-matched bone marrow donated by a parent and
without preliminary chemotherapy, if T-cells were cleansed from the donor blood
and the operation were performed within the early months of life. She also recommended that all babies be tested for the disease at birth.[101]

When HIV/AIDS (Human Immunodeficiency Virus/Acquired Immunodeficiency
Syndrome) erupted in 1981, it presented another Duke laboratory with an opportunity for a significant discovery. The viral disease, first noticed in New York and
California among homosexual men, soon revealed itself as a threat to a broad range
of the population, including intravenous drug users and recipients of blood transfu-
sions. As the fatal disease spread, it seemed that almost everyone was at risk, and
no cure was in sight. After a diagnostic test was devised, cases could begin to be
recorded and statistics compiled to reveal how many persons were afflicted and
how fast and where the disease was spreading. The death toll in the United States
for the 1980s and 1990s has been estimated at 440,000 cases. By 2003 forty million
people worldwide had contracted the disease.[102]

Little was known about the disease, however, when David W. Barry of Burroughs
Wellcome persuaded the Duke physician Dani Bolognesi and his associates Thomas
Matthews and Kemp Weinhold to devote a recent grant from the National Institutes of Health (NIH) to a search for a drug that could treat HIV/AIDS. In 1986
they found that AZT, which Burroughs Wellcome had earlier developed for another
purpose and which had proved useless at that time, was effective in prolonging the
lives of victims. The first trials were conducted at Duke and the NIH. Burroughs
Wellcome brought the drug to market in 1987, and it was hailed as a lifeline in an
otherwise bleak landscape. After more trials at Duke and elsewhere for the use of
AZT in combating the disease in children, the drug was approved for that use as

well in 1990.[103] In the early 1990s Dr. Bolognesi set up the company Trimeris Inc. to develop more AIDS treatments based on technology supplied by his laboratory.[104]

In 1987 Duke University established the AIDS Clinical Trial Unit (ACTU), funded by the NIH with $500,000 a year for ten years, under the supervision of Dr. John Bartlett, who became an expert in treating the disease. ACTU was to test new AIDS drugs and therapies. Two other units were also established, one to conduct basic research on the virus and to develop a vaccine against it, the other to evaluate the experimental vaccines as they were developed.[105]

The disease soon affected the Durham Health and Human Services Department when many of the men falling ill had no support to rely on as the illness incapacitated them, and could not pay for treatment. Dr. Janice Stratton and her assistant, Dr. Irving Hoffman, proposed that the city set up a clinic to treat HIV/AIDS and to educate the public about prevention. The clinic established by the city was staffed by doctors and clinical workers from the Lincoln Community Health Center under Dr. Evelyn Schmitt's supervision. Because Durham for a few years had the most cases of any metropolitan area in the state (in 1996 the city's HIV rate was triple the state average), the county health department distributed 200,000 condoms as an intervention policy for AIDS and for sexually transmitted diseases in general, a policy which, along with needle exchange, proved very controversial.[106]

Another county agency affected by AIDS was the Department of Correction. Stricter laws against possessing and trafficking in illegal drugs dramatically increased prison populations nationwide. Because many of the prisoners were intravenous drug users, they brought HIV/AIDS into the prison. The intravenous use of heroine and cocaine was rising along with the popularity of a powder cocaine and crack cocaine.[107] The prison became severely overcrowded. From 1983 to 1995 the number of prisoners in Durham increased from 3,496 to 10,122, far outstripping the average rise statewide. The county was forced to build a new jail at a cost of $43.5 million; it opened in March 1996. The hulking white mass, five stories high, with room for almost six hundred prisoners, comprised twelve small jails, containing forty-eight pods, where the prisoners could be separated by sex and seriousness of crime. Inmates infected with AIDS had to be given the medical care and expensive medications that treatment required.[108]

Durham County as a whole had its share of cases. From 1983 to 1990, 172 cases of HIV and 113 cases of AIDS were documented. These totals increased to 755 and 424 for the years 1991 to 1996. Better understanding of the disease and its means of transmittal, as well as education about prevention, behavior modification, and treatment, began to slow the spread of infection. The next years, 1997 to 2002, showed only 562 cases of HIV and 230 of AIDS in Durham County.[109]

Still, the disease was not soon going away, and people had to learn to live with it. Its presence changed forever the way health providers practiced. Rubber gloves and masks became obligatory for those in contact with human blood, or in danger of coming into contact with it. Before such precautions were adopted, there had been instances of accidental transmission of HIV/AIDS from an infected doctor or nurse to a patient and vice versa.

SOCIAL PROBLEMS

In the waning decades of the century a confluence of events and trends enormously increased the complexity of social problems in Durham: urban renewal had displaced many poor families and destroyed much low-cost housing; the Vietnam War had left many veterans physically or mentally ill, often addicted to alcohol and drugs, and consequently often homeless; the decline of the family meant increasing rates of divorce and illegitimacy, leaving children without the support and supervision of two-parent households and likely to live in poverty; the decline of traditional blue-collar jobs in tobacco factories and cotton mills as the economy shifted to biomedical and other research left hundreds of workers jobless, unable to fill jobs requiring an educated and skilled workforce; Hispanic immigration brought hundreds more unskilled workers competing for jobs; failing schools bred an increasing number of dropouts; and the construction of two interstate highways, I-85 and I-40, running through and converging near Durham provided fast corridors for drug traffickers and a place for them to rendezvous.

Under such an onslaught of needs, city and county services were strained beyond capacity. Although new programs, agencies, and offices to address these problems were devised, they never sufficed, and it fell to private charitable and religious organizations, often working with the local governments, to take up the slack.

HOMELESSNESS

Large and small cities had always had their share of vagrants and the homeless, but usually their small number lent them invisibility. In the 1970s, however, the number increased, and they became a permanent feature in metropolitan areas. By the 1980s, homelessness was so large a problem that attention had to be paid. As already mentioned, the Vietnam War had sent home a large number of veterans with physical and mental disabilities. An estimated 39 percent of the homeless were eligible for physical or mental disability payments. Many were never absorbed back into the fabric of society; they became incapable of supporting themselves. During Ronald Reagan's business-friendly administration (1981–89) efforts were focused on reducing the size of the federal government, which had ballooned with social programs during the 1970s. Funding for many programs was transferred to the states, and lack of state funding had the effect of actually ending the programs. Among the agencies and institutions affected were mental hospitals. At about the same time, medical researchers had come up with medication for some common mental illnesses, and it was thought more humane and less expensive for society to release the afflicted on medication back into the everyday world. In reality many without family or other support went off the drug treatment they required to function and joined the ranks of those living on the streets. Another group was just hard-luck victims who could not find or hold jobs, and a very few opted to be homeless.

Although homelessness is obviously a difficult subject to study because it is a moving target, in 2000 the homeless in Durham were estimated at close to four hundred on any given day, with an additional thirty-four homeless persons living on the street not counted in any of the agencies' shelters.[110] One organization that responded to the problem was Urban Ministries Inc., established in 1983. This was a nonprofit umbrella organization for a coalition of many churches seeking a means for their charities to be efficiently coordinated, operated, and funded. Its creation should be credited to the minister of St. Philip's Church, C. Thomas Midyette, who urged a response, and to Charles L. Steele IV, a church member who devised the ingenious plan and oversaw its implementation. The church acquired land adjoining its own and led a fund-raising campaign for $500,00 to build a shelter. The money was given to Urban Ministries, which built the shelter (the Community Shelter for Hope), leased it at a nominal fee from the church, and managed the program of activities. The already existing Presbyterian shelter program, which operated only during two months in winter, the Methodist clothing cupboard, St. Philip's soup kitchen, and various counseling services were all moved to the shelter building, which began operation in 1985. The Church League Basketball program also used the space. The city agreed to help subsidize the annual cost of running these vital services.[111] Two smaller agencies, Genesis House and Phoenix House, provided longer-term accommodations for a few homeless families while they worked out their problems.[112]

The community kitchen had begun in 1980 with a simple lunch, served five days a week on the premises of St. Philip's Church. From 1980 to 1999, while the number of the hungry and homeless ballooned, the remarkably able Betsy Rollins managed the soup kitchen. Although visually handicapped, she proved tireless and effective in garnering food supplies, raising funds, planning meals, and directing the entire operation as it grew, eventually supplying three meals a day every day. With the help of Senator Jesse Helms she was able to make nonprofit food programs for the indigent eligible for the same surplus foods as the public schools. This considerably eased the problem of supply. Her advocacy for the homeless won her appointments to President Reagan's Committee on World Hunger in 1983 and to his Task Force on Food Distribution. Her knowledge and experience made her a nationwide resource for similar programs.[113]

The Durham Rescue Mission, a private, nonprofit agency, provided food and shelter, job training, counseling, and help for homeless women and children as well as men, but with a religious component and behavior code unacceptable to many of the homeless. Ernie Mills and his wife Gail had established the mission in the 1970s. A small house on Main Street that accommodated twelve homeless men was the start of what became an extensive and very successful seven-month rehabilitation program, helping hundreds of the needy every year. Work and an evangelical Christian faith with strong social support formed the foundation of the program, but a missionary zeal and personal involvement by the founders accounted for much of its success. The mission undertook to serve anyone who came to its Thanksgiving and Christmas dinners, regardless of creed.[114]

Another charismatic reformer was Kevin McDonald, the founder of TROSA. Exclusively aimed at alcohol and drug addicts who wanted to recover their lives, it provided safe housing, social support, job training, and employment in a two-year program. Giving addicts back a sense of self-esteem and responsibility was an important component of the program's success. Those who completed the training received recognition and certificates at a graduation ceremony. TROSA began very modestly, with McDonald and a helper in an empty building provided by the city. They supported themselves as they renovated the building by running a potato-peeling business. Within ten years, under McDonald's inspired leadership and commitment, the organization had become the largest independent moving company in the state and also expanded into catering, furniture and upholstery repair, painting, bricklaying, and picture framing. It owned thirty properties and could house over three hundred residents in the recovery program and employ a staff of forty. The Ford Foundation recognized McDonald with its Leadership for a Changing World Award.[115]

The local government meanwhile was pouring resources into the most crime-ridden area of the city, described as Northeast Central Durham. A series of newspaper articles by different reporters shone a light on this troubled area and the considerable resources marshaled to improve it.[116] Once a stable working-class neighborhood, Northeast Central Durham had been declining for thirty years as traditional jobs in tobacco and textiles disappeared. The intersection of Driver and Angier streets had been the focus of a diverse neighborhood of southern whites and blacks interspersed with Italians and Russian Jews. More recently Hispanics had joined the mix.[117] Now drug trafficking, arson, and violence terrorized the inhabitants. Only 37 percent of families were headed by two parents. The unemployment rate was 15 percent. Teenage pregnancy and a high illegitimacy rate made for greater poverty and unstable families. Affordable housing was badly needed. Landlords had let their property deteriorate and were still charging unrealistic rents.[118]

Fifty-five agencies representing local government, foundations, and charitable and religious organizations rallied to the challenge, offering an array of programs, including Northeast Central Partners against Crime and the Urban Enterprise Corps, established with a donation of $1 million from the Kenan Trust to send newly graduated MBAs into the neighborhood to stimulate and support economic development. Other efforts were mounted to strengthen families, increase literacy, and provide learning programs for two- to four-year-olds. Night Flight offered evening recreation for teenagers directed by the Salvation Army, 4-H groups, and the Scouts at recreation centers with basketball courts. Duke University students volunteered hours of tutoring.[119]

In conjunction with business leaders, the county began a new program to provide career counseling and job training to the unemployed, primarily in Northeast Central Durham, with the aim of creating jobs and small businesses. Called Job Opportunities and Basic Skills (JOBS), it was operated out of the old bank building on Holloway Street.[120]

Perhaps in response to the Peirce Report, a series of newspaper articles published in 1993, Nannerl Keohane, who became Duke University's first woman president in that year, promised that the university would become involved with the city and do its share of volunteer work in the Northeast Central project as well as in other projects nearer home. The Peirce Report took a critical look at the Triangle and concluded that only the involvement of the universities and their cooperation with business and government could solve the area's serious social problems.[121] When Keohane spoke to the Greater Durham Chamber of Commerce in 1994 she claimed that already 75 percent of Duke students were engaged in some kind of charitable work. Later the university made loans for low-cost housing and gave its service employees opportunities for job advancement, education, child care, and health care. Having destroyed nearby neighborhoods as it expanded, the university tried to be especially sensitive to other adjacent poor neighborhoods that it might help.[122]

Affordable housing was vital to alleviating homelessness and poverty. The U.S. Department of Housing and Urban Development (HUD) had long poured money into the city through the Durham Housing Authority (DHA). Too often, however, poorly qualified administrators and malefactors in Washington and Durham had mismanaged or illegally diverted the money. Even when HUD and DHA were working well, as they did for long stretches, Durham lacked sufficient affordable housing, notwithstanding that private organizations besides banks often lent or gave money to city housing projects. Edgemont Elms, built around 1990 in the Northeast Central critical area, was built with funding from HUD, DHA, Development Ventures Inc. (a nonprofit subsidiary of DHA), Duke University, and six other entities. Duke's share was $1.2 million, a sum that had also been used to fund in part Edgemont Villages and Stratton Park.[123] Oxford Commons (1990) was built with money from the city, Duke, First Union Bank, and Cimarron Capital Inc.[124] In 1994 Duke University offered $2 million more at low interest to low-income families to purchase houses; $1 million went to secure $20 million in mortgages from Wachovia Bank and Trust Company. Duke employees were to be given preference for funding from the new loan. Administering it was Self-Help Credit Union, an independent organization.[125]

Independent nonprofit lending organizations such as these were set up by civic-minded citizens interested in helping to house those who needed a hand up. Jack Preiss was a notable example over many years. A professor of sociology at Duke, Preiss served on the city council from 1965 to 1969, where he was a crusader against discrimination in housing and other areas. In 1979 he was appointed to the board of the Housing Authority. He found a way for nonprofit organizations not under HUD to receive support from foundations for housing. These nonprofits could use the funding to provide other kinds of housing than those supported by HUD. Preiss's own Development Ventures Inc. became the first example.[126]

Development Ventures was involved in the Preiss-Steele project (1994) for the elderly (named for Jack J. Preiss and Alma G. Steele, board members of the DHA). Preiss together with Charles Markham and Roddy Tempest formed New Directions for Downtown Inc.[127] Preiss was also responsible for establishing the North Carolina Housing Trust Fund and the Durham Housing Bond Program. Preiss's long commitment to facilitating public housing for the elderly, disabled, and homeless won him several awards, among them the George Maddox Award for service to the elderly, a Leadership in Aging Award from the Duke University Center for the Study of Aging and Human Development, and the Life-time Achievement Award for

Advocacy from the North Carolina Interagency Council for Coordinating Homeless Programs.[128] Martin Eakes, a lawyer and another innovative entrepreneur for the poor, in 1980 established Self-Help, which provided loans to low-income and minority families to buy homes and start businesses. He also added a federally insured credit union. By 1995 Self-Help had grown to a $75 million institution with three other offices in the state.[129]

SEEDS (South Eastern Efforts Developing Sustainable Spaces Inc.), developed by Brenda Brodie, wife of the former Duke president H. Keith H. Brodie and Annice Kenan, began in 1994 in a modest way but soon flourished and spread. An effort in pursuit of beautification, education, and rehabilitation, it used nature and the land to teach residents of Northeast Central Durham how to plant a garden, raise vegetables and flowers, and market the produce. A two-acre empty lot rented for $1 dollar a year supplied the base for the experiment. The unemployed homeless men of Phoenix House supplied the labor with help from volunteers and became the beneficiaries of the skills they were taught and of the produce they grew. The program soon expanded to seven additional neighborhood sites and school gardens, and the produce was sold at the farmers' market. A greenhouse, model displays, classes on gardening and the environment, summer camps, and community compost bins were added as the program grew to become a supportive and imaginative force for good in the slow work of neighborhood rebuilding.[130]

MENTAL ILLNESS

In 1985 there were few programs to help adults battling mental illness to shape their lives into active, productive channels. Robert L. Dickens, Shirley Strobel, and others with mentally ill family members got together to construct a program that might answer this need. They estimated that at that time about fifteen hundred people in Durham could benefit from such a program. The program they devised and established, called Threshold, was based on Fountain House, a "clubhouse rehabilitation" program in New York City. Threshold's aim was to train the chronically mentally ill to live independently and was open to those eighteen to sixty-five, but not to drug or alcohol addicts. At its inception the incorporators estimated that up to forty persons might be accommodated in the rented house on Onslow Street. In 1994 Threshold acquired its own, larger quarters on Gary Street in East Durham. It supplied a sheltered, supportive environment in which participants could learn basic skills and perform simple jobs and become more self-sufficient. It also encouraged self-esteem and self-confidence. The clubhouse operated at first four days a week, with an occasional evening activity. While learning to manage time and money and relate to other people, the club members were taught to perform clerical duties, cook, serve lunch, put out a newsletter, and do similar tasks. Threshold then helped them find employment that used this kind of experience.[131]

At about the same time the county's mental health department began a treatment center for alcoholism and drug addiction called Oakleigh, consisting of an outpatient facility on Guess Road and an intensive-care facility close to the Durham General Hospital. Many of its patients had been formerly cared for at John Umstead Hospital in Butner, a facility for the mentally ill.[132]

Pockets of poverty in other parts of the city inspired programs intended for particular segments of the population. Two such efforts were aimed at school-age boys at risk of dropping out of school, becoming addicted to drugs or alcohol, joining gangs, or engaging in crime. Sports, especially basketball, were a magnet to draw youths in poor neighborhoods to safe, encouraging, disciplined environments where they could improve their self-esteem, find an outlet for their energy, and spend their free time. Like much of Durham's population, its youth was enthralled by the high level of basketball played by Duke University's teams during the late 1980s and 1990s. The Blue Devils gave Durham fans enormous satisfaction when one winning season after another ended in record performances.

This success was due to a fortunate hire in 1980, which brought Coach Mike Krzyzewski ("Coach K") to Durham. Born to a Polish immigrant family in Chicago, Krzyzewski emerged as a first-class coach with a sterling reputation and coaching experience at Indiana and West Point, his alma mater. After a few depressing seasons his Duke teams began to pile up record statistics in the National College Athletic Association (NCAA) and Atlantic Coast Conference (ACC). Winning games was not the only achievement of this remarkable man or the only reason for the fans' affection for his teams. In his coaching Krzyzewski instilled the importance of academic excellence and character development. Duke could be proud of its athletes' academic records. Coach K was voted national coach of the year twelve times and elected to the Basketball Hall of fame in 2001. His fame spread internationally when he coached the winning United States team at the 2008 Olympics.[133]

While an ambassador for Duke to the wider world, Krzyzewski was also a civic promoter and generous contributor to the underprivileged youth of the city. He was a major donor to the Emily Krzyzewski Center, named for his mother and built on ground provided by his church, Immaculata Roman Catholic Church. Situated on west Chapel Hill Street in a neighborhood of Hispanic immigrants and poor blacks, the center, in conjunction with other Durham social programs, offered tutoring, counseling, and coaching for underprivileged children of elementary and middle school age.[134]

A similar program, the Durham Eagles Athletic Association, a nonprofit organization chartered by Pop Warner Youth Football, was founded in 1994 to meet the needs of middle- and low-income minority youth of middle school and high school age in an effort to keep them in school and out of trouble. Coaches and mentors encouraged boys toward achievement in athletics as well as academic studies, setting up teams and competition among them. The association's reach increased every year; after beginning with only 41 boys, by 2000 it had grown to 135. A foundation was set up to raise money for scholarships for post-secondary education for boys who completed three years in the program, which eventually included basketball as well as football.[135]

Other groups—women and children—that formerly had been ignored or underserved were victims of domestic violence. Detection was always a problem with these victims, who could not or would not report their suffering. The conventional, fragmented attempts to deal with these cases were unavailing. Until statistics could be gathered, no one had an exact knowledge of the extent of the abuse. That changed for child abuse in the 1990s. A few pediatricians, disturbed by their inability to help these children in any permanent way, raised the alarm, and with the help of the Durham-Orange Medical Society and then other professionals concerned with abused children, began to devise a solution that would include all children in need and provide preventive services, early detection, and multidisciplinary intervention. NCCU, Duke, and UNC were appealed to and immediately took responsibility for heading the program. In 1996 the Center for Child and Family Health–North Carolina opened and brought to one location the myriad services of a holistic approach to the problem: medical, psychological, legal, and social. Collaboration in resolving the contributing elements of each case, as well as continuing study to develop and test new solutions, mounted a formidable and more successful attack against the complex and tragic reality of child abuse and of domestic violence in general.[136]

IMMIGRATION

During most of its history, while Durham was a place of constant and steady growth, the groups making up its population remained ethnically very much the same: whites, blacks, and Native Americans, with a sprinkling of Greeks, Italians, and Jews, long resident and well rooted in the community. All spoke English. In the 1970s local farmers began to hire migrant workers from Mexico and other Central American and Caribbean countries, and some of them remained. Internal political and economic upheavals in Central America and the Caribbean, along with increasing unemployment in both regions, initiated a long and still growing influx of needy people into the United States, at first into the southwestern states. What began as a trickle in Durham in the 1980s became a flood in the late 1990s. The census records tell the story. In 1980 only 1,279 Hispanics (0.84 percent of the total population) were counted in Durham County, mostly Mexicans but also including Cubans, Puerto Ricans, and other Hispanics. By 1990 the whole group had only grown to 2,054 persons (1.13 percent); but by 2000 the number had reached 17,039 persons (7.63 percent of the county's total population of 223,314). By 2006 Hispanics accounted for 11.5 percent of the total.[137] A high birthrate as well as a rising immigration rate accounted for the increase.[138]

North Carolina would not have seemed a likely choice for these immigrants, except that besides the usual, available agricultural work, jobs in construction were plentiful. The immigrants were drawn to the area when the Research Triangle began its dramatic expansion. While some who came were educated or skilled middle-class workers, and others had initially settled elsewhere in the United States, the majority were unskilled and poor; they obviously lacked health insurance, the English language, and skills for any but low-paying jobs. They needed all the help they could get. More than that, a large number were undocumented, a bureaucratic word for illegal aliens. Experts have estimated that in 2004, 45 percent of Hispanics then resident in North Carolina and 76 percent of those who had migrated to North Carolina between 1995 and 2004 were illegal entrants.[139]

Among the many local governmental entities affected by the new immigrants was the school system. There were few in Durham who could act as interpreters or teach in Spanish the special classes that had to be set up for the children. Even teachers of English as a second language were not that easy to find. In the school year 1997–98 there were 887 children enrolled in Durham public schools.[140]

The language barrier was the Hispanics' most serious problem. All governmental agencies finally had to address it and offer their services in two languages, including the issuing of all official notices, bulletins, and information in any form. Perhaps the language handicap proved most acute when the Hispanics came face to face with the criminal justice system—police, courts, and jails. The police department, like the schools and all the other official agencies, had to hire translators and when possible Spanish-speaking regular employees. It is understandable that in their economic plight, compounded by an alien culture, a language barrier, and ignorance of the laws, the newcomers were especially vulnerable to being drawn into illegal activities. Gangs were eager to recruit young men and even boys, offering membership in a group, protection, excitement, and money. Joining a gang seemed like an easy solution to a youth's problems, and some accepted the offer. For many of the same reasons Hispanic immigrants were also easy *victims* of lawbreakers.[141]

Despite the cost to the host county (and nation) in health, education, and social services, the Hispanic immigrants made a huge contribution in return. They filled necessary jobs that were the least desirable—road repair and construction, farm labor, garbage collection, domestic service (motels, hotels, private homes), and scullery jobs in restaurants and hotels. Increasingly they were also found as store clerks and small business owners. Their contribution to the economy of North Carolina by 2009 was estimated at $18 billion.[142] Their presence became obvious not only in service jobs but in the neighborhoods that serve them. Spanish stores sold ethnic products and conducted business in Spanish. Their influx was probably one of the biggest changes the county ever experienced.

The budgetary constraints of local government left vacuums of need for the immigrants. Volunteer and religious organizations stepped in to assist and ease the accommodation of both foreigners and natives. To bridge the cultural divide, many churches established services in Spanish and social groups to encourage friendship and support systems for the newcomers. They eased the transformation of foreigners into citizens.

DUKE UNIVERSITY

Duke University experienced consistent growth in size and achievement during this period, particularly its medical center. Forceful and visionary men such as the physician-administrators William Anlyan and Ralph Snyderman, who successively filled the role of chancellor for health affairs, gave the medical center the leadership it needed to grasp opportunities and pioneer new paths. Internal tensions, turf wars, and conflicting personalities among the many brilliant department heads caused administrative headaches but did not prevent innovative and successful outcomes.

The cost of health care occupied center stage as it took ever larger slices of the budgetary pies of federal and local governments, companies, and individuals. In the 1980s the Reagan administration had cut back federal spending on many public programs and research, and on subsidies for training physicians and community health clinics; these cuts affected the medical center. Because Duke University was the largest employer in Durham County, numbering twenty thousand employees in 1998, fourteen thousand of them in the medical center, what happened at Duke vitally affected Durham as a whole.[143]

When Terry Sanford took over the presidency of Duke in 1970 his aim was to make a widely respected regional institution into one nationally acclaimed, and he succeeded in part by increasing the university's base of potential donors, hence its working capital, and its visibility through the hiring of faculty stars.[144] By the time his hand-picked successor, H. Keith H. Brodie, was inaugurated in 1985, the university was ready to attempt the final step up to international recognition. It was probably not entirely chance that Brodie was a member of the medical center and head of the psychiatry department when Sanford appointed him chancellor of the university in 1982 and then groomed him as his own successor. In contrast to Sanford, Brodie was intellectual and introspective; while he lacked the political adroitness, personal magnetism, and common touch of Sanford, he possessed social polish and eloquence. Brodie preferred to operate behind the scenes instead of in the limelight.

Brodie continued to strengthen the faculty by making strategic hires, believing that this was crucial to Duke's rise to international stature, at the same time raising faculty salaries across the board.[145] He also initiated efforts to further racial integration of the university, and to commit it to community involvement. Brodie recognized that global political changes leading to the demolition of the Berlin Wall and the eventual breakup of the USSR—in effect the end of the forty-year cold war—provided opportunities for new international understanding, tolerance, and cultural exchanges. But as he witnessed the former communist countries being torn apart by ethnic, religious, and social strife, he realized that understanding, tolerance, and attention to our own population's diversity must be an important concern.[146]

On the home front Brodie instituted a campus-wide effort to hire more African American faculty members, setting quotas for all the departments. The goal proved elusive; he achieved only modest gains. He also appointed an African American vice-president for student affairs and established a black studies program to increase the pool of black students and encourage African American scholars to come to and remain at Duke.[147] Brodie offered Jean Spaulding, the daughter-in-law of Asa and Elna Spaulding and the first black woman graduate of Duke's medical school, a three-year residency in psychiatry. Later Dr. Ralph Snyderman appointed her vice-chancellor for health affairs. Later still she became a board member of the Duke Endowment.[148] Duke's first senior appointment of a black physician to its medical staff was in 1970: Dr. Eugene Stead hired Dr. Charles Johnson for the Medical Department.[149] In 1948, however, Dr. Robert E. Dawson had been the first black physician at Duke as an instructor in charge of the black interns from Lincoln Hospital who rotated through Duke Hospital.[150] Another important African American physician was Dr. Charles D. Watts, an adjunct clinical surgeon at Duke and the first black surgeon in Durham. He founded the Lincoln Community Center and was medical director of the North Carolina Mutual Insurance Company for twenty-eight years.[151]

Brodie strengthened already existing programs and established new ones on behalf of Duke's involvement with Durham. He appointed a vice-president for a division of public affairs to coordinate the various aspects of that effort. The medical center was already donating $30 million annually in services related to health.[152]

Brodie's belief in interdisciplinary research and teaching was reflected in his promotion of the enormous Levine Science Research Center (LSRC). Said to be the largest interdisciplinary research facility under one roof in the United States at the time it was completed (1994), it housed researchers from the medical center and others from the basic sciences, the schools of the environment and engineering, and the computer science department.[153] Brodie saw that the cross-pollination of ideas and their cooperative implementation was the way ahead for research and teaching.[154] He had already been involved in setting up the new School of the Environment (1991), which consolidated the former forestry school with programs in earth, marine, and environmental sciences, and the Institute of Statistics and Decision Sciences, another interdisciplinary research initiative.

By the time Brodie retired from the presidency in 1993, the university's endowment had doubled, thanks to a fund-raising campaign led by Joel Fleishman, and annual support had more than tripled, giving Brodie's successor, Nannerl Keohane, an institution poised for greatness.[155]

Brodie may have had a hand in choosing Keohane, Duke's first woman president, who proved a superb leader. Women seem to have had no trouble breaking through the glass ceiling in North Carolina, at least in academia. In 1997 Molly Corbett Broad was chosen to lead the state university system, comprising sixteen campuses, and in 1999 Marye Anne Fox was installed as chancellor of North Carolina State: each was the first woman to occupy her position.[156]

A deft and experienced leader, Nan Keohane made almost no missteps during her ten-year tenure, pleasing all her constituents, students, faculty, and administration by her remarkable abilities. She furthered Duke's commitment to the Durham community, renewed the black faculty initiative, and before retiring from the presidency in 2004 had begun an important study known as the Women's Initiative. She had had to face an unexpected slump in the medical center's own health and to depend on Snyderman to cure its ills while not always approving of his therapy.

Brodie had brought Dr. Snyderman back to Duke in 1989 to head the medical center. Seen in retrospect as "a transformational leader,"[157] Snyderman had begun his career at Duke in the 1960s as an intern and resident. His career in immunology returned him to the university in the 1970s, and he had only left in 1987 to join the research team at Genentech in California when he was recalled to Duke. Keohane's and Snyderman's tenures were banner years despite the rough spots. Keohane presided over a campaign that raised $2.3 billion in funds, empowering the university to extend its reach in many fields, while Snyderman presided over an unprecedented expansion of the medical center, which added the Bryan research building, the Center for Living, the Levine Center, the McGovern-Davison Children's Center, and two buildings devoted to genome research, his particular interest.[158]

Snyderman's responsibility for the Medical Center forced him to confront managed care and find a way to accommodate it while making the medical center profitable. Managed care, the biggest change in the nation's medical delivery system since World War II, initially slowed the rise in health care costs, but its side effects were uncomfortable. It cut into the profits of the Private Diagnostic Clinic and psychiatric services, took away patients' choice of their physicians, and sacrificed patient care to cost containment.[159] Snyderman eventually worked out solutions to these objectionable features, but not without some false steps and a great deal of internal contention. He realigned the long independent departments of the Medical Center with all the other units in one integrated system, at the same time greatly increasing the reach of the whole health care delivery system and establishing it as a business, of which he was the CEO. This union, achieved in 1995, was called the Duke University Health System (DUHS). Only the medical school and faculty and the Private Diagnostic Clinic were exempted. In 1998 the DUHS became independent of the university but was still controlled by the same trustees.[160]

To create this system Snyderman set about acquiring the Durham Regional Hospital and the Raleigh Community Hospital; he bought practices and set up satellite clusters of physicians, called Duke University Affiliated Physicians, throughout the area; these, along with the newly established clinics and urgent care units, would funnel patients to the Duke medical specialists and hospitals. DUHS branched out to provide as many kinds of health care as possible, for example home health care and hospice care, and eventually succeeded in stemming its losses and making the medical center profitable again.[161]

Managed care, which emphasized primary and preventive medicine, brought many more health providers into the profession, particularly women. New technology expanded the need for laboratory technicians, paramedical workers of all kinds, and nurses. In 1991 Snyderman reestablished the Duke School of Nursing, which had been eliminated as a financial savings strategy in the Reagan years; the school set up many different majors for a variety of career tracks, open to both women and men.[162]

Snyderman's perception that cell biology and genomics along with technology would propel medicine in the twenty-first century led him to venture into new terrain. He established the Duke Clinical Research Institute to handle large trials of innovative therapies. Already at hand to underpin the new institute was the computerized databank, established at Duke in the 1960s, to track cardiovascular cases. He also placed under institute control the records of the more recent (1990–93) comprehensive clinical trial known as GUSTO (global utilization of streptokinase for occluded arteries) that involved 41,000 patients in 15 countries. The institute became famous for its handling of large-scale trials and attracted world recognition and many participants for trials in other medical specialties, as well as huge profits.[163]

This was not the only new facility that Snyderman conceived of and set up. The Institute for Genome Sciences and Policy (IGSP), at the turn of the century, and the Duke Center for Integrative Medicine (DCIM) in 2004 incorporated the newest medical concepts of treating the whole person—body, mind, and spirit, using a whole range of conventional and nonconventional treatments. Snyderman saw that if genomics were to play an ever larger part in determining treatment, then social, political, and ethical issues had to factor into the decision.[164] Although Snyderman's vision laid the foundation for Duke's medical center in the twenty-first century, Keohane's cooperation and fund raising made its implementation possible.

TWO CURIOUS PROJECTS which Terry Sanford hoped to woo to North Carolina to add to the state's luster should be remembered: the Nixon Library and the Superconducting Super Collider. Fortunately these boons were averted. As already mentioned, Sanford's ambitions for Duke University had been to make it a world-respected and renowned institution. His strategy was to increase its endowment and fame through the prominence of its faculty and the wealth of its alumni. He no doubt saw as a coup on the path to his goal the acquisition for Duke and Durham of the presidential library of Richard Nixon, Duke's most famous (some said infamous) alumnus. Sanford negotiated behind the scenes and an offer was expected to be forthcoming. That plan was probably one of only a few miscalculations that Terry Sanford ever made. While he was a shrewd politician and had vast experience dealing with business and professional men, he had had little experience of intellectuals and university faculty. Sanford came rudely up against unexpected opposition in the Faculty Council. Its members were offended that he had not consulted them before going ahead with any move to achieve his end. They also, almost to a man, despised the president the library would honor. They foresaw that positioning the library on the Duke Campus, while of enormous benefit to a few historians and students, and no doubt a sure way to make Duke globally known, would create large invasions of visitors, vastly increased traffic problems, and unavoidably a shrine to an alumnus with whom they would rather not be associated. The faculty could only envision tourist buses and a holiday atmosphere invading their quiet, contemplative groves of academe. Contentious and acrimonious faculty council meetings made plain to Sanford and his administrators that a discreet withdrawal of the plan would be in everyone's best interest. The library eventually went to California on its own campus.[165]

A similar fate awaited the superconducting super collider, an $11 billion dollar experimental installation for which the federal government was seeking a site. When built the particle accelerator, or atom smasher as it was more popularly called, was expected to cover eight thousand acres, with a tunnel fifty-three miles in circumference one hundred meters underground. The government encouraged favorable offers and the states were busy wooing the project. In 1987 North Carolina was chosen as one of seven preferred locations, but residents near the site—which included portions of Durham, Person, and Granville counties, where the government had chosen to locate a huge installation, Camp Butner in World War II—were not at all eager to relive the experience. They were fearful of the harm they might suffer from radiation and other unknown scientific fallout, and they strongly objected to the prospect of having their quiet farmland and ancestral homes taken from them. Fortunately for them, the influence of Vice President George H. W. Bush prevailed, and the government settled on a site in Texas. After building fourteen miles of tunnels there, the whole project was discontinued for lack of funds in 1993.[166]

NORTH CAROLINA CENTRAL UNIVERSITY

Like every other institution North Carolina Central University underwent change in these decades, its fortunes rising in the 1990s with the country's general prosperity. NCCU was also experiencing a gradual evolution, from a historically black college to a racially integrated institution more like its sister units of the North Carolina university system. It was also playing catch-up for years of neglect before its consolidation in 1972 with the fifteen other state colleges and universities of the system. Under the new administrative system it was given a chancellor who answered to a president and board of governors that oversaw all sixteen institutions.

Progress very much depended on the individual leadership and character of its chancellors, which could vary considerably. In 1980 Albert N. Whiting was nearing the end of his seventeen-year tenure. From 1966 he had emphasized academics and high standards even with the straitened circumstances that the college still endured. In 1972 the art museum had been established and placed under the direction of an art historian, Norman Pendergraft, who gradually developed a select collection of works of African American artists and displayed temporary exhibits to acquaint students and the community with African American art. Whiting also built up the law school, which had been established in 1940.

LeRoy T. Walker succeeded Whiting in 1983 and served as interim chancellor until a successor could be found, but in grateful tribute he was retroactively named chancellor, without interim status. Walker had been chairman of the physical education department and director of public relations, but his administrative experience was far wider than that: he had been President John F. Kennedy's choice to head the Peace Corps in Africa. He was moreover a man of sterling qualities and brilliant leadership, who became nationally and internationally honored in the sports arena for his coaching of track and field. With Albert Buehler, noted track and field coach at Duke, he had arranged three international tract meets in Durham: the Pan-Africa-USA meets in 1975 and 1982 and the USA-USSR meet in 1974, each of which attracted many thousands of spectators. He was the first African American coach for an Olympic team and served as president of the United States Olympic Committee from 1992 to 1996. His athletes proved the effectiveness of his coaching: they numbered eighty-three All-Americans, forty national champions, and twelve U.S. Olympians, at least one of whom was a gold medalist: Lee Calhoun of NCCU. With Walker at the helm NCCU won attention and respect.[167]

In 1993 Walker was succeeded by Julius Chambers, another figure of national fame. Chambers was a civil rights lawyer and alumnus of NCCU. He had won renown as head of the NAACP's Legal Defense and Education Fund. Like Whiting he emphasized high standards and the importance of liberal arts as the vital center of the curriculum. He established a university book club for undergraduates and appointed leaders for discussion, encouraging academic discourse on a variety of subjects. He was determined to improve NCCU's academic standing, its physical plant, and its faculty. The sciences attracted his special attention, particularly biology. His monument on campus is the BBRI (Biomedical Biotechnology Research Institute), which opened in 1999. Its mission was research and education, especially concerning diseases that disproportionately afflicted African Americans and other minorities. Chambers attracted distinguished scientists and PhD fellows to teach and work with NCCU faculty and students.[168]

Chambers chose the former English department chairwoman Dr. Patsy B. Perry as a special assistant and gave her the task of revitalizing the old honors program by establishing an honors college for the most ambitious students, who were housed together and challenged by courses and seminars to develop reading, writing, and analytical skills. They had their own computer laboratory and were provided with culturally stimulating experiences, such as a weekend at a poetry symposium at Virginia Polytechnic Institute in Blacksburg and six weeks in Ghana to study its people and their culture. The honors students were required to attend all Lyceum programs on campus, to hear distinguished performers and speakers and then to review the performances.[169]

Chambers brought Harry E. Groves, the noted lawyer and expert on constitutional law, to be dean of the law school. A native of Colorado, Groves had already had a long, distinguished career before coming to Durham. Groves raised the school's standing, attracting an integrated body of students and winning considerable prestige for it.[170] Chambers was also particularly adept at raising money. He could persuade legislators, corporate heads, local officials, and private philanthropists to fund the projects he proposed: new named professorships, and new buildings and programs, as well as the upgrading and enlarging of old ones. The campus grew outward in all directions, often to the consternation and detriment of its neighbors.

Chambers was unquestionably helped in his ambitious plans by the times in which he served. The 1990s, after a rocky start, became more and more prosperous. There was excess money to be tapped into. Most of all, during much of Chambers's tenure the Board of Governors was chaired by the charismatic activist and NCCU graduate Ben Ruffin (1941–2006). When integration had become the law and local governments recognized their duty to make up for past mistakes and avoid further discrimination, experienced and skilled minority leaders such as Ruffin found important roles to play. Governor James B. Hunt appointed him to be director of the North Carolina Human Relations Council in 1977 and in the next year his special assistant for minority affairs. An indefatigable worker and advocate for housing, jobs, and education for the underprivileged, Ruffin was eventually appointed to the Board of Governors of the North Carolina Consolidated University and served as chairman from 1991 to 1998.[171]

That Henry M. "Mickey" Michaux had long represented Durham in the General Assembly at the same time was no small part of Chambers's success in winning large state appropriations for NCCU. The debt was acknowledged by the school's renaming of the School of Education for Michaux in 2008. The longest-serving representative in the House (twenty-nine years at this writing), Michaux was a dogged fighter for appropriations for black organizations and particularly for NCCU, his alma mater.[172]

Another graduate of NCCU who won fame outside the college was Alexander Rivera (1913–2008), a photojournalist of note because of his large portfolio of nationally important work during the civil rights movement and afterward his friendship with President Nixon. For fifty years on the front line of civil rights activism, he caught on film countless important incidents, places, and persons in that turbulent era. His connection with NCCU began in 1939 when James E. Shepard asked him to organize a news bureau while completing his undergraduate degree. After service in World War II Rivera began his newspaper career and made his name in photojournalism. He was brought back to NCCU as director of public relations and served in that capacity from 1974 to 1993.[173]

Perhaps the most illustrious faculty member that NCCU could claim was John Hope Franklin (1915–2009), who was offered a position by Dr. James E. Shepherd at the North Carolina College for Negroes in the early 1940s. Franklin was teaching at St. Augustine's College in Raleigh and had already to his credit a seminal book, *The Free Negro in North Carolina 1790–1860*. The Durham institution had a prestige among black colleges that Franklin was well aware of, however, and he accepted the offer. During the few years that he was in Durham he wrote another groundbreaking book and certainly his most famous one, *From Slavery to Freedom: A History of Negro Americans*. Franklin was by the end of his teaching career a towering figure in academia and black history. After his retirement from the University of Chicago, where he had headed the history department, he was recruited to Duke with a named professorship in 1983. He retired again in 1985 and continued to live in Durham, where he wrote an autobiography among other works of history and biography. In his long and very distinguished career, which included participation in the civil rights movement, the breaking of racial barriers in various positions, and repeated recognition in the form of awards and honorary degrees, including the Presidential Medal of Freedom in 1995, Franklin was finally honored by the creation of the John Hope Franklin Center for interdisciplinary and international studies at Duke University.[174]

NCCU entered the twenty-first century with a surge of building and an already greatly expanded campus and student body. Although finally a racially integrated institution, it was still mindful and proud of its long African American tradition. It was known and respected for its schools of library science, law, and nursing, and was embarking on flourishing new vocational tracks in biomedical and biotechnological sciences, ready to educate new generations of students for the future global economy and society.

RELIGION

As demonstrated above, Durham's churches could be counted on to respond to Durham's needs either through Urban Ministries Inc. or independently. While social outreach was always typical of religious organizations, it became a much more prominent feature of church agendas in the waning decades of the century. In place of the mainline congregations' exclusive, self-centered, club-like atmosphere in earlier decades, congregations became inviting, inclusive, outward-looking, and closer to those they wanted to help. This was not the only change they underwent. Church services became more informal, more interactive, and even more ecumenical, embracing popular culture and modern technology: guitars, drums, and other folk instruments and music as well as videos were used in services, which might be broadcast on radio or television or streamed over the internet. All churches in this period were probably in some degree modified by the Pentecostal/Charismatic movement that had caught fire in the 1960s and that was, in one writer's words, "barreling down Main Street."[175]

A comprehensive movement akin to the Great Awakening, perhaps a reaction to the modernism, secularism, and atheism of the late nineteenth century and early twentieth century, was sweeping over the country. Fundamentalist, evangelical, and addicted to more emotional, spontaneous forms of worship, the new religious tide had been growing all through the century. Holiness and Pentecostal as well as other kinds of churches gained many adherents. Based on the Bible literally interpreted as the center of their faith, these congregations also espoused conservative social agendas: anti-homosexual, anti-abortion, and anti-evolution, disguising their negativism in the code words "family values." The apostolic traditions of speaking in tongues, faith healing, and prophesying became earmarks of some new, independent churches and could even spill into historically established denominations, particularly the Baptists. This zeal threatened the separation of church and state, as some government buildings displayed crèches on their lawns and the Ten Commandments on their walls. It eventually invaded the corridors of power as well: politicians confessed to being "born-again" Christians and even to allowing their "faith" to influence their actions.

Like the cells of the human organism, religious organizations seem to have an inherent urge to split. Some old-line denominations split to form evangelical congregations within the same nominal tradition. For example, the Evangelical Presbyterian Church, founded in the United States in 1981, and the Evangelical Methodist church, formed in 1946, gained footholds in Durham. The mainstream denominations, which were watching their numbers shrink as members became disaffected with their old-line theology and staid devotional traditions, were also wrestling with social issues and splitting over abortion, gay marriage, gay ordination, and the like. In Durham the liberal Watts Street Baptist Church separated itself from the Baptist Southern Convention in 1992 and from the North Carolina Convention in 2004 over the homosexual issue.[176]

A new range of independent churches took root, usually sparked by individual, charismatic preachers in the mode of radio evangelists and televangelists such as Oral Roberts, Jerry Falwell, who intruded into the political arena, and Pat Robertson. The tendency toward independence of authority was of course in keeping with American character since its formative days; it was also very much a part of the current consumer practice of picking and choosing to suit one's taste. Religion became another consumer product. To expand their market and keep current, some of the new churches advertised themselves as interracial, multicultural, and family-oriented. They offered a complete array of services: seven-day-a-week day care, Sunday and weekday schools, adult, senior, and youth membership groups, small prayer groups, sports facilities, bookstores, counseling, and the like, all run like a business.

Durham did not escape these changes in religion's character and experienced a flurry of church building, particularly during the 1990s, because of the economic expansion of those years and a frenetic housing market which created new neighborhoods. Established, older churches as well as the new breed of churches built huge facilities in the new developments in the suburbs and the outlying countryside. The Evangelical Presbyterian Church of the Good Shepherd, Resurrection United Methodist Church, and Holy Cross, Holy Infant, and St. Matthew Roman Catholic churches were among the new congregations in new neighborhoods; Temple Baptist Church, Aldersgate United Methodist Church, Durham Mennonite Church, and the First Pentecostal Church exemplified older congregations' move to outlying locations. In 1994 Peace Covenant Church became the first church of the denomination Church of the Brethren to stake a claim in Durham, and in the same year Christ the King Moravian Church broke ground for the Moravian Church in North America on Hope Valley Road.[177]

Along with these new congregations appeared a new phenomenon: the mega-church, a church with a congregation of two thousand or more at a service, a charismatic preacher at its center, and an array of services such as those listed above. By century's end Durham could point to a handful of such churches. The first on the scene was probably Greater St. Paul's Missionary Baptist Church when Dr. W. T. Bigelow was pastor in the early 1990s. After his death, however, the congregation dwindled and no longer fitted the description. King's Park International Church on the fringes of the Research Triangle grew from the work of Ron Lewis as chaplain at UNC and N.C. State in the 1960s into an interracial, multicultural, evangelistic ministry by 1990, when it was organized as a Pentecostal church. It quickly gained members and with its missionary thrust started twenty-five churches around the world. By the end of the century its huge auditorium could accommodate over two thousand congregants at its Sunday services. It professed faith healing, miracles, prophesying, and speaking in tongues.[178]

An incipient mega-church was the Summit Church, a Southern Baptist organization that began as Homestead Heights Baptist Church. Multiple campuses (Brier Creek Parkway, Cole Mill Road, and West Club Boulevard) enabled it to reach large numbers of adherents.[179] In 2000 the old-time religion was new again in a big way.

Private Schools

The Christian fundamentalist fervor permeated education as well. The growth of private schools in this period represented two contradictory impulses—a desire for greater diversity and experimentation in education, and a need for a protected environment where undesirable influences could be excluded and certain kinds of information privileged. Two long-standing independent schools in Durham County already mentioned, Durham Academy and Immaculata, represented these two alternatives. In 1964 they were joined by a third school, Carolina Friends School, organized by members of the Society of Friends, notably Martha and Peter Klopfer. While technically in Orange County, the school was easily available to Durham residents and became well patronized by them. Its founding during the civil rights movement had nothing to do with white flight. To the contrary, the school was to be racially integrated from the start, and its founders wished to promote their philosophy of tolerance and peace in a time of intolerance and racial strife. While these three schools differed in their philosophies, they offered basic qualities that all parents wanted from independent schools: smaller classes, an atmosphere that promoted learning, and higher academic goals. Over the years these schools increased their student bodies and physical plant as the number of parents who could pay their tuition grew.

Private schools and home schooling noticeably increased during the integration of the public schools and on through the 1980s and 1990s.[180] A growing affluent population partially accounted for this, but many other factors contributed. White flight was a continuing one. The 1960s and 1970s in particular saw the beginning of so-called Christian schools. As they continued to increase in number, in 1980 a newspaper article asked, "Do They Serve Segregation?" The answer was that while technically the schools did not discriminate, some were "lily-white" and none had a black teacher.[181] An earlier report had suggested that Christian school graduates might be handicapped in applying to colleges because they usually followed the Accelerated Christian Education (ACE) curriculum, which was not accredited by any educational organization.[182] These schools were notable for their rejection of Darwinian evolution, which did not gibe with fundamentalist Christian belief, and their advocacy of "creationism" instead. Their questionable academic standing and social views did not deter the schools' continued popularity with the clientele they served. Most of these schools did not include the high school grades. Cresset Christian Academy, an offshoot of Cresset Baptist Church formed in the 1970s, became an exception.[183]

A slightly different kind of Christian school, not tied to any one church, was Trinity School, which described itself as nondenominational, though clearly dominated by Christian theology. Started in 1995 by Bill Cobey and David Spencer, it originally spanned preschool to fourth grade, with thirty-nine students. Peter Denton, Jr., attached to the Church of the Nazarene on Erwin Road, soon became headmaster.[184] In 1998 the school bought a twenty-six-acre tract on which to build a new campus able to accommodate all twelve grades and ultimately serve nine hundred students.[185]

Academic considerations, as always, came into play in the growth of private schools in these decades. First, there was widespread dissatisfaction with the public schools. Their test scores reflected the difficulties the teachers were having, as usual, overworked and underpaid. At the same time, college entrance competition began to increase dramatically, and students who wanted to go to good colleges had to compete at a higher achievement level. Furthermore, fear, hostility, and animosity between the races were palpable in public schoolrooms during the first few years of integration. The learning atmosphere was inevitably compromised for all children. Educational theories offered alternate systems of pedagogy. Among the large number of independent schools begun in the 1980s and 1990s were a number of Montessori schools. The Montessori Community School, an independent school, began in Chapel Hill but moved to Durham in 1980. At least one Montessori school in Durham, the former Morehead elementary school, became a charter school within the public system after enabling legislation was passed by the North Carolina legislature in 1996.[186]

The Duke School for Children emerged in 1984 from a previous incarnation as a preschool used as a teaching tool for the Duke psychology and education departments. Duke faculty members with school-age children, who had no quarrel with integration but were dismayed by the public schools, were allowed to transform the preschool into an elementary school. With the help of Terry Sanford, then president of Duke, the parents of the Duke School's children were permitted to build a structure for the initial grades on Duke University property in a hollow near Central Campus. As grades were added and the school body grew, they expanded the facility on the same tract. Interdisciplinary projects and innovative teaching cued to students' curiosity were its hallmark. Now nationally known for its strong teaching, the Duke School has become a model for mathematics instruction and for inquiry-driven methods of instruction. A new campus on Erwin Road awaits it.[187]

In 1991 dissatisfied parents established another independent school. Drawing from various neighborhoods and not tied to a particular church or philosophy, Triangle Day School began in the old sales and repair facility of the John Deere tractor company on Neal Road. Its aim was for small classes from kindergarten through the eighth grade, with an emphasis on academics.[188]

An innovative educational program that became a notable success and valuable resource for public and private schools alike was begun at Durham Academy in 1977. George Watts Hill donated generously to fund a special unit to help children with learning difficulties, particularly dyslexia, which was a problem for one of his stepchildren.[189] What started as an experiment became a notably successful ongoing program. It tackled all kinds of learning disabilities, including attention deficit disorder, recently diagnosed but widespread. Cathy Harkey initiated and supervised the program and enlisted specialists in learning problems to assist and advise her. At first located in an old farmhouse on Pickett Road adjoining the school, the Hill Center moved into its own large, specially designed facility on the opposite corner in 1999. Students divided their time daily between the Hill School and their own schools for as long as they needed to overcome their disabilities.

A New Institution

Housing for the elderly, as described earlier, evolved into new kinds of accommodations. The rather grim old people's home of the nineteenth century and the early twentieth began to wear a happier face for those who were not indigent and planned for retirement years independent of their families. One particular residential concept that began to proliferate at the end of the century was the continuing care retirement community (CCRC), which typically included independent and assisted living, usually with a component of medical care. For the "independents" all manner of activities were supplied: cultural, social, and physical, to stimulate and exercise mind and body. Residents could choose from a variety of apartment and cottage floor plans. All this came at a price, of course, which at first only a few elders could afford. The increasing affluence of the 1980s and 1990s, however, greatly increased their number, and commercial as well as nonprofit groups and religious organizations began to fill the demand.

As mentioned earlier, in Durham the Methodist Retirement Home was first to respond to this need in 1955, but in its earliest form it strongly resembled the outmoded old people's home, with barebones accommodations. During the 1970s and 1980s the home began to add apartments and cottages to its simple original accommodations, and in 1993 the Methodists bought a hundred acres in the Croasdaile development; by 1999 they had built an entirely new facility, with all the latest amenities.[190]

Duke University, which had long pondered the idea of supplying its retired faculty with accommodations, was actively considering such a venture when it was preempted by Dr. James D. Crapo, a Duke physician, and a group of his friends and neighbors on the Duke faculty. They bought a forty-six-acre site adjacent to the Duke Forest home sites, floated bonds, and by 1992 could offer a nonprofit organization, the newly built Forest at Duke CCRC.[191]

Simplified versions of the retirement community such as independent-living-only and assisted-living-only facilities, were also available. Yet the increased number of elderly and infirm in the population required local government as well as nonprofit and commercial groups to fill their needs, including day care centers and senior centers for those not confined to nursing homes, and facilities providing more extensive nursing and custodial care for others. Durham had examples of them all.

TAKING STOCK

The federal census of 2000 captured a moment in the history of a county still evolving. Of a total population of 223,314 persons, 187,035 lived within the city limits. Suburban housing developments pocked the former rural countryside, interspersed with patches of woods, old fields, small farms, and community hubs. In the northernmost reaches of the county lay large farms, forests, and tracts of undeveloped land. The historical communities once so self-conscious and self-contained could still be identified by road names, lingering representatives of original families, and remnants of commercial nodes, but their individuality was much diluted by newcomers without a sense of the past.

The proportions of African Americans and Native Americans in the population (39.5 percent and 0.8 percent) were not much changed from 1980, but the Hispanic presence had grown dramatically. With the unemployment rate at a low of 4 percent, it was no wonder that immigrants came to Durham.

The turning of the millennium caused considerable anxiety, almost as much as the coming of the year 1000 had done in medieval Europe, but for a different reason: daily life and the entire economy of the country had become dependent on computers, and it was feared that computers would be unable to accommodate the date change; many dire predictions were bruited about, and, as it turned out, needlessly.

In the previous twenty years Durham had also become a destination for visitors. Though no visitor statistics were recorded before the establishment of the Convention and Visitors' Bureau in 1989, in 1990 Durham had 2.3 million visitors, and ten years later 5.5 million.[192] Duke University, particularly its chapel, Medical Center, and gardens, and the Research Triangle accounted for many of those tourist and business visits, but Durham had other attractions. Besides the long-standing historic sites and a recent minor league baseball team in a new park, the 1980s and 1990s had remade the Museum of Life and Science and the Duke University Lemur Center, both science-based sites with great appeal to children.

A new director, Thomas Krakauer, arrived at the museum in 1985, and proved to be an energetic and creative director and educator. The next year a bond referendum awarded the museum $2 million to begin improvements of the facility, actually a whole new museum. By 1994 Krakauer had achieved many of the goals in his long-range plan, $9.8 million had been spent, and a superb butterfly house had just crowned his efforts. A three-story glass conservatory with several hundred tropical plants, birds, and frogs as well as butterflies, the house became a favorite site for visitors of all ages. In 2000 the museum also opened the Bayer CropScience Insectarium, with adjoining laboratories. There were also aerospace and geology exhibits, and educational exhibits focusing on the natural sciences and live animals, all in a seventy-acre tract. The museum had become a model interactive facility for the new century. Yearly visitation almost tripled, from about 108,000 visitors in 1985 to some 300,000 at the end of the century.

The other favored children's attraction was the Lemur Center, also newly focused and enlarged. Occupying eighty-five acres, the Duke center was the largest sanctuary in the world for lemurs, strange creatures known as prosimian primates, a species older than monkeys. Natives of Madagascar, they were becoming endangered in the mid-twentieth century as their natural habitat in the rainforests was gradually being destroyed by development. The collection at Duke began in 1966 with a group of ninety animals moved from Yale with the professor who had been studying them. At that time Duke did not have a clear sense of their value or a reason for their presence. With the growing environmental movement, however, and growing concerns about species extinction because of changes in the atmosphere and the economic development of third world nations, the Duke Center realized the importance of its collection and the need to study and preserve these animals. By the end of the 1990s the animals numbered well over two hundred and included, besides many varieties of lemurs, bush babies from Africa and lorises from India and Southeast Asia. A new variety, the golden-crowned sifaka, was identified by Dr. Elwyn L. Simons, the director of the center from 1977 to 2001. The animals were thought to be a subspecies of diademed sifakas when they were first brought to Duke in 1987, but in studying them Dr. Simons realized that they were an entirely different species. The Lemur Center drew many thousands of visitors each year. By 2000 its mission had an immediate urgency and an importance undreamed of at the time of the animals' arrival some forty years before.

Durham had become a success as a destination for visitors, with excellent and varied restaurants, shopping centers, motels, and hotels for almost any pocketbook, and a long menu of entertainment and sights to enjoy. But how did it rate as a home base? An objective summary could cite its geographic position between the mountains and the shore, its temperate climate, and its high employment rate as the county's fundamental advantages. Added to these were exceptional human resources. The Triangle could boast top national percentages of educated citizens along with highly ranked institutions of higher education.

High among Durham's assets was its flourishing artistic life and the artists who created it. Culturally Durham enjoyed its richest period to date. The flush late years of the twentieth century, with the exception of several short-lived financial downturns, continued to supply audiences and patrons for the arts. The already well-established arts organizations continued to operate and even thrive. Local governmental support increased with subsidized programs as well as costly renovations of three historic structures that housed cultural organizations: Old St. Joseph's A.M.E. Church, which housed St. Joseph's Foundation / African American Hayti Heritage Center (1991); the old City Hall, which housed the Durham Arts Council (1988); and the Carolina Theatre, for film and live performances (1994).

The Durham Arts Council and local government funding empowered and encouraged the arts. With a pair of annual festivals of its own—CenterFest, and Kwanzaa—the Durham Arts Council was gradually increasing its presence with programs that appealed to different segments of the population. It offered classes as well as gallery and performance space, juried shows, and even financial support. Its Emerging Arts program awarded modest stipends to unknown but promising young artists. This program was the inspiration of Ella Fountain Pratt, a lifelong supporter of the arts in Durham through her work as director of the Duke University Office of Cultural Affairs, where she was responsible for bringing to campus performances and exhibitions of all the arts, and through her tireless work for the Arts Council.

The Hayti Heritage Center dedicated the Lyda Moore Merrick gallery to exhibit space featuring African American artists. Its large, restored sanctuary accommodated performances of all kinds: lectures, drama, dance, and music. The center also developed an archive of local black culture. The Durham Public Schools nurtured artists by introducing art instruction in all the schools, most notably in the magnet School of the Arts. All these efforts bore fruit with increased numbers of practitioners in the arts, amateurs and professionals.

Durham's commitment to film was spurred in two ways: Duke University established the Center for Documentary Studies in 1990, and the Carolina Theatre became a popular regional and national venue for film festivals. The Duke program supplied essential instruction and opportunities for those interested in photojournalism as well as video and photography.

Nancy Buirski has been given credit for establishing the Double-Take Documentary Film Festival in 1998. It evolved into the Full Frame Documentary Film Festival (2002), which attracted international attention.[193] Its early success attracted a string of others in the following years devoted to specialized, niche films. The first such film festival was the North Carolina Gay and Lesbian Film Festival (1996), followed by Retrofantasma (1998), Nevermore Horror, Gothic, and Fantasy (2000), Escapism (2003), and others, each with an enthusiastic following.[194]

Durham Central Park, developed on the site of former tobacco warehouses, became the center of an active arts community in practical ways. The one remaining warehouse, Liberty, owned by Walker Stone, was refitted for artists' studios and rented at nominal rates. In the same neighborhood the George Watts Hill Pavilion for the Arts (2003), contributed by Central Carolina Bank (now SunTrust), housed the nonprofit Liberty Arts Corporation, a bronze-casting studio that supplied industrial equipment and space for sculptors, again at nominal rates. The benefactors behind this company were Jack Preiss, Walker Stone, Kate Dobbs Ariail, Frank DePasquale, and Francis Vega.[195] Across the street Vega Metals, established by Francis Vega and Neal Carlton, was a unique iron-casting studio. Besides working with artists whose designs needed to be translated into wrought iron, Vega and his partner created their own utilitarian art such as garden gates, railings, and fountains.[196]

Also at Durham Central Park was Claymakers Studio (2000), founded by Leonora Coleman in a building dedicated to sculpture studios, classes, workshops, and a store stocked with tools and materials for sculpture as well as books. Claymakers Studio contained firing equipment and gallery space to display art.[197] Several other clusters of artists' studios have taken shape in other restored downtown industrial buildings (Golden Belt and Venable Warehouse) in accordance with the city plan to reinvent itself as a center for art and entertainment.

Another art experiment was attempted in 1984: opera. Bringing together a formidable array of talent, a production of Bizet's *Carmen* proved exceedingly popular. The idea for a street opera originated with Mary and James Semans and was eagerly taken up by others who became crucial to its success: Ella Fountain Pratt, the Duke professor and composer Robert Ward, John Clum, professor and member of the drama program at Duke, the Arts Council member Barrie Wallace, and its director, Michael Marsicano. The Durham Symphony supplied the instrumental music, and the Savoyards and Choral Society the chorus. For the individual singing roles local singers were hired; Hilda Harris, a Durham native and star of the Metropolitan Opera Company, sang the title role.[198]

Buoyed by the success of this venture, some of those involved organized the Triangle Music Theater Association, but by the end of a decade some of its supporters had withdrawn and no permanent financial base had been put in place. The coup de grâce was administered by the weather: one summer five of the ten opera performances were rained out, and the company sustained a huge loss. Scott Tilley tried to continue the venture for a few years without success.[199] In 1999 Randolph Umberger, a professor of theater at NCCU, and Benjamin Keaton established the Long

Leaf Opera Company to perform works written in English. They have continued to produce three works a year, using singers beginning their careers.[200]

Two new instrumental groups formed in the 1980s added considerably to local classical music activity: the Mallarmé Chamber Players (1984), the inspiration of Anna Wilson, a flutist, and the Chamber Orchestra of the Triangle (1985), which was formed in St. Stephen's Church but became independent and under the direction of Lorenzo Muti. Both groups had flexibility to perform many varieties of instrumental works; the Mallarmé Players also ventured into combinations of music with the other arts. The venerable Chamber Arts Society and the Ciompi Quartet continued to present enthusiastically supported series of concerts.[201]

The revival of interest in folk music of all kinds—blues, gospel, country, and string band—stimulated many new musicians and combinations of musicians. Blues enthusiasts discovered a few survivors who had known the original Durham blues musicians and preserved the tradition. John Dee Holeman and Fris Holloway became stars, often performing at festivals and encouraging imitators to carry on the tradition.[202]

Jazz, with wide appeal in black and white cultures, was taken up by musicologists of both universities, who established courses in jazz and performing ensembles. NCCU's music department under Eugene Strassler introduced the subject in the 1960s. He brought Donald Byrd, the famous jazz trumpeter, to take charge of jazz studies. In the 1980s Dr. Ira Wiggins joined the department to teach jazz studies and develop jazz ensembles. He also established the annual NCCU / Grady Tate Jazz Festival.

At Duke, Frank Tirro was responsible for introducing jazz studies in 1977, and he later hired Mary Lou Williams to direct the jazz program there. Another notable jazz performer, Branford Marsalis, chose to settle in Durham in the 1990s and proceeded to teach at both institutions while he continued to perform worldwide.[203]

Gospel music, a combination of forms, had emerged in the years surrounding World War I in both black and white non-mainstream churches. In the 1980s and through the century Shirley Caesar, a Durham native, became widely known through performances and recordings as the "Queen of Gospel." She, like most gospel singers, thought of her music as a form of evangelism.[204]

Country music was always popular, and the mill villages were fertile ground for its growth. Durham had its share of songwriters who moved to Nashville and pursued successful careers as country music composers and performers. Notable names were John D. Loudermilk, Tom House, and Don Schlitz. The last won additional fame from his music and lyrics in the Broadway musical *The Adventures of Tom Sawyer*.[205]

Dance was an art form without a notable presence in Durham until the coming of the American Dance Festival in 1978 changed that. Over the following decades it continued to bring to Durham innumerable top performers of modern dance, along with hundreds of students to study, critics to observe, and audiences to enjoy and support the art. It generated dancers in the white and black communities eager to cultivate their talents.

Chuck Davis, a native of Durham, started his African American Dance Ensemble (1984) and had a huge influence worldwide. Dancers from his troupe formed other dance groups, some based in Durham. Other dancers associated with Davis joined top-notch groups elsewhere, such as Pilobolus and Shen Wei. Some notable professionals moved to Durham because of its nourishing dance activity and sophisticated audiences and performances: Carlota Santana, Carol Parker, and Laura Dean. Besides Davis, Durham produced Nancy Pinckney, who taught and developed dance at NCCU and was a highly regarded influence for dance in the black community.[206]

Duke's Institute for the Arts under its first director Cathy Silbiger strongly supported dance and persuaded the renowned Clay Taliaferro to become a professor of the practice of dance at Duke (1987–2007). Local dance companies and studios contributed to the surge in dance. The New Performing Dance Company (1975) and Nina Wheeler's School of Dance launched the careers of many dancers.[207]

The outdated accommodations of Page Auditorium at Duke prompted Charles Reinhart, founder and director of the American Dance Festival, to threaten more than once to take the festival elsewhere. That unpleasant prospect, along with economic forces and the city's desire to make downtown a center for the arts and entertainment, played a role in the willingness of local government to build the Durham Performing Arts Center (2008), which now serves much larger audiences more comfortably and conveniently.

Both universities encouraged theatrical performance through many decades. Duke undertook a number of schemes to produce student plays as well as to bring professional performers and productions to Durham. Summer Theater at Duke, produced by Professor John Clum from 1972 to 1984, mounted five to seven plays a summer in addition to the usual half a dozen during the school year. In 1985 a drama program under David Ball, independent of the English Department, initiated Broadway Previews at Duke in conjunction with the student union subscription series Broadway at Duke. This gave students the experience of classes with professional producers and actors and insight into the production and performance of the plays they were studying. Duke's contribution of two live-theater spaces in the new Bryan Student Center (1986) increased the opportunities for performances.[208]

In 1992 Richard Riddell became the first Professor of the Practice of Theater Studies at Duke, a named chair set up by Mary D. B. T. Semans and Dr. James Semans, and charged with setting up a department. Appropriate expansion of production space and opportunity for performances followed.[209]

At NCCU drama had long formed part of the English Department curriculum when in 1949 Mary Bohanon became head of a new department of dramatic art with its own faculty and course of studies. She served until 1964. The department and its number of annual productions gradually grew. With the coming of Randolph Umberger in the 1990s the department reached new heights recognized by its accreditation by the National Association of Schools of Theatre in 1997. It has since received the same imprimatur for musical theater.[210]

Nonacademic efforts at theater production also met with some success. Jeff Storer and Edward Hunt began the Manbites Dog Theater in 1987 to produce experimental theater. At various improvised locations through the years they have met with enough support to warrant their continued effort in a settled location on Foster Street.[211]

While no Durham author produced the great American novel, aspirants were not lacking and writers in general were numerous. Reynolds Price, after a nearly fatal brush with cancer in the early 1980s, produced an unprecedented and profuse stream of novels, plays, essays, translations, and memoirs, and by the end of the century his oeuvre numbered some fifty books. His most popular were *Clear Pictures* (1989), a memoir; *A Whole New Life* (1994), an account of his illness; and a novel, *Kate Vaiden* (1986), which won the National Book Award. New writers also broke into print, such as Clyde Edgerton, who made a splash with *Raney* in 1985, followed by *Walking across Egypt* in 1987. Southern stories with great humor followed unfailingly every two or three years. Another prolific writer was the Chilean Ariel Dorfman, included here by virtue of his long tenure at Duke (from 1985). An intellectual and often political writer in two languages, his many books—plays, novels, essays, polemics, memoirs—expressed his North and South American cultural experiences. *Death and the Maiden* (1991) and *Heading South, Looking North* (1998), both made into movies, are among his best-known works.

Joe Ashby Porter, who came to Duke to teach in 1980, wrote *Eel Grass* (1977) and other works of fiction and nonfiction, including several collections of short stories. In 2004 he won an award from the American Academy of Arts and Letters. Melissa Malouf, also at Duke, published a novel, a collection of short stories, and several one-act plays. David Guy, Elizabeth Cox, and Gwendolyn M. Parker (a native but not long a resident of Durham) also published novels, some of which have enjoyed more than local acclaim. Although she has written little besides a memoir and one novel, *These Same Long Bones* (1994), Gwendolyn Parker uniquely portrays the black experience in Durham from the point of view of a privileged black family. Poets are a rarer breed and their readers are rarer still. James Applewhite and Deborah Pope, also professors at Duke, published several volumes of poetry each. Pope's third collection, *Falling Out of the Sky* (1999) was nominated for a Pulitzer prize. As a way of marketing their wares, booksellers began to host readings by local authors, a pleasant and stimulating activity that became increasingly common and popular. On the whole, the climate for writers in Durham was receptive and supportive.

But Durham's artists and most capable intellects could not be counted on for public service. Local government and public schools did not commonly share in their talent or shine with the same luster. These occupations presented strong disincentives to the best qualified. Divisive, uncompromising opposing forces— minorities against majorities, developers against environmentalists, conservatives against progressives—jeopardized constructive action and tried the patience of the most motivated, who might have otherwise been attracted to serve in local government. Troubles with discipline, disadvantaged students, and administrative barriers frustrated innovative teaching. Besides, rewards were so much higher in the university and the corporate world of the Research Triangle.

There were other unpleasant realities. Durham had an unacceptably high crime rate and a huge prison population.[212] Gangs were increasing and undermining neighborhoods. Infant mortality was still shockingly high, particularly among nonwhites.[213] The illegitimacy rate for whites and blacks together, 38.1 percent of births, suggested that a large number of single-mother households depended on social services to survive.[214] This bleak picture was of course duplicated all over the nation; there was nothing peculiar to Durham except the severity of the problems. Unfortunately, whatever remedies were tried, no imaginative or successful solutions seemed to be forthcoming. Change in behavior cannot be legislated or socially engineered.

Wise voices and thoughtful action could often be detected behind the scenes, however, particularly in environmental concerns: reasonable controls on growth and land use, protection of open space and water resources, and respect for the past in historic preservation.

Although progressive leadership and social solutions were deficient, first-class cultural activities were not. As noted above, Durham enjoyed the finest music and was busily encouraging the other arts as well. There was nothing provincial about the influences to which Durham was exposed. The global economy and the availability of superior graduate education brought people from all over the world, attracting and producing experts in every field. As it entered the twenty-first century with its human potential and driving engines of medicine and technology, Durham could hope for increasing economic stability and an improving quality of life for all its people.

Appendix: Population Statistics
and Officeholders

Population Statistics for Durham County and Town

	Total Population	Urban	Rural	Rural Percentage	Nonwhite Percentage	Hispanic Percentage
1880	10,307	2,041	—	—	—	—
1890	18,041	5,485	12,556	69.6	40.6	—
1900	26,233	6,679	19,554	74.5	37.2	—
1910	35,276	18,241	17,035	49.3	35.1	—
1920	42,219	21,719	20,500	49.6	31.2	—
1930	67,196	52,037	15,159	22.6	35.0	—
1940	80,244	60,195	20,049	24.9	25.6	—
1950	101,639	73,368	28,271	27.8	33.3	—
1960	111,995	84,642	27,353	24.4	32.2	—
1970	132,681	100,768	31,913	24.1	33.0	—
1980	152,785	100,831	51,954	34.0	30.8	—
1990	181,835	154,580	27,255	18.3	39.1	1.1
2000	223,314	187,035	36,279	16.2	44.3	7.6

Note: As the county was not formed until 1881, no exact figures are available for 1880. Total was arrived at by adding the populations of Mangum, Lebanon, Durham, and Patterson Townships. When formed, Durham County did not embrace the entire landmass of each of these townships; consequently, the population was actually somewhat less than shown.

U.S. Congressmen from Durham County or Its Pre-1881 Territorial Equivalent

	Senators	Representatives
1823–27		Willie Person Mangum
1831–37	Willie Person Mangum	
1839–53	Willie Person Mangum	
1933–38		William B. Umstead
1945–48	William B. Umstead	
1967–72		Nicholas Galifianakis
1987–93	Terry Sanford	
1987–95		David Price
1997–present		David Price

Durham County Representatives and Senators in the North Carolina General Assembly

	Senate	House of Representatives
1881		Caleb B. Green
1883		R. C. Strudwick
1885		C. B. Green
1887		Thos. C. Oakley
1889		John T. Nichols
1891		Wm. M. Lowe
1893		Frank L. Fuller
1895		W. G. Vickers
1897	J. E. Lyon	John W. Umstead
1899		Howard A. Foushee
1901	Howard A. Foushee	R. G. Russell
1903		Jones Fuller
1905	Howard A. Foushee	J. Crawford Biggs
1907		James S. Manning
1909	James S. Manning	Young E. Smith
1911		Julian S. Carr
1913	Victor S. Bryant	Sumter C. Brawley
1915		Bennehan Cameron
		J. Edward Pegram
1917	Bennehan Cameron	J. E. Pegram
		Lennox P. McLendon
1919		Victor S. Bryant, Jr.
		Bennehan Cameron
1921	Bennehan Cameron	Reuben O. Everett
		Frank L. Fuller, Jr.
1923		R. O. Everett
		Victor S. Bryant, Jr.
1925	Wm. L. Foushee	Jacob E. Long
		James R. Patton, Jr.
		R. O. Everett
1927		Sumter C. Brawley
		R. O. Everett
1929	Sumter C. Brawley	Eugene C. Brooks, Jr.
		Victor V. Young
1931		E. C. Brooks, Jr.
		Victor V. Young
1933	John Sprunt Hill	Sumter C. Brawley
		R. O. Everett
1935	J. S. Hill	Victor S. Bryant, Jr.
		Oscar G. Barker
1937	J. S. Hill	same as 1935
1939		Victor S. Bryant
		Forrest A. Pollard
1941	Eugene C. Brooks, Jr.	same as 1939
1943	E. C. Brooks, Jr.	O. G. Barker
		F. A. Pollard
		S. C. Brawley

	Senate	House of Representatives
1945	Claude Currie	O. G. Barker
		Robert M. Gantt
1947	C. Currie	O. G. Barker
		Daniel K. Edwards
1949	C. Currie	D. K. Edwards
		R. M. Gantt
1951	Thos. B. Sawyer	Richard T. Sanders
		O. G. Barker
1953	C. Currie	same as 1951
1955	C. Currie	O. G. Barker
		Edward K. Powe III
		D. K. Edwards
1957	C. Currie	George Watts Hill, Jr.
		E. K. Powe III
1959	C. Currie	G. W. Hill, Jr.
		Ralph N. Strayhorn
1961	C. Currie	Eugene C. Brooks III
		Nicholas Galifianakis
1963	C. Currie	E. C. Brooks III
		N. Galifianakis
1965	C. Currie	W. Hance Hofler
		N. Galifianakis
1967	C. Currie	W. H. Hofler
		Wade H. Penny, Jr.
		Kenneth C. Royall, Jr.
1969	C. Currie	same as 1967
1971	C. Currie	George W. Miller, Jr.
		K. C. Royall, Jr.
		Willis P. Whichard
1973	Kenneth C. Royall, Jr.	Henry M. Michaux, Jr.
		G. W. Miller, Jr.
		W. P. Whichard
1975	K. C. Royall, Jr.	Pat Oakes Griffin
	Willis P. Whichard	H. M. Michaux, Jr.
		G. W. Miller, Jr.
1977	Willis P. Whichard	same as 1975
	K. C. Royall, Jr.	
1979	W. P. Whichard	G. W. Miller, Jr.
	K. C. Royall, Jr.	Paul Pulley
		Kenneth B. Spaulding
1981	William G. Hancock, Jr.	same as 1979
	K. C. Royall, Jr.	
1983	same as 1981	same as 1981
1985	Ralph A. Hunt	H. M. (Mickey) Michaux, Jr.
	C. Royall, Jr.	G. W. Miller, Jr.
		Paul Pulley
1987	R. A. Hunt	H. M. (Mickey) Michaux, Jr.
	K. C. Royall, Jr.	G. W. Miller, Jr.
		Sharon Thompson

	Senate	House of Representatives
1989	R. A. Hunt	H. M. (Mickey) Michaux, Jr.
	K. C. Royall, Jr.	G. W. Miller, Jr.
		Sharon Thompson
1991	R. A. Hunt	Paul Luebke
		H. M. (Mickey) Michaux, Jr.
		G. W. Miller, Jr.
1993	Wib Gulley	Paul Luebke
	Jeanne H. Lucas	H. M. (Mickey) Michaux, Jr.
		G. W. Miller, Jr.
1995	Wib Gulley	Paul Luebke
	Jeanne H. Lucas	H. M. (Mickey) Michaux, Jr.
		G. W. Miller, Jr.
1997	Wib Gulley	Paul Luebke
	Jeanne H. Lucas	H. M. (Mickey) Michaux, Jr.
		G. W. Miller, Jr.
1999	Wib Gulley	Paul Luebke
	Jeanne H. Lucas	H. M. (Mickey) Michaux, Jr.
		G. W. Miller, Jr.
2001	Wib Gulley	Paul Luebke
	Jeanne H. Lucas	H. M. (Mickey) Michaux, Jr.
		G. W. Miller, Jr.
2003	Wib Gulley	Jim Crawford
	Jeanne H. Lucas	Paul Luebke
		H. M. (Mickey) Michaux, Jr.
		G. W. Miller, Jr.
2005	Bob Atwater	Paul Luebke
	Jeanne H. Lucas	H. M. (Mickey) Michaux, Jr.
		G. W. Miller, Jr.
		W. A. (Winkie) Wilkins

County Commissioners

1881   G. A. Barbee, A. K. Umstead (Duncan Cameron), J. T. Nichols, W. Duke, S. W. Holman

1882   G. A. Barbee, Duncan Cameron, J. G. Latta, W. A. Jenkins, D. H. Paschall

1884   T. J. Holloway, W. K. Parrish, J. G. Latta, W. C. Mason, M. A. Angier

1886   W. C. Mason, A. J. Roberts, J. T. Nichols, W. A. Jenkins, M. A. Angier

1888   S. Scott, M. A. Angier, J. G. Latta, R. G. Tilley, W. H. Perry

1890   A. H. Stokes, P. H. Massey, K. Holloway, R. G. Tilley, W. H. Perry

1892   A. H. Stokes, P. H. Massey, R. G. Tilley, K. Holloway, Hugh Green

1894   T. W. Hopson, J. E. Suitt, J. G. Latta, W. G. Harward, C. B. Green

1896   W. D. Turrentine, J. B. Warren, J. G. Latta, W. G. Harward, A. D. Markham

1898   W. D. Turrentine, W. T. Redmond, J. G. Latta, W. G. Harward, A. D. Markham

1900   W. D. Turrentine, L. A. Page, J. W. Allen, W. G. Harward, H. H. Elliott

1902   O. K. Proctor, T. Lipscomb, J. W. Allen, J. W. Pope, J. T. Hampton

1904   O. K. Proctor, T. E. Belvin, J. W. Allen, L. C. Cole, J. T. Hampton

1906   Chris. Barbee, Charles A. Owens, J. W. Allen, F. M. Tilley, A. D. Markham

1908   J. D. Hamlin, T. E. Belvin, J. W. Allen, F. M. Tilley, L. B. Markham

1910   J. D. Hamlin, T. E. Belvin, Maynard Mangum, F. M. Tilley, L. B. Markham

1912	Chris. Barbee, J. T. Rogers, Maynard Mangum, G. W. Flowers, J. C. Nichols
1914	Chris. Barbee, John W. Holder, Maynard Mangum, G. W. Flowers, F. S. Thomas
1916	W. D. Turrentine, H. L. Carver, A. P. Carlton, G. W. Flowers, F. S. Thomas
1918	W. D. Turrentine, H. L. Carver, A. P. Carlton, C. M. Crutchfield, F. S. Thomas
1920	W. D. Turrentine, H. L. Carver, D. W. Stallings, C. M. Crutchfield, F. S. Thomas
1922	W. D. Turrentine, H. L. Carver, T. O. Sorrell, C. M. Crutchfield, E. A. Hughes
1924	D. W. Newsom, H. L. Carver, G. A. Crabtree, C. M. Crutchfield, W. G. Frasier
1928	D. W. Newsom, H. L. Carver, Cassam Tilley, R. E. Nichols, Sr., L. J. Kirkland
1930	C. W. Massey, H. L. Carver, J. H. Harris, R. E. Nichols, Sr., C. R. McHaney
1932	C. W. Massey, H. L. Carver, J. H. Harris, W. E. King, R. E. Hurst
1934	C. W. Massey, H. L. Carver, W. E. King, R. E. Nichols, Sr., R. E. Hurst
1936	G. F. Kirkland, Sr., H. L. Carver, J. H. Harris, R. E. Nichols, Sr., R. E. Hurst
1938	G. F. Kirkland, Sr., H. L. Carver, Otho A. McCullers, R. E. Nichols, Sr., R. E. Hurst
1944	G. F. Kirkland, Sr., S. L. Proctor, Otho A. McCullers, Luther G. Cheek, Robert L. Brame
1948	G. F. Kirkland, Sr., S. L. Proctor, C. L. Stone, J. P. McGuire (James Q. Davis), Robert L. Brame
1950	G. F. Kirkland, Sr., S. L. Proctor, F. H. Kenan, D. S. Scarboro, Robert L. Brame (J. Q. Davis)
1952	G. F. Kirkland, Sr., S. L. Proctor, F. H. Kenan, D. S. Scarboro, J. Q. Davis
1954	G. F. Kirkland, Sr., S. L. Proctor, F. H. Kenan, D. S. Scarboro, E. B. Clements
1962	G. F. Kirkland, Sr., S. L. Proctor, M. B. Fowler, D. S. Scarboro, E. B. Clements
1964	G. F. Kirkland, Sr., J. A. Ward, M. B. Fowler, D. S. Scarboro, E. B. Clements
1966	G. F. Kirkland, Sr., J. A. Ward, Howard Easley, D. S. Scarboro, E. B. Clements
1968	Darrell Kennedy, Asa T. Spaulding, Howard Easley, D. S. Scarboro, E. B. Clements
1970	Wm. E. Stauber, Asa T. Spaulding, Howard Easley, D. S. Scarboro, E. B. Clements
1972	Nathan Garrett, Wm. V. Bell, Howard Easley, D. S. Scarboro, E. B. Clements
1974–78	Elna Spaulding, Wm. V. Bell, Howard Easley, D. S. Scarboro, E. B. Clements
1980	Elna Spaulding, Wm. V. Bell, Howard Easley, R. Dillard Teer, E. B. Clements
1982	Elna Spaulding, Wm. V. Bell, Becky M. Heron, R. Dillard Teer, E. B. Clements
1984	Elna Spaulding, Wm. V. Bell, Becky M. Heron, R. Dillard Teer, Br. DeLoache
1986	Wm. V. Bell, Becky M. Heron, Louise McCutcheon, Josephine D. Clement, Al Hight
1988	Wm. V. Bell, Becky M. Heron, Ellen W. Reckhow, Josephine D. Clement, Al Hight
1990	Wm. V. Bell, Becky M. Heron, Ellen W. Reckhow, Mary Ann E. Black, Joe W. Bowser
2000	Philip R. Cousin, Jr., Becky M. Heron, Ellen W. Reckhow, Mary D. Jacobs, Joe W. Bowser
2002	Philip R. Cousin, Jr., Becky M. Heron, Ellen W. Reckhow, Mary D. Jacobs, Joe W. Bowser
2004	Philip R. Cousin, Jr., Becky M. Heron, Ellen W. Reckhow, Michael Page, Lewis A. Cheek
2006	Philip R. Cousin, Jr., Becky M. Heron, Ellen W. Reckhow, Michael Page, Lewis A. Cheek

Note: Names in parentheses represent those appointed to finish unexpired terms.

Durham City Mayors and Councilmen

1869   J. W. Cheek; R. F. Morris, A. M. Rigsbee, W. K. Styron, W. Y. Clark, William Mangum

1871   W. J. H. Durham (R. F. Morris); R. F. Morris, W. K. Styron, D. C. Parrish, J. W. Cheek, William Mangum

1872   E. J. Parrish (J. S. Carr); J. F. Freeland, J. E. Lyon, J. S. Carr, J. S. Lockhart, William Mangum

1873   W. J. H. Durham; W. K. Styron, William Mangum, A. M. Rigsbee, A. Walker (one missing)

1874–76 W. J. H. Durham; (records missing for aldermen)

1877   D. C. Parrish; J. L. Markham, A. M. Rigsbee, William Maynor, E. J. Parrish, William Mangum

1878   D. C. Parrish; E. J. Parrish, I. M. Reams, J. R. Day, William Mangum, J. C. Wilkerson

1879   D. C. Parrish; William Mangum, William Maynor, E. J. Parrish, J. W. Blackwell, R. W. Thomas

1880   I. N. Link; R. D. Blacknall, C. B. Green, William Maynor, L. E. Cooper, N. A. Ramsey

1881   D. C. Parrish; E. J. Parrish, T. C. Oakley, S. A. Thaxton (A. H. Stokes), G. W. Watts, William Mangum

1882   E. C. Hackney; R. W. Thomas, W. H. Rogers, W. H. Rowland, W. A. Lea, R. D. Blacknall

1883   D. C. Parrish (William Lipscomb); E. Morehead, S. R. Carrington, R. D. Blacknall, R. W. Thomas, L. Green

1884   J. F. Freeland; E. Morehead, R. W. Thomas, T. D. Jones, T. S. Christian, W. H. Rowland

1885   J. F. Freeland; W. H. Rogers, W. H. Rowland, W. L. Wall, R. D. Blacknall, R. W. Thomas, J. R. Blackwell, Q. E. Rawls

1886   J. F. Freeland; E. J. Parrish, J. S. Carr, G. W. Watts, C. C. Taylor, W. A. Lea, J. J. MacKay, W. J. Wyatt

1887   J. F. Freeland; E. J. Parrish, G. W. Watts, C. C. Taylor, W. A. Lea, J. J. MacKay (L. C. Anderson), W. J. Wyatt (J. S. Carr)

1888   W. J. Christian; T. D. Jones, C. M. Herndon, J. F. Corbett, R. D. Blacknall (J. S. Mangum), W. A. Lea, W. Duke

1889   W. J. Christian; T. D. Jones, J. W. Carlton, A. D. Markham, J. F. Corbett, J. S. Mangum, W. Duke (W. E. Foster)

1890   M. A. Angier; T. L. Peay, Leo D. Heartt, W. E. Foster, J. S. Mangum, T. S. Christian, S. R. Carrington, A. D. Markham

1891   M. A. Angier; H. J. Bass, M. H. Jones, J. W. Walker, J. M. Mangum, A. D. Markham, T. S. Christian, L. D. Heartt

1892   M. A. Angier; L. D. Heartt, T. S. Christian, J. M. Mangum, H. J. Bass, A. D. Markham, M. H. Jones, S. R. Carrington

1893   T. L. Peay; T. B. Fuller, S. R. Carrington, J. S. Mangum, L. D. Heartt, E. G. Lineberry, C. H. Norton, W. S. Slater

1894   Isaac Newton Link (J. W. Carlton); C. A. Jordan, W. H. Proctor, H. J. Bass, A. D. Markham, J. W. Walker, L. D. Heartt, J. W. Carlton (M. H. Jones)

1895   T. L. Peay; T. H. Martin, C. C. Taylor, Louis A. Carr, W. M. Yearby, A. D. Markham, M. A. Angier, T. J. Rigsbee

1897   Moses Ellis McCown; C. C. Taylor, W. A. Guthrie, John B. Morris, John W. Pope, M. G. Markham, C. A. Jordan, N. M. Johnson

1899	M. E. McCown; W. A. Guthrie, John B. Morris, N. M. Johnson, John W. Pope, C. C. Taylor, C. A. Jordan, M. G. Markham
1901	M. E. McCown; C. C. Taylor, J. B. Mason, Arch. Cheatham, Thomas B. Fuller, A. D. Markham, J. S. Carr, Jr., W. T. O'Brien, N. M. Johnson (W. H. McCabe)
1903	J. F. Freeland; W. J. Christian, L. C. Cole, T. B. Fuller, W. J. Holloway, W. H. Proctor, S. R. Perry, J. W. Pridgen, Q. E. Rawls
1905	Paul Cameron Graham; Henry Ernest Seeman, W. M. Fallon, T. S. Christian, J. S. Mangum, I. F. Hill, R. W. Vaughn, J. F. Wily, W. J. Griswold
1907	P. C. Graham; J. B. Mason, J. B. Warren, W. T. Pollard, T. S. Christian, J. D. Pridgen, I. F. Hill, Edwin H. Bowling, Norman Underwood
1909	W. J. Griswold; J. B. Mason, J. B. Warren, R. L. Lindsey, J. S. Perry, T. M. Gorman, J. E. Carpenter, John Sprunt Hill, J. J. Lawson
1911	Willis J. Brogden; John W. Pope, W. L. Umstead, John R. Proctor, J. T. McCracken, W. F. Carr, R. W. Vaughn, J. L. Morehead, J. C. Markham
1913	W. J. Brogden; Eugene C. Brooks, J. R. Proctor, Benjamin S. Skinner, John Sprunt Hill, M. Eugene Newsom, W. G. Bradshaw, J. D. Hamlin, W. T. Cole
1915	B. S. Skinner; J. G. Lawrence, J. D. Hamlin, J. T. Christian, John W. Pope, W. T. Cole, N. E. Green, Walter C. Bradsher, M. E. Newsom
1917	M. E. Newsom; Dolian Harris, Walter S. Lockhart, Waller Holladay, E. Lloyd Tilley, W. F. Carr, R. E. Hurst, W. P. Henry, W. T. Minor
1919	M. E. Newsom; W. S. Lockhart, J. T. Salmon, J. P. Royster, J. M. Manning, W. F. Carr, J. E. Carpenter, W. T. Minor, J. M. Lipscomb
1921	Dr. J. M. Manning; E. T. Rollins, R. T. Umstead, W. F. Carr, J. M. Lipscomb, John T. Salmon, Arthur M. Harris, J. E. Carpenter, J. J. Lawson
1923	J. M. Manning; J. T. Salmon, A. M. Harris, J. E. Carpenter, J. C. Markham, R. T. Umstead, J. M. Lipscomb, E. T. Rollins, W. F. Carr
1925	J. M. Manning; Richard E. Dillard, M. Freeland Markham, William F. Carr, F. A. Ward, William C. Lyon, Edward K. Powe, Jr., Young E. Smith, R. H. Crain, A. M. Harris, J. T. Salmon, J. C. Markham, J. E. Carpenter
1927	J. M. Manning; William Kenan Rand, A. M. Harris, J. E. Carpenter, J. C. Markham, J. A. Forlines, J. F. Pleasants, M. F. Markham, W. C. Lyon, Y. E. Smith, W. F. Carr, F. A. Ward, R. E. Dillard
1929	J. M. Manning; Kennie U. Bryan, George E. Isaacs, W. F. Carr, George Watts Hill, W. C. Lyon, Y. E. Smith, J. A. Forlines, J. F. Pleasants, A. M. Harris, W. K. Rand, J. C. Markham, J. E. Carpenter
1931	Delos W. Sorrell; J. Franklin Barfield, A. M. Harris, J. E. Carpenter, J. Ivan Beck, Aubrey P. Wiggins, G. W. Hill, W. F. Carr, Angus H. McDonald, G. E. Isaacs, W. C. Lyon, Y. E. Smith, K. U. Bryan
1933	W. F. Carr; J. T. Salmon, B. C. Woodall, Alonzo W. Cain, G. W. Hill, W. C. Lyon, Y. E. Smith, A. H. McDonald, A. P. Wiggins, A. M. Harris, J. F. Barfield, J. I. Beck, J. E. Carpenter
1935	W. F. Carr; J. F. Barfield, A. M. Harris, J. E. Carpenter, R. Thurman Taylor, A. H. McDonald, A. P. Wiggins, J. T. Salmon, B. C. Woodall, A. W. Cain, G. W. Hill (C. F. Williams), W. C. Lyon, Y. E. Smith
1937	W. F. Carr; W. K. Rand, B. C. Woodall (G. W. Munford), Benjamin F. Sewell, S. Parks Alexander (Richard S. Slattery), D. Russell Perry, Hurley I. Parrish, J. F. Barfield, A. M. Harris, J. E. Carpenter, R. T. Taylor, A. H. McDonald, A. P. Wiggins
1939	W. F. Carr; J. F. Barfield, A. M. Harris, J. B. Cole (R. L. Lee), R. T. Taylor, J. E. Strawbridge, A. P. Wiggins, R. S. Slattery, G. W. Munford, B. F. Sewell, W. K. Rand, D. R. Perry, H. I. Parrish

1941   W. F. Carr; J. F. Barfield, A. M. Harris, R. T. Taylor, J. E. Strawbridge, A. P. Wiggins, G. M. Munford, B. F. Sewell, W. K. Rand, Ernest C. Brown, M. F. Johnson, W. O. Moss, R. L. Lee

1943   W. F. Carr; J. F. Barfield, A. M. Harris, Arthur E. Burcham, J. E. Strawbridge, A. P. Wiggins, G. W. Munford, B. F. Sewell, W. K. Rand, E. C. Brown, M. F. Johnson, W. Otto Moss, R. L. Lee

1945   W. F. Carr; W. K. Rand, G. W. Munford, W. O. Moss, M. F. Johnson, E. C. Brown, B. F. Sewell, A. P. Wiggins, A. M. Harris, J. E. Strawbridge, R. L. Lee (James B. Cole), J. F. Barfield, A. E. Burcham

1947   W. F. Carr; J. F. Barfield, Walter A. Biggs, J. E. Strawbridge, A. M. Harris, John M. M. Gregory, Jr., D. H. Jacobs, G. W. Munford, W. K. Rand, W. O. Moss, M. F. Johnson, E. C. Brown, Benjamin F. Sewell

1949   Daniel K. Edwards (A. M. Harris); A. M. Harris, W. K. Rand, M. F. Johnson, Ernest R. Williamson, E. C. Brown, W. A. Biggs, J. F. Barfield, D. H. Jacobs, J. M. M. Gregory, Jr., B. F. Sewell, George Watts Carr, Jr., J. E. Strawbridge

1951   Emanuel J. Evans; E. R. Williamson, W. K. Rand, M. F. Johnson, Mary Duke Biddle Trent (later Semans), E. C. Brown, J. F. Barfield, E. G. Carlton, Kathrine Robinson Everett, J. M. M. Gregory, Jr., G. W. Carr, Jr., Marvin M. Fowler, B. F. Sewell

1953   E. J. Evans; E. R. Williamson, M. D. B. T. Semans, W. A. Biggs, E.G. Carlton, K. R. Everett, J. M. M. Gregory, Jr., G. W. Carr, Jr., M. M. Fowler, Clarence E. Whitefield, Floyd Fletcher, J. E. Strawbridge, Rencher Nicholas Harris

1955   E. J. Evans; Luther H. Barbour, G. W. Hill, Jr. (James E. Farley), Vance E. Fisher, Robert S. Rankin, W. A. Biggs, K. R. Everett, G. W. Carr, Jr., R. N. Harris, C. E. Whitefield, J. E. Strawbridge, Floyd Fletcher, E. R. Williamson (Alfred D. Atwater)

1957   E. J. Evans; L. H. Barbour, J. E. Farley, V. E. Fisher, R. S. Rankin, W. A. Biggs, K. R. Everett, J. E. Strawbridge, F. Fletcher, John S. Stewart, Charles L. Steel, B. R. Roberts (Scovill Wannamaker), R. Wensell Grabarek

1959   E. J. Evans; L. H. Barbour, S. Wannamaker (Southgate Jones, Jr.), J. S. Stewart, James R. Hawkins, K. R. Everett, V. Fisher, W. A. Biggs, R. W. Grabarek, R. S. Rankin (Bascom Baynes), J. E. Strawbridge, F. Fletcher, C. L. Steel

1961   E. J. Evans; L. H. Barbour, Eugene W. Carlton, J. S. Stewart, J. R. Hawkins, K. R. Everett, W. A. Biggs, Paul Alford, V. Fisher, Iley L. Dean, B. Baynes, F. Fletcher, C. L. Steel

1963   R. Wensell Grabarek; P. A. Alford, L. H. Barbour, E. W. Carlton, I. L. Dean, K. R. Everett, V. E. Fisher, F. Fletcher (Thomas M. Hunt), J. Tom Freeman, J. R. Hawkins, Samuel O. Riley, C. L. Steel, J. S. Stewart

1965   R. Wensell Grabarek; L. H. Barbour, E. W. Carlton, J. S. Stewart, J. R. Hawkins, K. R. Everett, P. Alford, V. Fisher, J. T. Freeman, T. M. Hunt, S. O. Riley (George A. McAfee), C. L. Steel, Jack J. Preiss

1967   R. Wensell Grabarek; E. W. Carlton (Allen D. Aldridge), J. S. Stewart, K. R. Everett, V. E. Fisher, P. Alford, C. L. Steel, T. M. Hunt, Jack J. Preiss, W. A. Biggs, Pat Oakes Griffin, Caldwell E. Boulware, William T. Coman

1969   R. Wensell Grabarek; J. S. Stewart, K. R. Everett, V. E. Fisher (Donald C. Christian), P. Alford, C. L. Steel, T. M. Hunt, Wade L. Cavin, W. A. Biggs, P. Griffin, C. E. Boulware, W. T. Coman, Allen D. Aldridge (M. W. Lynam)

1971   James R. Hawkins; J. S. Stewart, P. Alford, C. L. Steel, T. M. Hunt (Margaret Q. Keller), W. L. Cavin, P. Griffin, C. E. Boulware, D. C. Christian, M. W. Lyman (Murphy R. Boyd, Jr.), John E. Bugg, J. Leslie Atkins, Jr., A. Carroll Pledger

1973   James R. Hawkins; P. A. Alford, J. L. Atkins, Jr., C. E. Boulware, M. R. Boyd, Jr., J. E. Bugg, W. L. Cavin, D. C. Christian, P. Griffin (John C. Martin), Ralph A. Hunt, M. Keller, A. Carroll Pledger, C. L. Steel

1975   Wade L. Cavin; Edward Pope, P. A. Alford, Wade H. Penny, Jr., C. E. Boulware, M. R. Boyd, Jr., J. C. Martin, D. C. Christian, Isabelle Budd, R. A. Hunt, M. Q. Keller, A. Carroll Pledger, C. L. Steel

1977   W. L. Cavin; C. E. Boulware, O. Thomas Hudson, Jr., M. Q. Keller, Stewart Pickett, Jr., William C. Smith, Jr., Wade H. Penny, Jr., Clarence Brown (Carolyn Thornton), A. Carroll Pledger, R. Howard Harris (James W. Brown, Jr.), Isabelle Budd (Adrienne M. Fox), R. A. Hunt, J. C. Martin (Paul C. Bland)

1979   Harry E. Rodenhizer; James W. Brown, Jr., A. M. Fox, William Kimball Griffin, Jr., O. T. Hudson, Jr., R. A. Hunt, M. Q. Keller, S. M. Pickett, Jr., A. Carroll Pledger, Harwood T. Smith, W. C. Smith, Jr. (Judy Harward), Paul A. Vick, Barney H. West

1981   Charles B. Markham; Thomas H. Campbell, Jr., Jane S. Davis, W. K. Griffin, Jr., O. T. Hudson, Jr., R. A. Hunt, Chester L. Jenkins, Sylvia Kerckhoff, A. Carroll Pledger, Maceo K. Sloan, Harwood T. Smith, Paul A. Vick, Barney H. West

1983   Charles B. Markham; Richard C. Boyd, Thomas H. Campbell, A. J. Howard Clement III, Jane S. Davis, Lucy Virginia Engelhard, Lanier R. Fonvielle, Ralph A. Hunt, Chester L. Jenkins, Carolyn D. Johnson (Carolyn I. Thornton), Sylvia Kerckhoff (George S. Nixon), John E. Williams, Madison S. Yarbrough III

1985   Wilbur P. Gulley; Richard C. Boyd, Dr. Clarence P. Brown, Thomas H. Campbell, A. J. Howard Clement III, Jane S. Davis, Lucy Virginia Engelhard, Lanier R. Fonvielle, Chester L. Jenkins, Carolyn D. Johnson, Sylvia S. Kerckhoff (Peggy Watson-Borden), John E. Williams, Madison S. Yarbrough III

1987   Wilbur P. Gulley; Dr. Clarence P. Brown, Shirley A. Caesar, Thomas H. Campbell, A. J. Howard Clement III, Jane S. Davis, Lucy Virginia Engelhard, Chester L. Jenkins, Sylvia S. Kerckhoff, Oscar M. Lewis, Jr., Sandra V. Ogburn, Peggy Watson-Borden, John E. Williams

1989   Chester L. Jenkins; Dr. Clarence P. Brown, Shirley A. Caesar, A. J. Howard Clement III, Lucy Virginia Engelhard, Charles Grubb, Sylvia S. Kerckhoff, Oscar M. Lewis, Jr., Sandra V. Ogburn, Betsy Robb, Peggy Watson-Borden, John E. Williams, Diane Wright

1991   Harry Rodenhizer, Jr.; Dr. Clarence P. Brown, Howard Clement III, Virginia Engelhard, W. Kimball Griffin, Charles Grubb, Sylvia Kerckhoff, John Lloyd, Skip London, Sandra Ogburn, Betsy Robb, Isaac Robinson, Lorisa Seibel, Diane Wright

1993   Sylvia S. Kerckhoff; Howard Clement III, Virginia Engelhard, W. Kimball Griffin, Frank Hyman, Erick Larson II, Skip London, Floyd McKissick, Jr., Sandra Ogburn, Isaac Robinson, Lorisa Seibel, Diane Wright

1995   Sylvia S. Kerckhoff; Cynthia D. Brown, Howard Clement III, Tyrone (Ty) Cox, Virginia Engelhard, W. Kimball Griffin, Frank Hyman, Angela V. Langley, Erick W. Larson, Floyd B. McKissick, Jr., Paul Miller, Isaac A. Robinson, Diane Wright

1997   Nick Tennyson; Pamela L. Blythe, Cynthia D. Brown, Brenda B. Burnette, Howard Clement III, Tyrone (Ty) Cox, Virginia Engelhard, W. Kimball Griffin, Mary D. Jacobs, Angela V. Langley, Erick W. Larson II, Floyd B. McKissick, Jr., Paul Miller

1999　Nick Tennyson; Pamela Blythe, Brenda Burnette, Lewis A. Cheek, Howard Clement III, Tamare Edwards, Dan Hill III, Mary Jacobs, Angela V. Langley, Erick W. Larson, Floyd B. McKissick, Jr., Thomas Stith, Jacqueline D. Wagstaff

2001　William (Bill) Bell; John Best, Jr., Lewis Cheek, Howard Clement III, Cora Cole-McFadden, Tamara Edwards, Thomas Stith

2003　William (Bill) Bell; John P. Best, Jr., Eugene Brown, Diane N. Catotti, Howard Clement III, Cora Cole-McFadden, Thomas Stith

2005　William (Bill) Bell; Eugene A. Brown, Diane N. Catotti, Howard Clement III, Cora M. Cole-McFadden, James Michael (Mike) Woodard, Thomas A. Stith III

Note: Names in parentheses represent those appointed to complete unexpired terms.

Durham City Managers

1921–29	Radford W. Rigsby
1929	J. B. Iler (interim)
1929–35	Robert W. Flack
1935–43	Henry A. Yancey
1943	C. V. Jones (interim)
1943–46	Sterry J. Mahaffey
1946	C. V. Jones (interim)
1946–60	Robert W. Flack
1960–63	George Aull, Jr.
1963–79	I. Harding Hughes, Jr.
1980–82	Barry Del Castilho
March 1983–January 1997	Orville Powell
July 1997–December 2000	P. Lamont Ewell
May 2001–August 2004	Marcia Connor

Durham County Managers

1930–49	Dallas Walton Newsom
1949–84	Edmund S. Swindell, Jr.
1985–January 1991	John P. (Jack) Bond
August 1991–November 1995	George Williams
May 1996–March 2000	David Thompson
November 2000–present	Mike Ruffin

Durham County Clerks of the Superior Court

1881	W. T. Patterson (appointed)	1916	E. Lloyd Tilley (interim)
1881	J. J. Ferrell (elected)	1916–38	Wilbert H. Young
1882–85	William Jasper Christian	1938–62	James R. Stone
1886–89	Dewitt C. Mangum	1963–76	Alton J. Knight
1890–93	Caleb B. Green	1976–2002	James Leo Carr
1894–97	W. J. Christian	2002–present	Archie L. Smith III
1898–1916	Caleb B. Green		

Durham County Registers of Deeds

1881	William M. Lowe	1930–35	A. J. Barbee
1882	J. C. Wilkerson	1936–43	Walter A. Markham
1884–94	Paschall Lunsford	1944–59	R. Garland Brooks
1895–97	W. W. Woods	1959–76	A. J. Gresham
1897–1904	J. E. Suitt	1976–96	Ruth C. Garrett
1905–29	M. G. Markham	1996–present	Willie Lee Covington

Durham City Fire Chiefs

1882–86	Richard D. Blacknall	1905–9	Frank Maddry
1887–88	no information	1910–23	D. C. Christian
1889–91	Howard E. Heartt	1924–46	Frank W. Bennett
1891	Albert Kramer	1947–72	Cosmo L. Cox
1891–92	Moses Ellis McCown	1972/73–85	Joseph A. Letzing
1892–98	W. G. Bradshaw	1985/86–97	Nathaniel Thompson
1899	Howard E. Heartt	1997–98	William Bibby (interim)
1900–1903	J. Frank Maddey	1998–2005	Otis Cooper, Jr.
1903–5	W. H. Llewellyn	2006–present	Bruce T. Pagan, Jr.

Durham County Fire Marshalls

1980–95	Richard J. Sauer
1995–present	Jeffrey L. Batten

Durham City Police Chiefs

1880–81	J. B. Christian	1977–80	Theodore B. Seagroves
1881–82	D. C. Gunter		
1882–83	Moses Ellis McCown (W. C. Thaxton)	May 1980–1988	Talmadge H. Lassiter
		March 1, 1988– May 1992	Trevor A. Hampton
1883–84	J. R. Hutchings		
1884–87	Paul A. Brown	May 1992– June 30, 1997	Jackie W. McNeil
1887–94	W. A. Williams		
1896–1903	J. A. Woodall	June 30, 1997– January 20, 1998	H. Kent Fletcher (interim)
1903–16	J. F. Freeland		
1916–19	J. R. Pendergrast	January 20, 1998– January 31, 2002	Teresa C. Chambers
1919–21	George W. Proctor		
1921–30	Walter F. Doby	January 31, 2002– January 6, 2003	Steven W. Chalmers (interim)
1930–40	George W. Proctor		
1940–56	Hubert E. King	January 6, 2003– 2007	Steven W. Chalmers
1971–77	Jon Kindice		

Note: Early mayors acted as chiefs of police.

Durham City Public Safety Directors

1971	Jacob A. Jessup	1979–80	Nelson Fletcher (interim)
1971–76	Esai Berenbaum	1980–85	Talmadge Lassiter
1976–79	Barry Del Castilho		

Durham County Sheriffs

1881–84	James R. Blacknall	1930–58	Eugene G. ("Cat") Belvin
1884–86	Felix Donaldson Markham, Sr.	1958–70	Jennis M. Mangum
		1970–77	Marvin L. Davis
1886–88	John V. Rigsbee	1977–82	William A. Allen
1888–94	Felix D. Markham	1982–93	Roland Leary
1894–96	John V. Rigsbee	1993–94	Al Hight
1896–1906	Felix D. Markham, Sr.	1994–present	Worth Hill
1906–30	John F. Harward		

Superintendents of Durham City Schools

1882–94	Edwin W. Kennedy	1933–47	W. Frank Warren
1894–97	Clinton W. Toms	1947–57	L. Stacey Weaver
1897–99	W. W. Flowers	1957–75	Lewis Hannen
1899–1906	J. A. Matheson	1975–79	Benjamin T. Brooks
1906–11	W. D. Carmichael	1979–88	Cleveland Hammonds
1911–14	Ernest J. Green	1989–91	Dr. Hawthorne Faison
1914–23	Edwin D. Pusey	1991–92	Joyce P. Edwards
1923–33	Frank M. Martin		

Superintendents of Durham County Schools

1882–83	George W. Jones	1921–24	John W. Carr
1884–85	H. P. Markham	1924–43	Luther H. Barbour
1886–87	Rev. H. T. Darnall	1943–51	W. M. Jenkins
1888–90	C. C. Newton	1951–52	Lester A. Smith (interim)
1890–94	W. G. Vickers	1952–73	Charles H. Chewning
1894–96	R. B. Blalock	1973–84	J. Frank Yeager
1896–1919	Charles Wesley Massey	1985–89	Dr. Larry D. Coble
1919–21	Holland Holton	1989–92	Dr. Jerry D. Weast

Superintendents of Durham Public Schools

1993–96	Dr. C. Owen Phillips
1996–97	Ted Drain (interim)
1997–2006	Dr. Ann Denlinger

Notes

1 LAND FOR THE TAKING

1 *Laws and Resolutions of the State of North Carolina Passed by the General Assembly at Its session of 1881* (Raleigh, 1881), 272–82.
2 Boundary lines described in legislative acts establishing counties are jurisdictional and as such are only definitions, not legal boundaries. Except for the boundary between Durham and Orange counties made by a joint commission (the only method of establishing a legally defined boundary) and ratified 5 Aug. 1968, Durham County's boundaries have never been legally surveyed. Information obtained from Edmund S. Swindell, Jr., Durham County manager, Oct. 1984.
3 United States Department of Agriculture, Soil Conservation Service, in cooperation with the North Carolina Agricultural Experiment Station, *Soil Survey of Durham County, North Carolina* (n. p. [1977]), 1. Figures vary for the area of Durham County. The figure 299 square miles has often been used, for example by Hugh T. Lefler and Albert R. Newsome, *North Carolina: The History of a Southern State* (Chapel Hill, 1954), 713, and David LeRoy Corbitt, *The Formation of the North Carolina Counties, 1663–1943* (Raleigh, 1950), 94.
4 *Soil Survey*, 72 and Table 14.
5 "Extracts from the Letter-Books of Lieutenant Enos Reeves," *Pennsylvania Magazine of History and Biography* 21 (1897): 389–90.
6 Hugh T. Lefler, ed., *John Lawson's "A New Voyage to Carolina"* (Chapel Hill, 1967), 61.
7 George L. Bain and Bruce W. Harvey, *Field Guide to the Geology of the Durham Triassic Basin* (Raleigh, 1977), and information supplied to the author by Duncan S. Heron, Jr., Professor of Geology, Duke University.
8 Durham *Morning Herald*, 29 May 1975.
9 *Soil Survey*, 6–29, 37; W. M. Upchurch and M. B. Fowler, *Durham County Economic and Social* (n.p. [1915]), 11. Over 91 percent of Durham County soils are low in natural fertility.
10 United States Geological Survey Maps of Durham County, Northwest Quadrangle and Southwest Quadrangle, 1973.
11 Lefler and Newsome, *North Carolina*, 35.
12 Ibid., chapters 1, 3, 4.
13 William S. Powell, *The Proprietors of Carolina* (Raleigh, 1963), 6–7, 42–43, 56–57.

14 Lefler and Newsome, *North Carolina*, 156–57, 182–83.

15 Charles G. Sellars, Jr., "Private Profits and British Colonial Policy: The Speculations of Henry McCulloh," *William and Mary Quarterly*, 3d series, 8 (1951): 535–55; John Scott Davenport, "Early Settlers in the North Carolina Piedmont . . . on Lands Sold by Henry McCulloh within Granville's District, 1749–1763," *North Carolina Genealogical Journal* 4 (1978): 74–86.

16 Douglas L. Rights, "The Trading Path to the Indians," *North Carolina Historical Review* 8 (1931): 403–26.

17 Alexander S. Salley, Jr., ed., *Narratives of Early Carolina, 1650–1708* (New York, 1911), 28.

18 The basis for the identification of many of the Piedmont Indians with the Sioux Nation is linguistic, but the evidence is extremely scanty. James Mooney, *Siouan Tribes of the East*, Bulletin No. 22, Bureau of American Ethnology (Washington, 1895), 62–64; John R. Swanton, *The Indians of the Southeastern United States*, Bulletin No. 137, Bureau of American Ethnology (Washington, 1946); Frank G. Speck, "Siouan Tribes of the Carolinas as Known from Catawba, Tutelo, and Documentary Sources," *American Anthropologist* 37 (1935): 201–25.

19 William P. Cumming, ed., *The Discoveries of John Lederer* (Charlottesville, Va., and Winston-Salem, N.C., 1958), 27–28.

20 Paul Hulton, ed., *America 1585: The Complete Drawings of John White* (Chapel Hill, 1984), plate 36, "Indian Village of Secoton."

21 Carl F. Miller, "Archaeology of the John H. Kerr Reservoir Basin, Roanoke River, Virginia–North Carolina," *Inter-Agency Archaeological Salvage Program: River Basin Survey Papers*, Bulletin No. 182, Bureau of American Ethnology, ed. F. H. Roberts (Washington, 1962), 26–28.

22 Clarence W. Alvord and Lee Bidgood, eds., *The First Explorations of the Trans-Allegheny Region by the Virginians, 1650–1674* (Cleveland, 1912), 215–16.

23 Lefler, *John Lawson's "A New Voyage to Carolina,"* 60–62.

24 Douglas L. Rights, *The American Indian in North Carolina* (Winston-Salem, 1957), 114–19; Major C. R. McCollough and others, *Phase II Archaeological Investigations of Ten Specified Locales in the Falls Lake Reservoir Area, Falls Lake, North Carolina*, report prepared for the U.S. Army Corps of Engineers, Wilmington District, Dec. 1980, 72–73.

25 Samuel C. Williams, ed., *Adair's History of the American Indians* (Johnson City, Tenn., 1930), 235–36.

26 John Spencer Bassett, ed., "A Journey to the Land of Eden," *The Writings of Colonel William Byrd of Westover in Virginia, Esqr.* (New York, 1901), 283.

27 Joffre L. Coe, "The Formative Cultures of the Carolina Piedmont," *Transactions of the American Philosophical Society*, n.s., 54, pt. 5 (Philadelphia, 1964).

28 H. Trawick Ward, "A Review of Archaeology in the North Carolina Piedmont: A Study of Change," *The Prehistory of North Carolina: An Archaeological Symposium*, ed. Mark A. Mathis and Jeffrey J. Crow (Raleigh, 1983), 61–63. Archaeologists assign various dates to the periods of Indian culture.

29 Ibid., 63–65.

30 Ibid., 65–70.

31 Ibid., 61, 70–76.

32 *Herald*, 8 June 1975; William K. Boyd, *The Story of Durham: City of the New South* (Durham, 1927), 7–8.

33 The Research Laboratories of Anthropology at UNC keep lists of sites for each county. Most sites have been identified by surface remains only. An early effort at identification of potentially productive sites was an article by Burke and Frank Smith, "Archaeology in Durham County," in *Bulletin of the Archaeological Society of North Carolina* 1, no. 1 (Mar. 1934): 7–10. It describes various sites in Durham County

on the Cameron plantations and one site on Roxboro Road between the Little and Flat rivers. The *Herald* (13 July 1924) reported on extensive finds off Guess Road four miles north of Durham and (5 July 1944) on a collection of five thousand relics found by Charles Worley in the Flat River area of Fish Dam Road (now Cheek Road).

34 Ward, "A Review of Archaeology in the North Carolina Piedmont," 78–81.

35 Bennie C. Keel and Joffre L. Coe, "A Reconnaissance and Proposal for Archaeological Salvage in Falls Reservoir, N.C." (1970), and H. Trawick Ward and Joffre L. Coe, "An Archaeological Evaluation of the Falls of the Neuse Reservoir" (1976), reports deposited in the Research Laboratories of Anthropology, UNC.

36 McCollough and others, *Phase II Archaeological Investigations of Ten Specified Locales in the Falls Lake Reservoir Area, Falls Lake, North Carolina*, 66–67.

37 Ibid., 74.

38 Ibid., 68–76.

39 Ward, "A Review of Archaeology in the North Carolina Piedmont," 57–59; Roy S. Dickens, Jr., "In Search of Occaneechi: Archaeology and History of the Aboriginal North Carolina Piedmont," paper written for the Society for Historical Archaeology Symposium, Williamsburg, 1983, deposited in the Research Laboratories of Anthropology, UNC.

40 James B. Griffin, "An Interpretation of Siouan Archaeology in the Piedmont of North Carolina and Virginia," *American Antiquity* 10 (Apr. 1945): 324–25. Some of these artifacts are on display in the Research Laboratories of Anthropology, UNC.

41 "Answers at Occaneechi Town," *Carolina Alumni Review*, summer 1984, 10–13, 26, 28.

42 Mary Ann Holm, "Faunal Remains from the Wall and Fredericks [*sic*] Sites," and Kristen J. Johnson, "A Preliminary Statement on Plant Remains from the Wall and Fredericks [*sic*] Sites," papers written for the Society for Historical Archaeology Symposium, Williamsburg, 1983, deposited in the Research Laboratories of Anthropology, UNC.

43 Lefler and Newsome, *North Carolina*, 72–73; William K. Boyd, ed., *William Byrd's Histories of the Dividing Line betwixt Virginia and North Carolina* (Raleigh 1929), 169–79.

44 William P. Cumming, *North Carolina in Maps* (Raleigh, 1966), plate 6, "A New and Correct Map of the Province of North Carolina by Edward Moseley."

2 MOVING IN

1 William L. Saunders, ed., *The Colonial Records of North Carolina*, 10 vols. (Raleigh, 1886–90), 4:1115–16, 5:xxxii, 5:772, 6:579; North Carolina Land Grants, 2:219–23, 14:381; OCDB 2:128–31. The land Burrington bought had earlier been granted to William Little, Edward Moseley, John Lovick, and Robert Forster.

2 Hugh T. Lefler and Paul Wager, *Orange County, 1752–1952* (Chapel Hill, 1953), 19.

3 Saunders, ed., *The Colonial Records of North Carolina*, 4:xxi.

4 Lefler and Newsome, *North Carolina*, chap. 5, contains information on the settlers in the backcountry and the routes by which they came.

5 Zae Hargett Gwynn, *Abstracts of the Early Deeds of Granville County, North Carolina, 1746–1765* (Rocky Mount, N.C., 1974), 2, 12, 13; Ruth Herndon Shields and Mann Cabe Patterson, *Some Orange County, North Carolina, Families* (Chapel Hill, 1934), 1.

6 North Carolina Land Grants, 14:59.

7 Ruth Herndon Shields, Belle Lewter West, and Kathryn Crossley Stone, comps., *A Study of the Barbee Families of Chatham, Orange and Wake Counties in North Carolina* (Boulder, Colo., 1971), 162.

8 Saunders, ed., *The Colonial Records of North Carolina*, 4:597, 602, 801, 948.

9 Shields and Patterson, *Some Orange County, North Carolina, Families*, 1.

10 David Irvin Craig, *A Historical Sketch of New Hope Church in Orange County, North Carolina* (Reidsville, N.C., 1891), 4.

11 Robert W. Ramsey, *Carolina Cradle* (Chapel Hill, 1964), 123; OCR, Inventories, Sales, and Accounts of Estates 1:45; Mary L. Medley, *History of Anson County, North Carolina, 1750–1976* (Wadesboro, N.C., 1976), 40–41; Gwynn, *Deeds of Granville County*, 2; OCDB 1:159; B. Ransom McBride, comp., "The Inhabitants of Granville County, N.C., 1746, 1750," *North Carolina Genealogical Journal* 8 (1982): 28.

12 Bertie County Records, NCOAH, Bertie County Deed Book G:162; Adelaide L. Fries et al., eds., *The Records of the Moravians*, 11 vols. (Raleigh, 1922–69), 1:29, 145. Michael Synnott's will (OCW A:217) leaves land to a nephew Richard of Wapping, London. This is probably an old usage of the word *nephew* to mean *grandson.* Compare the will of Hugh Caine (A:235), in which the relationship is clearly defined.

13 Lord Granville Land Grant, Land Grant Office, plat of tract surveyed 19 Nov. 1751.

14 McBride, comp., "The Inhabitants of Granville County, N.C., 1746, 1750," 26–28.

15 Saunders, ed., *The Colonial Records of North Carolina*, 4:1322–24, 1336.

16 Walter Clark, ed., *The State Records of North Carolina* (Raleigh, 1895–1906), 23:383–84.

17 OCR, OCCM, June 1753.

18 Clark, ed., *The State Records of North Carolina,* 23:547.

19 Ibid., 819, 823, 828.

20 Ruth Blackwelder, *The Age of Orange* (Charlotte, 1961), chap. 2, describes county government in Orange County succinctly. Paul W. Wager, *County Government and Administration in North Carolina* (Chapel Hill, 1928), covers the same ground in great detail and for the state as a whole.

21 OCR, OCCM, June 1757, Nov. 1763, May 1764.

22 Ibid., June 1759, Sept. 1759, Nov. 1760, Feb. 1761, Aug. 1763.

23 Ibid., Aug. 1766, Mar. and July 1754.

24 John F. D. Smyth, *A Tour in the United States of America* (Dublin, 1784), 1:103.

25 OCR, OCCM, Oct. 1754.

26 Treasurer's and Comptroller's Papers, NCOAH, file 105.1. This list was published in the *North Carolinian* 1 (Dec. 1955): 103–8.

27 Saunders, ed., *The Colonial Records of North Carolina*, 5:24.

28 Harry Roy Merrens, *Colonial North Carolina in the Eighteenth Century: A Study in Historical Geography* (Chapel Hill, 1964), 76.

29 Lefler and Wager, *Orange County*, 19–20.

30 Saunders, ed., *The Colonial Records of North Carolina*, 5:1204; B. Ransom McBride, ed., "John Saunders' Journey to North Carolina—1753," *North Carolina Genealogical Journal* 5 (1979): 147; OCR, OCCM, Sept. 1757, June 1758, May 1763. The Moravians estimated the distance between Boggan's and Synnott's as eight miles (Fries, Moravian Records 2:518).

31 OCR, OCCM, July 1754.

32 Isak Dinesen, *Out of Africa* (New York, 1952), 157.

33 E. Lawrence Lee, *Indian Wars in North Carolina, 1663–1763* (Raleigh, 1968), 64. Chapters 10, 11, and 12 give a good description of the war in the South; Saunders, ed., *The Colonial Records of North Carolina*, 5:xxii–xxiii.

34 Lefler and Newsome, *North Carolina*, 169; Blackwelder, *The Age of Orange*, 39; Lee, *Indian Wars in North Carolina*, 65–71, 80; Saunders, ed., *The Colonial Records of North Carolina*, 5:xxvi–xxxi.

35 Saunders, ed., *The Colonial Records of North Carolina*, 5:853.

36 OCR, OCCM, Mar., June, Sept. 1757, Mar. 1758, deal with Indian matters.

37 OCW A:13.

38 Concise accounts of the War of the Regulation in Orange County may be found in Lefler and Wager, *Orange County*, chap. 4, and Blackwelder, *The Age of Orange*,

41–48. The Regulator movement in North Carolina took its name from that in South Carolina, but although both were backcountry movements, they had different complaints and objectives.

39 George R. Adams, "The Carolina Regulators: A Note on Changing Interpretations," *North Carolina Historical Review* 49 (1972): 345–52; Lefler and Wager, *Orange County*, 30–33; Saunders, ed., *The Colonial Records of North Carolina*, 7:671–72, 731–37, 758–66; Marvin L. Michael Kay and William S. Price, Jr., "'To Ride the Wood Mare': Road Building and Militia Service in Colonial North Carolina, 1740–1775," *North Carolina Historical Review* 57 (1980): 361–62, 376–77.

40 Lefler and Wager, *Orange County*, 25, 30–31; William S. Powell, *The Correspondence of William Tryon and Other Selected Papers* (Raleigh, 1980), 2:173.

41 Saunders, ed., *The Colonial Records of North Carolina*, 7:497, 8:515–16; Lefler and Wager, *Orange County*, 32, 34, 35–36.

42 Powell, *The Correspondence of William Tryon and Other Selected Papers*, 2:124.

43 Lefler and Wager, *Orange County*, 36; Saunders, ed., *The Colonial Records of North Carolina*, 8:241–44; Alan D. Watson, "The Regulation: Society in Upheaval," in *The North Carolina Experience: An Interpretive and Documentary History*, ed. Lindley S. Butler and Alan D. Watson (Chapel Hill, 1984), 105; Saunders, ed., *The Colonial Records of North Carolina*, 8:687.

44 Lefler and Wager, *Orange County*, 38; Powell, *The Correspondence of William Tryon and Other Selected Papers*, 2:733.

45 Powell, *The Correspondence of William Tryon and Other Selected Papers*, 2:729, 839; Florence Knight Fruth, *Some Descendants of Richard Few of Chester County, Pennsylvania and Allied Lines* (Beaver Falls, Pa., 1977).

46 Powell, *The Correspondence of William Tryon and Other Selected Papers*, 2:110–13, 769.

47 "Marking the Ramsgate Road" and "The Ramsgate Road," *North Carolina Booklet* 23 (1926): 57–62.

48 Boyd, *The Story of Durham*, 16–17.

49 Powell, *The Correspondence of William Tryon and Other Selected Papers*, 2:688, 689, 718, 731; OCDB 3:223–24.

50 Saunders, ed., *The Colonial Records of North Carolina*, 2:735.

51 A. B. Markham map, "Land Grants to Early Settlers in Old Orange County, North Carolina," 1973; Saunders, ed., *The Colonial Records of North Carolina*, 7:777; Lefler and Wager, *Orange County*, 173; Patrick Nicholson, *Mr. Jim: The Biography of James Smither Abercrombie* (Houston, 1983), 64. No documentation is given for the marriage of Abercrombie to John Booth's daughter. Presumably it was obtained from family tradition or records.

52 Cameron Family Papers, SHC, 11 Nov. 1768, 30 June 1787; John Scott Davenport, "Early Settlers in the North Carolina Piedmont . . . on Lands Sold by Henry McCulloh within Granville's District, 1749–1763," *North Carolina Genealogical Journal* 4 (1978): 85; OCR, OCCM, Nov. 1763; Powell, *The Correspondence of William Tryon and Other Selected Papers*, 2:792 and note; Cameron Family Papers, SHC, 11 Nov. 1768.

53 Powell, *The Correspondence of William Tryon and Other Selected Papers*, 2:630; Saunders, ed., *The Colonial Records of North Carolina*, 23:819–31, 844–46.

54 Saunders, ed., *The Colonial Records of North Carolina*, 22:441–42; Secretary of State's Papers, NCOAH, Legislative Papers, 1770–71.

3 THE AMERICAN REVOLUTION

1 Lefler and Newsome, *North Carolina*, 191.

2 John R. Alden, *The South in the Revolution* (Baton Rouge, 1957), 51–63.

3 Carole W. Troxler, *The Loyalist Experience in North Carolina* (Raleigh, 1976), 1–2.

4 Don Higginbotham, "Decision for Revolution," in *The North Carolina Experience,* ed. Butler and Watson.

5 Lefler and Newsome, *North Carolina,* 172.

6 Alden, *The South in the Revolution,* 169–71.

7 Higginbotham, "Decision for Revolution," 128.

8 Lefler and Wager, *Orange County,* 41–61.

9 Higginbotham, "Decision for Revolution," 130–31.

10 Lefler and Wager, *Orange County,* 45–46; William S. Powell, ed., *Biographical Dictionary of North Carolina* (Chapel Hill, 1984), 1:298.

11 Blackwelder, *The Age of Orange,* 52; Lefler and Newsome, *North Carolina,* 220–26; Lefler and Wager, *Orange County,* 42–45, 345–48.

12 Hugh F. Rankin, *The North Carolina Continentals* (Chapel Hill, 1971), 237.

13 Clark, ed., *The State Records of North Carolina,* 15:769.

14 Eli W. Caruthers, *Interesting Revolutionary Incidents and Sketches of Character Chiefly in the "Old North State"* (Philadelphia, 1856), 412.

15 Ibid., 418.

16 Josiah Turner, ed., *The Truth,* Mar. 1884.

17 OCR, Miscellaneous Records. This was published in the Hillsborough Historical Society *Newsletter* 15 (Apr. 1976) and *North Carolina Genealogical Journal* 3 (Feb. 1977): 48–51.

18 OCR, OCCM, May and Aug. 1777.

19 Lefler and Newsome, *North Carolina,* 232–35; Lefler and Wager, *Orange County,* 176.

20 OCR, OCCM, Aug. 1777.

21 Ibid.

22 Ibid., Feb. 1778, May 1778.

23 Ibid., Aug. 1777; Blackwelder, *The Age of Orange,* 56; A. B. Markham, Land Grants Map; OCDB 3:166.

24 Troxler, *The Loyalist Experience in North Carolina,* 37–38; Lefler and Wager, *Orange County,* 291–92; Blackwelder, *The Age of Orange,* 56–57; Treasurer's and Comptroller's Papers, NCOAH, Confiscated Lands, Box 4; British Records, NCOAH, American Loyalist Claims, Series 2, Audit office 13/91 and 13/100. The confiscation laws of 1778 resulted in the seizure of loyalist lands and their reselling for the state's gain. James Carrington the elder of Flat River was appointed one of three commissioners of confiscated property for the county.

25 Lefler and Wager, *Orange County,* 291–92.

26 Legislative Papers, NCOAH, 1779 Tax List. By 1782 the tax for refusal to bear arms in the war was fourfold (OCR, OCCM, Feb. 1782).

27 Jeffrey J. Crow, *The Black Experience in Revolutionary North Carolina* (Raleigh, 1977), 30, 31, 65.

28 Ibid., 55; Cameron Family Papers, SHC, 15 Feb. 1776.

29 Crow, *The Black Experience in Revolutionary North Carolina,* 55–63.

30 Cameron Family Papers, SHC, 15 Feb. 1776.

31 Ibid.

32 Rankin, *The North Carolina Continentals,* 62.

33 Ibid., 20, 63, 64.

34 Lefler and Wager, *Orange County,* 48.

35 Luther L. Gobbel, "The Militia of North Carolina in Colonial and Revolutionary Times," *Trinity College Historical Papers,* 13th series (Durham, 1919), 51–54.

36 These names have been taken from the sources that follow; the judgment that these men lived in what became Durham County is the author's. Ransom McBride, comp., "Revolutionary War Papers," *North Carolina Genealogical Journal* 4 (1978): 24, 26, 27, 28, 173: 5 (1979): 91, 93; 6 (1980): 176; 9 (1983): 90; 10 (1984): 111, 168, 169, 236; Daughters of the American Revolution, *Roster of Soldiers from North Carolina in the*

American Revolution (Durham, 1932), 449–50; OCR, OCCM, Aug. 1832, May 1835, Aug. 1848; Clark, ed., *The State Records of North Carolina* 22:55–92; Henry T. Shanks, ed., *The Papers of Willie Person Mangum* (Raleigh, 1950–56), 2:xi, 155–56; John Vickers and Thomas Scism, *Chapel Hill: An Illustrated History* (Chapel Hill, 1985), 14; John Goodwin Herndon, *The Herndons of the American Revolution* (Lancaster, Pa., 1950–52), 2:211; National Archives, Military Service Records, Pension Application file W9540 (Thomas Marcum), R6230 (Moses Leathers); Shields, West, and Stone, comps., *A Study of the Barbee Families of Chatham, Orange and Wake Counties in North Carolina*, 19, 165–66.

37 National Archives, Military Service Records, Pension Application file R6230.

38 OCR, OCCM, Aug. 1832.

39 National Archives, Military Service Records, Pension Application file S8185; OCR, OCCM, Nov. 1849. Carrington died in 1849 at the age of ninety-four. Thomas Marcum enlisted in the militia in 1781 as an artificer, a military name for a mechanic, under Colonel Thomas Farmer and Captain Elliott. He reenlisted for another three months under Captain Phillips. This time his unit was assigned to guard Hillsborough. He was discharged in November of that same year (Herndon, *The Herndons of the Revolution* 2:211). Isaac Hicks, later a mill owner on the Eno, also enlisted as an artificer (McBride, "Revolutionary War Papers," *North Carolina Genealogical Journal* 4 [1978]: 173).

40 McBride, "Revolutionary War Papers," *North Carolina Genealogical Journal* 5 (1979): 91; Cameron Family Papers, SHC, 17 Nov. 1781.

4 EIGHTEENTH-CENTURY ORANGE COUNTY

1 Saunders, ed., *The Colonial Records of North Carolina*, 6:614.

2 North Carolina Land Grants, Book 19, 455–60.

3 Saunders, ed., *The Colonial Records of North Carolina*, 7:288–89; Merrens, *Colonial North Carolina in the Eighteenth Century*, 53–54, notes considerable immigration from Virginia in the 1750s and 1760s.

4 Quoted by Merrens, *Colonial North Carolina in the Eighteenth Century*, 53–54.

5 Lefler and Wager, *Orange County*, 25.

6 Hugh Conway Browning, "Orange County and Hillsborough Items of History, The Families of Hugh and James Caine," unpublished typescript in the author's possession; Wirt Johnson Carrington, *A History of Halifax County* (Richmond, Va., 1924), for the Links, Carringtons, and Kennons; Lyman Chalkley, *Chronicles of the Scotch-Irish Settlement in Virginia* (Rosslyn, Va., 1912), for the McCowns, Lynns, and Shieldses; Churchill Gibson Chamberlayne, ed., *The Vestry Book and Register of Bristol Parish, Virginia, 1720–1789* (Richmond, Va., 1898), and *Vestry Book and Register of Saint Peter's Parish, New Kent and James City Counties, Virginia, 1684–1786* (Richmond, Va., 1937), for the Dezerns, Kennons, Majors, Masseys, Morelands, and Vaughns; George D. Colclough, *The Colclough Family* (Burlington, N.C., 1969); Durham *Recorder*, 19 Mar. 1907, for the Bowlings; Buxton Harris, "Remarks Addressed to My Children," photocopy in the author's possession, for the Hopkinses and Harrises; Herndon, *The Herndons of the American Revolution*; W. Mac Jones, ed., *The Douglas Register* (Richmond, Va., 1928), for the Bilboas, Dukes, Ellises, Harrises, Parrishes, Vaughans, and Wades; Paxson R. Link, *The Link Family: Antecedents and Descendants of John Jacob Link, 1417–1951* (Paris, Ill., 1951); Elizabeth F. McKoy, *Early New Hanover County Records* (Wilmington, N.C., 1913), for the Rogerses; Orange County Wills, Book D, 114–18 for the Trices; *The Parish Register of Christ Church, Middlesex County, Virginia, from 1653 to 1812* (Richmond, Va., 1897), for the Barbees, Kings, and Rhodeses; Shanks, ed., *The Papers of Willie Person Mangum*; Shields, West, and Stone, comps., *A Study of the Barbee Families of Chatham, Orange and Wake Counties in North Carolina*; Ruth

Herndon Shields, *The Descendants of William and Sarah Herndon of Caroline County, Va., and Chatham County, N.C.* (Chapel Hill, 1956); C. J. Stevens, ed., *Holloways of the South and Allied Families* (New Orleans, 1977); Arthur Mangum Tilley, Sr., *Tilley: A Brief Historical Sketch of the Name and Family of the Tilleys* (n.p., n.d.); Mary Ethel Tilley, *Carrington: A Brief Historical Sketch of the Name and Family* (Rougemont, N.C. [1943]); *The Truth*, Mar. 1884 (Suitts); George Ruford Turrentine, *The Turrentine Family* (n.p., 1954); Richard Baxter Umstead, *The North Carolina Umstead Lineage* (n.p., n.d.); interviews with Mildred Harris, Lucille Glenn, and Curtis Booker.

7 Boyd, *The Story of Durham*, 17–18.

8 These are the author's statistics. The ten landowners in Saint Mary's District with one thousand acres or more were Richard Bennehan, John Cabe, William Cabe, William Cain, John Carrington, Jr., William Chisenhall, James Critchen, Archer Harris, John Latta, Sr., and Samuel Turrentine, Jr. The seven in Saint Mark's District were Christopher Barbee, Daniel Booth, George Herndon, John Mitcham, Mark Patterson, William Pickett, and Thomas Price. In 1787 Christopher Barbee owned more land than anyone else in Orange County, 2,146 acres; Mark Patterson owned 2,031, George Herndon, 1,279, and Daniel Booth, 1,127.

9 These are the author's statistics. Wake County Records, Tax Lists, NCOAH.

10 Greene County, Georgia, Papers, Deeds, Book A, 28; A2, 2, 44; B, 9, 49, 152; C, 23, 29, DU-RBMSCL; [B.] Ransom McBride, comp., "Claims of British Merchants after the Revolutionary War," *North Carolina Genealogical Journal* 11 (1985): 25–43.

11 William Few, "Autobiography of Colonel William Few of Georgia," *Magazine of American History* 7 (1881): 343–44.

12 Merrens, *Colonial North Carolina in the Eighteenth Century*, 108, 120–21, 134.

13 Doug Swaim, "North Carolina Folk Housing," *Carolina Dwelling*, ed. Doug Swaim (Raleigh, 1978), 30–31.

14 Cameron Family Papers, SHC, 14 Aug. 1790; R. D. W. Connor, *A Documentary History of the University of North Carolina* (Chapel Hill, 1953), 1:296. The name Hardscrabble for the Cain plantation is first found in a letter dated 7 Feb. 1841 in the Tod R. Caldwell Papers, SHC.

15 Charles Richard Sanders, who almost bought the Brick House in the 1940s, is the source for the information about its construction, size, and layout; Cameron Family Papers, SHC, Nov. 1805.

16 OCR, Inventories, Sales, and Accounts, 1:9–10.

17 Ibid., 45.

18 Hugh Conway Browning, "Valley of the Eno, Some of Its Land—Some of Its People—Some of Its Mills" [1973], 61, typescript in the author's possession.

19 "An Eno River Calendar for 1972," July.

20 Browning, "Valley of the Eno," 70.

21 OCR, OCCM, NCOAH, Aug. 1786.

22 Cameron Family Papers, SHC, 24 Nov. 1785; OCR, OCCM, Aug. 1777; Walter Alves Papers, SHC, Oct. 1806.

23 OCR, OCCM, Feb. 1780, Feb. 1783, Feb., Mar., May 1791; OCDB 4:43. John Cabe built a mill on the Eno before he was granted in 1779 the tract on which it stood. The 304-acre tract today straddles the Orange/Durham boundary, but the sites of his mill, home, and graveyard are on the part in Orange County. Many other of his tracts, however, lie in Durham County.

24 OCR, OCDB 5:323; 9:221, 12:291. That Cain's mill existed before 1795 is inferred from a deed of that date that mentions Cain's Mill Road (OCDB 5:213).

25 Ibid. 38:341; Durham *Recorder*, 28 Aug. 1908.

26 OCW C:85.

27 Cumming, *North Carolina in Maps*, plate 7.

28 OCDB 1:133, 141, 12:291.

29 Ibid. 4:578 (Carrington's Mill Creek); OCR, Land Entry Book 1778–95, (Dunnagan's Mill Creek); Browning, "Valley of the Eno," 61 (Forrester's, later Warren's, Mill Creek).

30 Saunders, ed., *The Colonial Records of North Carolina*, 2:206.

31 Lefler and Wager, *Orange County*, 289–90; Few, "Autobiography of Colonel William Few of Georgia," 343–44.

32 One tract of Johnston's was called the Chapel tract. (Walter Alves Papers, SHC, Oct. 1806.) That a chapel was actually there is suggested by a notation in the Johnston and Bennehan Little River store accounts for 14 July 1775: "for work done abt [about] the Chapell" (Cameron Family Papers, SHC, vol. 9).

33 Lefler and Wager, *Orange County*, 297; Grady L. E. Carroll, ed., *Francis Asbury in North Carolina: The North Carolina Portions of the Journal of Francis Asbury* (Nashville, 1964), 50.

34 Carroll, ed., *Francis Asbury in North Carolina*, 48.

35 Thomas Mann Papers, DU-RBMSCL, Journal.

36 OCW A:223.

37 Ibid. C:13; OCDB 9:304, 10:266.

38 Interview with Mrs. Hubert Browning, 2 Mar. 1985.

39 Harley A. Chester, "A History of Mount Bethel Methodist Church" (n.p., n.d.).

40 Cameron Family Papers, SHC, Legal Papers, Box 28; OCDB 3:131.

41 OCDB 17:370.

42 Durham *Daily Sun*, 18 Oct. 1901; interview with Mildred M. Harris 18 Feb. 1985.

43 Few, "Autobiography of Colonel William Few of Georgia," 344. Since the Piper-Cabe schoolhouse is known to have stood near the ford where Few's mill had been, the school Few describes might have been that neighborhood institution.

44 Saunders, ed., *The Colonial Records of North Carolina*, 1:86.

45 *North Carolinian* 1 (Dec. 1955): 103–8.

46 *Heads of Families at the First Census of the United States Taken in the Year 1790: North Carolina* (Washington, 1908), 9; Lefler and Wager, *Orange County*, 96.

47 See Willie Lee Rose, *Slavery and Freedom* (New York, 1982), chap. 2.

48 Jean B. Anderson, *Piedmont Plantation: The Bennehan-Cameron Family and Lands in North Carolina* (Durham, 1985), 107–8.

49 Frederick Law Olmsted noticed differences in slavery on large and small plantations and in North Carolina as opposed to other southern states. For example, *The Cotton Kingdom* (New York, 1962), 148–49, 165.

50 Tod R. Caldwell Papers, SHC, 14 Apr. 1833.

51 For information on free blacks see John Hope Franklin, *The Free Negro in North Carolina, 1790–1860* (Chapel Hill, 1943).

52 *North Carolinian* 1 (Dec. 1955): 103–8; *Heads of Families . . . 1790: North Carolina*, 9; U.S. Census Office, *Second Census, 1800, Return of the Whole Number of Persons within the Several Districts of the United States* (Washington, 1802), 2K.

5 THE RIP VAN WINKLE ERA

1 Lefler and Newsome, *North Carolina*, 314–17, 322.

2 Ibid., 319–20, 323–24, 326.

3 The War of 1812–14 was an unpopular and divisive conflict. Planters who exported their produce, like the Bennehans and Cameron, felt the effect long before the war started when the American government resorted to embargoes to stop British predations on shipping. Duncan Cameron supported the war and was appointed a major general of the State Militia. He was in charge of raising and equipping troops in the various Piedmont counties that constituted the third district: Granville, Person, Orange, and Wake. The following men were officers of the Eno or Third Battalion of the

Orange Regiment of Militia, obviously an eastern Orange battalion. They signed a petition requesting that John Rhodes become the lieutenant commander and James Ray major of the outfit: Captains Zachariah Herndon, George Carrington, Herbert Sims, Abner Veazey, William Rhodes; Lieutenants Robert Harris, Edmund Herndon, J[ohn] Cain, Chesley P. Patterson, Chuzah Hopkins, Henry Lewis; Ensigns Ezekiel Trice, James Wood, Benjamin Rhodes, Samuel Turrentine, John Rhodes, Will Madison, J. Dixon. In addition David Parker, John Latta, Taylor Duke, Absalom Alston, William Carrington, and George Horton were eastern Orange men who were captains of companies. How many of these companies actually saw action is not known. Later Herbert Sims was colonel of the Hillsborough or First Regiment, and William P. Mangum was major of the Eno or Second Battalion of the same regiment. The battle fronts were largely coastal, and very few large-scale engagements occurred except in the Battle of New Orleans.

Besides the Cameron Papers, 13 Sept., 15 Sept., Dec. 1813, 25 July 1814, both the State Archives and the National Archives have documents relating to North Carolina troops. Six volumes of muster rolls in the NCOAH contain the names of the detached militiamen who served in the coastal defenses and in the army that assembled at Wadesboro to march south, but who never fought because the fighting in Louisiana had ceased before they started.

4 OCDB 13:268; 14:109, 151, 360; 15:382; 16:68, 345; 19:278, 282; 20:134; 21:167; 24:1, 2, 313; 25:10, 13, 242; 26:267, 322, 323; Wake County Deeds, Book T:201; 9:315; 11:13.

5 Cameron Family Papers, SHC, 30 June 1807.

6 For the total number of slaves on the Bennehan-Cameron plantations on the eve of the Civil War see Anderson, *Piedmont Plantation*, 95.

7 For the Great Revival see John Bruce Boles, "The Religious Mind of the Old South: The Era of the Great Revival, 1787–1805" (Ph.D. diss.), University of Virginia, 1969.

8 Boles, "The Religious Mind of the Old South," 271.

9 Ibid., 134–35.

10 Ibid., 139; David T. Morgan, Jr., "The Great Awakening in North Carolina, 1740–1775: The Baptist Phase," *North Carolina Historical Review* 45 (1968): 264–83.

11 Camp Creek Church Book [1852] in possession of J. Isaac Hill, Rougemont.

12 OCDB 14:107. John Welborn (Wilbourne) in his will (OCW D:553, 19 Jan. 1819) provided 100 acres for his slave Jeremiah, who was to be freed.

13 *Herald*, 22 Mar. 1942. The pews from Camp Creek Church are now in Rougemont's Primitive Baptist Church (interview with Mildred Harris, 4 Apr. 1982).

14 Bertha P. Shipp, Louis T. Stokes, and Beulah Walton, *A History of Cedar Fork Church, 1805–1970* [1970].

15 Curtis Booker, Durham, has a large collection of papers concerning the Leigh, Herndon, Hudgins, and other families in the southern part of the county, among which is the Hudgins bill.

16 Shipp, Stokes, and Walton, *A History of Cedar Fork Church*, 12.

17 OCDB 28:505. The first record book of this church is in the possession of Mrs. Wilmer Hunt, Durham.

18 Cameron Family Papers, SHC, Undated letters, Paul C. Cameron, folder 7.

19 Ibid., 30 June 1811. The existing Cain's Chapel in the same neighborhood is a Baptist church and may have been formed by black members who withdrew from Mount Lebanon.

20 Ibid., 5 Feb. 1818.

21 Ibid., 18 Aug. 1818.

22 Cameron Family Papers, SHC, 10 Aug. 1825, Dec. 1826, 21 Oct. 1827, 1 Aug. 1833, 25 May 1838; *Journal of the Proceedings . . . of the Protestant Episcopal Church in the State of North Carolina . . . 1827* (New Bern, 1827), 23; *Journal of the Proceedings . . . 1828* (Fayetteville, 1828), 9, 10; *Journal of the Proceedings . . . 1837* (Fayetteville, 1837), 9.

23 *Fletcher's Chapel Church* (Durham [1953]), Pamphlet Collection, D.U. Library; DCDB 8:153.

24 "Fletcher's Chapel United Methodist Church," a pamphlet printed for the dedication of the 1975 addition to the present church, in the possession of Ollie Nichols Carpenter. In 1980 the original church building was being used as a feed barn on the John Wesley Barbee homeplace near Fish Dam (formerly Cheek) Road.

25 Interview 10 Feb. 1984 with Thomas C. Rogers, then owner of the house, who had many family papers; *Herald*, 20 May 1984.

26 John Thomas Nichols Papers, DU-RBMSCL, volume of miscellaneous records, 47.

27 The Reverend Mark Nanney, "Andrews Chapel United Methodist Church: A Local Church History," in the possession of the church; Wake County Deeds, Book 18:164.

28 A. B. Markham, Land Grant Map; Wake County Records, NCOAH, Tax Lists, Lick Creek District, 1809.

29 Elizabeth Reid Murray, *Wake, Capital County of North Carolina* (Raleigh, 1983), 416, 661, 666.

30 Benjamin G. Childs, *Centennial History of Trinity Methodist Church* (Durham, 1961), 4; N.C. Railroad Collection, Private Collections, NCOAH, Map Book No. 3; OCDB 26:300.

31 OCDB 36:315.

32 The post-Revolutionary period must have seen the establishment of more crossroad stores than are now found in the records. By 1798 John Cain, a son of James and brother of William Cain, had a store which is mentioned in a road maintenance directive, but impossible now to identify.

33 Murray, *Wake, Capital County of North Carolina*, 256; Cameron Family Papers, SHC, 19 Feb. 1828; OCR, OCCM, Aug. 1838. Old coach routes are reflected in the scattering of "Stagecoach Road" or "Stage Road" names on modern maps.

34 U.S. Post Office Dept., "Records of Appointments of Postmasters, 1789–1929," microfilm copy, NCOAH.

35 Anderson, *Piedmont Plantation*, 13, 23.

36 OCR, Estates: Samuel Garrard, Willie M. Shaw; OCW E:159; Hillsborough *Recorder*, 7 May, 24 Sept. 1828. Midway was midway between Hillsborough and Oxford.

37 U.S. Post Office Dept., "Records of Appointments"; Hillsborough *Recorder*, 13 Sept. 1848; OCR, OCCM, Nov. 1847; interview with Mildred Mangum Harris, Bahama, 15 Mar 1985; Shanks, ed., *The Papers of Wilie Person Mangum*, 1:xxiii, 47–49; OCR, OCCM, May 1801.

38 U.S. Post Office Dept., "Records of Appointments." John J. Carrington's store lay on his 276-acre tract (OCCM, Sept. 1829; Shanks, *Mangum Papers*, 1:126–27, 210–11). Foreclosed mortgages on his land, including his home plantation, Stoney Retreat, and another tract with the intriguing name of Fiddleton, probably forced John J. Carrington to emigrate to Tennessee in 1831 (Shanks, *Mangum Papers*, 1:406, 570; OCDB 22:331, 334, 335, 337).

39 U.S. Post Office Dept., "Records of Appointments."

40 OCR, Estates Papers: David Parker, Sr., letter of David Parker, Jr., 5 Mar. 1840.

41 OCDB 13:239; OCR, Estates Papers: Allen Parrish.

42 Hillsborough *Recorder*, 11 Aug. 1830, 24 June 1847; Leathers, Latta & Co., Day Book, 1854–55, South Lowell, DU-RBMSCL.

43 OCR, Civil Action Papers, 1808, Herndon's bill to George Carrington, 1801–5; Herndon Family Papers in possession of Curtis Booker, Durham; OCR, OCCM, Nov. 1828; U.S. Post Office Dept., "Records of Appointments"; OCDB 26:67, 27:48, 29:306.

44 Hillsborough *Recorder*, 22 Aug. 1839.

45 U.S. Post Office Dept., "Records of Appointments"; OCR, OCCM, Nov. 1848.

46 Shields, West, and Stone, comps., *A Study of the Barbee Families of Chatham, Orange and Wake Counties in North Carolina*, 51, 133. Christopher Barbee, son of William, is

remembered primarily for his large gift of land to the University of North Carolina in its formative days. His homeplace, The Mountain, which would be today just inside Durham County line off Highway 54, is now the site of Meadow Mount, home of the David Saint Pierre DuBoses.

47 Interview with Curtis Booker, Durham, 5 Oct. 1983; Carolyn Satterfield, "Leigh Farm Gives View of Life of Yesteryear," *Sun*, 25 Apr. 1975.

48 Interview with Curtis Booker; Leigh Family Papers in possession of Curtis Booker, Durham.

49 Murray, *Wake, Capital County of North Carolina*, 104, 173.

50 Broadside, 1813, North Carolina Uncatalogued Broadsides, DU-RBMSCL.

51 Browning, "Valley of the Eno," 39–42, 50–53.

52 OCDB 16:65, 21:571, 22:18, 23:303, 306; 24:192.

53 Military Service Records, National Archives, Pension Application File S 8185.

54 U.S. Post Office Dept., "Records of Appointments"; OCR, Estates: Herbert Sims; OCDB 32:229.

55 Thomas Ruffin Papers, SHC, 11 Mar. 1832; Hillsborough *Recorder*, 9 Aug. 1838; NCOAH, Military Collection, Treasurer and Comptroller's Papers, 8–36; U.S. Post Office Dept., "Records of Appointments," West Point; U.S. War Department, *The War of the Rebellion, Official Records of the Union and Confederate Armies*, 70 vols. (Washington, 1880–91), Ser. 1, 47, Pt. 3, p. 250.

56 Cameron Family Papers, SHC, 2 Apr. 1836; Nov. 1839.

57 OCDB 16:171; OCW F:433.

58 Hillsborough *Recorder*, 10 Sept. 1834, 21 Oct. 1836; OCDB 27:162.

59 Buxton Harris, "Remarks Addressed to My Children," photocopy in possession of author; OCDB 27:357–58; OCR, OCCM, Feb. 1850; Interview with Mildred Harris, 24 June 1985.

60 OCW G:115; OCDB 35:78; Hillsborough *Recorder*, 17 Jan. 1855; Map of Durham County, "Southgate," 1887, copyrighted by L. Johnson, DU-RBMSCL; "Durham County, 1920," D.U. Archives.

61 Cameron Family Papers, Thomas D. Bennehan to his father, 31 July 1807; Hillsborough *Recorder*, 13 Sept. 1848.

62 OCW F:76; OCR, Marriage Bonds and Licenses.

63 OCW E:324, G:182, 469; 1860 Census, Orange County, Manufacturing Schedule; OCR, Estates: John D. Lipscomb.

64 Jean B. Anderson, "A Community of Men and Mills," *Eno* 7 (special issue, 1979): 30–33.

65 Shanks, ed., *The Papers of Willie Person Mangum*, 1:486.

66 Ibid., 41, 564–69.

67 Ibid., 204, 287; Cameron Family Papers, SHC, 1 July 1825. I have found no evidence to support the stories that Chavis visited the Camerons or that he was buried in the Mangum cemetery.

68 Cameron Family Papers, SHC, 10 Apr. 1816, 55; 21 Dec. 1816; OCR, Civil Action Papers concerning Land, Andrew Gray v. Thomas Wilson, 1826; Hillsborough *Recorder*, 27 June 1849.

69 OCR, Estates: Moses McCown, William Dilliard, Edmund Herndon; John Kelly Papers, SHC; Hillsborough *Recorder*, 3 Sept. 1846; OCDB 16:232; *Herald*, 6 Oct. 1935.

70 Blackwelder, *The Age of Orange*, 144–45; Hillsborough *Recorder*, 14 May 1840.

71 Lefler and Wager, *Orange County*, 83–84, 325, 350; Blackwelder, *The Age of Orange*, 76–77.

72 Shanks, ed., *The Papers of Willie Person Mangum*, 1:xv–xliii.

73 Cameron Family Papers, SHC, 19 Jan. 1842.

74 Shanks, ed., *The Papers of Willie Person Mangum*, 2:367–68.

1 Blackwelder, *The Age of Orange*, 85.

2 Lefler and Newsome, *North Carolina*, 329; "A View of the Internal Improvements Contemplated by the Legislature of North Carolina," Cameron Family Papers, SHC, Aug.–Sept. 1819.

3 Lefler and Wager, *Orange County*, 184.

4 Hillsborough *Recorder*, 10 July 1845. *Smut* denoted the sooty fungus growth of diseased wheat and other cereals.

5 McMannen Family Papers, DU-RBMSCL, Bible Records; Fourth Census of the United States, 1820, Orange County, N.C., 394 (microfilm); Cameron Family Papers, SHC, Feb. 1825, Jan. 1837, Aug.–Sept. 1853; Adolphus Mangum Papers, SHC, Diary.

6 Hillsborough *Recorder*, 22 Feb. 1844. A copy of this engraving is in the Crumpacker Family Papers, DU-RBMSCL.

7 Ibid., 4 Mar. 1846, 4 Oct. 1854. Local tradition attributes the naming of South Lowell to a New Englander connected with the mill. The 1850 census lists such a person, George G. Clement, mechanic, born in Massachusetts; OCDB 17:155, 34:394–95.

8 Ibid., 17 Jan. 1849; Elizabeth A. Persons, "South Lowell Male Academy and Its First Headmaster," Durham *Record* 1 (Fall 1983): 18–25.

9 Ibid., 27 Mar. 1850. The foundation of the dormitory may still be traced in the garden of the McMannen house.

10 Ibid., 30 Jan. 1850, 15 Jan. 1851, 22 Nov. 1854; interview with Mrs. Erna Perry, 30 Mar. 1971.

11 James Gill Papers, DU-RBMSCL, 1 Nov. 1852; see also 13 Mar. 1852; Mangum Papers, SHC, Diary, 4 Jan. 1857.

12 Hillsborough *Recorder*, 4 Oct. 1854; OCR, Estates: Bartlett Durham.

13 Hillsborough *Recorder*, 5 Apr. 1854, 28 May 1856, 13 Jan. 1864, 14 Feb. 1877; McMannen Papers, DU-RBMSCL.

14 Mangum Papers, SHC, Diary, 8 Feb. 1857; William K. Boyd Papers, Duke University Archives, Roxie J. Sasser, "History of Lebanon Township, Durham County, North Carolina."

15 Hillsborough *Recorder*, 30 Jan. 1850, 26 Oct. 1853, 19 May 1858; Seventh Census, 1850, Orange County, Free Inhabitants, 513 (microfilm); interview with Mrs. Perry.

16 Hillsborough *Recorder*, 2 July 1851, 1 Mar., 18 Oct. 1854, 5 Jan. 1856; Mangum Papers, SHC, 4 Apr. 1852; Shanks, ed., *The Papers of Willie Person Mangum*, 5:288. David Parker probably built the church. It already existed in 1844 (OCR, Estates: David Parker, deposition of Willie P. Mangum; see DCDB 1:5).

17 Mangum Papers, SHC, Diary, 15 July, 27 July 1852; Leathers Latta & Co., Day Book, DU-RBMSCL.

18 Mangum Papers, SHC, Diary, 28 July 1852.

19 Ibid., 3 July 1852; Durham *Morning Herald*, 19 Jan. 1930, 22 Feb. 1942; DCDB 5:143.

20 Murray, *Wake, Capital County of North Carolina*, 307. Murray locates the school in the Brassfield community, but the names of the trustees suggest the Fletcher's Chapel Church neighborhood. Another school (a subscription school) with the same name was established in the Fletcher's Chapel community in the 1880s.

21 The Wake County names are found in the census in the North Western District, an area that comprised far more than the areas of Oak Grove, Carr, and Cedar Fork townships now part of Durham County. Some names may be inadvertently included, therefore, that belonged to residents of parts of Wake not in Durham County today.

22 Amy Childs Fallow, *The Story of Duke's Chapel* (Durham, 1967); Virginia Gray, "A Goodly Heritage: The Dukes of Orange County," *Duke Alumni Register* 55, no. 5

(Sept. 1969): 18–21; John Alan Creedy, "Billie Duke . . ." Durham *Herald-Sun*, 13 July 1941.

23 Fallow, *Story of Duke's Chapel*; OCDB 46:315; DCDB 3:594; Johnson's 1887 map of Durham County.

24 Joseph W. Watson and C. Franklin Grill, *North Carolina Conference Historical Directory* (Raleigh, 1984).

25 Ibid.; Mangum Papers, SHC, Diary, 12 July 1856; Washington Sanford Chaffin Papers, DU-RBMSCL, Journal, 1862.

26 OCDB 35:307; 33:570.

27 Telephone conversations with Mrs. Otis Lee and Ran Whitley, Associate Pastor; *Herald*, 4 Apr. 1939.

28 OCDB 32:249; R. T. Howerton, Jr., "The Rose of Sharon Baptist Church," *Trinity Archive* 21 (1907–8): 187–95; N.C. Railroad Collection, NCOAH, State Agencies, Map Book 3, p. 20. The Piney Grove School District is shown on Silas Link's 1868 map of Orange County School Districts, DU-RBMSCL.

29 Browning, "Valley of the Eno," 43–44; Hillsborough *Recorder*, 7 Apr., 29 Sept. 1852, 14 June, 15 Nov. 1854, 11 June 1856.

30 Hillsborough *Recorder*, 15 Apr., 16 Dec. 1857, 20 Jan., 6 Oct. 1858, 8 May 1861; Browning, "Valley of the Eno," 45–46; OCR, Civil Action Papers, *Charles J. Shields v. Benjamin P. Sykes,* 1859; Eighth Census, 1860, Orange County, Manufacturing Schedule; Ruth Herndon Shields, "Some Notes about the Cabe, Shields, and Strayhorn Families," typescript in the author's possession, 12; Durham County Records, Civil Action Papers, NCOAH, J. H. Shields v. W. T. Neal, 1915.

31 OCR, Orange County Marriage Bonds, John C. Douglas and Rachel S. Lipscomb, 29 Jan. 1838; OCDB 34:92, 33:498; Hillsborough *Recorder*, 7 Apr. 1852; William James Webb, *Our Webb Kin of Dixie* (Oxford, N.C., 1940), 21; Robert and Newton Dixon Woody Papers, DU-RBMSCL, 11 May 1852.

32 Eighth Census, 1860, Orange County, Population Schedule, dwelling 986; Manufacturing Schedule.

33 Ronald A. Thomas, Martha J. Schiek, and Robert F. Hoffman, "A Report on Two Archaeological Surveys within Proposed Alternatives for a Reservoir for the City of Durham, Durham and Person Counties, North Carolina," unpublished report for the Army Corps of Engineers, Mar. 1982, II, 16–22, and figures II, 5 and 6; John Baxter Flowers III, *Orange Factory* (Durham, 1978), 17, 19, 23; Eighth Census, 1860, Orange County, 451–52 (microfilm). Cameron Family Papers, SHC, 1 Sept. 1864.

34 Flowers, *Orange Factory*, 25–26; Cameron Family Papers, SHC, Joseph Woods et al., deposition, 20 Sept. 1866, P. C. Cameron to Willard, 23 Sept. 1866, P. Southerland, deposition, 25 Sept. 1866, W. F. Vestal, deposition, 25 Sept. 1866, G. Pickard, deposition, 2 Oct. 1866, Willard to Cameron, 17 Oct. 1866; OCDB 37:402.

35 OCDB 42:165, 168; "A List of Cotton and Woolen Mills in North Carolina" (1879), Duke University Broadside Collection, DU-RBMSCL; DCDB 9:330; Hillsborough *Recorder*, 1 Sept. 1875; Sidney Willard Holman Papers, Private Collections, NCOAH, 30 June, 31 Dec. 1897, 25 Mar. 1899; Hillsborough *Recorder*, 1 Sept. 1875; *Tobacco Plant*, 24 July 1877; interview with A. G. Cox, Jr., 23 July 1984.

36 Flowers, *Orange Factory*, 27, 29, 31, 33; Benjamin N. Duke Papers, DU-RBMSCL, 6 Sept. 1904, 3 Apr. 1905; interview with A. G. Cox, Jr.; Sasser, "History of Lebanon Township," William K. Boyd Papers, D.U. Archives; *Herald*, 26 July 1917.

37 Hillsborough *Recorder*, 24 Jan. 1849, 3 Mar. 1852, 15 Nov. 1854; interview with Mildred M. Harris, 24 June 1985.

38 Seventh Census, 1850, Orange County, Manufacturing Schedule; Eighth Census, 1860, Orange County, Manufacturing Schedule; Browning, "Valley of the Eno," 57–58; OCDB 36:355; OCR, Estates: Barlett L. Durham.

39 OCR, OCCM, Aug. and Nov. 1850; Shanks, ed., *The Papers of Willie Person Mangum*,

5:314; OCDB 27:357, 358; 35:78; 39:272; 40:190; *The Southern Business Directory and General Commercial Advertiser* (Charleston, 1854), 390; Eighth Census, 1860, Orange County, Manufacturing Schedule; *Branson's North Carolina Agricultural Almanac, 1890* (Raleigh, 1890), 265; Ninth Census, 1870, Orange County, Manufacturing Schedule, Mangum Township. The Umstead and Walker mills are shown on Johnson's 1887 map of Durham County.

40 DCDB 5:143; OCDB 35:40, 61, 62; 36:153; 39:365; Eighth Census, 1860, Orange County, Manufacturing Schedule; Hillsborough *Recorder*, 25 Feb. 1863. In 1854 Bedford Vaughn [*sic*] was running the store at Stagville (*The Southern Business Directory* [1854], 390); interview with Mildred M. Harris, 24 June 1985.

The deeds that record the transfer of the mills to Lockhart and from Lockhart to Tilley give as a boundary "a pine at Roberts old Meeting House." A Roberts meetinghouse continued to function in that neighborhood; Silas Link's school district map shows a large section east of the Flat River as Roberts Meeting House District. Of this old church nothing is known. (Silas M. Link Map of Orange County . . . Common Schools and Townships [1868], DU-RBMSCL.)

41 Robert and Newton Dixon Woody Papers, DU-RBMSCL; Blackwelder, *The Age of Orange*, 83.

42 Blackwelder, *The Age of Orange*, 81, 83; Ninth Census, 1870, Orange County, Manufacturing Schedule, Mangum Township.

43 Bennehan Cameron Papers, SHC, P. C. Cameron to Joseph Roulhac, May 1854.

44 Hillsborough *Recorder*, 6 Dec. 1865; Seventh Census, 1850, Orange County, Agricultural Schedule, 1181, 1183 (microfilm); Eighth Census, 1860, Orange County, Agriculture Schedule, 21–22, 23–24, 45–46; interview with Curtis Booker; Blackwelder, *The Age of Orange*, 83. Southerland's cotton press and house (altered) on the Farrington road were both in the possession of John and Ola Foushee as of the 1980s.

45 Hillsborough *Recorder*, 17 Jan. 1821, 19 Mar. 1851; Seventh Census, 1850, 307; Lefler and Wager, *Orange County*, 122; Blackwelder, *The Age of Orange*, 10.

46 Blackwelder, *The Age of Orange*, 10.

47 Lefler and Newsome, *North Carolina*, 372.

48 Seventh Census, 1850, Wake County, Free Inhabitants, Northwestern Division.

49 Roy Brown, *Public Poor Relief in North Carolina* (Chapel Hill, 1928), 10–25.

50 Lefler and Wager, *Orange County*, 186; Blackwelder, *The Age of Orange*, 18, 141–42; Brown, *Public Poor Relief in North Carolina*, 25, 29, 33.

51 Brown, *Public Poor Relief in North Carolina*, 46, 47; Paul D. Escott, "Poverty and Governmental Aid for the Poor in Confederate North Carolina," *North Carolina Historical Review*, 41 (Oct. 1984): 463; OCR, OCCM, Feb. 1838, Feb. 1839.

52 Brown, *Public Poor Relief in North Carolina*, 50–51.

53 Ibid., 58.

54 Ibid.

55 Ibid., 48; Hillsborough *Recorder*, 7 Sept. 1853; OCR, Wills: Thomas D. Bennehan.

56 Mangum Papers, SHC, Diary, 19, 20 Jan. 1856.

57 Hillsborough *Recorder*, 10 Aug. 1843, 13 Sept. 1848, 12 Mar. 1851.

58 Ibid., 20 Jan. 1842, 13 May 1845, 19 Sept. 1849.

59 Mangum Papers, SHC, Diary, 26 July 1852, 15 July 1854.

60 Ibid., E. G. Mangum to A. W. Mangum, 12 Nov. 1851; Cameron Family Papers, SHC, 13 May 1849. The Methodists took up the temperance cause as they did morality in general. It was an uphill battle, for laxity had long been tolerated. Many men who were later pillars of respectability had been charged with fathering bastards, for example, General Francis Nash, William Cain, and Richard Henderson. Mangum would have known of the illegitimate children of Taylor Duke, his grandfather, of Willie Mangum, his great-uncle, of D. C. Parrish, of James Carrington, and of Nathaniel Harris. Mangum's diary tells of two local women reduced by prostitution to poverty,

and quotes the preacher Hezekiah Leigh's describing adultery as the "Steamboat to Hell." Mangum adds, "There is enough in five miles square around here to name the section Sodom."

61 Cameron Family Papers, SHC, 25 July 1850.

7 ORIGINS OF THE TOWN OF DURHAM

1 Shields, West, and Stone, comps., *A Study of the Barbee Families of Chatham, Orange and Wake Counties in North Carolina*, 115; OCDB 19:14; Wake County Records, NCOAH, Estates: Henry Dilliard c. 1804.

2 OCR, Estates: William Dilliard; Shields, West, and Stone, comps., *A Study of the Barbee Families of Chatham, Orange and Wake Counties in North Carolina*, 115.

3 OCR, Estates: William Dilliard; Shanks, ed., *The Papers of Willie Person Mangum*, 1:61.

4 OCR, Estates: William Dilliard.

5 U.S. Post Office Dept., "Records of Appointments of Postmasters"; OCDB 21:601, 22:159, 26:300; Childs, *Centennial History of Trinity Church*, 4; see also Lewis Blount, Map of Durham, 1867–68, Sept. 1923, DU-RBMSCL.

6 OCR, Estates: William Dilliard; OCW E:250, Will of Lydia Dilliard; OCDB 32:271; U.S. Post Office Dept., "Appointments of Postmasters."

7 OCR, OCCM, 1 Oct. 1832.

8 Since the post office was moved to Prattsburg in 1836 before Pratt bought the second Dilliard tract, his store must have been located on the dower tract (OCDB 19:124). William N. Pratt's body was first interred in the family graveyard off what is now Mt. Hermon Church Road but was apparently removed later, for his tombstone now stands at the head of an empty brick vault. OCDB 32:271; this land included "a large wheel in and attached to the gin house." I infer that the wheel was the large cotton press wheel mounted horizontally and rotated by a horse to turn the screw press. See also Lewis Blount, Map of Durham, 1867–68, DU-RBMSCL; N.C. Railroad Collection, State Agencies, NCOAH, Map Book 3, pp. 19–20; William N. Pratt and Company Ledger, 1857–67, DU-RBMSCL.

9 OCR, Estates: William N. Pratt; OCDB 37:450–52; OCW G:521; *Herald*, 11 Dec. 1912. Polly Redmond's obituary says that she was ninety-four years old and had lived with her son William Thaddeus Redmond on Burch Avenue.

10 Boyd, *The Story of Durham*, 27.

11 OCR, OCCM, May 1848; OCDB 33:266, 462–63, 36:270.

12 Lefler and Newsome, *North Carolina*, 365–66; "Report of the Chief Engineer [Walter Gwynn] on the Survey of the North Carolina Railroad, May 1851," *Xenodochy* 13, DU-RBMSCL. This report reveals the initial indecision about routing the railroad to Chapel Hill or Hillsborough. The choice of Hillsborough has been seen as a political one since that was the home of Governor Graham. The report suggests, however, that geographical and other engineering considerations—grades, cost, curvature, and distance—determined the route.

13 N.C. Railroad Collection, State Agencies, NCOAH, Deeds and Land Records, 1849–1952, Orange County.

14 *Herald*, 8 June 1919.

15 OCDB 32:249 (23 Nov. 1846).

16 Ibid. 33:474 (11 Dec. 1846); N.C. Railroad Collection, State Agencies, NCOAH, Deeds and Land Records, 1849–1952, Orange County, 11 Oct. 1880.

17 "Family Record," sheets from the family Bible of William Durham and Mary Snipes Durham, photocopies in the Durham County Library, North Carolina Collection; *Herald*, 15 Feb. 1924 (unveiling of Durham's portrait); R. O. Everett, "Dr. Bartlett Durham," *Herald*, 20 June 1937; OCDB 32:412.

18 Wyatt Dixon, "How Times Do Change," Durham *Sun*, 18 Sept. 1981.

19 OCR, Estates: Bartlett L. Durham; *Herald*, 11 Sept. 1915. Francis A. Stagg eventually became president of the North Carolina Railroad.

20 Hillsborough *Recorder*, 5 June, 7 Aug., 18 Dec. 1850, 26 May, 9 June, 30 June, 1 Sept., 17 Nov., 1 Dec. 1852.

21 OCR, OCCM, Aug. 1852; OCDB 35:221, 36:82, 83, 176; Hiram Paul, *History of the Town of Durham, N.C.*, 29; *Methodist Advance*, 9 Sept. 1880; OCDB 33:452.

22 Boyd, *The Story of Durham*, 30; Lewis Blount, Map of Durham, DU-RBMSCL; N.C. Railroad Collection, State Agencies, NCOAH, Map Book 3, p. 20; Durham *Sun*, 18 Sept. 1981.

23 Hillsborough *Recorder*, 20 July 1853.

24 Ibid., 6 June 1855.

25 OCDB 34:201; OCR, Estates: Bartlett Durham.

26 OCDB 35:334, 36:165; OCR, Estates: Bartlett Durham, William N. Pratt; OCDB 38:414, 44:329; *Tobacco Plant*, 28 June 1881. McMannen's house site would now be in the middle of the Mangum Street bridge over the "Buck" Dean Expressway.

27 N.C. Railroad Collection, State Agencies, NCOAH, Map Book 3.

28 John Spencer Bassett, "Old Durham Traditions," *Trinity Archive* 19 (1905–6): 161–70; A. B. Markham, Map of Land Grants to Early Settlers in Old Orange County, 1973; OCDB 31:99; OCW B:267, C:166, E:35, G:521.

29 OCDB 33:50, 476, 499; OCR, OCCM, Aug. 1850. The origin of the name Pin Hook for this site is obscure. Nannie May Tilley in *The Bright-Tobacco Industry, 1860–1929* (Chapel Hill, 1948), 298, explains the meaning of *pinhookers* in connection with that industry, but no activity of the kind was connected with the Pin Hook area, and the tobacco industry in Durham had not even been thought of when the name first appeared. Hillsborough *Recorder*, 27 Sept. 1871.

30 Hillsborough *Recorder*, 7 Jan. 1847; OCR, OCCM, Nov. 1847, May 1848; OCDB 34:143; Eighth Census, 1860, Orange County, Free Inhabitants, dwelling 1074. Seventeen persons are listed as residents of Robert Morris's household. The adjoining dwelling, that of Wright, had sixteen residents. Morris is identified as a farmer and Wright as a tobacconist. Thomas B. Morris, twenty-one years old, was listed as living with his father.

31 Paul's history says that Thomas B. Morris was Wright's partner; Boyd's history says Robert F. Morris was. Undoubtedly it was the elder Morris's money that was invested in the firm. Paul, *History of the Town of Durham, N.C.*, 60; Boyd, *The Story of Durham*, 29.

32 Paul, *History of the Town of Durham, N.C.*, 50–77.

33 Hillsborough *Recorder*, 14 May, 16 July, 13 Aug. 1828; Lefler and Newsome, *North Carolina*, 365–66. In 1854 the state subscribed an additional million dollars.

34 N.C. Railroad Collection, State Agencies, NCOAH, "Report of Col. Walter Gwynn, Chief Engineer of the North Carolina Railroad Company to the Board of Directors, Salisbury, 1856"; "Report of the Chief Engineer on the Survey of the N.C. Railroad, May 1851," *Xenodochy* 13, DU-RBMSCL.

8 VICTORY FROM DEFEAT

1 Cornelia P. Spencer, *The Last Ninety Days of the War* (New York, 1866), 169; Lefler and Newsome, *North Carolina*, 441–51.

2 Lefler and Newsome, *North Carolina*, 456, 477–78.

3 Ibid., 456; Blackwelder, *The Age of Orange*, 183–84.

4 Hillsborough *Recorder*, 15 Feb. 1860; Lefler and Wager, *Orange County*, 109; *Herald*, 29 Jan. 1928; *Tobacco Plant*, 12 Oct. 1888.

5 *Herald*, 29 Jan. 1928. The first site for the church in Durham, donated by Robert Mor-

ris, Umstead said, was not used for the purpose. An adjacent lot bought from William Green seemed more desirable and became the church's location. Ex-Governor William A. Graham and Henry K. Nash debated the question of secession in this structure (*Herald*, 22 Jan. 1923). In a letter to his sister William Mangum described their Durham quarters as an academy about a quarter mile from Durham (Shanks, ed., *The Papers of Willie Person Mangum*, 5:388).

6 Shanks, ed., *The Papers of Willie Person Mangum*, 5:380, 391, 398, 402–6, 756; Hillsborough *Recorder*, 11 Sept. 1861.

7 Louis H. Manarin and others, comps., *North Carolina Troops, 1861–1865: A Roster* (Raleigh, 1966–), 8:61–73; OCR, Estates: Wm. Lipscomb.

8 Manarin and others, comps., *North Carolina Troops*, 1:443–52; *Herald*, 11 Dec. 1929; Lefler and Wager, *Orange County*, 109–10; James E. Lyon is listed in both the church-bell battery and the Orange Grays.

9 Manarin and others, comps., *North Carolina Troops*, 2:170–77, 225, 8:358; *Herald*, 18 Nov. 1915; *Tobacco Plant*, 27 July 1888.

10 John T. Nichols Papers, DU-RBMSCL, Account and Memorandum Book, 1860–83.

11 Lefler and Newsome, *North Carolina*, 457; Lefler and Wager, *Orange County*, 109; Manarin and others, comps., *North Carolina Troops*, 4:294–305; *Herald*, 29 Aug. 1926, 23 Feb. 1936.

12 *Tobacco Plant*, 8 June 1888; Lefler and Wager, *Orange County*, 109; *Sun*, 31 Jan. 1900; Manarin and others, comps., *North Carolina Troops*, 4:368–80, 3:179; Boyd, *The Story of Durham*, 34.

13 *Herald*, 28 Aug. 1924; Robert F. Durden, *The Dukes of Durham* (Durham, 1975), 7–8.

14 *Compendium of the Eighth Census* (Washington, 1864), 210; Blackwelder, *The Age of Orange*, 79, 185; Eighth Census, 1860, Orange County, Slave Schedule; OCR, OCCM, Special Court of Magistrates, 17 Oct. 1863 and Nov. 1863, Aug., Nov. 1864; Escott, "Poverty and Governmental Aid," 463–75; Escott, *Many Excellent People: Power and Privilege in North Carolina, 1850–1900* (Chapel Hill, 1985), 57.

15 *North Carolina Christian Advocate*, 23 Apr., 20 May 1863; OCR, OCCM, Aug. 1864; Escott, *Many Excellent People*, 64; D. L. Corbitt and Elizabeth W. Wilborn, *Civil War Pictures* (Raleigh, 1961), 77.

16 OCR, OCCM, Jan. and Feb. 1865; Escott, "Poverty and Governmental Aid," 477–78; *Tobacco Plant*, 9 Oct. 1877; Boyd, *The Story of Durham*, 34.

17 John Hope Franklin, *From Slavery to Freedom: A History of Negro Americans* (New York, 1980), 216–19.

18 Ibid.; Thomas Ruffin Papers, SHC, Cameron to Ruffin, 24 Mar. 1863; Cameron Family Papers, SHC, 1 Jan. 1864.

19 Norman R. Yetman, *Voices from Slavery* (New York, 1970), 98–100.

20 Corneille A. Little Papers, DU-RBMSCL, "How We Lived during the Confederate War."

21 Ibid.

22 Spencer, *The Last Ninety Days of the War*, 30.

23 Ibid., 170.

24 Ibid., 171.

25 United Daughters of the Confederacy Scrap Books, Durham County Library, North Carolina Collection.

26 *The Memoirs of General William T. Sherman* (New York, 1931), 2:347–48; Boyd, *The Story of Durham*, 35; Blount, Map of Durham, 1867–68, DU-RBMSCL. The Bennett Place State Historic Site uses the conventional spelling of the name Bennett; the site's owner always wrote his name as Bennitt. Here the conventional spelling will be used for the site and Bennitt for the family members. A competing oral tradition says that William Mangum's house on now Chapel Hill Street served as Kilpatrick's headquarters.

27 *The Memoirs of General William T. Sherman*, 2:348–49.

28 *General Sherman's Official Account of His Great March through Georgia and the Carolinas* (New York, 1865), 193.

29 *The Memoirs of General William T. Sherman*, 2:352–57, 365–67; *War of the Rebellion: Official Records*, Ser. 1, 47:250.

30 William M. Vatavuk, "In the Shadow of Appomattox: The Surrender at Bennett Place," *Blue & Gray* (Apr.–May 1985): 45–56.

31 Arthur C. Menius III, "James Bennitt: Portrait of an Antebellum Yeoman," *North Carolina Historical Review* 57 (1981): 305–26; interview with Curtis Booker. M. B. Riggsbee remembered going out to see Mr. Bennitt long before there was a war because of the good horse-apple tree that grew there (Holeman Collection, Private Collections, NCOAH, Mary R. Holeman's collection of anecdotes for the Julian S. Carr United Daughters of the Confederacy Chapter); Menius, "The Bennett Place," report prepared for the Historic Sites Section, Division of Archives and History, July 1979; Governor William Holden Papers, NCOAH, James Bennitt to Gov. Holden, 5 Oct. 1868.

32 *Herald*, 19 Dec. 1906, 15 Oct. 1921; Menius, "The Bennett Place," 4; Governor William Holden Papers, NCOAH, Letters of James Bennitt to Holden, 5 Oct. 1868, Jan. 1870. (I am indebted to Harold Mozingo, site manager of the Bennett Place, for calling these letters to my attention.)

   The Durham *Globe*, 20 July 1893, reported the death of "the elder of the Bennett sisters." As there was only one Bennett daughter, Eliza, one of the two must have been a sister-in-law. Of them the paper said, "Uncompromising and unreconstructed, these two old ladies have lived on through the years that have past, in the same shambling style, letting time do its work on the home and themselves alike, all going down together."

33 Paul, *History of the Town of Durham, N.C.*, 25–26.

34 Boyd, *The Story of Durham*, 59–60.

9 FROM BUST TO BOOM

   1 John Richard Dennett, *The South as It Is: 1865–1866* (New York, 1965), 119.

   2 Benjamin Markham Papers, DU-RBMSCL, 11 Jan. 1866.

   3 Richard L. Zuber, *North Carolina during Reconstruction* (Raleigh, 1969), 7.

   4 Ibid., 6–9; Lefler and Newsome, *North Carolina*, 485, 487.

   5 Lefler and Newsome, *North Carolina*, 489–91, 494–95, 497–98; Lefler and Wager, *Orange County*, 116–19; William Woods Holden Papers, DU-RBMSCL, Bureau of Refugees, Freedmen and Abandoned Lands, Raleigh, 14 Dec. 1869; Pauli Murray, *Proud Shoes* (New York, 1978), 218–23; Allen Trelease, *White Terror* (Westport, Conn., 1971), 196, 218.

   6 Lefler and Wager, *Orange County*, 116–19; *Testimony Taken by the Joint Select Committee to Inquire into the Condition of Affairs in the Late Insurrectionary States: North Carolina* (Washington, 1872); William Woods Holden Papers, DU-RBMSCL, 4 Mar., 7 Mar., 28 July 1870; Austin Marcus Drumm, "The Union League in the Carolinas" (Ph.D. diss., UNC, 1955); Trelease, *White Terror*, 196, 197.

   7 Hillsborough *Recorder*, 2 Mar. 1870.

   8 Ibid., 18 Aug. 1869, 2 Nov. 1870; William Woods Holden Papers, DU-RBMSCL, 10 Jan. 1871; Mason Crum Papers, D.U. Archives, "Life and Times of Washington Duke"; Paul, *History of the Town of Durham, N.C.*, 89; Trelease, *White Terror*, 419.

   9 Lefler and Wager, *Orange County*, 192–93, 199; Lefler and Newsome, *North Carolina*, 540. New voting precincts also were designated, for example Bladen Springs at Thomas Lipscomb's home on Roxboro Road in the Mount Sylvan Church area.

  10 Lefler and Wager, *Orange County*, 194, 358; S. M. Link, "Map of Orange County as laid of[f] into Districts for Common Schools and Townships," DU-RBMSCL. Link's

map shows Mangum Township with nine school districts: Roberts Meeting House, Dials Creek, North East, Red Mountain, South Lowell, Bethel Meeting House, Lebanon Meeting House, and Orange Factory. The western boundaries of Durham and Patterson townships were farther to the west than they are today; consequently those townships once included areas that are not part of them today. The seven school districts in Durham Township were Pleasant Green, Band Box, Trice's Store, Hebron Meeting House, Piney Grove, Eno Meeting House, and Durham. Patterson Township comprised Mount Moriah, New Hope Creek, and New Comfort school districts.

11 Hillsborough *Recorder*, 18 Aug. 1869. The *Recorder* incorrectly reported the third member of the Durham school committee as H. H. Lewis.

12 Lewis Blount, Map of Durham, 1867–68, DU-RBMSCL; *Branson and Farrar's North Carolina Business Directory for 1866–67* (Raleigh, 1866); *Branson's North Carolina Business Directory for 1867–68* (Raleigh, 1867); *Branson's North Carolina Business Directory for 1869* (Raleigh, 1868), OCDB 36:448, 39:48; Boyd, *The Story of Durham*, 31.

13 OCDB 36:448, 39:48; Boyd, *The Story of Durham*, 31; OCDB 37:36.

14 OCR, OCCM, NCOAH, Nov. 1863; Blount, Map of Durham; *Branson and Farrar's Directory, 1866–67*; *Branson's Directory for 1867–68*; *Branson's Directory for 1869*; A. M. Rigsbee's bar was on the northeast corner of Main and Mangum streets. E. J. Parrish's bar was a few doors east of it. William Mangum's and Calvin O'Briant's bars were on the south side of Main Street in the same block, Mangum's on the corner, O'Briant's almost opposite Parrish's.

15 *Tobacco Plant*, 19 Jan. 1876; Hillsborough *Recorder*, 23 May 1877.

16 Boyd, *The Story of Durham*, 97–98; Minutes of the Town (of Durham) Board of Aldermen, Clerk's Office, City Hall, 4 Aug. 1869–1922.

17 Minutes of the Town Board.

18 Boyd, *The Story of Durham*, 32.

19 Minutes of the Town Board, 27 Aug., 18 Sept., 5 Nov. 1869, 1 Apr., 2 Dec. 1870, 22 May, 18 Sept., 1 Dec. 1871, 5 Jan., 2 Feb., 8 June 1872.

20 Ibid., 27 Aug., 18 Sept. 1869; Boyd, *The Story of Durham*, 99–100.

21 *N&O*, 5 Apr. 1896 (tobacco edition).

22 Minutes of the Town Board, 1 Oct. 1869.

23 Ibid., 9 Dec. 1870, 22 Feb. 1871; *Tobacco Plant*, 23 July 1878.

24 Lefler and Newsome, *North Carolina*, 531; Lefler and Wager, *Orange County*, 194–95; Zuber, *North Carolina during Reconstruction*, 59–60. Durham Township's 1870 school census showed 582 white children and 241 black (N.C. County Papers: Durham, DU-RBMSCL). The degree of poverty in the South came as a shock to the northern schoolteachers. "'It is startling to measure the real poverty of the South,' said one, . . . 'We have nothing like it in the North; we never have had anything like it'" (Henry Lee Swint, *The Northern Teacher in the South, 1862–1870* [Nashville, 1941], 63).

25 Zuber, *North Carolina during Reconstruction*, 23; Lefler and Newsome, *North Carolina*, 537–38; Daniel Jay Whitener, "Public Education in North Carolina during Reconstruction, 1865–1876," *Essays in Southern History*, ed. Fletcher M. Green (Chapel Hill, 1949), 89; Edgar W. Knight, "The Peabody Fund and Its Early Operation in North Carolina," *South Atlantic Quarterly* 14 (1915): 168–80; OCDB 37:329 (Association of Friends of Philadelphia purchase of lot 80); OCDB 37:453 (same group's purchase of one acre in Chapel Hill at the northwest end of Franklin Street); OCR, Board of Commissioners' Minutes, 12 Dec. 1868, enumerates six freedmen's schools in Orange County: 2 in Hillsborough, 1 in Cedar Grove, 1 at Bains, 1 at New Hope, and 1 at Durham, which had 30 pupils.

26 Boyd, *The Story of Durham*, 162; *Episcopal Methodist*, 11 Mar. 1868; *Tobacco Plant*, 19 Jan., 16 Aug. 1876, 24 July 1877, 28 May 1878, 23 Mar. 1880.

27 *Tobacco Plant*, 8 June 1880; Broadside Collection, DU-RBMSCL, "Red Mountain Male and Female School," 1877; Hillsborough *Recorder*, 17 Dec. 1862, 3 Jan. 1872; Tod R. Caldwell Papers, SHC, 28 Apr. 1868, James F. Cain to his sister Minerva; Round Hill Academy report card for Joseph Tilley, 10 Oct. 1879, in the possession of Mildred M. Harris.

28 *Herald*, 5 May 1940; Nichols Papers, DU-RBMSCL, Constitution of Trustees, Dayton Academy, 21 Mar. 1878; "The History of Oak Grove School," Oak Grove School Annual (1939), photocopy in the possession of Edna Carpenter Baker; *Herald*, 28 Nov. 1926; U.S. Post Office Dept., "Records of Appointments."

29 *North Carolina Christian Advocate*, 16 Sept. 1863.

30 *Tobacco Plant*, 4 July, 10 Sept. 1878; R. T. Howerton, Jr., "The Rose of Sharon Baptist Church," *Trinity Archive* 21 (1907–8): 191; "History of Rose of Sharon Baptist Church," photocopy in the author's possession.

31 *Herald*, 28 Nov. 1926, 2 May 1931, 9 July 1939; "The History of Roberson Grove Baptist Church," 1949.

32 Jay B. Hubbell, *Our First One Hundred Years: Yates Baptist Church, 1878–1978* (Durham, 1978); interview with Curtis Booker, 17 July 1985. The house in which Matthew Yates was born in western Wake County has been moved to the Yates Baptist Association campgrounds in Durham County on the Wake Forest highway. It will be restored and used as a museum (information supplied by Ruth Couch).

33 Childs, *Centennial History of Trinity Methodist Church*; "History of Trinity Church," *The Trinity League Record* 1, no. 2, Dec. 1894; DCDB 47:403; Methodist Church Papers, DU-RBMSCL, Historical Sketches, L. E. Thompson's questionnaire and *Journal of the Western Annual Conference of the Methodist Episcopal Church, South . . . 1890* (Statesville, N.C., 1891), 18; *Methodist Advance*, 1 July 1880; *Branson's North Carolina Business Directory, 1884* (Raleigh, 1884), 286.

In presenting the books to the church, Mrs. Brodie Duke said: "As many of you know, it was his long and cherished desire to build a church here for the worship of the true God. Near this spot, for years before his death, it was his great pleasure to preach to you and your fathers and mothers the glorious gospel of the grace of God under the shade of the trees" (*Methodist Advance*, 1 July 1880).

34 OCDB 43:80; Robert F. Durden's historical sketch of the church in *The Centennial Program of the First Presbyterian Church, Durham, North Carolina*; *Tobacco Plant*, 19 Jan. 1876; *Herald*, 14 June 1876.

35 Interview with Curtis Booker, 17 July 1985; telephone conversation with Miss Nannie Mae Herndon, 25 Nov. 1985; James Vickers and others, *Chapel Hill: An Illustrated History* (Chapel Hill, 1985), 42, 85.

36 OCDB 43:425; Robert Spence Tate, Jr., "A Study of Negro Churches in Durham, North Carolina" (B.D. thesis, D.U., 1939).

37 Telephone conversation with Mrs. Laura Torain, 17 Oct. 1985.

38 Boyd, *The Story of Durham*, 58–59, 60–62; Paul, *History of the Town of Durham, N.C.*, 26, 77, 139–40; *Herald*, 4 Mar. 1917; OCDB 36:187, 37:156; W. N. Evans, Jr., "History of the Tobacco Industry in Durham," *Trinity Archive* 33 (1920): 20. I am grateful to Marian K. O'Keefe for sharing with me the following information from the Colman Company about Durham mustard and their trademark for it. About 1720 a Mrs. Clements of Durham, England, originated a process of making a fine powder of mustard seed. The Ainsley Company of Durham, England (founded 1717), which used this process, made the name of Durham, England, synonymous with mustard just as Green and his successors were to make Durham, North Carolina, synonymous with tobacco. When Colman's of Norwich (originated about 1814) adopted a trademark for its Durham mustard in 1855, it chose the head of a shorthorn, or Durham, bull.

Whitted moved his manufacturing operation to Durham in the mid-1880s; his brick, three-story factory south of the railroad opposite the end of Queen Street is shown in the *Southern Tobacco Journal*, 25 Aug. 1888. (I am grateful to his descendant Hugh Whitted of Winston-Salem for bringing this to my attention.)

39 Boyd, *The Story of Durham*, 59; *Tobacco Plant*, 9 Oct. 1877; "Durham, the Magic Queen City of the Golden Belt," Raleigh *N&O*, 5 Apr. 1896 (tobacco edition). A descendant of Captain Ward related that one of Ward's daughters, Cora Lee, "remembered the Duke boys as they came to Durham on Saturday afternoons. They were always very, very clean, wearing blue overalls and homespun shirts and were very polite. One of the boys, Prodie [*sic*], asked Cora for a date, but her father thought she was too young [fifteen] to let young Duke come to see his daughter" (*The Heritage of Onslow County, North Carolina* [Winston-Salem, 1983], 452; OCR, Estates: J. R. Green; OCDB 40:451; Paul, *History of the Town of Durham, N.C.*, 26, 130, 134, 141; J. D. Cameron, "Durham and Its Tobacco Business," Hillsborough *Recorder*, 13 Feb. 1878.

40 OCDB 37:360; 1870 Census, Orange County, Agriculture Schedule, Mangum Township; interview with Mildred M. Harris; OCR, Estates: J. R. Green.

41 Boyd, *The Story of Durham*, 79, 83–85; Paul, *History of the Town of Durham, N.C.*, 93, 115–17; B. N. Duke Papers, DU-RBMSCL, 11 Dec. 1891, 10 June 1895; OCR, Estates: J. R. Green. Link sold out to the Dukes and became their employee.

42 Virginia Gray, "A Goodly Heritage: The Dukes of Orange County," *Duke Alumni Register* 55 (Sept. 1969): 21–23, (Nov. 1969): 18–21; *Determination by the Executors of James B. Duke, Deceased of Those Entitled to Participate in the Distribution to Be Made under Item vi of the Last Will and Testament of Said Decedent and of the Amounts They Are, Respectively, Entitled to Receive* (New York, 1927); OCR, OCCM, Aug. 1847; Hillsborough *Recorder*, 14 Oct. 1829; Durden, *The Dukes of Durham*, 4; OCDB 32:526, 35:219.

43 Durden, *The Dukes of Durham*, 4, 8–9; Durham County Wills, Durham County Courthouse, Will of Mary E. Lyon. Mary Lyon and her family lived with her father, Washington Duke. She left Caroline Barnes $500 in her will.

44 *N&O*, 5 Apr. 1896.

45 Ibid.

46 Frances Gray Patton, "The Town Bull Durham Built," *Holiday* (Dec. 1959): 97; Boyd, *The Story of Durham*, 83.

47 Paul B. Barringer, *The Natural Bent: The Memoirs of Dr. Paul B. Barringer* (Chapel Hill, 1949), 163–64.

48 Paul, *History of the Town of Durham, N.C.*, 104, 152; Durden, *The Dukes of Durham*, 15; Boyd, *The Story of Durham*, 83, 85. Paul's history says that the Dukes moved to town in 1872, Boyd's says 1874.

49 Hillsborough *Recorder*, 13 Feb. 1878, 11 Feb. 1874; Cameron Family Papers, SHC, 13 Mar. 1872; J. D. Cameron, *A Sketch of the Tobacco Interests in North Carolina* (Oxford, N.C., 1881), 57–59; Paul, *History of the Town of Durham, N.C.*, 114, 116; Boyd, *The Story of Durham*, 79–80; OCDB 42:157, 44:324.

50 Richard Harvey Wright Papers, DU-RBMSCL, 18 Feb. 1875; *N&O*, 5 Mar. 1929; Hillsborough *Recorder*, 13 Feb. 1878; Boyd, *The Story of Durham*, 79; OCDB 44:324; Cameron, *A Sketch of the Tobacco Interests in North Carolina*, 55–56; Hillsborough *Recorder*, 18 Apr. 1877.

51 Nannie May Tilley, *The Bright-Tobacco Industry 1860–1929* (Chapel Hill, 1948), 23, 64; Tobacco Institute, *North Carolina & Tobacco* (Washington, 1971), 26–29.

52 1860 Census, Orange County, Agriculture Schedule. Mangum Township produced 600 barns of tobacco in 1877 averaging 350 pounds each (Hillsborough *Recorder*, 5 Dec. 1877).

53 Tilley, *The Bright-Tobacco Industry*, 547–48. While the vast majority of slaveowners had fewer than ten slaves, a dozen or more Orange County men had substantially more. Some of these were Paul Cameron with 358 (not including 114 he owned in Person County), William N. Patterson, 132; J. N. Patterson, 106; William Cain's daughter,

Mary White, 76; John D. Lipscomb, 52; Joseph Woods, 44; Dr. James Cain, 41; John B. Leathers, 31; William N. Pratt, 28; Edmund Tilley, 19; Ellison Mangum, 18; and John Lockhart, 18 (1860 Census: Orange County, Slave Schedule).

54 Lefler and Newsome, *North Carolina*, 510–11.

55 Paul, *History of the Town of Durham, N.C.*, 133–37. Other sons of John Wesley Carr bore illustrious names: Robert Emmett and Albert Gallatin Carr.

56 Ibid.; Mena Fuller Webb, *Jule Carr: General without an Army* (Chapel Hill, 1987). President Andrew Johnson is said to have visited the Blackwell factory in 1869 (*Herald*, 19 Oct. 1905).

57 Paul, *History of the Town of Durham, N.C.*, 130–33; Boyd, *The Story of Durham*, 183–84; *N&O*, 5 Apr. 1896; Boyd, *The Story of Durham*, 117–18; Benjamin N. Duke Papers, DU-RBMSCL, W. T. Blackwell to B. N. Duke, 19 Oct. 1892, 10 Sept. 1893, 21 Dec. 1891, 2 Mar. 1896; *Herald*, 11 May 1936.

58 Cameron, *A Sketch of the Tobacco Interests in North Carolina*, 48–51; Boyd, *The Story of Durham*, 69.

59 Boyd, *The Story of Durham*, 69–70.

60 Ibid.; Paul, *History of the Town of Durham, N.C.*, 96–98, 144–48; *Tobacco Plant*, 30 Aug. 1879; *Herald*, 14 July 1929.

61 Ann Banks, ed., *First-Person America* (New York, 1980), 151.

62 Paul, *History of the Town of Durham, N.C.*, 98, 145; *Tobacco Plant*, 28 Mar. 1877; Cameron, *A Sketch of the Tobacco Interests in North Carolina*, 50–51; Durham *Recorder*, 28 May, 3 Sept. 1896; Banks, *First-Person America*, 153–55.

63 Boyd, *The Story of Durham*, 70; *Tobacco Plant*, 11 Jan. 1882.

64 *Branson's North Carolina Business Directory for 1877–78* (Raleigh, 1878), 233; *Tobacco Plant*, 28 Apr. 1875; Hillsborough *Recorder*, 2 Aug. 1875. The deathblow to the local water mills was a disastrous flood in August 1908 that destroyed or severely damaged all the mills on the three rivers. Before that freshet, the previous most damaging floods had occurred in 1792, 1847, 1868, and 1877.

65 R. G. Dun and Company, *The Mercantile Agency Reference Book . . . , Southern States. January 1878* (New York, 1878) 39; J. T. Nichols Papers, DU-RBMSCL, Diary; U.S. Post Office Dept., "Records of Appointments of Postmasters"; Hillsborough *Recorder*, 2 Aug. 1875; *Tobacco Plant*, 19 Jan. 1876. The Patrons of Industry movement reached North Carolina about 1873; local granges were established between 1875 and 1890. The following were in Durham County. Durham Grange: M. A. Angier and W. R. Vickers, masters successively, W. R. Vickers, secretary; Orange Grange: A. K. Umstead, master, G. W. Jones, secretary; New Bethel: William G. Latta, master, W. H. Carrington, secretary; Neuse River: Samuel T. Morgan, master, D. L. Belvin, secretary; Leesville Grange: J. M. Lynn, master, John W. Wiggins, secretary; Cedar Fork Grange: Sidney Scott, master, W. H. Edwards, secretary (Patrons of Husbandry, N.C., "A List of the Subordinate Granges of North Carolina with their Masters and Secretaries, 1875–1890," DU-RBMSCL).

66 Durham *Daily Sun*, 3 Feb. 1902. Brodie Duke's entanglements with women are well documented. In the early 1870s he was sued for breach of promise by Margaret S. Turner, with whom he admitted that he had cohabited since 1866, but he vowed that he had never intended to marry her whatever her expectations had been. She collected $500 damages. Brodie Duke married John A. McMannen's daughter Martha in 1874 and by her had three children, Baxter Lawrence, Mabel, and Pearl. Three other marriages followed: to Minnie Woodward in 1890, to Alice Webb in 1904, and Wylanta Rochelle in 1910. See Durham *Tobacco Plant*, 11 Apr. 1888; *Sun*, 26 Mar., 23 Dec. 1904; Durden, *The Dukes of Durham*, 85.

67 Dun, *Mercantile Agency Reference Book, 1878*; *Tobacco Plant*, 28 Apr. 1875, 24 Aug. 1887; Eli N. Evans, *The Provincials* (New York, 1973), 309. The Mohsbergs moved to Richmond in 1887 when the father's health began to fail.

68 Boyd, *The Story of Durham*, 116–17; Paul, *History of the Town of Durham, N.C.*, 137; Richard H. Wright Papers, DU-RBMSCL, 4 Apr. 1889.

69 "Durham Business Directory," ca. 1875, a single-page listing of merchants' advertisements, photocopy in the author's possession; information from Mrs. Egbert Haywood; *Sun*, 30 Nov. 1903; A. M. Rigsbee Papers, DU-RBMSCL. *Tobacco Plant*, 28 Apr. 1875; *Branson's North Carolina Business Directory for 1869* (Raleigh, 1869), 124.

70 *Tobacco Plant*, 2 Apr., 21 May, 23 July 1878; *Herald*, 14 June 1876; Boyd, *The Story of Durham*, 162.

71 Hillsborough *Recorder*, 27 May 1845, 29 Mar. 1876; *Tobacco Plant*, 14 Feb. 1872; Durham *Recorder*, 19 Jan. 1899; *Herald*, 22 Mar. 1876; Boyd, *The Story of Durham*, 233–36.

72 *Tobacco Plant*, 10 Sept. 1878.

73 North Carolina County Papers: Orange County, DU-RBMSCL, 1875 Tax List. The six black landowners in Mangum Township were Lewis Harris, Henry Chavis, Jr., Anderson Day, Henry Bass, Dennis Beasley, and William Bass. The five black landowners in Patterson Township were Tom Bass, Haywood and David Barbee, and Isham and Dick Marcom. The blacks who owned town lots in Durham were Jim Warren, Benjamin White, Isaiah Sparkman, Johnson Ray, Willis McCown, Green Leathers, Turner Henderson, Remus Gattis, and Luke Cameron. In Durham Township outside the town limits the black landowners were Verge Barbee, James Cozart, Haywood Day, Cannady Green, John Guess, Daniel Goodloe, Edward Hopkins, Dewitt Hopkins, David Justice, Monroe Jordan, Robert Justice, Manda Latta, David Lunsford, Samuel Miller, James Rencher, James Sudd, Lemuel Sowell, Anderson Turner, Alexander Watson, Paul Weaver, Gaston Weaver, and Matt Walker.

74 North Carolina County Papers, DU-RBMSCL, "Registry of Voters, Durham Election Precinct, 3 Nov. 1868."

10 A HOUSE DIVIDED: AN INDEPENDENT BLACK CULTURE

1 Pauli Murray, *Proud Shoes*, reprint (New York, 1978), 167.

2 J. G. deRoulhac Hamilton, *The Papers of Thomas Ruffin* (Raleigh, 1918–20), 4:35.

3 Ibid., 3:464.

4 John B. Boles, *Black Southerners, 1619–1869* (Lexington, Ky., 1983), 210.

5 Ibid., 208.

6 Federal Writers' Project, Slave Narratives: North Carolina, vol. 11, pt. 1, 324, Narrative of Addy Gill, microfiche, Duke University Library.

7 Lefler and Wager, *Orange County*, 122.

8 Bureau of the Census, *Population of the United States in 1860: North Carolina* (Washington, 1864), 353. Oak Grove Township, Wake County, which was later added to Durham County, contained a population of 2,591 persons. Cedar Fork Township, only a portion of which was added to Durham County at the time of the county's formation, contained a population of 1,715 persons (*The Ninth Census of the United States: Statistics of Population* [Washington, 1872], 224; *The Compendium of the Tenth Census of the United States, 1880* [Washington, 1883], 282). The figures are not broken down by race within the townships; therefore the author counted the blacks in the original records and subtracted those figures from the totals.

9 OCDB 45:567, Rosetta Holloway to John O'Daniel, 25 June 1877.

10 Joe A. Mobley, *James City, a Black Community in North Carolina, 1863–1900* (Raleigh, 1981), 44.

11 Gray's "New Map of Durham, 1881," DU-RBMSCL.

12 Markum Papers in the possession of Saint Joseph A.M.E. Church. Markum's own notes give the date of his purchase as 20 Aug. 1869. William Benjamin Markum,

The Life of a Great Man: Rev. Edian Markum and the Founding of Saint Joseph A.M.E. *Church, Durham, North Carolina* (Boston, 1941).

13 James T. Henry, "Negro Preachers of Durham," *Trinity Archive* 12 (Oct. 1898): 7; "Registry of Voters, Durham Election Precinct," 3 Nov. 1868, DU-RBMSCL, North Carolina County Papers: Durham.

14 Markum, *The Life of a Great Man.*

15 The freedom certificate is in the possession of the church. It has been reproduced in Elnora Kennedy's "Brief History of St. Joseph's A.M.E. Church" (1976). Pasquotank County Records, NCOAH, Miscellaneous Records: Records of Slaves and Free Persons of Color, 19 Oct. 1830, William L. Gregory to Charles Green, "I have never known a Spellman that was a slave."

16 Henry, "Negro Preachers of Durham," 7.

17 Markum, *The Life of a Great Man,* 13–14; *Herald,* 28 Apr. 1935; Henry, "Negro Preachers of Durham," 7.

18 Markum, *The Life of a Great Man,* 27–28.

19 Henry, "Negro Preachers of Durham," 7.

20 OCDB 40:374, 527, 572, 573, 576, 42:142, 45:567; OCR, Marriage Bonds and Licenses, Monroe Jordan and Anna Meeks, 6 Oct. 1868; SOHP, Walter Weare's interview with Conrad Odell Pearson.

21 Vickers Family Papers, DU-RBMSCL, 10 Feb. 1877; OCDB 39:51, 41:70, 494, 512, 42:164; DCDB 1:156, 178; *Herald,* 22 Jan. 1923. In 1874 Dempsey Henderson and his wife sold five acres to the Durham town commissioners for $125 specifically for a cemetery; see OCDB 46:61 (20 Dec. 1874). The commissioners were E. J. Parrish, Julian S. Carr, F. S. Tomlinson, J. W. Cheek, and W. R. Hughes. There is no documentation for the oral tradition that Carr gave two acres for the cemetery. The idea for the town purchase may have originated with him. In 1872 the aldermen had purchased from William H. Willard an unspecified amount of land for a graveyard. It cost $150 (Street Book, City Clerk's Office, 8 Oct. 1872).

22 OCDB 46:226; Murray, *Proud Shoes,* 225–27, 241–43, 267.

23 Tate, "A Study of Negro Churches in Durham, North Carolina." A. J. Corde, the minister, invited the Dukes to a service at which their own minister was to preach and added, "Our steeple is completed" (Benjamin N. Duke Papers, DU-RBMSCL [Apr. 1896]). The old building, now much altered, is used as a Holiness church.

24 Durham *Recorder,* 16 Apr. 1900; *Herald,* 31 Jan. 1918; Claudia Roberts, Diane E. Lea, and Robert M. Cleary, *The Durham Architectural and Historic Inventory* (Durham, 1982), 144; Murray, *Proud Shoes,* illustration of old Fitzgerald home (no page number), 238, 241–42.

25 OCDB 41:249; OCW G:521; Lewis Blount, Map of Durham, 1867–68 (1923). DU-RBMSCL.

26 Anderson, *Piedmont Plantation,* 94, 101; OCR, Marriage Bonds and Licenses: Monroe Jordan and Anna Meeks, 2 Oct. 1868; Negro Cohabitation Certificates, 1866–68; Cameron Family Papers, SHC, 10 ("Memo of the Birth of Negro Children Commencing June 1771"), July–Aug. 1841.

27 DCDB 25:492.

28 *Branson's Directory of the Business and Citizens of Durham City for 1887* (Raleigh, 1887); *Turner and Company's Durham Directory for the Years 1889 and 1890* (Winston, 1889); 1870 and 1880 Censuses, Orange County; *Herald,* 3 Oct. 1926.

29 Charles S. Johnson, *Growing Up in the Black Belt: Negro Youth in the Rural South* (Washington, 1941), 135.

30 Information provided to the author by William A. Clement, currently Grand Master of the Prince Hall Grand Lodge in North Carolina.

31 Boles, *Black Southerners,* 159.

32 Miles Mark Fisher, *Friends: Pictorial Report of Ten Years Pastorate* (Durham, 1943). Margaret Faucette's son Lindsey became a successful businessman in Durham. Born on the Norwoods' Occoneechee Plantation (later owned by Julian Carr) near Hillsborough, he began his career by driving a hack to carry passengers and freight to and from the station, but he soon acquired a fleet of hacks and then of trucks and eventually owned a principal dray service in Durham (Federal Writers' Project, Slave Narratives: North Carolina, vol. 11, pt. 1, 302–6; *Herald*, 30 Jan. 1977).

33 OCDB 45:85.

34 Fisher, *Friends*; *Daily Globe*, 8 Sept. 1891, 3 Apr. 1893; Durham *Recorder*, 26 Mar. 1896, 7 May 1896; B. N. Duke Papers, DU-RBMSCL, 8 May 1896.

35 *Globe*, 22 Aug. 1891; Durham *Recorder*, 13 Mar. 1908. Benjamin and Washington Duke agreed to give one-fifth of the building costs of the church provided the total did not exceed $7,000 and provided the members raised the rest (Durden, *The Dukes of Durham*, 104). In 1902 Benjamin and James Duke gave $2,000 to Saint Joseph's to enable them to clear the church's debt (*Sun*, 31 Mar. 1902). Roberts, Lea, and Cleary, *The Durham Architectural and Historic Inventory*, 113–14; Durham *Recorder*, 13 Mar. 1908; *Herald*, 26 Apr. 1935.

36 Tate, "A Study of Negro Churches in Durham, North Carolina."

37 OCW G:407; OCR, Estates: Jefferson Browning; *Herald*, 9 Aug. 1912, 21 Mar. 1917. Hickstown land had formed part of William N. Pratt's extensive holdings and was known as the Poole tract, for it had been previously owned by that family. Pratt's executor sold it to Robert M. Jones, who sold 100 acres of it to E. Hawkins Hicks in 1874. The tract was then described as lying on both sides of the railroad adjoining lands of Simeon Hester and Alsey Carroll (OCDB 43:201).

38 *Tobacco Plant*, 28 Mar. 1877, 14 Mar. 1888; *Globe*, 9 Feb. 1893; *Sun*, 18 Jan., 3 Mar. 1900; Murray, *Proud Shoes*, 26–27.

39 Federal Writers' Project, Slave Narratives: Alabama, 1:226, Narrative of Mildred Scott Taylor. See also, for example, ibid., North Carolina, vol. 11, pt. 1:286–88, Narrative of Tempie Durham. When she was 102 years old in 1937, she went to the post office to register for a social security number in anticipation of receiving an old age pension (*Herald*, 4 June 1937).

40 Hillsborough *Recorder*, 17 Dec. 1873.

41 Dennett, *The South as It Is*, 150–54; Lefler and Newsome, *North Carolina*, 479.

42 Lefler and Newsome, *North Carolina*, 501–2.

43 OCW G:521, H:70; OCR, Estates: Lewis Pratt; OCDB 41:272, 274, 267.

44 *Tobacco Plant*, 19 Jan. 1876.

45 Boyd, *The Story of Durham*, 159–61, 279–80; Walter B. Weare, *Black Business in the New South* (Urbana, Ill., 1973), 26.

46 Anderson, *Piedmont Plantation*, 126.

11 A COUNTY AT LAST

1 *N&O*, 9 Feb. 1881; *Tobacco Plant*, 6 Nov. 1877.

2 Boyd, *The Story of Durham*, 104–5.

3 Ibid.; *Tobacco Plant*, 15 Feb. 1881.

4 *Journal of the House of Representatives, 1881 Session* (Raleigh, 1882), 26 Jan.; Bennehan Cameron Papers, SHC, B. Cameron to Anne R. Cameron, 6 Apr. 1881.

5 *N&O*, 9 Feb., 10 Feb. 1881; B. Cameron Papers, SHC, Cameron to Emily Buford, 21 Jan. 1881; Cameron Family Papers, SHC, Richard Lewis to Paul Cameron, 7 Apr. 1881.

6 Boyd, *The Story of Durham*, 97; *Tobacco Plant*, 15 Feb. 1881; *N&O*, 14 Jan. 1881.

7 *Tobacco Plant*, 15 Feb. 1881.

8 *House Journal, Session 1881* (Raleigh, 1882), 26 Jan., 27 Jan.; *Senate Journal, Session 1881* (Raleigh, 1882), 28 Feb.; Boyd, *The Story of Durham*, 105–8.

9 Paul, *History of the Town of Durham, N.C.*, 29, 33–34; the governor's proclamation is reproduced in Boyd, *The Story of Durham*, 113.

10 Shanks, ed., *The Papers of Willie Person Mangum*, 5:762.

11 David Leroy Corbitt, *The Formation of the North Carolina Counties, 1663–1943* (Raleigh, 1950), 94–95.

12 *Laws and Resolutions of the State of North Carolina Passed by the General Assembly at Its Session of 1881* (Raleigh, 1881), 272–82.

13 Paul, *History of the Town of Durham, N.C.*, 38; Minutes of the Durham County Commissioners, 1881–89, Register of Deeds, Durham County Courthouse.

14 Minutes, Durham County Commissioners, 1881–89.

15 Ibid. Carrington had had a saloon in Durham for years.

16 Paul, *History of the Town of Durham, N.C.*, 40–43.

17 Boyd, *The Story of Durham*, 176; "As We See It," Broadside Collection, DU-RBMSCL.

18 "As We See It."

19 Paul, *History of the Town of Durham, N.C.*, 43–45; Boyd, *The Story of Durham*, 175–78.

20 Boyd, *The Story of Durham*, 179–83; *North Carolina Reports* 94 (Feb. Term, 1886): 577–82, *A. M. Rigsbee v. the Town of Durham*, 98 (Sept. Term, 1887), 92–98, *A. M. Rigsbee v. the Town of Durham and the School Committee of the Town of Durham.*

21 "To the Friends of Education in Durham, N.C., May 1, 1886." Broadside Collection, Rare Book Room, D.U. Library; Richard H. Wright Papers, DU-RBMSCL, S. F. Tomlinson to Wright, 30 July 1887; *Tobacco Plant*, 20 Oct. 1886, 24 Aug. 1887, 16 Nov. 1888; Thomas H. Houck, "A Newspaper History of Race Relations in Durham, 1910–1940" (M.A. thesis, D.U., 1941), 44.

22 James C. Biggs Papers, SHC, an address (c. 1950) on his recollections of Durham.

23 Paul, *History of the Town of Durham, N.C.*, 81–83, 227; *Tobacco Plant*, 4 Jan., 11 Jan. 1882, 10 Aug., 7 Sept., 28 Sept., 5 Oct. 1887; James H. Southgate, "History of Trinity Church," chapter 2, *Trinity League Record*, Jan. 1895; Childs, *Centennial History of Trinity Methodist Church*, 10; Durham *Recorder*, 25 Nov. 1881, 16 Mar. 1882; Elizabeth Anderson Persons, "South Lowell Male Academy and Its First Headmaster," *Durham Record* 1 (Fall 1983): 24.

   Dean secured as his assistant W. E. Burcham, an Englishman newly arrived in the United States. In the 1880s while the Burcham family was living at Redmond's Grove (the old Prattsburg area), he died of typhoid fever, leaving his French-born wife and five children. She obtained a position at Morning Sun Academy, where she taught music as well as the three R's to the younger children (Memoir of Willis T. Carpenter, a typescript in the possession of Mrs. Edna Carpenter Baker).

24 *Tobacco Plant*, 11 Jan., 15 Feb. 1882, 2 July 1885; Memoir of Willis T. Carpenter. Weatherly retired after thirty-three years of teaching, and operated the Mineral Springs Dairy (*Herald*, 19 Mar. 1939). A Miss Mary Cannady's school "at Persimmondale near Durham" is mentioned in *Tobacco Plant*, 20 Apr. 1887, but no other information about this school is available. Likewise Shipp and Jenkins's Academy, probably in Cedar Fork Township, has left only its name (Durham *Recorder*, 14 July 1886); William K. Boyd Papers, Duke University Archives, Roxie Sasser, "History of Lebanon Township, Durham County, North Carolina"; Hillsborough *Recorder*, 1 Sept. 1875.

25 In 1884 the elder Watts also invested in Morehead's bank (Eugene Morehead Papers, DU-RBMSCL, Morehead to his wife, 17 Apr. 1885); Boyd, *The Story of Durham*, 85–87; Durden, *The Dukes of Durham*, 18–19; B. N. Duke Papers, DU-RBMSCL, Legal Papers, 1891.

26 Paul, *History of the Town of Durham, N.C.*, 103–4; Boyd, *The Story of Durham*, 75–76; *Tobacco Plant*, 6 Apr. 1887.

27 Paul, *History of the Town of Durham, N.C.*, 111; Boyd, *The Story of Durham*, 87.

28 Paul, *History of the Town of Durham, N.C.*, 117; John D. Cameron, *A Sketch of the*

Tobacco Interests (Oxford, N.C., 1881); Boyd, *The Story of Durham*, 203; *Methodist Advance*, 22 Apr. 1880; *Tobacco Plant*, 2 Feb. 1887; Melton McLaurin, *Paternalism and Protest: The Knights of Labor in the South* (Westport, Conn., 1978), 62–63; Mason Crum Papers, Duke University Archives, "Life and Times of Washington Duke," manuscript of projected biography, chapter 8, p. 16; *N&O*, 5 Apr. 1896 (tobacco edition). One cigarette roller who had worked in Durham during that short sojourn was Sam Edelsohn, who was killed by a train in New Jersey in 1887 (*Tobacco Plant*, 2 Feb. 1887).

29 *Tobacco Plant*, 15 Sept. 1886; Paul, *History of the Town of Durham, N.C.*, 117–18.

30 *Tobacco Plant*, 11 Jan. 1882.

31 *Herald*, 17 Jan. 1926; Southgate-Jones Papers, DU-RBMSCL, Southgate Jones, "The Hand-Rolled Cigarette Industry," 22 Jan. 1945.

32 Durden, *The Dukes of Durham*, 19–25, 26–27.

33 Ibid., 23, 26–27, 32; *Globe*, 15 Oct. 1889; McLaurin, *Paternalism and Protest*, 63. For other inventors see Rufus L. Patterson Papers, SHC, 31 Oct. 1894; *Tobacco Plant*, 28 May 1878, 5 Jan. 1887. William H. Kerr, son of the state geologist W. C. Kerr, invented a bagging device eventually used in the Golden Belt factory, each machine of which could make ten to fifteen thousand bags a day (*Tobacco Plant*, 1 June 1887). Perhaps this invention inspired Carr to incorporate his bag-making company two months later. A later noteworthy inventor was John Thomas Dalton, whose connection with Durham began when Richard Wright bought an interest in his work of perfecting a bag-stringing device. He was successful in selling it to the Golden Belt Company in 1912. After that he worked for Wright inventing a machine to weigh tea, cut teabags, insert the tea, sew the seams, and attach the tags. Many other inventions followed for the tobacco industry, including a tie-boy that could tie bows in the bag strings. See B. W. C. Roberts and Richard F. Knapp, *John Thomas Dalton and the Development of Bull Durham Smoking Tobacco* (Durham, 1977).

34 Boyd, *The Story of Durham*, 90; Durden, *The Dukes of Durham*, 23.

35 Boyd, *The Story of Durham*, 89.

36 Durden, *The Dukes of Durham*, 24, 57–58.

37 Ibid., 29–36.

38 Cameron, *A Sketch of the Tobacco Interests in North Carolina*. In the 1870s W. K. Styron had gone into bag manufacturing in a small way and he had had to enlarge his factory in 1877, so successful had it become (*Tobacco Plant*, 14 Mar. 1877). Hillsborough *Recorder*, 11 Feb., 25 Feb. 1874, 19 Jan. 1876.

39 *Globe*, 11 July 1895; Durham Cotton Manufacturing Company Papers, DU-RBMSCL; *Handbook of Durham, N.C., 1895* (Durham, 1895), 41–42; Patricia Dickinson and Ruth Little-Stokes, "An Inventory of Edgemont and East Durham: Early Textile Mill Villages, Durham, N.C., 1980," Report produced by the Historic Preservation Technology Class, Durham Technical Institute, 1978–79, H2; B. N. Duke Papers, DU-RBMSCL, Letterhead 9 July 1894; *Manufacturers' Record* 10 (28 Aug. 1886): 80–81; *Sun*, 24 Mar. 1900. Carr's factory still stands, much altered, as do some of the mill houses (on Reservoir and Middle Streets), now cut off from the factory by the "Buck" Dean Expressway.

40 *Tobacco Plant*, 17 Aug. 1887; Durham *Recorder*, 29 Mar. 1900; R. H. Wright Papers, DU-RBMSCL, 5 Dec., 18 Dec. 1888.

41 Blackwood-Lloyd Papers, DU-RBMSCL, 13 Mar. 1884; *Tobacco Plant*, 29 Sept. 1886; *Herald*, 7 Oct. 1919.

42 *Tobacco Plant*, 27 Oct. 1886, 12 Jan., 19 Jan. 1887, 11 Jan., 14 Mar., 18 Apr. 1888; Souvenir Edition of the Durham *Daily Sun*, 23–25 July 1890; R. H. Wright Papers, DU-RBMSCL, 15 June, 3 Oct., 11 Oct., 17 Nov. 1887, 16 Aug., 22 Aug., 3 Dec. 1890, 18 July, 25 Aug., 29 Aug. 1893; *Globe*, 1 Jan. 1892, 27 Aug. 1891; *Hand-book of Durham, 1895*, 62.

43 R. H. Wright Papers, DU-RBMSCL, 17 Mar., 21 Mar., 9 Apr., 1 Dec. 1887; *Tobacco Plant*, 22 July 1885, 22 Dec. 1886, 13 July 1887, 4 Apr. 1888.

44 *Tobacco Plant*, 8 June 1880; OCDB, 46:109 (3 July 1879); Roberts, Lea, and Cleary, *The Durham Architectural and Historic Inventory*, 132, 133.

45 *Tobacco Plant*, 24 Nov. 1886, 9 Nov. 1887, 11 Apr. 1888; *Globe*, 12 Apr. 1893.

46 Interview with Wilkerson's daughter Maude Dunn, 29 July 1983; *Tobacco Plant*, 15 Dec. 1886.

47 R. H. Wright Papers, DU-RBMSCL, 27 Aug. 1888; *Tobacco Plant*, 22 Dec. 1886, 9 Mar. 1887, 7 Sept. 1888; Roberts, Lea, and Cleary, *The Durham Architectural and Historic Inventory*, 156; DCDB 10:456 identifies J. R. Blacknall's home.

48 *Tobacco Plant*, 6 July, 13 July 1887, 26 Feb. 1889.

49 Samuel P. Ashe, Louis R. Wilson, and Charles L. Van Noppen, *Biographical History of North Carolina* 5:290–91; Morehead Papers, DU-RBMSCL, 21 Sept. 1887; Paul, *History of the Town of Durham, N.C.*, 232, 238; *Tobacco Plant*, 2 Feb. 1887, 14 Sept., 7 Dec. 1888; *Globe*, 14 Sept. 1891; U.S. Post Office Dept., "Records of Appointments," East Durham; *Sun*, 1 Jan. 1900.

50 Phebe Stanton, Professor of Fine Arts at Johns Hopkins University and an expert on Augustus N. W. Pugin, kindly supplied the author with biographical information on Byron A. Pugin.

51 *Tobacco Plant*, 15 Dec. 1886, 26 Oct. 1887, 13 Apr. 1887. Pugin also built a house for C. M. Herndon on Dillard Street (*Tobacco Plant*, 22 Dec. 1886).

52 B. N. Duke Papers, DU-RBMSCL, 13 May 1887; Durden, *The Dukes of Durham*, 85, 171; *Tobacco Plant*, 11 Apr. 1888.

53 *Globe*, 11 June 1890.

54 *Tobacco Plant*, 17 Aug., 23 Nov. 1887.

55 Southgate-Jones Papers, DU-RBMSCL, Southgate Jones "Autobiography," 6–7; *Tobacco Plant*, 1 Feb. 1888; *Globe*, 6, 24 Apr. 1894; *Sun*, 20 Mar. 1900, 26 Apr. 1939; *Herald*, 14 June 1876, 29 Oct. 1914.

56 *Tobacco Plant*, 13 Apr. 1887, 5 Oct. 1888; *Herald*, 27 June 1926.

57 Cameron Family Papers, SHC, 24 Apr. 1889.

58 *Tobacco Plant*, 2 Mar. 1887; Southgate-Jones Papers, DU-RBMSCL, "Autobiography" of Southgate Jones, 11.

59 Boyd, *The Story of Durham*, 136, 138–40.

60 Ibid., 140–47; *Tobacco Plant*, 17 Aug., 21 Sept. 1887; Morehead Papers, DU-RBMSCL, Samuel T. Morgan to Morehead, 15 Sept. 1887.

61 Boyd, *The Story of Durham*, 148–49.

62 Paul, *History of the Town of Durham, N.C.*, 80; *Tobacco Plant*, 30 May 1877, 13 July 1880; 4 Jan. 1882, 13 July 1887, 7 Sept. 1888; Boyd, *The Story of Durham*, 304; *Turner and Company's Durham Directory, 1889–90* (Winston, 1889), 20; *Globe*, 17 Dec., 23 Dec., 1891, 6 Apr., 7 Apr., 8 Apr., 13 Apr. 1893, 11 July 1895; *Recorder*, 25 July 1896; *Sun*, 7 Oct. 1902.

63 *Recorder*, 25 July 1896; *Sun*, 7 Oct. 1902; Boyd, *The Story of Durham*, 304; *Herald*, 13 Apr. 1915.

64 Division of Water Resources, *The Water Supply of the City of Durham, North Carolina* (1981), 4; Boyd, *The Story of Durham*, 155–56; *Tobacco Plant*, 10 Nov. 1886. Heavy rains in February 1939 destroyed the old dam on Nancy Rhodes Creek, which had supplied the city with water until 1917 (*Herald*, 16 Feb. 1939).

65 *Tobacco Plant*, 24 Nov. 1886, 9 Nov. 1887, 11 Apr. 1888; *Globe*, 12 Apr., 27 May, 12 June 1893.

66 *Globe*, 16 June 1893, 1 Jan., 6 Feb. 1894; *Recorder*, 6 Oct. 1898; Boyd, *The Story of Durham*, 157; Gilbert C. White, *Final Report on the Establishment of Waterworks, Durham, N.C.* (Durham, 1917).

67 R. H. Wright Papers, DU-RBMSCL, J. S. Carr to Wright, 1 Oct. 1889, 23 Mar. 1891, also

Printed Materials, "Charter and By-Laws of the Durham Street Railway Company"; *Tobacco Plant*, 9 Mar., 13 July 1887; *Globe*, 8 Mar., 17 July, 20 July, 2 Aug., 4 Aug., 14 Aug. 1893; *Sun*, 5 Feb., 6 Feb. 1901; *Herald*, 26 Mar. 1912.

68 Charles E. Waddell Papers, DU-RBMSCL, "Fifty Years of Electrical Development in North Carolina," 1936; *Globe*, 3 Jan. 1894; *Herald*, 30 Aug. 1912, 23 Mar., 28 May, 6 June 1913, 27 June 1926; Boyd, *The Story of Durham*, 152; *Tobacco Plant*, 31 Aug. 1888.

69 *Herald*, 28 May 1944.

70 *Tobacco Plant*, 31 Aug. 1888; Morehead Papers, DU-RBMSCL, 1 May 1892; *Globe*, 23 Feb., 24 May, 15 June 1894; "Telephone Service in Durham," notes assembled by Sid Linton, public relations officer, General Telephone Company of the South; Chamber of Commerce Minutes, Durham Chamber of Commerce, 29 Mar., 1 Nov. 1917; *Herald*, 23 July 1919, 28 July, 22 Aug. 1920, 8 Mar. 1921, 10 Jan. 1926.

71 Paul, *History of the Town of Durham, N.C.*, 231; *Tobacco Plant*, 19 Jan., 31 Aug., 21 Sept. 1887, 11 Jan., 16 Nov. 1888; Boyd, *The Story of Durham*, 117; Morehead Papers, DU-RBMSCL, W. M. Morgan to Morehead, 31 Dec. 1887, 10 Jan. 1888; R. H. Wright Papers, DU-RBMSCL, William H. McCabe to Wright, 21 Sept. 1887, Thomas D. Wright to Wright, 11 Oct. 1888, Smith to Wright, 19 Nov. 1888. The exposition mentioned was an industrial fair, 10–12 Oct. 1888, held in Parrish's warehouse where forty-two exhibits boasted of Durham's progress. The whole town was in flags and bunting, and people came from all over the state to see "by far the grandest display of exhibits ever seen in the State." R. H. Wright Papers, DU-RBMSCL, T. D. Wright to R. H. Wright, 11 Oct. 1888; *Tobacco Plant*, 12 Oct. 1888. Among those who suffered by Blackwell's bankruptcy were E. J. Parrish, J. S. Carr, John L. Markham, and J. S. Lockhart, who had lent him over $100,000 (Peter Burke Hobbs, "Plantation to Factory," Master's essay, History Department, D.U., 1971, 31–32).

72 *Tobacco Plant*, 7 Sept., 9 Nov., 16 Nov. 1888; *Globe*, 27 Jan. 1893. Parrish's quick action recalls the model for his heroics, his father, and another event of the 1880s that marked it as a watershed in Durham's maturation. D. C. Parrish, who was certainly perceived as a founding father, died in 1883 during his seventh term as mayor. His death gave Durham its first ceremonial funeral and a realization that an era had ended. The funeral was held from Trinity Church, and the names of the pallbearers read like a who's who of Durham in that era. "During the funeral," Hiram Paul related, "every business house in town was closed, and the procession of carriages was three-quarters of a mile long. No man has ever lived among us who so entwined the affections of the people around him as did Col. Parrish." Through his daughters he had more than ties of affection to many townsmen; he was father-in-law to Julian and Albert Carr, Fielding Leathers, and John S. Lockhart (Paul, *History of the Town of Durham, N.C.*, 127–28; Broadside Collection, DU-RBMSCL, "A Statement by the Present Mayor and Town Commissioners").

73 *Herald*, 4 Oct. 1938.

74 Paul, *History of the Town of Durham, N.C.*, 84; *Methodist Advance*, 2 Nov. 1880; *Recorder*, 29 Nov. 1882; Boyd, *The Story of Durham*, 259. The first club with a purely social purpose seems to have been the Durham Pleasure Club, which was formed in the middle 1870s and met in the railroad office. Among other activities, they organized a hop (*Tobacco Plant*, 12 Apr. 1876).

75 Paul, *History of the Town of Durham, N.C.*, 242–43.

76 *Tobacco Plant*, 17 May 1881.

77 Ibid., 15 Feb., 3 May 1881, 5 Jan., 5 Oct. 1887, 15 Feb. 1888; *Recorder*, 16 Mar. 1882; Paul, *History of the Town of Durham, N.C.*, 83; *Turner's Directory, 1889–90*, 22–23.

78 *Tobacco Plant*, 28 Apr. 1875, 19 Jan. 1876, 9 Mar., 27 Apr., 8 June 1887, 23 May 1888; "Record of the Proceedings of the Central Prohibition Club of Durham, N.C.," DU-RBMSCL; *Sun*, 25 Feb. 1903; Lefler and Newsome, *North Carolina*, 599.

79 *Methodist Advance*, 18 Mar. 1880; *Tobacco Plant*, 8 Nov. 1881, 8 Feb., 15 Feb., 29 Feb.,

20 July 1888. *Turner's Directory, 1889–90* listed the Durham County Medical Society with J. M. Manning as president, J. A. Smith, vice-president, J. P. Monroe, second vice-president, J. D. Roberts, secretary and treasurer, and members A. G. Carr, N. M. Johnson, W. J. H. Durham, James F. Cain, and Thomas S. Vickers, presumably most of the medical fraternity in the county.

80 Robert C. McMath, Jr., "Agrarian Protest at the Forks of the Creek: Three Subordinate Farmers' Alliances in North Carolina," *North Carolina Historical Review* 51 (1974): 41–63, examines the Mount Sylvan chapter located six miles north of Durham. William Couch Papers, DU-RBMSCL, *Constitution of the Farmers' State Alliance of North Carolina* (Raleigh, 1889); Durden, *The Dukes of Durham*, 316; *Tobacco Plant*, 7 Mar., 21 Mar., 14 Dec. 1888; *Globe*, 24 July 1890, 2 Jan. 1893, 29 Jan. 1894; R. H. Wright Papers, DU-RBMSCL, John B. Morris to Wright, 4 Dec. 1891.

81 Samuel L. Adams, *Directory of Greater Durham, North Carolina, 1902* (Durham, 1902), 16; *Globe*, 2 May 1894.

82 *Tobacco Plant*, 6 July 1887.

83 Boyd, *The Story of Durham*, 261; *Herald*, 8 Mar. 1921; *Sun*, 15 Dec. 1910.

84 R. T. Howerton, "The Rose of Sharon Baptist Church," *Trinity Archive*, 21 (1907–8): 193; *Tobacco Plant*, 16 Mar. 1887; *Herald*, 26 Apr. 1953; *Globe*, 31 Oct. 1890.

85 *Globe*, 1 Nov. 1890.

86 *Tobacco Plant*, 1 June 1887, 1 Feb., 15 Feb. 1888; *Globe*, 24 May 1894; B. N. Duke Papers, DU-RBMSCL, Southgate to Duke, 9 Jan. 1894.

87 *Tobacco Plant*, 27 July, 10 Aug. 1887, 19 July 1881, 1 Feb., 8 Feb. 1888; "Church Directory of Temple Baptist Church," c. 1932, DU-RBMSCL, North Carolina County Papers: Durham; *Herald*, 6 June 1926. The First Baptist Church sent volunteers to hold prayer meetings and Sunday school for the new group first on Vickers Avenue, then on Milton Avenue, and finally in a vacant house on Duke Street owned by William T. Blackwell. A second church building was constructed in 1907. Another even larger church (dedicated 1956) and educational building, designed by R. R. Markley, now stand on the same site (*Herald*, 10 Feb. 1941); telephone conversation with Mrs. Ruby West, 10 Feb. 1986.

88 B. N. Duke Papers, DU-RBMSCL, 7 Jan., 1 May, 12 May 1886; Wyatt T. Dixon, *Ninety Years of Duke Memorial Church, 1886–1976* (1977); *Tobacco Plant*, 27 Apr. 1887. The old church building was sold to the Congregational-Christian Church, which used it until a new church, now called Pilgrim United Church of Christ, was built on Academy Road (1966). Methodist Church Records, DU-RBMSCL, Historical Sketches, "Historic Statements of Carr Church—Durham."

89 *Sun*, 20 July 1904.

90 Ibid.; *N&O*, 28 June 1936; Duke *Chronicle*, 8 Feb. 1931. For details of his Durham connection see Sterling Seagrave, *The Soong Dynasty* (New York, 1985), 28–43, 86–91.

91 Information kindly supplied by Mrs. Eunice Austin, Angier Avenue Church secretary; *Herald*, 16 Nov. 1924, 3 Dec. 1939.

92 OCDB, 46:346; *Methodist Advance*, 22 Apr. 1880; *Tobacco Plant*, 15 Feb. 1881.

93 Telephone conversation with Mrs. Elneda Britt, 30 May 1984 (Bethesda Baptist Church); *Herald*, 4 Aug. 1940, 26 Apr. 1953, 15 Jan. 1983; interview with the Reverend Tommy W. Jordan, 20 Oct. 1985 (Red Mountain Church), DCDB 1:5, mentions Shady Hill Church land. Curtis Booker supplied the data on Ephesus Church.

94 Robert W. Winston, *It's a Far Cry* (New York, 1937), 223.

95 U.S. Post Office Department, "Records of Appointments"; *Tobacco Plant*, 2 Mar., 30 Mar., 13 Apr., 13 July 1887.

96 *Tobacco Plant*, 20 Dec. 1881; U.S. Post Office Dept., "Records of Appointments"; interview with Mildred Harris, 3 Oct. 1975; Boyd, *The Story of Durham*, 140. (Charles) *Emerson's Tobacco Belt Directory* (Greensboro, 1886), 160, lists Hunkadora and the residents of that postal area.

97 Anderson, *Piedmont Plantation*, 57, 60–62; Cameron Family Papers, SHC, vols. 151, 152, 161; *Tobacco Plant*, 1 Mar. 1882.

98 U.S. Post Office Dept., "Records of Appointments"; *Globe*, 25 Jan. 1894. Edward E. Cooke, a grandnephew of William T. Cole, says that Cole wished the post office to be named Sylvan because his sister, S. E. Cole, had founded Mount Sylvan Church there in 1885; but this was not allowed for fear of confusion with Sylva in Jackson County.

99 U.S. Post Office Dept., "Records of Appointments"; *Globe*, 25 Jan. 1894.

100 Boyd, *The Story of Durham*, 232–46; Mary Westcott and Allene Ramage, comps., *A Checklist of United States Newspapers (and Weeklies before 1900) in the General Library [Duke University]* (Durham, N.C., 1936), 508–16; *Emerson's North Carolina Tobacco Belt Directory, 1886* (Raleigh, 1886), 150–51; *Branson's North Carolina Business Directory, 1884* (Raleigh, 1884), 24. Richard B. Fitzgerald bought the type and other equipment of the *Daily Reporter* to start a newspaper "in the interest of the colored race." No known copies survive (*Tobacco Plant*, 3 June 1885).

101 Winston, *It's a Far Cry*, 223; Boyd, *The Story of Durham*, 136.

102 *Globe*, 6 Nov. 1890.

12 THE APOGEE OF AN ERA

1 Earl W. Porter, *Trinity and Duke, 1892–1924: Foundations of Duke University* (Durham, 1964), 6–8; W. M. Upchurch and M. B. Fowler, *Durham County Economic and Social* (n.p., n.d.), 66; *Globe*, 19 June 1893.

2 Boyd, *The Story of Durham*, 170; Benjamin N. Duke Papers, DU-RBMSCL, 6 Oct. 1898. B. N. Duke was the first in the family to contribute to Trinity when he gave $1,000 in 1887 (*Tobacco Plant*, 10 Aug. 1887).

3 Porter, *Trinity and Duke*, 6; Durden, *The Dukes of Durham*, 93; *Globe*, 19 June 1893; *Tobacco Plant*, 19 Oct. 1887, *Herald*, 31 Aug. 1925 (Blackwell Park).

4 *Globe*, 10 Aug. 1891; *Herald*, 31 Aug. 1925. Besides the Trinity College building and various tobacco warehouses, Leary also built Michaels drug store at Main and Mangum streets (*Globe*, 26 Feb. 1892), Mangum and Son Company (*Globe*, 3 Sept., 24 Nov. 1891), Morehead School (*Globe*, 3 Nov. 1891), his own shingle-style house on Cleveland Street (*Globe*, 11 Jan. 1893), and Saint Joseph A.M.E. Church. See Roberts, Lee, and Cleary, *The Durham Architectural and Historic Inventory*, 74, 120.

5 Porter, *Trinity and Duke*, 29; *Globe*, 11 July 1895, 19 Mar. 1896.

6 John F. Crowell Papers, Duke University Archives, Crowell's "Recollections," 208; *Globe*, 23 Jan. 1895; *Trinity College, Durham, North Carolina, Catalogue for the Year 1896–97* (Durham, 1896), 94.

7 *Globe*, 30 Jan., 21 Mar., 23 Mar. 1894; Southgate-Jones Papers (uncatalogued), DU-RBMSCL, Mattie Southgate Jones's account of Durham organizations c. 1919; *Recorder*, 16 Apr., 8 Oct. 1896; *Globe*, 18 May 1894.

8 Records of the Up-to-Date Club, North Carolina Collection, Durham County Library, *Herald* (centennial edition), 26 Apr. 1953.

9 *Sun*, 26 Apr. 1939 (50th anniversary edition); Southgate-Jones Papers, DU-RBMSCL, Mattie Jones's account of Durham organizations; *Herald*, 26 Apr. 1953.

   Other publications of the 1890s were *Saturday Night*, 1893; *National Tobacco and Grocer*, the *Durham Review*, and *Trinity League Record*, all 1894; *Christian Educator* (a Trinity College publication) and *People's Advocate*, both 1896; *Daily Record*, 1898; and *Mount Zion Record*, 1899.

10 *Tobacco Plant*, 15 Feb., 17 May, 1881, 9 Mar. 1887; *Globe*, 24 Jan., 31 Jan., 14 Feb., 25 June 1894, 26 Mar., 23 Apr. 1896; *Recorder*, 16 Apr., 23 Apr., 30 Apr. 1896. The *Recorder*, 16 July 1896, reported that Julian Carr gave the site; its 16 Apr. 1900 edition reported that Miss Carr and Mrs. Thomas H. Martin gave the site.

11 Craven-Pegram Papers, DU-RBMSCL, 7 May 1896.

12 *Recorder*, 19 Jan. 1899, 16 Apr. 1900.

13 *Sun*, 23 Jan. 1900.

14 *Globe*, 2 Sept., 25 Sept. 1891, 4 Feb. 1893, 3 Mar., 19 July, 30 Aug. 1894; Morehead Papers, DU-RBMSCL, 14 June 1892, 3 Jan., 13 Jan., 30 Jan. 1894.

15 Southgate-Jones Papers, DU-RBMSCL, James H. Southgate's history of the conservatory in *Calendar of the Southern Conservatory of Music, Durham, North Carolina, 1901–02* (Raleigh, 1901); *Sun*, 10 Mar. 1900.

16 B. N. Duke Papers, DU-RBMSCL, Correspondence: 14 Sept., 12 Oct., 13 Oct., 31 Oct. 1899, Newspaper clippings: *Recorder*, 16 Apr. 1900.

17 *Sun*, 7 Feb., 12 Sept. 1900.

18 Ibid., 9 Apr., 13 June 1902; B. N. Duke Papers, DU-RBMSCL, 24 Apr. 1902; *Recorder*, 18 Jan., 20 Apr. 1909.

19 *Recorder*, 9 Jan. 1895, 14 Jan., 4 Feb., 11 Feb. 1897, 19 Jan. 1899, *Sun*, 1 Jan., 4 Oct. 1900.

20 *Recorder*, 9 Apr. 1896, *Globe*, 3 Nov. 1891, 10 Oct. 1895.

21 *Globe*, 27 May, 21 June, 11 Aug., 12 Oct., 13 Oct. 1893, 11 July 1895; *Recorder*, 7 May 1907; Richard H. Wright Papers, DU-RBMSCL, 2 Nov. 1885.

22 *Herald*, 22 Mar. 1876, 3 Sept. 1913, 2 Feb. 1922, 26 Feb. 1923; *Branson's North Carolina Business Directory for 1877–78* (Richmond, 1877), 231; *Recorder*, 27 June 1893, 20 Aug. 1896, 20 Oct. 1908, 24 May 1912; *Tobacco Plant*, 4 Jan. 1882; *Globe*, 11 June 1890, 7 July 1893, 11 July 1895; *Herald*, 3 Sept. 1913, 2 Feb. 1922, 26 Sept. 1923.

23 *Globe*, 25 May 1891, 2 Jan., 10 Jan., 12 Jan., 13 Jan. 1893.

24 Ibid., 31 Jan., 1 Feb., 9 Feb., 10 Feb., 12 Mar., 14 Mar., 3 Apr., 4 Apr., 15 Apr. 1893.

25 Ibid., 26 Jan., 2 Feb., 8 Feb., 10 May, 18 July 1893, 17 Oct. 1894.

26 *Recorder*, 16 Apr. 1896.

27 *Tobacco Plant*, 27 July, 12 Oct. 1887, 29 Feb. 1888; *Globe*, 5 Mar. 1894; *Recorder*, 25 Nov. 1900; *Sun*, 19 Feb. 1900, 10 Mar. 1903; James C. Biggs Papers, SHC, Address c. 1950 concerning his recollections of Durham in the 1880s; *Herald*, 13 Mar. 1912.

28 McMannen Family Papers, DU-RBMSCL, 1892; Jarratt-Puryear Papers, DU-RBMSCL, 8 May 1889; B. N. Duke Papers, DU-RBMSCL, 3 Mar., 12 Dec. 1892, 3 Jan. 1896, 3 Aug. 1898, 31 Jan. 1900; *Recorder*, 17 Dec. 1903; *Herald*, 13 June 1937; Durden, *The Dukes of Durham*, 86; *Globe*, 25 Jan. 1894. In 1876 Claudius Augustin Winfield Barham, the auctioneer, having got hold of a cure for hemorrhoids, "a malodorous salve," set his wife and daughter to manufacturing it in the attic. The next year he sold the rights to W. T. Blackwell and Julian Carr (Richard F. Riley, "The Case of the Unperceived U.S. Watermark," *American Philatelist* [Sept. 1977], 692–94). The imposing Tuscan villa that Alexander Jackson Davis built for Governor John M. Morehead became the Keeley Institute.

29 *Globe*, 6 May, 13 May 1893, 11 July, 27 July, 30 July, 25 Aug. 1894, 11 July 1895.

30 Minutes of the Durham Town Board, 1869–73.

31 *Sun*, 17 Feb., 19 Feb., 20 Feb. 1900, 5 Mar. 1901, 31 Mar., 7 Apr., 16 Apr. 1904. Angier's real name was Jonathan Cicero Angier.

32 *Globe*, 12 May 1894; *Recorder*, 20 Feb., 21 Feb. 1895. Watts nursing school was established in connection with the hospital.

33 Charles L. Van Noppen, comp., *In Memoriam George Washington Watts* (1922); *Herald*, 8 Mar. 1921; Roberts, Lea, and Cleary, *The Durham Architectural and Historic Inventory*, 266.

34 Pamela Preston Reynolds, "The Interaction between Public Attitudes and a Philanthropist's Dream: Watts Hospital, 1895–1976" (history honors paper, 1979), D.U. Archives; *Globe*, 9 Sept. 1889, 26 Sept., 16 Oct., 5 Dec. 1891, 11 Feb. 1892, 2 Nov. 1893.

35 *Globe*, 13 Nov., 15 Nov., 18 Nov. 1893.

36 Ibid., 15 Oct., 30 Oct., 23 Nov. 1891, 15 May, 16 May, 15 Nov. 1893.

37 Ibid., 23 Jan. 1892.

38 Ibid., 6 Nov. 1891, 20 Feb., 28 Apr., 13 Dec., 23 Dec. 1893, 12 Jan., 7 May, 18 June 1894, 11 July 1895. The Norfolk and Western Railroad bought Duke's beltline in 1900 (*Sun*, 15 Feb. 1900), *Souvenir Edition of the Durham Daily Sun, Complimentary to the North Carolina Press Association* [23–25] July 1890; R. H. Wright Papers, DU-RBM-SCL, 10 Dec., 21 Dec. 1892.

39 B. N. Duke Papers, DU-RBMSCL, 29 Jan. 1895, 9 Nov. 1896, 27 Feb., 21 Dec. 1897; *Recorder*, 16 Apr. 1900.

40 Durden, *The Dukes of Durham*, 128–30; B. N. Duke Papers, DU-RBMSCL, 8 Apr., 9 Apr., 20 Apr. 1892; Washington Duke Papers, DU-RBMSCL, 26 Apr. 1892; *Globe*, 13 Jan. 1894, 11 July 1895. For stockholders, construction, and management information see Erwin Cotton Mills Company Papers, DU-RBMSCL.

41 Durham Hosiery Mills Papers, DU-RBMSCL. S. W. Holman was manager for the Graham firm. The time book shows that in 1896–97 the workers made about four cents an hour, working from sixty-eight to seventy hours a week. *Globe*, 12 Dec. 1895.

42 *Sun*, 21 Feb., 28 Feb., 3 Mar. 1900. A soap manufacturing company, established by J. R. Blacknall, president, J. T. Pinnix, vice-president, and J. W. Walker, secretary and treasurer, made laundry soap, a softener, and a sizing soap used by the cotton mills (*Globe*, 18 July 1895).

43 Boyd, *The Story of Durham*, 93–94; *Globe*, 25 May 1891, 8 June 1892; B. N. Duke Papers, DU-RBMSCL, 26 Apr., 27 Apr., May 1892.

44 B. N. Duke Papers, DU-RBMSCL, 12 Mar. 1896, 6 Nov. 1899; Boyd, *The Story of Durham*, 94; *Sun*, 19 Feb., 1 Mar., 5 Mar., 28 Apr. 1900, 23 Mar. 1901; *Herald*, 28 July 1906; *Recorder*, 8 Nov. 1907.

45 *Sun*, 14 May, 31 Dec. 1900; *Recorder*, 19 May 1911; B. N. Duke Papers, DU-RBMSCL, 2 July 1900; *Sun*, 17 Apr., 15 May, 28 June 1901.

46 *Globe*, 5 July 1893, 17 Jan., 18 Jan. 1894, 6 Feb. 1896.

47 Ibid., 6 Feb. 1896.

48 Ibid., 5 July, 20 Nov., 14 Dec. 1893; B. N. Duke Papers, DU-RBMSCL, 8 Mar., 27 Nov. 1899, Sept. 1900; Durden, *The Dukes of Durham*, 74–76.

49 *Globe*, 27 Nov., 12 Dec. 1891, 21 Oct. 1893; B. N. Duke Papers, DU-RBMSCL, 5 Aug. 1895, 18 Aug. 1896.

50 B. N. Duke Papers, DU-RBMSCL, Correspondence: 20 July 1891, 10 Sept. 1894, 5 Sept. 1895, Oversize Papers: Plat of Duke Farm, 26 Feb. 1894, also undated and unsigned plat in 1895 folder; *Sun*, 3 July 1900; Southgate-Jones Papers, DU-RBMSCL, Southgate Jones's "Autobiography," 45–46, and Mattie Jones's account of Durham organizations.

51 Jeffrey J. Crow, "Cracking the Solid South: Populism and the Fusionist Interlude," in Lindley S. Butler and Alan D. Watson, eds., *The North Carolina Experience: An Interpretation and Documentary History* (Chapel Hill, 1984), 333–49; Lefler and Newsome, *North Carolina*, 547.

52 Lefler and Newsome, *North Carolina*, 546–47.

53 Ibid., 526, 529; *Globe*, 5 June 1894; B. N. Duke Papers, DU-RBMSCL, 9 Oct. 1892; *Tobacco Plant*, 31 Aug., 7 Sept., 5 Oct. 1888.

54 B. N. Duke Papers, DU-RBMSCL, 9 Oct. 1892.

55 Winston, *It's a Far Cry*, 177, 197, 200–201.

56 *Globe*, 4 July, 1 Aug., 15 Sept., 28 Sept., 8 Oct., 9 Oct. 1894; Lefler and Newsome, *North Carolina*, 550.

57 Lefler and Newsome, *North Carolina*, 552–53, 555–58; *Recorder*, 10 Dec. 1896. In 1896 the National (Prohibition) Party's nominee for vice-president was James Southgate (*Recorder*, 4 June 1896).

58 Lefler and Newsome, *North Carolina*, 559–60.

59 *Sun*, 11 Apr., 12 Apr., 14 Apr., 18 Apr., 20 Apr., 21 Apr., 20 July, 21 July 1900.

60 Ibid., 21 July 1900.

61 Ibid., 3 Aug., 6 Aug. 1900.

62 Robert McCants Andrews, *John Merrick: A Biographical Sketch* (Durham, 1920), 1–34; Walter B. Weare, *Black Business in the New South: A Social History of the North Carolina Mutual Life Insurance Company* (Urbana, 1973), 19–20, 50–51; *Sun*, 10 July 1901.

63 Weare, *Black Business in the New South*, 14–15, 32–38; Andrews, *John Merrick*, 43–46.

64 Frank H. White, "The Economic and Social Development of Negroes in North Carolina since 1900" (Ph.D. diss., New York University, 1960), 17–18; Weare, *Black Business in the New South*, 16n, 46, 46n, 48.

65 Weare, *Black Business in the New South*, 56–59; *Herald*, 31 May 1921.

66 W. E. B. Du Bois, "The Upbuilding of Black Durham," *World's Work* 23 (Jan. 1912): 336; Weare, *Black Business in the New South*, 52–55; *Sun*, 2 Jan. 1900; Winston, *It's a Far Cry*, 248.

67 Weare, *Black Business in the New South*, 79–80; Boyd, *The Story of Durham*, 219–20; Andrews, *John Merrick*, 46–47. Moore was one of four founders of the Old North State Medical Society (1887), the oldest black medical society in the world (White, "The Economic and Social Development of Negroes in North Carolina since 1900," 116).

68 Boyd, *The Story of Durham*, 221; B. N. Duke Papers, DU-RBMSCL, 6 July 1901.

69 Boyd, *The Story of Durham*, 221; *Paths towards Freedom: A Biographical History of Blacks and Indians in North Carolina by Blacks and Indians* (Raleigh, 1976), 60; B. N. Duke Papers, DU-RBMSCL, 1 Oct. 1902; Andrews, *John Merrick*, 46–47; Thomas H. Houck, "A Newspaper History of Race Relations in Durham, 1910–1940" (M.A. thesis, D.U., 1941), 151–56; John B. Flowers and Marguerite Schumann, *Bull Durham and Beyond: A Tour Guide to City and County* (Durham, 1976), 58; *Herald*, 16 Aug., 20 Aug. 1925.

70 B. N. Duke Papers, DU-RBMSCL, 22 Feb. 1900, 18 May, 13 Aug. 1901; *Recorder*, 15 Nov. 1907; Durden, *The Dukes of Durham*, 145–46; *Sun*, 12 Feb. 1900.

71 *Herald*, 26 Apr. 1953 (centennial edition): *Turner and Co.'s Durham Directory for the Years 1889 and 1890* (Winston, 1889), 24; *Globe*, 13 Feb. 1892.

72 *Globe*, 31 Aug. 1893; *Herald*, 26 Apr. 1953 (centennial edition). Additional information from F. H. Alston.

73 Jerome Dowd, "Rev. Moses Hester," *Trinity Archive* 9 (Feb. 1896): 283; *Globe*, 20 Dec. 1893; Craven-Pegram Papers, DU-RBMSCL, 31 Aug. 1940; *Sun*, 24 Sept. 1901; *Recorder*, 14 July 1908.

74 "Sierra Leone Missionary," *World for Christ*, 1, no. 4 (Apr. 1895): 1; *Globe*, 14 Sept., 15 Sept. 1893.

75 *Globe*, 16 Nov. 1893; B. N. Duke Papers, DU-RBMSCL, 27 Aug. 1894, 10 Oct., 12 Oct. 1895, 14 Nov. 1896, 31 July 1898, 1 Mar. 1900, 9 June 1900, 25 Apr. 1902, 15 Nov. 1905.

76 Two pamphlets both entitled "Mt. Calvary Baptist Church, Bahama, North Carolina," covering different years, were kindly lent me by Mrs. Caroline Mack through Mr. John Jones.

77 B. N. Duke Papers, DU-RBMSCL, 14 Nov. 1892; *Recorder*, 16 Apr., 9 July 1896; *Herald*, 13 Jan. 1906; William F. O'Brien, *The Memoirs of Monsignor William Francis O'Brien* (Durham, 1958), 71–88.

78 Boyd, *The Story of Durham*, 203–4; *Herald*, 26 Apr. 1953; *Recorder*, 13 May 1885, 5 Dec. 1895; Eli Evans, *The Provincials* (New York, 1973), 15–17.

79 B. N. Duke Papers, DU-RBMSCL, 9 Feb. 1894; *Herald*, 5 Dec. 1926, 4 Jan. 1942; Roberts, Lea, and Cleary, *The Durham Architectural and Historic Inventory*, 154. Thomas C. Atwood, an engineer from Massachusetts who came to Chapel Hill in 1921 and formed T. C. Atwood Organization, established a partnership with Arthur C. Nash, an architect from Washington, D.C., and in the 1930s with H. Raymond Weeks. H. Raymond Weeks, Inc. was bought out by Harris and Pyne. Atwood and his partners were responsible for buildings at UNC, Yale, Cornell, and other colleges, as well as

many structures of all kinds in Durham and vicinity. (Information from George C. Pyne, Jr., and Atwood's scrapbook in Pyne's possession.)

80 *Herald*, 19 July 1922; Roberts, Lea, and Cleary, *The Durham Architectural and Historic Inventory*, 102; Dixon, *Ninety Years of Duke Memorial Church*, 105; Boyd, *The Story of Durham*, 199.

81 *Sun*, 20 Dec. 1902; *Herald*, 24 Apr. 1914, 6 Jan. 1917; 16 May 1926, 21 June 1927; *Recorder*, 27 Aug. 1907; Childs, *Centennial History of Trinity Methodist Church*; Boyd, *The Story of Durham*, 200. Professor Childs listed another failed Methodist mission: South Durham, a Sunday school located at Cobb and South streets under R. F. Piper's supervision. See also *Recorder*, 11 July 1895.

82 *Recorder*, 25 Feb. 1908; *Herald*, 16 Dec. 1913; Joseph W. Watson and C. Franklin Grill, *North Carolina Conference Historical Directory*, 1984; Everette Latta Roberts, *History of Bethany M. E. Church, South, Durham, North Carolina* (1950).

83 *Herald*, 22 Nov. 1925 (Mt. Sylvan); *Globe*, 27 Aug. 1894; Watson and Grill, *Historical Directory*; Tilley and Moseley, *History of Rougemont Methodist Episcopal Church*.

84 Judy Hogan, "The Teller of Tales: From Homer's Ithaca to Durham County's Rougemont," Exhibit, 1983, North Carolina Collection, Durham County Library, Judy Blalock's narrative.

85 *Globe*, 23 Mar., 24 Mar. 1894; Richard B. Westin, "The State and Segregated Schools: Negro Public Education in North Carolina, 1863–1923" (Ph.D. diss., D.U., 1966), 75.

86 Southgate-Jones Papers, DU-RBMSCL, 30 June 1859.

87 N. A. Ramsey, ed., *Durham Almanac . . . 1896* (Durham, 1896), 34.

88 B. N. Duke Papers, DU-RBMSCL, 18 Dec. 1896, 27 Mar., 6 Apr. 1897; Durden, *The Dukes of Durham*, 105, 110; Records of the President, Trinity College, D.U. Archives, W. Duke to the Board of Trustees, 20 Apr. 1903. Later Duke rescinded the condition.

89 Westin, "The State and Segregated Schools," viii, 100–123.

90 Cameron Family Papers, SHC, 18 Feb. 1889; B. N. Duke Papers, DU-RBMSCL, 3 Nov. 1891, 8 Jan. 1892.

91 *Globe*, 22 Oct., 3 Nov. 1891, 8 Jan. 1892, 11 July 1895, 16 Apr. 1896, B. N. Duke Papers, DU-RBMSCL, 26 Sept. 1896, 19 June 1897; Ramsey, *Durham Almanac . . . 1892*, 69; *Sun*, 26 Apr. 1939 (50th anniversary edition), 1 Feb. 1985.

92 *Globe*, 2 June 1894, 20 Feb. 1896, *Recorder*, 28 Jan. 1897, 16 Apr. 1900; B. N. Duke Papers, DU-RBMSCL, 5 Aug. 1891, 5 Sept. 1898; *Sun*, 26 Apr. 1939.

93 *Globe*, 30 Oct. 1890, 7 Nov. 1891, 12 Jan., 16 Jan., 18 Jan., 25 Jan. 1892; "First Annual Announcement, Trinity High School, 1891–2," *North Carolina Pamphlets* 3 (nos. 21–33), in Duke University Library; Craven-Pegram Papers, DU-RBMSCL, 19 Sept. 1898; *Herald*, 5 Aug. 1922; Fran Summerell, "Trinity Park School, 1898–1922" (history honors paper, 1975–76), D.U. Archives; S. B. Underwood, "Joseph Francis Bivins," *Trinity Archive* 18 (1904–5): 1–10.

94 *Globe*, 6 Mar. 1894, 9 June 1894; *Sun*, 26 Apr. 1939.

95 Account of Milton Hill school by Mary Russell Harris, in possession of her daughter, Katherine Harris Reade.

96 Winston, *It's a Far Cry*, 174; *Sun*, 24 Nov. 1900; Porter, *Trinity and Duke*, 81.

97 Porter, *Trinity and Duke*, 82.

98 Winston, *It's a Far Cry*, 232–33.

99 *Sun*, 15 Oct. 1896; Louis R. Harlan, ed., *The Papers of Booker T. Washington*, 8 vols. (1972–84), 4:227–28. I am grateful to William E. King for bringing this incident to my attention.

100 Lefler and Newsome, *North Carolina*, 555–62; C. Vann Woodward, *Origins of the New South, 1877–1913* (Baton Rouge, 1970), 324, 350–52.

101 John S. Bassett, "Stirring Up the Fires of Race Antipathy," *South Atlantic Quarterly* 2 (1903): 297–305.

102 Joel Williamson, *The Crucible of Race* (New York, 1985), 259–61; Porter, *Trinity and Duke*, 99; Washington Duke Papers, DU-RBMSCL, 27 Jan. 1902.

103 B. N. Duke Papers, DU-RBMSCL, 13 Nov., 26 Nov. 1903; Porter, *Trinity and Duke*, 131–33. See also Bassett Papers, D.U. Archives.

104 B. N. Duke Papers, DU-RBMSCL, 30 Dec. 1903; Durden, *The Dukes of Durham*, 112.

105 *Globe*, 20 May, 30 May 1893.

13 SOCIAL CHALLENGES

1 Benjamin Duke first bought a corner house at Fifth Avenue and Eighty-second Street where he lived in New York until he built a house at Fifth Avenue and Eighty-ninth Street (*Sun*, 17 Apr., 28 June 1901; Durden, *The Dukes of Durham*, 169, 171).

2 A new industrial success had its beginning in 1910 when two pharmacists, Germain Bernard and Commodore T. Council, incorporated the B.C. Remedy Company to manufacture B.C. Headache Tablets. The originator of the pill's formula (according to his son, Professor A. C. Jordan) was Dr. A. C. Jordan, whose office was above the Bernard and Council drugstore and whose patients derived so much relief from Dr. Jordan's prescription that the astute druggists decided to patent it, with the doctor's permission. The company was dissolved in 1967. (W. C. Dula, *Durham and Her People* [Durham, 1951], 26; *Herald*, 8 June 1913; Book of Corporations 19:306, 543; Register of Deeds, Durham County Courthouse.)

3 Within the years 1901 to 1916 the following early Durhamites died: Sterling R. Carrington (*Recorder*, 28 Feb. 1901), Charles H. Norton (*Sun*, 4 Mar. 1901), William ("Tip") Lipscomb (*Sun*, 6 June 1902), Atlas M. Rigsbee (*Sun*, 30 Nov. 1903), William T. Blackwell (*Sun*, 13 Nov. 1903), Hiram V. Paul (*Sun*, 24 Apr. 1903), Alexander Walker (*Sun*, 24 Dec. 1904), William Mangum (*Herald*, 25 Nov. 1905), Washington Duke (*Herald*, 9 May 1905), Felix Markham (*Recorder*, 16 July 1907), N. A. Ramsey (*Herald*, 12 Sept. 1906), Virginius Ballard (*Herald*, 25 Nov. 1906), Louis A. Carr (*Recorder*, 23 Sept. 1909), James F. Lyon (*Recorder*, 21 Mar. 1911), John V. Rigsbee (*Herald*, 23 July 1912), Gabriel A. Barbee (*Herald*, 21 Aug. 1912), William Thomas Carrington (*Herald*, 16 Aug. 1913), James B. Warren (*Herald*, 16 Dec. 1913), James Southgate (*Herald*, 29 Oct. 1914), Caleb B. Green (*Herald*, 20 Aug. 1916), James H. Southgate (*Herald*, 30 Sept. 1916), William Anderson Guthrie (*Herald*, 15 Oct. 1916), and John E. Suitt, (*Herald*, 18 Oct. 1916). The Dukes were much harassed in their personal lives during the first decade of the new century. James's entanglement with Mrs. Lillian McCredy brought scandal. Soon after legitimizing their relationship (probably for his father's sake) he was forced to initiate divorce proceedings that made his most intimate affairs public knowledge (Durden, *The Dukes of Durham*, 160–65). Brodie Duke went through an even more lurid scandal with his third wife, Alice Webb, after he had divorced his second, Minnie Woodward, on charges of desertion. In 1910 Brodie was married again, to Wylanta Rochelle, whom he had sent to finishing school and with whom he eloped when she was eighteen (Durden, *The Dukes of Durham*, 162, 204; *Herald*, 9 May, 10 May, 11 May, 12 May 1905).

4 The large collection of Richard Harvey Wright papers in the Duke University Manuscript Department is the best source of personal and business information about Wright. The *Sun*, 3 July 1902, has a good summary of his career to that date. *Sun*, 26 Feb. 1901; *Recorder*, 3 June 1885; *N&O*, 5 Mar. 1929; Wright Papers, DU-RBMSCL, 21 Jan., 18 Feb. 1875, 17 Mar. 1886, 1886–89 passim; *Herald*, 5 Mar. 1929, 26 Apr. 1953; Boyd, *The Story of Durham*, 93.

5 B. N. Duke Papers, DU-RBMSCL, 13 July 1900, 6 June 1903; *Recorder*, 16 Apr. 1900 gives Watts as president of Pearl Mills and Erwin of Durham Cotton Manufacturing Co.

6 *Sun*, 1 Jan. 1901, 24 May 1902; Durden, *The Dukes of Durham*, 137–38.

7 B. N. Duke Papers, DU-RBMSCL, Erwin to Duke, 17 Jan. 1901; *Recorder*, 29 Jan., 19 Mar. 1909.

8 Julian S. Carr, Jr., "What Made Our Business Grow?" *System* 35 (Feb. 1919): 203, "Building a Business on the Family Plan," *System* 36 (July 1919): 48–49; *Herald*, 18 Mar. 1922.

9 Durham Hosiery Mills letterhead in the Edward J. Parrish Papers, DU-RBMSCL, J. S. Carr to Mrs. Parrish, 13 Jan. 1921, shows nine mills; Book of Incorporations, 1:397, Orange County Register of Deeds, County Courthouse, Hillsborough, lists a sixteenth mill. Boyd, *The Story of Durham*, 127, gives the number as fifteen factories at approximately the same date.

10 *Recorder*, 12 Feb. 1909; *Herald*, 22 June 1912, 14 May 1914; Julian Carr, Jr., "What Made Our Business Grow?" 201–7, "Building a Business on the Family Plan," 47–50.

11 *Recorder*, 16 June 1910; *Herald*, 27 Apr. 1913.

12 *Herald*, 8 Dec. 1914 tells of a government contract with the Carr mills for 300,000 soldiers' socks. Ibid., 13 Apr., 25 May 1915, 9 Jan., 19 Mar., 28 May 1916, 15 Jan. 1918.

13 Ibid., 22 Nov. 1919.

14 Harley E. Jolley, "The Labor Movement in North Carolina, 1880–1922," *North Carolina Historical Review* 30 (1953): 354–75. See also Melton McLaurin, *Paternalism and Protest: The Knights of Labor in the South* (Westport, Conn., 1978).

15 H. M. Douty, "Early Labor Organization in North Carolina, 1880–1900," *South Atlantic Quarterly* 34 (Jan. 1935): 261; *Journal of United Labor*, 6 Aug. 1887, 2468; J. B. Duke Papers, University Archives, Letterbook 1:47, Duke to D. B. Strouse, 16 Mar. 1888; J. F. Crowell Papers, D.U. Archives, Scrap Book 1890, Durham *Recorder* clipping, 6 Aug. 1887; Lanier Rand, "I Had to Like It: A Study of a Durham Textile Community," history honors essay, UNC, 1977, Appendix E, 83–85.

16 B. N. Duke Papers, DU-RBMSCL, C. A. Jordan to Duke, 22 Feb. [1893]; Crowell Papers, D.U. Archives, Scrap Book 1890, clipping from Durham *Recorder*, 24 May 1886 and another undated clipping concerning the facts of Strickland's life; Rand, "I Had to Like It," 85; Douty, "Early Labor Organization," 263; Jolley, "Labor Movement in North Carolina," 362.

17 *Sun*, 8 Aug., 17 Aug., 18 Aug., 20 Aug. 1900.

18 Ibid., 18 Aug., 29 Aug., 30 Aug. 1900.

19 Ibid., 3 Aug. 1903, 13 Dec. 1904; *Herald*, 25 Apr. 1905, 3 Sept. 1906; *Recorder*, 25 June 1907; *Herald*, 26 Apr., 27 Apr. 1913, 10 Sept. 1916. The Farmers' Educational and Co-operative Union attracted farmers at this time. J. D. Fletcher was president of the first Durham chapter (1909), W. H. Wilkins, vice-president, and S. M. Suitt, secretary-treasurer. This union, like the others, bore the marks of a fraternal organization. It stood for diversified, scientific, and businesslike farming. Durham County had fourteen Farmers' Unions by 1911 with a total membership of 300 (*Recorder*, 1 Aug. 1911).

20 *Herald*, 1 Oct., 10 Nov., 26 Nov. 1916, 9 Feb., 19 Aug. 1917.

21 B. N. Duke Papers, DU-RBMSCL, 29 Jan., 1 Feb. 1895; *Sun*, 31 Jan. 1901.

22 Lizzie F. Burch Papers, DU-RBMSCL, "Child Labor in N.C."; *Herald*, 6 Mar. 1913, 9 Aug., 3 Dec. 1916.

23 Lefler and Newsome, *North Carolina*, 591; Rand, "I Had to Like It," 46, 47, 66, 82.

24 Rand, "I Had to Like It," 66; *Sun*, 31 Jan. 1901.

25 *Recorder*, 14 Feb., 19 Sept. 1911; *Herald*, 18 Jan. 1912, 5 Apr., 14 June, 16 June 1914, 31 July 1915, 19 Dec. 1919. In 1914 G. E. and H. C. Rawls also adopted a profit-sharing plan for their twenty-one employees, mostly clerks in their department store. At the same time store hours were cut to eight daily, which meant opening at 9 A.M., later than others. Each sales clerk was to receive a percentage of the profits of the goods he sold in addition to a regular salary. Even the elevator boy was to participate in the dividends distributed every six months (*Herald*, 4 Feb. 1914).

26 Erwin Mills Company Papers, DU-RBMSCL, Profit-Sharing Committee Awards file, William A. Erwin to Benjamin Duke, 11 Mar. 1916, Alexander Sands to William A. Erwin, 11 Apr. 1916; Harriet L. Herring, *Welfare Work in Mill Villages: The Story of Extra-Mill Activities in North Carolina* (Chapel Hill, 1929), 110–11; *Herald*, 25 May, 18 July 1915.

27 Rand, "I Had to Like It," 66–67; *Recorder*, 15 Jan., 3 May 1907. William A. Erwin gave the money for the new Chapel of the Cross, built in Chapel Hill in 1925 (*Herald*, 15 May 1925).

28 In 1891 an antitrust suit was brought in Texas against American Tobacco alleging that the company forced grocers there to sell only American Tobacco products. Five years later James B. Duke and the directors of the company were indicted for "conducting a monopoly in the paper cigarette trade." (*Daily Globe*, 5 Dec. 1891. *Recorder*, 14 May 1896.) For a concise history of the corporate deals in the tobacco industry of James B. Duke and his associates see Durden, *The Dukes of Durham*, 56–81.

29 Ibid., 62–69; *Sun*, 13 Oct. 1904.

30 Durden, *The Dukes of Durham*, 77–79; *Sun*, 23 Mar., 19 Dec. 1901, 19 Apr., 29 Sept. 1902, 24 Jan. 1903; *Herald*, 26 Apr. 1953 (centennial edition). Durham's first and oldest tobacco manufacturer, the Robert F. Morris Company, was dissolved in 1904 and absorbed by the American Tobacco Company (*Sun*, 2 July 1904; *Herald*, 22 Jan. 1920).

    Duke and his associates formed the American Cigar Company in 1901. Cigar-making had been carried on in Durham in a small way in the 1890s. *Branson's Directory for 1897* listed the W. P. Henry, Samuel Kramer, and J. T. Mallory cigar companies. In 1900 S. R. Carrington started a cigar company and made the brands "Southern Beauty," "Sporting Club," and "Dead Shot."

31 Durden, *The Dukes of Durham*, 165–68; *Recorder*, 30 May, 1 Dec. 1911; *Herald*, 20 Feb., 27 Apr. 1912, 5 Sept. 1915, 21 Sept., 10 Nov. 1916.

32 *Recorder*, 13 Nov. 1908, 1 Dec. 1910.

33 Durden, *The Dukes of Durham*, 181–85; *Recorder*, 15 Dec. 1910.

34 *Recorder*, 3 Oct. 1911.

35 Margaret Battle Bridgers, "A History of Social Work in Durham County" (M.A. thesis, UNC, 1926), 1–21; *Recorder*, 31 July 1908; "Board of Charities and Public Welfare" (Durham [1923]).

36 Bridgers, "A History of Social Work in Durham County," 21–22; *Herald*, 10 Jan. 1913.

37 *Sun*, 12 Jan. 1901, 2 Aug., 4 Aug. 1902; *Herald*, 7 July 1914; *Recorder*, 11 Nov. 1909, 29 Dec. 1910; Murray, *Proud Shoes*, 252.

38 *Recorder*, 30 June, 15 Sept., 17 Nov., 29 Dec. 1910, 5 Sept., 26 Sept. 1911; *Herald*, 13 Feb., 8 Oct. 1912, 7 July 1914. An ironic footnote to Bowling's involvement with pellagra was his honorary LL.D. awarded by Union Christian College in recognition of his research into the disease, which, he claimed, was caused not by malnutrition but by a germ (*Herald*, 21 June 1923).

39 *Herald*, 22 July 1914; Murray, *Proud Shoes*, 252–54.

40 *Herald*, 4 Jan., 7 Jan., 10 Jan., 11 Jan., 26 Nov. 1913, 4 Mar., 2 June, 7 July, 14 July, 21 July, 22 July 1914, 29 Aug. 1915. The incorporators of Mercy Hospital were C. A. Adams, A. J. Pollard, W. C. Lindsey, J. B. Mason, R. O. Everett, and T. H. Scoggins; Record of Corporations, 2:478, Register of Deeds, Durham County Courthouse, 29 Oct. 1912.

41 James F. Gifford, Jr., *The Evolution of a Medical Center: A History of Medicine at Duke University to 1941* (Durham, 1972), 130–35; Julian M. Ruffin and David T. Smith, "Studies on Pellagra at the Duke University School of Medicine," in Seale Harris, ed., *Clinical Pellagra* (St. Louis, 1941), 194–247; Milton Terris, *Goldberger on Pellagra* (Baton Rouge, 1964), 3–16; *Herald*, 28 July 1957, 2 Nov. 1938.

42 In 1905 a joint city-county health officer had been appointed—Dr. Thomas A. Mann—

but he resigned in 1906, and the city reorganized its health committee with Dr. Mann as its own health officer (Roddey M. Ligon, Jr., *A Report on the Durham County Health Department* [Chapel Hill, 1960]). *Recorder*, 20 Aug., 16 July 1907; *Charter and Ordinances of the City of Durham* (Durham, 1908), chapter 15, section 35; Anderson, *Piedmont Plantation*, 207.

43 *Recorder*, 10 Dec. 1907; Van Noppen, comp., *In Memoriam George Washington Watts*; *Recorder*, 2 Dec. 1909.

44 *Recorder*, 17 June 1909; Ligon, *A Report on the Durham County Health Department*; *Sanitary Code of the Board of Health, Durham, North Carolina* (Durham, 1909).

45 *Recorder*, 22 Dec. 1910, 3 Feb., 7 Feb. 1911; *Herald*, 2 June 1912; 15 Feb., 21 Feb., 8 Apr., 6 May, 6 June, 13 Dec. 1913; Ligon, *A Report on the Durham County Health Department*; *Sun*, 2 Mar. 1939.

46 Minutes, Durham County and City Board of Health, May 6, 1918–Nov. 7, 1921; Durham County Health Department, unbound report of health director for 1914.

47 Southgate-Jones Papers, DU-RBMSCL, 15 June 1909, 1 Apr., 11 July, 18 Nov. 1911, 27 Mar. 1912, and unprocessed papers; *Recorder*, 24 Mar. 1911.

48 Southgate-Jones Papers, 19 Apr., 21 Aug. 1912, Southgate Jones, "Autobiography," 4, 10; Anderson, *Piedmont Plantation*, 45; Hillsborough *Recorder*, 3 Jan. 1855; *Globe*, 6 Apr. 1893, *Sun*, 14 Sept. 1900, 6 June 1902; *Herald*, 8 Jan., 12 Jan., 20 Oct. 1915, 12 Jan., 21 Jan. 1916.

49 *Recorder*, 3 Mar. 1908, 8 Dec. 1911; *Herald*, 11 Feb., 12 Feb. 1914; Southgate-Jones Papers, DU-RBMSCL, unprocessed papers.

50 *Herald*, 21 Jan., 23 May, 13 June, 7 July 1916, 22 July 1917. The *Herald*, 4 Jan. 1916, contains all the health services reports for the previous year.

51 *Recorder*, 3 Feb. 1910, 7 Mar., 21 Mar. 1911; *Herald*, 12 Oct., 21 Nov., 23 Nov. 1913, 4 Aug. 1914, 26 June, 18 July 1915, 19 July 1919.

52 Dr. James C. Johnson died of peritonitis in 1916 (*Herald*, 6 May 1916). Victor Bryant, "unsurpassed as a trial lawyer" and a law partner of Robert Winston, died at the age of fifty-three following an operation for appendicitis in 1920 (*Herald*, 2 Sept. 1920). Dr. Deryl Hart, head of surgery at Duke University, pioneered in combating septicemia in operations by the use of ultraviolet lights (Gifford, *The Evolution of a Medical Center*, 147–48).

53 *Recorder*, 14 June 1907, 6 Mar., 17 Apr. 1908; *Herald*, 5 Jan., 21 May 1912.

54 *Sun*, 20 Dec. 1901, 16 Jan. 1903; Jay M. Arena and John P. McGovern, *Davison of Duke* (Durham, 1980), 3.

55 *Sun*, 2 Jan. 1902; *Recorder*, 3 Jan. 1908; Lewis S. Gannett, ed., *The Family Book of Verse* (New York, 1961), 277–78.

56 *Sun*, 20 Dec. 1901; Weare, *Black Business in the New South*, 76; *Recorder*, 3 July, 31 July 1908, 14 Aug. 1908.

57 Andrews, *John Merrick*, 50–55; *Recorder*, 31 July 1908.

58 Weare, *Black Business in the New South*, 62–63, 78; *Sun*, 12 July 1901.

59 *Recorder*, 31 July, 7 Aug. 1908; Andrews, *John Merrick*, 56–57.

60 Booker T. Washington, "Durham, North Carolina, a City of Negro Enterprise," *Independent* 70 (Mar. 1911): 642–50; Weare, *Black Business in the New South*, 82–83.

61 Weare, *Black Business in the New South*, 79–81, 122.

62 *Recorder*, 18 Dec. 1908.

63 *Herald*, 11 May 1912, 30 June 1927, 12 Feb. 1928; *Recorder*, 30 May 1883; Weare, *Black Business in the New South*, 120, 122.

64 Rev. J. A. Whitted, *A History of the Negro Baptists of North Carolina* (Raleigh, 1908); *Recorder*, 5 Mar. 1907.

65 James E. Shepard, *New Plans for the Uplift of a Race* (n.p., n.d.); *Recorder*, 10 Nov. 1908, 16 Mar., 6 Apr., 8 July, 14 Oct. 1909.

66 *Recorder*, 7 July, 22 Dec. 1910; *Herald*, 22 Aug., 23 Aug. 1912, 15 Apr., 24 May 1913.

67 *Herald*, 26 Sept. 1915, 30 Aug. 1923.

68 Weare, *Black Business in the New South*, 105–6, 134, 138–39, 182; C. Horace Hamilton, "The Negro Leaves the South," *Demography* 1 (1964); *Herald*, 4 Nov. 1916; Durham Chamber of Commerce Minutes, 28 May 1917. Spaulding's and Moore's appearance before the Chamber revealed that 1,500 to 2,000 blacks had left Durham in the previous ninety days.

69 Williamson, *The Crucible of Race*, 115–40, 176–84, 306–10, 498; *Herald*, 22 Mar. 1917.

70 *Herald*, 6 Oct. 1905.

71 *Recorder*, 19 Mar. 1907, 6 Mar. 1908; *Herald*, 16 Nov. 1915, 12 Mar. 1916.

72 *Herald*, 30 Oct. 1914; *Recorder*, 28 July 1911; *Herald*, 19 Mar. 1913, 19 Oct. 1941.

73 *Recorder*, 24 Mar. 1908; SOHP, Piedmont Social History Series—Durham, interview with Hallie Caesar.

14 THE FACE OF CHANGE

1 *Sun*, 1 Mar. 1901; W. M. Upchurch and M. B. Fowler, *Durham County Economic and Social*, 20. Upchurch spoke to the Rotary Club in 1918 about his findings. Durham County, one of the smallest of the hundred counties in the state, at that time was 15th in population, 85th in birthrate, 10th in marriage rate, 19th in death rate, 2d in wealth, and 67th in farm value. Its per capita wealth for farm people was $210 per annum, while the national average was $994 and Iowa's was $3,386, showing how desperate Durham's farm conditions were. Durham did not feed her county or even her city. Durham headed the list, however, in real estate values with a per capita value of $2,907. *Sun*, 1 Mar. 1901; *Herald*, 20 Mar. 1918.

2 *Sun*, 5 Feb., 6 Feb. 1901.

3 *Globe*, 22 Aug. 1895; *Sun*, 11 July 1900, 25 Apr., 19 July, 5 Aug., 19 Aug. 1902; Wyatt T. Dixon, "How Times Do Change," *Sun*, 20 Sept. 1985. George Lyon Park, Lyon's practice range, was presumably a gift to the city for a baseball field before 1902 (*Sun*, 27 May 1902).

4 *Herald*, 23 July 1905; *Sun*, 21 Oct. 1983.

5 *Herald*, 2 May 1905, 1 Oct., 2 Oct. 1914, 17 Sept. 1923; information from Mrs. Philip W. Hutchings, Jr., James's granddaughter; Records of the U.S. Post Office Dept., "Records of Appointments"; *Sun*, 4 June, 31 Aug. 1904; *Herald*, 1 Oct., 2 Oct. 1914.

6 Ollie Nichols Carpenter and others, *Oak Grove School Annual* (1939), "History of Oak Grove School" (excerpt provided to the author by Edna Carpenter Baker).

7 *Sun*, 31 Oct. 1901, 1 Jan. 1902; *Recorder*, 30 Aug., 17 Sept. 1907, 17 Apr., 21 July, 25 Aug. 1908, 16 Apr. 1909.

8 *Recorder*, 21 July 1908; *Herald*, 7 June 1912, 12 Jan. 1916.

9 *Sun*, 19 June 1901; *Recorder*, 7 Aug., 11 Aug., 27 Nov. 1908, 20 May 1909, 24 Feb., 24 Mar. 1910; *Herald*, 11 Sept. 1915, 26 June 1938; Roberts, Lea, and Cleary, *The Durham Architectural and Historic Inventory*, 234–35. Stagg's house was named for the quarry in Vance County, owned by A. B. Andrews, where the stone for the house was obtained. Stagg had been private secretary to Andrews before he filled that office for Benjamin Duke (information supplied to the author by Marshall Bullock).

10 B. N. Duke Papers, DU-RBMSCL, Clippings; *Tobacco Plant*, 3 June 1885; *Sun*, 11 June 1900, 15 May 1902; *Recorder*, 13 May, 20 May 1909, 24 Feb. 1910; *Herald*, 19 July, 3 Dec. 1905.

11 Roberts, Lea, and Cleary, *The Durham Architectural and Historic Inventory*, 197–98, 214; see Southgate-Jones Papers, DU-RBMSCL, uncatalogued papers, "Map of North Durham, Property of B. L. Duke, April 1901." The plat shows the street now called Lamond as Lomond. No names are shown for the streets now called Buchanan, Watts, and Gregson. Oral tradition says that Gregson was first named Hated by Brodie

Duke so that the streets named in succession would read either Duke-Hated-Watts or Watts-Hated-Duke (*Herald*, 4 Mar. 1928).

12 Edward J. Parrish Papers, DU-RBMSCL, passport certificate, 1899, 31 Aug. 1904.

13 B. N. Duke Papers, DU-RBMSCL, 13 May 1897, 12 Mar., 13 Apr., 25 Apr., 22 May 1902; *Herald*, 14 Jan. 1905.

14 Parrish Papers, DU-RBMSCL, 18 Feb. 1907; DCDB 1:333, 15:532, 36:487, 488, 37:57. The Edward J. Parrish Collection contains many real estate papers concerning land companies, plats, individual deeds, and the like.

15 Parrish Papers, Parrish to T. A. Noell, 4 Dec. 1905. Richard Wright also built a country home on Roxboro Road in these years, Bonnie Brae Farm (*Herald*, 1 Feb. 1916).

16 *Sun*, 17 Feb. 1902; *Recorder*, 15 Oct. 1907; *Herald*, 28 May 1926. http://endangered durham.blogspot.com/2009/03/quail-roast-farm.html.

17 *Recorder*, 15 Oct. 1907; *Sun*, 14 July 1902; interview with Judge Sam Riley, 15 Feb. 1983.

18 *Herald*, 11 Aug. 1915; interview with Judge Riley; Chamber of Commerce Minutes, 18 July 1916; *Herald*, 23 Mar. 1913; telephone conversation with Mr. and Mrs. C. B. Weatherly, 8 May, 9 May 1986. Mineral Springs School takes its name from the nearby springs where the school obtained its water. They are now silted up.

19 *Sun*, 1 June 1903. The Temple building was so called because various fraternal organizations had their meeting rooms in its upper floors. Roberts, Lea, and Cleary, *The Durham Architectural and Historic Inventory*, 35, 36, 38, 40, 57; *Herald*, 12 July 1906, 2 Mar. 1913, 9 Aug., 20 Sept. 1914, 27 Jan., 31 Jan., 14 Mar. 1915, 30 Dec. 1916; *Recorder*, 22 Feb., 9 Aug., 6 Sept. 1907, 13 Nov. 1908; Chamber of Commerce Papers, DU-RBMSCL, pamphlet on Durham, 1906.

20 Roberts, Lea, and Cleary, *The Durham Architectural and Historic Inventory*, 56, 138, 148, 266; Elizabeth Lloyd M. Mansell, "The American Tobacco Company Brick Storage Warehouses in Durham, North Carolina, 1897–1906" (M.A. thesis, UNC, 1980).

21 *Recorder*, 3 Dec. 1896; *Sun*, 1 Aug. 1902, 6 May 1902; *Herald*, 9 Feb. 1917.

22 Record Book of Bute County 1767–1776, Minutes of the Court of Pleas and Quarter Sessions, NCOAH; Wake County Land Grant, 9 Aug. 1779, N.C. Land Grant Office; Records of Wake County, NCOAH, Deed Book G:31; information supplied to the author by Hazel Godwin, a descendant of Stephen Lowe; Lelia Lowe Godwin, "My Recollections of Lowe's Grove Baptist Church," Oct. 1969; J. R. High, C. C. Edwards, and S. J. Husketh compiled a short, untitled typescript history of the church in 1915; a copy in the possession of Robert Downey was supplied to the author by Hazel Godwin.

23 High, Edwards, and Husketh history; Lelia Godwin, "Recollections."

24 Information supplied to the author by Cynthia Gardiner, Public Relations Officer, Durham County Schools; *Recorder*, 19 May 1910; *Herald*, 19 Sept. 1912, 23 Feb., 26 Mar., 15 June, 22 Nov. 1913, 30 June 1915, 9 Aug., 1 Oct. 1922, 5 May 1940.

25 *Herald*, 7 Aug. 1913, 17 June, 30 June, 18 Aug. 1915.

26 Ibid., 10 Dec. 1915, 25 Apr., 2 Aug., 3 Aug. 1919, 5 May 1940.

27 William K. Boyd Papers, D.U. Archives, unnamed student papers on Lowes Grove; Boyd, *The Story of Durham*, 148–49.

28 *Sun*, 30 July 1902; *Recorder*, 10 Feb. 1910; U.S. Post Office Dept. "Records of Appointments," author's telephone interview with Lucille Glenn. Alexander M. Gorman was the editor of the temperance paper *Spirit of the Age*, and his son T. M. Gorman was first a printer-editor and later J. S. Carr's secretary. *Recorder*, 27 Feb. 1896; *Globe*, 5 Mar. 1896; *Sun*, 7 Oct. 1903, 26 Jan. 1904.

A Durham place name not found on maps is Wolf Den, located about 200 yards west and slightly south of the James A. Whitted school. It was "a small valley surrounded on three sides by steep banks and rocky cliffs" in which was the cave "extending 100 feet into the rocky bank." Unsuitable for tilling or building, the area remained unused for many years except as a place for picnics, revival services, and the like (*Sun*, 5 Aug. 1901, 21 May 1904; *Herald*, 5 May 1940).

29 See C. M. Miller, "Map of Durham County, North Carolina" [1910]; *Recorder*, 1 Jan., 12 Feb. 1907; letter from R. James Henderson to George C. Pyne, Jr., 23 Apr. 1984, photocopy supplied to the author by George Pyne. *Sun*, 9 Sept. 1901, 12 Apr. 1904; *Herald*, 19 July 1906, 5 Dec. 1913; telephone conversation with Mrs. Elneda Britt, 30 May 1984. The JOUAM Fred Green Council of East Durham had been organized in 1901 and by 1912 had 250 members. There were 21,000 members in North Carolina at that time. The order was patriotic and supported schools and orphanages (*Herald*, 16 Aug. 1912).

30 *Sun*, 1 July, 9 July, 16 Aug. 1902, 23 Jan. 1903; *Herald*, 19 Dec. 1904, 28 Apr. 1906; *Recorder*, 25 Jan. 1907; certificate of incorporation, 27 Apr. 1906, in possession of the chamber. The Merchants' Association, organized in April 1906, also provided strong civic leadership. P. W. Vaughan was the first president (*Herald*, 17 June 1923).

31 *Recorder*, 24 May 1907, 15 May, 17 July 1908.

32 *Herald*, 24 Mar. 1912, 20 Feb., 22 Feb., 20 Mar., 25 Mar. 1913; Southgate-Jones Papers, DU-RBMSCL 20 June 1912; *Herald*, 21 Aug., 30 Aug. 1912, 22 Aug., 16 Sept., 29 Sept. 1915; Chamber of Commerce Minutes, 21 Sept. 1917.

33 *Herald*, 4 Oct., 18 Nov., 20 Nov., 16 Dec. 1913.

34 Ibid., 14 Feb., 19 Mar., 20 Mar., 27 Mar., 7 Aug. 1912. On his farm Hill raised two herds of Golden Guernsey cattle to support his two dairies, first Croasdaile and then Hillandale. After Hill's death in 1961 his farm was partly developed by his daughter Dr. Frances Hill Fox and her husband, Dr. Herbert Fox, as a fashionable residential and commercial venture built around an eighteen-hole golf course. In the 1990s the development was expanded by her daughter Susan Fox Beischer and son-in-law George Beischer.

35 Ibid., 16 Apr., 28 Oct. 1913, 21 Mar., 13 Dec. 1914, 16 Oct. 1917; Record of Corporations, 2:459, 20 Mar. 1912. The incorporators were R. H. Wright, E. B. Lyon, J. S. Hill, W. J. Griswold, and E. J. Parrish.

36 *Sun*, 20 Mar. 1900, 3 Jan., 12 Jan., 17 Apr., 9 Sept. 1901, 18 Jan., 20 Jan., 9 Feb., 21 Feb. 1902; "Pledge Book of the Junior Order of United American Mechanics, 1910, 1915, 1919," DU-RBMSCL; *Herald*, 10 Jan., 16 Aug., 13 Sept. 1912, 14 Nov. 1915; *Recorder*, 19 Feb. 1909, 15 Sept. 1911; Chamber of Commerce Minutes, 8 Mar. 1917.

37 *Sun*, 2 May 1900, 1 Feb. 1901, 18 Jan., 9 Feb. 1902, 31 Mar., 12 Apr. 1904; *Herald*, 23 Nov. 1904; *Recorder*, 8 Dec. 1910; American Association of University Women Papers, DU-RBMSCL, "History of the Durham Branch of the American Association of University Women"; *Sun*, 23 June 1939; *Herald*, 23 Jan., 11 Feb., 13 May, 6 July, 17 Sept. 1915, 1 Oct., 9 Nov. 1916, 14 Mar. 1919; William K. Boyd Papers, D.U. Archives, papers on the DAR; *Herald*, 23 Jan. 1915; Hugh P. Brinton, "The Negro in Durham: A Study of Adjustment to Town Life" (Ph.D. diss., UNC, 1930), 435. The Volkamenia Club was organized by Dr. Moore. It met weekly from October to May to hear members' papers on literary or social topics. Its dues later provided a gold medal for excellence and a scholarship for NCC students and extra funds for black libraries. The Schubert-Shakespeare Club, perhaps a decade younger, focused on music and literature.

38 Bridgers, "A History of Social Work in Durham County"; *Sun*, 17 Feb. 1904; *Recorder*, 21 Feb. 1908, 9 Feb. 1909, 24 Mar., 4 Aug. 1910, 14 Mar. 1911; *Herald*, 11 July, 17 Nov. 1916, 23 Sept. 1917.

39 *Recorder*, 7 May 1907, 28 Feb., 6 Mar., 7 July 1908, 13 May 1909, 10 Feb. 1910, 20 Oct. 1911; *Herald*, 29 Feb., 12 Apr. 1912.

40 *Herald*, 17 Apr., 22 June, 20 July, 18 Oct. 1912, 15 June 1913. The Malbourne Hotel was enlarged in 1922 by the addition of fifty rooms over the adjoining Orpheum Theatre (*Herald*, 8 June 1922).

41 Ibid., 1 Aug. 1912, 8 Feb., 13 Feb. 1914, 10 Apr., 6 June, 15 June, 22 Oct. 1919, 17 Mar. 1921, 31 July 1941, 30 July 1943.

42 Ibid., 3 July, 4 July, 6 July 1915, 12 Jan., 16 Apr., 25 Nov. 1916. Both city and county jails were located in the new courthouse.

43 Ibid., 2 July, 3 July 1913.

44 *Recorder*, 29 Jan., 5 Feb. 19 Mar., 17 June 1909, 7 Apr., 20 June, 1 Sept. 1911, 17 Nov. 1910.

45 *Herald*, 26 Jan., 18 June 1913, 16 Jan., 24 Feb., 1 Aug., 15 Nov., 4 Dec. 1914, 27 Jan., 17 Mar. 1915.

46 William M. Shear, "The Background and Operation of the Council-Manager System in Durham, North Carolina" (M.A. thesis, D.U., 1951); *Herald*, 22 Apr., 24 Apr. 1917, 27 Apr. 1920, 7 Jan., 8 Jan., 10 Jan., 26 Jan., 13 Mar., 30 Mar., 28 June 1921.

47 *Recorder*, 10 Nov. 1910, 31 Jan., 7 July, 18 July 1911; *Herald*, 11 Sept. 1915; Anderson, *Piedmont Plantation*, 138. Particularly heavy rains in 1901 and 1908 gave the coup de grâce to water mills in the Durham area (*Sun*, 27 May 1901; *Recorder*, 28 Aug. 1908).

48 *Sun*, 17 June 1901.

49 *Herald*, 26 June, 3 July, 2 Dec. 1914, 2 Nov. 1915, 7 Mar. 1916.

50 Ibid., 3 Feb., 10 Feb., 17 Feb., 28 Feb. 1911.

51 Ibid., 20 Jan., 18 Mar., 24 Mar. 1914. Another result of the fire was a building code that prohibited frame structures in the city center and included other specifications to ensure safety and health (ibid., 26 Mar. 1915). In 1916 Hill Linthicum compiled a comprehensive building code that was endorsed by the North Carolina Association of Architects (ibid., 1 Feb. 1916).

52 Ibid., 24 Mar., 29 Mar., 1 Apr., 21 Apr., 19 Nov. 1914, 6 May, 25 July, 9 Oct., 19 Oct., 29 Oct., 8 Dec., 12 Dec. 1915; 31 May, 2 July 1916. In 1910 the county commissioners reached an agreement with Erwin Mills to allow the company to run water pipe along the shoulders of Erwin and Rigsbee roads to New Hope Creek in order to bring water to the mills and to West Durham. Although the land was surveyed and easements obtained, the line seems not to have been built. Instead the mills bought water from the city of Durham. A reservoir east of the old factory, only removed when the west side of Ninth Street was developed, was a remnant of that early water supply system (Erwin Mills Company Papers, DU-RBMSCL, Water Pipe Line and Electric Power Line to New Hope Creek file, 7 June 1910).

53 *Sun*, 11 Jan. 1900, 17 Jan. 1902; *Recorder*, 27 Oct. 1911; William E. King, "The Era of Progressive Reform in Southern Education: The Growth of Public Schools in North Carolina, 1885–1910" (Ph.D. diss., D.U., 1969), 20–22.

54 *Herald*, 13 July 1905, 28 Jan. 1912, 7 Jan. 1913, 12 Sept., 13 Sept. 1914, 6 May 1916, 1 Aug. 1919; *Recorder*, 19 Feb. 1907, 15 Sept. 1908, 23 June 1910.

55 *Recorder*, 6 Mar. 1908, 17 June 1909, 5 Sept. 1911; *Herald*, 23 Aug. 1914, 21 May, 25 June, 15 Dec. 1915.

56 *Herald*, 30 Sept. 1914, 3 Jan., 23 Jan., 2 Mar. 1915, 8 Apr. 1916; W. M. Upchurch and M. B. Fowler, *Durham County Economic and Social*, 66.

57 *Herald*, 5 Oct. 1916.

58 *Sun*, 17 Jan. 1902, 7 Aug. 1903; *Herald*, 28 Jan. 1912; 8 Apr., 6 May, 14 May, 5 Oct. 1916; 8 June 1919. Before the passage of the legislative act establishing rural school libraries, Walter S. Lockhart, who taught at South Lebanon school, established a library there in 1900 by private subscription (ibid., 8 June 1919).

59 Ibid., 14 Jan., 16 Jan., 8 Mar., 19 May 1912; 30 Mar. 1915; 6 Sept. 1916.

60 Ibid., 16 July, 11 Aug. 1916.

61 Ibid., 15 July 1905; 15 June 1906; *Recorder*, 13 May 1909; *Herald*, 30 Aug., 10 Sept. 1912; 24 Aug., 5 Sept. 1915; 11 Aug. 1918; B. N. Duke Papers, DU-RBMSCL, 19 Sept. 1906. Felicia Kueffner was a daughter of Rudolph Kueffner, a German chemist specializing in textile dyes. He was employed by the Durham Hosiery Mills and kept a close watch over his trade secrets; he was never without a black satchel in which, presumably, he carried his chemicals and formulae (Doris B. Tilley, "Durham's Early Lutherans," *Durham Record* 1 [1983]: 59; *Sun*, 14 Oct. 1901).

62 *Recorder*, 17 Mar. 1911.

63 Ibid., 7 Aug. 1908, 23 Mar., 13 May 1909; *Herald*, 3 Oct. 1915, 23 Nov., 29 Nov., 31 Dec. 1916, 6 May 1917.

64 Betty Irene Young, "Lillian Baker Griggs: Pioneer Librarian," *Durham Record* 1 (1983): 26–44.

65 Andrews, *John Merrick*, 60–62; *Herald*, 12 Aug. 1916, 14 Apr. 1940; Thomas H. Houck, "A Newspaper History of Race Relations in Durham, 1910–1940," 164.

66 *Sun*, 20 Dec. 1902; Robert F. Durden, "The Centennial Program Commemorating the One Hundredth Anniversary 1871–1971 of First Presbyterian Church, Durham, North Carolina"; *Recorder*, 15 Mar., 27 Aug. 1907; *Herald*, 4 Nov. 1904, 10 Sept. 1912, 6 Apr., 1 Nov. 1913, 3 Apr., 9 Aug., 8 Nov. 1914, 24 Oct., 31 Oct. 1915, 16 Apr., 22 July, 2 Dec. 1916, 15 Aug. 1923, 2 June 1935, 13 Oct. 1984.

67 DCDB 52:236, H. M. and Edna Amey to Henderson Grove Baptist Church, one acre, 21 Feb. 1917; telephone conversation with Mayme Perry, 3 Apr. 1986; Tate, "A Study of Negro Churches in Durham, North Carolina," 32, 39, 41, 43, 55, 62, 88.

68 *Herald*, 17 Sept. 1905, 26 Apr. 1953 (centennial edition); Durham *Recorder*, 24 Feb. 1910. Donald K. Routh, *The Story of the Eno River Unitarian-Universalist Fellowship* (Iowa City, 1979), 4, states that Durham Universalists organized in 1901 and had no pastor until 1908, when W. O. Bodell arrived to serve both Durham and the rest of the state.

69 *Herald*, 22 Aug. 1911, 9 Apr. 1916, 9 Oct. 1923, 20 Sept. 1925, 9 Mar., 22 Oct. 1930, 17 May 1931, 28 Oct. 1942. The author is grateful to George C. Pyne, Jr., for information obtained from the Episcopal Diocese of North Carolina. Deafness was hereditary in the family of Robina Tillinghast, a descendant of Samuel Tillinghast of Fayetteville, N.C.

70 *Herald*, 7 Jan. 1906; Durham *Recorder*, 3 Dec. 1907.

71 Arthur Burcham, "History of Saint Andrew's Episcopal Mission and Church School," typescript, 1961. (I am indebted to Albert Nelius for a copy of this history.) *Herald*, 7 Jan., 12 Sept. 1906; 26 Apr. 1953.

72 Telephone interview with Theo Clegg, 10 Feb. 1986; Murray, *Proud Shoes*, 250; Tate, "A Study of Negro Churches in Durham, North Carolina," 56.

73 The best source on the topic is Daniel J. Whitener, *Prohibition in North Carolina, 1715–1945* (Chapel Hill, 1945); *Sun*, 25 Feb. 1903; Lefler and Newsome, *North Carolina*, 571; *Recorder*, 23 July, 24 Dec. 1907, 28 Jan., 26 May 1908; *Herald*, 22 Aug., 22 Oct. 1914.

74 Hillsborough *Recorder*, 7 July 1875; *Tobacco Plant*, 15 June 1880.

75 *Sun*, 6 July, 7 July 1900, 1 Mar. 1901; *Recorder*, 11 June 1907, 31 July 1908, 16 Feb., 5 Mar. 1909, 19 May 1910; *Herald*, 15 Dec., 20 Dec., 24 Dec. 1912, 11 Nov. 1913, 5 Mar. 1914, 11 June 1917.

76 Porter, *Trinity and Duke*, 38, 176, 190–92; *Recorder*, 16 June 1910.

77 Porter, *Trinity and Duke*, 190–92, 217; *Herald*, 6 Nov., 7 Nov. 1913.

78 Porter, *Trinity and Duke*, 190–92.

79 Ibid., 91, 143, 171, 213; *Herald*, 11 Feb., 10 Sept. 1912, 5 June, 7 Nov. 1913, 9 May, 3 June, 28 June, 13 Nov. 1914, 18 July 1915; *Sun*, 17 Feb. 1902, 17 Aug., 18 Aug. 1904; *Recorder*, 4 Oct., 18 Oct. 1907, 13 Jan. 1911; *Annual Catalogue of Trinity College, Durham, N.C. 1904–05*, 108; *Annual Catalogue of Trinity College, Durham, N.C., 1910–11*, 155.

80 Porter, *Trinity and Duke*, 142; *Herald*, 19 Oct., 20 Oct. 1905.

81 Porter, *Trinity and Duke*, 219. Durham's only official hangings took place on 8 Feb. 1907. John H. Hodges, convicted of murdering his wife, and a black man named Jones, convicted of murdering Mrs. Jack Barker, were hanged after confessing that liquor was at the root of their crimes (*Recorder*, 25 Feb. 1906, 8 Feb. 1907).

1 *Recorder,* 15 Nov. 1907.

2 *Sun,* 13 July 1901, 13 Aug. 1902; *Recorder,* 2 June 1908; *Herald,* 8 Sept. 1925, 26 Sept. 1926, 25 Mar. 1928.

3 Anderson, *Piedmont Plantation,* 139.

4 Lefler and Newsome, *North Carolina,* 573–74; Franklin, *From Slavery to Freedom,* 328–31.

5 *Herald,* 27 May, 29 May 1917; Chamber of Commerce Minutes, 28 May 1917.

6 *Herald,* 8 Apr., 24 Apr. 1917; 30 Mar., 20 Apr. 1918.

7 Ibid., 6 Apr. 1917; Chamber of Commerce Minutes, 1 Mar., 31 May 1917; *Herald,* 15 Aug., 16 Aug. 1917. A history of the 120th infantry was written by Charles W. Perry of Company M, who had been a bookkeeper at Ellis Stone's store before the war (*Herald,* 14 Mar. 1919).

8 Wyatt T. Dixon Papers, DU-RBMSCL, World War I Diary; *Herald,* 12 Mar. 1919.

9 Chamber of Commerce Minutes, 31 May 1917; *Herald,* 30 Mar., 5 Apr., 19 July, 21 July, 19 Aug. 1917, 11 Aug. 1918; Porter, *Trinity and Duke,* 206–7.

10 *Herald,* 7 Apr., 12 May, 10 June, 13 June, 15 June, 19 June, 28 July, 29 July 1917, 16 Mar., 24 Mar., 3 Aug., 25 Sept., 15 Nov. 1918; Chamber of Commerce Minutes, 26 July, 1 Nov. 1917, 24 Jan., 14 Feb. 1918.

11 *Herald,* 9 Oct., 18 Nov., 1917, 30 Jan., 2 Feb., 5 July, 28 Sept., 17 Nov. 1918, 30 Apr. 1924; Dixon Papers, DU-RBMSCL, Diary.

12 *Herald,* 14 July, 27 Sept., 1 Oct., 4 Oct., 9 Oct., 12 Oct., 15 Oct., 16 Oct., 18 Oct., 17 Nov. 1918. Durham suffered a second Spanish flu epidemic in 1920 with somewhat fewer cases. Mrs. William A. Erwin, Jr., died in that epidemic (ibid., 22 Feb., 29 Feb. 1920). Between 1,500 and 2,000 men from Durham County were in the armed services during World War I. Of this number close to 100 were wounded, over 20 killed in action, and perhaps 50 others died of wounds or other causes. (These figures, obtained through the assistance of Gillian Ellis, Durham County Veterans' Service officer, are incomplete.)

13 Ibid., 29 Nov. 1918, 5 Jan., 12 Feb., 18 Mar., 20 Mar., 24 Apr., 27 Apr., 22 June, 2 July 1919, 24 Sept. 1920, 7 Aug. 1921. The three officers that Durham lost were Junius F. Andrews, Robert F. Mitchell, and Paul C. Venable (ibid., 22 Aug. 1920).

14 Ibid., 25 Apr., 26 Apr., 6 May 1919, 12 Nov. 1921.

15 Chamber of Commerce Minutes, 17 Dec. 1918, 7 Jan. 1919; *Herald,* 9 Apr. 1919.

16 *Herald,* 5 Mar. 1918, 7 Sept., 5 Oct. 1919.

17 Ibid., 27 Oct., 28 Oct. 1917; William J. Breen, "Southern Women in the War: The North Carolina Woman's Committee, 1917–1919," *North Carolina Historical Review* 55 (1978): 251–83.

18 *Herald,* 18 Oct. 1917.

19 Chamber of Commerce Minutes, 17 Sept., 23 Sept. 1918, 21 Mar. 1919.

20 *Herald,* 4 Apr., 18 Aug., 20 Aug., 26 Aug., 1 Oct., 6 Oct. 1920.

21 Ibid., 6 Mar., 28 Sept. 1924. There was also a Federation of Colored Women's Clubs, which had been formed under the leadership of the Civic League of Hayti. The league, in turn, had been stimulated to organize at Mrs. Jones's suggestion (Southgate-Jones Papers, DU-RBMSCL, among undated papers, "Address of Welcome to the Colored Women's Clubs of N.C.").

22 *Herald,* 1 Oct. 1916, 2 May, 14 May 1920, 19 Oct. 1921, 11 May 1923, 8 June 1924; Kemp P. Lewis Papers, SHC, Lewis to Thorn, 23 Feb. 1926.

23 Dolores E. Janiewski, "From Field to Factory: Race, Class, Sex, and the Woman Worker in Durham, 1880–1940" (Ph.D. diss., D.U., 1979), 224–25; this was published as *Sisterhood Denied: Race, Gender, and Class in a New South Community* (Philadel-

phia, 1985). Kemp P. Lewis Papers, SHC, Lewis to W. D. Carmichael, 23 Feb. 1926, Lewis to various others, 24 Feb. 1926.

24 *Herald*, 9 Nov. 1919, 27 Jan., 27 May, 2 Dec. 1923. Sallie Beavers was for many years principal of Morehead school.

25 Ibid., 19 Apr. 1920.

26 Ibid., 18 Oct., 5 Dec., 1917, 2 July 1918.

27 Ibid., 21 Jan. 1917, 2 July, 14 Sept., 19 Sept. 1918.

28 Ibid., 7 Aug., 12 Sept. 1919, 15 Oct. 1920.

29 Ibid., 31 Aug. 1920, 22 May 1921, 25 Jan., 12 Sept., 13 Oct., 19 Nov. 1922, 17 May, 19 May 1923, 28 June 1924.

30 Ibid., 21 Aug., 23 Aug., 24 Aug., 11 Sept. 1921.

31 Ibid., 7 Feb., 15 Feb., 2 Mar., 21 Sept. 1923. In 1928 the Klan gave up its masks, one of its most objectionable features, but the American Legion ordered the KKK float removed from the legion's parade (ibid., 22 Jan., 13 Nov. 1928).

Two surviving members of the original Klan, both Confederate soldiers, broke their silence in 1929: Major William Thaddeus Redmond (Pratt's illegitimate son) and state Senator James E. Lyon. Redmond had been in the Durham Klan and Lyon in the Eno Klan. Redmond told a reporter how they hanged Jeff and Dan Morrow, two blacks of the Cain Creek area, who had burned a barn. Another hanging of a black man, Wright Lipscomb, allegedly for assaulting a young white woman, occurred on the Johnson Mill Road. Redmond said that William L. Saunders was Grand Dragon of the North Carolina Klan and known on night-riding expeditions as "Spanish Bill" (ibid., 10 Mar. 1929).

32 Ibid., 8 July 1920.

33 Ibid., 11 July 1920.

34 Ibid., 14 July, 15 July 1920, 27 Jan. 1921, 14 May 1922.

35 Ibid., 25 Oct. 1921, 12 Feb. 1930.

36 Chamber of Commerce Minutes, 29 May 1917; *Herald*, 30 Jan. 1918, 27 May 1923; Franklin, *From Slavery to Freedom*, 340.

37 *Herald*, 23 Dec. 1920; Mason Crum Papers, D.U. Archives, "A Southerner Looks at the Race Question," chapter 17 of Crum's typescript autobiography, 247.

38 *Herald*, 25 Apr. 1922; Joel Williamson, *The Crucible of Race*, 248.

39 *Herald*, 17 Apr. 1920, 3 June, 23 July 1924; Weare, *Black Business in the New South*, 119–21.

40 *Herald*, 31 Dec. 1922; Weare, *Black Business in the New South*, 121–22.

41 Hugh Penn Brinton, "The Negro in Durham: A Study of Adjustment to Town Life" (Ph.D. diss., UNC, 1930), 257, 264. The census of 1920 also revealed that North Carolina had the highest birthrate in the nation (*Herald*, 2 Mar. 1921). Weare, *Black Business in the New South*, 126; Chamber of Commerce Minutes, 13 Dec. 1917; *Herald*, 30 Mar. 1923, 17 Jan. 1926. J. M. Avery was president of the league in 1916. John Z. Ayanian, "Black Health in Segregated Durham, 1900–1940," D.U. Archives, history honors paper (1982), 11, 13, 61, 64.

42 *Herald*, 12 Apr. 1925.

43 Ibid., 17 Feb. 1917, 8 May 1921, 27 Jan., 16 Feb. 1922, 20 June 1923; *Sun*, 20 May 1938.

44 *Herald*, 19 July 1919, 11 Dec. 1922; Minutes of the Board of Health, 11 Sept. 1923; Ayanian, "Black Health," 61, 40–41.

45 *Herald*, 2 Jan., 10 Mar., 9 Dec. 1921, 11 Feb., 12 Feb. 1922.

46 Ibid., 20 July 1919, 16 Nov. 1928, 17 May 1935.

47 *Tobacco Plant*, 8 Sept. 1875; *Globe*, 24 Oct. 1891; *Sun*, 12 Jan. 1900; *Recorder*, 20 June 1911; *Herald*, 6 July 1905, 5 Jan., 27 Nov. 1912, 4 June 1922, 16 June 1926, 10 June 1930; White, "The Economic and Social Development of Negroes in North Carolina since 1900."

48 *Herald,* 20 Oct., 22 Oct., 26 Oct., 15 Dec. 1922, 28 Jan., 3 July, 17 Aug. 1923, 13 Aug. 1924, 22 Apr. 1944; Minutes of the Board of Health, 6 Jan. 1919, 26 Jan., 5 Sept. 1921, 8 May 1923, 12 Aug. 1924; Report of Health Director, 1915.

49 *Herald,* 19 June 1921, 20 June 1923.

50 Ibid., 9 July, 17 July 1920, 21 Dec. 1922, 7 Jan., 30 Jan., 10 Feb. 1923; Chamber of Commerce Minutes, 4 Jan., 29 Jan., 1 Feb., 23 Feb. 1923; Porter, *Trinity and Duke,* 221–22.

51 *Herald,* 14 Jan. 1925, 21 Mar. 1926; Samuel Dace McPherson, Jr., *McPherson Hospital: Personal Recollections and a Brief History* (Durham, 2001).

52 Robin M. Williams and Olaf Wakefield, *Farm Tenancy in North Carolina, 1880–1935* (n.p., N.C. Agricultural Experiment Station, Sept. 1937), 11, 29; *Herald,* 30 Jan. 1918, 4 July 1923, 4 July 1926, 25 Apr. 1929; Chamber of Commerce Minutes, 19 Apr. 1917. B. N. Duke sold his farm of over 2,000 acres at auction in 1919 and 1920 (*Herald,* 30 May, 20 June, 28 June 1919, 21 May 1920).

53 *Herald,* 20 Apr., 22 June, 28 Aug. 1921, 15 Jan., 5 May, 2 Sept. 1922, 19 Oct. 1923, 8 July 1925. Everett was elected president of the cotton commission in recognition of his efforts in getting it established (ibid., 8 Dec. 1922).

54 Ibid., 22 Jan. 1923.

55 Ibid., 13 Mar., 15 Mar., 21 Mar. 1918, 27 June, 5 Aug., 8 Aug. 1919; Janiewski, "From Field to Factory," 219–21.

56 *Recorder,* 30 Oct. 1908; Arthur Vance Cole Papers, DU-RBMSCL, 26 Dec. 1919, 22 Jan., 7 Feb. 1920, 21 July 1922. Cole was a graduate of Durham High School (1901) and Trinity College (1905). He was the first principal of Lakewood School (1908) and taught until 1917, when he went to work for Liggett and Myers Tobacco Company. In 1922 he was editor of the *Southern Republican,* a short-lived weekly. After unionizing collapsed in 1920, he went into the import-export business in New York, then worked for the Durham Water Department, and then for the Internal Revenue Service. He studied law and was admitted to the North Carolina bar in 1932; thereafter he worked for the Federal District Court until he retired.

57 *Herald,* 15 June, 14 Aug., 20 Aug. 1919, 19 Jan. 1920.

58 Harley E. Jolley, "The Labor Movement in North Carolina, 1880–1922," *North Carolina Historical Review* 30 (1953): 354–75.

59 *Herald,* 4 May, 20 May 1919, 11 Aug. 1920; Boyd, *The Story of Durham,* 132–35.

60 *Herald,* 16 Nov. 1920, 4 Jan., 16 Jan., 24 Mar. 1921, 18 Mar. 1922; Herring, *Welfare Work in Mill Villages,* 202–5; Carr, "Building a Business On the Family Plan," 48.

61 *Herald,* 26 July 1922, 2 Feb., 4 Feb. 1923, 23 Apr. 1924. Kemp P. Lewis Papers, SHC, the agent Davenport to Lewis, 26 Mar. 1934; Spencer Miller, Jr., and Joseph F. Fletcher, *The Church and Industry* (New York, 1930), 213.

62 Rand, "I Had to Like It," 45.

63 Ibid., 42.

64 Letter of Lydia Evans Beurrier to author, 10 Mar. 1983, Lydia Evans Beurrier Papers, DU-RBMSCL; Janiewski, "From Field to Factory," 187, 200; Federal Writers' Project, SHC, "West Durham Cotton Mill," by Ida L. Moore. In the 1970s the Powe and J. Harper Erwin houses were rented, much deteriorated, to groups of counterculture youths who could live communally and cheaply while pursuing their careers in the arts, journalism, and the like. They gave the name Monkey Top, by logical extension, to their quarters on the ridge. This name was discussed in the newspaper, bringing to light much folklore and inaccurate information (*Herald,* 18 Oct., 19 Oct., 20 Oct. 1986; *Spectator,* 22 Oct. 1986). Powe descendants say that the house was never called Monkey Top when the Powes owned it (telephone conversation with Mary Louise Powe Gardner, 19 Oct. 1986).

65 Richard C. Franck, "An Oral History of West Durham: A Report Submitted to the Durham Bi-Centennial" (Durham, 1975), typescript in North Carolina Collection, Durham County Library.

66 Rand, "I Had to Like It," 70.

67 Kemp P. Lewis Papers, SHC, 19 Jan. 1926.

68 Miller and Fletcher, *The Church and Industry*, 213.

69 *Herald*, 24 Mar. 1924.

70 Ibid., 5 July 1921, 26 May, 5 July, 8 Dec. 1922, 1 Mar., 5 Mar., 9 Mar. 1923; Chamber of Commerce Minutes, 19 Dec. 1922, 4 Jan. 1923.

71 *Herald*, 16 May, 22 July, 16 Sept., 12 Dec. 1922.

72 *Globe*, 11 July 1895; Chamber of Commerce Minutes, 6 Sept. 1918; *Herald*, 3 July 1917, 29 July, 5 Aug., 26 Oct. 1919, 12 Apr., 15 Apr., 29 Apr., 14 Dec. 1924.

73 *Herald*, 5 Mar., 9 Mar., 10 July 1921, 29 Apr. 1922, 2 Jan., 7 Jan. 1923.

74 Ibid., 13 July, 29 July, 31 July, 4 Aug. 1924.

75 Ibid., 1 Mar. 1922, 22 July, 4 Oct. 1923, 23 Feb. 1924; Chamber of Commerce Minutes, 3 Mar., 21 Mar., 20 Oct. 1922. The Refuge property—twenty-two acres with an eleven-room house—had been the home of J. M. Arnette.
    While Young was Juvenile Court judge, the Durham cottage at the Stonewall Jackson Training School, a reformatory for boys in Cabarrus County, was established at his urging and that of other Durhamites (*Herald*, 5 Jan., 12 June 1921; Bridgers, "A History of Social Work in Durham County," 25).

76 Bridgers, "A History of Social Work in Durham County," 25–27; *Herald*, 22 Aug. 1923, 15 May, 30 Oct. 1924. The poor farm traditionally housed, among lesser offenders, prostitutes (who worked as laundresses and housecleaners) and tuberculosis and smallpox cases.

77 Southgate-Jones Papers, DU-RBMSCL, uncatalogued papers, Mrs. Jones's letter of resignation for the entire association and other papers relating to the Civic League.

78 *Herald*, 25 Apr., 6 July, 7 Nov., 10 Nov. 1916, 27 Sept. 1917, 15 Mar. 1918, 18 Dec. 1919, 6 July, 26 Oct. 1921; Betty I. Young, "Lillian Baker Griggs: Pioneer Librarian," *Durham Record* 1 (1983): 35–36.

79 *Herald*, 1 Oct. 1919, 2, 3 July 1921, 13 Apr. 1922, 1 May, 12 Aug. 1923, 17 Feb., 7 May, 15 May, 22 Nov., 7 Dec., 14 Dec. 1924.

80 Ibid., 19 July 1922, 22 Jan., 23 Sept., 30 Dec. 1923, 17 June 1924, 7 Jan. 1933, 26 Apr. 1953 (centennial edition); Southgate-Jones Papers, DU-RBMSCL, Julian S. Carr to Armour D. Wilcox, 6 Aug. 1923.

81 *Herald*, 23 Oct. 1920, 7 Jan., 31 Mar., 13 May, 17 July, 2 Sept., 18 Dec. 1921. In these years, too, came the Shriners (1921), the Lions (1922), a reorganized American Legion (1924), and the Carolina Motor Club (1924) (ibid., 7 Jan. 1921, 29 Nov. 1922, 15 June, 8 Aug. 1924). When a Big Star supermarket opened on West Main Street in 1938 with self-service and lower prices, it was advertised as innovative. Perhaps the earlier Piggly Wiggly store had not survived (ibid., 20 Oct. 1953).

82 Ibid., 15 Oct. 1934.

83 Ibid., 9 Oct. 1919, 10 Apr. 1920, 7 Sept. 1921, 28 May, 13 July 1924.

84 Kemp P. Lewis Papers, SHC, W. P. Budd and L. S. Booker to Lewis, 4 July 1926; *Herald*, 18 Sept. 1930, 7 Nov., 17 Nov., 25 Nov. 1933, 4 Dec. 1937, 11 June, 18 June 1939, 14 Feb., 9 Apr. 1941.

85 *Herald*, 8 June, 6 July, 1 Aug. 1919, 22 Jan., 15 June, 4 Dec. 1920, 12 Sept. 1923, 9 Oct. 1938.

86 Ibid., 13 June, 6 Oct., 21 Nov. 1920, 26 Apr. 1924.

87 *In Memoriam Julius Rosenwald, 1862–1932* (Raleigh, 1932); *Herald*, 11 Jan., 12 May, 13 July, 20 July 1923, 18 May, 23 May, 21 Sept., 16 Nov. 1924. Two Rosenwald structures survive: Russell School on St. Mary's Road and Bragtown School on Hamlin Road.

88 *Herald*, 30 Apr., 12 July 1921, 11 Feb. 1923; *Report of the Superintendent, Durham City Schools, 1914–1923* (Durham, 1923), 29–31. Miss Rogers is commemorated in the naming of Rogers-Herr Junior High School.

89 *Herald*, 21 Nov. 1924, 15 Feb. 1925, 12 Jan. 1929.

90 Ibid., 12 Nov. 1922.

91 Ibid., 14 Oct. 1921, 6 Apr. 1922; Southgate-Jones Papers, DU-RBMSCL, papers relating to the Civic League.

92 *Herald*, 13 May 1921. Washington Duke had given the building to James B. Duke, who had in turn given it to Mrs. J. Ed Stagg (ibid., 31 May 1922, 9 July 1922, 31 Dec. 1923, 15 June 1924).

93 Ibid., 25 Mar. 1922, 19 Aug., 11 Dec. 1923, 20 Nov., 31 Dec. 1924.

94 Ibid., 30 June 1921, 1 Oct. 1922; information about the Twaddells in the music file of the North Carolina Collection, Durham County Library; interview with Mrs. Vera Carr Twaddell, 15 June 1984.

95 Ibid., 10 Sept. 1922, 15 Oct., 9 Dec. 1921, 7 Jan., 13 Feb., 17 May, 27 June 1923. Morgan (1857–1920) organized the Durham Fertilizer Company (1895), which became the Virginia-Carolina Chemical Company, the largest fertilizer manufacturer in the world at that time. He was credited with turning the depleted and barren soils of the South into productive cotton plantations. He left a fortune estimated at sixty million dollars (*Herald*, 29 Mar. 1942).

96 Ibid., 13 Sept., 14 Sept., 19 Sept., 23 Sept., 8 Nov., 9 Nov. 1923, 23 Jan. 1924, 9 Apr. 1925. The speakers were Senator B. K. Wheeler of Montana, and Sherman's grandson Colonel William Sherman Fitch of Gulfport, Miss. Also seated on the platform was "a gray-haired darkey," symbol of the war's beneficiaries. Mordecai Ham, the evangelist, who had been conducting services in Durham at a newly built tabernacle at the corner of Main and Duke streets, offered the opening prayer.

    Another controversy erupted in 1934 when R. O. Everett proposed that statues of Johnston and Sherman be erected at Bennett Place. He defended the suggestion with the same argument that General Carr had used in 1923. Sherman's respectability and worthiness were vouched for by Johnston's friendship. Everett also stressed the symbolism of the place: unity, not just of North and South but of all peoples. Everett added, "There is room enough within that circle to remember the valor of our ancestors, and at the same time appreciate the worth of our opponents" (ibid., 11 Oct. 1934).

97 Ibid., 15 July 1923; Menius, "The Bennett Place," 13, 14. W. H. Proctor (1857–1921) was born in a house that had probably been built by his father, Kinchen Proctor, son of Richard. His birthplace may have been the one restored as the kitchen at the reconstructed Bennett Place rather than the house he later lived in, which is now the main house at Bennett Place. Frank Kenan donated the buildings, Nello Teer provided equipment for their removal to the Bennett Place site, the carpenters of Local 522 dismantled and prepared the buildings for moving, James J. Freeland provided materials for a smokehouse and fencing.

98 *Herald*, 12 Jan., 14 Jan. 1923, 10 May, 11 May 1924.

99 Ibid., 15 Oct., 16 Oct. 1920.

100 Ibid., 27 Oct. 1921, 14 June 1923.

101 Ibid., 17 Apr. 1921, 15 Feb., 20 Apr. 1924. The unveiling of the portrait was not Durham's final appearance in his town. Durham's American Business Club took the lead in the search and exhumation of his body from the Snipes family graveyard and its exhibition, perfectly preserved, to the public at the Hall-Wynne funeral parlor. Durham had been buried in a sealed iron casket (ibid., 28 June 1933). Six months later the ghoulish scene ended with reburial in Maplewood Cemetery, where the Durham-Orange Historical Society erected a large granite marker over his grave. Unfortunately his middle name and birth and death dates are incorrectly given there (ibid., 30 Dec. 1933, 2 Jan. 1934).

102 Ibid., 3 May, 4 May, 5 May 1924.

103 Ibid., 17 Feb. 1924.

104 Ibid., 14 Sept. 1924.

105 Ibid., 7 Aug. 1920, 29 Sept. 1922, 25 Sept. 1923.

106 Ibid., 12 Oct. 1923, 13 Jan. 1924.

107 Durden, *The Dukes of Durham*, 210–29.

108 Ibid., 229; *Herald*, 9 Dec. 1924.

109 *Herald*, 13 Dec., 30 Dec. 1924. The 1901 town boundary bisected the campus. The 1925 extension bisected the new West Campus, a mistake rectified two years later by the extension of the boundary around the perimeter of the campus. See Ben F. Lemert, *Economic Maps of Durham, N.C.* (Durham, 1938).

110 *Herald*, 10 Dec., 13 Dec. 1924. The vote was 3,865 for and 1,744 against extension. The expanded boundaries necessitated two additional city wards and two council members from each of those wards, increasing the city council from 8 to 12 members.

    Underscoring Durham's separation from her past were the deaths during these years of many men who had played important roles in that past: James R. Day in 1918, Brodie L. Duke, Frederick C. Geer, John Merrick, and Hill Carter Linthicum in 1919, Victor Bryant and E. J. Parrish in 1920, Henry Reams and George Watts in 1921, J. S. Carr, Jr., P. W. Vaughan, Arch Cheatham, and William Albert Wilkerson in 1922, Thomas B. Fuller, Dr. A. M. Moore, and James Russell Blacknall in 1923, and General Carr, Horace North Snow, William Gaston Vickers, and "Reuben Rink" (Jules Koerner) in 1924 (ibid., 16 Feb. 1918, 2 Feb., 8 June, 7 Aug., 7 Oct. 1919, 2 Sept., 23 Oct. 1920, 1 Jan., 8 Mar. 1921, 18 Mar., 25 Aug., 11 Dec., 31 Dec. 1922, 9 Jan., 30 Apr., 8 Dec. 1923, 27 May, 2 Sept., 24 Nov., 28 Nov. 1924).

16 ELATION AND DEPRESSION

1 Mason Crum Papers, D.U. Archives, "Autobiography," 223.

2 Robert L. Durden, *The Dukes of Durham*, 231.

3 Ibid., 233.

4 Ibid., 234.

5 *Herald*, 21 Nov. 1925.

6 Ibid., 2 May 1926.

7 Durden, *The Dukes of Durham*, 237–38.

8 *Herald*, 5 Apr. 1925.

9 Ibid., 3 May 1925. See also Trinity College–Duke University Real Estate Purchases and Sales, 1893–1955, D.U. Archives.

10 *Herald*, 3 July 1925; Durden, *The Dukes of Durham*, 244; Hillsborough Stone Quarry, Duke University Archives, Brest S. Drane, "Behind the Scene in Locating Stone for Duke University," *[State] Employment Security Commission Quarterly* 5 (winter 1947): 12; Eldon P. Allen and William F. Wilson, *Geology and Mineral Resources of Orange County, North Carolina* (Raleigh, 1968), 48; *Herald*, 13 Dec. 1925; Susan Block, "The Gothic Grande Dame's Golden Age," *Duke*, July–Aug. 1986, 2–7. Abele was also the designer of Harvard's Widener Library and the Philadelphia Museum of Art (Susan Cook, *Chronicle*, 10 Feb. 1987, 4). See also Julian F. Abele Biographical File, D.U. Archives.

11 *Herald*, 11 Oct., 13 Oct., 24 Oct., 28 Oct. 1925; Durden, *The Dukes of Durham*, 245–46; Edward C. Halperin, M.D., "Medical Origins of Duke University," *North Carolina Medical Journal* 48 (Dec. 1987): 664–66.

12 *Herald*, 24 Oct. 1925, 23 Oct. 1927; Durden, "Troubled Legacy: James B. Duke's Bequest to His Cousins," *North Carolina Historical Review* 50 (Oct. 1973): 394–415.

13 *Herald*, 25 Oct. 1925, 22 Jan. 1927; Durden, *The Dukes of Durham*, 245; James F. Gifford, Jr., *The Evolution of a Medical Center: A History of Medicine at Duke University to 1941* (Durham, 1972), 178–79.

14 *Herald*, 1 Feb. 1927; Seymour H. Mauskopf and Michael R. McVaugh, *The Elusive Science* (Baltimore, 1980), 72.

15 Mauskopf and McVaugh, *The Elusive Science*, 72, 87. The Scopes trial in Tennessee in 1925 had polarized church people and created difficult choices. North Carolina escaped Tennessee's ignominy, but for a while the outcome was in doubt when the Poole bill, outlawing the teaching of evolution or any theory linking man with any lower species, was introduced in the legislature. Representative R. O. Everett's motion to table lost. He then attacked the bill as an infringement of the rights of free inquiry and free speech. Throngs heard the debate on this emotional issue. The bill was defeated on the grounds that it treated a religious question not properly discussed in the legislature (*Herald*, 19 Feb. 1925).

16 Mauskopf and McVaugh, *The Elusive Science*, 91, 96, 160–61; *Herald*, 6 Feb., 19 Sept. 1937.

17 *Herald*, 5 June 1928, 13 July, 23 Oct. 1930. The cornerstone was later moved and incorporated into the foundation of the library. Marcus E. Winston was Duke Hospital's first manager (ibid., 13 Apr. 1930).

18 Durden, *The Dukes of Durham*, 235.

19 Oliver Goldsmith, "The Deserted Village"; Roberts, Lea, and Cleary, *The Durham Architectural and Historic Inventory*, 182; *Herald*, 22 Aug. 1937, quoting Huxley's article on Duke in a London journal, *Time and Tide*.

20 *Herald*, 7 July, 16 Oct. 1929, 7 May 1930, 30 Dec. 1931, 25 Jan. 1932, 7 May, 24 Dec. 1933, 2 June 1935; Durden, *The Dukes of Durham*, 241, 259.

21 Durden, *The Dukes of Durham*, 58–59; Rosa Mae Warren Myers Papers, DU-RBMSCL, B. N. Duke to Myers, 19 Apr. [1919].

22 Boyd, *The Story of Durham*, 280.

23 *Globe*, 26 Apr. 1893; *Herald*, 2 June 1935. All three Dukes had first been buried in the mausoleum that Washington Duke had built in Maplewood cemetery after the death of his daughter Mary Lyon. Designed and constructed by the W. F. Van Gunden Granite and Marble Works Company of Philadelphia, the building of the mausoleum was personally supervised by Van Gunden, who fell from the roof, striking his head, and died in June 1894 (B. N. Duke Papers, DU-RBMSCL, 31 May 1893; *Globe*, 6 June 1894). Other family members are still buried there.

24 Durden, *The Dukes of Durham*, 199, 248–50, 254–58; *Herald*, 30 Aug., 30 Oct., 14 Dec. 1925; 11 Apr., 3 May, 4 June 1926; 28 Apr. 1927; 9 Jan., 15 Jan. 1929.

25 Durden, *The Dukes of Durham*, 206–7, 259n; *Herald*, 25 Oct. 1935; B. N. Duke Papers, DU-RBMSCL, 1 Apr. 1896.

26 Mary Duke Biddle Foundation Papers, D.U. Archives. Mary Duke Biddle died in 1960 (Durden, *The Dukes of Durham*, 256); *Brighter Leaves*, 30–31.

27 B. N. Duke Papers, DU-RBMSCL, James S. Manning and Howard A. Foushee to Duke, 27 Feb. 1903, Manning and Foushee to J. E. Stagg, 13 May 1903; *Herald*, 7 Feb. 1931, 26 May 1935; DCDB 100: 186 (9 Jan. 1931). Stories in the *Herald*, 7 Feb. 1931 and 26 May 1935, relate that at the earlier date Mary Duke Biddle purchased the homestead and at the latter, donated it to Duke University. These seem to be in error as the deed shows the university as the purchaser in 1931.

Mrs. Biddle donated Four Acres, her parents' home, to the university (*Herald*, 26 June 1938). It was sold in 1960 to the North Carolina Mutual Life Insurance Company as the site for a new headquarters building.

28 *Herald*, 5 Feb. 1937. The 1939 centennial celebration of Trinity College brought to Durham such men as Sir William Bragg of the Royal Society, Dr. Eduard Beneš, former president of Czechoslovakia, and John Carter, Metropolitan Opera Company tenor, while the Woman's College symposium presented such eminent women as Marjorie Hope Nichols, dean of Smith College, Mary E. Woolley, former president of Bryn Mawr College, and Mary Allen, a jurist (*Herald*, 31 Mar., 1 Apr., 16 Apr., 21 Apr., 23 Apr. 1939).

29 *Herald*, 9 Aug. 1925, 5 June 1928; Kemp P. Lewis Papers, SHC, Lewis to W. D. Car-

michael, 26 Feb. 1926; Joseph J. King, "The History and Functions of the City Central Labor Union" (M.A. thesis, D.U., 1937).

30 The 1939 strike involved only 900 workers, but the rest of the employees were thrown out of work by the closing of the plant (*Sun*, 26 Apr. 1939). Janiewski, "From Field to Factory," 238–40; *Herald*, 17 Apr., 18 Apr., 26 Apr., 27 Apr. 1939; *Sun*, 26 Apr. 1939; Ann Banks, ed., *First-Person America* (New York, 1980), 140, 156; SOHP, Lanier Rand's interview with Ernest Latta, 1977.

31 Lewis Papers, SHC, broadside, 10 Mar. 1934, and correspondence from agent to Lewis, 25 Mar., 26 Mar., 27 Mar., 28 Mar., 29 Mar., 30 Mar., 31 Mar., 1 Apr. 1934, Lewis to Dr. W. DeB. McNider, 28 Aug. 1934; Janiewski, "From Field to Factory," 241–42; *Herald*, 20 May 1934.

32 Lewis Papers, SHC, 30 Sept. 1934; Janiewski, "From Field to Factory," 236, 241; *Herald*, 4 Sept. 1933, 24 Aug., 31 Aug., 4 Sept., 5 Sept., 7 Sept., 23 Sept. 1934; John W. Kennedy, "The General Strike in the Textile Industry, September 1934" (M.A. thesis, D.U., 1947). Another Durham worker, Frank Milnor, had also been killed in the Philadelphia strike and his body sent home for burial.

33 Janiewski, "From Field to Factory," 244; *Herald*, 4 Sept. 1934; Kennedy, "The General Strike."

William Gilliam, president of the Bull City Textile Union, S. H. Scott, president of the tobacco workers union at American, D. S. Upchurch, another tobacco union organizer, and W. B. Culbreth of the Liggett and Myers local were the Durham strike leaders, but the outside union leaders, Tom McMahon and Francis J. Gorman, were blamed for the strike's failure (*Herald*, 25 Sept. 1934).

34 *Herald*, 25 Sept. 1934; A. L. Fletcher, *Biennial Report of the [N.C.] Department of Labor, July 1, 1934 to June 30, 1936* (Raleigh [1936]), 10.

35 *Herald*, 21 July, 24 July, 2 Dec. 1935, 2 Dec., 3 Dec. 1937, 11 June, 19 June, 12 July, 2 Nov. 1939; Janiewski, "From Field to Factory," 245, 263.

36 *Herald*, 5 July 1927, 26 Mar., 27 Sept. 1931, 13 July 1975, 22 May 1982, 14 Dec. 1983; telephone conversation with Mrs. Louis Fara, 10 Nov. 1983.

37 *Sun*, 26 Apr. 1939.

38 Frances Gray Patton, "The Town Bull Durham Built," *Holiday* (Dec. 1959): 219.

39 *Herald*, 20 Nov. 1917, 28 Mar. 1922, 12 Aug. 1923, 1 Apr. 1928, 16 July 1935; A. V. Cole Papers, DU-RBMSCL, Printed Materials, "Where to Play in Durham."

40 *Herald*, 30 Jan., 23 May, 22 June 1926, 3 Feb., 26 June 1927, 13 Nov. 1928. Durham had to wait until 1957 for the next country club and golf development: Willowhaven, on Umstead Road.

41 *Herald*, 19 Jan., 12 Aug., 11 Nov. 1923, 9 May, 22 June 1924, 13 Nov. 1925, 21 Mar., 4 July 1926, 21 Sept. 1929, 27 Aug. 1940. Roberts, Lea, and Cleary, *The Durham Architectural and Historic Inventory*, 299–301. Booker bought large tracts of farmland and resold them to the Hope Valley development.

42 *Herald*, 15 Nov., 20 Nov., 18 Dec., 22 Dec. 1925, 20 June 1926, 3 Feb., 17 Nov. 1929. The Presley J. Mangum house, built probably in the 1880s, was moved to the Peabody Street end of the lot just before the end of the century to make room for the Sans Souci, a hotel and boarding house in succession.

A host of small, modestly priced developments had been attempted by investors outside the town limits beginning in the teens. The West End Land Company advertised land east of the country club on Club Boulevard. The Griswold Insurance and Real Estate Company and Southgate Jones and Company were agents for lots on Park Avenue in East Durham, an area only two blocks from the trolley line. In 1923 the Atlantic Coast Realty Company auctioned lots on Hyde Park Avenue in a development of James B. Mason called Sunnybrook. About the same time E. J. Parrish's and J. S. Carr's estates were advertising auction sales of adjacent tracts on Chapel Hill Road. Parrish's fifty-seven acres had been named Wawa Yonda and lay east of the main road (now in the 2400 block) extending to the Ward (later Long Meadow) dairy on James Street. Carrland Park was the former Vesson family farm across Chapel Hill Road.

43 Ibid., 3 Mar., 12 May 1929, 11 July 1930.

44 Ibid., 23 Feb. 1934, 2 Apr. 1935, 4 Mar. 1936, 10 Nov. 1937. A theater for sound movies ("talkies"), the Criterion, was built next to the new post office in 1932. It had mosaic tile and a fountain in the lobby (ibid., 1 May 1932).

45 Ibid., 24 May 1936; Roberts, Lea, and Cleary, *The Durham Architectural and Historic Inventory*, 44.

46 *Herald*, 8 Sept. 1929, 25 June, 5 Nov. 1933, 17 July 1934, 13 Oct. 1936, 2 Dec. 1939.

47 Ibid., 18 Oct., 27 Nov. 1925, 5 Dec. 1926, 24 July 1927, 4 Aug. 1940; Amy Childs Fallaw, *The Story of Duke's Chapel* (Durham, 1967).

48 *Herald*, 26 Aug., 28 Nov. 1926, 14 Apr. 1929, 3 Jan., 17 Jan. 1932, 4 Apr., 9 July, 27 Aug. 1939, 4 Aug. 1940, 25 May, 15 June, 14 July 1941; Wallace R. Draughon, *History of the Church of Jesus Christ of Latter-day Saints in North Carolina with a Detailed Record of the Church in Durham* (Durham, 1974).

49 Durden, *The Dukes of Durham*, 256n; *Herald*, 9 Jan., 10 Jan., 11 Jan., 15 Jan., 5 Mar., 8 Mar., 26 June 1929, 17 June 1932. Besides J. B. and B. N. Duke and Wright, other important residents died in this period: Bennehan Cameron (*Herald*, 2 June 1925), Moses McCown (11 June 1925) Eleanor Blackwell (Mrs. John L.) Markham (5 Aug. 1925), Rosa Bryan (Mrs. E. J.) Parrish (22 June 1927), Peyton H. Smith (27 Feb. 1928), Alvis K. Umstead (20 June 1928), Albert Gallatin Cox (8 Mar. 1929), Edward Knox Powe (29 Sept. 1929), Lavinia Blackwell (Mrs. J. D.) Pridgen, Sr. (5 Oct. 1929), William A. Erwin (29 Feb. 1932), Kate Morris (Mrs. Caleb B.) Green (7 Jan. 1933), James Edward Lyon (14 Jan. 1933), Dr. Neal P. Boddie (27 Jan. 1933), Dr. John M. Manning (31 Aug. 1933), Mrs. Gilmore Ward Bryant (4 Mar. 1934), Williamson W. Fuller (24 Aug. 1934), William Thaddeus Redmond (23 Feb. 1936), Mattie Southgate (Mrs. T. D.) Jones (14 Mar. 1936), Clinton W. Toms (30 Aug. 1936), Sarah Pearson Angier (Mrs. B. N.) Duke (3 Sept. 1936), James B. Mason (3 Sept. 1938), Reuben Hibberd (30 Sept. 1938), Dr. Norman M. Johnson (14 June 1940), William Gaston Pearson (1 Sept. 1940), William Preston Few (17 Oct. 1940), Thomas M. Gorman (29 Jan. 1941), Cassam Tilley (19 June 1941), Dr. George H. Ross (5 July 1941). All dates refer to the *Herald* issues in which the particular obituaries occurred, not to the dates of death.

50 Lefler and Newsome, *North Carolina*, 605–7, 611; *Herald*, 30 June, 24 Oct. 1929.

51 Alexander R. Stoesen, "From Ordeal to New Deal: North Carolina in the Great Depression," 382–404, in Lindley S. Butler and Alan D. Watson, eds., *The North Carolina Experience: An Interpretive and Documentary History* (Chapel Hill, 1984).

52 *Herald*, 23 Jan., 5 Feb. 1930, 25 Mar., 7 Dec., 12 Dec. 1932, 13 Jan., 8 Feb., 16 Feb., 8 Mar. 1933.

53 Ibid., 3 Dec. 1930, 11 Jan., 12 Aug., 3 Sept. 1931, 12 Mar. 1933.

54 Ibid., 2 May, 7 Oct. 1933, 28 Oct. 1934, 28 Apr. 1935, 24 Jan. 1943. The North Carolina Symphony began as a FERA-funded project (ibid., 17 Apr. 1935).

55 Ibid., 22 Oct. 1933, 27 Aug., 14 Sept. 1934, 21 Aug., 21 Oct. 1935, 4 Mar., 15 July 1936, 20 Feb., 3 Aug., 10 Aug., 12 Aug. 1938, 12 Mar. 1939, 13 Mar., 21 Mar., 21 May 1940.

56 Ibid., 25 July, 29 July, 1 Aug., 8 Aug., 2 Sept. 1933, 16 Jan., 17 Mar. 1934.

57 Ibid., 30 Dec. 1933, 16 June 1934, 13 July 1935.

58 Ibid., 9 Aug. 1935, 18 Jan., 5 Feb., 22 Feb. 1936, 22 May 1937, 9 Feb., 24 Apr., 17 Aug. 1938; Janiewski, "From Field to Factory," 251.

59 Lefler and Newsome, *North Carolina*, 617; *Herald*, 16 Oct. 1938, 25 Sept. 1989. By 1937 county homes or poorhouses were on the decline, their function having been largely assumed by the social security system that provided for the aged and indigent. Durham County continued its county home until 1969, taking care of mainly the physically and mentally incapacitated. When it was closed the residents were placed in

rest homes or nursing facilities (ibid., 2 July 1937, 24 Mar. 1987, obituary of Andrew S. Holt, Jr.).

60 *Herald*, 27 Oct. 1930, 21 Jan., 15 Dec. 1934, 6 Oct. 1939, 2 Jan. 1940, 16 June 1941; *N&O*, 13 Mar. 1938.

61 *Herald*, 25 Jan., 19 Sept. 1930, 1 Apr. 1935, 24 Apr. 1939, 11 May 1941.

62 Ibid., 5 Sept. 1931, 2 Feb. 1932.

63 Ibid., 7 Feb., 2 May, 14 May, 27 May 1933; Newman I. White, "Labor Helps Itself: A Case History," *South Atlantic Quarterly* 32 (1933): 346–64.

64 Stoesen, "From Ordeal to New Deal," 382–84; *Herald*, 29 July 1928, 1 Jan., 17 Mar., 1 July 1931.

65 *Herald*, 27 Mar., 8 Apr. 1931, 14 June, 29 June, 19 July 1932, 12 Apr., 1 July, 9 Aug. 1933, 14 Feb. 1939, 12 June 1942, 26 Apr. 1953 (Durham centennial edition); Lefler and Newsome, *North Carolina*, 612–13, 620; Stoesen, "From Ordeal to New Deal," 384. For additional information on the Taxpayers League see Mattie K. Goldberg Papers, DU-RBMSCL.

66 *Herald*, 4 Mar., 11 Mar. 1925, 21 Feb. 1926.

67 Ibid., 21 July 1926, 19 Mar. 1931, 13 July 1944.

68 Ibid., 14 July 1926, 5 May, 12 May, 19 May, 26 May 1929, 4 Apr., 8 May, 19 Aug., 2 Sept., 31 Oct. 1930, 12 July 1941; *N&O*, 18 Aug. 1930; North Carolina County Papers, DU-RBMSCL, Durham City and County: Dallas W. Newsom, "Durham County, North Carolina, A Decade of Progress, July 1, 1930 to July 1, 1940," a speech delivered to the Kiwanis Club. See Joseph S. Ferrell, ed., *County Government in North Carolina* (Chapel Hill, 1968), for a complete listing of the counties that had by then tried manager forms of government.

69 *Herald*, 8 May 1930, 14 Dec. 1932, 23 Feb., 24 Feb. 1933, 20 Jan. 1931, 7 Jan. 1936, 11 Sept. 1974; Warren J. Wicker, "Durham Rejects City/County Consolidation," *Popular Government* 40 (winter 1975): 27–28; James R. Hawkins Papers, DU-RBMSCL, City-County Government: Albert W. Kennon, "Report of the Durham City-County Charter Commission, 1960."

70 *Herald*, 10 Jan., 23 Feb., 20 Oct. 1934; Mamie Dowd Walker, "History and Progress of the Juvenile Court, City and County, Durham, N.C., Dec. 3, 1934–Dec. 5, 1949," NCC. The YMCA had formed a branch of the juvenile offenders association in 1914 to try to keep children out of jails and workhouses and to reform them (*Herald*, 2 June 1914).
   In 1931 Bradway established the first legal aid clinic in the South to help those who could not afford lawyers and to give students practical experience. Although the best law schools in the North ran such clinics, Bradway was opposed by the local bar, which looked on the clinic as unwelcome competition (*Herald*, 21 June, 21 Sept., 26 Sept. 1931). Duke's Law School was also a pioneer in establishing a student bar association. Richard M. Nixon, probably Duke Law School's most famous alumnus, was elected its president in 1936 (ibid., 2 May 1936).

71 *Herald*, 11 Oct. 1936, 19 Apr., 2 Dec., 4 Dec., 5 Dec., 6 Dec., 7 Dec. 1941; Walker, "History of the Juvenile Court."

72 Ibid., 20 May 1930, 18 Mar. 1932, 24 Mar. 1933, 11 Jan., 16 Jan., 12 May 1934, 11 June 1935, 15 July, 4 Aug. 1937, 8 Mar., 23 June, 18 Dec. 1938, 26 Jan. 1941; A. V. Cole Papers, DU-RBMSCL, Printed Materials, "Where to Play in Durham"; information supplied to the author by William A. Harrat of the city Recreation Department.
   In 1935 the chambers of commerce of Raleigh and Durham called for cooperation in seeking a state park halfway between the cities on Crabtree Creek. They applied for federal work-relief funds for the project which was the beginning of Umstead State Park (*Herald*, 12 June 1935).
   The Durham Foundation was organized as a perpetual fund for charitable and civic programs at a meeting of the Junior Chamber of Commerce, 4 Dec. 1939, when Eg-

bert Haywood was president. At that meeting Hill donated only the clubhouse, tennis courts, and six acres, reserving the golf links, which he donated later. Trustees were John A. Buchanan, Robert L. Flowers, Frank D. Bozarth, Gordon K. Ogburn, and Donnie A. Sorrell (ibid., 5 Dec. 1939).

73 Information supplied by William A. Harrat of the city Recreation Department. In 1925 the city improved its Flat River water supply by impounding the water with a dam (completed 1926). Although the city had been using Flat River water since 1917, it had had only a pumping station there, and the supply was not sufficient for the needs of the much expanded town. When Lake Michie, the reservoir, was filled it covered 550 acres. The dam, 1100 feet across Flat River, was designed by a Scot, D. McGregor Williams, who worked for the William M. Piatt Company, the builder. In 1930 Williams became assistant superintendent of the City Water Department and, after John Michie's death in 1939, succeeded him as superintendent (*Herald*, 15 Mar. 1925, 9 Dec. 1926, 9 Jan. 1927, 7 Nov. 1943). For complete information on Durham's old and new water systems see Allen Hazen and Charles Burdick, *Report: Extending and Improving the Water Works System, Durham, N.C., March, 1921* (Durham, 1921); Division of Water Resources, *The Water Supply System of the City of Durham, North Carolina* (Durham, 1981).

74 Susan Singleton Rose Papers, D.U. Archives; Boyd, *The Story of Durham*, 252. *Branson's North Carolina Business Directory . . . 1884* lists H. E. Seeman as a manufacturer of carriages.

Featured outings of the hiking club were the laurel and rhododendron slopes of the Eno River, Camp Hollow Rock on New Hope Creek, the Raleigh road, and the Nelson Pike (*Herald*, 14 May, 24 May 1931, 13 Nov. 1932).

75 *Herald*, 3 July 1927, 15 May 1928, 31 Mar. 1929.

76 Ibid., 19 May 1929, 21 May, 12 July, 26 July, 6 Oct. 1931, 22 Jan., 11 Sept., 1 Dec. 1932, 17 Jan., 23 Nov., 30 Nov. 1933, 17 Mar., 20 Mar. 1934, 12 Feb. 1942.

77 Ibid., 3 June, 2 July, 8 July, 1 Nov. 1936, 30 Apr., 10 June, 25 Aug. 1937, 18 Jan., 2 Mar. 1938.

78 Ibid., 30 Nov. 1938, 17 Aug. 1940, 2 Aug., 16 Sept., 17 Dec. 1941, 14 Mar. 1943; information supplied to the author by the Raleigh-Durham Airport Authority, 19 Nov. 1986.

79 Information supplied to the author by Isabelle Budd; Raleigh-Durham Airport Authority, *Raleigh-Durham Airport Long-Range Development Master Plan and Environmental Assessment, Technical Report Volume 1* [of 61], *March 1980.*

80 The doctors involved were Neal P. Boddie, E. H. Bowling, Ira J. Stone, William A. Strowd, and Elmer S. Waring (*Herald*, 17 Feb., 22 Apr., 26 Apr., 25 June, 27 June 1925, 1 Mar. 1931, 9 June 1932, 22 Apr., 28 Sept. 1939). Dr. Bowling's indictment in the narcotics case did not prevent his running (unsuccessfully) for mayor in 1935 with the endorsement of labor. Bowling promised union wages for all city employees if he were elected (ibid., 5 Apr., 30 Apr. 1935).

81 Pamela Preston Reynolds, "The Interaction between Public Attitudes and a Philanthropist's Dream: Watts Hospital, 1895–1976" (history honors paper, 1979), D.U. Archives, 20, 58; *Herald*, 9 Aug. 1931, 24 Mar. 1932, 20 Mar. 1934, 21 May 1935.

82 Reynolds, "Watts Hospital," 51–58; *Herald*, 14 Mar. 1929, 23 Jan. 1940, 10 Feb. 1985; Gifford, *The Evolution of a Medical Center*, 59.

83 *Herald*, 19 Dec. 1930, 26 Mar. 1938, 17 Dec. 1939; telephone interview with Dr. Lenox Baker, 9 Nov. 1986; Durham Bicentennial Commission Papers, DU-RBMSCL.

84 *Herald*, 15 June, 22 June 1930, 17 Mar., 10 June, 15 Oct. 1939. The YWCA had been running a summer camp for girls, Camp Hollow Rock, on the New Hope Creek for a number of summers up to the Depression (ibid., 2 June 1935). The YMCA Camp Sacarusa for boys (begun in 1920) was continued until 1938, when river pollution forced its closing (ibid., 26 Feb. 1931, 29 May 1932, 13 June 1937, 14 June 1938).

85 Ibid., 10 June 1940, 29 Oct. 1986 (50th anniversary of the Lions Club Industries, Inc. section).
86 Ibid., 20 Feb., 8 Aug. 1927, 1 Aug., 27 Nov. 1935, 5 Aug. 1937, 17 Dec. 1939; Board of Health Minutes, 12 Nov. 1935. One in six black babies born in Durham was illegitimate in 1927. In addition, one in twelve was born dead (ibid., 5 Aug. 1937; Board of Health Minutes, 12 Nov. 1935).
87 Ibid., 20 Aug. 1931, 13 June 1935, 19 Jan. 1939, 17 Jan. 1943.
88 Ibid., 8 Nov. 1927, 28 Apr. 1929.
89 Ibid., 2 Mar., 25 Mar., 8 May, 11 June, 7 Nov. 1938, 14 Nov. 1940, 13 Feb. 1944; information from Mrs. Gifford Davis, telephone interview, 10 Nov. 1986. Mrs. Davis had established a nursery school in 1932 in the Bivins Building of East Campus, Duke University, sponsored by the Education Department with a clientele drawn from town and gown. The first WPA nursery school was set up in 1941 at Southside school in West Durham (26 Jan. 1941). A year or two before, the Civitan Club (organized 1938) as its first project started a nursery school for the children of working parents in the basement of Y. E. Smith school (ibid., 26 Apr. 1953).
90 Herald, 11 Sept. 1940, 26 Apr. 1953 (Durham Centennial edition); interview with Mrs. Twaddell, 10 June 1983; Durham Bicentennial Commission Papers, DU-RBMSCL, Durham City and County Schools. The Twaddell School closed in 1966 (Herald, 3 June 1966).
    Mattie Louise Moore McDougald directed the first black kindergarten at White Rock Church in 1911–12 (ibid., 26 Apr. 1953, Durham Centennial edition). The First Presbyterian Church established a kindergarten in 1925 under the direction of Miss Marie Van Noppen (who was trained at the Horace Mann kindergarten school) assisted by Mrs. C. W. Toms (ibid., 26 Sept. 1925).
91 Herald, 22 Sept. 1935, 7 July, 4 Aug., 23 Aug. 1936; North Carolina Collection, Durham County Library, materials on civic organizations.
92 Herald, 7 Mar. 1937, 8 Mar. 1987; Grout Family Papers, DU-RBMSCL, Julia Grout, "Thirty-three Years with the Altrusa Club of Durham, North Carolina," 1967; information provided to the author by Dr. Lois Cranford and Jessie Pearson (Mrs. W. G., II). Rose Butler Browne (1899–1986), the wife of the minister of Mount Vernon Baptist Church, E. T. Browne, was an incalculable force for good in her community. Besides teaching in the Education Department of North Carolina College, which she also headed for a number of years, Mrs. Browne set up study groups for schoolchildren at the church every night where they were first served a nutritious dinner. She also organized a credit union in the church and successfully led the drive for an education building in which she started a state-approved nursery school. She persuaded the church to invest in a hundred acres on Boyce's Mill Road to provide a summer camp for the children (Rose Butler Browne, Love My Children [New York, 1969]).
    Scout troops for black boys had begun earlier. In 1942 there were 156 boys involved in troops under the leadership of J. M. Schooler. J. N. Mills was vice-chairman of the district (Herald, 17 Dec. 1942).
93 Herald, 22 Nov. 1931, 13 Sept. 1936, 20 May 1937, 18 Feb. 1938; information supplied to the author by Margaret McPherson and Susan Fox Beischer.
    Mrs. Catherine Groves Peele was executive secretary of the Family Service Association in 1941, and Mrs. Mabel Woodfork was supervisor (Herald, 24 Feb. 1941).
94 Herald, 13 Jan. 1927, 13 Nov., 18 Nov. 1932, 25 Feb. 1940.
95 Anti-lynching bills were repeatedly introduced in Congress, only to be obstructed by filibustering southern senators. None was ever passed into law (Herald, 11 Apr., 18 Nov. 1937, 7 Jan. 1940). "The Durham Fact-Finding Conference, Durham, 1929," NCC.
96 Herald, 30 Jan. 1927.
97 Ibid., 8 Jan. 1935, 18 Dec., 30 Dec. 1936; Carolina Times, 7 Aug., 21 Aug. 1937.

Hillside Park was the name given to the school at Umstead and Pine streets until 1950 when that school and Whitted school at the end of Brant Street exchanged names and student bodies. The former Hillside became Whitted Junior High and the former Whitted became Hillside High School.

Recognizing the need of a new cemetery for blacks, in 1926 the city bought from R. L. McDougald and others a tract of close to 25 acres on Fayetteville Road to which was given the name Beechwood Cemetery. It supplanted five older cemeteries, almost all full and lacking in maintenance and orderly arrangement: Violet cemetery (named for John Merrick's mother and donated by him, also known as Wolf Den cemetery because it bordered that area); Geer cemetery at the corner of the present Camden Road and Colonial Drive (sold by Jesse Geer to a cemetery committee headed by Willis Moore, John O'Daniel, and Nelson Mitchell); Fitzgerald cemetery on Kent Street; East Durham cemetery; and Hickstown cemetery, Crest Street (*Herald*, 29 July 1925, 19 Oct. 1926, OCDB 45: 89; *Durham, N.C. City Directory, 1922* [Richmond, 1922]).

98 *Herald*, 14 Feb., 17 Mar. 1933; SOHP, Walter Weare's interview with C. O. Pearson, 1979; Weare, *Black Business in the New South*, 226n, 235.

99 *Herald*, 19 May 1916, 18 Feb., 4 June 1925, 15 Feb., 20 Feb., 9 Mar. 1929. When taken over by the state, the college comprised eight buildings worth $135,000 and carried a debt of $19,000.

100 SOHP, Weare interview with Pearson. Much more complex maneuvering behind the scenes by both Spaulding and Shepard is evident in Spaulding's papers; see Weare, *Black Business in the New South*, 232–36.

101 SOHP, Weare's interview with Pearson; Weare, *Black Business in the New South*, 232–36; Thomas H. Houck, "A Newspaper History of Race Relations in Durham, 1910–1940," 51–56. The Old North State Bar Association for black lawyers was organized in Durham in 1935 (*Herald*, 23 Feb. 1935).

102 *Herald*, 14 Sept., 16 Dec. 1938, 27 June, 3 Sept., 4 Oct. 1939.

103 Ibid., 17 Mar. 1933; Kent Boyd, "Louis Austin and the *Carolina Times*" (M.A. thesis, NCCU, 1966).

104 *Herald*, 17 Mar. 1933; Boyd, "Louis Austin and the *Carolina Times*"; Daniel J. Singal, *The War Within: From Victorian to Modernist Thought in the South, 1919–1945* (Chapel Hill, 1982), 475–76.

105 Miles Mark Fisher, *Friends: Pictorial History of Ten Years Pastorate* (Durham, 1943), 28. Recreation for the black elite centered around the Algonquin Club and its tennis courts, organized in the 1920s. It later added food service and accommodated guests, becoming a focus of social life in Hayti until its demise in 1964. The clubhouse was located at Fayetteville and Morris streets.

106 *Herald*, 5 Apr. 1935; SOHP, Weare's interview with Pearson; Fisher, *Friends*.

107 *Herald*, 24 Jan., 11 May 1926, 6 Feb. 1929, 11 Dec. 1941, 24 Oct. 1943, 15 Apr. 1990. Donald C. Watson of Brooklyn was the first director.

108 Ibid., 20 Aug. 1935, 7 May, 11 May, 22 May, 15 July, 11 Aug., 26 Sept. 1937, 8 Mar. 1939; *Carolina Times*, 22 May 1937.

109 *Herald*, 12 May 1935, 26 Sept. 1937, 24 Aug., 26 Aug., 27 Aug. 1938. It was an era of statistics-gathering and surveys. In 1938 the Chamber of Commerce paid for an industrial and economic survey and the Family Service Association authorized a social survey (ibid., 22 Sept. 1938).

110 Ibid., 24 Aug., 16 Oct. 1938, 9 Apr. 1939, 27 Jan., 10 Mar., 18 Mar. 1940; *Report of the Real Property Survey of Durham, North Carolina, 1939–40*.

111 *Carolina Times*, 17 Nov. 1935, 16 Oct., 23 Oct. 1937; SOHP, Weare's interview with Pearson.

112 *Herald*, 9 Feb. 1935, 10 May, 12 May, 17 May 1936, 26 Apr. 1939; *Carolina Times*, 14 May 1938; Weare, *Black Business in the New South*, 240–46.

113 Boyd, "Louis Austin and the *Carolina Times*"; *Herald*, 30 May, 1 June 1937; *Carolina Times*, 5 June 1937. The following year Ellen Harris refused to move to the back of a bus when asked to by a white male passenger. After a conviction by both the lower and Superior courts, she won acquittal in the state Supreme Court. (*Carolina Times*, 14 May, 18 June 1938).

A short-lived competitor of the *Carolina Times* was the *Carolina Tribune*, started in 1927.

114 *Herald*, 23 June 1937; *Carolina Times*, 26 June 1937; Houck, "A Newspaper History," 141.

115 *Herald*, 30 May, 29 June 1938.

116 Bill Phillips, "Piedmont Country Blues," *Southern Exposure* 2, no. 1 (spring–summer 1974): 56, 60.

117 *Herald*, 3 Nov. 1986, obituary of Sippy Wallace.

118 Phillips, "Piedmont Country Blues," 58; Bruce Bastin, *Crying for the Carolines* (London, 1971), 12–14; Glenn Hinson, "Bull City Blues," *N.C. Bicentennial Folklife Festival Program Book*, 10–11, 45–47.

119 *Herald*, 24 June 1938; SOHP, Hinson's interview with Thomas Burt, 26 Oct. 1976, 6 Feb., 3 Nov. 1979; Sonny Terry, *The Harp Styles of Sonny Terry* (New York, 1975), 24; Phillips, "Piedmont Blues," 58; *Herald*, 1 Mar. 1938.

120 SOHP, Hinson's interview with Thomas Burt; Terry, *Harp Styles*, 120.

121 SOHP, Glenn Hinson's interview with Reginald Mitchiner, 15 Nov., 7 Dec. 1976, 7 Feb., 23 May 1979, for this quotation and those following.

122 After leaving high school Cole went into the army as a bandmaster during the Second World War (SOHP, Mitchiner interview).

123 *Herald*, 16 Feb. 1930, 28 Oct. 1931, 13 Mar. 1932, 1 Nov. 1935, 30 Oct. 1936, 12 Dec. 1937, 17 Apr., 9 Dec. 1938, 11 Feb. 1939, 25 Feb., 23 Apr., 23 Nov., 2, 12 Dec. 1940; information from Ruth and Richard L. Watson, Jr.

124 Undated letter [probably 1985], now in the possession of the author, from Mrs. Hunter to Mrs. Mayme Perry; program of the White House concert, photocopy in possession of the author; *Herald*, 7 May 1930, 4 June 1939.

125 *Herald*, 15 July 1932, 17 June 1934, 3 Nov. 1935, 20 Dec. 1936, 18 Oct. 1938.

126 Ibid., 23 July 1921, 26 Oct. 1925, 4 July 1927, 1 July 1928, 5 June 1939, 26 Apr. 1981 (Durham Centennial edition); *Carolina's Outstanding Sports Station, WDNC* (Peoria, Ill., 1941); W. C. Dula, *Durham and Her People* (Durham, 1951), 105, 165, 184.

127 *Herald*, 3 Oct. 1929, 25 Jan. 1931, 29 Nov. 1938, 3 Jan., 7 Jan. 1939, 1 Dec. 1941, 2 Jan. 1942.

17 WORLD WAR II AND THE END OF AN ERA

1 Theodore Draper, review of *Eisenhower: At War, 1943–1945*, by David Eisenhower, *New York Review of Books* 25 (25 Sept. 1986), 30.

2 *Herald*, 15 Feb., 10 July 1940; *Sun*, 1 Nov. 1940; interview with Mrs. Bernheim, 9 Jan. 1987.

3 *Herald*, 30 June, 19 July, 5 Aug., 23 Sept., 4 Oct., 16 Oct., 5 Dec., 13 Dec. 1940, 22 Mar. 1941. After the United States entered the war, a new draft law affected those aged 18 to 45. Florence Murray, ed., *Negro Handbook, 1946–47* (New York, 1947), 325, 364–65.

4 *Herald*, 4 Mar., 6 Mar., 1 Apr., 4 Apr. 1940, 18 Mar., 1 Apr., 13 Apr., 27 July 1941.

5 Ibid., 8 June 1941; Blackwell Robinson, ed., *The North Carolina Guide* (Chapel Hill, 1955), 202.

6 *Herald*, 20 Apr., 17 June, 16 Nov. 1941, 15 Nov. 1942, 23 Sept. 1943.

7 Ibid., 27 July, 29 July, 22 Aug. 1941.

8 Ibid., 8 Aug. 1941, 30 Jan., 1 Feb., 11 Feb., 22 Feb., 1 Mar., 15 May, 22 May, 5 Aug.

1942, 23 Jan. 1944; Clara Pugh Matthis, *The Unforgettable Years* (Durham, 1947). Former Mayor R. Wensell Grabarek was in the "Lightning" Division at Camp Butner, his introduction to the area.

9 *Herald*, 2 July, 7 July, 9 July, 9 Oct. 1942, 28 Mar., 30 May, 23 June, 24 Oct. 1943, 4 Jan., 20 Feb., 8 June, 11 June 1944.

10 Ibid., 12 July, 8 Aug., 4 Sept. 1942, 20 Feb., 21 June, 27 July, 12 Aug. 1944. A modern bus station had just been built on the site of the William Lipscomb mansion at the corner of Dillard and Main streets, but John A. Buchanan had retained title to the land and owned the new building (*Herald*, 4 Sept. 1942).

11 *Herald*, 22 May 1941, 25 Feb., 25 Apr., 29 Apr. 1943, 28 June 1944.

12 This and the following quotations are from SOHP, Glenn Hinson's interview with Reginald Mitchiner, 1976, 1979.

13 *Herald*, 9 May 1943.

14 Ibid., 9 May, 13 May 1943.

15 Ibid., 18 June, 16 July, 19 July 1942, 6 July 1944, 5 May 1985. Dr. Isaac Harris of Creedmoor, later a Durham practitioner, was head of surgery at the 196th General Hospital near Fairfoot, England.

16 Veterans Administration, Research Monograph 9, *County Veteran Population, 1966,* Durham County. The statistics in this monograph show 7,910 veterans in Durham County in 1966. With the addition of those who died in the twenty-year period 1946 to 1966 and the number that had moved elsewhere, the total would certainly be close to 10,000 persons (*Herald*, 1 Oct. 1944, 16 Nov. 1986).

17 One Durhamite won distinction when a liberty ship, built and launched in Wilmington, North Carolina, was christened the SS *John Merrick.* Three other illustrious blacks honored similarly were Frederick A. Douglass, Booker T. Washington, and George Washington Carver (*Herald*, 11 July 1943). William P. Few and James B. Duke also had liberty ships named for them (Joel A. Kostyu and Frank A. Kostyu, *Durham: A Pictorial History* [Norfolk, 1978], 117).

18 *Herald*, 3 Aug., 18 Oct., 26 Oct. 1941, 15 Feb., 7 Mar., 12 Mar., 13 Dec. 1942. Licenses to drive automobiles had been required since 1935.

19 Ibid., 8 Feb. 1942, 26 June 1944.

20 Ibid., 27 July 1941, 24 May, 11 July, 28 Nov., 6 Dec. 1942.

21 Ibid., 18 Dec. 1941, 12 Mar., 25 Apr. 1942. In 1943 the Wright Machinery Company (which merged with Sperry Rand Corporation in 1957) won a government award for excellence (it had been engaged in producing the Norton bombsight), and great publicity was given the ceremony held in the armory, attended by army and navy bands, and broadcast coast to coast (ibid., 27 Mar., 18 Apr. 1943).

22 Ibid., 14 Dec. 1941, 15 Jan., 30 Aug., 29 Nov. 1942, 28 Feb., 14 Mar., 31 Mar. 1943.

23 Ibid., 1 Oct. 1942, 6 June 1943, 5 July 1944.

24 Ibid., 20 Feb., 2 July 1944. After the Durham Community Chest was superseded by the United Fund in 1953, the chest's function of funneling funds to medical research was given to a new organization founded in 1955 by representatives of community chests and united funds all over the state. Called the United Medical Research Foundation, its president was Dr. James Semans and its secretary-treasurer, Paul Wright, Jr. It was particularly helpful in interim funding of research that would otherwise have been interrupted while awaiting new grants (ibid., 24 Mar. 1955; information from Dr. Semans, 25 Oct. 1984).

25 Ibid., 18 Jan., 28 Feb., 8 Mar. 1942, 13 Feb. 1944. The facility was closed in 1953 after the discovery of a new drug radically improved the treatment and cure rate of tuberculosis.

26 Ibid., 15 May, 9 July 1944.

27 Ibid., 10 Jan., 23 Feb., 26 Feb., 16 Mar. 1946.

28 Ibid., 18 Sept. 1949. Information provided by Triangle J Council of Governments;

Howard J. Sumka and Michael A. Stegman, "The Housing Outlook in North Carolina: Projections to 1980," N.C. Department of Administration report (June 1972), 82–83.

29 *Herald*, 16 Apr., 5 May 1943; 14 Apr. 1944, 28 Nov. 1982.

30 Ibid., 13 July, 19 July 1944; Conrad C. Haupt, "The Role of the Planner in Durham, North Carolina" (M.A. thesis, UNC, 1961); Minutes of the Durham City Council, Book T, 349, City Clerk's office; Durham City Planning Department, "A Governmental Center for Durham," 5; interview with former Mayor James R. Hawkins, 2 Mar. 1987.

31 Ibid., 9 Apr. 1949; telephone interview with Deryl Bateman, head of the county Planning Department, 16 Mar. 1987.

32 Ibid., 7 Nov. 1943; information supplied to the author by Mrs. Merrick and her daughter, Mrs. Charles Watts.

33 Ibid., 26 Apr. 1953; *A Quarter Century of Political Participation in North Carolina 1951–1976: A History of the League of Women Voters of North Carolina* (Durham, 1976).

34 *Herald*, 14 Aug., 15 Aug. 1945.

18 THE OLD ORDER CHANGETH

1 The title is taken from lines in Alfred, Lord Tennyson's "Morte D'Arthur": "The old order changeth, yielding place to new; And God fulfills himself in many ways, Lest one good custom should corrupt the world."

2 Robert J. Steamer, "Southern Disaffection with the National Democratic Party," *Change in the Contemporary South*, ed. Allan P. Sindler (Durham, 1963), 150, 170–72.

3 Lefler and Newsome, *North Carolina*, 627–29.

4 Among the many North Carolinians in President Truman's administration were two Durham natives, George Allen, a career diplomat and ambassador in turn to Iran, Yugoslavia, and India, and Daniel K. Edwards, an undersecretary of defense in 1950.

5 Lefler and Newsome, *North Carolina*, 697, 699. That education in the state was still poor was revealed by the 1960 census, which showed just under one-sixth of the population as illiterate.

6 Words from James Russell Lowell's poem "In Time of Crisis," used in the hymn "Once to Every Man and Nation."

7 Russell Clay, "Is Durham Lagging behind Other North Carolina Cities?" *Herald*, 22 Mar., 23 Mar. 1959. Rencher N. Harris (1900–1965), a Virginian, had come to Durham in 1921 as an agent for the Bankers Fire and Casualty Insurance Company. He had belonged to the Urban League in Chicago. A founder of the DCNA, he had appeared before the city council on behalf of many civil rights issues. He ran unsuccessfully for the city council in 1949. Rencher N. Harris Papers, DU-RBMSCL, and Olivia W. Cole, "Rencher N. Harris: A Quarter of a Century of Negro Leadership" (M.A. thesis, NCCU, 1967).

8 William R. Keech, *The Impact of Negro Voting: The Role of the Vote in the Quest for Equality* (Chicago, 1968), 106–9. Between 1950 and 1960 Durham's city population actually declined, for although the 1960 census showed a gain of 8,000 residents over the 1950 census, in that decade the city limits were extended to include over 9,000 additional inhabitants.

9 *Herald*, 18–27 Feb. 1952.

10 Clay, "Is Durham Lagging?" *Herald*, 23–28 Mar. 1959.

11 *Herald*, 6 Mar. 1959; Conrad C. Haupt, "The Role of the Planner in Durham, North Carolina," 91–95.

12 Haupt, "The Role of the Planner," 103–6.

13 Clay, "Is Durham Lagging?" *Herald*, 22 Mar. 1959; *Herald*, 29 Dec. 1951, 15 Apr. 1963; Evans, *The Provincials*, 10–13. In 1943 the Junior Chamber of Commerce voted "Mutt" Evans outstanding man of the year for his capacity for hard work, independent think-

ing, and integrity (*Herald*, 19 Jan. 1943). He was rated by some as Durham's most effective mayor because of his ability to create a consensus.

14 Between 1956 and 1959 the following suburban developments were taken into the city limits: Arnaldo division, Duke Forest (old section), Glendale Heights, Oakwood Park, Rockwood, Tuscaloosa Forest, and Wellons Village (Rencher Harris Papers, DU-RBMSCL, Board of Education folder [1959]).

15 Clay, "Is Durham Lagging?" *Herald*, 24 Mar. 1959.

16 *Herald*, 3 Dec., 8 Dec. 1960.

17 Telephone conversation with Del Amnott, longtime manager of Poplar Apartments, 20 Feb. 1987.

18 *Herald*, 21 July 1950. Mrs. Hanes's donation was supplemented by a federal grant. She was the widow of Dr. Frederick Hanes, chief of medicine in the medical school.

19 Ibid., 13 Jan., 15 June, 18 June, 15 Dec. 1950, 4 July 1952, 6 Apr., 19 Apr. 1953, 18 Sept. 1964.

20 "A Brief Chronological History of the Methodist Retirement Homes, Inc." typescript sent to the author by Mildred Cartee.

21 *The First Twenty Years: A History of the Duke University Schools of Medicine, Nursing, and Health Services, and Duke Hospital, 1930–1950* (Durham, 1952), 4; statistics for the Duke University Medical Center were supplied to the author by James F. Gifford, Jr.; *Perspectives* 1 (spring 1981).

22 Bruce Henderson, "A Diversified Durham," Charlotte *Observer*, 28 Aug. 1986.

23 "Entdecker der Reisdiät achtzig Jahre alt," *Berliner Tagespiegel*, 25 Jan. 1983; Burr Snider, "Fat City," *Esquire* (May 1973), 112–14, 174–82; Kathryn McPherson's variously titled articles on diets, *Herald*, 18–20 May, 25 May 1980.

24 *Herald*, 18–20 May, 25 May 1980. Dr. Richard Stuelke directed the Dietary Rehabilitation Center from 1972 to 1975, followed by Dr. Sigrid Nelius when Stuelke left to form his own program. Dr. Gerard Musante, who had headed the behavioral program at the Rehabilitation Center, also established an independent program, Structure House.

25 Ibid., 12 Jan. 1943.

26 Ibid., 28 Jan. 1943.

27 Ibid., 19 May 1946.

28 Lefler and Newsome, *North Carolina*, 626.

29 Lola Williams, "A History of Calvert Method School during the Headmistressship of Bess Pickard Boone" (19 May 1976), DU-RBMSCL, Durham Bicentennial Commission Papers; Leah Kim, "Durham Academy Has 50-Year History," *Herald*, 21 May 1983; Betty Hodges, "Durham Academy Alumni Reminisce about the Past," *Herald*, 25 Oct. 1983.

30 Information provided to the author by Durham Academy. In 1977 George Watts Hill funded the establishment of a center for children with learning disabilities, the Hill Learning Center, first located in an old farmhouse but after 1985 in a new building of its own.

31 *Herald*, 18 May 1946; Lefler and Newsome, *North Carolina*, 626.

32 Harry D. Hollingsworth, *Saint Luke's Episcopal Church, Durham, North Carolina* (Durham, 1981); William E. Stauber, *A History of Epworth United Methodist Church, Durham, North Carolina*; *Herald*, 14 July 1941, 11 Oct. 1942, 26 Sept. 1943, 26 Apr. 1953. Saint Luke's congregation built a new church on Hillandale Road in 1970.
    Bishop Henry L. Fisher claimed that he preached his first sermon in the Gospel Tabernacle on Piedmont Street in 1905 and became the founder of the oldest black Holiness group in the world (*Herald*, 13 June 1943).

33 *Herald*, 26 Apr. 1953.

34 Ho Laos ["the people"], *Saint Barbara's Greek Orthodox Church, Durham, North Carolina* ([Durham], 1970); Donald K. Routh, *The Story of the Eno River Unitarian-Universalist Fellowship* (Iowa City, 1979).

35 Lefler and Newsome, *North Carolina*, 136; Lefler and Wager, *Orange County*, 291.

36 Weston LaBarre, *They Shall Take Up Serpents* (Minneapolis, 1962), 3–10, 34–40; *Sun*, 16 Oct. 1948; *Herald*, 21 Oct., 2 Nov., 19 Nov., 20 Nov. 1947, 5 Apr. 1949.

37 *Herald*, 5 Jan., 24 Jan., 28 Jan. 1944.

38 Ibid., 15 June 1978.

39 Ibid., 18 Dec. 1958, 5 Mar. 1962.

40 David H. Rice, "Urban Renewal in Durham: A Case Study of a Referendum" (M.A. thesis, UNC, 1966); Al Wheless, "Durham Renewal, a $76.2 Million Tag," *Herald*, 8–12 Aug. 1976; Margaret Latimer, "Some Social Aspects of Urban Renewal," (M.A. thesis, UNC, 1964).

41 Rencher N. Harris Papers, DU-RBMSCL, Lincoln Hospital folder.

42 James R. Hawkins Papers, Watts Carr, Jr., to Hawkins, 18 May 1972; Downtown Revitalization Foundation, 3 Aug., 8 Aug. 1973; Bell Design Group, Bull Durham Business District (Raleigh, 1975), unpublished report prepared for Watts Hill, Sr.; Rice, "Urban Renewal in Durham."

43 Wheless, "Durham Renewal," *Herald*, 8 Aug. 1976.

44 Kostyu and Kostyu, *Durham: A Pictorial History*, title page, 173.

45 "History of Public Housing in Durham," fact sheet supplied to the author by James R. Tabron, Executive Director, Housing Authority of the City of Durham. Durham County did not have a minimum housing code until after the establishment of the County Planning Department and the adoption of a zoning ordinance in 1956. Before that complaints about county housing went to the Health Department.

46 Alex Hurden, "The Origin of the Damar Court Dispute," N.C. Fund report, 30 Aug. 1968, SHC.

47 Day Piercy, "The Greenberg Housing Controversy: A Case Study in Community Organization," N.C. Fund report, Aug. 1968, SHC.

48 Hurden, "The Damar Court Dispute." Duke University replaced its married student housing within a year or two with the units known as Central Campus Housing adjoining old Monkey Bottom.

49 "History of Public Housing in Durham." James Jackson ("Babe") Henderson prompted the formation of the Durham Business and Professional Chain (a kind of black chamber of commerce) in 1938 and was co-founder of the Durham Business College (telephone interview with J. J. Henderson, 25 June 1987); *Herald*, 8 Dec. 1952, 27 Aug. 1953, 13 Nov. 1978.

50 Lester M. Salamon, *Durham Urban Observatory Report: The Substandard and Rental Housing Market in Durham* (Durham, 1976); Dick Terry, "Public Action to Upgrade the Housing Stock of the Research Triangle Region, 1960–1970," DU-RBMSCL, North Carolina County Papers, Durham.

51 *Action* 7 (June 1968); *Herald*, 20 July 1968.

52 Louis R. Wilson, *The Research Triangle of North Carolina* (Chapel Hill, 1967); George Herbert, "The Research Triangle: An Early History," speech to the Watauga Club, 4 Mar. 1980, Romeo Guest Papers, DU-RBMSCL.

53 William B. Hamilton, "The Research Triangle of North Carolina: A Study in Leadership for the Common Weal," *South Atlantic Quarterly* 65 (1966): 255; Mary Virginia Currie Jones, "A 'Golden Triangle' of Research: Romeo Holland Guest—His Conception of and Involvement in the Development of the Research Triangle Park" (M.A. thesis, UNC, 1978).

54 Herbert, "The Research Triangle"; Herbert, memorandum, 11 July 1954; correspondence 1953–54, DU-RBMSCL, Guest Papers.

55 Herbert, "The Research Triangle," DU-RBMSCL, Guest Papers; Hamilton, "The Research Triangle of North Carolina," 266, 267.

56 "Summary of Land Purchased in Research Triangle Park, 5 June 1958," DU-RBMSCL, Guest Papers; Hamilton, "The Research Triangle of North Carolina," 261.

57 Luther J. Carter, "Research Triangle Park Succeeds beyond Its Promoters' Expectation," *Science* 200 (30 June 1978): 1469–70; Hamilton, "The Research Triangle of North Carolina," 271, 274. Hamilton suggests that Terry Sanford cashed in on his assistance to John F. Kennedy in the 1960 election by bringing the Park to Kennedy's attention and thereby securing the government agency installations there.

58 Information provided to the author by Ned Huffman, Executive Vice-President, Research Triangle Foundation.

59 Thomas Yancey Milburn Papers, Private Collections, NCOAH. Milburn practiced architecture in Durham from 1915 until 1926 and drew the plans of the following landmarks: First Presbyterian Church, courthouse, Alexander Motor Company, Masonic Building, King's Daughters Home, Durham High School, Carr Junior High School, Lincoln and McPherson hospitals, Erwin and Powe apartment houses, City Auditorium (Carolina Theatre), and the Nello Teer house (now owned by Duke University). George Lougee, "Potential of Research Park Cited by Retired Architect," *Herald*, 23 Nov. 1973.

60 Rencher N. Harris Papers, DU-RBMSCL, Board of Education, Industrial Education Center folder; William A. Clement Papers, SHC, Aug., Sept. 1958; *Herald*, 27 Apr. 1958.

61 Harris Papers, DU-RBMSCL, Hill to Milburn, 14 Aug. 1958; Hill to Fuller, 20 Aug. 1958.

62 Kostyu and Kostyu, *Durham: A Pictorial History*, 110–11.

63 Information supplied to the author by R. Edward Stewart, 6 Apr. 1987.

64 Janiewski, "From Field to Factory," 263.

65 Richard C. Franck, "An Oral History of West Durham." After annexing West Durham, the city was very slow to assume any responsibility for its improvement. The merchants on Ninth Street therefore formed an association to push for the paving and maintenance of streets.

66 Franck, "An Oral History of West Durham," interview with Frank DeVyver.

67 *Herald*, 3 Jan., 11 Jan., 23 Sept., 9 Oct. 1945, 3 Mar. 1946.

68 Ibid., 1 Apr., 3 Apr. 1951; Erwin Mills, Inc. v. Textile Workers Union of America, CIO et al., *South Eastern Reporter*, 2nd ser., 67 (1952): 372–74, 68 (1952): 813–16; Franck, "An Oral History of West Durham," interview with Frank DeVyver.

69 Information provided to the author by Marvin E. Baugh, Manager, Real Estate Department, Burlington Industries, Inc.

70 *Herald*, 1 Oct. 1944.

71 Cameron Family Papers, SHC, John D. Hawkins to Cameron, 5 July 1826.

72 Hillsborough *Recorder*, 7 Feb. 1872.

73 *Herald*, 12 Jan. 1964.

74 Ibid., 21 Feb. 1987.

75 After 1977 sales declined at Liggett and Myers, but wages there were the highest in the county at that time. The average tobacco industry employee earned $14,508 annually while the average textile worker earned $8,445. The average electronics employee, however, earned $19,700, an indication of how times were changing. In 1982 the services area of employment, including health, had the greatest potential and the greatest growth since 1977 (City of Durham Planning and Community Development Department, "Durham: Past—Present—Future," Nov. 1982, 219–22; *Herald*, 29 Oct. 1986).

76 Ven Carver, "The Last Warehouse," *Herald*, 14 Sept. 1986.

77 *Herald*, 7 Apr., 31 May, 28 June, 31 July 1951.

78 Ibid., 21 Aug. 1951, 10 Apr., 11 Apr., 24 Apr. 1957.

79 Ibid., 1 Mar., 20 Mar., 22 Mar., 4 May 1962; Jack Adams, "George Watts Hill, Baron of Durham, Chairman of the Boards," *Herald*, 25 Apr. 1982.

80 *Herald*, 23 Mar. 1964.

81 Interview with E. S. Swindell, Jr., 22 Apr. 1987; *Herald*, 9 Apr. 1949.

82 City of Durham Planning Department, "Durham: Past—Present—Future"; interview with E. S. Swindell, Jr. The city-county committee was largely responsible for bringing many new industries to Durham.

83 Winfield H. Rose, "Referendum Voting and the Politics of Health Care in Durham County, North Carolina" (Ph.D. diss., Duke University, 1973); interview with E. S. Swindell, Jr.; Pamela Preston Reynolds, "The Interaction between Public Attitudes and a Philanthropist's Dream: Watts Hospital, 1895–1976" (course paper, D.U., 1979), 93.

84 Rose, "Referendum Voting and the Politics of Health Care"; Hospital Study Committee Report, *Study of Durham County Health Facility Needs, Durham, North Carolina* (Durham, 1968); interview with E. S. Swindell, Jr.

85 Interview with E. S. Swindell, Jr.

86 Hawkins Papers, DU-RBMSCL, Jan. 1972, 3 Aug. 1973, 23 May 1976; Mark H. Webbink, "Durham Makes the Most of Revenue-Sharing," *Popular Government* 40 (winter 1975): 36–39. Durham got $25.4 million worth of value out of the $11 million gift. In addition to the government buildings, the money paid for forty-two miles of street paving, a wastewater treatment plant, sewer extensions, a firefighting training facility, fifty tennis courts, two city parks, and twelve neighborhood parks. The city had over $4 million left over for future needs. Lew G. Brown, assistant city manager, and T. L. Amick, city budget director, were responsible for this financial wizardry.

87 Information supplied the author by Richard J. Sauer, Durham County Fire Marshal.

88 *Herald*, 26 Apr. 1981 (centennial edition).

89 Ibid., 26 Feb. 1987.

90 Information supplied to the author by Carol Layh of Goodwill Industries, Inc.

91 *Herald*, 3 June, 4 Dec. 1953; Rencher Harris Papers, DU-RBMSCL, 1953.

92 Tami Hultman, "Edgemont," 7 Aug. 1968, N.C. Fund report, SHC.

93 In 1960 Edgemont had a population of about 6,500, slightly more black than white, with a median family income of $2,300 (the equivalent figure nationally was $4,976); 56 percent had less than five years of schooling; 63.4 percent of the housing was unsound or without plumbing (Sally Avery, "Public Welfare in Durham County" (course paper, D.U., May 1969).

94 An earlier food stamp program had been tried in 1941 for those on relief or receiving Social Security and for WPA workers (*Herald*, 2 Jan. 1941).

95 "Administration Manual of the North Carolina Fund," N.C. Fund Papers, SHC.

96 Information supplied to the author by Fred McNeill, Jr., Executive Director, Operation Breakthrough.

97 *Herald*, 7 Feb., 14 Apr. 1969; Greensboro *Daily News*, 19 Oct. 1967; Mike Nathan, "Community Organization in Edgemont," 29 May 1968, N.C. Fund report, SHC; Francis S. Redburn, "Protest and Policy in Durham, North Carolina" (Ph.D. diss., UNC, 1970), 78–79.

98 Cornelia Olive, "Clinic Caring for Poor," *Herald*, 22 Nov. 1969.

99 Information supplied to the author by Fred McNeill, Jr.; *Herald*, 11 July 1984.

19 CIVIL RIGHTS

1 The DCNA's accomplishment is reflected in Durham's voter registration figures from 1928 through selected years up to 1960. From fifty black registered voters in 1928 the number rose to 1,000 in 1935, the year of DCNA's organization, to over 13,000 in 1960, a figure equivalent to about 68 percent of eligible black voters. (William R. Keech, *The Impact of Negro Voting* [Chicago, 1968], 27.)

2 Weare, *Black Business in the New South*, 231n.

3 *Herald*, 22 June, 28 Oct. 1941; Weare, *Black Business in the New South*, 256.

4 *Herald*, 18 Feb. 1944.

5 Anticipating interracial tension because of the presence of black soldiers in 1941, Duke and UNC professors helped set up the Council against Intolerance (*Herald*, 8 Jan. 1941).

6 Ibid., 1 June, 5 June 1943, 9 July, 11 Sept., 16 Sept. 1944.

7 Weare, *Black Business in the New South*, 253; Gunnar Myrdal, *An American Dilemma* (New York, 1944), 842–50.

8 George B. Tindall, *The Emergence of the New South, 1913–1945* (Baton Rouge, 1967), 719; Weare, *Black Business in the New South*, 247n.

9 Benjamin Muse, *The Twentieth Century as I Saw It* (New York, 1982), 243.

10 Olivia W. Cole, "Rencher Nicholas Harris: A Quarter Century of Negro Leadership"; Rencher N. Harris Papers, DU-RBMSCL, Board of Education: 4 Mar. 1958, 18 June 1959.
   When airport extension plans came before the city council in 1955, Harris asked for the removal of "white" and "black" designations at the airport restrooms, basing his request on a federal law that prohibited the application of federal funds to racially segregated uses (Harris Papers, DU-RBMSCL, City of Durham, Airport, 1953–1956: Harris to R. Dillard Teer, 26 Oct. 1955).

11 William H. Chafe, *Civilities and Civil Rights* (New York, 1980), 77–82.

12 Author's telephone interview with William A. Clement, 15 Apr. 1987; Harris Papers, DU-RBMSCL, Letters: Petition to School Board, 11 July 1955, and Board of Education: "Summary of Board of Education Action on Application for Reassignment of 225 Pupils of the Durham School District, August 25, 1959," 28 Aug. 1959; Minutes of the Durham City Board of Education, 8:234 (28 Aug. 1959).

13 *Carolina Times*, 7 May 1960; *Herald*, 9 Aug. 1961, 15 May 1984; telephone interview with William A. Clement; Chris Howard, "Keep Your Eyes on the Prize: The Black Struggle for Civil Equality in Durham, North Carolina, 1954–1963" (honors paper, 1983), D.U. Archives, 71.

14 SOHP, interview of Floyd McKissick, Jr., by Jack Bass, 6 Dec. 1973.

15 *Carolina Times*, 4 June 1960; information supplied to the author by Mrs. Evelyn McKissick. The Richardsons had moved away before the case was decided. (Harris Papers, DU-RBMSCL, Board of Education: 29 Apr. 1960.)

16 Cole, "Rencher Nicholas Harris"; Harris Papers, DU-RBMSCL, Board of Education: 8, 15 Feb. 1960; Minutes of the Durham City Board of Education, vol. 8, 8 Dec. 1959. Harris resigned from the school board in 1962 because of ill health.

17 Minutes of the Durham City Board of Education, 9:285 (13 Jan. 1964); Capus Waynick et al., *North Carolina and the Negro* (Raleigh, 1964), 69; Henry Wefing, "30 Years Later in Durham," *Herald*, 13 May 1984.

18 Wefing, "30 Years Later in Durham," *Herald*, 13 May 1984.

19 Clipping file: The Links, North Carolina Room, Durham County Library; information to author from Dr. Patsy Perry. A second chapter of the Links, Triangle Park, was formed in 1984. Mrs. John Hope (Aurelia) Franklin was among the charter members.

20 Durham County School Board Minutes, 4 Apr. 1960, 24 June, 30 Aug. 1963. Unlike most blacks, Harris was in favor of consolidation as beneficial to the efficiency and quality of the schools. (Harris Papers, DU-RBMSCL, Board of Education: "The Matter of School Consolidation," 21 Oct. 1958.)

21 County School Board Minutes, 2 July, 3 Aug. 1964, 1 Feb. 1965.

22 Wefing, "30 Years Later in Durham," *Herald*, 13 May 1984.

23 *Herald*, 3 July 1971.

24 Ibid., 7 July 1972, 19 Sept. 1973, 18 Aug. 1984.

25 R. Taylor Cole, *The Recollections of R. Taylor Cole: Educator, Emissary, Development Planner* (Durham, 1983), 108, 155–94.

26 Harris Papers, DU-RBMSCL, Committee on Human Relations, 1956–1959: Petition to Mayor Evans (undated).

27 Information provided to the author by Shirley Strobel.

28 Howard, "Keep Your Eyes on the Prize," 11, 25, 33–34. Douglas Elaine Moore was one of the three Durham students in the Royal Ice Cream Company incident. (Information supplied to the author by Vivian Austin Edmonds.)

29 Allan P. Sindler, "Youth and the American Negro Protest Movement: A Local Case Study of Durham, North Carolina" (typescript, 1965), chapter 3, "The Durham Lunch-Counter Sit-ins of 1960," 22–35; Broadside Collection, DU-RBMSCL, "Don't Buy at These Stores"; Howard, "Keep Your Eyes on the Prize," 25, 30–36. The city had integrated its tennis courts in 1957, and in 1960 the first black played in a citywide tournament. (Information provided to the author by Edward Boyd of the NCCU Athletic Department, formerly of the city recreation department.)

30 Sindler, "Youth and the American Negro Protest Movement," 27; *Herald*, 24 Mar. 1961; Howard, "Keep Your Eyes on the Prize," 36f.

31 Howard, "Keep Your Eyes on the Prize," 47; Jim Peck, "A Carolina City—Fifteen Years Later," *CORE-lator* 98 (Nov. 1962).

32 Sindler, "Youth and the American Negro Protest Movement," 36–53.

33 Howard, "Keep Your Eyes on the Prize," 127–36; Waynick et al., *North Carolina and the Negro*, 67.

34 Howard, "Keep Your Eyes on the Prize," 129; *Herald*, 2 June 1963; Sindler, "Youth and the American Negro Protest Movement," 74 n45.

35 Waynick et al., *North Carolina and the Negro*, 69, 70, 75, 76; *Herald*, 2 June 1963. In the fall of 1963 Durham reported that 100 percent of its hotels and motels and 95 percent of its restaurants were desegregated (Chafe, *Civilities and Civil Rights*, 208).

36 Waynick et al., *North Carolina and the Negro*, 64, 71, 74; Ted G. Stone, "A Southern City and County in the Years of Political Change: Durham, North Carolina, 1955–1974" (M.A. thesis, NCCU, 1977), 88; Weare, *Black Business in the New South*, 231n; Sindler, "Youth and the American Negro Protest Movement," 47.

37 Sindler, "Youth and the American Negro Protest Movement," 48; Stone, "A Southern City and County," 93–100; Howard, "Keep Your Eyes on the Prize," 149–50.

38 Redburn, "Protest and Policy in Durham, North Carolina," 77–152.

39 Ibid.; *Herald*, 14 Apr. 1969.

40 Redburn, "Protest and Policy in Durham, North Carolina," 95–134.

41 *Herald*, 29 July, 16 Sept. 1967; Redburn, "Protest and Policy in Durham, North Carolina," 85.

42 *Sun*, 27 July 1967.

43 *Herald*, 2 July 1968; Redburn, "Protest and Policy in Durham, North Carolina," 151.

44 Author's telephone interview with A. J. Howard Clement III, 10 May 1987; Redburn, "Protest and Policy in Durham, North Carolina," 161–67.

45 Redburn, "Protest and Policy in Durham, North Carolina," 151–56, 165, 176–78, 185–94.

46 *Sun*, 13 Mar., 11 Apr., 22 May 1969. Fuller eventually went back to Wisconsin, where he became secretary of employee relations for the state.

47 *Herald*, 20 May 1970, 24 June, 26 Nov. 1971, 27 Mar. 1972, 26 May, 9 Sept. 1974, 18 Jan. 1980, 2 Apr. 1981; *Sun*, 6 Nov. 1979; Joel and Frank Kostyu, *Durham: A Pictorial History*, 110–11.

48 Cole, *Recollections*, 180–81; Harry Ross Jackson Papers, "Memorandum," D.U. Archives; Theodore Segal, "A New Genesis: The 'Silent Vigil' at Duke University, April 5–12th, 1968" (history honors thesis, D.U., 1977), D.U. Archives.

49 Segal, "A New Genesis," 37.

50 Cole, *Recollections*, 181–88; Jackson Papers, "Memorandum," D.U. Archives.

51 Don Yanella, "Race Relations at Duke University" (honors paper, Oral History Program, 1985), D.U. Archives, 26–46.

52 Yanella, "Race Relations at Duke University," 47–64, D.U. Archives; Allen Building Crisis—Papers, 1969, D.U. Archives.

53 *Action* 7 (Apr. 1968), 11 (June 1972).

54 Telephone interview with Mrs. Elna Spaulding, 30 June 1987.

55 *Herald*, 1 Dec. 1978.

56 Planning and Community Development Department, Durham, North Carolina, *Crest Street Redevelopment Plan, January 27, 1983*; Elizabeth Friedman, *Crest Street: A Family Community Impact Statement*, Policy Paper 2 of the Center for the Study of the Family and the State, Institute of Policy Sciences and Public Affairs, Duke University, 1978; *Herald*, 23 Sept. 1983.

20 ROUNDING OUT A CENTURY

1 Chamber of Commerce Papers, DU-RBMSCL, 1969–70.

2 Stone, "A Southern City and County in the Years of Political Change," 66, 181, 186–90. Two ministers, E. T. Browne and William H. Fuller, were allied with Spaulding in forming the Negro Voters League.

3 Stone, "A Southern City and County," 166, 194, 195, 203, 207, 217; author's interview with Margaret Keller, 14 Apr. 1987.

4 Charles R. Eilber, "Report Card: The First Year at the School of Science and Math," *Popular Government* 47, no. 2: 23–26.

5 "Outline of the History of the Battle for the Eno," *Eno* 1, no. 2 (fall 1973). Aside from the daily newspaper reports, the best accounts of the controversy are to be found in Timothy Sauls, "The Eno River Reservoir Controversy, 1966–1973: A Case Study of the Power of Public Opposition" (history paper, 1978), D.U. Archives, and Ed Martin, "Eno Association: Grassroots Politics for Conservation," *Herald*, 9 Apr. 1972.

The original Eno River dam protesters were Carl and Jean Anderson, Frederick and Mary Bernheim, Douglas and Frances Hill, Holger and Margaret Nygard, and Ann Zener. (Author's diary, 27 Aug. 1966.)

6 Rachel Carson, *Silent Spring* (Boston, 1962); *Herald*, 7 July 1975.

7 Author's telephone interview with Margaret Nygard, 5 May 1987; "Outline of the History of the Battle."

8 Telephone interview with Margaret Nygard. The Bernheims, Elizabeth Sunderland, and Mrs. Homer Dubbs donated land to the Nature Conservancy to be held for the proposed state park.

9 *Herald*, 31 Mar. 1968, 15 Mar. 1970, 9 Apr. 1972, 1 Nov. 1973; *Chapel Hill Weekly*, 2 June 1971; "Outline of the History of the Battle."

10 Author's telephone interview with Frank DePasquale, 12 Mar. 1987; "Outline of the History of the Battle"; *Action* 7, no. 3 (May 1967).

11 Author's telephone interview with William T. Coman, 12 Mar. 1987.

12 *Herald*, 16 Nov., 24 Nov., 5 Dec. 1972, 15 Apr. 1973.

13 The Governor's Commission on the Status of Women, *The Many Lives of North Carolina Women* (Raleigh, 1964); North Carolina Department of Administration, Commission on the Education and Employment of Women, *The Status of Women in North Carolina* (Raleigh, 1975), 105. See Jane DeHart Mathews, "The Status of Women in North Carolina," in Lindley Butler et al., eds., *The North Carolina Experience*, 427–51.

14 Author's telephone interview with Shirley Borstelmann, 21 May 1987.

15 Author's telephone interviews with Constance Renz, 19 May 1987, and Amanda Mackay Smith, 25 May 1987.

16 Telephone interview with Amanda Smith, 25 May 1987; *Herald*, 2 Dec. 1974.

17 *Herald*, 30 Dec. 1973, 4 Aug. 1974; information supplied by Miriam Slifkin of Chapel Hill; author's telephone interviews with Harriet Hopkins (27 Apr. 1987), Amanda Smith (26 May 1987), Ruth Mary Meyer (20 July 1987), David Bradley (10 May 1987), Miriam Slifkin (21 Apr. 1987).

18 Telephone interviews with Slifkin and Meyer.

19 Information supplied to the author by Miriam Slifkin, David Bradley, and Ruth Mary Meyer.

20 *Herald*, 2 Dec. 1974; telephone interview with Amanda Smith, 26 May 1987.

21 Information supplied to the author by Susan Fox Beischer, Norwood Thomas, Jr., and Lisa Harpole; *Herald*, 22 Nov. 1931.

22 Interview with Margaret Keller, 14 Apr. 1987.

23 Author's telephone interview with Nancy Laszlo, 28 June 1987; interview with Margaret Keller, 14 Apr. 1987.

24 Author's telephone interview with Peter Kramer, 18 Apr. 1987.

25 Telephone interviews with Peter Kramer and Anthony Mulvihill, 25 Apr. 1987. The chairman of the Mental Health Board who cast the negative vote to break a tie was H. Keith H. Brodie of Duke University.

26 Thomas C. Parramore, *Express Lanes and County Roads* (Chapel Hill, 1983), 65. The acronym "yuppies" stands for young upwardly mobile professionals, an aggressively ambitious new group in the population.

27 David L. Cohn, "Durham: The New South," *Atlantic Monthly*, May 1940, 614–19.

28 Leonard Sherwin, "A History of the North Carolina Museum of Life and Science" (Durham, 1986), North Carolina Collection, Durham County Library.

29 Ibid.

30 *Herald*, 22 Feb. 1941, 3 Oct. 1944; Alvah B. Davis III, "From Display Cases to Museum: The Use of Art and Artifacts in Teaching at Duke University, 1925–1975" (history course paper, 1975–76), D.U. Archives.

31 Ibid.

32 Author's telephone interview with Norman Pendergraft, Director of the North Carolina Central University Art Museum, 13 Aug. 1987; *Herald*, 21 Oct. 1970, 3 Nov. 1977.

33 "Summarized History of the Durham Art Guild, Inc., 1949 to 1969," a Twentieth Anniversary pamphlet, supplied to the author by George Pyne, Jr.; Ola Maie Foushee, *Art in North Carolina* (Chapel Hill, 1972), 153–54; telephone interview with George C. Pyne, Jr., 8 Mar. 1987.

34 Telephone interviews with Norman Pendergraft and Nancy Wardropper, 13 Aug. 1987, and with Edith Hassold, 16 Aug. 1989.

35 Biographical Files, D.U. Archives, concerning Broderson, Kremen, Pratt, Smullin, and Smith.

36 Durham Art Guild Archives, Durham Arts Council; Betty Hodges, "A Lifetime of Looking," *Herald*, 10 Oct. 1976; Jim Wise, "Edith London . . . Hitting It at 80," *Herald*, 2 Nov. 1984; Rubel Romero, "Dark Journeys," *Spectator*, 17 May 1984. (I am grateful to Professor Benjamin Boyce for bringing these articles to my attention.)

37 *Herald*, 28 Jan. 1932.

38 Ibid., 28 Jan. 1932, 4 Dec. 1933, 23 Sept. 1934, 9 Aug. 1935, 20 Oct. 1940, 30 Nov. 1941. Erwin died in 1972, aged 68 (ibid., 22 June 1972).

39 Ibid., 27 Feb. 1938, 1 Oct. 1939, 21 Jan. 1940.

40 Ibid., 12 Jan. 1941, 1 Mar. 1942.

41 Author's telephone interview with Mena Fuller Webb, 17 Aug. 1987.

42 Ibid., 7 May 1939, 2 Feb. 1941. See Kaj Klitgaard, *Art in America* (Chapel Hill, 1941).

43 Author's telephone interview with David A. Page, 18 Aug. 1989.

44 *Branson's Durham Business Directories*, various years.

45 Telephone interviews with David Page and Nelson Strawbridge, 4 May 1990.

46 *Herald*, 17 Feb., 2 Mar., 8 May, 10 Sept., 11 Dec. 1946; Durham Community Planning

Council, "Cultural Analysis of Durham's Assets in the Arts," 1966, 8–9; author's telephone interviews with Nancy Clark, 17 Aug. 1987, and St. Clair Williams, 18 Aug. 1987. At Duke University there were also the Duke Players (1931) and Hoof 'n' Horn (1936), clubs that performed drama and musical comedy.

47 Dorothy Newsom Rankin, "History of the Durham Civic Choral Society: Its First Thirty Years and a Few Recollections," 1979, D.U. Archives; information from Allan H. Bone.

48 *Herald*, 5 Sept., 5 Nov. 1976; author's telephone interview with Isabelle Samfield, 17 June 1987. By September 1976 the orchestra had fifty players, and it was able to play its first concert in November 1976.

49 Committee of the Chamber Arts Society, "Twentieth Anniversary Celebration," [1965], D.U. Archives, Chamber Arts Society Papers.

50 *Herald*, 18 Nov. 1983; information supplied to the author through Duke University Chapel.

51 Biographical Files, D.U. Archives, concerning Best, Bone, Hanks, and Kimbrough.

52 Durham Community Planning Council, "Cultural Analysis of Durham's Assets in the Arts," 1966, 8; Foushee, *Art in North Carolina*, 156; interview with Ella Fountain Pratt, 7 Mar. 1984; "Data Sheet on the Durham Arts Council for the 1982 Board Education Program."

53 Author's telephone interviews with Janice Palmer, 6 July 1987, and Ella Fountain Pratt, 29 Apr. 1987.

54 Telephone interview with Janice Palmer.

55 Author's telephone interviews with Jacqueline Morgan, 26 Apr. 1987, Ella Fountain Pratt, 29 Apr. 1987, and Julia Wray, 30 Apr. 1987.

56 Jack Anderson, *The American Dance Festival* (Durham, 1987), 181–83.

57 Author's telephone interview with Montrose J. Moses, 19 June 1987; *Herald*, 15 June 1978.

58 Priscilla Gregory McBryde, "Recognition of Former Presidents," a speech delivered at the Historic Preservation Society annual dinner, May 1983.

59 Ibid. The developers of Brightleaf Square were Terry Sanford, Jr., and Clay Hamner. Adam Abram developed the Warehouse.

60 Author's telephone interview with Margaret Haywood, 12 May 1987; *Herald*, 4 July, 5 July, 6 July 1976.

61 *Herald*, 26 Apr., 1 July 1981. A film about Durham's history was released later in the year.

62 Greater Durham Chamber of Commerce, *Economic Summary* (Durham, 1981).

21 CITY AND COUNTY TO MILLENNIUM'S END

1 *Action*, Feb.–Mar. 1981.

2 Ibid., Nov. 1981.

3 Ibid., Dec. 1982.

4 Ibid., Jan. 1983.

5 *Sun*, 29 Nov. 1985.

6 *DMH*, 4 Nov. 1981; Carolyn Thornton was the first African American woman to serve on the council, but she was appointed to the position in 1978 and did not seek reelection. The first elected female African American was Carolyn D. Johnson in 1983.

7 Ibid., 9 Nov. 1983, 6 Nov. 1985, 4 Nov. 1987, 5 Dec. 1989.

8 Ibid., 1 Jan., 4 Dec. 1990.

9 A Durham native with a Ph.D. from New York University, Allison taught physical education at NCCU from 1960 to 1974 and was a trustee from 2000 to 2001. She chaired the North Carolina Black Leadership Caucus (1980–84) and was director of the N.C.

Health Careers Access Program. (Jennifer Strom, "The Conflicting Agendas of Lavonia Allison," indyweek.com, 21 Nov. 2001; *H-S*, 26 Jan. 2008.)

10 *DMH*, 12 Dec. 1983, 1 Jan. 1984, 19 June 1985.
11 Ibid., 26 Mar., 21 Sept. 1982.
12 Ibid., 25 Aug. 1982; *Sun*, 15 Aug. 1984; Durham Voters' Alliance, newsletter, xii, no. 2.
13 *DMH*, 17 May 1985; *Sun*, 20 May 1986, 16 Oct. 1987.
14 *Sun*, 28 Feb. 1986, 4 Aug., 16 Oct. 1987; *Action*, Oct. 1983.
15 *N&O*, 9 June, 2 July 1985.
16 *Sun*, 10 May 1986.
17 *DMH*, 8 Mar. 1985.
18 The Brandonmill Group of Richmond, Virginia, was the developer. *DMH*, 21 Sept. 1983.
19 *Sun*, 2 Jan. 1985.
20 *DMH*, 5 Sept. 1984.
21 *Sun*, 8, 12 Jan. 1988. Clark also successfully opposed the superconducting super collider, discussed elsewhere, and an Eno River sewage plant.
22 *DMH*, 5, 6 Sept. 1984.
23 Ibid., 18 Oct. 1985.
24 Ibid., 16, 30 June 1985; *Sun*, 10 May 1985.
25 Ibid., 10 Feb. 1989; *N&O*, 10, 11 Feb. 1989.
26 Ibid., 8 May 1986.
27 Historic District Ordinance, 6 Sept. 1984; *DMH*, 10 Jan. 1985. The first board consisted of Leland Williams (the commission had been his suggestion), Robert Cannon, Frank DePasquale, Para Drake, David Lawrence, Myra Markham, Vivian Patterson, George Pyne, and Gwendolyn Simpson (information from Myra Markham).
28 *DMH*, 18 Apr. 1984.
29 Ibid., 12, 22, 25–27, 29 June 1986; *Sun*, 28 June, 12 Aug. 1986.
30 Ibid., 31 May 1983, 13 May 1984, 3 Oct. 1988.
31 *H-S*, 2 Apr. 1991, 30 Dec. 1992, 14, 24 Feb. 1995; *Action*, Mar. 1998.
32 *Sun*, 27 Sept. 1988.
33 www.sustainable.org/casestudies/sia-pdf.
34 *DMH*, 9 Oct. 1990. Another large bond referendum in 1996 was passed with no qualms. It included $35 million for streets, $5.5 million for an art center and museum, some $20 million each for housing and parks and recreation, and $5 million for public transportation. City Council Minutes, 21 Jan. 1997.
35 *H-S*, 14 Feb. 1991, 8 Sept. 1992
36 Ibid., 14 Mar. 1990, 15 Sept. 1991; *Sun*, 31 July, 16, 22, 23 Aug. 1990.
37 A fictional Durham Bulls team was the subject of the box-office success *Bull Durham* in 1988. The American Tobacco Co. left Durham in 1987, leaving eleven empty buildings in the Blackwell Street complex.
38 *Action*, Feb. 1980.
39 *H-S*, 15 Sept., 8 Oct. 1991, 11 Jan. 1992, 22 Feb. 1992; *Washington Post*, 20 July 1989.
40 *H-S*, 31 July, 15 Sept. 1991.
41 *DMH*, 14 Mar. 1990; *H-S*, 15, 21 Sept., 6 Nov. 1991.
42 *N&O*, 15 Nov. 1992.
43 *Sun*, 30 Apr. 1990.
44 *H-S*, 6, 7 Nov. 1993.
45 *Sun*, 31 July, 16, 22, 23 Aug. 1990; *H-S*, 22 Sept. 1992.
46 Information from Sylvia Kerckhoff and Bill Kalkhof; City Council Minutes, 15 Sept., 15 Dec. 1997.
47 *Action*, Feb. 1998, May 1999.

48 *H-S*, 25 Nov. 1992.

49 *H-S*, 8 Feb. 1994.

50 *H-S*, 15 Dec. 1993.

51 N.C. Gen. Stat. 14-409.

52 *H-S*, 9 Dec. 1998.

53 Ibid., 1, 9 Dec. 1998; interview with Sylvia Kerckhoff.

54 See Appendix for council and commission members.

55 *H-S*, 11 Oct. 1992.

56 Ibid., 29 Sept. 1992.

57 Ibid., 29, 30 Sept. 1992.

58 Ibid., 24 Oct. 1995.

59 *DMH*, 10 Dec. 1990.

60 Interview with Becky Heron.

61 *H-S*, 24 Nov. 1992.

62 Ibid., 31 Oct. 1993.

63 Jay Barnes, *North Carolina Hurricane History*, 2nd ed. (Chapel Hill, 2001), 172–204.

64 *H-S*, 23 June 1991.

65 *N&O*, 5 Feb. 1991.

66 *H-S*, 9 Jan. 1991.

67 Robert A. Parrish, "Neglected Common Interests: Durham's Struggle to Merge Its City and County Schools" (M.A. thesis, Duke University, 2001).

68 *H-S*, 14 Feb. 1991.

69 Ibid., 27 June 1991.

70 Ibid., 21 Dec. 1991.

71 Ibid., 20 June 1991.

72 Ibid., 12, 13, 14 Dec. 1991.

73 Ibid., 3 May 1994.

74 *N&O*, 18 Mar. 1994.

75 *H-S*, 12 June 1996.

76 Ibid., 12 Aug. 1994.

77 Ibid., 11 Feb. 1995.

78 Ibid., 19 Sept. 1994.

79 Ibid., 19, 24 Nov. 1992.

80 *Action*, Mar. 1997, Oct. 1998.

81 Parrish, "Neglected Common Interests."

82 *H-S*, 20 Oct. 2007.

83 htpp://people.forbes.com/profile/phail-wynn/75.

84 Information from Dorothy Borden.

85 Information from Barbara Smith.

86 James W. Cortada, *Before the Computer* (Princeton, N.J., 1993); I am indebted to Dr. Thomas M. Gallie for much information in this section on computers.

87 Alfred D. Chandler, *Inventing the Electronic Century* (New York, 2001).

88 Albert N. Link, *From Seed to Harvest: The Growth of the Research Triangle Park* (Research Triangle Park, 2002).

89 Frederick P. Brooks, Jr., James K. Farrell, and Thomas M. Gallie, "Organizational, Financial, and Political Aspects of a Three-University Computing Center," *Information Processing 1968*, 2 (1969): 923–27.

90 Louis T. Parker, Thomas M. Gallie, Frederick P. Brooks, Jr., and James K. Ferrell, "Introducing Computing to Smaller Colleges and Universities: A Progress Report," *Proceedings of the Association for Computing Machinery*, 12 (1969): 319–23.

91 Interview with Thomas M. Gallie, *Triangle Business Journal*, 23 Feb. 2007.

92 *Action*, May 1999.

93 Greater Durham Chamber of Commerce, *Communicator*, summer 1992.

94 Information about RTP can be found in Link's *From Seed to Harvest* and his earlier book *A Generosity of Spirit: The Early History of the Research Triangle Park* (Research Triangle Park, 1995).

95 Charles X. Larrabee, *Many Missions: Research Triangle Institute's First 31 Years, 1959–1990* (Research Triangle Park, 1993), 170; Link, *From Seed to Harvest*, 54.

96 *H-S*, 8 July 2002.

97 Hitchings and Elion shared their prize with the English researcher Sir James W. Black.

98 *Action*, Dec. 1982; Campbell, *Foundations for Excellence*, 323.

99 *N&O*, 19 Apr. 1992

100 Greater Durham Chamber of Commerce, *Communicator*, spring 1993.

101 "Early Marrow Transplant May Be Key to 'Bubble Boy' Disease Cure," www.docguide.com.

102 Jonathan Engle, *The Epidemic* (New York, 2006).

103 I am indebted to Dr. John D. Hamilton, chairman of Duke's Department of Infectious Disease, for information about Duke's efforts to combat HIV/AIDS.

104 Greater Durham Chamber of Commerce, *Communicator*, spring 1993.

105 "NIH Restores Funds for Duke AIDS Clinical Trial Unit," Duke University News Service, 28 Feb. 1992, http://dukespace.lib.duke.edu/dspace/bitstream/10161/640/9/ACTU.pdf.

106 *H-S*, 29 Dec. 1994, 29 Mar. 1996; interview with Dr. Janice Stratton.

107 Ibid., 21 Dec. 1991.

108 Ibid., 14 Feb. 1991, 3 Nov. 1992; *N&O*, 25 Apr. 1996.

109 Engel, *The Epidemic*, 291; *North Carolina 2007 HIV/AIDS Surveillance Report: Epidemiology and Special Studies Unit HIV/AIDS Prevention and Care Branch*, tables 2, 4.

110 "Homeless in Durham, Durham County, North Carolina," UNC School of Public Health Paper, 2000–2001.

111 Harold T. Parker, *The History of St. Philip's Episcopal Church, 1878–1994* (Durham, 1996), 265–68; *H-S*, 16 Dec. 1992.

112 *H-S*, 11 June 2001.

113 Parker, *The History of St. Philip's Episcopal Church*, 262–65; *Duke* (alumni magazine), May 1984; *N&O*, 18 Aug. 1991; www.wral.com/news/local/story/130184.

114 Andrea Higgins, *A Step of Faith: The History of the Durham Rescue Mission* (Durham, 2006).

115 *H-S*, 20 Feb. 1995; www.trosainc.org/about/history-vision.htby.

116 Ibid., 27, 28 Feb., 1, 2, 3, 4, 5 Mar. 1994.

117 Ibid., 27 Feb. 1994.

118 Ibid., 28 Feb. 1994.

119 Ibid., 1, 2, 3 Mar. 1994.

120 Ibid., 21 Sept. 1994.

121 Neal Peirce and Curtis Johnson, "The Triangle: A Future in Question," *N&O*, 19–26 Sept. 1993.

122 *Action*, Mar. 1994.

123 Interview with Dr. Jack Preiss.

124 *Sun*, 16 Oct. 1990.

125 Sanjay Bhatt, "Affordable Housing Loan Proceeds despite City Scandal," Duke *Chronicle*, 12 May 1994, http://media.www.dukechronicle.com/media/storage./paper/884news/1994.05/12.

126 Bhatt, "Affordable Housing Loan Proceeds despite City Scandal."

127 Interview with Dr. Jack Preiss.

128 Dr. Jack J. Preiss, "DHHS Employee Update," North Carolina Department of Health and Human Services, newsletter, Feb. 2005, http://www.dhhs.state.nc.us/newsletter/2005/feb/pdf.

129 *N&O*, 12 Nov. 1995.

130 www.seedsnc.org/history.htm.

131 *DMH*, 27 May 1985.

132 *Action*, Apr. 1984.

133 H. Keith H. Brodie and Leslie Banner, *Keeping an Open Door* (Durham, 1996), 17; *N&O*, 30 Apr. 1986; American Academy of Achievement, www.achievement.org/autodoc; Pete Thamel, "Playing as One, U.S. Basketball Is Once Again No. 1 in the World," *New York Times*, 25 Aug. 2008.

134 www.emily.org/faql.

135 http://www.durhamcares.org.

136 Interview with Dr. Thomas Frothingham; Thomas E. Frothingham, Matthew S. Epstein, Cheryl Amana, Lisa Amana-Jackson, Janis Ernst, Desmond K. Runyan, "Center for Child and Family Health: North Carolina," *North Carolina Medical Journal*, 60, no. 2 (Mar.–Apr. 1999): 83–89.

137 CensusScope (Durham County, N.C.), http://www.censusscope.org/us/s37/c63/chart_race/html; *H-S*, 11 Aug. 2007.

138 Census data analyzed by the Social Science Data Analysis Network (SSDAN), http://www.censusscope.org/us/s37/c63/chart_race-html.

139 John H. Kasarda, James H. Johnson, and Barbara Mason, "The Economic Impact of the Hispanic Population on the State of North Carolina," Kenan Flagler Business School, UNC, Chapel Hill, 2005, http://ime.gob.mx/investigaciones/2006/estudios/migracion/economic_impact_hispanic.

140 State Board of Education: Department of Public Instruction, *Public Schools of North Carolina Statistical Profile 1998*.

141 *H-S*, 15 Sept. 2008.

142 Kasarda, Johnson, and Mason, "The Economic Impact of the Hispanic Population on the State of North Carolina."

143 Campbell, *Foundations for Excellence*, 377; Greater Durham Chamber of Commerce, *Durham and Durham County, North Carolina, Economic Conditions* (1997).

144 Brodie and Banner, *Keeping an Open Door*, 37.

145 Ibid., 25, 40–1.

146 Ibid., 37, 119, 121–22.

147 Ibid., 28–32.

148 Campbell, *Foundations for Excellence*, 373–74.

149 Jim Rogalski, "Breaking the Barrier," *Inside Duke University Medical Center and Health System Archives*, 15, no. 4 (20 Feb. 2006), http://inside.duke.edu/ae.article.php?issueID=140 & ParentID=12502.

150 *N&O*, 30 Sept. 1990; *H-S*, 7 Apr. 2008.

151 *H-S*, 13 July 2004.

152 Campbell, *Foundations for Excellence*, 42–43.

153 Ibid., 341.

154 Ibid., 23, 85–86.

155 Ibid., 35–37, 40–41.

156 Women who succeeded in new places during this same period were Pamela Gann, who became the first woman to head the Duke Law School in 1988 (*N&O*, 14 Mar. 1988); Miriam Thomas, African American, a news anchor and reporter in 1982 for WTVD (*Carolina Woman: The Magazine for Women in the Triangle*, Mar. 1996); Jeanne H. Lucas, the first black woman in the North Carolina Senate (*H-S*, 11 Mar. 2007); and Julia Wheeler Taylor, who became president of the Mechanics and Farmers Bank in 1983, the first woman and first African American to head a Durham bank (clipping file: Biography, North Carolina Room, Durham County Library).

157 Brodie and Banner, *Keeping an Open Door*, 385.

158 *H-S*, 23 June 2004.

159 Campbell, *Foundations for Excellence*, 349.

160 Ibid., 349, 362–64, 375–76.

161 Ibid., 361–64, 370, 374–75.

162 Ibid., 327, 380.

163 In 2004 its profits were estimated to be $100 million a year. Ibid., 350–51, 354, 360–61.

164 Ibid., 387, 390.

165 Ibid., 313.

166 "Preliminary Inventory of the Superconducting Super Collider (SSC) Collection, 1986–88," North Carolina State Libraries, Special Collections Research Center, www.lib.ncsu.edu/nc.findingaids/00332; Jim Wise, "Rougemont Has Right Stuff to Become Real Town," *N&O*, 21 Jan. 2005.

167 Interview with Dr. Patsy Perry; clipping file: Biography, North Carolina Room, Durham County Library; *H-S*, 28 Apr. 2007; Durham Convention and Visitors Bureau. Major Past and Future Sports Events, http://www.durham-nc.com/planners/sports_events/major_events.php.

168 Interview with Dr. Perry.

169 Ibid., A native of Greensboro with a Ph.D. in English from UNC Chapel Hill, Dr. Perry became interim provost and vice-chancellor for academic affairs before she retired.

170 A graduate of the University of Chicago Law School and recipient of a Ford Foundation fellowship to Harvard, he served as dean of the National University of Singapore, which he helped to develop through a Ford Foundation grant of money for books and research projects. "Members of Alumni Will Be Recognized for Service," *University of Chicago Chronicle*, 24, no. 17 (26 May 2006), http://chronicle.uchicago.edu/050526/alumni.

171 *DMH*, 4 Mar. 1979; *H-S*, 8 Dec. 2006.

172 Michaux, a Durham native, after Army Medical Corps service in 1952–54 went into law and became under the Carter administration the first black U.S. attorney in the South since Reconstruction.

173 Rivera's house in Durham was declared of statewide significance by the state Office of Archives and History in an effort to save it from demolition by NCCU. *H-S*, 24 Oct. 2004, 2 May 2008.

174 Ibid., 26 Mar., 6 Apr. 2009.

175 Gary E. Gilley, "A History of the Charismatic Movement," Biblical Discernment Ministries, www.rapidnet.com/jHeard/bdm/Psychology/char/more/hist.htm.

176 Associated Baptist Press, 28 May 2004, www.abpnews.com.

177 See relevant web sites of individual churches.

178 *N&O*, 4 June 2006.

179 "Durham Church Spreads Gospel with DVDs," http://www.newsobserver.com/lifestyles/religion/story/1256727.html.

180 *N&O*, 27 Feb. 994.

181 *DMH*, 23 Apr. 1980.

182 Ibid., 21 Apr. 1980

183 Founded in the 1970s with the Cresset Baptist Church pastor Ned Matthews as headmaster, the school bought forty acres on Garrett Road that had been a gift to Duke University from Dr. W. Kenneth Cuyler. Information supplied by Guy Guidry.

184 Mr. Denton's information supplied to the author.

185 *H-S*, 9 June 1998.

186 Ibid., 12 Aug. 1994.

187 Ibid., 17 Oct. 2007.

188 Information supplied by Nicole A. Thompson, director of admissions.

189 Howard E. Covington, Jr., *Favored by Fortune* (Chapel Hill, 2004), 311, 329–30; *H-S*, 8 Oct. 2007.
190 "A History of Croasdaile Village" (brochure).
191 Mary Ruth Miller, Ph.D., "The Forest at Duke: A History (1992–2007)" (in-house publication).
192 Convention and Visitors' Bureau statistics.
193 *Brighter Leaves: Celebrating the Arts in Durham, North Carolina* (Durham, 2008), 233.
194 Ibid., 233–36.
195 Ibid., 209.
196 Ibid., 272.
197 Ibid., 204–5.
198 Ibid., 159.
199 Ibid., 159–61.
200 Ibid., 158.
201 Ibid., 156–7.
202 Ibid., 167.
203 Ibid., 134–35, 142.
204 Ibid., 162–3.
205 Ibid., 173.
206 Ibid., 109, 112, 114–15.
207 Ibid., 117–21.
208 Ibid., 186, 188.
209 Ibid., 190.
210 Ibid., 183, 185.
211 Ibid., 188–89.
212 Durham's crime rate, including property and personal offenses, was 6,980 incidents per 100,000 inhabitants in 2001, much higher than the state average. ("Durham Profile," www.idaide.com/citydata/nc/Durham.htm.)
213 Infant mortality (deaths under one year of age) for Durham County in 2000 was 8 per 1,000 live births for whites and 20 for nonwhites. (North Carolina Department of Health and Human Services, North Carolina Center for Health Statistics, http://www.schs.state.nc.us/schs/vitalstats/volume1/2000/county/durham.html.)
214 U.S. National Center for Health Statistics, *National Vital Statistics Report, 2000*, table 84; North Carolina Center for Health Statistics, http://www.schs.state.nc.us/schs/vitalstats/volume1/2000/county/durham.html.

Bibliography

MANUSCRIPTS AND PRIVATE COLLECTIONS

Advertising Collection, DUMD, Railroads.
Allen Building Crisis Papers, 1969, D.U. Archives.
Walter Alvis Papers, SHC.
American Association of University Women Papers, DUMD.
American Loyalist Claims, Series 2, N.C. Archives. Photocopies of originals in the Public
    Record Office and other British repositories.
Autry, William O., Jr. "Stagville Farm in the Upper Neuse River Basin: A Preliminary
    Evaluation of Archaeological Potential." Report, 1976, for Liggett and Myers, Inc.
    In the author's possession.
Rosa Lyon Belvin Papers, DUMD.
James Bennitt Papers, DUMD.
Bertie County Records, N.C. Archives, Deeds.
Mary Duke Biddle Foundation Papers, D.U. Archives.
James C. Biggs Papers, SHC.
Biographical Files, D.U. Archives.
William T. Blackwell Papers, DUMD.
Blackwood-Lloyd Papers, DUMD.
Book of Incorporations, Register of Deeds Office, Orange County Courthouse, Hillsbor-
    ough, N.C.
William K. Boyd Papers, D.U. Archives.
"A Brief Chronological History of the Methodist Retirement Homes, Inc., Durham, N.C."
    Pamphlet in the author's possession.
Broadside Collection, RBR, D.U. Library.
Frank C. Brown Papers, DUMD.
Browning, Hugh Conway, comp. "Information Relating to the Scarlett Family of Orange
    County, North Carolina." Typescript, n.d. In the author's possession.
———, comp. "Orange County and Hillsborough Items of History—The Families of Hugh
    and James Caine." Typescript, 1966. In the author's possession.
———. "Valley of the Eno: Some of Its Land—Some of Its People—Some of Its Mills."
    Typescript, 1973. In the author's possession.
"Victor Silas Bryant 1867–1920," North Carolina Collection, Durham County Library.

"Bull Durham Business District," Bell Design Group, Raleigh, 1975, unpublished report prepared for Watts Hill, Sr. James R. Hawkins Papers, DUMD.

Lizzie F. Burch Papers, DUMD.

Burcham, Arthur. "History of Saint Andrews Episcopal Mission and Church School," 1961. Typescript in the possession of the church.

Bute County Records, N.C. Archives, Record Book, 1767–76, Minutes of the Court of Pleas and Quarter Sessions.

Tod R. Caldwell Papers, SHC.

Bennehan Cameron Papers, SHC.

Cameron Family Papers, SHC.

Camp Creek Church Book [1852], in possession of J. Isaac Hill, Rougemont, N.C.

Willis Thomas Carpenter Memoir. In the possession of Edna Carpenter Baker.

Julian S. Carr Papers, SHC.

Washington Sandford Chaffin Papers, DUMD.

Chamber Arts Society Papers, D.U. Archives.

[Durham] Chamber of Commerce Archives, Chamber of Commerce.

Chamber of Commerce Collection, DUMD.

"Church Directory of Temple Baptist Church," c. 1932. DUMD, North Carolina County Papers: Durham.

William A. Clement Papers, SHC.

Arthur Vance Cole Papers, DUMD.

Constitution of the Farmers' State Alliance of North Carolina (Raleigh, 1889), in William A. Couch Papers, DUMD.

Convention of the Freedmen of North Carolina: Official Proceeding, NCC.

William A. Couch Papers, DUMD.

Mary Octavine Cowper Papers, DUMD.

Craven-Pegram Papers, DUMD.

"Crest Street Redevelopment Plan, January 27, 1983," Planning and Community Development Department, Durham.

John Franklin Crowell Papers, D.U. Archives.

Mason Crum Papers, D.U. Archives.

Crumpacker Family Papers, DUMD.

"Data Sheet on the Durham Arts Council for 1982 Board Education Program," Durham Arts Council Archives.

Day, Percy. "The Greenberg Housing Controversy: A Case Study in Community Organization," August 1968. North Carolina Fund Papers, SHC.

Dickens, Roy S., Jr. "In Search of Occaneechi: Archaeology and History of the Aboriginal North Carolina Piedmont." Paper read at the Society for Historical Archaeology symposium at Williamsburg, 1983. Research Laboratories of Anthropology, UNC.

Wyatt T. Dixon Papers, DUMD.

William C. Doub Papers, DUMD.

Benjamin Newton Duke Papers, DUMD.

James Buchanan Duke Papers, D.U. Archives.

Washington Duke Papers, DUMD.

Dulcan, Kris. "Juvenile Court: Durham, N.C., May 1971." DUMD, North Carolina County Papers: Durham.

Durham Art Guild Archives, in possession of the guild.

Durham Bicentennial Commission Papers, DUMD.

Durham Cotton Manufacturing Company Papers, DUMD.

Durham County and City Board of Health Minutes, Durham County Health Department.

Durham County Deeds, Register of Deeds Office, Durham County Courthouse.

Durham County School Board Minutes, County Board of Education.

"The Durham Fact-Finding Conference: Held in Durham, N.C. April 17, 18, and 19, 1929," NCC.

Durham Hosiery Mills Papers, DUMD.

William and Mary Snipes Durham. "Family Record." North Carolina Collection, Durham County Library.

W. J. Hugh Durham Papers, DUMD.

Charles W. Edwards Papers, D.U. Archives.

Erwin Cotton Mills Company Papers, DUMD.

"The Evolution of Lowe's Grove School and Community," 1913. William K. Boyd Papers, D.U. Archives.

"Facts About Durham" [1916]. Chamber of Commerce Collection, DUMD.

Federal Writers' Project Papers, SHC, interviews with workers in the tobacco factories and cotton mills.

Fletcher's Chapel United Methodist Church: A Pamphlet Printed for the Dedication of the 1975 Addition to the Present Church." In the possession of Ollie N. Carpenter.

Franck, Richard C., "An Oral History of West Durham: A Report Submitted to the Durham Bi-centennial," Durham, N.C., 1975. Typescript. North Carolina Collection, Durham County Library.

James Gill Papers, DUMD.

Godwin, Lelia Lowe. "My Recollection of the Beginning of Lowe's Grove Baptist Church," as written down by her daughter, Hazel Godwin, in the 1970s. In the possession of Hazel Godwin.

Mattie K. Goldberg Papers, DUMD.

Golden Belt Hosiery Company Papers, Private Collections, N.C. Archives.

"A Governmental Center for Durham," Durham City Planning Department, City Hall.

Graham, Donald. "An Archeological Reconnaissance of the Eno and Little River Confluence." Paper written for Anthropology 316, UNC, May 1973. Photocopy in the possession of the author.

"Grand Inaugural Horse Fair" (advertising flyer), NCC.

[Lord] Granville Land Grants, Secretary of State's Office, Raleigh, N.C.

Greene County, Georgia, Papers, DUMD (since returned to Greene County, Georgia).

Grierson, Mary (Mamie) J. "How We Lived during the Confederate War." Corneille A. Little Papers, DUMD.

Grout Family Papers, DUMD.

Grout, Julia. "Thirty-three Years with the Altrusa Club of Durham, North Carolina," 1967. DUMD, Grout Family Papers.

Romeo Guest Papers, DUMD.

Harris, Buxton. "Remarks Addressed to My Children." Photocopy in the author's possession.

Elizabeth Johnson Harris. "Life Records." In the possession of Mayme Harris Perry.

Harris, Mary Russell. "Account of Milton School." In the possession of Katherine Harris Reade.

Rencher Nicholas Harris Papers, DUMD.

Albert Bushell Hart Papers, DUMD.

James R. Hawkins Papers, DUMD.

John Franklin Heitman Papers, D.U. Archives.

Herbert, George. "The Research Triangle: An Early History." Speech delivered to the Watauga Club, 4 Mar. 1980, DUMD, Romeo Guest Papers.

Herndon Family Papers, in the possession of Curtis Booker.

"Hillsborough Manufacturing Company." Broadside Collection, RBR, D.U. Library.

Hillsborough Stone Quarry Papers, D.U. Archives.

"History of Public Housing in Durham [1949–1981]." Fact sheet, City of Durham Housing Authority.

"The History of Roberson Grove Church." Typescript, in the possession of the author.

"History of Rose of Sharon Baptist Church." Typescript in the possession of the author.

Hogan, Judy, ed. "The Teller of Tales: From Homer's Ithaca to Durham County's

Rougemont." Typescript from an exhibit, 1982. North Carolina Room, Durham County Library.

Governor William Holden Papers, N.C. Archives.

William Woods Holden Papers, DUMD.

Holeman Collection, Private Collections, N.C. Archives.

Holm, Mary Ann. "Faunal Remains from the Wall and Fredericks Sites." Paper read at the Society for Historical Archaeology symposium at Williamsburg, 1983. Research Laboratories of Anthropology, UNC.

Sidney Willard Holman Papers, Private Collections, N.C. Archives.

Hultman, Tami. "Edgemont." North Carolina Fund Papers, Report, 7 Aug. 1968, SHC.

Hurden, Alexander. "The Origin of the Damar Court Dispute." N.C. Fund Papers, Report, 30 Aug. 1968, SHC.

Jackson, Harry. "Memorandum." Report of 1968 Vigil, D.U. Archives.

Jarratt-Puryear Papers, DUMD.

Johnson, Kristin J. "A Preliminary Statement on Plant Remains from the Wall and Fredericks Sites." Paper read at the Society for Historical Archaeology symposium at Williamsburg, 1983. Research Laboratories of Anthropology, UNC.

William M. Jordan Papers, DUMD.

Keel, Bennie C., and Joffre L. Coe. "A Reconnaissance and Proposal for Archaeological Salvage in Falls Reservoir, N.C.," 1970, report. Research Laboratories of Anthropology, UNC.

Kennedy, Elnora. "Brief History of St. Joseph's AME Church." In the possession of the church.

Ku Klux Klan Papers, DUMD.

Mrs. Benjamin D. Lacy Papers, Private Collections, N.C. Archives.

Leathers, Latta, and Company Daybook 1854–55, DUMD.

Leigh Family Papers, in the possession of Curtis Booker.

Legislative Papers, N.C. Archives.

Kemp Plummer Lewis Papers, SHC.

Corneille A. Little Papers, DUMD.

Lowe's Grove Baptist Church History [c. 1915], by J. R. High, C. C. Edwards, S. J. Husketh. In the possession of Hazel Godwin.

George Leonidas Lyon Papers, DUMD.

Adolphus Mangum Papers, SHC.

Thomas Mann Papers, DUMD.

Benjamin Markham Papers, DUMD.

Hardy Massey Papers, Private Collections, N.C. Archives.

McBryde, Priscilla Gregory. "Recognition of Former Presidents." Speech delivered at the annual dinner of the Historic Preservation Society of Durham, May 1983. Photocopy in the possession of the author.

McMannen Family Papers, DUMD.

Menius, Arthur. "The Bennett Place." Report for the Division of Archives and History. Historic Site Section, July, 1979.

Methodist Church Papers, DUMD.

Thomas Yancey Milburn Papers, Private Collections, N.C. Archives.

Military Service Records, National Archives, Washington, D.C.

Minutes of the Durham City Board of Education, City Board of Education, Fuller School.

Minutes of the Durham City Council, City Clerk's Office, City Hall.

Minutes of the Durham County Commissioners, 1881–89, Register of Deeds Office, County Courthouse.

Minutes of the Town [of Durham] Board of Aldermen, City Clerk's Office, City Hall.

"Minutes or Proceedings of the Orange County Board of Common Schools, commencing Sept. 1845," SHC.

George W. Mordecai Papers, SHC.

Eugene Morehead Papers, DUMD.

"Mount Calvary Baptist Church, Bahama, North Carolina." Pamphlet in the possession of Mrs. Caroline Mack.

Benjamin Muse Papers, DUMD.

Rosa Mae Warren Myers Papers, DUMD.

Nanney, the Rev. Mark. "Andrews Chapel United Methodist Church: A Local Church History." Pamphlet in the possession of Andrews Chapel Church.

Nathan, Mike. "Community Organization in Edgemont." North Carolina Fund Papers, Report, 29 May 1968, SHC.

Newsom, Dallas W. "Durham County, North Carolina: A Decade of Progress, July 1, 1930 to July 1, 1940." Speech delivered to the Kiwanis Club, DUMD, North Carolina County Papers: Durham.

John Thomas Nichols Papers, DUMD.

North Carolina County Papers: Durham, DUMD.

North Carolina Fund Papers, SHC.

North Carolina Land Grants, Secretary of State's office, Raleigh, N.C.

North Carolina Railroad Collection, N.C. Archives, State Agencies.

North Carolina State Libraries, Special Collections Research Center, "Preliminary Inventory of the Superconducting Super Collider (SSC) Collection, 1986–88."

Orange County Deeds, Register of Deeds office, Hillsborough, N.C.

"Orange County, N.C., Tax List, 1875," DUMD.

Orange County Records, N.C. Archives, Board of Commissioners' Minutes, Census Records (1800–1870); Civil and Criminal Action Papers; Inventories, Sales, and Accounts of Estates; Land Entry Book 1775–1795, Marriage Bonds and Licenses; Minutes of the Court of Pleas and Quarter Sessions; Miscellaneous Records; Superior Court Minutes; Tax Lists; Wills (original).

Orange County Will Books, Orange County Courthouse, Hillsborough, N.C.

Ella Howerton Whitted Parks Papers, DUMD.

Edward J. Parrish Papers, DUMD.

Patrons of Husbandry, N.C., Papers. "A List of the Subordinate Granges of North Carolina with their Masters and Secretaries, 1875–90," DUMD.

Rufus L. Patterson Papers, SHC.

Planning and Community Development Department, Durham, North Carolina. "Crest Street Redevelopment Plan, January 27, 1983." In the possession of the department.

"Pledge Book of the Junior Order of United American Mechanics, 1910, 1915, 1919," DUMD.

William N. Pratt and Company Ledger, 1857–67, DUMD.

Arthur Marcus Proctor Papers, DUMD.

N. A. Ramsay Papers, SHC.

"Record of the Proceedings of the Central Prohibition Club of Durham, N.C.," DUMD.

Records of Corporations, Register of Deeds office, Durham County Courthouse.

Records of the President, Trinity College, D.U. Archives.

Records of the Up-To-Date Club, North Carolina Collection, Durham County Library.

"Registry of Voters, Durham Election Precinct," 3 Nov. 1868, DUMD, North Carolina County Papers: Durham.

"Report of the Health Director, Durham County," Durham County Health Department.

Atlas M. Rigsbee Papers, DUMD.

Roberts Family Papers, DUMD.

Susan Singleton Rose Papers, D.U. Archives.

Thomas Ruffin Papers, SHC.

"School Census, 1870, Durham Township." DUMD, North Carolina County Papers: Durham.

Secretary of State's Papers, N.C. Archives.

Sherwin, Leonard, "A History of the North Carolina Museum of Life and Science," 1986. North Carolina Collection, Durham County Library.

Shields, Ruth Herndon. "Some Notes about the Cabe, Shields, and Strayhorn Families." Typescript in the author's possession.

Shipp, Bertha Paschall. "Nelson Extension Homemakers' Club History, 1919–1970." In the possession of Bertha Shipp.

Robert Nirwana Simms Papers, DUMD.

Sindler, Allan P. "Youth and the American Negro Protest Movement: A Local Case Study of Durham, North Carolina." Paper, 1965. Bound copy in D.U. Library.

Southern Oral History Program Papers, SHC.

Southgate-Jones Papers (James H. Southgate Papers), DUMD.

"Souvenir Edition of the Durham Daily Sun Complimentary to the North Carolina Press Association Now in Session in Durham, N.C.," 23–25 July 1890. RBR, D.U. Library.

Street Book, City Clerk's Office, Durham City Hall.

"Summarized History of the Durham Art Guild, Inc. 1949 to 1969." Pamphlet in the possession of George C. Pyne, Jr.

Terry, Dick. "Public Action to Upgrade the Housing Stock of the Research Triangle Region, 1960–1970," DUMD, North Carolina County Papers: Durham.

Thomas, Ronald A., Martha J. Schiek, and Robert F. Hoffman. "A Report on Two Archaeological Surveys within Proposed Alternatives for a Reservoir for the City of Durham, Durham and Person Counties, North Carolina." Unpublished report for the U.S. Army Corps of Engineers, March 1982.

Tornquist, Elizabeth. "An Analysis of Durham Politics," NCC.

Treasurer's and Comptroller's Records, N.C. Archives, Confiscated Lands.

Trinity College—Duke University Real Estate Purchases and Sales, 1893–1955, D.U. Archives.

Bryan Tyson Papers, DUMD.

A. K. Umstead et al. "As We See It." Broadside, NCC.

Umstead, Richard Baxter. "The North Carolina Umstead Lineage." N.p., n.d. In the author's possession.

United Daughters of the Confederacy Scrapbooks, Julian Carr Chapter, North Carolina Collection, Durham County Library.

United States Post Office Department. "Records of Appointments of Postmasters, 1789–1929." Microfilm, N.C. Archives, Miscellaneous Federal Records.

Charles Van Noppen Papers, DUMD.

Vickers Family Papers, DUMD.

Vital Records, Durham Health Department.

Charles E. Waddell Papers, DUMD.

Wake County Land Grants, Secretary of State's office, Raleigh.

Wake County Records, N.C. Archives, Census Records, Deeds, Estates, Tax and Fiscal Records, Wills.

Walker, Mamie Dowd. "History and Progress of the Juvenile Court City and County, Durham, N.C., December 3, 1934–December 5, 1949," NCC.

Mamie Dowd Walker Papers, DUMD.

Ward, H. Trawick, and Joffre L. Coe, "An Archaeological Evaluation of the Falls of the Neuse Reservoir," 1976. Research Laboratories of Anthropology, UNC.

James Webb Papers, SHC.

William A. Wilkerson Time Book, 1919–20. In the possession of Dorothy S. Colvin.

Williams, Lola. "A History of Calvert Method School during the Headmistressship of Bess Pickard Boone." DUMD, Durham Bicentennial Commission Papers.

Robert and Newton Dixon Woody Papers, DUMD.

Richard Harvey Wright Papers, DUMD.

Adams, George R. "The Carolina Regulators: A Note on Changing Interpretations." *North Carolina Historical Review* 49 (1972): 345–52.

Adams, Jack. "A Farewell to Farms." *Herald,* 29 May 1983.

———. "George Watts Hill, Baron of Durham, Chairman of Boards." *Herald,* 25 Apr. 1982.

Adams, Sam L. *Directory of Greater Durham, North Carolina, 1902.* Durham, 1902.

Alden, John R. *The South in the Revolution.* Baton Rouge, 1957.

Allen, Eldon P., and William F. Wilson. *Geology and Mineral Resources of Orange County, North Carolina.* Raleigh, 1968.

Alvord, Clarence W. and Lee Bidgood, eds. *The First Explorations of the Trans-Allegheny Region by the Virginians, 1650–1674.* Cleveland, 1912.

Anderson, Jack. *The American Dance Festival.* Durham, 1987.

Anderson, Jean B. "A Community of Men and Mills." *Eno,* special issue (1979).

———. "The Federal Direct Tax of 1816 as Assessed in Orange County, N.C." *North Carolina Genealogical Journal* 5 (Feb. 1979): 14–23; 5 (May 1979): 114–21; 5 (Aug. 1979): 193–99; 6 (Feb. 1980): 37–47.

———. *Piedmont Plantation: The Bennehan-Cameron Family and Lands in North Carolina.* Durham, 1985.

Andrews, Robert McCants. *John Merrick: A Biographical Sketch.* Durham, 1920.

Anlyan, William G. *Metamorphoses.* Durham, 2004.

Annual Catalogue of Trinity College, Durham, 1904–05. Durham, 1904.

"Answers at Occaneechi Town." *Carolina Alumni Review,* summer 1984.

Arena, Jay M. and John P. McGovern, eds. *Davison of Duke.* Durham, 1980.

Ashe, Samuel P., Louis R. Wilson, and Charles L. Van Noppen. *Biographical History of North Carolina.* 8 vols. Greensboro, 1905–17.

Bailey, Snow, ed. *Dedication of the Edian D. Markham Memorial Building and Parsonage.* Durham, 1952.

Bain, George L. and Bruce W. Harvey. *Field Guide to the Geology of the Durham Triassic Basin.* Raleigh, 1977.

Banks, Ann, ed. *First-Person America.* New York, 1980.

Barnes, Jay. *North Carolina Hurricanes.* 3rd edn. Chapel Hill, 2001.

Barringer, Paul B. *The Natural Bent: The Memoirs of Dr. Paul B. Barringer.* Chapel Hill, 1949.

Bassett, John Spencer. "Old Durham Traditions." *Trinity Archive* 19 (1905–6): 161–70.

———. "Stirring Up the Fires of Race Antipathy." *South Atlantic Quarterly* 2 (Oct. 1903): 297–305.

———, ed. *The Writings of Colonel William Byrd of Westover in Virginia, Esqr.* New York, 1901.

Bastin, Bruce. *Crying for the Carolines.* London, 1971.

Benton, James C., et al. "Rebuilding Durham's Forgotten Backyard," *H-S,* 27–28 Feb., 1–5 Mar. 1994.

Bhatt, Sanjay. "Affordable Housing Loans Proceeds Despite City Scandal." *Duke Chronicle,* 12 May 1994.

Blackwelder, Ruth. *The Age of Orange.* Charlotte, 1961.

Block, Susan. "The Gothic Grande Dame's Golden Age." *Duke* (July–Aug. 1986): 2–7.

Board of Charities and Public Welfare. Durham [1923].

Boyd, William K. "Currency and Banking in North Carolina, 1790–1836." *Trinity College Historical Papers,* series 10, 52–86. Durham, 1914.

———. *The Story of Durham: City of the New South.* Reprint. Durham, 1927. First publ. 1925.

———, ed. *William Byrd's Histories of the Dividing Line betwixt Virginia and North Carolina.* Raleigh, 1929.

Branson and Farrar's North Carolina Business Directory for 1866–67. Raleigh, 1866.
Branson's North Carolina Agricultural Almanac, 1890. Raleigh, 1890.
Branson's North Carolina Business Directory for 1867–68. Raleigh, 1868.
Branson's North Carolina Business Directory for 1869. Raleigh, 1869.
Branson's North Carolina Business Directory for 1877–78. Raleigh, 1878.
Branson's North Carolina Business Directory for 1884. Raleigh, 1884.
Branson's North Carolina Business Directory, 1897. Raleigh, 1897.
Breen, William J. "Southern Women in the War: The North Carolina Woman's Committee, 1917–1919." *North Carolina Historical Review* 55 (1978): 251–83.
Brighter Leaves: Celebrating the Arts in Durham, North Carolina. Durham, 2008.
Brodie, H. Keith H., and Leslie Banner. *Keeping an Open Door: Passages in a University.* Durham, 1996.
Brooks, Frederick P., Jr., James K. Ferrell, and Thomas M. Gallie. "Organizational, Financial, and Political Aspects of a Three-University Computing Center." *Information Processing,* 2 (1968): 923–27.
Brown, Paul. "Hayti: It was 'Blighted' But It Bustled." *Herald,* 8 July 1979.
Brown, Roy. *Public Poor Relief in North Carolina.* Chapel Hill, 1928.
Browne, Rosa Butler. *Love My Children.* New York, 1969.
Burcham, Arthur. "History of Saint Andrew's Episcopal Mission and Church School," typescript, 1961.
Bureau of the Census. *Characteristics of the Population, Part 35: North Carolina, 1970 Census of Population.* Washington, 1973.
Butler, Lindley S., and Alan D. Watson, eds. *The North Carolina Experience: An Interpretive and Documentary History.* Chapel Hill, 1984.
Calendar of the Southern Conservatory of Music, Durham, North Carolina 1901–2. Raleigh, 1901.
Cameron, John D. *A Sketch of the Tobacco Interests in North Carolina.* Oxford, N.C., 1881.
——. "Durham and Its Tobacco Business." Hillsborough *Recorder,* 13 Feb. 1878.
Campbell, Walter E. *Foundations for Excellence: 75 Years of Duke Medicine.* Durham, 2006.
Carolina's Outstanding Sports Station, WDNC. Peoria, Ill., 1941.
Carpenter, Ollie Nichols et al. "History of Oak Grove School." *Oak Grove School Annual, 1939.* Durham, 1939.
Carr, Julian S., Jr. "Building a Business on the Family Plan." *System: The Magazine of Business* 36 (July 1919): 47–50.
——. "What Made Our Business Grow." *System: The Magazine of Business* 35 (Feb. 1919): 201–7.
Carrington, Wirt Johnson. *A History of Halifax County* [Va.]. Richmond, 1924.
Carroll, Grady L. E., ed. *Francis Asbury in North Carolina: The North Carolina Portions of the Journal of Francis Asbury.* Nashville, Tenn., 1964.
Carter, Luther J. "Research Triangle Park Succeeds Beyond Its Promoters' Expectations." *Science* 200 (30 June 1978): 1469–70.
Caruthers, Eli W. *Interesting Revolutionary Incidents and Sketches of Character Chiefly in the 'Old North State.'* Philadelphia, 1856.
Carver, Ven. "The Last Warehouse." *Herald,* 14 Sept. 1986.
Chafe, William. *Civilities and Civil Rights: Greensboro, North Carolina, and the Black Struggle for Freedom.* New York, 1980.
Chalkley, Lyman. *Chronicles of the Scotch-Irish Settlement in Virginia.* 3 vols. Rosslyn, Va., 1912.
Chamberlayne, Churchill Gibson, ed. *The Vestry Book and Register of Bristol Parish, Virginia, 1720–1789.* Richmond, 1898.
——, ed. *Vestry Book and Register of Saint Peter's Parish, New Kent and James City Counties, Virginia, 1634–1786.* Richmond, 1937.
Chandler, Alfred D., Jr. *Inventing the Electronic Century.* New York, 2001.

Charter and Ordinances of the City of Durham. Durham, 1908.

Chataigne's North Carolina State Directory and Gazetteer 1883–84. Raleigh, [1883].

Chester, Harley A. *A History of Mount Bethel Methodist Church.* N.p., n.d.

Childs, Benjamin G. *Centennial History of Trinity Methodist Church.* Durham, 1961.

City of Durham Planning and Community Development Department. *Durham: Past—Present—Future.* 1982.

Clark, Walter, ed. *The State Records of North Carolina.* 16 vols. Raleigh, 1895–1906.

Clay, Russell. "Is Durham Lagging behind Other North Carolina Cities?" (part 1 of an 8-part series of articles on Durham and its problems, each with its own title). *Herald,* 22–29 Mar. 1959.

Coe, Joffre Lanning. "The Cultural Sequence of the Carolina Piedmont." *Archaeology of the Eastern United States,* edited by James B. Griffin. Chicago, 1952.

———. "The Formative Cultures of the Carolina Piedmont." *American Philosophical Society Transactions* n.s., 54 (1964).

Cohn, David L. "Durham: The New South." *Atlantic Monthly,* May 1940, 614–19.

Colclough, George D. *The Colclough Family.* Burlington, N.C., 1969.

Cole, R. Taylor. *The Recollections of R. Taylor Cole: Educator, Emissary, Development Planner.* Durham, 1983.

Compendium of the Eighth Census. Washington, 1864.

Connor, R. D. W. *A Documentary History of the University of North Carolina.* 2 vols. Chapel Hill, 1953.

Constitution of the Farmers' State Alliance of North Carolina. Raleigh, 1889.

Corbitt, David LeRoy, and Elizabeth W. Wilbon. *Civil War Pictures.* Raleigh, 1961.

Corbitt, David LeRoy. *The Formation of the North Carolina Counties, 1663–1943.* Raleigh, 1950.

Cortada, James W. *Before the Computer.* Princeton, N. J., 1993.

Couch, William Terry, ed. *These Are Our Lives.* Chapel Hill, 1939.

County and City Data Book, 2000. Washington, 2001.

Covington, Howard E., Jr. *Favored by Fortune: George W. Watts and the Hills of Durham.* Chapel Hill, 2004.

Craig, David Irvin. *A Historical Sketch of New Hope Church in Orange County, North Carolina.* Reidsville, N.C., 1891.

Creedy, John Alan. "Billie Duke . . ." *Sun,* 13 July 1941.

Crow, Jeffrey J. *The Black Experience in Revolutionary North Carolina.* Raleigh, 1977.

———. "Cracking the Solid South: Populism and the Fusionist Interlude." *The North Carolina Experience: An Interpretive and Documentary History,* edited by Lindley S. Butler and Alan D. Watson, 333–49. Chapel Hill, 1984.

Cumming, William P., ed. *The Discoveries of John Lederer.* Charlottesville, 1958.

———. *North Carolina in Maps.* Raleigh, 1966.

DAR. *Roster of Soldiers from North Carolina in the American Revolution.* Durham, 1932.

Davenport, John Scott. "Early Settlers in the North Carolina Piedmont . . . on Lands Sold by Henry McCulloh within Granville's District, 1749–1763." *North Carolina Genealogical Journal* 4 (May 1978): 74–86.

Dennett, John Richard. *The South as It Is: 1865–1866.* New York, 1965.

Determination by the Executors of James B. Duke, Deceased, of Those Entitled to Participate in the Distribution to Be Made under Item VI of the Last Will and Testament of Said Decedent and of the Amounts They Are, Respectively, Entitled to Receive. New York, 1927.

DeVane, Steve. "Durham Church Leaves N.C. Convention over Handling of Homosexuality Issue." Associated Baptist Press, 28 May 2004, http://www.abpnews.com/index .php?option=com_content & task.

Dickinson, Patricia, ed. *An Inventory of the Cleveland Avenue-Holloway Street Neighborhood, Durham, N.C.* 1981.

———, and Ruth Little Stokes, eds. *An Inventory of Edgemont and East Durham: Early*

Textile Mill Villages. Report produced by the Historic Preservation Technology Class of 1978–79, Durham Technical Institute.

Division of Water Resources. *The Water Supply System of the City of Durham, North Carolina.* 1966, rev. 1981.

Dixon, Wyatt T. *How Times Do Change.* Durham, 1987.

———. *Ninety Years of Duke Memorial Church, 1886–1976.* Durham, 1977.

Douty, H. M. "Early Labor Organization in North Carolina, 1800–1900." *South Atlantic Quarterly* 34 (Jan. 1935): 260–68.

Dowd, Jerome. "Rev. Moses Hester." *Trinity Archive* 9 (Feb. 1896): 283–96.

Drake, Thomas M. and Philip B. Secor. *The Life and Service of St. Joseph's Episcopal Church: Fifty Years in the West Durham Community, 1908–1958.* Durham, 1959.

Drane, Brest S. "Behind the Scene in Locating Stone for Duke University." [State] *Employment Security Commission Quarterly* 5 (Winter 1947), D.U. Archives, Hillsborough Stone Quarry.

Draughan, Wallace R. *History of the Church of Jesus Christ of Latter-day Saints in North Carolina.* Durham, 1974.

Du Bois, W. E. B. "The Upbuilding of Black Durham." *The World's Work* 23 (Jan. 1912): 334–38.

Dula, William C. *Durham and Her People.* Durham, 1951.

Dun, R. G., and Company (later Dun and Bradstreet). *The Mercantile Agency Reference Book, Containing Ratings of the Merchants, Manufacturers, and Traders Generally, throughout the Southern States, January, 1878.* New York, 1878.

Durden, Robert F. "The Centennial Program Commemorating the One Hundredth Anniversary 1871–1971 of First Presbyterian Church, Durham, North Carolina." N.p., n.d.

———. *The Dukes of Durham.* Durham, 1975.

———. "Tar Heel Tobacconist in Tokyo, 1899–1904." *North Carolina Historical Review* 53 (Oct. 1976): 347–63.

———. "Troubled Legacy: James B. Duke's Bequest to His Cousins." *North Carolina Historical Review* 50 (Oct. 1973): 394–415.

Durham Almanac . . . , 1892. Edited by N. A. Ramsey. Durham, 1892.

Durham Almanac . . . , 1896. Edited by N. A. Ramsey. Durham, 1896.

"Durham Church Spreads Gospel with DVDs." *N&O,* 16 Oct. 2008.

Durham County Commissioners Public Hearing on the Superconducting Super Collider. [1988; video recording, held in Durham County Library].

Durham County Inventory: Critical Lands. [Durham,] 1985.

"Durham County, Population by Race." Census-Scope, http://www.censusscope.org/us/s37/c63/chart_race.html.

"Durham Fire Department History Page," http://www.angelfire.con/nc3/dfd/history.html.

Durham Illustrated (Special Souvenir Number, 1910), published by Durham Merchants Association.

"Durham Profile," www.idcide.com/citydata/nc/durham.htm.

"Durham, the Magic Queen City of the Golden Belt." *News and Observer,* 5 Apr. 1896.

Durham, N.C., Standard Metropolitan Statistical Area: 1970 Census of Population and Housing. Washington, 1972.

"Durham's Big Tobacco Factories." *Manufacturer's Record* 10 (28 Aug. 1886): 80–81.

"Early Marrow Transplant May Be Key to 'Bubble Boy' Disease Cure." *Doctor's Guide,* 5 May 1997, http://www.pslgroup.com/dg/25666.htm.

Eastland, Terry. "Parnassus for Humanists." *Change* 12 (6 Apr. 1980): 35.

Edmonds, Helen. *The Negro and Fusion Politics in North Carolina.* Chapel Hill, 1951.

Eilber, Charles R. "Report Card: The First Year at the School of Science and Math." *Popular Government* 47, no. 2, 23–26.

Emerson's Tobacco Belt Directory. Greensboro, 1886.

Engle, Jonathan, *The Epidemic*, New York, 2006.

Erwin, Carolyn K. "A Black Voice in Durham." *Ebony* (June 1973): 114.

Erwin Mills, Inc. *v.* Textile Workers Union of America, CIO et al. *South Eastern Reporter*, series 2, 67 (1952): 372–74; also 68 (1952): 813–16.

Escott, Paul D. *Many Excellent People: Power and Privilege in North Carolina, 1850–1900.* Chapel Hill, 1985.

———. "Poverty and Governmental Aid for the Poor in Confederate North Carolina." *North Carolina Historical Review* 41 (Oct. 1984): 462–80.

Evans, Eli N. *The Provincials: A Personal History of Jews in the South.* New York, 1973.

Evans, W. N., Jr. "History of the Tobacco Industry in Durham." *Trinity Archive* 33 (Oct.–Nov. 1920): 20–24.

Everett, Reuben Oscar. "Dr. Bartlett Durham." *Herald*, 20 June 1937.

Facts about the Textile Mills of the South. Comp. by Southern Textile Bulletin. Charlotte, 1921.

Fallow, Amy Childs. *The Story of Duke's Chapel.* Durham, 1967.

Federal Writers' Project. *These Are Our Lives.* Chapel Hill, 1939.

———. *Slave Narratives.* Microfiches in D.U. Library Published as *The American Slave: A Composite Autobiography*, edited by George P. Rawick. Westport, Conn., 1977–79.

Ferrell, Joseph S., ed. *County Government in North Carolina.* Chapel Hill, 1968.

Few, William. "Autobiography of Colonel William Few of Georgia." *The Magazine of American History* 7 (1881): 340–58.

"First Annual Announcement, Trinity High School, 1891–92." *North Carolina Pamphlets* 3 (nos. 21–33), in D.U. Library.

First Annual Report of the Bureau of Vital Statistics of the North Carolina State Board of Health. Raleigh, 1915.

First Presbyterian Church, Durham, N.C. *Centennial Program Commemorating the One-Hundredth Anniversary, 1871–1971.* [Durham, 1971.]

The First Twenty Years: A History of the Duke University Schools of Medicine, Nursing, and Health Services, and Duke Hospital, 1930–1950. Durham, 1952.

Fisher, Clyde O. "The Relief of Soldiers' Families in North Carolina during the Civil War." *North Carolina Historical Review* (1917): 60–72.

Fisher, Miles Mark. *Friends: Pictorial Report of Ten Years' Pastorate.* Durham, 1943.

Fletcher, A. L. *Biennial Report of the [N.C.] Department of Labor, July 1, 1934 to June 30, 1936.* Raleigh, [1936].

Fletcher's Chapel Church. Durham, [1953]. Pamphlet Collection, D.U. Library.

Flowers, John B., III. *Orange Factory.* Durham, 1978.

———, and Marguerite Schumann. *Bull Durham and Beyond: A Tour Guide to City and County.* Durham, 1976.

Foote, William Henry. *Sketches of North Carolina Historical and Biographical Illustrative of the Principles of a Portion of Her Early Settlers.* New York, 1846.

Forty Years 1887–1927. Durham, 1927.

Forty Years of Service to the Sick. Durham, 1936.

Foushee, Ola Maie. *Art in North Carolina.* Chapel Hill, 1977.

Franck, Richard. "William Erwin, His Cotton Mills Reflect History of West Durham." *The [Duke] Chronicle*, 23 Apr. 1976.

Franklin, John Hope. *The Free Negro in North Carolina, 1790–1860.* Chapel Hill, 1943.

———. *From Slavery to Freedom: A History of Negro Americans.* 5th ed. New York, 1980.

Friedman, Elizabeth. "Crest Street: A Family/Community Impact Statement." Policy Paper 2 of the Center for the Study of the Family and the State, Institute of Policy Sciences and Public Affairs, Duke University, 1978.

Fries, Adelaide L., et al. *The Records of the Moravians.* 11 vols. Raleigh, 1922–69.

Frothingham, Thomas E., Matthew S. Epstein, et al. "Center for Child and Family Health: North Carolina." *North Carolina Medical Journal* 60, no. 2 (1999): 83–89.

Fruth, Florence Knight. *Some Descendants of Richard Few of Chester County, Pennsylvania and Allied Lines.* Beaver Falls, Pa., 1977.

Gannett, Lewis S., ed. *The Family Book of Verse.* New York, 1961.

Gatlin, Douglas. "A Case Study of a Negro Voters' League: The Durham Committee on Negro Affairs in Municipal Elections." Political Studies Program, Research Reports, no. 2 (15 Mar. 1960).

Gifford, James F., Jr. *The Evolution of a Medical Center: A History of Medicine at Duke University to 1941.* Durham, 1972.

Gilley, Gary E. "A History of the Charismatic Movement." Biblical Discernment Ministries, Associated Baptist Press, 28 May 2004, www.rapidnet.com/jbeard/bdm/ Psychology/char/more/hist.htm.

Gobbel, Luther L. "The Militia of North Carolina in Colonial and Revolutionary Times." *Trinity College Historical Papers*, 13th series. Durham, 1919. Pp. 35–61.

Governor's Commission on the Status of Women. *The Many Lives of North Carolina Women.* Raleigh, 1964.

"The Governor's School of North Carolina." Winston-Salem, 1963.

Gray, Virginia. "A Goodly Heritage: The Dukes of Orange County." *Duke Alumni Register* 55, no. 4 (Sept. 1969): 20–23; 5 (Nov. 1969): 18–21.

Greater Durham Chamber of Commerce. *Economic Summary.* Durham, 1981.

Griffin, James B. "An Interpretation of Siouan Archaeology in the Piedmont of North Carolina and Virginia." *American Antiquity* 10 (Apr. 1945): 321–30.

[Groves, Harry.] "Members of Alumni Community Will Be Recognized for Service." *University of Chicago Chronicle*, 26 May 2005.

Gwynn, Zae Hargett. *Abstracts of the Early Deeds of Granville County, North Carolina, 1746–1765.* Rocky Mount, N.C., 1974.

Hall, Robert L., and Carol B. Stack. *Holding on to the Land and the Lord.* Athens, Ga., 1982.

Hall, Stephen P., and Robert D. Sutter. *Durham County Inventory of Important Natural Areas, Plants, and Wildlife.* [Durham,] 1999.

Halperin, Edward C. "Medical Origins of Duke University." *North Carolina Medical Journal* 48 (Dec. 1987): 664–66.

Hamilton, C. Horace. "The Negro Leaves the South." *Demography* 1 no. 1 (1964).

Hamilton, J. G. deRoulhac. "The Freedmen's Bureau in North Carolina." *South Atlantic Quarterly* 8 (1909): 53–67, 154–63.

———, ed. *The Papers of Willie P. Mangum.* 5 vols. Raleigh, 1957–60.

———. *Reconstruction in North Carolina.* New York, 1914.

Hamilton, William B. "The Research Triangle of North Carolina: A Study in Leadership for the Common Weal." *South Atlantic Quarterly* 65 (1966): 254–78.

Hand-Book of Durham, N.C., 1895. Durham, 1895.

Harlan, Louis R., ed. *Booker T. Washington Papers.* 8 vols. Urbana, 1972–84.

Hazen, Allen, and Charles B. Burdick. *Report: Extending and Improving the Water Works System.* Durham, 1921.

Heads of Families at the First Census of the United States Taken in the Year 1790: North Carolina. Washington, 1908.

Henderson, Bruce. "A Diversified Durham." Charlotte *Observer*, 28 Aug. 1986.

Henry, James T. "Negro Preachers of Durham." *Trinity Archive* 12 (Oct. 1898): 1–7.

The Heritage of Onslow County, N.C. Winston-Salem, 1983.

Herndon, John Goodwin. *The Herndons of the American Revolution.* Lancaster, Pa., 1950–52.

Herring, Harriet L. *Welfare Work in Mill Villages: The Story of Extra-Mill Activities in North Carolina.* Chapel Hill, 1929.

Higgenbotham, Don. "Decision for Revolution." *The North Carolina Experience: An Interpretive and Documentary History*, edited by Lindley S. Butler and Alan D. Watson, 125–46. Chapel Hill, 1984.

Higgins, Andrea. *A Step of Faith: The History of the Durham Rescue Mission*. Durham, 2006.

Hinson, Glenn. "The Bull City Blues." *N.C. Bicentennial Folklife Festival Program Book*, 10–11, 45–47. Durham, 1976.

History, Durham County Chapter, American Red Cross, State of North Carolina. Durham, [1919].

Hodges, Betty. "A Lifetime of Looking." *Herald*, 10 Oct. 1976.

———. "Durham Academy Alumni Reminisce about the Past." *Herald*, 25 Oct. 1983.

Hodges, Ed. "Those Saturday Nights." *Herald*, 8 July 1979.

Hofmann, Margaret M. *Colony of North Carolina 1755–1764: Abstracts of Land Patents*. Weldon, N.C., 1982.

Hollingsworth, Harry D. *Saint Luke's Episcopal Church, Durham, North Carolina 1956–1981*. Durham, 1981.

Holsey, Albon L. "The National Negro Business League—Forty Years in Review." *Crisis* 48 (Apr. 1941): 104–5.

Holton, Holland. "The History of Education in Durham County." *North Carolina Education* 11 (Jan. 1945): 243–47, 260–68.

"Homelessness in Durham, Durham County, North Carolina." UNC School of Public Health, http://www.hsl.unc/phpapers/durham01/durham/htm.

Howerton, R. T., Jr. "The Rose of Sharon Baptist Church." *Trinity Archive* 21 (1907–08): 187–95.

Hubbell, Jay B. *Our First One Hundred Years: Yates Baptist Church*. Durham, [1978].

Hulton, Paul, ed. *America 1585: The Complete Drawings of John White*. Chapel Hill, 1984.

Illustrated Durham, 1905. Kinderhook, N.Y., 1905.

In Memoriam Julius Rosenwald 1862–1932. Raleigh, 1932.

"Interview with Steven Chalmers by Alicia Rouverol." Southern Oral History Program Collection, Southern Historical Collection, Louis Round Wilson Special Collections Library, University of North Carolina, Chapel Hill.

Janiewski, Dolores E. *Sisterhood Denied*. Philadelphia, 1985.

Jensen, Howard E. "Durham's Unmet Needs." *Herald*, 18–27 Feb. 1952.

Jolly, Harley E. "The Labor Movement in North Carolina, 1880–1922." *North Carolina Historical Review* 30 (1953): 354–75.

Jones, W. Mac, ed. *The Douglas Register*. Richmond, 1928.

Jones, Yvonne V. "Black Leadership Patterns and Political Change in the American South." *Holding on to the Land and the Lord*, edited by Robert L. Hall and Carol B. Stack, 41–54. Athens, Ga., 1982.

Journal of the House of Representatives, 1881 Session. Raleigh, 1882.

Journal of the Proceedings . . . of the Protestant Episcopal Church in the State of North Carolina . . . 1827. New Bern, 1827 . . . 1837. Fayetteville, 1837.

Journal of the Senate, 1881 Session. Raleigh, 1882.

Kasarda, John H., James H. Johnson, and Barbara Mason. *The Economic Impact of the Hispanic Population on the State of North Carolina*. Chapel Hill, 2005.

Kay, Marvin L. Michael, and William S. Price, Jr. "'To Ride the Wood Mare': Road Building and Militia Service in Colonial North Carolina, 1740–1775." *North Carolina Historical Review* 57 (1980): 361–409.

Keech, William R. *The Impact of Negro Voting: The Role of the Vote in the Quest for Equality*. Chicago, 1968.

Kennon, Albert W. *Report of the Durham City-County Charter Commission*. Durham, 1960.

Kilgo, John C. "William H. Branson." *An Annual Publication of Historical Papers*. Series 4. Pp. 21–30. Durham, 1900.

Kim, Leah. "Durham Academy Has 50-Year History." *Herald*, 21 May 1983.

King, William E. [Pan-Africa–U.S. Games.] *Duke Dialogue*, 27 July 1993.

Klitgaard, Kaj. *Art in America*. Chapel Hill, 1941.

Knight, Edgar W. "The Peabody Fund and Its Early Operation in North Carolina." *South Atlantic Quarterly* 14 (1915): 168–80.

Kostyu, Joel A., and Frank A. Kostyu. *Durham: A Pictorial History.* Norfolk, 1978.

LaBarre, Weston. *They Shall Take Up Serpents.* Minneapolis, 1962.

Larrabee, Charles X. *Many Missions: Research Triangle Institute's First 31 Years, 1959–1990.* Research Triangle Park, 1991.

Laws and Resolutions of the State of North Carolina Passed by the General Assembly at Its Session of 1881. Raleigh, 1881.

Lee, E. Lawrence. *Indian Wars in North Carolina, 1663–1763.* Raleigh, 1963; reprint, Raleigh, 1968.

Lefler, Hugh T., ed. *John Lawson's "A New Voyage to Carolina."* Chapel Hill, 1967.

Lefler, Hugh T., and Albert R. Newsome. *North Carolina: The History of a Southern State.* 3d ed. Chapel Hill, 1973.

Lefler, Hugh T., and Paul Wager. *Orange County, 1752–1952.* Chapel Hill, 1953.

Lemert, Ben F. *Durham, North Carolina: An Economic Survey.* Durham, 1938.

———. *Economic Maps of Durham, N.C.* Durham, 1938.

Lewis, Marcus W. *The Development of Early Emigrant Trails in the United States East of the Mississippi River.* Washington, 1933.

The Life and Service of Saint Joseph's Episcopal Church: Fifty Years in the West Durham Community 1908–1958. Durham, 1959.

Ligon, Roddey M., Jr. *A Report on the Durham County Health Department.* Chapel Hill, 1960.

Link, Albert N. *Generosity of Spirit: The Early History of the Research Triangle Park.* Research Triangle Park, 1995.

———. *From Seed to Harvest: The Growth of the Research Triangle Park.* Research Triangle Park, 2002.

Link, Paxson R. *The Link Family: Antecedents and Descendants of John Jacob Link, 1417–1951.* Paris, Ill., 1951.

"The Little River." *Eno,* fall 2001, 9.

Locke, Alain, ed. *The New Negro: An Interpretation.* New York, 1969.

Lougee, George. "'Mama' Germino 99 and Going for 100." *Herald,* 22 May 1983.

———. "Potential of Research Park Cited by Retired Architect." *Herald,* 23 Nov. 1973.

Mabry, William A. "The Negro in North Carolina Politics since Reconstruction." *Historical Papers of the Trinity College Historical Society.* Series 23. Durham, 1940.

"Major Past and Future Sports Events." Durham Convention and Visitors Bureau.

Manarin, Louis H., and Weymouth T. Jordan, comps. *North Carolina Troops 1861–1865: A Roster.* Raleigh, 1966–.

[D. C.] *Mangum's Directory of Durham, 1897–1898.* Durham, 1897.

Markham, Mary Beth, and Jan Lamb, eds. "The Yellow House: An Oral History" [compiled by the class of 2002 of the Hill Center].

"Marking the Ramsgate Road." *North Carolina Booklet* 23 (1926): 57–60.

Markum, William Benjamin. *The Life of a Great Man: Rev. Edian Markum and the Founding of St. Joseph A.M.E. Church, Durham, North Carolina.* Boston, 1941.

Martin, Ed. "Eno Association: Grassroots Politics For Conservation." *Herald,* 9 Apr. 1972.

Mathews, Jane DeHart. "The Status of Women in North Carolina." *The North Carolina Experience,* edited by Lindley S. Butler and Alan D. Watson, 427–51. Chapel Hill, 1984.

Mathis, Clara Pugh. *The Unforgettable Years.* [Durham, 1947].

Mathis, Mark A., and Jeffrey J. Crow. *The Prehistory of North Carolina: An Archaeological Symposium.* Raleigh, 1983.

Mauskopf, Seymour H., and Michael R. McVaugh. *The Elusive Science.* Baltimore, 1980.

McBride, [B.] Ransom, comp. "Claims of British Merchants after the Revolutionary War." *North Carolina Genealogical Journal* 11 (Feb. 1985): 25–43.

————, comp. "The Inhabitants of Granville County, N.C., 1746, 1750." *North Carolina Genealogical Journal* 8 (Feb. 1982): 24–30.

————, ed. "John Saunders' Journey to North Carolina." *North Carolina Genealogical Journal* 5 (Aug. 1979): 146–49.

————, ed. "Revolutionary War Papers." *North Carolina Genealogical Journal* 3 (May 1977): 91–98; 4 (Feb. 1978): 24–29; 4 (Aug. 1978): 188–94.

McCollough, C. R., Quentin R. Bass III, William O. Autry, Jr., and Duane R. Lenhardt. *Phase II Archaeological Investigation of Ten Specified Locales in the Falls Lake Reservoir Area, Falls Lake, North Carolina.* Report of U.S. Army Corps of Engineers, Wilmington District, December 1980.

McKoy, Elizabeth F. *Early New Hanover County Records.* Wilmington, N.C., 1973.

McLaurin, Melton. *Paternalism and Protest: The Knights of Labor in the South.* Westport, Conn., 1978.

McMath, Robert C., Jr. "Agrarian Protest at the Forks of the Creek: Three Subordinate Farmers' Alliances in North Carolina." *North Carolina Historical Review* 51 (1974): 41–63.

McPherson, Kathryn. [Articles on diet programs in Durham, titled variously.] *Herald.* 18 May, 19 May, 20 May, 25 May 1980.

McPherson, Samuel D., Jr. *McPherson Hospital: Personal Recollections and a Brief History.* Durham, 2001.

Medley, Mary L. *History of Anson County, North Carolina 1750–1976.* Wadesboro, N.C., 1976.

Menius, Arthur C., III. "James Bennitt: Portrait of an Antebellum Yeoman." *North Carolina Historical Review* 58 (Oct. 1981): 305–26.

Merrens, Harry Roy. *Colonial North Carolina in the Eighteenth Century: A Study in Historical Geography.* Chapel Hill, 1964.

Miller, Carl F. "Archaeology of the John H. Kerr Reservoir Basin, Roanoke River, Virginia—North Carolina. *Inter-Agency Archaeological Salvage Program: River Basin Surveys Papers,* edited by F. H. Roberts. BAE Bulletin no. 182. Washington, 1962.

Miller, Mary Ruth. "The Forest at Duke: A History, 1992–2007."

Miller, Spencer, Jr., and Joseph F. Fletcher. *The Church and Industry.* New York, 1947.

Mooney, James. *Siouan Tribes of the East.* BAE Bulletin no. 22. Washington, 1895.

Morgon, David T., Jr. "The Great Awakening in North Carolina, 1740–1775: The Baptist Phase." *North Carolina Historical Review* 45 (1968): 264–83.

Murray, Elizabeth Reid. *Wake: Capital County of North Carolina.* Raleigh, 1983.

Murray, Florence, ed. *Negro Handbook, 1946–47.* New York, 1947.

Murray, Pauli. *Proud Shoes.* New York, 1978.

Muse, Benjamin. *The Twentieth Century as I Saw It.* New York, 1982.

"Museum of Life and Science in Durham, North Carolina," www.northcarolinatravels.com/museums/nc-museum-of-life-and-science/index/htm.

Muster Rolls of the Soldiers of the War of 1812: Detached from the Militia of North Carolina. Raleigh, 1873.

Myrdal, Gunnar. *An American Dilemma.* New York, 1944.

National Vital Statistics Report, 2000. Washington, 2001.

Nicholson, Patrick. *Mr. Jim: The Biography of James Smither Abercrombie.* Houston, 1983.

"NIH Restores Funds for Duke AIDS Clinical Trial Unit." Duke University News Service, http://dukespace.lib.duke.edu/dspace/bitstream/10161/640/9/ACTU.pdf.

North Carolina Board of Education, Department of Public Instruction. Public Schools of North Carolina: Statistical Profile, 1998. [Raleigh,] 1998.

North Carolina Department of Administration Commission on the Education and Employment of Women. *The Status of Women in North Carolina.* Raleigh, 1975.

[North Carolina Department of Health and Human Services, Division of Public Health.]

North Carolina Epidemiologic Profile for HIV/AIDS *Prevention and Care Planning, July 2007.* Raleigh, 2007

[North Carolina Department of Health and Human Services, Epidemiology and Special Studies Unit, HIV/AIDS Prevention and Care Branch.] *North Carolina 2007* HIV/AIDS *Surveillance Report,* tables 2, 4. Raleigh, 2007.

North Carolina Department of the Secretary of State. *North Carolina Government 1585–1979.* Raleigh, 1981.

North Carolina Reports 94 (Feb. Term 1886): 577–82, A. M. Rigsbee *v.* The Town of Durham, 98 (Sept. Term 1887): 92–98, A. M. Rigsbee *v.* The Town of Durham and the School Committee of the Town of Durham.

North Carolina's Research Triangle. Chapel Hill, 1980.

North Carolina State Center for Health Statistics, North Carolina Department of Health and Human Services. http://www.dhhs.state.nc.us/SCHS/data/county.clm.

O'Brien, William Francis. *The Memoirs of Monsignor William Francis O'Brien.* Durham, 1958.

Olive, Cornelia. "Clinic Caring for Poor." *Herald,* 22 Nov. 1969.

Olmsted, Frederick Law. *The Cotton Kingdom.* New York, 1962.

"Orange County, North Carolina, Tax List 1755." *The North Carolinian* 1 (Dec. 1955): 103–8.

"Outline of the History of the Battle For the Eno: A Chronological Guide." *Eno* 1, no. 2 (fall 1973): 5–9.

The Parish Register of Christ Church, Middlesex County, Virginia, from 1653 to 1812. Richmond, 1897.

Parker, Harold T. *The History of St. Philip's Episcopal Church, 1878–1994,* Durham, 1996.

Parramore, Thomas. *Express Lanes and Country Roads.* Chapel Hill, 1983. Vol. 5 of *The Way We Lived in North Carolina,* edited by Sydney Nathans.

Paths toward Freedom: A Biographical History of Blacks and Indians in North Carolina by Blacks and Indians. Raleigh, 1976.

Patton, Frances Gray. "The Town Bull Durham Built." *Holiday,* Dec. 1959.

Paul, Hiram Voss. *History of the Town of Durham, N.C.* Raleigh, 1884.

Peck, Jim. "A Carolina City—15 Years Later." *CORE-lator* 98 (Nov. 1962).

Peirce, Neal, and Curtis Johnson, "The Triangle: A Future in Question." *N&O,* 19–26 Sept. 1993.

Persons, Elizabeth Anderson. "South Lowell Male Academy and Its First Headmaster." *The Durham Record* 1 (fall 1983): 18–25.

Phillips, Bill. "Piedmont Country Blues." *Southern Exposure* 2, no. 1 (spring/summer, 1974).

Planning and Community Development Department, Durham, North Carolina. *Crest Street Redevelopment Plan, January 27, 1983.*

Population Profile: Durham County and the City of Durham. Durham, 2005.

Porter, Earl W. *Trinity and Duke, 1892–1924: Foundations of Duke University.* Durham, 1964.

Powell, William S., ed. *Biographical Dictionary of North Carolina.* Chapel Hill, 1984–.

———, ed. *The Correspondence of William Tryon and Other Selected Papers.* 2 vols. Raleigh, 1980.

———. *The Proprietors of Carolina.* Raleigh, 1963.

———. "William Johnston: Eighteenth-Century Entrepreneur." *The Durham Record* 1 (fall 1983): 5–17.

[Preiss, Jack J.] "Employee Update." Newsletter, North Carolina Department of Health and Human Services, Feb. 2005.

"Prospectus of Trinity Park High School." *North Carolina Pamphlets: Public Schools* 3 (nos. 21–33). D.U. Library.

"Quail Roost Farm." http://www.endangereddurham.blogspot.com.

A Quarter Century of Political Participation in North Carolina 1951–1976: A History of the League of Women Voters of North Carolina. Durham, 1976.

Raleigh-Durham Airport Authority. *Raleigh-Durham Airport Long-Range Development Master Plan and Environmental Assessment.* Technical Report 1 [of 61], 1980.

Ramsey, Robert W. *Carolina Cradle.* Chapel Hill, 1964.

"The Ramsgate Road." *North Carolina Booklet* 23 (1926): 61–62.

Rankin, Dorothy Newsom. "History of the Durham Civic Choral Society: Its First Thirty Years and a Few Recollections." Typescript, 1979.

Rankin, Hugh F. *The North Carolina Continentals.* Chapel Hill, 1971.

[Reeves, Lieutenant Enos]. "Extracts from the Letter-Books of Lieutenant Eno Reeves." *Pennsylvania Magazine of History and Biography* 20 (1896): 456–72; 21 (1897): 235–56, 376–91, 466–76.

"Report of the Chief Engineer [Walter Gwynn] on the Survey of the N.C. Railroad, Greensborough, May, 1851." *Xenodochy* 13, RBR, D.U. Library.

Report of the Durham City-County Charter Commission. Durham, Oct.–Nov. 1960.

Report of the Real Property Survey of Durham, North Carolina, 1939–40. Durham, 1940.

Report of the Superintendent, Durham City Schools, 1914–1923. Durham, 1923.

Report of the Superintendent of Public Instruction of North Carolina for the Year 1869. Raleigh, 1869.

Rhee, Foon. "Fifteen Years Ago: Tear Gas and Grievances." *The [Duke] Chronicle,* 13 Feb. 1984.

Rights, Douglas L. *The American Indian in North Carolina.* Winston-Salem, 1957.

———. "The Trading Path to the Indians." *North Carolina Historical Review* 8 (1931): 403–26.

Riley, Richard F. "The Case of the Unperceived U.S. Watermark." *The American Philatelist,* Sept. 1977, 692–94.

Roberts, B. W. C., and Richard F. Knapp. *John Thomas Dalton and the Development of Bull Durham Smoking Tobacco.* Durham, 1977.

Roberts, Claudia, Diane E. Lea, and Robert M. Cleary. *The Durham Architectural and Historic Inventory.* Durham, 1982.

Roberts, Everette Latta. *History of Bethany M. E. Church, South, Durham, North Carolina.* Durham, 1950.

Robinson, Blackwell, ed. *The North Carolina Guide.* Chapel Hill, 1955.

Rogalski, Jim. "Breaking the Barrier: A History of African Americans at Duke University School of Medicine." *Inside: Duke University Medical Center and Health System Archives,* 20 Feb. 2006.

Romero, Rubel. "Dark Journeys." *Spectator,* 17 May 1984.

Rose, Willie Lee. *Slavery and Freedom.* New York, 1982.

Routh, Donald K. *The Story of the Eno River Unitarian-Universalist Fellowship.* Iowa City, 1979.

Ruffin, Julian M. and David T. Smith. "Studies on Pellagra at the Duke University School of Medicine." In *Clinical Pellagra,* edited by Seale Harris, 194–247. Saint Louis, 1941.

Saint Barbara's Greek Orthodox Church, Durham, North Carolina. Durham, [1970].

Salamon, Lester M. *Durham Urban Observatory Report: The Substandard Housing Market in Durham.* Durham, 1976.

Salber, Eva J. *Don't Send Me Flowers when I'm Dead.* Durham, 1983.

Salley, Alexander S., Jr. *Narratives of Early Carolina 1650–1708.* New York, 1911.

Sanitary Code of the Board of Health, Durham, North Carolina. Durham, 1909.

Satterfield, Carolyn. "Leigh Farm Gives View of Life of Yesteryear." *Sun,* 25 Apr. 1975.

Saunders, William L., ed. *The Colonial Records of North Carolina.* 10 vols. Raleigh, 1886–90.

Seagrave, Sterling. *The Soong Dynasty.* New York, 1985.

Sellers, Charles G., Jr. "Private Profits and British Colonial Policy: The Speculations of Henry McCulloh." *William and Mary Quarterly*, 3d ser., 8 (1951): 535–51.

Seventh Census of the United States, 1850: Embracing a Statistical View of Each of the States and Territories. Washington, 1853.

Shanks, Henry T., ed. *The Papers of Willie Person Mangum.* 5 vols. Raleigh, 1950–56.

Shepard, James E. *New Plans for the Uplift of a Race.* N.p., [1908].

Sherman, William T. *General Sherman's Official Account of His Great March through Georgia and the Carolinas.* New York, 1865.

———. *The Memoirs of General William T. Sherman.* 2 vols. New York, 1931.

Shields, Ruth Herndon. *The Descendants of William and Sarah Herndon of Caroline County, Va., and Chatham County, N.C.* Chapel Hill, 1956.

Shields, Ruth Herndon, and Mann Cabe Patterson. *Some Orange County, North Carolina Families.* Chapel Hill, 1934.

Shields, Ruth Herndon, Belle Lewter West, and Kathryn Crossley Stone. *A Study of the Barbee Families of Chatham, Orange, and Wake Counties in North Carolina.* Boulder, Colo., 1971.

Shipp, Bertha P., Louis T. Stokes, and Beulah Walton. *A History of Cedar Fork Baptist Church, 1805–1970.* [1970].

"Sierra Leone Missionary." *The World for Christ* 1, no. 4 (Apr. 1895).

Sindler, Allan P., ed. *Change in the Contemporary South.* Durham, 1963.

Singal, Daniel J. *The War Within: From Victorian to Modernist Thought in the South, 1919–1945.* Chapel Hill, 1982.

Smith, Burke and Frank Smith. "Archaeology in Durham County." *The Bulletin of the Archaeological Society of North Carolina* 1, no. 1 (Mar. 1934): 7–10.

Smyth, John F. D. *A Tour in the United States of America.* 2 vols. Dublin, 1784.

Soil Survey of Durham County, North Carolina. Washington, 1924.

Southeastern Efforts Developing Sustainable Spaces (SEEDS). Corporate history, www.seedsnc.org/history.htm.

The Southern Business Directory and General Commercial Advertiser. Charleston, 1854.

Southgate, James H. "History of Trinity Church." *Trinity League Record*, Jan. 1895.

Souvenir Edition of the Durham Daily Sun Complimentary to the North Carolina Press Association Now in Session in Durham, N.C., 23–25 July 1890.

Speck, Frank G. "Siouan Tribes of the Carolinas as Known from Catawba, Tutelo, and Documentary Sources." *American Anthropologist* 37 (1935): 201–25.

Spencer, Cornelia P. *The Last Ninety Days of the War.* New York, 1866.

Stanford L. Warren Public Library. *Whetstone*, second quarter, 1964.

Stauber, William E. *A History of Epworth United Methodist Church . . . , Durham, North Carolina: The First Twenty-Five Years.* Durham, 1977.

Steamer, Robert J. "Southern Disaffection with the National Democratic Party." *Change in the Contemporary South*, edited by Allan P. Sindler, 150–173. Durham, 1963.

Steinberg, Michael. "Abandoned in Durham: Shelter System Harsh on Homeless." *Prism*, June 1996.

Stevens, C. J., ed. *Holloways of the South and Allied Families.* New Orleans, 1977.

Stoesen, Alexander R. "From Ordeal to New Deal." *The North Carolina Experience: An Interpretive and Documentary History*, edited by Lindley S. Butler and Alan D. Watson, 382–404. Chapel Hill, 1984.

Strom, Jennifer. "The Conflicting Agendas of Lavonia Allison." *Independent Weekly*, 21 Nov. 2001.

Sumka, Howard J., and Michael A. Stegman. *The Housing Outlook in North Carolina: Projections to 1980.* North Carolina Department of Administration Report, June 1972.

Swaim, Douglas, ed. *Carolina Dwelling.* Raleigh, 1978.

Swanton, John R. *The Indians of the Southeastern United States.* BAE Bulletin no. 137. Washington, 1946.

Swint, Henry Lee. *The Northern Teacher in the South, 1862–1870*. Nashville, Tenn., 1941.

"Telephone Service in Durham." Notes assembled by Sid Linton, Public Relations Officer, General Telephone Company of the South.

Terris, Milton. *Goldberger on Pellagra*. Baton Rouge, 1964.

Terry, Sonny (as told to Kent Cooper and Fred Palmer). *The Harp Styles of Sonny Terry*. New York, 1975.

Testimony Taken by the Joint Select Committee to Inquire into the Condition of Affairs in the Late Insurrectionary States: North Carolina. Washington, 1872.

Tilley, Arthur Mangum, Sr. *A Brief Historical Sketch of the Name and Family of the Tilleys*. N.p., n.d.

Tilley, Doris Belk. "Durham's Early Lutherans." *The Durham Record* 1 (1983): 53–64.

Tilley, Janet, and Charles K. Moseley. *History of Rougemont Methodist Episcopal Church*. N.p., 1980.

Tilley, Mary Ethel. *Carrington: A Brief Historical Sketch of the Name and the Family*. Rougemont, N.C. [1943].

Tindall, George B. *The Emergence of the New South, 1913–1945*. Baton Rouge, 1967.

Tobacco Institute. *North Carolina and Tobacco*. Washington, 1971.

Trelease, Allen W. *White Terror: The Ku Klux Klan Conspiracy and Southern Reconstruction*. Westport, Conn., 1971.

Trinity College, Durham, North Carolina, Catalogue for the Year 1896–97. Durham, 1896.

TROSA. Corporate history, www.trosainc.org/about/history-vision.htm.

Troxler, Carole W. *The Loyalist Experience in North Carolina*. Raleigh, 1976.

Turner and Company's Durham Directory, 1889–90. Winston, 1889.

Turrentine, George Ruford. *The Turrentine Family*. N.p., 1954.

Underwood, S. B. "Joseph Francis Bivins." *Trinity Archive* 18 (1904–5): 1–10.

United States Census Office. *Second Census, 1800: Return of the Whole Number of Persons within the Several Districts of the United States*. Washington, 1802.

United States Department of Agriculture Soil Conservation Service and the North Carolina Agricultural Experiment Station. *Soil Survey of Durham County, North Carolina*. N.p., [1977].

United States War Department. *War of the Rebellion: Official Records of the Union and Confederate Armies*. 70 vols. New York, 1865–1901.

Upchurch, W. M. and M. B. Fowler. *Durham County Economic and Social*. N.p., [1915].

Van Noppen, Charles L., comp. *In Memoriam George Washington Watts*. Greensboro, 1922.

Vatavuck, William M. "In the Shadow of Appomatox: The Surrender at Bennett Place." *Blue and Gray* (Apr.–May 1985): 45–56.

Veterans Administration. *County Veteran Population, 1966, Durham County*. Research Monograph 9.

Vickers, James and Thomas Scism. *Chapel Hill: An Illustrated History*. Chapel Hill, 1985.

Wager, Paul W. *County Government and Administration in North Carolina*. Chapel Hill, 1928.

Ward, H. Trawick. "A Review of Archaeology in the North Carolina Piedmont: A Study of Change." *The Prehistory of North Carolina: An Archaeological Symposium*, edited by Mark A. Mathis and Jeffrey J. Crow, 53–81. Raleigh, 1983.

Washington, Booker T. "Durham, North Carolina, a City of Negro Enterprise." *Independent* 70 (Mar. 1911): 642–50.

The Water Supply System of the City of Durham, North Carolina. Durham, 1981.

Watson, Alan D. "The Regulation: Society in Upheaval." *The North Carolina Experience: An Interpretive and Documentary History*, edited by Lindley S. Butler and Alan D. Watson, 101–124. Chapel Hill, 1984.

Watson, Joseph W., and C. Franklin Grill. *North Carolina Conference Historical Directory* [of Methodist Churches in Durham County]. Raleigh, 1984.

Waynick, Capus M., John C. Brooks, and Elsie W. Pitts. *North Carolina and the Negro.* Raleigh, 1964.

Weare, Walter B. *Black Business in the New South.* Chicago, 1973.

Webb, Mena Fuller. *Jule Carr: General without an Army.* Chapel Hill, 1987.

Webb, William James. *Our Webb Kin of Dixie.* Oxford, N.C., 1940.

Webbink, Mark H. "Durham Makes the Most of Revenue-Sharing." *Popular Government* 40, no. 3 (Winter 1975): 36–39.

Wefing, Henry. "Brown *v.* School Board: 30 Years Later in Durham." *Herald,* 13 May 1984.

Westcott, Mary, and Allene Ramage. *A Checklist of United States Newspapers (and Weeklies before 1900) in the General Library* [of Duke University]. Durham, 1936.

Wheless, Al. "Durham Renewal: A $76.2 Million Tag." *Herald,* 8–12 Aug. 1976.

White, Gilbert C. *Final Report on the Establishment of Waterworks, Durham, N.C.* Durham, 1917.

White, Newman Ivey. "Labor Helps Itself: A Case History." *South Atlantic Quarterly* 32 (1933): 346–64.

Whitener, Daniel Jay. *Prohibition in North Carolina, 1715–1945.* Chapel Hill, 1945.

———. "Public Education in North Carolina during Reconstruction, 1865–1876." *Essays in Southern History.* Edited by Fletcher M. Green, 67–90.

Whitted, J. A. *A History of the Negro Baptists in North Carolina.* Raleigh, 1908.

Wicker, Warren J. "Durham Rejects City/County Consolidation." *Popular Government* 40 (Winter 1975): 27–28.

Williams, Robin M. and Olaf Wakefield. *Farm Tenancy in North Carolina 1880–1935.* N.p., North Carolina Agricultural Experiment Station, Sept. 1937.

Williams, Samuel C., ed. *Adair's History of the American Indians.* Johnson City, Tenn., 1930.

Williamson, Joel. *The Crucible of Race: Black-White Relations in the American South since Emancipation.* New York, 1984.

Wilson, Louis R. *The Research Triangle of North Carolina.* Chapel Hill, 1967.

Wilson, William F., and P. Albert Carpenter III. *Region J Geology: A Guide for North Carolina Mineral Resource Development and Land Use Planning.* Raleigh, 1975.

Winston, Robert W. *It's a Far Cry.* New York, 1937.

Wise, Jim. "Edith London . . . Hitting It at 80," *Herald,* 2 Nov. 1984.

Wood, Clarence R. *A Study of Recreation Needs and Services in the Greater Durham, North Carolina, Area.* (1960).

Woodward, C. Vann. *Origins of the New South, 1877–1913.* Baton Rouge, 1951.

Woody, Robert H., ed. *The Papers and Addresses of William Preston Few.* Durham, 1951.

Yetman, Norman R. *Voices from Slavery.* New York, 1970.

Young, Betty Irene. "Lillian Baker Griggs: Pioneer Librarian." *The Durham Record* 1 (1983): 26–44.

Zuber, Richard L. *North Carolina during Reconstruction.* Raleigh, 1969.

DISSERTATIONS, THESES, AND MISCELLANEOUS PAPERS

Avery, Sally. "Public Welfare in Durham County." History paper, D.U., 1969. D.U. Archives.

Ayanian, John Z. "Black Health in Segregated Durham, 1900–1940." History honors paper, D.U., 1982. D.U. Archives.

Boles, John Bruce. "The Religious Mind of the Old South: The Era of the Great Revival, 1787–1805." Ph.D. diss., University of Virginia, 1969.

Boyd, Harold Kent. "Louis Austin and the *Carolina Times.*" M.A. thesis, NCCU, 1966.

Bridgers, Margaret Battle. "A History of Social Work in Durham County." M.A. thesis, UNC, 1926.

Brinton, Hugh Penn. "The Negro in Durham: A Study of Adjustment to Town Life." Ph.D. diss., UNC, 1930.

Cannon, Robert. "The Organization and Growth of Black Political Participation in Durham, North Carolina, 1933–1958." Ph.D. diss., UNC, 1975.

Cole, Olivia W. "Rencher Nicholas Harris: A Quarter of a Century of Negro Leadership." M.A. thesis, NCCU, 1967.

Davis, Alvah B., III. "From Display Cases to Museum: The Use of Art and Artifacts in Teaching at Duke University, 1925–1975." History paper, D.U., 1975–76. D.U. Archives.

Drumm, Austin Marcus. "The Union League in the Carolinas." Ph.D. diss., UNC, 1955.

Emory, Samuel Thomas, Jr. "The Durham Triassic Basin: A Study of the Agricultural Landuse of a Predominantly Non-Agricultural Region," M.A. thesis, UNC, 1958.

Haupt, Conrad C. "The Role of the Planner in Durham, North Carolina." M.A. thesis, UNC, 1961.

Houck, Thomas H. "A Newspaper History of Race Relations in Durham, 1910–1940." M.A. thesis, D.U., 1941.

Howard, Christopher D. "Keep Your Eyes on the Prize: The Black Struggle for Civil Equality in Durham, North Carolina, 1954–1963." M.A. thesis, D.U., 1983.

Hubbs, Peter Burke. "Plantation to Factory." Master's essay, History Department, D.U., 1971. D.U. Archives.

Janiewski, Dolores. "From Field to Factory: Race, Class, Sex, and the Woman Worker in Durham, 1880–1940." Ph.D. diss., D.U., 1979.

Jones, Mary Virginia Currie. "A 'Golden Triangle' of Research: Romeo Holland Guest— His Conception of and Involvement in the Development of the Research Triangle Park." M.A. thesis, UNC, 1978.

Kennedy, John W. "The General Strike in the Textile Industry." M.A. thesis, D.U., 1947.

King, Joseph J. "The History and Functions of the Central Labor Union." M.A. thesis, D.U., 1937.

King, William E. "The Era of Progressive Reform in Southern Education: The Growth of Public Schools in North Carolina, 1880–1910." Ph.D. diss., D.U., 1969.

Latimer, Margaret. "Some Social Aspects of Urban Renewal." M.A. thesis, UNC, 1964.

Lornell, Christopher. "A Study of the Sociological Reasons Why Blacks Sing Blues: An Examination of the Secular Black Music Found in Two North Carolina Communities." M.A. thesis, UNC, 1976.

Mansell, Elizabeth Lloyd. "The American Tobacco Company Brick Storage Warehouses in Durham, North Carolina, 1897–1906." M.A. thesis, UNC, 1980.

Nyeu, Ming Hwa. "A Study of the Durham Farmers' Mutual Exchange of Durham, North Carolina." M.A. thesis, D.U., 1933.

Parrish, Robert A., "Neglected Common Interests: Durham's Struggle to Merge Its City and County Schools." M.A. thesis, Duke Unversity, 2001.

Rand, H. Lanier. "I Had to Like It: A Study of a Durham Textile Community." Honors essay, Department of History, UNC, 1977.

Redburn, Francis S. "Protest and Policy in Durham, North Carolina." Ph.D. diss., UNC, 1970.

Reynolds, Pamela Preston. "The Interaction between Public Attitudes and a Philanthropist's Dream: Watts Hospital." History honors paper, D.U., 1979. D.U. Archives.

Rice, David H. "Urban Renewal in Durham: A Case Study of a Referendum." M.A. thesis, UNC, 1966.

Rice, John D. "The Negro Tobacco Worker and His Union in Durham, North Carolina." M.A. thesis, UNC, 1941.

Rose, Winfield H. "Referendum Voting and the Politics of Health Care in Durham County, North Carolina." Ph.D. diss., D.U., 1973.

Sauls, Timothy. "The Eno River Reservoir Controversy, 1966–1973: A Case Study of the Power of Public Opposition." History paper, D.U., 1978. D.U. Archives.

Segal, Theodore D. "A New Genesis: The 'Silent Vigil' at Duke University April 5th–12th, 1968." History honors paper, D.U., 1977. D.U. Archives.

Shear, William M. "The Background and Operation of the Council-Manager System in Durham, North Carolina." M.A. thesis, D.U., 1951.

Stone, Ted Gerald. "A Southern City and County in the Years of Political Change: Durham, North Carolina." M.A. thesis, NCCU, 1977.

Stukes, Thomas Sadler. "Hayti: A Study of White Economic Investment and Intervention in the Black Urban Poor of Durham, North Carolina." Major honors thesis, UNC, 1970.

Summerell, Fran. "Trinity Park School, 1898–1922." History honors paper, D.U., 1975–76. D.U. Archives.

Tate, Robert Spence, Jr. "A Study of Negro Churches in Durham, North Carolina." B.D. thesis, D.U., 1939.

Westin, Richard B. "The State and Segregated Schools: Negro Public Education in North Carolina, 1863–1923." Ph.D. diss., D.U., 1966.

White, Frank H. "The Economic and Social Development of Negroes in North Carolina since 1900." Ph.D. diss., New York University, 1960.

Yanella, Don. "Race Relations at Duke University." Honors paper, Oral History Program, D.U., 1985. D.U. Archives.

PERSONS INTERVIEWED FOR SECOND EDITION

Dorothy Borden
Howard G. Clark III
Peter Denton
Thomas E. Frothingham
Thomas M. Gallie
John D. Hamilton
Joseph Harvard
Rebecca Heron

Bill Kalkhof
Sylvia Kerckhoff
Louise Maynor
Patsy Perry
Jack J. Preiss
Hildegard Ryals
Herbert A. Saltzman
Janice Stratton

PERSONS INTERVIEWED FOR FIRST EDITION

William A. Amey by Glenn Hinson, SOHP
William A. Amey by author
Edna and Rudolph Baker by author
Bill Barbee by William O. Foster, Federal Writers' Project
Mary C. Bernheim by author
Curtis Booker by author
Thomas Burt by Glenn Hinson, SOHP
Hallie Caesar by Glenn Hinson, SOHP
Ollie Nichols Carpenter by author
Chester Clark by Glenn Hinson, SOHP
Josephine Clement by author
Albert G. Cox, Jr., and Mary Cox by author
Maude Dunn by author
Daniel K. Edwards by author
Hazel Godwin by author
Elise Evans Green by author
Mildred Mangum Harris by author
James R. Hawkins by author
Margaret Haywood by author
Betty Hodges by author
Patricia Hutchings by author
Tammy W. Jordan by author
Margaret Keller by author

Ernest Latta by Lanier Rand, SOHP
Lottie Lawrence by author
Leota Lowery by Mary Murphy, SOHP
Floyd McKissick by Jack Bass, SOHP
Lyda Moore Merrick by author
H. M. Michaux, Jr., by Jack Bass, SOHP
Dora Scott Miller by Beverly W. Jones, SOHP
Reginald Michiner by Glenn Hinson, SOHP
William D. Murray by author
Margaret Nygard by author
Lewis and Frances Gray Patton by author
Conrad Odell Pearson by Walter Weare, SOHP
Mayme Harris Perry by author
Ella Fountain Pratt by author
Samuel O. Riley by author
Thomas Rogers by author
Ernest Seeman by Mimi Conway
Catherine Stroud Shaw by author
Bertha Shipp by author
Asa T. Spaulding by author
Edmund S. Swindell, Jr., by author
Vera Carr Twaddell by author

PERSONS INTERVIEWED BY TELEPHONE OR CORRESPONDENCE
    FOR FIRST EDITION

F. Howard Alston
Del Amnott
Eunice Austin
Lenox Baker
Deryl Bateman
Marvin E. Baugh
Susan Fox Beischer
Lydia Evans Beurrier
Allan H. Bone
Shirley Hanks Borstelmann
Edward Boyd
David Bradley
Elneda Britt
Mrs. Hubert Browning
Isabelle Budd
Marshall Bullock
Nancy Clark
A. J. Howard Clement
William A. Clement
William T. Coman
Edward E. Cooke
Ruth Couch
Lois Cranford
Mrs. Gifford Davis
Frank A. DePasquale
Vivian A. Edmonds
Mr. and Mrs. Louis Fara
Mary Louise Powe Gardner
James F. Gifford, Jr.
Lucille Glenn
Lisa Harpole
William A. Harrat
Mildred Mangum Harris
Edith Hassold
James J. Henderson
Nannie Mae Herndon
Harriet Hopkins
Ned Huffman
Mrs. Philip W. Hutchings, Jr.
A. C. Jordan
Peter Kramer
Nancy Laszlo

Carol Layh
Mrs. Otis Lee
Evelyn McKissick
Fred McNeill, Jr.
Ruth Mary Meyer
Jacqueline Morgan
Montrose Moses
Anthony Mulvihill
Margaret Nygard
Marian K. O'Keefe
David A. Page
Janice Palmer
Jessie Pearson
Norman Pendergraft
E. K. and Sibyl Powe
Mary Walker and George Clinton Pyne, Jr.
Dorothy Newsom Rankin
Constance Renz
Hildegard and Clyde Ryals
Isabelle Samfield
Terry Sanford, Jr.
Richard J. Sauer
James H. Semans
Miriam Slifkin
Amanda Mackay Smith
Elna Spaulding
Phebe Stanton
R. Edward Stewart
Nelson Strawbridge
Shirley Strobel
Norman Thomas, Jr.
Laura Torain
Nancy Wardropper
Richard L. and Ruth Watson
Constance Merrick Watts
Mr. and Mrs. C. B. Weatherly
Mena Fuller Webb
Ruby West
Ran Whitley
St. Clair Williams
Julia Wray

NEWSPAPERS AND NEWSLETTERS

Action (newsletter of the Durham Chamber of Commerce)
Carolina Times
[Duke] Chronicle
Duke (university alumni magazine)
Durham *Globe*
Durham *Herald*

Durham *Morning Herald*
Durham *Recorder*
Durham *Sun*
Episcopal Methodist
Herald-Sun
Hillsborough *Recorder*
Methodist Advance
News & Observer
Clipping files, North Carolina Room, Durham County Library, Durham, N.C.

Index

AAUW (American Association of University Women), 234, 300, 306, 356
Abbott, R. B., 272
Abele, Julian, 282
Abercrombie, Charles, 27, 33, 44
Abercrombie, Robert, 19, 27
Abernathy, Ralph, 368
Abram, Adam, 410
Academic freedom, 201
Academy of Music, 173, 222, 228, 257
Adams, Mrs. Randolph G., 255
Adams, Randolph G., 255
Adkins, A. W., 191
Adshusheer (town), 11, 12
Adshusheer Indians, 6, 9
Agriculture: corn, 78; cotton, 79, 150, 264; Depression and, 296–97; emancipation and, 130–31; fertilizer, 152; organizations, 163; productivity, 230–31; reforms, 230; tobacco, 41, 79, 263–64; victory gardens, 326
AIDS, 420–21
Airport, 302–4
Alamance County, 18
Albemarle Sound, 5
Alcohol beverage control (ABC) stores, 325, 328, 341
Alcohol consumption, 83, 162, 177, 244–45
Alexander, Will W., 362
Ali, Muhammad, 375
Allen, David, 78
Allen, Fulton, 316–17
Allen, George G., 285
Allen, George W., 279
Allen, S. J., 126
Allen, T. N., 286
Allen, William L., 78

Allen family, 39
Allerby, John, 17
Allison, Lavonia, 380, 404
Alpha Woolen Mills, 75–76
Alston, Absalom, 85
Alston, Alice, 399
Alston, James, 23
Alston, John, 23
Alston, W. L., 57
Alston family, 39
Altrusa Club, 308, 356
Alves family, 53
America First, 321
American Association of University Women (AAUW), 234, 300, 306, 356
American Dance Festival, 399–400
American Federation of Labor, 264, 287
American Institute of Architects and Builders Association, 150
American Lung Association, 351
American Red Cross, 250, 262, 267, 294, 322, 324, 327–28
American Revolution, 29–37
American Society for the Protection of Refugee Children, 322
American Tobacco Company, 149, 181–83, 201, 209–10, 264, 288, 338, 351
Amey, Charles C., 133, 134, 219
Amey, Cornelius, 134
Amey, Mildred W., 308, 339
Amick, Larry, 383
Ancient Order of United Workmen Ehrlich Lodge No. 4, 163
Anderson, Abraham, 46
Anderson, Banks, 322
Anderson, Jane Rigsbee, 116

Anderson, Marian, 309, 318
Anderson, Roy, 366
Andrews, A. B., 151, 223
Andrews, John D., 248
Andrews, Junius F., 251
Andrews, R. McCants, 259, 315
Andrews Chapel Church, 56, 57
Angier, John C., 151; house of, 152, 209; store of, 153
Angier, Jonathan Cicero, 140
Angier, Malbourne A., 57, 114, 140, 154; chartered academy and, 115; death, 182; as elected official, 112; Fidelity Bank and, 160; as Hayti landowner, 132; Main Street layout and, 113; Malbourne hotel and, 235; opposition to schools, 144; as store owner, 91
Angier, Mrs. J. C., 253, 255
Angier, Sarah P., 286
Angier Avenue Baptist Church, 165, 272
Anlyan, William G., 338, 429
Annie Watts Hill Foundation, 388
Anson County, 16
Applewhite, James, 398, 447
Appomattox Courthouse, 99, 104
Arcade Hotel, 235
Arcade theater, 242
Archaeological Society of North Carolina, 12
Archaeology, 10–14
Architecture, 150–51
Arey, Beulah, 209
Ariail, Kate Dobbs, 444
Armfield, Joe, 248
Armistead, Lewis, 95
Armstrong, Joseph, 55, 64
Armstrong, W. H., 189
Armstrong family, 59
Arnette, J. M., 194
Arnold, A., 71
Art, 390–96, 443–44
Asbury, Francis, 46
Asbury Methodist Church, 292
Ashe, Hannah, 77
Ashe, Samuel A., 77
Ashley, William, 249
Ashley, Willis, 73
Ashley family, 55
Ashly, Robert, 35
Associated Charities, 271
Associated Press, 272
Atkins, General, 103
Atkins, John Leslie, 334, 336
Atkins, Mrs. M. T., 253
Atkins, Robert E., 229
Atlantic Monthly, 201, 390
Atwater, Ann G., 366–67
Atwood, Charles B., 311
Atwood and Weeks firm, 193
Auction Bridge Club, 234

Auctioneering, 352
Austin, J. F., 207
Austin, Louis, 315
Automobiles, 225
Avery, John M., 243, 259
Avery, Mrs. S. P., 220
Aycock, Charles Brantley, 186, 195, 226, 240, 334
Ayers report, 274

Backcountry: excavations in, 12; exploration of, 6–10; first landowners in, 15–18
Bagley, W. H., 141
Bailey, Frederick L., 277
Bailey, John P., 72
Baines, Bruce, 369
Baker, Lenox, 305
Baker, Quinton, 369
Baker, Richard, 322
Baker, Shirley, 322
Baldwin, Alice, 307
Baldwin, Mrs. J. J., 256
Ball, David, 446
Ball, Matthew, 70
Ballard, Virginius, 245
Ball family, 59
Bankers Fire Insurance Company, 219, 259
Bank of Durham, 160
Banks, 160–61
Banks, Abner, 133, 134
Banks, Judy, 135
Banner warehouse, 125
Baptist Female Seminary, 145
Baptists, 46, 54, 75, 116, 164, 191, 340
Barbee, Christopher, 117
Barbee, Dolphus, 229
Barbee, F. M., 126
Barbee, G. W., 93, 231
Barbee, Gabriel A., 143, 187
Barbee, Gray, 116, 219
Barbee, H. C., 233
Barbee, John, 40, 56, 94, 116
Barbee, John Wesley, 99
Barbee, Joseph, 17, 19
Barbee, Reuben, 85
Barbee, T. M., 143
Barbee, William, 17, 20
Barbee, William Matthew, 248
Barbee, Willis, 117
Barbee family, 21, 39, 55, 60, 229
Barbee's Chapel, 117
Barber, Margaret, 392
Barber, T. W., 231
Barbour, Luther H., 251
Barfield, Mrs. J. Franklin, 308
Barham, Claudius Augustin Winfield, 125
Barham, J. Q. A., 125
Barker, Mrs. Oscar, 327
Barnes, Alexander, 315

Barnes, Ernie, 393
Barnes, Jim, 125
Barnes, John Foster, 318, 399
Barnett, N. H., 364
Barringer, Rufus, 85
Barrow, W. W., 265
Barry, David W., 420
Bartlett Durham tract, 57
Baseball, 245, 273
Basile, Ann, 393, 394
Bassett, John Spencer, 93, 145, 163, 170, 199–201
Bassett, Richard Baxter, 170
Bass family, 80
Batchelor, Virganetta, 76
Battle of Guilford Courthouse, 32
Battle of Lindley's Mill, 31
Battle of Moore's Creek Bridge, 34
Bauer, George, 122
Bayh-Dole Act (1980), 419
Beasley family, 21, 55
Beavers, Sallie, 255
Beavers family, 57
Beck, Albert, 288
Beecher, John, 375
Beethoven, Ludwig van, 173
Bell, Bill, 412
Bell, Mrs. J. V., 330
Belvin, D. L., 143
Belvin Baptist Church, 116
Benevolent and Protective Order of Elks, 154,
    234, 324
Bennehan, Richard, 26, 27–28, 34, 35, 36, 40, 53,
    58; house of, 42
Bennehan, Thomas D., 53, 64, 82
Bennehan-Cameron Plantation, 49, 53, 134
Bennehan Mills, 61–62, 78
Bennehan's mill, 61
Bennett, Frank, 316
Bennett, George, 248
Bennett (Bennitt), James, 76, 93, 103, 104; cabin,
    105–6
Bennett (Bennitt), Lorenzo, 76, 98–99, 106
Bennett Place memorial, 276–77
Bennitt, Eliza, 106
Bennitt, James, 76, 93, 103, 104; cabin, 105–6
Bennitt, Lorenzo, 76, 98–99, 106
Bennitt, Nancy, 104
Bentonville battle, 104
Bentov, Marilyn, 387
Berea Baptist Church, 74, 75, 191
Berenbaum, Esai, 355
Berini, Tony, 290
Bernheims, Frederick, 322
Bernstein, A., 193
Bertie County, 17–18
Best, Michael, 397
Best Spanish Flavored Durham Smoking
    Tobacco, 94–95, 119

Beth-el Synagogue, 193
Bevington, Helen, 398
Bickett, Thomas W., 252
Biddle, Anthony J. Drexel, Jr., 286
Biddle, Mary Duke, 286
Bigelow, W. T., 438
Biggs, E. Power, 318
Biggs, James C., 145
Bilboa family, 39
Bill of Rights, 32
Bird family, 80
Bishop of Durham, 4
Bitting, N. D., 251
Bittle, Camilla, 398–99
Bivins, Joseph Francis, 198
Blackburn, William Maxwell, 398
Blacknall, James R., 143, 152, 153
Blacknall, Mrs. Richard D., 212
Blacknall, Richard, 143; house of, 104, 112; as
    physician, 71, 112; as Presbyterian, 116–17,
    208; as school promoter, 72; sons of, 152; as
    tobacco investor, 118
Blacknall, Richard D., 152, 154, 157, 158, 212
Blacknall Memorial Church, 243
Black Panthers, 374
Black power, 374–75
Blacks, 137–38, 161, 316; black code, 109; as
    candidates, 380; churches and, 117, 135–36,
    190–92, 340; in Civil War, 108; crime rate
    and, 221, 447–48; culture of, 139, 309, 343;
    Duke University and, 374; education and,
    196, 197, 220, 240–41, 275, 310–12, 348–49;
    employment of, 360–61, 377; free, 20, 34,
    50, 79–81, 108–10, 130–31, 134, 205; Great
    Depression and, 217–22, 293–94; hatred
    toward, 108; health and hospitals for, 189–90,
    260–62; lynching of, 221, 256, 257–58; migra-
    tion to North by, 221, 258; as millworkers,
    205; music culture of, 222, 309, 316–20;
    population statistics for, 21, 79–80, 129,
    131; as preachers, 135; protests by, 309–16;
    in Reconstruction, 108–10; Republican,
    259, 380; in Revolutionary War, 34; school
    desegregation and, 362–67; tobacco industry
    and, 134–35; voting rights and, 109–10, 315; in
    world wars, 249, 322, 324, 360, 361
Black Solidarity Committee for Community
    Improvement (BSCCI), 373
Blackwell, George R., 182
Blackwell, James W., 99, 160, 170, 182
Blackwell, William T.: as banker, 160; Black-
    well Baptist Church and, 164; as broken
    man, 203; business partners of, 123; business
    success of, 124, 127; Clingman Tobacco Cure
    Company and, 176; as county supporter,
    140, 142; Durham Real Estate Agency and,
    151; as Durham school supporter, 144–45; as
    father of Durham, 124; lawsuit against, 95;

Blackwell, William T. *(continued)*
  Main Street and, 113; mansion of, 151; as
  railroad owner, 156, 158; tobacco factory and,
  147; as tobacco jobber, 118
Blackwell Baptist Church, 164
Blackwell Company, 142, 147, 149, 162, 181–83,
  210
Blackwell Durham Tobacco Company, 124, 142;
  competition and, 148; need for cotton and,
  149; new owners of, 147; resale to American
  Tobacco of, 181–82
Bladen County, 18
Blake, Eubie, 318
Blake, Robert, 394
Blalock, Dewitt, 166
Blalock, R. B., 115
Blalock family, 55
Bledsoe, Jacob, 35, 93
Bledsoe, Lewis, 35
Bledsoe family, 53
Blind, programs for, 330
Blind, school for, 83
Blind Boy Fuller, 316–17
Blind Gary Davis, 316
Blind Sonny Terry, 316
Blomquist, Hugo L., 302
Blossom, A. C., 228
Blount, Lewis, 91
Blue Cross–Blue Shield of North Carolina, 305
Blues, 309, 316–18
Board of War, 31
Boddie, Leah, 308
Boddie, Neal P., 177
Boesch, C. F., 269
Boggan, Patrick, 17, 21, 43
Boggan, William, 17, 18
Bohannon, Joseph, 42–43
Bohannon family, 21
Bohanon, Mary, 446
Bolognesi, Dani, 420–21
Bonawit, G. Owen, 285
Bond, Jack, 412
Bone, Allan, 396, 397
Bonsack, James E., 148
Bonsack company, 149; cigarette machine and,
  148, 193, 204, 206
Bon-Ton theater, 242
Booker, Lyle Steele, 290
Booker Heights, 291
Boone, R. B., 180
Boone, T. A., 164
Booth, John, 27
Booth, Nash, 95
Booth, William, 93
Borden, Dorothy, 399–400, 416
Borland, Archibald, 93
Borstelmann, Shirley Hanks, 386
Bost, S. S., 244

Bostian, Carey, 346
Boston Tea Party (1773), 30
Bounds, Barbara, 400
Bouterse, W. M., 212
Bowie, James, 18
Bowles, Hargrove, 387
Bowles, James, 248
Bowling, Edwin H., 205, 213–14
Bowling, Hasten, 166
Bowling, James E., 194
Bowling, Mrs. William, 165
Bowling, Simeon, 166
Bowling, William, 18, 73, 126, 165, 213
Bowling-Emory Knitting Mill, 206
Bowling family, 39, 59
Boyce, H. Spurgeon, 354
Boyd, William K., 91, 274, 276, 292, 392; house
  of, 308
Boy Scouts, 234
Braddock, James J., 315
Bradley, David, 387
Bradley, Gail, 387
Bradshaw, George, 112, 133
Bradshaw, Herbert, 401
Bradsher, Walter C., 157
Bradsher, William, 161
Bradway, John, 300
Bragg, Beulah, 224
Braggtown Baptist Church, 292
Brame, Anita, 363
Brame, Claudette, 364
Bramham, William G., 239, 252, 273
Branson, William H., 150, 153, 164, 194
Branson Methodist Episcopal Church, 194, 272
Brassfield, Reuben, 99
Brassfield, Winny, 93
Brawley, Sumter C., 237, 299
Bridges, 238
Briggs, Thomas H., 141
Bright Leaf Council, 308
British-American Tobacco Company, 210
British Board of Trade, 5, 20
British War Relief Society, 322
Brittain, Joseph, 44
Broad, Molly Corbett, 431
Broderson, Robert, 393
Brodie, Brenda, 426
Brodie, H. Keith H., 426, 430, 431
Brogden, Mrs. Willis J., 255, 306
Brooklyn Dodgers, 273
Brooks, B. U., 251, 262, 274
Brooks, Eugene C., 274, 299
Brooks, Frederick P., 342, 417–18
Brooks, J. W., 152
Brooks, Mary Elizabeth, 326
Brooks, Paul, 329
Broughton, J. Melville, 333
Brown, Callis, 368

Brown, Frank, 222, 282
Brown, J. C., 261
Brown, Les, 318, 401
Brown, Lucille, 318
Brown, Wade, 352
Brown, William, 54
Brown, Wilson, 99
Browne, Rose Butler, 308
Browning, Dudley, 136
Browning, James, 136
Browning, Jefferson, 99, 136
Browning, Payton, 136
Browning, Simpson, 116
Brown v. Board of Education, 360
Bruce, N. C., 188
Brummer, Ella, 392
Bryan, William J., 185
Bryant, Gilmore Ward, 172
Bryant, Mrs. Victor, 253, 308
Bryant, Victor S., 187, 225, 275
Bryant, Victor S., Jr., 309, 357
Bryant family, 173
BSCCI (Black Solidarity Committee for
    Community Improvement), 373
Buchanan, Bessie, 267
Buchanan, Irwin H., 218
Buchanan, John, 226, 290
Buchanan, L. T., 115, 197
Buckley, Rebecca, 420
Buehler, Albert, 434
Buffalo Hill post office, 58
Bugg, E. I., 236
Buirski, Nancy, 444
Bull, Captain, 23
Bull, Squire, 112, 134
Bull City Red, 316
Bull City Textile Local 2155, 288
Bull Durham Company, 123–24, 150, 154, 233, 351
Bullock, G. L., 249
Bullock, J. M., 249
Bull trademark, 118
Bumpas, Robert F., 170
Bumpas family, 21
Bunch, Gideon, 21
Bunch, Micager, 21
Bunn, Hartman, 341
Burch, Frank P., 151
Burch, George, 211
Burcham family, 244
Burgess, T. H., 161
Burke, Governor, 31
Burke, Thomas, 32
Burnett, Frank G., 338
Burns, William L., 373
Burrington, George, 13, 15
Burroughs, John, 100, 138
Burroughs family, 232
Bush, George H. W., 434

Business and Professional Women's Club, 307
Business Men's League, 216
Busse, Barbara, 400
Butler, Emma, 308
Butler, General, 33
Butler, J. B. K., 190
Butler, Mrs. E. W., 324
Butner, Henry Wade, 323
Bynum, Gaston, 191
Byrd, Donald, 445
Byrd, William, 10, 13

C. C. Davis Company, 228
C. C. Hook and Sawyer Trust Building, 228
Cabarrus County, 190
Cabe, John, 32, 62, 65, 75, 93
Cabe, Robert M., 75
Cabe family, 39
Cablegram cigarettes, 147
Caesar, Shirley, 222, 445
Cain, James F., 99, 122, 141
Cain, Thomas R., 98
Cain, Thomas Ruffin, 45, 64
Cain, William, Jr., 64
Cain, William, Sr., 33, 36, 40, 67, 102; church,
    56; house of, 42; mill of, 44, 62, 64
Cain family, 39, 53
Cain's Chapel, 56
Cain's mill, 44, 62, 64
Caldwell, Edward, 213
Caldwell, Tod R., 110
Calhoun, Lee, 434
Calvary United Methodist Church, 116, 194
Calvert Method School, 339
Cameron, Bennehan, 141; Bennett Place memo-
    rial and, 276–77; as building supervisor,
    166; as chief marshal, 154; as government
    administrator, 248, 251; land sale to city by,
    239; as legislator, 237–38; Trinity Methodist
    Church and, 272
Cameron, Duncan (elder), 49, 53, 56, 84, 351;
    as Bennehan's executor, 82; Cain viewed by,
    67; politics of, 66; sawmills and, 62, 63; as
    store owner, 73; tobacco investments of, 121;
    tuberculosis and, 216
Cameron, Duncan (grandson), 143, 166
Cameron, John D., 128, 135, 167
Cameron, Luke, 133
Cameron, Mary Anne, 58
Cameron, Mary Ruffin, 50
Cameron, Paul, 49, 53, 55–56, 99; aid distrib-
    uted by, 100; college sports viewed by, 196;
    cotton growing viewed by, 79; emancipa-
    tion viewed by, 130, 139; land holdings of,
    141; Morehead Banking Company and, 127;
    optimism of, 84; railroad and, 95, 166; slave
    conscription and, 101; thefts from, 76–77;
    tobacco business and, 121, 122

Cameron, Thomas, 79, 122
Cameron, William, 99
Cameron family, 80–818
Cameron Grove Baptist Church, 243
Cameron Mills, 61–62, 63, 78
Cameron's Fish Dam store, 73
Cameron's New Mill, 61, 63
Campbell, Malcolm, 346
Campbell, Tom, 416
Camp Butner, 323–24
Camp Crabtree, 322
Camp Creek Primitive Baptist Church, 54
Camp Edward L. King, 295
Camp Julian S. Carr, 295
Campus Club, 234
Canada, E. W., 218
Canady family, 21
Canals, 69
Canterbury Club, 171, 172
Cape Fear River, 16
Card, W. W., 241
Carden, John S., 166
Carden family, 21
Carlton, Carrie, 349
Carlton, Eugene, 372
Carlton, Neal, 444
Carmichael, Stokely, 374
Carmichael, William D., 233, 245
Carnegie library funds, 271
Carolina Cinema Corporation, 400
Carolina Hosiery Company, 181
Carolina Mutual Life Insurance Company, 219
Carolina Piedmont: excavations in, 12; explora-
    tion of, 6–10; first landowners in, 15–18
Carolina Power and Light Company, 159
Carolina Slate Belt, 3
Carolina Theater, 272, 400
Carolina Times (newspaper), 310
Carpenter, C. W., 197
Carpenter, Duane, 126, 146
Carpenter, Lilly, 224
Carpenter, Willis, 146
Carpetbaggers, 109
Carr (town), 231
Carr, Albert Gallatin, 143, 163, 189, 226
Carr, C. M., 253, 290, 291
Carr, George, 261
Carr, George Watts, 290, 291, 311, 369
Carr, Isaac N., 261
Carr, John Wesley, 91, 123
Carr, Julian S., Jr., 204–8, 251, 265–66, 268
Carr, Julian Shakespeare, 202; as alderman, 113;
    as banker, 127, 160; Bennett Place memorial
    and, 276–77; character of, 123, 182–83, 189;
    charity of, 123–24; Clingman Tobacco Cure
    Company and, 176; as cloth and clothing
    manufacturer, 149–50, 181; Commonwealth
    Club and, 232; Commonwealth Manufacturing

Company and, 179–80; in Company K, 99;
    as county supporter, 140; death of, 278; as
    Democrat, 196, 237; Durham Consolidated
    Land and Improvement Company and, 159;
    Durham Cotton Manufacturing and, 150;
    Durham Traction Company and, 223; as gas
    company owner, 159; generosity to blacks of,
    218, 219; Golden Belt Manufacturing and, 150;
    as hotel builder, 174; Interstate Telephone and
    Telegraph Company and, 160; as land devel-
    oper, 151; as legislator, 237–38; mansion of,
    154–55, 291; mills and, 151; Morehead Banking
    Company and, 127; paternalism of, 175; as
    power company owner, 159; as publisher,
    167; as railroad entrepreneur, 156, 158–59;
    as tobacco manufacturer, 118, 123–24, 147;
    Trinity Church and, 123, 165; Trinity College
    and, 169, 171; unions and, 265–66; white
    supremacy and, 139
Carr, Lalla Ruth, 172
Carr, Lida, 176
Carr, Louis A., 160, 178, 225
Carr, Mrs. A. G., 171
Carr, Mrs. C. M., 253, 290
Carr, Snowden, 225
Carr, Warren, 367
Carr, Watts, Jr., 352
Carr, William F., 204, 206, 233, 289, 330
Carrington, Cynthia, 122
Carrington, George, 35, 36, 44, 62
Carrington, James, 36, 99, 111
Carrington, John, 36, 62
Carrington, John, Jr., 40
Carrington, John J., 59
Carrington, S. R., 143, 152
Carrington, Simeon, 98
Carrington family, 39, 59
Carrington's mill, 61
Carr Junior High School, 274
Carr Methodist Church, 164
Carrolina Hotel, 174, 235
Carrolina Roller Mills, 212
Carroll, Benjamin, 35
Carroll, Charles, 47
Carr Township, 2, 40, 57, 225, 231
Carson, Rachel, 382
Carson, Sidney, 154
Carter, Hill, 150
Carter, Mrs. Bayard, 324
Carter, Percival, 182
Carver, H. L., 254
Carver, Julia, 254
Carver, Thomas, 166
Cash, J. T., 185
Caswell County, 18
Caswell Hill (Caswell Heights), 152
Catawba Indians, 22
Catawba Power Company, 211

Cate, Benjamin, 18
Cavaliers Club, 232
CCC (Civilian Conservation Corps), 295
Cedar Creek Academy, 115
Cedar Fork Baptist Church, 54, 55, 57, 229, 292
Cedar Fork Rifles, 100
Central Prohibition Club, 162
Chaffin, Washington S., 74
Chamber Arts Society, 445
Chamber of Commerce: airport and, 302; army
    camp and, 323-24; consolidation and, 300;
    desegregation and, 370; economic develop-
    ment and, 348, 379; employment bureau of,
    294; formation of, 232-33; forms of local
    government and, 237, 268; jobs for blacks
    and, 377; low-cost housing and, 346; planning
    department and, 299; playgrounds and, 241;
    soldiers and, 249, 252; town history commis-
    sion and, 276; women and, 253
Chambers, Julius, 434-5
Chambers, Sidney C., 252
Chandler, Jeff, 396
Chang, Li Hung, 165
Chapel Hill and Durhamsville Plankroad
    Company, 69
Chapman, Thomas, 243
Chappell, Elbert, 252
Chappell, Fred, 398
Charity League, 308, 309
Charles II, king of England, 4
Chatham County, 18, 28
Chatham Knitting Mill, 207
Chavers, Howard, 81
Chavis, Howard, 81
Chavis, Jefferson, 81
Chavis, John, 65
Chavis family, 80
Cheatham, Arch, 215-16, 260
Cheatham, Geneva, 230
Cheek, Anderson, 93
Cheek, David M., 91
Cheek, James W., 94, 113, 119, 150; house of,
    112
Cheek, John W., 136
Cheek, Nash, 116
Cherokee Indians, 13, 22
Cheshire, Joseph B., 165
Chiang Kai-shek, 165
Child labor, 206, 207-8, 241, 250-51, 254-55
Children's Museum Association, 391
Childsburg (town), 21. *See also* Hillsborough
    (county seat)
Choctaw (racehorse), 248
Christian, J. T., 171
Christian, William Jasper, 99, 143, 164, 185
Christian Scientists, 293
Christmas, Matthew, 135
Church Bell Battery, 99

Churches, 45-48, 73-75, 135-36, 190-95,
    243-44, 272, 276, 292, 340, 436
Church Messenger (newspaper), 167
Church of England, 16, 45, 46. *See also*
    Episcopalians
Church of Jesus Christ of Latter-day Saints, 193,
    292-93
Church of the Immaculate Conception, 193
Churton, William, 18
Cigarettes, 147-48, 210. *See also* Tobacco
    industry
Ciompi, Georgio, 397
Ciompi Quartet, 445
Citrini, Tony, 290
Civic League, 215-16, 271
Civilian Conservation Corps (CCC), 295
Civil Rights Act (1866), 109
Civil rights movement: beginnings of, 360;
    school desegregation and, 300, 311, 335,
    362-67, 414, 430, 439-40
Civil War, 106-7; causes of, 97; deserters in,
    100; disease in, 99; inflation in, 100; Orange
    County and, 97-102; personal documentation
    of, 102-3; slavery and, 97, 101; speculation in,
    100-101; surrenders in, 99, 103-4, 105
Claiborn Hotel, 174, 235
Clapp's mill, 31
Clark, James G., 322
Clark, Jim, 406
Clark, Maggie, 255
Clark, Mrs. Kenneth, 327
Clark, W. R., 166
Clark, W. Y., 95, 113
Clark, Walter, 141, 199, 234
Classical music, 318-19, 444-45
Clay, Russell, 335, 336, 337, 343
Clement, A. J. Howard, III, 373
Clement, Josephine, 365, 411
Clement, William A., 364
Clements, Romulus, 91
Clements, Susan Ann, 91
Climate, 1-3
Clingman, Thomas L., 176
Clingman Tobacco Cure Company, 176
Clinton, Jesse, 119
Clinton, Mary Caroline, 119
Clinton, Rachel Vickers, 119
Closs, Morgan, 113, 138
Closs, Mrs. Morgan, 162
Clum, John, 444, 446
Cobb, J. S., 227
Cobb, James O., 286
Cobb, Mrs. J. O., 314
Cobeal, C. C., 133
Cobey, Bill, 439
Coble, Joseph F., 337
Coe, Joffre L., 12
Coggin, George T., 55, 71

Coggins family, 59
Cohen, E., 193
Cohen, Mrs. Louis D., 330
Colclough, J. M., 248
Colclough family, 39
Cole, Arthur Vance, 265, 267
Cole, Benjamin, 18
Cole, J. E., 185
Cole, Lanky, 318
Cole, Mrs. J. E., 295
Cole, Oliver W., 395
Cole, Sallie E., 194
Cole, William T., 166, 194
Coleman, H. G., 176
Coleman, Leonora, 444
Coleman, S. C., 310
Colens, Charles, 21
Colens, Samuel, 21
Colens, Thomas, Jr., 21
Colens, Thomas, Sr., 21
Colins, John, 21
Colley, Flora, 191
Collins, George P., 181
Collins, Trela D., 276
Colored Missionary Baptist Church, 136
Colored Primitive Baptist Church, 134
Colored Voters League, 259
Colton, Mrs., 115
Coman, William T., 373, 384
Comic strips, 272
Commercial Club, 235
Committee of Safety, 31
Committee on Community Relations, 370
Committee on the Affairs of Black People
    (DCABP), 300, 400. See also DCNA
Commonwealth Club, 163, 179, 232
Commonwealth Manufacturing Company,
    179–80, 194, 205
Commonwealth Methodist Episcopal Church,
    194
Communities, 57–61
Computer technology, 416–18
Confederacy. See Civil War
Confederate Navy, 100
Congress of Racial Equality (CORE), 361, 369
Connor, R. D. W., 237
Conservative Party, 111, 137
Constables, 20
Constitution Union Guards, 110
Construction industry, 150–55
Continental Congress, 31
Continental Line, 34
Continental Tobacco Company, 210
Conway, J. E., 243
Cook, W. D., 133
Cooke, Robert Bruce, 391
Cooleemee Cotton Mills, 204
Coon, Charles L., 274

Cooper, A. Derwin, 328
Cooper, Arthur, 383
Cooper, W. L., 180
Cooperative Association, 264
Coordinating Council for Senior Citizens, 356
Copley, Anderson, 93, 94
Copley, William, 94
Corbin, Francis, 5, 15
Corbinton (town), 21. See also Hillsborough
    (county seat)
CORE (Congress of Racial Equality), 361, 369
Corn farming, 78
Cornwallis, Charles, 31, 32
Cornwallis Heights, 291
Cornwallis Road, 26–27
Cotillion club, 234
Cotton farming, 79, 264
Cotton gin, 53
Cotton products, 76, 77, 149–50, 179–81
Couch family, 39
Coulter, Kenneth, 413
Council, Zeb V., 167, 171
Council of National Defense, Women's
    Committee, 252–53
Council of Relief and Unemployment, 294
Country music, 445
Courtney, William, 46
Covenant United Presbyterian Church, 191
Cowper, F. A. G., 341
Cowper, Mary Octavine Thompson, 254, 306–7,
    328
Cox, Albert Gallatin, 77, 126, 154
Cox, Clyde, 330
Cox, Elizabeth, 447
Cox, G. W., 315
Cox, J. W., 112
Cox, Laura, 147
Cozart, Joseph M., 57
Cozart, Thomas G., 57, 122
Cozart family, 55
Crabtree, Richard, 61
Crabtree's mill, 45, 63, 78
Craig, C. C., 191
Cram, Ralph Adams, 244, 272
Cranford, Dean, 246
Crapo, James D., 441
Creative Art Group, 393
Crest Street neighborhood, 377–78
Crossroads Presbyterian Church, 54
Crouch, E. L., 288
Crowell, John Franklin, 169–70, 196
Crum, Mason, 281
Cultural organizations, 161–62, 276, 391–402
Cunniggim's Chapel, 194
Cunningham, John S., 254
Cunningham, Mrs. John S., 253, 254
Cunningham, W. L., 212
Cut and Slash tobacco, 119

Dai, Mrs. Bingham, 393
Daily Dispatch (newspaper), 167
Daily Globe (newspaper), 153, 167, 171, 178–79
Daily Progress (newspaper), 167
Daily Reporter (newspaper), 167
Damrosch, Walter, 242
Dance culture, 399–400, 445–46
Dancy, John A., 219
Daniel, Dallas, 117
Daniel, John, 35
Daniel, Samuel, 44
Daniel, Thomas, 117
Daniell, William, 18
Daniels, Josephus, 199–200, 278, 339
Dann's warper, 150
Darnall, H. T., 117, 162
Darnell, Vernon, 172
Daughters of the American Revolution, General
    Davie Chapter, 234
Davenport, Thomas, 121
Davie County, 123
Davis, Archie K., 347
Davis, Blind Gary, 316
Davis, Brian, 410
Davis, Chuck, 445–6
Davis, Fred H., 327
Davis, Gifford, 322
Davis, H. C., 315
Davis, J., 261
Davis, J. Q., 300
Davis, James E., 403
Davis, Jane, 407, 416
Davis, Jefferson, 105, 202
Davis, Sam, 187
Davis family, 53
Davison, Wilburt, 217, 283, 304–5
Dawkins, P. W., 188
Dawson, Robert E., 430
Day, Fanny, 55
Day, Francis, 18
Day, James R., 118, 121
Day, Thomas, 80
Day, W. A., 188
Day, W. P., 121, 123
Day, William, 81
Day family, 80
Dayton (town), 126
Dayton Academy, 115, 126, 163
DCABP (Durham Committee on the Affairs of
    Black People), 300, 404
DCCC (Durham County Citizens Council),
    370–71
DCNA (Durham Committee on Negro Affairs),
    314–16, 342, 360–61, 363–64, 371
Deaf-mutes, church for, 244
Dean, James A., 70, 146
Dean, Laura, 446
Debro, Sarah, 101–2

DeKalb, Baron, 31
Delk family, 57
Dellinger, Ann, 415
Democratic Party, 137, 161, 184–87, 333, 379
Democratic Republicans, 67
Denny family, 21
Dental care, 261–62, 352
Denton, Peter, Jr., 439
DePasquale, Frank, 384, 405, 444
Depression (1921), 265–66
De Saram, Carole, 386
Desegregation: as law, 435; opposition to, 354,
    370, 374; of public accommodations, 367–70;
    of schools, 300, 311, 335, 362–67, 414, 430,
    439–40; token, 360. *See also* Segregation
Deshong, Lewis, 35
DeVyver, Frank T., 350
Dezern family, 39
Dial Creek post office, 58
DIC (Durham Interim Committee), 369–70
Dickens, Robert L., 426
Dickie, Zachariah, 194
Dike, James, 162, 167
Dillard, Henry, 85
Dillard, James H., 220
Dillard, Lydia, 85–86
Dillard, William, 85
Dillard, Willis, 106
Dilliard, Jefferson, 57, 65
Dilliard, Mary Jane, 65
Dilliard, Patsy, 65
Dilliard, William, 35
Dilliard, William Jefferson, 86
Dilliardsville (town), 85
DiMaggio, Joe, 273
Dinesen, Isak, 22
Dingley Tariff Act (1898), 181
Dix, Dorothea, 83
Dixie theater, 242
Dixon, Thomas C., 76, 221, 296
Dixon, Wyatt T., 250
Dobbs, Governor, 38
Dodson, J. A., 190, 218–19
Doherty, Henry L., 159
Dolby, Edward, 136
Dollar, James, 35
Dollar, Jonathan, 35
Dollar, William, 35
Donnell, Clyde, 260, 343
Donnelly, John, 285
Dorcas Club, 234
Dorfman, Ariel, 447
Doric Lodge of the Free and Accepted Masons,
    135
Douglas, John C., 76, 79
Douglass, Frederick, 395
Dowd, Jerome, 191
Dowd, John W., 121, 126

Dowd, Mamie, 171
Doyle, Arthur Conan, 284
Draper, E. S., 290
Driver, J. T., 174
Driver, Nancy, 174
Drug abuse, 221, 261, 304, 389, 420, 421
Drum, Barbara, 255
Du Bois, W. E. B., 188, 309
DuBose, Mrs. D. Saint Pierre, 309
Duke, Angier B., 232, 260, 285, 286
Duke, Artelia Roney, 119-20
Duke, Benjamin Newton, 77, 111, 119, 140, 263, 268; Bassett case and, 201; death of, 285, 293; Durham Railroad Company and, 156; Fidelity Trust Company and Savings Bank and, 160; generosity of, 124, 172, 183, 192-94, 197, 246, 260; hotel investments of, 235; houses of, 151, 153, 183, 225, 226; Keeley Institute and, 177; labor unrest and, 208; Lincoln Hospital and, 189; memorial to, 286, 397; North Carolina College for Negroes and, 311; relocation of, 182; Southern Power Company and, 159; textile mill investments of, 180, 203, 204; Trinity College and, 170-71; at W. Duke Sons and Company, 147
Duke, Brodie Leonidas, 119; bankruptcy of, 180; Bennitt's cabin and, 106; Commonwealth Manufacturing Company and, 180; death of, 235; early life of, 120; furniture store and, 143; Keeley Institute and, 177; land donations and, 164, 194, 216, 234, 241; remarriage of, 153-54; as tobacco manufacturer, 119, 121; weaknesses of, 127
Duke, Dicey Jones, 74, 119
Duke, Doris, 283, 284
Duke, Hardeman, 35, 36
Duke, James Buchanan (Buck), 119, 140, 263, 284, 285, 286; Catawba Power Company interests of, 211; employee profit sharing viewed by, 209; Lincoln Hospital and, 189; tobacco empire of, 147, 148-49, 209-11; treatment of workers by, 206; university endowment and, 278-83
Duke, John, 119
Duke, Mabel, 180
Duke, Mary Caroline, 119
Duke, Mary Elizabeth, 119
Duke, Mrs. Brodie L., 116, 171
Duke, Robert, 100, 106
Duke, Sarah P., 286
Duke, Sidney Taylor, 119
Duke, Taylor, 58, 74, 119
Duke, Washington, 147; charity of, 136, 139, 194, 196, 218; Confederate Navy and, 100; as county commissioner, 143-44; as education booster, 170-71; house of, 152; Main Street and, 113; Mount Hebron Temperance Society and, 83; ostracism of, 111; personal story of,

119-21; race relations and, 189; on tax list, 129; tobacco company of, 119, 146; tomb of, 285; Trinity College and, 170-71, 196; on voter registry, 129, 134
Duke, William, 35, 36
Duke, William J., 74, 83, 119
Duke Divinity School, 386
Duke family, 39, 59, 123
Dukeman, W. B., 201
Duke Memorial Methodist Church, 164
Duke of Durham cigarettes, 148
Duke Park, 301
Duke Power Company, 211, 408, 414
Duke's Chapel Church, 74, 292
Duke School for Children, 307, 440
Duke Symphony Orchestra, 397
Duke University: affordable housing and, 425; architecture of, 282; Army Finance School, 324; arts and, 318, 443-47; black power and, 374; building of, 281-87; computers introduced at, 417-18; as cultural inspiration, 318, 392, 394-400; desegregation efforts by, 366-67, 369, 370; economic impact of, 287, 402, 410; endowments of, 278-80, 283, 431; faculty housing at, 291; fine arts and, 392; in Great Depression, 293-95; health and medical research at, 338; hospital of, 325, 403; Lemur Center, 442-43; medical research at, 419-21, 431-33; name changed by, 279, 291; Naval College Training School, 324; public health and, 305, 337-38, 358, 389-90; Research Triangle Foundation and, 347; ROTC program at, 324; segregation and, 347; semiconducting super collider at, 433-34; sports teams of, 319, 427; student protest at, 375-76; visitors to, 442. See also Trinity College
Duke University Arts Council, 398
Duke University Press, 284, 302
Dun, R. G., 127
Dunagan family, 21
Dun and Bradstreet, 127
Duncan, Harmon, 319
Dunnagan, John, 18, 20
Dunnagan, Norman, 72
Dunnagan, Thomas, 18
Dunnagan family, 21
Duplin County, 16
Durham (city): airport and, 302-4; banking in, 160-61; building campaign in, 255; charter of, 237; city center of, 404-5; city limits extended by, 280; city planning in, 329-30, 406; commerce in, 127-29; construction industry in, 150-55; construction projects in, 92-96, 289-93; county courthouse in, 154; electricity and gas in, 159, 211; electric railway cars in, 158-59; entertainment in, 173-74, 222, 242, 272-73, 443-46; fire departments of, 157,

336, 355–56; forerunners of, 85; formation of, 111–12; government of, 268–70, 298–304, 334–35, 404–16; growth of, 112–13; health and hospitals in, 177–78, 188–90, 212–17, 260–63, 304–6, 337–38, 403–4, 426–28; homelessness in, 422–26; hotels in, 174–75; housing in, 313–14, 328, 329, 344–46, 371, 425–26, 440–41; immigration and, 428–29; landmarks of, 228–29; land values in, 151; music culture in, 172–73, 241–42, 316–20, 444–45; newspapers in, 128, 167, 171, 272–73; officeholders in, 454–60; organizations in, 161–67, 171, 232–36, 272; population statistics for, 128, 131, 141, 441–42, 449; public library in, 167, 171–72, 236, 242–43, 271, 354; race relations in, 137–39, 161, 221; railroad station in, 87, 91–92, 106; sanitation in, 215; schools in, 143–46, 186, 196–98, 240–41, 273–76, 298–99, 338–39, 414–15; slogan of, 403; social problems in, 175–78, 212, 328, 334, 356–59, 422; taxes in, 113, 128, 144, 268; telegraph and telephone service in, 159–60; tobacco industry and, 112, 118–26; trolleys in, 224; urban renewal in, 342–44; visitors to, 442–43; water supply of, 157–58, 228, 239
Durham, Bartlett Leonidas, 57, 75, 87, 90, 92, 112, 278; house of, 91
Durham, Columbus, 75, 116
Durham, Mary Snipes, 90
Durham, Matthew, 90
Durham, William J. Hugh, 99, 112, 177
Durham, William Lindsey, 90
Durham Academy, 339, 439, 440
Durham and Southern Railroad, 231
Durham Art Club, 234
Durham Athletic Association, 245
Durham Athletic Park, 273
Durham Auditorium, 272
Durham Babies Milk Fund, 308
Durham Bank and Trust Company, 124, 204
Durham Baseball Club, 273
Durham Board of Agriculture, 256
Durham Board of Education, 144
Durham Board of Health, 177, 215, 305
Durham Bulls Club, 245, 273, 409
Durham Business League, 260
Durham Chamber of Commerce, 232, 233, 237
Durham Chemical Fire Company, 157
Durham College, 374–75
Durham Committee for the Care of European Children, 322
Durham Committee on Negro Affairs (DCNA), 314–16, 342, 360–61, 363–64, 371
Durham Committee on the Affairs of Black People (DCABP), 300, 404
Durham Consolidated Land and Improvement Company, 151, 158, 159

Durham Cotton Manufacturing Company, 150, 204, 301
Durham County: annexation with Wake County, 238; boundaries of, 141, 142; charter of, 237; courthouse in, 154; environmental concerns in, 381–85, 408–9, 412–14; formation of, 1, 18, 28, 140–42; geography of, 1–4; government and politics in, 140–43, 184–87, 236–39, 298–304; historic sites in, 391–92; industrial development in, 347–49; land grants, 16; land values in, 151; liquor licenses, 143; newspapers in, 167; officeholders, 143, 449–53; population statistics for, 449; post offices in, 166–67; prison in, 143; rural expansion in, 166; schools in, 143–46, 239–41, 298–99; sewage treatment in, 353–54; technological expansion in, 347–49; Welfare Department, 212; zoning, 353
Durham County Board of Agriculture, 264
Durham County Citizens Council (DCCC), 370–71
Durham County Fair and Driving Association, 234
Durham County General Hospital, 354
Durham County Republican (newspaper), 167
Durham County Tuberculosis Society, 262
Durham Drug Company, 190, 218
Durham Dulcet Quartet, 222
Durham Electric Lighting Company, 159
Durham Farmers Mutual Exchange, 297
Durham Female School, 115, 197
Durham Fertilizer Company, 152, 178
Durham Festival Association, 242
Durham Garden Club, 308
Durham Gas Company, 159
Durham Glee Club, 162
Durham Golf Club, 234
Durham Gun Club, 234
Durham Health Department, 260–61
Durham Herald (newspaper), 128, 257, 272–73, 275, 335
Durham High School for boys and young men, 146, 274
Durham Hosiery Mills, 181, 204, 205, 209, 228, 265–66, 288–89, 326
Durham Hospital Association, 304–5
Durham House, 174
Durham Housing Authority, 314, 344, 371
Durham Interim Committee (DIC), 369–70
Durham Land and Security Company, 151
Durham Light and Power Company, 159
Durham Light Infantry, 99, 154, 202, 249
Durham Literary Society and Lyceum, 162
Durham Male Academy, 115, 145, 146, 197
Durham Memorial Baptist Church, 75
Durham Methodist Church, 164
Durham Negro Observer (newspaper), 218
Durham Nursery School Association, 307
Durham Primitive Baptist Association, 191

Durham Railroad Company, 156
Durham-Raleigh Aeronautics Authority, 303
Durham Real Estate Company, 151
Durham Redevelopment Commission, 342
Durham Savings Bank and Trust Company, 160
Durham School of Music, 162, 241
Durham Street Railway Company, 158–59
Durham Symphony Orchestra, 396
Durham Technical Community College, 415
Durham Telephone Company, 160
Durham Textile Mill, 218–19
Durham Theatre Guild, 396
Durham Tobacco Board of Trade, 119
Durham Traction Company, 159, 223, 265
Durham Triassic Basin, 3
Durham Warehouse, 124
Durham Water Company, 158
Durham Welfare Department, 270, 294, 297
Durham Women's Club, 254
Durham Woolen and Wooden Mills, 152–53
Durham *Workman* (newspaper), 167, 206
Duty, Martha (Patty), 72
Dyer, J. A., 243

E. M. McDowell and Company, 147
Eakes, Martin, 426
East Durham, 152–53
East Durham Baptist Church, 165
East End Methodist Church, 164
East Indian Company, 29
Eaton, Allen P., 136, 190
Eclectic Club, 234
Economic Opportunity Act (1964), 357
Edens, Hollis, 367
Edens, Mrs. Hollis, 307
Edgecombe County, 15
Edgemont Baptist Church, 243
Edgemont Presbyterian Mission, 243
Edgerton, Clyde, 447
Edisonia theater, 242
Edison incandescent burners, 150
Edmonds, Helen G., 365, 380
Edwards, Daniel K., 314, 334–35, 344
Edwards, John, 369
Edwards, Lewis, 133
Edwards, W. H., 261
Eisenhower, Dwight D., 332
Elder, Alfonso, 392
Elderly, 81
Electric power, 159, 211
Electric theater, 242
Elion, Gertrude Belle, 419
Elizabeth, queen of United Kingdom, 318
Elkins, W. S., 181
Elks (order), 154, 234, 324
Ellenwood, Everett, 389
Ellerby, John, 17
Ellington, Duke, 318

Elliot, George, 44
Ellis, Claiborne P., 366–67
Ellis, G. W., 231
Ellis, Thomas, 383
Ellis, W. B., 194
Ellis, W. D., 315
Ellis, W. F., 158
Ellis Chapel, 195
Ellis family, 55
Emancipation Day, 217
Embury, Aymar, 290
Emerson, Jordan, 161
Emmanuel A.M.E. Church, 133–34
Emory, J. H., 205–6
Emory, J. W, 205–6
Empie, Adam, 56
English settlers, 16, 17
Enoe-Will, 8–9
Eno Indians, 6–10
Eno Lodge, No. 21, 154
Eno Meeting house, 47
Eno River controversy, 381–85, 408
Eno Town, 7, 11, 12
Enterprise Land Company, 151
Environmental concerns, 381–85, 408–9, 412–14
Ephesus Baptist Church, 116, 166
Ephphatha Church, 244
Episcopalians, 117, 244, 340
Epperson, J. H., 215
Equal Rights Amendment (1972), 387
Equal Suffrage League, 234
Erwin, Eugene, 394
Erwin, J. Harper, 150, 203–4, 232, 244, 301, 394
Erwin, Mrs., 208
Erwin, William A., 150, 243; character of, 267–
    68; Commonwealth Club and, 232; as county
    food administrator, 251; Duke company and,
    180, 203–4; tuberculosis society and, 262
Erwin Auditorium, 266–67, 396, 400
Erwin Cotton Mills, 93, 177. *See also* Pin Hook
Erwin Mills, 204; Burlington Industries and, 378;
    closing of, 351; as employer, 207–9, 223, 269;
    incorporation of, 180; profit sharing and, 209;
    sale of, 338; union organizing at, 265–67,
    288–89, 350; in World War II, 326–27, 349–50
Erwin Square, 407
Escoffery, Philip, 310
Eubanks, George M., 248
Eubanks, Samuel, 248
Evans, Addie, 189
Evans, Emanuel J., 335, 336, 352, 367
Evans, John, 81
Evans, John W., 143
Evans family, 57, 80
Everett, Kathrine Robinson, 308, 335, 352
Everett, Reuben Oscar, 214, 237, 263, 277; Cotton
    Commission and, 264; as legislator, 268, 269,
    276; women's vote and, 234, 253, 256

Everett, Robinson O., 342
Evins, Elizabeth, 55
Excelsior Fire Company, 157
Exchange Club, 324, 326

Faddis's Tavern, 94
Fairbrother, Al, 175, 178–79
Fairbrother, Mrs. Al, 167
Fallon, William M., 210, 233
Falwell, Jerry, 437
Family Service Association, 309
Family Welfare Association of America, 309
Fanning, David, 31
Fanning, Edmund, 24, 25, 26, 66
Fara, Luigi, 290
Farley, James A., 291
Farmer, James, 361, 368
Farmers' Alliance movement, 163
Farmers Warehouse, 124
Farrell, James K., 418
Farrington, Vernon, 315
Farthing, G. C., 220
Farthing, J. T., 113
Faucette, Margaret, 136
Faucette, R. T., 121
Favorite Durham tobacco, 121
Fayetteville (town), 104
Federal Building, 228
Federal Emergency Relief Administration
    (FERA), 294–95
Federalists, 51, 52
Federated Ministers Association, 271
Federation of Women's Clubs, 216
FERA (Federal Emergency Relief
    Administration), 294–95
Ferettino, Peter, 290
Ferguson, Mrs. George B., 322
Ferrell, A. G., 116
Ferrell, Edward, 35
Ferrell, J. C., 99
Ferrell, J. J., 143
Ferrell, J. W., 185
Ferrell, James T., 99
Ferrell, Sallie, 255
Ferrell, Thomas, 91
Ferrell family, 39
Fertilization companies, 152
Few, James, 26
Few, William Preston, 41, 199, 246, 262–63, 274,
    278–86
Fidelity Trust Company and Savings Bank, 160,
    228, 235
Film culture, 400
Finley, Thomas D., 323
Fire departments, 157, 336, 355–56
Firkins, William, 222
First Baptist Church of Durham, 74, 75, 116, 292
First National Bank of Durham, 160, 228

First Presbyterian Church, 243
Fisher, George A., 314
Fisher, Miles Mark, 312
Fits, Harold M., Jr., 365
Fitzgerald, Charles T., 249
Fitzgerald, Richard Burton, 133–34, 161, 187,
    190, 218, 249
Fitzgerald, Robert G., 133–34, 244
Flagstad, Kirsten, 318
Flat River Church, 73, 74
Flat River Guards, 98
Flat River post office, 58
Flat River Union League, 111
Fleet, Florence, 197
Fleishman, Joel, 431
Fleming, Robert, 61
Fletcher, C. C., 231
Fletcher, Floyd, 300, 319, 346
Fletcher, J. D., 231
Fletcher, Wiley, 56
Fletcher Packhouse Debating Society, 231
Fletcher's Chapel Church, 56, 73
Flint, Thomas, 65, 146
Flintom, P. A., 126, 166
Flower, Lida Carr, 278
Flower, Lisa Carr, 278
Flowers (professor), 250
Flowers, Robert L., 279, 281, 282, 287, 305
Flowers, W. W., 197, 199, 233
Fluoride, 352
Folk housing, 41
Football ban, 246
Forbus, Ina, 398–99
Forbus, Sample, 304
Forest Hills Shopping Center, 336
Forrester, H. A., 212
Forrester, William, 18
Fort Bragg, 322–23
Fort Christanna, 10
Fort Henry, 7
Fort Sumter, 97
Fortune, Roma C., 244
Foushee, Howard A., 159, 173, 185, 225, 242, 398
Foushee, Ola Maie, 393
Foust, Robert L., 357
Fowler, M. M., 337
Fowler, Minerva, 132
Fowler family, 21
Fox, Marye Anne, 431
Franklin, John Hope, 436
Fraser, Lee B., 364
Fraternal organizations, 127–28, 135, 154, 162–63
Fredericksburg (battleship), 100
Free blacks, 20, 34, 50, 79–81, 108–10, 130–31,
    134, 205
Freedman's Bureau, 109, 111, 114, 115, 130
Freeland, J. F., 144, 154, 249
Freeland, William Johnson, 99, 177

Freeman, Burwell, 74
French and Indian War, 22–23
Friedan, Betty, 385
Friends, 30, 33, 340–41; schools of, 114; slave-holding viewed by, 34
Fuller, Bartholomew, 144, 162, 197
Fuller, Blind Boy, 316–17
Fuller, Caroline, 252
Fuller, Frank L., 184, 256, 276, 299, 348–49
Fuller, Howard, 358, 371, 372, 374, 375, 376
Fuller, Jones, 159, 227, 232, 237, 239
Fuller, Lillian, 256
Fuller, Mrs. Frank L., Jr., 327
Fuller, Ralph, Jr., 394–95
Fuller, T. O., 188
Fuller, Thomas B., 150, 207, 212, 233, 239, 242, 271
Fuller, Thomas C., 141
Fuller, Williamson W., 141, 144, 158, 226
Fuller Memorial Church, 243
Furlong, William, 74

Gage, General, 30
Galifianakis, Nicholas, 380
Gallie, Thomas M., 417–18
Gamble, Paul Dillard, 391, 393
Gantt, R. M., 352
Garden, Mary, 318
Gardner, Clarence E., 325
Gardner, O. Max, 294
Garrard, John, 62
Garrard, Samuel, 58
Garrett, Nathan T., 349, 358, 373
Garth, Sarah K., 330
Garwood, Thomas, 136
Gates, Albert L., 248
Gates, Henry T., 122
Gates, Horatio, 31, 32, 36
Gattis, J. W., 133
Gattis, Rubye, 371
Gattis, Thomas Jefferson, 199
Gay, A. W., 71
Geer, Frederick C., 36, 87, 90, 94, 112, 113, 119, 127, 156, 180, 243
Geer, Jesse, 112
Geer, Solomon, 112, 134
Geer Building, 228
General Assembly, 19, 31
General Electric, 403
General Telephone Company, 160
Genuine Durham Smoking Tobacco, 118
Geology, 3–4
George, William, 93
George II, king of Great Britain, 5
George VI, king of United Kingdom, 318
George Fuller Construction Company, 287
Georgetown Silk Mills, 326
George Watts Hill Pavilion for the Arts, 444

Gergen, John J., 417
German settlers, 16, 17, 30
Germino, Antonio, 290
Gibbs mill, 45, 63
GI Bill of Rights, 329, 333
Gibson, Charles, 18
Gibson, George, 18, 21
Gibson, Majer, 21
Gibson, Thomas, 18, 21
Gilbert, Katherine, 397
Giles, Deborah, 412
Gill, James, 71
Giobbi, Pete, 290
Girl Scouts, 308
Gladstein family, 147
Glass, Mrs. W. H., 255
Glasson, William H., 237
Glenn, Bonnie, 289
Glenn, R. B., 220
Glenn family, 39
Globe (newspaper), 153, 167, 171, 178–79
Globe Herald (newspaper), 171
Glover, Lynn, III, 3
God's acre plan, 192
Goins, Hinton, 81
Golden Age Society, 356
Golden Belt Club, 163
Golden Belt Manufacturing Company, 150, 181, 187, 204, 207, 208, 228, 289, 326
Goldstein, J., 127
Goldstein family, 127, 147
Gomez, Wanti, 259
Gooch, Haywood, 67
Gooch, Inez, 358
Gooch, J. R., 192
Gooch, Roland, 55
Goodloe, Daniel, 135
Goodloe, J. T., 218
Goodloe, Lewis, 134
Goodman, Benny, 318
Goodman, Jim, 409
Good Templars (order), 128, 162
Goodwill Industries of America, 356
Gorman, Mrs. Thomas M., 253
Gorman, Thomas M., 220, 226, 232, 253
Gorman Baptist Church, 292
Gospel music, 309, 318, 334
Gospel Tabernacle United Holy Church, 191
Grabarek, R. Wensell (Wense), 330, 336, 357, 369, 370, 372, 383
Gradwell, Isaac, 193
Graham, Frank Porter, 316, 333
Graham, George W., 181
Graham, Joseph, 31, 217
Graham, Paul Cameron, 181
Graham, William A., 97
Graham, William A., Jr., 99
Grand theater, 242

Grange Hall, 126
Grant, Ulysses S., 105
Grant Central Hotel, 174
Granville, Earl, 5–6, 17, 27, 37, 38
Granville County, 15, 18
Granville District, 5–6, 15
Gray, E. G., 249
Gray, Jane, 165
Great Depression, 281; blacks in, 293–94; government programs in, 294–96; unemployment in, 294–95, 297–98
Great Philadelphia Wagon Road, 16, 17
Great Revival (1801–5), 52, 54–57
Great Society, 357
Green, Caleb B., 128, 140–41, 143, 144, 161, 167
Green, James, 93
Green, John Ruffin, 115, 122, 128; tobacco factory, 106, 108, 112, 118–20
Green, Kate, 272
Green, Lucius, 122, 151, 160
Green, Major, 118
Green, Michael, 93
Green, William, 287
Green, William M., 56
Greenberg, M., 193
Greene, Nathanael, 2, 31
Green family, 229
Greenlaw, Alice, 387
Green Woods, 152
Gregson, Amos, 164
Gresham, Davis, 35
Gresham, William T., 99
Gresham family, 39
Grey Stone Baptist Church, 193, 292
Grierson, Mary J., 102–3, 106
Griggs, Lillian Baker, 242, 253, 392
Grissom, Eugene, 99
Griswold, W. J., 290
Grove, Roberson, 292
Groves, Harry E., 435
Guess, W. W., 79, 83
Guess, William G., 99
Guess family, 39
Guest, Romeo, 346, 347
Guildford College, 196
Guilford County, 18, 28, 32
Gulley, Wilbur, 404, 407, 416
Gun laws, 411
Gunn, Jimmy, 318
Gunter, D. C., 145
Guthrie, William A., 151, 182, 185, 239
Guy, David, 447

Hackney, E. C., 128, 167
Haid, Bishop, 192
Hailey, Ezekiel, 57
Halcott, John B., 154
Halcyon Literary Club, 234

Haley family, 229
Hall, Dawn, 389
Halliburton, Robert, 73
Halliburton, W. S., 151, 162
Halliburton family, 57
Hall (professor), 250
Hall, John H., 164
Hamilton, J. W., 100
Hamlet, George O., 251
Hamm, James W., 393
Hammonds, Cleveland, 365
Hamner, W. Clay, 406, 407
Hampton, Thomas, 383
Hampton, W. P., 98
Hampton, Wade, 104
Hampton family, 55
Hancock, John W., 57, 62, 65, 83, 91
Hanes, Elizabeth P., 337
Hanes, Frederic M., 286
Hanes, Robert M., 347
Hanks, John, 397
Hanks, Nancy, 400
Happer, Minnie, 171
Hardscrabble (Cain house), 42
Hardy, John D., 158, 239
Hardy, William N., 396
Hargrove and Meadows partnership, 78
Harkey, Cathy, 440
Harper, Walter, 346
Harrington, James S., 383
Harris, Alex, 395
Harris, Archer, 47, 63
Harris, Charles, 71
Harris, E. G., 315
Harris, Hilda, 444
Harris, John, 35, 248
Harris, Lucinda McCauley, 374
Harris, Marcus, 83
Harris, Mary Lucy Russell, 198
Harris, Nathaniel, 44, 47, 61, 63, 64, 78
Harris, Rencher Nicholas, 314, 335, 343, 349, 362, 364, 367, 376
Harris, Robert, 62, 63, 64, 67
Harris, Thomas, 81
Harris, Tyree, 19, 20; house of, 42
Harris, Williams, 83, 115
Harris family, 39, 53, 59
Harrison, William Henry, 67
Harris's mill (Nathaniel), 44, 61, 63, 64
Harris's mill (Robert), 62, 63, 64, 67
Hart's mill, 31
Haskell, M., 193
Haskins, Fannie, 135
Hassell, L. L., 174
Hastie, William H., 311
Hawfields Presbyterian Church, 54
Hawkins, James R., 300, 330, 344, 346, 369, 380, 401, 416

Hawkins, Reginald, 377
Hawkins, W. H., 243
Hayes, Henry, 373
Hayes, John B., 251
Hayes, Roland, 309, 318
Haynes, Willis, 57
Hayti, 132–33, 310, 343
Hayti Heritage Center, 405, 443
Hayti Mothers' Club, 308
Haywood, Margaret, 401
Health and hospitals, 176–78, 188–90, 212–17, 251, 260–63, 304–6, 337–38, 354, 403–4, 426–28
Heartt, Dennis, 128
Heartt, Leo D., 171, 177
Heartt, Mamie, 176
Heartt, Mrs. Leo D., 164
Heathcock family, 80
Hedgepeth family, 80
Heitman, John F., 197
Helms, Jesse, 380, 423
Henderson, Archibald, 234
Henderson, Dempsey, 133, 135
Henderson, Emma, 135
Henderson, James Jackson, 187, 314, 346, 371
Henderson, L. B., 261
Henderson, Richard, 25
Henderson, Sally R., 172
Henderson, Samuel, 248
Herndon, Adeline, 65
Herndon, Benjamin, 35
Herndon, Charles M., 165
Herndon, Coslett, 75
Herndon, Edmund, 55
Herndon, George, 44
Herndon, James, 35
Herndon, Lewis, 55
Herndon, Martha, 75
Herndon, Matchurine, 99
Herndon, William R., 57, 60, 86
Herndon, Zachariah, 35, 55, 60, 62
Herndon, Zachariah, Jr., 60
Herndon family, 39, 55, 60
Heroes of America, 100
Heron, Becky, 412–3
Hessee, Lena, 175
Hester, Benjamin, 78, 122
Hester, Moses, 191
Hester, Simeon, 99
Heyden, Siegfried, 338
Hibberd, Reuben, 155, 170, 193–94
Hicks, Hawkins, 136
Hicks, Isaac, 35, 44–45
Hicks, Joe, 248
Hicks, Rebecca, 93
Hicks, Thomas, 73, 112
Hick's mill, 61
Hickstown, 117, 152. See also Pin Hook area

High, G. H., 231
High, Isaiah S., 60
High family, 229
Highland Scottish settlers, 16, 30, 31
High Point Baptist Church, 229
Hill, Annie Watts, 388
Hill, George Watts, Jr., 329, 369, 370, 372
Hill, George Watts, Sr., 227; as city councilman, 300, 301, 302; donations by, 440; equal opportunity and, 349; Forest Hills Shopping Center and, 336; Hospital Care Association and, 305; as petitioner, 304; Research Triangle Institute and, 347; segregation and, 369, 370; as wartime fundraiser, 322; WRAM radio station and, 319
Hill, Jacob, 56
Hill, James W., 375
Hill, John, 55
Hill, John Sprunt, 214, 225, 227, 237; agricultural reform and, 230; as bank founder, 204; death of, 388; Durham Country Club and, 233–34; Durham Farmers Mutual Exchange and, 297; fluoride and, 352; as government administrator, 251; Hill Building and, 292; Homeland Investment Company and, 273; Home Security Life Insurance Company and, 405; as land donor, 269, 290; land sale by, 239; Lincoln Hospital and, 260; liquor control and, 341; Lowes Grove Credit Union and, 231; as road commissioner, 298; teacher training and, 311; zoning and, 353
Hill, Mrs. George Watts, 339
Hill, Mrs. I. F., 253, 255, 269
Hill, Mrs. John Sprunt, 251, 252, 253, 309
Hill, Percival, 182
Hill, Scott, 416
Hill, Watts, 405
Hillsborough (county seat): Durham and, 140; early names of, 21; as military center, 31; riots of 1770 in, 25
Hillsborough House, 94
Hillsborough Recorder (newspaper), 60, 75, 128, 167
Hitchings, George H., Jr., 419
HIV/AIDS, 420–21
Hobbs, Marcus, 376, 417
Hobgood, Burke, 233, 234
Hobgood, Mrs. Burke, 255
Hocutt, J. C., 115
Hocutt, Raymond, 310, 311–12
Hodara, Meneham, 261
Hodges, Jim, 370
Hodges, Luther, 333, 347, 363
Hodges, William, 35
Hoffman, Irving, 421
Hofmann, Josef, 318
Hogan, John T., 183
Hogg, James, 183

Hogg, Robina, 183
Holden, William Woods, 110, 132
Holeman, John Dee, 445
Holeman, Mary R., 103
Holeman, Richard, 72
Holeman family, 55
Holladay, Waller, 395
Holland, Alsey B., 74
Holloway, Fris, 445
Holloway, James, 99
Holloway, John N., 99
Holloway, Kinchen, 99
Holloway, Robert L., 228
Holloway, T. J., 185
Holloway, Thomas, 154
Holloway, William J., 76, 99, 161
Holloway family, 39, 57, 231
Holloway Station, 231
Holloway Street Baptist Church, 292
Holman, Mary, 241
Holman, Sidney Willard, 77, 126, 143, 158
Holman, W. C., 77
Holshouser, James E., Jr., 380, 385
Holt, Edwin M., 71–72, 98
Holtan, Holland, 269
Holton, Holland, 273, 307
Homeland Investment Company, 273
Homelessness, 422–26
Home Savings Bank, 204
Home schooling, 47
Home Security Life Insurance Company, 405
Hook, Charles C., 173, 225, 271
Hook and Sawyer firm, 157, 173
Hookworm, 216–17
Hope Valley project, 290
Hopkins, Alexander, 174
Hopkins, Everett H., 357
Hopkins, Harriet, 386
Hopkins, Susan, 174
Hopkins, William, 35
Hopkins family, 39, 59
Hopson, Sid, 231
Hopson, Tom, 258
Hopson, W. B., 231
Hopson family, 229
Horn, Joshua, 93
Horner, Edwin, 74
Horner, George, 35
Horner, Thomas Jefferson, 35, 73
Horner family, 55, 59
Horton cottage, 41–42
Horton Grove slave houses, 49
Hospital Care Association, 305
Hospitals: Durham, 176–78, 188–90, 212–17, 251, 260–63, 304–6, 337–38, 403–4, 426–28; Durham county, 354
Hotel Carrolina, 174, 235
Hotel Murray, 235

Hotels, 235
House, Robert, 316
House, Tom, 445
Howell, Jesse, 116
Howerton, Ella Mae, 209
Howerton, Ila L., 275
Howerton, R. T., 165
Howland, A. H., 157–58
Hudgins, John, 55
Hudson, Mrs. F. D., 165
Hughes (minister), 117
Hughes, Bradford, 134
Hughes, I. Harding, 355, 384
Hughes, W. R., 119
Hunkadora, 166
Hunt, Edward, 446
Hunt, James B., 418, 435
Hunt, James L., 393
Hunt, James T., 121–22
Hunt, Ralph A., 380
Hunt, Reuben H., 292
Hunt, Samuel, 136
Hunter, A. S., 318
Hunter, Archibald, 74
Hunter, George, 133
Hunter, Neil, 318
Huntley, H. W., 323
Husband, Fannie, 135
Husband, Herman, 24, 25
Husband, Sallie, 136
Husband, Sarah, 135
Huxley, Aldous, 285
Hyman, Mac, 398

IBM, 417, 419
Immaculata school, 193
Imperial Tobacco Company of Great Britain and Ireland, 210
Independent Hose Company, 157
Independent Order of the Knights of King Solomon, 191
Indian Ben, 23
Indian John, 7
Indians, 6–10, 13, 14, 22, 38
Indian Trading Path, 6, 11, 17, 19, 20
Industrial democracy, 265–66
Ingram, Merrick, 218
Ingram, Pearson, 218
Ingram, W. S., 218
Inns, 21
Insurance business, 154, 188, 219, 259
Intercollegiate sports, 196–97, 245–47, 273, 319, 427
International Missionary Alliance of New York, 192
International Textile Workers Association, 265
Interstate Telephone and Telegraph Company, 159–60

Invisible Empire, 110, 257
Ivey, Gregory D., 393
Ivey, Mary Frances, 327

J. A. Jones Construction Company, 337
Jackson, Abel, 146
Jackson, Andrew, 52
Jackson, George, 330
Jackson, J. E., 136
James, Leonidas, 224
James, S. T., 218
James Lumber Company, 224
James River squadron, 100
Jarvis, Thomas J., 142
Jazz, 309, 318, 445
Jeffers, Frances, 356
Jefferson, Thomas, 51
Jeffries family, 80
Jenkins, Chester, 404, 416
Jenkins, Jesse, 81
Jenkins, Lewis, 138
Jenkins, R. A., 118
Jensen, Howard E., 335, 356–57, 391
Jessup, Jacob A., 355
Jews, 127, 147, 193, 340
Jim Crow laws, 221–22, 258–59, 361
John Avery Boys' Club, 313
John Manning Camp, 234
John O'Daniel Hosiery Mills, 206
Johnson, Ann, 356
Johnson, Carlyle, 393
Johnson, Charles, 430
Johnson, E. A., 188
Johnson, Guion, 316
Johnson, J. M., 230
Johnson, J. Rosamond, 217
Johnson, James Weldon, 217
Johnson, Kate L., 395
Johnson, Lemuel, 166
Johnson, Lyndon, 346, 357
Johnson, N. M., 175
Johnson, Olivia, 209
Johnson, Samuel H., 45
Johnson, Stanhope S., 271
Johnson Motor Company, 175
Johnston, Gabriel, 15
Johnston, Joseph, 104–5
Johnston, William, 26, 27–28, 44, 46, 66
Johnston County, 15, 18
Johnston Riot Act (1771), 25, 26
Jones, A. J., 73
Jones, Alexander C., 73
Jones, David Curtis, 366
Jones, Frank, 74
Jones, George W., 72, 78, 79, 122, 126, 143, 144, 146
Jones, J. A., 141
Jones, Jasper, 133, 135

Jones, Joseph, 55
Jones, Lucy, 364
Jones, Mattie Southgate, 152, 171, 215–16, 271
Jones, Mrs. T. D., 254
Jones, Murray, 282
Jones, Murray, Jr., 394–95
Jones, Pride, 98, 110
Jones, R. M., 232
Jones, Randy, 393
Jones, Sam, 160
Jones, T. J., 188
Jones, Thomas Decatur, 124, 126, 151, 254, 384
Jones, Thomas T., 326
Jones family, 59, 80
Jordan, Abner, 134
Jordan, Brown, 113
Jordan, C. A., 151
Jordan, Cornelius, 133, 135, 136
Jordan, E. G., 161
Jordan, Emma, 135
Jordan, Monroe, 133, 134
Journal of Parapsychology, 284
Joyner, E. N., 167
Julian S. Carr Camp, 295
Junior League, 300, 308, 391
Junior Order of United American Mechanics, 232, 234
Just Come Four quartet, 222
Justice, David, 133, 135
Justice, John, 134
Justices of the peace, 19–20, 21–22
Juvenile Court Commission, 300

Kalkhof, Bill, 410
Keaton, Benjamin, 444
Keck, Charles, 285
Keeley, Leslie E., 177
Keeley Institute, 177
Keesee, Thomas, 406
Kelly, B. C., 265
Kelly, James A., 246
Kelly, Mike, 273
Kempner, Walter, 338
Kenan, Annice, 426
Kenan, Frank, 406
Kenan, Patrick, 416
Kendall, Helen, 393
Kendall and Taylor firm, 214, 225
Kennedy, Anneliesse, Markus, 387
Kennedy, Edwin W., 145, 179
Kennedy, John F., 332, 434
Kennedy, Robert F., 375, 393
Kennedy, William J., Jr., 313, 315
Kennon, Charles, 45
Kennon, John, 45
Kennon, Margaret Wannamaker, 307
Kennon family, 39
Kennon's mill, 61

Keohane, Nannerl, 424–25, 431–33
Kerckhoff, Sylvia, 407, 410, 411
Kerns, T. C., 251
Khedivial Tobacco Company of New York, 211
Kidd, C. R., 251
Kilbey, Marlyene, 386
Kilgo, John Carlisle, 189, 196, 199–200
Kilpatrick, Hugh Judson, 104, 106
Kimbrough, Steven, 397
Kimbrough family, 57
Kinchen, Alvis, 98
Kinchey, Ezekiel, 36
King, Andrew J., 111
King, C. C., 161
King, C. W., 225
King, Edward L., 295
King, J. H., 171
King, John, 73
King, M. N., 251
King, Martin Luther, Jr., 361, 368, 375
King, Nathaniel, 111
King, Thomas, 20, 40
King family, 55, 59
King's Daughters, 163, 212, 235
Kitchen, Dorothy, 397
Kitchen, Nicholas, 397
Kiwanis Club, 276
Klitgaard, Georgina, 395
Klitgaard, Kaj, 395
Klopfer, Martha, 439
Klopfer, Peter, 439
Knap of Reeds, 73
Knight, Douglas M., 375–76, 392
Knights of Labor, 147, 148, 161, 206
Knights of Pythias (order), 127, 154, 163, 234, 240
Knights Templar (order), 154
Koch, Robert, 216
Koerner, Jules, 147
Kornegay, Benjamin, 117
Krakauer, Thomas, 442
Kremen, Irwin, 394
Krynski, Elizabeth, 396
Krzyzewski, Mike, 427
Kueffner, Felicia, 241
Ku Klux Klan, 110–11, 256–58, 335

Labor unions, 206, 264–65, 287–88, 295, 350
Ladies Choice Scotch Snuff, 121
Laettner, Christian, 410
Lake, I. Beverly, 333
Lamb, Gideon, 36
Lampe, Harold, 346–47
Land grants, 16, 17–18, 38
Lane, Mrs. H. B., 291
Lane, N. M., 74
Langston, Jennie, 212
Laprade, William T., 282

Lassiter, R. A., 265
Laszlo, Nancy, 389
Latta, Elizabeth, 70
Latta, Ernest, 288–89
Latta, Hubert J., 235
Latta, J. E., 198
Latta, J. W., 100
Latta, James, 55, 70
Latta, Thomas, 55
Latta family, 59, 73
Latty, Ruth, 393
Laura Cotton Mill, 77
Law and Order League, 271
Lawrence, Mrs. James, 192
Laws, Candis, 135
Laws, Guilford, 98
Laws, Jonathan, 74
Laws, Thomas, 74
Laws, Thomas W., 161
Laws family, 21
Lawson, Dewey, 396
Lawson, John, 8–10
Lea, W. A., 124
League of Women Voters, 254–55, 300, 330–31, 380
Leak, Mrs., 208
Leary, Samuel L., 136, 157, 170, 197
Leathers, A. M., 185
Leathers, Elizabeth N., 59
Leathers, James S., 62, 71, 118
Leathers, John B., 59, 64, 70, 71, 78, 92, 122
Leathers, Moses, 35, 36
Leathers, Peter, 111
Leathers family, storehouse, 59, 73
Lederer, John, 6–7
Lednum, Mrs. Walter Lee, 240, 307
Lee, A. C., 287
Lee, Fitzhugh, 248
Lee, Goskin, 136
Lee, John I., 57
Lee, Malissa, 136
Lee, R. N., 211
Lee, Robert E., 103–4, 105, 200, 213, 248
Lee, William S., 211
Leftwich, George E., 318
Legislative actions: on compulsory education, 208, 240; on county formation, 1, 18, 28, 140–42; on Durham charter, 237; on Fourteenth Amendment, 109–10; on hospitals, 83; on land zoning, 330; on public schools, 65; on rural credits, 230; on school libraries, 240–41
Lehman, Harry W., 298
Lehman, Samuel, 193
Leigh, John, 60
Leigh, L. W., 166
Leigh, Richard Stanford, 60–61, 105, 126
Leigh, Sullivan, 60
Leigh family, 39, 61

Lemur Center, 442–43
Levitt, Isabel, 393
Levy, Jacob, 193
Lewis, James, 85
Lewis, Kemp Plummer, 255, 267, 287, 350
Lewis, Meriwether, 72
Lewis, Richard, 141
Lewis, Ron, 438
Lewter family, 229
Leyburn, E. R., 233
Libraries. *See* Public libraries
"Lift Every Voice and Sing" (anthem), 217
Liggett and Myers company, 121, 210, 264, 288, 351
Lincoln Health Center, 404
Lincoln Hospital, 216
Lindbergh, Charles A., 321
Lindsey, R. L., 313
Lindsey, W. E., 205
Link, Isaac Newton, 119
Link, Silas M., 65, 72, 111
Link family, 39
Links organization, 365
Linthicum, Hill Carter, 150, 266
Linthicum, W. H., 150
Lions Club, 276, 305
Lipscomb, Ethel Carr, 294
Lipscomb, George, 245
Lipscomb, John D., 64, 75, 122
Lipscomb, John M., 225, 233
Lipscomb, Thomas, 187
Lipscomb, William (Tip), 61, 64
Lipscomb, William L. (Tip), 61, 64, 72, 76, 98–99, 121, 126, 226
Lipscomb family, 39, 61, 62, 64, 78
Liquor licenses, 143
Literacy, 52, 64, 239
Literary Fund, 114
Little River Manufacturing Company, 77
Livengood, Mrs. C. H., 255
Lloyd, Thomas, 24, 205
Local Option Club, 162
Lochmoor Hotel, 235–36
Lockhart, John, 63, 72, 78, 79, 93, 227
Lockhart, John P., 99
Lockhart, John S., 113, 119, 125, 144, 156, 182
Locklear family, 80
Lodge, Oliver, 284
London, Edith, 394
Lone Jack Company, 149
Long, J. A., 77
Long, J. W., 217
Long, James Baxter, 317
Long, Johnny, 318
Lords Proprietors, 4
Lorillard company, 210
Loudermilk, John D., 445
Lougee, George, 228

Louis, Joe, 315
Louisburg Female Academy, 154, 293
Love, John, 258
Lovett, Willie, 404
Lowe, Edmund, 229
Lowe, Patsy Sorrell, 229
Lowe, Stephen, 229
Lowe, William M., 143
Lowe family, 229
Lowes Grove Baptist Church, 229–30
Lowes Grove Credit Union, 231
Lowland Scottish settlers, 17
Loyalists, 30, 33, 34–35, 37
Lucas, Arthur, 391
Lucky, Tom, 177
Lunsford, David, 134
Lunsford, James, 126
Lunsford, W. D., 119, 124
Lutherans, 340
Lynchburg and Durham Railroad, 77
Lynching, 221, 256, 257–58, 309
Lyon, Doris Elizabeth, 361
Lyon, E. B., 233
Lyon, Ed, 90
Lyon, Elizabeth Reeves, 393, 394
Lyon, George B., 225, 233, 239
Lyon, George Leonidas, 225
Lyon, Hugh, 93
Lyon, J. T., 116
Lyon, James Edward, 90, 99, 112; Bennett Place Memorial and, 276–77; Durham Railroad Company and, 156; house of, 153; schools and, 144; tobacco business and, 118, 119, 124
Lyon, Leonidas, 225
Lyon, Mary Duke, 172, 173, 216, 286
Lyon, Mary Washington, 91
Lyon, R. L., 159
Lyon, Robert E., 144
Lyon, T. B., 124
Lyon, Zachariah I., 119
Lyon farm, 112
Lyons, J. C., 192
Lynn family, 39, 57
Lytle, Archibald, 36

Maccaboy tobacco, 121
MacDuffie, J. F., 115
Macklin family, 80
Macon, Nathaniel, 52
Mahler, J. H., 228
Main Street Methodist Church, 164
Malbourne Hotel, 228, 235–36
Malcolm X, 374
Malcolm X Liberation University, 374
Malone, James, 93
Malouf, Melissa, 447
Manasse, Marianne, 393

Manataka Tribe of Red Men, 234
Mangum (town), 111–12
Mangum, Addison, 58, 72, 78, 126
Mangum, Adolphus, 71, 72, 74, 82–83, 84
Mangum, Amanda, 77
Mangum, Arthur, 66
Mangum, Bartlett, 152
Mangum, Benjamin Bradley, 229
Mangum, Charity, 67
Mangum, D. C., 144, 161, 185, 186
Mangum, Ellison G., 77, 84, 122; store, 58
Mangum, Hugh, 395
Mangum, Joseph, 74
Mangum, Leo, 273
Mangum, Martha, 115
Mangum, Mrs. K. R., 256
Mangum, Pattie, 98
Mangum, Presley J., 95, 99, 112, 126, 175
Mangum, Priestley, 65
Mangum, Solomon, 36
Mangum, William, 95, 112, 113, 138, 144, 152
Mangum, William Person, 58, 66
Mangum, William Preston (Willie): death of,
    98, 115, 122, 126, 142; diary of, 72–73; Dilliard
    viewed by, 85; donations by, 72; drinking
    problem of, 84; education viewed by, 64–65;
    house of, 67; law firm of, 58; as statesman,
    66–67, 68
Mangum brothers, 113
Mangum family, 39
Mangum Male Academy, 115
Mangum Street Methodist Episcopal Church
    South, 194
Manly, B. C., 141
Mann, T. A., 214
Manning, Isaac M., 161
Manning, Isaac M., Jr., 326
Manning, James S., 154, 159
Manning, John M., 141, 177, 232, 239, 257, 261
Manning, J. S., 159
Manufacturing, 75–79
Maple Camp of Woodmen of the World, 234
Maplewood Cemetery, 193
Marcom, Benjamin, 108
Marcom, George R., 108
Marcom, John, 65
Marcom family, 55. See also Markham family
Marcum, Charles G., 75, 287, 404, 425
Marcum, Thomas, 35
Marcum, Willis, 75
Marion, John H., 322
Markham, A. D., 185
Markham, Charles B., 75, 287, 404, 425
Markham, Charles G., 117
Markham, Edian, 123–33, 135
Markham, Edward, 132
Markham, Felix D., 99, 185
Markham, J. H., 231

Markham, J. M., 231, 272
Markham, J. W., 127, 272
Markham, John L., 74, 143, 197
Markham, Mary, 117
Markham, Robert, 133
Markham, W. S., 272
Markham, William Benjamin, 133
Markham, Willis, 75
Markham family, 39, 229. See also Marcom
    family
Markham's Chapel Missionary Baptist Church,
    117
Markley, R. R., 311
Markum, Edian, 123–33, 135
Markum, Maggie, 133
Markum, Robert, 133
Markum, William Benjamin, 133
Marsalis, Branford, 445
Marsh, Sarah, 191
Marshall, Jonas, 57
Marshall, Rosanna, 126
Marshall, Thurgood, 314, 364
Marsicano, Michael, 444
Martin, Elaine, 387
Martin, Frank M., 275
Martin, James, 34, 409, 414
Martin, Mrs. Thomas H., 172
Martin, Thomas H., 126
Mary Duke Biddle Foundation, 286, 397, 399
Mason, James B., 77, 111, 194, 239
Mason, Mrs. James B., 256
Mason, Mrs. S. P., 254
Mason, Thomas W., 154
Masons (order), 115, 126, 128, 135, 154
Massey, C. W., 240
Massey, Hardy, 99
Massey, Joe, 224
Massey, John, 74
Massey, Mrs. Pleasant, 256
Massey, Pleasant H., 163, 166, 184–85, 230
Massey, Rufus, 74, 99, 153
Massey, W. A., 198
Massey family, 39, 57
Massey's Chapel Church, 74
Matheson, Elizabeth, 395
Mathews, Frederick, 81
Matthews, B. W., 100
Matthews, James, 91
Matthews, Nina Horner, 296
Matthews, Thomas, 420
Maughan, William, 347
May, David, 389
May, Henderson, 92
May, Nancy Tuttle, 394
May, Orpah, 112
May family, 39, 57
Maynor, Dorothy, 309, 318
Maynor, William, 111, 145

Mayo, Mrs. Louis A., 357
Mayse, C. H., 192
McAden, Hugh, 21
McBroom, Grace, 255
McBryde, Angus, 306
McCabe, William Haywood, 154
McCabe family, 39
McCarthyism, 332
McCay Drug Company, 194
McClernan, Robert, 367
McCloud, Nola M., 327
McCormack, John, 318
McCown, John Cabe, 62, 126
McCown, Moses, 62, 228
McCown, Rachel, 62
McCown, Willis, 133
McCown family, 39
McCown's mill, 61, 77–78
McCoy, Cecil, 310, 311
McCoy, Vivian, 369
McCracken, J. T., 194, 261
McCullen, Arthur, 366
McCulloh, Henry, 5–6, 15, 17, 38
McCutcheon, Louise, 357
McDade, Ira, 248
McDonald, Kevin, 423–24
McDougald, Richard Lewis, 259, 314, 315
McDougall, Angus, 395
McDougall, William, 283–84
McDuffie, David G., 141
McFarling, John, 35, 36
McGary, Margaret, 339
McGhee, Brownie, 317
McGhee, Edward T., 252
McIver, Charles D., 145, 146, 195
McKissick, Andree Yvonne, 364
McKissick, Floyd, 364, 368, 369
McKissick, Joycelyn, 364, 369
McMannen, Amanda, 77
McMannen, Charles T., 71–72, 91, 92, 93, 176
McMannen, Elizabeth Latta, 93
McMannen, Hannah, 70
McMannen, John A., 70, 77, 79
McMannen, John Archibald, Jr., 64, 70–72,
    91–93, 96, 112, 113, 138, 176
McMannen, Leroy Dewitt, 71–72
McMannen, William Emmett, 98
McMannen's Chapel, 116
McNair, Ralph, 25
MCNC (Microelectronics Center of North
    Carolina), 418, 420
McNeal Pipe and Foundry Company, 158
McNeil, Judy, 386
McPherson, John W., 99
McPherson, Samuel, 99
McPherson, Samuel Dace, 263
McPherson, Samuel Dace, Jr., 263
McPherson, William, 99

McRae Rural Credits Bill (1915), 230
Meacham, Ethel, 330
Meadows and Hargrove partnership, 78
Mebane, Alexander, 20
Mebane, Charles, 196
Mebane, Jesse, 290
Mebane, Mary, 398
Mebane, Robert, 36
Mechanics and Farmers Bank, 218
Medlin, Leander, 349
Meherrin Indians, 13
Memorial Methodist Church, 164, 228
Menapace, John, 395
Mendelssohn, Felix, 173
Mental illness, 81–82, 426–28
Meny, Doranne, 386
Merchants Association, 235
Merrick, John, 136, 187–88, 190, 217–18, 330
Merrick, Lyda Moore, 330, 443
Merrick-McDougald-Wilson Company, 259–60
Merrick-Moore Memorial Park Association, 324
Merrick-Moore-Spaulding Land Company, 219
Merrick-Washington Magazine for the Blind, 330
Merrimon, Augustus, 141
Methodist Advance (newspaper), 167
Methodist Female Seminary, 145, 197
Methodists, 46, 54, 56, 114–16, 117, 194, 243, 246
Meyer, Ruth Mary, 387
Michaels, Matilda, 273
Michaux, Henry M., Jr., 300, 315, 380, 381,
    435–36
Michie, John C., 158, 239, 248, 250
Mickle, E. D., 243
Microelectronics Center of North Carolina
    (MCNC), 418, 420
Midway post office, 58
Midyette, C. Thomas, 423
Milburn, Frank, 236
Milburn, Thomas Yancey, 348
Milburn and Heister firm, 190, 228
Miller, C. M., 231
Miller, George W., Jr., 381
Miller, Justin, 300
Mills, 43–45, 61–64, 75–79, 98, 180–81, 204–8;
    strikes in, 288–89
Mills, Ernie, 423
Mills, Gail, 423
Mills, J. N., 218, 259
Mims, Edwin, 172, 199, 274
Ministerial Union, 216
Minor, Sidney W., 252
Minutemen, 31, 33
Mitchell, Edward, 117
Mitchell, John, 117
Mitchiner, Reginald, 317–18, 325, 342
Mitchum, B., 81
Moccasin Bottom, 137
Moderwell, Martha, 75–76

Mohsberg, A., 127
Mohsberg family, 127, 147
Moize, Adolphus, 74
Moize, Johnny, 74
Moize, Orford, 58
Moize, William H., 73, 126
Moize family, 55
Molina, Alexander, 396
Monk, T. Y., 164
Monk family, 55
Monro, James, 33
Moore, A. M., 218, 220
Moore, Aaron McDuffie, 187–90, 243, 330
Moore, Charles H., 240
Moore, Daniel K., 347
Moore, Douglas E., 363, 368
Moore, E., 249, 259, 260
Moore, G. Akers, Jr., 347
Moore, John R., 57
Moore, Sam, 55
Moore, Sampson P., 82
Moore, Willis, 136
Moore's Grove Primitive Baptist Church, 55
Moravian settlers, 18, 30, 31
Mordecai, Samuel F., 247
Morehead (principal), 203
Morehead, Eugene C., 153, 203; donations by,
    145; Durham Board of Education and, 144;
    Durham Electric Lighting Company and, 159;
    Durham Literary Society and Lyceum and,
    162; Durham Water Company and, 158; house
    of, 398, 400; Morehead Banking Company
    and, 127, 160; Morehead Hill and, 151; as
    railroad entrepreneur, 156; school committee
    and, 197
Morehead, J. L., 231, 233
Morehead, Margaret, 176
Morehead Avenue Baptist Church, 340
Morehead Banking Company, 127
Morehead City, 248
Morehead Hill, 151
Morehead School, 197, 240, 415, 440
Moreland family, 39
Morgan, J. D., 188
Morgan, Mark, 20, 21
Morgan, Samuel Davidson, 106
Morgan, Samuel Tate, 106, 152–53, 156, 178
Morgan, W. M., 127
Morgan brothers, 126
Morgan family, 21, 39
Moring, John M., 144
Morley, Meredith, 408
Mormons, 193, 292–93
Morning Herald (newspaper), 171
Morning Sun Academy, 73, 146, 163
Morris, Anita, 396
Morris, E. D., 265
Morris, Edward W., 119

Morris, Henderson, 93
Morris, Kate, 272
Morris, Robert F., 94, 111, 113–14, 115, 116, 138,
    272; farm of, 112; hotel of, 174; as landowner,
    132, 133; tobacco business of, 112, 118–19, 121,
    122
Morris, Thomas B., 94, 118
Morris, W. H., 143
Morrisville Plankroad, Tramroad, and Turnpike
    Company, 69
Moseley, Edward, 13–14
Moses, Constance, 400
Moses, Montrose, 400
Mothers' Club, 216
Moton, Richard R., 259
Mount Bethel Presbyterian Church, 292
Mount Bethel school, 72
Mount Bethel United Methodist Church, 47, 57,
    83
Mount Calvary Baptist Church, 192
Mount Calvary Christian Church, 191
Mount Hebron Church, 74
Mount Hebron Temperance Society, 83
Mount Lebanon Primitive Baptist Church, 55
Mount Pleasant Lodge No. 157, 126
Mount Sylvan Methodist Church, 194
Mount Tabor Church, 74
Mount Vernon Baptist Church, 190, 292
Mozart, Wolfgang Amadeus, 173
Mozart Musicale, 162
Muhammad, Elijah, 374
Mulattoes, 21
Mulvihill, Anthony, 389
Municipal Building, 173, 228
Murphey, Archibald DeBow, 53, 65, 66, 69
Murphy, A. F., 163
Murray, E. H., 235
Murray, Mrs. W. R., 254
Murray, Pauli, 130, 137, 213, 398
Muse, Mrs. E. G., 254
Music, 172–73, 241–42, 396–97; black, 222, 309,
    316–20; blues, 309, 316–18; church, 276; clas-
    sical, 318–19, 444–45; country, 445; gospel,
    309, 318, 334; jazz, 309, 318, 445
Muti, Lorenzo, 445
Mutual Company, 217–18, 219, 259

NAACP (National Association for the
    Advancement of Colored People), 361, 368,
    369
Nachman and Lehman store, 147
Nash, Willie, 393
Nation, Carrie, 245
National Association for the Advancement of
    Colored People (NAACP), 361, 368, 369
National Endowment for the Arts (NEA), 399
National Endowment for the Humanities (NEH),
    399

National Food Administration, 252
National Grange of the Patrons of Husbandry, 126
National Guard, Third Regiment, 249
National Industrial Recovery Act (1933), 287, 296
National Institute of Environmental Health Services, 403–4
National Labor Relations Board, 289
National Negro Finance Corporation, 259
National Organization for Women (NOW), 386–87
National Recovery Administration (NRA), 287, 288, 295
National Re-employment Service, 294
National Religious Training School and Chautauqua, 220
National Trust Company, 290
National Youth Administration, 323
Native peoples, 6, 10, 14, 38
NEA (National Endowment for the Arts), 399
Neal, Henry T., 93, 116
Needham, James, 7
Negro Braille Magazine, 330
Negro Business League, 312
Negro Civic League, 216
NEH (National Endowment for the Humanities), 399
Nelson, Ernest William, 397
Nelson, G. Murray, 270
Nelson, Sue, 386
Nelson, William, 75, 79
Neuse River Navigation Company, 69
New Bethel Baptist Church, 136, 191
New Canterbury Club, 234
New Durham tobacco, 190
Newell, William, 346
New Garden Board School, 196
New Hope Realty Company, 290
Newsom, M. E., 294
Newson, Dallas W., 299–300
Newspapers, 128, 167, 171, 272–73
Newton, George, 44, 63
Newton, William P., 286
Niccaulu, George, 289
Nichols, Archibald (Baldy), 83, 170
Nichols, John Thomas, 99, 126, 143, 163; house of, 57
Nichols, Margaret J. Halliburton, 99
Nichols, R. E., 115
Nichols, W. R., 126
Nichols family, 39, 57, 115; store of, 126
Nicholson, David, 57
Niemann, Thomas, 410
1900 brand tobacco, 190
NIRA (National Industrial Recovery Act), 287, 296
Nixon, Richard, 380, 433, 436

Noble Order of the Knights of Labor, 147, 148, 161, 206
Noel, T. A., 154
Norfleet, Grizelle, 305
Norfleet, Mrs. S. V., 243
Norfleet, M. T., 243
Norfolk Male Academy, 154
North, Mrs. Paul, 396
Northampton County, 15
North Carolina: archaeology of, 10–14; beginnings of, 4–5; in Civil War, 97–98; constitution of, 32; early accounts of, 6–10; ethnic diversity in, 30; government of, 52; land disputes in, 13; school system in, 274
North Carolina Central University, 392, 434–36
North Carolina Children's Home Society, 234
North Carolina Infantry Regiment companies, 98–100, 106, 249–50
North Carolina Legislative Council of Women, 254
North Carolina Medical Society, 262
North Carolina Museum of Life and Science, 391
North Carolina Mutual (newspaper), 218
North Carolina Mutual and Provident Association, 188
North Carolina Mutual Life Insurance Company, 188
North Carolina Railroad, 87, 95, 155–56; survey map of, *88–89*
North Carolina School of the Arts, 334, 390
North State Knitting Mills, 206
Norton, Charles H., 181
Norwood, Clem, 288
Norwood, James, 175, 183
Norwood, John, 100
NOW (National Organization for Women), 386–87
NRA (National Recovery Administration), 287, 288, 295
Nygard, Margaret Roger, 382, 413

Oak Grove Free Will Baptist Church, 272
Oakley, T. C., 144, 145
Oakley, Van Buren, 98
O'Briant, Calvin, 112, 113
O'Brien, Francis, 193
O'Brien, William T., 148, 152, 192–93, 227
Occoneechi Indians, 7, 10
Occoneechi Trail, 6, 11
Octavine, Mary, 306
O'Daniel, John, 133, 136, 205, 206
Odd Fellows (order), 154
Odell, J. A., 150
Odell, J. M., 150
Odell, W. R., 150
Odum, Howard T., 316, 346–47, 362
Ohlson, Mrs. John, 330
O'Kelly, William, 259

Oldham, Carvie, 346, 371
Oldham, Edward A., 167, 171
Old Orange County. *See* Orange County
Old Round Hill, 166
Olin High School, 154
Olive Branch Baptist Church, 115, 126, 292
Olmsted, Frederick Law, 285
Operation Breakthrough, 345, 357–58, 371
Orange Cavalry, 99
Orange County: boundaries of, 18–19; churches
    in, 45–48; in Civil War, 97–102; county seat
    of, 21; formation of, 18–22; French and Indian
    War and, 23; government of, 140–43; justices
    in, 19; land grants, 18, 38; map of, 2; migra-
    tion from, 40–41; mills in, 43–45; population
    of, 38–39, 79–80, 131–32; regulation and,
    23–28; Revolutionary War soldiers in, 35–36;
    schools in, 64–66; slavery in, 48–59; stagna-
    tion in, 52; system of government, 111
Orange Factory, 76, 79, 126, 166, 402
Orange Factory Methodist Church, 77
Orange Grays, 99
Orange Grove Church, 56
Orange Guards, 98–99
Orange Light Artillery, 99
Ormond, J. M., 282
Ornoff, Nathan, 394
Orphans, 81
Orpheum theater, 242
Our Durham tobacco, 119
Owens, P. Henderson, 60

Page, C. W., 57
Page, F. T., 218
Page, Jesse H., 115
Page, John, 93
Page, W. E., 249
Page, Walter Hines, 201
Page family, 55
Paine, Billany, 133
Paleo-Indian culture, 10–11
Palmer, Janice, 399
Pandora Club, 234
Parham, T. D., 315
Paris theater, 242
Parker, Abner, 59, 72, 73, 115, 216
Parker, Carol, 446
Parker, D. C., 67
Parker, David, 59, 72
Parker, Dudley, 99
Parker, Gwendolyn M., 447
Parker, Harrison, 59, 72, 78, 83, 100, 122
Parker, Jesse, 83
Parker, John W., 143
Parker family, 21, 59
Parks and recreation, 301–2, 330
Parrish, Allen, 59
Parrish, Ansel, 59

Parrish, Claiborn, 57, 59, 174
Parrish, D. C., 59, 67; as carriage-maker, 112;
    debating society and, 83; female seminary
    and, 72; as food distributor, 100; land transac-
    tions of, 93; as tobacco producer, 119, 122; as
    town board member, 113; as trustee, 71
Parrish, David, 122
Parrish, Edward J., 124, 125, 153, 154; as bank
    director, 160; Chamber of Commerce and,
    232; character of, 226; Country Club and,
    233; as county supporter, 140; courage of,
    161; estate of, 227; as hotel builder, 235–36;
    house of, 153; Japan and, 203, 226; as railroad
    entrepreneur, 156; real estate misfortunes of,
    182–83; as school opponent, 144–45; support
    for new county and, 140–41; tobacco cure
    medicine and, 176; as tobacco employee, 183;
    YMCA and, 164
Parrish, Eldridge, 117
Parrish, Mrs. Edward J., 234, 254, 256
Parrish, William, 63
Parrish, William B., 73
Parrish, William K., 98, 126
Parrish and Company (store), 73
Parrish Building, 153, 181, 209, 218
Parrish family, 39
Parrish's Arcade, 228
Parrish Stables, 217
Parsall Plan, 363
Patrick Henry Academy, 198
Patriotic Order of Sons of America, 234
Patrons of Husbandry, 163
Patterson (town), 111–12
Patterson, Emma, 71
Patterson, John, 17, 20, 43
Patterson, John Tapley, 33
Patterson, Mrs. Dave, 256
Patterson, R. A., 116
Patterson, Robert, 126
Patterson, William N., 111
Patterson, William T., 143
Patterson family, 21, 39
Pattishall, Charles, 277
Patton, Frances Gray, 398–99
Patton, Vicky, 400
Paul, Hiram V., 91, 106, 167, 206
Peabody Education Fund, 114
Peace Corps, 332
Pearl Cotton Mills, 180, 204
Pearsall, Thomas J., 363
Pearson, Conrad Odell, 310, 311, 314–15, 317, 364
Pearson, Cynthia Ann, 219
Pearson, H. J., 75
Pearson, W. S., 243
Pearson, William Gaston, 136, 161, 187–90, 197,
    218–19, 259–60, 277, 310
Peass, Abner, 56
Peay, Annie D., 172

Peck, Jim, 368–69
Peck, Mrs. Robert, 307
Peed family, 55
Peel, John A., 287
Peeler, Anthony Redwine, 93
Peeler, Benjamin, 93
Peeler, Pen-Tich-Eye, 93
Peeler, Samuel, 93
Pegram, George, 172
Pegram, J. Ed, 237
Pegram, William H., 136, 197
Pellagra disease, 212–14
Pendergraft, Norman, 434
Pendergrass, T. L., 231
Penn Construction Company, 159
Penny, J., 126
Penny, J. S., 143
Penny, S., 126
Pentecostal faith, 191, 340
Performing arts, 396, 399–400
Peritonitis, 217
Perkins, William R., 279, 285
Perlzweig, William, 214
Perry, Ben T., III, 342
Perry, Charles W., 252
Perry, George, 115
Perry, Joshua, 136
Perry, Patsy B., 435
Perry, W. H., 187
Person County, 18
Pettiford family, 80
Phillips (professor), 115
Phillips, P., 278
Piano and Vocal School, 241
Piatt, William M., 319, 323
Pickard, A. P., 73
Pickard, George, 76
Pickard, Mrs. Dallas, 339
Pickett, Stanford, 187
Pickit, Reubin, 54
Piedmont: excavations in, 12; exploration of, 6–10; first landowners in, 15–18
Piedmont Club, 272
Piedmont League, 273
Piedmont tobacco farms, 123
Pierce, T. B., 231
Pierson, Nancy Leigh, 105
Pierson, Richard, 105
Pinckney, Nancy, 446
Pin Hook, 93–94, 117, 136
Pinza, Ezio, 318
Piper, George, 99
Piper, William, 83
Planter mentality, 97
Pleasants, J. D., 186
Plucky Durham tobacco, 119
Pogue, E. H., 122
Polio, 306, 352–53

Polish Jews, 147, 206
Polk, Leonidas L., 176, 185
Pool, Isaac, 93
Poole, John, 166
Poole, W. R., 141
Poorhouses, 81–82, 143
Pope, Deborah, 447
Pope, George E., 166
Pope, Sidney, 116
Pope, Sidney M., 166
Pope, Simon, 57
Population statistics: for blacks, 21, 79–80, 129, 131; for Durham, 128, 131, 141, 289–90, 441–42, 449; for Durham County, 449; for mulattoes, 21; for Orange County, 38–39, 79–80, 131; for slaves, 21, 40, 48
Populist Party, 184–85
Porter, Joe Ashby, 447
Postal Telegraph Company, 159
Post offices, 58–61, 62, 85, 86, 126
Powe, E. K., 204, 209
Powe, E. K., III, 300
Powell, Benjamin E., 354
Powell, G. W., 219
Powell, Orville, 405
Pratt, Ella Fountain, 399–400, 444
Pratt, J. Fredd, 363
Pratt, James, 91
Pratt, Lewis, 112, 134, 138
Pratt, Mrs. Joseph G., 330
Pratt, Vernon, 393
Pratt, William N., 79, 86–87, 91–93, 93, 94, 112, 132, 138
Prattsburg (town), 85, 86
Preiss, Jack J., 425, 444
Prendergast, Father, 192
Presbyterians, 46, 117, 191, 194, 340
Price, Reynolds, 398, 447
Pridgen, J. D., 232
Primitive Baptists, 47, 55, 72, 73, 145, 164, 190–91
Prince Hall, 135
Prisons, 143
Pritchard, Jeter, 220
Privy Council, 30
Pro Bono Publico tobacco, 121
Proctor, John, 99
Proctor, Oswald Kinion, 234
Proctor, Sterling, 99, 113, 132, 133
Proctor, W. H., 224
Profit-sharing, 209
Progressive Music School, 241
Prohibition, 162, 244–45, 341–42
Protestants, 193
Provident Club, 175
Provincial Congress, 31–32, 35
PTA, 271, 308
Public accommodations, 367–70

Public libraries, 167, 171–72, 236, 242–43, 271, 276, 354–55
Pugh, John, 205
Pugin, Augustus W. N., 153
Pugin, Byron A., 153–54
Pulley, Paul, 381
Pupil Assignment law, 363
Pyle's Hacking Match, 31
Pyne, George, 393
Pyne, Mary, 393

Quail Roost Shooting Club, 227
Quakers, 30, 33, 340–41; schools of, 114; slave-holding viewed by, 34
Queen's Museum (college), 30

R. J. Reynolds, 210
Rachmaninoff, Sergei, 318
Radical viewpoint, 221–22
Radio, 319
Radmond, James K., 86
Railroads, 77, 84, 87–90; benefits of, 96; electric, 159; engines of, 95–96; expanded lines of, 156–57; industry and, 95, 155–56; Jim Crow laws and, 221–22
Raleigh, Walter, 4
Raleigh Board of Trade, 141
Raleigh-Durham airport, 303–4
Ramsey, N. A., 144, 195
Randolph County, 18
Raney, R. B., 305
Rape, Harvey, 369
Ray, James, 17
Ray, Johnson, 134
Ray, William, 35
Reagan, Ronald, 422, 423
Real Estate, Mercantile, and Manufacturing Company, 190
Reams, Henry A., 124, 136, 156
Reams, I. M., 124
Reckhow, Ellen, 412
Reconstruction, 108–13; education in, 114–15; equal rights and, 137; religion in, 115–17
Red Cross, 250, 262, 267, 294, 322, 324, 327–28
Red Cross Motor Corps, 308
Redding, Baird and Company, 155
Red Hat, Inc., 418
Redman, John, 34
Redmond, James K., 90, 99, 112
Redmond, William Thaddeus (Thad), 86–87, 90–91, 99, 126
Redmond's mill, 86
Red Mountain Church, 165
Red Mountain Female Academy, 72, 115
Red Mountain Male Academy, 115
Red Mountain school, 72
Red String, 100
Redwood County, 224

Reed, William, 23
Reese, Peewee, 273
Reeves, Enos, 2–3
Reeves, William, 17
Reformer (newspaper), 218
Register, Samuel, 159
Regulator (newspaper), 128
Regulator Movement, 24–26, 28, 29, 30
Reinhart, Charles, 446
Reinhart, H. W., 146, 162
Religion, 190–95, 243–44, 340, 342, 436–38; organizations, 163–64; persecution and, 16–17; in Reconstruction, 115–17; snake-handling sect, 341; Sunday schools, 164–66, 192
Remington, E. J., 248
Remington, W. F., 153
Rencher, Daniel G., 57
Renn, Joseph R., 224
Renn, Mrs. A. W., 165
Renz, Constance, 386
Republican Democrats, 51
Republican Party, 109, 110, 114, 128–29, 137, 144, 161, 184, 259, 379
Research Triangle Institute, 347, 419
Research Triangle Park, 346–49, 359, 403, 405, 419–22
Retirement homes, 337
Revell family, 80
Revivals, 52, 54–57
Revolutionary War, 29–37
Rex theater, 242
Rhine, Joseph Banks, 284–85
Rhine, Mrs. Joseph Banks, 330
Rhodes, Benjamin Cabe, 227
Rhodes, Elizabeth Cabe, 227
Rhodes, G. A., 161
Rhodes, George W., 75, 87–90
Rhodes, John, 35
Rhodes, Nancy, 227
Rhodes, Richard, 46
Rhodes, Termesia, 65
Rhodes, William, 20, 35–36
Rhodes family, 21, 39
Rialto theater, 242
Ricaud, T. Page, 165
Richard, William, 76
Richardson, Donovan, 174
Richardson, Elaine, 364
Richmond, Herbie, 191
Richmond, Jerry, 191
Richmond, Perryman G., 56
Richmond and Danville Company, 156
Rickenbacker, Eddie, 303
Riddell, Richard, 446
Rigsbee, Atlas M., 112–13, 114, 144, 145, 179, 197, 347; store of, 127
Rigsbee, Jesse, 35, 133
Rigsbee, John V., 162, 164, 185

Rigsbee, John W., 99
Rigsbee, Nancy, 224
Rigsbee, Robert, 230
Rigsbee, Thomas J., 116, 154
Rigsbees, Jesse, 127
Rigsby, Robert W., 237
Riley, Jefferson, 228
Riley, John Jefferson, 228
Riley, Mary, 21
Riley, Moses, 21
Riley, Sam, 228
Riley, Walter, 369
Rinehart, Charles, 400
Rink, Reuben, 147
Rip Van Winkle era, 52, 56
Ritch, Marvin L., 265
Rivera, Alexander, 436
Rivera, Hazel, 365
Riverview Methodist Church, 77
Roach, Edward, 258
Roads, 85, 231, 237–38, 339–40
Roanoke River, 7
Robbins, Daisy, 241
Robbins, Karl, 347
Robbins, Mary B., 327
Roberson, Foy, 272
Roberson, J. P., 116
Roberson, Mrs. Foy, 322
Roberts, Arthur, 244
Roberts, C. E., 272
Roberts, Charles B., Jr., 396
Roberts, David, 57, 98
Roberts, Elisha, 36
Roberts, Frank W., 115
Roberts, George, 54, 55
Roberts, Lewis, 73
Roberts, Oral, 437
Roberts, Willis, 56, 57
Roberts family, 55
Robertson, Jefferson, 81
Robertson, Pat, 437
Robinson, Charles M., 235
Robinson, James A., 167
Robinson, Kathrine, 308
Rochelle, Charles, 395
Rochelle, Sid, 248
Rochelle, Yancy, 93
Rockefeller, Nelson, 375
Rockingham County, 18
Rockwood, 291
Rodbell, Martin, 419
Rodenhizer, Harry, 380, 409
Rogers, C. M., 99
Rogers, Calvin J., 57, 73
Rogers, James F., 74
Rogers, James M., 377
Rogers, Maude F., 275
Rogers, Peleg, 73

Rogers, Robert I., 151, 179
Rogers, Will, 162
Rogers family, 21, 39
Rollins, Betsy, 423
Rollins, Edward T., 171
Roman Catholics, 192, 206, 340
Roney, Artelia, 119–20
Roosevelt, Franklin D., 294, 321
Roosevelt, Theodore, 247
Rosazza, John, 290
Rose, Jed E., 420
Rosenberg, Nelson, 394
Rosenthal, D., 193
Rosenwald, Julius, 274
Rosenwald Fund, 274, 306
Rose of Sharon Baptist Church, 74, 75, 90, 112, 116
Ross, Thomas, 33, 36
Rotary Club, 234, 270
ROTC program, 324
Rougemont (community), 229
Rougemont Methodist Episcopal Church, 194
Rough and Ready Club, 83
Roundabout Club, 234
Round Hill debating society, 83–84
Round Hill school, 72, 115
Rowan, Matthew, 20–21
Rowan County, 18
Rowland, W. H., 115
Rowland and Brothers, 79
Roxboro Cotton Mill, 77
Royal Arcanum (order), 154
Royal Arch (R.A.M.), 154
Royal Knights of King David (order), 188
Royall, Kenneth, 300, 357
Royall, Kenneth C., Jr., 381
Rubinstein, Arthur, 318
Rudolph, Paul, 348
Ruffin, Benjamin S., 346, 358, 375–76, 380, 435
Ruffin, Julian, 214
Ruffin, Thomas, 97
Ruffin, William, 350
Runkel Stock Company, 224
Rural War Production Training Program, 326
Russell, C. H., 243
Russell, Daniel L., 185, 380
Russell, Elbert, 341
Russell, Henry, 133, 134
Russell, John G., 126
Rutledge, John, 31
Ryals, Hildegard, 413
Ryan, Thomas F., 181

Sabin, Albert, 352
Sage, Mrs. Russell, 311
Saint Cecilia Society, 162
Saint Helen Hotel, 235
Saint Joseph's A.M.E. Church, 117, 136, 190, 229

Saint Mark A.M.E. Zion Church, 191
Saint Mark's tax district, 39–40
Saint Mary's Chapel, 56
Saint Mary's Roman Catholic Church, 192–93
Saint Mary's tax district, 39–40
Saint Matthew's parish, 18, 56
Saint Paul's Lutheran Church, 292
Saint Philip's Episcopal Church, 165, 228
Saint William's Roman Catholic Church, 193
Salem Chapel, 56
Salisbury occupation, 104
Salk, Jonas, 352
Salvation Army, 164, 212, 235, 297
Samfield, Isabelle, 396
Samuel, James B., 330
Sands, Alexander, 279
Sandy Creek Association, 24
Sandy Level Baptist Church, 292
Sandy Level Church, 74, 75
Sanford, Terry, Jr., 406, 407
Sanford, Terry, Sr., 333–34, 357, 381, 385, 400,
    406, 409, 430, 433, 440
Sans Souci, 175
Santana, Carlota, 446
Santon, Edward M., 105
Sarah P. Duke Gardens, 286
Saterfield, Agnes, 136
Satterfield, H. E., 261
Saunders, John, 21
Saunders, William L., 110
Sawyer, Frank McM., 173
Sawyer and Hook, 157, 173
Scarborough, Daisy E., 308, 313
Scarborough, J. C., 259, 308
Scarlett, John, 34, 86
Scarlett, Thomas, 36
Schenck and Warlick spinning factory, 61
Schields family, 39
Schlitz, Don, 445
Schmitt, Evelyn, 421
Schools, 47–48, 114, 239; academic freedom,
    201; for blacks, 196, 197, 220, 240–41, 310–12,
    348–49; for blind, 83; compulsory education,
    208, 240; desegregation of, 300, 311, 335,
    362–67, 414, 430, 439–40; in Durham County,
    146, 241, 298–99; in Durham (town), 143–46,
    186, 196–98, 240–41, 273–76, 298–99,
    338–39; financing of, 69, 72–73, 144, 298–99;
    graded, 144–46, 197; kindergartens, 307;
    merger of, 414–15; moonlight, 145; nursery,
    306–7; plight of, 186, 195–96, 240–41,
    273–76; private, 69, 73–74, 115, 144, 438–40;
    as public entities, 64–66, 69; subscription, 74;
    for women, 195–96, 197–98
Scotch-Irish settlers, 16, 17, 30
Scott, Abraham, 81
Scott, Anne Firor, 385
Scott, Edward M., 71, 100
Scott, F. W., 343
Scott, Kerr, 333, 339
Scott, Robert, 383
Scott, Sidney, 74
Scurlock, Larry, 364
Seaboard Air Line Railroad, 156–57
Searle family, 55
Sears, Frank, 135
Sears, John M., 176
Sears, Mordecai, 75, 79
Second Baptist Church, 164
Second Presbyterian Church, 194
Secoton (town), 7
Seeley, Emetta, 308
Seeman, Ernest, 302
Seeman, Henry E., 180, 302
Seeman, Mrs. H. E., 253
Segregation: challenges to, 309; civil rights
    movement and, 360; in Durham, 138;
    emancipation and, 137–38; lack of, 81, 131; in
    military, 322, 362; as political stance, 370–71;
    of public accommodations, 258–59. *See also*
    Desegregation
Select School of Music, 241
Semans, James, 357, 399, 444, 446
Semans, Mary D. B. Trent, 335, 346, 352, 356,
    444, 446
Sembrich, Marcella, 319
Semper Idem tobacco, 119
Separatist Baptists, 46
Servicemen's Readjustment Act (1944), 333
Sessoms, Carlie, 357
Settle, Thomas, 185
Sewage treatment, 353–54
Shacco Will, 10
Shackelford, Emmett W., 261
Shackelford, Walter, 395
Shady Hill Baptist Church, 165
Shady Hill Meeting House, 72, 74
Shakespeare Club, 171
Shakori Indians, 6, 9
Shands, Arthur R., 305
Sharp, Susie, 380
Shaw, Grover Cleveland, 382
Shaw, Willie M., 58
Shaw family, 57
Shelburn, William, 395
Sheltering Home Circle of the Kings Daughters,
    234, 235
Shepard, Augustus, 219
Shepard, Charles H., 218
Shepard, James Edward, 187–88, 218–20,
    219–20, 310–13, 361, 436
Shepard, Soloman, 112
Shepherd, Ferrell & Cheek Co., 91
Shepherd, George M., 75
Shepherd, John, 87, 92
Shepherd, Solomon, 91, 95, 113, 115

Shepherd family, 39
Sheppard, William B., 257
Sherman, William Tecumseh, 62, 104–5
Sherman Antitrust Act, 210
Sherron, John, 36
Shields, Charles J., 76, 79, 98–99
Shields, James S., 98–99
Shields, John Cabe, 75, 99
Shields, Joseph H., 99
Shields, William Thomas, 93, 98
Shiloh Church, 55
Shipman, Ellen, 286
Shipp, J. H., 231
Shively, Larry, 408
Shop Hill slave houses, 49
Shopping malls, 336–37
Shreve, Lamb, and Harmon firm, 292
Shuford (judge), 199
Siegel, David, 147
Siegel, J. M., 147
Sigmund, Charles A., 224
Silberman, Pauline, 399
Silbiger, Cathy, 446
Silver, Dot, 400
Simmons, Funivall M., 237
Simmons, Thomas J., 172
Simmons, William J., 257
Simon, Abram, 220
Simonetti, Vincent, 396
Simons, Elwyn L., 443
Simpson, George L., Jr., 347
Sims, Herbert, 62
Sims, Herbert H., Jr., 62, 99
Sims, Willie, 250
Sim's mill, 61
Singleton, Clyde, 125
Sioux Indians, 6–7
Sister Cities International, 416
Sixty-fifth General Hospital, 326
Slate Belt, 3–4
Slater, W. A., 232
Slaughter, J. F., 177
Slavery: Civil War and, 97, 101; free blacks and, 20, 34, 50, 79–81, 108–10, 131, 205; in Orange County, 40, 48–50; plantation, 49; population statistics on, 21, 40, 48; Revolutionary War and, 34; tobacco industry and, 122–23
Sledd, Andrew, 201
Small, Edward F., 148
Small, John E. G., 244
Small, Sarah Ann, 244
Smallpox epidemic, 215
Smith, Amanda Mackay, 387
Smith, Charles C., 243
Smith, David, 214
Smith, Dr., 99
Smith, Kathleen Godwin, 326
Smith, Lee, 313

Smith, Marian Wallace, 396
Smith, Mrs. Charles C., 307
Smith, Mrs. Y. E., 253
Smith, O. R., 160
Smith, Pat, 386
Smith, Peyton H., 157, 190, 248, 249
Smith, Susan Carlton, 394
Smith, Susan Gower, 214
Smithsonian Institution, 3
Smoky Hollow, 136–37, 176, 356–57
Smolensky, Joe, 193
Smoot, Willie, 172
Smullin, Frank, 393
SNCC (Student Non-violent Coordinating Committee), 361
Snow, Captain, 23
Snow, Horace N., 162
Snyderman, Ralph, 429, 430, 431–32
Social men's clubs, 272
Social work, 209, 356–59, 388–90
Sons of Liberty, 29
Sons of Temperance, 83, 91
Soong, Charles Jones, 164–65
Sorrell, A. M., 187
Sorrell family, 55
South Atlantic Quarterly (magazine), 201
South Carolina, 5, 97
Southerland, Fendal, 79
Southerland's sawmill, 62
Southern Association of Colleges and Secondary Schools, 197
Southern Association of College Women, 234
Southern Bell Telephone and Telegraph Company, 160
Southern Christian Leadership Conference, 361
Southern Conservatory of Music, 173, 241, 275–76
Southern Fidelity and Surety Company, 219
Southern Power Company, 159, 211, 278–79
Southern Public Utilities Company, 211
Southern Railway, 156, 344
Southern Tobacco Manufacturers' Association, 182
Southgate, Celestia (Lessie), 162, 172
Southgate, James Haywood, 128, 151, 152, 154, 155, 162, 164, 171, 201, 233, 281
Southgate, Mattie, 151
Southgate, Thomas Fuller, 268
South Lowell Female Academy, 71
South Lowell Male Academy, 70–72, 83
Sowell, Frank, 135
Spangenberg, Bishop, 18
Spanish-American War (1898–1899), 248
Spanish Flavored Durham Smoking Tobacco, 94–95, 119
Spanish influenza, 251
Sparger, Mrs. Samuel W., 327
Sparger, Samuel, 62

Sparger, Samuel W., 233
Sparkman, Katie, 135
Spaulding, Asa, 361–62, 369, 372, 377, 380, 381, 430
Spaulding, Charles Clinton, 187, 188, 243, 249, 256, 259, 310–14, 316
Spaulding, E. G., 315
Spaulding, Elna, 377, 411, 430
Spaulding, Jean, 430
Spaulding, Kenneth B., 381
Spaulding, Lewis, 249
Spaulding, Mae, 365
Speaker Ban Law, 334
Spears, Marshall, 301
Speed, Joseph, 251
Spelman, Edian, 132–33
Spencer, Cornelia Phillips, 103, 155
Spencer, David, 439
Spirituals and gospel music, 309, 318, 334
Sports, 196–97, 245–47, 273, 319, 427
Springs, mineral, 228
Sprunt, Mrs. Douglas H., 309
Stabler, Edward, 27
Stagg, Francis A., 74, 91, 96
Stagg, James Edward, 91, 225, 232, 233, 239
Stagg, Judith, 21
Stagg, Mary, 305
Stagg, Mrs. J. E., 254, 255, 256, 278, 302
Stagg, Radford, 166
Stagg, Thomas, 21
Stagg family, 21
Stagville Historic District, 12, 49
Stagville store, 53
Stallings, D. H., 231
Stamp Act (1765), 29
Stanfield, Lawrence, 252
Stanford, Lois, 308, 327
Stanford L. Warren Library, 243, 330, 355
Stanley, W. E., 212
State Normal and Industrial School, 195
Stead, Eugene, 417, 430
Stearns, Shubal, 46
Steele, Alma G., 425
Steele, Charles L., IV, 423
Steiner, J. F., 270
Stem, Rufus V., 248
Stephens, T. M., 162
Stewart, Benny, 318
Stewart, John S., 315, 363
Stewart, Pearson, 382
Stewart, R. Edward, 349
Stewart family, 80
Still, J. T., 299
Stokes, Alvis H., 115, 127, 153, 160, 190, 260
Stokes, Jeannette, 386
Stokes Hall, 143, 173–74
Stone, Luther G., 248
Stone, T. F., 405

Stone, Walker, 444
Stone, William, 397
Stone family, 55
Stoneman, George, 104
Stonewall Jackson Training School, 212
Storer, Jeff, 446
Strassler, Eugene, 445
Stratton, Janice, 421
Strawbridge, James E., 395–96
Strayhorn, William, 17
Strayhorn farm, 112
Streeter, Lacy, 368
Strickland, John, 248
Strickland, Junius A., 206
Strikes, 207, 288–89
Strobel, Shirley, 426
Strudwick, Clement, 394
Strudwick, Lucille, 394
Student Army Training Corps, 250
Student Non-violent Coordinating Committee (SNCC), 361
Styron, W. K., 112, 113
Styron, William, 398
Suffrage: for blacks, 109–10, 315; for women, 234, 253–54, 256
Sugar Hill, 176
Suggs, Simon, 40
Suitt, J. E., 231
Suitt family, 39, 57
Sullivan, Jane Wilkins, 396
Summerfield, Myer, 193
Sumner, Senator, 138
Sun (newspaper), 167, 186
Sunas, Ernest, 396
Sun Yat-sen, 165
Susquehanna Indians, 7
Swan, Herbert S., 299
Sweene, Henry C., 78
Sweeney's store, 73
Swindell, Edmund Slade, Jr., 353–54
Swindell, Edwin, 412
Sykes, Benjamin P., 75
Sykes, R. H., 232, 269, 272, 278, 299
Synnott, Michael, 17–18, 20, 21, 23, 44

Tabourn family, 80
Taliaferro, Clay, 446
Tapp, Bettie, 205, 213–14
Tar Heel Woman (magazine), 307–8
Tarrant, Julian, 336
Tate, Mark, 73
Tatum, J. A., 164
Taverns, 21–22
Taxation: Civil War, 100; in Durham, 113, 128, 144, 268; in Orange County, 20, 24, 39–40, 65; for schools, 144, 298–99; to support poor, 82
Taxpayers League, 298–99
Taylor, J. M., 192

Taylor, James D., 314, 315
Taylor, Vestal C., 323
Taylor, Zachary, 83
Tea Act (1773), 29
Teachers' Assembly, 163
Teer, Dillard, 329
Teer, Hubert, 251, 329
Teer, Mrs. Nello, 322
Teer, Nello, 257, 329
Telegraph and telephone service, 159–60, 252
Temperance movement, 83, 113
Tempest, Roddy, 425
Temple Baptist Church, 164
Terrill, Saunders, 316
Terry, Blind Sonny, 316
Terry, Marion, 161
Terry, W. S., 143
Terry family, 55
Tetanus infection, 217
Textile industry, 43–45, 61–64, 75–79, 98,
    180–81, 204–8; strikes in, 288–89
Thackston, James, 27, 34–35
Tharpe, William A., 53
Thaxton, Samuel A., 151
Theodore Gary Company, 160
Thetford, William, 44
Third Party, 161, 184
Third Provincial Congress (1775), 31
Thistlethwaite, Glenn, 324
Thomas, C. C., 324
Thomas, Durwood, 352
Thomas, James A., 285
Thomas, Katherine C., 339
Thomas, Norman, 288
Thomas, Octa, 175
Thompson, Clarence, 366
Thompson, Edwin, 180
Thompson, John G., 93
Thompson, M. Hugh, 315, 363
Thompson, W. W., 171
Thompson v. Durham County Board of Education,
    366
Thornburg, Murray, 327
Thorpe, Marion, 357
Thorpe, Rosa Hartwick, 155
Tidd, A. M., 393
Tillett, John, 116
Tilley, Adolphus, 195
Tilley, Allen, 98
Tilley, Doris Belk, 402
Tilley, Haywood, 64, 78
Tilley, Henderson, 73, 122
Tilley, John, 74
Tilley, Lazarus, 36
Tilley, Marcus, 195
Tilley, R. J., 166
Tilley, Scott, 444
Tilley family, 39, 59

Tillinghast, Robina, 244
Tilton, Edward L., 271
Tirro, Frank, 445
Tobacco industry, 112; advertising by, 148;
    brands of, 94–95, 119, 121, 148; in Civil War,
    106–7; construction for, 292; development of
    Durham County and, 141; Durham name and,
    95; employees of, 147–48; farming and, 41,
    79, 263–64; freed blacks and, 134–35; global
    expansion of, 210; health concerns and, 351;
    railroads and, 156; in Reconstruction, 117–26;
    reorganization in, 146–49, 181–83; statistics
    on, 123; unions in, 264–65
Tobacco Plant (newspaper), 128, 140, 167
Tobacco Workers International Union (TWIU),
    287–88
Tobacco Workers Union, 265
Tomlinson, Mabel, 176
Tomlinson, Mrs. L. A., 253
Tomlinson, S. F., 145, 154, 160, 162
Tompkins, D. A., 220
Toms, Clinton W., 172, 197, 210, 226, 228, 279
Toms, Clinton W., Jr., 327
Toms, Mrs. Clinton W., 324
Toms, Mrs. Clinton W., Jr., 255
Tourgée, Albion, 109
Townshend Act (1767), 29
Transportation: benefits of, 96; improvements
    in, 69. *See also* Automobiles; Railroads;
    Roads; Trolleys
Travellers Aid Society, 324
Trent, Mary Duke Biddle, 335
Trice, Chesley P., 75
Trice, Ezekiel, 55
Trice, James, 85, 93
Trice, James A. L., 191–92
Trice, John, 191
Trice, Noah, 75, 195
Trice, Pleasant, 195
Trice, Priscilla, 195
Trice, Richard, 316–17
Trice, Wilson, 316–17
Trice family, 39
Trinity Avenue Presbyterian Church, 194,
    292
Trinity College, 168, 169–71, 196, 198–201,
    246–47, 293. *See also* Duke University
Trinity Land Company, 151
Trinity League, 172
Trinity Park School, 197–98
Trinity United Methodist Church, 56, 57, 98, 123,
    151, 163, 164–65, 272
Trolleys, 223–24
Troy, Thaddeus, 212
True Reformer company, 218
Truman, Harry S., 331
Trumbauer, Horace, 292; firm of, 282
Tryce, G., 93

Tryon, William, 16, 25, 26–27
Tuberculosis, 215–16, 262, 305, 328
Tubman, Harriet, 312–13
Tucker, R. B., 141
Turnbull, L. B., 172, 194
Turner, Andrew, 75, 93, 94, 113, 132, 133; house of, 90–91
Turner, Israel, 93
Turner, John, 93
Turner, Josephine, 380
Turner, Josiah, Jr., 99
Turner, L., 90
Turner, Moss, 93
Turner, Nat, 80
Turner, William, 94
Turner and Hill store, 229
Turrentine, Sam, 98
Turrentine, W. D., 185
Tuscarora Indians, 9, 13
Twaddell, Vera Carr, 307
Twaddell, William Powell, 276, 318
Twine, L. D., 191
TWIU (Tobacco Workers International Union), 287–88
Tyler, Anne, 398
Tyler, John, 67

UDC (United Daughters of the Confederacy), 171, 257, 277
Umberger, Randolph, 444, 446
Umstead, Alvis Kinchen, 143, 144, 177, 229, 239
Umstead, Elisha, 73, 78
Umstead, John, 61
Umstead, John W., 194–95, 256
Umstead, Squire D., 63, 73, 83–84, 100, 122; mill of, 61, 78
Umstead, Walter, 349
Umstead, William Bradley, 303, 333
Umstead family, 39
Underwood, Norman, 271
Union Baptist Church, 191
Union Bethel Church, 133
Union Grove Church, 72, 74
Union League, 109, 111
Union Mills, 78
Unions, 206, 264–65, 287–88, 295, 350
Union Tobacco Company, 181–82
United Daughters of the Confederacy (UDC), 171, 257, 277
United Service Organizations (USO), 324
United Textile Workers Union, 288
Universalists, 244
University of North Carolina, Women's College, 195
Upchurch, Sidney, 111
Upchurch, W. M., 240
USO (United Service Organizations), 324

Vance, Rupert, 316
Vance, Zebulon Baird, 100
Van Noppen, Charlie, 151
Van Noppen, C. M., 151
Van Noppen, Johnnie, 151
Van Noppen, Leonard, 151
Vartanian, Nadine, 394
Vaughan, Bedford, 63, 73, 78, 79, 94, 111, 119
Vaughan, Caroline, 395
Vaughan, James, 44
Vaughan, Lida Carr, 254
Vaughan family, 39
Vega, Francis, 444
Verwoerdt, Julius, 405
Veteran's Hospital, 337
Vick, S. H., 219
Vickers, C. F., 161
Vickers, Gaston, 269
Vickers, George W., 75
Vickers, Henry Alonzo, 364
Vickers, Riley, 91, 93, 95
Vickers, Thomas, 112
Vickers, William Gaston, 146, 151, 185
Virginia-Carolina Chemical Company, 152
Virginia-Carolina League, 245
Virginia land dispute, 13
Volkamenia Club, 234
Voters League for Better Government, 335
Voting rights: for blacks, 109–10, 315; for women, 234, 253–54, 256

W. D. Hill Center, 373, 440
W. Duke Sons and Company, 146–47; American Tobacco Company and, 149; donations by, 157; formation of, 146–49; railroads and, 156
WAACS (Women's Army Auxiliary Corps), 327
WAC (Women's Army Corps), 332
Wade, Thomas, 17
WAFS (Women's Auxiliary Ferrying Service), 327
Wager, Paul, 299
Wahab, Henry W., 125
Wahab, Uriah M., 162
Wake County, 18, 28, 115, 141–42, 238
Walden, Mollie (Millie), 133
Walden, Stanford, 81
Walker, Alexander, 122, 124, 176, 177
Walker, Fielding Lewis, Jr., 210
Walker, James, Jr., 47, 61–62, 63
Walker, James, Sr., 47
Walker, LeRoy T., 393, 434
Walker, Mamie Dowd, 300–301, 313
Walker, Sallie, 63–64, 78
Walker, T. J., 228
Walker's mill, 61–62
Wall, George, 258
Wall, Monroe, 419
Wall, Mrs. John A., 307
Wallace, Barrie, 444

Wallace, George, 371, 380
Waller, Carter N., 63
Waller, James, 81
Wall Street Church, 258
Walter, Henry, 99
Walters, Fannie, 326
Walton, Epps, 186
Wani, Marsakh, 419
Wannamaker, William H., 282, 284, 313
Ward, J. J., 151
Ward, M. P., 185
Ward, Maggie, 224
Ward, Robert, 444
Ward, William P., 118, 120
Warner, G. Frank, 300–301
War of 1812, 53
Warren, Clem, 272
Warren, James B., 151, 157, 177, 185, 194
Warren, Julia, 308
Warren, Page, 161
Warren, Rosa, 266–67
Warren, Stanford Leigh, 243, 259
Warren, William, 40
Warren's Chapel, 194
Washington, Booker T., 138, 200, 218, 260, 361
Washington, George, 316
Washington, John, 330
Washington Duke Homestead, 286
Washington Duke Hotel, 271, 283, 344
Water supply, 157–58, 228, 239, 352, 353–54
Watkins, B. M., 251
Watkins, Basil, 301
Watkins, Frederick K., 310, 324
Watkins, J. L., 151, 152, 153
Watson, D. T., 188
Watson, Jeannette, 349
Watson, Lotan G., 65
Watts (principal), 203–4
Watts, Charles D., 365, 431
Watts, Constance, 365
Watts, George, 204; Commonwealth Club and,
    163, 232; donations by, 177–78, 189–90, 192,
    214, 216, 260; Durham Electric Lighting
    Company and, 159; Durham Fertilizer
    Company and, 178; Durham Gas Company
    and, 159; Durham Literary Society and,
    162; Fidelity Bank and, 160; hospital for
    blacks and, 189–90; houses of, 151, 225, 398;
    Interstate Telephone and Telegraph Company
    and, 160; Keeley Institute and, 177; liquor
    prohibition and, 245; Malbourne hotel and,
    235; municipal water supply and, 239; Pearl
    Cotton Mills and, 180; tobacco warehouses of,
    401; YMCA and, 164
Watts, George Washington, 146–47
Watts, Gerard S., 127, 146
Watts, Mrs. George, 262
Watts Hospital, 213–14, 229, 262–63; closing of,
    354; federal assistance to, 326; financial dif-
    ficulties of, 304, 354; segregation of, 371
Watts Street Baptist Church, 272
WAVES (Women Accepted for Volunteer
    Emergency Service), 327
Weatherly, Addison Cicero, 146, 240
Weatherspoon, J. R., 233
Weaver, James, 136
Weaver family, 57, 80
Webb, Garland E., 125
Webb, Henry, Jr., 18
Webb, Henry, Sr., 18, 21
Webb, James, 76, 79, 90
Webb, John Huske, 76
Webb, Luke, 191
Webb, Mena, 398–99
Webb, Robert Fulton, 77, 98, 125, 145, 165
Webb, Roulhac firm, 121
Webster, McCory, 272
Weddell, Mrs. F. L., 172
Weeks (architect), 311
Weil, Gertrude, 254
Weinhold, Kemp, 420
Welfare Club, 209
Wentzes, Robert, 396
West, C. B., 266
West, Marlon, 416
Westcott, Richard, 391
West Durham, 93, 152, 172, 197–98, 204, 251, 349
West Durham Baptist Church, 191, 193, 292
West Durham Methodist Church, 193
West Durham Mission, 243
Western Union, 159
West Point mill, 77–78
Wharton, R. L., 197
Wheat crops, 41
Wheeler, John H., 315, 346, 361–62, 363, 364, 369
Wheeler, Joseph, 101
Wheeler, Warren H., 364
Wheeler v. Durham City Board of Education, 364
Whichard, Willis, 381, 387, 404
Whidlin, Oliver, 244
Whig Party, 31, 65, 66–67, 69, 83, 95
Whitaker, J. B., Jr., 144, 162
Whitaker, William, 75
White, Gilbert C., 158, 239, 290
White, John, 7
White, Newman I., 297
White, Polly Sutherland, 101
White, Susanne, 400
White Brotherhood, 110
White Elephant Club, 272
White Man's Saloon, 138
White Rock Baptist Church, 117, 136, 190, 219
Whiteside, Jeanne, 393, 396
White supremacy, 110, 138, 139, 185–87, 257, 265,
    333, 335
Whiting, Albert N., 392, 434

Whitley, James, 395
Whitney, Eli, 53
Whitt, James, 112
Whitted, James A., 197
Whitted, James Y., 118
Wide-Awake Circle, 234
Widener, P. A. B., 181
Wiggins, Ira, 445
Wiggins, Mrs. A. P., 309
Wilburn, John, 54
Wilkerson, Albert Ernest, 152
Wilkerson, Sylvia, 398–99
Wilkerson, W. A., 143, 193
Wilkerson, William Albert, 143, 152, 193
Wilkerson Brothers warehouse, 125
Wilkerson family, 21
Wilkins, Roy, 368
Willard, William H., 76–77, 119
Willard Manufacturing Company, 77
Williams, A., 191
Williams, Amos, 364
Williams, Franklin, 222
Williams, J. B., 115
Williams, Mary Lou, 445
Williams, S. B., 243
Williams, Sylvester, 364
Williamson, E. R., 352
Willis, William, 392
Wills, Charles B., 250
Wilson, Anna, 445
Wilson, Edward N., 392–93
Wilson, Jordan, 191
Wilson, Rhea, 393
Wilson, Stephen, 47
Wilson, William L., 249
Wilson, Woodrow, 171
Wily, J. F., 228
Winston, Robert W., 168, 185, 188–89, 199–200, 226, 232
Winston-Salem All Stars Quartet, 222
Wise, J. A., 166
Wiser, Betty, 387
Witherspoon, Hiram, 93
Wittenberg, Frank, 405
Wolff, Miles, 409
Womble, Mrs. J. T., 115
Women, 252, 255; clubs for, 306–9; domestic violence and, 386, 427–28; feminist movement, 255, 385–88; schools for, 195–96, 197–98; voting rights for, 234, 253–54, 256; in world wars, 250–51, 326, 327
Women Accepted for Volunteer Emergency Service (WAVE), 327
Women in Action for the Prevention of Violence, 377
Women's Army Auxiliary Corps (WAAC), 327
Women's Army Corps (WAC), 332
Women's Auxiliary Ferrying Service (WAF), 327

Women's Christian Temperance Union, 162
Wood, Abraham, 7
Wood, Clarence R., 269, 301, 391
Wood, Frank H., 167
Wood, Hugh, 17, 18
Wood, John, 18
Woodard, A. A., 251
Woodburn, T. C., 128
Woodland Indian culture, 10, 11
Woods, Demsey, 55
Woods, J. S., 231
Woods, John, 36
Woods, Joseph, 122
Woods, W. W., 185
Woods family, 21
Woodward, James, 373
Woodward, Nola, 172
Woolen mills, 75–76
Wooten, Hattie B., 243
Works Progress Administration (WPA), 296, 307, 326
World War I: armistice, 251; black soldiers in, 249; memorials to, 251–52; recruiting in, 249, 250; unions and, 265; women in workforce in, 250–51, 252–53
World War II, 323–25, 328–31, 349–50; black soldiers in, 322; fear and, 327; fundraising for, 321–22; memorials to, 326; shortages in, 326–27; veterans of, 334; women in workforce in, 326, 327
Wortham family, 39
WPA (Works Progress Administration), 296, 307, 326
Wray, Julia, 400
Wright, Elizabeth Glover, 121
Wright, Glover, 121
Wright, John, 187–88
Wright, Mary, 293
Wright, Paul, 401
Wright, Richard, II, 301
Wright, Richard Harvey, 121–22, 127, 145, 178, 203, 216, 223, 271, 346; Commonwealth Club and, 232; Commonwealth Manufacturing Company and, 179–80; death of, 293; departure from American Tobacco Company of, 149; donations by, 270; Duke shares purchased by, 146; Durham Consolidated Land and Improvement Company and, 151; Durham Traction Company and, 159; Durham Woolen and Wooden Mills Company and, 152–53; heirs of, 302; house of, 226; Interstate Telephone and Telegraph Company and, 159–60; as park developer, 269; as salesman, 146, 148; strikers and, 288; Wright Machinery Company and, 204
Wright, Thomas Davenport, 204, 303
Wright, Wesley A., 94–95, 94–96, 118
Wright Refuge, 257, 270, 293

Wright Machinery Company, 204
Wright's Traction Company, 211
Wylie, Gill, 217
Wyngaarden, James, 404
Wynn, Alberta R., 241
Wynn, Phail, Jr., 415

X, Malcolm, 374

Yardley, Francis, 6
Yates, E. A., 170, 194
Yates, Matthew T., 116
Yates Baptist Church, 116
Yearby, W. M., 172
Yearby House, 174–75

Yirtle, Nancy, 415
YMCA, 164, 273
Yon, Pete, 290
York, Richard W., 100
Young, W. S., 218
Young, Wilbert, 270
Young, Y. E., 185
Young Men's Literary and Debating Club, 171, 234, 236
Young's Smut and Screening machine, 70
YWCA, 254–55, 271, 288, 312, 324, 356, 386

Z. I. Lyon and Company, 151
Zachariah I. Lyon and Co., 151, 211
Zion Tabernacle, 341

About the Author

Jean Bradley Anderson is a professional genealogist and a freelance contract researcher. Formerly a contract researcher for the
North Carolina Division of Archives and History, she was the
researcher for the prizewinning book series *The Way We Lived
in North Carolina.* She is the author of *Piedmont Plantation: The
Bennehan-Cameron Family and Lands in North Carolina, The Kirk-
lands of Ayr Mount,* and *Carolinian on the Hudson.*

Library of Congress Cataloging-in-Publication Data

Anderson, Jean Bradley.
Durham County : a history of Durham County, North Carolina /
Jean Bradley Anderson. — 2nd ed., rev. and expanded.
p. cm.
Includes bibliographical references and index.
ISBN 978-0-8223-4983-9 (pbk. : alk. paper)
1. Durham County (N.C.)—History. I. Title.
F262.D8A63 2011
975.6'563—dc22
2010039875